Bhagavad Gītā Demystified

by

Nithyananda

This book is a compilation of visionary spiritual talks delivered by Paramahamsa Nithyananda, to global audiences. Paramahamsa Nithyananda's morning satsang talks are viewed every day by over a million people worldwide, via web TV, video-conferencing and live telecast on na¬tional TV channels.

Bhagavad Gītā
Chapters 1 to 18

All meditation techniques, practices and procedures described or recommended in this book, are suitable for practice only under the direct supervision of an instructor, trained and ordained by Paramahamsa Nithyananda. Further, you should consult with your personal physician to determine whether those techniques, practices and procedures are suitable for you in relation to your own health, fitness and ability.

This publication is not intended to be a substitute for a personal medical attention, examination, diagnosis or treatment. Should any person engage in any of the techniques, practices or procedures described or recommended in this book, he would be doing so at his own risk, unless he has received a personal recommendation from his own physician and from an in¬structor trained and ordained by Paramahamsa Nithyananda.

Published by Nithyananda University Press

ISBN 13: 978-1-60607-161-8

A portion of the proceeds from the sale of this book will be towards supporting charitable activities.

Printed in India at
Print- O- Graph
Total Print Solution
97, Sultanpet, Banglore - 560 053
Phone : +91 80 425 303 12, 222 598 91

TRANSLITERATION AND PRONUNCIATION GUIDE

ॐ	oṁ	home	ॐ	oṁ	Rome
अ	a	fun	ट	ṭa	touch
आ	ā	car	ठ	ṭha	ant-hill
इ	i	pin	ड	ḍa	duck
ई	ī	feen	ढ	ḍha	godhook
उ	u	put	ण	ṇa	thunder
ऊ	ū	pool	त	ta	(close to) think
ऋ	r	rig	थ	tha	(close to) pathetic
ॠ	ṛ	(long r)	द	da	(close to) father
ऌ	ḷ	*	ध	dha	(close to) breathe hard
ए	c	play	न	na	numb
ऐ	ai	high	प	pa	purse
ओ	o	over	फ	pha	sapphire
औ	au	cow	ब	ba	but
अं	aṁ	**	भ	bha	abhor
अः	aḥ	***	म	ma	mother
क	ka	kind	य	ya	young
ख	kha	blockhead	र	ra	run
ग	ga	gate	ल	la	luck
घ	gha	log-hut	व	va	virtue
ङ	ṅa	sing	श	śa	shove
च	ca	chunk	ष	ṣa	bushel
छ	cha	match	स	sa	sir
ज	ja	jug	ह	ha	house
झ	jha	hedgehog	ळ	(Note 1)	(close to) world
ञ	ña	bunch	क्ष	kṣa	worksheet
त्र	tra	three	ज्ञ	jña	*
ऽ		unpronounced (a)	ऽऽ	"	Unpronounced (ā)

Note 1: "" itself is sometimes used.

* No English Equivalent.

** Nasalisation of the preceding vowel.

*** Aspiration of preceding vowel

CONTENTS

Bhagavad Gītā A Background

Bhagavad Gītā is a sacred scripture of the vedic culture. As with all scriptures, it was knowledge that was transmitted verbally. It was called *śruti* in Sanskrit, meaning something that is heard.

Gītā, as Bhagavad Gītā is generally called, translates literally from Sanskrit as 'Sacred Song'. Unlike *Vedas* and *Upaniṣads,* which are stand alone expressions, Gītā is written into the Hindu epic Mahābhārata, called a *purāṇa,* an ancient tale. It is part of a story, so to speak.

As a scripture, Gītā is part of the ancient knowledge base of the vedic tradition, which is the expression of the experiences of great sages.

Vedas and *Upaniṣads,* the foundation of *śruti* literature, arose from the insight and awareness of these great sages when they went into a no-mind state. These are as old as humanity and the first and truest expressions in the journey of man's search for truth.

Unlike *Vedas,* which were revealed to the great sages, or *Upaniṣads,* which were the teachings of these great sages, Gītā is part of a story narrated by Vyāsa, one of these great sages. It is narrated as the direct expression of the Divine.

No other epic, or part of an epic, has the special status of Gītā. As a consequence of the presence of Gītā, the Mahābhārata epic itself is considered a sacred Hindu scripture. Gītā arose from the super-consciousness of Kṛṣṇa, the supreme god, and is therefore considered a scripture.

Mahābhārata, literally meaning the great Bhārata, is a narration about the nation and civilization, which is now known as India. It was then a nation ruled by king Bhārata and his descendants.

The story of this epic is about two warring clans, Kauravas and Pāṇḍavās, closely related to one another. Dhṛtarāṣṭra, the blind king of Hastināpura and father of the 100 Kaurava brothers was the brother of Pāṇḍu, whose children were the five Pāṇḍavā princes. It is a tale of strife between cousins.

Since Dhṛtarāṣṭra was blind, Pāṇḍu was made the king of Hastināpura. Pāṇḍu was cursed by a sage that he would die if he ever entered into a physical relationship with his wives. He therefore had no children. Vyāsa says that all the five Pāṇḍavā children were born to their mothers Kuntī and Mādri through the blessing of divine beings. Pāṇḍu handed over the kingdom and his children to his blind brother Dhṛtarāṣṭra and retired to meditate in the forest.

Kuntī had received a boon when she was still a young unmarried adolescent, that she could summon any divine power at will to father a child. Before she married, she tested her boon. The Sun god Sūrya appeared before her. Karṇa was born to her as a result. In fear of social reprisals, she cast the newborn away in a river. Yudhisṭra, Bhīma, and Arjuna were born to Kuntī after her marriage by invocation of her powers, and the twins Nakula and Sahadeva were born to Mādri, the second wife of Pāṇḍu.

Yudhisṭra was born to Kuntī as a result of her being blessed by Yama, the god of death and justice, Bhīma by Vayu, the god of wind, and Arjuna by Indra, god of all the divine beings. Nakula and Sahadeva, the youngest Pāṇḍavā twins, were born to Mādri, through the divine Aśvini twins.

Dhṛtarāṣṭra had a hundred sons through his wife Gāndhārī. The eldest of these Kaurava princes was Duryodhana. Duryodhana felt no love for his five Pāṇḍavā cousins. He made many unsuccessful attempts, along with his brother Duśśāsana, to kill the Pāṇḍavā brothers. Kuntī's eldest son Karṇa, whom she had cast away at birth, was found and brought up by a chariot driver in the palace, and by a strange twist of fate, joined hands with Duryodhana.

Dhṛtarāṣṭra gave Yudhisṭra one half of the Kuru kingdom on his coming of age, since the Pāṇḍavā prince was the rightful heir to the throne that his father Pāṇḍu had vacated. Yudhisṭra ruled from his new capital Indraprasta, along with his brothers Bhīma, Arjuna, Nakula and Sahadeva. Arjuna won the hand of princess Draupadī , daughter of the king of Pāñcāla, in a *svayaṁvara,* a marital contest in which princes fought for the hand of a fair damsel. In fulfilment of their mother Kuntī's desire that the brothers share everything equally, Draupadī became the wife of all five Pāṇḍavā brothers.

Duryodhana persuaded Yudhisṭra to join a gambling session, where his cunning uncle Śakunī defeated the Pāṇḍavā king. Yudhisṭra lost all that he owned - his kingdom, his brothers, his wife and himself, to Duryodhana. Duśśāsana shamed Draupadī in public by trying to disrobe her. The Pāṇḍavā brothers and Draupadī were forced to go into exile for fourteen years, with the condition that in the last year they should live incognito.

At the end of the fourteen years, the Pāṇḍavā brothers tried to reclaim their kingdom. In this effort they were helped by Kṛṣṇa, the king of the Yadava clan, who is considered the eighth divine incarnation of Viṣṇu. However, Duryodhana refused to yield even a needlepoint of land, and as a result, the Great War, the War of Mahābhārata ensued. In this war, various rulers of the entire nation that is modern India aligned with one or the other of these two clans, the Kauravas or the Pāṇḍavās.

Kṛṣṇa offered to join with either of the two clans. He said, 'One of you may have me unarmed. I will not take any part in the battle. The other may have my entire Yādava army.' When the offer was first made to Duryodhana, he predictably chose the large and well-armed Yādava army, in preference to the unarmed Kṛṣṇa. Arjuna joyfully and gratefully chose his friend and mentor Kṛṣṇa to be his unarmed charioteer!

The armies assembled in the vast field of Kurukṣetra, now in the state of Haryana in modern day India. All the kings and princes were related to one another, and were often on opposite sides. Facing the Kaurava army and his friends, relatives and teachers, Arjuna was overcome by remorse and guilt, and wanted to walk away from the battle.

Kṛṣṇa's dialogue with Arjuna on the battlefield of Kurukṣetra is the content of Bhagavad Gītā. Kṛṣṇa persuaded Arjuna to take up arms and vanquish his enemies. 'They are already dead,' says Kṛṣṇa, 'All those who are facing you have been already killed by Me. Go ahead and do what you have to do. That is your duty. Do not worry about the outcome. Leave that to Me.'

Gītā is the ultimate practical teaching on the inner science of spirituality. It is not as some scholars incorrectly claim, a promotion of violence. It is about the impermanence of the mind and body, and the need to go beyond the mind, ego and logic.

Being blind, king Dhṛtarāṣṭra does not participate in the war. His minister Sanjaya uses his powers of clairvoyance to 'see' and relate to king Dhṛtarāṣṭra the goings on on the battlefield. It is in Sanjaya's voice that we hear Gītā, the dialogue between Kṛṣṇa and Arjuna.

All the Kaurava princes as well as all their commanders such as Bhīṣma, Droṇa and Karṇa were killed in battle. The five Pāṇḍavā brothers survived as winners and became the rulers of the combined kingdom.

This dialogue between Kṛṣṇa and Arjuna is a dialogue between man and God or *Narā* and *Nārāyaṇa* as they are termed in Sanskrit. Arjuna's questions and doubts are those of each one of us. The answers of the Divine, Kṛṣṇa, transcend time and space. Kṛṣṇa's message is as valid today as it was on that fateful battlefield some thousands of years ago.

Nithyananda explains the inner metaphorical meaning of Mahābhārata thus:

'The Great War of Mahābhārata is the fight between the positive and negative thoughts of the mind, called the *saṁskāras*. The positive thoughts are the Pāṇḍavā princes and the negative thoughts are the Kaurava princes. Kurukṣetra or the battlefield is the body. Arjuna is the individual consciousness and Kṛṣṇa is the enlightened master.

The various commanders who led the Kaurava army represent the major blocks that the individual consciousness faces in its journey to enlightenment. Bhīṣma, the grand patriarch of the Kuru clan, represents parental and societal conditioning. Droṇa, the teacher of both the Kauravas and the Pāṇḍavās, represents the conditioning from teachers who provide knowledge including spiritual guidance. Karṇa represents the restrictive influence of good deeds such as charity and compassion, and finally Duryodhana represents the ego, which is the last to fall.

Parental and societal conditioning has to be overcome by rebelling against conventions. This is why, traditionally, those seeking the path of enlightenment are required to renounce the world as *sanyāsin* and move away from civilization. This conditioning does not die as long as the body lives, but its influence drops.

Droṇa represents all the knowledge one imbibes and the teachers one encounters, who guide us but are unable to take us through to the ultimate flowering of enlightenment. It is difficult to give them up since one feels grateful to them. This is where the enlightened master steps in and guides us.

Karṇa is the repository of all good deeds and it is his good deeds that stand in the way of his own enlightenment. Kṛṣṇa has to take the load of Karṇa's *puṇya,* his meritorious deeds, before he could be liberated. The enlightened master guides one to drop one's attachment to good deeds arising out of what are perceived to be charitable and compassionate intentions. He also shows us that the quest for and the experience of enlightenment is the ultimate act of compassion that one can offer to the world.

Finally one reaches Duryodhana, one's ego, the most difficult to conquer. One needs the full help of the master here. It is subtle work and even the master's help may not be obvious, since at this point, sometimes the ego makes us disconnect from the master as well.

The Great War was between one hundred and eighty million people - one hundred and ten million on the Kaurava side representing our negative *saṁskāra*s (stored memories) and seventy million on the Pāṇḍavā side representing our positive *saṁskāras* and it lasted eighteen days and nights. The number eighteen has a great mystical significance. It essentially signifies our ten senses that are made up of five *jnānendriya* - the sensses of perception like taste, sight, smell, hearing and touch, and five *karmendriya* - the senses initiating action like speech, bodily movements, etc., added to our eight kinds of thoughts like lust, greed, etc. All eighteen need to be dropped for Self-realization!

Mahābhārata is not just an epic story. It is not merely the fight between good and evil. It is the dissolution of both positive and negative *saṁskāras* that reside in our body-mind system, which must happen for the ultimate liberation. It is a tale of the process of enlightenment.

Mahābhārata is a living legend. Bhagavad Gītā is the manual for enlightenment.

Like Arjuna many thousand years ago, you are here in a dialogue with a living enlightened master in this book. This is a tremendous opportunity to resolve all questions and clear all doubts with the master's words.

Introduction

In this series, enlightened master, Paramahamsa Nithyananda comments on Bhagavad Gītā.

Many hundreds of commentaries on Gītā have been written over the years. The earliest commentaries were by the great spiritual masters such as Ādi Śaṅkarācārya, Rāmānuja and Mādhava, some thousand years ago. In recent times, great masters such as Rāmakṛṣṇa Paramahamsa and Ramana Mahaṛṣi have spoken from Gītā extensively. Many others have written volumes on this great scripture.

Nithyananda's commentary on Bhagavad Gītā is not just a literary translation and a simple explanation of that translation. He takes the reader through a world tour while talking about each verse. It is believed that each verse of Gītā has seven levels of meaning. What is commonly rendered is the first-level meaning. Here, an enlightened master takes us beyond the common into the uncommon, with equal ease and simplicity.

To read Nithyananda's commentary on Gītā is to obtain an insight that is rare. It is not mere reading; it is an experience; it is meditation.

Śaṇkara, the great master and philosopher said:

'A little reading of Gītā, a drop of Gaṅgā water to drink, remembering Kṛṣṇa once in a while, all this will ensure that you have no problems with the god of death.'

Editors of these volumes of Bhagavad Gītā have expanded upon the original discourses delivered by Nithyananda through further discussions with Him. For ease of understanding for English speaking readers, and in their academic interest, the original Sanskrit verses and their English translation have been included as an appendix to this book.

This reading is meant to help every individual in daily life as well as in the endeavour to realize the ultimate Truth. It creates every possibility to attain *nityānanda,* eternal bliss!

The Great 'Why'

The Bhagavad Gītā opens with the great 'WHY', reflecting the personal crisis that we all face at some point of our lives.

We are drawn into the protagonist Arjuna's life at a crucial moment, when the renowned young prince is getting ready for a bloody battle against against a huge army consisting of his own family, cousin and teachers. Struggling with fears, a misconstrued sense of duty and an awakening consciousness, the young prince is caught in the dilemma of his life.

Even after five thousand years, Arjuna's dilemma is still alive in humanity's experience of life. Our questions are hardly different from Arjuna's -

- *Why are we here?*
- *Why do we do what we do in our lives?*
- *Why don't we find fulfillment, even after years of working for success in the world?*
- *Why do more and more challenges await us, even after we solve and overcome numerous challenges?*
- *How can we become spiritually mature and integrated individuals? Why is this path even required?*

This 'Why?' can be answered in a very simple way - *You are here to manifest your ultimate Possibility!*

But each one of you has to discover your own answer to this 'Why'. Any other answer can only be an inspiration for you to discover your own answer.

We can only move when we have the ability to handle this great 'Why'. Whether you know it or not, only your deepest conviction about your 'Why', only your deepest clarity about your purpose, can give you the inspiration, energy and courage to face life.

This great 'Why' is the seed of God himself! This seed is put inside you when you are sent to Planet Earth, so that you do not rest until you become a tree and bear fruit.

Please understand, every seed has an energy called veerya, which does not rest till it produces more seeds. Even if you eat the seed, you cannot destroy it, because that veerya still goes into your body and does its job in some other way!

The question 'Why' is the veerya put into your very DNA structure to help you realize yourself.

Just like Arjuna, you too will not be able to rest until you realize the meaning of the great 'Why' for you

Just as Kṛṣṇa addresses Arjuna's questions, Paramahaṁsa Nithyananda addresses the readers' questions and doubts, guiding us on the path of transformation, refusing to give up on us until we discover our full potential and live like gods on earth. As you read this book, you will find the presence of Paramahaṁsa Nithyananda guiding you to discover your own unique yet universal path to realization.

The Art Of Listening

Through the entire opening chapter of the Gītā, it is Arjuna who continuously speaks, while Kṛṣṇa listens, listens and listens!

Only an intelligent man will allow the other person to speak. We all continuously speak to each other, but a 'real' conversation does not happen. We simply carry out simultaneous monologues with each other. We are polite enough to pretend that we are listening, so that we will, in turn, be heard. You need intelligence to allow the other person to speak. You need intelligence to listen!

When you listen to others, you listen to yourself. And when you don't listen to others, you also don't listen to yourself. Are you getting it? Only when you listen to you, you will be able to listen to others. When you listen to others, you will also listen to YOU! Because any listening that happens, happens from the space of completion. Please understand, you can only listen when you are complete. If there is any incompletion in you, you will not be able to listen.

What is incompletion? For example, you are sitting here right now, hearing me speak, but you are not listening to me, you are thinking – 'I have not done this, I have not done that, this has not happened, that has not happened, I am restless' – that is incompletion. If you have such incompletions inside,be very clear, you will not be listening to me. You may be sitting here out of compulsion or some other reason, but you will not be listening to me. And when you don't listen, more and more incompletions happen. It is a vicious circle.

If you *listen*, especially to the words that come out of the space of completion of an enlightened being, you will suddenly see that the energy of those very words goes and changes your inner space. See, when you come to me and tell me about your problems, I give you my authentic *listening*. That is why you suddenly feel light; you suddenly feel that all your problems are not big anymore. It is the power of listening. Listening awakens your intuition. Listening awakens your innermost intelligence. *Listening is GOD!*

By His very listening, Kṛṣṇa is able to heal the restlessness in Arjuna, the incompletions in Arjuna. Kṛṣṇa is showing us the power of His completion, the power of His listening. He just listens while Arjuna empties himself. Now, the real Gītā can begin!

Arjuna's Root Pattern

Please understand, when Kṛṣṇa listens to Arjuna, He is interested in Arjuna's real problem, not what Arjuna is complaining about. And He is not interested in just expressing what He knows. He allows Arjuna to speak, so that He can go to the root of the problem and address the issue. He knows that once He allows Arjuna to express his problems, Arjuna himself can find a solution to them. And as Arjuna continues to speak, he exposes the root of his problem – his root thought pattern.

Let me define root thought pattern.

The first strong cognition you receive in your life, which influences you to continue to function based on the same cognition, is a root thought pattern!

When the first attack of any strong emotion happens in you and imbalances your whole cognition of life, giving birth to your mind, the pattern you develop from that moment is the root thought pattern. It is the pattern you develop when powerlessness takes you over for the first time in your life. Your pure cognition is imbalanced and your mind is born!

Listen! The way you behave, feel and respond, all come from this root thought pattern. It is the limiting cognition that happens in you and fills you at a very young age, overpowering you. Sometimes it is fear, sometimes it is greed, sometimes it is jealousy and sometimes it is the decision to prove yourself. Sometimes, it is just plain confusion and worry!

Throughout the initial chapters of the Gītā, Arjuna is operating out of his root thought pattern – his parental and societal conditioning - struggling with all the dos and don'ts that he learnt from society. The moment he sees that the enemy he has to fight are his own extended family, he is overcome by powerlessness and refuses to fight, lamenting, '*svajanam, svajanam*!' - my people, my people! The bonds of family were rooted in his very identity, and to Arjuna, to cut these bonds was to destroy himself! This was Arjuna's dilemma.

It is here that the Gītā begins, as Kṛṣṇa finally begins to speak.

In the succeeding chapters of the Gītā, Kṛṣṇa compassionately guides Arjuna, releasing him from his root thought pattern, guiding him to completion, leading him to the ultimate knowledge, enlightenment. Arjuna is re-established in jeevanmukti, living enlightenment.

Understanding The Essence Of KṚṢṆA'S Teachings Through The Four Tattvas

The essence of Kṛṣṇa's teachings in the Gītā can be understood through four simple but powerful universal principles, the four tattvas – Integrity, Authenticity, Responsibility and Enriching.

Let me define these principles.

1. Integrity (Sampoorti) is you fulfilling the word and thought you give to yourself and to others, and experiencing a state of 'poornatva' – completion with yourself and with life.

2. Authenticity (Shraddha) is you being established in the peak of your capability, and responding to life from who you perceive yourself to be for yourself, who you project yourself to be for others, and, what others expect you to be for them.

3. Responsibility (Upaayanam) is living and responding to life from the truth that you are the source of, and therefore, you are responsible for all happenings in and around you.

4. Enriching (Aapyaayanam) is you taking responsibility with integrity and authenticity, that you are committed to continuously enriching, which is expanding yourself and life, in and around you.

Any problem or conflict you have in your life can be handled very practically, efficiently and skillfully with these four principles. I can say with my entire experience that these four principles are the essence of all spiritual scriptures! They are the essence of life.

Now, I will summarize Kṛṣṇa's teachings through these tattvas.

Integrity - The Strategy For Success

Listen!

We all know honesty. Honesty is more like ethics, morality. But with the tattva of integrity, you are taking a step deeper than honesty. With honesty, you only have to honor the words that you give to others. With integrity, you also have to honor the words that you give to yourself. Honesty is not integrity. Integrity is honesty also.

It is very unfortunate that society teaches you to honor the words that you give to others, but forgets to teach you to honor the words that you give to yourself. The words you give to yourself are as important as - or more important than - the words you give to others. Because the flow of your life - the amount of contentment that you feel in your life, the degree of fulfillment that you feel in your life and the experience of fulfillment that you feel in your life - *everything* depends on the words that you have given to you!

Please understand, the words you give to yourself form the bone structure of your life. If you commit with yourself that you will become a doctor and you don't honor that word, and you don't even bother to complete that word inside your heart, then that word hangs inside you as a broken commitment given by you! Integrity is you not carrying the hangover of the commitments you have made, either to yourself or to others.

When you break the commitments you give to you, you lose self-confidence. The more commitments you give and break, the more your self-confidence is lost. You lose confidence in *you*!

When you break the commitments you give to others, it takes away their

When you break the commitments you give to others, it takes away their confidence in you. When you break the words you have given to yourself, you lose confidence in yourself. When you don't honor the words you give, and don't even bother to complete with them, the broken commitments that hang in your heart take away your self-confidence in life!

This is what happens to Arjuna on the battlefield.

Arjuna is a kshatriya by birth, a warrior, a Pāṇḍava prince. When the Pāṇḍavas decide to wage war against their Kaurava cousins, Arjuna is perfectly aware that this includes a large part of his extended family! Yet he makes the decision to fight as per his dharma, as per his path as a kshatriya. But when he enters the battlefield, he only sees 'friends', 'teachers', 'uncles' and 'relatives' leading the army, not the evil men who snatched away his kingdom and publicly insulted his brother and wife! Caught in the clutches of his parental conditioning, Arjuna instantly becomes powerless and decides to leave the battlefield.

By trying to escape from the battle, Arjuna falls completely out of integrity with his dharma as a warrior; he has slipped from his dharma. As a kshatriya, he should have had the courage to face his decision of waging war against the Kauravas. Otherwise, he should not have taken the decision for war! But by becoming powerless and preparing to leave the battlefield, Arjuna is out of integrity with his dharma.

This is what happens when you function out of your root pattern. You fall out of integrity with the words you give to yourself and others, and the root pattern takes over your response to life! The only way to come out of this is through completion.

Through His dialogues with Arjuna on sankhya YogaḤ and karma YogaḤ, the nature of life and the purpose of action, Kṛṣṇa helps Arjuna find the right understanding to complete with the limiting cognition created by his root thought pattern. Kṛṣṇa teaches Arjuna two key concepts – nithyam (the nature of the Eternal) and na tvam socitumarhasi (the pointlessness of grieving). By revealing to Arjuna the truth about his true eternal self, Kṛṣṇa helps him with the right understanding to go beyond all the arguments of his logic and complete with his root pattern.

Now, Arjuna is ready for the next lesson – Authenticity.

Discover Your Peak Capacity Through Authenticity

I am going to share an important concept here.

Listen!

You don't have just a single identity, as you imagine. You have four identities!

Please understand, what you consider as you has four dimensions -

1. *Mamakara* – what you believe as you
2. *Ahaṅkāra* – what you project to others as you
3. *Anyākāra* – what others believe as you
4. *Sva-anyākāra* – what you believe life to be for you

All these identities put together is YOU.

Authenticity is nothing but keeping all four identities in tune, and being in the peak of each parts of you. Usually, what you think as you - your mamakara - is always less than what you are, and what you project as yourself to others – your ahaṅkāra – is always more than what you are. Foryourself to others – your ahaṅkāra – is always more than what you are.

For example, you may experience yourself as a very fearful person, but you will always project yourself as strong and powerful. Rarely do people have a high mamakara and project a lower ahaṅkāra to others. And many times, the anyākāra that others have about you will be completely different from both your mamakara and your ahaṅkāra!

Authenticity is not just you living at what you think as your peak, or what you project as your peak, but also at what others think as your peak. Only when you stretch yourself to others' image and expectations about you do you express extraordinary capacities and miracle powers.

Every time you raise yourself and stretch yourself to fulfill others' anyākāra, you achieve completion. You achieve fulfillment. You achieve union. Liberation from your individual identity happens to you only when you raise yourself to others' anyākāra. When you stretch yourself to others' anyākāra, liberation from ahaṅkāra and mamakara happens!

You may think, 'I am responsible for what I feel as me, and what I project as me to others. But why should I take responsibility for others' expectations about me?'

As long as you think that you are stretching just because of others' expectation, you will carry continuous irritation, agitation and heaviness. Please understand this important truth. It is YOU who is sitting in the inner consciousness of those who have expectations about you, and making them expect these things from you! Some of your words and body language are responsible for them having that expectation from you. So whether you know it or not, accept it or not, you are responsible for others' anyākāra also.

Listen: when you are not ready to listen to your own heart and expand, the Divine helps you by creating the same expectation in others, so that you can expand! It is some part of you which is suppressed by you, which wants to realize itself, that goes and sits in another's heart and becomes their expectation about you, so that the suppressed part is realized!

At the root of mamakara is your jeeva – your soul, in which all of us are one. If you suppress it in one body, it simply comes out in another body. When you are suppressing your expectations about you in your own body, when you are suppressing your own mamakara for you, it simply comes out as anyākāra in another's body. Nobody else is forcing you. It is your own expectation about you, giving you one more chance! Now, it is no more somebody else's anyākāra. You are simply expanding to fulfil your own mamakara and ahaṅkāra.

Others' expectation about you is nothing but a reminder, another chance that the Divine gives you, that Bhagavan gives you, to realize yourself. When you realize that this is also your own expectation about you, you will have fulfillment!

The Bhagavad Gītā is a manifestation of Arjuna's suppressed longing to realize his own divine self.

In the early chapters, Kṛṣṇa shares His anyākāra for Arjuna. He urges Arjuna to realize his eternal blissful self. He gives him an intellectual understanding of this truth. Through the chapters of JñānakarmaSanyāsa YogaḤ and Sanyāsa YogaḤ, Kṛṣṇa guides Arjuna on the ways to achieve this. Kṛṣṇa then deepens Arjuna's understanding by revealing to him the deeper truths of death, renunciation and Sanyāsa.

Once this understanding has settled in Arjuna, Krishna leads him to the next tattva, Responsibility.

Responsibility – Waking Up To Your Highest Possibility

Krishna's teachings in the next chapter, Dhyāna YogaḤ, can be summarized in these words – 'Look in' and 'Take responsibility to raise yourself'.

Here, Krishna teaches Arjuna the techniques to go beyond the mind and senses and become liberated. He guides Arjuna to rise to the level of 'Eshwaratva' – leadership consciousness - and become like Himself.

That is why Krishna says,

uddharedātmanātmānam natmānam avasādayet |
ātmaiva hyātmano bandhurātmaiva ripurātmanaḥ ||

Translation: You are your own friend; you are your own enemy. Evolve yourself through the Self and do not degrade yourself.

By this, Krishna means - if you know the technique of how to raise yourself by yourself, you are the friend of your Self. If you let yourself down, you are the enemy of your Self!

Listen: Responsibility means thinking, feeling, acting and cognizing life from the truth that YOU are the source of everything; therefore, you are responsible for all happenings inside you and around you.

I know the big question you will all have now! You must be thinking, 'How can I be responsible for everything happening around me? I can be held responsible for what is happening inside me. How can I be held responsible for what is happening outside me? For example, if an accident happens in my life, how can I be responsible?'

Everybody asks this question.

Let me answer you.

- A person who does not feel responsible even for his own actions is an animal. He lives at a very low level of consciousness!

- A person who feels responsible for his own actions is a human being. He lives at the middle level of consciousness.

- A person who takes responsibility even for others' actions is divine. He lives in leadership consciousness, Eshvaratva.

Please understand, only when you feel that you are responsible for everything happening in and around you, you will start looking into the truth. You will start seeing the possibility for a solution. Only when you take responsibility will you even find the solution!

Listen. When you take responsibility, the higher energies express through you. Even if you take one step towards responsibility, the cosmos takes a thousand steps towards you, taking responsibility for you. When you are in the space of responsibility, both your inner space and your outer space support you. The whole universe supports you, because the universe experiences its fulfillment through the cognition of those who feel responsible.

Take responsibility in every situation. When you don't feel responsible, you are a drop in the ocean. When you feel responsible, you are the ocean in a drop! When you take responsibility, Eshwaratva – leadership consciousness - starts happening in you.

With responsibility, life happens to you. When you take responsibility for whatever is seen and experienced by you, that which is unseen and un-experienced by you takes responsibility for you! If you take responsibility for the known part of God and the world, the unknown part of God and the world takes responsibility for you. When God takes responsibility for you, you are God! You are an incarnation!

Krishna guides Arjuna to realize Krishna Consciousness through the tattva of responsibility. Krishna's teaching of responsibility culminates in ViŚvarūpa darŚana, where He blesses and enriches Arjuna with a glimpse of His Cosmic dimension - a foretaste of Arjuna's own enlightenment.

Enriching With Enlightenment

We now come to the fourth tattva – enriching. Let me define enriching once more.

Enriching is you taking responsibility with integrity and authenticity, that you are continuously committed to enriching, which is expanding yourself and Life, in and around you.

Enriching means infusing all these three tattvas continuously, in your lifeand others' lives!

You may ask, 'I can understand why I should enrich myself. But why should I enrich others?'

Listen. *Life happens to you with others!*

Please understand, every relationship you experience is just one dimension of you. It is your son who makes you a father, it is your wife who makes you a husband, it is your followers who make you a leader. Each significant relationship in your life is one dimension of you. And unless you fulfill all your dimensions, how can you be fulfilled?

Again and again, the ego forgets, the ahaṅkāra forgets, that all its joy comes only when it stretches itself to others' anyākāra, not when it fights with others' ahaṅkāra! You very conveniently forget this important fact, and take life happening to you with others for granted. You think, 'My brother has to behave like a brother, my father has to behave like a father, my teacher has to behave like a teacher,' without taking the responsibility or understanding that you should also fulfill your role! Why should the teacher to enrich the student, if the student does not take the responsibility of enriching the teacher?

The Bhagavad Gītā beautifully says – 'If you don't do yajña and give back to the Divine for what you receive, you are a thief!' It means that anything you receive from the Cosmos without enriching in return, is stolen!

Please understand, enriching means taking responsibility for everyone. I tell you, when you take responsibility for others, extraordinary powers start flowing through you! When you start enriching others, the whole Cosmos starts expressing through you. Whenever you enrich others, the energy that flows through you is cosmic energy. If you want to taste and experience cosmic energy, just start enriching others! The excitement you feel, the freshness you feel, the readiness happening in you, the joy happening in you and the inspiration happening in you is all cosmic energy, pure cosmic energy.

Just see Bhagavan, Sri Krishna - He is the ultimate embodiment of enriching. His very presence is enriching. Through the entire Gītā, he takes responsibility for Arjuna's inauthenticity, for Arjuna's confusion, without giving up on him. The entire Gītā itself is a manifestation of His enriching expression. Bhagavad Gītā is Lord Krishna's gift to the world, enriching generations with its timeless truths. Lord Krishna blesses Arjuna and humanity with the ultimate tools to look inward and explode in Divine Consciousness.

Again and again, Krishna beautifully says - 'To know your Self is to know God.'

What Krishna says is true for everyone. Whether you accept it or not, any idea that you have about yourself, other than the understanding that you are God, is low self-esteem! What you are lacking is just the awareness of the truth. Once you realize the truth that you are God, there is no difference between you and Krishna. You are enlightened.

Krishna is so compassionate that He expresses the whole Bhagavad Gītā just to prove this. That is what Krishna came to prove. He has no need to prove that He is God. His mission is to prove that YOU are God! His mission is to enlighten Arjuna, and through Arjuna, the rest of humanity.

Krishna's expression is the ultimate enriching, because he takes responsibility even for your enlightenment!

That is why He concludes the Bhagavad Gītā with the importance of completing with one's toot patterns and joyfully surrendering to Life. He simply says, 'Drop everything and surrender to Me.' the enlightened maser is nothing but concentrated Life!

When you drop your conflicts and surrender to His wisdom, He liberates you. This is the ultimate enriching!

Tattvas – Natural Flow Of Life

Please understand, these four tattvas are the very nectar pot of spirituality. They exist in our very DNA. They are the natural flow of life and they can solve ANY problem.

When you live these tattvas, you will find that

- With Integrity, the innate intelligence to expand is straightened and the space of positivity is awakened in you.
- With Authenticity, life continuously oozes in you. You experience the space of possibility.
- With Responsibility, you awaken to your true nature. Eshwaratva - leadership consciousness - blossoms in you.

- With Enriching, you establish your Existence into everything, and ultimately experience yourself as Brāhmaṇyam Bahuputrataam - the favorite inheritor of the Cosmos!

These four universal principles will continuously inspire, encourage and make you experience your ultimate possibility. When you live these tattvas, you will constantly expand and fulfill the very purpose for which the Bhagavad Gītā was delivered!

BHAGAVADGĪTĀ

Śāstras, Stotras, Sūtras

ARJUNAVIṢĀDA YOGAḤ

CHAPTER 1

Life will always be a mix of the good and the bad, the Divine and the evil. Choosing one over the other does not help. We need to go beyond both!

Beyond Scriptures

There are millions of scriptures and millions of books on planet earth. From time immemorial, human beings have created scriptures and still continue to create spiritual books. But Bhagavad Gītā is incomparable. Unlike any other, this book has penetrated human consciousness so deeply. Bhagavad Gītā is the unabridged dictionary and encyclopedia of spirituality. Spiritual literature can be classified into three categories. First we have *śāstras*: *śāstras* give us clarity about the goal of human life. They give intellectual understanding about the ultimate truth of man and God.

Śāstras logically and intellectually answer all major questions. Through them, we can be logically convinced to follow the ultimate path. There are many examples. The Ten Commandments, the śruti and smṛti of Hindu religion, the *Vedās, Upaniṣads,* Manusmṛti, epics such as Rāmāyaṇa, the Bible, Koran, Dhammapada of Buddha, Zend Avesta of Zoroaster, and the Jewish Kabbalah are śāstras. The second category of literature is *stotras.* It is the expression of someone who has realized the ultimate truth. The third type of literature, called *sūtras,* gives us techniques to realize the state of uniting with the Divine. *śāstras* give us intellectual understanding, *stotras* give emotional feeling, and *sūtras* give the being-level experience.

Śāstras are like signboards that explain the basics of life. People who are intellectually oriented need *śāstras,* intellectual scriptures. These people do not do anything unless they are intellectually convinced. We cannot say that because of this attitude they should not seek spirituality. Then we would be refusing to give spirituality to almost ninety percent of humanity. We should create a system through which we can reach every individual.

Our vedic seers created the *śāstras*. They logically taught us the path and the goal, and why we are asked to do all these things, why we need spirituality. All these major questions are answered logically and intellectually in *śāstras. Śāstras* completely take away our doubts. One thing we should understand about intellectual clarity is that unless we have complete intellectual clarity, our belief will be a pseudo belief; anyone can shake our faith. Our faith is almost like a building without a foundation. It will collapse anytime. The same will happen to us if we don't have the base of *śāstras.*

A person asked the great master Vivekānanda , 'Master, what is the importance of Veda and why should we study the scriptures?' Vivekānanda said, 'If you study the scriptures, all your faith and sincerity will become so strong that nobody will be able to shake you.' Otherwise, any fool can tell us that what we are doing is superstitious and we will start having doubts about ourselves. We may think we believe in something; but our faith or belief is not deep enough. Unless we have the deep foundation of *śāstras,* we will not be able to believe in anything.

I see all types of people who say they believe in what they think. One man said, 'Oh Master, I love the whole world.' Again and again, I tell people that to love the world is easy, but to love your wife is very difficult! We can always say Vāsudaiva Kuṭumbakaṁ - the world is my family. The problem is that we are not in tune with our own family. We think we love, but we don't really love. This is because we don't have the intellectual conviction. If we have only faith without intellectual clarity, our faith can be shaken by anybody. *Śāstras* give a base so that all our convictions, all our faith, can enter into our being and start working.

Devotion, a touchstone

Bhakti, devotion, is an alchemy process. It is as if a touchstone has touched us. Rāmakṛṣṇa says beautifully, 'If a touchstone touches any metal it becomes gold; just a touch of the stone is enough for any metal to be converted into gold.'

Devotion is a touchstone. The moment devotion touches us, we become divine. The problem is that we never allow devotion to penetrate our being. We may think we want the Divine, and as long as it is superficial, as long as it is under our control, things go well. The moment the devotion enters our being, and starts the process, we say, 'No, no. I think that is too much for me!' We stop at a certain point.

A small story:

A guy was an atheist. One day he fell from a cliff and was hanging onto a small branch. Slowly, the branch started giving way. The man started shouting, 'Oh God! I never believed in you, but now I do. Please save me!'

A booming voice from heaven said, 'Oh, my Son. Don't worry. Just let go of the branch and I will save you.'

Immediately the man responded, 'Is there anybody else out there who can save me?'

Our faith is just a show. God is only one of the many choices for us. If we don't have any other commitment, any other party on a particular day, we go to the temple. Until we have an intellectual conviction about life, God is just one more shop for us like Walmart and K Mart!

A small story:

There was a grandmother in a village. She went to the city to visit her five-year-old grandson who lived with his parents.

At bed time, she went to her grandson's room to wish him good night. The boy was praying.

She asked him, 'Do you say your prayers every night?' He replied, 'Yes.' She asked, 'And what about in the morning?' The boy replied, 'No. I am not scared in the daytime.'

This is our relationship with God. We remember God only when we need something. When things go well according to our chosen route, then

God is great, else throw away the God. If they pass the exams, they break coconuts in front of Ganesha temples, but if they fail, they break the Ganesha idol itself!

Our faith is pseudo if it is not life transforming. We do not allow devotion to work on us. A beautiful verse in the scriptures of Ved¢nta says: To clear your intellect, you must break your intellect. You must open your intellect and have a clear intellectual understanding about life, about spirituality, about everything. *Śāstras* give us that intellectual clarity, that intellectual understanding.

All the great devotional people like Caitanya, Rāmānuja and Mādhava had a strong intellectual base. Caitanya Mahaprabhu was a great Nyayaika philosopher. It is only when you reach the peak of logic, can you fall into the valley of love. All great masters who reached the peak of intellect had a strong śāstras base.

Next are the *stotras*. Stotra means expressing our love or devotion to our master or God. Many people ask, '*Swamiji*, why does Hinduism have idol worship?' Hinduism does not have idol worship. We worship through the idol; we do not worship the idol itself. When we stand in front of the idol, do we say, 'Oh stone! Give me a boon.'

No! We say, 'Oh God, please save me.' We worship through the idol. In Vaishnavism, the devotional stream of Hinduism, there is a beautiful word *arcāvatāra. Arcāvatāra* means incarnation of God. Incarnation means the Divine descending on planet earth. These idols are the incarnations of God. We worship through the idol.

When we stand in front of the idol and pour our heart out, this expression is *stotras.* All the songs written by great devotees like the Alvars, Nayanmars, Mīrā and Caitanya - are *stotras.*

People ask me, '*Swamiji,* sometimes I don't feel like chanting these *stotras.* Should I do it mechanically even if I don't like doing it?'

I say, 'Do it. You may feel it is a mechanical exercise at first. However, it will become your being once you start enjoying and experiencing what you express. It will become your feeling.' When you express your heart, it becomes stotra.

Next is *sūtras. Sūtras* give us the techniques to reach enlightenment. *Śāstras* are from the intellectual level. *Stotras* are from the emotional level. *Sūtras* are from the being level.

There are three kinds of human beings: head oriented, heart oriented and being oriented. To fulfill everyone, our enlightened sages have created three kinds of literature: śāstras, *stotras* and *sūtras*. Bhagavad Gītā is the only book that is a combination of śāstras, *stotras* and *sūtras* and something more! In Bhagavad Gītā, all three are combined, with something more!

Gītā is *śāstras*; it gives a clear intellectual understanding about life, soul, as well as the do's and don'ts. Just explaining dos and don'ts will not help. Giving the intellectual reason for it is necessary. Very few books give reasons why we should or should not do something. Gītā is the only book I know that gives a strong intellectual clarity and understanding about what we should do.

Within the vedic literature, our masters have chosen three books called 'prasthānatraya' that are the ultimate authorities in spirituality. They are the Brahma Sūtra, *Upaniṣads* and Bhagavad GĪtā.

Veda Vyāsa, an enlightened master, wrote the Brahma Sūtra. Many enlightened masters taught *Upaniṣad.* However, Gītā is directly from God, from a *pūrṇāvatār* - a perfect incarnation, Kṛṣṇa.

Kṛṣṇa – The *pūrṇāvatār*

Why is Kṛṣṇa considered the only perfect incarnation? Why can't he be just one more incarnation? First understand why incarnations come to planet earth.

> Rāmakṛṣṇa recounts beautifully: There was a beautiful paradise with many trees and varieties of flowers and fruit. Three friends were walking near this paradise. It had a big wall around it. One of

them climbed the wall and peeped inside.

He cried out, 'Oh my God! Such a beautiful place!' He jumped into the garden and started enjoying the fruit. The second man climbed the wall and saw the garden. He turned and said to the third man who was below, 'Dear friend, there is a beautiful paradise below. Come, I am going in.' Saying this, he jumped over and started enjoying the fruit. The third man climbed the wall and saw the paradise. He saw his two friends and understood the level of joy and bliss that they were enjoying. Then he said to himself, 'Let me go down and tell all the people about this beautiful paradise. I will bring them all to enjoy this garden.'

An incarnation is someone who comes down to tell others about the blissful place that he experienced. The man who descends from the Divine to express the bliss of that divinity is an incarnation. The person who returns to planet earth to tell you about divinity and to make you realize what he has experienced, is an incarnation. A scientist is one who creates a formula to understand things of the outer world. For example, Newton saw the apple falling from the tree. Suddenly some understanding came to him, 'Why is this falling? Why shouldn't it go up?' Newton glimpsed the truth at that moment. He analyzed and created the theory of gravity, a formula so that everybody could understand what happens when an object falls.

In the same way, an enlightened spiritual master is one who creates a formula to reproduce his inner world experiences. Meditation technique is the formula. An incarnation is one who can directly give the experience without even using the formula! He has descended to teach divinity to the world. Why is Kṛṣṇa a perfect incarnation? He has all the qualities needed to push human beings to divinity. He is called jagat guru – the guru who awakens. He is the teacher, the master of the whole universe.

The invocation verse of Bhagavad Gītā says:

I salute you, Lord Kṛṣṇa, teacher of the world,
son of Vāsudeva and
supreme bliss of Devakī, destroyer of Kamsa and Cāṇūra.

The verse says that Kṛṣṇa is the jagat guru. Jagat guru is the one who can help the whole world, all types of human beings at all levels, to reach the ultimate.

There are intellectual, emotional and being–level people. Incarnations like Śaṇkara, Buddha appeal only to the intellectual people. It is difficult for emotional people to relate with them. We can't imagine Buddha singing and dancing with a flute! Or Śaṇkara doing *rās-līla*! Emotional people relate to Mīrā and Caitanya Mahāprabhu; they are always singing, dancing and celebrating. An intellectual man can never understand Mīrā or Caitanya Mahāprabhu. He can see them dancing, but he cannot see for whom they are dancing.

People who are at the being level straightaway want the experience; they cannot relate to the intellectual or emotional incarnations. They are neither ready to analyze nor ready to believe. A person ready to analyze goes to *śāstras.* A person ready to believe is drawn to *stotras,* but a person who wants a straight experience wants the technology, the applied science. *Śāstras* are like the main theory, the basic science. *Stotras* are like the marketing department, publicity. *Sūtras* are applied science. They give straight answers. You need to understand a bit about this marketing department.

A small story:

One man died and reached Yamadharma's court for judgment. Yama is the God of death and justice. Yama said, 'You have committed some sins and you also have some merit. You are allowed to be in heaven and in hell. You have a choice. You can see both the places and choose what you want.'

The man agreed. He went to hell first. The people were so beautiful, dancing and singing. Computers and internet were available. Everything was so new, air-conditioned, and people were serving so many types of food. He wondered, 'What happened to hell?'

People in hell said, 'All the technical experts are here. So we updated the whole system. Now, everything is new.' Then the man said, 'Alright, let me go to see heaven.'

In heaven, he saw the same old saints with long beards, sitting on clouds and singing! Nothing new! He went to Yama and said, 'I think I will go to hell.'

Yama said, 'Please be certain. You cannot change your mind.'

The man said, 'I am sure. I will go to hell. It's so cool!'

As soon as he decided, a door suddenly opened and he fell into hell. He was shocked! There was the conventional hell - people being tortured by devils. He asked, 'What is happening? When I came half an hour ago, hell was different. Now the whole thing has changed.'

They all gathered around him and said, 'No, no. That was the promotional feature from our marketing department!'

Sometimes we are caught in the marketing department. Be clear about what is the truth and what is exaggeration. Please be very clear, when we go through the pur¢nas, the epic stories, we need to understand the spirit of the *purānas.* There is a big difference between fact and truth. *Purānas*, our epics, are truths. They lead us to the truth. So while understanding *stotras* we should understand the spirit of the *stotras.*

The next level people, the being-level people, want neither *shāstras* nor *stotras*; they straightaway want the applied science, technology. For them Śiva , the creator of Vijñāna Bhairava Tantra, is the answer. All the great meditation techniques He delivered are for being-oriented people. Zen masters are ideal for these people.

Kṛṣṇa can relate to people at all three levels. If you are intellectual, He is Gītā Kṛṣṇa. If you are emotional, you have Rādhā Kṛṣṇa, the beloved of Rādhā! He can sing and dance; He can give you the ultimate emotional fulfillment. For the being-level people, He offers the truth, Dhyāna Yoga – the path of meditation techniques - in the Gītā.

Kṛṣṇa is complete fulfillment. His very life is a technique that leads you to enlightenment. His body language is a *sūtra* for enlightenment. Understand that Rāma will lead you to dharma, righteousness. If you follow what Rāma did, you will have *dharma*, but with Kṛṣṇa, you will straightaway have *mokṣa*, liberation! His very being is a technique. That is why there is a word in the Bhāgavatam (ancient Indian epic) called '*līla dhyāna*.' Just remembering the *līla*, the playful pranks of Kṛṣṇa, is meditation.

The great sages were once disturbed by the singing and dancing of the *gopikās*, the cowgirls who were Kṛṣṇa's playmates. They thought, 'We sages are sitting with closed eyes trying to meditate with long faces and nothing is happening. These *gopikās* are so happy and always singing and dancing? What is really happening in that place?' So they went to Kṛṣṇa's birthplace Vṛdāvan to see what was happening.

So they came down to see the *gopikās*, but the *gopikās* did not receive them well, nor did they care to listen to what the sages had to say. They were happy and in total contentment in their reminiscences of Kṛṣṇa.

The sages asked, 'What is this? We are great sages. We have come all the way to see you and you are not even receiving us properly.'

One *gopikās* asked, 'Sages? Who are they?'

'We meditate in our heart on His feet,' explained one of the sages.

The *gopikās* said, 'Meditate on His feet? We are playing with His entire form! Come, we will show you how we play with Him. You say you are trying to remember Him. We are trying to forget Him! He is so much in our being. We are unable to forget Him.'

'You cannot forget Me,' says Kṛṣṇa

Many people ask, '*Swamiji*, should we remember you? Should we take you as our master?'

I tell them, 'Never make that mistake. If I am your master, you will not be able to forget me! That is the real scale to know if I am your master or not.' Only when you can't forget me, devotion has happened in you.

Kṛṣṇa appeals to the being level people who want an experience straightaway. Just by His will, He can give them that experience. He can give the experience of enlightenment to Arjuna just by showing him His cosmic form, *Viśvarūpa darśan*! Kṛṣṇa shows that He is in everybody and that everybody is in Him. Whether we are intellectually oriented, emotionally oriented or being level oriented, we can find our fulfillment in Kṛṣṇa. When the intellect ripens, it becomes intelligence; when emotion ripens, it becomes devotion; when our being ripens, we become enlightened. All these three modes of enlightenment find their peak in Kṛṣṇa. He can fulfill every being. Hence, He is called *jagat guru*, master of the whole universe.

Kṛṣṇa appeals to all kinds of people - the intellectual, the emotional, and the being-level people. He has keys to open all locks. He has created methods to give the spiritual experience to the whole of humanity. He has created the technology even for future generations. He is *nityānanda* – eternal bliss. Gītā is the ultimate scripture - *śāstra, stotra, and sūtra*.

When Kṛṣṇa says, 'Weapons do not cleave, nor fire burn the *Ātman*, water does not wet it and wind does not dry it,' - when He talks about the basic truths of life and spirituality, it is *śāstra*. He is giving intellectual knowledge.

When Arjuna says, 'Oh Lord, I bow down to you from the front, from behind, from all sides. You are infinitely mighty, pervading everything, you are the Ultimate,' Arjuna is expressing the stotra. He is expressing his devotion.

When Kṛṣṇa says, 'Whatever your thought is when you leave this body, absorbed in that thought, that alone you attain, Arjuna!' Here Kṛṣṇa provides Arjuna the technique, the most powerful *sūtra* that helps anyone to attain what he wants.

Bhagavad Gītā is the only scripture that combines the wisdom of *śāstras*, the depth of feeling of *stotras* and the practical reality of *sūtras*. It is a means to enlightenment for all, delivered by the master of masters.

Years ago, a man called Arthur Koestler wrote an article about Communism titled 'Yogi and the Commissar.' Arjuna is both the yogi and the commissar. As a yogi, he is deeply spiritual, centered within himself, aware of his moral and ethical obligations. As the commissar, Arjuna is the warrior, ready to avenge and impose control. He is the typical kṣatriya prince.

Only with enlightenment is it possible to continuously and consistently proceed with both these personalities without faltering. Arjuna falters as he faces his enemies on the battlefield of the great Mahābhārata War. His dilemma unfolds. He is now able to be neither a yogi nor a commissar. He sees his enemies and identifies himself with them. In front of him are his mentors, family, and friends. They are his extension, his lineage and his identity. He can no longer pretend that he is the ultimate warrior, the commissar, who can dispassionately dispatch them to death.

Arjuna's dilemma is the dilemma of humanity. It is an internal conflict between what we perceive as our value systems and beliefs, and what we feel we can actually do. Our value systems and beliefs are the saṁskāras that drive our decisions. The problem is these *saṁskāras* lie deep in our unconscious zone. We are not even aware of them.

Arjuna understood his *kṣatriya* code of conduct very well. This code demanded that he could not turn down a righteous challenge to fight and gamble. However, his deep-rooted attachment to his clan and lineage proved stronger than what he considered his duties to be. Those feelings were far stronger than his moral code of conduct.

Arjuna's *saṁskāras* were primal. They related to survival issues. By killing his clan members, he was in effect destroying a part of himself. No code of conduct was worth that destruction. That was his dilemma.

Each of us is caught in such a dilemma at one time or another. We are taught to follow certain societal rules and regulations. As long as our basic desires are in tune with these societal and religious rules and regulations, we have no problems, no dilemma. However, our dilemmas start when what we seek and the path we need to follow to achieve them violate these rules and regulations. Everyone, without exception, has inbuilt guilt for violating the commandments of religion and society. We fear that some unseen forces will punish us for these violations. Desire versus guilt is our dilemma, always.

In almost all cases, if the desires are strong enough, desires win. Rules and regulations can wait, we say. Let the worst come. We can always work out some means of appeasing these godly forces. We think, 'What are temples and priests for?' The truth is that society and religion encourage us to think this way. They know that no one can be controlled one hundred percent. 'Let us control them through fear and greed. If they were good all the time, it would be difficult to control them. We shall be out of business. They will deal directly with the unseen forces and not need us. So let us install rules and regulations that cannot be observed by most of them. People will violate them and stumble. Then we can control them through the fear of God.'

Such is the genesis of religious guidelines and societal regulations. Some religions are based only on such guidelines without any intelligent and acceptable reasoning to support the regulations. It is almost as though they are established so that we break them and feel guilty. Once we feel guilty, we are caught. In the spiritual sense, there is no such thing as sin. As the Tao religion says, good is mixed with bad; there can be no light without darkness, nor good without evil. When you become truly aware, you realize that there are no sins.

Whatever happens to us happens as a result of natural laws. The realized ones flow with that realization. When one has compassion for every living being, one can do no harm to another. There can be no sin. And therefore, there is no guilt either.

Arjuna's progress on this path of self-discovery is the path of Bhagavad Gītā. That can also be our path if we internalize the message of the Gītā. When there is no variation between what we wish to do and what we believe in, we act in total fulfillment and awareness. We have no dilemma. We are in fulfillment.

All of us are born with pre-existing desires. This is called *prārabdha karma.* They carry their own energy for fulfillment in that lifetime. We come down to planet earth with enough energy and resources to work out our *prārabdha karma.* There are three types of *karma: sañcita, prārabdha and āgāmya. Sañcita karma* is our complete bank of unfulfilled *karma*s, like our safe deposit or the files archived in our office vault. *Prārabdha karma* are those *karma*s that we have brought into this life, like files in filing cabinets that we access and work on regularly. *Āgāmya karma* is like the new files that we keep creating on our table – new *karma* that we create in every life. We must exhaust all three types of *karma*s to experience enlightenment. *Sañcita karma* is all that we have accumulated over many births.

When we are born, we bring enough energy to exhaust this *prārabdha karma.* In the time between death and the next birth, the body-mind system lapses into unconsciousness, into coma, as the energy leaves matter (the body). When the energy enters another body-mind, the memory of the *prārabdha karma* we have chosen for this birth is erased. Therefore, when we are reborn in another body, we no longer remember why we were born or with what purpose we have chosen this birth!

This is the root cause of our dilemma.

Incarnations and enlightened beings choose a conscious birth with full awareness of their reason for birth. Arjuna is not at that stage, nor are most of us. Fortunately, it is possible to become aware of our *prārabdha karma.* We can then work towards its fulfillment during the life without accumulating more *karma (āgāmya karma)* in this lifetime. By exhausting the *prārabdha* that we brought with us and by not accumulating more *āgāmya*, we reduce our *sañcita karma.*

These *karmas* or unfulfilled desires are also referred to as *saṁskāras*, the engraved memories stored in our unconscious zone that stir up our desires. *Vāsanas* or our mental setup are the mental patterns we carry over from previous births into the current birth. These three words can be used interchangeably for all practical purposes, although they do have separate, deeper meanings.

By understanding the nature and types of *saṁskāras*, *vāsanas* and *karmas* that we carry over into this birth, we can work towards their fulfillment. Then, our stock of *saṁskāras* diminishes.

The Ananda Spurana and Nithyananda Spurana Programs, the Life Bliss Level 1 and Level 2 courses, address these karmas. In both workshops, participants learn about their *saṁskāras*, what motivates their behavior and how to dissolve these *karmas*. In a sense, we begin to understand our opening balance of desires in this life, the *karma* we accumulate during this lifetime and how to work on and release them while alive.

These teachings are not meant for Arjuna alone. They are meant for all of us so that we dissolve our *saṁskāras*, resolve our dilemmas, and experience the ultimate truth.

Planet Earth Is A Battlefield

1.1 *Dhṛtarāṣṭra said:*
Sañjaya,
What are my sons and the sons of Pāṇḍu up to
On this holy land of Kurukṣetra, *eager and raring to fight?*

1.2 *Sañjaya said:*
Sire,
Seeing the Pāṇḍavā army in full formation,
Duryodhana approaches his teacher, saying:

1.3 *My teacher,*
Look at the great army of the sons of Pāṇḍu,
Expertly arranged by your intelligent disciple, the son of Drupada,

1.4, 1.5, 1.6 *Many are the heroes and mighty archers equal to Bhīma and Arjuna in war;*
Yuyudhāna, Virāṭa, and the great warrior Drupada, Dṛṣṭaketu,
Cekitāna, and the heroic king of Kāśī,
Also Purujit, Kuntibhoja, and the great man Śaibya; the valiant Yudāmanyu,
The formidable Uttamauja, the son of Subhadrā, and the sons of Draupadī , all great warriors.

1.7 *Best of the* Brāhmaṇas, *let me tell you about the powerful leaders who command my army, so that you know.*

It is significant that a blind man gave the opening statement of this great scripture. Not only had he lost the power of sight, but also the power of insight, the wisdom to distinguish between right and wrong.

'What are they doing?' he asked Sañjaya plaintively, 'These sons of mine, the hundred Kaurava princes, and those five sons of Pāṇḍu, the Pāṇḍavā princes?'

Dhṛtarāṣṭra's attachment to his sons, especially the crown prince Duryodhana, had blinded his powers of reasoning. Whatever his son did received his endorsement. From early adolescence, Duryodhana had been plotting to kill his Pāṇḍavā cousins. Although Dhṛtarāṣṭra pretended ignorance of his son's evil deeds, he was aware of what his son was up to.

Even when Duryodhana and his brother Duśśāsana went to the extreme extent of disgracing Draupadī , the wife of the Pāṇḍavā princes, by trying to disrobe her in the public court, Dhṛtarāṣṭra seemed powerless to act. When Duryodhana finally refused to give the Pāṇḍavās even a patch of land, still Dhṛtarāṣṭra kept quiet, thus ensuring that blood would be shed.

The sad part of the tale was that Dhṛtarāṣṭra was aware that he was following the path of evil and that it would result in the destruction of his clan. Yet he seemed powerless to act otherwise. Dhṛtarāṣṭra's tale is common to humankind. Often, we follow wrong paths even though we know it is wrong, almost as if under a hypnotic spell. We know that the result may not be in our best interests in the long run, but we can't stop ourselves. Gītā, therefore, begins from this premise, from where we find ourselves in our lives. It is not merely the fight between good and evil. It is about our inner conflict of being unable to do the right thing. It is about the lack of awareness, clarity and courage to follow the path of righteousness. Kṛṣṇa, the Superconscious, constantly looms over our being, yet we ignore this divine call within us, caught in the illusion that we will be eternally happy with what we choose to do instead.

Dhṛtarāṣṭra refers to the kurukṣetra, the site of this war, as a holy land, *dharmakṣetra*. People ask, 'How can a battlefield be called a holy land?'

You see, throughout the history of humanity many wars were fought. Almost all were created out of the belief that one party was morally right and the other wrong. In that sense, each battle was fought to restore righteousness, and so every battlefield was a holy site according to someone's belief. In the case of Dhṛtarāṣṭra, he had an additional reason. He implicitly recognized the divinity of Kṛṣṇa, whose mere presence on this battlefield conferred upon it the mantle of righteousness. Even in his confused state of thinking, there was enough clarity in Dhṛtarāṣṭra's mind to acknowledge the supremacy of Kṛṣṇa. This revealed itself in his choice of words. It was as if Dhṛtarāṣṭra knew that the fate of his Kaurava clan was sealed because they were opposing Lord Kṛṣṇa.

If Kṛṣṇa, the epitome of righteousness, was with the Pāṇḍavās, how could they lose? The tragic fate of Dhṛtarāṣṭra was that he knew that the destruction of his clan was inevitable, and yet he was powerless to do anything about it.

Sañjaya was Dhṛtarāṣṭra's minister and charioteer. By the grace of sage Vyāsa, Sañjaya was given the power to see whatever was going on in the battlefield so that he could faithfully convey the tragic happenings to King Dhṛtarāṣṭra and Queen Gāndhāri. His third eye, the centre of intuition, was opened, and not only could he see what was happening at a faraway location, but he had the power of intuition to know what would unfold as well.

We are all blind in one sense or another and Dhṛtarāṣṭra represents the majority of mankind in this aspect. Blindness in this case is the inability to discriminate between right and wrong along with the lack of desire to distinguish between them.

We can all be like Sañjaya, with our third eye open instead of being blind like Dhṛtarāṣṭra. This is one of the messages of Gītā. Becoming aware of our inner conflicts is the first step in opening the third eye, the energy center located between the eyebrows.

Before the war…

Duryodhana was the crown prince and, for all practical purposes, the king as well since his father was both blind and powerless to stop him. Duryodhana saw the soldiers of the Pāṇḍavā army arrayed in front of him. There were many ways he could have responded to the sight. He could have gloated, that surely he would destroy his cousins. He could have roared out in anger and in defiance. Yet, after seeing the army, he chose to approach his teacher and mentor, Droṇa, one of the commanders of the Kaurava army, to seek his blessings.

The move was to ensure that any blame for the outcome of the war would fall on Droṇa's shoulders; it was to hold him responsible more than to seek reassurance or blessings.

This is how most people act when they go forward with a plan of action, knowing fully well that it is wrong and can lead to serious consequences. They find something or someone else to blame. It is well understood that whatever follows will be unpleasant and what triggered it is their foolish action. Being blinded by fear or greed, they continue anyway. Then they take solace in the idea that they can lay the blame on someone else, however illogical or irresponsible.

Duryodhana understood the modern management concept of delegation. Like many managers today, he delegated so that he could abdicate responsibility. He was now exhibiting his mastery in this field of management. He was aware that there was no hope to win the war. However, his greed for power and wealth blinded him to a point where he could not face reality. He wished to change reality so that he could control the outcome. He could not take responsibility for the situation as it was, since he did not know how. All he could do was turn to his mentors and tell them they were responsible for ensuring his success.

Duryodhana's message to Droṇa on the battlefield was blunt. Droṇa was a *brāhmaṇa,* a scholar. He learned his skills of archery and warfare from his father, sage Bharadwaja. Drupada, the prince of Pāñcāla, was a fellow disciple of Bharadwaja, and he had promised his childhood friend

Droṇa part of his kingdom when he came to power. When Droṇa was in serious financial trouble and approached Drupada for help, Drupada insulted him and turned him away from his court. Droṇa became the teacher of the Pāṇḍavā and Kaurava princes. At the end of their training, he demanded his fees as a teacher, his *gurudakṣinā*, as was the tradition. Instead of anything material, he asked them to capture Drupada and bring the king to him. Of his disciples, only Arjuna was ready to do this. Arjuna did as he was asked and brought Drupada as his prisoner of war to his guru Droṇa, as a gift.

Droṇa released Drupada and handed his kingdom back. Drupada was mortified at his capture and submission to Droṇa. He went into deep penance and sought a child who would kill Droṇa. Dṛṣṭadyumna was born to Drupada as a result of this penance and he became, ironically, a disciple of Droṇa along with the Pāṇḍavā and Kaurava princes. Though Droṇa was aware of the background of Dṛṣṭadyumna's birth, he still accepted him as a disciple and trained him in warfare. Dṛṣṭadyumna became the Commander-in-Chief of the Pāṇḍavā army in this great war and Droṇa was one of the opposing commanders in the Kaurava army.

Duryodhana pointedly referred to Droṇa's lack of foresight in training his potential killer, who now led the opposing army. It was as though he was warning Droṇa not to be so trusting again. Duryodhana then pointed out the other great Pāṇḍavā warriors, such as Bhīma and Arjuna, who too were students of Droṇa, as well as a number of other great warriors fighting for the Pāṇḍavās.

Duryodhana then explained about the great warriors on the Kaurava side to Droṇa. Duryodhana was no longer a disciple addressing his mentor. Duryodhana alternately berated Droṇa for having trained the warriors of the opposing army and then pacified him by listing him at the head of his own great warriors.

Duryodhana was totally confused. He started off praising the strength of the Pāṇḍavā army. This was not because he genuinely wanted to, but mainly to point out to Droṇa the mistakes Duryodhana felt Droṇa had committed.

At one level, as a *kṣatriya*, Duryodhana did not have respect for Droṇa, a *brāhmaṇa* scholar. However, knowing the skill of Droṇa as a warrior, Duryodhana had no choice but to keep him on his side; it would have been too dangerous for Duryodhana if Droṇa took sides with the Pāṇḍavā princes.

At another level, Duryodhana had no trust in Droṇa. He always felt that Droṇa was partial to the Pāṇḍavā princes and that Arjuna was his favorite. Duryodhana knew that given the choice, Droṇa would not support him and considered him to be in the wrong. He also knew that Droṇa held Kṛṣṇa in great esteem and did not believe that Duryodhana could succeed in this war.

Duryodhana was in deep inner conflict. He had no sense of guilt going to war against his brethren for the kingdom. He believed that whatever he did was right. He was not a man given to deep thinking. However, Duryodhana had no trust in many of the great warriors who had taken his side. He knew that Droṇa, Bhīṣma, and Kripa, who were also the teachers of the Pāṇḍavā princes, did not want to fight the Pāṇḍavā army. They were compelled from a moral standpoint to fight for him and not as directed by their conscience. This was the source of his conflict and uncertainty.

It was also strange that at the beginning of the war Duryodhana chose to go to Droṇa and not Bhīṣma, his great grandfather and Commander-in-Chief. It was as if Duryodhana was afraid to tell Bhīṣma what he said to Droṇa.

Droṇa was a subject of the king to whom Duryodhana could talk abrasively. Bhīṣma, on the other hand, was his great grandfather, the one who had given up his chance to be king to fulfill his own father's moral obligations and to satisfy his father's lust. There was no way that Duryodhana could have said the same words to Bhīṣma at this stage of the war.

Duryodhana was not yet feeling desperate enough about the situation to confront Bhīṣma. At a later stage in the war when it became clearer that the Kaurava army was in deep trouble, Duryodhana approached Bhīṣma and blamed him for being partial to the Pāṇḍavā princes.

Ego Needs Support

1.8 *You, Bhīṣma, Karṇa, Kṛpa, Aśvattāma, Vikarṇa and the son of Somadatta,*
All always victorious in battle.

1.9 *Many other heroes there are who are prepared to lay down their lives for my sake; all well equipped with different weapons, and well experienced in warfare.*

1.10 *Our unlimited army is protected by Grandsire Bhīṣma,*
Their limited army is protected by Bhīma.

1.11 *Now all of you, wherever you are positioned,*
Promise full protection to Bhīṣma.

1.12 *Bhīṣma, the mighty patriarch of the Kuru dynasty and grandsire,*
Then blew upon his conch loudly, roaring like a lion and Duryodhana was joyful.

Duryodhana was a coward by nature. He was especially afraid of Arjuna and Bhīma, who were physically stronger and more skilled than he. He was only afraid of being overpowered by someone whose physical power was greater than his own.

Duryodhana felt secure only when surrounded by his cronies. His strength and valor arose from the feeling of being supported by his clan and the army around him. On the positive side, Duryodhana was an extremely generous friend who gave his all for someone he trusted. This quality had attracted strong men to him like Karṇa who swore undying loyalty. Even though Karṇa knew that Arjuna was his own brother, all he could say to his mother Kuntī was that she would finally be left with five sons, implying that one of her sons, either Arjuna or Karṇa, would perish in the war. Such was the loyalty that Duryodhana evoked in his friends.

Duryodhana now rightly went on to claim that there were a number of great warriors who would willingly lay down their lives for him. They were aware that Duryodhana was an immoral person but such was their commitment to him that it did not matter. Duryodhana then began to boost his own morale by saying that the power of the Kaurava army led by Bhīṣma was immense, whereas the Pāṇḍavā army with Bhīma as one of the commanders was limited in power. Duryodhana's reference to Bhīma alongside Bhīṣma was due to the fear of the oath that Bhīma had taken - to break Duryodhana's thigh and drink his blood to avenge the insult to Draupadī. Duryodhana knew that the only factor that could prevent it would be the protection of Bhīṣma. Duryodhana then addressed the Kaurava army, exhorting them to support their Commander-in-Chief Bhīṣma. In response, Bhīṣma blew his conch like a lion, making Duryodhana joyful.

Bhīṣma was the first Kaurava Commander-in-Chief and Duryodhana wanted to make sure that the entire Kaurava army was committed to his leadership. In the past, Duryodhana had not hidden his feelings that Bhīṣma was partial to the Pāṇḍavās. Now, however, the die was cast and Bhīṣma, the greatest warrior either side had known, was leading the Kaurava army. Duryodhana wanted to take no chances that his past hatred towards Bhīṣma would affect his assembled supporters. Duryodhana knew that he could not afford to antagonize Bhīṣma. Had it not been for his strong bonds of duty, Bhīṣma would have gone with the Pāṇḍavā princes and Kṛṣṇa. Duryodhana knew this.

Bhīṣma was the grand sire and patriarch of the Pāṇḍavā and Kaurava clan. He was born to Gaṅgā as Devavrata. He was the only surviving son of eight sons whom Gaṅgā had given birth to. When his father King Śāntanu wanted to marry Satyavatī, the daughter of a fisherman, Devavrata swore never to marry so that his stepmother Satyavati's children could have access to his father's throne. Satyavatī was the grandmother of both Pāṇḍu and Dhṛtarāṣṭra. Bhīṣma was highly respected for his valor and sagacity. It is one of the greatest ironies of Mahābhārata that wise men like Bhīṣma and Droṇa chose to be on Duryodhana's side, knowing fully well that whatever path Duryodhana was following was morally incorrect.

In the highest spiritual sense there is no right or wrong morally. Everything is neutral. Bhīṣma and Droṇa were highly learned in the scriptural truths. Moreover, they were fully aware that Kṛṣṇa was a divine incarnation. The very fact that Kṛṣṇa sided with the Pāṇḍavās was a clear indication to them how the war would unfold. They had no fears about their own deaths; and more importantly, they had no guilt about what they had embarked upon.

Men like Bhīṣma, Droṇa and Kṛpācārya trusted their awareness. Duryodhana was their prince and they were committed to him. They were certain that Duryodhana would perish and they would too, along with him. To these great warriors, dying on the battlefield was the duty of a kṣatriya, a warrior. What was more important to them was that they were rooted in the awareness of the present moment, carrying out their duty. Their awareness transcended the moral rights and wrongs established by society and religion. They disapproved of Duryodhana's insult of the Pāṇḍavā princes and Draupadī in the court but did not protest. They disapproved of Duryodhana's instigation of this war and yet took his side, knowing fully well that what lay ahead was destruction.

This was not foolishness or resignation. This was surrender to the inevitable, to the Divine. These great masters allowed Nature to take its own course and allowed themselves to be swept along with the tide. To relax and allow whatever happens to happen is the sure sign of an evolved spirit. Ordinary human beings have the freedom to think, choose, and act. As a result, they think they are in control of their destinies. In one sense they are; they make their decisions and act upon them. But it is their unconscious *saṁskāras*, the memories, value systems, and beliefs that drive them into and through all these decisions.

A cycle is created as the *saṁskāras* lead to certain actions and those actions in turn mould their mental set-up and reinforce these *saṁskāras*. Yet, a human being has the choice to break out of this cycle and live in freedom from his *saṁskāras*.

Go with the flow

It is our constant conflict with Nature that leads to our suffering. Most of the time our actions are driven by instinct, the unconsciousness, where the *saṁskāras* reside. It has been designed by Nature to cope with life or death issues. Unfortunately, this system gets misused for all other mundane issues as well.

If we learn to flow with Nature like the reeds in a river, we will always do the right thing. We suffer when we resist Nature. There are two ways to live life. One is to accept the world and life as it is, what in Sanskrit is termed *sṛṣṭi dṛṣṭi*. The other way is to try to make circumstances evolve according to our viewpoint, called *dṛṣṭi sṛṣṭi*. The first attitude, one of acceptance, brings happiness; the second, one of resistance, brings suffering. Resistance is an exercise doomed to encounter failure. In our lives we cannot change the attitude of our neighbor or our spouse. At best, we can transform ourselves, that's all. If we do that, it is enough!

All talk about revolutionizing the world is just useless talk. No revolution has ever succeeded in bringing about any significant, positive change. Revolutionaries who claim that they are against dictatorship become dictators themselves. That has always been history. Ironically, an enlightened master has no such freedom. He is a faithful channel of the universal energy, Parāśakti, the divine Existence. An enlightened being is in complete surrender to the Divine.

The scale that is applied to ordinary humans cannot measure the motives and actions of an enlightened being. Their actions are taken in a no-mind, thought-free state that flows constantly in the present with no expectations of what may happen in the future and no regrets about what has happened in the past. Their actions may seem immoral or at least strange when perceived through the lens of the rules and regulations of society. But they are beyond society.

Bhīṣma was of divine origin. He had the gift of living as long as he wanted and to die when he wanted. His integrity and morality were the standard for that era. Yet Bhīṣma kept quiet when Draupadī was to be insulted by being disrobed in front of the court . He did not act when Duryodhana denied the Pāṇḍavā princes even a patch of land. He chose to fight for Duryodhana. However, when Duryodhana requested that he lead the Kaurava army, Bhīṣma told him that the Pāṇḍavā princes were as dear to him as was Duryodhana. While he would wage war against their army, he could not take their lives. This was the condition under which Bhīṣma agreed to fight against the Pāṇḍavā army on Duryodhana's behalf.

Bhīṣma had repeatedly counseled Duryodhana against his evil deeds towards the Pāṇḍavā princes and Duryodhana was aware of how Bhīṣma opposed Duryodhana's acts. Yet, in this instance, Bhīṣma's compassion for Duryodhana overcame his distaste for his actions and behavior. Bhīṣma understood the desperate fears running through Duryodhana's mind and felt the need to reassure him. In response to these exaggerated claims of Duryodhana, Bhīṣma blew his conch as a sign of resounding affirmation of whatever had been said by Duryodhana. Sañjaya said that Bhīṣma's conch sounded like the roar of a lion, coming from the oldest and the bravest of all the warriors assembled on the battlefield. It was also an affirmation of Bhīṣma's own support to the Kaurava prince and the signal for the war to begin. Bhīṣma's conch was a celebratory signal, seeking victory.

The War Begins

1.13 *Conches, bugles, trumpets, drums, and horns all suddenly sounded;*
Their combined sound renting the skies.

1.14 *Seated on a magnificent chariot drawn by white horses,*
Kṛṣṇa and Arjuna sounded their divine conches.

1.15 *Kṛṣṇa blew on His conch, the Pañcajanya;*
Arjuna sounded the Devadatta and Bhīma sounded his great conch called Pauṇdra.

1.16, 17, 18 *King Yudhiṣtra, the son of Kuntī, blew his conch, the Anantavijaya; Nakula and Sahadeva blew the Sughośa and Maṇipuṣpaka.*
That great archer, the king of Kāśī, the great fighter Śikhaṇḍi, Dṛṣṭadyumna,
Virāṭa and the invincible Sātyaki, Drupada, the sons of Draupadī , and the others,
Such as the mighty-armed son of Subhadrā, all sounded their conches.

Conches, called *śankha* in Sanskrit, are the shells of mollusks that live in the sea. From time immemorial, Hindu scriptures have referred to the use of conches during ritualistic, devotional and celebratory occasions. Blowing the conch signified joy.

Each of the great warriors in the Mahābhārata War had his own, personal conch. Most of the great warriors also had their own flags that flew on their chariots, and their weapons, especially their bows, had great spiritual significance. The Divine often bestowed them upon the warrior after a long penance. It is said that even if his flag were masked by dust and distance, Arjuna's presence in any part of the battlefield would be known by the sound of his conch and the twang of his bow!

When Bhīṣma blew his conch in support of Duryodhana, the response was tumultuous on both sides. Every warrior on the battlefield took out his conch and blew his signature note. Of all the sounds that emanated at that moment, a few were heard above the rest. Kṛṣṇa sounded his Pañcajanya, which drowned all other sounds on the battlefield. It was an announcement that the Divine was already present with the Pāṇḍavā army.

Vyāsa, through Sañjaya, says that Kṛṣṇa sounded His divine conch. This is significant since Vyāsa attributes divinity only to Kṛṣṇa's conch, not to anyone else's. He refers to Kṛṣṇa as Mādhava, and later as Hṛṣīkeśā. Mādhava signifies that Kṛṣṇa is an incarnation of Viṣṇu, who is the husband of Lakṣmī, Goddess of wealth and fortune. In this context, it signifies that whoever Kṛṣṇa sides with would be invincible. Kṛṣṇa is then referred to as Hṛṣīkeśā, controller of the senses, the superconscious, who has created the māyā, the illusion that is this great war of Mahābhārata. Vyāsa implies that all that happens is a creation of Kṛṣṇa. For what purpose? The Divine truly has no purpose. The Divine IS, that's all.

Kṛṣṇa was Arjuna's charioteer. The chariot was a blessing from Agni, the fire god. His bow Gāṇḍīva was also a gift from Agni. Arjuna is referred to as Dhañanjaya, winner of wealth, in reference to his ability to generate the wealth needed by his brother Yudhiṣtra. Not to be outdone, Bhīma blew his conch Pauṇḍra, a fearsome sound that invoked dread amongst the Kaurava army. Here Bhīma is called Vrikodara, one with the stomach of a wolf. He was feared by his enemies for his strength and anger.

The other three Pāṇḍavā princes, Yudhiṣtra, Nakula and Sahadeva and then the great warriors, Drupada, Virāṭa, Sātyaki, Śikhaṇḍi, Dṛṣṭadyumna, Abhimanyu and others followed Bhīma's conch, all blowing their conches in celebration of their impending victory.

Each of these warriors had a great history. Yudhiṣtra, the eldest of the Pāṇḍavā princes, was born to his mother Kuntī through the grace of Yama, the god of justice and death, and was universally known as Dharmaraja, the king of truth, as he was always known to tell the truth. Nakula and Sahadeva were born to Mādri, the second wife of Pāṇḍu, through the grace of the Aśvini Kumāras, celestial beings.

Drupada, the king of Pāñcāla, was the father of Dṛṣṭadyumna and Draupadī , wife of the Pāṇḍavās. Dṛṣṭadyumna was born to Drupada, when he prayed to Śiva to give him a son who would match Droṇa in valor and vanquish him in battle. Virāṭa was the king in whose kingdom the five Pāṇḍavā princes and Draupadī spent a year in hiding. His daughter married Abhimanyu, Arjuna's son by Subhadrā, Kṛṣṇa's sister.

Śikhaṇḍi was born as Bhīṣma's nemesis, when Amba, a princess whom Bhīṣma captured as a bride for his stepbrother Vicitravīrya, immolated herself to be reborn to avenge her shame.

It is as if Sañjaya, the narrator of the incidents of war, repeatedly tries to impress upon the blind king Dhṛtarāṣtra the caliber of the Pāṇḍavā warriors and their glorious antecedents so that the shock of the impending disaster to the Kuru clan of Dhṛtarāṣṭra would not be so unexpected. Sañjaya specifically refers to these warriors as 'aparājita', invincible with the clear implication that they would be victorious in this war that they had embarked upon as well.

It is significant that as Commander-in-Chief, Bhīṣma's conch sound was responded to by Kṛṣṇa and not by anyone else. Kṛṣṇa's was a response to the challenge issued by Bhīṣma. It was an acceptance of the fact that whatever was thrown at the Pāṇḍavā army was being directly accepted by Him, Divinity Incarnate.

Kṛṣṇa, as the superconscious guide of the Pāṇḍavā princes, absolves them of any guilt or wrongdoing by taking upon Himself the responsibility for whatever is to happen. The rest of the Pāṇḍavā army, including Arjuna, follows His lead by blowing their conches.

Arjuna Falters

1.19 *This tumultuous sounding of the conches reverberated in the sky and the earth, and shattered the hearts of the sons of Dhṛtarāṣṭra.*

1.20 *Then, seated in his chariot, which bore the flag of Hanumān,*
Arjuna lifted his bow, fixed his arrows and looking at the sons of Dhṛtarāṣṭra spoke to Kṛṣṇa.

1.21, 1.22 *Arjuna said:*
O Infallible One, please position my chariot between the two armies and let me see the warmongers gathered here with whom I must wage this battle.

When Bhīṣma sounded his conch, it invited in return the resounding response of the conches of the Pāṇḍavā warriors. There is no mention by Sañjaya that Bhīṣma's conch or the accompanying sounds of drums and trumpets from the Kaurava army caused any concern amongst the Pāṇḍavā army. But with the roar of the conches of the Pāṇḍavā warriors, Sañjaya says that the hearts of the sons of Dhṛtarāṣṭra were shattered.

He says that the blowing of the conches created vibrations in the sky and upon the earth. The conches of the Pāṇḍavā princes and the great warriors were imbued with divine presence. The sound was filled with great spiritual power when activated by their owners. They created powerful vibrations affecting the environment. That is the uproar Sañjaya was talking about.

In the Hindu epics, one hears of references to weapons called 'astrā.' An astrā was not a physical weapon. It was a thought or a word that was given enormous power by its creator to destroy. These were *mantra*, sound wave technology that created vibrations or energy forces to destroy, the same as a nuclear device. Metaphorically speaking, these were meditative techniques to destroy the *saṁskāras* or engraved memories that resided within the individual.

The conches that the Pāṇḍavā warriors used were clearly successful in destroying the fantasies that the Kaurava princes nurtured in their minds. The purpose of sounding conches was to set the stage for the battle and to define its boundaries. The Pāṇḍavā princes and warriors had the comfort of knowing that they were doing what was right, both in their own hearts and in the eyes of God, since they had the support of Kṛṣna Himself. The Kaurava princes were afraid. All that motivated them was greed and envy. They did not have a divine purpose guiding and motivating them.

Sañjaya was able to see far beyond the superficial responses of individuals on the battlefield. He was able to fathom the subconscious and unravel the deep emotions and responses of the warriors. Whatever may have been the perceived reaction of the Kaurava army to the response from the Pāṇḍavā warriors, Sañjaya concludes that the Kaurava princes were demoralized. The armies went face-to-face. They were in military formation. The warriors on both sides were waiting for their commanders to signal the first move in the offense.

Arjuna was at the forefront of the Pāṇḍavā army. He blew his conch, Devadatta, at the same time as Kṛṣṇa. Arjuna had taken up his divine bow Gāṇḍīva, and fixed the arrow to it. However, instead of releasing the arrow, Arjuna looked at the Kaurava army in front of him, with all the Kaurava princes, his relatives and teachers. He then addressed Kṛṣṇa, his friend, mentor, divine guide and charioteer.

For the first time in this scripture, Arjuna speaks. Arjuna is not the mere hero of Mahābhārata in this Gītā scripture. He is the embodiment of all humanity. He is Narā, the human aspect of Nārāyaṇa, Lord Viṣṇu, who in turn is Kṛṣṇa. 'Infallible One,' said Arjuna to his friend and mentor, 'Please take me to a vantage point between the two armies so that I can see for myself whom I am fighting with. Who has taken up arms to fight and who are those I must be prepared to fight against. Kṛṣṇa, please show me,' he says. 'Show me whom I must vanquish.'

Arjuna already knew each one who was on that battlefield at Kurukṣetra. He had no confusion about whom he was fighting and whom he had to face. It made no sense at all for Arjuna to ask Kṛṣṇa at this last minute to show him clearly whom he was fighting against. It was as if he was hoping that at the last minute something would occur to change the course of events. If that were to happen, he knew that it could only take place through the grace of his charioteer, friend, and guide.

It is as if Arjuna was making a desperate plea to Kṛṣṇa, 'Please show me something that I do not know. Show me something that You alone know, Oh Infallible Divine. Take me there, where You will, and show me.'

Intelligence Questions

1.23 *Let me see those who have come here to fight,*
Wishing to please the evil-minded son of Dhṛtarāṣṭra.

1.24 *Sañjaya said:*
O descendant of Bhārata, being thus addressed by Arjuna,
Kṛṣṇa then drew up the fine chariot in the midst of both armies.

Arjuna is being called Guḍākeśā in this verse, the one who has transcended sleep, or the need to sleep. Sleep, here, refers to the unconscious mind. All our embedded memories and beliefs reside in our unconscious mind. Arjuna is being referred to here as one who has conquered his *saṁskāra*s, as a result of his total surrender to Kṛṣṇa.

Kṛṣṇa has been called Hṛṣīkeśā, one who controls the senses. The relationship between Kṛṣṇa and Arjuna is the highest form of interaction between the Divine and the human.

You see, for one who is caught in the sleep of unconscious living, this world of illusion appears utterly real and permanent. But the enlightened master has awakened to the level of pure consciousness and knows that this world is just another dream. When the disciple is able to completely trust the master's senses that this world is an illusion and not his own senses that give the idea that this world is real and is the source of his happiness, then the surrender is total. Kṛṣṇa's senses were controlled. He knew that what He experienced through them was not the source of His happiness and therefore He didn't run after sensual pleasures for His fulfillment.

Stages of surrender

When approaching the Divine or one's master, the ultimate step is one of complete surrender. This surrender happens in three stages. At the first level it is an intellectual surrender - the intellectual acceptance of what the master represents and what he means to you. A true seeker reaches this stage when he encounters the real master destined for him. At this stage, when the disciple meets the master, questions start dying down. It is as if answers come to one's mind even before the questions happen. Questions are a reflection of one's internal violence wishing to prove one's control over another person. We ask questions only to tell the other person that we know something. Rarely are our questions like that of an innocent child, who asks out of curiosity.

Intellectual surrender to the master replaces questions with doubts. Doubts are not violent like questions. They arise from a genuine need to know and to understand. Doubt and faith are two sides of the same coin. One cannot develop faith in one's master without having doubts about him. Despite his high level of surrender, one does see Arjuna initially in this state of questioning as well, perhaps as a lesson to us.

At the next level, one reaches the state of emotional surrender. The person feels a deep connection with the master. It is impossible to forget Him. His memory brings tears to one's eyes, tears of gratitude that are impossible to hide. Rāmakṛṣṇa says so beautifully, 'When thinking of the Divine or the master, if you have tears streaming down your cheeks, be very sure that this is your last birth.' Emotional surrender leads one close to liberation. At the final level, there is the surrender of the senses. One truly realizes Hṛṣīkeśā and gives up one's distorted sense of reality and embraces the truth of absolute reality. Arjuna is at that level of surrender and through the progression of the Gītā, we see Arjuna's transformation take place.

Arjuna calls Duryodhana evil-minded. When one's mind is filled with greed, lust, envy and fear, there is a single-minded focus on the potential material benefits of these negative and evil emotions. Duryodhana's objectives were very clear – to do away with the Pāṇḍavā princes and usurp the entire kingdom. Duryodhana was like an animal, operating out of instinct. He was not an intelligent man and did not suffer from doubts and guilt. He needed power, and whatever was the means to achieve that power he employed without any reservation.

A human being has a level of consciousness higher than that of animals. He can discriminate between right and wrong and has the free will to act based on such awareness. When a human behaves the way Duryodhana does, he is in the unconscious and unaware state. Mired totally in unawareness, the Kaurava warriors followed Duryodhana blindly. Arjuna, on the other hand, is in turmoil. As Kṛṣṇa brings the chariot to a stop between the two armies, in a metaphoric sense He brings Arjuna's mind to a steady state.

Duryodhana is operating out of his lower animal instincts. His moves are driven completely by his *saṁskāra*s. So strong is his delusion that the wise counsel of the few who told him the path he is following is a self-destructive one, falls on deaf ears. Arjuna, on the other hand, is in a twilight zone. Unlike Duryodhana, Arjuna has become aware of his *saṁskāra*s, and is working to free himself from their bondage. However, he is not in the zone of light yet.

The conflict between Arjuna and Duryodhana is the conflict that all humans face within themselves. It is a conflict between their deep unconscious desires driven by their *saṁskāra*s and the potential awareness of their consciousness. Which part wins depends on one's ability to surrender to the superconscious Divine or the master. A person born blind has no idea what sight is, what light is and what he is missing. Whatever he may think he is missing is based on what others tell him, not on any experience of his own. However, someone who has been born with sight and subsequently loses it will miss it. He would be afraid of that darkness, which a person born blind would never fear because that would have always been his experience.

Arjuna is in the state of a person who has had sight and has now lost it. He was an intelligent man but suddenly wondered whether what he was doing might be wrong and evil. So he is disturbed.

Duryodhana on the other hand has a mind that is always in darkness. He has never experienced true intelligence or awareness. Therefore, words like 'immoral' or 'unethical' would make no sense to him.

Arjuna's Dilemma

1.25 to 1.30

In the presence of Bhīṣma, Droṇa and other rulers of the world,
Hṛṣīkeśā said, Pārtha, behold all the Kurus who are assembled here.
There, Arjuna could see within the armies of both parties,
His elders, grandfathers, teachers, maternal uncles, cousins, sons, grandsons
And friends, as well as his fathers-in-law and well wishers.
When Arjuna, the son of Kuntī, saw all these friends and relatives present there,
He was overwhelmed with deep pity and said:
Kṛṣṇa, seeing my friends and relatives present before me, eager to wage war,
I feel my limbs trembling, my mouth drying, and my hair standing on end.
My bow, Gāṇḍīva, slips from my hands, and my skin burns.
I am unable to stand here any longer.
I am forgetting myself, and my mind reels.
I foresee only evil omens, O killer of the Keśī demon.

Kṛṣna parked the chariot between the two armies and said to Arjuna, 'Here are the people you wished to see.' Arjuna wanted to see those who were about to fight him and die. Kṛṣṇa, with no mercy at all, showed him that these were Arjuna's near and dear ones.

Assembled in front of Arjuna were grandfathers and great grandfathers such as Bhīṣma, his own teachers such as Droṇa and Kripa, uncles such as Śakunī, brothers and cousins as all the Kaurava princes were, friends and well wishers. At one time or another, each of them had been an object of affection and respect to Arjuna. Now, they were part of this enemy army.

As a *kṣatriya,* Arjuna was no stranger to death and violence. As long as those who faced him were his enemies, Arjuna had no difficulty in carrying out the execution. However, those in front of him now were his relatives - father, grandfathers, uncles, brothers, sons and grandsons. He could not bear to kill those whom he could relate with himself in one way or another. The bonds of family were rooted in his ego and to cut these bonds was to destroy himself. This was Arjuna's dilemma.

What follows now is a bunch of fantasies that Arjuna's mind weaves in an attempt to justify his dilemma. It is what the human mind conjures up time and again as its projection of the unconscious *saṁskāra*s, trying to justify its actions. Sañjaya says that Arjuna was overwhelmed with pity. Some translate this as compassion. True compassion is non-discriminatory. To the truly compassionate person, the whole world is an extension of his own self. Anything that hurts any object around such a person would hurt him and he too would feel the pain.

However, Arjuna's emotion was discriminatory. He felt pity only because they were his kinsmen and he identified with them. This was pity born out of *hiṁsā*, violence. True compassion arises from a state of absence of ego, where the feelings of 'I' and 'mine' have disappeared. It is a state of bliss. It happens when the individual self merges with the universal Self.

Arjuna's pity arose out of fear of losing his identity, his ego. He was mortally afraid. He claimed that his throat was parched, his hair was standing on edge and his divine bow was slipping from his sweaty hands. If one did not know Arjuna better, one would have considered him a coward. Arjuna was no coward. He was not concerned that he might be injured or that he might die. But he was afraid of breaking social and ethical laws. His values and beliefs, his *saṁskāra*s, told him that what he was doing was wrong and unacceptable. So powerful was this feeling, that he was reeling, quivering, dazed and unable to think or function.

Arjuna was frightened that he would be held responsible for the death of his kinsmen. Even if others did not blame him, he would regret his actions for the rest of his life. So great was this fear of potential guilt, that it drove Arjuna into behaving like a coward. All he could foresee was disaster and evil. At another, far deeper level, Arjuna was terrified of his own destruction. The moment one starts identifying with kinsmen, it is a material identification. It is an identification born out of possession. Possession is born of attachment, and leads to further attachment as well. There can be no feeling of possessing something unless one is attached to it.

People speak of attachment, liking and love. All these are valid only as long as a sense of possession exists. The moment the object of love turns around and displays independence and unwillingness to be possessed, the love disappears. Possession arises out of our survival need, from our *mūlādhāra cakra,* an energy center located at the base of the spine. Out of the need for possession, feelings of lust, greed and anger arise. We often feel, 'What I cannot have, let no one have.' It is also the deep-rooted desire for possessions, the feeling of 'mine', that gives rise to our identity 'I.' 'Mine' leads to 'I', not 'I' to 'mine.' This is why we cannot eliminate our identity until we transcend our attachment to or identity with all our desires and possessions. We need to dissolve the identification with the 'mine' first. Only then the 'I' disappears.

Arjuna is in this mood and frame of mind. It strikes him at the moment of waging war that what he is about to destroy are his own kinsmen, a part of his own identity. If he were to destroy them he would be destroying a part of his own self. It would be akin to committing suicide.

Arjuna's dilemma was an existential one. What is the point of eliminating others if it results in one's own elimination? It is a dilemma born out of partial understanding. If Arjuna were as unaware as Duryodhana, this doubt would have never entered his mind. Were he enlightened as Kṛṣṇa is, the answer would have been obvious. Arjuna was in between, hence his dilemma.

'Why should I destroy myself? For what purpose?' These are the questions that naturally follow this line of reasoning. Arjuna was far wiser than many modern philosophers in posing this as a doubt, but without venturing any answers. Arjuna is undergoing a process of transformation. The problem was that Arjuna was a thinking man unlike Duryodhana, or even his own brother Bhīma. This ability to think, to be aware, was what had got him into trouble now. Doubts assailed him. 'Am I really doing the right thing? Am I not destroying myself and all that I stand for when I wage this war against my own people?'

Arjuna had become a seeker of Truth. He wished to go beyond the *śāstras,* the *stotras* and the *sūtras.* He questioned them. Arjuna Vishāda Yoga, is the name of the first chapter of Gītā. *Vishāda* means grief, sorrow, despondency, despair, depression, dilemma and such. Here what we see is the dilemma that Arjuna was in, not knowing whether what he had been taught all his life and what he had believed to be true, was really true after all.

Kṛṣṇa is referred to by many names thus far. The word 'Kṛṣṇa' itself refers to His dark blue color. It also means existence and bliss, sat chit ānanda, and 'who provides salvation to those who surrender to Him.'

Keshava refers to the fact that He destroyed the demon Keshin. It also refers to his beautiful hair. The embodiment in Him of the holy trinity of the Hindu tradition (the Sanskrit words K referring to Brahma, A to Viṣṇu and Īśā to Śiva) is another meaning of this name.

Govinda is a combination of *go* referring to all living beings and *vinda* which means knower, Kṛṣṇa being the ultimate knower of the mind, body and being of all living creatures.

Rigors Of Conditioning

1.31 *I do not see how any good can come from killing my own kinsmen in this battle, nor can I, my dear Kṛṣṇa, desire any subsequent victory, kingdom or happiness.*

1.32 *What use is kingdom, pleasures or even life, Kṛṣṇa?*

1.33 *Those for whose sake we seek kingdoms, enjoyment and happiness*
Now are arrayed in this battlefield ready to lose their lives and wealth.

1.34, 1.35 *Even if I am about to be slain by my teachers, fathers, sons, grandfathers, maternal uncles, fathers-in-law, grandsons, brothers-in-law and all relatives,*
I would not like to slay them even to gain control of all three worlds.
Why then, Madhusūdana, would I wish to kill them for control of this earth?

Arjuna now started expressing his doubts with clarity. How could he seek happiness through destruction of his kinsmen, he asked. How could he desire power, possessions and pleasures through such action? And if he did gain those things as a result of killing his family, of what use would such a life be to him? Though Arjuna was in a dilemma, it was a dilemma born out of intelligence, not out of ignorance. Arjuna had been taught all his life to seek power, possessions and pleasure and he had done it. Up to this point, he had not come across a single situation where the cost of acquiring these had seemed to be greater than the accruing profit, the resulting enjoyment. For the first time in his life, he encountered a situation that forced him to evaluate his options.

'Do I forge ahead and destroy what is dear to me so that I get more power and possibly more pleasure?' he asks. This is a fundamental question that each one of us should ask ourselves. How often do we involve ourselves in activities for material benefits even though we know that these may damage our life or the lives of those we care about?

Life becomes mechanical for most people. Our past is vividly remembered and it is used to forget the present. If the past was sorrowful, we avoid it in the future. If the past was joyful, we try to replicate it. The problem is that life is not so predictable but we try to control it as if it is. The bigger problem is that we are so conditioned by our behavioral patterns that in spite of all precautions, we keep making the same mistakes. Our *saṁskāras*, our unconscious mind, is the root cause of this.

Very few of us stop to think and question the purpose of our actions. We are so busy just trying to keep up with our personal and professional commitments, that it never occurs to us to ask ourselves whether we are truly fulfilled. Our lives become a constant series of 'What next, what next?' It takes a lot of courage to stop and question our lives, our actions and society's plan for us. It takes inner fortitude to say to the world, 'Stop, I want to get off; I want to seek true inner bliss!' Sany¢sis are courageous people. They are not cowards who walk away from society because they can't succeed by society's rules. No! It takes enormous courage to escape from the materialism of the world with an attitude of seeking one's true purpose in life.

'What is the purpose of my life, Kṛṣṇa?' wailed Arjuna. Arjuna is now questioning himself, and his purpose when faced with the task of fighting against his kinsmen. The scene from his chariot has thrown him off balance! In his heart he knows that what he is about to do is correct. But when faced with the reality of actually killing those who have been near and dear to him, he loses his will. Why? Arjuna was afraid. Only a courageous person will have the confidence to open himself up so transparently and expose his innermost fears and seek help. Arjuna is a courageous man.

Arjuna was confused. Based upon all his training and society's guidance, he could certainly differentiate between right and wrong. His sudden confusion grew out of a concern that what he had been taught throughout his life might be wrong. Fortunately for Arjuna, his charioteer is none other than Kṛṣṇa Himself, Lord of all beings and knower of all! Only He can see what is at the heart of Arjuna's grief. Only He could provide the right solutions to Arjuna's dilemma.

Arjuna argues that the reason one would fight to gain power and wealth was for the sake of one's near and dear ones. However, his near and dear ones were the people with whom he should fight! He declared that even if they killed him, he would not consider killing them at any cost, even if he gained the possession of all three worlds as his reward. 'If I would not kill them for all the riches of the three worlds, why would I destroy them for the sake of earth, this one world, alone?' Arjuna questioned Kṛṣṇa.

Arjuna then calls Kṛṣṇa as Madhusūdana, which means the slayer of the demon Madhu. Arjuna implies that Kṛṣṇa may be a destroyer, but Arjuna himself would not like to be one like Him.

Arjuna's dilemma had now become more complicated. He now had gotten into justifications as to why he should not kill, justifications that have no merit from the standpoint of a warrior. Arjuna's initial dilemma was with his value system. It was created by the fact that his enemies were his kinsmen, teachers and friends. To any observer, his dilemma had validity. But now, he tries to convince himself through further arguments that actually lack strength. Arjuna's mind was playing tricks on him.

Arjuna said he would not kill even if he were to be killed. This is just a lie. It is his own loss of identity that would result from the destruction of his lineage that was bothering him. Arjuna then went on to say that he would not consider killing his kinsmen and teachers, even if he were offered all the three worlds of this universe in return. Why then, he queries, would the reward of just this planet earth be attractive to him?

Who was offering Arjuna the three worlds anyway? The notion was a pure figment of his overexcited imagination. If Kṛṣṇa had actually offered Arjuna the control of the universe, Arjuna's dilemma would have become far worse! However, posing it as a symbolic question as Arjuna did made him look noble.

He is consoling himself with the idea that the rewards of winning this battle are too small and that even if he were to be offered control of the universe, he would not be tempted. It is a safe position he is taking, since the chances of his being offered the control of the universe are infinitely small. What matters is that it calms his bruised mind and keeps the focus off the real source of his fear.

Time and again, people play this game with themselves and others. It starts when we cannot face the truth and therefore cannot tell the truth. So we camouflage the truth in a more acceptable presentation. Then we are caught in denial.

Arjuna was afraid to lose his own identity through the loss of so many well-established relationships in his life. However, that truth would hurt him and he was not prepared to see it. It might have been well hidden in his unconscious. For the majority of us, our identity lies in the roles we play, the responsibilities that we have, the worrying we do and the acceptance that we receive from others. Without these possessions and relationships to form the foundation of our personalities, without the foundation of 'mine', we feel lost and have no 'I.' Like us, Arjuna found it better to invent a host of other reasons to avoid facing the truth.

A senior government official, a devotee, once called me in the middle of the night, desperate to see me. 'I must see you now,' he said. 'I am so bogged down by problems and depressed, I may even commit suicide. I need to see you immediately.'

I talked to him for a while and managed to calm him down and suggested that he could come the next morning and that I would see him.

'No, no,' he replied. 'I cannot come tomorrow morning. I have urgent meetings that I cannot miss.'

A few minutes earlier, seeing me immediately was a matter of life and death to him. Now, his meeting in the morning was more critical!

We create illusions in our mind about the situations we face, about how critical they are to our existence. Then we create fantasies in our minds about what is going to happen to us, be it an imagined good result or a difficulty. We do everything except face the present moment with awareness.

Good Men Do Not Kill

1.36 *What pleasure will we get by destroying the sons of Dhṛtarāṣṭra, Janārdana? Only sin will overcome us if we slay these wrongdoers.*

1.37 *It is not proper for us to kill the sons of Dhṛtarāṣṭra and our friends.*
How could we be happy by killing our own kinsmen, Mādhava?

1.38, 1.39 *O Janārdana, although these men are consumed by greed and they see no fault in killing one's family or quarreling with friends,*
Why should we, who understand the evil of the destruction of a dynasty, not turn away from these acts?

Here is Arjuna's dilemma spoken plainly. He had two options and is looking to be convinced of one or the other. The first was that going to battle was wrong, especially against his kinsmen. Therefore he should cease and desist, walk away from the war before it starts. All his arguments up to this point were in this line of thinking. At the same time, Arjuna was open to the possibility that what he had set out to do was indeed correct, in which case he would go back into battle mode, as a true kṣatriya would do.

Arjuna's mind now brings up one more argument. Arjuna agreed that Duryodhana and his allies were the aggressors and wrongdoers. Whatever they had done to him, his brothers and his wife was unpardonable, and they needed to be punished for that. By all rights Arjuna would have been quite justified in attacking and killing those wrongdoers for what they had done.

'But,' Arjuna asked, 'Would one wrong be corrected by another wrong? How can I be happy killing my kinsmen, however justified I might be in doing that? Their misdeeds cannot be remedied by my misdeed and that would only make me miserable.'

There are two factors central to Arjuna's dilemma.

The first one is that of relationship. The problem that Arjuna faced is one that we all face when asked to do unpleasant things to people we know. It is always easier to criticize and punish people one does not know. With people one knows, there is a danger of breaking the relationship through perceived negative behavior, even when it may be fully justified. To face this factor in one's dilemma, one must first break the connection or develop a sense of detachment that allows right action without worrying about the consequences. As long as the path is right, whatever destination the path takes one to will also be right.

Over the ages, this sense of connection had been broken by religious and societal separation. More people have been killed in religious wars than for any other reason. When religion was deemed insufficient reason to kill, man found other 'rational' reasons to segregate and kill: color of the skin, language and cultural differences, territorial disputes and more. Anything that created the possibility of fear or threat was a good enough reason to discriminate and destroy.

We need to realize that no man is an island. We are interconnected at the spiritual level and at the cellular level too. Studies in molecular cellular biology by path-breaking scientists such as Bruce Lipton show that Darwin was wrong when he said we must compete to survive. In fact, we need to collaborate to survive. That is what cells do. They know intuitively that they are interconnected and are part of a larger system.

When we arrive on planet earth, we are open to all possibilities. As children, we are centered upon ourselves and open to all connections.

Over time, we build walls. We believe that these walls will keep us safe and that the connections that we have established inside the walls are ours to keep. Slowly, the open space we started with becomes a maze and we are lost inside! The silence needs to be broken. People need to communicate and collaborate instead of isolating themselves and competing. At the basic cellular level, it is now found that cells like to cluster together and form clumps that can communicate. It is found that cells communicate through their boundary membranes and not through their nuclei as had been assumed. Competition does not ensure survival; collaboration and communication does. However, when we work valuing only the results, our efforts become counterproductive. As long as this collaboration is for the collective good and collective survival, it is extremely effective. We must consider process and source along with the result.

The other factor that Arjuna faces is the problem of directness of action. If he shot an arrow and killed a kinsman, death was a direct result of his action. He had to look the victim in the eye before releasing his arrow. He was aware of whom he was killing and why. He felt the destruction within himself when he killed someone else.

Arjuna was affected by the combination of these two factors. It affected him because he was not a Duryodhana, who denied the consequences of his actions to himself and others or a Kṛṣṇa who would have taken responsibility for his actions, being aware all the time. His mind was pointing out that he might be doing wrong, but had not yet ascended into that state of awareness to be able to take responsibility for such actions. Arjuna was pleading with Kṛṣṇa, 'Please tell me, am I right? Should I withdraw from this battle?'

But now, he condemned the same fathers, grandfathers, teachers, uncles and friends that he had referred to so passionately a few moments earlier. These are the same people who he claimed to hold in great respect and affection and therefore did not wish to kill. He shifted gears now and moved from the position of not killing them because they were his flesh and blood to a greater moral position of not wishing to kill them because it was morally reprehensible.

Arjuna said that destruction of the lineage, the dynasty, is evil, and that he recoiled from such a deed even though his opponents had no such compunction, blinded as they were by greed. Arjuna's dilemma now jumps to a larger arena. It's no longer about individuals. It is about the destruction of a race that had existed for thousands of years, tracing its roots back to celestial beings. How could he be expected to carry out such a horrible act, he pleaded.

In Arjuna's mind this was a big doubt. Killing a few individuals, even if kinsmen, was a mistake. Killing a whole generation was a far bigger sin and now he was expected to destroy a whole race, the foundations of a proud and legendary dynasty. How could the future generations forgive him?

This was how the argument of Arjuna's dilemma shifted.

When Arjuna talks about the threat to his dynasty, it arises out of a fear of his own mortality. He has asked, 'Even if I am to die, as I must, should I not ensure the continuance of my dynasty that bears my signature, my identity, my DNA?'

The Plot Thickens

1.40 *With the destruction of dynasty, the eternal family tradition is destroyed too,*
And the rest of the family becomes involved in immoral practices.

1.41 *When immoral practices become common in the family, O Kṛṣṇa,*
The women of the family become corrupted,
And from the degradation of womanhood, O descendant of Vṛṣṇi, arise social problems.

1.42 *As these social problems increase, the family and those who destroy the family tradition are cast in hell,*
As there is no offering of food and water to their ancestors.

1.43 *Due to the evil deeds of the destroyers of family tradition,*
All kinds of rituals and practices of caste and family are devastated.

1.44 *O Janārdana, I have heard that those who destroy family traditions dwell always in hell.*

By now, Arjuna had become desperate. His arguments include the tragic impact this war would have on future generations and the entire Kuru race. The destruction of a noble lineage would bring about the decline in commitment to the rites and rituals that make society civilized and moral. Arjuna then elaborated upon these immoral and unrighteous acts.

He said that women in the family would become unchaste and that mixing with other castes would follow, resulting in children of mixed castes, which would be undesirable. Those who destroy family traditions would ruin all sacred practices and lead the families into polluted progeny, and such people had no place to go but hell. To understand what Arjuna said, it is important to understand the origin of the caste tradition in Hindu religion.

At the age of five, a child was given to the care of a spiritual master by the parents in the ancient Indian education system called gurukul. By living in close proximity to an enlightened master, the child's personality and expression were observed. These factors, along with any spiritual experiences before physical maturity, determined how the youngster was trained – either for *sanyās* (spiritual fulfillment) or for married life. The child's natural aptitudes formed the basis for the caste classification, *varṇāśrama*. *Brāhmanas* (priests/teachers), *kṣatriyas* (kings/warriors), *vaiśyas* (merchants/tradesmen) and *śūdras* (agricultural/service) are these four classes.

The Vedic gurukul system was not concerned with whether the child's parents were *brāhmaṇa* or *vaiśya*. The son of a *brāhmaṇa*, who had neither the aptitude nor the knowledge to be a *brāhmaṇa*, ceased to have the right and qualifications to be called a *brāhmaṇa*. Irrespective of parentage, the children were taught the Gāyatri mantra at age seven, which allowed their natural intelligence to blossom. Those whose ability leaned towards the spiritual path and who expressed this aptitude through personal development and experiences were trained in the scriptures. Others were trained in materially relevant arts and sciences so that they could re-enter the world with a mature, integrated personality.

Over time, this caste system was corrupted through human greed. Those who believed that they were doing more responsible work, and therefore were more respected, such as the *brāhmaṇa*s and *kṣatriya*s, decided to pass on their caste qualification to their children as if it was their birthright. Such a practice had no scriptural sanction.

Arjuna's doubts about caste pollution had no scriptural base or merit. What he referred to became the societal norm because of human greed. There were many instances of caste mixture even in the great Kuru lineage that Arjuna claimed would be destroyed. Satyavatī, his great grandmother, was a fisherman's daughter who his great grandfather, Śantanu, became infatuated with. Arjuna himself had wives who were not of *kṣatriya* lineage by birth.

Arjuna talked as if mired in total confusion when he linked practice of rites and rituals with morality and chastity. He talked about women becoming unchaste as a result of families not following rites and rituals. His logic was distorted. Rites and rituals, as prescribed in the scriptures, are an expression of one's inner awareness. They become useful when one is aware. Awareness is not created by blind practice of rites and rituals. How many people do we see muttering their prayers and *mantra*, rolling their beads while thinking of something else!

Arjuna voiced the sentiments of organized religion and priesthood, which derive their power and monetary base from such rites and rituals. They use these rites and rituals and their sole authority to perform them, as a factor of control over the masses. This is how, in each culture and religion, the power of the priestly class was established, as if they were the sole mediators to God.

Arjuna talked about ancestral worship and implied that the offspring of mixed caste have no right to make offerings to their ancestors, leaving them lost in the realms beyond death. Arjuna raises doubts on behalf of mankind and seeks clarification. There are no ancestral spirits waiting to be pacified by us. If the spirit is enlightened it merges with the infinite energy. If not, it gets reborn within three *kṣaṇa*s, three moments. Spirits do not hang around waiting to be pacified. Nor do they go to hell if they are not pacified.

Hell and heaven are in our minds. They are psychological spaces, not geographical places. We are in hell when we are depressed, guilty and in suffering. We are in heaven when we feel and express love, joy and gratitude. We pass through hell and heaven even as we live in our day-to-day lives.

The concepts of hell and heaven and sin were created to insert guilt and control people. Arjuna is not a fool. He understands all this perfectly. Yet, he voices his doubts as if ignorant and confused. He acts out of compassion for humanity when he articulates these doubts so that the divine Kṛṣṇa can answer them, to everyone's benefit.

A thoughtful man like Arjuna cannot talk about the lack of chastity of women without blaming the men who are equally responsible. He reflects here the superior attitude of men over the ages, those who have treated women with undue superiority. The doubts he voices are those of the society he lives in, and those doubts have not changed in thousands of years.

The Breakdown

1.45 *Alas, we are preparing to commit greatly sinful acts by killing our kinsmen,*
Driven by the desire to enjoy royal happiness.

1.46 *I would consider it better for the Kauravas to kill me unarmed and unresisting, rather than for me to fight them.*

1.47 *Sañjaya said:*
Having said this on the battlefield, Arjuna cast aside his bow and arrows
And sat down on the chariot, his mind overwhelmed with grief.

Arjuna was ready to give up. He was all set to run away from the battlefield and escape from the reality of his duty. He had convinced himself through his own illusory arguments that what he had embarked upon was pure evil and therefore he wanted no part of it. He said, 'I am ready to lay down my arms. Let Duryodhana and his men kill me.'

For a kṣatriya to say this means one of two things: either his act is one of total surrender or it is out of utter helplessness and confusion. As yet Arjuna was not in a mode of total surrender. It is neither fear of death nor fear of injury that compelled him to say what he did. He was also not in the mode of *ahiṁsā*, nonviolence. His arguments about killing his kinsmen being like killing himself were born out of his ego and not out of self-realization.

Arjuna's desperation arose from his dilemma, which was becoming more extreme by the minute. Arjuna was an intelligent man accustomed to the light of clarity but was now in darkness. He was torn between his duty as a *kṣatriya* prince and the scriptural codes of morality. Arjuna's distress was complete. He sat down, unable to bear the weight of his emotions. He put down his bow and arrows, which signified that he was out of the battle.

Arjuna's delusion was complete. He was as far away from reality and intelligent action as he could possibly get. The greatest warrior of his time, the greatest of men, was in the depths of despair due to his inner turmoil. The conflict between his upbringing and value systems, his *saṁskāra*s and what he was about to do by waging war against his kinsmen had reduced him to a pitiable wreck who now abandoned his weapons and collapsed inside his chariot. At this point, Arjuna was no example of a true *kṣatriya*.

Arjuna was now a true example of mankind. He was being human. He was experiencing the deep conflict between the unconscious *saṁskāra*s that were driving him and the reality of what he ought to do. The darkness that surrounded Arjuna at this stage was *māyā*, the illusion that prevents all human beings from perceiving the truth of Reality that pervades all our experiences. *Yā mā iti māyā*, that which is not real but appears as absolute is *māyā*. Māyā is not unreal in the sense that it does not exist. *Māyā* truly exists as reality. It veils, it covers Reality, the ultimate Truth.

Had Arjuna been Kṛṣṇa, had Arjuna been enlightened, he would not have been tormented by the play of his *māyā*. Had Arjuna been a Duryodhana or even a Bhīma whose individual consciousness was not awakened, he would have accepted the *māyā* without question and again not been tormented by it. But, Arjuna is intelligent. He is partially awakened, a seeker. He is in the presence of the greatest of all masters. He is struggling to rid himself of his *māyā* and seeks clarity.

It is Arjuna's ego that created the *māyā* in him. His own along with his conviction that he should preserve his lineage - all these factors created the illusion in him that he was something other than who he was. These created the doubt in him that he should do something other than what he was there to do.

All of us come into this world with no identity. As we grow we collect labels describing ourselves. We become so associated with the labels and their accessories that we forget who we really are. Our life is then about seeking fulfillment in the wrong places. We search for happiness in the external world because that is where we have been taught to look for fulfillment. We have not learned how to look within and experience it. Eternal happiness that constantly flows as bliss is always within you and not in material possessions, relationships or selfish philanthropy. It is a state of no-mind that you experience within yourself.

As very young children we were all in bliss. As we grow, as we learn from others, we are taught to shift our attention away from that bliss. In short, we learn how to stop feeling blissful. Just as we learned how to stop feeling blissful, we can also learn how to 'un-stop' that stopping of bliss. We can relearn how to connect with our blissful nature again.

That is the process Arjuna was going through. He had lost his awareness of inner bliss because of his *saṁskāra*s and was in the deep throes of despair. The process of relearning, the process of transformation at the hands of the master was about to begin. If we become aware of that process that the master takes His disciple through, if we follow that process carefully over the eighteen chapters, we too can become aware.

Śaṅkara says beautifully: If you imbibe even a little of Bhagavad Gītā, if you drink even a drop of Gaṅgā water, if you think even once about that great master Kṛṣṇa, you will never have to face death.

Thus ends the first chapter of the dialogue between ***Śrī Kṛṣṇa*** *and Arjuna, called* ***Arjunaviṣāda Yogaḥ****, in the Brahmavidya* ***Yogaśāstra Bhagavad Gītā Upaniṣad.***

BHAGAVADGĪTĀ

You are God

SĀṄKHYA YOGAḤ

CHAPTER 2

Make no mistake, you are divine!
Whatever state you are in now,
you are still divine within!
Let Krishna tell you
how to unleash your divine potential.

You are God

It is here that we enter into the real Gītā. It is from here that *Bhagavān* or God starts speaking.

Until now Kṛṣṇa was speaking as a man, as Vāsudeva Kṛṣṇa, in His human form. It is only from here that Kṛṣṇa speaks as *Parabrahma* Kṛṣṇa, in His divine state as *Bhagavān,* the universal Kṛṣṇa.

An important point we all need to understand is that only an intelligent man will allow the other person to speak. We all speak continuously to each other but a conversation does not really happen. We simply carry out simultaneous monologues with each other. We are polite enough to pretend that we are listening so that we will, in turn, be heard. You need intelligence to allow the other person to speak. Listen…

A small story:

A person was telling his friend that he had not spoken to his wife for a whole week. His friend asked him whether he was angry with her or if he had fought with her.

The man replied, 'No, I am afraid of interrupting her!'

Maybe because Kṛṣṇa is a male, he allowed Arjuna to speak! We speak continuously. Even when we keep quiet, we are not listening.

Kṛṣṇa does listen. He listens carefully and answers compassionately. Of the original 745 verses in Gītā, as part of the BhĪsma Purāna of Mahābhārata, He responds in depth to Arjuna's fifty-seven questions through 620 verses.

In the first chapter Kṛṣṇa does not say a word to interrupt Arjuna. He allows Arjuna to speak fully for one whole chapter. He keeps quiet even upon seeing the depth of Arjuna's confusion and depression. It is possible to become a successful businessman just by studying the first few chapters of Gītā. You can reach the peak of your profession just by learning the art of listening. A devotee once asked me, '*Swamiji*, how is it that you are able to answer so many questions?' There is only one secret to this. I know how to listen to the question, that's all. If you know the technique of listening, the reply is immediately ready in your being.

The problem is that we do not trust ourselves and our innate intelligence to respond to a question without preparation. That is why we start preparing the reply even before listening to the question. We are only interested in expressing what we know, not in addressing the real problem or even in understanding what the other person has to say. We hear mechanically at best; we never really listen.

Get to the real problem

Here, Kṛṣṇa is interested in the real problem and not interested in expressing what He knows. He allows Arjuna to speak so that He can go to the root of the problem and address the issue. One needs intelligence, or I may say enlightenment, to listen. Only an enlightened master like Kṛṣṇa can listen. In the first chapter He listens fully and completely. Even in the second chapter, He allows Arjuna to speak in many verses. He knows that once He allows Arjuna to express his problems, Arjuna can himself find a solution to them.

People come to me and say, '*Swamiji*, you know our problems; please give us the answer.' I ask them to state their problems clearly.

They say, 'You are enlightened, you already know our problems; please give us the answer.'

I say, 'Yes, I know your problem even if you don't speak, but you will not know your own problem if you do not speak!'

When you speak, the master listens. More importantly, you listen within yourself. All that is needed is to keep your mind open so that the transmission can take place. Even if you do not verbalize, you can visualize your needs and problems and this will be even more powerful than your speech itself.

People who have the rationality to compute time may wonder, 'Arjuna spoke for so long. Now Kṛṣṇa speaks for so long. How is it possible for these two to hold such a long conversation in the middle of a battlefield? What were all the others doing? Wasn't Duryodhana fed up or didn't he think that this was a good opportunity to get rid of Arjuna and Kṛṣṇa as they talked and wasted everybody's time?'

The logical mind cannot believe that a conversation can indeed take place in silence. People are not used to visualization. They lose this skill as they grow up. Children can visualize beautifully. That is why they can keep themselves busy talking silently to themselves and talking silently with imaginary friends. Education and logic rob us of this skill. At the higher level of communication your mind needs to be still to allow the grace to move in. This is the subtlest and most powerful of all communication. At this level communication becomes communion.

When they talk of great masters like Ramaṇa maharṣi communicating in silence, it was indeed true. To communicate, you don't need to use your mouth. The presence of the master will help still and open your mind. Answers will appear even before your questions are asked.

Intellectual seekers with years of questioning and doubting behind them, come to me and ask, '*Swamiji*, why is it that I come to you with hundreds of questions, but when I am in front of you there is no need to ask you about them? I feel as if the answers are already there!'

This is not imagination; this is the truth. Questions can only raise more questions. Questions are a reflection of your inner ego, which is violence. When you are in front of the master, a master you truly believe in, the first thing that happens is the melting of your ego. Therefore, questions also disappear. In their place the answers surface, though previously hidden by the veil of your ego and ignorance.

The truth is that the answers were all already there. Our ego would not allow us to accept and be aware of those answers. The master's presence dissolved the ego and let the answers out.

There is an interesting Zen story.

A soldier went with a problem to the master Nansen.

A man kept a goose in a bottle, feeding it until it grew too large to get out of the neck of the bottle. Now, how did he get the goose out without killing the goose or breaking the bottle?

Nansen said to him, 'Oh Officer!'

The soldier responded, 'Yes, master?'

Nansen exclaimed, 'There, the goose is out of the bottle!'

The moment the soldier addressed Nansen as master, accepted that he was his master, the goose, the ego, was out of the bottle, his body-mind!

Only when you open up to the master do you actually come to know your problem clearly and the answers come as if from nowhere. You can do it at three levels. You can converse and convey through words and the master will listen. At the next level you can communicate from the heart in silence; you can visualize instead of verbalizing in speech. Finally, you can commune in silence and the master will grasp this even more powerfully.

Here Kṛṣṇa allowed Arjuna to verbalize so that to begin with, Arjuna himself got the clarity to understand his problem. Once Arjuna expressed his confusion, he could relapse into silence and commune with the master.

A Zen Slap Awakens!

2.1 *Sañjaya said,*
As Arjuna's eyes overflowed with tears of pity and despair,
Kṛṣṇa spoke to him thus.

2.2 *Kṛṣṇa said,*
Wherefrom has this dejection descended on you at this critical time, Arjuna!
You behave unlike a nobleman and this will keep you away from realization.

2.3 *Do not yield to fear, Pārtha! It does not befit you.*
Drop this faint-heartedness and stand up, destroyer of enemies!

Arjuna was distraught with pity and despair. His pity was for his opposition that consisted of kinsmen, elders, teachers, relatives and friends. He despaired at the thought of what would happen if he did have to kill them. He collapsed in his chariot and let his bow and arrow slip from his hands.

Kṛṣṇa allowed Arjuna to exhaust himself physically, emotionally, and spiritually. Kṛṣṇa wanted to give Arjuna time to open his mind, heart, and being to Him, Arjuna's friend, guide and master, so that His answers would penetrate Arjuna's very being.

Then He spoke for the first time, as if opening His being directly. Kṛṣṇa says, 'My dear Arjuna, how have you acquired these impurities? They do not befit a man who knows the value of life at all. They lead not to higher planes but to infamy.'

'O Pārtha! Do not yield to this degrading impotence. Give up such petty weakness of heart and arise, O destroyer of the enemy.'

This is the direction of the whole of Gītā. Kṛṣṇa is the true Zen master and does not beat around the bush.

> A disciple goes to an enlightened Zen master and asks, 'Master, what is *Buddha*? How can I become *Buddha*? Please teach me.'
>
> The master slaps him hard on his face.
>
> He says, 'Master, I know that you do not do anything without a meaning. Please explain.'
>
> The master says, 'Fool, you *are* Buddha. Why do you try to become something you *are* already? You *are* already *that* and nothing else needs to be added to you. That's why I slapped you, to awaken you.'

Similarly, Kṛṣṇa gives the direction to the whole Gītā with this one 'slap'.

Kṛṣṇa knows that Arjuna is not depressed because of a spiritual search. It is just that he does not want a solution; he wants only support.

This is why Kṛṣṇa does not speak of spirituality in these two verses. Arjuna's problem originates from fear and worry. His *maṇipūraka cakra* (navel center) and *svādiṣṭhāna cakra* (being center) energy centers within the body are now completely locked due to worry and fear! Kṛṣṇa addresses Arjuna's deep fear straightaway without any philosophy and asks him to give up his foolish weakness so that he can get up and fight. He does not offer any consolation, just a straightforward scolding and a slap to awaken him!

Simple devotion and trust is sometimes enough

If Arjuna had been in the mood of devotional surrender that he reaches only later on, these two verses would have served as a technique for him. If Arjuna had been without fear and expressed full faith and devotion in Kṛṣṇa, these two verses would have been enough to get him up and going.

The entire Gītā would have been encapsulated here and there would have been no need to continue. There would be no need for eighteen chapters!

I spoke to you about *śāstra, stotra* and *sūtra* (wisdom, devotion and technique) in the first chapter. All three can be a means to enlightenment for people of corresponding aptitudes. At this point, Arjuna is in the state to be intellectually convinced and Kṛṣṇa employs *śāstra* as the right approach. Since he was not in the mood of *stotra,* not yet ready with devotion and faith, Kṛṣṇa had to create the *śāstra* or wisdom, to bring him to the *stotra* or devotion state. The whole issue was due to fear as well as worry and depression because of this fear. One needs to stand up to them to be rid of them.

There are many levels of fear: fear of losing our wealth and status, fear of losing a limb or our health, fear of losing our near and dear ones, and fear of the unknown or death. That is why Kṛṣṇa says that Arjuna is not behaving as an *ārya,* a word that can be interpreted as a nobleman, and in this case refers to a person who is aware. Arjuna is confronted with all the four fears: fear that he may lose whatever he possesses, that he may be maimed in the war, that he may lose his near and dear ones, and fourth, that he may lose his very life. These fears have in turn led to his worry. Kṛṣṇa directly addresses this worry and fear with the *śāstra,* the explanation of wisdom that is directed to the head, the intellect.

Later on in Gītā, in the eleventh chapter, after beholding Kṛṣṇa's cosmic vision, Arjuna realizes who Kṛṣṇa truly is. He is then overwhelmed with devotion. This devotion or *stotra* becomes the *sūtra* or technique to enlighten Arjuna. That stage is yet to happen. Since Arjuna is not yet in the devotional state, these words are only plain wisdom or *śāstra.*

Kṛṣṇa is not a philosopher. All philosophy is an attempt to convince the other to do what the philosopher wants of him. He wastes no time convincing Arjuna. He tries to give him the conclusion directly. However, as Arjuna is not in the mood to receive it because he is not mature enough to assimilate it, Kṛṣṇa needs to give Arjuna the experience.

There is a beautiful story in the *Upaniṣads*:

A disciple goes to the master and asks, 'O Master! Teach me *ātmajñāna* knowledge of the inner Self.'

The master says, 'Thou art that! *Tatvamasi*, You are God.'

The disciple, unable to believe this, thinks to himself, 'How can I be God? I am still afraid of my wife. I have all these problems and a thousand questions!'

Only when the master proves to him that the master himself is God, the disciple trusts the master's words. Kṛṣṇa does the same thing by repeating that He is all of this.

Kṛṣṇa later explains His glory and that all the deities and the *Vedās*, the scriptural wisdom, are worshipping at His feet; the whole world is in Him. He makes these incredible statements that would appear egoistic to a normal person. And yet Kṛṣṇa says all this even at the risk of being misunderstood. He repeats that He is God to make you realize that *you* are God.

You would not believe the words of ordinary people. You need to hear the words from a source of authority that has the right to say them. But as of now Arjuna is not able to take it all in. It is too much for him to grasp in his present condition. When masters prove their divinity and perform great deeds or miracles, they do not do so for their ego satisfaction. They do them so that you believe their words and experience that *you* are God. Once Kṛṣṇa proves His divinity, Arjuna believes His words and is ready to follow them.

Later on in the Gītā, Kṛṣṇa says 'I am the Divine. If you believe in Me, you too shall realize your inner divinity.'

It is this profound and yet simple message that has resounded so deeply in the hearts, minds and beings of generations of Hindus, in turn establishing the scriptural sanctity of Gītā.

Here all of Gītā is reduced to just these two verses by Kṛṣṇa.

He straightaway addresses and clears the point where Arjuna is stuck, in *rajas.* A man who is centered on *rajas* will work only for name and fame. A man who is centered on *satva,* goodness, who has neither greed nor lethargy, but a neutral attitude, will work out of compassion. A man who is centered on *tamas,* lethargy, will work only for sensual pleasures.

Duryodhana works only through *tamas,* which explains his cruel and gross behavior. Dharmarāja Yudhiṣṭhira works from *satva,* out of compassion. Here Arjuna is centered on *rajas*; therefore he is working only for name and fame. This is how Kṛṣṇa straightaway puts His hand on the tumor, the tumor that is the subtle ego working within Arjuna.

Fortunately for us, Arjuna is not intelligent enough to grasp everything immediately. Or rather, he acts as if he is not intelligent enough to understand these words. He has lived with Kṛṣṇa for more than thirty years so he must have some intelligence. He puts forth his questions and doubts not for himself but for the future generations and for the whole of humankind.

Let the problem remain simple

A small story I read in a magazine recently:

> There was a person who had an obsessive-compulsive disorder of tearing up whatever paper he laid his hands on. His family spent a lot of money and tried all possible treatments but nothing worked.
>
> One day they read in the newspaper about a young and innovative psychotherapist and decided to contact him. The therapist said he wanted to spend a few minutes alone with the patient. He and the patient simply walked up and down for a few minutes, after which the therapist returned and pronounced that the patient was now cured of his malady and could be taken home.
>
> His family was surprised when they found that he really was cured. Even after a year he was found to be perfectly alright. However, no one knew how the problem disappeared. The family returned to the

doctor to express their gratitude. They wanted to know what the doctor had really done to cure him of the problem that others could not solve.

He replied that he had simply asked the patient not to tear any more paper and that if he did so even once more, the patient would be brought to the doctor again, whereupon he would be thrown out of the window!

Most of the time our problems are very simple. We complicate them by analyzing them. When we verbalize and analyze a problem, we complicate it and give power to it. Our problems are not as big as we think they are. When we verbalize, analyze, label and categorize them, we have created a whole new problem that had not existed earlier in our being. This is how psychiatrists continue to invent new diseases!

You have only one mind. You can either use it to solve the problem or use it to create more problems naturally. Understand that if you are not solving your existing problems, you will be creating more problems. At the level of the mind, there is no position of simply standing, no *status quo* – you either climb or fall.

Here Kṛṣṇa is not creating any philosophy but gives the answer straightaway in just one line. However, since Arjuna is not mature enough, Kṛṣṇa must give an intellectual explanation. All Western philosophies begin with logical analysis and end with the conclusion. All Eastern processes begin with the conclusion and then give the analysis. Eastern masters are compassionate. They first give us the option of grasping the solution if we have the intelligence to do so. If we do not have the intelligence, they have no other option but to go into detailed explanation and analysis. They expect us to transform with just the trust in them. When they find that we do not have this qualification in us, they start the regular process.

Here Kṛṣṇa tries the first method of sudden enlightenment, the immediate liberation, but Arjuna is not mature enough to receive it or comprehend it.

Kṛṣṇa is God and so are you!

There are two ways in which people react to the sanctity and divinity of Kṛṣṇa in Bhagavad Gītā. To one set of people, Kṛṣṇa has no special qualification to be called divine and these people may not even believe in anything such as the divine. As atheists or agnostics, the only way such people can be convinced is initially through the rationale of the dialogue in the Gītā. The message of Kṛṣṇa is universal and timeless. For those that do not accept and understand, it just means that as of now, it is not their time to accept, understand and transform.

The laws of nature do not change just because we do not accept and understand them. The earth was always round and never flat and it always revolved around the sun and not the other way around. Societal leaders denied these truths and killed people for expounding these truths.

There is another class of people who say that there is only Kṛṣṇa, who is divine and all other divine manifestations have no relevance. One such group of people came to me very perturbed after I had spoken about the Gītā,. They said, 'From what you say, we see that you accept the divinity of Kṛṣṇa.' I said, 'Yes, I very much do. He is the *Pūrṇāvatār*, the complete incarnation.'

They complained, 'Then how can you worship Śiva in your ashram? We believe you have a Dakshinamurthy (Śiva) temple in your Bidadi ashram in India. How can you do this?'

I asked them, 'Have you read Anu Gītā, which is also another part of Mahābhārata?' They said, 'No.'

I then explained to them about Anu Gītā: After the war, Arjuna and Kṛṣṇa are together and Arjuna says, 'Kṛṣṇa, I do not remember all of what you taught me at the battlefield, when you delivered the Gītā to me. Can you please enlighten me again?'

Kṛṣṇa says, 'Oh, you have forgotten? I too have forgotten what I said then!'

Arjuna exclaims, 'Kṛṣṇa, how is that possible?'

Kṛṣṇa says, 'At that point I was *Parabrahma* Kṛṣṇa, the universal Kṛṣṇa. I was *Bhagavān.* I was the Superconsciousness. I was the Divine. Now, I am Vāsudeva Kṛṣṇa, son of Vāsudeva. So, I do not remember what I spoke to you as *Parabrahma* Kṛṣṇa. I shall try and remember.'

What he remembered and recounted was Anu Gītā.

Kṛṣṇa, as *Parabrahma* Kṛṣṇa, is the Divine energy, the formless *Brahman,* the same as Śiva, Viṣṇu or Devī. He is the ultimate Truth, the *Puruṣottama,* as are these other manifestations of the same *Brahman*.

It is only the ignorant cows of Kṛṣṇa who fight with the equally ignorant monkeys of Rāma, forgetting that Rāma and Kṛṣṇa are both the same energy. The ultimate energy behind all of them has no name and no form; that is the truth.

Throughout the Gītā, Vyāsa refers to Kṛṣṇa as *Bhagavān* to express His divinity. This is to emphasize the point that Kṛṣṇa is not just the mere charioteer of Arjuna, Pārtasārati, or Keśava, destroyer of the demon Keśin or Madhusūdana, destroyer of the demon Madhu, but that He is *Parabrahma* Kṛṣṇa, the supreme energy, who is formless and nameless.

This constant repetition is also to reinforce the concept that *you* too, like Arjuna, are God and no less.

Surrender is Not Based on Your Convenience

2.4 *Arjuna said:*
O killer of Madhu, how can I oppose in battle,
Bhīṣma and Droṇa, who are worthy of my worship?

2.5 *I would rather beg for my food in this world than kill the most noble of teachers.*
If I kill them, all my enjoyment of wealth and desires will be stained with blood.

2.6 *I cannot say which is better; their defeating us or our defeating them.*
We do not wish to live after slaying the sons of Dhṛtarāṣṭra who stand before us.

2.7 *My heart is overwhelmed with pity and my mind is confused about what my duty is.*
I beg of you, please tell me what is best for me. I am your disciple. Instruct me, as I seek refuge in you.

2.8 *Even if I were to attain unrivalled dominion and prosperity on Earth or even lordship over the Gods,*
How would that remove this sorrow that burns my senses?

Despite what Kṛṣṇa has said with total clarity, that Arjuna should get up and fight, Arjuna now recounts all his previous arguments. It is as if he hasn't heard Kṛṣṇa at all or not heard him correctly.

I must now tell you an important truth. Here Arjuna says, 'I am your disciple. Instruct me, as I seek refuge in you'. He means that 'My soul is surrendered unto you.' This is a lie. Had his soul been truly surrendered to Kṛṣṇa, he would simply have followed what Kṛṣṇa said and would not have waited for an intellectual explanation.

He says his soul is surrendered to Kṛṣṇa, but when Kṛṣṇa asks him to do His bidding, he is not ready to do so and is confused! Surrender out of confusion is not surrender, as you do not even know if you are doing the right thing. Understand that surrender after clarity of *śāstras,* or wisdom, is true surrender. Here Arjuna surrenders only verbally as he says that he is confused.

You must either do what you think is right or do as the master instructs. Here Arjuna wants the master to say what he wants to hear, not what the master wants to say.

Surrender first

Time and again, people come to me for advice and ask me, '*Swamiji,* I have this problem. Please advise me what to do. Whatever you tell me I shall do.' Then, if I ask them to come to the ashram for a few days or attend a meditation course because I know it will help them, they give me a dozen reasons why it cannot be done. They cite all other important tasks that they need to complete before they undertake anything that I suggest to them.

Some even say, '*Swamiji,* the time has to be right before we do that. Perhaps the time is not right.'

Nonsense… simply nonsense! Understand, you are not controlled by some unknown destiny that you can conveniently blame just because you cannot do something right. Your destiny is in your own hands.

Arjuna is asking Kṛṣṇa to tell him what he needs to do in the same way that I just described to you how people come and ask me. If what I tell them is in line with what they want, they will agree. So will Arjuna. Kṛṣṇa knows this only too well. However, only out of compassion, Kṛṣṇa continues to express and teach Arjuna the Truth. Here begins the *śāstra.* The two verses that Kṛṣṇa speaks are *sūtra,* techniques. But as Arjuna is not ready to receive them, he has to commence the *śāstra*, the background knowledge.

At this point Arjuna has not yet completely surrendered to Kṛṣṇa. He is in dilemma. He knows that his duty is to defeat his enemies and kill them if needed but his enemies are his kinsmen, his elders and his teachers. The relationship, the *saṁskāra* of his relationship with them, makes him hesitate. Arjuna brings up all that he knows from scriptures, from tradition and from hearsay, doing whatever he can to avoid the unpleasant decision to fight his own kith and kin.

Kṛṣṇa, fully aware of Arjuna's dilemma, moves forward in His mission to destroy that identity. The master is a surgeon who removes the cancer of ego. This is what Kṛṣṇa does throughout the Gītā dialogue. To give Arjuna credit, he stays through this surgery. Many weaker men would have run away from the operation theatre, this battlefield, with no desire to let go of their identities. The greatness of Arjuna lies in his determination to listen to his master and be guided by Him.

So he implores his master, 'Kṛṣṇa, please tell me what to do. I am your disciple. You are my refuge.'

It is this readiness to surrender to the master that redeems Arjuna and helps him win the war, which in reality is the war within himself.

If we are truly aware, we will see that this is the war each one of us is fighting every day. This is the war that we need to fight to drop our ego, our mind, and the identity that binds us to all the bondages upon this earth. Whatever we think is ours and whatever we think is 'me', is different from the truth. It is the master who can lead us through the path of this self-discovery, as Kṛṣṇa is now leading Arjuna. To be led, we need the attitude of true surrender.

Time Is Psychological, Not Chronological

2.9 *Sañjaya said:*
Arjuna then said to Kṛṣṇa, 'Govinda, I shall not fight,' and fell silent.

2.10 *Kṛṣṇa smilingly spoke the following words to the grief-stricken Arjuna, as they were placed in the middle of both armies.*

2.11 Bhagavān *said:*
You grieve for those who should not be grieved for and yet, you speak words of wisdom.
The wise grieve neither for the living nor for the dead.

2.12 *It is not that at any time in the past I did not exist; so did you and these rulers exist,*
And we shall not ever cease to be hereafter.

2.13 *Just as the spirit in this body passes through childhood, youth and old age,*
So does it pass into another body; the man centered within himself does not fear this.

Even though these are incidents of the past, I feel Kṛṣṇa should always be addressed in the present tense. He is still relevant to each of us today. We cannot say, 'Kṛṣṇa *was*' but 'Kṛṣṇa *is*'; not 'Kṛṣṇa *said*' but 'Kṛṣṇa *says*'.

Once again, having lamented about what he is being forced to do, and not wishing to do what he is expected to do, Arjuna, like a petulant child, sits down saying, 'I am not going to fight.' It is as if Arjuna is waiting to be persuaded. He is seeking an explanation.

If you worry for somebody living or dead, you cannot be an intelligent person. What are death and life after all? There are thousands, rather millions, who have lived and gone.

Someone once asked me, 'Why is it that natural calamities happen? Why is it that so many people die in wars and calamities? Why is God doing these things and why is God being mean?'

I told him, 'To give you an honest answer, I do not know. But if you insist on an answer, I can give you an answer the next time God calls for a conference. I can ask Him to give me an answer!'

These questions have no answer in Existence. The question is asked from a very low level, from your logic, but God is beyond your logic. You can never have an answer for these questions.

Only the ignorant worry about people who are living or dead. A truly intelligent person does not bother about death. Often people ask me, 'How was the universe created? Was it by Brahma, as Hindu scriptures say? Or was it created in six days by a nameless God as said in the Old Testament?'

I say to them what Buddha said thousands of years ago based on his personal perception. 'The universe,' Buddha said, 'has neither been created nor will it ever be destroyed. It always has been.' The universe created itself. It is the creation that embodies the creator and results in what has been created.

Our questions regarding the 'right' and 'wrong', questions of what happens around us, arise only when we feel threatened in some manner or another. Every person stricken with an incurable and fatal affliction such as cancer, would invariably ask the question, 'Why me?' If it is a young child, then certainly the parents, relatives, and friends are bound to question the justice and fairness of God.

What do we know about the fairness of God? What do we know at all about God? All we know and care about is our own welfare. Any concern about the rest of humanity occurs only after one's own comfort zone is managed. The creator is also the destroyer. What is created will be destroyed. We have no agreement with God that when we are born we will be assured of so many years of life along with the knowledge of the timing and nature of our death.

You are responsible for what happens to you

When you truly realize your Self, when you are enlightened, you will be aware of when you will die and how you will die. Living and dying are no longer issues in which you feel you need to play a part. They are progressions of Nature and, being enlightened, you flow with Nature.

We are just playing with words when we talk about *karma* and destiny, saying that they are responsible for everything that happens to us and for everything that we do. Let me tell you this: We are responsible for what happens to us. It is a misrepresentation of Nature's law to blame Nature for what happens to us.

Earthquakes and tsunamis occur because man has plundered Nature. We have ravaged the planet for our material benefit. Then we wonder why Nature misbehaves. Nature only behaves. She never misbehaves.

Nature does not guarantee that the person who creates havoc and destroys will suffer in that body. What one generation does to destroy Nature may impact another generation. From Nature's standpoint we never die. In whichever scene we reappear, we still bear responsibility for what we have done in an earlier scene. That's why questions of why a ten-year-old should die or contract cancer have neither meaning nor relevance. We are not normally aware of what one has done before and what one is therefore responsible for.

Some people question, 'Is it fair that we are held responsible for what we did in another lifetime and are not even aware of now?' What do we mean by fairness? What do we know of fairness except what we determine to be fair out of our own selfishness?

Sañjaya says Kṛṣṇa was smiling as He uttered these words. 'You Fool! You pretend to be wise and quote the scriptures. Who do you think you are quoting the scriptures to? What can you understand of what I Myself have said?'

Kṛṣṇa continues: 'Never was there a time when I did not exist, nor you and all these kings, and never in the future shall any of us cease to be.'

The essence of the whole Gītā begins with this verse. This is the gist of the whole Gītā. This is *ātmajñāna*, Self Realization. If you can understand this one verse, you can become enlightened straightaway and enter into eternal bliss.

Know your past, present and future

In Zen Buddhism, there is a beautiful meditation technique to achieve enlightenment.

You are asked to meditate on the face you had before your birth. The *koan* or *sūtra,* a technique for meditation, says, 'What was your face like before your father and mother were born?'

Upon meditating on this *koan* you realize that you existed in the past, exist in the present and will exist in the future. Your face and body may change but you continue to exist. If what Kṛṣṇa says is true, why are we worried about this life and about our death? You need to first understand the concept of the past, present and future to enable you to understand what Kṛṣṇa says.

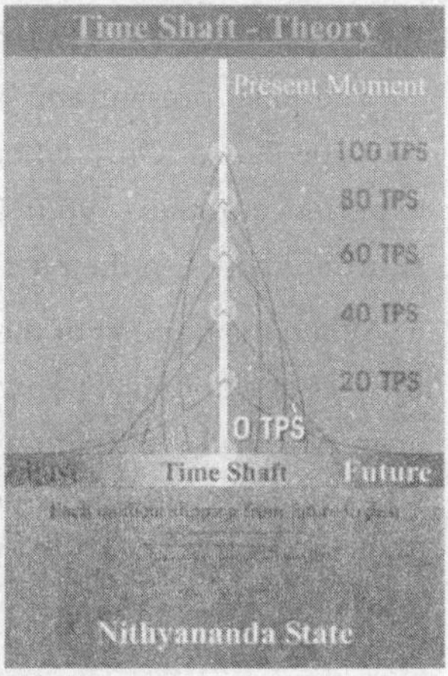

Let me explain this concept first.

Time is like a shaft continuously moving from the future on the right into the past on the left (see diagram). The future is continuously moving into the past from right to left every moment. The present is the point where the future and the past meet. Your mind as such is nothing but movements between the past and the future.

You cannot have any thoughts if you stop thinking about the past and the future. The more your thoughts shift from past to future or future to past, the higher the frequency of thoughts. Try to think of something in the present, you will find that you cannot. You can think of it only by taking it into the past or future. The higher the frequency of thoughts, the more you are caught in the physical and material world.

For example, if you have 100 Thoughts Per Second (TPS), it means you have jumped 100 times back and forth between the past and future in one second! The higher the frequency, the more you will be away from the present and the more problems will you have. If the number of thoughts reduces, you fall into the present moment.

The *Upaniṣads* talk of five body layers called *kośas*. When your frequency of thoughts is high, you are in the physical body or the grossest layer called *annamaya kośa*. When the frequency is a little less, you move into a higher energy layer called *prānamaya kośa*. When your TPS is say 60 (here the reference is just proportional), you move into the mental layer or *manomaya kośa*. When the TPS is still less, say 40, you enter the pleasure layer or the *vijñānamaya kośa*; you come a little closer to the soul. If you fall into the present moment, you are in the innermost layer, that is the *ānandamaya kośa*; you are *ātman* or the soul.

The past, present and future, all the three put together are eternal, *nitya* or *ātman*. Only when you come to the present moment do you experience *ātman* – your true Self, but as of now you are constantly shuttling between the past and future.

When the number of thoughts reduces, you will not even be aware of the passage of time. For example, when you are with someone you love, even two or three hours will seem like a short while. On the contrary, when you are with someone whose company is boring, even a short time seems very long. You will keep glancing at your watch and wondering why time does not move!

Time is more psychological than chronological. That is why, in our scriptures or *Vedās*, we have the word *kṣaṇa* to describe the unit of time. *Kṣaṇa* does not denote one second, but is defined as the gap or time interval between two thoughts. The larger the *kṣaṇa* or the gap between two thoughts, the more in the present we are. Each person's *kṣaṇa* will be different depending on how busy his mind is! When our TPS is lower, we will naturally be in ecstasy, in bliss. When the number of our thoughts is high, we are in hell. Hell and heaven are nothing but the number of thoughts that we entertain, that's all. That is why I say heaven and hell are not geographical places, but psychological spaces.

With a higher frequency of thoughts, you think you are the body. When the frequency of thoughts reduces, you think you are the mind and just emotion. When the thoughts become zero, you are there in the past, present and future; you realize you are *ātman* – Self. Only then can you realize what Kṛṣṇa says - You will be there forever. But right now the frequency of your thoughts is very high. You do not have the patience or the energy to understand who you are, your base and your nature. When you fall into the present moment, you experience that you were there in the past, are in the present and will be in the future. You realize you are eternal and not caught by the mind, jumping between the past and future.

Whatever dies can never live. Whatever lives can never die. Your deep consciousness says that something is living in you. You attribute this quality of life and consciousness to your body and mind. Do not misunderstand your consciousness to be your body and mind. You are not the body or the mind. As long as you are caught in the past and the future, you think that you are the body and mind. The moment you come down to the present moment, you experience that you are beyond the body, beyond the mind.

Here, Kṛṣṇa does not mean that we existed in the form that we are here now or that He was present always as Kṛṣṇa in the form we imagine Him to be, with a flute in His hand and a peacock feather on His head. He means that our spirits that are eternal always existed and will always exist as the divine, one with the universal energy, *Brahman*.

The gist of the second chapter is that you are the soul, that you are divine and that you are God.

The body passes through its seasons of childhood, youth, middle age and old age as the seasons of Nature do each year. Finally, it passes through death and the soul reappears, just as trees shed leaves in autumn and produce new leaves in spring. One does not grieve as one enjoys the pleasures of childhood, youth and middle age. Why then should one grieve the onset of old age and then death?

At death, the soul passes from one body into another body. It has three *kṣaṇa* to achieve this, each *kṣaṇa* being the time period between each thought. A person who is in a high thought-frequency state, a high TPS state, has a much shorter time to shift from one body to another compared to another person whose TPS is low, whose frequency of thoughts is low. A person in a no-mind, no-thought state has infinite time, as the time between thoughts is infinite. His spirit is at liberty to stay free without taking another body as long as he chooses, or more correctly, as the universe chooses.

All enlightened masters are in this category. When the spirit leaves the mind-body system, it becomes one with the universal energy.

Imagine a number of circles drawn on a whiteboard. Think of the whiteboard space as the universal energy. Individual body-mind systems are represented by the circles drawn on the whiteboard. The white space enclosed in the circles is the spirit and this is the same energy as the white space outside the circles. The space within is the individual soul and the space outside is *brahman*.

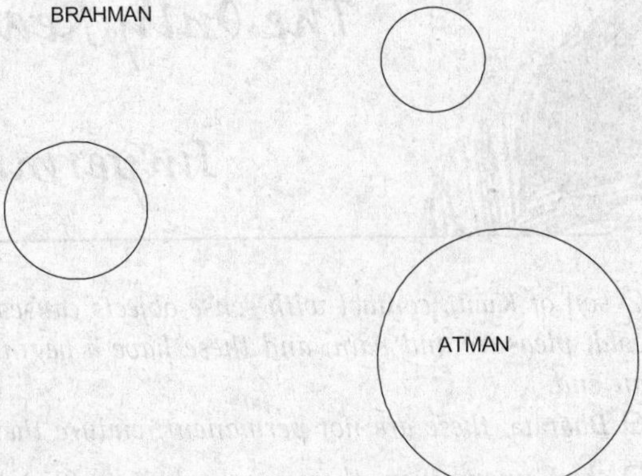

When a body-mind dies, when an individual dies, all that happens is that these perimeter lines get erased, that is all. The space within the circle merges with the space outside the circle. White merges with white. Energy merges with energy.

When the spirit, the energy, is ready to move into another mind-body system, it enters another circle. It is a continuous, ongoing process and a natural process. One who understands this process and accepts it is an integrated person. Kṛṣṇa refers to him as a '*dhīraḥ*', one who is firm, centered and aware.

The Only Reality in Life is Impermanence

2.14 *O son of Kuntī, contact with sense objects causes heat and cold, pleasure and pain, and these have a beginning and an end.*
O Bhārata, these are not permanent; endure them bravely.

2.15 *O chief among men, these surely do not afflict the man who is centered,*
Pleasure and pain are the same to him and he is ready for enlightenment.

2.16 *The non-existent has no being; that which exists never ceases to exist;*
This truth about both is perceived by those who know the Truth.

2.17 *Know It to be indestructible, by which this body is pervaded.*
Nothing can destroy It, the Imperishable.

2.18 *These bodies of material energy are perishable.*
The energy itself is eternal, incomprehensible and indestructible.
Therefore, fight, O Bhārata.

Kṛṣṇa says here that the sensory experiences are all temporary. Feelings of hot and cold, sweet and sour, wet and dry, experiences of pain and pleasure, as well as other experiences of like and dislike are all temporary. These experiences do not affect the centered person who is qualified to be enlightened.

Buddha refers to sensory experiences as *anicha* or impermanent and unreal. They are relative and based on time, space and individuals.

There are many *sādhu*s or ascetics, who stay in the higher reaches of the Himalayan mountains with very little clothing, in temperatures everyone would consider bitter cold. Renowned scientists from reputed institutions such as the Harvard Medical School have studied them. When Nature is accepted totally, heat, cold, rain, dryness and all these changes do not affect the body-mind system.

If we walk around without footwear, the earth that we walk upon becomes our friend. As long as we wear footwear with the intention of protecting ourselves from Nature, we are treating Nature as an outsider, an enemy. We can never be comfortable with Nature with this attitude.

One who is firmly grounded in himself is grounded in Nature. Kṛṣṇa says that such a person is qualified and ready for enlightenment. Such persons have brought their senses under control and as a result have their mind under control also.

What Kṛṣṇa says here, and what the wise sages of the East have understood for thousands of years, is only now being grasped by scientists and researchers. It is now accepted by medical science that the body-mind dies many deaths before its final exit. Cells within our body die in the thousands everyday and get reborn. Every single cell in your body-mind system, and therefore, every single bone, muscle, tissue, artery, vein, limb and body part is new, completely different from what it was two or three years ago.

The body-mind continually ceases to exist and gets recreated. It is not permanent. Separate from the body-mind system is our spirit that lives on eternally. The spirit remains the same throughout our life with no change despite all the changes in the body-mind system. It continues to be, to exist, even after our death. It lives on and is permanent.

When one understands this difference between what is eternal - *nitya,* and what is transient - *mitya,* one becomes a seer and knower of Truth.

Nitya and *mitya* do not translate into real and unreal. In the same way *māyā* or what is loosely translated as illusion, is not unreal. *Māyā* and *mitya* are real and perceived by our senses, but they refer to things that are not true, that are not lasting, that are not the ultimate truth. Truth here refers to the state of permanence, of being eternal. I say a living master is not present in the way that you feel and a dead master is not absent as you think. The presence of a dead master, an enlightened master who has left the body, is permanent and always real. A master is present in His absence as well.

Our perceptions through our senses may be real but not necessarily true. A dream is very real when it happens. You may get angry, frightened, excited, lustful, and such when you dream. Your body responds to the emotions that you feel in a dream and your senses react to what you observe in the dream. Yet the moment you start witnessing the dream, you awaken. You cannot dream when you become aware. The dream is not true though it seemed real when you were in it.

The same happens when you are awake and daydreaming, which is most of the time! You are awake but you fantasize. The fantasies are not permanent and you cannot do anything tangible with them. Even when you think you are fully awake, what you perceive through your senses may not be what you interpret it to mean. You judge whatever you perceive through your conditioned memories. All that you do is selectively put together pieces of what you perceive to support your judgment.

We are constantly caught in the experiences of the past, reliving them under the excuse of learning from them, but in actuality, we are caught in guilt, regret or pleasure from remembering the past experiences and memories with no ability whatsoever to do anything about them. The past is history. It is gone. Our intelligence, creativity, and bliss can be accessed only in this present moment, not in reviewing the past.

Our other mistake is to speculate about the future. The future is just as unreal as the past. If anything, it is more unreal, as it has not even happened. How can we control events of the future when we cannot control our next breath? The futility of our constant movement between past and future and back again is the greatest wonder of all. It is merely the stuff of our thoughts, supported by our belief that it is real. And it is the source of all of our suffering!

The only truth, the only true reality, is the truth of this very moment. As long as we focus on this present moment, we are truly aware and centered. The present moment alone is *sat*, truth, everything else is *asat*, untruth. One who realizes this and acts accordingly is enlightened, says Kṛṣṇa.

We are all made of body, mind, and spirit. The body is tangible; we can feel its boundaries. As long as we feel the body working smoothly, we say we are in good health. Our mind is subtle. We do not feel its boundaries. Yet, we feel the effects of the mind as thoughts, desires, emotions, etc. Mind and its intelligence are inbuilt into our cellular structure.

Recent studies have shown that it is our belief systems, which in turn arise from our experiences, that define the development of our mind and in turn influence the cellular structure. Earlier it was believed that genetic modifications to the cellular structure influenced the way we behaved. Now it has been proven that it is our behavior that leads to our beliefs and thereafter determines our genetics.

Even subtler is the spirit. What is this thing called spirit or soul? We cannot see it and we cannot touch it. Becoming aware of this subtle spirit or soul is just what Self-realization is all about.

In these verses, Kṛṣṇa says first that the spirit pervades the body. Secondly, He states that the body and mind are destroyed at death. Thirdly, He declares that the spirit does not die at death. Fourthly, He explains that the spirit is beyond our mental comprehension.

When death happens, bodily functions stop. The senses, which are a function of the mind, stop working. The brain, which processes thoughts, stops working. We can see the body-mind system degenerate. What we do not see is that there is something within us that does not perish at death. Kṛṣṇa clarifies here that this is the Self, the *Ātman,* the energy that never dies.

What is death? Is it the spirit's leaving the body that causes death, or is it that death forces the spirit into leaving the body? This spirit is energy. It is the energy of life. After death this energy moves from within the body that it occupied temporarily to the universal energy that surrounds the body.

Kṛṣṇa urges Arjuna to fight with the full understanding that what he thinks of as real is unreal, that what he thinks of as permanent is impermanent, and what he thinks he is about to destroy can, in truth, never be destroyed. Even if he wants to, Arjuna cannot destroy the imperishable spirit that lives on.

Arjuna's concern about the death of his kinsmen and elders arises out of his insecurity about his own death. He does not realize his true imperishable nature and therefore he is afraid of dying. By extension of this fear, he is afraid of others' deaths as well, especially at his own hands. Kṛṣṇa tells him that there is no such thing as death. He tells him that death is unreal.

All our lives we see people around us dying. We all know that death is the only certainty in this otherwise uncertain world. When we wake up from a dream, we don't mourn our dream lives, as real as they felt at the time. Do we? No. In the same way, when we awaken into the highest state of consciousness, we have the same experience that this 'real' life was only a dream. Even when the body perishes, we do not. It is impossible because we are eternal.

Kṛṣṇa is stating this reality straight out. He says firmly that there is no such thing as death. What dies is never really alive. What lives on has permanent existence anyway. What does have existence, what is truly real, exists now, has always existed, and will exist forever!

You Are Immortal!

2.19 *Neither understands, he who takes the Self to be slayer*
nor he who thinks he is slain.
He who knows the truth understands that the Self does
not slay, nor is It slain.

2.20 *The Self is neither born nor does It ever die. After having*
been, It never ceases not to be.
It is Unborn, Eternal, Changeless and Ancient. It is not
killed when the body is killed.

2.21 *O Pārtha, how can man slay or cause others to be slain,*
When he knows It to be indestructible, eternal, unborn,
and unchangeable?

2.22 *Just as man casts off his worn-out clothes and puts on new*
ones,
The Self casts off worn-out bodies and enters newer ones.

2.23 *Weapons do not cleave the Self, fire does not burn It,*
water does not moisten It
And wind does not dry It.

2.24 *The Self can neither be broken, nor burnt, nor dissolved,*
nor dried up.
It is eternal, all-pervading, stable, immovable and
ancient.

2.25 *The Self is said to be unmanifest, unthinkable and*
unchangeable.
Knowing this to be such, you should not grieve.

Kṛṣṇa directly addresses some of Arjuna's earlier doubts in these verses. Arjuna has claimed that destroying his relatives and his mentors will bring him untold grief, not only in this world but in future births as well. Kṛṣṇa explains to Arjuna that all his fears are misplaced. Therefore, no one can kill another person or be killed by another person from the vantage point of the absolute. Both are illusions.

There is no death in reality

The spirit that occupies the body lives on forever. It is the body, the sheath that covers it, that dies and is reborn. What Kṛṣṇa says here is radically different from what any other scripture has said. Kṛṣṇa is not saying, 'Be good and you will be taken care of when you die. If you are bad, you will suffer.' He says, 'There is no death!' That's all.

Just imagine that as an infant, you are cast away on an island with no other living being. As you grow older, will you have any idea of what it is to die? When you die you will not know anything. Here Kṛṣṇa is talking to someone who has witnessed death. So, He has to explain to him that death does not exist; it is a mere passage from one shell into another. Death is a transfer from one body into another.

It is the individual's attachment to the body that creates the illusion that the individual also perishes with the body. Attachment to the body is the most intense of all attachments. We also get attached to material possessions as well as our relationships. One who understands that all these attachments are temporary and are the cause of all our suffering, understands the truth.

In some cultures, people are bred on the belief that one's life ends at death. This belief leads to desperate behavior, as if there is no further time for the individual to seek happiness. Hell and heaven have been created based upon this concept of having a single life and the permanence of death. They are used by these cultures to control people through fear and greed. Once a person understands that death, like birth, is merely a passage and sees the continuity of being, the fear of losing one's identity disappears along with fears of sins and hell.

This is why religions that accept the continuance of life after death, as Hinduism and Buddhism do, breed a culture of tolerance amongst their followers. There is no rush to live and extract the maximum juice out of one's life in a single birth. Those who understand this spiritual truth preach acceptance, inclusion, and compassion, and they have no desire to convert others to their beliefs.

It is easy to misinterpret these verses and propose that if there is no one really killing or being killed, and then nothing stops us from mindlessly killing. That is not what Kṛṣṇa intends.

Arjuna fully understands the implications of killing, and that, as a *kṣatriya,* it is his *dharmic* code of conduct that requires him to slay his enemies. Here Kṛṣṇa reveals a more subtle level of truth to him that he hasn't yet grasped. Arjuna shies away from killing, not because of his conviction of *ahimsā,* non-violence, but because he identifies with the people he has to destroy. His hesitation is from ignorance, attachment and fantasy, not from the wisdom of non-violent compassion.

Kṛṣṇa's message to Arjuna is as it would be to someone who has to uphold *dharma* at all costs, and in today's context that would apply to a soldier or a policeman. However, it would not be a blind acceptance of orders that would compel such people to take lives. It would not be killing for gain and it would not be killing out of fear that one would be killed. It would be an ultimate action, born out of the knowledge that such destruction is needed for universal good and that such destruction would lead to creation.

You may ask, 'If nothing is destroyed and nothing can be destroyed, is there no sin in killing at all? Is Kṛṣṇa indifferent to mass violence?' No, He is not. For one thing, Kṛṣṇa speaks as an enlightened master from an existentialist perspective and says that even when the body perishes, the spirit lives on, and therefore, there is no death.

Violence and killing are not merely physical acts. They are psychological compulsions being acted out in the physical realm. A person with Hitler's mindset but without Hitler's power would have behaved similarly but on a smaller scale. The ruler of a country who orders warfare against others is the violent one, even if he hides behind his throne. Violence of the mind carries on as the *vāsana*, or mindset, after death. The spirit is violated by this attitude of violence.

A violent man is always a coward. He does not have the courage to face the truth. He does not have the sensitivity to treat others as he expects to be treated. In modern times, violence has increased because it is so much easier to kill than to work through problems and find solutions.

Most often we do not even have to face the person we want to kill. We can fire a pistol or a rifle; we can throw bombs; and if one is a ruler with power, he or she can press a button or convince a nation that unleashing havoc is the best option available. We do not have to face the consequences of what we are doing and can pretend we know nothing about it. We can even pretend that we are committing these acts in the name of God and righteousness.

When we become aware, when we become conscious that the person next to us is actually an expression of the energy of God, how can we possibly respond with violence? It has nothing to do with whether someone is family, part of our culture, part of our religion or part of our nation. It does not matter if the other person shares our history, habits or beliefs. The other person may oppose all that we believe in. Yet he is as much a part of this universe as we are.

That is why Kṛṣṇa says, 'O Pārtha, how can man slay or cause others to be slain, when he knows It to be indestructible, eternal, unborn, and unchangeable?'

If this message of Kṛṣṇa is truly understood, there can be no violence in this world, no killing at all. You will not even kill an insect. You will not kill even in self-defense, because once you are in awareness, your awareness is transmitted to the other being and that being will not even attack you.

Once in Oṁkāreśvar, a forest region, I saw a huge bear when I got up from meditation. It was very close to me. I felt no fear. The bear looked at me and walked away. I have come across deadly cobras many times. They just look and go away. When I feel no fear, and therefore no enmity towards them, they understand and accept. All this talk about killing others in self-defense is a lie.

All the nations in this world claim they have standing armies because they need to defend themselves. The right to defend is enshrined in all self-respecting constitutions. So, if everybody is only defending, who then is offending? Does anyone think about that?

You are imperishable

Kṛṣṇa continues:

Just as man casts off his worn-out clothes and puts on new ones, the Self casts off worn-out bodies and enters newer ones. Weapons do not cleave the Self, fire does not burn It, water does not moisten It, and wind does not dry It. The Self can neither be broken, nor burnt, nor dissolved, nor dried up. It is eternal, all-pervading, stable, immovable and ancient.

These verses are amongst the most quoted verses of the Bhagavad Gītā. Here, in very few words, Kṛṣṇa expounds upon the entire truth of life and death, mind, body and spirit. He clarifies why we should accept death gladly, as a matter of fact and course, instead of grieving over it. He says this so simply that even an innocent child can understand this truth.

Do we grieve over a dirty shirt that we have cast away when we know we will have a new one? Do we say, 'Oh, I am so attached to this shirt. I cannot let it go. Let me keep wearing it. I shall be heartbroken if I have to take off this shirt'. If only we understand that a body needs to be changed when it grows old, in just the same way as with the dirty shirt, there would be no grief, no attachment.

An understanding of the truth that Kṛṣṇa unveils here is the key to immortality. It is the doorway to enlightenment. 'Do not fear death,' Kṛṣṇa says, 'neither yours nor that of others. It is the disappearance of this material body. You are beyond this material body. Even if the body perishes, you live on so you do not have to worry or fear.'

What survives death is the sacred spirit in you that can never be destroyed. It is pure energy. How can you destroy energy? Science states that energy can only appear in another form; it cannot be destroyed. It is the energy that creates the elements. It is the energy that has always been and will be, never created, never destroyed. It is unchanging, neutral, eternal and all pervading.

'When you are that spirit, that energy,' asks Kṛṣṇa, 'what is there to grieve about? When you are the Divine yourself, what can you fear? What can you want? What more can you ask for?' This explanation holds good for every one of us. We are divine. We live on despite what we see to be the destruction of our body and identity. Once we understand this truth, nothing can disturb us.

'Weapons cannot cleave It, fire cannot burn It.' If only the so-called leaders of this world understood what Kṛṣṇa is saying! Then, there would be no need for the United Nations, Peace Days, Friendship Days and so on. Everyday would be a Peace Day.

At the heart of all torture and killing is fear and greed. When we sincerely contemplate these teachings and these verses of the Gītā in particular, such concerns dissolve and we live peacefully with others and ourselves.

If you are courageous, you will face anyone and state your case. In the event that you cannot convince the other person, you will accept the situation and walk away. It is when we get opinionated, fixed in obsessive beliefs and become intolerant of other beliefs, that we become afraid. We become afraid that we may lose our identity. That insecurity and fear of loss of identity is greater than the fear of death. So we respond violently. To avoid being killed, we kill.

Once we understand what Kṛṣṇa says, that death is like changing a worn-out garment, our fears will disappear. If we are truly wise, this false identity itself will disappear. Why do we need that garment at all? Then there is no need even to worry about that change. We can live blissfully with the garment and relax from it when the time comes. Going beyond the garment is going beyond the attachment to the body-mind. It is going beyond the cycle of life and death, the cycle of *samsāra*. It is the ultimate relaxation.

Death is But a Passage

2.26 *O mighty-armed, even if you should think of the soul as being constantly born and constantly dying,*
Even then, you should not lament.

2.27 *Indeed, death is certain for the born and birth is certain for the dead. Therefore, you should not grieve over the inevitable.*

2.28 *O* **Bhārata**, *Beings are unmanifest in their beginning, unmanifest again in their end, and seemingly manifest in their middle state.*
What are we grieving about?

2.29 *One sees It as a wonder, another speaks of It as a wonder, another hears of It as a wonder.*
Yet, having heard, none understands It at all!

2.30 *O* **Bhārata**, *This that dwells in the body of everyone can never be destroyed;*
Do not grieve for any creature.

Sometime ago when I was delivering a discourse in India, news arrived that my father had died. I continued with the discourse. Later that night, many of our disciples traveled with me to Tiruvannamalai where the body lay. If you see the videos of this event, you will find that my mother never once cried. She was a very traditional person, brought up in a rural environment that sets great importance on how one should behave socially. When one's husband dies one is naturally heartbroken; especially as in the case of my mother and father, who were very close to each other. His departure would have been a great loss to her. She understood the meaning of these verses without my ever having to explain them to her.

When I told her that my father is now in the energy form that is eternal, she trusted my words implicitly and joined me in celebrating his release. Many of our followers have seen the video recording of this event. They could see Kṛṣṇa's words in action and get over any fear that they may have still had about death. Many have overcome their fear and grief of death and instead have learned to celebrate death.

We are not talking about philosophers and saints here. We are talking about very ordinary people whose lifestyle was all about fear of death and grief at death. They understood that the spirit lives on after the body perishes, and death is indeed an event to celebrate and not to grieve. It is only the scholars, who have a mere intellectual understanding of what the Gītā says, with no trust in Kṛṣṇa, who still suffer from the fear of death. Kṛṣṇa's words are not about logic; they are about trust in the master and the eternal truths.

The celebrated Greek philosopher Socrates was sentenced to death because Greek society could not accept his views and his constant questioning attitude. Since he refused to reject his own philosophy, Socrates was sentenced to death. As he calmly awaited his death, his disciples asked him, 'Master, are you not afraid of dying?' Socrates said, 'There are two possibilities. One, that there is indeed life after death. In that case I shall continue to exist in the same form. The other is that there is no life after death. In that situation I shall not be aware of anything that would happen after death. In either case, what is there to worry about?'

Whether the spirit goes to a region called hell or another region called heaven is as debatable a point as whether there is an undying spirit at all, or whether that spirit reincarnates. You may believe whatever you like to believe. Occidental religions don't believe in the cycle of life and death. They seem to believe that death is once and for all. Even then what is there to worry about?

A deeply disturbed woman approached Buddha one morning. She brought the body of her dead son to Buddha and said, 'Master, they tell me that you are the only one in this world with the power to revive the dead. Please give life back to my son.'

Buddha knew that no words of His could console the mother. He merely said, 'Mother, please bring me a handful of mustard seeds from any household that has not experienced death so far and I shall revive your son.'

The woman went door-to-door seeking a handful of mustard seeds. Every household she visited was only too glad to give her what she asked for. However, they all said that they too had suffered such a loss in their household.

She came back to Buddha and said, 'Master, I now understand that death is inevitable and that there can be no life without death. Thank you for teaching me this invaluable truth. I would like to sit at your feet for the rest of my life.'

Bringing the dead back to life is not a miracle. It can be done under certain circumstances, but to transform individuals and to instill truth in them is indeed the miracle that only a true master can perform.

Many of us do believe that life is a wonder; truly so. Life is wondrous! We do not understand how life is created. We may have a biological explanation as to how a new life is created. Even today there is no absolute proof as to how the universe was created. All one has are theories such as Big Bang, etc. What was there before the Big Bang? No one knows.

Buddha rightly observed, 'The universe creates itself. It always was and always will be.' No one knows as well, how the first life form originated. Again, there are only theories. The explanation for 'abiogenesis', creation of life from non-living matter, has no scientific proof as yet. The first life form just seems to have happened. One fine morning or evening or night, the first amino acid, the first life block, seems to have sprung up from nowhere.

From time immemorial this has been the human quest. What happens after life, or more correctly, after death? Conversely, what were we before we were born? The cycle of life and death is a mystery and a wonder. Quantum Physics and Molecular Biology are making rapid advances in this area and it is possible that there would be some 'proof' soon.

Those who are confident enough to accept the truth of the eternal nature of the spirit are fortunate. They are blessed. Those who fight and grieve are the wretched, the miserable. You cannot fight life or death. They are both beyond you, out of your control. You can marvel at them and be happy and joyous. Or you can keep questioning them and be miserable. This is the choice and free will you have.

The illustrious King Yayāti lived for hundreds of years. *Bhāgavatam*, the Hindu epic, says that when Yama, the god of death, came to Yayāti at his appointed time to die, Yayāti begged to be allowed to live on. He said he had not lived life enough and he needed more time. Yama relented and said that if one of his sons would give Yayāti the rest of his life, then he could live that long. Using the life span of his son, Yayāti lived many more years. Finally the realization dawned on him that no matter how long he lived, his desires would never cease and that fulfillment would never happen through material enjoyment. Yayāti gave himself up to Yama once he realized this truth.

It is not death that frightens us. It is leaving our desires and unlived life that frightens us.

The problem is that we do not know how to live a fulfilled life, how to genuinely enjoy ourselves so that our desires are fulfilled. To be truly joyful, to be eternally blissful, is to understand the truth that you are indestructible, that your spirit lives on. Death is not an end; it is a passage of sorts. The truth is that the spirit is not satisfied with mere material pleasures. The more you enjoy through your senses, the more the need for enjoyment. Discontentment with material pleasures alone is hardwired into the human psyche.

Spirituality is the total understanding and enjoyment of life - materially, physically, emotionally, relationally and in all senses without discontent and with responsibility. This enjoyment and responsibility arise out of awareness of the present moment. That is when our mind stops flitting from the past to the future, from regrets to speculation. The present moment is the only moment when we are truly alive and awake. The rest of the time we are in deep sleep, even if our eyes are open. We are in virtual death. Funnily, the walking dead are afraid to die.

If we don't believe in God, we still need to accept that there are no answers to what we were before we were born and what we will be once we are dead. It is still a mystery with no answers except from the great *ṛṣis*. This understanding can only come with the understanding that we live on in spirit.

A Zen master was asked, 'Now that you are enlightened, what is the difference in your perception of things around you?'

The master said, 'Before enlightenment, I saw a mountain as a mountain and a river as a river. During the process towards enlightenment the mountain was not a mountain and the river was not a river. Now again, the mountain is a mountain and the river is a river.'

The master here means that before he set out on his spiritual journey, he just saw the physical forms of the mountains, rivers, etc. But once he started experiencing the energy behind them, he saw them all as manifestations of the very same energy.

Kṛṣṇa says whatever is permanent and real was intangible before it became tangible and again it will become intangible. Everything is in a state of becoming something else. At every moment we die and are reborn; millions of cells in our body-mind system die everyday and are reborn. Yet, through all this change there is continuity.

Code of The Samurai

2.31 *You should look at your own duty as a kṣatriya.*
There is nothing higher for a kṣatriya than a righteous war. You ought not to hesitate.

2.32 *O Pārtha, happy indeed are the kṣatriya who are called to fight in such a battle without seeking;*
This opens for them the door to heaven.

2.33 *If you will not fight this righteous war, then you will incur the sin of having abandoned your duty and you will lose your reputation.*

2.34 *People, too, will remember your everlasting dishonor, and to one who has been honored, dishonor is worse than death.*

2.35 *The great generals will think that you have withdrawn from the battle because you are a coward.*
You will be looked down upon by those who had thought much of you and your heroism in the past.

2.36 *Many unspeakable words would be spoken by your enemies reviling your power.*
Can there be anything more painful than this?

2.37 *Slain, you will achieve heaven; victorious, you will enjoy the earth.*
O son of Kuntī, stand up determined to fight.

2.38 *Pleasure and pain, gain and loss, victory and defeat – treat them all the same.*
Do battle for the sake of battle. You shall incur no sin.

Kṛṣṇa works on Arjuna at two levels. Here, Kṛṣṇa addresses Arjuna's fears about killing his relatives and elders and teaches him that what he considers to be the end of life for these people is just one step in their journey.

Kṛṣṇa explains to Arjuna why, from a societal point of view, he should not run away from the battlefield, but instead, stay on and fight like a warrior should. Kṛṣṇa here addresses Arjuna as the *kṣatriya*, the warrior.

In each society there are groups of people who are the designated protectors of that society. They are the warriors who defend their country. In the same manner, there are others who are designated the clerics and priests, the teachers, the traders, and so on.

When Kṛṣṇa refers to Arjuna as a *kṣatriya*, he is referring to the entire personality of Arjuna, the great warrior. Arjuna is the quintessential warrior, the samurai who knows no fear, and yet is now disturbed by issues of whether he is doing right or wrong by fighting against his kinsmen. The code of the *kṣatriya* is a professional code. Rights and wrongs no longer apply.

Kṛṣṇa says, 'Fight! You are a *kṣatriya*. By fighting as your duty demands, you earn merits and go to heaven. If you run away from this war you will be dishonored, and for a *kṣatriya*, dishonor is far worse than death. If you are defeated and slain you will ascend to heaven. If you are victorious, you will enjoy material benefits in this world itself. Therefore, fight as it is your duty as a *kṣatriya*.'

Kṛṣṇa says to treat pain and pleasure, gain and loss, victory and defeat all the same. He says to fight without worrying about the outcome. 'Isn't fighting and killing people a sin?', you may ask. Then why is it that Kṛṣṇa not only encourages Arjuna, but actually forces Arjuna to fight and kill? There is no logic here. Kṛṣṇa's exhortation is beyond human rationale. It is not what you do that matters. It is who you are that matters. An enlightened master can do no wrong even if he kills because when he kills, it would be with awareness and not for personal benefit. There can be no violence in his actions, only ultimate good. On the other hand, any average person, even while doing an act of kindness, may be doing something wrong.

Kṛṣṇa is not worried about what you do; He is only concerned about who you are. If your actions are innocent of motives, whatever you do is right. If what you do is motivated by fear and greed, pain and pleasure, victory and defeat, you can do nothing right in the sense that it will leave a lingering impression in your inner space.

What if you were in a totally strange place for a very short period and you knew that nothing you did would have any repercussions? Would you have any inhibitions based on what your conditioning had been? What happens when the fear of loss of reputation and loss of identity disappears? Will you be the same person? What happens when you have an Aladdin's lamp with a genie that makes all your dreams come true? How long will the excitement last when you know that whatever you wish will happen? Will your greed still last?

Fear and greed are strong motivators because we are not centered; we do not know who we are. Here Kṛṣṇa is breaking that mould. Act without fear and greed, He says. Do not worry about consequences. This injunction is against all societal and religious conditioning.

Kṛṣṇa, as the transcendental *Parabrahman,* is not concerned with the practical and societal consequences of Arjuna's walking out of the battlefield. He is only concerned about the impact that will have on Arjuna's inner self. If Arjuna had truly been steeped in *ahiṁsa,* non-violence, Kṛṣṇa would have never attempted to persuade Arjuna into violence. In these verses, Kṛṣṇa is trying to get Arjuna to transcend his conditioned actions based on fear and greed relating to the killing of his kinsmen. He is trying to get him to act without worrying about the outcome.

What Matters is Experience, Not Knowledge

2.39 *What has been taught to you concerns the wisdom of Sāṅkhya. Now, listen to the wisdom of yoga.*
Having known this, O Pārtha, you shall cast off the bonds of action.

2.40 *There is no wasted effort or dangerous effect from this.*
Even a little knowledge of this, even a little practice of yoga, protects one from great fear.

2.41 *O Joy of the Kuru, all you need is single-pointed determination;*
The thoughts of the irresolute are many, branched and endless.

2.42 *Foolish ones speak a lot, taking pleasure in eulogizing the words of* Vedās, *O Pārtha, saying, 'There is nothing else.'*

2.43 *Men of little knowledge are very much attached to the flowery words of the* Vedās *that recommend various fruitful actions for elevation to heavenly planets, resulting in high birth, power, and so forth.*
Being desirous of sense gratification and opulent life, they say that there is nothing more than this to living.

2.44 *Those whose minds are diverted by such teachings and who cling to pleasure and lordship*
Are not determined or resolute and are not fit for steady meditation and samādhi.

2.45 *O Arjuna! Be you above the three attributes that the* Vedās *deal in; free yourself from the pairs of opposites and be always in sattva (goodness),*
Free from all thoughts of acquisition or preservation, be established in the Self.

2.46 The sage who has known the Self has little use for the vedic scriptures as these are like a pool of water in a place that is already in flood.

Kṛṣṇa begins his teachings of *Karma Yoga* to Arjuna in these verses. These verses should be read carefully by those who believe solely in scriptural authority, based on their superficial understanding of what has been said.

Kṛṣṇa unequivocally says here, 'Forget the *Vedās*.'

He says, 'All the knowledge contained in the *Vedās* is of as much use as water in a flood to one who has realized himself. The *Vedās* are limiting; they concern the three attributes, *satva, rajas* and *tamas*, the attributes of calmness, aggressive action and lazy inaction. The time has come now to move beyond these attributes, at least move from *rajas* into the state of *satva*, calmness.'

'Do not quote to Me what the scriptures say,' Kṛṣṇa says. He continues, 'Do not tell me about what you should do and should not do in this life through rituals and practices that will please the deities and ancestors so that you will benefit materially in this life and spiritually in some after-life. All this is for people with limited understanding of their own Self, people who have not experienced the Truth. These are the people who still hanker after fulfilling sensual pleasures and achieving name and fame.'

'Move beyond them to the single-pointed determination of yoga that I shall teach you,' Kṛṣṇa says, 'and be established in a state where you are no longer concerned about creation, preservation and destruction. You will be beyond these and reach the state of *Parabrahman*.'

Only a master, the master of the universe, can say such things and get away with it! Kṛṣṇa's authority as He speaks these words is compelling. He is casting away the divinely transmitted scriptures, the *Vedās*, to instill truth in the mind of Arjuna. It is the truth as spoken by the Divine who Himself has all the knowledge contained in the *Vedās*.

Kṛṣṇa refers to that truth here in these verses, the truth of the highest energy. 'Do not be carried away by the apparent ritualistic approach of the *Vedās* as propounded by half-learned scholars,' the master says; go beyond; go beyond duality. All these seem to bring joy but are transient; that joy is the brief intermission between periods of sorrow. Go beyond and seek the firm truth of the ONE, the union, that is yoga,' He says to Arjuna.

'There is something beyond the superficial understanding,' Kṛṣṇa says, 'that will take you beyond the three human attributes of *satva* (calmness), *rajas* (active action) and *tamas* (passive inaction) and into liberation arising out of true understanding. At that stage you will be beyond creation, preservation and destruction, as these would have no meaning in the understanding of the permanence of the ultimate energy.'

Kṛṣṇa finally says, 'Once you understand and realize *Brahman*, all the knowledge of the *Vedās* that you quote so passionately will be of as much relevance to you as a lake in the midst of an ocean.'

Kṛṣṇa is leading Arjuna step by step, as if teaching a baby to walk. One by one the master demolishes Arjuna's arguments and fears, dispelling his dilemma. These first baby steps address Arjuna's intellect, for that's all Arjuna has been using until now. Kṛṣṇa shows Arjuna how inadequate and meaningless his intellectual knowledge is. It is all borrowed, with no experiential backing. He now seeks to lead him into experiential knowledge.

Act Without Worry About The Result

2.47 *You have a right only to work, but never to its outcome.*
Let not the outcome be your motive; but do not move into inaction.

2.48 *O Dhañanjaya! Do what you have to do with no attachment to outcome, being centered in yoga.*
Be balanced in success and failure. Evenness of mind is yoga.

The entire teaching of Bhagavad Gītā can be summarized in the above two verses. The sheer brilliance of the wisdom of the universal master is reflected in these verses. Whenever I get a chance, I refer to these verses to explain how one should lead one's life.

Kṛṣṇa says many, many things in these few words. He says, 'You have the right and responsibility to work. You have no responsibility or right to the results of that work. Do not focus on the result and make it either an object of greed to chase or fear to stay away from. Do what you have to do with a centered mind without worrying about whether you will succeed or fail.'

Nothing more can be said or ever needs to be said about why and how one should perform.

Many people wrongly communicate these verses and misunderstand these verses. There are people who stay away from work that they fear may end in adverse results. As long as the results can be positive either to themselves or others, they will carry out what they are assigned sincerely. But when they think that something bad may happen, they will stop doing whatever they are doing. There are others who feel that doing nothing and disengaging from all action is the best solution, since all actions result in reactions and they accumulate *karma*. Kṛṣṇa says, 'Stop! Who do you think you are? You are here to do My work. You have no right to take the results that are Mine.' Awareness of what Kṛṣṇa says here is the solution to almost all our day-to-day problems. Do what you have to do without worrying about the results.

Many of you in corporate life are focused on results. You will do something only if you think it will be effective. You get caught in the result even before you start. So how do you define what is effective? For whom should it be effective?

Ninety percent of the time effectiveness is interpreted as something that benefits our self interest. Even if it benefits the organization, we do it because our performance will be recognized and we will be rewarded. We also do it because we are afraid we may be punished if what we do does not produce results. All institutions, whether corporate, societal, or religious operate on this principle of greed and fear to make us do what they want and to prevent us from doing what they do not want us to do.

Walk the talk

You are not true to yourself when you say one thing and do another. You do not walk your talk. When I ordain teachers of my practices and mission, I tell them only one thing: Walk your talk.

When you walk your talk and your talk is true, then you do not have a problem, but if the talk itself is untrue, then your walk and your actions will also be untrue. Ultimately, it is all about the truth, your awareness, and being in the present moment. If what you preach comes from awareness and the truth of your own experience and you act in accordance with that truth and awareness, then there is no differentiation between thoughts, words and actions. All will be true.

What Kṛṣṇa says here is the law of Nature. Nature just acts. Nature does not think about successes or failures, rewards or punishments. People ask me, '*Swamiji*, why is nature so cruel? Why are there natural disasters? Why do young children die?' The answer is what Kṛṣṇa gives. Nature goes about its job without any thought about what the end result will be. The problem is that we do not understand the laws of Nature. We measure natural actions by our yardstick of logic.

You will then ask me, 'How do we know what to do? How do we know what is the path of righteousness? How do we know what our *dharma* is? Do we decide we are a *kṣatriya*, therefore we should fight and kill and not worry about who dies, or do we decide we are a *vaiśya*, a business person, in which case our *dharma* is to make money without worrying about how we make it?'

No, Kṛṣṇa is not talking about acting in selfishness; the universal master is talking about acting in awareness. He says, 'Be centered in yoga and drop all attachment to results; do what you have to do.' Yoga is your realization of your own Self, your realization that you are divine. When you perform with this awareness and with no expectations, you will do what is right and just.

Suffering happens when we link our thoughts

Our thoughts are unconnected, illogical and unpredictable. It is only when we link thoughts together that problems start and suffering happens. Ninety percent of what we observe and experience is never recorded by our conscious memory; it just slips into our unconscious. Within the ten percent of what we retain, what stays in our memory is always that which falls outside the pattern. If it is part of a normal pattern we will almost always ignore and forget the event. If your spouse is always in a grumpy mood, it is no surprise if he or she is in a grumpy mood today too. But if your spouse is especially caring and loving today, then that would be a miracle and noteworthy!

The trouble is that our mind picks up these exceptions, because that is what it remembers and uses to form a pattern. It then expects that exception to happen again. When it does not happen we are unhappy; if it does, we are happy until the next time when it does not happen. Do not link thoughts and create a shaft of thoughts. Unclutch from your thoughts and automatically the mind will drop. This is the way to stay in the present. Unclutching is not about being idle. You can be doing nothing and yet occupy your mind fully. That is what they mean by saying that an idle mind is the devil's workshop. When you have nothing to do, you end up creating fantasies.

With a no-thought mind comes great awareness and energy; idleness or lethargy is far from that. A confused and furiously overworked mind is constantly occupied with chatter and fantasies that can result in apathy and idleness. When you are unclutched, you are in present moment awareness. When you are in the present moment, regrets of your past and expectations of the future are absent from your mind. Fear or greed does not influence you and the outcome. You do what is right naturally and easily.

That is why Kṛṣṇa says that you must act in the present moment. He says, 'Do not get attached to the results of your action, nor get attached to inaction, thinking that it could be an easy way out of this problem.'

Stand up And be Counted

2.49 *O Dhañanjaya, centered in yoga, balanced in success and failure, act with no attachment*
Such evenness of mind is called yoga.

2.50 *O Dhañanjaya, beyond the yoga of wisdom is action.*
Wretched are those whose motive is the outcome; surrender yourself to wisdom.

2.51 *Endowed with the wisdom of evenness of mind, move away from both good and evil deeds in this life;*
Devote yourself to yoga. Skill in action is yoga.

2.52 *The wise, having abandoned the outcome of their actions and possessed of knowledge, are freed from the cycle of birth and death.*
They go to the state that is beyond all sorrow.

2.53 *When your wisdom takes you beyond delusion,*
You shall be indifferent to what has been heard and what is yet to be heard.

2.54 *When you are not confused by what you have heard and your wisdom stands steady and unmoving in the Self,*
You shall attain Self–realization.

He says, 'Act without attachment. Do not worry about success or failure in results. Center yourself in the wisdom that takes you beyond action and the desire for fruits of action. Once you are centered in wisdom you will act wisely. Once you give up attachment to results, you will be freed from the cycle of birth and death and you will be beyond sorrow.' He then adds, 'When you are centered in wisdom you will no longer be deluded by what you hear, be it from the scriptures or other elders. You are then liberated.'

Kṛṣṇa's words resonate even today and are perhaps far more relevant today. We are bombarded by information on all sides twenty-four hours a day, whether we like it or not. When something is stated repeatedly, especially by an authority, we tend to believe and accept it without reservation. No one even needs to force you to believe; your brain can be washed without any pressure, without coercion. This is also what all political, religious, and corporate marketing teams do to convince you about their products and services.

The first response of most of us is to believe rather than doubt. If we are told again and again from childhood onwards that we must listen to elders and figures of authority, we grow up tending to do just that. It also happens that when what we see fits our fantasies, we don't bother to question. Institutions use this power with great effect upon us. All religions and cultures have some book or other that is believed to be divine in origin and which must be obeyed implicitly. Does our inner experience tell us that whatever such a book says is even relevant to us today?

The vedic scriptures, the *śruti,* divine in origin, and the *smṛti,* rules and regulations laid down later by Manu and other sages, make no such claims. In fact, vedic scriptures have both the humility and the arrogance to challenge us to transform ourselves according to the needs of the day, but stipulate that we first experience what is said. Vedic scriptures are not dead knowledge that is a burden for us to abide by, but rather living guidelines that lead us into wisdom and liberation.

'So,' Kṛṣṇa says, 'let the *Vedās* say what they want. You may hear whatever you must, but put what you hear, see, and read to the test of wisdom to go beyond delusion.' He is the source of the knowledge, and yet He asks him to experiment and be guided by his inner wisdom, not by what he merely hears.

What courage, what authority! Only one who is so sure about the truth can say, 'Do not listen to what I say and how I act, but listen to your inner voice of truth born out of your own awareness and experience.'

Kṛṣṇa is taking Arjuna on the path of enlightenment through simple steps. He says, 'Don't be inactive; do what you need to do. Do it with no expectations and no attachment to results. Do it with a centered mind and in wisdom. Do it with the wisdom of your own inner calling and not because of something you have heard. You will then go beyond all suffering and be liberated.' These steps are so simple that everyone can practice them; in fact every one *should* practice them. Stay fully centered in the experience of the present, and based on the truth of that experience, act. You can never go wrong. I promise you that.

Follow That Man!

2.54 *O Keśava! What is the description of one who stays in the present moment and is merged in the awareness of truth and wisdom?*
How does one of steady wisdom speak, how does he sit, how does he walk?

2.55 Śrī Bhagavān *said:*
O Pārtha, A man who casts off completely all the desires of the mind and is satisfied in the Self by the Self,
He is said to be one of steady wisdom.

2.56 *He whose mind is not disturbed by adversity, and who in prosperity does not go after other pleasures,*
He who is free from attachment, fear or anger is called a sage of steady wisdom.

2.57 *His wisdom is fixed on one who is everywhere without attachment,*
Meeting with anything good or bad, and who neither rejoices nor hates.

2.58 *As the tortoise withdraws its limbs from all sides, when a person withdraws his senses from the sense-objects,*
His wisdom becomes steady.

2.59 *From the body, the sense objects turn away, but the desires remain;*
His desires also leave him on seeing the Supreme.

Arjuna is now curious and wants to know more. He asks Kṛṣṇa, 'You are telling me all this; that is wonderful. You tell me that I must perform without expectations and attachment and that I must be centered in wisdom. I would like to live that way and move on the path of wisdom. Pray, tell me what kind of a person is this, the one who is always in awareness in the present moment? How does he behave, walk and talk? Let me model myself on him.'

Arjuna has realised that whatever he said earlier had arisen from his confusion. When Kṛṣṇa tells him to behave in a manner befitting the code of the warriors, it makes good sense to Arjuna, since this is the conditioning that he has been brought up in. However, when Kṛṣṇa tells him to do what he has to do without being concerned about the outcome, Arjuna is confused. He has rarely done anything in his life without first thinking about what is going to happen as a result of his action.

Arjuna is the greatest of marksmen. He is conditioned to first define his target and then act. Kṛṣṇa has confused him totally now. Kṛṣṇa says, 'Release your arrow; where it lands is my business.' Arjuna has enough trust in Kṛṣṇa not to ignore this instruction from the Divine. So he asks, 'What kind of a person is not concerned about the result, whether it is good or bad, painful or joyful, and how do I identify with such a person?' Arjuna is asking Kṛṣṇa for the specifications of the person he should emulate so that he too can become what Kṛṣṇa wants him to become. This is the basis of modern day Neuro-Linguistic Programming!

Kṛṣṇa responds, 'This man is free from desires and emotions. He has neither greed nor fear. He is always centered in himself. Pleasures through the senses do not interest him. He has withdrawn his senses from the external world and has focused them inwards, directed them towards that supreme Truth that is beyond all pleasures, attachments, emotions and sense objects. Once he realizes that truth, even the longing for that truth leaves him.'

Seeking the Unattached

'Nirmohatve niscalatatvam,' says Ādi Śaṅkarācārya, taking a cue from the master. It means: Absence of desires leads to a clear and still mind, steeped in wisdom. When there are no desires, there are no emotions such as joy, elation, depression, sadness, anger, disappointment, jealousy, that normally arise from the fulfillment or non-fulfillment of such desires. When the mind is without fear and anger, without expectations of success and failure, the unattached mind seeks that which is unattached. The desire for the objects disappears as truth dawns.

This universe is responsible for all of us. We exist not because of our actions and ourselves but in spite of them. When we let go, when we listen to the universe, it gives us all that we need to live with abundance, but the problem is that we don't listen. We do not stop with our needs but get greedy with our wants as well. There is no way all our wants can be fulfilled without taking away the needs of other beings in this universe.

The law of the jungle operates beautifully without man. Animals act based on needs and not on wants. A lion kills because it has to eat, not because it sees another lion killing. It would kill only to appease its own hunger or when its own life is threatened. Once the human being enters the scene, this equation changes. Man engages in wanton killing without caring about what he needs. Unlike animals, man no longer expresses his innate intelligence.

Kṛṣṇa aptly provides the example of the tortoise to illustrate how to withdraw one's senses inwards. The tortoise follows its instincts to obey nature; it lives in the present moment. It moves when its sensors report that there is no danger and it withdraws completely when it senses threat. Its entire cycle of life is tuned to the wisdom of nature. It is not an active and adventurous living being, but it is celebrated in all ancient cultures for its longevity and steadiness. Man is obviously a different being from the rest of the animals. He alone has the power to decide whether to follow the wisdom of nature inherent in him as in all other beings, or reject it to be 'unintelligent'. An animal, when it indulges in any act, whether of mating, caring, killing or saving its own life, does all and any of these with tremendous focus. The animal always lives in its present moment. Not so the human. For the human, his mind is never where his body is.

Corporate people ask me how to make right decisions. It is simple. When you focus intensely on the job at hand and make a decision based on the information available at that moment, your decisions will always be right. The universal energy guides you in your decision when you settle into yourself, focus inwards and withdraw your senses as the tortoise does.

What do you all do instead? Half the time you postpone decisions because you are afraid of the consequences of the decision. So things happen that are out of your control and that do not favor you. The other half of the time you are led by greed and prejudices based on past experiences and future fantasies, and you decide with no relevance to issues of that moment. You never do anything with complete awareness.

When you do whatever you do with one-hundred percent focus, you are in awareness. You become God!

Monkeys in Your Mind!

2.60 O son of Kuntī, the turbulent senses carry away the mind of a wise man,
Though he is striving to be in control.

2.61 Having restrained them all, he should sit steadfast, intent on Me.
Whose senses are under control, his mind is steady in the present.

2.62 When a man thinks of objects, it gives rise to attachment for them.
From attachment, desire arises; from desire, anger is born.

2.63 From anger arises delusion, from delusion, loss of memory, from loss of memory, the loss of discrimination, from loss of discrimination, he perishes.

2.64 The self-controlled man, moving among objects with his senses under control, free from both attraction and repulsion, attains peace.

2.65 All pains are destroyed in that peace, for the intellect of the tranquil-minded soon becomes steady.

2.66 A person not in self-awareness cannot be wise or happy or peaceful.
How can there be happiness to one without peace?

2.67 He loses his awareness of the present moment when his mind follows the wandering senses,
Just as the wind carries away a boat on the waters.

Kṛṣṇa continues to explain to Arjuna how difficult it is to control the senses and what happens when one loses control of the senses.

It is like this: Once a monkey spotted a jar full of nuts. The jar was big and heavy with a long and narrow neck. The monkey put his hand into the jar and grabbed lots of nuts, but he was unable to withdraw his fist from the jar! He thought he was trapped with his hand in the jar!

He didn't realize that all he needed to do was to let go of the nuts and he would be free. His greed enslaved him!

Kṛṣṇa says that our senses are turbulent, and however much we try to control them, they stay out of control. Even some of the greatest sages, the *ṛṣis*, have been known to succumb to sensual pleasures. There is the legendary story of *Viśvāmitra*, a great sage, who, in the midst of his intense penance, was seduced by the celestial maiden Menakā.

Do you think the gods above have no other business than sending young women down to disturb people who meditate? In that case, I am sure that all men will start meditating from tonight without any compulsion from my side!

Nothing of that sort will happen, so don't start meditation for this reason. It was the suppressed fantasies of *Viśvāmitra*'s mind that took the shape of the celestial nymph. His senses were out of control. Hindu scriptures have referred to *brahmacarya* as a prerequisite to spiritual evolution and many misinterpret this to be celibacy. *Brahmacarya* is not merely celibacy; it is more than physical celibacy; it is living in reality without fantasies.

Kṛṣṇa says that the only way is to focus one's mind on Him once the senses are under control and the mind is steady. The mind cannot be stopped. Thoughts cannot be stopped as long as the body exists. You can only focus your mind on something that transcends sensory pleasures and it will become quiet by itself.

A small story:

A man who was intent on spiritual progress went to a master and begged him to teach him how to control his mind. The master tried to explain that the mind cannot be controlled in the manner he was seeking, by stopping his thoughts, but he wouldn't listen. Fed up, the master gave him a bottle of some liquid and told him to drink three drops three times a day.

The man asked, 'That's it? It will control my mind?'

The master said, 'Just one thing, make sure you don't think of a monkey when you drink the medicine.'

'Oh, sure, quite simple!' said the man as he walked out. At the door he turned and asked, 'By the way, in case I do think of a monkey, what should I do?'

'Take a shower,' said the master, 'and try again.'

As soon as the man went home, without wasting time, he took out the medicine and opened his mouth to drink it. Just then he remembered the master's warning - and remembered the monkey! 'Oh, my God!' he said to himself, 'Now I have to take a shower. What else to do!'

You can guess the rest of the story. Each time he opened his bottle of medicine, monkeys invaded his mind and all he did was keep taking showers.

It got to a point where as soon as he got out of the shower, thoughts of monkeys arose in his mind.

He ran to the master and pleaded, 'Forget the medicine and the powers. Just get rid of the monkeys, please!'

You can never destroy thoughts or suppress them. You can only witness thoughts and not get involved in them and gradually the mind will settle down. When you settle into the present moment with no expectations and no attachments, you will find that your mind becomes quiet and your senses slow down.

Fall into the present moment

Kṛṣṇa says that from attachment springs desire, from desire arises anger, from anger arises delusion, from delusion comes loss of memory, and from loss of memory develops loss of discrimination which then leads to one's destruction. The only way to stop this, the Lord says, is to control one's senses, center oneself in the present and surrender to Him, the universal energy, and achieve everlasting peace.

Go through each of these stages laid down by the master. The path will be crystal clear. Each one of us develops attachment, liking, hatred and dislike for many things based upon our experiences. These likes and dislikes stay in our unconscious memory and even without any conscious awareness on our part they drive us into actions through desires or into inaction through fears. When the desires are fulfilled, there is temporary satisfaction; then the desires grow. When the desires do not get fulfilled, we are disappointed, we get angry.

We should be angry with our own selves for having had the desires or for not having worked wholeheartedly towards fulfilling the desire, but we actually get angry with other people whom we think are responsible for our failures. Rarely do we admit that we are the cause of our failures. We normally say, 'Why admit our fault when there are literally millions out there who can carry it for us?' So we create fantasies and delusions about shifting responsibility and gradually erase the memory of our own responsibility for our actions.

The vicious cycle is now almost complete. The moment we fail to take responsibility for our actions, we lose all our powers of intellectual discrimination between right and wrong and resign ourselves to being unaware and engaging in unconscious behavior. This is a one-way road to disaster.

Kṛṣṇa reveals two very important truths here in the last two verses. One is that you can never be peaceful unless you are aware and conscious. The other is that you cannot be aware if you are led by your senses. Therefore, as long as your senses lead you into what you think is a pleasurable journey, you cannot really be happy or peaceful. It is just another trick your mind is playing on you.

There are many who come and ask me, '*Swamiji*, I am so happy just fantasizing. I fantasize about you. It is truly blissful. Yet you say not to do that. You ask me to drop your form. Why?'

Even fantasizing about me or fantasizing about your *iṣṭadevatā*, your favorite god, is not going to lead you to happiness. When you lose that form, you will be in depression.

Your happiness is not real happiness. It is just a gap between two periods of sorrow. All this happens when you fantasize about the master also. Imagine your plight when you fantasize about other material objects and desires that can only lead you into more greed. Every single thing that you receive as inputs through your senses is processed and colored by the filter of your mind and ego, and you get to know only what they want you to know.

Your mind is constantly flitting between the future and the past in the form of thoughts. That is what thoughts really are, the journey of your mind between past and future and back, again and again. This journey never stops all through your life unless you make a serious attempt to stop it. On its own, your mind would never want to stay in the present moment, which is the only moment of truth. Your past is the dumping ground of all your regrets and guilt. There is no greater sin that you can commit than carrying these regrets and guilt. Committing an act labeled sinful by society and religion is less of a sin; carrying the guilt of having committed it is the real sin. That is what carries you into hell, even as you live in this world.

There is no hell in some afterlife. Do you think God has no other job except to chronicle each and every deed and thought you had in your life, mark them good and bad, give you marks and, like a schoolteacher, send you to suffer in hell because you had poor marks? He has no time for all that! Hell for you is what you suffer in this life while living. You suffer with guilt, regret and remorse. You *live* in hell in this life; you don't *go* to hell after you die.

Or your mind dwells in the future, a future that does not exist. You speculate and dream creating stories and arguments, planning a case for your future. How much of what you plan is based upon the present reality? There is nothing wrong at all if you are grounded in reality and plan to progress in that reality. That is what I call chronological planning. Chronological planning is necessary if you live in the material world. I do it too. For example, it is planning your day, with what time you will wake up, what time you will have the meeting at the office, what work you will complete during the day, etc. But most of the time what you plan has nothing to do with reality.

You either worry about things that you have no control over and plan how to escape such worries, or desire things not in your reach out of sheer greed. Our senses aid us very ably in these worries and desires. They make us believe that all this is real and make us react to situations as if they are real. It is the same way that we get up from a nightmare sweating profusely out of fear. In the same manner, these projections of our mind appear real to us even when we are fully awake.

Kṛṣṇa says, 'Get away from your senses; escape from their control; ground yourself in the awareness of the present moment. Only then can you be at peace.'

What is this present moment? What is this awareness? When our mind stops moving back and forth between the past and future, it will by itself land in the present moment. The present moment is what we are doing now. If you are reading this book, don't half-read this book and half-listen to music; don't half-read this book and half-watch television; don't half-read this book and half-talk with someone.

Either focus completely on what you are reading or don't read at all.

When did you really eat last? When I mean eat, I mean eat with full focus on the eating. When was the last time that you can remember each morsel that went into your mouth, without reading a book, watching television or talking to someone, without the food's going into your mouth on auto pilot? If we treat food as junk, it turns into junk in our stomach. So instead of giving us the energy that it should, it makes us want to nap.

The next time you do anything, focus completely on what you are doing at that moment. If you are brushing your teeth, just focus on how the brush moves and how the paste tastes. Stop thinking about the meetings later at your office or getting your children ready for school, or whatever it is that you need to do a few minutes or hours later.

When you settle into the present moment, you are out of the clutches of your senses and mind. You will still see and hear, but none of what you see and hear will divert you from what you are focused on. You will be aware of only what you are doing in that present moment. This is what we call meditation. Meditation is nothing but being focused completely on what you are doing at a particular moment. This is what Buddha calls mindfulness.

Wake Up!

2.68 O Mighty-armed, his knowledge is therefore steady whose senses are completely detached from sense objects.

2.69 The self–controlled man is awake in that which is night to all beings.
Where all beings are awake, it is night for the sage who sees.

2.70 Just as all waters enter the ocean, he attains peace into whom all desires enter, which when filled from all sides, remains unmoved; not the desirer of desires.

2.71 The man who moves about abandoning all desires, without longing,
Without the sense of I and mine, attains peace.

2.72 O Pārtha, this is the state of Brahman; none is deluded after attaining this.
Even at the end of life, one attains oneness with Brahman when established in this state.

In His concluding words in this chapter, Kṛṣṇa clarifies to Arjuna once again, how to reach liberation, how to become one with *Brahman*, which is one's true and natural state. We have seen that a person not centered in self-awareness and led by his senses cannot be peaceful or happy or wise. A person who is in control of his senses is firmly in control of his mind and emotions. Only such a person is truly awake.

We all think we are awake but are we really? We live in daydreams even if we are awake. We pretend that we are awake, that we are intelligent, that we are thinking and that we are making the right decisions. The only occasion when we are truly awake is when we are in the present moment, when we are aware of what we are doing at that point in time. A person in such awareness is whom Kṛṣṇa calls a '*muni*', a realized being living in the present. Such a person is always awake, whether physically awake or asleep.

Kṛṣṇa says that such a person is in sleep when others are awake. The realized person, although he may appear to be living and actively participating in the activities of the same world that we live in, is, in reality, in a state of passive alertness. This means that his senses are not immersed in worldliness and he is centered in his Self. He is dead and asleep to this world because he has moved beyond his senses. A truly realized person is also awake when others are asleep. Even in his sleep, he is aware, in what is called the state of *supta chittam*.

The '*muni*', one who is still, in silence, is one who is in total control of his senses. When the senses are controlled, when the ego is out of action, all thoughts and desires are just witnessed. The '*muni*' does not get involved in these thoughts and desires. He does not even try to stop or suppress them, as he knows it is impossible. He just lets them be. An enlightened being watches the world go past, just like the ocean watches impassively as other waters merge into it.

We are all enlightened because we are all a holographic part of the reality of the universe, *Brahman*. All that we lack is the awareness of the truth of our enlightenment. There is no path to enlightenment because we already are enlightened. All that is needed is the awareness of our enlightened state.

What prevents you from realizing that you are enlightened is your ego. This ego is not necessarily about any arrogance. It is the perception of who you think you are; it is the collection of thoughts, experiences and emotions that go to make up that 'I' and 'mine'. Your identity is that of the body and mind, not of your spirit. Therefore, it perishes with your body and is transient. This identity with the transient reality of who you think you are and what 'yours' is, is *māyā*.

Māyā is the illusion that creates a barrier between you and your awareness of your enlightened state.

A person who is in control of his senses, his mind and thoughts, lives in the present moment, in full awareness of his true nature and is one with *Brahman.* He is the only one who is truly awake, not the rest of us who think we are awake. We are all still in deep sleep. Such a person who is self-aware is fully awake even when he is asleep.

People with a strong consciousness of 'I' live out of their blocked *mūlādhāra cakra,* the root energy center. They are at the very beginning of their spiritual evolution. Their main concerns will be about their own survival and the survival of their species and they are caught in lust, anger and greed.

The person with a strong attachment to 'mine,' the possessions belonging to the 'I', constantly lives in fear of losing these possessions. Such people live out of their blocked *svādiṣṭhāna* or spleen *cakra* - the energy center that gets locked due to fear. They live in insecurity of losing possessions, of losing identity, and finally, of death.

Energization of the *mūlādhāra* and *svādiṣṭhāna cakra,* and moving the energy up through the *anāhata* or heart *cakra* to the *ājñā* or third eye *cakra* (the energy center between the eyebrows which is the seat of intelligence) opens up people to the reality of looking at others and the rest of the universe as themselves and finally dropping the ego - one's identification with 'I' and 'mine'.

Then, true surrender to the universe and identification with one's true nature occurs, and enlightenment happens. You then do become God!

Kṛṣṇa completes His description of the person established in yoga whose profile Arjuna has asked for. Kṛṣṇa concludes by saying that a person steeped in yoga is centered in reality and is one with *Brahman.* He says that this person is liberated even if he were to reach that state at the end of his life.

I tell my disciples time and again, 'I am not here to prove my divinity. I am here to prove *your* divinity.'

This is the timeless message of Kṛṣṇa. This is the message of Bhagavad Gītā.

Arjuna's confusion is slowly reducing. Actually, it is good to be confused. It is much better to accept that one is confused than to live in the delusion that one knows everything. Arjuna had the courage to come out and tell Kṛṣṇa his fears and doubts. This is the first step towards clarity. How long it takes for that clarity to emerge doesn't matter. One is on the path, and that is what matters.

Thus ends the second chapter named **Sāṅkhya Yogaḥ** *of the* **Upaniṣad** *of* ***Bhagavad Gītā****, the scripture of yoga dealing with the science of the Absolute in the form of the dialogue between* ***Śrī Kṛṣṇa*** *and Arjuna.*

BHAGAVADGĪTĀ

Beauty of Purposelessness

KARMA YOGAḤ

CHAPTER 3

Life is to enjoy living, not to chase goals. There is no real purpose to life; life in fact is purposeless. Once we create goals to reach, we create sorrow to follow.

Beauty of Purposelessness

The whole of Existence, the whole universe, is purposeless. Of course, it is very shocking to hear this. From a very young age, we are taught and socially conditioned to believe that life has got some purpose. We are always made to run towards some goal, towards some purpose.

'What is life without purpose?' you may ask. We feel that any activity, let alone one's entire life, has to have a purpose. Only then does it become meaningful. The purpose is what drives us.

You will say I am confusing you. 'All our life we have been brought up to believe that we are here for a purpose. As children we are expected to do well at school, and later at college. Once we grow up, we are supposed to get married and bring up our children. In each phase of our life, we have specific guidelines that society has set up for us. How can we let go of them, let others down? How can we believe that there is no purpose to life?'

The more you run towards a goal, the more you are considered a successful person. From birth, again and again, you are taught that life has a purpose and a goal. Understand that this is not the truth of Existence. Life does not need a defined goal to make living worthwhile, meaningful and happy. It is the absence of goals in life that makes living worthwhile.

The Universe has no purpose. It just is. A river runs downhill towards the ocean because it is its nature to run downhill. Our life has no purpose. We were born to live, to enjoy life and to be happy. Instead, we set ourselves up for unhappiness by setting goals based on fantasies. In the process, we stop enjoying life.

The more you run towards the goal, the more you miss life itself! A person who is continuously bothered about goals will never be able to enjoy his life. He lives in the future and ignores the present. When we are in the present moment, the here and now, we do not need a goal to guide us. Just the awareness of the present moment will help us decide what needs to be done at each point in time. As long as the path is right, whatever destination we reach will be right.

However, we constantly worry about the future, relating it with our past.

We continuously postpone our happiness without enjoying the present moment. For example, when you are studying you think, 'When I get a job, I will be happy.' When you have your job you think, 'After marriage my life will be happy.' After marriage, you think, 'When I have kids and my own house, I will be happy.' After you have kids and your own house you think, 'When the kids grow up and all my responsibilities are over, I will be happy.' By the time your kids are settled, by the time your responsibilities are over, when you want to relax, your being is so conditioned to running that you can't relax!

With this mental attitude, we are constantly running to stay in the same spot. Happiness is where we are not where we think we should be.

We do not understand what it is to relax. When I tell people to relax during meditation, they ask me, '*Swamiji*, please give us detailed guidelines about how to relax!' We feel we need to lose our happiness before we can start searching for it. The tension of running behind something has become a part of our conditioning. Resting is no longer a relaxation anymore.

When we run behind goals, all that seems to matter is the achievement of that goal. Any sacrifice seems to be worth it. We don't even feel connected to people around us when we run behind our goals. When we rest at the end of our lives, we will feel lonely because we have been conditioned to associate ourselves with some activity or the other all our life.

The more you run, the more titles you receive. You are called a 'multi-dimensional personality.' Only a person who has deeply experienced himself is a multidimensional personality. Only he understands himself and his many personalities, and is comfortable with all of them. Only a Kṛṣṇa can be a multidimensional personality.

A person who runs to satisfy society can never experience peace. Society wants you as it thinks you should be, not as you are. If you are useful to society in some way, then you are rewarded; otherwise you are made to feel inadequate. You are respected just based on your title, not for what you are. The more titles you have, the more respect you get. The more useful you are to society, the more you are respected.

Life is purposeless. Whatever you think of as the goal of your life, even if it were fulfilled, do you think you will be fulfilled? No! You will only look for the next goal. As each goal is fulfilled, another springs up in its place. There is not even time to appreciate or enjoy what you have achieved. There is always a feeling of discontentment. You run not because your being wants to but because society drives you.

> A person came to me and said, 'Earlier I used to smoke and drink. My wife used to fight with me all the time. She would connect anything and everything to my smoking and drinking and blame me. If the kids did not study well, she would say, 'You are a drunkard. That is why they are not studying well.' If something went wrong in the house, again she would find some way of connecting it with my smoking and drinking. I was continuously blamed this way. I was totally disturbed. So finally, somehow, I gave up smoking and drinking.'
>
> I asked, 'Oh! Is she happy now?'
>
> He said, 'No! Now she is unhappy that she is not able to complain about anything anymore!'

When you have something or someone to blame, you can always put the responsibility on them and feel comfortable. When you can't put the responsibility on someone else, you suffer. It is easy to escape reality by putting the responsibility on someone else. Here, Arjuna is doing the same thing by asking Kṛṣṇa this question in the third chapter of the Bhagavad Gītā. Arjuna is shifting responsibility away from him.

To Act Or Not To Act

3.1 *Arjuna said:*
O Janārdana, O Keśava, Why do You make me engage in this terrible war,
If You think that knowledge is superior to action?

3.2 *My intelligence is confused by Your conflicting words.*
Tell me clearly what is best for me.

3.3 *The Lord said,*
'O sinless Arjuna, as I said before, in this world there are two paths;
Self-knowledge for the intellectual and the Path of Action for the yogi.

3.4 *A person does not attain freedom from action by abstaining from work,*
Nor does he attain fulfillment by giving up action.'

A few days ago, a young man came to me and asked, '*Swamiji*, should I marry as per my wish or should I listen to my father?'

I said, 'Listen to your father's words and go for an arranged marriage.'

He asked, 'Why Swamiji? Won't I be happy if I marry as per my wish?'

I told him, 'If you have enough courage to take the blame yourself for anything that happens later, go for a love marriage. Otherwise, with an arranged marriage, at least you will have somebody you can blame for anything that happens!'

If you marry as per your wish, you can't blame anybody if such a situation arises! If you go for an arranged marriage, after two to three years, even if things don't work out well, you can always put the blame on someone else.

Understand, I am not advocating this mode of behaviour. I am only telling you what is happening in today's world. Generally, with your own decision you can't blame anybody. But if you decide to follow others, even though the decision to follow them is your own decision, you can blame the other person and escape.

Arjuna is still very much in this mode. He is confused as to what he should do. He tells Kṛṣṇa, 'I do not understand what you are saying. First, you tell me to fight. Then you tell me to shed anger. You say I must kill my enemies, who are my elders and relatives, but then you say I should not worry about the end result.' Arjuna says, 'All I need to know is whether I should act or not. You say that knowledge is superior to action, and yet, you say I must act. What should I do?' he asks.

What Arjuna leaves unsaid is, 'What use is knowledge if it cannot be used in action?' Arjuna is a warrior, not a scholar or a philosopher. He says, 'Cut out all this superficiality; tell me the truth as it is. Tell me what I should do.' True to his conditioning, Arjuna is uncomfortable when he is not engaged in some action.

Your whole life is purposeless, but again and again, you are conditioned to run towards something. You are continuously made to feel that you are not good enough. Whatever you think of as your purpose in life, whether it is money or relationships or whatever, even if you have complete fulfillment in that dimension, you will not rest!

Someone told me this, I believe a management consultant said it, 'If you place a ladder somewhere and climb as fast as you can, you will quickly reach the top of the ladder. But unless the ladder is placed where you want, where you reach will be of no consequence!' Climbing as fast as you can is *efficiency*. Placing the ladder where you want is *effectiveness*. It does not matter where you place the ladder, as long as you enjoy the climb!

The trouble is that we spend the entire climb obsessed about where we will reach and what we will do there. If we spend that time enjoying the journey, any destination we reach will be the right destination. The destination is not important; the journey is. The goal is not important; the process is.

A small story:

A man met his friend on the street. His friend was nearly in tears. So he asked him, 'What happened? Why do you look so sad?'

His friend replied, 'Three weeks ago, my uncle died and left me fifty thousand dollars.'

The man replied, 'That's not bad.'

His friend said, 'Wait till you hear the rest. Two weeks ago, my cousin died and left me ninety-five thousand dollars.'

The man exclaimed, 'Hey, that's great!'

His friend said, 'Last week, my grandfather passed away. I inherited almost a million.'

Now this man was really curious. He asked, 'Then why are you so sad?'

His friend replied, 'This week - nothing!'

We continuously pursue material goals. As a result, we never relax within ourselves. That is the reason why even in old age when we want to relax, we are unable to relax. Have you seen a single man above seventy relaxing? Never! At the most he will be watching the television. People can never sit with themselves! If they have company, they would talk about their golden past or else they would be watching the television or reading the same old newspaper.

A man who can't sit with himself misses one of the major dimensions of his being. Continuously running, thinking that there is some purpose to life, his whole being will be in a state of tension, conditioned to running.

Life has no purpose. Even if you achieve whatever you want, you can't take it with you when you leave the body. Nothing will come with you. Understand, there is no exchange offer. No matter how much money you give in this world, you cannot have a single rupee in heaven.

A small story:

A millionaire was on his deathbed. He distributed his property among his three sons and told them, 'Each of you should put a million rupees in my coffin when I die.'

All three agreed. One was an accountant, another was a doctor, and the third was a lawyer. After the father's death, the first son said, 'I should be honest. Father has given me so much property.' Saying so, he put a million rupees cash in the coffin.

The second son came and said, 'I should also be honest. Let me put my share.' He put in his share of one million rupees.

The third son came. He put in a cheque for three million rupees and took back the two million rupees his brothers had put in and said, 'I am paying for all three of us. Let him cash this cheque and spend it!'

The third son understood. You can't carry anything to the next world.

As of now, this material world is multi-colored as you enjoy it with all your senses. The moment you leave the body, the same world will appear black and white, flat and uninteresting. When you are dreaming, your dream looks very real. When you are awake, this world around you looks like reality and the dream looks dull and in black and white. But there is no scale to measure which is reality and which is a dream.

A small story:

A great Zen master comes out of his bedroom one morning and suddenly starts weeping.

His disciples ask him, 'What is this, master? You are an enlightened man. How can you weep? What happened?'

He says, 'Last night I dreamt that I was a butterfly.'

The disciples laugh and say, 'It was only a dream. Why do you bother? Forget about it.'

The master says, 'No, no! Now I have a big problem. I don't know whether I am a Zen master who dreamt that he became a butterfly or whether I am a butterfly is who is now dreaming that it has become a Zen master!'

There is no scale to prove whether the dream is reality, or what you think as reality is really the reality. We don't know! Right now you may be dreaming that you are sitting in a temple and listening to the Gītā! We don't know!

People tell me, 'But everyday when we enter into a dream, we are not entering into the same dream, Swamiji. On the other hand, everyday when we return to reality we are entering into the same reality. So with this scale we can say which is reality and which is a dream.'

See, in one night's dream you can live even twenty years of life, right? In that twenty-year span, you are in the same consistent dream, is it not? Then why can't your dream be reality, because of its consistency? This whole time span, which you think is reality, may be part of one dream! When you leave the body, all that you see now as multi-colour will become black and white.

Nothing can be carried with you at the time of leaving the body. You can't encash your cheques! You can't talk to your relatives. If you speak, they will run away! Your car will not be useful to you anymore. When you are not able to take anything with you, what is the purpose of life then? The moment you understand that life is purposeless, you will realize the meaning of living.

Life has no purpose, only meaning

Purpose means goal orientation. You always keep running behind the goal and suddenly one day you just drop dead! The more goal-oriented you are, the more you will miss life. When I say 'meaning', I mean that living itself becomes meaningful. Come to this present moment and the path itself is life. There is no such thing as, 'In the end you will be happy.' Life is lived in a very superficial way because you think life has a purpose. Be very clear: the man who works just for his salary, for him only the payday will be a beautiful day. He sells his twenty-nine days every month for that one day of happiness.

I don't say, 'Don't take your salary.' But let it not be the only goal in your life. That is what Kṛṣṇa means when He says you can do only your duty, you have no right to its fruit. If you think of the fruit, you will lose the joy of doing, living! The meaning of living is experienced only when you understand the beauty of purposelessness. It is the essence of the Gītā! There are two things you need to understand from this. One, He says, 'Let your inner space not be contaminated by the purpose of life.' When you close your eyes, what comes into your mind is your inner space. If your inner space is filled with the purposes of life, you are running behind something that will never give you fulfillment.

By nature, your inner space is filled with blissful energy, eternal bliss. The more you free your inner space of other furniture or 'purposes,' the more you empty yourself of goals, the more space for the bliss. For example, this room is filled with space or ether. The more furniture you put in it, the more space will be unavailable. The more furniture you bring in, the more ether will be pushed out; the ether energy will be less.

In the outer space, if you furnish your home, it will look very nice. But if you furnish your inner space, it will look very ugly. Let your inner space be filled with bliss! The more inner space you create, the more blissful your life will be. That is what Kṛṣṇa means by saying, 'Don't be attached to results.' If you continuously think about the result, you will never be able to perform your action completely; you will never enjoy the path. Not enjoying the path is the worst hell you can be trapped in.

Again and again Kṛṣṇa says, '*Paritrāṇāya sādhūnāṁ vināśāya ca duṣkṛtām dharma saṁsthāpanārthāya saṁbhavāmi yuge-yuge.*' It means: I come down again and again to save the innocent and good people, and to destroy the evil-minded people.

People ask me, 'You say *dharma* (duty) is the only thing to be practiced, but in our lives, we see people who are not living according to *dharma* are living happily with more property and wealth. Why is that?' Understand, they may have more things in the outer space, but never think they are happy in their inner space. When does someone not follow *dharma*? When he follows his ambition! Ambition causes you to commit all possible mistakes and sins. Such people are already in hell. It is not that we commit sins and go to hell. No! We commit sins because we *are* in hell. If you are happy and blissful, you will never disturb others. If you are unhappy, naturally you will vomit that violence on others. Just because of their ambition, they miss the whole life. The very ambition is enough punishment.

You can easily miss life by having a purpose to life. If you have salary as the purpose, you will miss twenty-nine days of your life just for that one day, your payday. Unless your working itself becomes ecstasy, you cannot experience what Kṛṣṇa says in this verse: *karmaṇyevādhikāraste mā phaleṣu kadācana*

Purpose can be fulfilled, but through purpose, your life can never be fulfilled.

When you carry purposes in your life *you* are not living, *purposes* are living through you. In your childhood somebody gives you some purpose like, 'You should become a lawyer or a doctor.' You are given a purpose and that purpose is fulfilled through your life, but *you* will never feel fulfilled.

Your fulfillment is completely different from the fulfillment of your purpose. If you want to experience fulfillment, listen to what Kṛṣṇa says here.

Kṛṣṇa is the first and the last master who declared the Truth as it is. There are two things to understand. People who are active in the outer world know the techniques to achieve success in the outer world. People who are active in the inner world know the techniques to achieve success in the inner world.

But Kṛṣṇa knows both! He is the only master who is an enlightened man and a king as well. He knows the technique to achieve total success in the outer and inner worlds. He teaches about keeping your inner space in eternal bliss and keeping your outer space in ultimate luxury. That is life in totality. The entire Gītā is only about this one idea: how to furnish your outer space with the ultimate luxuries and how to keep your inner space in the ultimate bliss.

You can't expect this from a Buddha because Buddha gave up the outer space. He lived with just three pieces of clothing. He lived the life of a monk. So he taught how to remain simple and blissful.

But Kṛṣṇa lived as a king; only He can give a manual for practical spiritual living. With all other masters, their manual is useful only for monks in monasteries. Only Kṛṣṇa's manual is useful for people who are living a regular lifestyle.

Here Kṛṣṇa says, 'Not merely by abstaining from work can one achieve freedom from action.' You can't achieve freedom from action by moving away from work.

Abstaining from work or moving away from work cannot give you freedom from action. To have freedom from action, your inner space should become empty. You need to remove furniture from your inner space. Renouncing furniture in the outer world is not going to help you. The idea that life has a purpose should be renounced. That is why Kṛṣṇa says, 'Just by outer renunciation, perfection can never be achieved.'

One more thing, if you renounce the outer world, you will be thinking about the outer world all the more. The outer world will fill your inner space even more.

A small story:

An enlightened master and his disciple were walking near a river. They were supposed to cross the river to go to their monastery. On the way, a young lady wanted to cross the river, but was afraid to do so. She asked the master, 'Master, can you help me cross this river?'

He said, 'Why not? Please come.'

He just lifted her, crossed the river, left her on the other bank, and continued walking towards the monastery. The disciple was observing the whole scene. He was not able to digest what he saw. He was angry within. Maybe he was jealous!

After reaching the ashram he was not able to control himself and asked his master, 'Master, you are a *sanyāsi* (monk). How can you touch a woman and carry her across the river?' The master turned, smiled at him and said, 'I left her long ago. Why are you still carrying her?'

Renouncing in the inner space is the real thing to be achieved. That is what Kṛṣṇa says here. Once you have renounced in the inner space, it doesn't matter what you do in the outer world. Nothing will touch you.

It Is Human Nature To Act

3.5 *Surely, not even for a moment can anyone remain without doing anything.*
He is always in action, despite himself, as this is his very nature.

3.6 *He who restrains the sense organs, but who still thinks of the objects of the senses, is deluded and is called a hypocrite.*

3.7 *He who begins controlling the senses with the mind and performs selfless work through the organs of action is superior, O Arjuna.*

3.8 *Do your prescribed work, as doing work is better than being idle.*
Even your own body cannot be maintained without work.

Usually people ask, '*Swamiji*, you say that life is purposeless. Then I may as well just lie down and relax. Who will give me food? Who will pay my bills?'

Let me tell you, you can never lie down forever. You may lie down for the next four or five days or maybe for a week maximum. After that, you will not be able to lie down. By your very nature you will work. When I say life is purposeless, I am not asking you to just lie down and relax. All I am saying is, 'Let your body and mind work without disturbing your inner space. You don't have to sell your inner bliss to have outer comforts.'

Kṛṣṇa gives the assurance here, 'By your very nature, your body and mind will work; if you just keep quiet that is enough; they will function beautifully.'

Somebody asked me, '*Swamiji*, how can I do the right thing? How should I train my mind to do the right thing?' I told him, 'Just keep quiet. Automatically your body and mind will do the right thing. If you just get out of your system, that is enough, the Divine will get in.' All we need to do is just get out for the Divine to enter.

By their very nature your body and mind know the right thing to do. The problem however is that you never trust your body and mind. All you need to do is keep quiet, relax from your ego. Don't think your inner space is needed for the outer work. The person who understands what *nitya* (eternal) is, and what *anitya* (transient) is relaxes into Existence and is always in eternal bliss.

Kṛṣṇa says, 'A *karma yogi* is a person who relaxes into *nitya ānanda* and does his work.'

Just relax into your inner space, and automatically you will be guided. You always think, 'If I relax mentally thinking that life is purposeless, how will I know what is right and what is wrong? How will I finish my work on time?'

Be very clear, when you worry about what is right and what is wrong, you will commit big blunders instead of small mistakes. One who doesn't bother makes small mistakes, but the one who continuously worries will commit big blunders. And I tell you: to take this leap of faith needs courage. Even if you make one or two mistakes, what is wrong?

Taking the risk and jumping, and living without worrying, is the courage to enter into spiritual life. When you take the jump, you will naturally make some small mistakes. Putting up with those mistakes is what I call penance. Penance is nothing but accepting the small mistakes that you make when the conscious transition happens in your being. When babies learn to walk, they always fall the first few times. But just because of that, can you say they should never walk? No! Even if they make one or two small mistakes, they have to stand up and start walking. Those small mistakes of falling and trying to stand up are the penance done to learn how to walk.

In the same way, when you start trying to live without the ego, initially you may commit mistakes. But don't worry about that. Have courage and just enter into the zone of no-ego, the zone of eternal consciousness. Decide, 'From today onwards I will live without worrying. Life is too short to be spent worrying.' Don't bother about the goals - just drop them. The moment you understand the beauty of purposelessness, all the wounds in your inner space will be healed. You will fall into the comfort of eternal bliss.

'A man who keeps his senses under control, but who is not able to keep his inner space under control is called a pretender, a hypocrite,' says Kṛṣṇa.

The quality of your life will be judged based only on the quality of your inner space. When you leave your body and enter into your next life, nobody is going to keep accounts of what type of car you drove, in what type of house you lived or what your bank balance was. No! These details don't count. How you lived, what was the quality of your inner space, this is what you will carry forward with you. That is why the scriptures state, 'You are going to carry with you only the *saṁskāra* (engraved memories), the *karma* (unfulfilled desires) and the *vāsana* (mindset) of your inner space - not the outer space.'

> A beautiful story from Rāmakṛṣṇa Paramahamsa, the enlightened master from India:
>
> A monk was living in a temple doing meditation and preaching the glory of the Lord. Opposite to his dwelling lived a prostitute who was busy all day long. She was deeply devoted to the Lord. No matter what her business was, she was immersed in the silent contemplation of His glory. She and the others from her group would serve the temple by singing and dancing in front of the deity.
>
> Everyday this monk would notice everyone who entered the prostitute's house, what time they entered and left, how many people entered. He would keep track of everything because he had no other work. He maintained a complete diary of who came, who

left, who visited regularly, who came once in a while or often. The whole day he thought about what was going on in her place.

But the prostitute lived in a different way. She thought, 'This is my natural duty given to me in this life. I don't know any other profession. For my food I have to live this life. But please save me, O Lord! Let my mind and heart always be at Your feet.' She was deeply devoted to Kṛṣṇa. Her inner space was filled with the Divine.

Life went on. After many years, suddenly, both the monk and the prostitute died on the same day. They reached Yama Dharma's (Lord of death) court for judgment. First, the prostitute came in. Yama Dharma saw her list of sins and merits and said, 'Alright! Don't worry. You lived all your life thinking of the Divine so you can go to heaven.' She was sent to heaven.

It was then the monk's turn for judgment. The moment the monk arrived, Yama Dharma said, 'This is your list of sins and merits. Throughout your life you thought about the wrong things, so you must go to hell.'

The monk started shouting, 'How dare you send me to hell!'? He was a professional preacher, so he knew how to shout! He started shouting, 'I will sue you.'

Yama Dharma said, 'Relax! Up here in heaven we don't bother about what you do in life; we bother about how you live. Through your body you lived a pure life. Look at planet earth and see how your body is being honored.'

There the monk saw that his body was being honored like that of a celebrity; people were falling at the feet of his body. Big garlands and worship was offered. It was receiving great respect. Yama continued, 'Through your body you lived a pure life; your body is now getting the rewards. But through the mind, you lived an impure life; so you have to go to hell.'

Yama continued, 'Similarly, she lived an impure life through the body. Look at her body.' Nobody was there even to care for the corpse. Because she was a prostitute there was no one even to do the last rites. The scavengers just came and dragged the body and dumped it somewhere. Yama continued, 'See! Through the body she lived an impure life. Her body is suffering. But through the mind she lived a pure life, a divine life. She is therefore going to the Divine.'

It is important how you live in your inner space.

Master your senses

Please be very clear, again and again Kṛṣṇa declares:

karmendriyāṇi saṁyamya ya āste manasā smaran |

indriyārthān vimūḍhātmā mithyācāraḥ sa ucyate || 3.6

If you can't clear your inner space, even if you control your body or your senses, you are just a hypocrite. Your life will not be a blissful life. The meaning of living is bliss, not purpose. The more you think about purposes, the more worries you create and the more you try to squeeze the most out of life. When you try to squeeze the maximum out of life, it just slips through your fingers.

Life is like a river. If you place your hands in the river and keep them open, the river will always be there in your hands. But if you try to hold it, you will have only empty hands! If you just allow it to happen it will continuously flow through you. The moment you try to possess it, you will have only empty hands.

The moment you experience in your inner space that nothing is going to be with you permanently, a deep healing, a breeze enters your consciousness. Your whole inner space is healed. This one understanding that life is purposeless, that whatever you achieve is just nothing, and that nothing is going to be with you, is enough.

A small story about Alexander:

Alexander the Great can never be called 'the Great.' Please be very clear: never teach your kids that he is great. Then you are inspiring them to commit violence. Unconsciously, you are putting all these ideas into their heads. Of course, he did one good thing. He met an enlightened master in India. Somehow, his teacher in Greece gave him the idea, 'Bring one enlightened master and the *Vedas* from India, and I will change the whole society.'

So Alexander decided he would take at least one enlightened person from India. Somehow he met an enlightened person. He invited him, 'Please come to our country.'

The master just laughed and said, 'No, no! I don't want to come anywhere; I am happy here.'

Alexander said, 'No! Please come. I will give you a big palace. Here you are living like a beggar without clothes or food. Please come with me. I will give you a big palace and all the comforts.'

The master just laughed and said, 'No. I am quite happy here, I don't want to come.'

You know the next step a king will take. First, by he tried to entice him. When it did not work out, his next step was to convince the master through fear. He simply took his sword out, pointed it at the master and said, 'If you are not ready to come, you will be killed.'

Faced with the naked sword, the master just laughed. Please be very clear, laughing now is very easy, but laughing when faced with a naked sword is very difficult, especially when the person who is holding the sword is a king - because if he kills there is nobody to even question him.

But in front of the naked sword, the master straightaway looked into the eyes of Alexander and said, 'Fool! You are a liar.' For the first time Alexander was shaken. He asked the master, 'Are you not afraid?'

The master replied, 'Afraid of what? You can never kill me. You may destroy this body, but you cannot kill me.'

That is the courage and confidence gained by the spiritual experience as we study in the Gītā:

nai 'naṁ chindanti śastrāṇi nai 'naṁ dahati pāvakaḥ I
na cai 'naṁ kledayantyāpo na śoṣayati mārutaḥ II 2.23

It means: *Ātman* or the soul cannot be killed; the soul cannot be destroyed; it cannot be burned.

This had become an experience for the master. That is why he had such courage and confidence. He just laughed.

Slowly, Alexander started thinking, 'If he can laugh in front of my naked sword, how courageous he must be!' For the first time he was shaken because he had never seen anybody who could laugh in the face of death. Even *he* was afraid.

All the so-called great warriors are cowards. They live in constant fear of death. That is why they kill others. Alexander was totally shaken. He was shocked to see the courage of this master. He asked him, 'Please tell me something. How are you so courageous, so bold?'

The master asked him in return, 'Tell me, why did you come to India?'

Alexander replied, 'To conquer India.'

The master continued, 'After that, what are you going to do?'

Alexander replied confidently, 'I will conquer the next country.'

The master again asked, 'After that, what are you going to do?'

Alexander continued, 'I will conquer the next country.'

The master persisted, 'And after that?'

Alexander replied as if the answer was obvious, 'I will conquer the whole world.'

The master questioned further, 'After that?'

Alexander replied, 'I will relax and enjoy.'

The master said, 'Fool! That is what I am doing now!'

The master said, 'Don't you see that that is what I am doing now? *Why* do you need to go around and conquer the whole world to relax and enjoy? That is what I am doing now right in front of your eyes!'

Only a man who has understood the impermanence of life can relax and surrender totally even in the face of death. The master gave a glimpse of the Truth to Alexander.

That is why Alexander said to his ministers, 'After my death, during the funeral procession, please let both my hands hang out of the coffin, visible to all. Let people know that even the great Alexander could not carry anything with him.'

You need to understand three things. The first is the courage and confidence when they are kings. Why is it that the former are put in an asylum and the latter are respected? If the person is cunning enough to convince others about what he says, he is respected and given a throne. People who are innocent, people who are not able to frighten others into accepting what they say, are put in the asylum, that's all. In Existence, there is no mad person and there is no king. Both are one and the same.

A small story:

A man in India suddenly started thinking and claiming that he was Jawaharlal Nehru. At that time, Jawaharlal Nehru was the Prime Minister of India.

If he had only been claiming, it would have been okay. He started dressing like him. Then he started writing letters to all the officials and signing them, 'Jawaharlal Nehru.' Naturally, he was taken to an asylum and treated for six months.

After the treatment, he started behaving normally. The doctor said, 'I think you can be discharged now.' The day he was about to be discharged, fortunately or unfortunately, Jawaharlal Nehru himself visited the asylum.

They brought this man to Nehru and introduced him. 'Sir, he is the person who used to claim he is Jawaharlal Nehru.'

After the formal introduction, the man asked Nehru, 'Who are you?' Nehru said, 'I am Jawaharlal Nehru.'

The patient said, 'Please stay here for six months. They will cure you!'

Understand that there is no difference between these two. Somehow one is able to convince others that what he says is the truth. The other one is not able to convince people, that's all!

Never think that having comforts in the outer world will give you inner fulfillment. All developed countries are filled with depression. They have the best roads, the best dams, the best bridges, the best infrastructure, but their people are depressed. If you want a peaceful inner space, you need to work for it. You need to understand the dynamics of your inner space.

Understand your inner space

Here, Kṛṣṇa gives you the technology to reclaim your blissful inner space. Let us see how we work. This graph represents your being. Material life is the horizontal line and spiritual life is the vertical line. You continuously worry about whether to go on this (horizontal) path, or that (vertical) path.

You are always stuck somewhere on the horizontal line or somewhere on the vertical line. You try to move but you are always caught in the dilemma of whether to go this way or that way. Whatever you choose, whether material life or spiritual life, you will always feel you are missing the other part. As long as you live with the mind, you will have this problem.

Just like how people have goals in material life, they have goals in spiritual life too. There are so many people who say, 'I should meditate for seven hours daily. I should become enlightened. I should become that, I should do this, I should be that.' Be very clear, goals in material life or

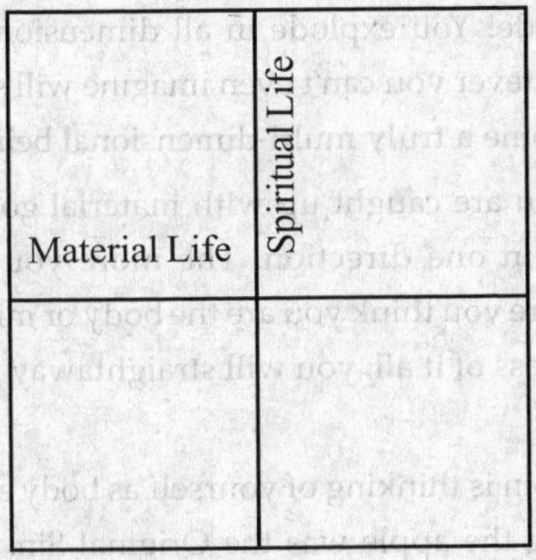

spiritual life - both make you mad. If you want to become mad, continuously think of some goal. It is the easiest way to go mad! But if you can just withdraw into your being, you will forget about the goal. And you can still work. By withdrawing into your being, you stop trying to locate a purpose somewhere all the time and running towards it.

The person who runs behind the material goals will always feel he is missing the spiritual goal and the religious man feels that he is missing the material life. That is why the so-called religious men and rich men are always trying to be together. Both feel that they have missed the other aspect in their own lives. The person who travels along the horizontal line feels he is missing the spiritual life and the person who travels along the vertical line feels he is missing the material life. Both try to fulfill each other cerebrally.

The materialist fulfills the spiritualist's ideal and the spiritualist fulfills the materialist's ideal.

The man who realizes the purposelessness of both these goals just falls back into his being. When you realize that whatever you consider the goal of your life is ultimately meaningless, that very moment the glamour is gone, the need for perspiration is gone and you stop running.

Mind you, it is not inspiration; it is perspiration that you give up! The moment all respect for the purpose is gone from your life, you will simply fall into your being. One important thing: the moment you fall into your being, you explode! You explode in all dimensions. Whatever you can imagine and whatever you can't even imagine will start happening. Only then do you become a truly multi-dimensional being.

As long as you are caught up with material goals or spiritual goals, you travel only in one direction. The more you are caught up with purposes, the more you think you are the body or mind. When you realize the purposelessness of it all, you will straightaway fall into the depths of your being.

The Original Sin is thinking of yourself as body and mind. Don't think that Adam eating the apple was the Original Sin. No! Why should we suffer for Adam's sin?

Actually, this single verse is enough for an individual to get enlightened.

Then why am I speaking on all the verses? It is only because there are so many kinds of individuals. These are different keys for different individuals, which is the reason for explaining all the verses. If you can just look into yourself and understand this one verse for your own self, it is enough. Whenever I speak, understand that I am speaking to you. Don't prepare notes in your mind to repeat to somebody else. Don't think, 'I should go and tell my husband; he really needs it.' When you do this, you are sure to miss the experience yourself!

Just allow this one idea to work on you: the truth of the purposelessness of life. You can just close your eyes and think, contemplate for two or three minutes: 'What is really the purpose of my life? Why am I doing what I am doing? Where am I going? What is happening?' If your inner eye opens, if your inner space experiences the beauty of purposelessness, that is enough. You will fall into your being. As of now, you can experience neither material nor spiritual life because when you are here, you are looking there and when you are there, you are looking here. You never experience either in a solid way.

Your mind is not where your body is. The grass on the other side of the river always looks greener. Only when you experience the beauty of purposelessness will you be able to understand what Kṛṣṇa says throughout *Karma Yoga*. 'Relax!' This one idea can transform your way of thinking, working and living. When you understand there is no purpose of life, you will start enjoying every single moment; you will start living intensely in every single inch of your body. Every moment will become meaningful.

If you think the whole has a purpose, then the part loses its meaning. When you realize that the whole has no purpose, the part will become meaningful. Your life everyday, your living, your sitting, your walking, your standing, everything will become a joyful experience. That is why they say *sat chit ānanda*, which means 'The bliss of the very existence.' You don't have to think that at the end of your life you will have bliss. No! Your very *existence* is blissful. But you need to take steps towards that bliss.

By nature, man has to work. The senses *have* to be engaged in some action. Even if you try and control them and do nothing externally, the very act of restraint is an action in itself. The choice is really about how to work. Here, Kṛṣṇa gives the answer to that. He says that we should perform work with devotion and without any attachment to the results. When we work, our thoughts are on the future, we are not in the present moment. Am I right? Then how can we perform to our fullest potential? How can I say that I am doing my work with full devotion if my mind is not totally merged with the task at hand? It's not possible.

When do you get worried or afraid? When there is expectation, and an unconscious desire to achieve something as the result of an action. Kṛṣṇa says, 'Drop the very desire. Drop the very expectation.'

We wonder, 'How can we function if we drop expectations?' I am not saying that you should not plan and or you should do something without thinking. I am saying, 'Plan, but plan chronologically, not psychologically.'

You see, there are two things: chronological planning and psychological planning.

Chronological planning is planning on a timescale. You decide you to get up at a particular time, finish your morning routine by a particular time, reach the office at a particular time, finish the list of tasks you planned at the office by a certain time, and so on. This is a practical way to organize your work in such a way that it can give the best results. This is fine.

But what do we do? We don't stop at this. We review the plan in our head over and over again, thinking in different ways about whether we will be able to manage it. We keep supposing, 'What if this happens? What if that happens?' In the name of contingency planning, we just worry. We are thinking about how to handle something if the plan does not go as expected. Instead, if we apply our awareness to the problem in an objective way, the solution will be visible.

But we complicate the whole process. We get worked up and introduce a complex negativity in the whole thinking process. We start worrying about what the possible unknowns are that have not been accounted for in the plan, and what not! Psychological planning boosts your ego. It makes you feel great and worthy.

Kṛṣṇa says, 'One who does devotional work without attachment, and controls the senses, is superior to one who merely pretends to be in control of his senses and acts in renunciation.'

There are people of the intellectual type, philosophers, well versed in all the scriptures, who look down upon the devotional practitioners! They believe that their dry understanding of the non-duality of the Self is superior to that of those who fall at the feet of the Divine. Kṛṣṇa firmly says, 'No, it is not so!'

Kṛṣṇa says that what makes the difference is your lack of expectations, the sense of purposelessness that defines your state. *Sanyās* (renunciation) is a state, not a label. The state of renunciation is not a state of doing nothing. Even if you sit still in one place, you are sitting, you are breathing, are you not? The internal functions in your body are happening. Maintaining this very body requires that work be done.

The breath that you take in carries *prāna*, the life energy that sustains you. Constantly, air that is laden with *prāna* goes in, leaves the *prāna* inside and comes out. This is also an action being performed to sustain the body. So, you cannot say you are not doing anything.

You may think that it is better not to do any work rather than analyze what work you should do, how to do it, whether it will suit you etc. You can take this as an excuse for laziness, for your *tamas. Tamas* means laziness, lethargy. When Kṛṣṇa says, 'I am not the doer, it is just the senses performing the actions according to their nature,' you say, 'Why should I even bother to do anything? '

Be very clear, by your very nature, you will act. Your body and mind are forced to do something by their nature. Just try to sit with a completely blank mind, with no mental activity, not thinking about anything. Just relax and try this simple exercise. You will initially try not to think about anything and be aware if any thought comes to your mind. But, after a few moments, you will find yourself having some thought, about something from the past or the future. Some random thought about something will pass through the mind.

By nature, your mind will think about something or the other. If you try to force silence upon your mind, you will be forcing a dead silence, the silence of suppression. How long can you sustain that? The moment you drop your guard, mind will express its nature and start the wandering.

So, neither expression nor suppression is the solution. It is better to be aware of the nature of the senses and the mind, and be engaged in work with a sense of devotion. Be aware that when you are in action, it is the senses acting. Then you will not get attached to the action or its result. Then you are free; you are liberated from the bondage of action. Action binds you only when you consider yourself the doer and have expectations about things being a certain way.

Selfless Service Liberates

3.9 *Work has to be performed selflessly; otherwise, work binds one to this world.*
O son of Kuntī, perform your work for Me and you will do it perfectly, liberated and without attachment.

3.10 Brahma, *the Lord of creation, before creating humankind along with selfless sacrifice said, 'By this selfless service, be more and more prosperous and let it bestow all desired gifts.'*

3.11 *The celestial beings, pleased by this sacrifice, will also nourish you; with this mutual nourishing of one another, you will achieve supreme prosperity.*

3.12 *Satisfied with the selfless service, the celestial beings certainly bestow upon you the desired enjoyments of life. He who enjoys the things given by them without offering anything to the celestial beings is certainly a thief.*

3.13 *Those who eat food after selfless service are free of all sins. Those who prepare food for sense enjoyment do grievous sin.*

There are two techniques by which one can liberate oneself from attachment to work. One is by telling oneself, 'I am not the doer.' The other is by surrendering the fruits of one's work to the Divine. This is the technique that Kṛṣṇa talks about here. He says, 'Perform your work for Me and you will do it perfectly, liberated and without attachment.'

When you do work as a sincere, humble offering to the Divine, the very attitude of this surrender will make you do the job perfectly and you will be liberated. When you are excessively bothered about the results, you actually think you are the doer of the action! That is why you get attached to the work and its results. This is when you start getting stressed and tense about results. Naturally you are not performing at your optimum level because so much of your valuable energy is getting wasted in being tense. Then how will you be able to get your job done properly?

I always tell people, 'When you are afraid to make small mistakes and are over-cautious, you end up making big blunders.' This doesn't mean you can be careless about your work. I am only saying that you should have the courage to make mistakes, and then can you learn from them. Only then have you seen both sides of the coin. You will have seen the perspective of both sides. Otherwise, just at the crucial time, you will make mistakes. You will have this courage only when you are not attached to the ownership of tasks and results. When you see that Existence is purposeless and you are living in the loving, caring arms of Existence, you will relax and surrender to that very Existence. You will function at your best.

A beautiful story:

A person who had faced a lot of trouble in life felt that he had had enough of his life. He ran away to the forest and wanted to find an enlightened master and achieve liberation. He searched day and night but was not able to find anybody.

Then he decided, 'Whoever comes along this road first, whoever I meet on this road first, I shall accept as my master, that's all. I am going to follow his instructions. Oh God, I know you are here. Send me a proper person and guide me. That's all I ask.'

He sat down and waited patiently. After two days, a thief came running that way. The man went and caught hold of the thief's feet saying, 'Oh master, please save me. You are my God. Please give me instructions on how to become enlightened.'

The thief said, 'What is this? Leave me! I am a thief. The palace guards are chasing me; I just robbed the palace.'

The man said, 'No! You are my guru. You have to guide me on the path towards enlightenment.'

The thief said, 'Fool! Don't you see I have all these stolen items with me? Let me go. Otherwise, I will kill you.'

The man said, 'I don't know all that. All I know is that you are my guru; teach me.'

The thief thought, 'Now, what can I do?' Then he said, 'Alright, you say I am your guru. Then listen to me. Will you do whatever I say?'

The man said, 'Yes, surely I will.'

The thief said, 'Sit down and close your eyes. Don't open your eyes until I come back and tell you to open your eyes.' The man sat with all sincerity, his eyes closed, and the thief immediately ran away. The man continued sitting for hours. Then slowly, days passed, then a week passed; a month passed by. The man sat without food or water, absolutely still. The story says, seeing the depth of his sincerity, Lord Śiva appeared before him and gave him enlightenment!

Understand, it has a beautiful meaning and a truth behind it: utmost sincerity is enough. Nothing else is needed. Surrender has tremendous power. Whether you surrender to an idol or to a person or to your guru, or even a rock, is not important. What is important is surrender itself.

Surrender and relax

Vivekānanda says beautifully: 'When you pray to God, your prayers actually awaken your own inner potential and it showers blessings on you.' Even if you see this logically, surrender helps you to simply relax and when you are relaxed, you can work beautifully with intelligence.

A small story:

There was once a bank cashier who used to take the entire bag of cash home everyday and bring it back with him the next morning. He had done this for a month and could not do it anymore.

He found himself trembling all the way while driving back home and was not able to sleep at all with the money in his custody. He finally asked his boss to relieve him of the job since he could not bear the stress any longer.

His boss told him that even if the money were to be lost, he would not be blamed and he could continue with his job. The cashier slept peacefully from that day onwards.

What was the difference in him? He was doing the same job, but why was the fear and tension not there anymore? It was because the responsibility had been shifted to a higher authority. This is surrender! Do your duty, leaving the responsibility of the results to Existence. Have trust in the intelligence of the life force.

This is the energy that runs all the galaxies and the entire universe. Imagine, is it possible for so many billions of stars and planets to move in such a beautiful order even if you had the most modern traffic control system in place? Such a beautiful order!

A very beautiful story from the Indian epic Mahābhārata:

King Yudhiṣtra performed a great sacrifice after the battle of Kurukṣetra was over. He gave very rich presents to the poor. They were all impressed by the grandeur of this sacrifice. They praised him saying, 'We have never seen such a great sacrifice in our lifetime.'

Just then, a small mongoose appeared. Half of his body was golden and the other half was brown. He rolled on the ground where the sacrifice was performed. He then exclaimed with sorrow, 'This is no sacrifice at all. Why do you praise this sacrifice?'

The priests were aghast and angry, 'What! You silly mongoose! Did you not see the sacrifice? Thousands of poor people have become rich. And millions have been sumptuously fed. So many jewels and clothes have been distributed!'

The mongoose replied, 'That may be a big sacrifice for you. But to me the sacrifice offered by the poor brahmin was much bigger.'

'What brahmin and what sacrifice are you talking about? We never heard of this!' said the priests.

The mongoose continued, 'There was a poor brahmin in a village. He lived in a small hut with his wife, son and daughter-in-law. Once, there was a great famine. The whole family starved for days on end. One day, the poor man brought some food home. When they were ready to eat, they heard a voice at their door. The brahmin opened the door and found a guest at the doorstep.

The brahmin said, 'O Sir! Please come inside. Please have some food.' He gave his portion of the food to the guest. The guest said, 'Sir, I am still hungry. I have been starving for the last fifteen days.'

The wife gave her share also to the guest. The guest ate this portion also, but he was still hungry. The son said, 'Father, please give him my share also.' The guest ate this and yet he remained dissatisfied. The wife of the son said, 'O Sir, please have my portion too.' The guest ate this portion also and was fully satisfied. He then blessed the poor brahmin and his family and departed in great joy.

I entered the hut that day and found that four persons had died of starvation. A few grains of rice were found on the ground where the guest had eaten. I rolled myself on those grains. Half of my body became golden. Since then I have been traveling all over the world to find another sacrifice like that. Nowhere have I found one. This sacrifice of Yudhiṣtra has not turned the other half of my body into gold. That is the reason why I say that this is no sacrifice at all.'

The sacrifice that Kṛṣṇa refers to comes from a true sense of surrender to the universe. Only when we give to others by denying ourselves, it is a sacrifice. That is why most of the charitable work done by people, even with good intentions, does not fit into the essence of what Kṛṣṇa says here. Of course, it is better to give to others rather than foolishly stuff yourself. But when you give at your own expense, by sharing what you also need, you function at the level of the universal energy; you function as part of the principle of *Vasudaiva kuṭuṁbakaṁ,* meaning 'The whole world is my family,' as said by Kṛṣṇa. You operate out of compassion. There is no expectation that you will go to heaven if you give and to hell if you don't. That's why, I tell people, 'Do not donate anything to the mission with the belief that I will help you pass through the gates of heaven. First of all, there is no heaven, and second, I am not its gatekeeper!'

There is a joy, a bliss that enters your being when you act out of sacrifice, selflessly. The bliss is always there, but you start experiencing it only when you are free from the filtering ego.

This was the principle on which various sacrificial rituals came into existence in the *vedic* culture. These were instruments of mass meditation. The energy of the cosmic space *(ākāśa)* was captured by the vibrations of the air created when the *mantra*s were chanted. This energised air fuelled the sacred fire in the sacrificial fire pit (*homa kuṇḍa)*. This energy was transferred to pots of water by physically linking the pots to the fire pit through many threads. This energised holy water was then sprinkled on bodies, deities and the earth to complete the energy cycle. All five energy points: space, air, fire, water and earth were connected through such a ritual to benefit humanity!

It was only a metaphoric offering of all that was sacrificed to the fire. During these rituals, great kings and nobles who performed the rituals gave to those who lacked material wealth. These rituals helped to maintain material balance.

But, as the mongoose said, even the *rājasūya yāga* of Yudhisṭra, performed to celebrate his victory, lacked the spirit of sacrifice of the poor brahmin family. So give away what you need, not what you do not need!

Senses And Sins

3.14 *All beings grow from food grains, from rains the food grains become possible, the rains become possible from selfless sacrifice.*

3.15 *Know that work is born of the Creator and He is born of the Supreme.*
The all-pervading Supreme is eternally situated in sacrifice.

3.16 *O Pārtha, he who does not adopt the prescribed, established cycle lives a life full of sins.*
Rejoicing in sense gratification, he lives a useless life.

This metaphorical explanation in a few verses actually has a deep meaning about life, about how we connect with life, how we depend on the universe, and how we affect the whole universe. Our relationship with the activity of Nature is a very deep one. Our actions are like offerings offered in a fire sacrifice. Our activities are not just movements of the limbs.

A physical action is a gross action, something that can be seen on the physical plane. Thoughts, mental actions, are subtler and they cannot be seen on the physical plane. When we perform a sacrifice, we perform certain invocations to the higher energies. So, we attract corresponding effects for our actions. Our actions are like offerings in a sacrifice. When the actions are in tune with the flow of Existence, it is like offering ghee (clarified butter) into the fire. When we do not flow in tune with Existence, it is like offering mud into the fire. You know the kind of smoke that comes out of the fire when you offer ghee and the kind of smoke that comes when you offer mud. Just as how from the quality of the smoke you can determine the quality of the offering you gave to the fire, the result of your actions can be determined from the quality of your actions. The quality of the end result is based on our input, our offerings.

Kṛṣṇa says that rains become possible from sacrifice. Rain is a grosser form of energy that is activated by the subtler energies, which are influenced by our actions, thoughts and vibrations. Rain is the cause for the growth of food grains. Food is needed to sustain our bodies and minds, which give rise to further action. So you see this cycle now, of how the subtle energy manifests itself in the grosser world and how the actions in the grosser world affect the subtler elements.

If we just understand this, we will realize that everything that we do and experience is caused by our own actions. We invite our destiny. As we sow, so shall we reap. Our body-mind is highly influenced by our thoughts and words. Bliss attracts fortune. You may wonder, 'Fortune can bring us bliss but how can bliss bring us fortune?'

In India, when any new activity is started, the first thing that we do is sit for a few moments, close our eyes and remain in a meditative mood. We try to bring about some kind of an energy play or transformation inside us. Over the years, this has become a prayer and a ritual. That is a different issue. But the first thing that we do is sit down and try to kindle the energy flow in us. When the energy flow in us becomes harmonious, it has the property of influencing external incidents. Whether you believe it or not, accept it or not, want it or not, you are deeply connected to Existence. You are an integral part of Existence.

Every subtle movement or subtle thought in one part of the universe causes a counter-effect at that same moment elsewhere in the universe. Our thoughts and energy flow have the capacity to create and attract incidents and people of the same nature. What I have said here is one of the age-old truths expounded by our *ṛsis*, sages in the *Upaniṣad, vedic* lore. It is interesting that modern science is coming up with some startling evidence that reveals some of these truths now.

Dr. Masaru Emoto, a Japanese doctor and research scientist renowned for his book, *The Hidden Messages in Water,* conducted extensive experiments on water samples taken from all over the world.

He took similar samples of water and exposed the water to different influences. To one set of samples, he spoke positive words such as 'love' and 'gratitude' and recited Buddhist chants. To another set, he spoke words such as 'anger' and 'war.' Then he froze the different water samples so that he could photograph their crystal form.

In the samples that had been exposed to positive energy, beautiful clear crystals were formed, like diamonds! The water exposed to negative energies did not form into crystals; they looked like a tumor: dark, cloudy and without any distinct geometrical pattern.

Several hundred experiments were conducted to prove the effects of the vibrations created by our words and thoughts on matter. Water being the most common molecule in our bodies, we can now see the obvious and dramatic effect our thoughts have on others and ourselves! It doesn't stop there. Our thoughts have the capacity to affect the oceans and the seas.

Recent research by Russian scientists throws an entirely new light on how our DNA can be influenced and reprogrammed by words and frequencies. They did experiments where they superimposed certain frequencies onto a laser ray and with it influenced the DNA frequency and thus the genetic information itself!

Science is beginning to touch what our *vedic* seers have declared thousands of years ago about collective consciousness. What we do in any plane, physical or mental, affects our consciousness. And since we are all a part of the common fabric called Existence, our consciousness is a part of the collective consciousness, which also gets affected by our thoughts and actions.

Weather is strongly influenced by earth resonance frequencies, and the same frequencies are also produced in our brains. When many people synchronize their thinking, the individual consciousness synchronizes and affects the collective consciousness. So we can actually even influence the weather by our thoughts. This is what Kṛṣṇa means when He says rains are caused by sacrifice. It is a metaphorical statement. When a large number of people synchronize and focus their thoughts with no expectations and with full faith in the abundance of the universe, the universe responds. Rain falls, grains grow, and abundance results.

It has actually been revealed by various studies that when a number of people focus their thoughts on something similar, like during communal celebrations or a football world championship, then certain random number generators in computers start to deliver ordered numbers instead of random ones!

Also understand, that all the so-called natural calamities are nothing but the effects of global negative thoughts.

From a young age, we have been trained in 'mathematical logic,' never in 'Existential logic.' Mathematical logic is very straightforward and should not be applied to matters like life and relationships. It will only cause chaos. With it, we will always look to conclude with a 'good' or 'bad' judgment. There is something beyond and deeper than this - and that is Existential logic. This comes with a mature understanding and flowering from within.

Your thoughts and energy directly affect your body, your cell structure, your decisions, and your capacity to fulfill your decisions, the outer world incidents, and even accidents. Currently, you are always centered in either greed or fear. It becomes very easy for others to exploit you because of this. You create a mental setup that attracts similar incidents to your life. You also corrupt your energy flow in this way. If you can change your mental setup from this type to one of bliss, then your energy flow will start brimming, and your thoughts will be much clearer and you will be more in the present moment.

When you do this, you have every power to control external incidents because you and Existence have a very deep connection at the energy level. This is the thread that you need to catch in order to understand that bliss attracts fortune. When you are blissful, when your mental setup is in the present, always joyful, you will automatically attract all good things to yourself. When you throw a pebble into a lake, ripples start from that point to the edge of the lake. So also, your thoughts have a permanent effect on the universe.

Every action has an effect. Using the same principle, I can say that you can actually create the desired effect by just visualizing it. For example, if you meditate, if you visualize you *are* bliss, bliss is bound to happen in and around you as an effect. It would seem that the cause has created the effect. But in life, cause and effect are actually a cycle, each generating and being generated by the other.

This is the endless cycle that Kṛṣṇa refers to when He says that work originates with the Creator, who in turn originates from the supreme Existence, and therefore all sacrifices are from the Supreme to the Supreme. When we are in the mood and mode of surrender, we no longer retain our identity. We are one with Existence.

Act Without Attachment

3.17 One who takes pleasure in the Self, who is satisfied in the Self and who is content in his own Self, for him certainly, no work exists.

3.18 Certainly, he never has any reason for doing his duty or not doing his duty in this world.
He does not depend on any living being.

3.19 Therefore, one should work always without attachment.
Performing work without attachment, certainly, man achieves the Supreme.

3.20 King Janaka and others attained perfection by selfless service.
To guide others, you too must act selflessly.

Our Eastern masters have declared again and again, 'You *are* bliss.' When you are bliss itself, what more can you ask for? When you understand and experience this truth, you are enough unto yourself. Then nothing exists for you to achieve because you are already the ultimate thing you can achieve!

As of now, you are running behind something out of greed, thinking that when you achieve that, it will give you bliss or you are running away from something out of fear, thinking that it will take away your joy. Both of these motivations, running towards something and away from something, become irrelevant when you understand that you are a part of this loving Existence which is taking care of you every moment. Do you think you can be alive even for one moment if Existence does not want you to be alive? The very fact that you are alive proves that Existence wants you here, now, in this form, in this place. This is the ultimate cause for celebration! What more do you want? Existence is continuously providing for each and every one of your needs. Your suffering and struggle is only because you don't trust that you are being provided all that you need by Existence.

People often look at my feet and tell me that I have such smooth and soft feet. They do not know that I have wandered thousands of miles with no footwear in all possible types of terrain. Understand, when you walk upon Mother earth with great respect and love, She will simply cherish you.

I never wore footwear in early years of life. Even now, when I enter Tiruvannamalai, I don't wear footwear. When I used to go to college by bus, I would put on shoes only after the bus left Tiruvannamalai town, and would take them off when it entered the town again. It is a holy land that one must fall in tune with. Many of our followers take off their shoes when they are in this town.

Once I was on an elephant safari on a jungle path. The guide showed me a path that was used by humans. It was alongside the one on which the elephant was walking. The guide's path had no grass on it. The guide said that where man walks, no grass grows, but where the elephant walks, the grass does not die!

We human beings have lost touch with ourselves and with nature. That is why we experience nature unpleasantly. Even in our prayers there is no gratitude, there is only asking. We have become beggars. Also, you are not satisfied with how Existence chooses to take care of your needs. You look at others and have a big list of wants based on what others have. You fail to understand that each of us is unique and has been provided with exactly what we need. Instead, you start looking at what others have and want that also. Greed sets in.

This is how you waste your entire life running behind desires. We are focused only on the outer world. As long as the outer world is responsible for your happiness, there can be no permanent happiness. The person who is centered does not depend on external causes or people for enjoyment. Constantly, the fountain of bliss is happening within him. He *is* enjoyment itself! Actually, the fountain of bliss is happening spontaneously in each of us. We always think that joy or happiness can happen only for some reason. On the other hand, we feel we can be sad for no reason. No! It is you who is stopping the fountain of bliss from happening in your being every moment.

The first level meditation program, Ananda Spurana Program, (Life Bliss Program Level 1) which deals with the seven *cakras*, the seven energy centers in our body, is all about 'stopping the stopping' of the fountain of bliss. The second level program, Nithyananda Spurana Program (LBP Level 2) reinforces this and shows you how to keep this fountain of bliss happening eternally in you.

> Kṛṣṇa says a beautiful thing: King Janaka was a beautiful example of a true *karma yogi*, a man of continuous and selfless action. He was a king. He ruled a kingdom and yet was unattached, liberated. Janaka was a model king who was untouched by the external world. Once, an ascetic went to the court of King Janaka and saw how he was neck-deep in the activities of his kingdom. He then thought to himself, 'Janaka seems to be a materialistic person. He is entrapped in so many worldly matters.'
>
> Janaka understood what the ascetic was thinking. Janaka called him and asked, 'What kind of an ascetic are you? Instead of being happy and content within yourself, you are trying to find fault with others? This is a grave sin especially for an ascetic. For this, you will be hanged to death next week.' Now, the ascetic was terrified. He spent sleepless nights thinking of the gallows. Daily he dreamt that his neck was being tied to a rope. He became very thin and pale.
>
> Janaka sent a servant to call him on the day of the execution. The ascetic trembled and fell on the ground, unable to stand before the

king. Janaka offered him some fruits and a cup of milk. He ate the food, but his mind was on the gallows.

Janaka asked him, 'How do you like the taste of the milk now? Is it good? Did you relish your food these past seven days?'

The ascetic replied, 'Oh king! I did not feel any taste in the food that you offered me just now. My mind is only on the gallows all the time.'

Janaka said, 'Just as your mind is always on the gallows, so also my mind is always fixed on the Divine, though I am involved in worldly activities, discharging my duties as a king. Though I am in this world, I am out of the world. Work for the world, unattached like myself.'

I tell you, only when you are completely detached can you be completely involved. Otherwise, your very sense of ownership and emotional attachment will be a hindrance to plunging headlong into the task. Only when you work without internalizing the incident can you perform the task in the best way, without expectation and without being concerned about the results.

Leader Consciousness

3.21 *Whenever action is performed by a great person, others follow.*
They follow the example set by him.

3.22 *O Pārtha, there is nothing that I must do in the three worlds.*
Neither am I in want of anything. Yet, I am always in action.

3.23 *If I did not engage in work with care, O Pārtha, certainly, people would follow My path in all respects.*

3.24 *If I do not work, then these worlds would be ruined. I would be the cause of creating confusion and destruction.*

3.25 *Even the ignorant do their work with attachment to the results, O Bhārata, the wise do so without attachment, for the welfare of the people.*

Here, Kṛṣṇa talks about the practical aspects of why a leader needs to act in a responsible manner.

There is a difference between the state of a leader and the status of a leader. Most of us want the status of a leader, not the state. When you achieve the status of the leader, it is ego-fulfilling and you feel great. Most politicians are great examples of this status. They exert the power of their position on others. They were a little more dominating and a little more convincing than the people whom they were trying to dominate. It is not that they were more intelligent or more capable.

The *state* of the leader is something totally different. It is the state of the leader that affects people, whether it is people under a political leader or in an organization in the corporate world under a CEO. Problems of all kinds, ranging from stress to discontentment and violence, result because the leader has achieved the status and not the state.

I always tell my disciples, 'Practice what I teach you. Don't just preach what I teach. Only by example can you inspire others to follow you.' It is easy to utter words and talk about what you have understood intellectually from my teachings, but that understanding is very shallow.

Deep understanding happens only with experience. Only then does your understanding become complete. Then you are unshakeable in your conviction. Otherwise, if the understanding is based on somebody else's experience and not on your own, there is always the possibility that somebody can shake your belief. The roots of conviction are not deep and strong enough to withstand all kinds of questions.

There are three types of people: the disciples (or the followers), the masters, and the leaders (or guides). The disciple is one who has not yet experienced the teachings of the master but who is interested and has embarked upon the path. He needs some guidance on the path. He does not yet know how to practice what is being taught.

The master is one who has had and is in the ultimate state. Out of compassion, he shows people the path to reach his state. It is not necessary for the master to practice what he preaches because he is beyond the common rules of conduct.

A small story:

There was once a Zen master who would advise people not to smoke. But he himself would smoke everyday.

One day, a disciple asked him, 'Master, how can you tell people that they should not smoke when you yourself are smoking?'

The master replied beautifully, 'Understand, I am not in the same state, the same plane, as the person whom I am teaching.'

Masters need not follow what they tell you to do to reach their state because they are in a completely different state altogether. Whatever they may do physically is done in a state of complete awareness.

Even though I always tell people that they need to be aware and completely present when they eat, you will see that I never concentrate on my food when I eat. When I eat, I will be reading something or talking to someone.

For you, you have to meditate to be aware of the food that you take, so that you eat only as much as needed. But for me, if I am aware, I will not be able to eat the amount of food my body needs. I have to distract myself and remove the awareness and only then the food will go inside! An enlightened being's system is very different from an ordinary person's system. That is why things that apply for ordinary people cannot be applied to an enlightened being.

A leader is someone who is in between the master and the follower. He has not yet reached the ultimate state of the master but has had glimpses of that state. He is not as inexperienced as the follower. He is the bridge that leads the follower to the master. I always tell the teachers of the mission that it is their responsibility to practice what they teach because they are the bridges leading the people to me.

Practice gives understanding

One more thing: It is not that you need to practice just so that others get inspired. Understand that the very practice will give deep understanding to you. That is the first effect, the actual result. Being an inspiration to others will be just a byproduct. It will result automatically from the confidence that you radiate in your body language and words when you teach people out of the strength of your own conviction.

In these verses, Kṛṣṇa beautifully explains what walking the talk means. He says there is nothing in the three worlds for Him to achieve, no duty that binds Him. Even though He has nothing to gain, lose or even to do, He is constantly engaged in action. Why? Because people look up to Him as God, they will simply follow the path He sets. He is now responsible for leading them on the correct path. If He did not engage in action, people would follow His example and fall into inaction or *tamas*.

Every year, I take people to the Himalayan mountains. It is a lifetime experience to be in the lap of Nature. Just seeing and living in the Himalayas for fifteen days will bring a powerful transformation. In the Himalayas, we do various types of rituals at various places, at the *cār dhāṁ* (the four sacred pilgrimage centers in that area). Of what use are the rituals to me? But I do them for you so that you understand their significance and you get inspired to do them and benefit from them.

After enlightenment, I came from the Himalayas to be amidst the people. I could have just stayed there happily and blissfully. But I came here because people need to be guided on the right path. That is why masters come to planet earth - to guide people.

Seeing me work constantly, being intensely involved in work, whether it is administration or giving discourses or planning upcoming activities or whatever the action may be, people are inspired to be engaged in work constantly, blissfully enjoying every moment. I don't have to give you my words. You can see me and learn from my body language much more than from my words. I give you words only to silence your mind so that you can absorb my energy. Else you will be chattering inside yourself and will miss my message.

As Kṛṣṇa says, I need to be careful what I do for the sake of those who follow.

The problem is, what I do is my experience. Unless you experience it yourself, it cannot become your truth. So the same action will have a completely different meaning and effect when done by a disciple than when done by a master. But if you follow the master's teachings and watch his body language, you will imbibe enlightenment itself.

For example, look at a simple teaching by Buddha, 'Watch your breath.' This very simple *vipāsana* meditation technique has led thousands of people to enlightenment.

But look at a seemingly powerful discovery of the principle behind the atom bomb: nuclear fission. It was a great truth, but when it came into the hands of an ignorant person who did not understand the implications of it, it resulted in so many countries piling up so many atomic weapons that the earth can now be destroyed several times over!

It is the energy behind the action that decides the quality and the effect of the action, not the action itself. You must have seen that there are some people who can get away with anything, even something that would normally appear as a disrespectful action. It is because there was no negative attitude or vengeance behind the act.

Children get away with so many things like even hitting you, and you actually enjoy it. Can you imagine feeling like this if an adult hits you? The innocence of the child, the honest simplicity of the child's act, the energy of the child, its intelligence, is completely behind the action. This is unlike an adult whose intellect may be behind the act, the mind is behind the act, but the intelligence is not there because there is a certain unconscious vengeance in the act.

Masters act out of pure compassion in whatever they do. That is why even when I scold people, the person does not carry vengeance towards me. Scolding is for your good, for your ego to be removed. It will seem painful because your ego, which you have been thinking is you, is being pulled out. But your being understands that it is for your good. There is pure compassion even in scolding. That is why in the very next moment after scolding, I can be completely different, showering love. It was just complete truth at that moment, pure compassionate energy. That is why it can switch to loving emotion the very next minute. Every instance is pure in its own way.

But what happens when you get angry with someone and scold him, say you scold your child, for example? The anger takes over you. Instead of you controlling the anger, *it* controls you because you are not conscious during the action.

You are driven by your memories of similar incidents in the past and you react with more anger than this current act deserves. Anger is also energy but you need to handle it with respect. Just like you respect money and never overpay someone, when you realize the power of the anger energy, you respect it and do not pay the other person more anger than necessary.

If you give just the right anger energy, it can be transformational, but your negative attitude behind the action creates an undesired result and the person carries a certain vengeance towards you which even he may not be conscious of. Be very clear, the other person's vengeance is the result of your very own vengeance, which you did not realize was there in your action because you were not completely aware when you were scolding.

I always tell people, 'When I am compassionate, I cheat you. When I scold you, I teach you. Either way, you grow.' When I scold you, you are jolted into the present moment. Suddenly, in a flash, you get the awareness that you have been missing. The energy behind my words is purely for your transformation. There is only pure compassion. There is no vengeance against anyone or any vested interest for myself.

Role Of The Wise Ones

3.26 Let not the wise disturb the minds of the ignorant that are attached to the results of work.
They should encourage them to act without attachment.

3.27 People, confused by ego, think they are the doers of all kinds of work while it is being done by the energy of Nature.

3.28 One who knows the Truth, O mighty-armed one, knows the divisions existing in the attributes of Nature and work. Knowing well about the attributes and sense gratification, he never becomes attached.

3.29 Fooled by the attributes of Nature, those people with less wisdom or who are lazy become engaged in actions driven by these attributes.
But, the wise should not unsettle them.

An ignorant man says to himself, 'I shall do this action and thereby enjoy its result.' A wise man should not unsettle this belief. Instead, he himself should set an example by performing his duties diligently but without attachment. If the wise man condemns the actions performed with attachment, the ignorant person may simply decide to neglect his duties.

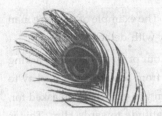

It is like this. Can you explain to a child that his toys are not precious? No! The child will never be able to understand that. It has to grow and automatically its attachment to toys will drop when maturity happens. Similarly, the ignorant person can first do the action only with attachment. But upon seeing the wise person being unaffected by his own actions and being always blissful, naturally, the ignorant one will get curious and want to know the secret behind happiness. The example of the wise man will automatically pull him towards work with detachment.

Take the example of relating to God. All our prayers to God are asking God to fulfill some desire or to protect us from something. It is okay to start a relationship with God like this. When you get what you asked for, your trust grows and you start feeling gratitude towards Him. This is important.

In the beginning, it is very difficult to feel grateful to God for all that has been given to you. So if you ask a person who has not eaten food for three days to meditate, will he be able to? No! His needs are different. You will be foolish, if you try asking him to meditate. What he needs now is some means to get food and then he can be told about meditation.

When a person is doing work and expecting results, the wise person should not disturb him. At least the person is working and not sitting idle! He is in *rajas,* which is better than *tamas* (laziness). He needs to be guided from *rajas* to *satva,* a state of calmness born out of action without any expectations. That is the job of a master.

We are all governed by our basic attributes, or *guṇa.* The mental set-up from previous births, *vāsana* determines nature and attributes in this birth. The desires born out of *vāsana* carry their own energy for fulfillment. If you are conscious of your *vāsana,* you will be able to fulfill them. Once fulfilled, these *vāsana* and *karma* get dissolved. One who reaches this state of awareness of fulfilled desires also realizes that he is not the doer. The potter's wheel keeps turning around even after the potter has ceased to turn it when the pot is finished. The *vāsana* or desires with which you took this body and mind will make the body-mind go through whatever activities it was made for.

Actually, your desire to lead life in a particular way is what creates the corresponding mental setup. You are the one who chooses to live life in a particular way, and once you decide this, your body supports this decision and acts accordingly. This mental setup that you create to live life in a particular way is your *vāsana,* or the seed of *karma.*

You are the one who chooses, but any choice comes with effects and side effects. Sometimes when you see the side effects, you feel that you don't want this way of life. It is too costly; it is creating more unwanted effects than you were expecting. Then you say what you are getting is due to fate or destiny. Actually, you are the one who chose it in the first place.

A small story:

> Once a man went to a restaurant and ordered various items: hamburgers, steaks, pasta, drinks, ice cream, and so on. He had a hearty meal and relaxed. The waiter brought the bill.
>
> The man took a look at the long bill and exclaimed, 'But didn't order for this bill!'

When you eat, you don't think about the bill, but the bill comes only as a result of all that you ate in the restaurant. You don't have to order it separately. Similarly, in life, all that you undergo are the effects of your own actions. You are not aware of what those effects can be because you perform the actions unconsciously. To understand, 'I am not the doer,' this concept of 'I' and 'mine' needs to be understood. The concept of 'I' itself comes from the concept of 'mine.' We always think it is the other way around. But if you look deeply, our idea of what we think of as 'ours' is what defines what we think of as ourselves. Just imagine, if your possessions, your status, your wealth, your relations all are taken away from you, what will you think of as you? How will you define yourself? Your idea of 'I' is also relative, is it not?

Many devotees feel that they are just touching a soft pillow when I embrace them during *ānanda darśan* (transfer of bliss energy). Sometimes they feel nothing and they are shocked. Basically, enlightened beings are just energy. In this plane, in these dimensions of space-time, you see them in this form. You see them in this six-foot form as say 'Nithyananda', but in truth, this 'Nithyananda' does not exist. It is just energy. There is no 'I.'

When you get attached to anything, when you internalize external incidents, you start creating suffering for yourself. When you understand that it is the mind and the senses doing what is in their nature, you become detached from your body-mind and do things with the clear understanding that what is happening is just the mind, body and senses doing their job.

When you don't understand this, you get caught in what you are doing, you get emotionally attached to incidents and people, and you start living without awareness because your energy is being wasted in getting stressed out and getting emotionally upset over things.

Do As I Teach

3.30 Dedicating the results of work to Me, with consciousness filled with spiritual knowledge, without desire for gain and without sense of ownership, without being lazy, do what you have to do.

3.31 Those pers ons who execute their duties according to My injunctions and who follow these teachings faithfully, without envy, become free from the bondage of actions.

3.32 But those who do not regularly perform their duties according to My teaching are ignorant, senseless and ruined.

Next Kṛṣṇa makes an important point. He clarifies one more point. Kṛṣṇa says: Those persons who execute their duties according to My injunctions and who follow this teaching faithfully, without envy, become free from the bondage of actions.

Here you need to understand two things. He says, 'according to *My* injunctions.' It means that when you enter into your being, whatever your being says is Kṛṣṇa's words. When he says *My* injunctions, He means the injunctions from the *ātman,* injunctions from the being.

When you drop the goals and fall into your being, the Divine will guide you and you will become an instrument in His hands. As long as you follow the goals set by society, you will be carrying a social conscience. The moment you drop social conditioning you will drop conscience and start living with consciousness. Social conscience is different, spiritual consciousness is different. If you live with goals, you will carry a social conscience in your life. If you realize the beauty of purposelessness you will carry spiritual consciousness in your life.

'The man who lives according to his consciousness, believing in and having *śraddhā* (faith) towards these teachings...' This is the first time Kṛṣṇa says '*śraddhā*'. Why? *Śraddhā* cannot really be translated as faith. In English, there is no equivalent for *śraddhā*. *Śraddhā* does not mean just faith. It means faith plus the courage to execute the idea. The courage to experiment with the idea is *śraddhā*. Here Kṛṣṇa says, '*śraddhāvanto anasūyanto*,' the person who executes the teachings with *śraddhā*, with the courage to follow. Why do we need courage to follow the teachings?

A small story:

A man born blind goes to the doctor and asks, 'Doctor, will you help me gain my eyesight?' The doctor says, 'Don't worry. I will perform an operation. You will get your vision and after that you can walk without your stick.'

The blind man asks, 'Doctor, I understand you will do an operation. I understand I will have my eyesight restored. But how can I walk without my stick?'

In the same way, I tell you, just live without purpose and goals; you will be able to walk without the stick. The stick is nothing but your planning and worrying. You never believe that you can live without worrying. By and by, worrying has become a part of you. When I say you can live without worrying, you will say, 'No, no! How is it possible? If I don't worry what will happen to my children, my house? Be very clear: Your life is going smoothly in spite of you, not because of you!

When you have the courage towards these teachings and start living without purpose, only then will you realize that you don't need the stick to walk. You will enter into the depths of your being. Whatever you think now as a spiritual life or a material life, both will lose their meaning and you will enter into a new dimension of life.

When you experience the purposelessness of life, both material and spiritual lives drop you and you enter into 'Quantum Spirituality' or eternal consciousness. You are then in eternal bliss. Only then you understand that you don't need worries to live. You don't need your mind. Until you reach the being, you need to have *śraddhā*. Until you gain your vision, you must have *śraddhā* and lie down on the operating table. You need to allow the doctor to work on you. That is the reason Kṛṣṇa says, '*śraddhāvanto anasūyanto*.' When you follow My teachings with *śraddhā*, you will be liberated. You will not be caught in the cycle of life and death.

The next word is a beautiful word: '*anasūyanto*,' which means 'without envy.' We all think, 'My brother has purchased two houses. My sister got a new car. How can I live like this?' The moment you get such thoughts, what happens? All your spirituality, all your purposelessness just disappears. You are again in the same rat race. Kṛṣṇa says, 'without envy.' Envy is the thing that again and again puts you in the same rut. The problem with the rat race is that even if you win, you are still a rat!

The power of illusion

There is a beautiful idea from *Tantra* about *māyā śakti* (the power of illusion). Illusion makes us all dance with just this one stick called jealousy. Have you seen the guys who make money using monkeys in India? On the roadside, they do a small show with monkeys. They carry a small stick. With that they make the monkey do whatever they want it to.

In the same way, the power of illusion is making you run as it wants with just one stick called jealousy, envy or comparison. The moment you compare, you just jump into the same path again, the same rut which I call the purposeful life. Then you become a *karmi*, not *karma yogi*. The man who lives in eternal consciousness and allows his body and mind to work according to their nature is a *karma yogi*. That is one who has espoused action without attachment as the ultimate renunciation. The man who acts out of jealousy and comparison, enters into social conditioning. He is caught in the rat race, and is called a *karmi*, one who is focused on action arising from greed.

The man who is driven by jealousy is a *karmi,* and the man who allows the eternal consciousness to drive him is a *karma yogi.*

When we do things out of comparison, we do only foolish things. Those who do not perform their duty according to Kṛṣṇa's teachings, those who are driven by comparison, will not attain Self-knowledge. They are again and again driven by greed and comparison. Our performance will definitely fall short of our potential when we compare because now we are using someone else's productivity as our measuring stick. We might be capable of accomplishing much more than what our neighbor has done, but now we are setting our sights on his achievements!

> A small story:
>
> A Christian and a Jew were living across from each other. They were great rivals. If the Christian made a rose garden in front of his house, then, within twenty-four hours the Jew would bring in a new rose garden. If the Jew painted his house white, within twenty-four hours the Christian's house would also be painted white.
>
> Suddenly, one day a new Mercedes Benz was standing in front of the Jew's house. The Christian somehow found the money and bought a Rolls Royce within twenty-four hours. He parked it outside his home and started sprinkling holy water on it.
>
> The Jew saw this from his house and asked, 'Hey! What happened to you? Why are you sprinkling water on the car this morning?'
>
> The Christian said, 'I am baptizing it.'
>
> Now the Jew was in big trouble! What to do? That evening he was seen cutting the exhaust pipe of his Benz with a hacksaw blade!

If you understand, understand. If you have not understood, ask the people who are laughing!

If you do things out of jealousy you will end up doing only these types of things. Understand, each of us is unique. There is no need to compare with any other person. The main problem is that you compare only with the nearest person, your neighbor or brother. You don't compare yourselves with Bill Gates, do you? Why? The problem is your *worry* about failure. That is why you aim only at reachable goals, and compare only with those people in your immediate world. Again and again, this comparison brings up the whole social conditioning in you and eats away your whole life. Just like how the whole earth is destroyed by the ocean at the time of the final deluge, in the same way, just this one concept of comparison destroys your whole life.

Jealousy and comparison have no absolute existence. There are two levels of reality: comparative reality and existential reality. If you build your life based on existential reality, you will never suffer. If you build your life based on comparative reality, you will be continuously suffering until your death and even after death. But, if you build your life on existential reality, you will live your life blissfully in eternal consciousness, as a *karma yogi.*

By nature, a person with a body and mind has to act in oneway or another. If you follow your nature, you can be comfortable and flow in tune with Existence. When you are relaxed, you express yourself beautifully. When you become possessed by greed or fear and try to be what you are not, you suppress yourself. For example, if you see someone who irritates you, what is your reaction? If you are in a position to show your irritation, you will do so. You will make your irritation known to the person because you are not afraid of losing anything. But, if this person is your boss, then you are afraid to make your irritation known because he holds the power to affect your job. So you suppress your emotions.

Neither expression nor suppression is the solution. The solution is to infuse awareness and understanding into this process. Your reaction of irritation is not because of anything the person has done. If you just look a little deeper, you can see it is how *you* choose to react that decides what you feel about the person. You choose to get irritated by what he is doing.

Why should you allow yourself to get worked up about the other person's actions? Also, it may not even be that the person has done something that you think is irritating. Your irritation is because you are already biased by your past perception about him. You have decided unconsciously this is what he is going to do and you get irritated even before he comes close to you.

That is why I say that awareness is the key. If you are aware of what is happening both within you and outside you, you will not be controlled by your unconscious. You will be able to see clearly when biased emotions arise or unconscious reactions arise. You don't need to suppress the emotion or express it. The awareness will itself bring the emotion under your control.

Do Your Duty

3.33 *Dedicating the results of work to Me, with consciousness filled with Me, even the wise person acts according to the modes of his own nature, for all living beings go through their nature. What can restraint of the senses do?*

3.34 *Attachment and repulsion of the senses for sense objects should be put under control.*
One should never come under their control, as they certainly are the stumbling blocks on the path of self-realization.

3.35 *It is better to do one's own duty, even if it is in a faulty manner, than to do someone else's duty perfectly.*
Death in the course of performing one's own duty is better than doing another's duty, as this can be dangerous.

3.36 *Arjuna said, 'O descendant of Vṛṣṇi, then, by what is man forced to commit sinful acts, even without desiring, as if engaged by force?'*

3.37 *The Lord said, 'It is lust and anger born of the attribute of passion, all-devouring and sinful, which is one's greatest enemies in this world.'*

Here, it is important to understand what duty means. If I have to do my duty, I need to know how to identify my duty.

The idea of duty is different for different people. The term 'duty' is impossible to clearly define. We have always been trained by society to consider certain acts as duty, some as good and others as bad. We are brought up with certain ideas of duty. For example, it is our duty to help elderly people. It is our duty to follow principles of truth, non-violence, non-stealing and such tenets. But how many of us have experienced the beauty of implementing them?

Then there are certain principles that get handed down depending on the religion we follow. For example, a starving person who finds a piece of meat has no problem eating it if he is a non-vegetarian. On the other hand, a vegetarian would feel it is his duty not to touch meat even if it means losing his life. In some religions, you can marry only once but in some other religions, you can marry multiple times. These are all socially defined duties.

One thing we should remember is never to judge the customs of other people by our standards. There is no common standard for the universe. What Kṛṣṇa talks about here is not socially defined duty or conscience. He is talking about consciousness.

Vivekānanda talks about a sage, a yogi in India. He was a peculiar man; he would not teach anyone. If you asked him a question, he would not answer immediately. However, in some days, in the course of a conversation, he would bring up the subject and throw wonderful light on it. He once told Vivekānanda the secret of work, 'Let the end and the means be joined into one.'

When you are doing any work, do not think of anything beyond that. Do it as the highest worship, and devote your whole energy to it at that time. The right performance of duty at any point in life, without attachment to the results, leads us to the highest realization. The worker who is attached to the results grumbles about the nature of the duty. To the unattached worker, all duties are equally good. He welcomes what he has to do, irrespective of the nature of the job. He approaches every act with the same enthusiasm and liveliness and becomes completely involved in the task at hand.

In the great epic Mahābhārata, there are actually three versions of the Gītā: Bhagavad Gītā and Anu gītā, both delivered by Śri Kṛṣṇa; the third and equally important one is called Vyādha gītā, the song of a butcher.

A butcher delivered this Vyādha gītā a man who is considered a sinner or a *candāla* (low caste person) delivered this great scripture.

There lived a great yogi, a person with special powers but who was not yet enlightened. He was a highly egoistic person. He was meditating under a tree in a forest. A bird sitting on the tree relieved itself and the droppings fell on the yogi. He was disturbed and angry. He opened his eyes and looked at the bird. The bird was killed by his powerful gaze. The yogi felt very proud of what he had done.

He then went on his daily round of begging for alms. He came to a house and begged for food. The lady of the house called out from inside the house and asked him to wait as she was serving her husband. The yogi was upset. He thought to himself, 'Foolish woman! She is serving her husband and making a great yogi like me wait!'

Suddenly he heard the lady's voice again as if in answer, 'I am not like the bird in the forest to be killed so easily. Your powers are useless against me, so relax!'

The yogi was shocked! The lady actually knew not only what he was thinking, but also about what had happened in the forest! The yogi apologized to the lady when she came out to give him food.

He asked her, 'Mother, how did you know what I was thinking? And about what happened in the forest? Please teach me how I can also achieve this.'

She replied, 'You have attained *śakti* (power) but not *buddhi* (intelligence). Go to the butcher who is down the road and he will teach you.' Now the yogi was even more surprised. He thought, 'How can an ordinary butcher teach me anything about *buddhi*?'

He quietly took the lady's counsel and went down the road to the butcher's shop. When he reached the butcher's shop, he saw that the butcher was busy cutting up the meat of the animals that he had just slaughtered. He could not imagine how he could learn anything from the butcher. But he wanted to have intelligence, so he approached the butcher and asked, 'I was told by a lady living nearby to ask you about intelligence. Can you explain to me how to attain intelligence?'

The butcher explained how he himself had achieved intelligence, the ultimate experience. All he did to achieve it was to do his job with complete awareness and total involvement. He did his job with complete intensity and used the money that he earned to take care of his aged parents, which he did with equal devotion and involvement.

Just the very doing of his duty liberated him. The nature of his work, the act of slaughtering animals, was not important. The attitude with which he did it, the sincerity, was what mattered. You may be doing the greatest acts of social service and in the eyes of society you may be a great man. But if the attitude behind the act is not positive, the action is just hypocritical.

Each of us is unique in our capabilities. Accordingly, our duties are also different. If you try to imitate others, you will be making the mistake of following somebody else's path, which is not natural to you. You see, comparison literally rules our lives. We waste our time and energy analyzing the other's growth. When we use our energies for our growth without comparing with others, we do our duty according to our nature.

These verses on *karma yoga* by Kṛṣṇa have been misused by some to defend the caste, or *varṇa* system in the Hindu tradition. They say that what Kṛṣṇa means is that one should not swerve from one's *varṇa dharma*, the duty of one's caste. They do not understand the origin of the caste system.

*Brāhmaṇa*s were the scholars and priests. *Kshatriya*s were the soldiers, nobles and kings, ambitious and physically strong. *Vaishya*s were the business community. *Śūdra*s were the workers, the servers who were physically able and skillful.

In the *vedic* culture, a child was taken to a *gurukul* (the ancient system of living with and learning at the feet of the master) before the age of seven.

The master then took care of the child until the child reached adulthood. He taught the child based on its abilities. If the child had the aptitude to become a scholar he was trained in scriptures, and became a *brāhmaṇa*. If the child was aggressive and courageous, he was trained in martial arts, and became a *kṣatriya*, meaning warrior, and so on.

The children were trained based on their *guṇas*, not birth. Over time, this system was manipulated and degenerated into a classification based on heredity. One needs to understand Kṛṣṇa's injunction in the *vedic* educational context.

Arjuna then asks Kṛṣṇa why even a centered person is led to commit sinful acts, as if forced by unknown powers. Arjuna's question is the eternal dilemma of expression or suppression.

For example, if you see a beautiful woman and you feel attracted to her, you feel this is not correct according to what society has taught you and you try to suppress your feelings. Can this work? If you try to suppress something, it will surface again with more intensity.

We are always conditioned by society, which teaches us that anyone with passion is a lower human. Understand, there is no lower or higher person. Only a transformation of energy needs to happen. The people who pretend to be moralists are either afraid to express their lust or they feel guilty about expressing it. So they go about preaching others that being lustful means you are a lower person. The moment you think you are a lower human, you start fighting with that feeling. Then it becomes very difficult to get out of that and for the transformation to happen. What you need to do is bring in awareness and allow the transformation to happen.

The alchemy

What needs to be done is to have understanding and awareness. Then the base energy of lust can be transformed into the higher energy of love like alchemy. Alchemy is the process of changing any base metal to a higher metal. In alchemy, first the impurity is removed from the base metal. Then something is added to it, and finally, the base metal undergoes the process of transformation into the higher metal.

First, the impurity should be removed from lust, which is an animal emotion. Our lust is contaminated by all kinds of fantasies. We live with a solid cerebral layer of fantasies collected from the media. Even when you are in a relationship, you are relating from this layer. Your lust is contaminated by guilt and desire. Either our conditioning makes us feel guilty and so we withdraw, or the intense desire to continue makes us indulge excessively, only to make us feel guilty again. It is a vicious cycle of pulling and pushing, the result of which is that the lust is simply contaminated.

Always, the moment you fulfill your fantasy, you are engulfed by guilt. That is why sex makes you feel guilty. Your family and society instill the first sense of guilt in you when you are a child. Then you master the art of creating guilt for yourself! Understand, anyone who wants to have control over you, first instills guilt in you. They make you feel you are inferior. Then, automatically, you follow what they are saying. When you indulge in desires and become prone to guilt, you are caught in a vicious cycle. That is why you don't go deep into your desires, fulfill them and come out liberated, but keep coming back with more and more craving. If you go deep into it, you will flower out of it!

In earlier times, people were able to drop their lust by the age of forty. They related directly with their husband or wife without any fantasies. They were able to move deep into lust and come out of it. In Indian marriages, there is a beautiful verse that priests make the couples recite. The meaning of the verse is, 'In the eleventh year of marriage, let the wife become the mother, and the husband the son.' What it means is, let the relationship reach the ultimate fulfillment.

The ultimate fulfillment for a woman is when she expresses the motherliness in her. The ultimate fulfillment for the man is when he comes back to the innocence of the child. So, by the eleventh year, let the relationship mature to such an extent that both the husband and wife attain the ultimate fulfillment.

First, the impurity in lust needs to be removed so that a deep friendship can be added at the being level. Only then can alchemy happen. When you feel deeply connected to a person, there will be no need for physical proximity to that person. You will feel happy and satisfied with just the feeling of connection with him or her. This connection will not suffer with separation or anything else.

For the final transformation of lust into love, the relationship needs to go through the process of patience and perseverance. You need to be patient for the other person to accept the transformation you are going through. Give the other time to understand that this is not just a superficial, temporary change. Then he or she will automatically be transformed as well.

Here Kṛṣṇa refers to lust and anger, both born out of passion. When the other person rejects your lust, it turns into anger against that person. Anger is again a tremendous energy that we misuse because we do not understand and respect it.

Greed, anger and lust are all rajasic qualities that arise from passion and aggression. They arise from the blocked *mūlādhāra cakra*, the root center. These are instinctive emotions that we inherit from our animal ancestors. The *mūlādhāra cakra* is common to animals and humans.

Indulging in these base emotions keeps a human being in bondage to his sensual and instinctive nature. This is the reason Kṛṣṇa classifies these as the root causes of sin. A human being endowed with consciousness rises above these instincts. The meaning of a human life is the realization of one's superconscious nature. Anything that stands in the way of Self-realization is a sin.

Control The Senses

3.38 *As fire is covered by smoke, as a mirror is covered by dust, or as the embryo is covered by the placenta, So also, the living being is covered by lust.*

3.39 *The knowledge of the knower is veiled by this eternal enemy in the form of lust, which is never satisfied and burns like fire, O son of* Kuntī.

3.40 *The senses, the mind and the intelligence are the locations of this lust, which confuses the embodied being and veils the knowledge.*

3.41 *Therefore, O Chief amongst the descendants of* Bhārata, *in the very beginning, control the senses and curb the symbol of sin, which is certainly the destroyer of knowledge and consciousness.*

3.42 *It is said that the senses are superior to the body. The mind is superior to the senses.*
The intelligence is still higher than the mind and the consciousness is even higher than intelligence.

3.43 *Knowing the Self to be superior to mind and intelligence, by steadying the mind with intelligence,*
Conquer the insatiable enemy in the form of lust, O mighty-armed one.

Just as the smoke veils the fire, just as the dust on the mirror masks your reflection, and just as you cannot see the embryo when it is covered by the placenta in the womb, we are not able to see our true nature of bliss because we are caught in base emotions like lust.

In the hymn *Bhaja Govindaṁ*, Ādi Śaṅkarācārya, the enlightened sage from India says beautifully, 'Do not be excited by looking at the breasts and navel of women. Do not be overcome with lust. Think to yourself again and again that these are of flesh and will perish with time.'

Lust is linked intimately to the survival of the species. Without lust, there can be no mutual attraction between genders, no reproduction, and no continuity of the human race. This basic survival instinct is lodged in our *mūlādhāra cakra*. Eighty percent of our spiritual energy is locked in this energy center. When this *cakra* is blocked we behave out of instinct, like animals. In the case of animals, their highest energy center is the *mūlādhāra cakra*. In humans, this *cakra* is the starting energy point. When this *cakra* is energized and unlocked, we learn to live in intelligence as we are truly meant to live.

Once a person reaches physical or sexual maturity at adolescence, it is very difficult to control the effects of lust arising out of the *mūlādhāra*. One needs to be spiritually awakened before sexual maturity so that the energy can flow upwards towards the *sahasrāra* or the crown *cakra*.

The *mūlādhāra cakra* is the seat of all fantasies, primary amongst them being sexual fantasies. These fantasies are the ones that Kṛṣṇa says are like the dust on the mirror, completely clouding our judgment. We live based on these fantasies and live towards fulfilling these fantasies, rather than accepting life as it is.

When the Hindu myths say that Menakā, the celestial nymph, came down to disturb the penance of the great sage Viśvāmitra, the metaphoric significance of that is that Viśvāmitra's *mūlādhāra* was still blocked, giving rise to sexual fantasies.

Awareness in the present moment is the key to unlocking the *mūlādhāra* and dissolving lust. Only the awareness of the present moment brings you in touch with reality and dissolves your fantasies.

In the Śiva sūtra, Śiva tells His consort Devī, 'In a marriage, four people coexist.'

Devī is shocked. She asks, 'There is just husband and wife. Why four?'

Śiva explains, 'There is the wife, and the husband's fantasy of the wife. There is the husband, and the wife's fantasy of the husband.'

As long as there are four in a marital bed, it will be an orgy, not a love affair. When you bring yourself into the present moment, fantasies of the past disappear. Fears and speculations about the future vanish. You are exposed to the reality of the present. Only in the present moment can lust be transformed into love.

Kṛṣṇa closes His dialogue with Arjuna in this chapter with these words, 'Be aware that you have a higher intelligence. Use that intelligence to control your senses and curb your lust, which is your most dangerous enemy on the path to awareness.'

Please note that Kṛṣṇa does not say, 'Arjuna, come here, I shall help you. I shall help dissolve the lust in your body and mind. You can then be at peace.' To practise what Kṛṣṇa teaches, the senses have to be in control. They cannot be suppressed. Anything suppressed waits for an opportunity to explode. The mind and senses cannot be suppressed. However, they can be transformed. When we realize that life has no purpose, that the meaning of life is to enjoy the path, the journey, we learn to give up attachment to end results. We drop expectations. We move into the present moment. We become aware.

This is the whole essence of *karma yoga*. Drop your attachment to the goal and live a happy life. Live life blissfully. You will achieve the Supreme.

So let us pray to the ultimate Divine, *Parabrahma* Kṛṣṇa, to help us understand and imbibe His message. May He help us experience the eternal consciousness, the eternal bliss, *nityānanda*!

Thus ends the third chapter named **Karma Yogaḥ** *of the* **Upaniṣad** *of* **Bhagavad Gītā**, *the scripture of yoga dealing with the science of the Absolute in the form of the dialogue between* **Śrī Kṛṣṇa** *and Arjuna.*

BHAGAVADGĪTĀ

Path Of Knowledge

JÑĀNAKARMASANYĀSA YOGAḤ

CHAPTER 4

Logic can never lead you to Self-realization.
Dissolution of logic will.

Path Of Knowledge

The human psyche longs for continuance. Continuation and perpetuation of one's identity is of utmost importance to us. We trace our lineage back as far as we can go in memory and records and look for something noteworthy there. We ensure that our heirs are well taken care of, especially the weak ones in the family. There is a general anxiety on the account of our own lineage.

People ask me, 'When was this universe created? How and why?' I tell them that the next time God calls for a conference, if I am invited, I shall ask this question and find out the answer! As far back as I can see this universe has existed. As far into the future as I can see this universe continues to exist. It has been there forever and will be there forever. No beginning, no end.

The form and identity that we are familiar with is perishable. It is matter, subject to creation, destruction and re-creation. But the universe is formless energy. It transforms into matter and again back to energy. That energy is imperishable. This energy, the energy of the universe, is the same energy that is within us. It is indestructible. It cannot be destroyed by a weapon, burnt by fire, dried by the wind, or wet by water. Whatever we see as destruction to the body-mind system is actually the conversion of matter back into energy.

All religions may not accept this principle of the energy in man and the universe as eternal. Views of religions change as new knowledge arises. Scientists now agree that matter and energy are inter-convertible in time and space. Advances in Quantum Physics have shown that sub-atomic particles can appear in different forms and shapes depending on when they are viewed, how they are viewed, and who views them. For example, people think that materialization of objects is magic or trickery. No! It is just simple science. It is converting matter into energy, moving the energy and converting it back to matter. This can be demonstrated with the help of Kirlian photography.

I showed the *ashramites* (those who live in the ashram) how this can be done. I made them count the number of *rudrākṣa* necklaces that they had in a cupboard. I produced one from the air as if miraculously and showed it to them. Then I sent them back to count the number of necklaces in the cupboard. They found there was one less in the cupboard!

Understand, no matter can be produced from nowhere. It can only be produced out of energy. Fortunately this energy source is infinite in the universe. This universe is constantly growing. There is not even a known theoretical limit to its size.

The very first verse of the first Hindu scripture, *Īśā Vāsya Upaniṣad,* says that 'out of energy arises all matter.' Upon reading this verse Albert Einstein the famous physicist said, 'It is only now that I could establish that energy arises from matter. Even thousands of years ago these sages knew that matter arises from energy. Science has yet to establish this. The last frontier of science is the threshold of spirituality.' It is important to understand that the constant factor in us, as well as in the universe, is this energy that is eternal. Once we understand that there is no separation between the universe and us, all our confusion will be at rest. There will no longer be any fear of death or the greed to acquire and hoard wealth. After all, the energy that is who we are is forever. Once we understand and accept this, we are in eternal bliss, *nithyānandam*!

4.1 *The Lord said:*
'I taught the sun god, Vivasvān, the imperishable science of yoga and Vivasvān taught Manu, the father of mankind and Manu in turn taught Ikṣvāku.'

4.2 *The supreme science was thus received through the chain of master-disciple succession and the saintly kings understood it in that way.*
In the course of time, the succession was broken and therefore the science as it was appears to have been lost.

4.3 *That ancient science of enlightenment, or entering into eternal bliss, is today taught by Me to you because you are My devotee as well as My friend.*
You will certainly understand the supreme mystery of this science.

You need to understand that Kṛṣṇa is just thirty-two years old when He makes this statement! He is just thirty-two years old. Physically His body is only thirty-two years old, but He says, 'I gave this knowledge to Sūrya, the sun god.' Of course, this is very difficult to understand! With ordinary logic you cannot make any meaning out of this statement. But Kṛṣṇa goes on to say other things. In the next statement He says: The science as it was, appears to have been lost.

These two verses should be understood clearly. The first thing is that the truth is not new. It is eternal and beyond time. Only things that are described based on time can be said to be new or old. Anything new will become old one day. Anything old was new at one time. Eternal means it is there from time immemorial.

Here, this science of enlightenment is eternal or *nitya.* It is neither new nor old. The first thing that needs to be understood is the first glimpse. If you allow my words to penetrate you, then straightaway they can give you the first glimpse of enlightenment. They can lead you to the first step of ultimate liberation. Understanding the purposelessness of life will wash away all its pressures and burdens from your being, whether they are physical or mental. You are liberated in that same moment.

Kṛṣṇa doesn't give you any technique that works over lengthy periods of time. There are other techniques that work over long periods of time.

You will have to practice them forever. Your son or your daughter may get the result!

Kṛṣṇa says, 'No!' He says, 'Now, here or nowhere!' All His techniques straightaway give you the experience. If you can allow that one idea of purposelessness into your conscience, that very moment the breeze of enlightenment enters your heart. The healing of your being starts. Healing of *bhāva roga,* emotional diseases, and healing of *samsāra roga,* the disease of birth and death, start.

Five thousand years ago Kṛṣṇa says, 'I gave this science to Sūrya, the sun god and the sun god instructed Manu. The sun god is Vivasvān. Vivasvān instructed Manu, the father of mankind. Manu passed this wisdom on to Ikṣvāku. Here, Kṛṣṇa gives the succession, the lineage through disciples. He gives the lineage, the master-disciple lineage. 'In the course of time, the science of yoga was lost,' He says.

You should understand why this science was lost. When a disciple who listens is not sincere or is not ready, naturally the technique becomes a ritual. Understand that there is only one difference between technique and ritual. When done sincerely, even an ordinary ritual becomes a great meditation technique. When done without any sincerity or understanding, then even a meditation technique becomes a ritual. The only difference between a meditation technique and a ritual is sincerity.

'In the course of time, the science was lost.' He has used a beautiful phrase, 'The supreme science was taught, and the supreme science was delivered.' You don't lose that supreme science in just one generation. In the course of time, even a single unenlightened disciple is enough to destroy the whole science.

The problem is, when your master creates a big movement and you succeed him without having the necessary qualification. People who ascend the throne only because they are the successor are the most dangerous people. They have everything except enlightenment. One who creates a movement, creates it only out of energy and enlightenment. But for someone who succeeds the founder, the whole movement is a gift. The whole setup was created by somebody else and the successor just represents him. The successors are like librarians, not masters. Librarians are good but they can only preserve books, nothing more than that.

A story from Zen Buddhism:

A disciple of a great master talks about Zen to his followers. An enlightened master comes to him and says, 'You yourself have not become enlightened. What right do you have to teach others?'

Out of ego he says, 'Don't you know? I am the disciple of the great master.'

The Zen master laughs and says, 'If you wash the cup in which you had tea, will that water have the same taste as tea?'

So, if a person is just a successor it is dangerous. He carries just the book and not the knowledge. That is why Zen masters destroy their books when they leave the body. If you have Zen in your life, if you have achieved enlightenment, then you can teach. Otherwise keep quiet. In the course of time people who were not enlightened, entered this field and corrupted it. So the science was lost. That is why, time and again, our *Upaniṣad*s insist upon going to a living master.

All our books are only manuals. *Vedas* are the only books that are courageous enough to declare that they cannot give you enlightenment. If you want the ultimate experience, you have to go to a living master. What do all medical books say in the end? Consult your family doctor! You can't take medicines by merely reading a medical book. You can't take medicines from someone who is not a doctor. In India, compounders, the doctors' assistants, are the ones who prepare the medicines. In the course of time they would learn that for a headache you should take the yellow tablet, the green tablet for back pain, and so on. They would know the color of the tablet for a particular disease. Taking medicines from a compounder and learning from unenlightened masters are one and the same.

A compounder may, at the most harm, your physical body. But an unenlightened master can destroy you life after life. This is because the whole purpose is lost if you have missed even a single crucial point.

Spirituality – the ultimate luxury!

Here Kṛṣṇa says,

Evaṁ paraṁparā prāptam imaṁ rājarṣayo viduḥ I
sa kāleneha mahatā yogo naṣṭaḥ parantapa II 4.2

One important thing, He says, '*rājarṣayo viduhu*', meaning, this science was given to kingly saints.

If you attended yesterday's lecture, you would know that the science He taught was Quantum Spirituality, which gives you both material and spiritual wealth. Had it been only for ordinary saints, he would have emphasized only on the inner world. Had it been only for the kings, he would have emphasized on the outer world. But here He says, 'Kingly saints'. The science is delivered to enlightened masters who are kings. Only they can preserve the science as it is. Be very clear, only an enlightened person who is a king, or a king who is enlightened can know the totality of spirituality.

People again and again ask me, 'What should we do for the poor?' I say, 'Give food and medicines for the poor. Serve them.' Only a rich man who has enjoyed material wealth can understand the meaning and relevance of spirituality. Poor men who have not seen the outer world wealth can only beg in front of God. They cannot understand the ultimate spirituality. Only someone who has enjoyed the outer world thoroughly realizes its emptiness. Only he can enter into the inner world. Only a king can be utterly frustrated. Only he can enter into enlightenment because he knows there is nothing in the outer space that can fulfill him. He has seen all possible comforts and pleasures.

There is a huge difference between a religious and a spiritual person. When you know God has got the *śakti* (power) to give whatever you want, religion starts. When you understand he also has the *buddhi* (intelligence) as to when to give you what you want, then you enter into spirituality! We all believe that God has the power to give us what we want, but we don't trust that he also has the intelligence to give it at the right time! That is why we beg and beg! Only a person who trusts that God has both the power and intelligence can enter into spirituality.

Here, Kṛṣṇa uses the words 'Kingly saint.' Only a person who has lived fully in the inner space and the outer space can experience the truth of the totality. When a person who is not sincere enough to realize this truth enters into the system he corrupts it. So, Kṛṣṇa says, 'In the course of time, the science was lost.'

In the next verse, Kṛṣṇa says:

Sa evā 'yaṁ mayā te'dya yogaḥ proktaḥ purātanaḥ |

bhakto 'si me sakhā ceti rahasyaṁ hy etad uttamam || 4.3

He says, 'I am telling you about this very ancient science of the ultimate enlightenment or entering into eternal bliss, and being my devotee and my friend, you will understand the supreme mystery of this science.'

Understand, one cannot tell this ultimate truth to a person who is not ready. I repeat, this truth cannot be delivered to a person who is not ready.

Again and again, people ask me during many of my meditation programs, '*Swamiji*, please talk about your enlightenment.' I never speak about my spiritual experiences to people unless I know them well. I wait. If intimate experiences are shared when you are not ready, you always doubt and spoil things for yourself. If you have courage, you will straightaway question the experience. If you don't have that much courage, you will just think, 'Alright, this is one more story! I have heard one thousand stories. Leave it.'

Either one of the two things will happen. The spiritual experiences cannot be shared just for nothing. If it is shared, it should be a source of inspiration for you. It should transform your life. Then it is worth sharing.

By sharing the spiritual experience, if it gives you the courage to take the same jump, if you also feel, 'I should also experience the same joy and bliss. I should not postpone it.' If it becomes a source of inspiration for you, then it is worth sharing. Otherwise it is of no use.

There was a great master in South India. He wrote a set of poems on Śiva. He did not even write, he just sang the verses for Śiva. Close disciples who lived around him requested him to put it in writing, so that it could be useful to society. He said, 'No, they are my intimate love letters to my Lord. How can I release this to the public? It is my intimate expression, my personal relationship. How can I publish it?'

If, for example, you see somebody for the first time and he straightaway starts asking you personal questions, won't you feel it's rude? Indians are the only people who do that. They don't bother to introduce themselves or get acquainted. Straightaway, they will ask personal questions. It takes a little intelligence to understand this social etiquette. You need to understand that you can't share your personal experiences right away with anybody and everybody.

In the same way, the master says, 'When somebody asks you about your personal life, you can open up only when you are intimate with him.' Only then conversation happens. If both are prejudiced, a conversation can never happen.

I always tell people in a marriage, in the first year, the man speaks and the woman listens. In the second year, the woman speaks and the man listens. The third year onwards, both speak and the neighbors listen! The conversation never happens! Only arguments happen. As long as the other person is in a mood for arguments, the *satya* (truth) cannot be expressed.

The master says, 'It is my intimate relationship with God. How can I share that with the public? I cannot.'

Then one disciple, who considers himself intelligent asks, 'Why? When you can share it with us, why can you not share it with the world?'

Then, the master says, 'By becoming a disciple you have become a part of me. Only a person who has become a part of me can share these poems. Physically you may be another body, but mentally you are in tune with me, completely ready to receive me. You have become like a womb, ready to receive the divine energy. This is the reason I share my experience with you.' Unless you enter into a deep receptive mood, you cannot receive the ultimate truth. It is beyond logic. Initially when you start to teach the truth, it starts with logic. But after some time, you have to leave logic behind. Otherwise, you can't reach the Divine. You can't talk to God through logic. You cannot relate with him in prose. Only in poetry you can relate with God. That is why, all over the world, whether it is Eastern or Western culture, Hinduism or Buddhism or Christianity, whenever it comes to prayer, it is only through songs and poems.

If you want the divine relationship to happen, you need love. Here, only one who has become a part of the master can receive the master's experiences. That is the reason the master says, 'I share my songs with you, because you have become me. I cannot share this with the public.'

There was another great saint called Manickavasagar in Tamil Nadu, South India. Throughout his life he sang about Śiva, but he never wrote or recorded his poems. Once, Śiva himself came down as an old man and said, 'O Manickavasagar, I have heard that you sing beautiful songs about Śiva. Why don't you recite them for me? I am your disciple.' Manickavasaga was in an ecstatic state. So in that ecstasy, he started singing everything. Śiva himself recorded the songs!

After recording, Śiva signed the palm-leaf document, 'Recited by Manickavasagar, written by Ambaravanan', Śiva Himself! He placed the palm leaves at the entrance of the temple and disappeared. The next day morning the priests saw the leaves. Suddenly, they realized the signature said, 'Manickavasagar recited and I myself recorded this.' Until the end, till his death, he never recorded his songs. Then all the disciples went and asked him, 'Oh master, please give us the meaning of all these songs.' He walked straight into the temple, pointed to the Lord and said, 'He is the meaning.' He walked and disappeared into the deity.

Unless you become a part of the master, it is very difficult to understand his message. That is why Kṛṣṇa says, 'Arjuna, this supreme science, the technique of entering into eternal bliss is today told by me to you, because you are my devotee as well as my friend and can therefore understand the transcendental mystery of this science.'

When you speak the ultimate truth to someone who is not ready, he not only misunderstands, but also creates trouble for others. But with the right person, even a lie told by him will be good for society. To whom it is delivered is important, rather than whether it is the truth or a lie. With the wrong person, even a great truth like *advaita* (non-duality), 'I am God', may make him think he is God and he will start doing all nonsensical things. With the wrong person, even great truths will become harmful. A wrong person can never understand the truth told by Kṛṣṇa. For example, Kṛṣṇa says, 'I am God. Surrender unto me.' If the person is not devoted, if he has not understood Kṛṣṇa, he will think, 'What an egoistic person! How dare he tell me to surrender to him!' Naturally, instead of understanding Kṛṣṇa he will create more trouble for Kṛṣṇa.

Beyond your logic lies devotion

Here, the qualification to receive the truth is devotion. If you have heard all the things I have said in the other three chapters of the Gita, it is expressed logically. Until this point, I am able to bring both logic and spirituality together. Now, the time has come when I have to express the truth as pure truth. Be very clear, great things can never be expressed by logic, because logic is not sharp enough!

Somebody asked me, '*Swamiji*, why don't you prove God logically?' I told him, 'If I can prove God logically, then logic would become God!' Logic will become greater than God. God is great because He cannot be proved by logic. He is beyond your logic.

Here, Kṛṣṇa is going to speak about something that is beyond logic. This is where you leave your logic behind and become completely open. Sit in a totally passive mood, open up your being and be ready to receive. One thing, with logic either you will understand everything or you will not understand anything. There is no other danger. But with deeper teachings, you either understand or misunderstand. The teachings which Kṛṣṇa is going to deliver now are much deeper, much more subtle than the teachings which were delivered in the previous chapters. That is why He says, 'Now I am telling you these secrets just because you are my devotee and friend, just because you are near and dear to me. You are my own.' That is the reason He uses the word *bhaktosi*. He says, 'You are my devotee, and you are my friend.' *Sakha* means friend.

Now Kṛṣṇa enters into the deeper level truths, where you need to come down from your head to your heart, where you need to sit with your whole being and listen to the truths. Here, He gives a warning, *rahasyaṁ hyetaduttamaṁ*. 'I am giving you these secrets, the mysterious science of realizing the ultimate, my dear friend and devotee, Arjuna.'

So, now let us enter into the science that is taught by Kṛṣṇa. Let us begin with a small prayer to Kṛṣṇa:

vasudeva sutaṁ devaṁ kamsa cāṇūra mardanaṁ I

devakī paramānandaṁ kṛṣṇam vande jagad guruṁ II

Understand, *Vedānta* always emphasizes on three things: *śravaṇa*, *manana* and *nididhyāsana*. *Śravaṇa* means listening. *Manana* means contemplating on it. *Nididhyāsana* means expressing or experiencing it in your life. Here, these truths do not need these three steps. Just listening is enough to experience them. *Śravaṇa* is enough; proper *śravaṇa* becomes *nididhyāsana*. All you need to do is to sit with a completely open being, with complete openness, with a completely relaxed feeling.

These words are uttered for your sake, not for the sake of the master. So we will just take a few minutes to meditate on Śrī Kṛṣṇa, the great enlightened master. Let us pray to Him to allow His words to penetrate our being and reside in our consciousness. Let Him lead us to eternal bliss.

Just take a few minutes, close your eyes and intensely pray to Him to lead us to the experience. Give us the understanding. Let Him raise our inner space by His presence. Let Him enlighten our consciousness.

I Am Reborn, Age After Age!

4.4 *Arjuna said:*
'O Kṛṣṇa, you are younger to the sun god Vivasvān by birth.
How am I to understand that in the beginning You instructed this science to him?'

4.5 *The Lord said:*
Very many births both you and I have passed.
I can remember all of them, but you cannot, O Parantapa!

4.6 *Although I am unborn, imperishable and the lord of all living entities,*
By ruling My nature I reappear by My own māyā.

4.7 *When positive consciousness declines, when collective negativity rises,*
Again and again, at these times, I am reborn.

4.8 *To nurture the pious and to annihilate the wicked,*
To re-establish righteousness I am reborn, age after age.

Kṛṣṇa starts His message here. He delivers it as a response to Arjuna's question when he asks, 'The sun god is elder to you by birth; he is so much your senior. How am I to understand that in the beginning you delivered this science to him?'

Arjuna and Kṛṣṇa are almost equal in age. Suddenly, Kṛṣṇa says that thousands of years ago He gave this science to the sun god! This is very difficult to understand. Moreover, Arjuna lived with Kṛṣṇa for a long time. He has seen the human side of Kṛṣṇa, all of Kṛṣṇa's *līlā* (plays) and moods. So now, it is very difficult for Arjuna to believe Kṛṣṇa's words.

This is exactly the same trouble that all disciples who live around enlightened masters face. They find it very difficult to understand the Divine descending and walking on the planet earth in human form.

Arjuna struggles to understand. How can the Divine descend? How can Kṛṣṇa declare, 'Thousands of years ago, I gave this science to Sūrya?' It is very difficult to understand. If I suddenly make a statement, 'A hundred years ago, I taught all these things to the masters who were there.' It is very difficult to believe. And naturally questions will arise. Here the same thing happens. Arjuna thinks, 'How can he say this? How can I understand?' But of course, he has become a little polite. So he says, 'How can I understand?' instead of, 'How can you say this?' Here Arjuna is ready to believe, but wants some explanation.

Kṛṣṇa declares His Divinity

Whenever enlightened masters descended on planet earth, they faced this trouble. When Rāmakṛṣṇa declared that one who came as Rāma and the one who came as Kṛṣṇa, the same person has now come down in the form of Rāmakṛṣṇa, he was called mad! People did not respect him. But there were a few qualified people who received his words and transformed their lives. They established the truth of his statement.

See, all movements can be started in two ways. One is the political movement with huge numbers of followers. For the person who leads, the more the number of people, the more powerful he feels and makes all kinds of claims. These movements, over a period of time, slowly dwindle in quality and quantity. Once the founder dies, the movement dies. The second type of movement is the spiritual mission. When the masters declare the truth, the quantity may not be there, but the quality is present. Only a few selected individuals listen to those truths.

When Rāmakṛṣṇa made his declaration, hardly a few were ready to trust him. Those few transformed their lives. It started as a slow, small thing, but exploded into an international mission. When it started, only sixteen disciples were there. Today, millions of people worship him as God. These spiritual missions start in a very small way, but expand and explode. Political movements start in a very big way, but slowly die down. For a political speech you need quantity. The more the number of people present, the stronger the speech. But for a spiritual discourse, you need quality. The more intense the people, the more deeper the truths are revealed!

For a political person, the inspiration is in numbers. In how many newspapers has it been covered? It matters to him how many newspaper cuttings he can collect. But for a spiritual person what matters is the number of ego-cuttings he does to liberate people. For a political person it is the paper cutting, for a spiritual person it is the ego-cutting.

I always tell people, my best discourses are given always to small, close devotees. Because when you speak the truth to an intimate group, it will be straight and shake the whole being. It will transform your whole life. That is why Rāmakṛṣṇa, whenever he wanted to speak deep truths, would close the doors and call his monastic disciples and he would speak only to them. He would not speak to the public.

This very Gita was delivered to only one person. But today billions read and practice it. For all the Hindus, this is the basic book. Only one person heard Kṛṣṇa. Today the whole world uses it. So, to express the truth, the quality of the person who hears is important, not the quantity of persons.

Now Kṛṣṇa starts to answer this question. He says, 'O Arjuna, many, many births both you and I have passed. I can remember all of them, but you can't.' Kṛṣṇa first says, 'We have both passed through many births that I remember, and you do not.' Then He says, 'Although I am unborn, imperishable, and the lord of all living entities, I reappear by my original *māyā,* by controlling my nature.'

ajo 'pi sann avyayātmā bhūtānām īśvaro 'pi san |

prakṛtiṁ svām adhiṣṭhāya saṁbhavāmyātmamāyayā || 4.6

I think this is the first time He declares his divinity! All this while, Kṛṣṇa was only playing the role of *ācārya* (teacher), giving Arjuna the intellectual knowledge. For the first time, He declares the truth about His nature. He reveals His divinity. This is the point where Kṛṣṇa starts to speak the ultimate truth as it is. Kṛṣṇa opens up, saying, 'Although I am unborn and my transcendental body never deteriorates and although I am the Lord of all living entities, I still appear in every millennium in my original transcendental form.'

Three things we need to understand here. First, He says, 'I am unborn. I never take birth. I am the ultimate *Parabrahma* (cosmic or divine energy).' I don't think any one else has declared so clearly. Even Jesus said, 'I am the Son of God.' Here, Kṛṣṇa straightaway declares, 'I am God.' Of course, it does not mean Jesus is not God. At one point, maybe to some close disciple he declares, 'The Father and the Son are one and the same.' When the disciple is mature, the master is understood.

Here, Kṛṣṇa declares, 'I am unborn, *ajopi*, eternal consciousness, and my transcendental body never deteriorates. You can always relate with me. I am unborn and I never die.' Understand, that which never takes birth can never die; that which takes birth, only such can die.

Somebody asked me, '*Swamiji*, can dead masters teach us? Can we relate with the masters who have left the body, like Paramahamsa Yogānanda, Mahavatar Babaji, etc.?' Someone asked me, 'If I pray to them, can they show me the truth?' I told him, 'Dead masters are not dead as you think. When they were alive, their presence had a body. When they are dead, their presence has no body. Having or not having a body is in no way going to affect their presence. They are eternally available to you. All you need to do is just turn towards them. They are always available to the whole of humanity.'

It is very difficult to understand masters, because whether they have the body or not, their presence is unchanged. If you reach out with intensity, even if they don't have the body, you will be able to relate with them. You will be able to talk to them. When you don't have intensity, you will miss even a living master.

Understand, Kṛṣṇa says, 'I am the Lord of all the entities. But I still appear in every millennium in my original transcendental form, using my own *māyā* (Illusion). Because of my *māyā,* I assume the body and come down. I assume the body and incarnate myself.'

Kṛṣṇa means that He happens on the planet earth again and again in many forms to guide the people. Ordinary human beings are in the clutches of *māyā* due to which they take birth. But Kṛṣṇa has *māyā* itself under His control and takes birth due to His own wish! But we repeatedly miss Him. We are all conquerors of Buddha, Kṛṣṇa, and Rāmakṛṣṇa. That is why we are here on this planet earth! But again and again, He has to come down to lift us and guide us.

Kṛṣṇa's promise to come again and again

The next two verses, if they are understood, then all the spiritual scriptures can be realized. Here He declares: whenever there is a decline in individual consciousness, whenever the collective unconsciousness increases, *Dharma samsthāpanārthāya,* to establish the righteousness of the eternal consciousness, *sambhavāmi yuge yuge,* I myself appear, millennium after millennium. Only a master like Kṛṣṇa can declare the truth so clearly. He keeps the whole thing open for the future. He keeps the possibility of enlightenment open for the future.

People often ask me, '*Swamiji,* are there more enlightened masters on planet earth?' I tell them, 'Surely. There are thousands of enlightened masters available. Don't think I am the only one.'

Only a courageous man can declare the truth as it is. If you are in business, you cannot stand other similar shops in your city. You would not even give out the address of similar businesses. Only if you are honest, can you declare that other things are available.

People often ask me this question, '*Swamiji,* if I take initiation from you, can I go to another master?' I tell them: 'Not only can you go, I also encourage that you go. Pluck flowers from all the beautiful gardens and make a beautiful bouquet for yourself!' The human ego is such that it needs to be beaten by more than one person to die! So go wherever it is possible and learn the best things.

Only a courageous person like Kṛṣṇa can declare the truth, *saṁbhavāmi yuge yuge,* which means that He keeps the possibility of enlightenment open for planet earth. This verse is a promise to entire humanity. In science, the principle of entropy states that the energy level of every system, including the universe, degrades with time. So it is with consciousness. Over time individuals start losing their positive consciousness, and collective negativity builds up.

One must understand that the consciousness is always individual. When one is conscious, one accepts all of humanity in the same manner as oneself; yet, each individual needs to be aware of his own consciousness. On the other hand, negativity or unconsciousness can be collective. A whole nation can become collectively unconscious as Germany did under Hitler.

In history, over many thousands of years, each time such collective unconsciousness has built up there has been deliverance. There is a cycle of positivity and negativity, up and down, over time. Righteousness is restored eventually. This is Kṛṣṇa's promise.

To Know Me Is To Be Liberated

4.9 One who knows or experiences My divine appearance and activities does not take birth again in this material world after leaving the body
But attains Me, O Arjuna.

4.10 Being freed from attachment, fear and anger, being filled with Me and by taking refuge in Me,
Many beings in the past have become sanctified by the knowledge of Me and have realized Me.

4.11 I reward everyone, I show Myself to all people, according to the manner in which they surrender unto Me,
In the manner that they are devoted to Me, O Pārtha!

4.12 Men in this world desire success through activities and therefore they worship the gods.
Men get instant results from active work in this world.

This is a very strange statement. He says, 'One who understands the nature of My appearance and activities will be liberated from this birth and death cycle.'

How can it be? Just now He said he is birthless and deathless. *Ajopi.* Now He says, 'If you understand the truth of the transcendental nature of My appearance and activities, once you leave the body, you will not take birth and death like ordinary humans do. You will also achieve the same transcendental nature.'

We will start with an incident from Bhagavān Ramaṇa maharṣi's life, an enlightened saint from India. Everyday his devotees used to sing some songs in his presence. There is a song called, '*Ramana Satguru*', which means

'Praising Ramaṇa maharṣi, an enlightened master.' When the song was sung, Ramaṇa himself used to enjoy and sing along with the devotees! Somebody asked him, 'What is this? You are an enlightened person, you yourself are singing your own name. What do you mean by this?' Bhagavān says, 'Fool! Why are you reducing Ramaṇa to this six-foot body? Why are you reducing me to this six feet body?' This is a deep, very subtle thing. He says, 'Just as you see this body from a distance, in the same way, I too see this body. I don't associate myself with this name and form. That is the reason why, just like you, I too enjoy singing the name.'

An egoistic person, at least in public, will not show that he enjoys praise, because if he does people will see that he is egoistic. He will never be open. Here, Ramaṇa maharṣi is totally open. He says, 'Just like you I too enjoy name and form, because I don't feel this is me. The name is just getting repeated, that's all.'

> Another incident: One of Ramaṇa's disciples, Muruganar wrote '*Ramana Puranam*'. It is the *stotra* (verses in praise) of Ramaṇa maharṣi. He wrote a few lines and somehow he was not able to write further. So he just brought the paper and put it at the feet of the master and said, 'Bhagavān, I am not able to write.' Ramaṇa maharṣi says, 'Alright, you go, let us look into it tomorrow.' The next day when the disciple came back, he saw that the poem was completed.
>
> Ramaṇa maharṣi himself wrote and completed it! The disciple was surprised. Bhagavān himself had written his own praises! Later, when the disciple published it, Bhagavān saw that he had put a small footnote: 'From this line onwards it was written by Bhagavān himself', just so that the devotees would be aware that those particular verses were Bhagavān's own words.
>
> The first copy of the book was taken to Ramaṇa maharṣi. He saw the book and the footnote: 'From this line onwards it was written by Bhagavān himself.' He turned to the disciple and asked, 'Oh! Were the other lines written by you then?' Bhagavān goes on to tell him, 'When you wrote all those verses, it was I who wrote through you.

As such, you cannot think about me. You cannot write about me. What do you know about me? Unless I express myself through you, you cannot know anything about me.' Only a man who has disappeared into the divine consciousness can write his poem.

In the Bhāgavatam, Kṛṣṇa himself sings, 'I am the Lord,' just like how He now says, *bhutānām ishvaropi*, I am the Lord of all living beings!

A mere boy from Brindāvan, a cowherd boy from Brindāvan says this! You should not look at Kṛṣṇa from today's perspective. Now, because of time, we have accepted Kṛṣṇa as God. But this was said when he was alive, when people did not realize him as God. When Rāma lived, only the *saptarṣi*s (the energy of seven sages that controls the world) knew that He was an incarnation. Similarly, when Kṛṣṇa was alive, very few people recognized who He was. At least Rāma lived a controlled life; he is easy for people to accept. But Kṛṣṇa lived such an ecstatic and spontaneous life, it is very difficult to realize who He is!

For a so-called religious person, it is very difficult to realize Kṛṣṇa. But He says, *bhutānām ishvaropi,* I am the Lord of all living entities. Somebody asks Ramana, 'Why are you expressing your own glory?' Bhagavān says, 'If I don't speak about myself, you can never understand me. Unless I reveal myself, you can never realize me. Just out of my compassion, I express the truth, I express myself.'

It is like this: You are caught in a traffic jam on the road. You ring up your friend who is traveling ahead of you on the same road and ask him, 'How is it there? Is there a traffic jam? Can I come by the same road or should I take some other road?' Will he not have the simple courtesy to guide you? He will surely have that basic courtesy to guide you.

With the same courtesy, Kṛṣṇa is revealing His truth to all of us. Here, when He says, 'I am God, I am the ultimate,' He says there is a possibility, 'When I can achieve, why not you?' He shows the possibility. He gives us the courage and encourages us. Here He says, 'When I can achieve, why not you?' It is like a seed afraid of rupturing to become a tree. The seed feels, 'What if I break and the tree doesn't happen? I will die.' But the tree tells the seed, 'Unless you break, I cannot happen.' The seed says, 'No, no, no, let the tree happen, then I will open.' But the tree says, 'No, no, first you have to open, only then I can happen.' The problem between the tree and the seed continues endlessly.

It is necessary for somebody to give a little courage to the seed. A tree that was a seed once and now has become a tree can give that courage, 'Be courageous. Open. Just like me you will also become a tree.' In the same manner, Kṛṣṇa gives courage to us, 'You can also become God, like me. You can also experience the truth like me.'

When He says, 'I am the Ultimate,' He expresses the possibility. He reminds us of our potentiality and inspires us to experience the same bliss. He shows us the way of truth, which we need to experience. When Kṛṣṇa reveals this truth, understand, Kṛṣṇa is not egoistic. He is expressing His true nature out of compassion for His fellow travelers. The senior tree encourages the junior seed to open up and become a tree. It says, 'Don't worry, I have become a tree. You can also become like me.' It is an assurance.

That is why again and again I tell you that when He declares Himself as God, He means, 'You too are God.' He gives you the courage to enter into the same experience. When enlightened masters say 'I', they don't have any meaning behind that 'I'. Only the divinity speaks. For you, 'God' is just a word with no solid meaning. But when you say 'I', you attribute a solid meaning to it, you have a solid identity. But when you say 'God', your understanding is not supported well by any experience. With enlightened people, when they say 'God', it is based on solid experience and when they say 'I', it has no meaning. It is an empty word for them.

There was a great enlightened master, Nisargadatta maharāj who lived in India. Somebody went to him and asked, 'Master, you say enlightened people don't have *karma*. But how can you do all your activities if you don't have *karma*?' He said, 'I am not doing anything!' The disciple asked,

'No, you are speaking to me. How can you speak if you don't have *karma*?' Nisargadatta maharāj said straightaway, 'I am not speaking to you!'

He was speaking, yet he said, 'I am not speaking to you.' It is very difficult to understand! He continues, 'Because you wanted me to speak, the speaking is happening through this body. There is nobody inside.' He was just like a hollow bamboo. When the breeze enters a hollow bamboo, it comes out as music. When you become like a hollow bamboo, whatever words come out of your mouth become *mantra*, sacred syllables. Your form becomes *yantra*, the tool of liberation, and your whole life becomes *tantra*, a technique for liberation. Your words are *śāstras*, scriptures. Your form is the center for *stotras*, devotional prayers, and your life is the *sūtra*, the technique. Your very life is a technique.

Here, when Kṛṣṇa says, 'I', it is just the Divine.

Then the disciple asks Nisargadatta maharāj, 'What do you mean by *I*?' Maharaj says, 'Because there is no other word, I use 'I'. But unlike yours, this 'I' is supported by experience. When you say 'God', it is not supported by experience.' But when you say 'I', it is supported by solid experience. You feel it. For you 'God' has no meaning. It is some imagination created through what you read in books; something that you heard when you were a child. But when enlightened people use 'I', it has no meaning for them.

Here, when Kṛṣṇa says 'I', it is pure emptiness. Just the Divine, the pure energy speaks through Him. That is why He can courageously declare in a battlefield, *bhutānām ishvaropi,* I am the Lord of all beings. Sitting in a home comfortably, where you have all the security and protection, and declaring, 'I am God' is very easy. You don't need to prove anything. But Kṛṣṇa is making this statement in a battlefield, where His life itself is at stake. One arrow is enough to kill him. Yet He boldly declares, 'I am God.' What courage behind His words! It can come only from a deep conscious experience.

Earlier I told you the story of Alexander threatening an enlightened master with his sword, and the master laughing fearlessly at Alexander in response. Only an enlightened man can laugh in front of a sword. Imagine if somebody is holding a gun to you and demanding your wallet, will you be able to laugh? Impossible! But here, this person is able to laugh in front of Alexander's sword. The courage that comes out of truth is the courage that comes out of solid experience. One important thing which the *Vedānta* scriptures give you is the courage to live, to face life and death, to face Existence.

Understand death first

One of the great disciples of Swami Vivekānanda , Sister Nivedita asks him, '*Swamiji*, if I come with you what will you teach me? What will you give me?' Vivekānanda says, 'I will teach you how to face death.' That is the ultimate teaching. Here, Kṛṣṇa gives that ultimate teaching.

In these two verses, He says,

yadā-yadā hi dharmasya glānir bhavati bhārata I
abhyutthānam adharmasya tadā 'tmānaṁ sṛjāmyaham II 4.7

paritrāṇāya sādhūnāṁ vināśāya ca duṣkṛtām I
dharma saṁsthāpanārthāya saṁbhavāmi yuge-yuge II 4.8

Then the next statement is very strange:

janma karma ca me divyam evaṁ yo vetti tattvataḥ I
tyaktvā dehaṁ punarjanma nai 'ti mām eti so 'rjuna II 4.9

It means, if you understand the secret of My birth and death, you will be liberated from birth and death, Arjuna. How? Let us see the secret of the birth and death of Kṛṣṇa, how we all go through the birth and death cycle. Now, just as Kṛṣṇa made the statement, 'I tell you this because you are my devotee and friend', now I have to make the same statement to you again. I am going to speak on something that is beyond logic, pure experience. Before speaking, I take an oath: Whatever I speak is the truth.

Whenever something beyond our logic is uttered, we never receive it completely. If we are courageous, we question and argue. If we don't have that much courage, we don't allow it to enter us. We don't believe it. It is always an argument, sometimes open, and at other times, in the mind. If we can't express it openly, we continuously repeat the same words in the mind. That is why, before entering into the truths, I tell you that what I speak is the truth. If you can, receive it. There is a possibility of transformation, because here I speak the truth that is realized only by experience, which cannot be logically true.

There is a website on NDE, Near Death Experience (http://www.nderf.org). A doctor has researched for 30 years on this Near Death Experience. Let me first describe what Near Death Experience is. People who are declared clinically dead, after four or five hours, sometimes come back to life. The doctor who created this website traveled worldwide meeting people who came back to life after being declared medically dead. He met about several thousand people - from Buddhists to Christians to Hindus to Muslims - and collected their reminiscences about death.

Different religions describe death in different ways. Some say you will reach heaven if you have *puṇya* or merits and hell if you have sinned. Some say there will be a special *puṣpaka vimānam* (mythological aircraft) sent from Śiva's abode and you will be taken to Śiva's place. The Kaṭhopanishad says you will enter a tunnel and see a thumb-sized light, which is your soul when it leaves the body. There are so many explanations as to how death happens, and how your spirit enters into the next body.

This researcher has categorized and researched for years. In the end he makes an important statement, 'I have studied so many Near Death Experiences. I can tell only one thing: Only when people are alive, they are Christians, Hindus, Muslims, etc. When they die, they all undergo the same experience.' All of them undergo the same experience which is described in the Kaṭhopanishad.

Here, Kṛṣṇa beautifully explains that people belong to different religions only when they are alive. When they are dead they all follow the path described in Kaṭhopanishad.

See, when you leave the body, the moment the physical body dies and relaxes, the soul leaves the body. At that time, what you perceived as the highest pleasure in your life surfaces. If you thought eating was the highest pleasure, then naturally while leaving the body you will think, 'I should take a body which will continuously help me to eat.' You go through all the choices and decide to take a pig's body. Whichever occupies the maximum inner space, you decide your next birth based on that. It is clearly the conscious decision of your soul.

Here Kṛṣṇa says, 'I am telling you the mysterious ultimate science, oh my dear devotee and friend.'

Understand, now I made a few statements: 'You take birth based on how you lived in the previous birth. Birth and death are your conscious decisions.' We will now analyze these statements with questions and answers. Only then will we be able to internalize them. I always encourage people to ask questions, because only when you question will you be able to relate with the idea.

Never think that by asking questions you will look like a fool. If you ask a question you may look like a fool. If you don't, you will remain a fool! Better to look like a fool, than be a fool.

We will analyze this whole concept, the secret of birth and death. The moment this truth is understood, you will immediately see that life is a blessing. This life is your decision, please be very clear, including poverty. Everything is your decision. When we take birth, we take birth based on our fear and greed. On one hand, greed pushes us, 'Let me become the son of a rich man.' On the other hand, our own fears say, 'No, no, I can't take on so much responsibility.' Along with money comes a big responsibility of protecting it. That is why goddess Lakṣmī, the goddess of wealth, is handed over to Lord Viṣṇu, the Protector! Most of the time we don't want to take up responsibility; we want only enjoyment. That is where the trouble starts. A person who is ready to take on the responsibility as well as the enjoyment, will never miss. He will never be deprived.

If you understand this secret clearly, this very moment you will feel that life is a blessing and not a curse. But we always blame life. We think we can develop on the existing creation. Surely God is much more intelligent than us! Whether it is your life or Existence, He has done the maximum that can be done. Because we don't understand the mystery behind our decisions, we continuously blame life and the person who gave us this life.

Let me narrate an incident that happened in America. A little boy of about seven years had autism. He was brought to me for healing. His parents requested me, '*Swamiji*, please help him become alright.' I put my hand on his head and started healing. Immediately, the boy started talking to me in Tamil, my mother tongue. That family, neither the boy nor the parents, knew Tamil. The parents were shocked. They didn't know that he was speaking Tamil. He simply started talking fluently in Tamil. Normally he would utter only one or two words. He said, 'Stop healing.' Using Tamil slang, he very crudely told me to stop healing. I was shocked to hear him speak such crude Tamil words.

Then I asked him, 'Why are you asking me to stop healing? Who are you?' Then he said, 'I am the owner of this body. I didn't want to take the responsibility of leading a regular life - attending school, making money, and all. That is why I took this affliction. I took this decision of autism consciously. I just want to enjoy.' Throughout, he spoke in Tamil. I don't know how you will believe this. Because this is personal, I cannot give his name and reference. But this really happened. Then I asked him, 'Alright, but why did you take birth through such nice people? Why did you come down as a son to them?' Then he replied, 'I took birth in their family *because* they are nice people! They will not abandon me. Had it been someone else, they would have abandoned me and not have taken care of me. That is why I took birth in their family.' In the end, he forcefully removed my hand from his head. Then I said, 'Alright. I cannot interfere in anybody's decision or life.'

The greatness of God is that He gives you the freedom to be in bondage if that is your choice. Even if it is the ultimate freedom He does not force you. He gives you the freedom to be in bondage if that is your choice. And in the end, I did not heal him.

Your birth is based on your fear and greed. But an enlightened master's birth is based on love and compassion. That is the whole secret. That is why Kṛṣṇa beautifully says, '*Ātma māyayā*, because of my own energy I take birth. Just out of my love and compassion, I land on this planet earth.' The next question is this: How can we be liberated by knowing this truth? How will it help us? Understand, when I say *death*, I don't mean just dying at the end of life. I also mean, every night's sleep is your birth and death. Every night when you go to sleep, you die and take birth again when you wake up. You go to the causal body in deep sleep and come back.

As of now, every morning, how do we come back to life? Just look deeply. What happens when you wake up? First thing, the moment you become aware that you are awake a thought based on either greed or fear hits you. Maybe you want to meet somebody, or you want to meet some deadline. Immediately you jump out of your bed. If you have analyzed your waking up, how you assume this body every morning, that moment is actually your taking birth. The moment when you take the body matters. Early morning, with whichever thought you enter into the body, that thought is going to play a major role in your consciousness for that entire day.

But an enlightened master assumes the body out of compassion. He comes back every day just to share himself with the whole world. If you understand this once and alter your thoughts at the time of waking up, the very quality of your consciousness can be changed. It is just like how a camera works. The moment when the lens is opened, whatever scene is in front of the camera eye is recorded on the film. That will remain forever. Similarly, during the first moment of consciousness, the thought that you have while entering into the body plays a major role on your consciousness for the whole day.

So when you get up from bed, let the first thought be of love and compassion. Get up only to express your life in bliss. The moment you become aware of yourself, express, 'Oh Lord, it is so beautiful! You have given me one more day!' See don't think life is your birthright. I have seen many people taking things for granted. Before they get the job, they say, 'If I get that $10,000 per month salary, I will feel blessed.' The moment they get the job, in one month they think it is their birthright. Birth itself is not your right. It is a pure gift. The word birthright is completely wrong. You can't inhale or exhale even for a moment unless the Divine allows you. So every day is a blessing. When you get up from bed, assume the body with gratitude to the Divine. The quality of your whole consciousness will change and you will become an incarnation.

You too can become God

Here I am giving you the technique to become Kṛṣṇa, to become an incarnation. When you assume the body out of love and compassion you are an incarnation. Your whole life will then become pure eternal bliss. If you assume the body out of greed or fear, you are a man. Understand, your whole life is purely your responsibility. Nobody has forced anything on you!

People always ask me, 'Then why do we get into accidents, *Swamiji*?' See everything, including your accidents, is your choice. I am making a bold statement now: everything, including accidents, is your choice. You can raise questions. Only then you will understand this truth in a much deeper way.

Here Kṛṣṇa gives us a technique to attain Him. If we live in such a way as to be free from the attachments born out of anger and fear, then we can attain Him. All actions create their own reactions. When we sow a seed, it sprouts and becomes a plant. Thus it is in the order of Existence, that every action has its own reaction or effect. It is quite difficult to escape the clutches of this cause-effect cycle. Here Kṛṣṇa gives a technique to cut these *karmic* bonds, to escape and realize the reality.

Actions that are free from fear and anger do not create bonds. They lead us towards elevated consciousness. Fear and anger lead to bondage. Attachments are our bondage to the future based on experiences of the past. We have unfulfilled desires that we hope to fulfill. We get attached to the possibility of these results. When they happen the way we want, there is temporary satisfaction, and more wishes and attachments arise. When things do not happen the way we want them to, we are depressed. We strive again. Either way it is a never-ending cycle that brings sorrow in the end. When we let go of attachments and perform actions with no expectations, we enjoy the path of action. There is no stress regarding the results, since there is no attachment.

Kṛṣṇa offers a way out. He says, 'Be drowned in Me; you will have no anger, no fear. All your actions will be without bondage and you can realize Me.' He is not telling us, if you do this, something good will happen. He straightaway gives the positive assurance. 'Do it, you will achieve! Not only a few, many people have done so and have realized Me.'

Masters are like mirrors reflecting us. If the devotee prays for wealth, he gets it. If he wants healing he is granted it. To the devotee who only wants to realize God He shows him the way to ultimate reality. If you visit our ashram, you will see that there is something there for everyone. We have prayers, fire rituals, devotional songs, yoga, meditation, service, etc., for all kinds of people from all walks of life. For one who believes in worship, we have temples. For the one who wishes to attain through yoga, there are various yoga programs. For those on the path of knowledge, there are enough meditation techniques. Only in this manner can we raise the consciousness of society.

We cannot hope to transform society through any mass movement. It can happen only through individual transformation. When such transformed people act together, it will have the same power as a laser beam. I always say that each devotee and disciple is unique. The way I treat each one is unique. What I tell one person is not applicable to another. I warn my disciples, time and again, not to advise someone else based on the advice I have given them. It will only cause more confusion.

Here, Kṛṣṇa reaffirms that He will take care of the need of every one of His devotee. Only the most compassionate being will make this statement. Now it is left to the devotee to have some wisdom as to what to approach the master for. Kṛṣṇa explains here why non-attachment is so difficult. It is in our nature to look for success in whatever we do. Nothing wrong in it, but what creates problems is the illogical attachment to the expectation of success. We become so obsessed with what we desire that the expectation consumes us. This shows that our mindset has not changed in over five thousand years. Even then they were looking for material success. When they prayed to God they prayed to fulfill their expectations of material success.

Kṛṣṇa is the greatest psychologist who ever lived. He has measured human nature accurately. What we want is tangible and instant results. In His days, when the *saṁskāras* were relatively fewer, people had a different concept of time. There was much less aggression. Yet the master uses a term '*kshipraṁ*', instant. Now the master is talking about humanity: past, present and future. He says you normally pray to God only to seek unfulfilled material desires and all that you think will bring you happiness. All your actions are based on material success. Such activities bear instant results. Whether you understand it or not, your prayers also produce instant results. It does not mean that whatever you pray for is instantly granted. God, fortunately, has far more wisdom than we have. He uses His *buddhi,* wisdom, to grant what He deems appropriate.

However, the result of your actions, *karmaphala,* is instantaneous. When religions talk of *karma* (action) and *karmaphala* (the outcome of such action), they speak in terms of merits and sins, *pāpa* and *puṇya.* They tell you that you will go to hell if you accumulate sins, and to heaven if you gain merits. They try to control you through fear of hell and greed of heaven. There is no hell or heaven. They are both states of your mind, not locations in some distant future in God's land.

When you think good thoughts and do good deeds you feel good, you are in heaven. When you think and act evil, you feel evil and you are in hell. This is the cosmic cause-effect principle. You are what your intent is; you become what your intent is. *Karma* acts instantly, here and now. It is not some slow grinding of the wheels of God. You live in the tormented mindset of a sinner or the blissful mindset of a sage depending on what you think and do. Do not blame others for your actions.

Karma is in your hands. You have freedom of thought and action. It is not merely guaranteed by your national constitution, but by God's own constitution. What you sow, you shall certainly reap.

Understand And Be Unaffected By Action

4.13 Depending upon the distribution of the three attributes or gu´as and actions, I have created the four castes.
Yet, I am to be known as the non-doer, the unchangeable.

4.14 I am not affected by any work; nor do I long for the outcome of such work.
One who understands this truth about Me also does not get caught in the bondage of work.

4.15 All the wise and liberated souls of ancient times have acted with this understanding and thus attained liberation.
Just as the ancients did, perform your duty with this understanding.

4.16 What is action and what is inaction, even the wise are confused.
Let Me explain to you what action is, knowing which you shall be liberated from all ills.

Here Kṛṣṇa says, 'I have created the four castes depending upon the distribution of the three *guṇa*s or attributes.'

'*Guṇa*' means 'attribute' or 'quality' that we are born with. It is also a reflection of the *vāsana,* mindset with which we are born. There are three basic *guṇa*s: *satva* or purity, *rajas* or activity, and *tamas* or inactivity. People quote this verse whenever they want to make the caste system more solid. They say, 'This system has been given by the incarnation Himself.' Kṛṣṇa uses the words, 'depending upon the distribution of the three *guṇas*,' and not, 'depending upon birth.' There are basically four kinds of people; the character of the person will be of that *guṇa* which is more dominant in him. He says, 'Based on the *guṇa* one is born with, I decide on his *varṇa,* his caste.' The *varṇa* system was four-fold consisting of the *Brāhmaṇa*s, *Kshatriya*s, *Vaishya*s and the *Shudra*s. Based on the skill sets, the children in ancient *gurukul* (a school run by an enlightened master) were trained into either one of the four *varṇa*.

Over time, this system was manipulated. Those who believed that they had a better *varṇa* decided to make it a hereditary right. Earlier, the son of a *brāhmaṇa* could not be a priest, if he was unsuitable, or the son of a *kshatriya* to be a warrior, if he was inadequate. Kṛṣṇa states very clearly that only the one who transcends these three *guṇas*, a *triguṇa rahita* can reach the higher levels of consciousness. When a desire is fulfilled, it no longer creates ripples in the mind. Desires that get fulfilled are the basic needs one is born with, the *prārabdha karma.* We acquire all other desires by comparing ourselves with others. These are wants, not needs. Existence has no way of fulfilling such wants.

Ramaṇa maharṣi says beautifully: The universe can fulfill the needs of all its inhabitants, but it cannot fulfill the wants of even one person. Wants only grow and grow. Wants and greed stop only with death. Even then they continue to haunt us as the mental attitude, the carried-over *vāsanas*.

When one works out of basic need, he acquires no *karma.* A poor man with just one pair of footwear is happy that he does not have to go barefoot. Till that footwear is worn out, he has no need for another one. In comparison, many of us acquire dozens of shoes, many of which we rarely wear. These purchases born out of our wants can never be fulfilled. Once they are acquired, we seek the next acquisition. The cycle goes on. Have you ever seen a rich man enjoying his meal like a hard working manual laborer does? The rich man will be more worried about his illnesses than the quality of the food in front of him.

Only a person who has taken a conscious birth, is aware of his *prārabdha karma.* Only he can extinguish his *karma* by fulfilling this list.

Kṛṣṇa, the ultimate master has no *karma,* no unfulfilled desires, and no attachment. So it is with every enlightened master. His so-called desire gets fulfilled as it arises. When I desire food, it appears. When I need to sleep, I rest. There is no gap between my desire and its fulfillment and no trace of that desire after its fulfillment. The fulfillment is complete. Therefore, there is no *karma.*

This is the lesson every master tries to teach his disciples. Work from your needs, act without attachment. You shall attract no *karma* and be liberated.

Action In Inaction And Inaction In Action

4.17 *The complexities of action are very difficult to understand.*
Understand fully the nature of proper action by understanding the nature of wrong action and inaction.

4.18 *He who sees inaction in action and action in inaction, is wise and a yogi,*
Even if engaged in all activities.

4.19 *He who is determined and devoid of all desires for sense gratification, he is of perfect knowledge.*
The sages declare such a person wise whose actions are burnt by the fire of knowledge.

4.20 *Having given up all attachment to the results of his action, always satisfied and independent,*
The wise man does not act, though he is engaged in all kinds of action.

Here, Kṛṣṇa says that the person who sees inaction in action and action in inaction has attained transcendence. When you see that it is your senses doing the activities and the mind creating the false sense of identification of you with the action, then you have attained transcendence. You are no longer in the clutches of the mind. The mind makes you attached to something and repulsed by something else. When you are free from the mind you do actions because the senses, by their very nature have to perform their functions. Yet, you are free from the bondage of action, because you do not have any identification with the action; you do not have any emotional attachment to anything. So naturally, you are liberated and you can do things most beautifully without expecting any particular result. This is what it means to be 'unclutched'.

If you observe your mind keenly, you constantly connect all your thoughts and create some links in your mind. For example, the headache that happened ten years ago, five years ago and yesterday, are all independent experiences. For easy reference, you categorize all these into one category like how you file documents in your office. But slowly, you start believing that all these experiences are connected. When you start believing they are connected you create a shaft.

You connect all the painful memories and create a pain shaft and conclude, 'My life is suffering.' Now when you started believing that your whole life is a suffering, you created a pain shaft and are waiting only for painful incidents in your life, so that you can elongate that shaft. Understand, whatever you believe, is what you enhance within you. That is why vedic *ṛṣi*s, sages, say that you create what you want. You will wait unconsciously for painful incidents to strengthen your belief.

Secondly, whenever you add the painful incidents unconsciously you will elongate that shaft, even though you may want to consciously end the pain. If you believe your whole life is a shaft of joyful experiences, constantly you will be in fear whether the joy will continue. Understand these are two big dramas that you enact with yourselves. You forget that you can neither break the shaft nor elongate it, because the shaft itself does not exist! It is your own imagination. When you started archiving all the incidents in your life for the sake of easy reference, by and by you started believing that they are really connected. When you thought life as a pain shaft you tried to break it; when you thought it was a joy shaft, you tried to elongate it. You can neither break it nor elongate it, because the shaft itself does not exist.

Just try this experiment:

Sit down for ten minutes with a pen and paper. Now, just start jotting down whatever thoughts come to your mind. Do not edit your thoughts;

write them down as they are. Do not judge yourself or try to control your mind. Without judging, write down whatever thought occurs. Now, read what you have written. You can see for yourself how unconnected and illogical your thoughts are! One moment you would think, 'I should go to my office tomorrow,' then the next moment you think, 'No. I should wake up and then decide,' then, 'What should I do about dinner tonight?'

Have you seen how bubbles rise up in a fish tank? There is a gap between one bubble and the next. But the gap is so small that it looks like a continuous stream. Similarly, the thoughts in your mind are independent; they appear connected because the gap between them is very small. By their very nature, thoughts are independent.

For example, if you see a dog in the street, you remember your pet when you were a child. Then you remember your teacher, then the place where your teacher used to stay, and so on! The dog and the teacher are not connected in any way, but your mind simply flows. If you look a little deep, you will understand that your thoughts are illogical, independent, and unconnected.

When you believe your mind is logical, you have created the first 'original sin' for yourself. Understand, by nature you are unclutched. Connecting thoughts is like trashing all your emails and then picking up some emails from the trash and reading them again. When I say trash mails, I mean the thoughts that have left you already. Every moment you are renouncing thoughts. A new thought can appear only when the old thought has been renounced. But even after renouncing them you try to create a shaft with them. You feel that some valuable thoughts have been dropped in the dustbin, so you pick up those thoughts and try to create a shaft.

First, understand that you are creating a shaft, and fighting with it, either to elongate or break it. Second, you don't even have to unclutch yourself from the shaft, because the shaft is imaginary. By your very nature, if you stop creating a shaft, you are unclutched.

Then you would start asking, 'If I unclutch how will I take care of my things? Will I not just lie in bed and waste my life?' I ask you, 'Why should you not go to your job? The moment you say that you will not go to work, it means you have some vengeance against your job. That is why the moment you get some excuse you want to escape from your job!'

I always tell people, 'Fine, don't do anything; just be unclutched; for how many days will you be lying in your bed?' Maybe ten days, till all your *tamas* gets exhausted. *Tamas* is one of the three attributes of purity, activity and inactivity. Until your *tamas* gets exhausted you will lie there, but after that you will start working and you will naturally start moving! So do not be afraid that if you are unclutched, you will not follow your daily routine.

This is what Kṛṣṇa means by action and inaction. You cannot by nature be inactive. You will daydream. You will try to escape from reality because your mind is clutching onto an easy dream shaft.

When you truly unclutch, without any attachment to the past and future, you will realize that you are full of energy. You will *have* to do something. That 'something' will be dictated by your present moment awareness. See, what you think as 'you' is not necessary to run your day-to-day life. This is the basic truth. If you just observe yourself, if somebody is happily independent of us, we can't tolerate it. Constantly we need to feel needed. That is why we expect people to project their sufferings on us and we, too, project our sufferings on them, so that we feel important.

People ask me, 'Constantly I repeat positive affirmations that I should stop smoking, but it is not working. Why, *Swamiji*?' All these creative visualizations create more trouble. Because in the very words, 'I should stop smoking', 'smoking' and 'I should stop' contradict each other. You end up empowering 'smoking' as much as you are empowering 'I should stop'! Instead you should say, 'Let me have only healthy habits' or something totally positive without even the word 'smoking' in it. Similarly, if you have a headache, instead of empowering the thought of the headache, if you decide to have a glass of water, which is a fresh thought, it will replace the thought of headache. Once you keep replacing the thoughts, you break free from the headache-based thought patterns and eventually expel the headache from your system itself.

You may ask me, 'How can it be so simple, *Swamiji*?' It *is* simple. You are constantly taught that it is not so simple. You may question, 'But *Swamiji*, the thought of the headache may come back, then what to do? Understand, your faith is what brings it back. You are so faithful towards the 'headache,' that you forcefully drag it back into your system. Think of it this way, if it comes back, it can go also, is it not? Why don't you celebrate those moments in which it left you? Why do you constantly remember the moments when it came back?

People ask me repeatedly, 'I fail when I try to unclutch *Swamiji*.' I ask them, 'Why are you connecting your past failure with your present failure?' When you connect all the past failures, you create one more shaft, 'failure'. All your past failures are independent events. Just relax and stop connecting, and suddenly you will see a deep healing, a deep peace happening in you. Suddenly you would have dropped out of the constant running. Just relax. When you drop from this whole game, you will suddenly realize that the whole thing is just a psychodrama.

Unclutch from your thoughts

Try this simple meditation:

Just close your eyes and sit. Whatever thoughts arise, just witness them. Just do not connect them with other thoughts or create a shaft, simply unclutch. If you feel bored, unclutch from that thought as well. Just sit, be unclutched. Do not create, maintain, or destroy any thought. Try this for a few minutes and you will see the effect for yourself. Kṛṣṇa says that to understand what action is, you need to understand what inaction is. In my programs I tell people, 'To understand what is meditation, you need to understand what is not meditation.' I spend a day and a half explaining what is not meditation and less than half a day explaining what exactly is meditation.

When you unclutch, you are seemingly in inaction. However, the removal of the various pain and pleasure shafts, releases so much energy that you are now actively passive. You are at the height of potential energy, ready to release it for whatever purpose you decide in that moment. If instead, you actively daydream, caught in pain or pleasure shafts, then you are seemingly active and busy, but totally useless. In fact, you are counterproductively busy, pushing yourself deeper into more suffering.

In the process of unclutching, you transcend both action and inaction. You successfully destroy the false notion of connection between the thoughts and rest in the present moment. In this unclutched condition, you are active and yet not attached to any activity. You are truly in Kṛṣṇa consciousness. All suffering and pain arise when we associate ourselves with the senses and the mind. The real Self in you is eternal, timeless, never changing. It is like this, when you see the clouds drifting in the clear sky, is the sky actually changing? No! The sky is like the canvas over which clouds drift across, sometimes completely covering the sky behind them, and sometimes drifting apart to reveal the sky behind. Just like this, due to illusion, it appears as if the Self is being affected by the emotions and the perceptions of the senses.

If you see yourself in a clear lake, what you see is what is being projected, right? Just like that, in the lake of the Self, whatever quality is projected is what you will see. The reflection has no reality, no solid existence. Actually, the Self is permanent. The Self in you, me, and everyone, is the same. When everything is *You* what is there to fear? Everything is you. Enjoy this world in its many forms and manifestations. However, enjoy without getting caught in attachment. Our treacherous senses create addictions that overwhelm us. The more we have, the less we enjoy, and yet we cannot do without them. True wisdom is to step back from the dictates of the senses.

Have you seen someone trying to sell a painting? You can see the seller busy trying to convince people, to get the best bargain. But only someone who is neither interested in buying nor selling can really enjoy the painting.

A small story:

There was once a stag standing in front of a lake with its young one. The stag was looking at its own reflection in the water and telling the young stag, 'Son, look at what we have been endowed with - long horns, strong feet, and sharp eyes. We are truly powerful.'

Just as the stag was talking, a dog jumped in front of the stag. The stag, in a split second, just leapt and ran instinctively out of fear.

Then the young stag asked its father, 'Father, what is the use of being powerful if we have to run away from the dog?'

When we are faced with a testing situation, we forget all truths that we learnt. That does not mean that we do not accept the truth. It is just that we feel we are not strong enough to experience it. We need to persevere till it becomes an experiential reality in our lives. If you have the right ideals, you will reach the truth much faster. When you take the help of those who have seen the truth, it is more intelligent to experiment with the techniques that they advocate.

We are taught that we are sinners. But the vedic sages have time and again declared that we are the children of immortality. Let us be open to positive thoughts rather than continuously repeating negative, self-defeating thoughts to ourselves. Understand, the positive thoughts are the great truths that our sages have experienced. Hence they encourage us to·experiment and experience, as well. With them come the energy and power of the experience that is possible for every one of us.

When we are blissful and centered within ourselves, we would never see anything disturbing outside. That is what Kṛṣṇa says here: Be involved completely in the action yet be detached, independent and satisfied within. Then you can function spontaneously, flowing in tune with Existence. Life then becomes a celebration. Every single thing that you do will be an act of joy. Your joy will no longer be dependent on what society says or thinks about you or your actions.

Whatever we do or think, we are subconsciously seeking approval from the people around us in some subtle way. We are very keen to earn a good name from everyone. If you analyze deeply, you will see that you are not at ease without the endorsement of the people around you. If you just sit down and note how many things you do to get a good name, you will realize that eighty percent of your actions are for getting someone's approval. It is like a signature campaign. In a big register, you make various columns and then you go to your wife, friend, brother, etc., and ask for their signature under their columns. Of course, all these people also come to you for your signature in their registers.

Why do we bother so much about others' opinions about us? The reason is we know ourselves only through others' opinions of us. Second, when others give us their approval and attention, they are actually giving us energy. Attention is energy.

When you are dependent on external sources for energy, it means that you are psychologically handicapped. With psychological handicap, you don't even know that you are handicapped. You would have seen children building castles with cards and then enjoying by collapsing those castles. Like this, we build our self-image with people's opinions of us. The image looks beautiful until someone withdraws their certificate. Then the castle simply collapses and you feel miserable. At least the children build castles with their own cards. But we build our castles with others' certificates. We work hard so that people don't remove their certificates. This is how we get enslaved.

Because you don't know anything about yourself, you turn to society for an answer. And society happily labels you, 'You are good-looking', 'You are a failure', and so on. Just like how a parcel without an address is pushed from place to place, we move around, collecting the stamps that society puts on us. By and by we forget that we are not the labels but the stuff inside the parcel.

The sage Aṣṭāvakra says beautifully, 'Bondage is when the mind longs for something, grieves about something, rejects something, holds on to something, is pleased or displeased about something. Liberation is when the mind does not long or grieve about anything, does not reject or hold onto anything, is not pleased or displeased about anything. Liberation is when the mind is not entangled in the senses. When there is no 'me', that is liberation. Don't hold on to anything or reject anything.'

Equanimity In Success And Failure

4.21 *The person who acts without desire for the result; with his consciousness controlling the mind,*
Giving up all sense of ownership over his possessions and body and only working, incurs no sin.

4.22 *He who is satisfied with profit which comes of its own accord and who has gone beyond duality, who is free from envy,*
Who is in equanimity both in success and failure, such a person though doing action, is never affected.

4.23 *The work of a liberated man who is unattached to the modes of material nature and who is fully centered in the ultimate knowledge,*
Who works totally for the sake of sacrifice, merges entirely into the knowledge.

4.24 *The offering, the butter offered to the supreme in the fire of the supreme is offered by the supreme.*
Certainly, the supreme can be reached by him who is absorbed completely in action.

4.25 *Some yogis worship the gods by offering various sacrifices to them,*
While others worship by offering sacrifices in the fire of the supreme.

A sense of ownership over possessions or your body is the same thing. What are your possessions? You came with nothing at all. In the same way, you will leave this world empty-handed. Can you say that all your possessions will accompany you when you leave this body? No!

Understand, your life itself is a gift of Existence. How then can you claim that anything else is your possession?

Real knowledge comes only by experience. The moment you imbibe any dimension of truth in any way, it can do wonders for you. Vivekānanda says beautifully, 'Even if you memorize all books in all the libraries of this world, it will not help you in any way other than increasing your ego about the bookish knowledge that you have. Instead of having a whole library in your head, just realize five concepts in your heart.'

I tell you, use only one idea and imbibe that in your being. Your life will be transformed by a single idea. In Tamil Nadu, South India, they describe beautifully the lives of 63 enlightened masters in Periapurānam, a Tamil literary work. If you study the lives of those masters, you will find some masters did not really do anything. They just plucked flowers and offered them to God. Yet they achieved enlightenment! It is not what you do that is important; it is the attitude with which you do. When they did the act of offering flowers, they were true and honest to the action.

You may ask, 'We also offer flowers everyday. The only thing we get is the extra expense of buying the flowers!' The problem is, we are not honest. When these masters plucked flowers for God, they were totally devoted to the thought of the Lord. When we pluck to offer to a favorite deity, we are thinking of something else. I have seen these people who regularly chant the 1000 names of the gods as in the Viṣṇu sahasranāma. Even while chanting, they keep looking at the number of the verse they reached. They are desperate to see how much remains to be completed.

The intention decides the energy behind the action. In fact, some of the latest research shows how our DNA can be influenced and reprogrammed by words and frequencies. When a number of people focus their thoughts on something similar, like the football World Cup, certain random number generators in computers start to deliver ordered numbers instead of the random ones.

All the so-called natural calamities are the effects of global negative thoughts. Your thoughts and energy directly affect your body, your cell structure, your decisions, your capacity to fulfill your decisions, the outer world incidents, even accidents. You create a mental setup that creates and attracts similar incidents to you.

If you can change your mental setup from greed and fear, which is what we have normally, to one of bliss, or *ānanda*, then your energy flow will start brimming and your thoughts will be much clearer and more in the present. When you do this, you have every power to control the outer world incidents because you and Existence have a very deep connection at the energy level. When you are blissful, when your mental setup is not one of worry, fear and greed but one that is in the present, always joyful, you will automatically attract all good things to yourself.

One more thing: All our minds are not individually separated pieces of the universe. They are all one and the same. All our minds are interlinked. Not only interlinked, they directly affect each other. This is what I call the 'collective consciousness'. Though each one is independent in his consciousness, when one is conscious of one's true nature, one feels as if one is part of the whole universe.

You are a part of the collective consciousness

Each one's thoughts straightaway affect others around them. Your thoughts are more infectious than your cold. If you catch a cold from someone, you may suffer physically for a few days and then get over it. But when you catch thoughts from people, not only do you suffer mentally but you suffer forever, also.

Not only are those who are staying around you touched by your thoughts, everyone who is living on the planet earth is touched by your thoughts.

The next truth: Not only at the mental level are you connected; even at the deeper conscious level you are connected to every other being. Your body is not just one body. Actually, there are seven layers or bodies.

The first layer is the physical body. The second is the pranic body. There are seven such energy layers or bodies. These energy layers can be represented as concentric circles, with the physical layer as the outermost circle and the seventh layer, the nirvanic body as the innermost.

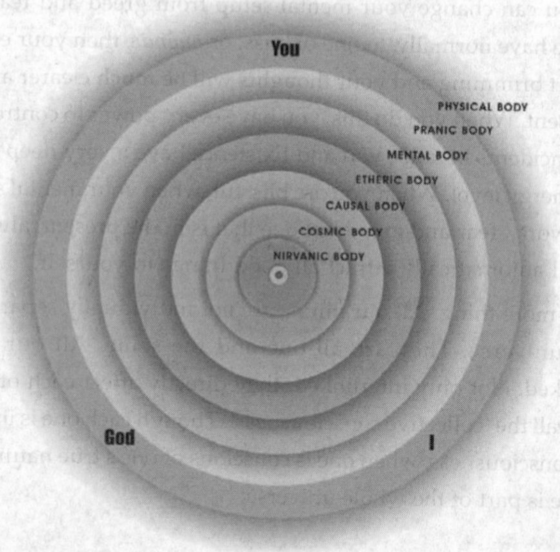

The first four layers are related to the physical body-mind system. They store engrams related to desires, guilt, and pain experienced during that lifetime. The fifth layer is experienced during deep sleep and when leaving the body. The sixth layer is associated with happy memories and the seventh layer is the ultimate consciousness. Now, at the physical layer, you, God, and I can be represented as three different points in the outermost concentric circle. At the physical level, the distance between these three is more. At the pranic level, the distance is reduced. At the mental level, the distance between you and me is still reduced and so is the distance between you, God, and me. When you go deeper and deeper, these three entities finally merge into one at the innermost nirvanic layer.

At the deepest point of all these layers, God, you, and I are one. There is no distance between the three.

Once you become aware and realize that you are a part of the collective consciousness, you realize that you do not have a separate ego. You think you own your individual identity. In Existence there is no such thing as a separate individual identity. Once you know this truth, you go beyond pain, suffering, depression, and diseases. As long as you are individually conscious, you will be continuously suffering.

There is a beautiful saying:

Mind as a rule is a fool
When it is hot, asking for cool
When it is cool, asking for hot
Always asking for what is not!

When it is cool, you resist. You think you are different from Existence. I have seen *sanyāsī*s living in the Himālayas, almost nude in the snow. I have myself lived in such conditions, but the body was never disturbed. I never had the feeling of separation from Nature. When you think you are different from the atmosphere, you start resisting it.

The other day I read an interesting interview with a man who survived his jump into the Niagara Falls. If you have been to the Niagara Falls, you can understand the enormity of the fact that someone survived jumping into it. I cannot imagine someone surviving that jump. He says beautifully, 'When I jumped, I became a part of Niagara Falls. I felt like I was a part of it. I never felt that I was different from the Falls.'

When you are in tune with the collective consciousness, Nature will protect you. As long as you think you are different from Nature, it will protest. A very simple thing that you can practice now; if you are feeling cold, just relax and witness the area you are feeling cold. Just say to yourself, 'I am not going to resist Nature. Let me relax.' Consciously decide. You will feel the body relaxing and will become completely comfortable.

The Universe is a hologram of which you are a part. Just as in a hologram every single part of a hologram reflects the totality of that hologram, even if it is split, you reflect the totality of the Whole that is the Universe.

Wherever you want to achieve success in a social or in an economic context, only when you fall in tune with the whole group, with the collective consciousness, will you be able to achieve what you want. As long as you feel you are an individual, you will be resisted and you will be resisting. If you disappear into the collective consciousness, you will be taken care of. You will attain complete success socially and economically, and will also experience deep fulfillment. As long as you resist the current, whether it is your workplace or your house you will continuously be creating hell for yourself and for others.

Even in the physical layer, if you think you are separate, then you are inviting disease. In the mental layer, if you think you are separate, you will be sowing seeds of violence. With collective consciousness, you unify, but with individual consciousness you dissect, you cut things into pieces. At the soul level, if you think you are an individual, there is no possibility for any spiritual growth.

First thing, at the physical level, you are not an individual. Your body and the body of the sun are directly connected. Any change in the sun makes changes in your body. Any change in your body can change the body of the moon. Even if you are not able to logically relate to this, it is true.

In the mental layer also, you are not alone. Any thought created in your mind goes and touches someone else. Any thought sown by someone can touch you and affect you. It is like ripples in a lake. If you are creating a strong wave, you will be creating an impression with your thought. You will be leading and inspiring others with your thought. If your thoughts are not solid enough, other waves will impress you.

Either you live like a leader or you will be a follower. There is no in between. You always think, 'I will not be a leader, I cannot do that much;

I will not be a follower either; I shall maintain my own stand.' This is simply impractical. Either you lead or you follow.

At the spiritual level, the moment you understand that you are deeply connected to the whole universe, not only do you experience bliss, but you really start to live, opening many dimensions of your being. See, with just one body, you can enjoy so much. If you disappear into the collective consciousness, you will experience so many dimensions, that you cannot even imagine!

During the Indian festival of Holi, Rādhā and the *gopī*s experienced the collective consciousness of Kṛṣṇa. This is called as *rās līlā.* It is not something where Kṛṣṇa had a relationship with so many women. What actually happened was that He gave the experience of collective consciousness to the whole group of *gopikā*s and Rādhā. This collective consciousness is God.

Throughout our second level meditation program - LBP Level 2 course, you will realize that you are not only a part, but you *are* the collective consciousness. Layer by layer when we go deeper, you will realize that you are just one with everything. Your health improves and you start feeling the well-being in all the other layers.

You are like an onion. The onion thinks it has got something solid but when it is opened layer by layer, it is empty. Similarly, you think that you are individual consciousness, but if you peel the individual layers, you will experience that you are nothing but the collective consciousness!

In LBP 2, we open your minds. You are asked to write about your pains, desires, guilt and pleasures. You will not be showing your notes to anyone else. By writing them down, you are opening your minds in my presence. When your minds are open, I can heal them. Healing simply happens. In the same way, if you open your mind, it can be healed. In LBP 2, your pains, pleasures, guilt and desires are opened up. When they open up, you experience God.

We are all taught from childhood to work towards goals in life. We are expected to live up to the expectations of our parents, later our teachers, much later our spouses, and finally our children. Understand, the purpose of life is to enjoy life. But how can we enjoy life if we get saddled with a bagful of goals and obligations? Life is about enjoying the journey of life. When the path is right, when you enjoy the path, the destination is always right; it will always be enjoyable. The very path itself is the goal. When you realize this, you relax into the present and are not affected by success or failure.

Understand that the goal of life is like a mirage. It does not exist in reality, but it continuously creates illusions of its existence. Live life every moment in bliss, and you can see the tremendous difference it makes to the very quality of your life.

A small story:

> This has happened according to the mythological stories in my native place, Tiruvannamalai. The story goes that once Śiva appeared as an infinite column of light to settle a dispute between Brahma, the Creator, and Viṣṇu, the Sustainer, as to who was greater. As per Śiva's orders, Brahma had to find Lord Śiva's head and Viṣṇu was asked to find Śiva's feet. Whoever found their part first would be declared the greater one. This story has a beautiful meaning. Brahma is the consort of Sarasvatī, the goddess of knowledge. Viṣṇu is the consort of Lakṣmī, the goddess of wealth. The story says that Brahma started searching for the head. Viṣṇu started searching for the feet. Viṣṇu came back after some time and accepted, 'I am not able to find Your feet; please forgive me. I only now realized that it is an impossible task!' Brahma also realized he would not be able to find Śiva's head. So he took a flower as a false witness to testify that he had touched and brought it from Śiva's head. He cheated.

You need to understand the story: Viṣṇu is the embodiment of wealth. Brahma is the embodiment of intellect. Neither by wealth nor by intellect can you achieve enlightenment. If you travel in the line of wealth, you will get frustrated, you will face depression of success, and you will become really humble. This is symbolized by Viṣṇu surrendering first. But if you travel in the line of intellect, you will never accept that you are defeated. This is symbolized by Brahma bringing a false witness in order to escape defeat.

If you travel in the path of material success in the outer world, at least at one point you will experience depression of success and understand the futility of your pursuit. But the person who travels in the line of intellect, he will not even be able to understand that he cannot achieve. The intellect becomes so subtle that it will bring false claims to say that he has achieved it. Those false claims are only these false flowers, the false witnesses. The ultimate knowledge can be reached only through sincerity, not through intellect or wealth. Then you are not caught in running behind the senses, behind the inner world or the outer world.

Know The Meaning Of Sacrifice and Be Purified

4.26 *Some sacrifice the hearing process and other senses in the fire of equanimity*
And others offer as sacrifice the objects of the senses, such as sound, in the fire of the sacrifice.

4.27 *One who is interested in knowledge offers all the actions due to the senses,*
Including the action of taking in the life breath into the fire of yoga, and is engaged in the yoga of equanimity of the mind.

4.28 *There is the sacrifice of material wealth, sacrifice through penance, sacrifice through yoga*
And other sacrifices, while there is sacrifice through self-study and through strict vows.

4.29 *There are others who sacrifice the life energy in the form of incoming breath and outgoing breath,*
Thus checking the movement of the incoming and outgoing breaths and controlling the breath.

4.30 *There are others who sacrifice through controlled eating and offering the outgoing breath, life energy.*
All these people know the meaning of sacrifice and are purified of sin or karma.

4.31 *Having tasted the nectar of the results of such sacrifices, they go to the supreme eternal consciousness.*
This world is not for those who have not sacrificed. How can the other be, Arjuna?

4.32 *Thus, there are many kinds of sacrifices born of work mentioned in the Vedas.*
Knowing these, one will be liberated.

In all these verses Kṛṣṇa talks about the various types of sacrifices. 'Sacrifice' is not just the *act* of giving, but the *attitude* of giving. Otherwise, you may follow all rituals according to the scriptures, but will miss out on the real intent for which the act had to be done.

A beautiful story from the Bhāgavatam, the ancient Hindu epic:

Once, Kṛṣṇa was playing with his friends. After playing, his friends were tired and asked Kṛṣṇa for food. Kṛṣṇa replied, 'Go to the nearby hall where learned priests are performing a great ritual to attain heaven. Tell them that you have been sent by me and request them to give you some cooked rice.'

Kṛṣṇa's friends did as they were told. The *brāhmaṇas* were all caught up in the rituals and did not know the intent of the sacrifice. They did not give the boys any food. Kṛṣṇa's friends returned disappointed and narrated what had happened. Kṛṣṇa, on hearing about the foolish *brāhmaṇas*, just laughed and said, 'Now, go to the innocent wives of these *brāhmaṇas* and ask them the same thing.'

The friends once again did as they were told. The ladies, on hearing that they had been given such a wonderful opportunity to serve, gathered all the food from their houses and rushed to feed Kṛṣṇa and his friends.

The very act of service, the welcoming attitude is what is important.

There is a beautiful verse in the Mahābhārata that says, 'A guest comes with all the gods. If the guest is honored, so are the gods; if he goes away disappointed, the gods are disappointed too.'

That is why in Sanskrit, we say, '*atithi devo bhava*', the guest is God. When somebody comes unexpectedly also, serve him. That is a real welcoming attitude. The word used for ritual giving in Sanskrit is '*dāna*', which means sharing, imparting.

The true meaning of sacrifice lies in the meaning with which it is done. Here Kṛṣṇa mentions many forms of sacrifice. He talks of sacrifices of material wealth, yoga, and penance - a combination of material, physical, mental, and spiritual sacrifices. When a person does these at some cost and pain to himself, they would be genuine sacrifices. Otherwise they would merely be meaningless rituals.

However, even that which is given away by someone who can afford what he is giving, if done with good intentions, would result in gains to that person. His very intention would alter his mindset and liberate him. A person who does not believe in sharing his wealth will not only not enjoy his wealth in this life, but will also suffer in future births as a result of his mental makeup.

When one sacrifices whatever is dear and whatever is difficult to give away, he enters a completely different plane of sacrifice, one that liberates the person. Such a person enters a plane of true non-attachment, leading to liberation.

You Are No Sinner

4.33 O conqueror of foes, the sacrifice of wisdom is superior to the sacrifice of material wealth.
After all, all activities totally end in wisdom.

4.34 Understand these truths by approaching a spiritual master, by asking him your questions, by offering service.
The enlightened person can initiate you into wisdom unto you because he has seen the truth.

4.35 O Pāṇḍavā, knowing this you will never suffer from desire or illusion,
You will know that all living beings are in the supreme, in Me.

4.36 Even if you are the most sinful of all sinners,
You will certainly cross completely the ocean of miseries with the boat of knowledge.

Here Kṛṣṇa advises the seeker to sacrifice one's knowledge at the feet of the master, to experience the ultimate Truth. A master is one who has experienced the truth. He can simply transfer his experience of truth to you by communing with you.

In Sanskrit, there are three beautiful words to describe this. You are born in the *bhū garbha,* the womb of the mother; this signifies your physical birth. The teacher with his love and teachings gives birth to you in the *hrid garbha,* the womb of the heart. The master gives birth to a completely new you, a transformed being in the *jñāna garbha,* the womb of knowledge. You then become re-born, *dvija*!

All you need to do is be open to the master. He can elevate you to the same experience as his.

Surrender transforms

Buddha says,

Buddham śaraṇam gacchāmi
Dhammam śaraṇam gacchāmi
Saṅgham śaraṇam gacchāmi

This means,

I surrender to Buddha, the enlightened master
I surrender to Buddha's teachings
I surrender to Buddha's mission

Actually, the master lives in all three: the body, his teachings, and his mission. One third of the master's energy is in the physical body. The other third is in the teachings, and another third is in the mission.

Nithyananda is *nitya-dhyāna-ānanda,* all in one. *Nitya,* the master in the body as Nithyananda, *dhyāna,* my message of meditation, and *ānanda,* my mission of bringing forth the fountain of bliss that is lying latent in you. All the three together constitute the energy called Nithyananda. Understand that.

It is easy to follow the master in his physical form because masters are so alluring and attractive by nature and they do not expect you to give them anything in return. The next level is to follow the master's teachings. This is slightly more difficult because you not only have to listen to his teachings, but also follow them. Though it is only for your own growth, your laziness *(tamas)* causes you to not do this. The final level is where you give your life to spreading the master's teachings. This is the most difficult, since it requires from you the ultimate commitment for life.

And I tell you, when you take up the responsibility of the mission, you will realize that what seemed to you as a load, as a responsibility, is actually a blissful experience. The moment you stand up to take up the responsibility, you will find that the divine energy flows through you and you express yourself most beautifully.

When you surrender your mental faculties to serve the mission, you become like a liquid, molded into shapes created by the master. He creates the molds for each of you to grow according to your needs and abilities. At the being level, when your being surrenders to the master, you become a part of the master. You no longer carry any separate identity. This process of transformation automatically happens when you surrender to the master, his teachings and his mission. The master tirelessly and compassionately pushes you in different ways so you can also experience and be in the same state of eternal bliss as he is.

The *Vedas* also clearly declare that a master is needed. You may have access to all the books, the recorded teachings of all the great masters. But you have only the words; where is the body language? For example, Yoga as it is taught now has been reduced to just a form of physical exercise. Physical health is just one of its benefits. Yoga as taught by Patañjali was a means to enlightenment. But the body language of Patañjali no longer exists; only his words exist. You need a living master who is in the same consciousness as Patañjali, to convey the underlying essence of the words.

There is a beautiful verse in the Guru Gītā which says, 'The guru just wipes off with the big toe of his left foot your fate which Brahma wrote on your forehead.' An astrologer may be able to predict your future, but a master can simply change your future. He is one with Existence, which is operating this whole universe. Can the energy that runs the planets and stars not have the power to handle your life?

See, it is very easy to relate with a dead master. You can easily escape by just worshipping him. You can just say, '*Amayaṁ anahankāraṁ arāgaṁ amadaṁ tatha…*'; 'I offer my non-attachment to you', 'I offer my ego to you.' But, if you tell me that, I will simply catch your neck and say, 'Hey! Where is your non-attachment? Where is your ego? Surrender it!'

A living master will be constantly working on you, to show you your true Self. So just be open to the master's energy. He will lead you from ignorance to bliss. The master does not differentiate between who is good and who is bad. He is not bothered about whether what you do is considered meritorious by society or sinful. He is simply compassion personified. See, knowledge makes all the difference. Here, Kṛṣṇa says beautifully, 'Even if you are the most sinful of all sinners, you will certainly completely cross the ocean of miseries with the boat of knowledge.' The concept of sin does not exist. It is a creation of man-made institutions, or religious and political organizations to control others through fear. In all such institutions you will find all are not judged by the same standards.

The Original Sin is merely one of forgetting our true divine nature. Animals do not care whether they are animals or divine. They eat when they are hungry, mate when nature guides them, and sleep when they are tired. In that sense, they are one with Nature. But humans eat when they don't have to and watch television long after they are tired. Sex has become a form of entertainment. We have corrupted our true nature through misuse of our intellect. That is the sin we have committed.

When you have the true knowledge of what you are doing, the knowledge itself will make the action divine. Automatically, you will cross the ocean of miseries because misery itself is a result of ignorance of your true self. When 'spirit' is added to a 'ritual', it becomes 'spirituality'. When wisdom is blended into the ritual, it truly becomes a prayer.

Doubt Destroys

4.37 *Just as a blazing fire turns firewood to ashes, O Arjuna,*
So does the fire of wisdom burn to ashes all actions, all your karma.

4.38 *Truly, in this world, there is nothing as pure as wisdom.*
One who has matured to know this enjoys in himself in due course of time.

4.39 *A person with* śraddhā *(courageous faith) achieves wisdom and has control over the senses.*
Achieving wisdom, without delay, he attains supreme peace.

4.40 *Those who have no wisdom and faith, who always have doubts, are destroyed.*
There is no happiness in this world or the next.

4.41 *O winner of riches, he who has renounced the fruits of his actions, whose doubts are destroyed, who is well established in the Self, is not bound by his actions.*

4.42 *O descendant of Bhārata, therefore, stand up, be established in yoga.*
Armed with the sword of knowledge, cut the doubt born of ignorance that exists in your heart.

A small story:

Once, a blind man went to a doctor to see if he had any hope of getting his eyesight back. The doctor checked him and said, 'Yes, I can do an operation to restore your eyesight. Then, you can drop your stick and start walking.'

> The man replied, 'Doctor, I understand I will get back my eyesight, but how can I walk without the stick?'
>
> The blind man does not even know what it means to be able to see. The doctor has to do the operation to give him back his eyesight, then automatically he will drop the stick.

Similarly, it is only when you drop the mind, you really start 'seeing'. Your ego stops filtering and adding tones to what your senses experience. Your baggage of *samskāras* dissolve, and the new 'you' is born. You are reborn. All your actions then arise out of intuition, from the superconscious state, the state of truth, where no mind can exist.

The Power of *śraddhā*

In the next verse Kṛṣṇa uses '*śraddhā*'. Actually, *śraddhā* means faith plus the courage to execute the idea. When you have the knowledge and the courage to follow the teachings, then you can achieve the ultimate. When Galileo declared that it is the earth that goes around the sun, contrary to the then existing Christian belief, he was persecuted. In his writings, he actually has a footnote, 'We can deny this, but since the earth and sun are not Christians, they will continue to move the way they do, irrespective of Christian beliefs!'

Look at Patañjali: He boldly declares that all that he says in the Yoga Sutras is completely open to experimentation and verification. He invites you to try out these in your life and if you learn something more from that, his work is open to editing. That is the beauty of our system; it is a living system open to being updated.

Of all religious and spiritual doctrines, it is only the scriptures of the *Sanātana dharma,* the eternal path of righteousness, as the Hindu philosophy is called, that allow themselves to be updated. The *Vedas* and the *Upaniṣads* are truths to be understood and followed only in awareness. There are no punishments if one does not follow them, nor is one condemned as a sinner if one doesn't follow them. Nothing was sacred just because it was uttered. All that we follow blindly today as traditions came through societal interpretation. It is for us to sift through these truths with conscious awareness.

Once tested, proven, and accepted, we need to have the *śraddhā* to practice these truths. With *śraddhā* you make the effort to conquer your senses, and direct your mind towards the truth.

In the next few verses, Kṛṣṇa says that there is no happiness for those who always have doubts and who have no knowledge and faith. He uses the word 'always'. See having doubts is natural; as long as you have the mind, doubts will be there. But you need to go beyond it.

In the Śiva sūtra, Devī asks, 'O Śiva, what is your reality? What is this wonder-filled universe? What is this life beyond form pervading form? Let my doubts be cleared.' Beautifully she expresses her whole state of mind. If you say, 'Let my questions be answered', you want only intellectual answers. But Devī says, 'I am not bothered whether you give me techniques or words, but let me be free from doubts.'

When questions become a quest, when the urge becomes urgent, you start speaking in this language. Actually, the moment you decide 'I will wait forever', things will simply start happening for you! As long as you are in a hurry, you stop things from happening in you. The moment you decide to wait, things will simply start happening, and you don't have to wait anymore. Just allow the master to do the operation and give you back your true Self, and automatically you will drop what you are not.

Kṛṣṇa refers here to the stages in the master-disciple relationship. The first level is purely intellectual, doubt-based. 'Doubt-based' refers to the negative doubts that you have about the master. It is like you are telling yourself on seeing the master, 'Eh! What is he going to sit and do? How is he able to mobilize such a big crowd at such a young age?' and so on. The next step is intelligence. You tell yourself, 'Why not attend this program and see what he is really doing?' The intellect is becoming intelligence. You are giving a little space for the master.

If you continue to start looking in, from intelligence, to intelligence combined with emotion, then you will feel like a friend towards the master. Go deeper and you will feel like the master is like a father or mother or lord or teacher. You feel respectful towards him. And then, the relationship becomes pure emotion. You will feel a deep connection like a mother and son.

Then, after that, it is purely a being-level relationship, the deep connection to the beloved, the *madhura bhāva.*

And suddenly, you will see, he is beyond the beloved. You experience the *mahā bhāva* or the guru-disciple experience. That is what I call *'Tat tvam asi'*. *'Tat tvam asi'* means 'That art thou'. It means you *are* the master. When you go beyond doubts and faith, into the realization of the formless energy that is you, then you find yourself.

Thus ends the fourth chapter named **Jñānakarmasannyāsa Yogaḥ** *of the* **Upaniṣad** *of* ***Bhagavad Gītā****, the scripture of yoga dealing with the science of the Absolute in the form of the dialogue between* ***Śrī Kṛṣṇa*** *and Arjuna.*

BhagavadGītā

Live All Your Dimensions

Sanyāsa Yogaḥ

Chapter 5

Seeking more and more
does not lead to happiness.
It leads to only depression.
Then what leads to happiness?

Live All Your Dimensions

If we look closely at our lifestyle, what we accept as normal is actually chaotic and crazy. But we have been conditioned to it since childhood so we are not even aware of this. From an early age we are taught certain beliefs and habits that cut deep grooves in our mind. The rest of our lives we follow these furrows and tracks of thinking. In Indian villages, even today, they grind oil seeds in a traditional expeller powered by bullocks. These bullocks are tied in such a way that they walk in circles to crush the seeds inside the expeller. If we analyze the way we live, we are very much like these bullocks! We get caught in a rut and we go around driven by our senses and memories. We unconsciously follow the same routine day after day, year after year.

Even when we think we are breaking the routine and doing things creatively, we are still driven by our unconscious mind. Nearly ninety percent of our mind exists in the 'unconscious' zone, where all our deep memories are stored. These engraved memories stored in the unconscious mind make decisions on our behalf, even though we are completely unaware of it. What we think of as an intuitive decision is actually an instinctive decision from our unconscious.

Understand the difference between intuition and instinct. Instinct is the unconscious mind. It is the deeply grooved habit patterns that are encoded in the genes and DNA. Animals are driven by instinct. The instinctive action of the unconscious is of crucial value to our survival. Intuition, on the other hand, is a superconscious state of the mind. It is a state of living and being in the present moment and is developed through meditation. Intuition allows us to explode in all directions while instinct restricts us to the furrowed path of our conditioned, unconscious memories.

By nature we are multi-dimensional, intuitive and enlightened. We only lack the awareness of this potential. In the verses that follow, the master tells us how to break away from our bondage and become multi-dimensional and reach our true state.

Throughout the Gītā, Kṛṣṇa talks about yoga. Yoga is the same as *samādhi.* Yoga means 'uniting' - uniting with our true nature. When we unite with our true Self, we become multi-dimensional. There are no limitations. We can be both spiritual and materialistic.

5.1 *Arjuna said:*
Oh Kṛṣṇa, you asked me to renounce work first and then you ask me to work with devotion.
Will you now please tell me, one way or the other, which of the two will work for me?

5.2 *Kṛṣṇa says: The renunciation of work and work in devotion are both good for liberation.*
But of the two, work in devotional service is better than renunciation of work.

5.3 *He who neither hates nor desires the fruits of his activities has renounced.*
Such a person, free from all dualities, easily overcomes material bondage and is completely liberated, Oh Arjuna!

5.4 *Only the ignorant speaks of the path of action to be different from the path of renunciation.*
Those who are actually learned say that both action and renunciation lead to the same truth.

If you look at it, it will seem like Arjuna was playing a game. A king could never have been so ignorant. There is no other book that is so clear, so direct. There is no other master who is so straight in giving the instructions. After all the explanation given by Kṛṣṇa previously, Arjuna asks, 'Oh Kṛṣṇa, first of all, you asked me to renounce work and then again you recommend work with devotion. Now, tell me clearly, which of the two is more beneficial?'

We will never get an answer if we start thinking about which would be more beneficial. Before we evaluate the benefits of something, we should be clear about the scale we want to use to measure the benefits. The scale we use for measuring success is a very important thing. Unless we know the scale, we cannot arrive at any conclusion. Even jumping to a conclusion should be done with clear intelligence. Jumping to a conclusion without intelligence is like falling out of an airplane without a parachute! We just wouldn't know where we will land.

Before measuring life in terms of success or failure, one should know how this success is to be measured first. If we are going to measure our life with a scale of dollars, then we have to work only for dollars. So, from morning to evening we would work only for that goal. But you see, by the time we reach evening, the very scale changes! We start our life using a certain scale and after a few years we measure again using a totally different scale.

It is fortunate that the scale changes. If we grow with every mistake in life, then the scale with which we measure success in life should also change. If it does not change, then we will start the next life from ground zero. It is an endless game unless we learn lessons and move on. If the scale with which we measure our success changes in the right way, it shows we are becoming mature. If the scale stays at the same level of acquiring wealth, then we can expect unhappiness. This is because there is no end to accumulating money or any material wealth. First of all, we set high standards for ourselves in terms of material comfort. Even if we achieve these, we are not successful in our own eyes because we would have extended our target by comparing with others. Out of greed we keep saying, 'What next, what next'. There is no end to this.

At the end of our lives, we feel we have not done enough. Then we again start the whole game of a fresh birth and life from square one with the same limited maturity. Understand: If money or worldly comfort is our only scale, then again and again we would feel that we could have done a little more. We would always feel that we missed out in life. There is no absolute scale that defines success especially in monetary terms. For any amount of money that we have, we would be happier with a dollar more.

The Yakṣa's Jar

Let me tell you a small story:

A king's barber used to live a very happy life. Every morning he would go to the palace to shave for the king. He would get ten gold coins for it and would return home. He led a very happy and peaceful life without any worries. One day when he was returning from the king's palace, suddenly he heard a booming voice, 'Dear Son, do you want forty gold coins?'

The barber said, 'Forty gold coins? What am I going to do with them? My expense is ten gold coins and that is enough. I don't need anything more.'

The booming voice said, 'I will give you twenty-four hours to think. You can go home, think and come back tomorrow to tell me. If you decide 'yes', I shall give you a magical jar full of gold coins.'

This poor barber should have at least kept quiet about this. He went and opened his mouth to his wife! She started to scream, 'You fool! You should have brought that jar. She raved and ranted saying 'Throughout my life, I am wearing the same *sarees* (traditional attire of Indian women) and jewelry. You never indulged me. What have I enjoyed after marrying you?'

I tell you, marriage is a three-ring circus: One is the engagement ring, next is the wedding ring and the third is suffering!

When she started shouting at him, the barber said, 'Alright. Don't worry. The booming voice has given me time till tomorrow morning to decide. Tomorrow morning, I will talk to him and get the jar.'

The next day morning, he told the voice, 'Please give me that jar.' Immediately, a *yakṣa* (an astral being) appeared before him and said, 'Have this jar. This jar has got 990 gold coins, just 10 gold coins less than 1000.'

The guy brought the gold jar back to the house. He was very happy that he could spend it for at least 99 days if he spent ten coins per day. But the moment his wife got the jar, she said, 'What is this? The jar is not overflowing. There is something missing.' He said, 'This is the way I got the jar. The *yakṣa* told me that it is a little less.'

She started worrying, 'Had it been full, how nice it would have been!' The next day, when the barber came back, she hurriedly grabbed all the ten gold coins that he earned and put them in the jar. She wanted the jar to overflow. But to her surprise, again the jar was not full.

The barber's wife now started becoming restless. She waited anxiously for the next day's wages to fill the jar. The next evening, again, she took the money from the barber and put them into the jar. Again, it was a little short from being full. This went on continuously for a week. She stopped giving food to the barber and cut all expenses. In a week's time the barber had become tired and dull and it showed on his face. The king started enquiring, 'What happened? You used to look so fresh. For the last week, you seem very tired. You have started worrying. What happened to you? Did you accept the *yakṣa's* jar?'

The barber was shocked at hearing this. He said, 'Oh king, how did you know?'

The king said, 'All those who are suffering in this country have one thing in common. They accepted the *yakṣa's* jar at some point in time.

The king said, 'When you go back home, get rid of the *yakṣa's* jar if you wish to be happy again.'

The man did so and lived happily again from that day on.

What the king said applies to all of us. Go back home and see if you have *yakṣa's* jar. If you do, get rid of it. If you are worrying, then there is every chance that you have the *yakṣa's* jar. Of course, when I say *yakṣa's* jar, I mean it may not literally be there in your house. But it will surely be there in your head. Sometimes *yakṣa* hands over the jar in the form of a bank balance! The *yakṣa's* jar is made out of the Brahma *kapāla,* one of Lord Brahma's head that Lord Śiva holds in his hand, which simply swallows anything that is put into it, asking for more. The *yakṣa's* jar makes us believe that we are not complete. Our head makes us think continuously that we are not enough unto ourselves.

However much we may have, we will feel it is not sufficient. Our mind will take everything for granted. *Yakṣa* refers to a person who has got wealth, but neither does he enjoy it nor does he share it with the world. When accumulation of wealth is done greedily, there is never an end because there is always scope for more. And secondly, when one is so preoccupied about accumulating, enjoyment never happens. The greed of wanting more and more and the fear that the saved balance will deplete hinder true enjoyment of the wealth.

I always tell people, 'Either you do *dāna* (charity) or you achieve *mahādāna* (the final and grand sacrifice or death). If you do *dāna* you share a little along with enjoying yourself. Else, you will achieve *mahādāna,* which means you will leave everything and go away once and for all when you die.

Ramaṇa Maharṣi says beautifully, 'Before achieving it, even a mustard seed will look like a mountain.' It will seem that without it, your life will not move. It will seem as if that is the basic and most important thing for your life. 'Once you achieve it, even a mountain will look like a mustard seed.'

The mind is such, that before achieving, even a trivial thing seems so important and huge in our lives like the mustard seed that initially looks like a mountain. Suddenly, once it is achieved, even a mountain will look like a mustard seed. This is because something else looks like a mountain now. We get caught in the trap of achieving and lose the ability to relax and enjoy what we have achieved.

Karma or Sanyās?

Here, Arjuna asks:

'Now, will you please tell me surely, which of the two: *karma*, action, or *sanyās*, renunciation, is more beneficial?'

All of us ask this question to ourselves. Be very clear, our mind itself is a dilemma. It will be alive as long as we are caught between any two extremes. The moment we come to any single conclusion we will be liberated. We will be ignorant as long as we are moving from one extreme to the other. Don't say, 'Ignorance is bliss.' If ignorance is bliss, then why do so many people suffer on this planet earth? Innocence is bliss, not ignorance. Innocence means we will not carry a scale with which we are continuously measuring our life. Ignorance means we will have a scale but we will not be able to fulfill our life according to our scale. If we neither have a scale nor have a goal, then there is no problem.

What we need to understand is that we have made our mind a dilemma, a disease. Man starts and ends his life with dilemma. I can't even say 'ends'. He will even be in a dilemma about whether or not to end it! But death comes and his life is just taken away from him. Here, Arjuna is in a dilemma as to which of the two is more beneficial for him. If we look into our entire life as a utility, then we are creating our own hell. Understand, life *itself* is a benefit. There are people who have achieved all that they wanted in life but still feel a deep void in them. This is what I call 'depression of success'. They feel something is lacking and are unable to comprehend what it could possibly be.

This is because they ran the race of life without any self-inquiry. So when they stop running or when suddenly they can't run anymore, they fall back into themselves and find that they are out of sync with their own being. This is what becomes depression or disease. So if you constantly look for some benefit from life, if you don't achieve it, you will feel life is a failure, and if you achieve it, you are bound to face the depression of success. Either way it is trouble.

Life itself is a benefit. If we constantly try to see which of two things is *more* beneficial, it means we have a pure business mind. Our whole life cannot be managed as a business. At some point we need to relax from the business mind. I always tell people, 'For at least half an hour per day, do something that will not get you money - like some painting or writing.' When you start painting, don't think of a big gallery with your paintings! For at least thirty minutes, do some creative work without bothering about how to show off your artwork to people.

Even before starting to paint, we will think, 'My friend will come home. I will show this to him and explain how I developed this concept.' You will decide how to bore your friend with your plans. Now think a little about my plight. I visit so many houses in a year. In some of the houses, where I go, they start giving me a commentary on the whole house. They start from the entrance and say, '*Swamiji*, this photo is from this temple from this city and I bought it in 1962…' People just love talking about such things. Similarly, when you start writing a few poems, don't start thinking of a Pulitzer Prize or the Nobel Prize. No! Without thinking about any benefit, just do something just for the sake of doing it. You will see that during that half hour, you will fall into your very being!

You can also go to some place of worship and start cleaning it without any big expectations in return. Serve food for people without thinking of how to derive some benefit from it. Even while volunteering, we do it so that we can tell others about it. So at least for thirty minutes do something that will not give any external benefit to you. If you can just use thirty minutes from your life for this, you will start tasting the real essence of life. I promise that these thirty minutes will lead you to Kṛṣṇa consciousness. They will be the only useful time in your life.

There are many people who listen to these discourses so that they can repeat it to others. I am not saying don't do that. But allow it to sink into you first. When you stop looking for benefits, you will start tasting life. You will come alive. Life is not and cannot be a business. Here, Arjuna is stuck because he thinks that life is a business. See, Kṛṣṇa is so compassionate. Literally, inch by inch, He guides Arjuna. He uses at least one hundred verses to explain this one concept of *karma sanyāsa yoga*. He comes down to the plane of Arjuna and gradually transforms him by reiterating the same teachings in different ways.

The question concerning *karma* and *sanyās*, duty and renunciation, has existed from time immemorial, and each time it has been answered. Yet the question remains. Somebody asked me the other day, 'Why is the Gītā still relevant today, although it was uttered at least 5,000 years ago?' I said, 'Because we never learned.' History simply repeats itself because man has not learnt his lesson.

The unconscious process never comes to the conscious energy. Man as such is governed by the unconscious. He is not even aware of what he is after most of the time. That is why he goes on and on but never achieves. But by the time he gets what he wanted, he wants something else. So there is a constant restlessness and depression. By merely flooding awareness into this depression you can get out of it. If you just move through your depression with awareness, in the process you will become enlightened. But we are scared to confront our own selves and allow our unconsciousness to take over and rule us instead of boldly seeing it through.

Life is the greatest master; it continuously teaches us. But we never learn from it. We never mark the spot where we stopped our journey in this birth. At least if we mark the place in this life, saying, 'I covered this much distance. In the next birth I will continue from where I left last,' if we do that much, it is enough. When I say birth, I do not mean just the totality of our life. Each day and night is also a birth. We die and are reborn everyday!

Every day or every week, consciously decide, 'Let me learn one lesson today.' Tell yourself, 'I will allow one understanding to enter into my consciousness this week.' If you allow one understanding to enter into your consciousness every week, your life will become blissful.

If you decide every weekend, 'I have traveled this much distance. Let me stop here and mark it.' Next week, you refer back to where you had left and say, 'Yes, this week I will start from here.' If you do this much sincerely, your whole life will be transformed.

But the problem is that we always mark the wrong places.

A small story:

Two friends rented a boat and went fishing. One day, they managed to catch a hundred fish. One of them instructed his friend, 'Mark this place. Next time we will come straight here and directly start fishing here.'

The next time they were about to set out for fishing again. One of them asked the other, 'Did you mark that place?' The other replied, 'Yes, I put the cross mark in the boat.'

The first one said, 'What a fool you are! If we don't get the same boat, what will we do?'

We also mark, but on the boats, not in life. We never mark where we should in the bigger picture of our lives. These markings of desires and worldly goals continuously get washed away and new markings take their place. We forget that these markings are temporary and do not reflect the growth within. What truly matters is inner transformation. If we are aware of what we are doing and what our pitfalls are, we can learn from them. But again and again we end up making the same mistakes. The person who commits the same mistake on a larger scale becomes a typical leader. One who does it on a smaller scale is a follower. The leader hides the mistakes, whereas the follower justifies them. That is the difference between a leader and a follower.

Even if you allow a single lesson to penetrate and work on you, your whole life will be transformed. I always tell my *brahmacāris* and *brahmacārinis* (young unmarried boys and girls training on the path of *sanyās*) and our *ashramites* (other ashram residents) to do at least new mistakes every time! Honestly, we are not so intelligent or creative as to even commit new mistakes. Even if you merely decide not to do the same mistake once again, your whole life will be transformed. But we do only the same kind of mistakes because our mind works in the same recorded route. This route is an engraved memory. If we take up the life of either *karma* or *sanyās* based on a recorded memory, we will never achieve bliss.

Let us analyze these paths of *karma* and *sanyās*. *Karma* is normally done out of greed and desire and *sanyās* out of a fear of life. When you are not ready to take the risk, you renounce everything. That is the first reason for *sanyās*. When a person is bogged down by the responsibilities of life, he takes *sanyās* as an easy escape. In the name of renunciation, he covers the deep fears. Then we have people running after material wealth, in the name of *karma*. Both categories of people are not going to achieve the eternal bliss.

On the entire planet earth, only three types of human beings exist: One who has surrendered to greed, one who has surrendered to fear, and the one who has surrendered to the supreme intelligence. The person who has surrendered to greed is caught in the *mūlādhāra cakra* (root energy center at the base of the spine). He literally becomes a slave to greed.

Understand and surrender

There is a beautiful *Upaniṣad* story:

There are two birds on the same tree. One bird, a fulfilled being, is sitting calmly, enjoying the silence. The other bird is sitting a little below, busily pecking at the fruit. It keeps flitting from place to place trying the fruit. It enjoys when the fruit is tasty and suffers when it is not. It continuously oscillates between enjoyment and suffering. Suddenly, this bird looks up and sees the bird that is sitting silently and thinks, 'How is this bird so calm and beautiful? Let me go and talk to him.' Slowly the small bird moves towards the peaceful bird.

As it goes nearer to the other bird, the small bird continues to taste more fruit and suffer. Suddenly, when the small bird is close enough to the other bird, it realizes that the other bird is nothing but its own self, which is silently watching the small bird getting distracted and suffering with sour fruit! The small bird simply becomes one with the other bird.

In the same way, as long as you are a *jīvātman,* an ordinary soul, you struggle between fear and greed. The moment you realize that there is something untouched by fear or greed inside your being, you start traveling towards it. When you get nearer and nearer to it, you realize that you are that *consciousness*. Here, Kṛṣṇa explains the same thing: We are caught between fear and greed. Either we surrender to fear or to greed.

Arjuna asks here, 'Which is more beneficial for me?' Keeping track of accounts is good in business but not in life. In life, accountants will be the worst failures. They can't live because they will be continuously calculating.

Some people come and ask me, 'Why should I surrender to the Divine? If I surrender, what will I get?'

Understand that if you don't surrender to the Divine, you will be surrendering to your fear or greed. I am not asking you to surrender to the Divine just to get something out of it.

An accountant can never be happy. If at all he is happy, he won't be an accountant; he must be simply an intelligent person!

A small story:

A man wants to employ an accountant. He interviews a candidate for the post and asks him, 'Can you do double entry?' The accountant says, 'I can do even triple entry, sir.' The man asks, 'Triple entry. What is that?'

The accountant says, 'The first entry consists of the original accounts showing the actual income. This is for the person who has put more money in the company. The second entry is for showing a small profit for the person who doesn't come to the company regularly.'

He continued, 'The third entry is for showing loss for income tax purposes. So I can do triple entry!'

Triple entries may be good for business, but when it comes to life, it doesn't work out. Life is beyond calculation.

The moment we ask, 'What will I get by surrendering to the Divine?' we miss the whole idea of surrender.

Venkaṭeśvara (an Indian deity) holds the *cakra* (discus) in one hand. It represents fear. In the other hand, He has the *śankha* (conch), which represents success. The conch is blown when you achieve success. This represents greed because man is constantly seeking success in everything and is never satisfied.

If you don't surrender to Venkaṭeśvara's *pāda* (feet) and His *pāduka*, His sandals, you will surrender to His conch and discus. You will surrender to fear or greed if you don't surrender to His energy. Those who constantly approach God for fulfillment of their desires or for refuge for their problems are surrendering to greed and fear. Only very few surrender to the feet of Venkaṭeśvara, which is the ultimate surrender.

Our whole life is spent running behind greed or fear. The path of *karma yoga,* seeking liberation through action, happens because of greed. The path of *sanyāsa yoga,* seeking liberation through renunciation, happens because of fear. Neither the path of *karma* nor the path of *sanyās* will help unless we change our very attitude. Don't bother about whether you are a *karma yogi* or a *sanyās yogi.* The attitude with which we approach life is what is important.

Repeatedly, Kṛṣṇa is focusing on the attitude, the being. If we don't know the root cause of our actions, why we are living with *karma* or why we pick up *sanyās,* we will not be able to solve our problems.

A small story:

A person goes to a bar, drinks too much and collapses. The bartender comes and kicks him in the back to wake him up. The next day, the same story repeats. The same person comes, drinks, and again falls down. Again the bartender comes and kicks him in the back to wake him up. On the third day, again this same person comes and says, 'Just give me soda. I don't want anything else.' The bartender asks, 'Why?'

The guy replies, 'I've realized that drinking gives me back pain.'

Be very clear, when we don't know why we are having a problem, we can never solve it! Our suffering is only because of our wrong attitude. And I tell you, with this wrong attitude, any path will only feel like a punishment. With the right attitude, any path will feel like a true blessing.

If you decide to enter into *karma,* just enjoy doing the *karma* and drop the goal. Realize that life itself is beautiful. On the other hand, if you decide to take up *sanyās,* then drop the goal of *sanyās,* which is renunciation. The *karma yogi* runs towards the goal, the *sanyāsi* runs away from the goal.

Kṛṣṇa says, *sāṅkhya yogou prithagbālaḥ pravadanti na panditaḥ.* Indirectly He tells Arjuna that he is still ignorant. Only the ignorant man says that *karma yoga* is different from *sāṅkhya,* the *sanyās.* Here, *karma* and *sanyās* are equated to *karma yoga* and *sāṅkhya yoga.*

The experienced say that both *karma* and *sanyās* lead to the same truth. If we drop the greed in *karma yoga* and the fear in *sanyās*, we will drop into the eternal consciousness. Through both, when we have the right attitude, we will achieve what we are supposed to achieve.

Kṛṣṇa says here, 'Only the ignorant person says that one is superior to the other. Both the paths are one and the same.' A person who is courageous enough, takes the life of *sanyās*. A person who wants to share his life takes the life of *karma*. It is up to us. What is important is having the right reason and the right intent. It is our being and not the 'doing' that is important. The man who is doing just for the benefit of having will never be able to enjoy life because even when he is having, he will be doing.

The man who is established in his being will enjoy both doing and having at the same time. Just by being, he will enjoy both doing and having. All we need to do is a simple technique. Let all our mental thoughts and physical deeds be directed towards gratitude to the Divine. Don't work out of fear or greed, because with whatever we achieve out of greed, we are not going to be fulfilled. It is like pouring ghee (clarified butter) into the fire. It will only create more desires and make our senses weak and tired.

In the same way, our laziness born out of fear will only make our mind restless. We may do things physically, but our mind will continue to worry. If we become a *karma yogi* out of greed, our senses will be weakened. If we become a *sanyāsi* out of fear, the whole day we will be worrying.

A simple truth:

When a man doesn't have money, the problem is money. When he has money, the problem is sex. When he has sex, the problem is comforts. When he has comforts, when everything goes well, he starts worrying about death. Something or the other will always be going on in his mind.

Don't think that all the people sitting in the Himālayas who have become *sanyāsi* are in bliss. No! Unless they change their attitude, they cannot experience bliss. Bliss is directly related to our attitude. Our whole life will be in doing and having if we are caught in fear and greed. If we surrender ourselves to the being, doing and having both will happen to us with tremendous ecstasy.

Never work out of greed because whatever we achieve is going to be taken away at the time of death. Never become silent out of fear because there is nothing really to lose. Whether we are afraid or not, everything is going to be taken away at the time of death. So in either case, why not just be blissful?

This is a beautiful story:

One man went to Rāmakṛṣṇa Paramahamsa and asked for money as a blessing. Rāmakṛṣṇa usually never blessed anyone for money. This man went to Rāmakṛṣṇa and asked, 'Master, please bless me that I should have wealth.' Finally, Rāmakṛṣṇa blessed him.

This man used to collect paper from the roads and from the houses. He used to make his money and living by selling it. The way Rāmakṛṣṇa blessed him, something drastic happened in his life. Within ten years, he became the owner of a very big newspaper called Ānanda bazār patrikā. If you are from Calcutta, you will know about this newspaper. The founder of Ānanda bazār patrikā is a disciple of Rāmakṛṣṇa. Rāmakṛṣṇa just blessed him, 'You will have wealth.' Even today, this newspaper is in circulation.

He didn't have children. At the end of his life, he said, 'Oh God! Now I realize my mistake! I asked for wealth from my master. Throughout my life, I worked like a donkey. I created the whole thing and I will now be leaving it and going away. I worked and worked for somebody else to enjoy this wealth now.'

So, if we work out of greed, surely we will repent some day.

Why do you think parents are so possessive of their children? Parents have some vengeance inside. They think, 'I worked and created this wealth for my child. So he must obey my words.' The possessiveness comes because you have suffered and created the wealth. If the wealth is created without suffering, it will be graceful when we give it. We will not bind or torture the recipient in any way. We will write our will clearly, in an open way.

Why do you think people always write their will secretly? It is so that they can dangle the carrot so that the son or daughter is continuously behind them until they die and the will is read.

People come and ask me, '*Swamiji*, I hear that the parents' *karma* will come to the children. Is it true?' The sins or the merits of the parents will not come to you. But their mental setup will influence you. This is because they will try to force their mental setup on you. They will expect you to live the way they want you to.

We always try to fulfill our ambitions through our kids. If we want to become a doctor and if do not succeed, we try to fulfill our ambition through our kids. If we do that, we will destroy their life. We will be sharing not only our wealth but our suffering also.

If the person is not able to torture the son or daughter who has received his wealth, he will start suffering himself. He will suffer thinking, 'I am leaving all these things, placing trust upon my son. I don't know what will happen.' When he dies, he will have the worst death. He will be like a yakṣa. He will come back and sit on that property. He will not let even his son enjoy that property.

I have seen many litigation cases where the parents give their wealth to their kids. But even after thirty or forty years, the kids will not be able to enjoy that wealth. It means the property is guarded by a yakṣa. Neither will the man enjoy it nor will he allow others to enjoy it. And God knows when the high court will pass the judgment.

If the wealth is created out of a pain-body, you will transfer the pain body also to the next generation along with the wealth. It should be created out of a relaxed mood, or without any strong motivation.

One important thing: Working without motivation is completely unheard of today. All psychologists, psychiatrists and scientists emphasize that we cannot work without motivation. That is why there are so many motivational gurus today. These people have come to the conclusion that 'work without motivation is not possible,' after analysis on diseased patients, but not on enlightened beings. They never encountered an enlightened person. That is why they say that work without motivation is impossible.

I tell you, work without motivation is the only real work. It will never make us tired! Every moment we will be ecstatic. Further, Kṛṣṇa gives a meditation technique in this chapter. Until the fifth chapter, He was giving only intellectual advice, śāstra. Kṛṣṇa now thinks that Arjuna has become mature or realizes that without some technique, it is impossible to relate with Arjuna. Kṛṣṇa realizes, 'If I don't give him a technique, I cannot escape from him!' Masters give meditation techniques in two situations. The first is when they see the person is mature enough. The other is when the person is constantly questioning them without transforming.

So I don't know whether Kṛṣṇa thought that Arjuna had become mature or He thought, 'Let him at least sit quietly for a few minutes with closed eyes!'

Devotion Above Action

5.5 He who knows, knows that the state reached by
renunciation and action are one and the same.
The state reached by renunciation can also be achieved by
action. Know them to be at the same level and see them as
they are.

5.6 Renunciation without devotion afflicts one with misery,
Oh mighty-armed one.
The wise person engaged in devotion attains the Supreme
without delay.

5.7 The person engaged in devotion, beyond concepts pure
and impure, self-controlled, and who has conquered the
senses is compassionate and loves everyone.
Although engaged in work, he is never entangled.

5.8, 5.9 One who knows the truth, though engaged in seeing,
hearing, touching, smelling, eating, going, dreaming,
and breathing knows that he never does anything.
While talking, evacuating, receiving, opening, closing, he
considers that the senses are engaged in gratification.

---

yat sāṁkhyaiḥ prāpyate sthānaṁ tad yogair api gamyate I
ekaṁ sāṁkhyaṁ ca yogaṁ ca yaḥ paśyati sa paśyati II 5.5

One who knows that the state reached through *sāṅkhya yoga* and *karma yoga* are one and the same and that the position reached by *sāṅkhya yoga* can also be achieved by *karma yoga*. He sees both of them on the same level and sees things as they are.

Beautiful verse!

All of us are not always *karma yogi* sor always *sanyāsi*s. When a *sanyāsi* surrenders himself to greed, he is a doer. And when a *karma yogi* surrenders to fear, he is a *sanyāsi*. So whenever we make an optimistic decision, we are a *karma yogi*. Whenever we make a pessimistic decision, we are *sanyāsi*.

Who is an optimist and who is a pessimist? An optimist is a man who created the airplane. A pessimist is a man who created the seat-belt. In life you play both roles. Here, both can lead to the same goal if the attitude is pure. But understand: anything created out of greed will create more greed. Anything created out of fear will create more fear.

Whenever our body is moved by a particular emotion, that emotion gets settled inside our system. It will be created again and again in our system. Jiḍḍu Kṛṣṇamūrti, an enlightened master from India, made a wonderful statement about emotions. He said, 'If you can, try to remain centered without moving your body when a particular emotion rises in you, without co-operating with it. Within eleven times, or I can say within eleven emotional upsets, if you have managed to be this way, you will be liberated from that emotion.'

For example, if you are caught in lust or fear, then just eleven times, whenever that emotion arises, don't allow your body to co-operate. Don't allow your body to flow with that emotion. Within eleven times, you will be liberated from that emotion.

You may think, 'What is this, *Swamiji*? Just eleven times! Is it so easy?' Yes. It is easy. All great things are easy. Only we complicate them because we don't believe in anything that is easy.

A small story:

A person goes to the doctor and asks, 'Doctor, how much will you charge to pull this tooth out?' The doctor says, 'Ninety dollars.' This person asks, 'Ninety dollars just for a two minute job?'

The doctor says, 'I can do it more slowly if you like!'

We don't believe in simple things. We want to complicate things. Actually, I think with all the 'factor-of-safety' ideas, Kṛṣṇamūrti said to do this technique eleven times. He might have been afraid of lawsuits! If somebody practices fewer times and they don't get the result, they may sue him! Maybe that is why he says eleven times.

But honestly, eleven times is too much. When that emotion rises in you, just don't cooperate. Let your body not go behind that emotion whether it is anger or irritation or depression or lust or fear or anything. Within three or four times, you will be liberated from that emotion. You will have the key now in your hand: how not to be taken away by that emotion, how to be centered in your Self. Whether it is anger or fear or greed, it gets more power if your body also cooperates with it. With whatever emotion your body moves, that emotion gets recorded inside your system. And that emotion will become much more intense.

There is a beautiful movie, *'What the Bleep Do We Know?'* In that movie, they beautifully show the idea that I have just conveyed to you. Don't think I have some contract with the moviemakers to promote it! No! Once, two of our devotees invited me for a show in New York. I said that I would come if it would finish in fifteen minutes. They said that no show would finish in less than three hours. I said, 'Then it is not for me.' Fifteen minutes is the maximum time I can watch any show. So I didn't watch that. But somehow I watched this movie *'What the Bleep Do We Know?'*

I am surprised at how these people sit for hours together in front of the television. And they will continuously eat something while watching. The snack box will be full before the program starts. When the program is over, that box will be empty and the stomach will be full. This is such a dangerous habit. It will lead to obesity.

Rāmānujācārya, the Indian philosopher says beautifully, when it comes to '*āhāra-śuddhi*', 'purity of food', when you eat something, you digest not only the food but also the thoughts that you have while you are eating. So your eating should be done like worship. Never ever eat watching the television or reading the newspaper. We already have enough of *tamas* -

laziness - in our system. With this habit, the laziness energy will be significantly enhanced.

Never eat with negative thoughts. And those of you who cook or serve the food, please don't complain at that time. In India, usually only at the time of serving, the wife will start complaining about everything. Never complain when you serve or when you cook because the thoughts will also enter the food and will settle down into your system.

I can never watch anything for more than fifteen minutes. Somehow, I watched this movie, 'What the Bleep Do We Know?' I will explain a concept from that movie. It is actually a truth from *Vedānta*. They say that whenever some emotions happen within your system, it is like a shower of rain that happens in your being. There are particular cells that catch these emotions. For example, if you are angry, there are particular cells that catch that anger emotion and start reproducing themselves as well. Each cell will create at least four or five more cells that can catch this emotion.

An important truth is that the basic quality of life is reproduction and expansion. This is the survival instinct governed by the *svādiṣṭhāna cakra,* the fear energy center within our body. Reproduction is governed by the *mūlādhāra cakra,* the sex energy center in our body. The two are closely associated.

The cells that catch the anger emotion start reproducing and each cell creates five or six more cells. Next time, when the anger shower happens, all these new cells will catch the same emotion and become the size of the original cells. Now, they will also start reproducing. The third time, when the shower happens, all these cells catch the emotion and start storing it. That is why, every time when we are showered with the same emotion, it becomes stronger and stronger and we are not be able to control that emotion.

The first time anger is showered on us, if we are affected for ten minutes; then the next time it will become twenty minutes. The third time, it will become half an hour. This is how the emotion becomes stronger and stronger. When we cooperate with these negative emotions in our being we create the same type of mood in us. Not only will the emotion get recorded in us, we will express the same thing on others also.

Go beyond greed and fear

If we are working to strengthen our greed, we will radiate the emotion of greed. If we strengthen our fear, we express fear and torture others with it. Warriors are caught in fear. That is why they torture others. Actually they are the most cowardly people. A real warrior is one who has conquered his being.

Now, take a few minutes to sit and analyze, 'Throughout this life, I was driven by greed and fear. What have I achieved? Where do I stand?' Consciously think and allow this idea to work on you. Decide, 'From today, I will not do anything out of greed or fear.' Immediately the fear will rise in you, 'What will happen to my bills and my house? Who will repay the mortgages? Who will feed my kids?'

Understand, you have enough energy to maintain yourself without fear and greed. You need to trust that you don't need fear or greed to run your life. You have enough potential energy to live and achieve what you want.

Mahāvīra, another great enlightened Jain master from India, says, 'When you come to planet earth, you bring enough energy to fulfill all your desires.' You already have enough fuel. You always think, 'If I stop fueling myself with fear or greed, I may stop working.' No. There is enough reserve of fuel in you. But psychologists can never believe that unmotivated action is possible because they have never seen a Buddha.

Repeatedly, the psychologists come to a conclusion, 'Only with motivation can a man work.' What motivation have birds got to sing? But modern day psychologists are so focused on sex that even for *that*, they give a meaning! They say that the bird is calling for its partner. They can't see anything as it is.

That is why here, Kṛṣṇa says:

yaḥ paśyati sa paśyati

One who is beyond the pull of fear and greed is the only one who can see things as they are. If you are caught in fear or greed, you will see things only as *you* want to see them, not as they are.

For example, on seeing a beautiful, tall building, a man who is caught in greed will think, 'If I have at least one building like this, how nice it will be!' The man caught in fear will think, 'I should not see these things. They stress me out. I should stay only in the forest.' But only a person who is liberated from these two emotions will see it as it is.

yaḥ paśyati sa paśyati

He will see what IS.

Analyse: 'Throughout my life, I was pushed and pulled by greed and fear. Do I want to continue that?' As Mahāvīra says beautifully, 'You don't need energy from greed or fear.' For someone conditioned by society, it will be very difficult to believe this truth.

I know you are all sitting here out of politeness, thinking, 'He is speaking. Let us listen. What can be done?' Just because you are sitting, it is not that you trust my words. I know that. In your whole past, whatever your age may be, you lived fueled only by fear and greed. Now just give ten days for Mahāvīra. Decide that for the next ten days you will trust Mahāvīra's words - You don't need fuel from fear or greed because when the Divine sent you to earth, He sent you with whatever you will need.'

In India, when the daughter gets married, they send a whole set of household items, from a broomstick to a car. And they give a dowry too. I don't know when India will come out of this dowry system. If any of you have taken dowry and if you want a spiritual life, then the first thing you need to do is return the dowry to your in-laws house or give it to your wife.

If you keep that dowry in your house, *Lakṣmī,* the goddess of riches, will never fill your house with Her full blessing. See, there are two things.

Lakṣmī has two manifestations - the outer comfort and the inner bliss. The man with the dowry in his house will never have the inner *Lakṣmī*. He may think he has the outer *Lakṣmī*. What is the difference between the poor man and the rich man? The poor man sits on the ground and worries while the rich man sits on the sofa and worries.

Just as a daughter is sent with everything to the in-laws' house, in the same way the Divine sends you to this planet with everything you will need. In Vedānta this is called *prārabdha karma*. When you come down you bring enough of energy for your senses and body to acquire whatever it needs to live blissfully. The only problem is you don't trust that you have brought everything. And after coming down, you accumulate more desires from others.

If you are born with ten desires, you get enough energy to fulfill those desires. But after coming down, you collect more desires and start working to fulfill those desires as well. Work out only your desires, not the desires or standards of others.

Decide clearly, 'Let me not be fueled by fear or greed.' Just ten days for this idea is enough. Decide that you will work only out of your joy and bliss. It will transform your life. Anyway, I am going to be here even after ten days. If it does not work out, come and catch me! Just living ten days out of joy and bliss rather than fear and greed will transform your whole life and liberate you from all bondage.

When you practice this, for the first few days you will feel a little unsettled. Say 'No' to any desire or fear that comes up. Initially, you will feel some emptiness but don't worry. In a few days you will settle well with the emptiness, the new system. That emptiness is what Buddha calls *śūṇya* or *nirvāṇa*.

Just for ten days decide, 'I will work only out of joy and not let fear or greed enter my mind.' Don't worry when you fail a few times. Starting this way is much better than staying in fear of failure. So start! You will soon know the trick of the trade. If you never start, you will not even know where you are a failure. Honestly, this will transform your whole life. Don't be bothered about the initial feeling of emptiness. If one of the people with whom we are living dies, we will always feel that we are missing something, because we don't have anybody to nag us. But it will settle in a few days.

So for the next ten days when you practice this, you will initially feel that you are missing something, because we are used to fear and desire continuously nagging you. But don't worry. You will soon settle into that new consciousness and become a new personality. It is important you trust that you have enough energy to run without fear and greed. Only when you are a child, you need fear or greed to make you work. Now, you are all grown-up. If you still need fear or greed, then you have grown only physically and not mentally.

One more thing: in just ten days, you will not lose your wealth. If you think that you will lose your wealth by practicing this for ten days, then that wealth is not worth having. The earlier it is lost, the better it is for your being. Just remove the tremendous stress and load from your inner space. Decide, 'For ten days, I will do all my action out of deep bliss, out of a settled mood.'

If you practice this, the constant irritation that remains in you without your knowledge will disappear. Knowingly or unknowingly, you carry constant irritation in you that is just waiting to burst, to explode. For any small thing, you simply explode. You shout, 'Don't you have sense? Why are you doing that?' Look into yourself: how many of you can honestly understand and agree that you carry that constant irritation in you? Raise your hand. *(A few raise)* Others are not honest! Don't think you are not carrying it. Everyone carries it. This irritation we carry in our inner space is because of fear and greed.

Let you be liberated from this uneasiness today. That uneasiness is what I call *dis*-ease, that *dis*-easiness between you and your being. We carry this dis-ease because we are putting the wrong fuel in our engine. If the wrong fuel is added into our engine, a different type of sound and smoke will be emitted!

A small story:

A husband and wife were traveling by car. They stopped at a signal. Suddenly, next to them they saw a Mercedes Benz. The husband said, 'Last night, I dreamt that I was driving a beautiful Mercedes Benz car.' The wife said, 'Yes, yes, I heard the engine sound!'

Sound sleep: Sleep for them and sound for others!

If we are carrying constant irritation in us, then the fuel is not pure. So decide that just for ten days, you will not put the fuel of fear and greed in your vehicle. You will suddenly feel a new enthusiasm, a causeless auspicious energy. This causeless auspicious energy is called Śiva in Sanskrit. It is possible to live with reasonless, unmotivated energy. Only two things are needed: First, the trust that you have that energy. Second, actually start living it. Only these two things are needed to reach divine consciousness. When we work with the causeless auspicious energy, we are Śiva, else we are śava (dead body).

Here, Kṛṣṇa does not refer to renunciation the way we traditionally understand it. Normally we think renunciation is giving up everything, especially responsibility. When we use 'renounce' we exclude something. When we try to renounce the world, we are renouncing the creation of Existence. Actually, we see what is creating trouble and decide to renounce it. It is our attitude of fear and greed that causes all the trouble. The mental setup needs to change. Running away from material pleasures due to fear of facing reality cannot be called renunciation.

Just sit down for five minutes and see how you perceive situations in those five minutes. With awareness, look at everything that you think and do. When you come to an understanding of your own self you are able to live as a witness to everything that goes on in and around you, unaffected by situations and people.

If we do things fuelled by greed and fear, we are hypocrites. Even renunciation will be a farce. It will lead to misery. Just decide not be fuelled by greed or fear. Simply live with reality, the present. When we are ecstatic unto ourselves, we live completely in the moment, totally involved in what we are doing. Then we become the action itself. We no longer exist as the doer. That is when we have truly renounced, renounced the sense of 'I am doing', the ego. Then we are true *sanyāsi*s.

But we don't want to renounce the mind that creates fantasies and gets us worked up. All we need is to experience that behind the shallow emotions in the periphery, at the very core of our being, is a solid, silent center, absolutely unaffected by external incidents. It is a pure witness to everything that goes on and is eternally pure.

You see, renunciation is going beyond all desires, including desirelessness, not just material desires. The desire to attain God is also a desire. The moment we say, 'I want to achieve liberation,' we are holding onto that desire. It is still a desire; something that the mind hankers after, something in the future and not in the present.

When we desire something, we are working in the plane of the mind. It is only when we drop all desires that we are completely in the present, beyond the clutches of the mind. Only then we see reality as it is. Otherwise, we always live in the world of our illusions, *māyā*, because the future is unreal; it is an illusion.

The present can never be comprehended by the mind because it is way beyond logic. The mind can only philosophize. It cannot experience. And the truth or God or Divinity can only be experienced. It is beyond the small purview of the mind.

Vivekānanda said that, to him, Rāmakṛṣṇa was greater than God Himself. God was just a concept in Vivekānanda's head. Rāmakṛṣṇa, his guru, was a living master who gave Vivekānanda the experience of God. The guru is therefore even greater than God Himself because he is the bridge for man to experience God.

All our desires can be based only on what we know or what we imagine based on what we know. How can we desire God or enlightenment, which we never knew? We can always desire enlightenment in a way that fits our limited understanding, but that is still our imagination.

Experience your true nature

We can never possess enlightenment. Only enlightenment can possess us. It happens when we drop all desires. Actually, it is our true nature beyond purity and impurity. Whether we accept it or not, believe it or not, we are bliss. Our true nature itself is self-control. When we realize and experience that our being is pure bliss, the other emotions automatically drop.

When we allow ourselves to be our true nature, to be bliss, we live spontaneously and respond with intelligence instead programmed unconscious reactions. Then there is no need of controlling the senses. They will be under the control of the Ultimate.

In the Mahābhārata war, Kṛṣṇa drives Arjuna's chariot. The horses represent the senses held in control by the divine charioteer. He drives the being, represented by the warrior, in the body represented by the chariot, towards victory, towards bliss. When the individual consciousness surrenders to the Divine, the Divine controls the body-mind-spirit and steers one towards one's true nature, bliss.

Society teaches us from a very young age what is right and what is wrong. So, we have programmed reactions to everything. We see a situation and react in the manner we have been taught. We only react, not respond. We react by looking up our database of the past, referring to the reaction of people then. If what we did was appreciated, we will react in the same fashion. If it was not appreciated, then we will now react in a manner acceptable to others. This is what happens all the time.

We have forgotten what it is to respond with intelligence. No situation can be exactly the same as before. Can a river flow in exactly the same way at two different points? No! Life is like a river, continuously changing. Existence is energy. Every moment is unique.

We see it from the limited perception of our mind and organize life into different categories. We say, 'These are pleasant situations, those are unpleasant situations, this is good, that is bad.' It is not Existence that makes these distinctions but us. If we allow this understanding to penetrate we, we can simply relax. We will then allow our consciousness to respond.

Have the courage to live life with intelligence, with consciousness and awareness. Just this small change in attitude can do wonders for you! When the intelligence happens, the compassion also descends. Compassion for the whole world automatically happens because you see yourself in every one. That is why masters can feel only compassion and responsibility towards the whole world.

When we flow in tune with Existence, we become a channel for the divine energy to flow through us. If the bamboo can remain hollow, it will become a beautiful flute. The air from the lips of the Divine will come out of the flute as heavenly music. Instead, if the bamboo is blocked with the dirt of ego, it will be used only for carrying a dead body! These verses of Kṛṣṇa are very powerful, but often misinterpreted.

Many people use them conveniently to justify their actions. It is like you commit a murder and then claim you didn't do it, but your hands did it! Be very clear: Not being the doer does not mean we totally give up responsibility for our actions. It means that we are so involved in the action, and we do it out of the blissful energy in us. You must have noticed, when certain people act in a seemingly disrespectful manner, they still don't come across as disrespectful. The energy behind the action is what decides the effect and the perception of the action.

Even in our ashram, I sometimes reprimand my ashramites. But not a single person has left the ashram because he or she was fired! When masters scold, the energy behind the firing is only of compassion. It carries tremendous power of transformation. It will simply rid us of the blocks and tumors in our system, and we can simply flower.

When we are complete and total in what we do, our whole intelligence, our whole energy will be behind the act. When we are truly involved in any action, we become the action. The action and we are no longer separate. On the other hand, if we do something without being fully involved, our energy is not completely behind the action. Energy is intelligence. So, when our energy is not total, be very clear, our intelligence is not completely behind the action.

When the energy behind the action is total, we will always propagate the blissful energy in our action. That is why even watching the breath technique given by Buddha can be so powerful. But even a seemingly big action of moral good does not have the desired energy and effect.

Another very important thing: Every moment, every action should be done with awareness. That is true meditation. Many people claim that they have been meditating for thirty or forty years. Actually they have only been sitting with closed eyes, doing some breath control. That is why even after many years of meditation, the person inside remains exactly the same.

Meditation is actually a quality that needs to be added to our life. It should permeate the attitude with which we perceive everything. When we infuse awareness into every action, we are in meditation. We can be aware only when we can distance ourselves from what is happening. The moment we get involved, we can no longer be the witness. Then we can never see things as they are. It is just like this - when we are in the dream, we don't realize it is a dream. We think it is reality. But the moment we wake up, we realize that it was just a dream.

The way we are living life now is exactly the same. We live in the dream of future and past. The present is the actual reality. When we realize this, we simply wake up to the true reality from the dream of illusion. Then, we understand that we are something beyond the senses, mind and body. With this awareness we become blissful.

Controlling the Mind

5.10 *He who acts without attachment, giving up and surrendering to the eternal consciousness,*
He is never affected by sin, in the same way that the lotus leaf is not affected by water.

5.11 *The yogis, giving up attachment, act with the body, mind, and intelligence,*
Even with the senses for the purpose of self-purification.

5.12 *One who is engaged in devotion, gives up attachment to the outcome of one's actions and is centered, he is at peace.*
One who is not engaged in devotion, and is attached to the outcome of one's action, becomes entangled.

5.13 *One who is controlled, giving up all the activities of the mind, surely remains in happiness in the city of nine gates (body),*
Neither doing anything, nor causing anything to be done.

Time and again Kṛṣṇa talks about detachment. This is the whole crux of the Gītā. This detachment is renunciation. You can give up all material possessions and move into a forest, but if the mind still hankers for those possessions, then renunciation has not happened. One can be very much in the material world, busy with wheeling and dealing, and yet be totally detached about the outcome. Action without attachment is renunciation. It is only this renunciation that leads to liberation.

If you see the lotus flower, it grows in a dirty pond. The flower is so beautiful, that when someone looks at it, the dirt around it is hardly noticed! Similarly, when you can be neck-deep in the activities of the world and yet be unaffected by what goes on, then you have reached the goal of renunciation.

A beautiful story about Svāmi Brahmānanda, a direct disciple of Sri Rāmakṛṣṇa Paramahamsa:

One day Svāmi Brahmānanda was meditating in Brindāvan. A devotee came and placed a costly blanket before him as an offering. Svāmi Brahmānanda said nothing. He just silently observed what was going on.

A couple of hours later, a thief came by, spotted the blanket, came up to him and took away the blanket. Still, the Swami watched in the same way, silently, with no reaction.

Some of the junior disciples were very perturbed that a costly blanket given to him by a devotee had been stolen. However, it made no difference to Brahmananda.

He was so centered in himself that the outer world incidents did not affect his core in any way. When we can become like this, we will not get caught in the sway of emotions.

The basic truth behind imbibing this sense of centeredness is really this: Existence is a loving mother, providing all that we need. When this understanding happens, we surrender to Existence. The wave drops into the ocean, blissfully aware that it is a part of the ocean. This surrender needs to happen out of a deep understanding and not as a compromise. There is no point in blaming destiny. We have a free will. We have to accept the flow of life with the true understanding that we are being taken care of.

One more thing you must know is that to whom or to what we surrender is not important. What is important is the surrender itself.

Swami Vivekānanda says that all our prayers to God do only one thing: they awaken our own inner potential energy. When we pray intensely, our own inner potential energy is awakened and it showers its blessings on us in the form that we believe as God. Having the understanding that Existence cares for us and surrendering to it is the ultimate intelligence. It is the key to a life of bliss.

Witness and transform

Repeatedly, Kṛṣṇa emphasizes that life happens only when we live as a witness to everything that happens around us. We should not let outer incidents affect our inner space. When we live this way, all our troubles simply disappear.

Of course, the way in which we live automatically creates a transformation in others too. We then attract incidents that fall in tune with our desires and thoughts. When we are blissful inside, whatever happens outside will also be blissful. This is because what we project outside is what is inside us. It has been scientifically proven that the results of experiments conducted by different researchers under identical conditions vary depending on the mood of the scientists. In a study of elementary particles such as quarks, scientists were amazed that the behavior of these particles varied with different observers. What we see is our reality. If we see without wishing to change anything, we are in tune with reality.

Even the same situation will be seen in a completely different way when we witness. Automatically, no emotion can sway us because we are no longer operating from the mind, analyzing and categorizing. Our state is in no way affected by what others say or do. Then, we are masters unto ourselves.

We are never totally involved in anything that we do. Do we completely enjoy the food when we eat? Most often we are worrying about something when we are eat. We are actually dumping food into our system without awareness. That is why we overeat. Be very clear, with intelligence just being aware of what we are putting into our system is enough to control what and how much we are eating.

The person who is aware, who is completely involved every moment feels hunger in every cell of the body when it happens. He lives it totally. When food is before him, he enjoys every morsel of the food completely. Every cell of his body feels satisfied. Just like having the sense of taste is very natural when we eat with awareness, so it is with all the senses.

A small story:

Once a man went to a Zen master and asked him, 'Master, please tell me what is meditation.'

The master replied, 'When I eat, I eat. When I sleep, I sleep.' The man was perplexed. He asked the master, 'Master, you are saying what *you* do. But, please tell me what meditation is.'

The master replied, 'This is meditation. If you can eat totally when you eat, if you can sleep totally when you sleep, you are in meditation.'

Just being totally involved in whatever we do is meditation. Enjoying the present moment is meditation. You must have experienced in your own life that when you are intensely involved in something, you go deep into it and forget yourself. When you have an intense headache, just try doing something interesting very deeply; your headache will go away.

Or you can even try another method where, like a witness, you intensely watch the energy flowing to the head to heal it. Just look at the energy flow with full curiosity like a complete outsider. Allow the energy flow to that area and work on it. You can use this technique to dissolve physical pain in any part of your body. Focus on that part with curiosity and without thinking about the pain. Initially the pain may seem to increase, but soon it will disappear.

When we go deeply into any emotion, we cease to exist. This is what we mean by 'totality.' This moment when 'you' disappears, you may experience for a just a few seconds in your current lifestyle. But if you work on being intense and total in everything, it will happen more often and for longer periods. Soon, you will master the art of doing work intensely, independent of what goes on outside.

Here, Kṛṣṇa gives us a technique to realize who we are. By giving up attachment to the sense objects and dropping all false identifications with the body, senses and mind, we can live life with intelligence, and this leads us to self-purification.

Kṛṣṇa tells us that our job is only to do the work, not to be concerned about the results.

We need to keep doing things because we have so much loving energy inside us. When we are like this, we are not bothered about the results. When I say we are not bothered about the results, I mean that we don't expect results because we are continuously moving and expressing our blissful inner energy. We are just flowing joyfully with real love.

When we identify ourselves with our body, mind, and ego, we alienate ourselves from the rest of Existence. Instead of playing our role in the divine drama as an actor, we start thinking that we *are* the character and actually go through all the emotional turmoil that we were just supposed to enact. We become entangled and miss the joy of the drama.

In the same way, when we just do what we have at hand without being bothered about the result, we are always happy. Once we start thinking about the result, we lose the joy of doing what we are doing at this moment. When we are established in ourselves, we are automatically in peace irrespective of anything that exists or does not exist around us.

> Once a man went to Ramaṇa Maharṣi, enlightened master form India, and said, 'Bhagavān, I want peace!'
>
> Ramaṇa replied, 'From your own statement, just remove the word 'I', remove the word 'want' and what remains is peace!'

All our want for peace is all a want. We don't know how to be satisfied as we are. Just think, how can we want something like peace that by its very nature has the absence of want as the criterion to be able to exist? When we want peace, we create desires in us. That desire drives us to do various things to get peace and we once again start to worry about the results of those actions. These worries take us away from peace and then again we want peace. This is a vicious circle. When we drop the idea of wanting peace, when we can just *be* and let Existence take care, peace automatically happens. Absence of want is the criterion to be peaceful.

Some people say that they want to be left in peace without worries. The peace they are talking about is a lifeless and dead peace. It is a peace that they crave because life is too much for them to handle. They haven't got solutions for how to handle life so they just want to escape.

Real peace is something that is in us all the time irrespective of what is going on outside. We are simply happy unto ourselves. Our peace is in no way related to or dependent on the people and situations around us. It is the bliss that we feel inside ourselves. When peace is born out of bliss, it keeps us as well as others in a peaceful state. When we are satisfied with ourselves, we do not depend on anything external to be peaceful.

Actually, with modern man, because of all the influences from media and the Internet, a cerebral layer has formed. He relates only with the fantasies collected from the media. He lives in an imaginary world and does not see what he really has. He is always dreaming. Even if the dream gets fulfilled, the moment it gets fulfilled, the mind will start running behind a new imagination. Only then it can survive.

We don't understand that tomorrow comes only as today. When the tomorrow comes as today, we simply miss it because we are now looking at tomorrow once again! But when we work without unnecessarily thinking about the result, all our energies will be used towards realizing the goal. The power of desire, *icchā śakti,* will be converted to the power of action, *kriya śakti.* The desire may initially be a goal, but what is important is the path and not the end result. The goal is merely a byproduct.

Suppose a child is playing with some small toy and you bring him a new big toy. If you take away the small toy from his hands, what will the child do? He will start yelling and crying. Even if you explain you have a much better, bigger toy, will he listen? No! Just give him the new toy and suddenly, it will forget the old one and start enjoying the new one.

In the same way, Existence also tries to give us a big toy - the whole of Itself! Enjoy it to the fullest. Your mind will always tell you that the small toy, your little dreams, is most important. Just for a few days, try to drop your fantasies and expectations. Just enjoy every moment and every thing that Existence has created. Start observing simple yet wonderful things like the sunrise in the morning or the chirping of the birds and so on. Just these few moments will show us what it is to enjoy life without a reason.

The city of nine gates

In these verses, Kṛṣṇa refers to the body, which has nine gates to the external world: the two eyes, two nostrils, two ears, mouth and the two organs of evacuation.

Here, Kṛṣṇa does not refer to not doing anything out of laziness and indulgence. Actually, if we become intensely lazy, we will be in meditation! This is a deep mental laziness where the mind has been stilled. It has stopped all activity, but the body moves according to the will of the Divine. We will be in the midst of intense activity and yet not doing anything.

The mind separates the doer from the action. In the conventional sense, when we say lazy, we refer to the body. The body is lazy but the mind is completely active creating and linking unrelated thoughts. When the mind becomes lazy, instead of the body, we drop the mind also. That is when we stop identifying the action as being separate from ourselves.

Kṛṣṇa is talking of being so completely involved in something that we become the action itself. First, we become the witness to the action; only then can we become completely involved in it. Then the doer and the action merge into each other. It is the conscious experience of the bliss within us through the action that actually gives us happiness and bliss.

A small story:

A dog found a piece of bone. It started chewing on the bone, but the piece was very dry. It chewed and chewed and after some time, its own gums started bleeding from rubbing against the dry, hard bone. The dog was very happy to finally taste blood.

It licked the bone even more, making more blood ooze from its own mouth. Little did the dog realize that the blood it was enjoying was its very own!

When we realize through experience or understanding that bliss is within us, we will get over our misconception that external pleasures give us joy. When we really understand that we are already all that we want to be, we have reached the ultimate goal. Until then it will be a struggle to achieve what we already are.

The enlightened boy sage from ancient India, Aṣṭāvakra, taught the enlightenment science to Janaka, the king of Mithilā and Sīta's father, saying: 'Righteousness and unrighteousness, pleasure and pain are purely of the mind and are no concern of ours. We are neither the doer nor the reaper of the consequences, so we are always free. We are the one witness of everything. The cause of our bondage is that we see the witness as something other than this.'

You see, when we leave the ownership to someone else, we are free. The burden is not ours. That is when we can be blissful. As long as we think we are the owners, we always have to face the worry that comes with ownership. Let the universe take care and you carry on with your work!

A beautiful story from the life of Buddha:

A disciple of Buddha was going to spread the message of Buddha. The monk was not enlightened though.

Buddha called and told him, 'I have to say this because you are not enlightened yet. You are clear, you speak well, and you can spread the message. You may not be able to sow the seeds but you may be able to attract a few people to come to me. But use this opportunity also for your own growth.'

The monk asked, 'How can I use this opportunity?'

Buddha said, 'There is only one thing that can be done in every opportunity and that is watchfulness. You will sometimes find people irritated by you because you have hurt their ideologies and prejudices. Just remain silent and watchful. You may have days when you cannot get food or even water because the people are against you. Watch your hunger and thirst. But do not get annoyed. What you will be teaching people is of less importance than your own watchfulness.

If you come back to me watchful, I will be immensely joyful. What ultimately matters is whether you yourself have found the solid basis of witnessing. The rest is all insignificant.'

Buddha clearly says to be watchful of all your actions. Only when we witness our actions as a third person, do we not associate any kind of emotion either to our action or to its result. Whatever goes on outside does not affect us because we do not associate any emotion to any of it.

Also, what is important is that we practice what we preach. Only that will lead to the true understanding. When we walk the talk we will automatically inspire others to follow. We will simply inspire people. The inspiration will be just a by-product while our own transformation will be the joyful end-result.

Cleansing Ignorance With Knowledge

5.14 The master does not create activities or make people do or connect with the outcome of the actions.
All this is enacted by the material nature.

5.15 The Lord, surely, neither accepts anyone's sins nor good deeds.
Living beings are confused by the ignorance that covers the knowledge.

5.16 Whose ignorance is destroyed by the knowledge?
Their knowledge, like the rising sun, throws light on the Supreme consciousness.

5.17 One whose intelligence, mind and faith are in the Supreme and one who has surrendered to the Supreme,
His misunderstandings are cleansed through knowledge and he goes towards liberation.

Here Kṛṣṇa says, 'I do not create activities or make people do or connect with the fruits of the actions. All this is done by the material nature of humans.'

Kṛṣṇa is talking about the creation of the universe itself. Nothing in this universe can be created or destroyed. When I say 'nothing,' I *mean* NOTHING. Everything that exists has always existed and will continue to exist in some form or other. Science also says the same thing that matter and energy are inter-convertible and energy can never be destroyed. The *Veda* has already said what science has now understood. The last line of science is the first line of the *Upaniṣads*.

The end or the beginning?

The Īśāvāsya Upaniṣad opens with, '*Īśā vāsyaṁ idaṁ sarvaṁ*', meaning, 'All that exists arises from energy'. Now, after much research, Quantum Physics has concluded that matter and energy are one and the same. But thousands of years ago this was the first statement in the Isavasya Upanishad, which says everything is energy.

People ask me, 'Who created this universe?' I tell you, the universe itself is the Creator, the created and the creation. Both the creation and the Creator are one and the same; they are both divine.

We consider what we see and wonder who created this universe that has a form. We believe that there has to be some stronger energy that created what we perceive as the universe. We fail to understand that every bit of matter is energy. So when everything is energy, there is no difference between the Creator and the creation. Both are divine. The difference is because of the way we perceive them. This is *līla,* the divine play. The un-manifest, formless energy made itself manifest in the creation. The universe created itself.

We cannot answer the question 'why,' for the answer lies in the realm of logic. If we get caught in the 'why', we will be stuck with it forever. Instead, explore the 'what'. Try to understand what we really are, what is this universe and when we get the answer to just that question of what we are, the question 'why' itself disappears.

Bhagavān Ramaṇa Maharṣi's meditation technique was to probe with, 'Who am I?' This is also the basis of Zen koans like 'imagine your form before your birth' or 'focus on the sound of one hand clapping.' These questions cannot be answered logically. Our mind cannot comprehend these things at all.

God created man in His own mould so that He could experience Divinity. You see, God as pure energy cannot see the Divinity outside of Himself. Everything exists as a part of Him. Can you say how you feel your hand from inside your body? No! On the other hand, can you describe how you feel when you touch your own hand with the other hand? You will have some feeling, do you not? You can feel it because from outside, your two hands are separate; you can perceive them as different parts of your body.

Similarly, God can experience and express Himself through man. Now, just like one hand in itself cannot understand that the hand it is touching is a part of the same body, similarly, man cannot understand that he is a part of God. What does it take for the hand to understand that the other hand is actually a part of the bigger whole called the body? It takes the understanding that the entire body is a single entity with the different parts of the body being integrated in it.

Similarly, it takes the understanding of our consciousness to see that we, the individual consciousness, are an integral part of the collective consciousness. The individual ego can never understand the truth that it exists as a part of the Whole. The ego has to dissolve for the truth to be understood.

If we want to see our own beauty, we can do that only when we see our own reflection in a mirror. The mirror in which God sees Himself is man. Man can experience and express the divine in him. The game of life is all about man is trying to realize the Divine in himself and the Divine trying to express itself through man.

What Kṛṣṇa teaches here is actually a technique. The Western master,Gurdjieff used this technique very often. He would create situations to master this technique of being unperturbed by external incidents. You would enter a room where a group of people would be sitting and something would be done to make you angry. It would be done so naturally that you would not realize the situation was being set up.

Others would join in to enhance the disturbance and right at the point where you are about to explode, Gurdjieff would shout, 'Remember, remain undisturbed!' The disturbance cannot disappear suddenly because it is a physiological happening. Your hormones have been released into your system; the body has been poisoned. Even though the anger cannot go away immediately, your awareness will dissipate the effect of the anger.

An ashram is a spiritual laboratory. Constantly, such situations will arise and you will go through the entire gamut of emotions in response to them. But when you go through these with awareness, you will have the tremendous, deep experiential realization of an undisturbed, silent core within you. Then the next time you are being swayed by emotions, you will remember this and become aware. Only when you are unconscious and ignorant you come under the sway of emotions.

A small story from the life of Buddha:

Buddha was passing by a village. The villagers were against the teachings of Buddha and a few of them insulted him. Buddha just listened and then said, 'I have to reach the next village. If you have finished with whatever you had to say to me, I can move. Or if you have something more to say, while returning, I can stop here. You can come and tell me.'

The villagers were surprised. They could not understand why Buddha did not react in an angry or defensive manner. They said, 'But we have been shouting and insulting you!'

Buddha said, 'You can do that. But if you are looking for any reaction from me, you have come too late. Ten years before, if you had come with these words, I would have reacted. But now I have become a master of myself. You cannot force me to do anything.'

This is what is meant by 'being centered'. You are no longer a slave to your emotions, or to others. Otherwise, anybody can shake you. You won't be integrated and whole.

Kṛṣṇa separates morality from spirituality in these verses. I tell you, heaven and hell are purely psychological. They exist only in our heads. You don't commit sin and then go to hell. You commit sin because you *are* in hell. When you are not aware, and do things unconsciously, when you are disturbed and not at peace with yourself, you are in hell. The quality of your inner space is what decides whether you are in heaven or hell.

Somebody asked Buddha, 'If you don't have compassion in your life, what kind of hell do you get?' Buddha replied, 'No punishment can be given to such a man who has no compassion because he is already in hell!'

I tell you, live with consciousness. Live with awareness and you can never make a mistake. Morality is just skin-deep. The so-called moralists have their rules and regulations for the whole society because they lack the understanding and the intelligence to live life spontaneously.

Understand, there is no such thing as virtue or sin. Everything is energy. Energy cannot be categorized as good and bad. Emotions such as lust and anger are also energy. These so-called base emotions arise due to our own ignorance. When our awareness and understanding transform the base emotions, they become higher emotions. Lust's becoming love is the ultimate alchemy.

Consciously decide that you will face every moment with deep awareness. The very decision will transform your life. Not only will we feel total and complete, we will radiate the bliss to others as well.

A beautiful story:

Naropa, an enlightened master, was asked by someone when he became enlightened, 'Have you achieved liberation now?'

Naropa replied, 'Yes and no, both. Yes, because I am not in bondage. No, because the liberation was also a reflection of the bondage.'

The liberation existed as long as the concept of bondage existed. Both are just individual concepts that exist as long as the other exists. They are opposites and they will remain as long as the mind exists. As long as the mind exists, liberation and bondage cannot exist independently.

For example, when you have a headache, why do you want to get rid of it? It is because you have experienced a state of headache-less-ness before. If you never had a headache, would you ever yearn to be in a state of no headache? No. You won't even perceive a state as having or not having a headache because you don't even know such a thing as headache exists. A thing can be felt by the mind only in contrast, in opposites.

That is why Naropa says, 'Yes and no both.' He says that now he is beyond bondage and liberation both because the mind that perceives these opposites is no longer there to judge these, to categorize these.

We are in ignorance when we think that liberation is some state that we need to achieve. The moment we want to possess something, it will simply slip from our hands like how water simply slips from our hands the moment we close our fist tightly.

The light of knowledge dispels the ignorance and we realize the state in which we have always been. Understand, ignorance, just like darkness, has only a negative existence.

If I want to take this microphone in front of me out of the room, I can easily remove it, can I not? But if there is darkness inside the room, can I physically remove it? No! I can bring light into the room and the darkness disappears. But I cannot remove the darkness directly. This is what I mean by something having a negative existence. Just like the rising sun removes the darkness of the night, the light of knowledge dispels the darkness of ignorance.

What is that ignorance that we need to remove by bringing in the light of knowledge? Whatever we do in life, we want to be happy, right? But the strange truth is, we are already pure bliss. I am not saying we have achieved bliss. I am saying we *are* bliss. Each one of us is pure bliss. The problem is we are not ready to accept this ultimate truth and relax, because the moment we accept this, we no longer have a separate personality. Desire or fear no longer exist. How then can the ego drive you?

The ego needs us to be a solid entity for it to exist. The mind always yearns to be occupied, running after something. Only then can it survive. When we are pure bliss, we have nothing to run after because we are complete unto ourselves. We have no identity because we have merged into Existence. This is too much for the ego to handle. The mind therefore plays a very cunning game to keep us engaged in some pursuit, material or spiritual.

If we look deeply, we can see clearly that it is we who choose to stay in suffering. We think that we want bliss, but deep down, we choose to stay with our ego.

Surrender leads to liberation

Kṛṣṇa gives us another technique to liberate ourselves.

He says surrender leads to liberation, and it happens when one's intelligence is focused on Him.

When we believe there is a life force conducting this universe and taking care of us, we relax. When we relax, we can live and function at our optimum potential. We can express our creativity and live spontaneously. This is surrender. This is the knowledge that cannot be taught or picked up. The master can simply transmit it when our being is ready to receive it.

All we need is the faith to allow the supreme intelligence to guide us. The knowledge removes the ignorance. All our problems are due to ignorance. Whether it is fear or greed or worry or anger, all these emotions are able to control us because we are not aware. When we bring a deep awareness into anything, the solution simply stands out. When we go deeply into any emotion with deep awareness, we can flower out of it. This is true knowledge.

I tell you, at the times of extreme doubt, doubt your ego. Never doubt the master. The master is the only truth you can cling to when all else gives way. The master is the only one who can guide you when everything seems to be confusing. At the start of the war, Arjuna is utterly confused but has the intelligence to listen to Kṛṣṇa in that time of extreme doubt.

Surrender can happen at different levels. Bodhidharma said,

Buddhaṁ śaraṇaṁ gacchāmi
dhammaṁ śaraṇaṁ gacchāmi
saṅgaṁ śaraṇaṁ gacchāmi

This means,

I surrender to Buddha's form
I surrender to Buddha's teachings
I surrender to Buddha's mission

Understand that the master lives in all three, the body, his teachings and the mission. They come to dispel the ignorance of seekers out of sheer compassion for the whole of mankind. Only a third of the master's energy is in the physical body. The other third is in the teachings and another third is in the mission.

Nithyananda is *Nitya-Dhyāna-Ānanda* all in one. *Nitya,* the master in the body as Nithyananda; *Dhyāna,* my teaching and blessing of meditation; and *Ānanda,* my mission of bringing forth the fountain of bliss that is lying latent in you. All the three together constitute the energy called *nityānanda.*

When you surrender at the physical level, you surrender your physical self, your comforts to the master, to spread his teachings and mission. On the mental level, surrender means surrendering your intellect to serve the master and the mission. You surrender your mental faculties, mental pursuits to serve the mission according to the needs of the mission.

The third level is the being-level surrender. At this level our being clearly recognizes the call of the master. We become a part of the master. We just merge with Existence that the master is an embodiment of. The process of transformation has converted water, the liquid, into formless steam. Like steam, we explode in all directions.

We now transcend the mind and express our limitless potential. This is the ultimate state in which a master lives every moment and to which He tirelessly and compassionately pushes us in different ways so that we can also experience and be in the same state of eternal bliss.

The Dog and the Dog-Eater

5.18 *One who is full of knowledge and compassion sees equally*
The learned brāhmaṇa, *the cow, the elephant, the dog and the dog-eater.*

5.19 *In this life, surely, those whose minds are situated in equanimity have conquered birth and death.*
They are flawless like the Supreme, and therefore, are situated in the Supreme.

5.20 *One who does not rejoice at achieving something he likes nor gets agitated on getting something he does not like,*
Who is of steady intelligence, who is not deluded, one who knows the Supreme, is situated in the Supreme.

5.21 *One who is not attached to the outer world sense pleasures, who enjoys in the Self, in that happiness,*
He is self-connected and engaged in the Supreme and enjoys unlimited happiness.

Kṛṣṇa succinctly explains the neutrality and equanimity of Existence. Existence has no favorites. All comparative and hierarchical definitions are manmade.

Kṛṣṇa says there is no difference between a human and an animal, and that there is no difference between those we consider to be saints and those we consider to be sinners. A learned scholar, the priest and the *brāhmana* should be seen as equal to an animal or a person who eats dogs.

He says that the dog and the eater of the dog are the same.

This is what Śaṅkara means when he sings the six verses of his Ātma Śatakam. 'I am not the enjoyer. I am not the enjoyed. I am not the enjoying. I am beyond all that; I am just the embodiment of Śiva.'

This is one of the most beautiful messages from Śaṅkara. 'I am not the doer, I am not the deed, I am not the doing,' he says. 'I am just the witness, beyond all these.'

When we go beyond all three, all connotations disappear. The eater and the eaten merge. We reach the source. There is just you, your being.

Animals and plants do not differentiate and discriminate. Except in man-made fables, animals do not think of one animal as superior and another as inferior. The lion is a king only to us, not to other animals. There are many animals that are not afraid of the lion.

> A king was depressed with all his responsibilities and went to Buddha seeking advice. Buddha sent him with a disciple into the nearby garden and told him to look at the cactus plant and the rose bush that were growing next to each other.
>
> The king came back puzzled. He asked what was there to see. 'I saw the tree and bush, that's all. What else?'
>
> Buddha said, 'Neither is the cactus plant jealous of the rose bush whose flowers every one admires, nor is the rose bush complaining that people pluck all its flowers while the cactus plant is left unharmed. Each of them is centered in their own uniqueness. There is no comparison. There is no envy. There is no unhappiness.
>
> The king realized how foolish he was for complaining about his responsibilities. He thanked Buddha and left in peace.

Existence continuously showers bliss upon each of us. Only we are not open to receive it. Existence sees everyone as equal. It does not discriminate. Everyone is a part of the same Existence. Similarly, masters see the whole world as one with their own selves. That is why they can only show compassion to anyone and everyone.

Every atom is divine

External appearances are ephemeral. When we see the eternal being as the core of every one of us, we will realize the inherent divinity in each of us. This knowledge, gained through the experience of the Self, results automatically in deep compassion towards the whole of Existence.

Classifications of lower species and higher species are all made by society and not Existence. Only the human beings think that they are more intelligent than the rest of Nature!

A small story:

One night, a thief knocked on the door of a monastery located in the middle of a forest. The master opened the door and allowed the man to spend the night in the monastery.

The next morning, the thief thanked his host and asked for his permission to leave. He also confessed to the master that he was a thief and had burgled the palace the previous night. The master was aghast.

He started weeping loudly, 'What a great sin I have committed by allowing a thief to spend a night in my monastery! I also gave him food. What can I do to make up for my sin?'

At that time, he heard a voice from the sky, weeping even louder than him, 'You are upset and weeping because you have looked after him for one night. What about me? I have been looking after him everyday since he was born!'

The master had begun feeling holier than others because of which he looked down upon the thief as a less holy person. God never differentiates between a sinner and a saint.

Every atom on earth is divine. When we just realize that this very life is a divine gift to us, our attitude changes from taking things for granted to one of gratitude to Existence for everything!

With every breath that you take every moment, the life energy flows into you and keeps you alive. We take for granted the life energy that goes in through our breath. The mind continuously runs after 'more and more'.

If we make two lists: one list of what we have, what Existence has showered upon us, and a second list of what we *really* want to have to feel happier, we will quickly realize how much longer the first list is. Have we ever strongly considered what our life would be like if we did not have even a small limb that we take so much for granted? Can you imagine the limitations we would have without a toe or thumb, not to speak of our eyes or ears?

We take so much for granted. We always crave for more. We are here as gifts of Nature. Instead of being grateful to Existence for what we have been showered with, we complain about what we do not have.

Remember that when God does not grant us what we seek, He is doing it out of deep compassion and wisdom. He does not grant many of our prayers because He knows what we need far better than us. That is why it is better to be careful about what you wish for, because you may get it! We ask for something because we see someone else enjoying that same thing. That creates envy and desire in us and we too seek the same. For all you know, that person may be suffering with whatever you are coveting!

The Divine is far wiser. The Divine knows what we really need. There is a huge difference between what we want and what we need. We do not realize the difference. The Divine does.

For the next couple of days, just try living with the attitude of gratitude, and with deep awareness. Automatically, you begin to experience every person as a unique creation of Existence. Just decide consciously that you will respond with love for the next couple of days, whatever may be the situation. Just the very attitude change will bring tremendous peace and relaxation into you.

Kṛṣṇa says, when you look at every single thing without favoritism or attachment, then you are a true renunciate, a true *sanyāsi.*

Death – only a passage

Can you look at death and birth in the same manner? We celebrate birth, we mourn death. Why?

Both are passages. The cycle of life is continuous. We move seamlessly from birth through living into death and again into birth. It is just that in this life, we do not remember what happened in the period between our death in our previous birth and our birth this time. That loss of memory is for our own safety.

We are perturbed by that loss of memory. If we understand that death is no different from birth, there will be no fear. This can happen when we have the experience of death while we are still alive. This is what we teach in our programs. An important thing: Our perception of death changes our way of life.

Death is feared by most of us because it is considered a discontinuity. When we realize that death is just a continuation in some other form, we will not fear death. Then the joy of birth and the sadness at death will both be seen as the same.

A small story about Socrates:

The Greek society killed Socrates by forcing him to drink the poisonous juice of the hemlock herb. Just before he drank the poison, one of his disciples asked him, 'Master, are you not afraid of dying?'

Socrates replied, 'Why should I be afraid? I know that only two things can happen after death. Either I will continue to exist in some other form or name, in which case there is nothing to worry about. Or I will cease to exist after death, which means nothing remains to worry! So either way, there is nothing to fear!'

Our idea of birth and death is a clear mirror of how we look at various situations in life. That is why understanding about birth and death is actually fundamental to leading a life of realization.

Aṣṭāvakra, the boy sage from India says, 'Seeing this world as pure illusion, and devoid of any interest in it, how should the strong-minded person feel fear, even at the approach of death? Equal in pain and in pleasure, in hope and disappointment, equal in life and death, and complete as you are, you can find peace.'

Understand, one who knows that what he sees is illusion will not fear death. As long as we hold on to this illusion created by the mind, we have a feeling of losing it when we think of death. When we see pain and pleasure as the same, we will be free from the fear of death. Because then we realize that nothing is taken away from us when death comes.

Enlightened masters' experience about death teaches us a lot. Bhagavān Ramaṇa Maharṣi got his enlightenment through a conscious experience of death.

When Bhagavān was a young boy, one day he was just lying on his bed in his uncle's house in Madurai in India. Suddenly, he felt that death was coming upon him.

He had two choices: to resist the feeling or go through it with acceptance. He chose to go through it. He became enlightened after he experienced the process of death.

In our second level program, the Nithyananda Spurana Program (NSP), the Life Bliss Program Level 2, we go into the complete understanding of death, what happens exactly when we die. We teach you to experience the process of death and to understand how and what happens, so that there is no mystery and, therefore, there is no fear.

Though we know from the moment of our birth that our life will culminate in death, we never try to visualize or welcome it. At least once if we go through our fear of death with deep consciousness, we will lose our fear for death automatically.

Bhagavān was courageous enough to allow the process of death to happen. He saw the parts of his body dying clearly, one by one. Slowly, his whole body was dead. He saw his body turn into ashes.

Suddenly, he realized that something remained even after that. At that moment, it hit him that he was pure consciousness! He was simply a witness to the whole thing!

That knowledge was tremendous and it never left him. When he came back into his body, he was Bhagavān Ramaṇa Maharṣi, an enlightened master! When we get over the cycle of greed and fear, we can be in equanimity in all situations in life. It is then we have touched our core, our real Being.

Kṛṣṇa goes on to explain the characteristics of one who is supreme. He says that one who is of steady intelligence, one who does not get caught in the play of opposing emotions like pleasure and pain, is truly not deluded and is established in the Supreme.

What do we need to know to get out of the whirlpool of emotions?

If we look deeply, we will see that all our emotional blocks are born of an expectation for a certain thing to happen in a certain way. We live in a virtual world and when there is a gap between reality and imagination, the trouble starts. The greater the gap, the more disappointment and frustration we experience. We start to like or dislike something based on this gap. We create all negative emotions and forget about our innate blissful nature because we constantly fantasize about how things should be. The likes and dislikes are a product of the mind, not of the being which is just bliss.

Beautifully, Kṛṣṇa says, 'An object of enjoyment that comes of itself is neither painful nor pleasurable for someone who has eliminated attachment and desire.'

This is actually a *sūtra* that Kṛṣṇa gives. If we put our attention neither on pleasure nor on pain, but between the two we actually go beyond both and we can transcend the play of the mind. Understand that both pleasure and pain are of the mind and not the being. They are based on our *saṁskāras* from our past. Instead of trying to hold onto pleasure or run away from pain, just witness it. Then, we can transcend this nature of the mind.

For example, if you have a headache, don't resist it. Just witness and accept it. As the tree is there, as the night is there, so also the headache is there. On the other hand, if you are very happy, don't try to cling onto it.

Whether it is happiness or pain, just be a witness to it. In fact, this is the whole principle behind the 'middle path' of Buddha. He endorses neither indulging in pleasure nor abstaining from it. Be involved but be aware. When we are aware, we can never be unconsciously pulled into it. Then we are always the master.

When we are not aware, we get caught in the cycle of guilt and desires because after the desire gets fulfilled, we go through guilt for having succumbed to the desire. But we did not live the desire fully with awareness, so we can't get out of it either. Next time, the desire happens again and again we go through it incompletely and then feel guilty. The only way to get out of this vicious cycle of desire and guilt is to go through the desire with awareness.

Normally we either suppress or express our desires. Because of past *saṁskāra,* we think the experience would be painful, and so we suppress the desire. This is because of negative associations imposed on us by society. If it is seen to be pleasurable, we go into the experience willingly and we express our desire.

Suppression only temporarily blocks access, but that desire will rise with renewed vigor again. Even when expressed, the desire will rise even after repeated expression because we rarely experience anything with awareness.

In expression of a desire, once we experience a desire with full awareness, whether related to food, sex or material desires, we will find that the desire is fulfilled and we will transcend the desire.

This is what I term *karma. Karma* is unfulfilled desire that makes us repeat the same experience again and again. Once we experience the situation with awareness, in that present moment, we will transcend our Karma. We will be supreme.

Tune in to bliss

Kṛṣṇa advises us to turn inwards into our Source away from our senses.

By nature, we are tuned inwards. By conditioning, we lose this capability to turn inwards. We have seen that most children are blissful and able to be what they are. Then, unfortunately, they grow up to be adults! They lose their bliss and natural response to turn inwards. Society teaches them to trust their senses. Over time, they become slaves to their senses and fall into the trap of sensual pleasures. Once caught in this trap, it is difficult to get out.

One who indulges in sense pleasures is caught in the push and pull of desires and guilt. Our mind is like a monkey moving from one desire to another. Until that desire is fulfilled, it will look like the most important thing, and after it is fulfilled, it will seem the most insignificant. This is how we get caught in the web of sense pleasures.

Again and again, we look outside for solutions to keep us happy. If we see our list of desires, most of them are borrowed from others. We will be totally happy with our car until our neighbor gets a new car. We constantly update our desires by looking at what is going on outside, and we start believing that fulfilling these desires will give us what we define as happiness or pleasure. So to fulfill these desires, we keep on running the rat race, not knowing what exactly *we* want.

We are looking for solutions outside. However, the real solution lies inside. We need to be able to connect to our true self. The true source of pleasure is not outside us. We should realize that we are blissful by nature. The correct place to look for pleasure is within us. If we realize this, we will always be centered in ourselves. He who is free from being and non-being, who is contented, desireless, and wise, even if in the eyes of the world he does act, does nothing.

We must have seen, on the surface, a madman with tremendous laziness will look very similar to a mystic in deep bliss. They may seem very similar, but inside they are complete opposites.

A madman is lazy and is lying around with many things on his mind. A mystic, however is completely relaxed because he is centered in his being with no mind. To us he may seem the same as a madman. But the mind of the mystic is not doing anything. He is complete unto himself.

When we are situated in the core of our being, we are not shaken by the emotions that happen on the periphery. It is like a rock that is standing still in the ocean unperturbed in spite of lashing waves.

The happiness arising from our very being is unlimited because no external agent can stop it. The *ānanda spurana* (fountain of bliss) is eternal (*nitya*).

With societal conditioning, we block the energy centers in our body-mind system that connect us to the Existential energy that is our primary source of energy. When these centers get blocked through conditioning, we lose that bliss, that ease. We become dis-eased.

These energy blocks are the root cause of all our illnesses. Through the use of meditation techniques, we teach people how to unblock and energize these energy centers called *cakras*, so that we can experience that bliss again. That is why this program is called *Ānanda Spurana*; *Ānanda* is bliss, *spurana* is to gush. The bliss we blocked out starts gushing again. Somewhere, we stopped the bliss flow. We teach how to stop the stopping and let bliss flow within you again.

The Path To Self Realization

5.22 The intelligent person surely does not enjoy the sense pleasures, the enjoyments that are sources of misery and are subject to beginning and end.

5.23 Before leaving this present body, if one is able to tolerate the urges of material senses and check the force of desire and anger,
He is well-situated and he is happy in this world.

5.24 One who is happy from within, active within, as well as illumined within, surely is a yogi (united in mind, body and spirit)
And he is liberated in the Supreme, is Self-realized and attains the Supreme.

5.25 The holy men whose sins have been destroyed are working for the welfare of other beings,
Those who are self-restrained and have cleared all their doubts and dualities attain the eternal happiness of God, nityānanda (eternal bliss), of Divine.

5.26 They who are free from lust and anger, who have subdued the mind and senses,
And who have known the Self, easily attain liberation.

Kṛṣṇa says that sense pleasures are bound to end. They are just temporary. Generally, we are controlled by what happens outside us. Our happiness is created by something outside of us - a pleasant situation, or the presence of someone we like, and so on. When we experience happiness due to some event outside us, be very sure, sadness is around the corner. We will soon experience sadness once that external source is taken away from us. We think we are happy because of this event or because of that person. If these things are taken away from us, we are left with sadness. It is like a pendulum swaying from the one extreme of happiness to the other extreme of sadness.

In our programs, we asked participants to imagine a state of great happiness and stay with it for a while. After that experience, they described what they went through. Invariably it was happiness related to a person or an event; the happiness was brought about by the sense perception.

Now, when we ask them to remove that event or person from their imagination, there is deep sorrow. They feel they have lost something. That is how temporary happiness or sorrow is for all of us. Happiness and sorrow are caused by our sense perception and judgment based on the sense perception. That is why the same event that may be joyful to one is sorrow-filled for another. It is our attachment to that person or event that creates the sorrow or happiness. The incident by itself is neutral.

There is a beginning and an end to these states of sorrow and happiness. But bliss is something that continuously happens in us for no reason. It does not depend on external sources. It is inside us. Once we are centered in ourselves, we are always in bliss. When we are constantly experiencing the inner joy, whatever happens outside does not affect us.

Happiness or sadness happens because of the sense pleasures that are again a result of our mind and ego. Our ego is the actual cause of our misery. Maya, or illusion, impermanence, is really the ego. *Yā mā iti māyā*: that which does not exist but which troubles as if it exists is *māyā*. We don't see reality as it is because we are all the time looking at life through glasses tinted with our biased perceptions picked up from societal conditioning.

When we start watching these sources with awareness, we break our attachment to these external sources. When we are aware of what we really want, this dependency on sense pleasures breaks. We start taking things as they come.

I am not saying you should not enjoy the joy that you get from external sources. No. All I am saying is to be aware of it when it happens. Do not attach your internal state of joy to these sense pleasures.

Kṛṣṇa now gives us a beautiful technique to reach that ultimate state of Kṛṣṇa consciousness.

He is saying exactly what I said earlier. If at least once we settle inside our being when we are attacked by the emotions of desire and anger, without moving our body, without cooperating, without being taken away by that emotion, we are well-situated. This means that we achieved what has to be achieved; we are blissful in this world.

Purpose of body and mind

People ask me again and again, '*Swamiji*, what is the purpose of this body and mind?'

The purpose of body and mind is only one thing: to achieve, to learn how to experience joy without body and mind.

If we can learn to have happiness, bliss, without the body and mind, we have achieved the purpose of the body and mind! After that, we can live without the body and mind.

The person who is able to live without the body and mind is a *jīvan mukta* - a person living enlightenment. Even if the body and mind are with him, he will not be touched by them. He has no use for them. If we don't have any need for it, will you go to Los Angeles? No. Unless you have some reason, you will not go there.

In the same way, unless you have some reason, you will not assume this body. If you had a single glimpse of bliss without this body and mind, this body and mind would never disturb you. Even if they are there, it will be following you.

It is like this: If you don't know how to put the brakes on when you are driving the car, it means you are not driving the car, the car is driving you! Without reading the owner's manual and learning to drive, if you sit in the car, you will not know how to start or to stop or apply the brakes properly. Then the car will be driving you.

So read the owner's manual before getting into the vehicle. The Bhagavad Gītā is the owner's manual for your body and mind. If you read the owner's manual before getting into the body and mind, you will be able to stop when you want to stop. You will not repeat the life and death cycle.

Here Kṛṣṇa says: The man who is not moved, who can tolerate the urges of the material senses, check the force of desire and anger, is well-situated, and he is happy in this world. He knows where he is. He knows his place.

In this world, many of us don't know our place. That is why we experience that we don't feel we belong to this life. We feel uprooted.

> A small story:
>
> In a dark theater, during the intermission, one man went out, came back with popcorn and Coca-Cola. He came near a woman and asked, 'Did I step on your foot a few minutes ago?' She said, 'Yes. As a matter of fact, you did.'
>
> The man said, 'Thank you. Then this is my row!'

You don't know your place! You have to identify your place only through these sources. Only a person who has gone beyond greed and fear can relax into his being. Only he will know what his place is on this planet earth.

If we don't fuel our being with fear and greed, suddenly, we will see a new clarity. We will start working out of divine consciousness. Just decide, 'Whatever I do out of greed will only result in more greed. This is getting nowhere. Enough!' In the same way, if we are escaping from something out of fear, decide, 'Alright, how long can I escape? This fear will attack me in some other form. If I am afraid of this now, later I will be afraid of something else. So let me face it now.'

It is just the fear, not the object that you are afraid of. You may escape anywhere but you will carry the canopies of fear and greed with you. Wherever you go for a picnic, you open your own little canopy. There are many places for great escapes today! They claim that the world's happiest places are the theme parks with all those roller coaster rides and water rides. People even took me to these places in the name of entertainment. After seeing those places, I felt really sad. These places show how much depression people are carrying within them. If so much entertainment is necessary, it means that there is so much depression in the people.

By his very nature, man doesn't need much entertainment. If we need so many things to make us happy, there is something seriously wrong in the whole system. We need to repair it.

Again and again, Kṛṣṇa declares, 'Let you work out of bliss.' And I tell you, if you work out of bliss, you will create bliss for yourself and others; you will never know what tiredness is.

Let me tell you honestly that I still can't understand the meaning 'tiredness'. How can you have tiredness? Tiredness is the inner contradiction between the *icchā ṣakti* (power of desire) and *kriya ṣakti* (power of action). Inside, there is a deep problem. Your greed and fear are attacking each other. If we feel tired, it means there is a big war going on inside us. The person whose consciousness is clear can never experience tiredness.

In my young age, when I was in college, I used to sit and meditate for four hours each in the morning and evening. My roommates would ask me, 'How are you able to sit for so many hours?' And I used to tell them, 'What is there? It is my body, my mind. If you want, can't you sit? If you can't even sit with your body and mind, what are you going to achieve?'

Why do we feel tired? We feel tired when we are not integrated within ourselves. One-half of our being wants to express itself, but we have suppressed it for various societal reasons. The other half of our being is what is expressing itself in the manner that we are forcing it to.

Because we constantly have to put in effort to be what we naturally are not, we become tired at some point. When we become tired, the suppressed, unconscious half of us starts dominating. Be with complete awareness rather than suppressing yourself, and there will be no unconscious half to fight with. Then where is the question of feeling tired?

We feel tired only when we are not completely involved in what we are doing. Become complete, integrated, and whole. Then you can never feel tired, whatever you may do.

See for how long are you able to sit here listening to me. How is it that you are not feeling tired now? It is because when I speak, I speak from my being, with totality. When I speak with totality, automatically, you receive my energy totally also.

This is the state from which enlightened masters operate. That is why there is no sense of tiredness in them even though they are intensely involved in what they do every moment.

We feel tired only when there is a gap between what we are doing and what we want to do. When we are driven by greed for something, we are caught up in the goal and the goal is something we want to achieve. Or we are driven by fear of something; we want to escape from the object of fear and hence, here also, we are not completely involved in what we are doing.

Honestly, I am not able to understand how a man cannot sit with himself. It is our body and our mind after all. You are not able to sit because you continuously pour the wrong fuel into your system.

We are continuously chasing power. The power hunger in us is so high that we are always running after something to get control over it. Understand, first let us get our body and mind under our control. Then, automatically, we can get anything under our control. If our body and mind are not under our control, whatever we wish to control will never come under our control.

One thought of greed or fear is enough: our body just runs. Let the body and mind be completely under our control.

Here is a beautiful *sūtra,* a beautiful technique from Kṛṣṇa to enter into the supreme consciousness:

Just be happy from within. Smile as an expression of the love in your being. All of us are so used to living an artificial life that we have forgotten our being. Every moment, we are continuously either in greed by running after our desires or in fear by continuously running away from something. Our happiness in every moment is measured only by either greed or fear.

This means we are not actually experiencing the moment. We are continuously in the web of greed and fear. We can enjoy something totally only when we are totally in the present moment. When you are in the current moment, you are in a state of bliss that is not affected by the past or future. It is always there.

Naturally, the current blissful moment will give birth to future moments of bliss. We enter a virtuous circle rather than being caught up in the vicious cycle of fear and greed in which we are now caught.

Why do we run behind our desires or why are we afraid of something? It is because we think that life has some goal to be achieved and we continuously run towards it. Understand, life itself is the goal. The path itself is the goal. If we think that the goal and the path are different, then we will only run towards the horizon. Can we ever touch the horizon? The more we run the further it recedes from us. The horizon is imaginary, an illusion.

If we are running behind a goal in life, we will be disappointed at the end of life. But when the path itself is the goal, every moment is blissful. The goal is achieved every moment of our life.

The self-realized one is active and happy because he is completely in the present moment, living in reality. The divine energy blissfully flows through him and he no longer needs to derive energy for his activities from desire or fear.

Here, Kṛṣṇa refers to the state in which we are in the peak of activity yet in the ultimate relaxation. Such a state is indeed possible and is the only state in which we can really be involved in which we can be completely satisfied and blissful in what we are doing.

Responsibility

When we are tuned fully inwards, we are one with Existence, and we have transcended all *karma*. We are then in *nityānanda*, eternal bliss. When we feel genuine love for others, we will take up more and more responsibility to share that love with as many as people as possible.

When we are tuned inwards, we live in the present; past and future do not exist for us. When we are in the present, we are one with Existence. We encompass everything. In this state, we are at the height of spontaneity. Spontaneity is being responsive to everything around us. Nothing is excluded. We expand and cover.

The more responsibility we take up, the more we expand. If we keep shouldering responsibility, we will expand and the divine energy will automatically flow in us. And we can take up more responsibility only when we feel overflowing energy in us.

Usually whenever we are asked to do something, the mind creates a dilemma. We start analyzing intellectually and logically. So at the end of it, we act out of greed or fear.

As long as we intellectually weigh the situation for good and bad, the mind exists. We have to cross this barrier. The dilemma of wanting or not wanting to do something should not come at all.

Many times when people come to me and I ask them to do something, just by the very way they say, 'Yes, I will do it,' I can tell whether they really want to do it or not! Our response to take up a responsibility is shaky when our mind operates. We should take up responsibility spontaneously. The ability to respond spontaneously is what I call responsibility.

Only when we go beyond the mind, we see the absolute oneness and synchronicity of the entire Existence. Only then will we take up responsibility. When we reach this state, there is no mind that is acting. We are in a state of deep relaxation or bliss. And this will create the ability to spontaneously respond when we are in this state.

When we feel genuine love for others, we will take up responsibility because we want to share that blissful love with others around us. Only when we work out of bliss, will we do good things for others. When there is no dilemma, when we take up responsibility spontaneously, there is no expectation, no fear and no greed on our part. We will always be giving.

If we are working out of fear or anger, fear or greed, even if we do good things, they will end up only in trouble. They will not end up as a service.

Know Me and Be in Bliss!

5.27, 5.28 Shutting out all external sense objects, keeping the eyes and vision concentrated between the two eyebrows,
Suspending the inward and outward breathes within the nostrils and thus controlling the mind, senses and intelligence,
The transcendental who is aiming at liberation becomes free from desire, fear and the byproduct of desire, fear and anger, all three.
One who is always in this state is certainly liberated.

5.29 One who, knowing Me as the purpose of sacrifice and penance,
As the lord of all the worlds and the benefactor of all the living beings, achieves peace.

Here, the 'Me' refers to the supreme witnessing consciousness, the Kṛṣṇa consciousness and not the six-foot Kṛṣṇa frame.

I always tell people, the outer guru is needed only to kindle the inner guru. Once the inner guru, the consciousness, is awakened, the outer guru needs to be dropped. Just like after burning the dead body, the stick that is used to stoke the wood to burn the body is dropped into the same pyre, so also the outer guru needs to be dropped.

For the first time, Kṛṣṇa gives a beautiful technique to move your energy from fear and greed to divine consciousness.

Your fear is rooted in the *svādiṣṭhāna cakra* while your greed is rooted in the *mūlādhāra cakra.* Kṛṣṇa gives us the technique of elevating ourselves from these two *cakras* to the *ājñā cakra* at the brow center, where the eternal consciousness resides. When we have elevated ourselves to *ājñā*, we go beyond our ego or mind.

We are all caught in the *mūlādhāra* and *svādiṣṭhāna*. That is why, continuously, we have a tensed feeling. We will be continuously holding our *mūlādhāra* and *svādiṣṭhāna* tightly. Just feel yourself in your *mūlādhāra*. You will see that you are tightly holding yourself.

Kṛṣṇa explains how to relax that area, how to get the *amṛta-dhāra* (flow of nectar) from the eternal consciousness. Shutting out all external sense objects, keeping the eyes and vision concentrated between the two eyebrows, suspending the inward and outward breaths within the nostrils and thus controlling the mind, senses and intelligence, the transcendental who is aiming at liberation becomes free from desire, fear and the by-products of desire, fear and anger - all three. One who is always in this state is certainly liberated.

First, He gives the technique to enter into that state. Then He says, if you can stay in that same state, you are liberated.

Now, at least, let us try to have a glimpse of this state. I will guide you step by step through this meditation.

Please try to enter into that state.

MEDITATION

Please sit straight and close your eyes. Let your head, neck and backbone be in a straight line. Intensely pray to that ultimate energy, *Parabrahma* Kṛṣṇa, to give the experience of this meditation to us.

First thing, visualize that all your senses are completely shut. Visualize that your eyes are completely closed. Don't allow any visualization inside your being. Not only should you close the eyelids, you should close the eyes also, because sometimes we continue to see things from behind the eyelids. Visualize that your eyeballs have become completely dark. You are seeing only darkness in front of you.

Visualize your ears are shut. Visualize your sense of touch is shut. Visualize your smelling capacity is shut. Visualize your face to be shut. Feel deeply that all the five senses have been shut down.

Inhale and exhale as slowly as possible. Slowly, let your nostrils blow out the air. Let your consciousness reside between the two eyebrows. In a very relaxed way, let you be aware of the space between your two eyebrows. Don't tense yourself. Just be very relaxed.

Let your *mūlādhāra cakra* located at the base of your spine be relaxed. Let your *svādiṣṭhāna cakra* below the navel center be relaxed. Let your whole consciousness come up to the *ājñā cakra,* which is between the eyebrows. Let you relax in the *ājñā cakra,* between the eyebrows.

Visualize cool, soothing light in the *ājñā cakra,* in the space between the eyebrows. Relax in the *ājñā cakra* between your two eyebrows.

Forget all other parts of your body. Forget about the body, mind and the world; remember only the *ājñā cakra,* the space between the two eyebrows. Relax in the same state in your *ājñā cakra.*

Go deeply into the *ājñā cakra.* Visualize a beautiful, cooling, soothing light in the *ājñā cakra.* Let you experience beautiful, blissful light in the *ājñā cakra.* Let your awareness be in the *ājñā cakra* in a very relaxed way; let your consciousness rest in the space between the two eyebrows.

Let you relax in the same space of eternal consciousness. Let your intelligence be awakened. Let you work from your eternal consciousness. Let you have the pleasant awareness of the *ājñā cakra.*

Let you all have the grace of the divine consciousness. Let you be established in the eternal consciousness. Let you all be in, with and radiate eternal bliss, *nityānanda.*

Om śanti, śanti, śantihi...

Om tat sat

Relax. Slowly, very slowly, you can open your eyes.

Try to remain in this same mood at least for the next ten days.

Understand: Don't concentrate by force. Have a pleasant awareness. When you keep the pleasant awareness around your *ājñā cakra,* your whole energy will be directed towards the eternal consciousness. You will receive energy from eternal consciousness, from immortality, *amṛtatva.* You will be driven from above by the eternal consciousness. If you are driven from below by fear or greed, you are man. If you are driven from above, you are God.

Let you learn the science of how to connect yourself with the divine energy, how to be driven by the divine consciousness. Let you function through the eternal consciousness.

Thus ends the fifth chapter named **Sanyāsa Yogaḥ** *of the* **Upaniṣad** *of the* **Bhagavad Gītā**, *the scripture of Yoga, dealing with the science of the Absolute in the form of the dialogue between* **Śrī Kṛṣṇa** *and* **Arjuna.**

BHAGAVADGĪTĀ

Look In Before Coming To Any Conclusion

DHYĀNA YOGAḤ

CHAPTER 6

You are your best friend and
you are your worst enemy.
Whether you wish to degrade yourself
or enhance yourself
is in your hands.

Look In Before Coming To Any Conclusion

We will start with a small story:

A Hollywood director was shooting a big-budget movie in a deserted area.

In the middle of a day's shooting when the sun was shining brightly, an old Native American Indian appeared on the set and whispered hoarsely to the director, 'Tomorrow rain,' and went away. The director took no notice of the man until it so happened that on the next day it poured and no shooting was possible. The director still did not link the Indian's words with the rain.

Again, after one week the same Indian appeared and said, 'Tomorrow storm,' and disappeared. This time, too, the director and others took no heed of what this strange man said. Exactly as the Indian predicted there was a big storm the next day. The director had to cancel that day's shooting, also.

The Indian appeared a few more times with his predictions. After noticing that his predictions came true each time, the director was really impressed.

He told his assistant, 'We can save a lot of money with the help of this man. Get that old Indian no matter what it costs. We will pay him and keep him with us.'

After three weeks the Indian disappeared and didn't come back for over a month. The director was very upset and sent out search teams. They finally located the Indian and brought him back to the sets.

The director asked him sincerely, 'Please tell me about tomorrow's weather. I have to shoot an important scene and the set is very expensive. I am relying on you to tell me about tomorrow.'

The old man just shrugged and said, 'Don't know about tomorrow; my radio is broken.'

Look in before coming to any conclusion! This is the message for today.

In this chapter Arjuna is not asking any questions to Kṛṣṇa. Kṛṣṇa continues His answers from the previous chapter.

6.1 *Bhagavān says:*
One who performs actions without being attached to their outcome is an ascetic. He is a religious performer of the purification of mind.
One who has stopped performing any actions, one who doesn't accept the sacred fire and doesn't perform his rituals, is neither an ascetic nor a karma yogi, a sage immersed in action.

6.2 *O Pāṇḍavā, renunciation leads to the state of yoga where one is linking oneself with the Supreme. This union with the Divine can happen only when you renounce self-interest.*

6.3 *A person who initially wants to start practicing the yoga system laid down by the sages should carry out all activities in line with that system. Activities for all other reasons will cease.*

6.4 *One is said to have attained the state of yoga when, having renounced all material desires, He neither acts for sense gratification nor engages in result-oriented activities.*

Kṛṣṇa continues with what He said earlier. He says, the person who is not attached to the fruits of his action is an ascetic and a *karma yogi.* Understand, *karma,* the state of action, or *sanyās,* the state of renunciation, is directly related to your being. Being a *sanyāsi,* a renunciant monk is a state and not a status. It is a state of mind.

If one is a *karma yogi,* one goes about his work without any expectations. This is done even in the midst of one's life as a householder. In the same manner, it is immaterial whether one dons saffron robes to be an ascetic. One can wear all the outer trappings of a monk and still be fully attached to the *saṁsāra māyā,* the illusion of life.

In the verses of Bhaja Govindaṁ, Ādi Śaṅkarācārya, an enlightened master of ancient India, says this beautifully about the ascetic who cheats the world and himself. He says, 'The ascetic may have his hair knotted, or shave his head bald, he may pull out his hair one by one in penance, or may wear saffron robes, but he does not see, even though he has eyes. He does all this only to fill his belly! '

One's attitude alone matters.

People repeatedly ask me, '*Swamiji,* should we renounce everything to achieve enlightenment? How can we lead our day-to-day life and yet hope to achieve spiritual progress?'

I tell them, 'No! Just renounce what you don't have, not what you have. That is enough.' We fantasize about all that we do not have. But we live with all those things mentally. The problem is not what we have, it is what we don't have. Renouncing what you don't have will solve all the problems. Then you will start living intensely with what you have.

One of the major problems we bring upon ourselves is that we chase desires and possessions. And once we have achieved what we want, we don't enjoy it. We simply move on to the next chase. It is as if the enjoyment is only in the chase and not in the possession itself. The present has no meaning to many of us. Because of this we miss reality. It is the illusion of the speculative future that draws our interest and causes misery to us.

Brahmacarya – The marriage to Existence

There is a beautiful word in Sanskrit: *brahmacarya.* It has no equivalent in English. The word has often been translated as celibacy. But celibacy is not the right equivalent for *brahmacarya.* This word never existed in

English because the very idea of *brahmacarya* never existed. *Brahma* means Existence, reality. *Carya* means, 'living like'. *Brahmacarya* refers to a person who lives like the gods, who lives with Existence, who lives with reality.

Brahmacarya does not mean one who is unmarried. In the course of time it was translated as celibacy. It is one of the four stages of life as defined by the scriptures. It is the stage in which a young student learns at the feet of the master, in the *gurukul,* the vedic system of schooling. It starts at the age of seven when the parents hand the child over to a master. The child stays with the master until early adulthood. At the end of this period, depending upon the child's aptitude and skills, he or she moves on into life as a *gṛhasta,* a householder, or a *sanyāsi,* an ascetic. This period of *brahmacarya,* under the master's guidance in one's early years, provides the background to shed fantasies and live life in reality.

In today's world most of us live with fantasy. We don't live with the reality of our existence. From the time we start interacting with the external world, even from our childhood, we are exposed to different forms of media. They continuously flood us with fantasies.

A young girl of ten came with her parents to my ashram. Just for fun I asked her whom she would marry when she grew up. She named a popular film actor who was already married with children. If Rāma and Sīta had lived in today's world, with all the fantasies being thrown at them, even they would have been tempted to indulge in fantasies!

In our lives, we search for the ideal life partner with great vigor and determination. Nature has intended that we pursue this relationship actively in the interest of the survival of the human race. Everyone is searching for an ideal person who matches their fantasy. Even if we find someone who matches our so-called ideal, when we start living with the person, life will slowly reveal that the template that we have so carefully built over many years is different from the person with whom we are living. The template can never be matched because the template itself is just a fantasy.

A small story:

Once there was a couple who was married for fifty years. Everybody including their daughter was surprised as to how they managed to stay together for fifty years. One day, the daughter asked her mother about this.

The mother replied, 'Oh, it is no big deal. You just close your eyes and imagine it is not happening to you. That's all!'

Understand! This is what is happening in marriages most of the time. We do not accept our spouse as he or she is. We live with our own fantasies and not the real spouse. Though we live in the same house, how many times do we look into each other's eyes? The reason is that there is always a screen of fantasy between our spouse and us. We are not ready to accept life as it is.

There is a book: *Men are from Mars, Women are from Venus*. There are so many things that the author has expressed that we can see in our lives. I feel we should find some other title for the book. Venus and Mars are too close. They are from the same galaxy!

Anyway, our life is filled with fantasies about how our would-be should be, and what we should do if reality does not match fantasy. We are continuously chiseling the other person and the other person is continuously chiseling us, with the hope that the other will match the ideal. All the sounds heard in our house are that of the chisel and hammer. We can chisel a stone and make a beautiful sculpture. But can we chisel a living being?

In the Śiva sūtra, Śiva tells His consort Pārvatī, 'In the bed of a married couple, there are four people.' Then He explains, 'There is the husband and the wife, and the fantasies of the husband about his wife, and the fantasies of the wife about her husband.' Such a marriage is not a marriage.

When we start chiseling a living being we create more trouble for ourselves and for the other person. A person who is mature enough to live with reality, with the real situation, has achieved the state of *brahmacarya.* He accepts the present moment for what it is. So just drop your fantasies. Live with reality. That is *brahmacarya.*

Here, Kṛṣṇa says, 'Just renouncing the sacred fire and not performing one's duty does not mean one is an ascetic.' In those days fire was the basis for everything, whether it was cooking or spiritual practice. I can replace the word 'fire' with 'cell phone' for today's world!

In this age, we can say, 'Don't think that by sacrificing the cell phone and laptop you become a *sanyāsi* or a great *karma yogi.*' Just like how cell phones and the laptop have become a basic necessity today, in those days *agni* (fire) was a basic need in life. Our ancient *ṛṣi*s (mystics) knew the techniques of relating to the higher energy through fire, just like how we use the cell phone to communicate.

All of science is based on using light particles, whether in the term of electricity, atomic energy, or other forms of energy. Everything is about handling light particles, but with different formulas. Whether it is our fan or iron or a microscope or a video camera, everything can be reduced to the technique of handling light or electro-magnetic particles. Scientists worked on light energy and created all these objects. Our eastern sages worked with sound energy and created all their products. We actually had the *puṣpaka vimāna* (flying chariot) and we did really have the *brahmāstra* (nuclear weapon). Everything is true.

But in the course of time we lost the technology. Since the technology was lost, the existence of these things is being questioned today. People now believe that all these things are just mythology, epic stories. No. Just because we have lost the key and are not able to open the lock, don't think there is no treasure.

The entire collection of scriptures, the *Vedas,* consists of the techniques to tune oneself to work with sound particles. The ancient sages were able to relate to higher energies and communicate with vibrations through fire. Whether it was Sañjaya, King Dhṛtarāṣṭra's minister, who saw the Mahābhārata war through telepathy, or the *puṣpaka vimāna* (the flying chariot), or *brahmāstra* (the ultimate fire weapon), these were all true.

When the cultural invasions of India took place, these techniques were lost.

I have seen a *sanyāsi* create fire by just uttering a few words. Even now, at *Kumbhamelā* (the holy river festival that occurs once in twelve years in India), we can see *sanyāsis* who bury their heads inside the earth for more than twenty-four hours. There are so many people who can play with sound energy.

Ten years ago at the Haridwar *Kumbhamelā* , I saw a *sanyāsi* floating in the air with people watching him in awe. I have also seen a *sanyāsi* sitting on a board full of sharp nails.

Understand and renounce

So here, Krṣna says that just by renouncing fire, a person cannot become a *sanyāsi*. Similarly, here I can say that just by renouncing our cell phone in life, we cannot become a *sanyāsi*. The attitude needs to be changed. To truly renounce, the mind has to renounce thoughts. Usually, wherever our body is, our mind is elsewhere. To bring the mind to where the body is, renouncing the inner chatter is the starting point of renunciation.

Thoughts cannot be suppressed. The more we suppress, the more they erupt. We cannot control the mind in a traditional manner. We need to constantly bring ourselves back to where our body is, to the present, away from the dead past and the unborn future. Renunciation of the past and future, by bringing our mind to focus on the present, is true renunciation.

This renunciation does not happen by giving up objects of material welfare such as fire and the cell phone. It also does not happen by giving up what we think is superficial to spiritual progress, such as rituals. Giving these up without bringing in the true awareness of consciousness is not renunciation.

Renunciation of material things without renouncing desires is of no value. It has been said that when the great sages went into deep meditation the gods above would get terrified, especially Indra, who was forever getting into trouble with these sages! The great *ṛṣis* were all householders. So Indra would try to disturb them by tempting them. Even great *tapasvis* (men with the experience of long meditative penance behind them) were not immune to these temptations.

Ravi Varma, the King of Travancore, made a very famous painting of the great sage Viśvāmitra being tempted by the celestial nymph Menakā. In the painting Viśvāmitra is holding his hands up shielding his eyes to prevent himself from seeing Menakā. But the fingers are spread wide so that he could peep through his fingers!

All these are metaphorical stories. There are no celestial nymphs or heaven or Indra. If Indra were to send down a celestial nymph each time someone meditated, all men would immediately take up meditation! It is only our inner fantasy that comes out as Menakā. Just sit, meditate, and you will see! You need to renounce fantasies. These fantasies are the creation of the mind, which conjures up all these visions to keep you occupied.

We may think that we are in control of our mind. But actually our mind controls us. This is what Kṛṣna means by *sankalpa,* self-interest, because the mind wishes to satisfy the senses that it operates and controls. By visualizing, by hearing, by smelling, by tasting, by touching through the sense organs, our mind wants us to experience pleasures that will keep us under its hold.

Only when we renounce the mind's control by going beyond the senses can we become a true renunciant. 'Control your senses and still your mind so that you can reach Me,' He said.

Only when we do renounce this so-called identity will we perceive our self as the supreme Self, which is our true identity. An ordinary person sees his own self as the body, mind, memories, senses, and the identities that he creates for himself. These are the channels through which we can project ourselves onto the outer world.

Normally we create two identities. One is the *Ahankāra* - the identity that we project to the outer world. This is based on our achievements in society, our profession, our possessions, etc. The second is *mamākara.* It is the identity we project to our inner self. This identity is usually based on our attitudes and our self-esteem.

Through a combination of these two identities we create an image about ourselves that we hold on to with deep conviction and belief. Our true Self is beyond this image. As long as we allow our senses to feed us, we will be controlled by our mind.

Renunciation of these fantasies is yoga. Yoga is the state when our desires dissolve. We unite with our true Self in this state and there is no gap between the Divine and us. Whether we believe it or not, accept it or not, want it or not, we *are* God. All we can do is experience and express it or we can just continue to struggle and fight with it. This is the truth.

A small story:

A man was informed that his wife had just fallen into the river. He ran to the river to save her.

To everyone's surprise he jumped into the river and started swimming upstream, against the current.

The onlookers shouted to him and called him a fool. They asked him, 'Why are you swimming against the current? Your wife has been carried with the current downstream.'

The man said, 'You don't know my wife. Even in the river, she would go only against the current!'

We can be like a rock in the water, forever resisting the flow of the water. The river pounds the rock, eventually reducing it to sand that settles at the bottom. Or we can be like the reed that bends and flows in whichever direction the water flows. There is nothing that the water can do to the reed. By giving in to the water flow, the reed rests in the water.

This is what Christ was referring to when He said, 'The meek shall inherit the earth.' He was not saying that we should be cowards and then eHe would deliver the world to us. Meekness here is a virtue that allows us to flow with the current and flourish. It is the ability to know that, it is the universe, not us, in control. Meekness is wisdom. The wise shall inherit the earth.

In Sanskrit there are two terms, *'Dṛṣṭi sṛṣṭi'* and *'Sṛṣṭi dṛṣṭi'*. *Dṛṣṭi sṛṣṭi* means to look at the world as it is and take life as it comes. *Sṛṣṭi dṛṣṭi* is just the opposite. We want the world running according to our fantasies, instead of accepting the reality of the world. This is a sure recipe for disaster.

We can either move against the current, believing that we control our destiny, and struggle all the time. Or we can flow with the current, surrender to the Divine and be in bliss. Whether we go against the current or go with it, we are in the water. Whether we realize it or not, we are Divine. When our desire for external sensual pleasures is controlled, we experience the divinity within.

Yoga – uniting the body and mind

This is the state of yoga that Kṛṣṇa talks about, where there is no suppression. Instead, there is transformation. The path is no longer towards self or sensory satisfaction. In fact, there is no 'towards' or 'goal.' The goal is the path itself.

Kṛṣṇa says next, 'A person who initially wants to start practicing a yoga system laid down by the sages should carry out all activities in line with that system. Activities for all other reasons will then cease.'

Today, the true meaning of yoga is lost. Yoga is not about physical exercise or sweating in high temperatures. It is a journey into the inner Self, towards the Self.

Patañjali, the great sage who authored Yoga sūtras, laid down an eight-part system called Aṣṭāṅga yoga. Today this is being misinterpreted as 'eight steps of yoga'. These eight limbs need to be practiced concurrently. There is no purpose in practicing only two of the eight parts: *āsana*, physical postures, and *prāṇāyāma*, breath control, which is how it is done today.

In Patañjali's Aṣṭāṅga yoga, bliss is the goal and the path. Have you seen any yoga practitioner enjoying what he is doing? They are grimacing all the time, forcing their bodies and torturing themselves. Yoga as it is practiced now only breeds ego. There are many varieties of Yoga: Deluxe Yoga, Super Deluxe Kundalini Yoga, Instant Enlightenment Kriya Yoga!

Patañjali's Yoga is a way of life. Starting with inner and outer regulation, *yama* and *niyama,* his system cleanses our body, mind, and spirit. Just *yama,* one of the eight limbs, has five parts, one of which is *satya,* or truth. If we practice this sincerely, it will lead us into enlightenment. Another is *brahmacarya,* or walking in tune with reality. Actually, we need to be in the eighth state of *samādhi* to truly be able to practice even one of the *yama* principles with awareness.

The yoga system is a parallel system. When each of its parts is acted upon with awareness, we will attain *samādhi. Ahiṁsā,* non-violence, is another part of *yama.* Religion teaches non-violence as a moral injunction: Only if we are non-violent will we reach heaven, else we will end up in hell. Understand, it is very difficult to practice any morality. If we are successful, then we will be schizophrenic. When we understand and practice, it will never be a discipline. It will be just falling in tune with Existence.

In reality, there is no hell or heaven. *Ahiṁsā* should be practiced out of deep understanding. Only then will we radiate it in our very walk and talk. Even animals will be attracted to us. One of the other rules in *yama* is *satya,* truthfulness. Truthfulness can happen in us only after we have experienced *samādhi,* or enlightenment, the eighth limb. Until we attain enlightenment, whatever we think of as the truth is only a perception, not reality. We perceive the world with our 120-degree vision and our gathered societal knowledge, conditioning, etc. It is only when we reach enlightenment that we will be able to perceive Truth as it is. The rules of *yama* and *niyama* (moral discipline) will only be established firmly after we have experienced *samādhi* .

To realize our divine nature, ancient mystics have created this wonderful eight-fold formula of the yoga system. Yoga in modern days is practiced just for health reasons. Good health is just a by-product of practicing yoga, not the end. The actual reason that our wonderful sages created this formula, was to create the divine experience within anyone who used the formula. This formula has to be practiced as prescribed for one to realize the divine nature of one's self. Once we become intensely tuned to the eight-fold formula, it will become an integral part of our being.

When we practice yoga to meet with the Divine, we will not treat yoga as an activity to be performed on a daily basis; we will live and breathe yoga. It will influence any activity that we perform. For example, if we are speaking to someone, we will constantly be aware of the need to speak the truth. If we are performing an activity, our awareness will be completely on that activity. Even modern man can become a yogi by applying these principles to every single activity he performs. When this happens, all material activities will automatically cease.

I was taught Aṣṭāṅga yoga by a great yogic master. He started training me when I was barely three and he was then already nearing one hundred years of age. I truly believe that he was a descendent of Patañjali, he was so much in tune with the Yoga Sūtra*s* of Patañjali. I hated a lot of what he made me do then. He made me climb pillars in the Aruṇācala temple in Tiruvannamalai with one hand behind my back! But it was this training that allowed my body to withstand the rigors of my spiritual wandering through the country and the Himalayan mountains, in search of enlightenment.

Now, I teach Aṣṭāṅga yoga, as it was taught to me, with the additional insight of Patañjali's vision. I call it Nithya Yoga. The path and purpose of Nithya Yoga is bliss. It is bliss arising out of the merging of body, mind, and spirit. It is the process of *uniting* the body, mind, and spirit. We should understand one important thing about yoga. For whatever purpose, with whatever intention we move our body or bend our body, that intention is completely inserted or recorded into our body and mind. This may seem startling but it is the truth from my experience.

Whatever intention or *saṁskāra*, you hold when you move your body, that *saṁskāra* will get inserted into you and will start expressing itself in your body. For example, if you move your body with the intention that you will have health, in whichever way you move your body, including just sitting, health will simply happen.

This leads us to another important conclusion: The method in which we do postures in yoga is not important. It is the thought with which we move our body that matters. The body itself is made out of memories. We are an expression of our own self-hypnosis. Our memories are recorded in our muscles, as well.

Here is a simple technique to experience this truth: For just ten minutes in the morning, visualize your whole body as a bliss-bag filled with bliss. Then move the body in whatever way you want. The body will start working, experiencing, and expressing the bliss.

When we reach the state of yoga, we are in a meditative state of bliss. All desires for sense gratification cease. There will be so much bliss bubbling up from inside that there will be no need to look for an outer object, person, or location for fulfillment. The desire to run after goals will automatically drop. This bliss is independent of the external world. It is beyond the body and the mind. This state of bliss can radiate and flow out to touch outer objects, but the outer objects cannot influence this inner bliss!

Are You Your Friend Or Your Enemy?

6.5 *You are your own friend; you are your own enemy. Evolve yourself through the Self and do not degrade yourself.*

6.6 *For him who has conquered the Self, the Self is the best of friends.*
For one who has failed to do so, his Self will remain the greatest enemy.

6.7 *For one who has conquered the Self, who has attained tranquility, the supreme is already reached. Such a person remains in this state, in happiness or distress, heat or cold, honor or dishonor.*

6.8 *A person whose mind is contented, because of spiritual knowledge, who has subdued his senses and to whom stone and gold are the same, and who is satisfied with what he has, he is said to be established in self-realization and is called an enlightened being.*

6.9 *A person is considered truly advanced when he regards honest well-wishers, affectionate benefactors, the neutral, the mediators, the envious, both friends and enemies, the pious and the sinners, with equality of mind.*

'You are your own friend; you are your own enemy. Evolve yourself through the Self and do not degrade yourself.'

In this verse, Kṛṣṇa says:

'One must deliver himself with the help of his own being and not degrade himself. The being is the friend of the conditioned soul and his enemy as well.'

You are your own friend and you are your own enemy. If you know the technique of how to lift yourself by yourself, you are a friend of your Self. If you let yourself down, you are an enemy of yourself.

A small story:

There was a big spiritual organization. A monk was sent to a remote tribal area to perform service. Suddenly the headquarters received a lot of complaint letters about that monk.

After reading the complaint letters, the president said, 'We have posted the right person. Don't worry.'

The secretary was puzzled and asked him why he thought this despite all the complaints received.

The president replied, 'If we are getting complaints, it means that he has already started working. At least something is happening.'

When we start anything new, we will always have three phases. The first is resistance. The second is avoidance without caring or resisting. The third is acceptance. Similarly, when we start doing anything inside our system, we start growing in the same way.

First, resistance: We will repeatedly forget. We will try to create complications and all possible arguments. I have seen that many people, when they are unable to follow the teachings of Kṛṣṇa, will go ahead and start blaming Kṛṣṇa saying, 'What Kṛṣṇa are you talking about? He was always flirting. He was always with women. What type of a person was He?' We can easily escape Kṛṣṇa by criticizing Kṛṣṇa.

When we can't practice these teachings, we start justifying ourselves. Since we are unable to follow, we start criticizing Kṛṣṇa. This is the best way to escape and avoid the teachings of Kṛṣṇa. When our being resists, if we allow the resistance to grow, we are our worst enemy. This is what Kṛṣṇa means by saying, 'May you lift yourself by yourself.' If we don't, we will be our worst enemy. It is up to us to help ourselves as best friend or to hurt ourselves as our worst enemy.

Nobody can hurt you or help you unless you allow him or her to. May you lift yourself to your Self. If you have failed or forgotten while practicing these words, don't worry. Again and again, lift yourself. Don't feel depressed or guilty.

The last teaching of Buddha was: *ātma deepo bhava,* 'May your Self be the guiding light.' When Buddha was about to leave his body all his disciples asked him, 'Master, please give us your ultimate message.' Buddha said, 'Let you be the light, the guide unto yourself. Let your being guide you.' Here Kṛṣṇa says the same thing: May you lift yourself by yourself.

Just the other day, I came across an advertisement on the internet called 'Super Deluxe Kundalini Yoga' for $240. They sell a by-pass circuit by which your *kuṇḍalini* energy will be raised to the *sahasrāra chakra* (the crown energy center) automatically. All you need to do is to allow them to do the by-pass connection. Then your *kuṇḍalini* will stay in the *sahasrāra* forever. I was simply shocked! How can someone else awaken your *kuṇḍalini*? Enlightened masters can awaken our latent energy, but only with our own effort can we stay in that same state. Only we can help ourselves.

> Someone went to Buddha and asked, 'Master, you know that enlightenment is the ultimate thing. Why don't you give that to all of us?'
>
> Buddha said, 'Oh, you want enlightenment? You think I should give enlightenment to everybody? Please go around and survey how many people really want enlightenment.'
>
> By that evening the man returned after conducting an extensive survey in that city and said, 'Master, only two people want enlightenment.'
>
> Buddha said, 'Please bring them here, let me give it to them.' The man said, 'No, they are not ready to come all the way here from their houses. If you can send it to them, they are ready to receive it.'

Nobody really wants it! And even if we do, we want it as one more item in our showcase. We are not ready to risk anything for enlightenment. Whenever people come to our houses, we can say, 'This is from Delhi. This is from New York. This statue is from Japan.'

Just like that, we can say, 'Oh... this enlightenment... do you know that Master, Nithyananda? He gave it to me. He was giving a Gītā discourse that I attended and he just gave it to us. How does it look?'

Buddha said, 'Existence is so great that It gives you the freedom to be in bondage. It is your choice. If liberation is forced, even liberation is not liberation. So you have one-hundred percent choice to be liberated or to be in bondage.'

Here, Kṛṣṇa says, 'May you liberate yourself by yourself. If you help yourself, you will be the greatest friend for yourself. If you don't, you will be your worst enemy.' This is an important verse. This has to be understood well.

From blah to Bliss

When you get up every morning ask your mind, 'What do you want today?' If your mind chooses bliss, just tell your mind, 'Be blissful. That's all!' This single conscious decision can change the quality of your life. Just decide to do this for 24 hours. People will immediately think, 'Let me decide for my whole life today itself.' No! You will forget. You will be back at the same point where you started. Decide only for one day. Only then will you be able to maintain it. Otherwise you will have the same old natural face.

A small story about this natural face:

The head of a monastery was teaching the young novices to preach. He was giving them tips on how to speak in public.

He said, 'When we speak our whole body should express what we are saying. Our face should express the idea. When we speak about heaven our eyes should sparkle and our whole body should show the bliss; we should express the joys of heaven clearly. Our face should shine.'

He continued, 'When we speak about hell we can just remain as we are. People will understand!'

At least in our life, let us not maintain the long face as our natural face.

Vivekānanda said, 'If you are depressed, don't come out of your room. There is enough suffering in the world.'

When we conquer the mind, happiness and distress are both one and the same, and we are not touched by them. Kṛṣṇa says, 'For one who has achieved the supreme bliss, for him happiness and distress, heat and cold, honor and dishonor are all the same.' Throughout this chapter Kṛṣṇa emphasizes this one idea, 'senses.' How can happiness and distress, heat and cold, honor and dishonor be the same for a man? How do we reach that state? Throughout this chapter He speaks about conquering the senses.

First, we need to understand that when I say conquering the senses, I don't mean controlling or destroying the senses. If we try to control or destroy the senses, we will only struggle more.

Kṛṣṇa says beautifully, 'For one who has conquered the self.' When he says Self, he means the whole setup, the mind-intelligence-ego, where the decision-making is happening. When we just try to conquer the senses, we will fail again and again. We automatically think that it is impossible, and lose confidence. We need intelligence to progress in this path.

A small story:

A man wanted to go on a vacation to Juhu beach in Mumbai. He started to travel and kept going. After one week he came back.

His friend asked, 'Did you go to Juhu beach?'

He said, 'No, I was not able to find it.'

His friend asked, 'Did you not see any sign on the highway?'

The man replied, 'Yes, there was a board but it said Juhu Beach left, and I thought the beach had left so I came back.'

We need intelligence to traverse this path. If we try to work from the wrong side, from the side of the senses, we will never be able to succeed. If we try to create more pressure in the cooker, we will not be able to open the cooker lid. First, we need to put out the fire, the energy source. The ego is continuously supplying energy to our senses. What we need to do is to work at the level of the mind, not at the level of the senses.

For example, if we fast for one day, that night in our dreams we will be feasting! Our body has got its own balance. If we avoid something, it has to supply and rejuvenate itself. If we are hungry, we can't sleep. In order to continue to be in the state of sleep, we should be made to believe that we are not hungry. So, the unconscious energy creates a dream as if we are feasting. Whenever we deprive ourselves, our unconscious energy will satisfy itself in the dream state, because in the dream state, there are no cops or anyone else to control us. We can do whatever we want.

Understand, if we suppress something it will automatically express itself in our dreams. Dreams are nothing but expressions of our suppressed desires and fears. Not only that, they expresses themselves in a perverted way. If we enjoy with the senses we will never become tired. But when we suppress our senses, our being suffers in our dreams. We can see very clearly, if we have a nightmare, even when we wake up, for hours we continue to be in that same mood and our whole being feels shaken.

Now there is a new concept called 'fear stroke'. These are imaginary fears, such as seeing a rope in the dark and imagining it to be a snake, or imagining ghosts lurking in dark corners, or the sudden ringing of the telephone, etc. We get them in dreams, too. If we are suffering at the dream level, then there is something seriously wrong at the mind-intelligence level. We are trying to control the senses instead of controlling the mind. Instead of removing the fire, we are trying to create more pressure in the cooker. All we need to do is to work on the mind to stop the supply of fuel to the senses.

Here Kṛṣṇa says, 'For one who has conquered the mind.' This applies to one whose mind has learned the right processing. If our intelligence and memory are filled with past memories, we cannot make correct decisions. Sometimes, our mind makes decisions in a very funny way.

When you see me, if you have had any problems with any other *swami* or any other person who was wearing this same color robe in the past, suddenly that memory will be awakened. Then the intelligence is not even ready to think. Immediately our ego gives the order to leave. This is what we call prejudice.

Many times we make a judgment and then collect arguments to support our judgment. We are caught in this network. A man who is not driven by his senses has the ability to make decisions with clarity. If the area of the *citta* (intelligence) is clear, then automatically our senses work properly and we make the right decisions.

The fountain of Bliss is within you

We can achieve bliss by controlling the mind and not the senses. Only by changing the leader, can we change the servants. The mind is the master who is making decisions and leading the senses. So all we need to do is work on the mind, not on the senses.

Kṛṣṇa says, 'One who has conquered the mind achieves the *Paramātman* (divine Self).' We don't need to achieve bliss. It is always there within us. If it has to be achieved, there is every possibility it can be lost. If it can be lost, what is the guarantee it will be there forever? If something is our very nature, it becomes easy. If it has to be achieved, then there is every possibility that after ten days it may be lost.

The fountain of bliss is continuously happening in us. Unless we have the bliss energy in us, we cannot inhale and exhale. But we stop the bliss fountain again and again. All we need to do is stop the stopping process. We don't even need to create anything or achieve anything. Kṛṣṇa says that we just have to conquer the mind, because the Self has been already achieved and we are with it. There is nothing to strive for.

Here is a small story to explain how happiness and sorrow are in no way related to the outer world, but to the inner world.

An old man went to a nearby city only for some work. When he was coming back to his village, from a distance he suddenly noticed that his house was on fire. He started shouting, screaming, rolling on the ground, and weeping.

His son came to him and said, 'Dad, don't worry. Don't you remember, we sold that house just yesterday?'

Immediately, the old man sat up and wiped his tears. The sorrow just disappeared.

In ten minutes his other son came to him and said, 'Dad, yes, we sold it, but we have yet to get the money.'

Again the man started rolling on the ground and weeping, 'Oh, I don't know what I will do now. I don't know who will care for me. I don't know how to save myself.'

Some ten minutes later, his wife came on the scene and said, 'Don't worry; just this morning I saw that the money was deposited in our bank account.'

Again the man got up, wiped his tears and became perfectly normal!

Here it is, the same situation and the same person, but the suffering happens only when he thinks that the house is his. It is just thinking that something is 'mine' that causes the suffering.

One day I was going for a walk on the beach. One of our devotees said, '*Swamiji*, I think we should have a cottage here. It would be very nice. We can come out and enjoy the breeze.'

I asked him, 'Are we not enjoying ourselves now? Why do you need a cottage here to enjoy? Just enjoy yourself now!' But the mind never enjoys unless we possess it. The man who possesses and tries to enjoy will never be able to enjoy. By the time we own the cottage we start worrying, 'I think I should have this kind of furniture or that arrangement.' Or we have already started thinking about another cottage in some other place.

Ramana Maharishi was a great devotee of Aruṇācala, the sacred hillock in Tiruvannamalai, my birthplace. Someone who visited him for the first time said, 'Master, what a beautiful place this is! The Aruṇācala hill is so beautiful!' Ramana Maharishi said, 'Just be here for three days, all these ideas will disappear!' In just three days we take things for granted. The person who enjoys only by possessing will never enjoy. The person who enjoys will not bother about possessing. It is just our mind. Sometimes the mind will not allow us to enjoy something unless we know for sure that it is ours. And at other times when we know it is ours it creates suffering. Suffering or joy is created only by that one link, the mind. If that link is disconnected, the whole process will happen beautifully.

The only difference between an enlightened person and us is that one missing link! It's not as if he has two big horns. There is no other difference between an enlightened person and us other than this mind, which continuously thinks, 'What is in it for me?' If we delete that 'I', we will become Christ! Don't start from the senses; start instead from the ego, the mind.

We always complain that our senses are corrupting us. No, *we* are corrupting them. We abuse them. See, even at two a.m., we still watch our soccer game on television. When the advertisements come on, our eyes would close automatically, but we continue to watch the rest of the game. We abuse our eyes because we want to enjoy ourselves.

It is the same story with the *gongura chutney* (extremely spicy South Indian side dish). Our tongue burns and our eyes water, but we continue to put large quantities of it into our mouth! Just the mention of it is enough; I can see how many mouths are salivating just now! We abuse and disrespect our senses. It is we who are disturbing our senses. It is this 'What is there for me?' that destroys the whole thing. This is where the whole trouble starts. All we need to do is control the mind, not the senses.

Another simple thing: hot and sweet tastes are just one and the same. Just try this simple experiment: stretch out your tongue and concentrate on it. Visualize that you are walking on your tongue. Then take a chili and a sugar candy. Touch one corner of your tongue with the chili and the other corner with the sugar candy. Deeply witness what happens. You will see that when you touch with the chili and when you touch with the sugar candy, both feel one and the same! From this we can understand that if we go a little deeper into our system, the experiences of hot and sweet are identical.

The trouble starts only when we put a label on it saying, 'This is hot. This is not good for me,' or 'This is sweet. I like this.' Actually both are one and the same. Based on our recorded memory, we start thinking that this is not good for me, as a result of which we really begin to feel that it is not good for us.

Understand, our thoughts create our senses. We create what we want to have. Our thoughts are so powerful that they can just change the whole body. For example: just think of a person who took money from you and has not returned it. Immediately we experience something happening in our system. Our blood boils, our blood pressure, heart rate and pulse rate rise. A single thought can change the whole chemistry.

Our body is created only by our thoughts. In India there is a great science called *sāmudrikā lakṣaṇa*. Just by seeing the face, the body, the way a person stands or sits or walks, a trained sage can tell the quality of the mind. This is because the sage knows the secret that the mind creates the body. The body is the outer expression of the mind. The mind is the inner experience of the body. If our mind changes, our body can be changed and our whole system can be changed.

A man whose mind is clearly reprogrammed according to spiritual ideas can completely change his senses. The entire sense experience can be changed. All we need to do is to reprogram our mind to look in.

And Kṛṣṇa says one more important thing about heat and cold. I don't know how you will believe this, but I have seen people living in the Himalayas with just two pieces of clothing. I myself lived in the Himalayas and I used to sleep on the snow with this same cotton dress. It is difficult to believe, but true. All we need to do is stop resisting.

Just try this experiment: the moment you feel the cool breeze, don't create the idea that you will catch cold or may have wheezing. Just don't create such words. These days, you have learned all big negative words. The more words you know about diseases, the greater the possibility of getting them! Whenever we repeat something, we create that quality in ourselves.

> Here is a simple experiment you can do:
>
> Close your eyes and repeat ten times: '*Śānti*, *Śānti*, *Śānti*,' you will have peace inside (*Śānti* means peace in Sanskrit). The only thing, your wife's name should not be *Śānti*! By just repeating '*Śānti*', the quality of peace will start happening in you. In the same way, if you repeat the names of diseases, you will start creating those diseases with you.

Recently, I went to the AAPI (Association of American Physicians of Indian Origin) convention. There they showed me a book containing their research work. One such study shows that in medical colleges, if lessons are being taught about a particular disease, more than forty percent of the students start showing symptoms of that disease. The reason for this phenomenon is that the students are continuously thinking about those symptoms. Whenever we hear about a disease, the first thing we tend to do is to check if we have those symptoms.

Since the students are constantly meditating on the symptoms, forty percent of them express the same. Whatever we think, we express. We need to work on the mind. Then our whole system will be purified and our senses will be reconstructed. Kṛṣṇa gives us a beautiful technique to work on the mind.

He says one more important thing, 'Honor and dishonor will be the same.' This is very difficult to believe. We can even accept that hot and sweet can be the same. But honor and dishonor, how can they be the same? One word is enough to get us angry.

Attention is energy

Someone asked me the other day, '*Swamiji*, why do we bother so much about others' opinions?'

We bother about others' opinions because we know ourselves only through the opinions of others. If everybody says, 'You are beautiful,' we get that certificate. If everybody says, 'You are great,' we get that certificate. We collect all these certificates and build our personality with them.

In our Life Bliss Program, the first session is about this. It is about why we get depressed, or repeatedly fall into a low energy state. It is because others' certificates are our energy source. We don't have any self-respect. If others' opinions about us are good, we think we are great; else we immediately lose our self-esteem.

Christ says, 'Love thy neighbor as thyself.' But we don't even love ourselves. That is why there is so much of hatred. That is the reason for the wars all around us. I tell people, if we want to live, we must learn how to be with ourselves. As of now, our source of energy is others' opinions. If somebody tells us, 'You are really great,' we may act humble and say, 'No, no, I am not,' but inside us we want them to go on and on.

We are constantly fuelled by others' opinions and work to get them. Just meditate on this one thought. This is a great technique that can liberate us. Don't worry about what others are thinking about you. Because they also worry about what you might think of them! If we meditate on this one statement, it will completely liberate us from this problem of honor or dishonor. Be very clear, if we are bothered about somebody's opinion, directly or indirectly, he is also bothered about our opinion. It is just a give-and-take game.

Kṛṣṇa says, 'A person whose mind is content because of spiritual knowledge, who has subdued his senses and to whom stone and gold are the same, and who is satisfied with what he has, is said to be established in Self-realization and is called an enlightened being.'

First we should understand why Kṛṣṇa is speaking of all these qualities of a master. Why is he explaining all these qualities? These qualities are techniques. If we practice them we will also reach the same enlightened state.

Be very clear: an enlightened master's word is a *mantra* that will transform us. His life is a *tantra,* a technique that will transform us, and his form is a *yantra,* a sacred image to be meditated upon. His actions, if replicated in our life, will create the same quality of consciousness in our being. For example, if we listen to music that comes from the heart, like traditional Indian classical music, we will have that same experience as the great saints who composed it. If we listen to music that comes from the *mūlādhāra* (sex center) it will create the same lustful mood in us. If we meditate on some expression, we will have the same experience behind that expression. Experience leads to expression, and expression leads to experience.

There are research reports on art therapy. Once, several mad people were given canvas and paint and asked to paint. They just did whatever they wanted. We can imagine how they painted! But the surprising thing is, they experienced a complete recovery within a six-month period. This is because they painted and the catharsis occured. They threw everything out. When catharsis happens, naturally people get healed.

And the next amazing thing is that the doctor who was doing the research on this art therapy found certain patterns. He found that those who became mad because of money all painted in the same manner. People who had become mad because of relationships all painted in the same way, and people who had become mad because of loss of name and fame painted in the same way.

A small story:

A man went to a mental asylum, to see what was happening in there. The doctor took him around the hospital. In the first room, he saw that one person had written a name all over the walls in blood: 'Latā,' 'Latā,' 'Latā.' He was chanting, 'Latā, Latā, Latā.'

The man asked the doctor what had happened to this patient. The doctor replied that he had wanted to marry some girl called Latā, but was not able to. That is why he became mad. The tour continued and the man was shown many different kinds of people in different rooms.

One patient was attempting to swim on the floor; another was hanging from the ceiling, and another was walking on all fours.

In the end, he came to the last room, where another person was chanting, 'Latā, Latā, Latā.' In this room too, the walls were covered with 'Latā'. The visitor enquired whether this patient was also in love with Latā.

The doctor replied, 'No, he actually married Latā! That is how he went mad.'

So, there are so many reasons why someone can become mad.

All men who become mad because of an obsession with money, paint and draw in the same way. The reason is, only what is inside comes out. In the process of painting, which is really a form of catharsis, they throw onto the canvas whatever is inside their unconscious. And the last and most important part of this story: the doctor who was reviewing all the paintings became mad!

There are three things we need to understand here: First, experience comes out as expression.

Second, the quality of experience and the quality of expression are very closely associated. And third, and most importantly, if you concentrate on the expression, you will reach the experience. Here, repeatedly, Kṛṣṇa speaks about how an enlightened person lives and the qualities that an enlightened person expresses, so that we can meditate on it. When we begin imbibing these ideas, we can reach the consciousness of an enlightened being. When we contemplate upon these ideas, we start expressing them naturally, and they sink into our being.

The winner of the senses

Kṛṣṇa says repeatedly, '*Vijitendriyaḥ*' (one who has subdued his senses). He gives us a method to solve the problem and go beyond. All we have to do is understand where we are caught and where our problems lie. Our whole trouble is in the mind, the intelligence and the ego.

In this diagram, beyond the ego we have the *ātman,* the Self. Just the presence of the *ātman* makes our ego work. The whole trouble begins when we judge for ourselves and start thinking, 'What am I going to gain from this?' If the ego and the intelligence are removed from the system, the self starts radiating its energy directly through the senses. That is why enlightened people have sharp senses. Whether it is their vision or

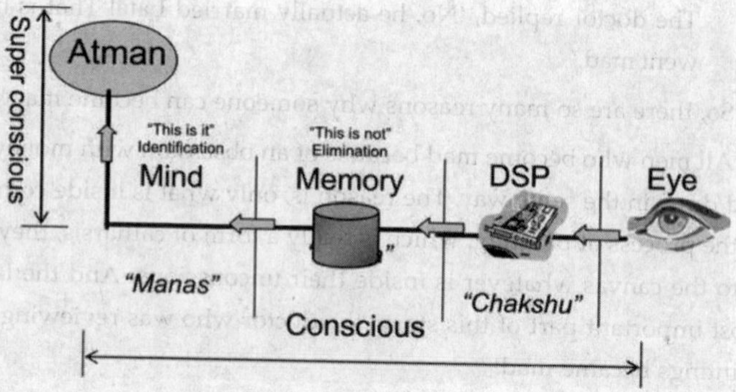

hearing, it will be sharp and deep because it is not corrupted by the ego. Only a person whose being is clear will have pure senses. A man who continuously uses his senses abuses them. He will not have energy or *tejas* in his senses.

The first thing that happens to a man who has abused his senses is the loss of his sense of smell. If we have lost our sense of smell, then we need immediate emergency treatment! We need to be admitted into the ICU of spirituality. We need meditation immediately. When our mind is under our control we develop equanimity. This happens when we reach enlightenment. When we become enlightened there is nothing to be achieved. Our being will start respecting everyone automatically.

Here 'equal' is used, but the exact translation should be 'unique'. We respect everyone as a unique being. Treating everyone equally is one thing. Treating them as unique is another. When we understand that each person is unique, we respect him or her. Sometimes when we say we treat everyone equally, we start disrespecting everybody equally! Instead of raising others to a higher level, we bring ourselves down.

Rāmakṛṣṇa Paramahamsa, an enlightened master from India, was such a humble soul. If anybody came to see him, he would first do *namaskār* (bowing down with hands folded to show respect for the other person) even before they paid their respects to him. Once, an egoistic man, a well-read scholar came to see Rāmakṛṣṇa. A man who has read all the scriptures and not become enlightened has a lot of ego. He knows the tricks of the trade, but he does not have the capital or courage to do business.

Rāmakṛṣṇa as usual, bowed down before this well-read scholar who came to meet him. The scholar told the people standing around, 'After all, he is younger than me. He can bow down to me, no problem.' Rāmakṛṣṇa said, 'By doing *namaskār,* I raise you to my level. But by accepting it in an egoistic way, you try to bring me down to your level!' So be very clear, when we treat people equally, we may bring them to our level. When we understand that every being is unique, we will begin respecting every being. We will understand that every being has its own unique place.

We are not all the same. God is an artist not an engineer. That is why He painted each one of us so differently. If He were an engineer, He would have just ordered ten thousand pieces of Mr. India or one million pieces of Miss Universe so all of us would look the same. But He is an artist, not an engineer. When we understand that each one of us is unique, we will start respecting every being.

One more thing we need to understand is that even our enemy is necessary for our life. We have possibly learned thousands of things from our enemies. Without them we wouldn't have achieved what we have achieved. When we are depressed we can remember our enemies. Then we can come out of our depression and start fighting again! We don't know in what ways people contribute to our life.

A small story:

There was a great *sanyāsi* who was highly respected all over the world. Suddenly one day, his close disciple found out an important secret about him. The disciple happened to be in the *sanyāsi*s private quarters and saw that he had his divorced wife's photograph in his room.

The disciple asked the *sanyāsi*, 'Master, I thought you were such a great person. I never expected that you are harboring such family attachments in your life. Why do you still have her picture in your room?'

The *sanyāsi* just laughed and replied, 'Whenever I want to give up this life of *sanyās*, I just look at her photograph and I get the courage back to sustain this lifestyle immediately!'

So we don't know who is playing what role in our life!

Even our enemy might be playing an important and helpful role in our growth. We can't say why somebody is necessary in our life and why somebody is not necessary. Just like our friends, our enemies also play their role in our lives. When we understand that each and every being is unique, we will see everyone in the same way. Kṛṣṇa here says about 'the pious and the sinners'. Be very clear there is no such thing as sin, except calling human beings 'sinners'. Kṛṣṇa rightly states that the enlightened being sees only divine consciousness in everyone and so can never label anyone as being pious or a sinner.

Understand: God accepts each one of us as we are. The society created the idea of sin and merit. Immediately the next question will be, 'Then can we do whatever we want?' A man who understands this spiritual science will never disturb others. Again and again I tell people, our sin and merit should be based on our understanding, not out of greed for heaven or fear of hell. Let discipline happen to you as a natural flowering. If we are afraid of the police and follow the traffic rules, then whenever we don't see a police car, we are tempted to press the accelerator.

Actually stepping the wrong way is a deep temptation. Breaking rules can be exciting, especially when something is forbidden. It becomes really attractive. The forbidden fruit is always tasty.

Let our morality not be based on fear and greed. That is why in Patañjali's *Yoga sūtras,* there is a beautiful word *yama. Yama* means discipline. It also means death. If we understand that our life is going to end in death, we start thinking and meditating upon death. We will automatically be disciplined. In Sanskrit, the same word translates as both death and discipline. Let our discipline happen only out of understanding of death and not out of fear or greed.

Controlling The Mind

6.10 *A yogi should always try to concentrate his mind on the supreme Self.*
Remaining in a secluded place, he should carefully control his mind without being attracted by anything and should be free from the feeling of possessiveness.

6.11 *In a clean and pure place, he should establish his seat by laying* kuṣa *grass, a deerskin and a cloth one over another, neither too high nor too low.*

6.12 *Sitting firmly on that pure seat, the yogi should practice the purification of the self by controlling the activities of the mind and the senses.*

6.13 *Holding the body, head and neck steady, looking at the tip of his nose without looking in any other direction.*

6.14 *Let him sit with an undisturbed mind, free from fear and in tune with Existence, controlling the mind, focusing it on Me and making Me the supreme goal.*

In these verses Kṛṣṇa gives directions for the practitioner of yoga, the *yogi*. There are instructions about both the state of the mind and the state of the body.

Kṛṣṇa stresses the importance of controlling our senses repeatedly. Why? Senses are our doors to the external world. As long as they are open and uncontrolled, we are immersed only in the external world and it is impossible to understand our true reality. We may become a great scientist or a wealthy businessman by observing the outer world, but never an enlightened person. For this path, looking inwards is the only way.

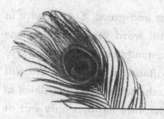

Controlling the senses requires controlling the mind, which in turn requires control of thoughts. If we analyze our thoughts for a few minutes, we will find that there is no connection between one thought and another. By their very nature our thoughts are illogical, unconnected, and irrational. Thoughts keep swinging from past to future and back to the past.

Unclutch and become liberated

We need to do two things to control our thoughts. First, we need to stay in the present moment by refusing to move to the past or future, and second, we need to disconnect thoughts. I call this unclutching. We need to be aware that thoughts are not inherently connected. We connect them into a shaft of joy or sorrow that do not exist at all. So unclutch and become liberated. Just witness thoughts. Detach yourself from the regrets of the past and the speculations about the future and you will automatically rise into the present.

Understand, we cannot live without desires. If anyone tells us that we can reach enlightenment through elimination of desires, it is incorrect. First of all, we are already enlightened. We are just not aware of it. If we are already there, how can we achieve it? Second, desires are energy. We cannot inhale and exhale without the desire to live. Simply dying will not give us the experience!

When Buddha talks of desires being sorrowful, he means that the attachment to desires brings sorrow. That is what Kṛṣṇa talks about here - dropping the attachment and possessiveness. It is the feeling of 'mine,' that creates the feeling of 'I,' not the other way around. Our identity is made up of all the things that we desire. Once the feeling of 'mine' disappears, it is possible to shed our identity as well. When we are free of the feeling of 'mine' and 'I', when we are not attached or attracted to external objects, when we are not led by our senses, we have steadied the mind and senses. To facilitate this, Kṛṣṇa stipulates the conditions.

We should go to a secluded place. Why? When all is said and done, in the house there will be some disturbance or other. A secluded place is really just a means to move us away from these disturbances.

The *kuṣa* (a type of grass considered ideal to sit on and meditate), deerskin and all those things are like insulation, so that the earth will not absorb the energy we create. But now we don't have to bother about that, since we usually sit in a chair, raised a little from the ground. It should be comfortable. The most important thing to be aware of in any meditation is to be relaxed. We cannot meditate in discomfort. *Sthira* (stable) and *sukha* (pleasurable) are the basic essentials of any meditation posture.

Here Kṛṣṇa gives three more instructions:

1. Head, spine and neck should be in a straight line.
2. We should fix our eyes on the tip of the nose. Then, naturally our awareness will settle on the third eye. Our concentration will settle on the *ājña cakra* (the brow energy center).
3. We should meditate on 'Me' as the supreme goal.

These are simple, commonsense instructions. Keeping the head, neck and spine, all in one line, prevents us from dropping off to sleep. It also helps in the upward flow of pranic energy, the life-giving energy.

A small story:

In Chennai, South India, there was a famous preacher. He was well known but boring. People used to go to sleep listening to him. On the day he died, a bus driver from Chennai also died. In Chennai, bus drivers are like Yama, the god of death. They drive buses just to terrorize people. People both inside and outside the bus pray for their own safety.

When they both arrived at the gates of heaven, the driver was speedily ushered into heaven's first class suite. The preacher found himself escorted to a hot and humid space, very similar to the Chennai climate.

> The preacher started screaming, 'There is no justice in the land of Yama. I, a great preacher, am being led to hell, while this driver goes to heaven. Will someone give me justice?'
>
> Yama heard his screams and explained, 'Here, we go by the end result caused by you on planet Earth, irrespective of what you might have been doing as a profession. When the driver drove, fearing for their lives, many people remembered God and prayed to Him sincerely. You, on the other hand, through your preaching only put people to sleep!'

That is why I am always afraid with you people. When I talk and teach you meditation, you doze off. Just think, Yama may say the same thing to me! So at least for my sake, keep your eyes open.

Whether we close our eyes fully or half close them, it is important that we disconnect from the external world. When the eyes are focused on the tip of the nose, they are not looking at external objects and ninety percent of sensory inputs are cut off. In addition, the focus is on the third eye between the brows, which, when energized, dissolves the ego block.

Finally, Kṛṣṇa says, 'Focus on Me.' He means our true Self. If we like, we can meditate on the form of Kṛṣṇa with a flute and peacock feather. But I always prescribe going beyond the form. Go into your being. Of course, when we enter into our third eye, automatically we will go beyond the form. We will start meditating on the formless energy that is beyond the form.

Neither Too Much Nor Too Little

6.15 Always practicing control over the mind and established in the Self,
The yogi attains peace, the supreme liberation and My kingdom.

6.16 Yoga is neither eating too much nor eating too little,
It is neither sleeping too much nor sleeping too little, O Arjuna.

6.17 One who is regulated in food, rest, recreation and work, sleep and wakefulness can reduce misery.

6.18 When the mind is disciplined and one is established in the Self, free from all desires,
Then one is said to be established in yoga.

6.19 As a lamp in a place without wind does not waver,
So also the yogi whose mind is controlled remains steady, engaged in yoga, in the Self.

Kṛṣṇa talks here about control of the mind and being established in the Self. The first line of Yoga sūtras starts with *'yogaḥ citta vṛtti nirodaḥ.'* It means: Yoga is cessation of the mind.

The very first line gives the path and the goal of yoga. The word yoga means uniting with the Divine. To reach the Ultimate, the goal and the path is the practice of Yoga. The goal is uniting with the Ultimate and the path is dropping the mind, which means going beyond thoughts. See, we are spiritual beings having a human experience, not human beings having a spiritual experience. This is the truth. All we need to do is go back to the source and realize our true nature.

The mind pulls us towards the temporary happiness that we experience by pursuing sense pleasures. For example: there might be some particular sweet that we like. When we eat it, for a few minutes our mind stops thinking about it. There is a sense of peace when we are eating the sweet. Actually, the peace is because the number of thoughts has come down for those few minutes. But we think the peace we experience is due to the sweet itself.

Understand that there is nothing wrong with liking the sweet. But if we think that the sweet is the cause of our fulfillment, then the problem starts, because the next time the same sweet may not give us the same experience of fulfillment. The experience of fulfillment has nothing to do with the object of experience.

In the same way, if we hold on to an object that we think gives us bliss, we will create an attachment to that object. But the experience of bliss is in no way related to the object. It is beyond attachment to any object, material or spiritual. When we are happy due to some person, the momentary joy comes because the number of our thoughts comes down when we meet the person. But the bliss itself comes only from our own being and not from the person whom we met. In fact, it continuously happens within us, irrespective of anything that goes on outside. Then why do we not feel the bliss continuously? It is because we are under the control of the mind.

We can stop the stopping of the fountain of bliss that is happening every moment in us. When I say 'eternal bliss', what do I mean? '*nitya*' or 'eternal' means the past, present, and future all put together, because it is beyond time. It is beyond time. But the eternal can be touched only in the present. Being in the present is what eternity is. The only reality is the present. So bliss can be experienced only in the present.

When we are completely in reality, in the present, we are completely in tune with Existence and we are in bliss. The present blissful moment gives birth to the next moment, which will also be blissful. But if we try to look for bliss in the future, it will never happen. So accept reality here and now and be blissful; automatically the future will also be blissful.

Bliss is like the water in a river. We can keep our hands open in it and enjoy it. But if we try to hold the water with closed hands, it will simply flow away from us. If we want to be in eternal bliss, we need to be blissful this very moment. We should not bother about whether we had bliss in the past or whether we will have it in the future. Just be blissful now.

When Kṛṣṇa talks about the mind and the senses being controlled, He is not talking about suppressing the mind and the senses. People who claim to renounce the world and its material aspects still cling to desires. Their efforts only result in misery. Instead of directing our senses towards external objects, all we can do is turn our focus inwards and experience inner joy. Once the senses and the mind discover this inner joy, on their own they will give up their attachment to external pleasures. Suppression never works; what works is transformation.

To be balanced in whatever we do and to act without attachment is the path of a *yogi*. For any activity, moderation is needed. This is what Buddha meant by the 'middle path.' Understand, when we are aware we will be sensitive in all our actions. The awareness will show us what is conducive to our system.

Yoga manuals will not tell us what Kṛṣṇa tells Arjuna here. Guidelines on sleeping too much or too little, or eating too much or too little, are in no way a prescribed method for yoga. Controlling or regulating the senses does not mean we should suppress the senses. Eating too much will only make us lethargic. Eating too little will make us crave more food. If we sleep too much, it will lead to laziness and lethargy. If we sleep too little, we will end up feeling tired because the body-mind is not rejuvenated enough.

How do we know what is too much or too little? Here, Kṛṣṇa actually refers to our body intelligence. The body has intelligence to maintain itself. But we do not trust our inherent body intelligence. We run our body according to our desires and senses. Otherwise, why would we stay up late at night watching television when our eyes are already tired and our body is begging for some sleep? Why would we overeat? Has anyone ever seen an animal overeat? They eat according to their body intelligence. When the body signals that it needs food, they eat. When the body signals that it needs sleep, they sleep. The problem is that we have forgotten how to relate with our own body intelligence.

After eating we should feel energetic, but we feel lazy and sleepy after lunch. It is because we do not eat the right type and amount of food. We eat much more than what we need. Just try this for a few days: When you eat, eat just enough until you are about full but not completely full. When you feel you can eat one more handful of rice or food, stop. Try this for a few days and you will see a difference.

Similarly, we do not need to sleep for as long as eight hours as most of us do. Even science has established that there are periods in our sleep - the dream and deep-sleep-states-that determine our holistic health. The deep sleep state is what rejuvenates us. Actually, it is in the deep sleep state that we access the causal body, the *kāraṇa śarīra* from where we derive our energy. This state can be achieved through meditation as well. In the course of an eight-hour sleep cycle, we are in the deep-sleep state for only a couple of hours. That is why even a few minutes of meditation can actually refresh us as much as a few hours of sleep, because we access the same energy of the causal body through meditation.

Once the mind comes in between and demands either too much sleep or too much eating or fasting, we are ignoring the body intelligence. We should trust our body intelligence and just try living by becoming sensitive to the body.

Kṛṣṇa talks about *āhāra* in these verses. *Āhāra* in Sanskrit means food. It is the food that is taken in through our five senses and not just the mouth.

Pratyāhāra, one of the eight parts of yoga, is the control of sensory inputs. It means going beyond these *āhāra,* beyond the sense objects, so that the higher level of consciousness can be awakened. When we move away from the senses and experience bliss. What we experience through the senses can be called pleasure or joy. Pain is bound to follow this temporary pleasure. Bliss is beyond the pairs of opposites like pleasure and pain. It is internally generated.

The main aim of all our yoga and meditation techniques is to reach the level of our being or '*nityānanda*' or 'eternal bliss.' As of now, we are running after something in the outer world, because we think it can give us what we are ultimately looking for, bliss. Bliss is actually what we are running after, but we think it can be achieved through money, comforts, relations. We do not realize that all these objects only give us temporary states of pleasure and happiness. Our inherent nature is bliss and that is the reason why we are constantly searching for this state of bliss. When we realize that bliss is happening inside us all the time, the desires will drop automatically.

When we are aware of our actions, we can never be addicted to anything. The addictions cannot exist if we are conscious and aware when we engage in the action. We try to suppress the desire instead of being aware, and that is where the problem starts. When we repeat the words 'I want to quit smoking,' we are actually empowering 'smoking' without even being aware of it. What we speak, what our mind thinks gets inscribed in our body and our body gets prepared to execute it. So we should not use the word *'smoking'* again and again.

Addiction has power over us because of the feeling of regret or unfulfillment. As long as we are not aware that we need not carry guilt for anything that we have done, the addiction will persist.

Guilt is the greatest sin we can commit and carry. Whatever we did in the past we did with the wisdom we had then. We realize it was a mistake because now, we have updated intelligence to realize it. So drop that guilt. When we drop the guilt that we have been shouldering, many of our repetitive negative behavior patterns stop automatically.

Moreover, we cannot consciously send something harmful into our system. As long as we drink or smoke as a ritual, it becomes an addiction. To those who come to me for help with addictions, I say, 'Smoke as much as you want. Drink as much as you want. But do it with awareness.' In a few days, they come back and say they cannot smoke or drink anymore. That is because the innate body intelligence refuses to cooperate with the disastrous activity.

Awareness is the key to bring the mind under control. Normally, our mind oscillates between the past and the future just like the flame of a lamp that's wavering in the wind. When the same lamp is placed in a windless place, it stops flickering. By nature, the mind is in dilemma. We cannot suppress it or control it just by allowing it to wander either. All we can do to still the mind is to stop bothering about it and just witness it. So just relax.

Be in the present

All our desires and fears arise because we feel that life has some purpose. Understand that life has no purpose. It has only meaning. Life has no goal; the path itself is the goal. Enjoy the path. Enjoy life as it comes. Understand that the way we are living life in our world of fantasies is actually like living in our dream world. Each of us has a web of desires, and we try to protect our ego in this web. Only when we break out of the web and drop the ego, can we even see what life really is. Otherwise, we will only be projecting our imagination. When we realize the purposelessness of life, we can drop our desires and fears, we can plunge into reality.

The moment we decide to stay in the present, the mind stops oscillating. When the mind stands still in the present, we reach the state of 'no-mind'. In this state of 'no-mind' we don't create, sustain, or destroy any thought. We relax from all these three things into the state of no-mind.

Our mind is like a lake. When we throw a stone in a lake, many ripples will be created. If we want to stop these ripples, we cannot put our hand in the lake to try to smooth out the ripples. This will only cause more ripples. This is what we end up doing when we try to still our minds. We try to still our minds by trying to destroy and suppress thoughts. We can never be successful this way. If we just relax and watch our mind with complete awareness, then no new thoughts will be created.

In India we say that God has three roles - creator, sustainer and destroyer. Brahma is called the Creator, Viṣṇu the Sustainer, and Śiva the Rejuvenator. With respect to our thoughts, when we stop performing these roles of creation, sustenance, and rejuvenation, we become *Parabrahma* – supreme Self.

There is a beautiful story described in Bhāgavatam, the story of the various incarnations of Viṣṇu, the Hindu god:

> The demigods were oppressed by the demons and appealed to Lord Viṣṇu for help. According to His directions, the demigods were to churn the ocean of milk using the Mahā Meru mountain as the staff and Vāsuki, the serpent, as the rope. During the churning, many products emerged out of the ocean of milk including an elephant, a horse, a divine chariot and many other divine things. Then, a deadly poison emerged, that threatened to take the lives of everyone. Śiva came to their rescue by consuming the poison Himself. He did not completely take it in. He just held it in His throat. That is why he is referred to as Nīlakaṇṭha, the one with a blue throat.

This is actually a metaphysical representation. Life is like the churning of the ocean of milk where we are churned, pulled by desires and fear. There are various products that emerge out of the churning (decisions and choices we make in life). Some of these products appear pleasing while others like poison appear dangerous. When we exist without taking in the poison or throwing it out, meaning without running towards the desires or running away from the fears, we become Śiva and live life blissfully, irrespective of what comes our way.

Self Is Satisfied By The Self In The Self

6.20 In yoga, the mind becomes quiet and the Self is satisfied by the Self in the Self.

6.21 Supreme bliss is grasped by intelligence transcending the senses.
The person who knows this is based in reality.

6.22 By attaining that Supreme, one does not consider any other gain as being greater. By being established in the Supreme, one is not shaken by the greatest misery.

6.23 When yoga is practiced with determination without deviating, the misery by contact with the senses is removed.

6.24 Giving up completely all the fantasies born of the mind, one can regulate all the senses from all the sides by the mind.

Krsna talks about two important things: practice with determination and practice without deviating from the prescribed way. Both are key elements to the experience of yoga. After a few days of practice it is easy to fall into inertia, *tamas,* and give up. Our mind has been programmed with our old routine for years and will draw us back to the old ways. This is where determination is needed. Determination driven by the curiosity and the quest to see and experience the truth is what will give us the energy to practice yoga.

The other important element is practice without deviating from the prescribed way. We (Nithyananda Mission) are re-introducing, re-presenting yoga in the form of Nithya Yoga, the yoga of eternity. I can say re-presenting because it is a new teaching method. The method has evolved but the system, the truth itself, is the same as the original system offered by the great master, Patañjali. His system is so complete that we can't add even a single word to the techniques. It is the experience of Truth and Truth cannot be developed. All we can do is help evolve the teaching of Truth to suit the current minds. The system itself cannot and need not be changed.

Kṛṣṇa emphasizes here that yoga should be practiced in the prescribed way. All eight parts of yoga need to be practiced simultaneously and not sequentially as interpreted today. Even one part of Patañjali's Aṣṭāṅga yoga will take many lifetimes to achieve, given the modern man's mindset.

Satya, truth, is a part of *yama,* the first of the eight steps of Aṣṭāṅga yoga. If we consistently practice truthfulness alone, we will reach *samādhi,* the state of liberation. Our thoughts, words, and actions become pure and truthful only when we are enlightened. This is what Kṛṣṇa means when He says, 'Self is satisfied by the Self in the Self.' All of this has to happen together. When one aspect is fulfilled, all others also become fulfilled. This is the state of *pūrṇa,* complete fulfillment. Nothing can be taken away from it or added to it that would make any difference to its completeness. One becomes centered in bliss.

These days, yoga is a fashion statement. The people doing yoga and those teaching it don't know the true purpose of yoga. I believe in many parts of the world, cosmetic surgery is accepted socially. Similarly, in some other parts, being a student of yoga is a necessary qualification for social acceptance.

So, today there is hot yoga, temperate yoga, cold yoga, very cold yoga, and so on. All these do not lead us to the truth. Very little can be gained spiritually by doing only the physical postures and breathing exercises. They may provide some physical health benefits in the short term if done carefully. But actually, unregulated breathing exercises and physical contortions can do more harm than good.

Kṛṣṇa talks about moving into reality, transcending the senses and the mind. The way yoga is practiced in many places, one is moved away from reality into a fantasy world. The senses and the mind wander aimlessly. We should neither suppress nor pursue our desires. We need to understand what is happening and how it is happening.

A small story:

Buddha had several thousand disciples whom He used to address every morning. One day He brought a tightly knotted rope with Him and asked, 'Can someone untie this knot?'

Many disciples came and they tried pushing and pulling at the rope but the knot only became tighter.

Finally, one disciple came up, looked at the knot for a while, and then undid the knot.

We need to look at the knot to see how it has been created. Once we do that, we have to simply reverse the process of creating the knot. Instead, if we simply pull and push the knot will only become tighter. The way out of the mind is also through the mind and not by avoiding it. Awareness is the key through which all our emotions can be handled.

Take fear for example. What do we do when we feel afraid of something? The moment we are faced with the object of fear, we try to escape. The next time you are afraid, try this: instead of running away, just try looking at the fear consciously with full awareness. Do not try to suppress it or run away from it. When you look at fear with awareness, you will see that the fear does not exist as you thought it existed. Because we don't know the object or situation fully, we fantasize about how it could be and how it could affect us, and build up our fear.

When we bring the light of knowledge upon fear, ignorance is removed and we get the courage to see the object as it is. Because now, since there nothing is hidden, our mind cannot fantasize about the unknown.

So understand, our fears are nothing but negative fantasies.

The same also applies to greed. We start running after the next desire before one desire is even fulfilled. 'What next? What next?' becomes our chant. After fulfilling a desire, have we stopped to think whether we have achieved what we wanted? Have we stopped to enjoy what we just fulfilled? If we sit and contemplate sincerely over one desire after fulfilling it, by now we would have gotten out of the vicious cycle of desires.

Can we ever drink water from a mirage? Running after the fantasies created by the mind is just like running after a mirage or running after the horizon. We can never achieve bliss by running behind these fantasies because these fantasies have no existence in reality.

Be In The Self And See The Supreme

6.25 Gradually, step-by-step, one should become established in the Self,
Held by the conviction of intelligence, with the mind not thinking of anything else.

6.26 From wherever the mind becomes agitated due to its wandering and unsteady nature,
From there, one must certainly bring it under the control of the Self.

6.27 The yogi whose mind is peaceful attains the highest happiness;
His passion is pacified and he is free from sins as he is liberated by the Supreme.

6.28 The yogi always engaged in the Self and free from material contamination
Is in touch with the Supreme and attains the highest happiness.

6.29 The yogi sees the Supreme established in all beings and also all beings situated in the Supreme.
One established in the Self sees the Supreme everywhere.

Here Kṛṣṇa says that we need conviction and intelligence to be established in the Self. Why does He talk about conviction? Understand that intelligence cannot happen without a strong conviction. That is why our eastern sages have given us the treasure of the *śāstras*, scriptures that give the intellectual understanding, conviction, and commitment to this process. Logically, we will be clear about the questions that naturally arise. 'What is the path? What is the goal? Why do we need spirituality?' All these questions are answered logically. The conclusions are given to us. *Śāstras* are the scriptures that take away all our doubts completely.

saṁśaya rākśasa nāshana astraṁ

It means 'doubt is a devil'. Once a doubt enters our mind, until we clear it, we can't rest. Unless we have complete intellectual clarity, even if we believe, our belief will be a pseudo-belief. Anyone can shake it. Our faith will not have a strong base.

Somebody asked Vivekānanda , 'What is the importance of *Vedas* and why should we study the *śāstras*?'

Vivekānanda said, 'If you study the *śāstras*, all your faith, all your sincerity will become so strong nobody can shake your faith and sincerity.'

Otherwise, any fool can tell us that what we are doing is superstitious and we will start questioning ourselves, 'Am I really doing superstitious things? What am I doing?' We will start having doubts about ourselves.

Understand, we don't really believe our belief. We think we have faith, but our faith is shallow. It will not be deep unless we have the foundation of intellectual conviction. A man who doesn't have intellectual conviction, and just faith, can be shaken by anybody. *Śāstras* give us this intellectual understanding, so that all our convictions can enter into our being and start working.

If we see all the great devotees of the Lord - Caitanya, Rāmānuja, Mādhava - all of them had a very strong intellectual base. Caitanya Mahāprabhu was a great philosopher of logic. Once we reach the peak of logic, only then can we fall into the valley of love. Till then, we are not qualified to fall in the valley of love.

There are different ways to learn and develop conviction. We can learn from our experiences, as well as those of others. We need a strong conviction for spirituality to flower in our lives. Only then can we stay on the path without faltering. If we do anything with knowledge about the science of the whole action, then the activity becomes a meditation.

When the science is lost and only the activity remains, it becomes a ritual. When the juice of wisdom is not in the activity, it becomes a ritual, and we become religious nuts. When we add the juice of wisdom, we become spiritual fruits! When we commit an act without knowing the science behind it, we make that activity a ritual. We need to add 'spirit' to the 'ritual'. Then it becomes 'spirituality'!

We can start with simple things. We can try to infuse awareness into simple actions in our everyday life like eating, taking a bath, and driving. Gradually, when the awareness extends to more actions and to more moments of our life, we can see that such awareness results in bliss, because we are living more in the present moment. Only in the present can we experience that our true nature is bliss.

We need to bring the light of awareness into everything we do. This state of complete awareness, which can be practiced in every one of our daily activities, comes out of a deep internal conviction arising out of our innate intelligence and understanding that we must return to our true nature.

Persevere and succeed

Now, Kṛṣṇa is emphasizing an important spiritual quality, perseverance. What happens most of the time to most of us is that when we realize we need to change, we try a few times and then give up thinking we cannot do it. We expect the mental setup that we have created and solidified to be broken and restructured almost instantly. We need to be more patient and persevere in our efforts for the real change to happen.

So what if we fail sometimes? Why don't we look at the positive side and see that we succeeded a few times as well? Naturally, when we start trying we will be aware and successful a few times, and we will be unaware a few other times. Why do we want to count the failures and feel depressed? We can also look at the successes and feel inspired. That is a much smarter approach!

Once the conviction is there, nothing can stop us except our own mind. The mind is like a faithful servant reproducing whatever it has been fed. All along we have been feeding the mind negative memories of failure. Naturally the mind will recollect and present the same instances of failure. When we want to measure the strength of a chain, we measure the strength of the weakest link in that chain. But we cannot apply the same logic to measure ourselves.

When we measure our lives based on our failures, on our low energy moments, we take a wrong reading of ourselves. We cannot do with our lives what we do with the chain.

Why can't we give credit to ourselves for the successful moments of our lives? We have been conditioned by society to consider ourselves weak beings. We have been taught to feel guilty. The more we remember negative decisions or mistakes, the more guilt we create for ourselves. It only creates low energy. We should just decide that we will not be trapped in this cycle of guilt and desire.

We need to measure ourselves by our strongest moments, when we displayed extraordinary awareness, compassion, and other such divine qualities. We have shown to ourselves what we can achieve if we try. A human being is the sum of his greatest moments. He is a spiritual being who thrives on his strengths.

One more thing that you should understand is that you attract 'like' incidents in your life. The energy of one frequency attracts the similar frequency. Pain attracts pain. Joy attracts joy. Bliss attracts fortune. If we are joyful, we will create joyful people around us. We will create a beautiful community around us. If we are suffering, then naturally we will attract only that type of people around us. It is for us to decide what we want to attract.

If we tune our mind to a positive attitude and to positive things, we start attracting positive situations and people. We start meeting blissful friends and start creating blissful situations. We start creating a blissful life. We must persevere in our efforts to change our attitude and we will see the results in front of our very eyes. Failures are merely tests to verify our mettle. Irrespective of how many times we may fail, with complete faith we can totally believe in that inner strenght that we all possess. Then we shall succeed. This is what is meant when Kṛṣṇa says the true *yogi* reaches the state of ultimate happiness, the state of eternal bliss and divine consciousness, by his identification with the Absolute.

In the next verse, Kṛṣṇa talks about passion and sins. Passion is nothing but a deep attachment to something for the pleasure that it gives. Usually we associate passion, sin, and such terms with deeds that we classify as right or wrong. But here, Kṛṣṇa does not talk about sin in the way society teaches us. There is no sin except the sin of connecting thoughts and thinking that we are logical beings. That is the original sin.

When we are unaware, we commit sin because we are not aware of what we are doing. So the key is to be aware every moment and not to condemn ourselves as sinners. It is we who choose everything in our lives. But since we do not participate in this process with awareness, we call it 'fate'. We are the ones who commit the actions, but we don't want to accept that fact when we get the results.

Somehow we choose to do whatever we want to do and then blame everyone else for the consequences. When we infuse awareness into our actions, automatically the very awareness will ensure that we do the right things. We don't need to depend on society to teach us the right things.

Conscience is a very poor substitute for consciousness. Live according to your intelligence and awareness. If you depend on others, even after becoming an adult, it means you are not mature. Anything done out of conscience does not have the conviction of experience to back it. That is why it is never done whole-heartedly, because your intelligence is not behind the action.

Once a man asked me, '*Swamiji,* I know I should do certain things but I am not able to do them when I need to. For example, the other day I was traveling in a bus and an old man got onto the bus. I knew I should get up and offer my seat to the man, but I started to think that I myself had such a long way to go, and that if I got up I would feel tired after some time. I just thought about it and couldn't get myself to get up and give my seat to the old man. Later I felt guilty about it.'

I told him, 'It is because you have not had the deep experience of joy when you give your seat to another person. Even if you have given your seat before, you have given it half-heartedly. Now, try doing the same act with an attitude of experimentation, thinking, 'Let me try this.' Try doing it as an experiment, with complete involvement. Just do the action with the curiosity of a child.'

Have you seen a child doing anything, like looking at a flower? A child will look at the flower with his entire body. The eyes will look at the flower with curiosity. The hands will feel the flower and the nose will enjoy the smell of the flower. We should try to look at life in a similar way. Many of us have not experienced the joy of serving someone whole-heartedly. On the other hand, if we are smokers, do we need somebody to convince us to smoke? No! Smoking has become our experience. That is why we don't need to depend on somebody else to convince us about it.

When we are in bliss or the highest happiness, we can never commit any sin, because we are aware and conscious. Then the divine hand that is orchestrating every single event will guide every one of our actions.

What does it mean to be freed from all past sinful reactions? Our past reactions are nothing but our past memories, along with the associated emotions, deeply inscribed in our unconscious zone. Understand, a reaction is different from a response. A reaction to anything is always due to our past memories. We can see in our own lives how many times this has happened and we may not even have noticed. Our son comes home late from school one day and we would have already decided that he was in some bad company or has gone to some movie. When he returns, we are ready with our judgment based on some incident in the past and are not even open to listen to him. As soon as he walks through the door our tone and actions become accusatory. Perhaps he stayed back to study in the library, but we are not ready to accept this. We have already formed our judgment.

Whenever we hold on to any past incidents, our actions are bound to be impacted by them. On the other hand, if our action arises from a spontaneous decision based on the present situation, then we are 'responding' to the event or incident or person. When we are in bliss, our actions will be only a response. Have the courage to make decisions without referring to these past incidents, because every single incident is a brand new one. How can we compare what is happening now with what happened before? Every moment we are changing. Our intelligence is being constantly updated. Then how can we analyze the present situation through the lens of the past? We must give up all regrets of the past and immerse ourselves in the present moment.

Kṛṣṇa says that the realized person sees the Supreme in everyone and everything. The ***yogi*** is in touch with the higher Self and is in bliss. When we experience the Truth, we see everything in ourselves, and ourselves in everything. In fact, in my first spiritual experience at the age of twelve, this is what I clearly saw.

When I was twelve, I was playing with this technique of just watching where thoughts came from. At that age I didn't even realize it was meditation. One day, at the foothills of Aruṇācala, in my hometown of Tiruvannamalai in South India, I was sitting on a rock just playing with this technique that I had been practicing for two years. Suddenly, something happened; something opened within me. I felt as if I was being pulled inside. Suddenly, I could see 360 degrees in all directions. My eyes were closed but I could see everything in front of me and behind me. Not just that, I felt that whatever I was seeing was all me. I could see myself in everything - in the trees, in the rocks, in the ground, in the hills, everything!

An enlightened person sees no difference between himself and the rest of the universe. His boundary does not end where his physical body ends. In fact, now with Kirlian photography, we can even check the auric body. For ordinary people, the aura just surrounds the physical body but when you are one with the universe, the aura extends infinitely. The *viśvarūpa darshan* (vision of the cosmic form) that Kṛṣṇa gives Arjuna is the glimpse of the same Truth, where Arjuna sees that Kṛṣṇa is one with the universe.

Through Quantum Physics studies, the scientific community has come to the conclusion that everything in the universe is energy. All our minds are not individually separate pieces of the universe. They are all interlinked and directly affect each other. This is what I call collective consciousness.

In the ultimate sense, the moment we understand that we are deeply connected to the whole universe we start experiencing bliss and living it. Many dimensions of our being start opening. Right now we are stressed out and disturbed because we think of ourselves as individual egos. If we disappear into this collective consciousness, we will experience so many dimensions that we cannot even imagine right now!

When we see an enlightened master, we understand how all encompassing he is. He never excludes anything or anyone. He is just pure love. When we see every human being as a part of God, then that is real worship. Real worship is seeing everything as God, seeing our neighbor as God. Deep inside, society is actually against Existence or God. The best way not to follow anything is to start worshipping it. Society escapes in the name of worship.

Society would never approve of us if we were to let go and love every plant and animal with endless love. It will tell us that we are mad. It will approve only of societal love, love governed by give and take. But I tell you, we must keep loving with all our hearts and expand to see Existence in everything.

The root of God lies in seeing Him in everything. People are afraid to go to the roots and so they delude themselves in superficial layers. Have the courage to go deep inside and love. We will start feeling the common thread of Existence in all that we see. We will understand that all that we see are illusory happenings held together by the real thread that is Existence. Automatically we will start loving everything in the same way because we will see only Existence in everyone and everything.

Controlling The Wavering Mind

6.30 *For one who sees Me everywhere and who sees everything in Me, for him I am never lost nor is he lost to Me.*

6.31 *He who is in oneness with Me in all respects, worships Me situated in all beings and remains present in Me.*

6.32 *One who can feel the happiness or misery of others equally as he can feel his own happiness and misery is the supreme yogi in My opinion, O Arjuna.*

6.33 *Arjuna said: O Madhusūdana, I am not able to see this system of yoga as told by You, owing to the mind being restless and not steady.*

6.34 *O Kṛṣṇa, the wavering mind is agitated, strong and firm. I think it is difficult to control the mind just as it is difficult to control the wind.*

6.35 *The Lord said: O mighty-armed son of Kuntī, it is undoubtedly difficult to control the wavering mind, but by practice and detachment, it can be controlled.*

Here, Kṛṣṇa gives a promise. He says that for anyone who sees Him in everything and who sees everything in Him, He is always available. What Kṛṣṇa means by 'Me' is the Kṛṣṇa energy, the divine consciousness. See the Divine in everybody and everything and automatically, you will relax. You will no longer fight, because you will see everything around you as a part of the Divine, including yourself. Who is there to fight with and what should you fight for? You will simply relax.

Existence is waiting with open arms to engulf us, only we need to let go. When we are ready to feel the embrace of Existence, we rise into a higher plane of consciousness. We enter into a space we never even knew existed. With Existence we always fall in to rise.

All are one

People ask me, 'How can we tell that you are the right master for us?'

I tell them simply, 'If I am truly your master, you can never forget me. I will be there even in your dreams!' The relationship between a master and a disciple is one of pure love. When we are truly in love, we see the object of love in everything around us. The master fills every pore of our being. We don't need to ask, 'Are you my master?' We just know! He has touched us at our core, because to him, there is no separation. An enlightened person can empathize with everyone, because he experiences himself as everyone.

An incident from the life of Vivekānanda :

One night, Vivekānanda woke up at two a.m. and woke up his disciples. His disciples were anxious and wanted to know what was happening. Vivekānanda said that he was feeling a lot of pain and that in some part of the world there was a natural calamity happening that was causing him the pain. The next morning, the newspapers carried the news of a terrible earthquake in the Fiji Islands that consumed many lives. Vivekānanda was sensitive to a calamity that happened in some corner of the world thousands of miles away!

What happened in Vivekānanda is what we call empathy. It is not sympathy.

Sympathy is a very superficial word. We are all capable of sympathy. When someone tells us that they are suffering, we make some noises and just confirm their suffering for them. That is sympathy. We affirm to them that their worries are big, so we actually give them a subtle ego boost.

What an enlightened master feels is empathy. Empathy is when we feel another's suffering in our own being. The other person does not have to tell us he is suffering. We simply know, because the Existential energy in us feels it. Masters are one with us because they are one with Existence and we are a part of Existence.

When we realize the sense of oneness with the entire universe, we experience a tremendous overflowing of love and compassion for every being without discrimination. That is why we can see that masters are such an ocean of infinite love and know only how to give. They are one with Existence and cannot see anyone as a separate entity because there is no separateness.

It is only our senses, mind, and logic that perceive information, and categorizes and analyzes it to create the separateness. As long as we use our logic, we will be excluding and judging. Existence is simply beyond our logic. Only when we drop our logic, mind, and ego can we merge with Existence and become whole and start seeing that everyone is an extension of the same life force, with just different expressions.

Just as the fingers on the hand and the toes on the feet belong to the same body, we will be able to see that everyone is a part of the same universal energy. This is when true compassion, empathy, and service towards everyone can happen. Until then we will only be using our logic, mind, ego, and conditioning to serve others.

When we realize the oneness, we will express our unconditional love towards everyone without discrimination. Our very walk and talk will start radiating so much bliss that our very presence will start healing others. We will become a blessing for planet Earth.

There are a few disciples who have internalized me so much, imbibed me so much that they express me in everything that they do. People who come to the ashram are amazed to see these people who walk like me and talk like me. Some people think that these disciples are doing it to show off. No, they are so much in tune with me that they reflect my body language. My presence is in them.

Kṛṣṇa goes further to explain the state of an enlightened person. He says that the enlightened person will feel the happiness and pain of another person as equal to his own. For him, everything is a part of him. His boundary does not end with the boundary of his own physical body. What does Kṛṣṇa mean when He says that the enlightened person feels happiness and distress equally in himself and in others? First, he said that the enlightened person is beyond the opposites.

It is like this: say there are two trees in a forest. Now, if one tree falls on the other, we can say that the tree on which the other tree has fallen feels the impact of the falling tree. Now, say the tree actually feels the entire forest as a part of its own self. Can we say that it will feel 'another' tree falling on it? When everything is a part of its own self, where is the idea of 'other'? When the idea of 'other' disappears, then where is the pain? The idea of pain is relative. The enlightened person is just immersed in enjoying Existence. No separate identities exist. These terms and concepts exist only as long as one feels separate.

A *yogi* in the state of superconsciousness will watch everything in Existence without judging or labeling it. He will be in a state of complete celebration of life. Existence is only love. Yet, the compassion of the master is such that he feels the experiences that others undergo and empathizes with them. The master's state of equanimity is not disturbed, and yet he feels the pain and joy of others.

This expression of collective consciousness is what Kṛṣṇa has described as *vasudaiva kuṭumbakaṁ.* It means that the world is our family and we should feel for the rest of the world as we would for our immediate family. When we exist in this state of consciousness, we are true *yogi*s.

Arjuna introduces the word 'difficult' here. Be very clear, the moment we categorize something as easy or difficult, we have made it that way. People ask me, '*Swamiji,* is *brahmacarya* difficult?' I tell them, it is neither easy nor difficult. It is just a way of life. Even if we say it is easy, it means it is a little difficult!

For example, now I am sitting here. If I had arthritis, sitting would be difficult. But if I were standing for a long time, sitting would be easy. This is just comparative reality. In the same way, yoga is a way of being. When we complicate things by using words, we make it difficult for ourselves, just to fulfill our ego.

After listening to Kṛṣṇa about controlling the mind, Arjuna expresses his doubts about being able to still the mind. Here, Arjuna is asking about problems that will be faced by future generations as well. His question is not just an individual's question.

People ask me, 'Why is Gītā relevant even today?' Because the questions asked by Arjuna are the same questions that we ask today and the answers of Kṛṣṇa are also relevant even today. The questions are the fundamental quest of the individual and the answers are the eternal Truth. Kṛṣṇa, the energy and His teachings, are the timeless Truths. The doubt that Arjuna has raised is even more applicable to the modern man. In the present age, there is so much materialism and exposure to fantasies through the media. We have become more complex than our forefathers because of this cerebral layer that has formed with all the fantasies bombarding us from all directions.

We are not ready to spend some time or do simple, practical techniques in the inner world because we are so caught up in the outer world. We are in a constant rat race. Arjuna cannot understand how to practice yoga, given the unsteady and wavering nature of the mind. Five thousand years ago, even though there was no infiltration by media on the scale that we have now, Arjuna expressed his doubt about how to handle the mind.

Here, Arjuna addresses to Kṛṣṇa his concerns about the mind being so strong and obstinate that it sometimes overcomes the intelligence. The first and foremost thing is to accept that we have a problem. The next thing is to understand how the problem is created. That is what Arjuna does here. It is only then that we can overcome the problem. If we ignore or run away from it, we can never resolve the problem.

So the first thing to accept is that our mind does flicker and oscillate. We then need to understand how it flickers or oscillates. For this we need to watch the mind. This is meditation. The very act of watching and being aware of the mind will take us beyond the mind.

Here, Kṛṣṇa has to answer from the same plane that Arjuna asks the question. Arjuna says that the mind is wavering and difficult to control. Kṛṣṇa has to give Arjuna a technique. He has to support the idea that it is difficult to control the mind. Now, if He tells Arjuna that this problem is a creation of his mind, Arjuna will not understand. Kṛṣṇa has to give a technique for the mind to play with.

The Path to Self-realization

Masters give meditation techniques so that we try all of them and ultimately realize we are bliss, and that there is nothing to be achieved. But if I tell you that right away, you will not believe me. Your mind will create all kinds of contradictions. Kṛṣṇa also has to give a solution for the questioning mind. He emphasizes perseverance and penance. Don't think penance means going to the Himalayas and meditating and fasting. Penance is persevering with conviction until we experience the Truth.

Kṛṣṇa also gives the technique to master the mind - detachment. Here we need to understand 'detachment'. Whether we say ego or mind, it is just the collection of thoughts. Thoughts can exist only in relationship to our identity and the past or the future.

In the present, we cannot have thoughts because the moment we think, that very moment, the present has slipped into the past. The mind moves only because it is attached to the past or the future, constantly driven by fear and greed. Either we fear losing the carefully constructed identity we have created for ourselves, or we are greedy to develop a better image of ourselves in the eyes of society. We create two identities, one for ourselves, and the other to project to the outer world. The mind is in constant fear and greed about maintaining and developing these identities.

The mind becomes so attached to these identities that it is constantly reviewing past incidents or it is constantly planning the future to protect these identities. This constant pre-occupation of the mind with the past and future is the root cause of the oscillation and movement of the mind. The mind is always in such constant preparation that it never lets us stay in the present moment. Staying in the present moment means total insecurity. It requires that we be ready to embrace the present without planning for the future or reviewing the past. This seems like a great danger for our ego. The mind is not prepared for that.

Actually, our identities are only a collection of opinions and ideas from the people around us. We are always trying to maintain this ego and carefully run our lives according to its opinions and ideas. It is as if we are constantly walking a tightrope. The pole in our hands is our ego and the rope is the path and framework laid out by society. We are constantly trying to get the applause of the audience, society.

This false image that we have constructed about ourselves is the root cause of all misery. I tell you, any identity that we create about ourselves that is less than the idea that we are God, is a false identity. It is an inferiority complex. If we have the courage to drop these false identities about ourselves, then we can embrace the Divine. Detachment is the direct technique that Kṛṣṇa is suggesting here. Detachment from the ego or the identities will lead to detachment from desires. This is detachment from the past and future. This is being 'unclutched'.

Where Do I Go Without Yoga?

6.36 For one whose mind is uncontrolled, it is difficult to attain yoga in My opinion.
But, it is practical to achieve control over the mind by appropriate means.

6.37 Arjuna said: O Kṛṣṇa, if a person is engaged in yoga with faith but does not attain yoga because of the wavering mind, what destination does he achieve?

6.38 O mighty-armed Kṛṣṇa, does the person who deviated from the path perish, torn like a cloud without any position?

6.39 This is my doubt, O Kṛṣṇa, and I request You to dispel it completely. Certainly, there is no one to be found other than You who can remove this doubt.

6.40 The Lord said: O son of Pritā, the person engaged in activities for good does not meet with destruction either in this world or the next life; he never faces degradation.

Here, Kṛṣṇa explains that it is possible to achieve control over the mind. Actually, having an experience of *satori* or the first glimpse of bliss is not a big thing. It is easy. But to stay in that same space and consciousness needs preparation of the body and mind. To express and radiate that high energy through the body, our body and mind need to be prepared with yoga. This is why sage Patañjali created yoga. The problem is that now only the verbal language of Patañjali remains, but the body language is absent. Only his words are there. That is why there are so many mutated forms of yoga today.

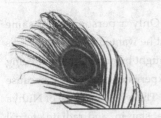

But how much can words convey? Only a person in the same consciousness as Patañjali can convey what he wanted to convey. This is what Nithya Yoga is all about. It is yoga taught by an enlightened being who can convey the body language, the experience of Patañjali, because he is in the same consciousness as Patañjali. The whole purpose of Nithya Yoga is to prepare the body to experience, stay in, and radiate eternal bliss. Its purpose is to 'unclutch' and enlighten.

Here, Arjuna again asks the questions we all will have in our minds. What happens if we start with faith, but somewhere we fail in controlling the mind? Be very clear, initially we *will* face failure in our attempts to control the mind. If we don't experience this, we should check ourselves because we may be fooling ourselves with whatever we are doing!

Enlightenment is possible for all kinds of people

Here, Arjuna wants Kṛṣṇa to give an assurance that enlightenment is possible for all kinds of people. Actually, at the very root of Arjuna's question is the mind that is generating the fear and making him believe that it is hard to find the no-mind state. The mind does not want to lose its existence. The mind always looks for a reason to convince us that we cannot carry on our lives without it.

In our day-to-day life we face the situation that Arjuna faces here. Even with activities that we have carried out successfully many times in the past, we feel nervous when we start again. Even before we begin, we start imagining the worst. Actually, it is okay to imagine the worst. Then we are prepared to face the worst situation. I tell people that to overcome fear and face fear, it is good to imagine the worst-case scenario. Visualize it fully, relive the experience fully, and the fear will disappear.

The future is not ours to see. The goal as we imagine it does not exist. There is no purpose to life. The meaning of life is to live. If only Arjuna was comfortable with just practicing the techniques that Kṛṣṇa showed him, he would not be asking such questions. Arjuna still does not believe Kṛṣṇa, his master. He has heard and intellectually understood the meaning of what has been said. But he has not imbibed the master's words. Arjuna has yet to learn.

Kṛṣṇa assures Arjuna by saying that there is no destruction either in this life or the next life for one who is on the path of yoga. Here, Kṛṣṇa is giving a wonderful assurance for all of us that even a small amount of practice of this yoga will save us from the cycle of birth and death. Any yoga practiced will give us tremendous benefit. The very intent to practice yoga itself means that we have gained knowledge about the problem of the mind.

One important thing: Any movement of the body with a strong intention will cause that intention to get deeply inscribed into our bodies and muscles. If the intention is a desire to become one with our true identity and drop our false identity, it will get deeply inscribed in our body and automatically the body will start moving towards that one goal. This is a very important thing to understand. If we move our body with the thought of bliss, the bliss emotion gets ingrained in our system. If it is anger that moves our body, the anger emotion gets ingrained.

There is a wonderful movie, *What the Bleep Do We Know?* Using principles of Quantum Physics, the film visually explains this truth from *Vedānta* very nicely. It says that whenever we experience an emotion in our system, it is like rain. The emotion pours like rain and certain cells catch onto those emotions. For example: When we are angry, there are particular cells that catch the anger emotion and start multiplying. They affect other cells that also catch onto the anger emotion and multiply. As the process replicates, the anger emotion is strengthened.

This happens every time we get angry, and with every episode the emotion becomes stronger. Like this, it is possible for us to replicate bliss as well. It is up to us to choose what type of emotion we want to be ingrained in our system. All that we need to do is to intend to be joyful and joyful cells will keep reproducing. This process cannot stop. We will be full of joy.

We can try this when we meet people we do not particularly like. Just smile at them. However embarrassed we may feel, we should just smile. Not the plastic smile that only covers the lips, but a smile from our heart with warmth, so that the smile spreads to our eyes. See what happens. All our negativity will disappear. In addition, any negativity that we create in others will also disappear and they will respond with the same smile.

In our programs on energizing of the *cakra*s, I advise people to respond always from the *anāhata cakra,* the heart center, to everyone, in all situations. When our *anāhata* is unblocked, we are capable of pouring out unconditional love. Spread that love around and you will find that the negative emotions of people who approach us with anger, fear, or jealousy will be consumed by the energy of love that we unleash.

Rare Birth Of A Yogi

6.41 *The person who has fallen from yoga after many years of living in the world and doing virtuous deeds takes birth in the house of the virtuous and prosperous.*

6.42 *Or the yogi certainly takes birth in a family of wise people. Certainly, such a birth is rare in this world.*

6.43 *O son of Kuru, on taking such a birth, the person gains the intelligence of the previous body and tries again to attain yoga.*

Kṛṣṇa talks about how we choose everything in our lives, including our birth, parents, etc. This truth may seem difficult to believe. Our birth is an incident and we choose all its details. We must understand that it is only we who program and design everything and everybody in our life, including our parents and environment. Our choice of the next body is based on the way we have lived our life in this body.

This phenomenon happens again and again. Whatever we choose at the moment of death will become reality in the next birth. Some people think that they will remind themselves of the Almighty, in the last second of their lives. But that will never happen unless we make that a habit throughout our life. If we repeat 'Coca-Cola' our whole life, we cannot think of Rāma or Kṛṣṇa during our last moments!

Here, Kṛṣṇa gives the assurance to the whole of humanity that a person who has performed virtuous activities takes birth in a family of wise people or in a prosperous family. His pious activities will earn him a place among the higher worlds. After dwelling there for a while he will take birth in the family of righteous people to once again enable his spiritual seeking.

We can choose our body and the time that we wish to be born. When we live our life running behind our greed and desires, naturally, at the time of our death also, we will not be ready to leave the body. The body will be tired of running behind desires continuously, but the mind will not be ready to leave. So we will leave the body in the pain and suffering of this push and pull of desires and fear. If we can just relax into the present and take life moment by moment, we will leave the body in a relaxed way, peacefully.

Once we leave the body, in three *kṣaṇa*, three moments, we get into a new body and are reborn. *Kṣaṇa* is the time gap between two consecutive thoughts. If we have been constantly running after our desires, the *kṣaṇa* will be really small for us. When we learn to relax into the present, the *kṣaṇa* is much longer. In three *kṣaṇa*s, we take on the new body to fulfill whatever desires were unfulfilled in the previous body. Here, Kṛṣṇa says that on taking birth, we gain the intelligence of the previous body and continue the journey where we left off.

Death is not the death that happens at the end of our lives. It happens every day and night. Every night, we go from the physical body to the dream body and causal body. In the morning, we enter the physical body again. We die and take birth again.

Every day we leave the body. We go to the causal body when we fall asleep. Every day we die. When we wake up, we come back. As of now, every morning, how do we come back to life? What happens at the time when we get up from bed?

First thing, usually, the moment we gain awareness, either a thought based on greed or fear will hit us. There will be thoughts based on greed, such as 'I need to get this today,' or thoughts based on fear, such as 'I have to finish this work today in the office. Will I be able to?' Immediately, we will jump out of our bed. The moment we assume our body, that moment is a moment of taking birth.

Early morning, the thought with which we enter into the body is going to play a major role in our consciousness. Just as the thought with which we leave the body on dying decides the kind of body we will assume in our next birth, in the same way, every day the thought with which we get up in the morning and assume this body decides the quality of that day, that life. If we understand this once and alter our thoughts at the time of waking up, we will alter the whole consciousness.

When we get up from bed, let the first thought be related to love and compassion. Get up only to express life in bliss. Let us assume the body with gratitude to the Divine. If we do this, we will become a divine incarnation! Kṛṣṇa is actually giving a technique on how to enter into Kṛṣṇa consciousness. The man who assumes the body out of love and compassion is an incarnation. If we assume the body out of greed or fear, we are human. Early morning, let the first thought be of love and compassion. Our whole life will become pure eternal bliss. Our whole life will be lived with a different, enlightened consciousness.

Become A Yogi

6.44 *Due to the practice in his previous life, he certainly gets attracted automatically to yoga and he is inquisitive about yoga and transcends the scriptures.*

6.45 *A yogi by trying and practicing, after many births, is cleansed of all sins and achieves the highest state.*

6.46 *A yogi is greater than the ascetic, than the wise and the person who works for the fruit of action. So, become a yogi, O Arjuna.*

6.47 *Of all yogis, one who always lives in Me, thinking of Me, who worships Me in full faith, he is considered engaged in Me.*

Kṛṣṇa is describing the process of the human experience. We think we can experience bliss through the body and mind; that is why we assume the body. When we realize that bliss cannot be experienced through the body or mind, we know that going beyond the body is the only way to experience it. Then we will not assume the body. Assuming the human body is simply our choice.

People ask me, 'Why do we choose to have the human experience?' That we should find out for ourselves. *Why did we assume this body?* I asked the question and I got the answer. Ask the question yourself and pursue it as a quest and you will get the answer. You will be enlightened.

We claim that we want to experience the ultimate and want to be enlightened. If we really want to be enlightened, there is nothing that can stop us. As of now, enlightenment is last on our laundry list! When the urge becomes urgent, when the question becomes a burning quest, then we get the answer. There is no other way.

In these verses, Kṛṣṇa says that whatever we have learned in one life does not get wasted. We start from where we left off. Our mindset in one birth continues into another. If we keep practicing, we will be cleansed of all sins and reach the highest state. Such a person, Kṛṣṇa promises, will reach Him.

At the end of the day, what Kṛṣṇa implies is this: We need to do our bit. We need to practice yoga, the path that leads to self-awareness, with dedication, perseverance and conviction. There is no short cut. Once you do your bit, the master promises deliverance. He promises that you will be one with Him.

MEDITATION

Now it is time to tune ourselves to that highest teaching given by Śrī Kṛṣṇa in this Dhyāna Yoga. We will enter into the meditation.

Please sit straight and close your eyes. Keep your head, neck and spine, all three in a straight line. Inhale and exhale as slowly as possible and as deeply as possible.

Slowly, in a relaxed way, bring your awareness to your *ājñā cakra*. Concentrate between the two eyebrows. Bring your awareness between the two eyebrows. Remember and pray to that energy that came as Kṛṣṇa, that is guiding us and helping us in our life. Pray to that energy that gave us the Bhagavad Gītā.

Meditate on the pure light energy. If your mind wanders here and there, don't worry. When you remember, bring it back again and relax in your *ājñā cakra,* between your eyebrows. Don't concentrate. In a very relaxed way, be aware of the *ājñā cakra,* the space in between the two eyebrows.

(a few minutes pass)

Slowly, very slowly bring your mind to your heart and meditate on your heart center. If you want, you can touch your heart center with the hand and feel it. Try to bring your awareness to the heart center. Try to remember the heart center. Forget all other parts of your body; forget your mind. Just become the heart center. Just be in the heart center. Inhale and exhale as slowly as possible.

May you experience your pure inner space. May you experience the eternal bliss, *nityānanda*.

(a few minutes pass)

Om Śānti, Śānti, Śāntihi

Relax. Slowly, very slowly, open your eyes.

We may wonder how a simple technique like this one can lead us into our Self. Please understand that we always live in the head. Start living from the heart. We will then start acting from intelligence. When we start acting from the heart, we don't calculate. The 'I' disappears, and naturally our senses become sensitive. Too much of the energy that is supplied to the heart is taken away by the mind. The fuel supply to the mind will be reduced and the fuel supply to the heart will be increased.

So continuously remember this heart region, the *anāhata cakra*. Naturally, we will have awareness in the *ājñā*, also. In the last session, Kṛṣṇa gave the technique to be in the *ājñā*. Today, He says start with the *ājñā* and come down to the *anāhata*. This is because in the heart, there is a possibility of much more happening. The possibility is much greater in the heart. Kṛṣṇa says, 'Let you be in the heart.'

Look in! You will realize 'You are That.' Just look in, you will experience eternal bliss, *nityānanda*. Let us pray to that ultimate energy, *Parabrahma* Kṛṣṇa to give us all eternal bliss, *nityānanda*.

Thus ends the sixth chapter named* Dhyāna Yogaḥ *of the* Upaniṣad *of the* Bhagavad Gītā*, the scripture of Yoga dealing with the science of the Absolute in the form of the dialogue between* Śrī Kṛṣṇa *and Arjuna.

BHAGAVADGĪTĀ

Understand And Evolve

JÑĀNAVIJÑĀNA YOGAḤ

CHAPTER 7

All living beings are caught in the duality of attachment and aversion. The great Master Krishna explains how to move out of this bondage.

Understand And Evolve

To begin with, let us see why Kṛṣṇa has given us this chapter. Again and again Kṛṣṇa speaks the same truth. Nothing else is spoken. Then what is the need for so many chapters?

People can say that Kṛṣṇa is repeating Himself. They may ask, 'How many times must He say that the spirit is indestructible, or that all work must be done without expecting returns or that one must surrender to Him to reach salvation?'

People ask me, '*Swamiji,* how many days will it take for us to learn meditation?'

I tell them, 'To learn meditation, two minutes are enough. To learn what meditation is not, you need ten days!'

Kṛṣṇa knows that Arjuna is just like us. He represents the sum total of humanity. To explain to a man or woman what needs to be done, and why it is right is not enough. The human mind will find a hundred reasons why ninety-nine other things are just as good. So the master must also tell why the other ninety-nine things are not the straight path, and why we must stick to those things that the master prescribes.

That is exactly what Kṛṣṇa does. He does this so that the one option that He outlines sinks deeply into Arjuna's consciousness and therefore into the consciousness of every individual who reads the Bhagavad Gītā.

There is a beautiful philosophy in India, *nyāya śāstra,* or the scripture of logic. According to this, any statement has two lines of logic. The first line of logic is regular logic; *nyāya* means regular.

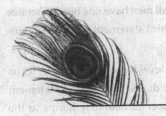

For example, if I make the statements, 'All men have one head. Socrates is a man,' we can easily conclude that the third statement will be: Socrates has one head. This is simple logic.

There is another kind of logic, a higher level logic. For example, let us say the first statement says, 'There are two doors.' The second statement says, 'One door is open.' An average person immediately jumps to the conclusion that the other door is closed. However, in this kind of logic we cannot jump to conclusion based on the first two statements. The second door may also be open. We don't know. We cannot come to any conclusion unless we are told that the second door is closed.

So that the listener, reader and disciple do not make mistakes in the understanding, the master ensures that we know which door is open and which door is closed. It is not left to assumption on the basis of the disciple's intelligence.

But the master does not explain for that reason alone. When the truth sinks into us, it should sink in without a trace, without any resistance. When something is not fully explained and our mind detects options, it starts on its own trip. It moves away from what is being explained. Instead of focusing on the substance of what is said, the mind gets constantly distracted and tired. A tired mind makes mistakes.

Usually in life we make mistakes when we jump to conclusions using the first kind of logic when we should have made those decisions using the second kind of logic. The moment somebody makes a statement, 'You don't have compassion,' we immediately become defensive and say, 'Do you mean to say I am cruel? We don't have to jump to such a conclusion. He made a statement, 'You are not compassionate.' We don't have to immediately think, 'You mean I am cruel? You mean I am violent?' When we jump to conclusions, we create trouble not only for ourselves but also for others. Many times we make this mistake.

When we handle our mind without awareness, we make this mistake. The words that we repeat inside our system create our whole life. If our mind jumps to illogical conclusions like this, naturally we create problems for others and trouble for ourselves. When we are unaware we always jump to these types of conclusions.

Ordinary masters express their philosophy with the second kind of logic, which is why there is so much misunderstanding. However, Kṛṣṇa is a *jagat guru* (master of the universe). He knows the minds of all possible types of human beings. He knows the problems of logic. He is delivering this message in such a way that we cannot jump to conclusions. He makes all the three statements. He says, 'There are two doors, the first door is open, the second door is closed.' There is no need for us to assume! He protects us from ourselves.

If we are allowed to jump to conclusions, we miss the truth and the whole message. Here Kṛṣṇa does not allow us to jump to conclusions. That is why He repeats the same truth in each chapter from a different level of logic each time. He makes the same statements, but from a different level of logic so that the people who hear it will not miss the message.

One In A Billion Reaches Me!

7.1 *Kṛṣṇa says,*
Arjuna, Listen to Me, you can know Me completely and without doubt by practising yoga in true consciousness of Me,
With your mind attached to Me.

7.2 *Let Me explain to you in detail this phenomenal and absolute knowledge along with its realization;*
By knowing which, there shall remain nothing further to be known.

7.3 *Out of many thousands of men, hardly one endeavors or strives to achieve the perfection of self-realization;*
Of those so endeavoring, hardly one achieves the perfection of self-realization, and of those, hardly one knows Me in truth or reaches that state of oneness with Me.

7.4 *Earth, water, fire, air, ether, mind, intelligence and false ego*
All together these eight constitute My separated external energies.

7.5 *Besides these external energies, which are inferior in nature, O mighty-armed Arjuna, there is a superior energy of Mine.*
This comprises all the embodied souls of all the living entities by which this material world is being utilized or exploited.

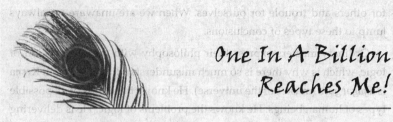

Again and again people ask me, '*Swamiji*, why did you choose to speak on the Bhagavad Gītā? Why not on books like Aṣṭāvakra Gītā, Patañjali's Yoga Sūtra, Brahmasūtra or the *Upaniṣad*? I tell them that the Gītā expresses the truth in totality. Kṛṣṇa has created keys for all kinds of human beings. He fulfills every need of every human being.

He says, 'Listen, Arjuna, by practising yoga in full consciousness of Me, with mind attached to Me, you can know Me in full, without doubt.' In this statement, Kṛṣṇa uses the word 'Me' three times. Having read that, a psychologist will conclude that Kṛṣṇa is egoistic. A person might hate Kṛṣṇa because he feels Kṛṣṇa is egoistic. Again and again, Kṛṣṇa declares, 'Surrender to Me. I am everything.' We should understand here that He is expressing His glory. The person who hates Kṛṣṇa thinking He is egoistic, misses the truth expressed by the Gītā. In the same way, a person who loves Kṛṣṇa gets caught in His form and misses the juice of the Gītā!

Whenever people are caught in the form, they worship the form and slowly start saying, 'Gītā is great. Kṛṣṇa is God. He can express all these things, but surely it is not for us. It is not practical.' In this way, they create a distance between themselves and Kṛṣṇa. They worship the Gītā instead of practising it. If we have a pot full of milk and we worship it but never drink it, will we get the benefit of the milk? Understand, unless we drink the milk, we will never get the benefit of the milk.

Unless we imbibe Kṛṣṇa, we cannot get the benefit of the Gītā. That is why I always tell people, Jews have avoided Christ by crucifying Him, and Hindus have avoided Kṛṣṇa by worshipping him and putting His photo on the wall. When we don't imbibe Kṛṣṇa's teachings in our lives, worshipping Kṛṣṇa is nothing but crucifixion. It's a cunning method of escaping from the truth.

The people who crucified Christ at least carry the guilt that they made a mistake, but these people who hang Kṛṣṇa on the wall don't even carry that guilt. In a nice and cunning way they have escaped from Kṛṣṇa. People who hate Kṛṣṇa think He is egoistic. And people who love Kṛṣṇa are caught in His form. Only a person who experiences Kṛṣṇa realizes the Gītā.

Approach the Divine the right way

Anyhow, this chapter is about how human beings approach the Divine, why they approach the Divine, and at what level they approach the Divine. There is a beautiful saying in the Bible, 'God created man in his own mold.' But I tell you, 'Man created God in his own mould.' We approach the Divine in the way we want It to serve us.

At what level do we approach the Divine? How do we grow in maturity? Kṛṣṇa answers these questions in this chapter. Here He says, 'Out of many thousands of men, *one* may endeavor for perfection, and out of those who have achieved perfection, hardly *one* knows Me in truth.' He says, 'out of thousands'. He should say 'out of billions'. In those days, the population must have been less, which is why He says 'out of thousands'. Now we should say, 'Out of billions, *one* may endeavor for perfection.'

manuṣyāṇāṁ sahasreṣu kaścid yatati siddhaye |
yatatām api siddhānāṁ kaścin māṁ vetti tattvataḥ || 7.3

Among millions of men, one man may endeavor for perfection, and out of those who achieve perfection, hardly one knows Me in truth.

There are millions of people out there, but only a few hundred are present today to listen to this Gītā discourse. And out of these few hundred, only a few will hear it as it is expressed. We may even hear, but don't think we actually listen. Never think that we really listen.

I request people to never repeat to someone else what I have said. If you do repeat it, then please tell them, 'I heard these things.' Never say, '*Swamiji* said'. Many times we miss much of what is said. Modern scientists say that we observe hardly two percent of the things that happen around us. It is as if you have a hundred-page storybook, and you try to reconstruct the whole novel with only two of its pages. How true will it be to the original? In the same way, you remember hardly two percent of what I say. With that two percent, if you try to reconstruct this whole discourse, naturally it will be your discourse, not mine. So be very clear, you might sit here. However, it doesn't mean that you listen. If you want to tell people what I said, please always say, 'I heard Nithyananda say this.' Don't say, 'Nithyananda said...' Because of your assumptions you jump to conclusions, and miss what is actually being said.

The master is always ready to share his experiences. That is his mission in life. The infinite compassion that fills an enlightened being is forever bursting to be let out to share. That is why Kṛṣṇa says that He is now ready to explain. The question is whether or not Arjuna is ready to listen. Are we ready to listen today, now?

Why does Kṛṣṇa say that a few try, and of those who try, very few succeed? Remember that He is talking about Self-realization, about understanding who we are. Why is it so difficult even to try? We do not want to try because we are afraid. We are restless in any form of silence. If I am silent for a few minutes after I sit down before an audience, the entire audience becomes restless; they start fidgeting.

Why do we find it difficult to meditate? Why is it so difficult to give half an hour a day to ourselves? Why would we rather read the same old newspaper again and again? Understand, all these are because we are afraid of being with ourselves. Why are we afraid of being with ourselves? We must ask and answer these questions ourselves.

If Self-realization means going back to where we came from, and where we came from is a state of bliss and divinity, then why are we afraid to be with ourselves? The truth is that we have forgotten where we came from. Nothing in the way we are brought up and 'educated' tells us that we come from bliss and we can regain that bliss. Society has its own self-interest in not letting us be aware of this truth. If we realize how easy it is to be blissful and return to our original state, no one can control us. But society, religion, and political and family structures operate on the principle of control.

The moment we realize who we are and we are liberated, these institutions cannot make us do what they want us to do. So they give us carrots and they wield the stick. They give us recipes in the form of laws. From childhood we are conditioned to avoid looking too deeply into ourselves because if we do, we may find the truth and be liberated. Then there will be no need for our churches and temples, priests and politicians. They make us afraid that there will be anarchy if we do not obey their directives.

Why would there be anarchy if we realize the truth about ourselves? It is because we will be filled with awareness and such awareness will remove all fear and greed in us. We will no longer need external inducements to make us happy. No one and nothing can control us. We will be liberated. That is a great threat to society.

Most of society doesn't know these deeper truths and even the ones who know it conveniently avoid it because it is too much of truth for practicality. This is how society puts generation after generation of people in deep illusion. It is most convenient to them.

Ādi Śaṅkarācārya, the great Indian saint says beautifully in the verses of his song Bhaja Govindaṁ, *kā te kāntā, kaste putraḥ*... meaning, 'Where is your wife, where are your children when you finally depart?' You leave alone. You came alone and you will leave alone. Even your wife, who loved you dearly, is afraid of you once your body becomes cold.

So if we need to follow the truth, we must look after ourselves. We must be selfish. We need to be selfish to enter into this path of Self-realization. However it is selfishness born out of the desperate need to be *selfless*. When we reach our center or our core, we become one with humanity. Then there are no differences among us. That is why even our spouses will be unhappy if we realize ourselves, because they cannot possess us any more. At that point they must share us with humanity. But they won't understand that the love of Self-realization is infinite and that there is only growth in sharing.

The path to Self-realization is the path of aloneness. It is not a lonely path; it is an 'alone' path. We are all in one; that is what being alone means. From being fragmented, we become whole. From being islands, we become the universe.

This is the knowledge that Kṛṣṇa offers humanity. Out of His deep compassion He says, 'Please listen to Me and realize your Self and be liberated.' One in a million may heed His words and start on this path. Of that only one in a million will eventually find his own Self, and thus find Me. Is the path so difficult? No, it is not. Why then does it seem so difficult? We find the external world so attractive that we rarely stay on course in our internal voyage of self-discovery. It is always easier to blame other people and remain where we are than to step on the path of change.

Buddha compares our mind to a monkey, always jumping from point to point. This is where we differ from animals. Animals and plants also have intelligence and emotions as proven by science. However they do not have monkey minds, even monkeys don't! Animals work with Nature. They eat when they are hungry; they sleep when they are tired. Human beings, on the other hand, have a powerful tool with which they can either redeem themselves or destroy themselves. And invariably, they work against Nature.

Throughout the Gītā, Kṛṣṇa talks about how to control the mind. All we need to do is to follow the guidance of this universal master. Without any doubt, surely we can then become that one in a thousand or one in a million. But to follow Him, we need to understand Him.

In these verses Kṛṣṇa explains who He is. Kṛṣṇa explicitly separates Himself from His manifested energies in these verses. What we perceive as manifested energies - the five natural elements and the three inner elements of mind, intelligence and ego - are His energies no doubt, yet they are not Him.

The manifest and the unmanifest

Puruṣa and *prakṛti* are considered the operative principles of the universe in the Hindu philosophical systems of Sāṅkhya and Vedānta. *Puruṣa* and *prakṛti* are unmanifest energy sources, *puruṣa* being inactive and *prakṛti* capable of being active. Everything else arises from these two elements when they operate together.

Prakṛti gives rise to the cosmic and individual intelligence and the five natural elements. The Taittirīya upaniṣad explains that the cosmic energy gave rise to etheric energy or *ākāśa,* which pervades the universe. From etheric energy the energy of air or *vāyu* or air that sustains us in our body-mind system as the carrier of pranic or life energy.

From the energy of air arises the energy of fire, *agni. Āpas,* the energy of water, arose from the energy of fire. *Pṛthvī,* the energy of earth arose from the energy of water. The Taittirīya upaniṣad goes on to say that it is from the earth energy that plants, herbs and food were created, from which came human beings. Within the human being is the intelligence that is a hologram of the cosmic intelligence. The energy cycle is now complete.

This energy tree, from its subtlest beginning to the grossest manifestation, is also the story of creation. Ten thousand years ago, sages of our ancient vedic culture propounded these truths with no external devices to aid them. They intuited them, as they looked inward rather than outward. Our vedic rituals were full of meaning. Today they are condemned as old fashioned and meaningless activities because we lost the link to their meaning. Spirituality is nothing but spirit infused into rituals.

The fire rituals are methods to transfer the energy from the ether to earth, from the cosmos to the individual. Of all the energies in the five natural elements, we can directly access the energies of earth, water, fire and air. We eat, drink, warm ourselves and breathe with these energies. However, we cannot directly access the etheric energy due to the barrier of our mind.

Meditation is the key to imbibe the etheric energy of the cosmos. *Vedic* fire rituals are mass meditation processes: meditation for dummies! We just need to be there to absorb the energy, even if we do not have the capacity to meditate.

The cosmic intelligence is reflected in the human as the mind. The mind in turn uses the senses to access the external world. Each of the senses - sight, hearing, smell, taste and touch - are related to the natural elements. Ether is linked to sound or the ears; air is linked to touch and the skin; fire is linked to color and form, and so to sight and the eyes; water is linked to taste and the tongue; earth is linked to smell or the nose.

The mind receives information through the senses of perception, and executes decisions through the senses of action. When the senses are denied access to the external world, which is their sustenance, the mind shuts down. Thoughts cease! Ego is a creation of the mind. It is an illusion and not the truth. True realization of the Self is achieved when the ego is shed and when the mind stops. Then, inner intelligence awakens to the cosmic intelligence.

Here, Kṛṣṇa refers to ego as *ahaṅkāra.* It is our identity that we project outwards. It is always in excess of what we think of as ourselves. There is another side to our ego, called *mamakāra,* which we project inwards; what we think of as us inside us. This *mamakāra* is always lower than what we think ourselves to be.

The perpetual gap between this outer projection and inner projection creates stress, suffering and dis-ease within us. When we realize our Self, we realize that we are divine and nothing less. Anything that we think about ourselves that is lower than this is low self-esteem. We are above the energies that constitute us. All that we lack is the awareness of this truth. Our natural state *is* to know ourselves. Once we realize the truth that we are God, there is no difference between Kṛṣṇa and us. We are enlightened. That is what Kṛṣṇa came to prove. He has no need to prove that He is God. He doesn't care if we know it or not. His mission was to enlighten Arjuna, and through Arjuna, the rest of humanity. His mission is to prove to us that we too are God!

I Am The Thread!

7.6 *Know for certain that everything living is manifested by these two energies of Mine.*
I am the Creator, the Sustainer and the Destroyer of them.

7.7 *O conqueror of wealth [Arjuna], there is no truth superior to Me.*
Everything hangs upon Me, as pearls are strung on a thread.

7.8 *O son of Kuntī [Arjuna], I am the taste of water, the radiance of the sun and the moon, the sacred syllable Oṁ in the vedic mantras.*
I am the sound in ether and ability in man.

7.9 *I am the original fragrance of the earth, and I am the heat in fire.*
I am the life of all living beings, and I am the penance of all ascetics.

'I am the thread,' He says. 'I am the thread, the *sūtra*, the technique on which all Existence is strung.'

What a beautiful analogy! That is why He is the *sūtradhāra*, the controller and director of the cosmic play! Nothing can be created, sustained or destroyed in the absence of His energy.

People often ask me why I call myself Swami, speaking in the third person. They question me as to why I dress up in these ways and allow myself to be photographed. I tell them that I do not even identify with this body. This skin itself is alien to me. There is no difference between this skin and other coverings. So how does it matter? I look at myself the way you look at me, as a witness! Or the way you and I look at an idol. If this body is dressed well, I feel good - the same way you feel good seeing it dressed up.

God – an idea?

For you, God is just an idea. You think of God and attribute various concepts to Him. You talk about Him in the same manner in which you would talk about a friend or relative. To you, your identity is real. Without this identity you are lost. Your identity is your reality. 'I' is what makes you alive. To me, God is reality. I live with God every moment. The body, mind and the body-mind identification do not exist for me. It is only a concept! Therefore, when I refer to myself, I refer to that body-mind the same way that you refer to it. I too call it Swami or whatever!

I cannot move a finger without permission from Existence, from that *Parabrahma* Kṛṣṇa, that cosmic Kṛṣṇa. You may think, 'This sounds nonsensical. He says he is enlightened and then he says there is nothing that he can do; he can do only as Existence dictates.' Whether you understand it or not, whether you accept it or not, this is the truth.

My disciples know that when someone with deep faith in me comes with a problem, I say, 'I'll take care.' If it is someone who is yet to develop that deep faith, I say that I shall meditate or pray to Ānandeśvara for him or her! They go away happy to hear that. When I say, 'I shall take care,' I just pass it on to Existence. It is for Her to take care. Because I have that immense faith in Her, She always obliges!

People know that the rosary that they wear, the string of *rudrākṣa* beads or red sandalwood beads, is not a mere rosary. It is their hotline to connect to Existence. When someone is desperately in need of help of some sort, they simply hold onto the rosary and pray. The results are always instantaneous.

All this has nothing to do with me. It has to do with Existence. The moment I feel that it is a result of my penance, it will stop happening! There is nothing that 'I' can do. There is nothing that this energy can do.

The great master says, 'I am not what you see. I am not the energy that is manifested. It is not this six-foot Kṛṣṇa with a flute and peacock feather that makes things happen. It is the formless energy beyond Vāsudeva Kṛṣṇa (Kṛṣṇa, the mortal being, the son of Vāsudeva). It is *Parabrahma* Kṛṣṇa (Kṛṣṇa, the cosmic energy)'.

When we see a necklace or garland, do we notice the thread? If it is a pearl or diamond necklace we may get it threaded in gold, but still we rarely notice the thread unless it snaps and all the pearls and diamonds spill on the floor. Then, we blame the thread!

Kṛṣṇa says, He is the unseen thread without which no rosary can exist. He says He is the unseen essence without which there can be no substance. Have you ever wondered how this universe operates? There are billions of planets like ours, thousands of galaxies and many universes. We need traffic lights and policemen to control traffic on our roads. In the Milky Way there are no policemen to control the movements of planets and stars. Yet they move unerringly!

Can you imagine the intelligence that controls multiple universes? How is there such discipline and order in that seeming chaos that no one is in charge of? No one is responsible, or is someone? On the other hand, within this small body of ours we try to control everything. Yet we can predict nothing about it. Despite all the order that we impose, there is chaos sometimes! Control can never bring order. Only freedom brings about order. The ultimate chaos is the cosmic Kṛṣṇa; He is also the ultimate order too.

The beauty of Kṛṣṇa's teaching in the Bhagavad Gītā is the depth to which He goes to make everything crystal clear to Arjuna. It is as if Arjuna is a child and He is the parent or teacher. For the Lord of the universe to take the trouble to ensure complete understanding shows the depth of His compassion.

Kṛṣṇa explains that He is the essential quality in each of the elements; also that He is the *praṇava mantra* - primordial sound - *'Oṁ'* and the radiance of the sun and moon.

Life in any form cannot exist without the energy of cosmic Kṛṣṇa. But living within this energy field we lose sight of this energy. Kabir, the mystic poet said hauntingly, we are like fish that are immersed in life-giving water yet cry out saying, 'We are thirsty.' Kabir advises: Fool, become aware! You cannot be a fish in water and be thirsty!

Here, Kṛṣṇa goes to such depths to explain that He is everything and above everything. He is the Creator - Brahma, the Sustainer -Viṣṇu and the Rejuvenator - Śiva. He is all and above all.

I Am Eternal

7.10 *O son of Pritā, I am the eternal source of all creatures, the intelligence of the intelligent, and the brilliance of all those who are brilliant.*

7.11 *I am the strength of the strong, and I am the procreative energy in living beings, devoid of lust and in accordance with religious principles, O lord of* Bhārata.

7.12 *All states of being - be they of goodness, passion or ignorance - emanate from Me.*
I am independent of them but they are dependent on Me.

7.13 *The whole world is deluded by the three modes (goodness, passion and ignorance), and thus does not know Me.*
I am above the modes and unchangeable.

7.14 *My divine energy, consisting of the three modes of material nature, is difficult to overcome.*
But those who surrender unto Me can cross beyond it with ease.

7.15 *Those miscreants who are foolish, lowest among mankind, whose knowledge is stolen by* māyā *(that which is not real), and who have taken shelter in demonic nature, do not surrender unto Me.*

'I am the procreative energy,' says the Lord. 'I am the seed of all living beings.' He makes no excuses, no apologies.

He says, 'I am that procreative energy but without the fantasies of lust.' How can one be a Creator, if one cannot procreate?

Many of our great sages in the past, the *ṛsi* and *maharṣis,* such as Vasiṣṭa and Vyāsa were householders with wives and children. Yet they were enlightened. Other than Hanumān and Ganeśa all our deities are married! Kṛṣṇa is reputed to have had 16,008 wives!

How can the life form continue without procreation, without the sex act? For celibacy to happen naturally, the first spiritual experience must happen before adolescence, so that the life-giving sex energy moves upwards as transcendental spiritual energy. People who have this spiritual awakening because of their *prārabdha karma* (desires one is born with) are the *Paramahamsas.* Celibacy happens to them naturally.

To force celibacy after adolescence is difficult. It must be done under supervision. Otherwise the so-called renunciate monk, the *sanyāsi,* will pretend to follow celibacy. Inside he will be filled with fantasies, ready to explode. The word *brahmacarya* means 'moving in reality'.

It is said that once Kṛṣṇa was crossing the river Yamuna with a group of *gopīs,* women devotees. The river was in spate. Kṛṣṇa said to Yamuna, 'If it is true that I am a *brahmacāri,* part and let me walk across.' The river parted and Kṛṣṇa walked to the other bank.

A *sanyāsi* who watched this was dumbstruck. 'Kṛṣṇa, a *brahmacāri?* He walks with these women who are His lovers, and He says He is a *brahmacāri* and the river parts for Him! How can this be?'

That is what Kṛṣṇa explains here. Fantasies are the root cause of our problems. With each fantasy coming true, more fantasies arise. We can never be in reality. To be in reality one must be in the present moment. When you are in the present moment you are Kṛṣṇa. When we hanker after the past and speculate about the future, we slip into fantasies. We are no longer within the boundaries of our body. This way of living will lead only to suffering. All you need to do to be blissful is, renounce your fantasies. You do not need to renounce what material things you have with you.

Enjoy your wealth, enjoy your work, and enjoy your spouse and children. Enjoy what is your due. Just stop fantasizing about what you do not have. Stop running after more acquisitions; stop and take time to enjoy what you have acquired.

Move into the present, here and now, into reality, and you will be a *brahmacāri*!

Beyond the *guṇas*

In these verses, Kṛṣṇa talks about the *guṇas,* the natural attributes.

Prakṛti, the energy that manifests in the universe, has three elements called *guṇas.* When *prakṛti* is in equilibrium, it is pure potential energy. When it is disturbed, the *guṇas* come into operation. Rarely is only a single element or *guṇa* present in a person. It is almost always a mixture. The three *guṇas* that Kṛṣṇa refers to are *satva, rajas* and *tamas,* commonly translated as goodness or calmness, passion or aggression and ignorance or inaction.

The interplay of these *guṇas* creates the functioning of the mind and through the operation of the mind, activity. *Guṇa* does not refer to the state of a person. It causes that state to happen. *Satva* by itself is not goodness or calmness. It is the building block that leads to calmness.

When one transcends the *guṇas,* as Kṛṣṇa says about Himself, one becomes a *triguṇa rahita.* Such a person is no longer influenced by the mind and its actions. Even an incarnation, needs to initially be born with some *guṇa* infused into that being. It is like this; we cannot make jewelry out of pure gold. We must alloy it with copper.

In the same way, even an energy source that has transcended the three *guṇas* needs to have some *satva guṇa* infused in it to be born into this planet. Similarly, as Vāsudeva Kṛṣṇa, the son of Vāsudeva, He has some *guṇa* at play in Him.

Remember that Bhagavad Gītā is rendered by *Parabrahma* Kṛṣṇa, the cosmic Kṛṣṇa, and not by Vāsudeva Kṛṣṇa. So He boldly says, I am beyond the *guṇas.* He says, I am the *paramapuruśa,* the Supreme being, who sets *prakriti* into play, and I am beyond its influence.

We can see the interplay of the *guṇas* in people as they move through this material world. People are generally more in a state of *rajas* -

aggressiveness with passion, with various proportions of *satva* and *tamas*. *Rajas* is needed to create and is the predominant *guṇa* of action.

Especially when you move into an ashram environment, committed to a life of renunciation and detachment, many fall into a deep state of *tamas*, inaction. It is a state of inaction where all your suppressed opposition to your earlier life of meaningless activity surfaces and forces you into sheer inactivity. You may sleep long hours, disinclined to do anything. However, this is a passing phase. All these suppressions surface and dissolve. You then move into *satva*. It is surprising that one falls into *tamas* before moving into *satva*, yet it happens. A person steeped in *tamas* is the one who does not surrender to Kṛṣṇa. Such a person is in deep darkness and ignorance, unaware of his potential. He is no better than an animal.

Māyā, illusion, is also the interplay of the *guṇas*. It is a collection of our fantasies. Just as darkness needs light to destroy it, we need awareness to destroy *māyā*.

> In Bhāgavatam (the Hindu epic that describes Lord Viṣṇu's various incarnations, and especially His incarnation as Kṛṣṇa), there is this story.
>
> Nārada is the greatest devotee of Viṣṇu. He forever sings His praise and has nothing else on his mind. Over time Nārada became conceited about being the most celebrated devotee. As a true master, Viṣṇu took action.
>
> He called Nārada and asked him to fetch a pot of water. Nārada rushed to do it. Suddenly he was in front of a house asking for water. A beautiful maiden came out with water and Nārada fell instantaneously in love with her. He married this girl and they raised children together.
>
> One day there was a great storm. The house and the entire surroundings were flooded. The rushing water carried Nārada and his family away. Soon they were separated and his family died. Nārada wailed and screamed for help.

Suddenly he heard a voice, 'Nārada, where is my water? What happened to you?'

Nārada awoke, as if from a great sleep, and saw Viṣṇu smiling at him. He said, 'Even my greatest devotee is not immune to *māyā*!'

As long as the mind is active, no one is immune to *māyā*.

Four Pious Men

7.16 *O best among the Bhārata [Arjuna], four kinds of pious men begin to render devotional service unto Me.*
They are: the distressed, the desirer of wealth, the inquisitive, and those searching for knowledge of the Absolute.

7.17 *Of these, the wise one who is in full knowledge and ever united with Me through single-minded devotion is the best.*
I am very dear to him, and he is dear to Me.

7.18 *All these devotees are indeed noble; one who knows Me, dwells in Me.*
Being engaged in My mission, he attains Me.

7.19 *After many births and deaths, he who knows Me surrenders to Me, knowing Me to be the cause of all causes and all that is.*
Such a great soul is very rare.

Kṛṣṇa now goes deeper. Before entering into this subject, I bow down to the system that has been created by the *ṛṣis* (sages), which has made the whole spiritual science a reality.

In these modern times, abusing the social system created by the *ṛṣis* has become a fashion! Especially in Southern India, abusing the vedic system and *swamis* has become the trend. If you want to show you are educated or an important person, abuse our vedic system. You can immediately gain popularity.

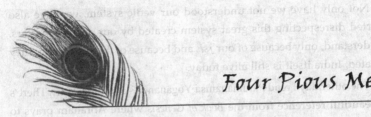

Not only have we not understood our vedic system, we have also started disrespecting this great system created by our ancient masters. Understand, only because of our *ṛṣis* and because of the system that they created, India itself is still alive today.

The other day I read Paramahamsa Yogānanda's autobiography. There's a beautiful reference from the *Book of Genesis* where Abraham prays to God. He requests God not to destroy a particular piece of land. God says, 'If I find ten good people in that land, I will not destroy that land.'

From this statement, you will understand why India is still alive. India is still alive and that's the greatest miracle of God. And it's all because of these ten people.

No other culture has survived or lived for such a long time. All other cultures that came into existence along with or after the Indian culture knew how to fight and build empires and big cities in a professional way. They were great warriors! Yet they were unable to survive. Today those cultures are not alive. Of the Indian culture, the Indian system, we have at least 10,000 years of recorded history.

There's a beautiful book by Swami Prakāśānanda Sarasvati about the history of religion in the Indian culture. According to him, the Indian culture is trillions of years old. And we have at least 10,000 years of recorded history of the Indian culture. No other country has been invaded as much as India. Yet, no country has been invaded by India. India stayed within its boundaries. India was again and again invaded, but it never invaded anybody. At the end of the day, this is the only culture that is still alive! Only because of this vedic system is Indian culture alive today.

Another important thing we need to understand is that 'Man is a social animal.' He creates some form of community or other. You cannot say that the United States does not have some form of community system. In other countries also the community system is there. However, these community systems are based upon money.

When I went to Brazil, I gave a discourse to a large company called Petrobras. One man asked, 'How do you justify the community system in

India? The high caste people look at the low caste people in a disrespectful way. How do you justify this?'

There are a few issues in Indian culture. Indians missed the spirit with which the community system was developed, and started following the letter. However, the whole community system cannot be labeled wrong because of a few mistakes. For example, if someone has a tumor in his body, the tumor must be operated on and removed. You cannot straightaway kill the person!

And it is we who committed mistakes, and now we are abusing the whole system.

I told him, 'Yes, one or two mistakes happened. But look at the developed countries. If you enter an airplane and walk to the economy class past the first class, watch the way the first class passengers look at you! Just by observing, you can see how disrespectfully they look at you.'

Don't think there is no community system in other countries. In every country, there is a community and class system.

The Indian community system

The vedic *ṛṣis* at least created the system based upon intelligence and wisdom. In other cultures, the community system was created based upon money and power.

In countries where the rulers are *kṣatriya*s (warrior class), they create the community system based upon power. The more powerful someone is, the more respected he is. In other countries, the business class people, control the whole system. There the more money someone has, the more he is respected.

India is the only country where people who respected intelligence and wisdom created the whole system. So that is why, in India, the more wisdom a person carries, the more spiritual he is, the more he is respected.

The whole social system was created based upon sharing. Let me describe the spirit with which the whole system was created, and how we abused it. First, the whole system is based upon our character. It is based upon our *guṇas* (nature), our attitude towards life. A person who works driven by fear belongs to the working class called *śūdra*. A person who works out of greed, belongs to the merchant class called *vaiśya*. A person who works to get attention or to prove that he is superior, belongs to the *kṣatriya* community. A person who works out of gratitude, expressing his bliss, is a *brāhmaṇa*. This was how people were categorized in those days.

Everybody must contribute something to society. A person may share his time if he has nothing else to share. Such a person is a *śūdra*. He belongs to the working class. A person who shares products, has time and intelligence to create products and share them is a *vaiśya*.

The person who shares confidence, who gives courage to the whole community, is a *kṣatriya*, a warrior! He unites the whole group as a community in a solid way by sharing his confidence. The person who shares his knowledge, bliss or spiritual wisdom, is a *brāhmaṇa*.

This type of division is completely based on the role we play in the community. In no way is it related to our birth. This is the spirit with which the whole system was created. Here nobody is higher and nobody is lower as it is practised today. In the course of time, one or two mistakes happened. But because of that we can't say that the whole system is wrong.

caturvidhā bhajante māṁ janāḥ sukṛtino 'rjuna **/**
ārto jijñasurarthaarthī jñānī ca bhārata ṛṣabha **// 7.16**

'O best among the Bhārata, four kinds of pious men begin to render devotional service unto Me: the distressed, the desirer of wealth, the inquisitive, and he who searches for knowledge of the Absolute.'

Here Kṛṣṇa talks about those who approach the Divine and the ways in which they approach the Divine. Man is centered on seven basic emotions. Basically we live and work based on these seven emotions: greed, fear, worry, attention-need (name and fame), comparison and jealousy, ego and the last one, the seventh emotion, deep discontentment.

These are the qualities with which man lives and works. Every moment, we work based upon these seven emotions. These seven emotions are seven energy centers that supply energy to us. Everything we do in life is rooted in one of these seven emotions.

If we are centered on greed, Goddess Lakṣmī (goddess of wealth) appeals to us. Or we continuously run behind Kubera (Lord of wealth) and perform Kubera *pūjā* (worship of Kubera); we continuously repeat the concept of Kubera. When we feel we are missing something, we try to get fulfillment by creating our own God and approaching Him in that mold. We try to get fulfillment by approaching the Divine with the same emotion, the same feeling that we miss in our being.

One more thing: When we become mature, we approach the same Lakṣmī as Jñāna Lakṣmī (goddess of wisdom as wealth)! We pray to the same goddess to give us wisdom, to give us knowledge.

According to our maturity we see the Divine. Understand, there's nothing wrong in approaching the Lord from greed. There's nothing wrong in starting our life with prayers for boons. However, we should not end our life also with prayers for boons. It's a good start, but a bad end! Vivekānanda beautifully says, 'It's good to be born in the church, but not to die there.' Before we die, we must realize the other dimensions of the Divine.

In prayer, we pray to God; in meditation, we become God! Prayers give us immediate results. Praying to the Divine is not wrong, yet it is not enough. Whereas in meditation, we become that higher principle or the Divine to which we constantly pour out our prayers. This is permanent.

The Divine is nothing but our own reflection. The more we understand, the more we grow and relate with the Divine in a more mature way. Otherwise we are confused and caught like a drunkard.

A small story:

A man returns home very late, completely drunk. He's not able to walk. He somehow makes his way into the house, stumbles over a table and breaks a piece of glass. Not only does he break a piece of glass, the glass cuts him badly. He goes to the bathroom and tries to bandage himself, looking in the mirror. Then slowly, without making a sound, he enters the bedroom and falls asleep.

The next morning, his wife starts her enquiry, 'What happened? What did you do last night?'

He replies, 'I didn't do anything. I am okay.'

The wife says, 'No, tell me why you were late.'

He says, 'I went and had a few drinks.'

She says, 'That's ok, but did you hurt yourself?'

He says, 'No, I did not hurt myself.'

She asks, 'Then why did you put so many bandages on the mirror?'

Instead of putting the bandages on himself, he put the bandages on the mirror!

If we are drunk, if we are unaware, we land up doing the same thing! We would do everything to the mirror. We miss where we are supposed to work. Catching the mirror and catching the form is one and the same. Catching the form is nothing but catching the mirror. If we put the bandage on the mirror, we can never be healed. The mirror should be used to find out where to put the bandage on us. We cannot heal ourselves by putting bandages on the mirror.

In the same way, we should use God or the Divine like a mirror to find out where we have a problem. The healing work should be done on us, not on the mirror. Don't miss and try to do the healing work on the mirror. If we do that we will miss the whole thing.

This reminds me of another story, a true incident.

A small-time astrologer used to visit the Bangalore ashram. Suddenly, one day he came to the ashram in a car.

I asked, 'What happened? Suddenly you have a new car. Did you win a lottery?'

He replied, 'No *Swamiji*, it's the grace of Lakṣmī *yantra* (Lakṣmī *yantra* refers to an instrument giving wealth). It's because of Lakṣmī *yantra*,' he said.

I asked him, 'Who gave you the *yantra*? I have never heard of something called Lakṣmī *yantra*. Who gave it to you?'

He said, 'Nobody gave it to me *Swamiji*. I give it to people!'

Whether the person who received Lakṣmī *yantra* became rich or not, the person who made money selling it became rich!

So be very clear: Starting life with prayers is okay, it is a good start, but it is not the right place to end.

We choose God based on our emotions

At the next level, the person is centered on fear and so he worships gods who will protect him. He does the Sudarśana homa (Sudarśana homa refers to the fire ritual done for general protection), or he continuously does Mṛtyuñjaya *homa* (fire ritual done to avoid untimely death and improve longevity) for protection. He continuously goes about worshipping some planet or god. That's why tribal gods have big swords. People who are fear-centered worship gods with weapons. All this is okay, nothing wrong, but it is not the place to stop.

The third level is approaching the Divine because of worry. The mixture of fear and greed is worry. We pray to the Divine, 'Please help me stop worrying.' At this point, we may do yoga or meditation for the sake of peace. The next level is based on attention-need. We approach the Divine for the sake of name and fame. Not only do we pray to the Divine, we gradually start representing the Divine also. If you go to India, you will see that the people who run temples behave almost like God. It's a big problem. The person who runs the temple thinks he is God because he takes care of the whole thing. That's where the problem starts.

I tell people: unless you are mature, never take up the task of running a temple. One person asked me, 'I don't believe in spirituality. However, I want to run a temple as a social service. I want to do it as a social service. Shall I do it?' I told him, 'Never make that mistake! If you are not spiritually mature and you enter this work, surely you will trouble yourself and others. By and by, it will become a pure name and fame game! And naturally you will not only hurt yourself, you will hurt others too. Never take up the responsibility unless you are spiritually mature.'

There's a beautiful ritual performed during the installation of a deity in a temple, called *prāṇa pratiṣṭha*. The scriptural instruction is that the person who installs the deity must be enlightened or else he will receive the collective negativity of the people who pray in that temple. It may be a frightening idea, but it is true. The person who takes up this job without spiritual maturity will naturally end up with name and fame problems, creating problems for others and himself. He puts himself in the place of the Divine and acts on behalf of the Divine.

The people who stand and pray in front of God, the deity, are gullible because they are caught in fear and greed. You can easily exploit them. They are searching for a solution. So naturally you can take them for a ride. That is the reason why repeatedly, it is emphasized that only an enlightened person should run a spiritual organization.

If we give a spiritual project to a person who has only the attitude of a businessman, he turns the whole thing into a business. The Divine cannot be brought under accounts and mathematical calculations! The whole thing loses its spirit. The original spirit and inspiration with which the whole thing was created will not be realized. That is why masters emphasize again and again that we need spiritual maturity before we enter into these activities.

The next is comparison and jealousy. People always compare themselves with others and feel jealous of the others' position and wealth. Such a person can never rest. Why do we feel like running continuously? Why are we in a hurry?

There is a beautiful verse that says, 'Just as a monkey-charmer makes a monkey dance using a stick, *māyā* or illusion, makes us dance with a single stick called jealousy.' With one stick, *māyā* makes us dance. The moment we think somebody has more than we do, we hurry. We are in a hurry!

A small story:

A man entered a bar and ordered five drinks. Without pausing, he gulped down all five glasses.

The bartender asked him, 'Why are you in a hurry?'

The man replied, 'You would also be in a hurry, if you had what I have.'

The bartender asks sympathetically, 'What is the problem? What do you have?'

The man replied, 'Only fifty cents.'

If we are in a hurry, please be very clear, we have only fifty cents. We don't trust ourselves. That is why we run. We don't trust our energy. We want to grab and finish everything. We don't want someone to see that we are inadequate.

We don't need to run. If we are centered on jealousy and comparison, again we approach the Divine from that angle and only for that purpose. I have heard some people who run temples in India say, 'Only in my temple, we have a hundred foot high tower; we have diamond crowns and twenty-four carat gold crowns. I have this, I have that!' With the Divine also, people boast and compare.

In San Jose, I visited a devotee. He took me to his prayer room and started explaining about each of the ten photographs that were there. For each photo he gave at least half an hour's explanation.

He said, 'No copy of this photograph exists anywhere else on planet earth.'

I asked, 'How is that possible? There must be at least a few prints.'

He said, 'No! All other prints are destroyed! This is the only print available.'

Expressing the Divine

It is hard to imagine the extent of foolishness people go to and what type of things they do if they are caught in jealousy and comparison. We need to realize that each of us is unique. God is an artist. He sculpts each of us with His hands, lovingly and uniquely. Therefore, each one of us is different.

When we approach the Divine with the mentality of jealousy and comparison, we are caught again. People ask me, '*Swamiji*, in our epics, we read about gods and goddesses fighting out of jealousy and greed, out of anger. What do you say about that?'

Those epics were written for people caught in jealousy, so that they could relate with them. Don't think that the Divine has done those things. Even rituals are done only so that people feel comfortable with God and they start coming closer to Him. When people witness the ceremony of Gods getting married, they feel comfortable and safe. They feel, 'Yes, I can relate with Him now. He is like me.' You see, unless the Divine is expressed in our language, we will not be able to relate with It. That is why these stories are written.

Next is the person who is centered on ego. The person who is centered on ego tries to get name and fame for himself. He starts claiming that he is divine without expressing the qualities of the Divine. That is why there's a beautiful *Upaniṣad* verse that says: If you are divine, express it by your quality. Let people recognize it by your quality, not by your words.

What you do speaks for you; what you speak will not do anything for you. What you do, the way in which you work, speaks for you. Your words will not work for you. There's a short, beautiful *Upaniṣad* called Paramahamsa Upaniṣad. It says that a *Paramahamsa* should not wear the saffron robe. Technically speaking, I am not supposed to wear this saffron robe. They say we are not respected the way we are meant to be respected if we wear this saffron robe. By our very *quality*, we should be respected. The divine qualities expressed in our life, that alone should be respected, and not this robe.

Yesterday there was a question: How do we know if a person is egoistic or he is a real spiritual master?

A person who is egoistic can only play with words. Only a person who has achieved enlightenment can radiate the energy to reproduce the same experience in you. If you get the experience, then be very clear your master is enlightened. He is the embodiment of spiritual experience and knowledge. If you get the words but not the experience, then the person or the path you are following is not the ultimate.

Words are like the menu card. Experience is like the food. If you go to a restaurant and they give you a menu card and say, 'Here is the menu card, but the food is not available here,' can you call that a restaurant? No! The menu card is not enough; your hunger cannot be satisfied by it. In spiritual life we cannot stop with just the menu card.

The person who has approached the Divine with ego always tries to represent the Divine without having the solid experience himself. That is why the *Upaniṣads* again and again emphasize experience. If we don't experience, be very clear there's something seriously wrong with the person whom we are following.

I always tell people, if you have not experienced anything with me, please follow some other person. It is easy to put the blame and responsibility on the disciples and continuously blame them by saying, 'You are not qualified, you are not practising perfectly, and that is why you have not had any experience'. This is a cunning way of cheating the disciple and evading the truth. The disciple comes to a guru because the disciple has not yet experienced. And the guru says, 'You are imperfect and that is why you do not have spiritual experiences.' To learn this, one doesn't need a guru: a spouse is sufficient! Anyway, this is what the spouses tell each other continuously.

A true master will reproduce in you the same experience that happened in him, no matter what your condition is. A scientist is a person who creates a formula to reproduce what he experienced in the outer world. A spiritual master or a mystic is a person who creates a formula to reproduce his experience in the inner world. For example, Newton saw an apple fall from a tree and he understood something. He created a formula to reproduce the same understanding in everybody else. Likewise, a master or a mystic creates formulae or techniques to reproduce the same experience that happened in him in everybody else.

I always tell people: if you have not experienced anything by attending our meditation programs then something is wrong with me, not with you. Forget about me; carry on with your life. You may meet some other master.

I am enlightened only if you can experience my enlightenment, not otherwise. Before that, it's a mere menu card that will not remove your hunger. What you hear is only the menu card. Aim directly at the Divine.

The person who approaches the Divine with ego gets everything and boosts his own ego. He becomes more egoistic by getting all the knowledge. These are the most dangerous people. Instead of surrendering their ego to the Divine, they strengthen their ego with their knowledge.

A small story:

A king went to the forest to hunt. Suddenly he saw more than fifty trees with the target marked circles within circles, like a bull's eye. In the center, there was an arrow. There were target marks and an arrow pierced exactly in the center. He saw so many target marks and the arrow was exactly in the center in all of them. He wanted to find out who had mastered the art of archery. 'Who is this person? He must be a great master. He must be like Arjuna,' he thought to himself.

Suddenly he saw a young boy with bow and arrows; the same colored arrows that he saw on the target marks.

He asked him, 'Are you the person who shot the arrows?'

The boy replied, 'Yes, I am the person.'

The happy king congratulated him saying, 'From this day onwards, I appoint you as commander-in-chief of my army. I appreciate your mastery over archery, your power, and your capacity. Please tell me how you mastered such a great art at such a young age.'

The boy replied, 'It's simple. First I shot the arrow, and then I marked the circles. That's all!'

If we approach the Divine with ego, we do the same thing. Instead of aiming at the center, we shoot arrows and then create the circles. When we approach the Divine with ego, instead of surrendering our ego, we strengthen our ego with knowledge.

Approach the Divine with gratitude

The next level is the ultimate level. In this level, we go to the Divine with the attitude of gratitude. We feel so grateful, so deeply connected to the Divine that our whole life changes.

We move from the first level of greed, where we pray to boon-giving gods, to the next level of fear where the gods who can protect us appeal to us. The next is worry. Buddha appeals to us if we are centered on worry because he appears to be so peaceful and calm. To the person who is centered on name and fame, gods who give name and fame appeal the most.

In the same way as with gods, people also approach masters from all these various levels.

I have seven kinds of people who approach me: *One*, people who approach me out of greed; *two*, people who approach me out of fear; *three*, people who approach me out of worry; *four*, people who approach me for name and fame; *five*, people who approach me out of jealousy and comparison; *six*, people who approach me out of ego, to strengthen their ego by saying, 'I am a disciple of Paramahamsa Nithyananda. I am close to him. He knows my name,' finally, *seven* - there are a few, very few who approach me out of gratitude.

There's one more problem with people who approach me out of greed. Not only do they have greed, they also have their own ideas and fantasies about a master. Also, I face a big problem because of my young age. Let me narrate to you an incident that happened in our India ashram:

> One day I was sitting outdoors in the ashram. I was sitting alone, without my turban. Nobody was around me. Our ashram is located next to a forest. I was sitting there on a small rock, enjoying the cool breeze. One well-read, elderly scholar came to me and asked, 'I want to meet Swamiji. Where is he?' I told him, 'Please go and sit in the Ānanda Sabhā (meditation hall). He will come in half an hour's time.' He went and sat in the meditation hall.
>
> He went and sat in the hall. After half an hour, I wore my turban and *rudrākṣa* rosary and went there and was about to take my seat. This man said, 'No! I want to meet the big Swamiji. I want to meet *Guruji* (master).'
>
> I said, 'Please forgive me. In this ashram I am the *swami*. Whom do you want to meet?' He said, 'I have heard about Paramahamsa Nithyananda. He healed my cousin. I want to see him.' Then I told him his cousin's name and the disease he had and that I had healed him. I told him, 'I am Paramahamsa Nithyananda.' You will be surprised; he was not ready to believe me. He just stared at me.
>
> Then I said, 'Usually, *swamis* don't carry any ID card (identity card) in India. Still, if you don't believe me, look at that photograph (on the ashram signboard). See the name, and see that face. I am that *swami*! I can't say anything more to convince you.'
>
> You will be surprised! He said, 'I am not ready to learn from you.' He did not speak to me, and also went away. Because of his strong fantasies and imagination about what a guru should be like, he was not able to even relate with me!

When we have such strong fantasy about things, we will not be able to relate with reality. That man said, 'I have nothing to ask you about,' and he went away. People who come with fear will never be able to get rid of that fear. They will be stuck with that because fear itself is a fantasy.

At different levels, people approach the master or God. The more mature we are, the more we will feel connected to that person who will give us fulfillment. When we become mature, when we are above fear and greed, we will approach the same master, the same God, with more maturity, with more intimacy. We will feel deeply connected to him.

In Bhāgavatam (an Indian epic), we learn about five different attitudes with which we normally relate with a master or God:

1) *Dāsa Bhāva* - seeing God as a master and oneself as a servant, as with Hanumān who saw Rāma as his master and served Him as a path for liberation.

2) *Vātsalya Bhāva* - seeing God as a divine child, as with Yaśodā who saw Kṛṣṇa as her son.

3) *Sakha Bhāva* - seeing God or the master as a friend, the way Arjuna related with Kṛṣṇa.

4) *Mātṛ Bhāva* - seeing God or the master as a father or mother, the way Rāmakṛṣṇa related with goddess Kālī (representation of the divine Mother).

Rāmakrsna really felt goddess Kālī to be his mother. He always tasted the food before offering it to Her. The temple organizers scolded him, 'No, you cannot do this. It is sacrilegious! You cannot offer food to God after you have tasted it.'

Rāmakṛṣṇa said, 'If you say that, I will leave the temple. But I cannot give food to my mother unless I taste it first. Unless I know it is good food, I cannot give it to Her. I have no problem in leaving the temple and worshipping from outside. But I will not stop what I am doing.'

Rāmakṛṣṇa deeply felt that goddess Kālī was his mother.

5) Finally, the fifth attitude is *madhura bhāva* - seeing God as a beloved, the way Rādhā saw Kṛṣṇa. This attitude needs a tremendous maturity. Only if we experience the consciousness which is beyond the body, can we relate with the Divine with the attitude of a beloved, *madhura bhāva*.

According to our maturity, our attitude differs. The more mature we are, the more the gratitude happens. The less the maturity, the more we fill our life with prayers. Prayer is greed; confession is fear!

That is why I say, 'Gratitude is the greatest prayer, and 'Thank you', the greatest *mantra.*'

When we go beyond prayer and confession, we experience gratitude. We experience the Divine. Kṛṣṇa explains how we can grow step-by-step, how we can reach the ultimate maturity.

Let us see how Kṛṣṇa explains. What is the technique Kṛṣṇa offers us to grow in maturity and experience eternal consciousness?

caturvidhā bhajante māṁ janāḥ sukṛtino'rjuna **|**
ārto jijñasurarthārthījñānīca bhāratarṣabha **|| 7.16**

Based on how we approach the Divine, the community system is created. How much we share with society depends on how mature we are. With the same maturity, we approach God also.

If we miss money, we go to the God who gives money. If we miss knowledge, we go to Sarasvatī (the goddess of knowledge), who gives knowledge. If we feel insecure, we go to the god who protects us, Mother Durgā or Kālī. If we miss spiritual experience, the ultimate experience, then we go to the divine incarnations, the ultimate expressions of the Divine.

Kṛṣṇa says, 'Four types of people come to Me - *caturvidhā bhajante māṁ.*' He explains the four types as four communities. The first are the people who are distressed, i.e., the working class or *śūdra.* The second are the people who desire wealth, i.e., the business people or *vaiśya.* The third are inquisitive people who continuously enquire, continuously ask, '*Tataḥ kim*? *Tataḥ kim*? *Tataḥ kim*?' (What next? What next? What next?) A *kṣatriya,* for example, never rests because he constantly asks, 'What next? What next? What next?' The fourth is the person who searches for knowledge of the Absolute: He is a *brāhmaṇa.*

'All four come to Me, all four reach Me, but from different levels.' From different levels all four go to the same God, but they will experience Him in different ways. You will experience the Divine according to your maturity. As long as you are caught in fear or greed, you go only to those types of gods. You will be attracted to only those types of gods.

It is easy to go to a temple and pray, but difficult to go to a master and meditate. It is for mature people. In the temple we see thousands; but in spiritual places, we see a few hundred.

Spirituality is a luxury!

Spirituality is a luxury; only a few intelligent people can afford it! The price of spirituality is the limit of our suffering! Only if we have had enough suffering can we afford to get into spirituality. It is only for people who have suffered, or who have understood that they have suffered. There are two things. It is not only the suffering but also the understanding that we suffer. This understanding is intelligence. It happens even beyond age and experience. Just a glimpse of life is enough if this intelligence is there; we will understand how suffering happens and we will not get caught in it! Both, the suffering and the understanding, are needed to enter into spiritual life.

The person who approaches Me out of love and gratitude, is the best person, for I am dear to him and he is dear to Me. By this one verse, Kṛṣṇa ends the whole conversation, the whole concept.

Kṛṣṇa says, 'Starting at different levels is okay, but don't stop there.' We can start or take off from any level. However, we should not stop and stagnate there. It is like failing to proceed to the second standard from the first. It takes many lifetimes to understand and achieve this maturity. When I say it takes many lives, some think, 'Let me take some more lives and become mature.' Now, that's a big problem. Whenever we speak, we must make things very clear, otherwise you can't imagine how many different ways people will interpret it!

A small story:

Once, a great scholar recounted the story of Hariścandra. Most people in India know the story of Hariścandra, a king who lived to uphold the truth and sold his wife for the sake of the truth. Just to keep his promise, he sold his wife. Such was his greatness.

The scholar narrated the whole story. After narrating the story, he asked one person, 'What did you understand from this story?'

The person said, 'Master, I understood that truth is the most important thing in life. We should give up everything for the sake of the truth. Truth is the ultimate.'

The scholar was pleased. He asked the next person, 'What did you understand?'

The man said, 'Master, I understood that in an emergency, it is okay to sell your wife.'

From the same story, two people have two different understandings! So be very clear, don't miss the understanding.

A common saying is, 'As many masters, so many paths.' However I say, 'As many disciples, so many paths!'

The master may utter the same truth to his disciples, yet each understands and interprets in his or her own way depending on the maturity of the person receiving the truths. Hence the attitude with which one approaches matters a lot. Based on that one experiences the Divine differently.

Here Kṛṣṇa says, 'Out of these, the wise is always devoted to Me. He is the best person.' To start with, you can start at any level, yet you must strive to reach the Ultimate. And one more thing that I want to make clear is, please don't think, 'Oh! Kṛṣṇa says it will take many lives; let me take some more lives and become mature.'

No! If you can enter into the knowledge this moment, the experience can happen to you this very moment. You don't need to postpone. Every moment is a new birth for you. Every moment is death. The outgoing breath is death, and the incoming breath is birth. So be very clear, every moment you die and take birth. This moment can be a new birth for you.

The person who understands this truth takes a new birth. He is called *dvija.*

A person who is initiated is called *dvija* in Sanskrit, which means twice born or reborn. All *sanyāsi* are twice born or *dvija*. They are the reborn people. 'Reborn' refers to taking a new birth at the being level. They become newborn beings. So understand that in this moment, a new birth can happen to you.

Kṛṣṇa says: *ahaṁ sa ca mama priyaḥ* - He is dear to Me, and I am dear to him. Kṛṣṇa says beautifully that He is in you and you are in Him. The moment you understand this ultimate Truth, you become the Divine. All you need to do is change your attitude. There is one more thing you must understand. The master or the Divine is in you only when you engage yourself in service to Him. Sitting in front of the master or the Divine, just enjoying the form, is not the service Kṛṣṇa talks about. Then you are only chasing Him from a purely selfish motive.

When you devote yourself to the divine mission, you become a devotee. That is when you become dear to Him. Your worship is no longer selfish. It is towards the mission of the Divine, in whatever form. I tell my followers: Stop sitting in front of me, gazing and waiting for words to drop. Work for my mission. Help me transform people. As long as you sit and gaze, you chase me. When you work for my mission, I chase you. I shall always be with you.

When the scriptures say, 'Follow the master,' they advise you to follow the teachings of the master, so that you can be the master too. They tell you to follow the institution of the master, his community. When we follow these three, the master, his teachings and his mission, we are on the path to liberation. Only after many births and deaths can we relate to an enlightened person. We will not be able to relate to an enlightened master unless we undergo many births and deaths.

I told you about the seven steps in spiritual progress: 1) go around many temples, perform many rituals, pilgrimages, etc 2) do rituals by yourself 3) concentrate and pray to one God 4) instead of rituals, chant verses in praise of God 5) instead of chanting, visualize His form and meditate upon it 6) instead of meditating on any form, fall into that same consciousness, realize that the form and your soul are one and the same, that God and the soul are one and the same 7) experience reality!

People take hundreds of lives to achieve this maturity. Kṛṣṇa says: *sa mahātmā sūdurlabhaḥ* – indeed, very rare is it to see such souls who have achieved that maturity. It is easy to relate with gods in the temple because they don't demand discipline from us. We can pray to Him, do whatever we want, and think He has blessed us and go away. However, relating with a living enlightened master is difficult.

People ask me, 'Why do masters become popular after their death?' After death, all masters become popular because it's easy to cheat ourselves with a photograph. We can keep His photograph and do whatever we want and think these are His teachings. There is nobody to question us. We can do whatever we want and project everything as His blessings, and we can play with the photograph. That is why dead masters become popular.

And most importantly, we don't have to give up our ego with dead masters. We don't need to surrender. That is why there will be large crowds with dead masters and temples. All we need to do is think that we have done everything and that we are blessed. But with a living master, we need to transform our life. We need to experience the truth. He will not let us rest. He will haunt us until we realize the truth. He will not fulfill our ego.

I always tell people, 'Dead masters are dead. The living master is death!' The living master will be death for us, for our ego. We cannot play our games with him. We must grow and become mature beings. He awakens us.

Somebody asked the enlightened sage Ramana Maharishi, 'If this whole world is *māyā* (illusion), I see the master also in the same dream, I see the enlightened person also in the same dream. I see You also in the same dream. How is it going to help me?'

Ramana Maharishi said, 'If we see a lion in our dream, what happens? We wake up immediately. In the same way, if we see a master, be very clear, we wake up from our dream! The master is a *siṁha svapna* - lion-dream or nightmare!'

The living master is a nightmare!

Living masters are nightmares. That is why we are afraid. People are afraid to come near a living master. We can't play the same game with him.

Only a person who has understood, after many, many births and deaths, one who has matured, who has enough knowledge, surrenders to Me, surrenders to the living master', says Kṛṣṇa.

In India, especially in Tamil Nadu, kids play with wooden dolls. They have four to five dolls. For one doll, they will drape a *sari* and call it as mother. Another they will dress in a *dhoti* and call it father; then brother, then sister and so on. And they start their game. They say, 'Mother is cooking,' and they take the mother doll and make it stand near the toy kitchen. They say, 'Father is going to office,' and place the father doll in a small car, and they will drive it too. They will make honking sounds, 'peem… peem…' to give an effect of a real life scenario, and take the car to office. And then, after a few minutes they will say, 'Sister is going to school.' They will place the sister doll in the toy car and move it around. They will cry and make sounds as though the sister cries because she doesn't want to go to school.

They will enact the scenes of the game. Then they will say, 'Now it is evening, sister comes back from school.' They will bring the sister back. They will bring the father back and say, 'Father comes back from office.'

This seems like a game for kids. But please understand, you play the same game in your life. You catch somebody and say, 'You are my mother, you are my father, you are my wife, you are my husband, you are my son, you are my sister, and you are my brother.'

And if that doll doesn't behave according to your frame you say that it is not a good doll and throw it away. Sometimes, children hurt themselves with dolls and complain that the doll hurt them. They cry. In the same way, when somebody doesn't behave according to your frame, you feel they hurt you. You want all the people in your life to play their role the way you want them to play. When it does not happen, you feel hurt. Suddenly, you die. You leave the body.

When you go to another place, in your next birth, you again catch one more set of dolls and start the same game. Sometimes you bring dolls into the game, sometimes you throw dolls out of the game, sometimes you fire them and sometimes you pamper them. If you don't have enough dolls, you get some cats or dogs to play with.

Suddenly, again you die. When you die again, you assume another body. With that body, you catch one more set of people and play the same game! Again and again, you play the same game. Only a person who is a little mature thinks, 'How many times will I play this same game? How many times will I do this same psychodrama?'

The whole thing is a psychodrama! You have an agenda. Society has taught you that, as a father or a husband or a son, you should behave in a certain manner. As long as you follow the agenda, you are considered a good citizen. When even once, you don't follow that agenda, you are not respected. All the other dolls kick you out of the gate. You are not invited to parties. They boycott you and then suddenly one day you realize, 'How many times am I doing the same drama; again and again, the same game?'

The person who understands that he is playing the same game again and again, has achieved the real intelligence about what is happening. Then naturally you surrender. 'You surrender unto Me', says Kṛṣṇa.

Kṛṣṇa says, 'One who understands that the cause of all causes is Me, realizes the ultimate divine. He realizes thus, 'How many times will I play the same drama?' Until this realization, the whole thing is repeated again and again without end, without the experience.

'The person who has understood, who has knowledge of this truth, surrenders unto Me, surrenders to the master, an enlightened being, knowing Me to be the cause of all causes and all there is. Such a great soul is rare.'

Only a person who has achieved this knowledge relates with the master in the real sense. There's a beautiful verse that says, 'Even if you have *seen* an enlightened master *once*, you will become enlightened.' Some people ask me, 'Why haven't I become enlightened yet, *Swamiji*?' Be very clear, 'Never think that by seeing me through your eyes, you can see the Divine. You can see my form, but not me. Even if you have seen many enlightened masters, never think that you have seen them. Just by looking through your eyes, never ever think that you have seen them.'

Even if you have seen them, the attitude with which you have seen them plays a major role. If you went to them with greed or fear, then you have approached a demigod and not an enlightened master. Only if you go with an attitude of love and gratitude, understanding and maturity, only then do you see an enlightened person. The moment you see an enlightened being AS HE IS, you WILL become enlightened. There's no doubt about it.

I Am In Your Heart!

7.20 *Those whose discrimination has been distorted by various desires, surrender unto deities.*
They follow specific rules and regulations of worship according to their own nature.

7.21 *I am in everyone's heart as the super soul.*
As soon as one desires to worship some deity, I make his faith steady so that he can devote himself to that particular deity.

7.22 *Endowed with such a faith, he endeavors to worship a particular demigod and obtains his desires;*
In reality, these benefits are granted by Me alone.

7.23 *Men of limited intelligence worship the demigods and their fruits are limited and temporary.*
Those who worship the demigods go only to the planets of the demigods, but My devotees reach My supreme planet.

He says: I am in everyone's heart as the *Paramātman* (super soul). As soon as one desires to worship a particular deity, I make his faith steady so that he can devote himself to that particular deity.

Please understand that when He says 'deity' or 'demigod', He doesn't mean the Supreme. Even if you approach Kṛṣṇa out of fear or greed, you approach only a demigod. When He says the word demigod, He means the attitude with which we approach the Divine; *how* we approach the Divine. With the right approach, even if you approach a demigod, he will be supreme! He will give you enlightenment. With the wrong approach, even if you approach Kṛṣṇa, you will have only material benefits.

There's a beautiful story from Kṛṣṇa's life.

A rich man prayed to Kṛṣṇa to become a king. Twice a day, morning and evening he repeated, 'Kṛṣṇa, Kṛṣṇa.' He always asked Kṛṣṇa thus, 'Kṛṣṇa, please give me a kingdom. Kṛṣṇa, I want to become a king.'

There was another poor lady, who had only one cow. With that milk she made a little butter and some sweets and offered it to Kṛṣṇa. The whole day she sat and chanted Kṛṣṇa's name.

Suddenly one day Kṛṣṇa appeared and responded to both of them. This man, who had asked for a kingdom, became a king. And in the case of this lady who prayed everyday to Kṛṣṇa, her cow died.

Nārada asked Kṛṣṇa, 'What is this, Kṛṣṇa? That man who repeats your name only twice a day has been made a king by you. This lady who remembers you twenty-four hours a day, got deprived of her only cow. Is it fair?'

Kṛṣṇa says, 'That man only wants the kingdom. I am a utility to him. So I blessed him with what he wants. But for her, I was her whole life. There was only one small hindrance that stood between her and Me, and that was the cow! I removed that hindrance also. Now she has come to Me and completely become Me!'

Whatever our approach to the Divine is, it plays an important role in our spiritual progress. If we approach Kṛṣṇa out of fear or greed, we worship a demigod. It is not wrong, but it is not enough. That is not the place to stop. It is a good place to have a visa, but not to have a green card or citizenship. Here, the planets or palaces of demigods are good places to visit, but not the right place to stay.

Kṛṣṇa says, 'Because I am in everyone's heart as the super soul, the moment you desire to worship some demigod, I shall make your faith steady, so you can devote yourself to that particular deity.'

Stages of seeking

Let me describe how a seeker usually travels through all these paths and eventually reaches the ultimate. When you start as a normal seeker, you hear about all kinds of rituals like *pūjā* (worship) and *homa* (fire ritual). You hear that a particular *pūjā* will give a certain benefit and you start doing these things. On Friday, you fast for Devī (the divine mother), on Saturday, you fast for Bālāji (another name for Lord Viṣṇu), on Sunday you fast for some other god, on Monday you fast for Śiva, on Tuesday for Skandha (another name for Lord Subrahmaṇya), on Thursday for the guru (the master), and so on.

Then slowly, you not only go to all these *pūjās* and *homas*, you also go to many different temples. After some time, you understand that these rituals and trips to the temples are too much. Then you think, 'Why let somebody else do these things for me? Let me directly do it and relate with the Divine.' You start your own shrine in your prayer room in your own home. This happens when you become a little mature. You think that you should feel directly connected to the Divine.

The first grade in spirituality is going around visiting all the temples, watching all the types of offerings. The second grade is doing it yourself. The third grade is realizing, 'The Divine is there in all the gods, in all the forms. But I feel more attracted towards this one god. So let me concentrate on worshipping the Divine in this form.' Having one form and offering only to that form is the third grade. The fourth grade happens when you think, 'More than these types of offerings, sounds imbued with energy is more powerful. Let me chant the sacred verses.'

Understand: surrendering through the body is *pūjā*; surrendering through words in chanting verses in praise of the Lord is *japa*; surrendering through the mind is *jñāna* - wisdom or knowledge of the Self. So here you think, 'Why not chant the name of God?' You start repeating the name of your favorite deity.

At every level, different gods, different gurus or masters appeal to you. When you are at the level of going to pilgrimage places, people who guide you to these pilgrimage centers appeal to you. When you go to Sabarimala (a famous pilgrimage spot in South India), you call the person who leads the trip *guru swami*. He appeals to you.

When you come to the level of *pūjā* and *homa*, other people who also do these rituals appeal to you! The person who teaches you *pūjā* appeals to you. He becomes your guru. Next, when you come to the level of focusing and offering to only one deity, the deity becomes your guru. Next, when you come to the level of chanting verses, the person who teaches you the verses appeals to you. He becomes your guru.

Next, after some time you think, 'Why only repeat this verse? Why not do some meditation?' Now the person who teaches you meditation appeals to you. Meditation is again *saguṇa brahman*, which means meditating on a form. This is the next grade.

Then, when you sincerely meditate, He Himself appears. He gives you His *darśan* (vision) and guides you to the higher level of practice. He guides you to the right master. Sometimes He gives you *darśan* and guides you; sometimes He automatically makes you feel connected to your master.

Only a person who has come to this level can feel directly connected to an enlightened master. Until you reach this level, until this maturity happens, you cannot straightaway feel completely connected to an enlightened person.

You need to go through all five steps, only then will you feel completely connected to a living master. When you come to the stage where you meditate on a single form, the master happens in your life. The form upon which you meditate and your own form are expressions of the same divine energy. So the master puts you into real meditation. This means turning towards your own consciousness, your own being or soul. He gives you the technique to realize your being. This is the sixth level.

The seventh grade, the ultimate grade, is when you experience that *You are That*. You achieve enlightenment!

This is the usual route that seekers travel on, starting from the first grade, moving to the second grade, and ending with experiencing the

Self. Now find out in which grade you are in and try to go to the next level. That is all you need to do.

Here Kṛṣṇa says, 'Because I reside in everyone's heart as the super soul, when somebody desires to worship a demigod, I make his faith steady, so that he can devote himself to that particular deity.' When you approach the Divine even from the first level, He helps you.

When you start, you are like 18 carat gold. Nothing is wrong with that but you need to be put into the fire a little to become 22 carat gold. Then you reach a living master. Then slowly you become 24 carat gold, and you become enlightened. Unless you have gone through the earlier steps, it will be difficult to relate to a living master.

This morning, one man came to visit me and started speaking to me. He expressed his confusion after having read many books. He said, 'I am now more confused than before.' In the Gītā, after a few chapters, he says, 'Oh Kṛṣṇa, I am now more confused than before hearing the Gītā!' Understand, this clearly means that you have done your spiritual practice well! Understanding that a particular practice is not helping you is the right help derived from the practice!

Buddha teaches meditation to one of his disciples. The disciple tries his best to meditate and comes back and says, 'Buddha, I am unable to meditate!' Then Buddha says, 'Don't worry. Understanding that you are not able to meditate is the purpose of this meditation. You have done it. That meditation has served its purpose. Now forget about it and come to the next step.'

Sometimes these techniques make us mature by giving us the understanding that we are unable to do the technique. That understanding is a big maturity. Approaching the Divine in some form is the first step, or the first level. There's nothing wrong in that, but don't stop there. Here Kṛṣṇa says, 'I make his faith steady, so that he can devote himself to that particular deity,' which means that he can grow in that particular attitude. There is the possibility of growth.

Kṛṣṇa says, 'Even if you approach Me with an attitude of fear or greed, I fulfill your needs. It is My own energy that fulfils them, so that you grow, and you come up to the next level.' If you receive boons through demigods, do not think that those deities are responsible for it. All these are granted by the ultimate energy, the Existential energy. But you are not expected to stop with these boons. You are expected to grow further.

When you approach the Divine, first God gives the *śakti* (energy) to turn your dreams into reality. Then He gives the *buddhi* (intelligence) to realize that reality itself is a dream!

That is what He says here: When I bless you, according to your maturity and based on the way in which you approach the Divine, I give everything.

There are many educated individuals who question me about the wisdom of idol worship and rituals.

> A small story:
>
> A disciple was massaging Vivekānanda's feet. A follower, a young student, came to Vivekānanda, prostrated at his feet and said, 'I adore you. I adore you because you despise all these superstitions about idol worship and bathing in the Ganges. You are truly educated.'
>
> Vivekānanda roared at him, 'You Fool, what do you know about my beliefs. I pray everyday to *Ma* Kālī and bathe in the Ganges. Shed all your notions that worshipping idols is foolish and learn how to pray.'
>
> Soon after, an elderly scholar came to Vivekānanda and said, 'Master, you are the greatest. Whatever you have said about learning the scriptures and going to temples is so powerful. I wish everyone would talk like you do.'
>
> Vivekānanda said to him, 'What do you know about the scriptures? Is there any point in reading all this outdated material? It only makes your ego stronger. Stop this nonsense and meditate.'

After the scholar left, the shocked disciple massaging his feet asked Vivekānanda, 'Master, I am confused. You have just reversed your position with these two people. What should I do?'

Vivekānanda said, 'Just keep your mouth shut and massage my feet. That is good for you.'

When you go to a temple and worship an idol, you might feel that you are praying to a stone. As your awareness grows, you will realize that the idol is not just stone; it is energy. Without much effort, you will start feeling the energy inside the temple.

Why do you think millions of people visit holy shrines in Tirupati or Vārāṇāsi or Tiruvannamalai? A few hundred people can be misled, but not millions, and that too without any enticement. They go because they feel relieved. They feel the touch and they feel the 'energy connection'.

Hindus worship *through* the idols, not the idols themselves. Our rituals address the energy behind these idols. Only faith can make us understand this. We need to go through this stage of form worship before we realize the formless. Otherwise we will all be intellectual monsters. Religions that condemn idol worship without understanding the philosophy behind such worship breed confusion that leads to destruction.

In every form of learning we need to advance step by step. Only if we are an exception can we be promoted to university education without attending high school. Such exceptions are rare, and prove the rule. When we consider idol worship meaningless, it only means that we are foolish and ignorant. The minute science advances and a scientist measures the energy vibration of our temples and proves that these are centers of energy, the same people will be queuing up at the temples.

It does not matter whether it is a Hindu temple, a Christian church, a Buddhist pagoda, a Muslim mosque or even a river or mountain. When millions of people congregate to celebrate the Divine and offer gratitude, any place becomes a place of worship. Every twelve years, tens of millions of people gather by the sacred river Gaṅgā in India to celebrate *Kumbhamela.* As these people bathe in the river with deep conviction, gratitude and prayers, the river gets purified and in turn purifies them. It is a deep bio-spiritual interaction that raises the energy of the planet and the universe.

When Kṛṣṇa says, 'He goes to the planets of the demigods,' He talks about space and experience. If we worship some god out of greed, we will be continuously caught in greed. If we worship some god out of fear, we will be always in that fear. If we worship the Divine out of love and gratitude, we experience a totally different space.

Hell and heaven are not geographical; they are psychological. Depending on our particular mood, we create our own hell or heaven wherever we go. We all know how to create hell! Now all we need to know is how to create heaven. He says: Men of small intelligence - people caught in greed or fear, attention-need or worry - worship the demigods. Of course, sometimes we worship the demigods; sometimes we approach Kṛṣṇa or the ultimate God with the same attitude – the attitude of asking. If we carry the attitude of greed, whether we worship Kubera, the god who gives money, or Kṛṣṇa, in effect we worship only a demigod. It is the attitude that makes Kṛṣṇa either the ultimate god or a demigod. It is we who create the attitude. It is we who create the energy. By worshipping demigods, we attain demigods.

This is an important *sūtra,* a technique. It says:

antavattu phalaṁ teṣāṁ tad bhavati alpamedhaśāṁ |
devān devayajo yānti madbhaktā yānti mām api || 7.23

It says that when we get boons from demigods, they are temporary. God will bless us with wealth when we ask Him. But we need intelligence to preserve it. So be very clear, when we receive anything out of energy, without having the maturity to receive and sustain it, it is only temporary. If we have enough intelligence and maturity to have wealth, then naturally, we would have created it. Because we don't have *buddhi,* wisdom, we ask God to give us *śakti,* energy. If we get *śakti* without *buddhi,* it will only be temporary.

That is what Kṛṣṇa says: If we get *śakti* without *buddhi*, it is temporary. It will not remain with us. That is why He says that boons derived from demigods are temporary, not permanent. And if we continue to worship them, we are stuck with them. We create that kind of energy in our inner space. We live with that kind of energy in our being.

He makes one more statement: *madbhaktā yānti mām api* - My devotees attain Me.

Then He says these words: If you approach Me with the ultimate attitude, with the attitude of love and gratitude, you achieve Me. The greatest attitude is gratitude. If you approach Me with gratitude, you experience Me.

Gratitude – The greatest attitude

Again and again people ask me, '*Swamiji*, when I have so many problems, how can I be grateful?' See, we continuously pray, 'Oh God, please give me a diamond ring.' Do we feel grateful that He gave us the finger to wear the ring? No! The finger is not our birthright. There are thousands of people who don't have hands or fingers. It's not our birthright.

We continuously pray intensely, in all possible ways, 'Oh God, give me this. Oh God, give me that.' But we never feel grateful for the things that are showered on us. This very life is a blessing!

Can we say that our life has been given to us as payment for some job that we did in Vaikunṭa (abode of Lord Viṣṇu) or Kailāś (abode of Lord Śiva)? No! It's not as if we worked for one hundred years in Kailāś, and earned a check that says, 'Alright, have seventy years of life.' If we work in the army, they give us money to study. It's not like that; we did not get life as a salary. It's a pure blessing showered on us.

Every breath is a blessing! This very life is a blessing. Continuously we miss things that are not part of our possession. But we never experience the things that are showered on us by the Divine.

Each of us has a big list of things that God has not given us and we also have a big list of things that God has given us. If you take a paper and pen and start writing these lists, both lists will be endless. Every moment of our life is a gift from the Divine.

If we honestly list the things that are not given to us, it will be an endless, infinite list. If we earnestly make a list of the things given to us, that will also be an endless, infinite list. Now it's up to us whether to look at the list of things not given to us and constantly feel miserable and live in hell, or look at the list of things showered on us and be in heaven. The second way makes us feel deeply grateful. We feel grateful and create our heaven. It is up to us to create hell or heaven. It's purely our choice.

Kṛṣṇa says, 'These men of small intelligence worship demigods. Their results are temporary.' We continue to live that way. When we feel life is a blessing and we approach the Divine with deep love and gratitude, not only do we experience divine consciousness, Kṛṣṇa says: They achieve ME. They attain ME.

There's another verse where Kṛṣṇa beautifully says: 'If you ask for something, I will give you that. If you don't ask for anything, I will give you Me.' People say, 'Who wants Him? We want Him only as a utility, not Him. As long as He serves our purpose, things are okay. So we don't want Him.' People want only solutions. They don't want the Divine.

No One Knows Me

7.24 *Unintelligent men, who do not know Me perfectly, think that I, the Supreme personality of Godhead, the* Bhagavān, *who was impersonal before, have become a human being now.*
They do not know that I am imperishable and Supreme, even when I assume the body.

7.25 *I am never revealed to the foolish and unintelligent, covered as I am by My divine power*
The ignorant do not know Me, unborn and eternal.

7.26 *O Arjuna, as the Supreme personality of Godhead, I know all that has happened, all that is happening, and all that is to happen.*
I also know all living entities; but no one knows Me.

7.27 *O scion of Bhārata [Arjuna], O conqueror of the foe, all living entities are born into delusion, overcome by the dualities of attachment and aversion.*

Unintelligent men, who do not know my supreme, illimitable and immortal form, assume my illimitable form as manifested.

Here is another important verse. When He says earlier, 'My devotees achieve Me, attain Me,' naturally Arjuna would have had the doubt: are you one more demigod? Naturally Arjuna would have had this obvious doubt.

So Kṛṣṇa gives the explanation: 'Unintelligent men think I am just this form. Only an intelligent man understands that I am immortal. Even when I assume this form, I am that same consciousness. I have not become an ordinary human being by assuming a human form.' He declares, 'I am the same even when I assume a human form. Don't think I am one more demigod.'

He says, 'I am unborn, immortal, illimitable, even when I assume this form. Even when I assume this form, I am that same ultimate divine. I am not an ordinary man.' This is an important statement. This statement is made to declare His enlightenment and to express clearly and explicitly, 'I am enlightened. I am the embodiment of the ultimate consciousness.' The problem is that the person who is receiving this is not mature enough to recognize it as such.

People ask me again and again, 'Why is Kṛṣṇa repeatedly declaring that He is enlightened?' That's a big problem. If you talk about something again and again, people tend to think that something is wrong with that.

There is a proverb in Tamil: If you wear a new ring, you always gesture with that hand because you continuously show it off. If you wear a new earring, what will you do? You shake your head to show it off!

If you speak about something again and again, there's something wrong with that thing. This is how a spiritually immature person will misunderstand what is said.

Arjuna is approaching Kṛṣṇa out of fear and greed. When the Gītā started, Arjuna approached Kṛṣṇa out of fear and depression, and also out of greed. Next he experiences fear. He is afraid of what will happen in the war. So initially, even Arjuna sees Kṛṣṇa as a demigod. That is the reason why Kṛṣṇa now declares His glory, or His true form.

He says, 'All types of people come to Me. I fulfill them at different levels, to encourage their faith and to help them grow. But only intelligent people understand, that even if I assume this body, I am the Ultimate, I am enlightened. Unintelligent people think by seeing my body, by seeing my form, that I am not the Divine. So please be very clear: I am THAT.' He makes a clear statement again and again, so that Arjuna understands.

We need to understand two important issues here. First, the formless energy of Kṛṣṇa defines His supremacy. Second, in whatever form the formless is expressed, it is divine. It is the awareness of that divinity in Him that makes Kṛṣṇa divine, the supreme master. If that awareness happens in you, you will be in Kṛṣṇa consciousness. The intelligence Kṛṣṇa talks about is the intelligent awareness of one's own divinity. They are both one and the same.

I say to my disciples, 'Till you become enlightened, you will have no clear awareness of who I am. Till then you try to reach me only out of fear or greed, however slight it may be. It is only when you are enlightened and are in the same awareness as me that you open up to me in sheer gratitude.'

That is the intelligence that Kṛṣṇa speaks about. When that intelligence exhibits itself, when that awareness surfaces, then and only then true recognition of the Divine happens. That true recognition happens when you recognize the Divine within you.

How to recognize divinity?

Kṛṣṇa asks: How can you recognize divinity when you are covered in ignorance? How can you recognize Me when you are not aware? Out of the thousands who come to me, tens of thousands, the vast majority seeks favors of one kind or another. Even those who do not look for material benefits may aspire to that intangible peace and bliss.

It is the rare person who comes without asking anything. It is not even seeking a benefit, tangible or intangible, that leads such people. It is an awareness of what they need to be and where they need to be. They are attracted like iron filings to a magnet. It is a call from their being which leads them to me.

In Mahābhārata, the Indian epic, the Pāṇḍavā princes could recognize the reality of Kṛṣṇa. No one needed to coach them for it. On the other hand, their cousins the Kaurava for the most part denied Kṛṣṇa. They rejected and ridiculed Him. Duryodhana, who was offered the first choice by Kṛṣṇa to choose either Him unarmed or His Yādava army, chose the utilitarian army! That was all Duryodhana could see. That was his level of awareness, steeped as he was in ignorance.

Arjuna jumped at Kṛṣṇa's offer. All Arjuna wanted was Kṛṣṇa, His presence, not His army, not His divine powers, nothing else.

It is a choice that all of us need to make, whether we wish to be Duryodhana or Arjuna. It is not a difficult choice, as our being and our awareness will determine it. It will not be a choice at all. It will be a happening.

'No one knows Me,' says the master. How true!

'Don't take me for granted,' says Kṛṣṇa. 'Do not put me in a frame for I shall not stay there,' He says.

Can you know Nature? Each time you think you know, Nature does things differently. Then you say Nature is cruel. Nature is Nature. It just is.

So is Kṛṣṇa. The compassion of the master is beyond our frames of time and space. So we cannot fathom what that means. When a *tsunami* kills a thousand people, we weep. When we pray and then win a lottery, we make a donation to the temple, very pleased. Divine compassion is not related to these. It is the truth that is beyond time and space.

Those who stay around me have experienced that whatever I say is the truth and it happens. They don't question me, not because they are afraid. What is there to be afraid of? What control can I have over them? They are free to leave any time they want. In fact, I tell them the only thing that causes me to pause is when a disciple leaves me, because then I have lost the chance to help him. So actually, they know enough to blackmail me if they wish to!

But they don't. Instead they do not question me when I am seemingly irrational, angry or inconsistent. They know the way enlightened beings flow. They recognize that and they simply follow. They know that when I tell them something, it is truth that is not constrained by time and space.

Over two years ago when I went to the Himalayas with a group of disciples to the *cār dhāṁ* pilgrimage centers, I had asked them to say to the local religious authorities that I am a *Mahāmanḍaleśwar*. This title is given to the leader of a very large religious organization. It is more than a title; it confers spiritual leadership, like being canonized as a saint. Without questioning, they announced that a *Mahāmanḍaleśwar* had arrived. As a matter of fact, no one questioned them. They accepted the statement and gave the due respect when I visited the temples.

Recently in 2007, I was at the *Ardha Kumbhamelā* at Prayāg in Northern India. It normally happens every four years. However, this time the sacred river Gaṅgā reversed Her direction, and this happens once in every 144 years. So it was more significant and ninety million people gathered for a dip in the holy river. I went with a large group of disciples.

In every *Kumbhamelā,* the first right to dip on the day of the royal bath is given to the naga sect, which is a special sect, and among them the Nirvāṇi akhāda, the naked monks. During part of my wandering days before my self-realization, I had been with a group of these monks and they had accepted me as their own. Now at the *Kumbhamelā* they conferred upon me the title of *Mahāmanḍaleśwar* of their sect, just a few days prior to the day of the royal bath, and also gave me the first right to enter the Gaṅgā on that special day. Amongst the disciples was one who was present two years earlier during the Himalayan trip. He couldn't believe how the words he had heard from me were manifesting themselves now! He brought up the topic and I explained to him that it had nothing to do with what I had said. It is just the way Existence wants things to happen. What is spoken through enlightened beings is what Existence directs, and there can never be a contradiction in that.

The Truth is unpredictable because it is not bound by time and space as we know it. Truth cannot be known unless we are in truth ourselves. We cannot know Kṛṣṇa unless we are in Kṛṣṇa consciousness.

Kṛṣṇa consciousness is not about going around chanting *Hare Kṛṣṇa, Hare Kṛṣṇa*. True Kṛṣṇa consciousness needs no words because the experience is beyond expression. One who experiences it does not express it.

Fear and greed are what drive us, says Kṛṣṇa. That is the delusion that leads us away from Him. Attachment and aversion, *rāga* and *dveṣa,* form the duality, the polarity of human life. Even at the fundamental cellular level, biologists have shown that this tendency is exhibited. If you place a single cell in a Petri dish and place a drop of nutrient, it is attracted to it and moves towards it. If you place a drop of toxin in the same dish, the cell moves away from it. If on either side, you place drops of nutrient and toxin, the cell remains immobile.

At the cellular level, attraction aids in growth and aversion in survival. A cell can either grow or protect itself. At the multi-cellular level with higher intelligence, human beings act in the same way as the primary cell. They get attached to what they think is good for them and flee from what they think is not good.

Unfortunately, what works well at the cellular level does not work so well at the human level simply because humans have greater intelligence. Cells obey Nature and are directed by Nature to recognize instinctively what is good and what is bad. They also automatically accept the consequence.

Humans are different. They refuse to accept what Nature tries to tell them and indulge in or avoid activities or objects based on their logic. Logic overriding Nature always leads to suffering.

Shedding attachment and aversion is the first step to awareness. Attachment and aversion are based on our *saṁskāra* or engraved memories. Based on these *saṁskāra,* we try to define our future. The problem is that these *saṁskāra* operate at an unconscious level and drive us from unawareness to unawareness. Therefore, we end up acting instinctively, but unlike our cellular brethren, without listening to Nature.

Human beings are given intelligence so that they can rise above instinct and logic and operate out of intuition. This intuition is born from awareness. It comes through meditation. With awareness, we understand that there is truly nothing that we can be attached to, since everything is impermanent. As I said earlier, every moment of our life is a psychodrama.

The same is true of aversion. It arises from insecurity and fears. Every occasion that we are afraid, we actually die inside us. If we shed our fear of death, we lose all our fears.

When we move into awareness, through meditation, we settle within the boundary of our body-mind and we enter the present moment. When we are in the present moment there is no duality of like and dislike, attachment and aversion. We respond to each event as it unfolds with clarity, with intuitive intelligence, and we are always right.

No Sin, No Virtue

7.28 *Persons who have acted virtuously, whose sinful actions are completely eradicated and who are freed from the duality of reality and unreality,*
Engage themselves in My worship with firm resolve.

7.29 *Persons who are striving for liberation from the cycle of birth, old age and death, take refuge in Me.*
They are actually Brahman *because they comprehend everything about activities that transcend these.*

7.30 *Those who know Me as the supreme Lord, as the governing principle of the material manifestation, who know Me as the one underlying all the demigods and as the one sustaining all sacrifices,*
Can, with steadfast mind, understand and know Me, even at the time of death.

Kṛṣṇa talks here about *pāpa* and *puṇya*, sinful and meritorious acts. The concept of sin and merit itself is a delusion, one of duality. At the level of Kṛṣṇa consciousness there is no *pāpa* or *puṇya,* no sin and no act of merit. All are the same.

Your immediate question will be, 'Can I do anything I want? Can I kill, maim, annihilate, and be a Hitler?'

When you reach Kṛṣṇa consciousness you will not be a Hitler. It is impossible. At the level where you are now, it is necessary to follow some regulations because you still operate in duality. You operate from attachment and aversion.

Unfortunately, instead of these statements being guidelines for self-awareness as they were intended to be, they have become tools in the hands of institutions to control us, whether they are religious, political or societal.

Every year, I take a group of disciples to the Himalayan mountains on a pilgrimage, and the first stop is Ṛṣīkeśa. Here I make them take the *sanyās* vows prescribed in *yama* of Aṣṭāṅga yoga. It is for their own protection and guidance. These five vows are *satya, ahiṁsā, asteya, aparigraha* and *brahmacarya. Satya* is truth in thoughts, word and action; *ahiṁsā* is not harming anyone in thought, word and action; *asteya* is not coveting, not stealing what belongs to another; *aparigraha* is living with minimal needs; *brahmacarya* is living without fantasies. They take these vows after a dip in the sacred river Gaṅgā and participate in a *vraja homa,* a fire ritual of purification. For the next two weeks they wear the saffron cloth that I give them. These vows are for self-discipline and they lead one to awareness.

Kṛṣṇa addresses mortal beings here, in the form of Arjuna. So He talks about doing virtuous acts and avoiding sinful acts. He says to go beyond the duality of sin and virtue. This is only possible when we become aware.

In the verses of the famous Bhaja Govindaṁ, Ādi Śaṅkarācārya says hauntingly, 'Birth and death again and again; lying in a mother's womb again and again. This ocean of repeated birth and death is so difficult to cross. Please save me, O Kṛṣṇa!'

The greatest philosopher that Hinduism has known, prays to the greatest master that the universe has known, 'Save me from this endless cycle of *saṁsāra,* the cycle of birth and death.'

To know that one needs to be saved from this cycle needs great wisdom. To seek the feet of the master who can lead you to that liberation needs great wisdom and awareness.

You can be born again and again and still think that you are being born for the first time, and that this is the only life that you have. With this knowledge, you focus on this life and want to extract the maximum juice out of it. You run after everything possible, as if there is no tomorrow. You live in a fantasy world.

Please understand that this is not your only life. This body is not who you are. All this is temporary. What you chase is a dream. One day you will wake up and discover that this life is nothing but a dream.

You are above this body-mind. What you are returns after death. When you understand this cosmic truth, you are liberated. At some point in time, you do not wish to be part of this psychodrama anymore. You ask, 'What for?' just as Śaṇkara plaintively asks Kṛṣṇa, 'Again and again, without end, I come and I go. Please save me from this useless journey; let me be with You.'

Kṛṣṇa ends this chapter with the prescription for how to know and understand Him and how to reach Him.

It is never too late

Even at the time of death, He says, even if all your life you lived a dissolute life, if at the point of departure you realize your folly, that is enough to redeem you. The mere recognition of that can save you. His compassion is unlimited. He promises: Knowing Me at the time of death, even at the time of death, will lead you to Me.

Please understand that this is not so easy as it seems. If you have been ruled by greed and fear throughout your life, then nothing can change suddenly at the time of death. You will be full of the same fantasies that you were obsessed with throughout your life. Your last thoughts will be on those very same things.

A small story:

A recently bereaved widow went to a medium to contact her husband's spirit.

All she wanted to know was to whom he had lent money when he was alive. She knew that he was a miser. He died suddenly without leaving a record of what people owed him, and she knew he would suffer wherever he was if she did not do something about the collection.

Sure enough, the medium responded, 'Our neighbor owes me a hundred dollars. The man living opposite our house borrowed five hundred dollars…' The list was long and went on for a while.

When the medium stopped, the widow asked, 'Is that all?'

The medium responded, 'Oh, I forgot. I owe Bill a thousand dollars.'

The widow hurriedly told the medium, 'I don't think this is my husband,' and she left the place!

We cannot change our nature at the last minute. Gandhi died with the name 'Hey Rām' on his lips when he was assassinated because Lord Rāma's name permeated his whole being all his life. It could never have been otherwise.

If we want to die with the thought of the Divine uppermost in our mind, we must cultivate the habit of remembering Him now. We should start understanding Him today. Then and only then will we know and understand Him at the time of death.

Some may ask, 'What is the need to understand and know Kṛṣṇa, whether at the point of death or before? If I do the right things in the right manner, why should it make any difference whether or not I understand and know Kṛṣṇa?'

Please understand that Kṛṣṇa speaks about our understanding and about knowing ourselves. He talks about the need for us to understand who we are.

The ultimate master resides within us. The external master, be He Kṛṣṇa or Nithyananda, is a guide to make us understand, know and accept the master within us. Yes, it may be possible in rare cases for that wisdom to dawn on us at the point of death, but it is not common. Someone who constantly seeks that truth will continuously search for that master within, and has a better chance of making that connection, earlier rather than later in life.

Kṛṣṇa in His deep compassion says, 'Even if that happens at the point of death, I shall redeem you.' He does not want us to miss that chance, even if we have not thought about Him all our lives. He wants us to discover the master within. Even if we do that at the point of our last breath, it is okay with Him.

So, let us pray to the Ultimate Kṛṣṇa to give us the intelligence and awareness to realize the truth about ourselves, to give us this experience of eternal bliss - *nityānanda.*

Thus ends the seventh chapter named **Jñānavijñāna Yogaḥ** *of the* **Upaniṣad** *of **Bhagavad Gītā**, the scripture of yoga dealing with the science of the Absolute in the form of the dialogue between **Śrī Kṛṣṇa** and Arjuna.*

BHAGAVADGĪTĀ

The Art Of Leaving

AKṢARABRAHMA YOGAḤ

CHAPTER 8

Death is our ultimate fear.
Anyone who claims not to be disturbed
by the thought of death is only lying.
Nithyananda answers all the questions
you have been afraid to even ask!

The Art Of Leaving

In this chapter, Kṛṣṇa speaks about death. He gives us an insight into how death can become liberation and celebration. Death is the end of life as we understand it or don't understand it! The moment we understand it, it becomes a liberation and celebration.

Death is a celebration!

Death is not the end of life. It is the climax of life. End is different from climax. The moment we think that death is the end, we try to figure out what happens next. We start worrying about death. The shadow of death happens even when we live.

A person who does not understand death dies even when he is alive. A person who understands death lives even when he dies. Death or life depend on our intelligence. When we have clear intelligence, we live our death. When we don't know, we die even when we live.

The fear of death haunts everyone from birth. All religions sprang up from this one fear, this one question: Why do we die? What happens after we die? Most religions answer in such a way that they can control us through the fear of death and the greed of escaping death. They talk about sins and merits and threaten us with hell and entice us with the promise of heaven. None of these really exists. Heaven and hell are not physical or metaphysical locations; they are merely states of our mind.

Death is a passage. It is a passage in a journey that continues. We do not live and die once; we live again and again. As Kṛṣṇa says, the undying spirit casts off bodies as one casts off garments and puts on new ones. The spirit within is immortal. The spirit within us is part of the cosmic energy and lives on, whereas the bodies that it assumes perish.

Enlightened masters of the vedic tradition experienced the state beyond life and death and have provided us with guidelines about how to achieve the same state. However, they expressed this to a select audience of disciples in a language coded for the understanding of those mature enough to work with that knowledge.

Here Kṛṣṇa, the greatest of all enlightened masters, out of His infinite compassion, provides this knowledge in a form that anyone can understand. All one requires to imbibe this knowledge, is an open mind and the willingness to work sincerely and with dedication.

When we understand the art of living, the process of leaving becomes a celebration. When we understand that this life and the departure from this life is a single journey in a continuous cycle of birth and death, there is no urgency in living this life and there is no fear in leaving this life also. When we understand that what we do in this life and how we do it determines how we are reborn, we will have a far greater understanding of how to lead this life.

Arjuna starts here with questions:

8.1 *Arjuna said:*
O my Lord, O supreme person, what is Brahman? *What is the Self? What are result-based actions?*
What is this material manifestation? And what are the demigods? Please explain all this to me.

8.2 *How does this Lord of sacrifice live in the body, and in which part does He live, O Madhusūdana?*
How can those engaged in devotional service know You at the time of their death?

These are two beautiful questions! Of course, when I translate them into English, much of the taste is lost! We do not have the right words in English for many beautiful words expressed by Arjuna. A single word has many meanings in Sanskrit. The moment I translate, I give only one dimension, a single dimension of the verse.

An important thing we should understand about the Sanskrit language is that it is not only linguistic, but also has importance at the phonetic level. Just the vibration of the words can transform our whole inner space. The sound changes the energy of the place and the inner space of those who hear it or are chanting it.

We should understand the concepts called *padā* and *padārtha*. For example, when I say the word 'cow,' immediately a figure appears in our mind – an animal with four legs, a tail, head and two horns. The word is called *padā*, the figure is *padārtha*. What happens in our mind when we hear the word is *padārtha*. In all languages the distance or gap between *padā* and *padārtha* is significant.

In Sanskrit the connection is immediate; the result is instantaneous. That is why I tell people to listen to Sanskrit devotional verses for at least 10 minutes a day. It does not matter whether you understand it or not. Just listen to any Sanskrit verse for at least 10 minutes every day. The very energy of the vibrations will purify your body.

There is something called *śabda tattva*, the principle of sound. When air travels from our navel area to the throat, the *śabda tattva* changes the air into words. If this element is not there, only air comes out; no words come out. In other languages the more we use *śabda tattva*, the more tired we become. However in Sanskrit, the *śabda tattva* strengthens us. The more we chant, the more energetic we become! It is like the generator automatically re-charging the battery and the battery running the generator. It is completely interconnected.

The Sanskrit language strengthens the *śabda tattva* that converts air into sound or words. This is why it does not matter whether or not we understand it. Modern day research proves that the vibrations of the verses have the effect of removing impurities. This is why masters ask us to offer different types of worship which are the means to chant verses in Sanskrit. When we chant, we simply heal ourselves.

Here, Arjuna asks beautifully, 'O Lord! What is *Brahman*? What is Self? What are result-based actions? What is this material manifestation? What are demi-gods? O Madhusūdana! How do You live in the body, and how can those engaged in devotion, those who are practicing the eternal consciousness, know You at the time of death?' He continuously poses these questions.

I had seriously wondered how Arjuna, a *kṣatriya* (warrior) who ruled a kingdom, could ask the same questions again and again in different ways! Yesterday I read a version of Mahābhārata. That version says that Arjuna is also an embodiment of Kṛṣṇa: the incarnation of *Narā* and *Nārāyaṇa*. These are two different energies of Lord Viṣṇu; one manifested as Arjuna and the other as Kṛṣṇa. The whole drama happened so that the Gītā took shape for humanity! Otherwise, even the disciple with the least consciousness would not have asked so many questions, again and again.

One thing we should understand is that when we have so many questions, we are not ready to wait for answers. We are simply expressing our confusion. It is almost a catharsis. Here Arjuna asks so many questions. However, the main question is: How does a person who is engaged in practicing Your teachings know You at the time of death?

Here starts the whole teaching of Kṛṣṇa. He reveals the secrets of death.

One thing I want to tell you: The West has spent all its energy to understand life. The East has spent all its energy to understand death. Nobody has gone so deeply into, or achieved such deep experiences of death, as our *ṛṣis*, sages have. These masters have done a great service by bringing the knowledge of death to the people who are living.

People ask me, '*Swamiji*, why should I know about death? Knowing about life is enough; after all I am still young.' The word 'death' creates fear in people. They are ready to listen to any other subject. However, when it comes to death, they think, 'Why should we know about death? If we know about life, it is enough.'

Our understanding about death impacts our understanding about life. Life and death are two sides of the same coin. In the East, all religions talk about many births. Most Western religions talk about a single birth. This concept of reincarnation has influenced Indian society so deeply that nobody bothers about time! They are so relaxed. Till 10 o'clock in the morning, people sit in teashops! If we ask for anything, they say, 'Not today, tomorrow; if not tomorrow, next birth!' They have eternity in front of them because somewhere they know they will come again. They are in no hurry and therefore do not run behind anything.

In the West, whatever they desire to achieve, they must finish achieving within 75 to 80 years. They do not have time. They either live now or never because there is only birth according to them. That is the reason why people run and run!

Our understanding about death influences our whole social structure. Our whole thinking system, our whole mentality can be transformed with the right understanding about death. I gave a single example about how the idea of reincarnation influences Eastern society and how the idea of one birth influences Western society. Thousands of such examples can be given.

The idea and understanding of death is much more important than the understanding of life. Whether we understand life or not, it remains the same. But the moment we understand death, the whole quality of life changes.

If we experience even an intellectual understanding of death, it is enough to transform our whole way of thinking. That is why the moment we think of *Yama,* god of death, our whole life has *yama,* or discipline. The Sanskrit word *yama* means both 'death' and 'discipline'. For your convenience, I pronounce it a little differently; yet the spelling is the same.

Understanding of death, instills discipline

The first technique of sage Patañjali in his work - Yoga Sūtra, is *yama*. And death is also *yama*. If we understand death, a strange but honest discipline will happen in our life. Why do I say 'strange but honest?' It is because discipline as we know it is hypocrisy. But the discipline that is *yama* is a new kind of discipline, which is strange yet totally honest.

Yesterday a person asked me a question. He was well read in Bhāgavatam, the Hindu epic that describes the incarnations of Viṣṇu. He asked, '*Swamiji*, Kṛṣṇa is enlightened and He was a *brahmacāri*, celibate; but He made love to Kubja. How is that possible?'

The name Kubja can be found if we read Bhāgavatam very deeply. She is supposed to have been the maidservant of Kṛṣṇa. Somebody who had read Bhāgavatam very deeply asked this question. What he said was true. There is a record in Bhāgavatam that Kṛṣṇa lived with Kubja. *Brahmacarya* does not mean celibacy. I have not said that Kṛṣṇa is celibate. I said Kṛṣṇa is in the consciousness of *Brahman*. Here we translate the word '*brahmacarya*' to mean celibate. The moment we translate it, the meaning is lost. Kṛṣṇa's inner space was totally pure, untouched.

Let me tell you a small story:

Once Vyāsa, the ancient sage of India attended a function. After having a feast at the function, on his way back, he came to a river which he had to cross in order to reach his monastery. He stood before the river and said, 'If I am sincere in my *ekādaśi* fasting, let this river give way so that I may cross over.' *Ekādaśi* refers to the eleventh day of the moon's cycle when normally people fast.

The moment Vyāsa uttered those words, the river gave way. Vyāsa crossed it followed by his devotees and they reached the ashram.

The devotees were astonished and asked, 'What is this? You enjoyed a feast just a few hours back. Yet, when you asked the river to give way on the condition that you have been sincere in your *ekādaśi* fast, the river gave way! How can this be?'

Vyāsa replied, 'When you eat with the consciousness that you are not the body, you never feel that you are touched by food. You never feel that you are eating, digesting, living. The body ate; I do not know anything about it.'

Of course, it is difficult to understand this concept. We can easily cheat ourselves with this idea. The problem with all great truths is, there is the danger of our misusing and abusing them. Take atomic energy; we can use it to serve the whole of humanity. Or we can destroy humanity with that same energy. This truth is like atomic energy; we can use it or abuse it.

People ask me, 'How can I find out whether I am living in the out-of-body-consciousness or not; how can I live like Vyāsa?' Understand, when we reach the state of Vyāsa, we will not have this question. Vyāsa says he is fasting after having eaten a feast because he does not feel connected to his body. He is untouched. His inner space is so pure and filled with bliss.

If we read Rāmakṛṣṇa Paramahamsa's life, we will know that he did different kinds of spiritual practices. As far as I know, Rāmakṛṣṇa is the only master who has performed so much penance. He also practiced *tantra sādhana*, which aims at harnessing and transforming our powerful sensual energies as a means to enlightenment. An ordinary person straightaway falls if he does *tantra sādhana*.

The greatness of Rāmakṛṣṇa was that his inner space was never touched. His inner space was so pure and filled with bliss that he completed *tantra sādhana* successfully. *Tantra sādhana* is supposed to be done with many conditions, yet he achieved and successfully completed it because his inner space was pure.

Going back to the question, 'How can you say that Kṛṣṇa is a *brahmacāri*?' Please understand that His inner space was so pure that He was never touched by body consciousness. Let me tell you one more thing: It is not easy to live with so many women as he did, and yet survive! When a single man or woman enters our life, we understand how difficult it is to adjust and live. The other person seems to naturally create hell for us. Here we see somebody living with many persons, and yet remaining blissful. This shows that His inner space was pure and radiating bliss.

The person whose inner space is filled with bliss will never be touched by any impurity. The moment we understand the depth of it, we will understand this concept.

A small story:

A *sanyāsi* (monk) goes to the Indian king Janaka who is supposed to be an enlightened king and one who enjoyed both the material world and spiritual enlightenment. The *sanyāsi* questions him, 'How can you say you are enlightened when you enjoy the benefits of worldly life?'

*Sanyāsi*s are jealous of people who enjoy life! If you experience bliss within you and consciously leave the world to enter monastic life, you will never feel jealous. If you have escaped from the outer world thinking that you will find something worthwhile in the inner world, and there too the experience has not been solid, you start wondering what to do. You have neither the inner space of bliss nor the outer possessions. You are stuck.

Such people console themselves by abusing householders. They say to them, 'You are too attached to everything. You are not doing this, you are not doing that....' That is why from time immemorial, people who took the *sanyāsi* life condemn the householder's life. Have you seen a householder jealous of a *swami*? You will never find one. Yet I have seen hundreds of people who took *sanyāsi* who are jealous of householders because they feel something is missing in their own lives.

So this *sanyāsi* asked Janaka, 'How can you say you are enlightened and have both material and spiritual enjoyments?' Janaka said, 'Please stay in my palace for a few days. I will talk to you after that. Right now I am busy, a party is going on, so I cannot talk about philosophical things now!'

Accordingly, arrangements were made for the *sanyāsi's* food and stay. However, above his bed a sharp knife hung, suspended on a thin thread. The *sanyāsi* asked, 'Why do you hang this knife exactly over my head?' The palace workers said, 'We do not know, but these are our king's orders. You must sleep here.'

Throughout the night the *sanyāsi* sat up, awake, thinking when the knife might fall on him.

The next morning Janaka asked, 'O *swami*! How are you today? Did you sleep well?'

The *sanyāsi* said, 'You know what you have done! Why do you then ask? How can I sleep when a knife hangs over my head? How can I think of sleeping?'

Janaka laughs and says, 'When death is in front of you, your whole life changes. However, although I know death is in front of me, I am unaffected. That is the difference. Just because of one knife you are unable to enjoy the beautiful bed and all these luxuries. Yet even though all these things are there externally, my inner Self is not touched. It is pure because I know clearly that at any moment death can happen. Because I live with this moment-to-moment awareness of death, I enjoy the material world fully without getting caught in it.'

That is why I said, 'Yama can make a strange, yet honest *yama* in your life. Death can instill a strange but honest discipline in your life.'

Understand death, intellectually. Your whole thinking will change. You will not leave this place as the same person. Your being will be transformed.

Kṛṣṇa starts with the secrets. He explains the secrets of death.

Your Last Memory Follows You In Your Next Birth

8.3 Bhagavān *said:*
The indestructible, transcendental living entity is called Brahman *and His eternal nature is called the Self.*
Actions pertaining to the development of the material bodies is called karma, *or result based activities.*

8.4 *Physical nature is known to be endlessly changing.*
The universe is the cosmic form of the supreme Lord, and I am that Lord represented as the super soul, dwelling in the heart of every being that dwells in a body.

8.5 *Whoever, at the time of death, quits his body remembering Me alone, attains My nature immediately.*
Of this there is no doubt.

8.6 *Whatever state of being one remembers when he quits his body,*
It is that state one will attain without fail.

Before going into what happens at the time of death, let us understand how we assume the body, how we live through it and how we leave it. Please understand that we create our whole body out of our fear, greed, guilt and our engraved memories *(saṁskāras)*. The problem is that once we have created the body and live our life, we do not live out only the *saṁskāras* that created this body. We acquire more. For example, we take $10,000 and go downtown to buy things that we need. On the way, we meet a friend with whom we go Disneyland and blow up all the money. Finally, when we go downtown to buy what we need, we are broke. Now, with the credit card we buy what we want to buy, come back and live our life just to pay credit card bills. We then feel that we do not have sufficient things. We have fulfilled our friend's desires through our body using our time, money and energy.

In the same way, when we came down to planet earth, we came with enough energy to work out our *saṁskāras*. *Karma* refers to the unfulfilled desires that we create over many births, which pull us back again to take birth and fulfill them. We have three types of *karma* - *sañcita, prārabdha* and *āgāmya. Sañcita karma* is our complete bank of unfulfilled *karma*s like our safety deposit or the files archived in our office vault. *Prārabdha karma* are those *karma*s that we have brought in this life, like files in filing cabinets which we access and work on regularly. *Āgāmya karma* are like the new files on our table that we keep creating – new *karma* that we create in every life. We must exhaust all three types of *karma*s to experience enlightenment. *Sañcita karma* is all that we have accumulated over many births.

When we are born, we bring enough energy to exhaust this *prārabdha karma*. Then why do we feel that this life is not sufficient? The problem is that after coming down, we forget what we came for and accumulate more and more desires from family, friends and society. For example, if our neighbor wears a new *sari*, we think, 'I should also get one.' We try to work out her desire. Naturally we run short of money, energy and everything.

When we live out others' desires in our life, we feel deeply discontented, because the energy that we brought with us will become insufficient. After coming down to planet earth, we forget what *saṁskāra*s we brought and we collect more and more desires from society.

So much social conditioning happens through advertisements. All advertisements make us poor. The advertisers become rich, no doubt, but we become poor. Ideas are continuously put into our head, especially advertisements that touch the *mūlādhāra,* the root *cakra,* the sex energy center. Anything related to sex appeal is recorded in our system.

That is why whether it is soap or shampoo, it is promoted with the undertones of sex appeal. We automatically ask for that product when we shop. Yet we forget one thing: when we pay $2, we get only the soap and not the model who posed for the soap in the advertisement! But when it was recorded, both the soap and the model are recorded together in our system.

Whatever is recorded in the *mūlādhāra* energy center is so deep that we unconsciously act in accordance with it. As long as we fulfill our own desires, it is fine. However, when we live out others' desires, the problem starts. In the next verse, Kṛṣṇa goes slightly deeper into this.

Kṛṣṇa says here, 'O best of embodied beings! The physical nature that is constantly changing is called *ādibhūta* or the universal form of the Lord, which includes all the demi-gods. For example, the nature of the Sun and Moon is *ādidaiva.* As the supreme Lord represented as the super soul in the heart of every embodied being, I am called *ādiyagna.*'

We have seen how we are ruled by our desires at every step. This gives us a background against which to understand the secret of death. When we understand why we take birth, it is easier to understand what happens when we leave the body. Here Kṛṣṇa throws light on the physical matter in front of us. If we deeply understand this, our desire to 'possess' automatically drops.

Let us take this chair you are sitting on. To our knowledge, there is some solid object placed at this location. However, if we go one level deeper, this solid plastic can be broken down into many particles that make up this plastic. Now if we go one step further, we see that there are atoms and molecules. We can keep dividing into smaller and smaller particles and there is no end to it. And more than ninety percent of the volume within each particle is empty space.

Modern science has proven that matter and energy are mutually convertible. You see, this solid object that our eye sees is not solid. It is pure energy. This physical matter is energy and it constantly changes because of the fluid nature of energy. That is what Kṛṣṇa says:

adhibhūtaṁ kṣaro bhāvaḥ

This physical or material nature constantly changes. Understand, because of the fluid nature of energy, it constantly moves. Change is the only certain thing. That is why everything around is temporary. We think something is permanent and hence we try to possess it.

Everything that we call matter is energy and it constantly changes. This truth was given by inner scientists or *ṛṣis* thousands of years ago. This truth was declared not only in the Gītā but in the *Upaniṣads* also. All physical matter is energy and it keeps changing. In the last verse, we talked about our desires. Why do we run behind materialistic desires? Why do we constantly operate from the *mūlādhāra cakra*? It is because we do not have a good understanding about the physical world. If we understand this verse, we will understand the futility of running after the fulfillment of material desires.

When we look at something, we think of it as a physical object. We think we can possess it. This is where the problem lies. Our ego sees the material world as only matter, and it asks for more and more of it to keep under its control. We fail to see that it is all energy and energy cannot be kept in one place. Energy is universal. The physical object that we see is a manifestation of the universal energy.

There is a wonderful movie called *What the Bleep Do We Know?* If you get a chance, please watch this movie. It talks about Probability Theory. We see this chair here because our mind wants to see it here. There is every possibility that this chair may not be present here. Our mind creates a high probability for its presence here. There are energy waves and these waves manifest as physical matter. When we understand this, we can understand the futility of holding onto something or running after something.

One more thing, this is our pattern with people as well. We are continuously looking for someone to possess. When we have someone, we hold onto that person. If that person leaves, we feel terrible. When a close family member passes away, we feel depressed. Why?

It is because we hold onto them as if they are physical matter like the television, refrigerator, car and air conditioner. If our car meets with an accident, we feel sad. We feel that we have lost something. In the same way, when someone passes away, we feel that part of us is lost. We feel depressed.

I do not say that we should be insensitive to relationships. I mean we should stop being possessive. Understand that everything and everyone is created out of the same underlying energy. Kṛṣṇa says clearly in this verse: Everything, whether living or non-living, is an embodiment of the supreme soul. When we understand this, we see the truth that we are a part of everything around us. There is no difference between you and me, this chair and me or that tree and me. We see ourselves in everything.

When we understand this great truth, a new dimension of ourselves is revealed to us. Our compassion towards everything grows a thousandfold. By being compassionate to others, we are being compassionate to ourselves because everything is one. Please understand this great truth. This completely changes the way we perceive our desires, our fantasies. Kṛṣṇa answers all the questions with a single technique.

The secret of death

Here, Kṛṣṇa reveals the secrets of death. He says, 'Whoever dies remembering Me alone at the time of death will attain Me at once.' What does He mean when He says, 'remembering Me alone?' He says, 'Whoever, at the end of his life, quits his body remembering Me alone, at once attains My nature. Of this there is no doubt.'

Why should He say the words *nāstyatra samśayaḥ*? Why should He say, 'there is no doubt?' He emphasizes, 'this is the truth.' He takes an oath.

We have a meditation program lasting two days on this *sūtra,* called Nithyananda Spurana Program. In India we conduct it for four days. Here I do it as a two-day program because people are unable to take 4 days off. Here, in America, even if God comes, He must come on the weekend! Otherwise people will say, 'Please give me your card or email me; I will get back to you.' The whole program is based on this single verse. Before starting the discourse on death, I always take the oath, 'I hereby state that whatever I say is the truth,' because there are some truths that cannot be logically expressed. You need a little patience to listen.

The big problem with our mind is that we question, refute or straightaway don't want to listen to anything not presented in a logical form. Otherwise, we hear it as one more story. It will not go into our being. We think, 'Anyhow, I have come all the way, let me sit and hear what he has to say.' We allow the speaker to speak; however, we do not listen.

That is why, before I talk about death, I say, 'Hereby I promise that whatever I am going to say is pure truth. If you are interested, take it, digest it and transform your life. If you are not, it is ok; it is up to you; it is your choice.'

Kṛṣṇa says *nāstyatra samśayaḥ*, because He is going to speak something that is beyond logic. When we want to understand the outer world, we need logic. When we want to know about the inner world, we need a master who takes us beyond logic. Logic gives us the outer world; it cannot give us the inner world.

Here Kṛṣṇa says *nāstyatra samśayaḥ*: Have no doubt, what I am speaking is the truth. Please wait. Let Me finish the calculation, then you will understand. For now assume that 'X equals 2.' At the end of the calculation, you agree that X should be substituted with 2, but at the start, you need to believe the master's word and patiently wait until he works it out and shows you.

Until it becomes an experience for you, for a few minutes you need to accept the master's word as it is. When you finish the calculation, naturally it becomes your understanding. Then you naturally see the truth behind the words.

So Kṛṣṇa says:

'Whoever, at the end of his life, quits his body remembering Me alone, at once attains My nature. Of this there is no doubt.'

Why? Why does He say, 'remembering Me?' and that too 'alone?'

In Mahābhārata there are at least 100,000 stories. One story goes like this:

There was a king who lived for a hundred years. Then Yama, the god of death comes and tells him, 'Your life is over, O King, come now, it is time, let us go.' The king says, 'What is this? You gave me such a beautiful kingdom, such a beautiful life, such wonderful wives, kids; you have given me everything. 100 years is too short to enjoy this life. Please bless me with 100 more years.'

Yama explains that no extension is possible. The king continues to plead, 'No, please bless me with another 100 years.' Yama says, 'Alright, if one of your sons gives his life, I will extend yours as an exchange offer.' Somehow one son agrees to give his life for his father and the king gets 100 more years.

After 100 years when Yama appears again, the king does not realize that his time is up and says, 'What is this? I asked for 100 years and you have come so soon.' Yama tells him that 100 years are over. The king pleads again, 'Please help me somehow; I did not realize that 100 years are gone. Please give one more extension.' Yama tells him it is too much and that a second extension is not possible. However the king begs Yama to let him live a few more years. Finally he gets one more extension.

The next time when Yama comes, again the king is in the same mood. Now Yama gives a beautiful teaching. He says, 'By pouring oil on it, you can never put out the fire. Now it is time, you must come.' The king understands and follows Yama.

In the same way, by chasing our desires, we can never feel fulfilled. Only more desires will come up. When we acquire more and more desires from the outer world, we naturally feel that life is not sufficient, that we had not been given time or resources to fulfill these desires.

Understand that if we have lived 70 years, at the end of our life, when we leave our body, the whole 70 years appear before us as a flash, as a fast-forward movement so that we can make the decision about our next birth. Now, we have *karma* that we brought with us but have not enjoyed or experienced, as well as *karma* that we accumulated from society in this birth, but have not exhausted. I want to give you one more understanding: *karma* or *saṁskāra* means any desire that is not completely experienced by you. By nature you are a fulfilled being. But whenever you do not fulfill any action completely, with totality, you create a hangover. You create a recorded memory of that action, a *saṁskāra*. A *saṁskāra* is not merely a dead memory stored in your unconscious mind; it has the power to make you repeat that action again and again till the desire is fulfilled.

Now you are going to decide a few important things: birth, type of parents and family, whether to choose a male body or female body. All these decisions are taken by your consciousness, under the influence of *karma* collected when you lived on planet earth.

One important thing you should understand is that even sense enjoyments look like enjoyment because from a young age you are taught that it is enjoyment. An important research report about the lifestyle of a group of African tribal people said that they do not know anything called joy or sense pleasures. They eat everything, they taste, they smell, they listen, they see, they have the sense of touch, everything. However, they do not have the idea that something is a pleasure and so they do not run after it. They are not conditioned to chase pleasures.

Before I continue telling you about these African people, let me share another example of how social conditioning works. During my days of wandering, I lived near Oṁkāreśvar in Madhya Pradesh with a small group of tribal people. I was really surprised about the way they lived. Not a single person there was depressed. This is the truth, the honest truth. Human beings *can* live on planet earth without getting depressed!

I lived with them for months. I was surprised that not a single person in that village was depressed, and nobody ran behind sense pleasures. I was surprised and thought to myself, 'How come these people lived without running behind sense pleasures?' It was because they had not been taught that there is something called sense pleasure. The basic corruption had not happened.

We read in the Bible that the relationship between Adam and Eve is the original sin. I tell you, whether the relationship is the original sin or not, I do not know. But when we are taught that something is a pleasure and therefore should not be done, it is then that sin starts.

One more thing - when I was with these tribal people in Madhya Pradesh, I lived in a small temple in the center of the village. While wandering about one day I came upon a small hut. A pregnant lady entered it. Half an hour later, she came out with a newborn baby! There was no pain, no attendant, no doctor, no medicine, no screaming. Within half an hour she walked out with a baby.

I was shocked! Of course, I could not ask her anything because I did not know their language. After one month, another pregnant lady did the same thing. Within half an hour she came out with a baby. Now it was too much! I asked the local priest who came to the temple, 'How does this happen? Don't they have pain?'

He asked in surprise, 'Pain? Why pain?'

I was surprised! They do not have pain at the time of delivery. The idea that women should have pain during delivery does not exist in their society. Not only that, nobody suffers from menopause problems. Nobody suffers from any gynecological disorders.

I enquired about their lifestyle. Then I understood that they respect women a lot in their culture. Women are never disrespected. They are never told that they become impure during their monthly periods. Women are never taught that they are lower than men. The moment a girl comes of age, she is honored and told, 'Now you are qualified to become a mother.' She is respected. People fall at her feet and she touches and heals them. They believe that if a woman touches and blesses them during her menstrual period, they will be healed. Because the conditioning is totally different, nobody suffers any pain there.

In the so-called civilized society today, women are disrespected. They are taught, 'You are not pure now; don't stand here, don't sit there.' Especially in India, it is real torture. Because of the wrong conditioning, women suffer pain. If they are not conditioned in this way, they will never feel pain.

Getting back to the research on the African tribal people, the research scholar says, 'They don't know anything called pleasure.' Because of that, they do not run after pleasure. Social conditioning divides everything into pleasure and pain. Even this decision – 'What kind of life will I choose in my next birth? What kind of body will I take?' - is based upon your social conditioning.

You decide to achieve whatever you think is the highest thing in life. Whatever you consider the highest ideal of your whole life, only that comes to your mind when you leave the body. Kṛṣṇa says, 'Whatever state of being one remembers when he quits his body, O son of Kuntī, that state he will attain without fail.'

Death is a mere passage

What exactly happens at the time of leaving the body? When a person leaves the body, he goes through seven layers of his being. The first and the outermost layer is the physical layer. When a person leaves the body, it creates tremendous pain in his whole system like 'thousands of scorpions stinging at a time.'

I am frightening you. Even though it hurts, it is better to tell the facts now. At least we will be better prepared for the journey. Whether we will take it or it will be forced upon us we don't know, but we must make this journey.

There will be tremendous pain at first. We may ask, 'Why pain?' It is because our being wants to stay in the body, but the body cannot host the being anymore. There is no need for our being to leave unless the body is completely tired or exhausted. If death starts happening, it means the body is completely exhausted, or damaged. In natural death, the body is exhausted while in an accident, the body is damaged.

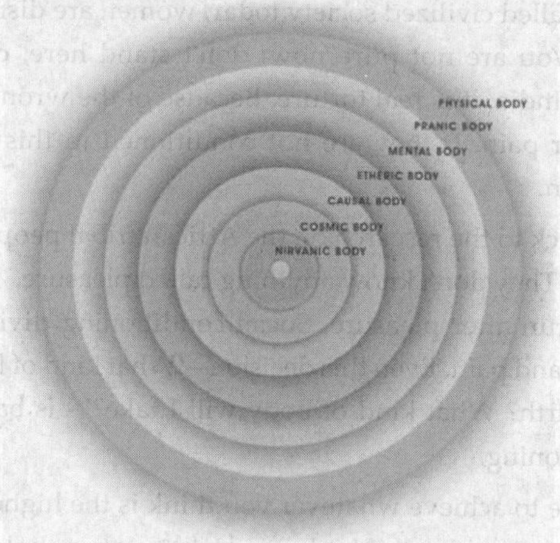

Understand: You know the pain that we experience when we cut our finger. What would the pain be like if we extend the same thing to our six-foot body? Naturally there will be tremendous pain. But one thing: there is an automatic painkiller mechanism. The moment the pain becomes unbearable, we fall into coma to escape pain. But the problem is, we also die in unconsciousness when we are in coma. That is the worst thing, because we will remain unaware of why we took this birth, and we will not be able to make the decision about the next birth consciously. That is the reason Kṛṣṇa says: *yaṁ yaṁ vā 'pi smaran bhāvaṁ;* in whatever state you are at the time of leaving the body, you will achieve that state without fail. If we are unconscious at the time of leaving the body, then naturally, we come back as beings which do not have a high level of consciousness.

The moment we leave the physical body, we go to the next level, the *pranic* body. The *pranic* body refers to the layer responsible for the inhaling and exhaling of *prāna,* the life giving energy in our body. It is filled with all our desires. Our *prāna* and desires are closely related. If our desires change, immediately the circulation of our *prāna* changes.

Similarly, if we change the circulation of *prāna,* our whole mind changes. Our mind and *prāna* are closely connected. That is why people inhale and exhale, pull and push with their breath at the time of leaving. The body says, 'I can't host you anymore; go out.' But the being says, 'But I have so many desires. I must live in this body.' The tug of war happens between body and being.

Next we move to the mental layer, *mana śarīra.* All the guilt that we harbored is in this layer. Guilt is regret about the past. Desire is expectation about the future. Guilt is regret about the past. Guilt is: I have not lived in this way - thoughts about the past. Desire is: I should live like this - a thought about the future. Understand, guilt is nothing but the emotion created in our being when we review our past decisions with updated intelligence.

Let me give you a small example. At the age of seven we are playing with our toys. Our mother comes and calls us for dinner, 'Come and eat.' We say, 'No, I don't want to eat; I want to play.' By force our mother takes away the toys and pulls us to come and eat. Immediately we say, 'You go and die; give me my toys, I want to play.'

At that moment, the toys look most important to us. We feel that toys are more important in life than our mother. But as we mature, we understand that this isn't true. Once we mature, if we think, 'O what a grave mistake I made. I shouldn't have said those words to my mother. It is a big mistake. How important the mother is! But I never thought of it at that time!'... If we create guilt in this fashion, there is no point or utility in it. At that moment as a young child, we had only that much intelligence. Now, our intelligence has been updated. If we review our past decisions with updated intelligence, we create only one thing: guilt. When we review our past decisions with updated intelligence, we create guilt.

If God gives us one more life, we will make the *same* mistakes that we made at seven years of age because we will have only that much intelligence at that age. Now just because our intelligence has been updated *now,* we can't review our actions and create guilt in ourselves about what we did earlier. We had such and such data and we had only that much intelligence to process the data at that time. Based on that, we made the decision. Now the intelligence to process the data has been updated; our software has been updated. Because our software has been updated, we now say, 'Oh! I made the wrong decision at that time; I am suffering from guilt.' This does not make sense.

Guilt is a wedge inserted in our being. It creates uneasiness between you and your being. It is the worst sin. Guilt is the only sin on planet earth, nothing else. We can never achieve morality through guilt. People ask, '*Swamiji*, how can I become a better person without guilt?'

Be very clear: We can never become a moral person through guilt. Instead, guilt becomes such a load on us that we repeatedly make the same mistake. If we have deep guilt about smoking, we can never quit smoking because the habit is strengthened when the guilty thoughts are continuously repeated in our system. Whatever is continuously repeated in our consciousness becomes strong; we never grow out of it.

In Rāmāyaṇa, there is a character called Vāli. He obtained a boon from Lord Śiva that whomsoever stands in front of him to fight him, half of that person's power would go to Vāli. If we stand in front of Vāli, half of our power goes to Vāli! Naturally Vāli will win. Understand, our guilt is like Vāli. The moment we fight the smoking habit, we empower the habit and struggle with it. Then how can we come out of it?

Bernard Shaw says beautifully, 'Quitting smoking is easy, I have done it many times!' We can continue to quit many times. But we never get out of the habit. We are caught in the rut that guilt creates. If we remove guilt, at least our personality will be integrated and we will naturally become pure and energetic. All immoral behavior is because we don't have enough energy. The person with plenty of energy is always pure. In society we have a wrong idea that people who are full of energy do nonsensical things. No!

Doing immoral things means a person *wants* energy through that action. Understand, even our sense enjoyments are in the same league. We feel that we will get energy or feel blissful through that action. If we create guilt, the whole thing sits in the mental body and when we leave the body it becomes a big obstruction.

The next layer we cross is the etheric body where all the painful experiences of our life are stored.

These four layers are hell. When the energy crosses these four layers: physical body, pranic body, mental body and etheric body, the being undergoes hell. Understand hell is not situated in a place above our heads. It is in these four layers, comprising all our desires, guilt and painful experiences.

During our life in the body, if we have kept these four layers clean, we will never enter hell. If we clean these layers through meditation, we will not have problems at the time of leaving the body. We will have a clear highway. That is what Kṛṣṇa says: This is the path on which a man can easily leave and liberate himself, and also the path on which he can suffer and destroy himself. Both ways are now shown by Kṛṣṇa. These are the major obstructions when we leave the body.

After these first four layers, the three inner layers where all our blissful memories are stored are called heaven. Even if we are stuck there, we need to move on. Even our *puṇya,* merits, are *karma*. Even that will not allow us to become enlightened. We may feel good, ecstatic, for a few days. After that our mind takes that also for granted. In the case of heaven also, we will take it for granted after a few days. When we take it for granted, the trouble starts and you have to come back to take another body, another birth.

Be Sure To Reach Me

8.7 *Arjuna, think of Me in the form of Kṛṣṇa always, while continuing with your prescribed duty of fighting.*
With your activities dedicated to Me and your mind and intelligence fixed on Me, you will attain Me without doubt.

8.8 *He who meditates on the supreme person, his mind constantly engaged in remembering Me, not deviating from the path, O Pārtha,*
Is sure to reach Me.

8.9 *One should meditate on the supreme as the one who knows everything, as He is the most ancient, who is the controller, who is smaller than the smallest, who is the maintainer of everything, who is beyond all material conception, who is inconceivable, and who is always a person.*
He is luminous like the sun and, being transcendental, is beyond this material nature.

8.10 *One, who at the time of death, fixes his mind and life breath between the eyebrows without being distracted, who by the power of yoga and in full devotion engages himself in dwelling on Me,*
He will certainly attain Me.

In the first two of these verses Kṛṣṇa says, 'Arjuna, you should always think of Me. You should always be in My state of consciousness even when you are doing your regular duty. Let your mind and intelligence be fixed in My consciousness. You will attain Me without doubt.'

Again He uses the words, 'without doubt', *asamasyaḥ* 'Without doubt, you will achieve Me.'

One important question we may ask, 'Anyhow, I have to think of Him at the time of leaving the body, so why bother now? Let me lead my life now. At the time of death, I will think about Him.' Please be very clear, these verses answer that question. We cannot think about Him *then* unless we think about Him *now.* When we live our whole life repeating the words, 'Coca-cola, Coca-cola', suddenly at the end of our lives we will not be able think of Rāma or Kṛṣṇa. No!

Whatever we think during our whole life, the same thought will come to us in the end also. At the time of death, we will not be able to remember. Our consciousness will not be under our control at that time! At the time of our death, the totality of our whole life comes up. Whatever we spent the maximum energy on, that file will come up first. We can't do anything in that moment. Only the thought that we lived with intensely throughout our life will come up at that moment. That is why He says, 'Even when you do your duty, may you be absorbed in Me.' This means that when we live, we should try to continuously be in the witnessing consciousness, the Kṛṣṇa consciousness.

The supreme witness

The next question: 'How can I be in the witnessing mode when I live my regular life?'

Start in a simple way. When you drive, when you sit, when you talk, see what is happening inside and outside you. You don't need to close your eyes. At least while driving, please don't close your eyes! Just move away from your body and see what is going on in your mind and your being.

When you talk to someone, witness how he talks and how you respond. Even before he finishes his statement, notice how you are ready to jump on him with your own opinions! See how you prepare your speech before he finishes his statement. Witness continuously. You will see the influence of desires, guilt and pain on your being automatically disappears.

The moment you create a gap between you and your body-mind, the suffering disappears. Suffering is due to attachment to your body and mind. All your sufferings disappear the moment you witness. Actually, you may fail the first few times. After you face failure, you think, 'It is difficult, I cannot do it,' and you create an idea that it is difficult.

Somebody goes to Ramana Maharshi, the enlightened saint from India, and asks, 'Master, is *ātma vidya* (knowledge of the self) difficult?' He says, 'The word *difficult* is the only difficulty.' He sings beautifully in Tamil, *'Aiyye ati sulabham atma viddai, aiyye ati sulabham' - Oh! So easy! The knowledge of the Self is so easy!* He sings beautifully, 'To achieve money you must work, to achieve name and fame you must work, to achieve anything else you must work. To achieve the knowledge of the Self, you need to just keep quiet. Nothing else needs to be done.' Such a simple thing; a few moments of witnessing consciousness is enough.

Now don't start calculating, 'From tomorrow onwards, 24 hours a day I will be in the witnessing consciousness.' Then you will become frustrated if you are unable to be that way. Even if you stay in that consciousness for five minutes, it is a big blessing. When you experience the relief that happens when you remain as the witness, even once or twice, you can see how the stress disappears from your being. Then you will automatically stay in that same state, because now you have tasted it. Then you will come back to the same mood again and again.

Rāmakṛṣṇa says, 'If you give a little bit of *abhin* (an opium variant) to a peacock one evening at four o'clock, the next day exactly at four o'clock, it will be in front of your house!' In North India they give *abhin* to peacocks to make them dance. Similarly, if we experience the relaxation that happens when we witness the body and mind, we will automatically come back for that peace, again and again. If we feel witnessing is difficult, witness that thought also. Go into the consciousness of your being. Experience *samādhi* so that all hindrances disappear. You will experience the ultimate, eternal consciousness.

In the next verse Kṛṣṇa says, 'At the time of death, fix your mind between the eyebrows.' He adds, 'without being distracted and with devotion.' See, all this is not in our control at the time when the life force is about to leave the body. But if we have led a life in such higher consciousness, this automatically happens at that time! When Kṛṣṇa talks about the space between the eyebrows, He speaks of the higher *cakra* or energy center in the body.

Our mind is nothing but a bunch of conditionings. All these conditionings influence us at the time of death. How do we condition our mind? If we think that eating is the best thing in life, when we leave the body, what comes in front of us? All kinds of food and the McDonald's arches!

If we are taught that eating is the greatest pleasure in life, we would only see food when we leave this body. Then the last thought will be, 'Let me take a body that will help me eat more and more. Let me take birth in a family where I will be given food, where I will not have any other responsibility.'

We call for the archived files. From all the experiences of our past, we choose what we think is best and what we have worked for all our life. Based on that, we make a decision, 'Alright, if I want to eat, this is the right country.' There we will spend our next life, in *tamas*, in dullness, not doing anything, in just pure laziness.

A small story:

A man goes to a doctor and says, 'Doctor, please examine me. I don't feel like doing anything. I feel dull.'

The doctor thoroughly examines him. The man says, 'Doctor, please tell me in plain English, what is my problem?'

The doctor says, 'If you ask me, in plain English, you are 'lazy'. Nothing else is the problem.'

The man says, 'Ok, now tell me the medical term for it; I will go and tell my wife!'

If we have lived that kind of a life, that same laziness will make the choice for us when we take the next body. If you want to see the ultimate laziness, come to the Himalayas. You can see strange kinds of laziness. That is why Vivekānanda says openly in his lectures, 'The people who eat and sleep in the name of *sanyās*... make them stand up, and simply beat them!' Pure laziness!

> A man tells his friend, 'If only somebody would invent a machine that does all our work when switched on: laundry, cleaning, cooking, ironing, giving us a bath and putting on clothes! How nice it would be if the machine did everything at the flick of a switch!'
>
> His friend replies, 'How much nicer would it be if the machine also automatically switched itself on and off!'

This is what I call the peak of laziness! Be very clear, we actually *spend* energy when we are lazy. Don't think we are not spending energy. Have you heard the phrase, 'tired of sleeping?' Many people are tired of taking rest. If we sleep for more than ten hours, we will be tired of taking rest.

To be tired of taking rest is *tamas*. If we have lived life completely in *tamas*, we naturally decide, 'Anyhow, the ultimate thing in life is sleep. Now what type of body is the right body - whether pig or buffalo or human being? What type of family should I take birth in?' We make a decision. The whole calculation happens based on our own data, the data that we have collected.

As I said, at the time of leaving the body, the whole data appears before us in a single flash - *āgāmya* (acquired) file, *sañcita* (bank balance) file and *prārabdha* (current) file. Based on the files, we decide, 'What should be my next birth?' The moment we decide, we enter that kind of body. Because we are so attached to the body and mind, we cannot live without a body for more than three *kṣaṇa*s. *Kṣaṇa* is not chronological time. It is the gap between one thought and the next thought. For most of us, *kṣaṇa* will be a few microseconds because of our endless stream of thoughts.

While still in the body, if we have experienced 'thoughtlessness' at least once, (thoughtlessness means being alive without a sense of body and mind), if we have experienced thoughtless awareness, if we have been in universal consciousness for a single moment without the body and mind, that is what I call s*amādhi.*

Here is a small diagram to explain what exactly I mean by the word 'thoughtlessness'

	With Thoughts	Without Thoughts
With Consciousness	Waking	Samadhi
Without Consciousness	Dream	Deep Sleep

The four states of consciousness

In our life, we experience two states of being and two levels of mind. For example, now, while we are awake, we have thoughts. In deep sleep, do we have thoughts? No! So the two possibilities for the mind are with thought and without thought. In the same way, in the being, there can be 'I' consciousness and no 'I' consciousness. As of now, while we are awake and talking and moving, we have the idea of 'I' all the time, that of 'I' consciousness. In deep sleep, the 'I' consciousness does not exist. These two levels of consciousness and the two levels of mind and thought overlap each other and create four states of being in us.

The state with thoughts and with 'I' consciousness is the waking state, *jāgrat,* in which most of us are now (not all, some of us are in the dream state – sleeping already!) The next state is when we have thoughts, but 'I' consciousness is absent. This is the dream state - *svapna.* In the dream state, the frequency of thoughts will be more than the frequency of 'I' consciousness. That is why we are not able to control our dreams. When we are awake, the frequency of 'I' is more, that is why we can control our thoughts; we can do anything we want. If we can have the dreams of our choice, we know what kind of dreams we will have! Dreams are not in our control. So we have thoughts but no 'I' consciousness. The flow of thoughts happening in our being is the dream state.

In the next state, neither 'I' consciousness nor the flow of thoughts exists. This is deep sleep or *suṣupti.* The three states are *jāgrat, svapna, suṣupti* – conscious, sub-conscious, unconscious.

There is a fourth state that we have not experienced in our life, where we have no flow of thoughts yet we have 'I' consciousness. This is *samādhi,* thoughtless awareness, *turīya avastha, ātma jñāna, brahma jñāna,* Self-realization, *nirvāna, ātma bhūti,* state of the Divine, *nitya* consciousness, eternal bliss!

All these words refer to the state where we have pure awareness but no thoughts, where we exist without body and mind. In *Jāgrat, svapna, suṣupti,* we live with the body and mind. In *jāgrat,* we live with the the *sthūla śarīra* or gross body. In *svapna,* we live with the *sūkṣma śarīra* or subtle body; understand in the dream state also we assume a body. That is why we are able to travel in our dreams. For example, we fall asleep in Los Angeles but suddenly dream we are in India! In deep sleep, we assume the causal body or *karana śarīra.*

In *turiya* state, we experience boundarylessness, bodylessness. We have pure 'I' consciousness, but without thoughts. Vivekānanda says, 'If you experience even a single glimpse of this consciousness when you are alive, the same thing automatically repeats when you leave the body. You leave the body in *samādhi.*'

All spiritual practices directly or indirectly aim at achieving this state where we exist with the awareness of 'I', but without the consciousness of body and mind. That is why Kṛṣṇa says that if we experience at least one moment of consciousness beyond the body and mind, we can choose our next life in a relaxed way.

If we have not lived a single moment of our life without the feeling of being the body and mind, we cannot be without the body and mind once we die. So once we die, we immediately try to catch hold of another body without bothering about which body we are getting into. It's like we are late for a train, so we run and jump onto the first train that we see, not thinking about where it's headed. We rush and get into some body or the other and come down to planet earth yet another time.

After coming down, we again forget the purpose of assuming the body. The whole thing is confusion leading to confusion and more confusion. If we have experienced a single moment of complete rest and thoughtless awareness, naturally when we leave the body, we will be in the same state. This state is also called 'bodyless' awareness because when we are in *turiya* state, all the three bodies do not touch us; neither the gross body nor the subtle body nor the causal body touches us. We experience awareness that is beyond the three bodies.

If we have experienced this thoughtless awareness for even a single moment earlier, we will have the required clarity in the end. We will have the patience to work with our data files before assuming the next body. Sometimes, if we decide to take birth, we can even take a conscious birth, like the great masters!

Kṛṣṇa says *yogabraṣtha*. We take birth in a family that will be conducive to our spiritual growth. Kṛṣṇa says that only very rarely do souls take birth in this type of family. I have rarely seen parents who do not object when the son does spiritual practices. If your family does not object, then be very clear, there is every chance of your being a *yogabraṣṭha!*

Otherwise, I have seen even religious parents creating obstacles if their son wants to enter into spiritual life. They say, 'Go to temples but not to ashrams!' As long as you go to temples, it is ok because you grow to the level where your parents are. But if you grow beyond the maturity of the parents, it is something that they cannot digest. Very rarely do souls take birth in families where they will not be disturbed. When I left home for my *parivrājaka* (wandering *sanyās* life), I was just 17 years old. I told my mother that I was going, that I wanted to live the *parivrājaka* life, I wanted to taste *sanyās* life.

She started weeping. So I asked her, 'Do you mean that I should not go?'

She said beautifully, 'No, I don't want to stop you. But I am not able to digest the idea of your leaving, so I am weeping.' Even today I am grateful to my parents because they did not stop me. Not only that, from a young age I did all sorts of things. Sometimes I used to spend the night meditating in the graveyard in the outskirts of my village! Any other parents would not have tolerated it. Yet somehow the atmosphere was such that I was able to continue my spiritual practice.

If your family and surroundings do not disturb you, then, you have taken a conscious birth - you are a *yogabraṣtha.*

But if you have not experienced a single glimpse, a single moment of thoughtless awareness, you cannot live without the body and mind once you die. So within three *kṣaṇa*s, you take birth in some way or the other.

Even one glimpse of consciousness, when you live without the body and mind is enough. All I try to do is give you a single glimpse of consciousness, thoughtless awareness.

Actually, if you achieve one glimpse of thoughtless awareness, you achieve whatever has to be achieved in life. If you have not achieved that, then whatever else you achieve is not ultimately useful.

Remember Me Constantly

8.11 *Persons who are learned in the Veda and who are great sages in the orders of renunciation, enter into the* Brahman.
Desiring such perfection, one practices brahmacarya. *I shall now explain to you the process by which one may attain liberation.*

8.12 *Closing all the doors of the senses and fixing the mind in the heart*
And the life breath at the top of the head, one establishes oneself in yoga.

8.13 *Centered in this yoga practice and uttering the sacred syllable Om, the supreme combination of letters, if one dwells in the Supreme and quits his body, he certainly achieves the supreme destination.*

8.14 *I am always available to anyone who remembers Me constantly*
Pārtha, because of his constant engagement in devotional service.

Kṛṣṇa gives different ways to attain *Brahman* or God or ultimate consciousness. He says that people learned in the *Vedas* attain *Brahman.* This does not mean that we read the *Vedas* and forget about them. Kṛṣṇa speaks at a far deeper level.

If someone is completely immersed in the scriptures, his thoughts will continuously be along those lines even at the end of his life. That is what Kṛṣṇa means by His words 'Immerse yourself in the scriptures'. Keep reading some scripture or the other and imbibe its truth. It will have a tremendous impact on you.

Even if we do not understand the deeper meanings of these scriptures, it is ok. These scriptures are energy hubs. When we read them, the sound that is generated cleanses our inner being. That is the power of those verses. They will transform you.

If you listen to *vedic* chants, you will see they are chanted in a specific way. When they are chanted, they completely cleanse our system, our inner being. Most of us are not aware of this, yet they carry that energy for us.

If we visit the ancient temples in India, we will see that the sanctum sanctorum is very peaceful. When we enter that place, automatically our being too becomes peaceful. Why do you think that happens? This is because, when the priest chants, the sound of the chants energizes everything in the place.

One more thing, these scriptures talk about realizing the Self. They are guides to enlightenment. So when we read them, we will get into that mood of enlightenment! Our mind will be tuned to that frequency.

It is like this: When we come out of a movie theatre after watching a movie, our mind keeps processing the scenes of the movie, is it not? It tries to recollect the various scenes. For one or two days, we experience a hangover. In the same way, when we read these scriptures, even if we don't completely understand them, we will experience a hangover. We will continue to think about what they say - enlightenment, Self … these thoughts will come into our mind again and again.

Similarly, when our thoughts are always directed towards Self-realization, our thoughts will be of enlightenment at the time of death also.

Kṛṣṇa says, when we read the scriptures, when we practice its lifestyle, we practice *brahmacarya. Brahmacarya* is commonly misinterpreted as celibacy. *Brahman* means the Self and *carya* means to walk the path. So *brahmacāri* means one who follows the path to attain the Self.

A small story:

There was an old sea captain who was telling a story from his adventures to a group of people at a party.

He said, 'Once, I was shipwrecked on the coast of South America, and there I came across a tribe of women who had no tongues and were very wild.'

One lady said, 'My goodness! They couldn't talk?'

The old captain replied, 'No they couldn't talk, and that was what drove them wild.'

Be very clear. Suppression does not lead to transformation. It only creates depression. Suppression of desires is very dangerous; it is like a volcano ready to erupt anytime and we won't even know it.

Our inner space must be cleansed, free from fantasies and we should strive to merge with the *Brahman*. That is *brahmacarya*.

All great truths were told by different masters in different ways, yet the truths remain the same. Here Kṛṣṇa talks about the deeper meaning of Yoga. Yoga means the continuous process of uniting our mind, body and soul. Patañjali, the father of yoga, talks about this verse in his Aṣṭāṅga yoga. Aṣṭāṅga yoga means eight limbs of yoga and two of these limbs are *pratyāhāra* and *dhārana*. These two parts talk about what Kṛṣṇa mentions.

Now, how do we bring about that continuous process of uniting body, mind and soul? What should we do? You see, our body-mind system reacts to different external situations. These external situations are like food, *āhāra* to our system and our five sense organs are the points through which we take in this food.

Our mind functions because we give food to our mind through our senses. We react to situations and our mind is continuously occupied because of this. We are again and again jumping from past to future and back to past.

Pratyāhāra means getting ourselves out of the clutches of these senses. It does not mean that we physically shut down our senses. Even if we close our ears and mouth, there is inner chatter, is it not? Even if we shut down our senses physically, our mind functions. When I say, 'Close the doors of your senses,' I mean, 'continue to hear everything going on outside but do not process anything. Whatever comes, just witness.' That is the only way we can close the doors of our senses. Neither suppress thoughts nor create thoughts. Just watch them.

We cut the continuous flow of inputs from our senses when we increase our awareness. The number of thoughts, TPS, drops slowly as awareness rises. This is what Kṛṣṇa means by closing all the senses. When we do this, our awareness becomes more and more concentrated on the present moment. We focus on our divinity. We automatically fall into the present moment. Awareness of our breath becomes more acute. We feel life energy or *prāna* filling our system.

This is called *dhārana,* the single-minded focus. We can focus on the life-force energizing our system when we increase our awareness and close all the inputs from our senses. We automatically unite mind, body and spirit. This is yoga.

Again and again Kṛṣṇa emphasizes this truth so much. He continuously tells Arjuna the importance of the last thought before death. These are not mere words to be read and not put into practice. People have used these words and left their bodies gracefully. Thousands of enlightened beings have constantly thought about God. They have expressed their undaunted devotion in so many carefree ways. People realized the power of that devotion only after these enlightened beings left their bodies, completely merging with the cosmos.

Kṛṣṇa says the people who reach Him are those who remain continuously on the path of yoga, continuously fixed upon the Divine without deviation. Kṛṣṇa asks us to be in that consciousness all the time. The problem is when an enlightened master says, 'Think of Me all the time,' we question, 'What kind of an egoistic person is He? Why should we think of Him?'

Actually, our ego plays the game. We think Kṛṣṇa is exploiting us when He advises us to be in Kṛṣṇa consciousness. Many people think I am exploiting them when I make such statements. They think I profit from all of this.

Be very clear, Kṛṣṇa, or any enlightened master, only asks us to keep our inner space completely free of desires. Our thoughts are generally related to greed and fear. We keep piling up desires because our thought patterns are of greed and fear. When we die, our soul re-experiences these desires making death painful. An enlightened master has seen this process and He wants everyone to know the secret of mastering the art of leaving.

That is why Kṛṣṇa says again and again: When we direct our thoughts to the Divine, our whole being is filled with gratitude to the Divine.

When we think of the Divine, we should do so out of gratitude, and not out of greed or fear. Be very clear that thinking of God out of greed or fear will not help us. Our thoughts about God, our devotion to the Divine should be out of pure gratitude to Existence.

Brahma's Day And Night

8.15 After attaining Me, the great souls who are devoted to Me in yoga are never reborn in this world.
This world is temporary and full of miseries and they have attained the highest perfection.

8.16 From the highest planet in the material world down to the lowest, all are places of misery wherein repeated birth and death take place.
One who reaches My abode, O son of Kuntī, is never reborn.

8.17 By human calculation, a thousand ages taken together is the duration of Brahma's one day.
His night is just as long.

8.18 From the unmanifest all living entities come into being at the beginning of Brahma's day.
With the coming of Brahma's night, they dissolve into the same unmanifest.

Now He says, 'After attaining Me the great souls who are steeped in yoga never return to this temporary world which is full of miseries, because they have attained the highest perfection.'

The understanding of this science, the very intellectual understanding, gives the inspiration to experience truth and naturally leads us to the ultimate Truth.

Here Kṛṣṇa says, 'If you achieve this state, you never come back.' He inspires us to enter that state. The only job of an enlightened master is to make everyone realize the truth that he himself has experienced. There is no ulterior motive.

People again and again look at an enlightened master with suspicion. They suspect foul play. Understand: A person who remains at the inner source of bliss never cares for anything external. He does not need external sources of happiness.

That is the reason he does not see the world as a collection of miseries. You see, an enlightened master may not get food for days, yet he is always blissful. Even in such situations, the only things that he experiences are gratitude and compassion. He is neither attached to sorrow nor to happiness. He is detached from both to the same degree.

He is always in a state of gratitude to the universe. Worldly things do not affect him. Happiness and sorrow are not in his dictionary.

> A small story:
>
> The Sufi master, Javed paid gratitude to God five times a day. Once he and his followers were wandering through several villages where Sufism was not accepted as a religion.
>
> In the first village, people accused them of begging, and threw meager alms at them. In the next village, the people refused to give them any alms.
>
> On the third day, the village they visited was so hostile that the villagers drove them out with sticks and stones.
>
> That night as usual, the master knelt down and offered gratitude to God. His disciples watched. It was too much for them. They could not understand why their master was thanking God when they were hungry, thirsty and miserable.
>
> They cried out, 'Master! For three days we have gone without food! Today we were driven out of that village like dogs! Is this what you offer gratitude for?'
>
> Their master looked at them and said, 'You talk about three days of hunger! Have you thanked God for the food you have received for the past thirty years? My gratitude is not based on receiving or not

receiving anything. It is an expression of deep joy and love in my being; it is a choiceless and prayerful expression.'

An enlightened master looks at misery and happiness with total gratitude and surrender to the universe. He surrenders everything that he has and gets, to Existence. He says, 'Let Existence take care.' There is a great relief inside when that state of surrender happens. We suddenly light up in joy.

We consider something as misery because we think we are responsible for that something. That is why, when something does not happen according to our expectations, we see it as misery. But an enlightened being simply flows. Whatever comes, he accepts it and surrenders it to Existence.

Beyond karma

In the next verse, Kṛṣṇa talks about the misery-filled world and we see how good deeds cannot get us out of the cycle of birth and death. Kṛṣṇa says here:

'From the highest planet of *Brahmaloka* in the material world down to the lowest, all are places of misery wherein repeated birth and death takes place. But one who attains Me, one who attains My being, one who attains My consciousness, never takes birth again.'

Even if we reach the cosmic layer of *Brahmaloka,* the land of the Divine, we must come back and take birth again. It means that even if we are full of good intentions and good deeds, even if we are attached to good things, we must come back into a body.

Even if we are caught in doing good deeds, we return. Our good deeds, *puṇya,* cannot give us enlightenment. I tell people, 'Even if you give money for my ashram, I cannot give you a speed pass to enlightenment!' Be very clear, unless *you* achieve at least one moment of thoughtless awareness, nobody can save you from the cycle of birth and death.

Some people believe that when they give money to institutions, they receive a receipt and a pass to heaven. They are buried with the receipt so that they can show the receipt to the gatekeeper of heaven who will let them in!

Honestly at least I don't have such a system with this institution. Let me be very clear! I never tell people, 'Do charity and good acts and I can get you into heaven.' Do things out of love and gratitude with no attachment, and you will be in heaven as a result of your mental setup.

I tell people, 'Even if you give money to my ashram, I cannot give you any speed pass; nothing can be done. This is the honest truth.' People ask, 'Then why do you build ashrams and temples?' I build them because they are laboratories where the spiritual sciences can be practiced, where people study and imbibe great truths to practice them in their lives. They are inner-science laboratories.

Do charity and good acts with the consciousness that you are engaged in research in the inner sciences in these laboratories, just as the *ṛṣis* of the great vedic tradition did. Don't do it for some special ticket to heaven.

Don't expect that if we do these things for Lord Viṣṇu, He will send a special flight with a *garuḍa* (eagle) emblem when we leave the body, and the celestial beauties, will take us there. Nothing of that sort happens! If we expect these things to happen, we will only sit and wait. No such thing will happen! Whether we acquire sin or merit, we suffer when we leave the body. Both are *karma*.

Then what is to be done? When we live in the body, at least once, by meditating or by surrender, experience one glimpse of thoughtless awareness.

Work intensely for it. If we achieve one glimpse, it's over. That one glimpse acts like a torch and guides us through these seven layers when we leave the body. We will just slide through all seven layers. If we achieve that one glimpse of consciousness, we achieve what has to be achieved; everything else is a waste. All merits and sins - nothing comes with us. We will be judged only by this one glimpse of *samādhi*, the ultimate truth.

Again and again Vivekānanda says, 'If you achieve even a single glimpse, you leave your body in that experience.' The intense experience of Self-realization will come up at the time when we leave the body. At the time of death, our whole life is played back to us in a fast-forward mode in a few seconds. And only the important scenes appear in multicolor; all others scenes appear in black and white. If we have had the *samādhi* experience when we were alive, that alone will appear in multicolor; all other things will fade away in the background.

And naturally, we stay in that state and leave the body. One more thing - if there is a scratch on a videotape, the tape gets stuck in that place when it runs in fast-forward mode, is it not? So when the fast-forward happens, the remainder of the tape is erased. Similarly, thoughtless awareness is the *stuck* point in our life because in that space we never had a thought. We will be stuck there and whatever fast-forward happens beyond that, all the *karma* associated with it will be erased, washed away!

It is like a virus entering our software; the more we try to operate the software, the more the virus destroys the software. Similarly, thoughtless awareness is the divine virus for our *samsāra sagara* – ocean of worldly life, for the software that is our mind.

Don't think that the mind is intelligence. The mind is just programmed software. For example, let us say we experience anxiety every morning because of office-related worries. The funny thing is, eventually we start experiencing the same depression even on the weekend when there is no office to attend! Then we tell our mind, 'No, this is the weekend. I don't need to think about those things.' But every weekend, our mind goes back to the same mood because our mind is pre-programmed software.

One glimpse of consciousness in our lifetime is enough. Then there will be no need to take the next birth. We assume the body and mind only if we believe there is something to be enjoyed or achieved through the body and mind. When we are in this body, if we work on our engraved memories, *saṁskāras*, and come out of them, we will liberate ourselves from their influence, and hence from the cycle of re-birth.

Actually, you do not normally become aware of these *saṁskāras*. In our Second level program, Life Bliss Program Level 2, we take you through techniques to uncover them first. You write down and analyze all that has happened in your life and all that you have stored in the various energy layers. You analyze: What is the root of your desires? What are your own desires? Which desires are borrowed?

For instance, guilt is initially imposed on us by society. Later we master the art of creating guilt and continue to create it for ourselves! Next, pain and suffering. Society creates a scale deciding what pain is and what suffering is. We then actually turn our whole life into suffering by measuring it with that scale. In the workshop, we work deeply on these things - on every emotion related to engraved memories or *saṁskāras*.

If we are stuck with guilt, we can never enjoy our desires. When we don't enjoy our desires, we create more guilt. Then again we cannot enjoy our desires. This becomes a vicious circle.

Experience His *līla*

As of now, understand this one thing: Experience His consciousness, the witnessing consciousness in which Kṛṣṇa stays and plays the whole game of life. That is why Kṛṣṇa's life is called *līla* – cosmic play; *Kṛṣṇa līla*. It is not history. It is a cosmic play.

For ordinary human beings, after they die, their life will be written as history. For incarnations, their life itself is a script that has already been written; they just come down and enact it! They play the whole game. That is why their life is called *līla*. If we achieve the witnessing consciousness, our whole life becomes *līla*. We know the script and we are ready.

Kṛṣṇa conveys one thing: All we need to do is work to achieve a glimpse of thoughtless awareness. He says further:

'By human calculation, the thousand ages taken together form the duration of Brahma's one day, and such also is the duration of his night.'

One year for us is one day for the *devatas*, demigods. Only when we achieve the consciousness of *nirvāṇa* – thoughtless awareness, will we not take re-birth. Here He says a beautiful thing about *kṣaṇa*.

At the time of death, our soul has three *kṣaṇa*s to take another body. If we have lived a restless life, our *kṣaṇa*s will be in microseconds. If we have lived a peaceful, blissful life and achieved at least one glimpse of thoughtless awareness, our *kṣaṇa* can be even two or three hundred years. It can extend to two or three hundred years, because it is the gap between one thought and the next thought. So *kṣaṇa* is relative and depends on our state of mind.

Time is actually psychological. If we sit with a friend with whom we are comfortable and joyful after three or four hours, we suddenly notice the time and say, 'Oh! I don't know how the time has passed by so quickly!' At the same time, if we sit with somebody with whom we don't feel comfortable, we will keep looking at the watch and think, 'Why is the watch not moving? The time is simply dragging on.'

The number of thoughts that happen in our mind decides the time consciousness. If thoughts are less, even after ten hours, we will not feel that ten hours have passed. If the number of thoughts is more, two or three minutes will seem like years.

> A small story:
>
> A lady goes to the doctor for a check-up. After a thorough examination, the doctor says, 'I'm sorry. I have bad news. You may live only six months more at the most.'
>
> She says, 'What is this? What should I do now?'
>
> The doctor says, 'I have one suggestion. Marry an accountant.'
>
> She asks, 'Will that cure me?'
>
> He says, 'No, no. But then the six months will seem very long.'

One year of human life equals one day of the *devata*s, demigods, because their thoughts per second (TPS) is very less. That is why the deity Naṭarāja in the temple at Chidambaram in South India, has only six prayer offerings throughout the year. Normally, the worship is carried out six times a day in other temples. But this temple is supposed to be where the *devata*s worship the Divine, so the worship is carried out according to their time!

The six offerings of worship required for the deity are conducted in our one year because our one year is one day for the deities or *devatas*. *Devatas* refers to those whose TPS has come down, who have had a glimpse of *samādhi*. If our TPS is low, we too are in heaven. If our TPS is high, we are in hell. Heaven always looks brief; hell always looks eternal, because of the number of thoughts.

When we are in the body, if we have had a single glimpse of thoughtless awareness - the experience of meditation, then automatically this consciousness comes up at the time of leaving the body, and we will have two benefits. We can choose to become enlightened and not take another birth, or we can choose the right place to express and work out our *karma*, to live as we want. We have both choices if we experience thoughtless awareness while living.

My Supreme Abode

8.19 *Again and again the day comes, and this host of beings is active;*
And again the night falls, O son of Pritā, and they are automatically annihilated.

8.20 *Yet there is another nature, which is eternal and is beyond this manifested and unmanifest matter.*
It is supreme and is never annihilated. When all in this world is annihilated, that remains the same.

8.21 *That supreme abode is said to be unmanifest and indestructible and is the supreme destination.*
When one gains this state one never comes back. That is My supreme abode.

8.22 *Son of Pritā, the supreme person, who is greater than all, is attainable by undeviating devotion.*
Although He is present in His abode, He is all-pervading, and everything is situated within Him.

Kṛṣṇa explains how transient this material world is. In our concept of time, we see things as permanent, but when we operate in a different zone of space and time, all this becomes temporary.

Our ignorance makes us think that all that we see is real and permanent. Once we understand that this entire life and the world around us is impermanent, we see everything from a completely different angle.

In our concept of time and space, we see material things as permanent. We want to have ownership over everything that is available. And the problem is everyone wants the same thing! We are like cats fighting over a piece of bread. One more thing you should know: We want to hold onto this body for as long as we can. Even at sixty or seventy, many people go in for plastic surgery to look young. Why? They do not want to accept the truth that the body is impermanent.

When you look around, you see that the earth is stationary. When you look from the moon, you see the earth moving. When you go beyond the moon, you see that the moon also moves. Once we raise ourselves to higher dimensions, we see the actual truth. As long as we limit ourselves to this space, we think the earth is stationary. When we change our reference point in space and time, we realize that all we think of as permanent, ours, is not permanent.

This is what Kṛṣṇa says. We believe in a concept of finite time and limited space and we cling to that without realizing what is beyond this dimension.

We are greedy to accumulate more and more material pleasures because we see them as real and permanent. That is one side. On the other side we fear that they will be taken away from us. Both greed and fear are the main sources of our misery. We run, not for the joy of running, but because greed makes us run towards something that we want to possess, and fear makes us run away from something that seems to take away our possessions.

When we live in bondage of fear and greed, we continuously build *saṁskāras*. First of all, we are not trying to fulfill our true desires or *prārabdha karma*. Then on top of that, we build a whole new set of desires. In our concept of time and space, we think things are permanent. We think we own them and should take care of them and control them.

When we understand that at higher dimensions, all that we see is destroyed and created continuously, we realize the futility of holding onto even our own body.

Kṛṣṇa says that in all this creation and destruction, only one thing is neither created nor destroyed, and that is the 'ultimate consciousness'! What we think of as an age is a fraction of a second to Brahma and everything we see as permanent is being made and destroyed every time

Brahma blinks. Do not analyze the literal meaning of this. Do not analyze how it is possible. Do not worry about how many hours, how many seconds make one day of Brahma? Do not worry about what is Brahma's time or what is Viṣṇu's time or what is Śiva's time or Kṛṣṇa's time. Kṛṣṇa refers to the concept of time and space as it exists in the ultimate consciousness, and as an enlightened master experiences it.

Appreciate the deeper meaning. Understand that whatever we see is transient. It is like putting our hand in a river and trying to hold the water in our hand. What happens? The river flows past, and our hand is empty. Once we realize this truth, our whole idea about time and space will change. We will see everything around us in a different light and understand the futility of the rat race.

The abode of no return

The secret to liberation is what Kṛṣṇa gives here – 'One who attains My abode will never return.' The abode where one will not return to refers to the state of the being when it transcends joys and sorrow. Kṛṣṇa repeatedly talks about focusing one's thoughts on the Divine. The only way to think of the Divine at the time of our death is by thinking about Him all the time. At that time, suddenly we cannot think of God in the midst of such pain and suffering. It is impossible.

That is why Kṛṣṇa insists upon continuous devotion to the Supreme. When we live in a state of continuous devotion, our last thought will be of the Divine. Our last thought determines our next birth. There is no doubt about it.

You see, thousands of thoughts come to us every minute. Let as many thoughts as possible be of God. Let us immerse ourselves in thinking about the supreme soul. This purifies our inner space. Throughout the day, how many times do we think of God? Maybe before a meal, or before going to bed. Otherwise, it's only when we face some problem, that we think of God! But how many times do we think of some film actress or actor? Everything in the newspapers, on television or on the internet is about something with which we are not really connected. We take many such things into our system, and all our thoughts revolve around them.

Out of thousands of thoughts, less than one percent is probably related to God. Everything else is related to something external. Every thought is energy and we waste more than ninety nine percent of our energy on something that is not really needed for us. If we can channel this energy to look inward, we explore a new dimension of our Self.

We are ready to do anything other than think about God or our Self. We think it is a waste of time. We do something only if we feel we will get something from it. But if we analyze our thoughts carefully, we are not thinking of anything productive.

Most of the time, we justify ourselves saying, 'Why think of God? What will we get? I have better things to think about like work and my studies.' These are mere justifications. If we sit and write down our thoughts, we will see that we are not thinking about anything productive. Our thoughts are completely illogical and random.

So why not think about God? When we are completely immersed in thoughts of God, our inner space is cleared. We are preparing our Self. At the time of death, these thoughts will liberate us. Constantly thinking about God helps when our soul passes through the energy layers at the time of death.

Passing In Light

8.23 O best of the Bhārata*, I shall now explain to you the different times*
When passing away from this world, one returns or does not return.

8.24 Those who pass away from the world during the influence of the fire god, during light, at an auspicious moment, during the fortnight of the waxing moon and the six months when the sun travels in the north,
And those who have realized the supreme Brahman *do not return.*

8.25 The mystic who passes away from this world during the smoke, the night, the fortnight of the waning moon, or the six months when the sun travels in the south,
Having done good deeds, goes to the cosmic layer and returns.

8.26 According to the Vedas*, there are two ways of passing from this world —one in light and one in darkness.*
When one passes in light, he does not return; but when one passes in darkness, he returns.

In these few verses, Kṛṣṇa describes at what time one can achieve enlightenment, how one can achieve enlightenment and how to reach that state. He also talks about how people come back into this cycle of birth and death.

He says:

Those who know the supreme Divine attain that Supreme by passing away from the world during the influence of Agni, the fire-god, during light or at an auspicious moment of the day, also during the fortnight of the waxing moon or during the six months that the sun travels in the north, referred to as *uttarāyaṇaṁ*.

Understand, these are not chronological calendars. If it were a chronological calendar, then at *uttarāyaṇaṁ* time, all of us can commit suicide and be done with it!

All these things have metaphorical meanings. When He says *uttarāyaṇaṁ,* He means when our mind is totally balanced. In the Mahābhārata war, in the Hindu epic Mahābhārata, it is said that Bhīṣma waits for *uttarāyaṇaṁ* to leave the body. Don't think he waited for January. He waited until his mind settled down from the agitations.

He had fallen in battle and was down on a bed made of arrows. He must have felt agitated. He must have felt, 'My grandson, for whom I did everything, did this to me.' He would have been disturbed. So he waited until the agitation settled down. That is what is meant by the words, 'he was waiting for *uttarāyaṇaṁ.*'

Don't think these are chronological concepts. If they were then the millions of people who die in those six months will become enlightened. Enlightenment is not an accident! It is a pure conscious choice.

So be very clear, when He says *agnir jyotiraḥ suklah,* He means if we are conscious... *agnir jyotiraḥ...* means when your being is conscious... when your being is fully alive, awakened, naturally you go up. (*suklah* means going above, *Kṛṣṇa* means going down)

If we live, throughout life centered on the eyes, our energy leaves through the eyes. If we live throughout life centered on the tongue and eating, the soul leaves through the mouth. So if we live throughout life centered on higher consciousness, our energy leaves through the *sahasrāra,* the crown *cakra,* the energy center on the top of our head.

Kṛṣṇa says *brahma brahmavido janah.* He means that if we have always lived with our attention focused towards higher consciousness, we will travel in that path and disappear into *Brahman.* We will become enlightened.

So be very clear, these conditions are psychological. Bhīṣma waited until his mind settled. He waited until he felt completely peaceful, till he was able to forgive everybody and reach conscious awareness. Then he entered enlightenment.

Next, Kṛṣṇa says that the person who passes away from this world during the night, the fortnight of the waning moon or those six months when the Sun travels in the south, referred to as *dakṣināyanam*, reaches the Moon but comes back again.

Again, this is also psychological. They can't say that in these six months nobody can become enlightened. They can't say, 'During the six months of *dakṣināyanam* the enlightenment gates are locked, no entry. Only at *uttarāyaṇaṁ* time, the gates are open. Come at that time.' No! They can't say, '*Dakṣināyanam* time is non-working hours and only *uttarāyaṇaṁ* time is working hours.' There are no working hours for enlightenment. It is purely because of the conscious choice of one's being.

Kṛṣṇa says that according to the *Vedas*, there are two ways to pass from this world: one in light and one in darkness. When one passes in light, he does not return, but when one passes in darkness, he comes back again.

What does Kṛṣṇa mean by light and darkness? They refer to the levels of consciousness one has reached. If a person leaves the body without knowing what drove him all along - his *saṁskāras*, his desires, fears, guilt, etc., which we call engrams - then this ignorance is what He refers to as darkness.

When we become aware of these and are free from them, we leave the body and become liberated. This is what He means by light. He says that when this happens, the being does not return to the body.

Be Fixed In Devotion

8.27 O son of Pritā, the devotees who know these different paths are never bewildered.
O Arjuna, be always fixed in devotion.

8.28 A person who accepts the path of devotional service transcends the results derived from studying the Vedas, *performing austerities and sacrifices, giving charity or pursuing pious and result-based activities.*
At the end he reaches the supreme abode.

In the last few verses Kṛṣṇa summarizes the essence of the whole chapter. He says, 'O son of Pritā, the devotees who know these different paths are never bewildered. Therefore O Arjuna, be always fixed in devotion.'

He means that a person who understands the different paths that a spirit can take while leaving the body will always be prepared for death. He immerses himself in devotion throughout his life so that he becomes liberated. Kṛṣṇa first gives Arjuna an intellectual understanding of the whole death process. He clearly tells him that the last thought while leaving the body governs the path that the spirit chooses when entering the next body.

Again and again He emphasizes that this thought cannot be divine unless we spend our entire lives in devotional service. When I say devotional service, devotion is more important than service. I tell people, never give money in charity because some priest told you that it is a good thing. I do not say, 'Don't do charity work.' I am only saying, 'Let it just be a natural expression of yourself, not with any expectation.'

We have a head to think with and a heart to feel with. We do not need to refer to society every time to decide what to do and what not to do. Do not work in the name of 'devotional service' to please someone else or society. If you expect something in return, then it is not devotional service. If it springs purely out of devotion, the act itself should be the reward.

A small story:

Bodhidharma goes to China. The King of China was devoted to Bodhidharma. The king did a lot to spread Buddhism in China. He built many temples and ashrams, and spent lots of money trying to get people to follow the path.

When Bodhidharma entered his palace, the king welcomed him and asked, 'Buddha, I have done so much to spread Buddhism in my country. What will happen when I die? Will I reach heaven?'

Bodhidharma replied, 'You will reach the worst hell.'

The king was shocked! Understand: The king's question contained an expectation of return for his charity. He did service hoping that Bodhidharma would recognize and reward him.

I tell people, every day for just half an hour, work without expecting anything in return. It could be anything. If you make a painting, don't calculate, 'Oh, how many people will appreciate this!' Without such calculations, immerse yourself in some work for half an hour.

You will suddenly see a new space open up inside you. When you work without expecting anything in return, just for the joy of doing it, you will see how liberating it is. Gradually, when this becomes ingrained in you, you will enjoy whatever you do much more. You will no more bother about who thinks what about you.

Kṛṣṇa says, 'Performing austerities and sacrifices, giving charity or pursuing pious result-based activities will take a person to the supreme abode.'

While doing each of these activities, it is the attitude that matters most, not the action itself. Kṛṣṇa says, if one engages in activities with devotion, then He will be there at the time of one's death.

He has given intellectual knowledge until now.

Let us pray to that ultimate energy, *Parabrahma* Kṛṣṇa, to give us intelligence and the experience of thoughtless awareness, witnessing consciousness, *ātma jñāna*, the eternal bliss, *nityānanda.*

Thank you.

Thus ends the eighth chapter named **Akṣara Brahma Yogaḥ**, *of the* **Upaniṣad** *of* ***Bhagavad Gītā****, the scripture of Yoga dealing with the Science of the Absolute, in the form of the dialogue between* ***Śrī Kṛṣṇa*** *and Arjuna.*

Death: The Ultimate Liberation And A Cause For Celebration

Editor's note:

Nithyananda's father, Śrī Nitya Arunācalānanda attained enlightenment and left the body, what we call Mahā samādhi, on 12 November 2006. This is the account of a disciple present on that occasion.

It was the third and final day of the Aṣṭāvakra Gītā discourses in Bengaluru.

The topic that evening was Enlightenment: Have it! *Swamiji* expounded so authoritatively on the *sūtras* (aphorisms) of the boy sage, Aṣṭāvakra. The mesmerized audience listened to the flow of words. It was suddenly interrupted by a coughing bout from *Swamiji*.

He asked for water, drank it, and continued talking.

There was another interruption. *Ayya* (Secretary to *Swamiji*, for Indian affairs) came flying onto the stage. He went behind the sofa and whispered something to Him. *Swamiji* covered the mic with his one hand, listened calmly to *Ayya* and made a facial gesture that seemed to convey, 'I'll take care' or something to that effect. The talk resumed. Then to the audience's utter consternation, he gestured to *Ayya* to come onstage again. More whispered conversation followed. There was stillness and finality in *Swamiji*'s body language. *Ayya* left, the talk continued and progressed to the end. The effect was electrifying. No one left his seat during the discourse. Spontaneous applause followed. Then the long serpentine queue for *Swamiji*'s blessing started.

I sat in the balcony watching the flow of events. Little did I know that one soul had already taken the offer of enlightenment. As the long line of people was shortening, I went down to the entrance to take my allotted place. Just then *Ayya* came and said, '*Amma, Swamiji's* father has attained *mahāsamādhi* (final liberation). All of us are leaving for Tiruvannamalai as soon as *Swamiji* finishes. Please round up all *ācārya*s (teachers) and healers and gather them at one place. At no point should your body language reveal what I have just now conveyed to you. *Swamiji* wants you to remain calm and act with spiritual maturity.'

That set the tone for the unimaginable events that followed. Enlightened beings are compassion incarnate. *Swamiji* blessed each and everyone in the queue taking as much time as he would in the normal course of events. After blessings, very smoothly *Swamiji's* car moved away with His mother beside Him in the center seat and His brothers occupying the rear seat. Mini buses were arranged for *ashramites*, healers and *ācārya*s. Barring a few people, most of them did not know where we were going. The ones who didn't know were delighted by the turn of events. They were traveling out of Bengaluru and would be in *Swamiji's* company… that was enough!

When we reached Tiruvannamalai, one of the ashramites stopped the bus, went down and picked up fresh garlands for us to place on the coffin. In the wee hours of the morning of 13th Nov 2006, the bus stopped at the entrance to Rajarajan Street where *Swamiji's* maternal parents lived. A passing thought struck me that young ***Raja***sekaran had lived on ***Raja***rajan street and was destined to be a ***Raja***sanyāsi…*Raja* meaning King - royalty to the manner born. It looked like Existence had planned very meticulously. (*Swamiji's* original name was **Raja**sekaran) The orchestration was truly exquisite!

We got down quietly and in a single file walked solemnly into the house. *Swamiji* sat in the *veranda* (porch) with some male relatives. He radiated a serene calmness. The minute He saw us, He remarked about us, 'For the first time I see these people really serious!' And then He addressed us, 'Go inside. Pay respects. Be with my mother. See to it that no one disturbs her. I don't want anyone wailing and weeping and creating scenes.'

We stepped into the hall and saw a lot of people seated there. To the left of the main doorway was the glass coffin. One after the other, in a silent procession, we placed garlands on the coffin and paid respects. I looked at the face and found it to be utterly calm. It echoed the final relaxation. Somehow, I couldn't connect with the fact that this inert body was a living person to whom I had spoken just two days earlier in the ashram. I had bid him goodbye and said that we would see each other during *Jayanti* celebrations, *Swamiji's* birthday celebrations in December-January. In his usual manner, he invited me to Tiruvannamalai for the *Karthigai Deepam* festival... '*Ellarum vaango*', 'all of you please come for the festival of lights.'

Yes, everyone came - but not for the festival. Little did we know that we had been invited for a celebration, the likes of which we had never seen in our lives before. I found the atmosphere to be strange. I couldn't put my finger on it. Then it suddenly dawned on me that no one was crying! Everyone sat quietly. I had witnessed many deaths in my family. The ambience had always been one of great grief. Wailing, shouting and calling out to the departed is the rule rather than the exception. And this was repeated with the arrival of every new relative.

I had no doubts that *Swamiji* was the single controlling factor.

We sat around *Amma* (*Swamiji's* mother) who was an inspiration to watch. She sat on the floor, next to the sofa in which *Swamiji* sat. There was an air of innocence and dignity in her demeanor. She aligned her wishes to whatever her son said. She exhibited a total childlike trust in Him. As she simply and beautifully put it: '*Swami ennodu irrukumpodu vera enna ma ennakku venum? Avar ellamay patthuparu, ma.*' (When *Swamiji* Himself is with me, what more can I ask for? He will take care of everything, *ma*.)

She showed a high level of spiritual maturity that is rare for a person, especially a woman born and brought up in a small, closed society.

I understood why *Swamiji* had chosen her to be His mother. He had mentioned that India's energy attracts higher-level beings and acts as the spiritual incubator for them when they descend on planet earth. In a similar way, I felt *Amma*, due to her extreme innocence and unshakeable spiritual strength was the womb, the incubator that had radiated the innate capacity to receive and nurture an enlightened being's exalted energy.

The whole day was suffused with an air of spiritual fervor. Even as people were trooping in to pay respects, the young ascetics, the *brahmacāri*s of the ashram, looking so majestically resplendent, performed *pūjā* in *Swamiji's* presence and with His participation: *Guru pūjā, Vraja homa, Nitya kirtans, ārati* and other ceremonies, as directed by *Swamiji* Himself.

Swamiji explained, 'When *Ayya* came up on stage and informed me that my father was no more, I paused awhile and related to his energy. I clearly saw that before his death, my father had gone into an enlightened state and had stayed there for at least 21 minutes. He had attained *mahāsamādhi*, the great liberation! Then he had relaxed beautifully into the all-pervading consciousness. I told *Ayya* to relax and carry on with the necessary arrangements. In those few moments of relating, I did whatever had to be done at the initial stage for the soul to move on. I had to take care of the people who had come for my blessings at the discourse. They too need me.'

Only a person in the *Paramahamsa* (supreme) state can be so unattachedly compassionate and unconditionally available at all times for those who seek Him, no matter what the situation. In those few moments, the teachings of Aṣṭāvakra - *you are by your nature unattached, renounced, liberated; you are the all-pervading, witnessing consciousness* - had been expressed through *Swamiji's* sheer body language.

The profound truths of the scriptures must be lived. Here, before our eyes was a living example. All of us - devotees, disciples, healers and *ācārya*s - were shown what it means to 'practice what you preach'. Masters do not teach. Their life is their teaching. If you are alert and awake around the master, you can learn within moments what years of poring over great philosophies cannot teach you.

Every now and then, *Swamiji* would go out, sit in the *veranda*, watch arrangements being made to receive people and speak with relations and friends. In those moments of reminiscing, he said with great fondness, 'My father was a V.I.P. (Very Important Person) in his own right in this town. Because of his innate generosity of spirit and his helping nature, he managed to have a great following. He was so considerate to everyone. Even the last moments he spent on planet earth have been done with care and consideration! In the same way that he did not disturb me when I was a mere boy on the spiritual path, so too in death he has chosen to cause me the least disturbance. In my busy schedule, I am relatively free for the next three days. He has chosen to rightly leave his body now! He could have gone when I was in America or during the *Ananda Ula* tour. What would have happened to all the programs, all the arrangements? Simply a beautiful soul! I have blessed him with the ultimate gift of enlightenment. His energy will never again be converted to matter. He has left his body smoothly, without pain. He is relaxed and relating with me. *Amma, nee kavalai padadhey, naa pathikirain.* (*Amma,* you don't worry. I will take care.)'

So saying, *Swamiji* stood up, walked to the glass coffin and very lovingly, with a beautiful smile on his face, blessed his father's body and energy. He would repeat this often, throughout the day.

The gentry of Tiruvannamalai were being exposed to the joyous dignity of death.

Hearing Him talk and watching His utterly relaxed, confident and authoritative body language, I realized we were sitting in a live classroom. He was living the truths that He had spoken of on so many occasions, in all those meditation programs. He showed us the way to receive death, the way to handle the dead and the living. No book can give this understanding, this kind of confidence.

I understood why He was particularly careful to maintaining a deeply joyous atmosphere. Why was He insistent that no one should weep and wail? As far as my understanding goes, when the soul leaves the body it is essential that the atmosphere is light, suffused with spiritual understanding, awareness, and a mood of deep celebration. Then we make it easier for the soul to move on smoothly to the next dimension.

This is the greatest gift of love we can give to anyone. This is the ultimate act of selflessness.

When we cry, when we grieve, we create such a heavy atmosphere that the soul struggles to leave. We cause an obstruction. This is the greatest act of cruelty that we can commit. And all the while, we suffer from the misconception that if we weep, we tell the departed how much we love him.

Actually, if we look deeply and honestly within ourselves, we see that we cry for the loss, the void that the person's death has caused in *our* life. Because, if we appreciate that death is the climax of life and not the end, we too will celebrate with that understanding. Then where is the room for tears?

When evening, s*andhya kāl,* arrived, the *ārati* – the offering of lit camphor and wicks, was performed to the sound of tinkling bells and the rhythmic clapping of the gathering. Everyone participated with great fervor. I sat next to the coffin. Each time I turned my gaze to my left, I looked directly at the face. I was surprised that at no time did I feel disturbed by this physical proximity to the dead body. In fact, more often than not we forgot that the body was there. Though it was placed in the center of the room, it was not holding centerstage. There was no exhibition of grief or trace of morbidity to keep us focused on the body.

I realized that as *Swamiji* was constantly keeping the group occupied with some aspect of spirituality, the mind was diverted from its habitual pattern of response to such situations. Our energies, instead of being tight and confined to our boundaries through fear and grief, were expanding and relating to the high level of enlightened energy present in the room. The moment of death can be a process of deep alchemy for the dying and the living. Since this blessed soul had attained *samādhi,* the energy it radiated, combined with the powerful vibrations of an enlightened master's presence, had the power to transform all those tuned to it. This was exactly what *Swamiji* was working on.

He did not want us to miss this huge opportunity that Existence was offering us.

In between all these extraordinary activities, *Swamiji* kept the normalcy of day-to-day activities going. We went for breakfast, came back, drank coffee served with polite hospitality, and then got into vehicles and performed *giri-vala* (circumambulating Aruṇācala, the holy hill of Tiruvannamalai). We went for lunch, had a shower; in short, the ordinariness of day-to-day life carried on. This in no way showed disrespect to the departed soul.

On the contrary, it showed an extremely mature understanding that death was one more event in life. It could be as simple as changing our old, worn out clothes for something new. That act of changing is death, that's all. If, while living, we had learnt the art of changing then we would carry the same attitude with us while dying. If we wish to die well, all we have to do is learn to live well.

Live fully, moment to moment, as if each moment is our last one. Then there is no room for regrets. We will have the spiritual understanding that death is neither frightening nor fascinating, as some naively think. It is simply a fact of life, which creates a great opportunity for the most profound and beneficial inner experiences to happen. It carries with it the potentiality to be the moment of final illumination.

Early next morning, around 5.30 am, we gathered in the main hall. *Swamiji* asked that the body be given its final bath and draped in *kāvi vastra* (saffron cloth usually worn by *sanyāsis*). At that moment I remembered: Once when *Swamiji* was returning from a tour of South India, his father jokingly told his eldest son, who too had come to visit the ashram, *'seekaram vaa da... sami varadukulla namba kazhambalam...paatarna nambazhayum samiyara panniduvaru...'* (Come quickly. Let us leave the ashram before *Swamiji* arrives. Otherwise, if He sees us, He will make us also *sanyāsis*!) It looked like Existence has a great sense of humor. She had the last laugh. I am sure that *Swamiji's* father would have joined in the laughter.

I noticed that there had not been any change in the physical condition of the body. Death had arrived on 12th evening and now it was 14th morning. The body was as intact as it had been on the first day that we had seen it. No doubt it was kept on ice; yet not a single change had happened, considering the low level of sophistication of that glass coffin and the heat of Tiruvannamalai. The face radiated the same sereneness; there was no odor of decay. The use of *agarbattis (*incense sticks*)* and room fresheners had stopped long ago.

I mused silently: Was it *Swamiji's* energy? Or was it the vibrations of the *pūja* and *ārati* performed at regular intervals? Or was it the group energy that was so profoundly calm and elevating? Perhaps it was a direct reflection of the *samādhi* state into which Śrī Arunācalānanda had entered before leaving the body completely. The separated ego with all its sense-residues had been transformed and purified at the moment of the final exit. So there was no odor. Only lightness and the bliss of the liberated soul suffused the air that we were breathing. It could be all these aspects acting together. I honestly didn't know. This was not time to seek clarifications. That understanding will happen when the need arises, automatically, without any kind of seeking or prompting. And of course, my ego never got tired of musing.

Once the necessary rituals were completed, *Swamiji* asked everyone who was not a healer or *ācārya* to pay respects and leave the room. Then, closing the doors and windows firmly, He asked Śrī Nitya Kīrtanānanda to play *ānanda darśan* music.

The room exploded to the beat of '*bomma bomma tha thaiya thaiya thaka…*' with everyone singing and clapping. *Swamiji* danced joyously, throwing tremendous energy all around. There was a great buildup of heat in the closed room. Then, He placed his *ājñā cakra* (energy center between the eyebrows) on His father's *ājñā cakra.* He then uttered the *mahāvākya* (great declaration)*: tat tvam asi, tat tvam asi, tat tvam asi, ahaṁ brahmāsmi,* *ahaṁ brahmāsmi, ahaṁ brahmāsmi* (Thou art That; I am the ultimate reality). Energy transfer must have surely taken place.

I cannot even begin to understand its meaning. Then, with absolute grace, He removed His turban and put it on His father's head. A *rudrākṣa* rosary was placed around his neck.

The moments that followed are frozen in time in our memories. Something in me gave way. I felt an ecstatic connectivity.

Śiva was no longer a mere concept for me. He danced before my eyes. I realized that the updated version of Śiva *is* Nithyananda. It blew my mind. Something in me died forever, for something else to bloom.

Later, just before the doors were opened to let people in, one healer echoed the feeling in all our hearts when he said, '*Swamiji*, if this is how death is going to be, I am ready to die now!'

The next moments were all about history being created in Tiruvannamalai. For the first time women were allowed to accompany the funeral procession to the cremation area. The bier was lifted onto the flower-bedecked vehicle. With *Swamiji* leading the way, women sang the beautifully evocative devotional lyrics of the *Arunachala Aksharamana Maalai* (the soul stirring hymn to Aruṇācala Śiva, composed by the enlightened master Bhagavān Śrī Ramaṇa Maharṣi) accompanying it on its last earthly journey.

The most poignant and unbelieving scene was that of *Amma*, the wife of the departed soul, walking alongside the vehicle, rhythmically clapping her hands to the beat of the devotional song. I do not think this happens in any strata of society, let alone in a small temple town like Tiruvannamalai. What astonishing courage! What progressive thinking, done not as an act of defiance or with the need to score some socially relevant points, but simply as an expression of implicit trust, inner steel and dignified grace!

When we reached the cremation area, *Swamiji* informed us that this was the land gifted by *Amma*'s father to start a Dhyanapeetam Center in

Tiruvannamalai. He revealed to the gathering that the first person to attend the Nithyananda Spurana Program and get enlightened before leaving the body was His father. It was only befitting that the body of a realized soul should be cremated here. When the pyre was readied, the mortal remains of Śrī Nitya Arunācalānanda Swami were placed on it. The way the body was positioned was symbolic. At one end was the sacred Aruṇācala Hill. At the other end was *Swamiji*, the enlightened master! The formless and the form on either side.

Can anyone ask for greater protection than this?

As the final moments arrived for the curtain to be drawn on this drama, people were given flowers to offer at the feet of the departed soul one last time. Then, *Swamiji* informed the gathered crowd that as a *sanyāsi* who had cut all family ties, He couldn't perform the last rites of his father as a son would traditionally be expected to do. However as a guru, it was His responsibility to conduct the rites of passage for His disciple. *Swamiji* recalled that when He had asked His father what kind of help he needed, His father had answered simply: '*Swami irunda podum.*' (If You are there, that is enough.)' *Swamiji* told us, 'At that moment, He became my disciple! That complete, total trust is enough. Nothing else is needed!'

Swamiji also declared that in the future, Nov 12th of every year, the death anniversary of Śrī Nitya Arunācalānanda Swami, will be celebrated within the Nithyananda Order as *Mahāparinirvāṇa day,* the day of enlightened souls, in memory of those who attain enlightenment and leave the body under *Swamiji's* grace. He promised that no matter where His disciples died, His presence would be there to perform the last rites. With such an amazing promise thundering in our beings, the last, lingering fear of death seemed to melt away…

This was a promise from none other than Śiva Himself.

As His father's energy had traveled directly from a conscious state to a superconscious one, without slipping into the unconscious coma state, and had remained in that exalted level for 21 minutes, he had become enlightened. Therefore, he could not be treated in the normal way. Also, since he had been conferred with *antima sanyās* (final renunciation and enlightenment) the body had to be cremated with honors conferred upon enlightened souls.

It was like a spiritual salute of honor to a departed war hero.

Just before the pyre was lit, *Swamiji* called His mother and brothers, and gave them each a sandalwood log to be placed on the mortal remains of the energy that had been a husband and father for many years. There was finality to that act. Then with cries of '*Śrī Nitya Arunācalānanda Swami Ki Jai*' (Hail to Śrī Nitya Arunācalānanda Swami) rending the air, *Swamiji* performed *ārati,* lit the funeral pyre and consigned it to flames, all with flowing grace and compassion.

The last cameo shot that I remember is of *Swamiji* putting His arm around His mother and hugging her to His side, acknowledging her trusting innocence and spiritual strength and courage.

He stood tall with His biological family around Him - son, brother, master, God.

I offer the writing of this whole experience as an act of deep gratitude, and as an expression of my love and respect to each and everyone reading this. If anything, it was your deep longing to 'experience the experience' that made this sharing possible.

In Nithyananda

MNM

BhagavadGītā

Secret Of Secrets

Rājavidyā-Rājaguhya Yogaḥ

Chapter 9

Logic can never
lead you to Self-realization.
Dissolution of logic will.
Devotion and trust are the keys
to this dissolution.

Secret Of Secrets

We are now at the halfway mark of the Bhagavad Gītā. Arjuna started in total confusion and dilemma. His questions were varied and repetitive. It was as if he did not listen to what Kṛṣṇa told him. As I said, questions arise from inner violence. They arise from the ego to prove one's correctness.

These questions gradually morph into doubts. Doubts are essential for any seeker. Doubt and faith are two sides of the same coin. Without doubt, we cannot develop faith. Blind faith is based upon social conditioning and will collapse under pressure. Real faith develops in the seeker when he sincerely questions spiritual truths. Raising sincere doubts before an enlightened master actually does a lot to integrate a person and strengthen his faith.

Kṛṣṇa sees the change happening within Arjuna. He feels Arjuna's inner violence and conflict is clearing up and that his individual consciousness is opening. The master is ready to change gears now and take the dialogue to the next level that is needed to address this change in attitude.

Now Kṛṣṇa reveals to Arjuna the greatest of all secrets, the secret about Himself.

Eternal And Easy

9.1 *Krṣṇa said:*
Arjuna, you trust Me and you are not envious of Me; I shall therefore impart to you this profound and secret wisdom and experience;
This will free you of all miseries of material existence.

9.2 *This knowledge is king of all knowledge and the greatest secret of all secrets.*
It is the purest knowledge, sacred, and gives direct perception of Self-realization.
It is eternal and easy to practice.

9.3 *Those who have no faith in this knowledge cannot attain Me, O conqueror of foes;*
They will return to birth and death in this material world.

Krṣṇa assures Arjuna with these verses. He says, 'My dear Arjuna, because you are never envious of Me, I shall impart to you this most confidential knowledge and realization, knowing which, you shall be relieved of the miseries of material existence.'

Krṣṇa says, 'Because you are never envious of Me.' Depending on the context, this verse can be taken to mean 'Because you are not envious of Me' or 'Because you have trust in Me.'

We may wonder how Arjuna could be envious of Krṣṇa. You don't know the ways in which the human mind works, especially since in our generation, we think of Arjuna as a human and Krṣṇa as divine. We accept Krṣṇa as God. However, when Krṣṇa was alive, people did not always accept that He is divine. In addition, Arjuna and Krṣṇa were close friends, so Arjuna treated Krṣṇa as a human and related to Him with human emotions.

We should first understand the background to understand this whole chapter as it is expressed.

The utimate knowledge

The very idea that Arjuna might be envious of Krṣṇa may make us surprised.

Honestly, whenever the masters were in the body, people never respected them. This problem always existed. Only after they left the body did people worship them. Actually, it is easy to worship a photograph, since no sacrifice is required. However, it is never easy to worship a living being. The living person will always be questioned and envied.

There is a beautiful one-liner:

During his life the grandfather is forced to live in the family outhouse. After his death he is brought into the house and respected, as a photograph!

As long as he is alive, he lives in the outhouse. Especially in India, every village home has a front porch. As long as he is alive, he lives there, or on the verandah in city houses. When he is dead, his photo is kept inside the prayer room. When he is alive, he has no place inside the house! However, once he dies, his photograph has a respected place inside the home.

Similarly, when a master is alive he is never understood, respected, or received. When he has left the body, it is easy to worship him.

A beautiful incident:

A group of devotees from Caitanya Mahāprabhu's (an enlightened master from India) birthplace, Māyāpūr, came to Rāmakrṣṇa. They told him, 'Oh master, we missed Caitanya Mahāprabhu. We could not see him. If we had that fortune, we would have become enlightened. We would have experienced devotion to Krṣṇa.'

Rāmakṛṣṇa laughed and said, 'When Caitanya was alive, many people went to him and complained, 'Oh Caitanya! We missed Kṛṣṇa. We could not see Kṛṣṇa. If we had seen Kṛṣṇa, we could have enjoyed the devotion, the energy!'

Rāmakṛṣṇa says, 'Open your eyes and see. Caitanya is here. Just as people went to Caitanya and talked about Kṛṣṇa, you come here and complain that you have missed Caitanya.'

Whenever masters are alive, it is difficult for people to accept their divinity. However, once they leave the body, people say, 'We missed Rāmakṛṣṇa,' 'We missed Ramana maharshi,' and so on. We complain about what we missed. We never realize what we have.

Here Kṛṣṇa says, 'Because you are never envious of Me, I will give you the ultimate secret.'

Understand, Kṛṣṇa is giving the ultimate secret. Once we know this secret, then there is no difference between the Divine and us.

In the business world, the leader usually never gives secrets to anyone. Corporate people maintain secrets. Here Kṛṣṇa says, 'I am not going to maintain any secrets. I am going to open the whole thing.' He says that knowledge is free. It is up to us to use it.

There is an important thing that people who live around the master should know. By and by, these disciples, instead of trying to achieve the state of the master, try to achieve the status of the master. State is different from status. The enlightened state of the master should be achieved, not the status that his enlightenment confers. When we work for status, we are in trouble.

Once I went to a college for a public lecture. It was a meditation program in Tamil Nadu. One young boy questioned me, 'Why should you be respected so much? After all, you are my age.' Of course, it is true. I am barely a few years older than him. He asked, 'Why do they shower so many roses at your feet when you come?' In India, spiritual masters are usually received with flowers wherever they go.

I had tried my best to advise the organizer of the program, 'Don't do these things. Don't offer flowers, especially since it is a college. Naturally I will face such questions,' yet the organizer, a devotee, wanted to somehow show his devotion. He took care of the arrangements and ensured there were flowers. The boy directly asked, 'Why should so many flowers be showered at your feet? Why should you be respected so much?' Of course it is jealousy.

The first thing I told him was this: 'I tried my best to avoid these arrangements. However, they have done it out of devotion. You only see the flowers that are showered now. You don't know how many thorns these feet have crossed and how many austerities this body has endured. So don't be envious of the status. Be envious of the state. Try to achieve the same state in which I live. Then you will be showered with everything. Achieve the state, not the status.'

When you see the status, you will be caught in jealousy. If you see the state, I will become an inspiration for you. I will be a role model. You will think, 'When he can achieve this, why not me?' I tell people that the one and only difference between an ordinary and an enlightened being is that an ordinary man is sleeping while an enlightened person is awakened. The consciousness is the same.

Understand, 'Whether you believe it or not, accept it or not, realize it or not, you *are* God. You have two choices. You can either sleep as long as you want to without experiencing this truth, or you can make the conscious choice to experience your enlightenment. But the truth is, 'You are That.'

Here, Kṛṣṇa says, 'Because you never try to achieve my status, I am trying to give you my state.' The person who never tries to achieve the status of the master achieves the state of the master. First, state comes. Then, status follows. If we try to create the status, the state will never be achieved.

Rāmakṛṣṇa says, 'First God, then the world.' The world is like a shadow. Status is like a shadow. If we run after it, we can never grab it, no matter how much we chase it; however, if we walk on the path, it simply follows. The outer world is like a shadow. Even if we run after it, we will never be able to catch and hold onto it. Go towards the state, status will follow you.

Here Kṛṣṇa says, 'Because you are never jealous, never envious of My status and Me, I give you the ultimate secret of this state.' And I tell you, this *is* the ultimate secret. And He says, 'Knowing which, you shall be relieved of the miseries of material existence.'

What are the miseries of material existence? Whether we have something or not, it is misery. If we don't have, then the misery is, 'I don't have.' If we have, then we have the misery, 'I must protect it.'

The king of all knowledge

Yoga means achieving. *Kṣema* means protecting or preserving. Both are miseries. Whether we have or not, it is misery.

Kṛṣṇa says that the miseries of having wealth and not having wealth, both disappear by knowing this secret. This is the ultimate secret that needs to be understood. Knowledge of this secret liberates you.

He says, 'This knowledge is the king of all knowledge. The greatest secret of all secrets, it is the purest knowledge and because it gives direct perception of the Self by realization, it is the perfection of religion. It is everlasting and it is joyfully performed.'

See, religion or a spiritual path should have three characteristics. First, it should clearly describe the goal of life. Next, it should clearly give you the path to achieve the goal. Third, it should make you happy to travel in that path. The path itself should be joyful.

A small story:

Some herbal doctors advertised with billboards claiming they can cure anything. One doctor's billboard said he could cure all diseases that we know the names of, as well as all diseases that we don't know the names of. He put up a billboard with all these claims. One person came with a disease.

The doctor asked, 'What is your disease?'

This person said, 'I don't know the name. Please diagnose it yourself.'

The doctor tried his best to diagnose. However, he was unable to determine the disease. But he had put up the big advertisement, so he had to cure. There was no other way. So he gave some medicine. The medicine was: 'Swallow a crowbar without it touching your teeth and drink three liters of water. You will be cured!'

What kind of medicine is this? The medicine clearly shows that the person will not be cured! In the same way, our solution or path should not be impractical. If it is impractical, naturally, we cannot practice.

So here, Kṛṣṇa says, 'It is eternal,' meaning that the result that we achieve is everlasting. It is easy. We don't need to struggle for it. All we need to do is to realize the secret.

If it is going to help so much then why is it a secret? Why not let the whole world use it? It is important for us to understand this point.

The ultimate knowledge is not for the masses. Masses always get stuck with small things and shallow entertainment. If we run a cinema theatre, you can see how such a big crowd gathers! Only a few hundred people are here today because we built only a temple. Temples are for the chosen few. We need intelligence to enter spirituality. It is not for everyone.

Yesterday one lady asked, '*Swamiji*, my husband does not accept or understand the path of spirituality that I am traveling. Coming to this program is important to me. However, it is difficult for my husband to come to terms with it. Do you have a suggestion to help bridge this gap?'

How to make the husband or wife spiritual? When people ask me this question, I laugh and ask them, 'If I knew this secret, do you think I would have become a *sanyāsi* and renounced the material world!' Honestly, the answer is that it has to happen on its own from within the person.

All you can do is give him some intelligence about life. Please don't ask him to meditate or come to the temple. Talk to him about life. Ask him, 'What kind of a life are we leading? What are we doing? Again and again, we are caught in the same rut.' All we can do is to give intelligence about life in this fashion. Nothing else can be done.

Only by intelligence can a man come to spirituality. That is why this is preserved as a secret. If this spiritual intelligence is given to all, without bothering about the qualifications of the receiver, the person who receives will harm himself and others, also. First, he harms himself if he has not completely understood it. For example, what will a criminal do if he is told, 'You are God.' He will think, 'I am God. So let me do whatever I want to.' He misuses the knowledge. He abuses it and harms himself.

A person who experiences God radiates compassion, simplicity and innocence. Divine qualities express through him. We see a beautiful innocent shine in him. He never hurts anybody.

If we are relaxed, blissful, in a good mood, and our co-worker makes a mistake, do we shout at him? No. We will say, 'Alright, leave it. What to do?' However, if we are in an irritable mood, then nobody needs to make a mistake. We shout at everyone for no reason. We are just waiting to burst.

Our mood decides our action. If we are blissful, we never do anything wrong. If we are in a hellish mood, we always make mistakes.

Don't think people go to hell after making mistakes. No! We make mistakes because we are in hell. We do the right action because we are blissful. If this knowledge is given to all, including those who don't have the maturity, naturally they harm themselves and others. They say, 'I am God. I will do whatever I want.' That is why this knowledge is kept as a secret.

It is like terrorists knowing the secret of the atom bomb. It is dangerous for them *and* the world. Similarly, this is the secret of the inner world. If the person who is not qualified knows this secret, it is dangerous for him.

That is why He says, 'this king of secrets is the king of knowledge.' Kṛṣṇa reveals the secret only to qualified people.

Christ declared, 'I am the Son of God.' It is true, what Jesus declared is from the experience of his enlightenment. He experienced heaven. That is why He clearly expressed, 'I am the Son of God.' But there was only one thing there: He spoke about the inner kingdom. The people thought that He was trying to snatch the outer kingdom from the rulers. Jesus spoke about a totally different truth; people understood it in a totally different way. For this He was crucified. The whole thing is a simple misunderstanding!

In this chapter Kṛṣṇa says, 'I am something more than God. Whatever you think of as God rests in Me. All created beings rest in Me.' But He is not crucified, because He declares this truth to a person who understands and accepts it. We need to see whether a person is mature enough to receive the truth before we share it.

Here, Kṛṣṇa says it is a secret, because it can be delivered only to a person qualified to receive it. However, these chapters are intimate secrets delivered only from the master to a qualified disciple who really wants the knowledge.

One person asked me, '*Swamiji*, please teach me about God. Give me enlightenment.' I told him, 'See, it is time for *prasād* (food offered to God and eaten by devotees with His blessings). Please go and eat in the ashram. They will give you *prasād*. Please, eat and come back. I will talk to you in the evening session.'

He immediately said, 'No *Swamiji*! I must leave by the next bus. I only have half an hour left. In this half an hour please tell me about God.'

In half an hour what can I tell him and what will he understand? God cannot be given like instant coffee! Coffee can be instant, but not God! We need to realize God; we need a little patience. The more we hurry, the more we will delay. Speed is not the technique for the inner world. The more we hurry, the more we delay. The hurrying postpones the experience. It will not let us relax. That is why Kṛṣṇa says that these secrets can be told only to a person who is really intimate, and desires to know.

Beautiful words! All our scriptures are called *Upaniṣad*. Even Gītā is called *Upaniṣad*. The word *Upaniṣad* literally means 'sitting down near someone'. It refers to the teaching style of a traditional vedic school or *gurukul* of ancient India, where students sat by their master to learn. This is how knowledge was imparted. It was transmitted in close groups in a trusted environment. It was a communion of beings wherein the experience of one was experienced by the other.

The path to Self-realization

In our home we keep everything prepared for our worldly life: a bed, the kitchen, a dining table. We also collect luxurious things like jewelry. Whatever we need for the worldly life and comforts, we collect and store.

Just as we collect things for the outer space, we need to collect knowledge for our inner space: life solutions. If we feel depressed or if we face some adverse situation, how are we to react? We need knowledge of the inner space to handle it.

Collecting life solutions is what Kṛṣṇa calls *jñāna yajñya.* What is *nitya* (eternal) and what is *anitya* (temporary)? What is *satya* (truth) and what is *asatya* (falsehood)? Acquiring all this understanding is *jñāna yajñya.*

Jñāna refers to higher knowledge and *yajñya* refers to the purification process that leads to this higher knowledge. What Kṛṣṇa means through *jñāna yajñya* is the spiritual path that leads one to Self-realization. This realization of the deepest truths about oneself happens through a combination of two things: understanding about similar spiritual experiences by observing others, and our own efforts to contemplate upon these experiences so that they are reproduced within.

Please focus on the life solutions offered by great masters while gathering knowledge. I request that people read books that give life solutions for at least half an hour every day, books of Rāmakṛṣṇa, Vivekānanda , books of great masters. We have the book *Guaranteed Solutions* based on my teachings in the Life Bliss Programs. Spend at least half an hour every day reading books based on the life and teachings of enlightened masters.

If we can't spend half an hour reading, then listen to audio CDs in the car. In the USA we spend at least one hour a day driving. Even to shop for basic groceries we drive at least one hour. Don't waste that time. Always have some audio CDs that give life solutions in the car.

It is not that it must be my lectures. Read, watch, or listen to anything that gives insight into leading a better life. Let that one hour become your spiritual journey. Add more and more life solutions into your inner space.

I tell you one thing: A life solution may suddenly come up at the time of need and can reduce the depth of your depression. The moment a life solution erupts from our inner consciousness, the depth of our depression can be immediately reduced. The low curve is straightened out and we move up in spirit. That is why I am telling you to make driving your *jñāna yajñya*. Let that time be used for collecting life solutions. Whether you understand everything or not, just listen. Let that become your habit. Automatically those life solutions stay in your inner space. You will be surprised how they will come to your aid when you need them!

If we don't spend time finding life solutions, we spend time finding problems. Even if we don't have problems, we will create problems! If we have problems, we worry. If we don't have problems we think, 'Today everything is going well. I don't know what will happen tomorrow!' We strongly believe that if we have no problems today, we will have problems tomorrow. It becomes a strong faith in us.

Whether we have problems or not, we worry. Better not to allow the mind to worry. Listen to something that gives life solutions. Let that hour become *jñāna yajñya* in our lives.

Kṛṣṇa says that doing *jñāna yajñya* is one step. Understanding that the whole cosmos is energy is one step. If we understand that whatever exists is energy, automatically fear will be taken away from our being. The next question is, 'How can we say that whatever exists is energy, *Swamiji*? It is impossible. All these things are good to listen to, but are not practical to practice!'

Our mind never accepts that these things can be practiced and experienced. So Kṛṣṇa continues. He goes on talking and comes out with the basic secrets.

Here Kṛṣṇa gives the qualification of people who can attain Him. When I say 'Him', it is the universal energy I am referring to. In the first two verses Kṛṣṇa says, 'It is a great truth that I am going to tell and it is a secret that I am revealing to you.' Now He lets Arjuna know what kind of people can know the secret.

He says people who do not have faith in His teachings go back to the path of rebirth without attaining Him. He says the qualification required is to have faith in His teachings. Only those people can come out of the vicious cycle of birth and death.

Faith is one of the most important things, especially in the spiritual path. Whenever an enlightened master speaks, every word he utters is the Absolute Truth.

There are three possible levels of faith you put in what a master says. With the first level, you can have doubt. You doubt what I say, because you can't comprehend what I say.

You can have doubts. Only if you have doubts, you question what I say. However, you should find out if those doubts are genuine, or is it your mind playing a game. As long as you question to know the truth out of curiosity, it is fine. In my discourses, I encourage people to ask questions and to raise doubts. Only then can you fully internalize.

The second level is when you believe whatever I say. This is dangerous. Believing whatever I say without understanding and experiencing it for yourself is dangerous. This creates a weak foundation. If someone questions you on your belief, you will be unable to stand by it.

I know lots of people who call themselves my devotees. When I ask whether they meditate, they stammer, 'No *Swamiji*. There is no time.' Then they say, 'But I pray to you everyday, *Swamiji*. I offer fresh flowers and incense sticks.' They talk as if they do me a big favor. They are believers. Only when they meditate will they experience what I speak about.

The third approach is trust. When you trust me, you accept what I say even though you have doubts. However, you are willing to break that wall and try to experience what I am saying. You build your foundation and make it strong, because you trust me. This is the way faith should develop. First you trust me, then you try exploring the truths I share and when you have a glimpse of the truth, you believe me with a stronger foundation. Now nobody can shake you, because you have developed a strong base. You have done the work yourself.

Here, Kṛṣṇa talks about faith in *dharma,* His teachings. When Kṛṣṇa says *dharma,* He means anything that leads us to a higher level of consciousness. Man without consciousness is an animal, a *dānava.* In Hindu epics there are two types of people: *mānava* and *dānava,* humans and non-humans. The first category has faith in *dharma* and a higher level of consciousness. *Dānava* are animals. They do not have faith in any *dharma,* so their level of consciousness is low.

The only difference between man and an animal is the seed of consciousness implanted in us. We must water this seed and allow it to germinate. We must nurture this sapling to flower into a fully-grown tree. We need faith in *dharma* for this tree of consciousness to happen in us. Kṛṣṇa clearly says that we must allow consciousness to flower in us, and in order to do that we must have faith in *dharma.*

When we have internalized His *dharma* in everything that we do, our consciousness automatically blossoms. When we reach that state of consciousness, we merge with universal consciousness and then we are free from the cycle of birth and death.

So Kṛṣṇa gives a technique. He says, 'Have faith in *dharma* and it will lead you to the Ultimate.'

Rest In Me

9.4 *The entire universe is pervaded by Me, in My formless form.*
All beings are based in Me, but I am not in them.

9.5 *Look at My mystic powers!*
I create and sustain all living entities but do not depend on them, nor do they depend on Me.

9.6 *As the mighty wind, blowing everywhere, always rests in eternal space,*
All beings rest in Me.

9.7 *O son of Kuntī, at the end of every age all beings merge into Me,*
At the beginning of every new Age I create them again.

9.8 *My material nature creates the beings again and again.*
They are controlled by My material nature.

It is time to reveal the secrets. Kṛṣṇa starts: 'By Me, in my formless form, this entire universe is pervaded. All beings are in Me but I am not in them.'

Before entering further into this verse, the meaning of the verse should be understood.

I want to tell you about my meeting with Charles Townes, a Nobel Laureate and a great scientist. He discovered something related to LASER and MASER.

I asked him, 'How did you discover? How did this truth happen in your being?'

He answered, '*Swamiji*, to tell you honestly, I was relaxing in a park in Washington. It was early morning, about six a.m. I was supposed to give a lecture on this subject to a group that day at nine a.m. I tried my best to recollect everything. I was completely frustrated, because I could not achieve much. Suddenly like a revelation, as an intuition, the conclusion was revealed to me! The whole truth came into my consciousness. I discovered it! I immediately penned down what I got.'

And he says, 'I then realized I had a difficulty: I knew the conclusion, the truth, but not the steps! I didn't know the logical steps to arrive at that conclusion! So after that, I needed to think and develop the logical steps. Only then could I present it to others. Like an intuition, suddenly, it happened. It had been revealed to me.'

Even Albert Einstein said, 'The theory of relativity was revealed in deep meditation. It was like sitting on the edge of a light particle and traveling in space. It came as an intuition.'

Actually, even this experience is not a big thing. The truth, the important thing is this: I asked Charles Townes, 'How did you feel when it happened to you, when the revelation happened to you?' Because what he experienced was intuition just as our sages experienced.

He said, '*Swamiji*, I don't know how to exactly express those things; however, one thing is certain: from that moment onwards, I know for sure that the whole universe is intelligence!'

This is the truth! The whole universe is pure intelligence, not dead matter. It is not an accident. It can respond and react to our thoughts. This is an important and basic understanding. The moment we understand that we are inside the energy that is intelligence, we immediately settle into a deep relaxation.

The moment we experience, we understand that we are under the guidance of an intelligent energy. We don't need to struggle or stress ourselves. We don't need to torture ourselves with insecurity problems and with unnecessary worries.

Actually, all our problems and stresses arise because we think *we* do everything. We think *we* are responsible for everything that happens around us. We think the universe runs because of us. Understand, the universe runs in spite of us! We should understand that the universe is intelligent and it responds to our thoughts. We can unload all our troubles, including the extra responsibility of thinking that *we* do everything.

This does not mean that we just sit and relax and say, 'Okay, the universe is intelligence. It will take care of everything.' This is laziness and escapism. We still must do what we need to do. We should still work; however, we can enjoy the process. You see, we think of the results all the time and never enjoy the process of doing that work. When we enjoy the process and trust the universal intelligence, thoughts of fear and greed will disappear. We will let the universe take care of the results. Kṛṣṇa says elsewhere, 'You do what you have to. But surrender the results to Me.' When He says 'Me,' He refers to the universal consciousness or intelligence.

This is what Kṛṣṇa means in the next verse when He says that the beings do not depend on Him, nor does He depend on them. Of course, it is clear that the universe does not depend upon us, yet, how can He say that we do not depend upon the Universe? What He means is this: it is not a passive and lazy dependence of letting everything happen while we sit idle. It is an active understanding. One does what one must do as part of his life process but without attachment and ownership.

One way or the other, we are in this universe. Because the universe is intelligence, it responds to our thoughts. It makes things happen. Since we are part of this universe, just flow with the energy of the universe. If this understanding penetrates our life, it is enough!

If we know the universe is intelligence, we never question how life unfolds. We don't say, 'I am moral. But I see people who don't live morally living luxuriously. Yet I always suffer!' We never have these frustrations because we know the cosmic intelligence will take care ultimately. Whoever is immoral will naturally face the consequences, because intelligence takes care. In the same way, if we are honest, integrated, and living a spiritual life, we will live a beautiful life.

Don't think the cosmos is just matter. If we think the cosmos is matter, we are materialistic. If we understand that the cosmos is intelligence, we are spiritual.

The only difference between the materialistic and spiritual person is that the materialist thinks the whole thing is material. The spiritual person understands that the whole thing is energy. When we understand this, a tremendous relaxation and bliss consciousness happens to us.

Understand that bliss is not just a mood. It is our very consciousness. One devotee asked, 'Bliss comes and goes, what to do?' I explained, 'You are having initial glimpses of bliss. Through your mind, you are trying to touch the bliss. Just relax, that's all.'

Once we understand this secret, a deep relaxation happens to us. In such a deep relaxation we straightaway experience bliss consciousness.

Kṛṣṇa says, 'By My formless form, this entire universe is pervaded. All beings are in Me.' He speaks of cosmic intelligence.

Be very clear, such a big Universe is moving and happening. All the planets move around the sun. Each planet has its own moons. Now the latest discovery is a planet called sedna in our solar system, further away from Pluto. They have also discovered a neighboring solar system called Cygnus that has three suns.

So now we cannot say *nava graha,* (nine major heavenly bodies as defined in Hindu mythology) we must say *dasa graha* (ten major heavenly bodies)!

There are so many suns, moons and planets. However, each one travels in its route properly. No traffic police! Accidents are rare. Unless intelligence runs the whole thing, do you think things can happen so beautifully? And even on this planet earth, see how the whole thing is beautiful! Everything is in order. Only wherever human beings live, there is chaos! Even in chaos, the Divine creates order.

We need to understand that the whole universe is intelligence. This intelligence responds to our thoughts. When we imbibe this, then we naturally experience a deep peace. As long as we believe the world is material, we create more and more violence because we live materially. Materially means that we must snatch from others. Only a person who experiences, who understands that the whole thing is energy, intelligence, only he can relax.

Let me repeat the next verse. He says, 'Understand that as the mighty wind blowing everywhere rests in the sky, all created beings rest in Me.' Please understand this concept. He says, 'Just as the wind rests in the sky energy.' We know earth is energy. Take a stone. If a stone is thrown at us, we know the energy behind that stone. We know the energy of water. Whoever knows about the waters that devastated New Orleans knows the energy of water! Next is *agni*, fire. All of us know the power of fire. Next, air: storms, hurricanes, tornados. We know the power of air.

In the same way, *ākāśa* (space or ether) is also energy. We do not know the power of *ākāśa*, because it does not directly impact our lives. The collective energy of the universe is *ākāśa*. It is also related to collective negativity, collective poison.

When the earth element is disturbed only one person suffers. For example, if our food is poisoned, we alone suffer. If water is poisoned, the whole region, whoever uses it, suffers. If whatever creates fire in us is corrupted, a big group suffers. We can use medicines as an example for fire because medicines keep the fire inside us alive. To keep us healthy, we need medicines. If medicines are corrupted, people who take the medicines suffer. If chemicals pollute the air, the whole country suffers. But if space, *ākāśa,* is polluted, the whole world suffers.

Corruption at higher levels of energy creates suffering for more and more people. The higher the level of energy that is corrupted, the number of people suffering is more. Our thoughts corrupt space. Because ether or space is so subtle, we cannot feel the happenings in the space of ether. We feel the happenings in the other four spaces: earth, water, fire, and air;

however, we fail to understand that space is also energy, a power. The subtler it is, the more powerful and energetic it becomes.

Levels of space

There are three levels of space. The first level is *ghaṭākāśa,* which is contained within our body. We limit our whole understanding of everything around us to this body. We think we are only this body and nothing else. This is the lowest level.

The next level is *cidākāśa.* This space refers to what our mind perceives as the world. Let's say we are sitting here but our mind is in Los Angeles. Then that (Los Angeles) becomes our *cidākāśa,* the space perceived by our mind. The space that our mind operates in is *cidākāśa.*

The third, and final level, is *mahākāśa.* The whole cosmos forms the *mahākāśa.* This is the ultimate level. This is the level where everything that we see as different becomes one.

Now, if something happens inside our body, we immediately feel it. If we are hurt, we see the blood flow. We clearly see and feel any disturbance or event in *ghaṭākāśa.* This event happens at a gross level.

When we go to the next level, *cidākāśa,* events that change this space are subtle. Our thoughts affect *cidākāśa.* Whether we believe it or not, our thoughts have a huge effect on the external world. Every thought is energy. It manifests as something in the external world, but we are unaware of the effect. The effect is subtle. That our mind cannot see what happens is because of those thoughts we entertained.

So, as we advance one level higher, the changes become more subtle, but the effect is more powerful. In *ghaṭākāśa,* the effect is limited to our body. In *cidākāśa,* our thoughts affect the space around us. The effect is more widespread.

Now the highest level is *mahākāśa.* This level is subtler than *cidākāśa.* Any change here affects the whole universe. When we enter this space, we realize the Ultimate Truth. We merge with everything, with the whole cosmos.

The fifth element, ether, is like *mahākāśa*. Actually they are the same. Ether is everywhere. The problem is we don't know it. *Mahākāśa* pervades everything. We are just not aware of it. This space takes any shape and any form. Even in a vacuum, it is there.

Understand this: If water is compressed by a compressor it becomes energy. If air is compressed by a compressor it can even move a train. In the same way, if ether is compressed in a particular space, again that becomes energy.

Like earth, ether can be handled. It can be used in different forms and shapes. Certain techniques allow us to use the ether energy to its maximum level. When ether is put in one particular size – inside that room or inside that space – whoever lives there will be controlled by that ether and the ether is in turn controlled by them. Their thoughts affect the ether and the ether affects their thoughts.

This concept of using the energy of space, or ether, is the basis of *vāstu śāstra,* an ancient vedic science related to the science of architecture. We can live in harmony with the universal energy by constructing dwellings in a manner that fits in with the spatial energy of the universe. *Vāstu śāstra* lays down details for where various activity spaces should be located in a dwelling, as well as the direction. It tells where the kitchen should be located in a house, where fire resides, and so on.

Kṛṣṇa says, 'How the wind rests in the space, in the same way the universe rests in Me.'

Don't think space is emptiness. It is energy. Just as the air rests in the space, our being, the whole universe including our being, we all rest in the Divine. Kṛṣṇa says, 'All beings rest in Me.'

Can you see why Kṛṣṇa calls all that He is speaking of a secret? He is being very careful as to whom He is telling this secret. He wants to tell all this to a qualified person, Arjuna, who is both a friend and a disciple. He knows now that Arjuna is ready to take in this secret.

Actually, till this point Kṛṣṇa has slowly prepared Arjuna. Now He knows Arjuna is ready to take in some truths of this universe. In these two verses, Kṛṣṇa talks about the creation and destruction of the universe. He makes bold statements. Only an enlightened master can make such bold statements because he speaks from experience. Some people do not agree with what I say. They think their own understandings are correct. When they tell me, '*Swamiji*, how can you say that? In so-and-so book, it is written like this,' I laugh and let it pass.

First of all, they did not understand what exactly was written in those scriptures and then they tell me I am wrong. What can be done? Even if I argue, they won't listen. All the old people are dangerous! Here Kṛṣṇa makes bold statements and truths and He knows Arjuna is ready to take in those truths. He talks about the creation of the universe. In the first verse Kṛṣṇa says, 'The whole material manifestation enters into Him when the universe is destroyed and He projects it again to create the universe.'

Understand that when Kṛṣṇa says, 'The universe enters Me,' He refers to the cosmic Kṛṣṇa, the cosmic consciousness. Let us try to understand this very deeply.

For a long time, the Big Bang theory was used to explain the creation of the universe. It said that there was a big ball of fire and an explosion. After the explosion some smaller parts cooled down to become planets, meteors and asteroids. Bigger parts stayed on as stars and suns. In the theory of evolution on planet earth Darwin talks about how life originated.

However, modern scientific findings go towards what ancient Indian scriptures, the *Upaniṣads*, said thousands of years ago. According to the *Taittirīya upaniṣad*, first there was ether. From ether, came air. From air, came fire. Then water appeared, and finally earth appeared. From earth, other living beings appeared.

Actually, this order shows the process of evolution from a subtle form of energy to a gross form. We feel gross forms through the senses, however, as it goes to subtler forms of energy, we must experience it. As the energy goes from gross to subtle, the way we experience it changes. Earth is tangible matter; ether is intangible energy. The subtlest form of energy is ether and we can only experience this through meditation.

Kṛṣṇa says at the end of each age, called a *kalpa* in Sanskrit, the materially manifested Universe, with all its creations, merges back into Him. If we analyze the Big Bang theory, the first question we ask is, 'Where did the ball of fire come from?' The Big Bang theory does not answer this fundamental question. However Kṛṣṇa answers this question in these verses. Science has now proven that the vacuum has something in it. The subtlest form of energy, ether, is present in the vacuum.

This whole Universe was created from ether and it goes back into ether again. All that we see outside as the material world is the manifestation of this subtle form of energy. The material world is the gross form of energy that we can see.

When Kṛṣṇa says, 'All material manifestation enters Me,' He means, it enters the universal consciousness. Everything we see and feel using our senses is part of the universal consciousness. The problem is that we see it only as matter.

If we see things as matter, we are caught up in that level only. As long as we think that they are matter, we run after them. Our mind says, 'These things will make you happy. Go and get them.' When we get this thought, the rat race starts, and our suffering starts.

When we understand that whatever we see and feel are only material manifestations of the subtle energy, we operate in a different plane. We see the futility of the race we are running. We realize that they are a projection of our own inner self.

All material things that we see are a manifestation of our inner self. Our desires and thoughts are projected as the materials that we see. However, in actual fact, there is no such thing as material, separate, and independent things. Everything is one; everything is energy.

Kṛṣṇa says that only He can create and destroy this universe at His will. This whole universe is a manifestation or a projection of our own self. Someone said, 'We make our own world.' This sentence has a deep meaning. All that we see as the world or universe is what we create. All relationships are projections of either our insecurities or our desires. We create our world through our needs or desires. Only an enlightened being sees the real truth, as it is. Once we understand everything is a mirror image of our own self, we become enlightened.

In these two verses, Kṛṣṇa says this truth clearly. Every material manifestation is created by Him and goes back into Him. He says only He can create and destroy it at His will, which means the world that we see, the universe that we perceive, is a projection of our own Self.

How To Be Unattached

9.9 *O Dhañanjaya, all this work does not bind Me.*
I am ever unattached and indifferent.

9.10 *The material nature of* prakṛti *works under My direction,*
O Son of Kuntī, and creates all moving and unmoving
beings through My energy of māyā.
By its rule this manifestation is created and annihilated
again and again.

9.11 *Fools deride Me when I descend in the human form.*
They do not know My transcendental nature and My
supreme dominion over all that is.

9.12 *Those who are thus deluded are demonic and atheistic.*
In their deluded condition, their hopes for liberation, their
result-oriented actions and their culture of knowledge
become false and useless.

Being attached or bound to what we do or what we have is a major hurdle in realizing our Self. Kṛṣṇa is not bound to this universe. This is the reason, He says, that keeps Him unaffected when the universe is created and when it is destroyed.

The whole universe is being born out of Him and it is getting destroyed. Even then He is not affected, because He is not bound to the universe. It is because He is a mere spectator.

Let us understand this in the context of daily life. When we start to internalize these great truths in small things that we do, a great change happens in us. Kṛṣṇa speaks in terms of the universe being created and destroyed from universal consciousness. We can apply them to day-to-day activities.

When we understand this truth, we feel a great sense of liberation. You see, we become attached or bound to what we have. We think that all we have is ours. When we create that attachment, we create a strong bond. Then the problem has started.

Drop your attachment

Our material possessions create greed and fear in us. We attach so much importance to them that getting more and more of them becomes our only goal. Naturally when we have so much, we create a fear of losing them. The problem is we associate ourselves with material possessions. Again and again, we run after them and forget who we are. So many people are in the rat race. They spend their lives accumulating money. And at the end of their life, they regret: they wonder what they have done in their lives.

This is one kind of attachment. There is another kind of attachment. We are attached to people. We create strong bonds in relationships. We start possessing people. It becomes so strong that we suffer when someone dies. We become so dependent on persons that our whole life seems to lose meaning when they die.

Actually, in this kind of bondage, we define ourselves based on the opinions of other people. We energize ourselves based on others. So we constantly hold on to that relationship because it gives us energy. So when a person dies, we feel depressed because whatever we were holding to very tightly was the source of energy for us. Now it is no longer there. So our whole system is shaken.

Now there is the third kind of bondage. It is related to our thoughts and emotions. Whenever something happens, we start linking it with our past and start fantasizing about the future. When a thought arises, we link up that thought with other thoughts.

None of the thoughts are linked to each other. We create a shaft binding all these thoughts. Each thought is like a bubble in a fish tank: unrelated, unconnected and disjointed. However we create a shaft and link them up. We attach ourselves with that shaft and start experiencing them. We let the thoughts control us.

In the same way, we create a shaft of all our pains and all our joys. If we see that our pain shaft is longer than the joy shaft, we conclude that we had a painful life. Otherwise, we say we have a happy life. Yet if we look deeply, each of the pains is completely unconnected and disjointed.

For example, the headache that you experience today is not related to the headache that you had one week ago. The headache that you had one week ago is not related to the headache that you felt one month ago. But we connect all these and say we have always had headaches. We create a shaft through all these pains and come to a conclusion.

Here Kṛṣṇa says He is neutral. How do we get ourselves unconnected from these attachments? Please understand that being unconnected from material possessions does not mean you leave everything and go away or break your relationships. Being neutral or unconnected has a deep meaning: it means being a spectator. When you watch a movie, you watch something on the screen. Do you become an actor in that movie? No. You watch it and let it go.

In the same way, when we watch as a spectator, we get detached from our attachments. When we watch our materialistic wealth, we will not run after it. When that is the attitude, the universe starts showering. The results happen of their own accord. The materialistic wealth comes on its own.

In relationships, also, we must be a spectator. When we stop seeing someone as a possession and when we become a spectator to the relationship, our dependency on that person and expectations from that person drop. Then there is no give and take in the relationship. There is only giving. The relationship becomes stronger.

When we become a spectator to our thoughts and emotions, we feel a great sense of liberation. All we have to do is break the shaft that we create between different unconnected thoughts and emotions. When we see thoughts like passing clouds in the sky, we stop associating ourselves with them, we are no longer controlled by them.

Being a spectator to thoughts does not mean that we suppress or destroy thoughts. By being a spectator we remain unaffected and unattached to what happens in and around us. This is the truth. If we can internalize this completely, we will be enlightened this very minute!

Kṛṣṇa says that, although He is a mere spectator, everything happens under His supervision. Here He shows His authority. He says the material world is created and annihilated according to His will through the power of *prakṛti*, Nature, and the energy of *māyā*, Illusion. Kṛṣṇa wants to clearly get this idea across to Arjuna. The whole material manifestation is a projection of the energy of universal consciousness. This is what is reflected within us in our individual consciousness. We create what we see and what we wish to see.

Kṛṣṇa says, 'I am the supreme power.' Everything happens under His supervision. Whatever happens is a drama of creation and annihilation, through Nature and Illusion. Kṛṣṇa, the director and producer of this cosmic drama, stands unmoved as a spectator.

This truth is reflected within us, too. We create and destroy ourselves. Everything, our happiness, our pains, our fantasies, our sorrows, our relationships are created by us. If we see from a higher level, we influence the whole universe. Kṛṣṇa shows how powerful our inner Self is. Whether we believe it or not, it is the truth. We create everything that we see, feel and hear. That is the power of our inner Self. Yet we do not stay detached the way Kṛṣṇa does.

Our thoughts and inner chatter have a tremendous impact. The cosmic consciousness responds to our thoughts. What we think and how we think affects what happens around us.

You have seen people who always shout and yell at others. Some people keep shaking their legs. All this happens because of inner restlessness. If something goes wrong, we blame others. All this is because there is so much restlessness inside us. However instead of looking inside, we blame others.

We see negativity around us because there are negativities inside us. Because of such thoughts inside us, we project them outside by becoming irritated at small things. This is how we create our own world. Because of our thoughts and inner chatter, we create a world full of negativities outside.

When we observe children, they are always blissful. In children there is no inner chatter. The world they project or manifest outside is blissful. They create a beautiful world, because they do not have negativities inside them. Understand, a person is blissful not because of what happens outside him: it is because of what is inside him.

One more important thing: there is a difference between being happy and being blissful. Happiness happens inside because of external factors. If suddenly the external source disappears, our happiness also disappears. So our internal state is affected by an external source. The outer world is affecting our inner world.

Being blissful does not depend on external sources. If we are at peace internally, we express that bliss. No external event affects this state. Bliss is eternal; happiness is temporary. When we are blissful inside, we project the same bliss outside. When we are in that state, we enjoy everything that happens outside us.

As we enjoy the external material manifestation of our inner bliss as a spectator, it is fine. When we try to possess that bliss, that bliss is gone. It disappears because our mind has come in. So in this verse Kṛṣṇa tells us clearly that we create our own world. The material manifestation is solely because of our inner Self, and nothing external is responsible for it.

In the next verse He says, 'Fools deride Me when I descend in the human form. They do not know My ultimate nature, eternal nature, as the supreme Lord of all that is.'

Here Kṛṣṇa uses a strong word: 'Fools.' Enlightened masters don't edit their words. They speak the truth as it is. Usually, normal people edit because they fear others' opinions. See, normally in all your minds, three processes happen: first, words are created, then edited, and then finally presented. In masters, these three processes don't happen. Straightaway what is created is presented.

One American university professor, who attended many of our discourses, said, '*Swamiji*, you are speaking continuously for hours. How are you able to continuously speak without notes?' Please be very clear, here also in front of me, only the verses are there. I see these verses in front of me so that the original pronunciation is not lost. If you have attended earlier discourses, whether it is a four-day program or five-day program, I never use notes. This is the first time I am keeping something in front of me. This is the first time I am commenting on Sanskrit literature. So I keep the Sanskrit verses in front of me.

He asked me, 'How are you able to continuously speak?' I told him, 'Because the process is easy in me. I don't edit. I don't have the three mechanisms: creating words, editing, and presenting. Usually, for all people, these three mechanisms have to happen.'

Then he asked one more question, '*Swamiji*, speaking for hours is different. For me, I must prepare three hours even for a one-hour lecture. If I must speak one hour on the ideas or the concepts I am supposed to present, I must prepare for three hours. I know for sure that you don't have time to prepare for so many discourses.'

In our meditation camps, sometimes the program is eighteen hours long per day. For eighteen hours people listen to the talks and meditate. In India the same program is for four days, about forty hours or more. He said, 'How can you prepare for such long discourses? How do you speak without preparation?'

I told him, 'You prepare because it has not become your experience.' Then I asked him, 'If somebody asks your name do you look at your notes and tell them your name?' Your name has become your experience, your being. So you immediately respond. Similarly, whatever I speak is from my experience. So I don't need to prepare. Because it is my experience, I spontaneously express it.

One more thing, why do people fear public speaking? Why do they again and again prepare and rehearse? They fear that they may speak what they really think! They want to express only polished words. They fear they may utter words that they are thinking. That is why they again and again prepare.

Only for a person whose inner chattering has become pure, his thinking becomes pure. That person can talk in a relaxed way for hours in public. To speak in public, that too in a relaxed and casual way, we need our inner being to be in a pure way. Otherwise, continuously we must edit.

If we edit and speak, within half an hour or one hour, we are tired. We do not radiate the same energy. We cannot be relaxed.

Masters don't edit; they express whatever they think. Because their thinking has become so pure, they don't need to edit. Even if they use sharp words, they are spoken to awaken you.

Here Kṛṣṇa uses the word, '*mūḍhaḥ*', meaning 'fool'. He gives a jolt to the ego. 'Fools deride Me when I descend in the human form. They do not know My eternal nature as the supreme Lord of all that is.' He says, 'When I land in the world in the human form as a master, people, fools, deride me. They don't understand.'

Why masters descend?

He again and again tells this to Arjuna, 'Don't think that just because I am in the body, I am your friend. Don't think that I am the person who was sitting in Brindāvan (the place where Kṛṣṇa spent his infant years), who is your own friend. I am the energy that takes care of the whole world. I have come down in this form to liberate all of you. So only fools deride Me, fools miss Me. Don't miss, Arjuna, understand the ultimate nature of Me and liberate yourself.'

In these verses, Kṛṣṇa tells some interesting truths. These were true during His time and they are true today. When an enlightened master is in his body, people do not accept him. They do not even want to accept that he can be an enlightened master. However, when the master is no longer in the body, people visit his final resting place, offer flowers, and do all kinds of things. This has happened to all enlightened masters.

You see, over time, it has become worse. When I am in the ashram in Bidadi, many people come with speculation. They have questions about what I say, what I wear, and everything I do. They say, 'You are so young. How can you be enlightened?' Some say, 'If you are enlightened, why do you wear a golden *rudrākṣa* necklace? Why do you charge money for courses?' They have questions and questions and questions. These same people will come to my final resting place after one hundred years and offer flowers on it. They will accept me as their guru then.

Kṛṣṇa says, 'Fools lose Me when I come in human form.' He calls them fools. This is the truth. When an enlightened master is in human form, we do not accept him as a master. Only after the master leaves the body do we pay our respects to the master. Why do people again and again do this?

You see, when the master is still in human form, our mind sees him as another human being. We see him like another person. Then our ego comes between him and us. It reasons, 'He is another human like me. Why should I listen to him?' All these questions come. We decide we don't have to follow another human being and go back.

See, a simple act of ego makes us miss a living enlightened master. Our mind always boosts our ego and keeps us away from an enlightened master. Our being wants it, however, our mind and ego create a strong wall of questions between the master and us. If there is a continuous inner chatter in us when we approach a master, our mind and ego take over our being. We miss the opportunity.

And one more thing, some people know that a person is a master. They know what he says is good for them, however, they escape. This is because they know that the enlightened master can see through them. They do not want anybody to know what a mess they have created in themselves. They want to escape that transformation.

We should understand why an enlightened master comes to earth. If we know this, we will not miss Him. If we understand that, then we can let our being experience the master's energy.

A small story from Rāmakṛṣṇa:

> Three men walk near a village. They see an orchard. One of them jumps into the orchard to see what is happening. He sees a big party going on inside. He sees so much joy and bliss inside the orchard. This man also starts enjoying. He forgets about the two men outside the orchard.
>
> After some time, the two men, who stand outside, get impatient. The second man says, 'Let me go and see what happened.' He enters the orchard. He sees people dancing, singing, enjoying. However, before he joins the party, this man thinks he should tell the third man standing outside the orchard about what he has seen. He has concern for the third man. So he tells the third man what is going on inside the orchard and runs back into the orchard and joins the party.
>
> Now this third man goes in. He sees the bliss everyone is in. He thinks, 'I should tell everyone in the village about this: everyone should enjoy.' So he tells everyone in the village and brings them into the orchard.

Enlightened masters are like the third man. They have experienced the truth, the bliss. They are the embodiments of compassion. They want everyone to know the truth. The only aim of an enlightened master is to get everyone enlightened. There is no ulterior motive of the master.

People ask me lots of questions. Why this? Why that? People look at me with suspicion. If I suggest to them to attend some course, they think I will make money. They run away thinking I want to convert them to a *sanyās*. They do not understand that an enlightened master is beyond all that. They miss the opportunity of being with a master, because of their own ignorance.

In the case of a normal man, when he takes birth, he carries over desires from his previous birth (*vāsanas)*. However, an enlightened master does not have desires or *vāsanas*: he is in a no-mind state. His spirit can merge directly into the universal energy. Whenever there is a need on planet earth, the energy of the enlightened master is sent down to earth with a mission to fulfill.

Be very clear, nobody can help when we create a wall of doubt between the master and us. The master can help only if we allow the master to take charge. As long as we hold onto our ego, we remain a fool. If we meet an enlightened master that is the best thing that can happen to us. Now it is up to us to take advantage of it or miss it. Kṛṣṇa tells everyone: if you miss an enlightened master, you are a fool. If we think out of ego that an enlightened master is like any other human, we lose the chance of knowing the truth: we lose the chance for enlightenment.

Worship Me In Any Form But With Devotion

9.13 O son of Pritā, the great souls who are not deluded know me as unchangeable.
They are devoted to Me as they know I am the cause of all creation.

9.14 Those with firm resolve perpetually worship Me with devotion.
They sing My glories, striving with determination, prostrating to Me,

9.15 Some worship Me by acquiring and spreading wisdom of the Self.
Others worship Me in my non-dual form, or dual form, or universal form.

Kṛṣṇa speaks about *bhakti* or devotion in these verses. You see, devotion can be one of the most powerful ways to reach God. Many saints showed the world the path of devotion. Caitanya Mahāprabhu was devoted to Kṛṣṇa. He sang songs and danced in ecstasy while singing about Kṛṣṇa. Mīrā was another devotee of Kṛṣṇa who was in love with Him. Mīrā's devotional songs, *Mīrā bhajans,* are sung even today to show her devotion towards Kṛṣṇa.

Devotion is one of the most powerful ways to reach God, however, it depends on how we express devotion. Many people go to temples. Some people have a habit of going to a particular temple every week. Going to temples becomes a fashion statement.

Making mechanical visits to the temple is just a sort of ego. We mostly go to temples to ask for something. We make business deals with God. As long as God gives what we want, he is our God, otherwise, He is no longer God. Our prayers should express our devotion, gratitude, and love to God. All great devotees of Kṛṣṇa and Rāma showed complete gratitude and love. When devotion reaches that state, they reach the ultimate consciousness.

Devotion or knowledge?

Prayers are powerful, however, we should not get stuck at prayers. They are good for initial stages. When we pray, we are stuck in words. We should go beyond words. Our devotion should help us see the ultimate energy behind the idol of Kṛṣṇa or Rāma.

Actually, complete devotion puts us in a completely different plane. When we show our devotion to someone, we surrender ourselves to him or her. Have you heard the story of Prahlāda?

> He was a young boy less than ten years old. His father Hiraṇyakaśipu does intense penance and asks Brahma, the Creator for a boon. He asks to be made immortal. Brahma says that is impossible. Hiraṇyakaśipu then comes up with lots of conditions such as: he should not be killed by an animal, a bird, a human, or anything living or non-living, either during the day or the night. Brahma grants him that boon.
>
> Hiraṇyakaśipu thinks his boon covers all the ways in which he might be killed, so he declares himself to be God. He asks all the people in his kingdom to worship him as God. So people worship his idol. All the chants include his name. Hiraṇyakaśipu's son, Prahlāda, turns out to be a great devotee of Lord Viṣṇu. He is a little boy, yet, his devotion to Viṣṇu is strong.
>
> His father is not happy about this. He tries to persuade Prahlāda, but, it is of no use. The more Hiraṇyakaśipu talks to his son, the more intense Prahlāda's devotion becomes. Hiraṇyakaśipu then tries to get Prahlāda killed through various ways. Prahlāda worships Viṣṇu

with such great devotion that Viṣṇu saves Prahlāda every time. His devotion is deep. Even when he is about to be executed, he prays to Viṣṇu with gratitude and love. His devotion is that of surrender rather than a prayer asking Viṣṇu to save his life. This is the story of Narasimha *avatār*, the incarnation of Viṣṇu, in which He is half-lion and half-human.

Kṛṣṇa continues to explain to Arjuna the ways in which people worship Him. Here he talks about the path of *jñāna*, knowledge: those following the path of knowledge try to worship Me by acquiring and propagating knowledge.

Understand, mere accumulation of knowledge only increases ego. It does not give enlightenment. Internalize the knowledge by meditation and contemplation, and relate it to experiential wisdom. Then the breeze of joy will flow into your life.

Many people read many books and scriptures. They have shelves filled with books. They will show off their library of books to whoever visits their home. Many people discuss spirituality and have debates over this subject. Debates are not wrong, but the motive with which they discuss should be correct. If they discuss to show others how much they know, then they are debating purely out of ego. Please be very clear, if we show off our knowledge to show how much we know, there is no use of that knowledge.

The only way knowledge in the scriptures helps us is through experience. Instead of debating, apply it in day-to-day activities. See the results on yourself first. Only when we experience it, we have the right to speak about it to others. Till then, they are mere words.

Meditation helps us here, especially in the path of *jñāna* or knowledge. You see, in the path of devotion all we have to do is pray to some form. We must completely surrender. Actually that is difficult. In the path of devotion at least we have someone to whom we can pray and look up to.

In the path of knowledge, there is no reference point. There is nothing called you and He. In the path of devotion, there is a clear separation between Krṣṇa and us. Here, Krṣṇa says that everything is Krṣṇa. Everything is one.

When we meditate, we connect to our inner space. The scriptures, the *Upaniṣad,* talk about microcosm and macrocosm. Actually, they are one and the same. If we talk about this knowledge without experience, all our knowledge is only words. The difference happens when we experience that truth. During meditation, we merge with the cosmic energy. We enter that space where our inner space merges with the outer space.

In the path of devotion, even if we meditate on the form, after a point we will see that there is no form. We experience the same thing as in the path of knowledge. Nothing is better than the other. The great enlightened master Śaṅkara who spoke on non-duality, wrote poems on devotion also. Swami Vivekānanda was an intellectual being, yet, he saluted the devotion of Rāmakṛṣṇa's disciple, Gopale Ma, a devotee of Krṣṇa.

This is what Krṣṇa says in this verse, 'Some worship the form, some worship the formless. There are many ways to worship Me.'

There are many different ways people worship the Divine. We have customized paths for our personal growth. So naturally wherever one is, one can grow and reach the level we are supposed to reach. There are all sizes of ladders, all kinds of steps. He gives options among the different paths: worshipping through singing the glories of the Lord, or cultivation of knowledge, and offering everything at the feet of God.

I Am Immortality And Death!

9.16, 17, 18, 19

I am the ritual, I am the sacrifice, I am the offering, I am the herb, I am the mantra, *I am the clarified butter, I am the fire, and I am the oblation.*

I am the supporter of the Universe, the father, the mother, and the grandfather. I am the object of knowledge, the sacred syllable 'Oṁ', and also the Ṛg, the Yajur, and the Sāma vedas.

I am the goal, the supporter, the Lord, the witness, the abode, the refuge, the friend, the origin, the dissolution, the foundation, the substratum, and the immutable seed. I give heat. I send, as well as withhold the rain.

I am immortality as well as death. I am also both the Eternal and the temporal, O Arjuna.

Kṛṣṇa says in specific terms what He is. He is the creation of the act, the actor, and the action. He is the fire to which the sacrifices are made. He is also the offering, and He is the sacrifice as well. He is the seer, the seen, and the seeing, all in one.

He tells Arjuna that everything has come from Him. Everything that we see is *Parāśakti* or universal energy.

Great masters like Ramana, Rāmakṛṣṇa, Sadā Śiva Brahmendra, lived in this realization. Many people could not relate to the experience of these masters or to the expression of their experience, so they considered these masters mad.

All are *Brahman*

We are all *Brahman*. Divine energy fills and overflows in all the places. This is what Kṛṣṇa says in these verses. Whatever name we may give It, It is present everywhere. When we worship some idol or form, we actually worship the formless energy behind that idol. People ask me, 'Why do we keep your photo in front of us and pray to it? Why can't we meditate on the formless?'

I tell them, 'First start meditating on the form, then you can go to the formless.' Our mind is like a drunken monkey, jumping from here to there. We need a form to bring our mind to the present. Once we master this, meditating on the formless becomes easier. Meditating on the form should only be a starting point. We should understand that we are worshipping *through* that idol and not the idol itself. Actually, it is religions that give shapes and forms to this divine energy.

Thousands of years ago, our sages have clearly said in the *Upaniṣad* that everything is energy and everything arose from energy. Now it has been proven scientifically that there is ether even in a vacuum. This energy is all-pervading. Only recently has science understood this truth. We now know with the help of powerful tools that 99.99% of an atom is empty space with continuous vibrations. Each and every body is filled with energy. Today science says, 'Everything is filled with energy.'

Our enlightened masters expressed it this way, 'God is energy and He fills all space and is omnipresent.' This energy can only change form; it cannot be destroyed. You see, when we switch on a light, electrical energy is converted into light energy. In the same way, universal energy is everywhere. Once we realize this great truth, we see that everything around us is the same as us. When I say everything, I mean everything is Kṛṣṇa, everything is *Brahman*.

Go To Heaven

9.20 *Those who practice the vedic rituals and drink the soma juice worship Me indirectly, seeking the heavenly pleasures.*
They go to heaven and enjoy sensual delights.

9.21 *Once they have thus enjoyed heavenly sense pleasures, they are reborn on this planet again.*
By practicing vedic rituals as result-oriented actions, they are bound by the cycle of birth and death.

9.22 *When you reside in My consciousness, whatever you lack I give*
And whatever you have, I preserve

9.23 *Even those who worship other deities, they too worship Me,*
O son of Kuntī, but without true understanding.

9.24 *I am the only enjoyer and the only object of sacrifice.*
Those who do not recognize My true transcendental nature are born again and again.

Kṛṣṇa says that people who read scriptures, the *Vedas*, and who perform pious ritualistic activities based on scriptural injunctions with the aim of acquiring merits, enjoy heavenly pleasures. But, they fall back into the cycle of life and death after they finish enjoying these pleasures.

You see, many people do lots of rituals and read scriptures. This surely helps elevate them to a higher plane of consciousness, however, they are still caught in the cycle of *saṁsāra,* birth and death. By reading scriptures and performing different rituals, we will enjoy the pleasures of *Indra loka,* the heavenly pleasures. When the rituals are performed with that objective, we will again enter the vicious circle of birth and death.

Kṛṣṇa speaks about the attitude with which we read scriptures or perform rituals. Scriptures have immense knowledge. Rituals have immense power. They are meditations, yet, they are useless if done with fear and greed.

Many people fear that if they do not perform certain rituals, they will go to hell. Another class of people operates with greed. They donate large sums of money thinking that the gates of heaven will be eternally open for them. They even get their names carved on the temple walls.

Please understand that when we do pious activities with fear or greed, though we see some transformation, we will go back to where we started. That is what Kṛṣṇa means by *Indra loka,* the momentary transformation or elevation of our state.

When we perform certain rituals: when we do *pūjā,* or prayer, or we read scriptures, it should become a meditation. Our ego, our fear, and our greed should not come in the way. Do things with intensity.

The next verse is the main core that reveals the secret. Kṛṣṇa tells Arjuna and all of us: 'Those who always worship Me, those who always reside in Me, *ananyāscintayanto mām ye janāḥ paryupāsate,* people who have become Me, people who reside in eternal consciousness: to them, I carry what they lack and I preserve what they have. I personally take care of them.'

Understand, no other incarnation has revealed this truth so clearly. He says, 'If you reside in eternal consciousness, divine energy, bliss consciousness, I take care of you in all ways. I give them whatever they want spiritually and materially and I take care that it stays with them. I take care that nobody takes it away from them.' This is a beautiful statement and assurance.

It is not only an assurance; it is also a promise. The strange thing is that He says we will have everything and nothing will be lost. It is difficult to believe! 'How can I have what I want by meditating?' This will be the immediate question.

We create our world

Please be very clear. Now in the modern day, Quantum physics, science, clearly proves our thoughts create the universe. If we reside in eternal consciousness, we create our own universe. The universe responds to our thoughts.

> A small but important experiment that I read in a magazine:
>
> A professor did an experiment using three rose bushes. They were the same height, same kind. He kept them in three different rooms. He entered the first room and used beautiful words, 'You are beautiful. You are nice. I'll protect you. Why do you need thorns?' He gave assuring and caring words.
>
> Next he went to the room that had the second plant. He did not do much. He looked and came back: neither negative nor positive.
>
> To the third plant, he cursed, 'What nonsense are you doing? You are ugly.' He created negative energy with his words.
>
> He continued this experiment for twenty-one days. He studied how plants respond to thoughts as a research.
>
> The report is shocking. The first plant that received positive words doubled in size and had no thorns! I saw photographs of that plant. There were no thorns on that rose plant just because he gave the assurance, 'I'll protect you. Why should you protect yourself?' Can you imagine a rose plant without thorns!
>
> The second to which he spoke neither positive nor negative words was a normal rose plant. It experienced normal growth. The third plant, to which he spoke negative words, died. He repeated the same experiment in different places. The third plant that received negative thoughts, died all the times.

Sir Jagdish Chandra Bose, an Indian Nobel Laureate, proved that plants are alive with 'feelings.' They are capable of responding to our thoughts and emotions. This experiment proves that Existence, the outer world, responds to our thoughts.

Each of us is not an island. Our outer life and inner life are deeply connected. If we live a spiritual life, we automatically attract only spiritual friends. Our outer world also becomes spiritual. All other relationships drop by themselves.

Many devotees tell me, '*Swamiji*, nowadays I am unable to go to a party. Even if I go, I have nothing to talk about. What is there to talk about at a party? Same stock market, or who ran away with whom, who is going with whom, who is staying with whom. Nothing useful.'

And everybody feels that they know some secrets. They call somebody and say, 'Don't tell anybody. This is only for you.'

Not only that, just telling her will not do: we must extract a promise that they wouldn't tell anyone. Then after ten minutes, even the dog on the street will bark with the news!

Existence cares for you

Anyhow, understand, Existence responds to our thoughts. Only based on our thoughts, we create relationships, friends, society, our circle, and naturally, our whole world.

Again and again, *Vedānta* says, *dṛṣṭi-sṛṣṭi,* we create what we see. We create the universe from the angle of our vision. When our *dṛṣṭi* (vision) changes, the *sṛṣṭi* (world around us) changes too. By changing our vision, we change the world around us.

See, whatever slide we place in front of a projector, that will appear on the screen. If we place the slide of God, the picture of God appears on screen. If we place an actress, that actress appears on the screen. Whatever we use as a slide appears on the screen. The screen represents the physical planet earth. Whatever we keep in front of our consciousness, we project that in our life, our world, and our experience.

The slide determines the scene on the screen. Our mentality decides the way we perceive the world, the way we experience the world. A small change in the slide changes the scene. A small change in our mind changes our whole world. The screen remains the same: The backdrop screen is the same, however, the scene changes.

Similarly, if the thoughts in our inner space change, the whole universe changes. The whole universe responds, the whole of Existence responds to our inner space.

Kṛṣṇa says:

'When you reside in My consciousness, whatever you lack I give, and whatever you have I preserve.'

You may think, 'Yes *Swamiji*, we understand when you say the universe responds to our thoughts. How can we get what we want?'

Please understand that the moment we change our thoughts, the moment our inner space changes, automatically we attract good things. If we tune our television to BBC, we see the BBC channel. If we tune it to ABC, we see the ABC channel. Similarly, if we tune our consciousness to bliss continuously, even material wealth will shower on us.

We may think, 'How can this be possible? What kind of words is *Swamiji* giving?' I tell you, it may look difficult now, but start experimenting. I honestly tell you: I declare from my own authority, this verse is the solid truth.

I can say this with authority, because I experienced this truth for nine years. I tell you, this is a promise by the Divine. Nine years I lived in utter insecurity. I know Kṛṣṇa still proves His words. His words are guaranteed, *yogakṣemaṁ vahāmyahaṁ*, He does!

Let me tell you a small incident that happened in my own life during my days of spiritual wandering, before the incident of enlightenment.

I was staying in Haridvār at a place called Kankhal. I was doing spiritual practice. Every day morning, I went for alms to places where they feed monks. In so many ashrams they give alms to monks. I used to get my food, eat two or three *rotis* (Indian bread), and then start meditating.

Suddenly, one day I fell sick. I had a high temperature and diarrhea. I could not walk. I thought, 'What can be done? Alright! Let it be.'

Suddenly, a young *sanyāsi* came from nowhere and gave me food. Continuously for three to four days, he came. He brought food and medicine for me. I asked him, 'Who are you? Where have you come from?' He said, 'Oh, my name is Śaṅkar. They call me Śaṅkar Maharāj. I stay at an ashram called Sadhana Sadan. This ashram is nearby.' He pointed towards a distant place and said that is where he stayed. Everyday he brought me food and medicine till I recovered. He came for at least four days. Because he came everyday, I talked with him. We became acquainted.

I saw that he wore a beautiful pen with a diamond in it. It was a beautiful pen! I was surprised at how a monk got a diamond pen. I asked, 'What is this, *Swami*?'

He said, 'This is a diamond pen. Some devotee gave it to me. It looks nice, so I wear it.' Anyhow, I did not bother about it.

After several days, when I returned to normal, he stopped coming. By then I was okay. Then I thought, 'I must go and see him.' I felt I must thank him. After a week, when I became completely alright, I started walking.

I went to this ashram and asked an elderly person sitting there, '*Swamiji*, I want to see Śaṅkar Maharāj.' The swami said, 'Śaṅkar? Who are you talking about?' I said, 'I want to see Śaṅkar, a young *swami*. I met him two to three days ago. He came everyday and brought me food. Is this Sadhana Sadan?'

This swami replied, 'Yes, this is Sadhana Sadan. In our ashram, there is only one Śaṅkar. Go to the temple and see. He is the only Śaṅkar Mahārāj we have!' He pointed towards their temple.

I tell you, what I am telling is the truth. When I entered the temple, I saw a Śiva deity as a white marble statue with a cloth draped on His upper body, and wearing the same diamond pen on Him!

Of course, tears rolled down from my eyes. So much gratitude overflowed. Later, I asked the temple priest, 'How did this pen come to Śiva? Who put a pen on Śiva's statue?' He said, 'One week ago, a devotee came and offered the pen. It looked nice and he said it was a diamond pen. We just wanted to decorate Śiva with diamond jewelry. So we put the pen on Him.' It was the same pen! The very same diamond pen!

I asked, 'Who gave a pen to Śiva?' Other jewelry, we can understand, but a pen?

He replied, 'I don't know. A devotee came and offered this pen. I asked, *Why should a sanyāsi have a diamond pen? I will give it to God instead.* So I put it on Śiva. I just inserted it into Śiva's clothes.'

He then continued, 'For the last few days all the food offering, *prasād* that we place in front of Him, disappears. I suspect that rats have been eating the food. So now I am careful. I sit for a while after placing the food for Śaṅkar Mahārāj.'

I did not want to tell him that I was the rat who ate Śaṅkar Mahārāj's food!

During the 2006 Himalayan trip I searched for this ashram and Śaṅkar Mahārāj's temple with my devotees. After many years, it was still the same, the same temple and the same Śaṅkar Mahārāj; but no diamond pen now!

Of course, I do not ask you to believe the whole thing, because of this one incident. But you can experiment in your life. You may say, 'This is your experience. How can this be truth for us, *Swamiji*?' An ordinary mind doubts.

Let me tell you that your consciousness has the quality to create miracles in your lives. What you need, you will receive. Continuously, miracles are happening.

Let me try to show you how miracles might have happened in your lives. You might have noticed, when the telephone rings, you suddenly remember a friend's name. When you pick up the phone, that same friend is on the line. Or at times, somebody knocks on the door. You remember some person and open the door and that very same person stands there. This is what I call the power of coincidence! These are miracles in their own way.

In each one of us, the power of coincidence, the power to create, exists. All we need to do is open that. Understand that we have the power to create the coincidence.

Trust that your consciousness is connected to the universe. Continuously, the universe cares for you. The Divine waits for you. It responds to your thoughts.

We create what we want. We have the power to create the world when we are conscious, when we are in the waking state. When we can create a world in the dream state, can't we create that in the waking state? We can do it.

Even now, we create our world. Next question, 'If we are creating our world, why do we create so many miseries, *Swamiji*?'

The answer is simple. We do so because we have vested interests in our sufferings. Somewhere we feel comfortable when we suffer. When our inner consciousness changes, when we reside in eternal consciousness, we automatically attract the power of coincidence. We attract the power of coincidence.

The moment we understand that the whole universe is pervaded by the Existential energy of Viṣṇu, we attract Lakṣmī, Viṣṇu's consort, who represents wealth! When we understand that the whole universe is divine, when we experience Viṣṇu, meaning when we experience eternal bliss, we attract Lakṣmī, wealth!

Bliss attracts fortune

There is a beautiful *mantra* in Tantra *śāstras*: '*ānanda kāmaprānaha*' that means 'Bliss attracts fortune.' When we create a blissful inner space, automatically we attract external wealth.

Tell me, what creates wealth? We need three things: clear thinking, a creative mind, and the ability to make spontaneous decisions. The ability to respond spontaneously to any situation is responsibility. Only these three create wealth and preserve wealth. If we enter the bliss space, all three automatically happen to us. Then wealth will be created around us and it will stay with us. Wealth can come simply by creating a blissful inner space and such wealth stays with us.

Please be very clear, whomsoever wins through a lottery never preserves it! Without knowing the value of it, they simply blow it away. When wealth comes by intelligence, it stays with you. When we take care of our inner space, automatically, the outer space showers on us. Existence responds to our inner bliss and blesses us. Never think that the universe is mere matter. It is live intelligence.

People ask me, '*Swamiji*, I am searching for a guru. I feel inspired to do spiritual practice, but I need a guru.'

I tell them, 'If your search is intense, God sends you the guru. He never misses His responsibility. If you do not have the right guru, then something is seriously wrong with your seeking.' If our seeking is proper, straightaway the master happens in our life. He never delays. The Divine never delays.

All we need to do is change our inner space. The first thing is to understand this secret. Once we enter spiritual life, once we decide we want to lead a spiritual life, all our worldly things are taken care of by the Divine.

We may ask funny questions, '*Swamiji*, from today onwards if I stop working, will I have everything?'

If we enter the spiritual life, we will never think of dropping our work. We will only drop our *worries* about work. Then we will work in a much better way. We will have tremendous confidence, 'The whole of Existence protects me. I am a friend of this Whole.'

When we understand that we are a friend of the whole of Existence, even after death we will not disappear, because we know we will be there in the universe in some form, that there is nothing to worry about.

Plato, a disciple of Socrates, recorded the conversations of Socrates. All of you must read the conversations between Plato and Socrates. They asked Socrates, 'Are you not afraid of death?'

Socrates says, 'Only two things can happen. The first thing: I will be alive after I leave the body in some form, in some way, somewhere. In that case, why should I be afraid? The second thing: I may not exist. Then there will anyway be no one left to feel fear! If I exist, why should I fear? If I am not going to exist, then who is there to suffer? Either way there is no need for fear.'

Of course, this answer is logical. But I tell you this from experience: it is practical. From experience I tell you, we never perish. We continue to exist, in some form, somewhere. Even if we become enlightened, we become a pure conscious energy. We will be there, everywhere. We never die when we understand that Existence is intelligence.

Life After Life

9.25 *Those who worship the deities will take birth among the deities; those who worship ghosts and spirits will take birth among such beings; those who worship ancestors go to the ancestors;*
Those who worship Me will live with Me.

9.26 *Whoever offers Me with love and devotion a leaf, a flower, fruit, or water,*
I will accept and consume what is offered by the pure-hearted.

9.27 *O son of* Kuntī, *all that you do, all that you eat, all that you offer and give away, as well as all austerities that you may perform,*
Give them as an offering to Me.

9.28 *You will be freed from all reactions to good and evil deeds by this renunciation,*
You will be liberated and come to Me.

Here, Kṛṣṇa talks about the life that we lead now. He talks about the birth that we will take next. Understand that our present life is a result of our previous life. This is the truth. There is life after death as long as we are not enlightened.

Once we are enlightened, we merge into universal consciousness. Until then we take birth and go through the process of life and death.

Kṛṣṇa talks about the kind of life that we lead now. The last thought that we have at the time of death determines our next birth, next life. If we think of money, we will be reborn as a rich man or as a dissatisfied man who always thinks about money. If we think of food, we will be reborn as a glutton or a pig. If we think of lazily relaxing, we will be reborn as a buffalo.

This is the truth. Actually we need not go to the extent of life and death. We see this in daily life itself. Our last thought affects our first thought. Every night we die and every morning we take birth. During the day, when we are in the waking state, we use our gross physical body or *sthūla śarīra* to carry on with our activities. When we sleep, if we have dreams, we use the subtle body or *sūkṣma śarīra* to travel to the places that we see in our dreams. When we are in deep sleep, when we have no dreams, then we are in our causal body or *kāraṇa śarīra*.

When we sleep at night, we actually change bodies. We are not aware that this happens. In our dream, we have created a world in which we live. Our gross body is on the bed, while our subtle body is active in the dream. In the same way, the causal body is active during the deep sleep state.

We see that our last thought before sleeping affects our first thought upon waking. If we come back from the office with a frustrated mood about our boss, we wake up with the same mood in the morning. If we sleep with a blissful smile on our face, we will be happy the next morning. This is the reason we are asked to pray before we sleep at night. When we pray with full awareness, we enter a meditative and blissful state. When we sleep in a blissful state, we wake up in the same state.

One more thing you need to know is that whatever feeling we wake up with in the morning, that same feeling stays with us throughout the day. If you wake up dull in the morning, you will be dull throughout the day. If you wake up energized, you will be active and energetic throughout the day.

I tell people, 'When you wake up, dance your way to the bathroom! Feel the toothpaste on your teeth, feel the water on your body when you bathe. Bring in full awareness to every action. Start the day with a blissful thought. For that, we must sleep also in a blissful mood.

Exactly what happens everyday during sleep is exactly the same thing that happens during the time of death. Rāmakṛṣṇa says beautifully: When we die and take the next birth, the soul just changes clothes. During death, the soul sheds the cloth and in the next birth, it puts on a new cloth.

The process of sleep and the process of death are not different. During the process of death, the soul passes through seven energy layers. The next body it enters depends on the *vāsana,* or the carried-over desires that it comes with from the previous life. It takes up a body that can help shed that *vāsana* in the next life.

The body that we take now is dependent on the *vāsana* or carried-over desires of our previous birth. Our soul always tries to merge with the colorless and formless universal consciousness. However, the *vāsana* creates a slight tinge on the soul and it cannot completely merge with the universal consciousness. So the soul takes up another body that can help remove this tinge and help it merge.

Now it is up to us how we make use of this lifetime. We can either fulfill our unfulfilled desires of the previous life or we can build new desires in this life and stay in the cycle of birth and death. The kind of life that the soul chooses in the next life depends entirely on the *vāsana* and the last thought at the time of death.

People ask me, '*Swamiji,* I was not inclined towards spirituality and meditation, however, when I did the meditation I felt like I had been doing this for a long time. What is it?'

Understand you may not have done any meditation in this life. But you see a deep connection with meditation, because you might have meditated in your previous life.

You see, our next life depends on our last thought in this life. That does not mean that throughout our life we can think about money and food and suddenly at the time of death, we can say, 'Rāma, Krṣṇa.' If we think about money, name and fame throughout our entire life, naturally we will only think about money when we leave the body.

When we are continuously aware of the Existential energy, when we continuously meditate on It, we will have only the same thought when we leave the body, also. And It will ensure that our next birth takes us closer to this energy and liberates us from the cycle of birth and death.

In simplicity lies greatness

He says next: 'If one offers Me with love and devotion, a leaf, flower, fruit, or water, I will accept it,' He says, 'The Existence, the Divine is so alive that It responds to even simple things.'

Please be very clear. He doesn't say, 'I accept only big things.' He says, 'Even simple things, I accept.'

That is the greatness of the Divine. He is very simple. Please be very clear, simplicity is the real greatness.

There is a small beautiful saying in Zen:

A Zen disciple was behaving very humbly, respecting everybody. The master told him, 'Don't be so humble, you are not that great!'

To be humble, you need to be great!

Simplicity is the great quality of the Divine. He says, '*patraṁ, puṣpaṁ, phalaṁ, toyaṁ*. Just a leaf, a flower, a fruit, a little water... simple things are enough. I accept it. I am pleased. I respond to it.'

He says in the fourth verse of this chapter:

mayā tatam idam sarvaṁ jagadvyaktamūrtinā

'I am all-pervading, great, ultimate, divine.'

Now He says, even though He is all-pervading, even though He is big, He accepts any small thing given with love and devotion.

Even if we know somebody is big or great, we can't relate with him unless he relates with us, unless he comes down to our level. Real greatness is not only being great. He must be able to relate with everybody. Otherwise, even if he is great, what can be done about it?

Many people in India know that great masters are there. They tell me, 'Yes I know they are there, *Swamiji*. But how can I relate with them? I can't relate with them. I have no way to establish communication with them.'

Here, Kṛṣṇa creates a way, even for ordinary people to relate with Him. On the one side He declares with authority His greatness. On the other side He shows us how to relate with Him. He says, 'Even if you offer a leaf, flower, fruit or water with love, I accept it. I relate with it.'

That is why, from time immemorial, enlightened masters are requested to live by begging, so that people can relate with them. In India, *sanyāsis* live by begging. Even Buddha lived by begging, so that we can relate with Him. When we give food, we talk to Him and relate with Him, we feel that He is like us.

Modern day psychology has a beautiful term, 'zeroing down the distance.' Here, Kṛṣṇa zeroes down the distance completely.

First, Kṛṣṇa proves that the whole cosmic energy is intelligence. The moment we understand it is intelligence, we relax from all tension and insecurity. As long as we think the world is material, matter, we feel like protecting ourselves from it. The moment we understand that we are a part of the Whole, the Whole that is the intelligence that responds to our thoughts, which responds to our being, which responds to our consciousness, we relax into enlightenment!

I tell people, this verse is the lazy man's guide to enlightenment! Understand that the universe is intelligence. It responds to our thoughts, deeds, and consciousness.

When we give cookies to our child and he opens it, we say, 'Give one to Mommy!' It is not that we don't have a cookie or we want it, but if the child gives it to us, how happy we feel! We feel connected. And we know he wants to connect to us: he wants to relate with us.

Similarly, when we offer something to the Divine, don't think that He does not have it and so you are offering. He is the one who gives everything to us in the first place! But when we offer, we show to the Divine: I want to connect to you. We show a green signal for the Divine to enter into our space.

He is always ready. The Bible says, 'Knock and the door shall open.' I say, 'God is knocking, just open!' *We* don't need to knock: *He* is knocking. Just open. Naturally we will be ushered in.

I tell people, 'Don't go to the temple empty-handed. Take at least two or three fruits or whatever you have. Always offer something to God. Always offer something to the Divine. By giving to the Divine, you express a willing attitude to relate with Him. When you offer it to the Divine, He accepts it and He relates.'

Again and again, out of His compassion, Kṛṣṇa reveals truths and techniques to Arjuna to liberate himself. That is the job of an enlightened master. He comes down to the earth to liberate as many as He can.

In these verses, Kṛṣṇa asks Arjuna to surrender everything to Him. I tell you, surrendering to an enlightened master is the easiest way to become enlightened. If we can surrender every action to the supreme Self, we experience a great sense of liberation.

We constantly worry. We always think of the future or past. Why do we do that? We think we do everything. We boost our ego when we do things successfully. When they do not go according to our plan, our ego is hurt. Our ego is working continuously. It is either getting excited or getting hurt. We again and again think of ways to stop our ego from getting hurt.

We do not understand that by letting go, by surrendering to the Existential energy, we will be free. All our burdens will be gone. We do not realize this. All enlightened masters have spoken about surrender. It is the easiest way, however, we make it the most difficult due to our ego.

Levels of surrender

There are three levels in which we can surrender to the Existential energy. The first level is surrender of our actions. Whatever we do, good or bad, surrender them to the universal energy. Kṛṣṇa clearly says this in these verses, 'All your reactions to good and evil will be taken care of, if you offer all your actions, all your austerities to me.'

When worship is done, when you chant verses, do it with full surrender to the Divine. Do it as if it were your last prayer. Feel the prayer. Put in your complete awareness and surrender it to the Divine. That should be the feeling when you do anything.

Not just prayers, everything that we do should be done with that level of surrender. When we surrender, we feel light. Our efficiency goes up. This is true! When we surrender our actions, we are not bothered about what will happen in the future. When we surrender our actions to the Divine, we put our entire burden on His shoulders. Whatever good or bad happens, He is now responsible and we also know that He can never do anything wrong.

The second level of surrender is that of intellect and mind. The first level is easier compared to this. Surrendering our mind is more difficult, because it is not in our hands. You see, we can see our actions. We can say, 'O God, I have surrendered my actions to you.' But now will our mind keep quiet? No. It will keep saying, 'No, no, no. How can you do that? How can you not think about your future?' Our mind continuously analyzes!

One more thing. When I speak great truths, your mind analyzes them. It thinks, 'What is He saying? How is that possible? I can't think of completely surrendering myself to the Divine.' Your mind always looks for opportunities to hold you back. It again and again logically analyzes using the intelligence it has.

Our mind, based on its limited intellect, cannot comprehend certain things. When I say there are eleven dimensions in our system, you think, 'What are you saying, *Swamiji*? How is it possible?' This is what I mean by surrender of mind and intellect. When you surrender your mind and intellect to the universal energy, you experience great truths. When you do not surrender, you are stuck. Once you surrender, you experiment and you see quantum progress.

The third and the most difficult level of surrender is that of the senses. If the master says something, the disciple takes it as it is. That is the level of surrender. When we reach this level of surrender, we are one with the Divine. The Divine takes cares of us.

Kṛṣṇa says this clearly. Every enlightened master makes this promise. When we surrender ourselves to the master, to the Divine, to the universal energy, it takes care of us. When we offer all our actions to the universal energy, It takes care of us. The entire burden on our shoulders is offloaded. We are free from all the results of our actions. This is the promise of every enlightened master.

Anyone Can Reach Me

9.29 *I dislike no one, nor am I partial to anyone. I am equal to all.*
Whoever is devoted to Me is a friend, is in Me, and I am also a friend to him.

9.30 *Even if the most sinful person engages himself in devotional service,*
He is to be considered saintly because he is properly situated.

9.31 *He quickly becomes righteous and attains lasting peace.*
O son of Kuntī, declare it boldly that My devotee never perishes.

9.32 *O son of Pritā, anyone who takes shelter in Me,*
Women, traders, workers, or even sinners can approach the supreme destination.

9.33 *How much easier then it is for the learned, the righteous, the devotees, and saintly kings*
Who in this temporary miserable world engage in loving service unto Me.

9.34 *Fix your mind on Me, be devoted to Me, worship Me, and bow down to Me.*
Thus, uniting yourself with Me by setting Me as the supreme goal and the sole refuge, you shall certainly come to Me.

An enlightened master wants nothing from this world. After realizing the supreme knowledge, he is beyond material pursuits, what can he want from anybody? He is here out of his compassion to awaken mankind into this reality.

A true master is never envious of anybody. Envy enters us when we think that somebody else has something we do not have and something that we want. There is nothing wrong with desiring something because we need it. See, each one of us is born with a certain set of desires and we bring with us the energy to fulfill them, also.

Mahatma Gandhi says beautifully, 'The universe has enough to satisfy each man's needs, however, it does not have enough to satisfy a single man's wants.' Our needs become wants when we look at others and accumulate their desires into our own list.

If you notice in life, most of our actions are governed by comparing our lives with others. Buddha says, 'Nothing exists but in relationship.' See, all adjectives of good, bad, tall, thin, ugly, beautiful, come when you compare with others, right? Imagine you are alone on an island and there are no other human beings. You are by yourself. Would these adjectives make sense or have relevance to you?

Something is good, because something else is bad in comparison to that. So, our lives are run by constant comparison with those around us. Naturally, when someone has something that we like, and which we do not have, emotions like envy and jealousy are bound to come. They have to.

When we have a clear view about what we really want, then we will spend all our energies in fulfilling those needs, without worrying about what others want or think.

In this verse, Kṛṣṇa says that he does not dislike anybody. He also says that He is not partial to anyone. Normally, in our lives we are partial to those who are helpful to us. From childhood, we are taught to love those who are potentially useful in our lives. We make friends based on what we get back in return.

Everything has been reduced to a business transaction. If someone is nice to us, we are nice to them. If someone says something that hurts us, they become our enemies. We are vulnerable to the outside world, to what others say and do. We place people on different pedestals depending on how they behave with us.

See, an enlightened master wants nothing. He gives constantly. He radiates love, because that is his true nature. A river flows happily from one region to the other all the way from the hills to the ocean. It meets various kinds of stones and grass along the way. All kinds of people bathe in it: even buffaloes bathe in it. Does the river differentiate?

Does the river say, 'No, I will give water only to such and such a person?' No! A river flows continuously, happily, without bothering about who comes in contact with it. The same is the case with an enlightened master.

Now Kṛṣṇa says, 'If one is engaged in devotional service, then even if he commits the most abominable actions, he is considered saintly. He quickly becomes eternal and attains eternal consciousness. O Kaunteya, son of Kuntī, declare it boldly, that My devotee never perishes.' He goes on to say that His devotee never perishes.

He says, 'Not only I am declaring to you, you declare to the whole world, My devotee never perishes.'

He says, 'He who quickly becomes righteous and understands this truth enters into eternal bliss, eternal consciousness, O son of Kuntī, Kaunteya: declare it boldly, *pratijānīhi* means 'declare it boldly', that my devotee never perishes.'

Understand that Existence is intelligence. You will never die because you will be in Existence somewhere in some form. This body may move, however, *you* will be there forever. When we understand the whole cosmos is intelligence, our whole life will be blessed with what we want.

And I tell you a practical thing. Decide, 'From today I will live in a blissful mood, in a blissful way, in utterly relaxed consciousness.' You will attract wealth.

When we really, intensely understand this truth: the whole universe is energy, the whole Existence is energy, please be very clear, yoga and *kṣema* (success) happen in our life.

When we understand this truth, not only in this world, wherever we go, we are protected. We relax into the consciousness that Existence continuously protects us, takes care of us.

When we think that the Whole is our enemy, we will be continuously antagonizing it. When we understand that the Whole is our friend, we will relax and enjoy the whole of Existence.

Understanding rituals

The whole chapter reveals this single secret: that is the cosmic energy, the whole universe, is intelligence. It responds to our thoughts and again and again, It answers our dreams, our thoughts, and our very consciousness.

Again and again, Krṣṇa talks about the correct understanding of rituals and sacrifices made in front of God. We see numerous people going to the temple. They take one hundred and one coconuts and break them in front of the deity. In the Tirupati temple of Lord Venkaṭeśvara, people offer their hair as a sacrifice. If we offer hair and pray and come back home, nothing is going to happen.

When we sacrifice something, it represents the surrender of our ego. When we sacrifice our hair in Tirupati, we surrender our ego to Lord Venkaṭeśvara. When we break a coconut, the shell of the ego is broken into pieces.

However what generally happens? When we do some sacrifice, we proudly tell people that we did this and we did that. Our ego gets boosted. When we do such sacrifices, we think we did something great. All the sacrifices that we make are only to boost our ego.

If a sacrifice is made with complete gratitude and surrender, it is fine. When it is made out of ego, there is no use.

I take a group of people to the Himalayas every year. We meet priests in the temples there who say, 'If you offer a cow to Śiva, you will go to heaven.' For that offering, the priest charges lots of money. When we go the next year, we see the same cow being offered again! Understand how many times the same cow is offered to Śiva and how much money this person makes out of it.

Sacrificing in temples has become a business today. People who act out of ego make a business deal with God, 'I will donate so much money for the temple: leave one spot for me in heaven.' That is the way sacrifice is done in temples. Another class of people sits outside the temple and makes money from sacrifices. They say that they will make sure that the donor will be given a red carpet welcome at the gates of heaven if he or she makes a donation.

People ask me, 'Are sacrifices wrong? Is worship and sacrifice for a particular deity wrong?' No, it is not wrong. We should understand that we are not worshipping or sacrificing to that one particular deity. We must go beyond that. When we make a sacrifice from our being, we merge with the Existential energy. We do not see a difference between one deity and the other. Every deity will then appear the same.

Everything is Krṣna or Rāma or Jesus or Buddha. This is what Krṣṇa says here. He is the only enjoyer of all sacrifices. When we understand His transcendental nature in everything around us, any small thing that we give from our whole being to even a rock becomes a sacrifice. That rock need not be carved into a statue of Krṣṇa or Śiva. We need not name it because we see the energy behind that rock.

These two verses must be carefully understood. If not, they can be conveniently used as a justification to do whatever one wants. See, Krṣṇa does not give a license to do whatever we want here.

If we are classifying an action as good, bad, saintly, or sinful based on guidelines laid down by society or someone else, then be very clear we operate at the conscience level. No action is good or bad in itself. The entire situation should be considered. The act may remain the same: the situation might have completely changed.

There is a deeper layer of operation called consciousness. Conscience is different from consciousness. In consciousness, we become spontaneous. When consciousness flowers, we know what needs to be done and what is right at that point in time. When this happens, even if an action seems to violate the norms of society, it is always for the good. It may not be evident to society, but a person operating from consciousness can never do anything against the benefit of humanity. Kṛṣṇa killing demons may appear like the act of a criminal. Yet He established truthfulness and justice by doing it.

Please understand that when devotion matures, consciousness flowers. Devotion may seem different from knowledge when it is not ripe. Kṛṣṇa says that His devotee never perishes. Devotion is not simply offering worship daily to Kṛṣṇa's photo, lighting camphor, lamps, and offering garlands. When one is a true devotee of Kṛṣṇa, he becomes Kṛṣṇa. He experiences Kṛṣṇa consciousness. The ultimate consciousness is where no good, bad, evil, or virtue exists.

Devotion, knowledge, and wisdom appear to be different when they are not ripe. When they mature, they become the same. One experiences true wisdom at the peak of devotion or peak of knowledge.

Kṛṣṇa says, 'Anyone can reach Me through devotion, whether they are women, traders or workers, or even sinners.' He makes a point that there is no pre-qualification. Even in the age of Kṛṣṇa, there was a distinction between various trades as well as between men and women.

Someone asked Ramana maharshi whether he was qualified to enter a spiritual path. Ramana asked him, 'Are you still breathing?' Taken aback the man said, 'Yes.' Ramana said that was qualification enough. If he was alive, he was qualified.

Kṛṣṇa's message is the same. All one needs is devotion to attain Kṛṣṇa consciousness. The point Kṛṣṇa makes here is that irrespective of caste, a person who has faith and devotion to Him can attain Him. A person may follow any profession: if his inner space is cleansed, he can attain and experience Kṛṣṇa consciousness.

All practices like meditation and rituals, cleanse the inner space. When this space is cleansed, transformation automatically happens. It is a shame if a person claims to practice meditation for many years, yet there is no transformation inside. Many times people tell me, '*Swamiji,* I have been meditating for twenty five years.' They tell me this proudly. I tell them, 'What a shame, if even after twenty five years of meditation, this remains your state!'

In the last verse of this chapter Kṛṣṇa says, 'Engage your mind, always thinking of Me.'

Please understand that the whole universe, the whole cosmos, is intelligence, and it responds to our thoughts, it responds to our consciousness, to our very being.

Let me narrate an incident from my life:

> Some time after enlightenment, I was sitting in a forest in Tamil Nadu. There was a big snake lying just next to me. I had my eyes open but was resting in the universal consciousness, in a meditative mood. Several hours must have passed before I came out of my meditative state and the first thought that came to my mind was, 'Oh, it is a snake.' As long as I was in the meditative state, I did not think of the snake. You will be surprised that as soon as the thought of the snake came to my mind, the snake began to realize that I was a man! It looked up, put down its hood and moved away. The fear in me triggered the fear in the snake.

The entire universe responds to each and every thought that we have. So we must be careful about what we think. A continuous stream of random thoughts, worries, fantasy, etc., goes on in us all the time. It is like a continuous television going on inside and we have misplaced the remote control to stop it!

See, our inner space reflects the outer incidents. The entire universe responds beautifully to each and every thought. When the thought patterns are positive, only positive incidents are attracted.

If we are constantly worried and fear that we will fall ill, we attract incidents that make us fall ill again and again. Similarly, if we are constantly happy and blissful, we attract blissful events and happy people in our lives. When Krṣṇa says, 'Engage your mind in always thinking of Me,' He speaks about cleansing the inner space. When our mind is engaged in thinking of the Divine, we become divine. The moment we understand this, we relax into eternal bliss.

Let us pray to the *Parabrahma* Krṣṇa, the Divine consciousness, the cosmic intelligence, to make us understand this secret and experience the outer space and the inner space with eternal bliss, *nityānanda*. Thank you!

Thus ends the ninth chapter named **Rājavidyā-Rājaguhya Yogaḥ**, *of the* **Upaniṣad** *of the* ***Bhagavad Gītā****, the scripture of Yoga dealing with the Science of the Absolute, in the form of the dialogue between* ***Śrī Krṣṇa*** *and Arjuna.*

BhagavadGītā

You Are The Ultimate

Vibhūthi Yogaḥ

Chapter 10

I am the Creator,
the Created and the Creation.
All else is illusion.
Know Me and be liberated.

You Are The Ultimate

This chapter, the tenth chapter of the Bhagavad Gītā, is called *Vibhūti Yoga,* the yoga of divine manifestations. In this chapter, Kṛṣṇa explains His glories. In the last chapter, He explained the ultimate secret of how to feel deeply connected with the whole of Existence. Now He goes on at length, and in great detail explains how He is the Ultimate and how He expresses Himself.

An enlightened being has no identity. His only identity is the merged identity with the universe. When Kṛṣṇa, the ultimate master, talks about Himself in this chapter, He talks from the perspective of *Parabrahma* Kṛṣṇa, the cosmic Kṛṣṇa and not Vāsudeva Kṛṣṇa, the son of Vāsudeva, the mortal Kṛṣṇa. The entire Gītā is delivered from Kṛṣṇa's cosmic consciousness. In this chapter especially, He is at the peak of His cosmic consciousness, before He reveals Himself as that consciousness to Arjuna in the next chapter.

Every word that the great *Jagatguru,* the universal master utters here, is a gift to Arjuna and to humanity. The verses in this chapter are the authority on which the Bhagavad Gītā rests. It is these verses that make the Gītā a sacred scripture.

10.1 *Lord Kṛṣṇa said:*
Listen again, Oh Arjuna! You are My dear friend,
Listen carefully again, I shall speak further on knowledge for your welfare.

Please understand, a master's relationship with his disciple is in many forms. Usually it is described in five forms.

The most basic relationship between a master and disciple is that of a master and a servant, *dāsa bhāvā*. The relationship of Hanumān with Rāma represents this type. Another is the relationship of a mother with her child, *vātsalya bhāvā,* as in the case of Yaśodā to infant Kṛṣṇa. The third is the relationship of a child with the mother, *mātru bhāvā,* like the relation of Rāmakṛṣṇa to Mother Kālī.

The fourth relationship is that of friendship, *sakha bhāvā,* feeling that the master is the closest friend. The fifth is that of the beloved, *madhura bhāvā,* like the relationship of Rādhā to Kṛṣṇa.

Here, Kṛṣṇa refers to the fourth relationship, *sakha bhāvā,* as exemplified by His friendship with Arjuna. He is the master to His disciple Arjuna as well as Arjuna's friend.

In the last chapter, Kṛṣṇa gave the technique or the understanding of feeling deeply connected with the Whole, with Existence. He told Arjuna that He is revealing the greatest of all secrets to him because Arjuna is His dear friend. Now He explains the next step.

Usually, as an individual ego, we see the Whole as our enemy. We are like small waves in a big ocean. However, suddenly, the wave starts thinking that the ocean is its enemy. When it is created, while it exists or when it drops, the wave is connected to the ocean. However, the wave thinks that it is in some way different from the ocean. Not only that, the wave starts fighting with the ocean. For the wave to realize that it is fully connected to the ocean, it must be consumed by the ocean. The ego must dissolve. The individual identity of the wave must disappear. This is the first step to enlightenment.

We live in the illusion of our self-created identities. Each wave relates to another wave but not to the ocean. It adopts another wave as its father, mother, wife or child and relates with them. However, ultimately, each one of these related waves disappears into the ocean, just like the wave itself.

Yet, the impermanence of its own existence as a wave, as well as the impermanence of other waves around it, to whom it feels related, does not sink in easily. It is difficult when we are a wave, to see beyond ourselves, to our connection to the ocean. We must rise beyond the individuality of our existence as a wave dsee that we are part of the larger ocean.

Our ego makes us think that we are the center of the world, and we try to protect our status constantly. For anybody else, our ego has no meaning. Everyone has far greater concerns in their lives. They are worried about themselves. They don't have time to think about us.

A small story:

The enlightened Japanese master Suzuki wept profusely when his master passed away. Someone asked him, 'You are enlightened. You shouldn't be crying over your master's death.'

Suzuki replied, 'My master was the most extraordinary man on planet earth.' The person asked him, 'What was so extraordinary about him?'

Suzuki replied, 'I have never seen such an extraordinary person who thought he was the most ordinary.'

The thing about enlightened people is that they think they are ordinary. And the thing about unenlightened people is that they think they are extraordinary! When we feel that we have undergone maximum suffering, our ego feels good; we feel we are extraordinary. Only when our enemy is big, do we feel big. When our enemy is small, we feel small. For the same reason, if our suffering is big, we feel good and our ego is satisfied. We measure life by the amount of our suffering. That is why, we constantly torture others, as well as ourselves.

Suzuki's master was extraordinary because he thought he was the most ordinary person, whereas everyone else in this world thinks he is extraordinary.

When people have depression, they feel big. If we look deeply, everyone thinks he is extraordinary because he thinks his problems and his arguments are the greatest. A man who feels ordinary and believes in simplicity, gives respect to everybody's arguments. He knows how to put himself in another's shoes.

Because of our ego, we think that we are extraordinary and that a lot of things happen in this world because of us. We are all unique creations of Existence, but we are not responsible for the world. The wave cannot attribute to itself the power of the ocean. It must realize that it is a part of the ocean. Instead, if it tries to separate itself from the ocean, it is a futile effort.

All of us think that the world runs because of us. Please be very clear that the world does not run because of us. It runs in spite of us! Fifty years before our birth, don't you think the world was running as it is now? Fifty years hence, do you think the world will stop because you are not here?

> Ramana maharshi describes a beautiful story:
>
> A man was traveling on a train carrying his luggage on his head. A fellow passenger asked, 'Why are you carrying your luggage on your head? You can put it down and sit peacefully.'
>
> The man replied, 'It would be too heavy for the train!'

Little did he realize that even now, the train was not only carrying him, but his luggage as well! In the same way, the Divine not only takes care of you, it also takes care of your mind. But you always think you are taking care of yourself. That is the foolishness of the mind.

We are waves of the Divine. We are part of this Whole. We cannot exist as an island. We cannot be an isolated existence. We exist in the cosmic Whole just as the wave exists in the vast expanse of the ocean. The ego gives us the feeling that we are individual, separate and isolated whereas the reality is that we are a part of this Existence, in it and supported by it.

The maze of illusion

There are two ways in which we can live. First, we can embrace and welcome reality, in which case our ego must dissolve, because only then can we face reality. Please understand that this reality is God. God is not some entity hidden in some remote corner of the universe or in the sky. He is the reality around us.

The second way of living is how most of us live: We create a shell, a dream world around ourselves to defend a false ego that has no substance in reality. This is what is meant by *māyā* - illusion. In Sanskrit, there is a beautiful explanation of this term *māyā*: *Yā mā iti māyā*. That which does not exist but which troubles us as if it exists is *māyā,* illusion!

Since we are hidden in this capsule of our unreal world with our ego as the center, we cannot feel the immediate presence of God, who is actually the closest to us.

The *prānā* (vital energy) that is going inside our body and coming out is not our property. It is the property of Existence. *Prānā* is not the air that we breathe in and out. *Prānā* is the vital energy carried in the air that we breathe. Air is a mere vehicle to carry the *prānā*. Just like a truck carries and delivers material for the construction of a house, air acts as a carrier for the vital energy, *prānā*. We do not need air to survive. We need *prānā* to survive.

Constantly, the air goes in, leaves the *prānā* inside and comes out. Constantly, we take *prānā* through the air from the cosmos. If the incoming breath carries more *prānā* than the outgoing breath, we are going towards life. Then, we expand, we strengthen our body and we strengthen our energy. If the outgoing breath carries more *prānā* than the incoming breath, be very clear, we are going towards death.

Understand that whatever we think of as our being cannot function if *prānā* doesn't go in and come out.

Again and again, we think that we end where the physical boundary of our body ends, and anything outside that boundary constitutes the external world. This physical boundary is not our boundary. We think that whatever is outside the physical boundary of our body constitutes Existence and that it is our enemy.

Since you consider Existence to be your enemy, you continuously try to protect yourself from others. Look at yourself carefully, and you will notice that you always look at people with the attitude, 'Why has he come? What is he going to steal from me? What is he going to take from me? How will he exploit me?'

Continuously, you are in a protective mood, trying to protect yourself from others. The moment you see somebody, you start the calculation, 'Why is he here? What should I do before he does something to me?' You defend yourself. You are always calculating because you feel threatened by the existence of the other. The moment you think Existence or the Whole is your enemy, you become defensive. Defending is a polite word for offending. All over the world, the military forces of all countries are called defensive armies. Then who is offending? Every country claims that its army is an army for defending itself. Then who is really offending?

The idea of defending is a subtle way of offending. When you feel the Whole is your enemy, that everybody except you is your enemy, you spy continuously and fight constantly.

The fighting mood creates an increasingly violent feeling in you, with more and more restlessness. The first thing Kṛṣṇa teaches as *rājavidya rājaguhyaṁ* (Secret of Secrets), is that Existence is not your enemy. It responds to your thoughts. It continuously cares for you. It is intelligence.

Please be very clear: If you live with the attitude of enmity, even when you live, you will be dying. When you live with the attitude of enmity with the Whole, you will constantly be tortured. When you live with the feeling of friendliness, with the attitude that Existence is your friend, that Existence is your own, you feel a deep easiness.

Above all, more than the easiness, you will feel deeply connected to Existence. Even if the wave thinks that it is different from the ocean and starts defending itself from the ocean, it will ultimately fall into the ocean, however much it tries to defend itself!

By its very nature, the wave starts in the ocean, exists in the ocean and falls into the ocean. If it understands that it is a part of the ocean, it will be utterly relaxed. It will live a blissful life. If it fights the fact, it will fight with the ocean. But eventually it has to fall into the ocean.

The ultimate secret that Kṛṣṇa wants to reveal is that Existence, *Parāśakti, Brahman,* is your friend, not your enemy. It is intelligence and it responds to your thoughts. This is the first understanding. Next, in this chapter, Kṛṣṇa says, 'I am That.' He says, 'I am the whole of Existence.' In the next chapter, He gives the experience of the cosmic consciousness to Arjuna. These chapters lead Arjuna step-by-step to an elevated consciousness.

In the previous chapter, Kṛṣṇa says, 'Don't have enmity with Existence.' In this chapter, He says, 'I am the same energy. Not only don't you need to have enmity, you can have deep love.' In the previous chapter He says, 'Drop your enmity against the universal energy, *Brahman* and *ātman.*' Now, He explains how to feel connected to Existence. In the next chapter, He gives the cosmic experience. In the *Viśvarūpa Darśana Yoga,* He gives the experience to Arjuna that He is in the whole cosmic consciousness.

First, He removes enmity, then, He creates the feeling of connectedness. Finally, He gives the *advaitic* (non-dual) experience. These three chapters lead Arjuna step-by-step. They elevate Arjuna from a low level to a higher level.

Let us study this scripture with intense devotion and deep sincerity. Along with Arjuna, we will grow. We will not miss it.

Kṛṣṇa says, 'For your benefit, because you are My dear friend, I shall speak to you further, giving knowledge that is better than what I have already explained.' Kṛṣṇa explains His glory not for His own sake but for Arjuna's sake. Kṛṣṇa does not explain His glory to show His ego.

You need to understand an important thing: The ego of the king is based upon how many people accept him as king. The more the number of people who accept his ego, the greater his ego will be. Suddenly, if all the ministers, all the warriors and all his citizens are taken away from him, what will happen to his kingdom? What will happen to his kinghood?

He will lose the base, he will lose the very idea of kinghood, and he will not be a king anymore. His ego will be totally shaken.

Ego needs support

A beautiful story:

The great saint called Dakṣiṇāmūrti Swamigal lived in Tamil Nadu. He lived the life of a *Paramahamsa* (enlightened one). The sky was all that covered his body. He never wore clothing. He lived like a child, in bliss.

One day a king came to meet him. Swami was sitting under a big tree meditating blissfully. The king expected Swami to stand up and receive him with respect. Swami however did not bother. He did not care about the king. The king egoistically said, 'What! You are an ordinary beggar. I am a king. Don't you know how to respect me?'

The Swami laughed and said, 'Actually, you are the beggar. You are begging respect from me. You feel respected only when somebody gives you respect. However, I don't feel respected when somebody gives me respect nor do I feel disrespected when somebody doesn't give me respect. Whether somebody respects me or not, it is not in any way related to my consciousness. I do not ask you why you are not respecting me. I am not bothered about that. The moment you ask, you are a beggar.'

Then he continued, 'Your personality or ego could be shaken if your army and all your ministers leave you. Oh king, your being is dependent upon somebody else.'

That is why it is said that when Buddha begged for alms, He looked like a king and the kings looked like beggars! Outward possessions cannot make us regal. The inner bliss that radiates makes us regal.

Be very clear, that is why leaders are always in trouble. Never think leaders lead us. We lead the leaders. The honest truth is that as long as we accept them as a leader, they will be our leader. Just as we are concerned about their ideas, they are also concerned about our opinions. Continuously, they are bothered about our ideas.

Dakṣiṇāmūrti Swamigal says, 'You are a king as long as your citizens accept you. So naturally, directly or indirectly, you will be begging your citizens to accept you because your consciousness is dependent upon them. In my case, that is not true. Whether somebody accepts or not, I am blissful! I am a *Paramahamsa*. My *Paramahamsa*-hood can never be taken away from me. But your kinghood can be taken away from you. So be sure that the moment you ask for respect, you are a beggar. I am not.'

A clear truth is that the person whose ego is enriched by more and more citizens is a politician. He is an egoistic person. But an enlightened man reveals himself for the sake of the disciple's understanding. Here, Kṛṣṇa does not speak about Himself out of ego. Whether Arjuna accepts it or not, Kṛṣṇa is Kṛṣṇa.

Kṛṣṇa was in a blissful state even before Arjuna became His disciple. Kṛṣṇa will be in a blissful state even after Arjuna becomes His disciple. Irrespective of whether Arjuna is His disciple or not, Kṛṣṇa is in the same blissful consciousness.

One important thing: In the next chapter, Arjuna says, 'Oh Kṛṣṇa! Forgive me. I called You by Your community name: 'Hey Kṛṣṇa, Hey Yādava, Hey Saketi! I called You by Your first name. I called You by Your community name.' In India, if you are a very close friend to a person, only then you call him by his community name. Arjuna says, 'I called You by Your community name: Yādava (Kṛṣṇa's community). I called You Kṛṣṇa, Yādava and I called You my friend! I called You by these names thinking that You are my friend, a normal human being like me. But now, I understand. You are the God of gods. You are Mahādeva (supreme God). Forgive me please, I beg of You! You must forgive me and accept me as Your disciple. Forgive me for my ignorance. I did not know Your greatness, please forgive me!'

Because of this statement, Kṛṣṇa's ego does not become big. Please understand: Kṛṣṇa was safe. He had all the glory from day one until the very end. Even with all His glory, He allowed Arjuna to call Him by His first name and community names. He never said, 'Don't you know who I am? How dare you call me by my first name?' He never carried a business card!

Carrying a business card is the biggest problem. Observe how people behave. Wherever they go, the first thing they ask is, 'Do you know who I am?' We carry a business card. We give this card to whomsoever we meet.

Not only that, there is an important thing to be understood about this: Never think that your business card is wallet-sized. It is a huge billboard's size! Just because you can't carry that, you carry a small version. Your business card is the size of a billboard. Because you can't carry it wherever you go, you carry it in a small way. After giving that card, you say, 'I am this; I am that.' Kṛṣṇa never carried a business card. Kṛṣṇa never bothered about it.

A small Zen story:

The governor of a Japanese province came to visit a celebrated Zen master. The governor, as was the custom, sent in his business card through an attendant. The master read the card, 'Suzuki, Governor of Kobe Region.'

The master said, loudly enough so that the governor could hear, 'Tell that idiot I have no time to meet a governor!'

The disciple took the card back to the governor. The governor was an intelligent man. He crossed out the word 'Governor' and sent it back saying, 'Suzuki wants to meet the master to seek advice.

The Zen master happily received him!

A master cares nothing about business cards or who you are or what your status is. He is only concerned about the state of your being.

Even when Arjuna was talking to Kṛṣṇa in a friendly way, He was humble. Kṛṣṇa responded to Arjuna in the same way that Arjuna spoke to Him. Suddenly now, Arjuna says, 'Kṛṣṇa! I didn't know You were such a great person. You are God Himself. Please forgive me.'

Even after this, Kṛṣṇa does not become egoistic. He says, 'Don't worry. Don't bother about that.' He is simple. He is humble.

Before the experience, at the time of the experience and after the experience, Kṛṣṇa is the same. Only Arjuna undergoes a tremendous change. Before the Gītā started, at the time of the Gītā and after the Gītā, Kṛṣṇa is the same. But before the Gītā, Arjuna was different. At the time of the Gītā, Arjuna was growing. After the Gītā, he was a totally different man.

Here, Kṛṣṇa does not explain His glories out of ego. He explains to give Arjuna an understanding. He explains so that Arjuna will experience Him. When Kṛṣṇa says, 'I am,' He means the cosmic consciousness, the egoless being and the enlightened energy.

Again and again, He expresses the glory of enlightenment, the glory of *ātmajñāna* (knowledge of the Self). That is why He is so confident and clear. With such clarity, He explains, 'I am Everything.' Even to utter these words, you need courage. No normal man can say, 'I am God' to somebody else. If he does, the next day he will be in a mental asylum with a special seat reserved for him!

Here, Kṛṣṇa is courageous enough to declare His state, and the person who is listening experiences it.

What is the science? What does it take for an enlightened person to declare himself as enlightened and as God? What do we need as a disciple, to experience that as the truth?

Many hundreds of enlightened masters declare this truth again and again. Sometimes the people who listen to them become enlightened like Arjuna or Vivekānanda . Sometimes the disciple is hurt and disturbed by the statement and crucifies the master.

Rāmakṛṣṇa said, 'The one who came as Rāma, who came as Kṛṣṇa, is residing in this body as Rāmakṛṣṇa.' He boldly declared this, not when he was healthy, but when he was suffering from throat cancer. He affirmed, 'Who came as Rāma, who came as Kṛṣṇa, has come down in this body as Rāmakṛṣṇa.' These words did something in Vivekānanda . It was then that Narendra became Vivekānanda .

When Kṛṣṇa declared, 'I am God,' Arjuna became enlightened. How? What do you need to create this experience?

Existence cares for us

See, be very clear that the experiences of Kṛṣṇa, Christ, Buddha and Mahāvīra , are all one and the same. As the enlightenment experience, it is the same. When they express the enlightenment, why are there different reactions? When they express their enlightenment and declare their divinity, some people become enlightened and some run away.

How can we also become enlightened when we listen to Kṛṣṇa's words? How can we listen? How can we have that benefit? How is that to happen? With what mood are we supposed to receive the words?

When people who hear this declaration of truth, the glory, *vibhūti*, are egoistic and aggressive, they crucify the master. If they are egoistic but not aggressive, they run away.

Arjuna, Kṛṣṇa's disciple, is totally in love with Kṛṣṇa. He has totally surrendered to Kṛṣṇa. He is not ready to suspect anything. By now, he is clear. His head has stopped working. His logic has stopped analyzing.

This truth should be declared only to a person who is totally, intimately related and feeling connected to the Divine.

Arjuna has completely surrendered to Kṛṣṇa. What is surrender? When we hear the word 'surrender', we think that it is the easiest thing to do since we don't need to do anything. For example, if we meditate, we need to do something. But if we need to surrender, we think we don't need to do anything. Hence, we think it is easy.

This is because we think about surrender in a totally different way compared to what the masters mean by the word 'surrender'. When we use the word 'surrender', we only say that we have surrendered. We do not really surrender.

When you surrender, you cannot choose to react. When you surrender, the egocentric 'I' totally disintegrates. Please understand: The egocentric 'I' is eccentric.

When you surrender, you will be bubbling with joy and bliss. You will be like a kid. Have you seen an ugly child? Even in the poorest country, the kids are beautiful. On the same count, have you seen a single adult who is beautiful? Enlightened people are like children, bubbling with bliss. They are called *dvija* (born again). After the death of the ego, it is a new birth. The father and mother give us our first birth. The second birth is given by God and the guru. This helps you relate to Existence.

If you understand that Existence is your friend and It deeply cares for you, you will not feel the need to live according to a script. Instead, you will have tremendous courage and trust in yourself to live life spontaneously. Then, instead of re-living life and reacting to life based upon past memories and experiences, you live life with spontaneous responses to situations. If you live in a simple way, you don't need a script. If you live based upon the truth, you don't need to remember the lies that you told your friend the last time in order to maintain them.

Every moment, we project what we are not. Once we project this false image, we need a script to remember what we have projected. We are so careful not to make small mistakes that we make the biggest blunder of all - living according to a script and enacting the same drama over and over again!

Please understand that Existence constantly cares for you. Trust the intelligence in you. Accept and welcome life as it flows.

Kṛṣṇa says, 'If you continuously merge in Me, I will take care of all your needs and necessities. You will be My responsibility.'

In the last chapter Kṛṣṇa promises: *yogakṣemaṁ vahāṁyahaṁ*: My responsibility is Yoga, to get the things that you need, and *kṣema*, to take care that they remain with you. *Vahāṁyahaṁ*: He makes this promise: He says, 'I will take care of you spiritually and materially. You shall not lack anything. You will always be in bliss.' You may wonder how this is possible. When you surrender to the Divine, your higher consciousness will be activated, and you will have the intelligence and courage to live everything.

The ultimate intelligence is first understanding that Existence cares for us, and secondly, surrendering to that Existence. Realizing that Existence is not a brute force or power but an intelligent energy, is the key to a life of bliss.

When we surrender the mind, we go from 'mind' to 'no-mind' state. The mind actually arises from possessiveness. *Tantra* says that the ego is based upon possessions. Look deeply, and we will see that the origin of our mind lies in whatever we think of as ours. Our idea of 'mine' creates the sense of 'I'. Most of us think that from 'I,' the 'mine' arises. No! It is from the sense of 'mine' that 'I' arises. The root of the tree of 'I' is 'mine'.

Just surrender everything that you think of as 'mine' to Existence. Let Existence take care of you. Surrender not only your pain and suffering but also your responsibility. This does not mean that you stop doing household work or going to office. You continue to do so, but with the mood of utter relaxation. Surrendering yourself is a clear, conscious decision.

Decide consciously that from this moment, you will surrender everything at the feet of God, to the energy that runs this whole world. We don't need to believe in any name or form. Trust the energy pervading the universe and trust it to run your life.

Now, even after we surrender, at some time, a doubt will naturally arise in us whether we have totally, actually surrendered. Understand that the divine intelligence gave us the intelligence to surrender in the first place and that same divine intelligence has given us this doubt to doubt our surrender. Surrender the doubt also at the feet of the divine energy. So do not wait to change and become perfect before surrendering. No! Surrender yourself as you are, consciously, totally. Surrender deeply and your whole being will be flooded with new bliss.

True love is divinity

Kṛṣṇa says,

mahābāho śṛṇu me paramaṁ
vacaḥ yat te ahaṁ priyamāṇāya
vakṣyāmi hitakāmyayā

Because you are My dear friend, and you are deeply connected to Me, I am revealing this truth to you.

Let me explain a few basic things. Actually, when we feel deeply connected to some person, the person will almost look like God. We will feel so deeply related. If we feel deeply connected to the person, no matter whether it is our husband, wife, kids, parents or our master, he will look like God. Whatever he does, we will feel that he is divine.

Why do you think the eternal lovers Ambikavati and Amravati, Devadās and Pārvatī, Laila and Majnu, Romeo and Juliet, felt that the other person was God? They almost felt as if their partner was divine. They gave their life for the other person. Why?

When we feel deeply connected, when we feel deeply related, when we are in love with another being, that other being will look almost like God. Look at the great Mīrābāi. She was so much in love with Kṛṣṇa who was not even physically in front of her. Yet, she felt so deeply connected to Him. She talked to Him, sang His praises and became totally immersed in Him. When Mīrābāi was given poison, she even drank that, totally surrendering herself to Kṛṣṇa. The power of her love and devotion was such that even a deadly poison had no effect on her!

Vivekānanda describes a *nāgā sanyāsi* who lived in a cave. All kinds of wild animals surrounded the area, including snakes. He had many snakebite marks, but he was so connected to Existence that he welcomed snakes! All we need is the attitude of deeply connecting through the heart.

The problem is that we have forgotten how to connect through the heart. All our relationships have become superficial. Now, the wife is no more a wife. In the modern day society, the husband is no more a husband. He is just a boyfriend. She can be with him as long as she wants. She can leave him when she doesn't want him anymore.

Be very clear: In Sanskrit, we don't have an equivalent word for divorce. The idea never existed! In Hindu marriages, no divorce is allowed. We take an oath in front of *agni* (fire), 'As long as you are alive, as long as I am alive, I will support you.' Both partners take this oath in front of *agni* . The *agni* is inside our body. The *Jatarāgni*, which is the digestive fire inside our body, is represented by the *agni* in the ritual fire outside.

As long as this fire is inside our body, we will be alive. The moment this fire in our body disappears, our body will be in fire in the cremation ground! Either the inner fire is in our body or our body will be put into the outer fire.

In front of this fire as witness, we take the oath, 'Hereby I commit, as long as this body is alive, I will support you. As long as this body is alive, you will take care of me.' It is a commitment of a lifetime.

Sanskrit doesn't have an equivalent word for divorce because the concept did not exist at that time. With the cultural invasion of the so-called developed cultures, the materialistic cultures, changing the wife, house and car has now become a fashion. Once in three months, the house, car and wife become outdated.

Some time ago, a man asked me to bless his divorce. In India, a master is not only a spiritual person, he is also marriage-broker, stockbroker, financier, counselor, psychiatrist and a doctor! Masters are supposed to do all these things. Whatever decisions are advised by an enlightened person are for your good. Out of compassion and responsibility for the world, the master acts.

I asked this man to tell me the real problem before I gave advice. I always try to patch up differences between people. One should have a strong case before going for a drastic step.

The man replied, 'One day when my wife brought me hot coffee in the morning, she spilled it on me. The fight started from there.' He then went back down his memory lane to give all his arguments against her.

Some communities in India follow a custom at the time of marriage where the bride and groom compete to find a ring dropped in a pot of water. It is done more for fun. Whoever grabs the ring will have it. The man exclaimed, 'Right from that time, she spelled trouble for me. She scratched my hand while playing that game.' Look at the mentality! He has forgotten all the coffee she has brought him everyday before he wakes up. He feels no gratitude for that. Instead, he blames her for spilling coffee.

We forget the arguments that go against our judgment and pick up those that support it. If you scan your life and see how many times you do this, you will understand what I am saying.

The outer world is a projection of the inner world and the eye projects it. Whatever is visible as the outer world is a mere projection. For instance, if there was a scene in a movie we did not like, we would not be able to change it by clearing the screen. Instead, we need to switch off the projector or change the reel. Likewise, we try without success to change things in the outer world. Our frustration and depression are due to our attempt to manipulate the screen rather than the projector.

We fantasize about a holiday on a beautiful beach in Hawaii as ultimate bliss. However, when it happens, our thoughts are not of the beach but of our office and deadlines! I tell people that if we sit in the house and worry, it is homework. If we sit in the office and worry, it is work and if we sit on the beach and worry, it is vacation! The mind is the same, only the location is different. How can we change the mental state by changing the place? We are engaged all the time in changing the status, not the state.

We need to change the state, not the status. When we begin to change the state, we work with the projector and make progress, but changing our status is like working with the screen. Changing our wife, house or car is like working with the screen and it does not help us. Changing our mind and therefore our fantasies is the only way.

When we don't pass judgment on others, we reach the state of acceptance, the state of compassion. When intelligence happens, we reach the stage of acceptance. Acceptance is the first step and not the final step. When we welcome people and situations, compassion happens. *Beloved* means being loved, not 'body love.'

What is the difference between intellect and intelligence? Intellect is always prejudiced. Intelligence is always fresh. When we pass judgment and collect evidence to substantiate our decision, it is intellect. When we first collect evidence and pass judgment without bias or prejudice, it is intelligence.

In fact, this is a true scientific attitude: We need the urge to know the truth, the perseverance to gather data and the courage to follow the conclusion. Patañjali's Yoga sūtras is an excellent example of a true scientist's research report. We need to embody these values to do justice to the scientific attitude.

Many people do not have the courage to follow their results. Galileo declared that the earth goes around the sun, which challenged the widely held Christian belief of a heliocentric world. He was persecuted. In his writings, he added the footnote, 'We as Christians can deny this but since the earth and sun are not Christians, they will continue to move the way they do.'

So even from the scientific perspective, we need to analyze data with an unbiased perception before we conclude, before we judge.

Ninety nine percent of the time we make the judgment and collect arguments to substantiate our judgment.

Look at your life and see how your mind works. How do you act in your daily life? The vast majority of the time, your judgment is ready. For example, your son comes home late by a few hours. You make a judgment about him. You will not accept any of his explanations. They can't shake your judgment. On the contrary, you pick arguments to support your decision. After that incident, whatever he does, you will be biased by your previous judgment.

Similarly, after living with your wife for a few months, you create a concept about her. Then, whatever she does, you pick only those arguments that are necessary for your already formed judgment.

Whenever we try to live for our judgment, our ego, and our decisions, we make our life miserable. And we make the lives of others miserable also. Most of the time, others do not create the miseries we face. Just to prove our ego, we create them. We may not even derive any benefits from them.

Whenever we think too much of ourselves, we believe only in our judgments and lay the blame on others. When we understand that we are simple beings, we start seeing the arguments clearly before passing judgment. We start making decisions in our lives in the right way and our relationships with others also change.

Most of the time, when we are attracted to a person of the opposite sex, we say it is love. If it is someone else's emotion, we call it lust. Or when we become angry, we say it is for the other person's good. Yet, if others become angry with us, we say they have ego.

People boast about their deeds to me but quickly add that they are only informing me and not boasting. When others boast, we say it is ego. But we justify when we say the same thing by calling it information. We use different arguments for others. We put on one set of lens when we look at the world and another set when we look at ourselves.

Actually, we have forgotten how to relate through the heart, the intense way of relating. Our relationships have become superficial. We don't really know the meaning of the term, 'falling in love'.

Whenever Rāmakṛṣṇa worshipped through *pūjā,* he felt that Devī was present. He never felt that the statue was a stone. He felt the presence of Devī. When we deeply fall in love, even a stone can become God and guide us. When we don't feel connected, even if God comes down, we will ask for His business card! If we strongly feel connected, if we know how to open ourselves, a stone can become God and guide us. That is what happened to Rāmakṛṣṇa. He spoke to Kālī Devī. He talked to Devī directly.

Let me tell a beautiful story that happened in Rāmakṛṣṇa's life:

Rāmakṛṣṇa was the priest in the Devī temple. He used to taste the food before offering it to Devī. All the temple authorities told him, 'No! You cannot do this. That is sacrilegious.' Rāmakṛṣṇa said, 'I don't know all these things. I feel that She is my mother. How can I offer the food unless I know that it tastes good? And if you don't want me to offer, I will stand outside and offer. But I will offer.'

They agreed, 'Alright, do whatever you want.' Not only that, when he decorated the idol of Devī, he placed a small thread near Her nose to see whether She was breathing or not, whether She was alive or not. And the story says, the thread moved due to Devī's breath. He felt Devī everywhere.

The descent of the Divine

There is another beautiful story you should know and this is the solid truth. Please understand: It is the truth.

In Bengal, devotees adorned the wrists of Devī in the Dakṣiṇeśvar temple with bangles made out of conch shell. Devī Kālī has four hands: Two are *'abhaya hasta'* and *'varada hasta'* - 'protecting hand' and 'providing hand' respectively. In the third hand, She holds the *khadga,* sword. In the fourth hand, She holds the *munda,* the head of a demon that represents the human ego.

Actually, this is a philosophical representation. It means: By cutting our ego with the sword of knowledge, She protects and takes care of us.

It is easy to put a bangle on three of the hands of this Devī statue. In the hand that holds the sword, the sword can be removed and the bangle can be slid on. In the protecting and giving hands, the bangle can be slid on. However, the fourth hand of Devī holds the head of the demon. In that hand, we cannot put the conch bangle over the demon's head nor can we remove the head and slide it on.

One day a devotee brought four bangles for Devī. Within half an hour, Rāmakṛṣṇa somehow decorated each of Devī's wrists with one of the four bangles. Even though it was physically impossible, Devī's fourth hand was now wearing a bangle! Neither was the statue's hand broken nor was the bangle broken.

The devotee was surprised, shocked. This incident is mentioned in the reminiscences of Rāmakṛṣṇa, written in original Bengali by the close devotees, the householder disciples of Rāmakṛṣṇa.

The devotee asked, '*Swamiji*, how did you put the bangle on Devī? Did you break it and paste it?' Rāmakṛṣṇa said, 'No.'

The devotee asked curiously, 'Did you break the statue?' Rāmakṛṣṇa said, 'No.'

The statue is made of black marble. Neither was the stone statue broken nor was the bangle broken but the bangle was on the hand of Devī! The devotee was shocked. He asked, 'How did you do it?'

Rāmakṛṣṇa asked, 'What is the problem? I told *Ma* (mother), 'Mother, drop the head for a few minutes. She dropped the head. I put the bangle on. I gave her the head back. She started holding it again; that's all!'

Please understand: If you visit the Dakṣiṇeśvar Temple in Kolkata, please don't miss seeing that bangle. That bangle is still there. Somehow, by divine grace, I had the chance to go into the sanctum sanctorum and I saw the bangle at close quarters. Still, it is a mystery as to how Rāmakṛṣṇa put on the bangle. One thing is sure: Neither the statue nor the bangle was broken.

The energy is such that even a stone can respond! We should never think that the deity in the temple is stone. It is *arcāvatāra*: descent of the Divine into the deity for the purpose of worship. Never think it is stone. It can straightaway respond to us.

Honestly, when I first read that reminiscence, I did not believe it. I was a strong intellect before enlightenment. I am the kind of person who never believes easily. I never trust anything. I prefer to verify and do crosschecking. I thought, 'One more story. Alright, leave it.'

In North India, we can go inside the sanctum sanctorum. Even in Kasi, in the Viśvanāth temple, we can touch the Viśvanāth deity and make offerings. There is only one condition: We must first take a bath and then enter the sanctum. When I went to the Kālī temple, the priest took me inside. I touched the bangle and rotated it. The bangle is made of conch-shell and it rotates. Neither was there a cut nor was the statue broken. It is still a mystery!

Be very clear: When we feel connected, when we know how to open ourselves, when we know how to surrender, even stone can become God and guide us. When we don't know how to open, how to surrender, even if God comes, we will ask for His identity card. We will be unable to relate with Him.

Now, all we need is the mood of being deeply in love with Kṛṣṇa, deeply connected to Kṛṣṇa, deeply related to Kṛṣṇa. If we can open ourselves to Kṛṣṇa when He describes His glories, it will not be words. We will feel it.

First, Kṛṣṇa removed the enmity between *jivātma* (Self) and *paramātma* (supreme Self). Arjuna is the *jivātma.* Kṛṣṇa is the *paramātma.*

We may not be aware but we continuously maintain enmity with *paramātma,* Existence. That is why we suspect life. We have fear about what will happen in the next moment. We are afraid of life because we don't believe what is going to happen the next moment will be good for us. We don't trust Existence.

All life insurance policies are only because we don't trust Existence. Understand, life insurance is not life insurance. It is death insurance. Real life insurance is devotion to the Ultimate. Understanding that Existence is taking care of us is the real life insurance. It is the only life insurance. All other things are death insurance that goes to our families, who are waiting for it! So that is not life insurance. That is death insurance.

A small story:

A young child was playing on the beach. He wanted to wade into the ocean. His mother ran after him and said, 'Don't go into the ocean. Play in the sand. Don't go into the water.'

The boy asked, 'Why? Daddy is going into the water. Why are you not stopping him? You are stopping me.' The mother said, 'He is insured!'

So please be very clear: All our insurance is death insurance. It is not life insurance. Understanding that Existence is taking care of us, and that it is not our enemy, is the only life insurance we need.

One more thing: When we have the deep love - the connection with Existence, even when we die, we know that He knows where to keep us. We will be utterly relaxed. Even after death, we know He will protect and guide us. So now itself, our mind should be prepared to fall in tune with this energy; to obey, to surrender to the ultimate will. Now itself, our body and mind should be prepared.

If we live life fighting with Existence, our life will be hell. Nothing else can be done. All we need to do is know how to feel connected.

First, Kṛṣṇa removes the enmity between the individual Self and Existence. Now, He explains the glory of Existence. Next, He gives the experience that the individual Self and the supreme Self are the same.

Step-by-step, He leads Arjuna from *viśiṣṭādvaita* (a school of thought that says that the individual self is a part of Existence, with its own attributes) to *dvaita* (duality - a school of thought that says that the individual self is separate from Existence), to *advaita* (non-duality - a school of thought that says that the individual self is an integral part of Existence), to beyond *advaita* to *anubhūti,* experience. He leads Arjuna to a spiritual experience step-by-step. I spoke earlier about the three essential identities in our lives. These are: *jīva* - individual Self; *jagat* - the world in which this Self lives, and *Īśvara* - Creator of *jīva* and *jagat,* or in other words, God.

Initially, we see these three as separate entities, just as the water drop sees itself as separate from the ocean. There are different approaches in Hindu philosophy as to how the individual Self can reach the Creator, the Divine. The concepts of *viśiṣṭādvaita* and *dvaita* are based on a separation between the Self and the Creator, with deep devotion connecting the two. Devotion leads the Self to the Divine and an understanding of the Divine. Yet they remain separate. It is like the water drop realizing it is part of the ocean and yet separate.

Advaita philosophy integrates the Self and the Creator into one non-dual entity, of which *jagat,* the world, forms a part. So the three seemingly separate entities merge into one. *Advaita* says that separation is an illusion, *māyā,* and that true realization of the non-dual aspect of the Self and the Divine leads to liberation and enlightenment. These are different ways of looking at the same situation. None of them is wrong.

Kṛṣṇa leads Arjuna from the concept of separation into the understanding of integration. Kṛṣṇa makes Arjuna understand that nothing stands between him and Kṛṣṇa, except his level of understanding.

Please be very clear: These are not contradictory. Many people ask me, '*Swamiji,* is *dvaita* or *advaita* right? Is *viśiṣṭādvaita* or *dvaita* right?' They are not contradictory. They complement each other. They lead us step-by-step to more and more understanding. They lead us step-by-step to the ultimate spiritual experience.

In India, this clash between *advaita* and *dvaita* is a big fight. Is the Śaṅkara *bhāṣya* (Śaṅkara's commentary) big or is Rāmānuja *bhāṣya* big? Śaṅkara was the founder of *advaita* philosophy and Rāmānuja founded the *dvaita* philosophy. The problem is that supporters of these scriptures have not studied either of them deeply. If we study deeply, we will understand that they say the same thing in different languages.

All enlightened masters speak the same thing in different ways. If we surrender, we will have the same experience of *advaita-anubhav,* non-duality experience. If we achieve the non-duality experience, we will have deep surrender.

The man who has achieved *advaita-anubhava* has tremendous devotion. For example, the verse of Śaṅkara says:

bhaja govindaṁ bhaja govindaṁ
govindaṁ bhaja mūḍhamate
samprāpte sannihite kāle
nahi nahi rakṣati ḍukṛñkaraṇe

Śaṅkara says, 'Oh Fool! May you start meditating on Govinda (God) now. May you start remembering Govinda now. *Nahi nahi rakṣati ḍukṛñkaraṇe* means: When *Yamadharma,* the Lord of death comes, intellectual knowledge will not help you. Your intellectual knowledge will not guide you.

A great *advaita-jñāni,* sage of non-duality experience, will be a great devotee. And a great devotee will be an *advaita-jñāni*! Both are one and the same. Only those who have not realized the experience argue.

> Rāmakṛṣṇa tells this beautiful story:
>
> Four people approach a water tank. One person says, 'I am going to drink *tanneer*, meaning water in Tamil. The other person says, 'No! In that tank, there is only water. *Tanneer* is not there.' The third person says, 'No, I am going to drink *paani* (water in Hindi).' The fourth person says, 'I am going to drink *neeru* (water in Kannada).'
>
> One person says, 'No, my grandfather told me that there is only water.' The other person says, 'My grandfather constructed this tank. He says it is *tanneer*.' Another person says, 'My grandfather has all the knowledge. He said it is *neeru*.'
>
> The four people start fighting without even going near the tank, without seeing the tank, before ever reaching the tank. They kill each other and die.

If they had had enough patience to peer into the tank, they would have understood that the four words mean the same thing. What they meant by water, *tanneer*, *paani* and *neeru* are one and the same. However, these people did not have that much patience.

If we experience it, we will understand that Rāmānuja, Śaṅkara, Buddha and Madhvācārya are all one and the same in their experience.

A small story:

A *Vedānta* bookstall at a book-fair was selling the Brahma Sūtra *bhāṣya* and the Rāmānuja *bhāṣya*. An elderly *puṇḍit*, a scholar well read in the scriptures, stopped by and saw one volunteer standing in the store.

He wondered how much knowledge this salesman had of these books. He asked the volunteer, 'Do you know the difference between the Śaṅkara *bhāṣya* and the Rāmānuja *bhāṣya?*'

The volunteer replied, 'Forty-five rupees, sir!'

All he knew was the price and not what was inside those books! To him the difference was a dollar.

If you go inside *dvaita* and *advaita* philosophies, both show the same knowledge, wisdom and experience. All we need to know is how to open ourselves and surrender to this Existence. Then we will experience at the level of our being that Existence is taking care of us. Please be very clear: If Existence doesn't want us here, we cannot be here even for a single moment. Even for a single moment, we cannot be here. There is no reason for Existence to keep us alive. If it is keeping us alive, we are wanted. We are wanted in this form, in this way, in this place. That is why we are still alive.

God continuously cleans all the garbage. He never waits. Everyday He clears away all the old things. He is the perfect energy that maintains cleanliness. They say that cleanliness is next to Godliness. I say that cleanliness *is* Godliness. It is not next to Godliness.

Trust even if you are exploited

Unless we are needed, we will not be kept alive. Just by being alive, He proves that we are needed. We are wanted. We are not an accident. We are an incident. Don't think that we are alive as an accident. We are an incident. When we understand that we are an incident, we feel deeply connected. We open ourselves to Existence.

I tell people: Trust, even if you are exploited. You may say, 'What is this, *Swamiji*? What kind of teaching are you giving? You are asking us to trust even if we are exploited.'

Be very clear: There are two kinds of lives. One is living completely with trust, and the other is living completely with an insecure feeling. The person who lives in insecurity may have more wealth. He may have two or three more sofa sets, two or three more beds, a little bigger house, yet he can never rest. The person who lives with the insecure consciousness may have more comfort, but he will never be blissful.

On the other hand, the person who lives with deep trust in Existence, may have less comfort, but he never misses that comfort. People who trust Existence are always showered with blessings. They will live like God on planet earth. They will live like a flower on planet earth. They will be a blessing for the whole planet. The earth is alive because of a few people who live radiating this trust, who live radiating the divine grace.

In Genesis, God says to Abraham, 'If ten good people are found in a country, I will not destroy that land.' India has been invaded so many times. Yet the culture is alive. It exists in spite of the invasions, in spite of all the trouble. Nobody can shake it. Nobody can touch it because it continuously produces enlightened masters! As long as India produces enlightened masters and supplies them to the world, it will not be destroyed.

You see, each country contributes something to humanity. For example, the western society contributes to the social structure. They work with so many different social structures. Germans contribute to the medical field. They have done so much research in medicine. The Japanese contribute to the field of technology. The Chinese contribute to the level of production. In some way or the other, every nation contributes.

India contributes by creating enlightened masters! For anything else, we can go to other countries. For spirituality, we must turn towards India. All the great spiritual cultures were born and nurtured in India. All the spiritual cultures have had their basis and inspiration from India.

We should trust, even if we are exploited. Even if we are exploited, when we live with trust, we live like God on planet earth. After all, we are going to live on this earth for a maximum of seventy to eighty years. In those seventy to eighty years, why should we continuously torture others and ourselves? When we live with an insecure consciousness, we torture others and ourselves.

One more thing that is important for us to know: If we defend ourselves because of our insecurity, we will not only offend others but we will also miss the joy of living on planet earth. If we trust even if we are exploited, how much will we lose? All that we possess is nothing more than a sand castle.

According to the Hindu mythological stories, Vyāsa lived longer than any other man. Someone asked why he didn't build a house. Vyāsa replied, 'After all, I am only going to live for a few years. Why should I build a house? Why waste my time?'

A Zen koan says, 'Children build sandcastles on the beach until the evening. Before they go back home, they simply destroy them without a care.' However, we build castles with costly things, and we are so serious about it; that is the only difference! We take things too seriously. Children have intelligence, not seriousness.

If we can, let us live with the completely relaxed mood of deep trust. Then our life will be like a flower. Our presence will be a blessing. Our existence will save planet earth. No matter what crosses our path, we will just be living and enjoying. It is a blessing.

What have we brought here to lose? Our insecure consciousness is nothing but ignorance of the truth. What are we going to carry with us after death? Nothing! A simple truth: Neither have we brought anything nor are we going to take back anything.

While we are here, we can relax and trust that Existence will provide for us. If the energy moving inside our body can convert bread into blood, can't it bring bread to us? Just to convert bread into blood mechanically, it has been said that we need an industry that measures three miles long. Yet, the whole process happens inside our body without our conscious effort.

Our brain receives information, analyzes, understands, and responds. This entire process that is happening inside our brain would need a computer at least three stories high that would create a sound equal to at least ten generators!

When people tell me, '*Swamiji*, my mind is too noisy, I don't feel the silence or peace,' I tell them, 'For the amount of work done by your mind, it is very silent! Never think it is noisy.'

The big problem is that we don't trust our energy. We don't trust the cosmic energy. When it can convert bread into blood, can't it help us with our small things? Can't it give us the intelligence to bring bread, sustenance into our lives? It can guide us. It can give us enough intelligence to bring bread for our life. When the energy can move planets and run the whole universe, can't it take care of us?

> Let me narrate to you a real incident:
>
> Śāradā devī, the wife of Rāmakṛṣṇa, opened a charitable hospital in Calcutta. There were two counters: one counter where medicines were given free for the poor and another counter for people who could afford to buy medicines.
>
> One employee of the hospital complained to Śāradā devī, 'Mother, even rich people stand in the counter for the poor and take advantage of the free medicines. What should we do about this?'
>
> Śāradā devī replied, 'Don't be concerned. When a rich man stands in the line for the poor, be assured that he is also poor, and give him medicines. Even if he has money, he is a poor man. He has come here as a beggar.'

She makes a beautiful statement, 'Outer wealth doesn't make one rich or poor. It is the inner attitude that matters. If you live with trust, even if you are exploited, even if you lose your comforts of the outer world, you will live like God on this planet earth. You will simply float. You will never merely walk. You will become a divine person.'

I am asking you to trust Existence, not based upon my intellectual knowledge but from my personal experience. If you believe me, if you trust my words, when you trust Existence and relax from your tensions, headaches, worries and problems, be sure that you will be taken care of. Miracles will happen in your life. When you put your energy totally on trust, something happens in you. An alchemy takes place in you.

A small story:

Once there was an enlightened master. One day he went to bathe in the river leaving his shawl on the riverbank. His student was passing by. He saw the shawl and thinking that someone might steal it, decided to guard it till its owner retuned.

When the master came looking for his shawl, the student asked, '*Swamiji*, under whose care did you leave your shawl? It could have been stolen!'

The master replied, 'I left it under His care who gave you the task of guarding it!'

Understand, when you surrender, there is utter relaxation in you and your responsibilities are shifted to a higher authority. This is surrender. Do your duty and leave all of the responsibility to Existence. She will take care!

The moment we live with trust, we are liberated. Nothing hurts us anymore. If we live with the truth, we beautifully live even our death because we trust that Existence will take care of us even then. If we live without trust, we will be killed by the fear of death. Every moment, we will be dying. With trust, even in our death, we will be living, celebrating!

Here, if we can relax and feel deeply connected to what Kṛṣṇa says, we will experience the state that Kṛṣṇa expresses when He tells us about His glories.

I Am The Source

10.2 *Neither the hosts of deities nor the great sages know My origin, My opulence.*
I am the source of the deities and the sages.

10.3 *He who knows Me as the unborn, without beginning, and supreme Lord of all the worlds,*
Only he who has this clarity is wise and freed from all bondage.

Kṛṣṇa says, 'Neither the *devatas* (gods) nor the *ṛṣis* know Me.' He means that neither people who work in the line of comforts and luxury nor the people who work in the line of religion and *tapas* (penance) know Him. 'But, I am their origin.'

Whether we live a spiritual or a materialistic life, our root is our consciousness. We should understand an important thing: Whenever Kṛṣṇa says, 'Me, Me, Me,' He is referring to the enlightened consciousness.

Let me narrate a real incident:

I was invited to a conference by a group of Kṛṣṇa *bhaktas* (devotees). I can't say devotees as the word devotee is a beautiful word. They were more like fanatics. I went humbly, politely and in a friendly way.

Suddenly, they confronted me and started arguing. They asked me, 'Do you believe in the Gītā?' I said, 'Yes, Gītā is the ultimate book. I respect it and I worship it.' They questioned me, 'Then why do you worship Śiva?' I was shocked. They asked me, 'You should worship only Kṛṣṇa. Why are you worshipping Śiva? Why do you put *vibhūti* (holy ash) on your forehead? Why you wear *rudrākṣa* (fruits of *rudrākṣa* tree)?'

I asked them, 'How does respecting Śiva and wearing *rudrākṣa* contradict respecting and following the Gītā?' They said, 'No. Kṛṣṇa says in the Gītā, 'I am everything,' so how can you worship Śiva?' I was surprised.

I said, 'When Kṛṣṇa says 'I,' He means the *Parabrahma svarūpa* (universal Self) of Him. He means the formless consciousness of His being. He represents the universal energy. He doesn't mean the six-foot form with the flute and peacock feather. The form is beautiful as long as it leads you to the formless. If He means the six-foot form, how could He say that He taught this knowledge to Vivasvān? He says, 'I gave this knowledge to Ikṣvāku. I gave this wisdom to Sūrya.' He says, 'I gave this knowledge to Ikṣvāku. And from there, it came down to Manu.' He says again and again, it is He who gave this knowledge to these great people who lived thousands of years before Him!

When the Gītā was delivered, Kṛṣṇa was thirty-two years old. If He was speaking about His form, how could He say, 'I gave this knowledge to Sūrya. I gave this knowledge to Manu?' When Kṛṣṇa says 'I', He means the cosmic consciousness.

Immediately, the people who were arguing asked, 'How can you say the form and energy are different? When He says 'I,' He means the form also.'

I explained, 'I do not want to disrespect Kṛṣṇa's form. When the form represents the energy, the form is also energy, no doubt. But it is not that you cannot worship another form. You don't have to become a fanatic.'

One person started arguing, 'How can you say that when Kṛṣṇa says 'I', He doesn't mean the form but He means the energy?' Then, I had to refer to another important scripture, the Anu Gītā that was delivered in the Mahābhārata after the Bhagavad Gītā.

After the war is over, Arjuna asks, 'Kṛṣṇa, please tell me whatever You taught me earlier. I remember the essence but I forgot the words because You taught me the whole thing during the war. I have forgotten the words. Please repeat them once more. I want to listen to those great teachings.'

You will be surprised but Kṛṣṇa says, 'Arjuna, not only you, I have also forgotten.' He says:

na cākhyaṁ tanmayā bhūyastataḥ

bhaktom aśeṣataḥ param hi

brahma rati yoga yuktena tanmayaḥ

This is in the Mahābhārata in *Aśvamedhika Parva.*

Kṛṣṇa says, 'Arjuna, I can't give the teachings again because they were said in that high spiritual, eternal consciousness. At that time, I was in that high, eternal consciousness. I was radiating My enlightenment. That very enlightenment spoke through Me. The universal consciousness spoke through Me. The universal energy expressed itself through Me. That is why all those teachings came out. I represented the universal energy, the universal consciousness at that moment. Now, I cannot give you the same teachings again.'

He says that these things are expressed in that high, eternal consciousness. Please understand that when Kṛṣṇa says 'I', He means the enlightened energy, the universal consciousness. However Kṛṣṇa recollected a few things from what He told and delivered to Arjuna what is called the Anu Gītā.

When I quoted this verse, the senior religious *puṇḍits* (scholars) arguing with me said, 'You look young, but you seem to be well read. We cannot argue with you!'

The greatness of *Sanātana Dharma* – the religion of eternal righteousness later called Hinduism - is that it doesn't propagate the religion or produce fanaticism.

Whether you worship Kṛṣṇa, Christ, Muhammad or Buddha, it does not make a difference. Please continue to worship whomever you believe in and whomever you connect with, that's enough. Be intense in your path. Nothing else needs to be done. There is no need for fanaticism because all forms are representations of the same divine energy.

There is a question here from the audience: 'I am a worshipper of formlessness, the formless energy. Can I become your disciple and follow *dhyāna* (meditation)?'

Only *then* can you become my disciple!

Only if you are the worshipper of the formless, can you become my disciple. There is a strict instruction for my disciples that they should not meditate on my form. If you have done any of our meditation camps, you know. There is a strict instruction: You cannot meditate on my form. You should not meditate on my form.

And be aware, if any guru tells you to meditate on his form, escape from him. You are falling into the net. You are falling into indirect slavery. Never, never, do that. You will slowly get exploited. Spiritual slavery is the worst slavery. Never be caught in that.

The basis of spirituality is that it should lead us to liberation. In spirituality, if we are caught in slavery, then even God cannot save us. Never meditate on my form.

In our healing initiation, the third level program, there is a clear instruction: You cannot meditate on my form. The form will be here today and gone tomorrow. It will disappear tomorrow. How long will forms be here? Forms can never be here forever.

Form is a representation. Understand: It is like the finger pointing to the moon. I am telling you, 'There is the sun. There is the moon!' Instead of looking at the sun or moon, if you catch hold of my finger, you miss what I am showing you! You miss what I represent. When the finger points to the moon, if you catch the finger, you miss the moon.

In the same way, the master represents the divine consciousness. If you catch His form, you miss the Divine. Never be caught in the form. I tell people: Never meditate on my form. If somebody tells you to meditate on his form, be very clear that he is exploiting you. Escape. Save yourself.

All I want you to understand is that when Kṛṣṇa says 'I', He means the universal consciousness.

In the next verse, He uses the word *mūḍhaḥ,* fool. Again He uses the word 'Fool'. He says only someone who is free from all the sins understands Him. Again and again, what does He want to convey? what does He expect as a qualification from us in order to experience Him?

Where exactly are you missing it?

There is one more question: '*Swamiji,* again and again, you say all we need is one simple understanding. Exactly, what am I missing? Tell me. I think I have that understanding. I almost feel I am around the corner. Yet, I am unable to experience what Kṛṣṇa says. What am I missing? Where am I missing? Please tell me.'

As I was telling you, what and where exactly do we lack? The person who asked this question is totally frustrated. He says, 'Everyday at the end of the lecture, you bring everything to the one point that the inner being should be transformed. Exactly what am I lacking? Please tell me.'

Everyday I stop at that subject, so that you will ask this question. Now, I can tell exactly where you are lacking. First, the thirst should be created. The quest should be created. Then, the quest should be answered.

When the question becomes a quest, you speak in this language. When the urge becomes urgent, you speak in this language.

A small story:

Once there was a college student who was very weak in Math. She somehow wanted to pass the Math exam. So she went to her Math professor's office. She closed the door and went up to him. She looked deeply into his eyes and said meaningfully, 'I will do anything to pass in this exam… anything.'

The professor also looked deeply into her eyes and asked, 'Will you really do *anything* to pass the exam?'

'Yes,' replied the girl.

'Will you… study?' the professor asked.

Our interest in spirituality is similar to this. Our seeking is only this much. Many seekers are just like window shoppers. Window shopping is just walking along the street and seeing what's there. Many seekers are window shoppers. They go from master to master.

Going from master to master is not wrong. It is perfectly alright. However, not learning from anybody is wrong. Again and again, I tell people, 'Go to all the gardens, but pick flowers and make a beautiful bouquet.'

But what do we do? We don't pick flowers from any garden. That is where the problem starts. A lot of people are just window shoppers. They go around. They don't do anything. They act as if they are seekers. Above all, they want to satisfy themselves that they are seekers. This is hypocrisy.

Either put your whole effort into seeking, or forget it and carry on with life. If you say that you are trying to pick up a book, but you don't pick it up, what does it mean? It is just cheating.

Rāmakṛṣṇa says beautifully, 'If somebody's hair is burning, will he keep quiet? Will he say, 'I have no time now. I still have many more years. Later on, I can take care?' The moment there is fire on a person's head, he tries to put out the fire. He runs towards water.

Exactly where are we lacking? Because we feel too much ego in our being. When Kṛṣṇa says He is God, we feel He is egoistic. For example, if I suddenly say, 'I am God,' what will you naturally think? 'This guy has gone crazy and he has too much ego.'

Please understand: When you say the word 'I', the meaning is different from when a master says it. When you say the word 'God', the word is empty for you. When you use the word 'God,' it is just a superficial understanding for you. It has no solid truth behind it. When you say the word 'God', it is some collected thoughts about whatever you have read or heard or whatever you think about God, that's all. It is not a solid truth or experience for you.

Whereas when you say the word 'I' or your name, there is a solid meaning and experience behind that word for you. But when you say 'God', there is no solid meaning behind that word. When it comes to enlightened masters, the word 'I' has no solid meaning. It is vague, superficial. However, the word 'divine' or 'enlightened' or 'God' has a solid meaning. It is their very experience.

Just because you have ego, you think that masters too have ego and end up missing their expressions or teachings. Just let go your ego and listen to the master's words intensely.

I know, I can see how this whole scene of the Gītā between Arjuna and Kṛṣṇa would have happened. After Kṛṣṇa's teachings, Arjuna completely and totally melted in front of Kṛṣṇa.

Kṛṣṇa explains, 'Oh my dear! Understand, I am everything. I have come down. I have happened in this body to liberate you.'

Immediately, the man who is centered on fear, says, 'If you are everything, do all these things for me. Alter this world.' If he is centered on greed, he says, 'If you are everything, give me all these boons.'

The moment the master says he is God, the moment Kṛṣṇa says He is God, if you are centered on greed, you catch him and ask him to give you all the boons. You start begging, 'Give me this, give me that, give me this, and give me that.' You start begging. If you are centered on fear, again, you catch him and say, 'Please protect me from this. Protect me from that.'

The moment we demand, divinity disappears because we have brought in the business consciousness, the business mind. The attitude that exists between the master and us plays a major role in our experiencing Him as divine and our experiencing ourselves as divine.

Many people say, '*Swamiji*, if my son is healed, I will give you so much money. If my daughter is healed, I will give you this property.' I start laughing!

First of all, I never asked them for anything. Second, the moment we start bargaining, the whole beauty of the relationship is gone. For healing to happen, a special bridge is necessary. The bridge or a deep connection, a deeply connected feeling is required. A deep love is necessary.

The moment we bring in the business mood, it is over! As soon as we start bargaining, neither can I heal nor can the person being healed receive the energy. The bridge is disconnected. There is no bridge anymore. If that bridge is there, even without seeing me, you can be healed. You don't need to even see me. You don't need to be in my presence.

Surrender – a deep passive waiting

Continuously, again and again, I receive emails from all over the world, '*Swamiji*, you gave me *darśan* (vision) and removed my sufferings. *Swamiji*, you gave me *darśan* and healed me. *Swamiji*, you appeared in front of me and answered my question.' Then they ask, '*Swamiji*, are you aware of the times when you appear and give *darśan* to us?'

Now, let me tell you clearly, honestly: I do not know when the *darśan* is happening. Let me break the business secret. Let me tell the whole truth as it is. Just because of your trust, deep love and devotion, the cosmic energy guides you by giving *darśan* using this form, that's all. I rent this body to the Divine. Because I disappeared, because my ego disappeared, the Divine uses this form to guide you. Over! Otherwise, it is totally between you and the cosmic energy. I cannot involve myself. I have no say. I cannot appear for any specific person and say, 'He is my favorite!' No! I cannot show favoritism. It is not under my control.

It is between your attitude and the Divine. It is your ability, your attitude to receive, that creates the bridge. Again and again, I tell people: All I can do is, go back and download the information regarding the *darśan* that you had, and tell you what exactly happened, when you had the *darśan* and what instruction was given to you. I can go back, download, bring that information and give it to you. That's all. I have no other say over it. I have no control over it.

With all enlightened people, this is what happens. The moment I claim that I gave *darśan*, the whole thing is over. The moment I declare it is I who appeared, the whole thing is over. Then, the Divine will stop using this form.

As long as I am clear that this is not me and it is *Parāsakti,* Existence, using this form, She continues to use this flute to play Her songs. She continues to use this form to carry on with Her mission. She continues to use this form to bless Her devotees.

When I say *Parāsakti,* I mean the cosmic energy. Don't think there is a lady with four hands! It is the cosmic energy. She does Her job using the forms of people who have surrendered their form to Her. Because I vacated, She lives in my body.

All you need to do is just get out of your system. The Divine will get in. If you get out of your system, the Divine will get in. Again and again, I tell people it is not me who gives the *darśan.* I don't give visions and it is not related to me. I don't even know when exactly it happens.

All I can say is that when you come back and tell me what happened, if you tell the place or date, I can download and see that file. I can search and bring the file back and tell you in a detailed way what exactly happened. Nothing else is in my control.

The big problem with the spiritual process is that you will have what you want only when you drop the idea of having that. That is where the problem starts. A deep, passive waiting without knowing what is going to happen, is passive surrender. That is total surrender. The moment you decide, 'I will wait forever,' things happen.

As long as you are in a hurry, you are agitated. You stop things from happening in you. It is like trying to get the lotus to blossom. What do you do? You open the petals by hand. Will it be a flower? It will never be a lotus flower. The lotus flower blooms by itself, when the sun's rays pierce it. Give a little space to yourself so that your being blossoms.

The moment you decide to wait, things start happening. You don't need to wait anymore. You must wait until you decide to wait. Then, the moment you decide to wait, you don't need to wait anymore.

A beautiful story:

Nārada, a devotee of Viṣṇu, was going to *Vaikunṭa* (abode of Lord Viṣṇu). On the way, he saw a yogi sitting in meditation. The yogi asked Nārada, 'Oh Nārada, please ask Viṣṇu how long I must wait before I become enlightened?' Nārada said, 'Surely I will ask,' and he went on his way.

Next, Nārada encountered a man who was jumping and dancing under a tree. He asked Nārada, 'Oh Nārada, please ask Viṣṇu when I will have his *darśan*.' Please be very clear, he never asked when he would become enlightened. He asked Nārada when he would have Viṣṇu's *darśan*, His vision. He said, 'Ask Him to grace me. How long should I wait for His grace?' Nārada said, 'Surely I will ask, don't worry.'

Nārada went to *Vaikunṭa* and came back with the replies. The yogi asked him what Viṣṇu had said. Nārada said, 'Viṣṇu said you must wait four more *janma* (lives) to become enlightened.' The yogi fell into depression, 'Oh, four *janmas*! What will I do?'

The person who was dancing, jumping around asked Nārada, 'What did Viṣṇu say?' Nārada said, 'He said you must wait for as many *janmas* as there are leaves on this tree. Then you will have His *darśan*. Only then His grace will fall upon you.'

As soon as he heard this, the man said, 'Oh! He gave me the assurance that He will grace me! That is enough.' He started jumping and dancing again.

The moment he uttered this, there was a stroke of lightning and the Divine descended. The man became enlightened.

So understand, deep patience and the decision to wait is surrender.

In my life, as long as I was doing meditation, I never became enlightened. As long as I was doing all the practices, penance, I was so agitated. Nothing happened. Actually after my enlightenment, I came to know that because of the penance, I had postponed my enlightenment. To tell you honestly, at the age of twelve, I had become enlightened. I did not know that I had become enlightened. I tried to hold on to the experience. I tried to possess *nitya ānanda,* eternal bliss. The moment I tried to possess it, it started slipping away, like wet soap.

The day you decide to wait, things happen. In order to wait, you will need absolute trust.

Arjuna had the courage to trust totally in Kṛṣṇa and let go, which was why he had the *vishvarūpa darśan,* the cosmic vision of Kṛṣṇa. We must have the energy to let go, to allow the dark night to happen to us. Only if we have trust in the master can the ultimate gain happen to us.

The master George Gurdjieff had strange techniques to enlighten disciples. He had a rule that anybody engaged in any activity, on hearing his cry, 'Stop!' should immediately stop whatever he or she may be doing, sit down and meditate. He had a stream inside his ashram. Once three disciples were in the stream when he cried 'Stop!' However, no sooner than he had cried out, the water in the stream began to rise. Frightened, two of the disciples rushed out of the water. The third continued to meditate. His ego drowned with his body and a new being floated.

We need to trust in order to experience the unknown space. At that moment, we have only the master to hold onto. We must accept the new experience happening to us, and deeply trust that the energy to transcend our old personality is entering us.

Kṛṣṇa emphasizes the feeling of connectedness. Feeling deeply connected to the master is the basic need to understand this truth. That is why the east gave so much importance to the guru, the master.

There is one more question here:

I Create You

10.4,5 *Intelligence, knowledge, freedom from doubt and delusion, forgiveness, truthfulness, control of the senses, control of the mind, happiness, distress, birth, death, fear, fearlessness, non-violence, equanimity, satisfaction, austerity, charity, fame and infamy, all these qualities of living beings are created by Me alone.*

10.6 *The seven great sages and before them, the four great Manus, come from Me,*
They arose from My mind and all the living beings populating the planet descend from them.

10.7 *He who knows all this glory and powers of mine, truly, he is fully united in Me;*
Of that there is no doubt.

If you understand this first verse, you can immediately relax. Kṛṣṇa says, 'Whatever you have, whether you have a good name or a bad name, it is created by Me.' Then be certain that whatever you have is a gift from the Divine.

Kṛṣṇa asks us to accept life as it is. Only when we accept ourselves as we are, can we accept others. Only then we will feel deep friendliness with others. Deep friendliness with others *is* spirituality. Understand that spirituality is honest and deep friendliness with others.

Friendliness and honesty is spirituality

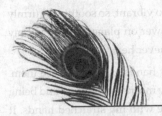

Love is the flowering of our consciousness. Whenever our consciousness expresses itself through the heart, compassion happens, lust becomes love. The touch will become so vibrant, so soothing. I firmly believe that love is the greatest healing power on planet earth. I tell my healers, 'If you can't spread love, you can never heal.'

When people meet me, I stretch out my hands as soon as I see them. Many feel strange. They feel that spirituality means seriousness and being reserved. Here I am reaching out to people with my stretched hands. It doesn't match the picture of spirituality or the spiritual person that they carry in their heads! According to them, spirituality is never associated with sharing or loving.

People from various backgrounds visit our ashram for healing: young and old people, cancer and HIV patients, and people with various other disabilities. If a person has pain in the leg, naturally I get up from my seat and touch their leg to heal. After all the foot is just another part of the body.

An elderly, traditional and conservative *Swami* gave me friendly advice about this practice. He remarked, 'You are a *Swami*. It is unbecoming of a *Swami* to come down from his seat and touch someone's feet. It is against the tradition.' I replied politely, 'The very seat and the cloth which I wear (saffron robes) mean compassion. I acquired this seat because of my compassion. I am not here *for* the seat.'

Spirituality means flowing. Spirituality means spreading love and compassion. Whenever we serve out of compassion, we never feel that we have served. We feel that we have been given an opportunity to serve.

Whether we believe it or not, as of now, we have a deep enmity or hostility towards others. We may smile at others like models posing for the camera. We may smile, but we never feel friendly. We keep a safe distance and play a safe game because we never feel any real friendliness with others.

To correct this, the first thing you need to do is accept yourself as you are. Some people tell me, 'I am unable to accept myself as I am, *Swamiji*. What can I do?' I tell them, 'At least accept that you are unable to accept yourself, that is enough.'

If we accept that we are unable to accept ourselves, it is enough. We will drop from the mind. We need to accept ourselves as we are. Otherwise, if we are unable to accept ourselves as we are, at least accept that we are not able to accept ourselves as we are. That very acceptance will open a new consciousness in us.

Forgiving others and forgiving yourself are one and the same. Jesus says, 'Love your neighbor as you love yourself.' Unfortunately, we don't even love ourselves. So how can we love others?

When we torture others with our judgment and prejudices, we torture ourselves, too. We use the same sword to kill others and to commit suicide ourselves. The same mind deals with others as well as with us.

When Kṛṣṇa says, 'Happiness and distress, birth and death, fear and fearlessness, non-violence and equanimity, satisfaction, austerity, charity, name and fame, fame and infamy, all these various qualities of living beings are created by Me alone,' He means accept your life as it is.

The moment we accept life as it is, we experience divinity in everything. We don't exclude anything. The moment we accept, a cognitive shift happens in us. As of now, the cognitive process happening inside our mind, the cognition agent, is centered on enmity.

The moment we accept ourselves, we accept the whole world. Then, the cognitive shift happens in us. The cognition that happens inside our system will be centered on bliss. Then we experience the whole thing as divine.

Kṛṣṇa explains His glory. He says, 'I am everything.' He declares, 'I am the universal consciousness. The person who truly knows My glories and powers, engages in *yoga*, the union of individual consciousness with the divine consciousness, and undoubtedly attains liberation.'

The *saptarṣis*, the seven sages that Kṛṣṇa talks about, are not seven old men with flowing beards sitting in meditation and penance, waiting for something to happen. From my experience, this is the energy field that drives this universe. This energy field referred to as the *saptarṣis* has the intelligent power to make decisions that determine the course of the universe.

During my *parivrājaka,* wandering days before enlightenment, I lived for several months in Tapovan, beyond Gangotri and Gomukh, in the Himalayan mountain range at a 17,000 feet altitude. Even now, no roads lead to Tapovan and there are no permanent structures to stay in. I lived like many other *sanyāsis,* staying in caves, covering myself with jute cloth and newspaper in the winter and eating whatever fruits were available. Tapovan is referred to as Shambala, heaven on earth. It is the point from which one can move from the material earthly plane up to the spiritual plane.

Kṛṣṇa refers to the *saptarṣis* as the universal consciousness that was born from His mind, from Him, the Primal Source and Primal Creator. He is the *saptarṣis.* His energy decides what enlightened beings should do, and directs their actions. Every movement that I make is governed and decided by this energy.

In Hindu mythology, *Manus* are the children of Brahma, the Creator. There is a lineage of *Manus,* fourteen *Manus,* who populated the earth. Each *Manu* ruled for a period. The collective period of all fourteen *Manus* equals one *kalpa,* one day in the life of Brahma. In Sanskrit, all humans are termed *Mānava,* meaning those descended from *Manu*.

As the universal consciousness, Kṛṣṇa is all in one. He is the Creator, Sustainer and Rejuvenator. He is Brahma, Viṣṇu and Śiva. He also transcends all three as the *Parabrahman,* the supreme superconsciousness.

One needs to do nothing except understand and accept what Kṛṣṇa is. The master says that belief and understanding alone liberates us. Nothing more is needed.

Experience The Light

10.8 *I am the source of all the spiritual and material worlds. Everything arises from Me.*
The wise, who know this, are devoted to Me and surrender their heart to Me.

10.9 *With mind and lives absorbed on Me, always enlightening one another and talking about My glories, the wise are content and blissful.*

10.10 *To those who are always engaged in Me with love, I give them enlightenment by which they come to Me.*

10.11 *Out of compassion to them, I destroy the darkness born out of their ignorance by the shining lamp of knowledge.*

Now, instead of understanding these statements of Kṛṣṇa intellectually, we should try experiencing them. In the deep meditative mood, let us feel connected to the *Parabrahma* Kṛṣṇa, to our very life source, to our very life energy.

Let us enter into meditation, because all the following verses in this chapter must be experienced. They cannot be understood. There is nothing much to understand.

Later Kṛṣṇa says, 'Amongst the *ṛṣi*, I am Nārada. Among the months, I am Margazhi. Among the rivers, I am Gaṅgā. Among the fish, I am Makara.' He explains His glories at length.

We may think, 'Why does He explain these things in a detailed way?' He makes us understand, wherever we see the glory, wherever we see the

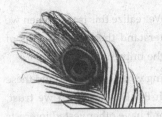

Divine radiating, there lies the greatness. We realize this is true when we start experiencing, when we deeply understand these basic truths of accepting ourselves and connecting with the universe.

We experience life as divine and a blessing when we understand these things. It happens when we connect with the Divine, when we trust, when we completely open up, when we don't have other vested interests and when we do not beg for anything from life.

As long as we are begging for things in the hope that, 'with this, I will feel blissful,' or 'with that, I will feel blissful', we will ask only for this or that. Only when we understand, 'I want just Him, nothing else. I want the pure experience of the Divine, nothing else,' we experience the whole of Existence in a totally different way. The cognitive shift starts happening in us.

I can imagine how Arjuna felt when Kṛṣṇa revealed these things for the first time, inch by inch. 'Oh Arjuna, I am that. I am this. I am everything.' Arjuna may not have said anything, but he surely must have felt that he was expanding.

Understand this example: You and your husband were ordinary people when you were first married. Slowly, your husband entered politics and became a mayor. After five years, he became governor, a well-known person. Already, you feel connected to him since he is your husband. Now, he becomes a famous person or you understand him as a big person. You deeply feel the gratefulness or the gratitude to him because his expansion has helped bring about yours.

In the same way, Arjuna already felt deeply connected to Kṛṣṇa as his friend. Now, he understands the glories of Kṛṣṇa. Kṛṣṇa reveals His glories to Arjuna.

See, when your husband became governor, you also expanded because you are connected to him. You rejoice. A husband's power is a source of joy for wives. For men, money is the source of joy. When the person to whom you are connected expands, you also expand. When he achieves the glory and becomes great, you also become great.

Viṣṇu, whose incarnation Kṛṣṇa is, wanted to teach a lesson to his disciple, Nārada. Nārada considered himself to be Viṣṇu's greatest devotee. Viṣṇu pretended he had a headache. His devotees brought him all kinds of medicines, which he tried and pronounced useless. He told them, 'The only substance that will cure my malaise is the dust from the feet of a true devotee.'

Nārada and the great sages were shocked. How could they allow the dust of their feet to fall on their master's head? 'It will be a sacrilege,' they argued. One day Viṣṇu pretended to become annoyed. He told Nārada, 'Get out of My sight. Go to the *gopīs* in Brindāvan and tell them what I said and seek a solution.'

When Nārada reached Brindāvan, the *gopīs* were so busy with their chores that they would not talk to him. Nārada explained, 'I have come from *Vaikunṭa*.' They were not impressed. He told them, '*Vaikunṭa* is the home of Viṣṇu.' 'Who is Viṣṇu?' they asked. Nārada said, 'Viṣṇu is Kṛṣṇa.'

As soon as he uttered the word Kṛṣṇa, they gathered around Nārada and asked him in one voice, 'How is our Kṛṣṇa, our darling?' Nārada said, 'He is suffering from a headache.' They asked, 'What can we do? We cannot let our Kṛṣṇa suffer.' Nārada told them that Viṣṇu had asked for the dust from the feet of one of his true devotees.

One *gopī* immediately removed her upper cloth. She placed it on the ground and all the *gopīs* danced upon this cloth to collect the dust from their feet. Folding the cloth, not worried that she had nothing covering her breasts, the *gopī* said, 'Here take this to our Kṛṣṇa. We do not know which of us is His true devotee. So this has all the dust from all our feet. Go now and give it to Him.'

Nārada asked, 'Aren't you worried that you are giving Kṛṣṇa the dust from your feet to put on His head?' In one voice, the *gopīs* answered, 'Are you crazy? He, our Lord and Lover, is suffering and has asked for the dust from our feet. If it would cure Him, we are ready to dance on His head! We shall give our lives for Him.'

Nārada, humbled, returned to Vaikuṇṭa with the *gopi's* upper cloth filled with dust from their feet. Viṣṇu took the cloth in His hands, smelled the dust and pronounced Himself fully cured. The sages, *devas* and Nārada watched in amazement.

'What did they tell you, Nārada?' He asked. 'Did they give useless reasons and advance futile arguments as to why they could not apply the dust from their feet on their Lord and master, as you all did?'

Nārada hung his head in shame.

Even to this day all main entrance steps to Viṣṇu temples have the imprint of feet carved upon them. These imprints represent the feet of devotees whose feet dust Viṣṇu covets more than all the crowns He is adorned with!

Kṛṣṇa says, 'With mind and lives absorbed on Me, always enlightening one another and talking about My glories, the wise are content and blissful. To those who are always engaged in Me with love, I give them enlightenment for which they come to Me.'

Kṛṣṇa here talks about *satsaṅg,* the collection of people whose hearts, minds and bodies are immersed in Him. They are the ones who can talk about nothing except Him, who are filled with bliss and love for their Lord and master. He promises He will provide them the intelligence to enlighten them and bring them to Him.

I keep telling my devotees about the importance of *satsaṅgs.* These are regular get-togethers where people listen to the master's words, dance to the *kīrtans* and go home with refreshed and reinforced memories of their master. Everyone who attends *satsaṅgs* regularly can tell you that the master is present with them, wherever they may be, however many *satsangs* there may be, at that particular moment.

An ashram is an intensified *satsaṅg* that is forever, twenty-four by seven. That is why I motivate groups of people to form ashrams, spiritual communities, where they can follow their spiritual quest with one-pointed minds. Ashrams are not cults like people in the West fear. Cults can be created whether you have communities or not. Gangs are cults. Do gangsters live in an ashram?

We are eligible to be part of an ashram community when we are deeply in love with our master. The motivation to live in an ashram is neither fear that he will hurt us if we leave, nor greed that he will take us to a non-existent heaven if we stay. Rather, it is love born out of this present moment. We must have shed our entire ego and surrender ourselves to the One who has already surrendered himself. Only then the process works. Otherwise, it is just the blind leading the blind, which is a cult.

Here Kṛṣṇa talks about such an environment, an ashram. An ashram is not a serious center of penance with old people meditating in painfully distorted postures. Come to one of our ashrams and see for yourself. No one will be serious. They will be laughing all the time. They are not like Nārada and the sages engaged in intellectual arrogance. They are the *gopīs* who are in love with their master; with their entire being filled with love for Him.

At the ashram, each one does what he can. No one forces them to do anything. They can sit in meditation with eyes closed for twenty-four hours. No one will bother them. No one will ask them why. No one will complain that they are not doing anything. But the energy of the master provides them with intelligence. It does not allow them to waste themselves in frivolous activities.

A monastery is not an ashram.

There is a hierarchy in a monastery. There is order. There are rules, regulations and norms as to how much work each person must do. An ashram has no man-made rules and regulations. No one measures how much one person does and how much another does. Outwardly there is chaos. There is no equality in terms of responsibility or duties, but there is uniqueness. Each person does what he is best suited for.

In an ashram, one does not work out of fear, greed, motivation or necessity. An ashramite, a resident of an ashram, works out of gratitude.

Once we start to measure what people do and start comparing, we create a political organization, not a spiritual organization.

A man who works out of fear and greed, is a *śūdra*. The man who works out of attention need is a *vaiśya*. The man who works out of jealousy or comparison to prove that he is superior to others, is a *kṣatriya*. The man who works out of gratitude is a *brāhmana*.

People are not equal. Each one comes with his own *karma* (unfulfilled actions) and a particular attitude. As long as the master is there, He takes care of everything. When the master is not there, the whole thing becomes *dharma*, righteousness. When the master is there, everything becomes *mokṣa*, liberation. That is the difference between *dharma* and *mokṣa*. Work for *mokṣa*. That is the difference between an ashram and a monastery.

My mission is for people to live together focused on spiritual evolution; to be self-funded, self-managed and self-sustaining, operating with one mission, that of transformation of oneself through meditation. Soon people will find out how much better this system works compared to their normal lifestyle.

I say to all of them, as Kṛṣṇa said: *Those who are always engaged in Me with love, I give them enlightenment, by which they come to Me.*

The master defines Himself in the last verse: *I destroy the darkness of ignorance within them, with the shining lamp of wisdom, through my compassion.*

The Sanskrit word guru, meaning master, has two syllables: *gu* refers to darkness and *ru* to light. The master leads the disciple from darkness into light with compassion. This darkness of ignorance is the identification that one has with one's self, one's material attachments and material possessions. This identification surely leads to sorrow since this attachment is for things that are fleeting and not for something long lasting.

Wealth gets created overnight and disappears just as quickly. Relationships, however sound, last only as long as the body lasts, most often far less since the mind is even more fleeting in holding onto relationships. Nothing that exists in this world, nothing that is of material creation, can last eternally. Our impression that material possessions and attachments last, comes from ignorance. This ignorance is born of self-identity, ego.

The master is the only person who can dispel that darkness. Only He can light up that wisdom within you in order for you to realize that you are already one with Existence and therefore need nothing from this material world.

Your master gains nothing from teaching you. He gains nothing from enlightening you. He does it out of sheer compassion, so that others may experience the same bliss that He constantly experiences.

Know Yourself By Yourself

10.12 *Arjuna said:*
You are the supreme Truth, supreme sustenance, supreme Purifier, the Primal, Eternal and Glorious Lord.

10.13 *All the sages like Nārada, Asita, Devala, and Vyāsa have explained this.*
Now You are personally explaining to me.

10.14 *Oh Keśava, I accept all these truths that You have told me.*
Oh Lord, neither the gods nor the demons know You.

10.15 *Surely, You alone know Yourself by Yourself,*
Oh Perfect One, the origin of beings, Oh Lord of beings,
Oh God of gods, Oh Lord of the world.

10.16 *Only You can describe in detail Your divine glories by which You pervade this universe.*

10.17 *How may I know You by contemplation?*
In which forms should I contemplate on You, Oh Lord?

10.18 *Tell me in detail of Your powers and glories, Oh Janārdana.*
Again, please tell for my satisfaction as I do not tire of hearing Your sweet words.

Arjuna becomes the perfect disciple. He has no doubts about whatever Kṛṣṇa has said to him so far. It only corroborates what the great sages have said. All that Arjuna seeks is that his Lord and master tells him more about Himself, His glories, 'I just need to know how I should approach You, how I should see You. Tell me more, I can never tire of listening to Your words.'

Arjuna is in love with His master. When you are in such deep love as Arjuna is now, and as the *gopīs* were with Kṛṣṇa in Brindāvan, there is nothing to be said. There is nothing even to be heard. Whatever Arjuna says is merely to keep his end of the dialogue going. Arjuna knows that there is no need for Kṛṣṇa to say anything now. Yes, he would be delighted if Kṛṣṇa were to speak of His glories, His *līla.* However, Arjuna is in such a state of meditation, ready for his ultimate experience, that whatever his master says or does would not matter to him.

Therefore, when Arjuna asks the Lord to talk about His glories that no one else understands, Arjuna is not requesting on his behalf, He is requesting on behalf of humanity. Arjuna would have been perfectly happy to sit in silence, in deep meditation upon Kṛṣṇa. And in His compassion, Kṛṣṇa would have eventually revealed Himself to his chosen disciple. However, the rest of humanity would not have benefited from a revelation that came to Arjuna alone. Hence Arjuna requested that Kṛṣṇa speak about His glory.

Arjuna wants to know about *Parabrahma* Kṛṣṇa, the ultimate superconscious being. He does not want to know about his friend and charioteer, Vāsudeva Kṛṣṇa, the son of Vāsudeva.

Arjuna is in the mood of the perfect devotee and disciple. Anything that he can hear about his master is nectar to his ears. He is in a state of complete immersion.

> Rāmakṛṣṇa asked Vivekānanda, 'If you were a fly and you were on the rim of the cup of nectar, what would you do?'
>
> Vivekānanda said, 'Sip from the cup, of course, what else?'
>
> 'You Fool!' said the master, 'You should fall into the nectar and submerge yourself! When would you ever get this opportunity again?

Arjuna is on that verge of immersion. His intellect has almost disappeared. He needs the last nudge, so to speak.

You too, as the reader, make your plea to *Parabrahma* Kṛṣṇa, the *Jagatguru*, so that He may tell you about His glory, and so that you may meditate upon His glory with single pointed focus of the mind. As He promised, He will provide the light of wisdom for you to be enlightened.

I Am The Beginning, Middle And End

10.19 *Kṛṣṇa said, 'Yes, Oh Kurukṣetra, I will talk to you surely of My divine glories;*
But only of the main ones as there is no end to the details of My glories.

10.20 *I am the Spirit, Oh Guḍākeśā, situated in all living beings.*
I am surely the beginning, middle and end of all beings.

10.21 *Of the Āditya, I am Viṣṇu. Of the luminaries, I am the bright sun.*
Of the Marut, I am Marīcī. Of the Nakṣatras, I am the Moon.

10.22 *Of the Veda, I am the Sāma veda. Of the gods, I am Indra.*
Of the senses, I am the mind and in living beings, I am the consciousness.

10.23 *Of the Rudra, I am Śaṇkara and of the Yakṣa and Rākṣasa, I am Kubera, god of wealth.*
Of the Vasu, I am fire and of the peaks, I am Meru.

10.24 *Of the priests, understand, Oh Pārtha, that I am the chief Bṛhaspati.*
Of the warriors, I am Skandha. Of the water bodies, I am the ocean.

10.25 *Of the great sages, I am Bṛgu. Of the vibrations, I am the Oṁ.*
Of the sacrifices, I am the chanting of holy names. Of the immovable objects, I am the Himalayas.

There is no way to describe the Divine fully because the Divine pervades every bit of this entire universe. When it exists in every atom, when it is the essence of all that exists, how can we describe or comprehend it in its entirety?

So Kṛṣṇa explains the main manifestations that give a glimpse of the unfathomable Divine.

Kṛṣṇa refers to Arjuna as Guḍākeśā, meaning one who has conquered sleep! He implies that Arjuna has overcome sleep, signifying darkness or ignorance. Therefore Arjuna is ready to receive what Kṛṣṇa is about to deliver. Throughout the Gītā, Kṛṣṇa refers to Arjuna by different names. Each one is appropriate within a particular context. Sometimes He calls Arjuna - Kaunteya or Pārtha, meaning that he is the son of Kuntī. Kuntī in Mahābhārata is the epitome of patience and forbearance. No one suffers like she does. When Kṛṣṇa addresses Arjuna as the son of Kuntī, it is in the context of advising Arjuna to be patient and listen carefully. While addressing Arjuna here as Guḍākeśā, one who is in the light, having conquered sleep, Kṛṣṇa readies Arjuna for liberation.

Kṛṣṇa declares that He is everything that really matters. Kṛṣṇa says that He is the ultimate consciousness in all beings and He is the beginning, middle and end of all beings. He declares that He pervades the entire space and time and beyond.

Kṛṣṇa is both the macrocosm and the microcosm: the *Brahmāṇda,* cosmos and the *pindāṇda,* individual being. His energy permeates all living and non-living entities and He decides upon their nature.

> Young Prahlāda was subjected to an inquisition by his demonic father Hiraṇyakaśipu. His father asked, 'You speak about Nārāyaṇa all the time and refuse to give up even when I command you to do so. Where does Nārāyaṇa live? Where is he now?'
>
> Prahlāda replied, 'He may be in this twig lying on the floor. He may be in this pillar next to you. He is everywhere.'
>
> Hiraṇyakaśipu kicked the pillar in fury daring Nārāyaṇa to appear. Nārāyaṇa appeared in the form of Nṛsimha, half-man half-lion!

Prahlāda trusted fully that Nārāyaṇa was everywhere. He did not have one iota of doubt about it.

When Prahlāda was being challenged by Hiraṇyakaśipu to show Nārāyaṇa anywhere, it is said that Lord Viṣṇu (Nārāyaṇa) suddenly started preparing to leave Vaikunṭa, His abode, when Lakṣmī, His spouse asked, 'Lord, where are you going?' Viṣṇu smiled and said, 'I have no idea where this devotee of mine, this young boy Prahlāda, is planning to call me from. Wherever he calls from, I need to appear from there!'

Not only does the Lord reside everywhere, He will also go to any length to ensure that His true devotee's words don't go futile!

In this universe, there are twelve planes of existence. These are a combination of the factors of length, breadth, depth, time, space and consciousness. At best, we are aware of the first five and that, only partially too. It is difficult for those in the human plane to comprehend even time and space fully. We can only exist in one aspect of time and space in relationship with the three dimensions of length, breadth and depth.

Quantum Physics now recognizes that fundamental particles can exist simultaneously in different locations at the same time. Matter can transcend time and space. Matter and energy can exist beyond the bounds of time and space.

A master is one who can transcend time and space and reach consciousness. Kṛṣṇa, the great master, is in the twelfth plane, that of pure consciousness. He is beyond all dimensions, beyond time, and beyond space. He is the beginning and He has no beginning. He is the end and He has no end.

He is the Creator. He is the Created. He is also the Creation. In this huge canvas of the universe, He is the canvas. He is the paint. He is also the stroke of the brush and He is the painting. There is nothing that He is not.

The only way to understand even a part of Him is to become immersed in Him.

When great Sufi masters went into ecstasy, they were immersed in that consciousness that pervades everything. When Rāmakṛṣṇa even heard the name of Mother Kālī, he went into ecstasy.

In the Chandogya Upaniṣad, Āditya is a name of Viṣṇu in His Vāmana *avatāra*. In the ten incarnations of Viṣṇu, Vāmana is the fifth incarnation as a small brahmin boy.

When King Bali of the demon race was performing a series of fire rituals to attain supremacy over the universe, the demigods requested Viṣṇu to save them from Bali and prevent Bali from conquering the universe.

On King Bali's last fire ritual, Viṣṇu appeared as a small brahmin boy. The king, as per the custom, respectfully welcomed the brahmin boy and offered to give anything that he wished for. The king's guru, Śukrācārya, realized that Vāmana was Viṣṇu disguised in order to foil the plans of the demons to achieve supremacy over the worlds. He warned Bali. However, the king had to keep his promise. Out of full respect for the brahmin, Bali asked him to take whatever he wanted. Bali angered his guru for honoring the brahmin boy instead of taking his warnings. Vāmana asked King Bali to give him three steps of his land as his property. Once Bali consented, Vāmana grew from the size of a small boy to a huge figure. He stepped over the entire earth in a single footstep. In the next step, he stepped over the heavens.

Having thus conquered the worlds, Vāmana asked Bali where he could place his third step. Having nothing else to offer, Bali offered Vāmana his own head. Vāmana placed his foot on Bali's head.

The story symbolizes how arrogance and pride leads to one's downfall since all possessions are temporary and of no inherent value. Surrendering only to the Divine, to the ultimate consciousness, leads us to liberation.

Kṛṣṇa says that among the Maruts, He is Marīcī. The Maruts are the thought-gods associated with power and knowledge. Marīcī is the father of sage Kaśyapa, who is the father of the Maruts. Many Ṛgveda hymns are dedicated to the Maruts. The Maruts aid the activities of Indra, the representation of the mind. This is a metaphysical representation of the power of thoughts that originate from the mind.

A common representation of the Maruts in the Ṛg Veda is a flock of birds. This symbolizes the power of thoughts that influence the recipient. When a person radiates positive thoughts, he is receptive to similar thoughts and attracts similar incidents in his life. If we are blissful, people with a similar attitude will be attracted towards us. If we are dull, lethargic and depressed, the same type of people will be attracted towards us.

Thoughts and desires are energy. They contribute towards shaping our actions and lives. Everyday we create our bodies, minds, actions and our reality by our thoughts. We are what our thoughts are.

We are fully responsible for what happens around us, even though we may be unaware of the implications of our thoughts. That is why it is important to become fully aware of ourselves. Our thoughts and actions influence not just us but the entire world. It may be hard to believe logically, but a butterfly flapping its wings can cause a tsunami in another part of the world!

Next, Kṛṣṇa says that He is the sun amongst all the shining objects, and among the stars He is the moon. We may say that the moon is not a star. We would be factually correct. Kṛṣṇa refers to the influence that the moon wields upon earth and humans. It is scientifically established that out of all celestial bodies around planet earth, the two most important influences are the sun and the moon. No one doubts that the sun is a star, and that it is the brightest object that can be seen.

The moon influences the tides of the ocean as well as the tides of the human minds. Of all planetary, non-planetary and solar bodies that surround us, with the exception of the sun, the moon exerts the greatest influence on us both in a broader planetary sense, and in an individual sense.

People have mood variations depending on the phases of the moon. New moon and full moon days dramatically influence our emotional well being, for good and for bad. Being the physical mass closest to the earth, the gravitational force of the moon affects each of us deeply. The moon influences far more than its size would suggest, or its classification as a satellite would have us believe.

This is why the Hindu astrological and astronomical systems consider the moon to be a planet. This belief is not based on whether the moon revolves around the earth as a satellite instead of around the sun as a planet. It is based on the effect that the moon has on human beings and upon planet earth.

All we need to do is experience Kṛṣṇa

In *vedic* astrology, the stars, are the different positions in the sky that the moon passes through in a cycle of 27 to 28 days. These stars are referred to as the wives of the moon. This is why Kṛṣṇa refers to Himself as the moon amongst the stars, that He is the pride of the stars.

Recently, I read that the moon may have been a planet in our solar system. The article said that the moon and the earth were of similar size and collided. Consequently the size of the moon was reduced and it became caught in the gravitational pull of the earth as a satellite. Kṛṣṇa certainly knew more than what we know now!

Kṛṣṇa declares that amongst the *Vedas*, He is the Sāma veda. The *Vedas* are the timeless truths expounded by the *ṛṣis* as the expressions of truth experienced by them. These are the revelations of the truth experienced through intuition by the seers. There are four *Vedas*: ṚgVeda, Yajur Veda, Sāma Veda and Atharva Veda.

Each *Veda* consists of four parts: *mantra-saṁhita* or hymns, *brāhmaṇa* or explanations of *mantras* (or rituals), *āranyaka,* forest books which give the philosophical meaning of rituals, and the *Upaniṣads,* essence of the *Vedas*.

The Sāma veda is a collection of hymns in praise of *agni* (fire), *Indra* (king of the gods) and *soma* (drink of the gods). While the Ṛg Veda is the oldest *Veda*, Sāma veda is the basis for all musical systems of India. The basic notes of all music, not just of Indian music, originated with Sāma veda. The seven notes, which are the fundamentals of all music all over the world, were derived from Sāma veda, which even today is sung, and not recited.

The Ṛg and other *Vedas* may be recited only by a few scholars today, but Sāma veda is heard everywhere. It is the essence of Carnatic and Hindustani music forms, the two major classical music forms of India. As the essence of music, Sāma veda is also the essence of dance forms.

One does not need to understand music and dance. It is enough to indulge and experience. So it is with Kṛṣṇa. All we need to do is experience Him.

Among the gods, Kṛṣṇa says He is Vasava (Indra), the king of gods.

The five senses, *jñānendriya,* namely sight, hearing, smell, taste and touch, originate from the mind and are of the mind. Without the mind, the senses cannot function. He says He is the subtlest and most powerful, the mind. In living beings, He is the life force, the consciousness, not merely body and mind.

Rudras are the elemental powers worshipped by the Ṛg Veda. The word *Rudra* means to cry. Metaphorically the *Rudras* were worshipped to obtain some gain. When in deep anguish, if one prays to one of the *Rudras* in awareness, it was believed to bring results. There are eleven *Rudras*: Aja, Ekapāda, Ahirbudhnya, Vīrabhadra, Girīśa, Śaṅkara, Aparājita, Hara, Anakaraka, Pināki, Bhaga and Śambhu. Śaṅkara is the doer of good. Śaṅkara is also the precursor to Śiva in the evolution of the Hindu constellation of divinity. Śiva means auspiciousness; auspiciousness born without a reason. Wherever Śiva is, good happens for no reason. Of the *Rudras,* Kṛṣṇa says He is Śaṇkara.

Yakṣas are celestial beings considered to be the creators of wealth. The king of the *Yakṣas* is Kubera, the god of wealth. *Rākṣasas* too are celestial beings of a negative nature of hoarding power and wealth. *Yakṣas* and *Rākṣasas* are keepers of wealth. They do not enjoy wealth. Of the *Yakṣas* and *Rākṣasas,* Kṛṣṇa says He is the god of wealth, the king Kubera.

The *Vasus* are the attendants of Viṣṇu. They represent various aspects of Nature. The Brhadāraṇyaka Upaniṣad mentions eight *Vasus*: *agni* (fire), *pṛthvī* (earth), *vāyu* (wind), *antarikṣa* (space), *āditya* (light), *dyaus* (sky), *candramas* (moon) and *nakṣatrāṇi* (stars). Kṛṣṇa says among the *Vasus,* He is the formless fire.

Meru is the golden peak, the metaphoric abode of gods, and its foothills are the Himalayas. It is also said to represent the spine of humans. Amongst the peaks, Kṛṣṇa says He is the majestic *Meru.*

Bṛhaspati is the priest of the gods. He dispels darkness and ignorance and destroys the enemies of the gods. Among the warriors, Kṛṣṇa says He is Skanda, the supreme General of the forces of gods. Skanda is the son of Śiva and Pārvatī, who destroyed Tārakāsura, the demon who, along with his hordes of demons, tormented the *devas*. This is a metaphysical representation of the Divine as the supreme General of the being, vanquishing the senses, desires and ego.

Of the water bodies, Kṛṣṇa says He is the mighty ocean, infinite in expanse and essential to all life forms. In fact, it is the origin of all life forms.

Of the great sages, Kṛṣṇa says He is Bṛgu, one of the *saptarṣis* (seven sages who form the cosmic energy). Bṛgu is believed to have been created by Brahma to aid him in the creation of the universe.

Of the vibrations, Kṛṣṇa says He is the transcendental *OM. OM* is the primal sound from which the universe manifested itself. It is the *praṇava,* the mystic symbol.

The symbol of OM - ॐ contains three curves, a semicircle and a dot. Out of the three curves, the upper curve symbolizes the waking state, the lower curve denotes deep sleep and the right curve denotes the dream state. It thus represents the three states of individual consciousness. The dot represents the fourth state of consciousness, *turiya*, complete awareness. The semicircle represents *māyā*, illusion, and separates the dot from the three curves. But the open semicircle represents the Absolute which is unaffected by *māyā*.

Of the different types of sacrifices, Kṛṣṇa says He is the *japa* or chanting of holy names.

Of the immovable objects in the world, He says He is the mighty and majestic Himalayas. The Himalayas, literally meaning 'the abode of snow', is home to hundreds of peaks, including the highest peak in the world. Some great rivers originate in it and flow through it, including Gaṅgā, Yamunā, Brahmaputrā and Indus.

The Himalayas have a great unique spiritual significance as well. *Kailāś*, the home of Śiva, is the representation on earth of the metaphorical *Meru*. The Himalayan mountains are the spiritual incubator of the world. The Himalayas are truly a powerful energy field.

For thousands of years, millions of *sādhus* (sages) have lived there and left their bodies from there. When enlightened masters leave their bodies, the result of their penance, the energy of their spiritual penance, is not carried by the spirit. They leave this energy behind in their bodies. Imagine how much energy is in the Himalayas, where so many enlightened beings have left their bodies! We should be thankful to the Himalayas since their positive energy balances the collective negativity in the world.

When Kṛṣṇa says, 'I am the Himalayan Mountain out of all unmoving things,' I can feel the energy of Kṛṣṇa in these mountains. Everyone who has been with me on my trips to the Himalayan Mountains has felt it at some point or another. They are blessed. They have been in Kṛṣṇa consciousness!

I Am The Lion

10.26 *Of all the trees, I am the Banyan tree and of all the sages of the gods, I am Nārada.*
Of the Gandharvas, I am Citraratha. Of the realized souls, I am the sage Kapila.

10.27 *Of the horses, know me to be Ucchaiśravas born of the nectar generated from the churning of the ocean.*
Of the elephants, Airāvata and of men, the king.

10.28 *Of the weapons, I am the thunderbolt. Of the cows, I am Kāmadhenu;*
For begetting children, I am the god of love. Of the snakes, I am Vāsuki.

10.29 *Of the serpents, I am Ananta. Of the water deities, I am Varuṇa.*
Of the ancestors, I am Aryamā and of the ones who ensure discipline, I am Yama.

10.30 *Of the Daitya (demons), I am Prahlāda and of the reckoners, I am Time.*
Of the animals, I am the king of animals (Lion) and of the birds, I am Garuḍa.

Kṛṣṇa says among the trees He is the banyan tree. The banyan tree develops its root-like structures from the branches. These grow into the earth as secondary roots. The metaphysical meaning of the banyan tree is that, just as the banyan tree grows its roots upside down unlike other trees, the spiritual person shuns the illusory outer world, the world that most people run after. Instead, he goes inwards towards the Absolute.

In a later chapter Kṛṣṇa says that the leaves of the banyan tree are the *Vedas*. He who knows this tree is the knower of the *Vedas*.

Of all the spiritually enlightened masters, the *ṛṣis*, Kṛṣṇa says He is Nārada. Nārada is considered the greatest of all devotees. His mind is immersed in remembering Viṣṇu, forever chanting 'Nārāyaṇa, Nārāyaṇa'. Kṛṣṇa identifies Himself with His greatest devotee.

Of the *Gandharvas*, the celestial beings, Kṛṣṇa says He is Citraratha. *Gandharvas* are celestial beings skilled in music and they are guardians of the *soma* juice – the nectar of the divine beings. Citraratha is the king of the *Gandharvas*.

Among the Self-realized persons, Kṛṣṇa says He is Kapila the sage, the author of the Sāṅkhya system of philosophy, which deals with the elements of the physical universe and the spiritual world. Kapila is also considered an incarnation of Viṣṇu.

Ucchaiśravas is the legendary snow-white horse that emerged during the churning of the ocean of milk described in the Bhāgavatam.

> According to the story, the *devas*, the good, oppressed by the *asuras*, the evil, appealed to Lord Viṣṇu for help. Viṣṇu directed the *devas* to churn the ocean of milk upon which Viṣṇu rests, using *Meru*, the mountain, as the staff and Vāsuki, the serpent, as the rope. Viṣṇu became the base as a tortoise upon which *Meru* rested. Since the *devas* did not have the strength to do the job alone, they took the help of the *asuras* promising them a share in whatever materialized.
>
> During the churning, various divine entities emerged. Among these were the divine horse, Ucchaiśravas, and the four-tusked king of the elephants, Airavata, whom Indra took as his mount.
>
> As part of the churning process, a deadly poison *alahala* also emerged that threatened to take the lives of the *devas* and *asuras*. Śiva came to their rescue and drank the poison.
>
> Finally, the nectar of immortality emerged. Viṣṇu, in the form of a beautiful damsel Mohini kept the *asuras* occupied, while He allowed

the *devas* to drink the *amṛt,* nectar of immortality, and become invincible.

This is a metaphysical representation, signifying how we are pushed and pulled by desires in our lives. From this churning in our life, various products emerge. The nectar of immortality emerges when we offer our entire being to the Divine, as we go beyond the push and pull of desires, beyond life and death. Then we dwell in ultimate bliss. There may be obstacles in the path. Yet, the master supports and protects us during our churning, as we endeavor to realize the ultimate state. Just as Śiva drank the poison that emerged as a result of churning the ocean, the master holds the disciple steady as the unconscious *saṁskāras* rise to the surface during our spiritual maturing.

Kṛṣṇa says, among the weapons, He is *vajra,* the thunderbolt. This is the weapon of Indra, king of the demigods. Viṣṇu is considered to be present in the *vajra.* Indra was specifically given this weapon - the thunderbolt, for a purpose. Kṛṣṇa does not choose His own weapon, the *cakra,* the mighty discus. Instead he used Indra's *vajra* that was made from the bones of the great sage Dadhici, who gave up his life to destroy the evil Vṛtrāsura.

Among the cows, He says He is the sacred cow, Kāmadhuk, or Kāmadhenu, which also emerged during the churning of the ocean. In the Hindu way of life, the cow is worshipped for her essential utility. Kāmadhuk is considered to be the cow that grants all wishes and is the mother of all cows.

Kṛṣṇa says, for begetting children, He is the god of love, the basis for procreation.

He says He is the Vāsuki of serpents. Vāsuki is the king of snakes. Vāsuki was used as the rope and he wound himself around *Meru,* the staff, for churning the ocean of milk.

Kṛṣṇa says, among the *nāgas,* non-poisonous snakes or creatures of the nether world, He is Ananta, the many-hooded serpent who forms the bed of Lord Viṣṇu. He is said to support all the planets, including the earth, on his various hoods.

Among the water beings, Kṛṣṇa says He is Varuṇa, the god of the mightiest water body, the ocean.

Among the ancestors, Kṛṣṇa says He is Aryamā, one of the *Ādityas*, who presides over a planet occupied by the energy bodies of our ancestors.

Of the ones who ensure discipline, Kṛṣṇa says He is Yama, the Lord of death. Death is the perfect equalizer of all beings. Death is the only certain thing in the life of all beings and it treats everyone exactly the same whether they are big or small, rich or poor. So the Lord of death, Yama, ensures perfect discipline. The Sanskrit word *yama* means both discipline and death. *Yama* is the first of the eight paths of Patañjali's Aṣṭāṅga yoga.

Of the *Daityas*, Kṛṣṇa says He is Prahlāda. The *Daityas* are considered to be a race of beings that warred against the demigods. Prahlāda was the son of a powerful Daitya King, Hiraṇyakaśipu. Hiraṇyakaśipu did severe penance and obtained a boon that he could not be killed by either man or animal, at night or in the day, either inside or outside his abode, on earth or in space and neither by animate nor inanimate weapon.

Upon receiving this boon, Hiraṇyakaśipu was convinced that he was immortal. He believed there was no way in which all these conditions could be fulfilled; therefore he believed that death could never touch him. He became arrogant and attacked the *devas*.

However, his son Prahlāda was a pious child. Hiraṇyakaśipu could not tolerate that his son was a staunch devotee of Lord Viṣṇu, someone he despised. He was furious to see Prahlāda chant Viṣṇu's name day and night. In his fury, Hiraṇyakaśipu made multiple attempts to have his son killed by pushing him off a cliff, trampling him under an elephant and making him sit on a burning pyre.

Hiraṇyakaśipu's attempts were futile since each time Prahlāda prayed to Viṣṇu in complete surrender and escaped the punishment untouched.

I mentioned this story earlier but I will elaborate on it a bit more now. Once, when Prahlāda extolled the glories of Viṣṇu, Hiraṇyakaśipu furiously asked him, 'If you claim that Viṣṇu exists everywhere, does he exist in this pillar as well?' Prahlāda calmly and confidently replied, 'Yes, he very much exists in the pillar.' This was too much for Hiraṇyakaśipu. He charged at the pillar and smashed it.

To his utter surprise, a figure that was half-man and half-lion emerged from the pillar. Consequently, it was neither man nor animal. It was twilight time. Hence, it was neither day nor night. The pillar was located at the threshold of the exit of Hiraṇyakaśipu's palace. So it was neither inside nor outside his abode. The figure, Nṛsimha held Hiraṇyakaśipu in his hands, placed the terrified king on his thighs so he was neither on earth nor in space. In this state, Nṛsimha tore into Hiraṇyakaśipu's stomach with his claws, thus killing him by neither an animate nor inanimate weapon!

All the conditions granted to Hiraṇyakaśipu in the boon had been honored and still death could grab him! Viṣṇu, as the incarnation of Nṛsimha, killed Hiraṇyakaśipu and proved once again that He is always available to take care of his devotees.

The young Prahlāda is a supreme example of devotion. His life is the example that total surrender to the Divine is possible and that such surrender leads the Divine to completely care for His devotees, in all situations and at all times.

Of the reckoners, Kṛṣṇa says He is *Kāla*, Time itself. Time is the ultimate reckoner. No being exists who can beat Time. Irrespective of who it is, Time always moves on. It cannot be stopped by anyone.

Of the animals, Kṛṣṇa says He is the Lion, king of the jungle.

Among birds, He says He is Garuḍa, king of birds, the eagle who is the mount of Lord Viṣṇu.

I Am Rāma

10.31 *Of the purifiers, I am the Wind. Of the wielders of weapons, I am Rāma.*
Of the water beings, I am the Shark and of the flowing rivers, I am Jāhnavi (Gaṅgā).

10.32 *Of all creations, I am surely the beginning and end and the middle, Oh Arjuna.*
Of all knowledge, I am the Spiritual knowledge of the Self. Of all arguments, I am the Logic.

10.33 *Of the letters, I am the 'A'. Of the dual words, I am the Compounds and surely I am the never-ending time.*
I am the Omniscient who sees everything.

10.34 *I am the all-devouring Death and I am the Creator of all things of the future.*
Of the feminine, I am Fame, Fortune, Beautiful speech, Memory, Intelligence, Faithfulness and Patience.

10.35 *Of the Sāma veda hymns, I am the Bṛhat Sāma and of all poetry, I am the Gāyatrī.*
Of the months, I am Mārgaśīrṣa and of the seasons, I am Spring.

10.36 *Of all the cheating, I am Gambling. Of the effulgent things, I am the Effulgence.*
I am Victory, I am Effort, and I am the Goodness of the good.

10.37 *Of the descendants of Vṛṣṇi, I am Vāsudeva Kṛṣṇa. Of the Pāṇḍava, I am Arjuna.*
Of the sages, I am also Vyāsa and of the thinkers, I am Uśāna.

10.38 Of rulers, I am their Scepter. Of the victorious, I am Statesmanship. Of all secrets, I am also Silence. Of the wise, I am Wisdom.

Of the purifying elements, Kṛṣṇa says He is the formless and pure wind. The wind pervades the other elements such as earth, water and fire and removes impurities.

Of the wielders of weapons, He says He is Rāma, the seventh incarnation of Viṣṇu. Rāma defeated Rāvaṇa, the demonic ruler of Laṅkā who abducted his wife, Sīta. Rāma was a righteous ruler and chosen heir to his father's throne. Yet, Rāma went into exile to uphold his father's vow. Rāma is considered the greatest archer ever known. Of the ten incarnations of Viṣṇu, Rāma is the incarnation just prior to Kṛṣṇa.

Of the aquatic beings, the fish, He says He is the Shark, the most powerful and feared.

Of the rivers, He says He is Gaṅgā. The river Gaṅgā is worshipped in India as goddess Gaṅgā. Millions of people pray in the waters of the Gaṅgā everyday. On its banks, millions of people gather everyday to offer *pūjā* to Gaṅgā and to take a holy dip in the waters. The sage Jahnu swallowed Gaṅgā as She rushed down the Himalayas into his ashram. Bhagīratha begged the *ṛṣis* to release Gaṅgā. That is why Gaṅgā is known as the daughter of Jahnu and has the name 'Jāhnavi'.

As Gaṅgā descends from the Himalayas to the plains, there are multiple places of pilgrimage where people revere the river and offer daily prayers. Gaṅgā is considered to be the river that descended from the heavens. Millions of people standing and praying in the waters have energized the whole river and explains why Gaṅgā has the inexplicable ability of cleansing Herself.

Let me share a factual observation recorded in the reminiscences of the British who ruled India. When the British traveled by ship from England to India, their water became spoilt during the long journey.

However, on the return trip from India to England, the water from the Gaṅgā remained pure even after reaching England. The research showed that the Gaṅgā water had the miraculous power of cleansing itself.

Of all the creations, Kṛṣṇa says He is the beginning, the middle and the end, thus establishing that He is all that existed, exists and will exist. He is the creator, created and creation.

Of the various branches of knowledge, He is the ultimate spiritual knowledge, Self-realization. Other branches of knowledge result from intelligence. Only Self-realization requires intuition and something beyond.

Of all arguments, He says He is the logic that binds everything together.

Of the letters, Kṛṣṇa says He is the first letter, the origin of all that is spoken and written. Of the dual words, a class of words in Sanskrit, He is the compound word. He affirms He is never-ending time and the Creator of this universe, Brahma.

Kṛṣṇa says He is the Creator and Destroyer.

Of the feminine qualities, He says He is the seven *Devīs*, goddesses, who impart fame, fortune, beautiful speech, memory, intelligence, faithfulness and patience. In Sanskrit all these qualities have feminine nouns to represent them. He says these attributes in women come from Him.

Kṛṣṇa said in an earlier verse that among the *Vedas*, He is the Sāma veda that contains beautiful songs and hymns. Now, He says, among these hymns, He is the Bṛhat Sāma, a unique melody.

Of all poetic meters, He says He is Gāyatrī. Various invocations and prayers in the *vedic* literature are set to Gāyatrī meter, including Devi Gāyatrī, Rudra Gāyatrī, etc. This meter is 24 syllables, usually in 3 or 4 lines.

This verse can also be translated to mean that Kṛṣṇa says, 'I am Gāyatrī amongst the *mantras*.' *Mantras* are the sacred syllables that create awareness of the divinity within our inner space. The very vibrations created while chanting the Sanskrit *mantras* purify the mind-body system and raise the energetic frequency. Here, Kṛṣṇa states that Gāyatrī is the greatest of the *mantras.* Its popularity has been evident from the earliest *vedic* times. This was the first *mantras* taught when the child entered a *gurukul,* the traditional *vedic* schools of the enlightened masters.

Gāyatrī literally translated means 'the song that emancipates'. Gāyatrī is an invocation to the ultimate intelligence. This prayer creates self-awareness:

Om bhūr bhuva suvaḥ
tat savitur vareṇyam
bhargo devasya dhīmahi
dhiyo yonaḥ prachodayāt

Freely translated, this means:

We bow to You, that Ruler of physical, mental and spiritual planes,

That which is beyond all, the supreme Brilliance,

May You kindle our inner awareness!

It is a prayer to the supreme intelligence to awaken our inner intelligence.

Gāyatrī is not merely a prayer or a *mantra.* It is far more than that. It is a *tantra,* a technique that can create tremendous awareness and intelligence in our being. *Mantra* means the syllable that shows the way to go beyond joys and sufferings of the world. *Mantra* makes us more centered. *Tantra* is more than that. It is an instant delivery system.

Generally, religions condition us from childhood by installing in us value systems and beliefs, our *saṁskāras* – past engraved memories. Gāyatrī is a technique that completely liberates us from our *saṁskāras.* Gāyatrī gives complete freedom and thus a new way to think. It is like a torch to guide one on one's path. Children were taught this *mantra* from early childhood in ancient times so that they could be free from their *saṁskāras.*

Gāyatrī is not about giving someone a belief or prayer to be chanted to any gods or during any form of worship. It is a pure technique that can lead to pure intelligence.

Continuous meditation on this *mantra,* just continuous recitation of this *mantra* with awareness, directly leads one to the ultimate intelligence.

Gāyatrī mantra says, 'Let us meditate on the energy which awakens the intelligence in our Being. Let that intelligence help us meditate on It.'

Contemplate the meaning of Gāyatrī mantra. This *mantra* creates a beautiful vibration inside our being. Repeating the *mantra* mentally and letting the *mantra* sink into our being is like planting a seed in our being that will lead to thousands of fruits in the outer world as well as in the inner world. It gives us what we want along with giving us the inner space in which we don't want anything.

Among the months, Kṛṣṇa says, He is the month of Mārgaśīrṣa, November and December in the Gregorian calendar. In India, these months bring joy to people as they are the time when grains are collected from the fields. Also, the month has a lot of spiritual significance because the auspicious days of *Vaikunṭa Ekādasi* fall in this month. This month in the divine calendar is the early morning time, the *brahma muhūrtaṁ,* and the most auspicious part of the day. This is the time recommended to focus on worship.

Among the seasons, Kṛṣṇa says, He is spring. Nature is at the pinnacle of Her creation in spring with new blossoms on trees and pleasant weather, which is neither too hot nor too cold. Spring thus signifies life, growth and the beginning of the cycle of life.

Kṛṣṇa declares that of all vices, He is gambling. Even in the vices He says He is present! Anybody who deludes himself by thinking that He is not present in 'unvirtuous' activities should realize that the Divine exists everywhere and in all activities and things.

By this, Kṛṣṇa also refers to the fact that Yudhiṣṭra's vice of gambling brought about this Great War. Known as the wisest of all men, the most righteous being, Yudhiṣṭra, the Pāṇḍava prince, had one vice that brought him down. That was his weakness for gambling.

Kṛṣṇa says, He is the effulgence that is the essence of all radiant things.

He declares He is the Victory of the victorious, the effort needed to succeed, and *satva,* Goodness, amongst the attributes.

Kṛṣṇa's father, Vāsudeva, was a member of the Vṛṣṇi or Yādava race. Amongst the Vṛṣṇis, Kṛṣṇa says He is the ultimate, Vāsudeva Kṛṣṇa. Amongst the Pāṇḍavās, He says He is the arch bowman, Arjuna.

Of the sages, He says He is Vyāsa, author of the great epic Mahābhārata that includes the Bhagavad Gītā. Vyāsa is also referred to as Veda Vyāsa, the compiler of the *Vedas* who split one *Veda* into four *Vedas* so that the common person could understand the knowledge in the *Vedas.*

Of the thinkers, Kṛṣṇa says, He is Uśāna, also known as Śukra, guru of the *asuras,* celestials with a negative bent of mind.

Kṛṣṇa says, 'I am the scepter, the *daṇḍa,* the rod of punishment of the King.' As a master, Kṛṣṇa wields the *yoga daṇḍa,* the divine staff of wisdom. A ruler is not merely a refuge for his subjects, but also the rule giver, the disciplinarian. So too is the master.

There Is No End To My Glories!

10.39 *Also, of whatever beings exist, I am the Seed, Oh Arjuna.*
There is nothing that exists without Me in all creations, moving and unmoving.

10.40 *There is no end to My divine glories, Oh Parantapa.*
What has been said by Me are examples of My detailed glories.

10.41 *You should know that whatever glories exist or anything beautiful and glorious that exists, all that surely is born of just a portion of My splendor.*

10.42 *Of what use is it to know about the many manifestations of this kind, Oh Arjuna?*
I pervade this entire world with just a part of Myself.

Kṛṣṇa says to Arjuna, 'Enough has been said. You can take no more. Whatever I have said, whatever more I can say, will only be a drop in the ocean, a small fragment of what I am. There is nothing that is not Me, nothing that can exist outside of Me, and nothing that has not been created from and by Me.'

He has given the background to Arjuna, so that Arjuna is prepared to see His formless form. Arjuna is now in a mode of total surrender and deep gratitude.

Now, let us also experience these words of Kṛṣṇa in a mood of absolute surrender and total gratitude.

Close your eyes, and meditate on the divine glory of Kṛṣṇa.

Express deep gratitude for whatever way your life has been elevated. Express deep gratitude to whoever has helped you achieve health, wealth and education. Each and every one of these are expressions of the Divine.

Remember every one of them for the reasons they were in your life. Remember all of them, who helped you to flower in your life. Remember all of them with love and respect, with love and gratitude.

Remember your mother who gave you this body. She is the embodiment of the Divine, *Parabrahma* Kṛṣṇa. Give her your gratitude.

Remember your father, who gave you life. Feel him and give your gratitude to him.

Remember all the teachers and professors, who gave you education. They are embodiments of the Divine.

Feel deeply grateful to all of them for their contribution to your life and to your being.

Whoever has helped you to grow economically, whoever contributed to your economical growth, directly or indirectly, remember all of them and give your gratitude to them. Feel deeply connected to all of them.

Whoever gave you mental strength and understanding about life when you needed it, whenever you were depressed, whoever gave you courage when you were in a low mood, remember all of them. They are embodiments of the Divine, representatives of the universal consciousness. Remember all of them and give them your gratitude.

Whoever helped you grow spiritually, whoever helped you grow in spiritual understanding, remember all of them. Give them your gratitude. They are representatives of the Divine. Give them your gratitude for giving spiritual understanding, for adding something to your life.

Whoever helped you with understanding on the level of material wealth or spiritual growth, remember all of them and offer them your gratitude.

Ultimately, give gratitude to the divine energy, *Parabrahma* Kṛṣṇa, who gave all this intelligence and understanding to us in our life.

Just drop yourself and become one with the cosmic energy. May you become part of the whole universe, part of the energy that is moving the sun, moon and planet earth.

OṀ śānti, śānti, śāntihi

Relax. Now open your eyes. Continue to spend at least the next few hours in this mood of surrender. Drop yourself. You will see this experience works miracles in your being. It can transform you.

Forget about yourself. Drop yourself and let the Divine, let this cosmic energy prevail. Let Him be. Let the Divine be. This surrender mood can transform your whole consciousness. It can make you experience the ultimate truth that Kṛṣṇa explains here: His glories, His *vibhūti*, His divine glory.

When you are blissful, whatever you see looks divine and glorious. May you reach that bliss.

Let us pray to *Parabrahma* Kṛṣṇa, the universal energy, Existence, to guide us all and to give us all the experience of eternal bliss, *nityānanda*.

Thank you!

Thus ends the tenth chapter named **Vibhūti Yogaḥ** *of the* **Upaniṣad** *of* **Bhagavad Gītā**, *the scripture of Yoga, dealing with the science of the Absolute in the form of the dialogue between* **Śrī Kṛṣṇa** *and Arjuna.*

BHAGAVADGĪTĀ

Kṛṣṇa: The Cosmic Window

VIŚVARŪPA DARŚANA YOGAḤ

CHAPTER 11

How does one experience
Universal Consciousness?
What exactly happens?
What basic qualification
does one need for this experience?
Krishna explains with His very Presence!

Kṛṣṇa: The Cosmic Window

In this chapter, Kṛṣṇa shows His cosmic and divine form to Arjuna. Kṛṣṇa gives Arjuna the experience of universal consciousness. For the first time, Arjuna is about to experience Kṛṣṇa's divine form. Of all the chapters in Bhagavad Gītā, this chapter, *Viśvarūpa Darśana Yoga* -Vision of the cosmic form, has a very special significance. Elsewhere He speaks with the authority of *Parabrahma* Kṛṣṇa, but He is still present as the mortal Vāsudeva Kṛṣṇa form. Now, at Arjuna's request, He reveals His true cosmic Self to Arjuna.

In the previous chapter, along with Arjuna we too heard the glories of Kṛṣṇa, the complete expression of the Divine. Kṛṣṇa declares, 'Amongst the stars, I am the moon, amongst the *ṛṣis*, I am Nārada; whatever is best, I shine in that.'

Kṛṣṇa is not boasting that He is the best. All that He conveys is that whatever there is, is manifest in Himself. He is the very essence of Existence. Enough words have been said. It is now time to demonstrate. Kṛṣṇa proves who He is by giving a solid experience to Arjuna. The difference between an enlightened person and an egoistic person is that an egoistic person also declares what he perceives to be a fact, but only the enlightened person can give the experience itself. A mortal can talk, that is all he can do. He has no experience to back it up.

Our entire existence as we know it is unreal. So therefore, what can be true about it? We have no control over the next breath we take. We have no control over what will happen during the course of our lives. Yet we believe we are in control of the whole of our lives.

Divine or delusion?

Hiraṇyakaśipu, the Indian demon king, thought he was God and he made his subjects chant his name, '*Hiraṇyāya namaḥ*'. Kṛṣṇa also stated that He was God. The difference between the two was that Hiraṇyakaśipu could not give the experience to his subjects. He told them, 'Either believe that I am God or I will kill you!' He threatened his subjects into this behavior, whether or not they actually believed he was God. Please understand that conversion by blood or bread does not help. While both of them declared they were gods, Kṛṣṇa could actually prove it. He could give the experience of universal consciousness to people!

No great master believed in spreading his words through fear and greed. All great masters spread their words through unconditional love and compassion. That is the only way truth can spread.

Unfortunately, the disciples who followed these spiritual masters were not always masters themselves. They were there to establish business practices in the form of religions. They were organizers, not leaders. Fear and greed became handy tools of organization and propagation, since these followers did not have the experience of truth within themselves.

How to find out whether a person is a master? How to establish whether a person is enlightened or just egoistic? This is the scale: If he can give the experience, then whatever comes from him is the truth. Here Kṛṣṇa shows clearly that He *is* everything. He demonstrates His divinity to Arjuna. Kṛṣṇa walks His talk in this chapter.

In the *Bhāgavatam* (ancient Hindu epic) there is a beautiful verse that the *gopī* (female cowherd of Brindāvan), sings to Kṛṣṇa, who is everything to her clan:

tava kathāmṛtaṁ tapta jīvanaṁ
kavibhirīritam kalmaṣāpahaṁ
śravanamaṅgalam śrīmadātatam
bhuvi gṛhṇanti te bhūritā janāḥ

'O Kṛṣṇa, *tava kathāmṛtaṁ*...Your words and the words uttered about You are *kathāmṛtaṁ*, words of immortality, words of nectar, words both on You and by You. Just by listening to these words, You create auspiciousness in us.

'These words are worshipped and expressed as the highest truth by the great *ṛṣis* (sage to whom the *Vedas* were revealed). We who have experienced You, feel the joy again and again by speaking about You. You rejuvenate our whole being. Just by listening to these words about You and by You, we are transported to a different plane.'

If you have fallen in love with Kṛṣṇa, this is the chapter to know Him and enjoy Him. Here in this chapter He does not give any teachings. All intellectual teachings are over. Do's and don'ts are all over. He gives the experience directly: 'I am everything.' He gives the experience of the ultimate universal consciousness and the realization that He is present in everything. Arjuna experiences the universal consciousness. This whole chapter is pure experience.

The first thing we need to understand is whether it is possible to have the experience of the universal consciousness. Secondly, what is the basic qualification to experience it? Thirdly, what really happens inside our being during such an experience? These three things we shall understand from this chapter and explore the wonderful possibility of experiencing Kṛṣṇa as the cosmic window.

Live beyond logic

In the previous chapter, Kṛṣṇa gave the intellectual explanation that He is the Ultimate. More than an intellectual expression, I may say that this is an expression given to a person who is deeply in love. Kṛṣṇa can be God only when a person achieves the maturity of Arjuna. The truth should be declared only when a person is qualified and mature. Only when you reach the maturity of Arjuna, can you experience the divinity of Kṛṣṇa. When you feel deeply connected to a person, he looks divine even though he may be quite ordinary in reality.

Śiva says in Tantra that when one drops one's fantasies, he becomes Śiva and his wife becomes Uma. He reaches the state of *Śivatva,* the state of Śiva, and she reaches the state of Devi.

How does one attain enlightenment living a normal life?

In the Śiva Sūtra, Śiva says there is nothing wrong with a husband and wife living a normal conjugal life, but they need to drop their fantasies about one another.

When we live without fantasies, the other person looks like God. Śiva asks you to throw out the frame of fantasies so that then you can see everybody as God. What does not fit is your frame; your ideas of how others should behave. Because the frame does not fit, you wish to change the face! It is like cutting the foot to fit the shoe! Alter the shoe, not the foot! You are intelligent if you do the latter, but what most of us do is the former.

We have our own imagination of how our wife, husband, son, daughter, brother, boss, and friend should be. We try to fit them into that frame and suffocate them when they don't fit. That is why the other always suffocates us. That is why you need your space.

The space you require is the space for your fantasies. Over time this space becomes unlimited, because your fantasies grow. We cannot accept another person for what he or she is. The natural self of the other person threatens us. From childhood we have grown with ideas about what we should be and what everyone around us should be. We have clear ideas about how our would-be should be!

When you are deeply connected with the other person as they are, when you can accept anybody as he or she is, you establish a divine relationship. However, to do so, you must first learn to accept your own self as you are. When you are continuously engaged in chiseling, your job has no end. You can never be happy by chiseling the outer image. You can be happy only by dropping the image, the template, about the other person.

A small story:

Once there lived a couple married for fifty years. They were being interviewed on television.

The interviewer asked the old man, 'How old is your wife?'

He replied, 'She is ninety-two and I hope she lives for a hundred and ten years.'

The interviewer asked, 'How old are you?'

The old man said, 'I am also ninety-two and I hope to live for hundred and eleven years.'

The interviewer was surprised and asked, 'Why do you want your wife to live to a hundred and ten years and you for hundred and eleven?'

The old man replied, 'To be honest, I want at least one year of peace!'

Just understand, when you try to chisel each other constantly, you will only cause unhappiness in your life. But when you accept everyone as they are, the whole world appears as God.

This can be achieved in two ways. Firstly, by your own *tapas*, your spiritual penance, you acquire maturity by undergoing this experience repeatedly. You need to keep dropping your fantasies about other people. You need to stop creating fantasies about others, and accept them for what they are.

Secondly, a master can also give you this experience by infusing tremendous energy in you, by bringing you to his own frequency. But even to retain the energy of the master, you need a certain level of maturity. This is what happens here in this chapter. The frequency of Kṛṣṇa's cosmic form is too much for Arjuna to bear and he cries out to Kṛṣṇa to resume his normal form.

A small example: The other day I was watching the disaster caused by the hurricane Katrina, in USA on television, when one of the *ashramites* asked me why such calamities were taking place.

I tried to explain to them that it is something like driving your car or SUV, and incidentally it goes over a small anthill. As far as the ants are concerned, this is a natural calamity for them. They may call it 'Hurricane SUV!' But as far as you are concerned you are not even aware of this disaster. You are just driving the SUV. Can you relate with the ants in this incident or say that driving over their anthill was pre-destined?

Their logic and yours are completely different. Neither can they question you, nor can you answer them.

So when we question hurricane Katrina, it is like an ant questioning the SUV car owner! We can only conclude, 'This is all God's will.' The kind of explanation any organized religion gives is also this! No organized religion can ever give a reasonable answer to such happenings. No logical answer or explanation can ever be given for these experiences. No justification can be given that it is pre-destined and such. There is no logical answer as to why thousands of people die for no reason.

The frequency, logic, perception, and concepts of the ants are completely different from ours, just as ours is again completely different from the cosmic consciousness. Just like how you do not even know that your vehicle has killed thousands of ants, the cosmic energy or consciousness is not even aware of a happening like Hurricane Katrina! The frequency of this consciousness is in a completely different dimension. From the cosmic level, what happened in New Orleans, is something like a mug of water spilling onto an anthill, washing away the ants.

It is not possible to comprehend what that level or frequency is. What is possible is for us to raise the frequency of our will or consciousness to be one with It, to learn to live with It, and experience It. Neither God nor your wife can be understood; just learn to live with them!

The ants cannot question you as to why you spilled the mug of water on them. If their level of frequency is 10, your level is 100, and the universal consciousness is infinity. Logically, nothing can be done. Please understand, anyone who is trying to give a logical explanation is simply cheating. Anyone who attempts to explain logically why there are so many natural calamities, why death, why the misfortunes in life, why someone is high or low, has simply created one more philosophy.

If the person is charismatic, has a way with words, he will have created a new philosophy and cheated a group of people. One does not need to be very intelligent to cheat people, because people are not as intelligent as you think! This is probably why great philosophers convince others, but they themselves are not convinced.

I know a great atheist who chanted God's name when he lay dying! The very act of trying to convince and convert others testified to the fact that he was not convinced himself.

Please be aware that conversion is an intellectual and psychological crime. A converted person has one face superficially and his internal unconscious being is not in tune with it. The two conflict with each other and he becomes a schizophrenic. And preachers, who convert others without any deep personal experience of the Divine, always fall into the worst kind of depression. They punish themselves by their own acts.

One person from Oklahoma who was associated with us, was a reverend of the clergy. He enjoyed our programs and eventually went on to become a teacher of our meditation programs. I had never asked him to convert himself to our religion. To begin with, I myself do not have any religion! There is no need, because what I teach is pure *satya,* the Truth.

It is like this: The light bulb was invented by Thomas Edison. We cannot say that the light bulb belongs only to Christianity, since Edison happened to be a Christian! It belongs to humanity. Similarly the truth of the inner light given by Kṛṣṇa, like the light bulb, belongs to humanity and not to any particular religion. It is not necessary to convert to any religion. It is enough if you understand the truth and live your life happily and intensely.

I met a preacher engaged in violent conversion of people in India. Not having had the experience of truth himself, this preacher, who was engaged in converting others, had fallen into depression. He wanted to meet with me in private, so I agreed.

He wanted healing from me and after a few days of healing, he felt much better. I asked him the reason why he was engaged in such a violent practice. He replied that when he spoke, so many people listened to him and this gave him a sense of power. He then felt convinced that what he was teaching was the truth! I share this incident to show that when a person preaches without experience, he is simply trying to solidify his own confidence. Don't be fooled.

People who are trying to convert others into their faiths by greed and fear have no faith in themselves. If they did, there would be no need to convert others. Their own faith would transform others and make them realize the truth of their experience. Instead, somewhere deep within, they believe they are sinners. So they are keen to prove to others that they too are sinners, whether they wish to believe this or not.

Spiritual truths should transform, not convert. Spiritual truths should make a Christian a better Christian, a Muslim a better Muslim, and a Hindu a better Hindu. Those who try to force others into converting their religion, by convincing them that they are sinners, are the biggest sinners themselves. They have no redemption.

That is the difference between Kṛṣṇa, the incarnation, and Hiraṇyakaśipu, the demon. Here the difference between Kṛṣṇa and Hiraṇya is that the latter tries to preach and convince others of his ideas and convert them to be his followers. He is just trying to play the game when he himself does not have the experience. Kṛṣṇa gives the experience directly. When He declares that He is God, it is not for Him to satisfy His ego, but for us to experience the truth. He tells Arjuna that He is uttering these words for Arjuna's sake.

Let us now go into the verses and examine three questions:

Can universal consciousness be experienced? What is the basic qualification for this experience? What happens when one experiences it?

These three questions are explained beautifully by Kṛṣṇa in this chapter.

I Wish To See Your Divine Form

11.1 *Arjuna says: O Lord! By listening to Your wisdom on the supreme secret of Existence and Your glory, I feel that my delusion has disappeared.*

11.2 *O Kṛṣṇa! I have heard from You about the creation and destruction of all beings,*
Also Your inexhaustible greatness.

11.3 *Puruṣottama ! You have declared what You are, O Lord supreme,*
I wish to see the divine form of Yours.

11.4 *If You think it is possible for me to see it, then please, O Lord of Yoga and all mystic power,*
Show me Your form of eternal universal Self.

In the minds of many, Kṛṣṇa is considered an incarnation. It is in this chapter that Kṛṣṇa reveals Himself as not just an incarnation, but as also the very source from which everything flows. He is the source of all sources, the cause of all causes, the source of all the worlds and universes.

Arjuna has already heard from Kṛṣṇa about everything that he needs to do. Arjuna's questions have all disappeared; his doubts and delusions have dissolved. In the previous chapter, Kṛṣṇa explains to Arjuna who He really is.

Despite the faith that Arjuna has in Kṛṣṇa, he has doubts, too. Doubts and faith are two sides of the same coin. You cannot have one without the other. At the intellectual level, Arjuna had shed his doubts. At the emotional level, he had shed his doubts. But at the being level, at the very core of his being, Arjuna was still troubled by what he was about to do.

Arjuna has no one else to ask but Kṛṣṇa. Intuitively, Arjuna sees his own Self in Kṛṣṇa. *Narā,* the man, meets *Nārāyaṇa,* the Divine. Arjuna knows at the depths of his being that Kṛṣṇa, and Kṛṣṇa alone, can provide the answers to the doubts that have risen within him.

Can universal consciousness be experienced?

Step by step, Kṛṣṇa clears Arjuna's doubts. First, Kṛṣṇa addresses Arjuna's doubts of the intellect. Kṛṣṇa explains to him the misconceptions that Arjuna has from the literal reading of the scriptures and what he has understood to be right and wrong. 'All the people in front of you are already dead,' says the Lord, 'I eliminated them long ago; why are you then worried? Do what you need to do.'

And now, finally, the time has come for Arjuna to see Kṛṣṇa as He truly is. Arjuna is standing on the last step. He beseeches, 'My delusion has been dispelled and I am now aware of Your divinity. Please show me now who You really are.'

And yet, Arjuna still hesitates. He wants to know, but he is not sure if he can bear to experience the truth. He says one phrase clearly, 'If you think I can behold Your form,' which indicates that there is already some fear in him.

It is not important what others think; what is important is what *we* think. *We* should be ready to take the responsibility and face whatever comes. Even simple truths or experiences cannot be given so easily, since the receiver must have the maturity to hold what he has received. In one of our publications titled, '*Swamiji as We Know Him,*' there is a chapter, 'In the Arms of the Master.' It tells the story of how one of the devotees was constantly nagging me for an experience, much like Arjuna asks here. I advised the person to meditate but the person insisted on a personal experience. The experience is not like a coconut to be given away! The receiver has to have the maturity to hold it. This went on for six months and she would not listen; she kept on asking. Then I eventually decided it was time.

In the narration of the account, she says that she felt her base itself being shaken. She felt herself being without boundary and cried out to me to stop because she could not take it anymore. For two days she was bedridden and she went on to say that I was thoughtless to have given her what I did!

Here Arjuna says, 'If you think I can behold your cosmic form, My Lord, show me Your unmasked, manifested universal Self.' Please understand, before entering into the experience, you must have the courage to take whatever comes.

There are people I know, who after meditating for about a year, start experiencing the state of boundarilessness. They get frightened and shaken and afraid of losing themselves. I tell them that the meditation itself was to give them the experience of boundarilessness. It is like taking all the trouble to invite a guest to your house and when he does arrive, you are surprised at his arrival! Invariably, when people have the experience for the first time, they are shaken and try to escape.

This is also the case with people who practice chanting intensely. When the Divine starts giving them the experience, they are shaken by fear, and stop. When you are meditating on the Divine, a chant, or God, do not try to escape when you get the vision or *darśan.* Please understand that the Divine will never disturb you, only your fear disturbs you. When you have the experience, have the courage to go with it. With the Divine, nothing is too much.

Rāmakṛṣṇa asks Vivekānanda, 'If you see the *amṛtasāgara,* the ocean of nectar, how will you drink from it?'

Vivekānanda says he would become a fly, sit by the edge of the ocean and begin to drink it slowly. Rāmakṛṣṇa says, 'Fool! Jump into it and drink!'

Vivekānanda fears that he would die if he did that. Rāmakṛṣṇa says beautifully, 'It is the ocean of nectar, how will you die?'

Amṛta means nectar, that which guarantees immortality. By drinking it you cannot die. How would you die by jumping into the ocean of immortality?

Here, Arjuna says, 'If you think I can behold your cosmic form…' Arjuna wants the experience, but puts the responsibility on Krishna. He wants the sweet, but not Diabetes! Of course, the divine sweet can never make you a Diabetic.

> I had occasion to visit Melkote, the place where Rāmānujācārya the Indian saint had lived.
>
> The *prasād* (food offered to the Lord and distributed to the people) was so tasty and intensely sweet. I feared that the devotees would have become diabetic but was surprised when I was told there was no diabetic in the entire village, although everyone consumed the *prasād* daily! Understand, food offered to God gets energized and becomes *amṛta* or nectar. What we chant while offering the *prasād* cleanses and energizes it.

I would like to tell you about important research done on water. I have mentioned this before but it is so important that it is worth repeating here.

In the movie, *What the Bleep Do We Know?*, the recently released book, *The Hidden Messages in Water*, is discussed. A Japanese doctor Dr. Masaru Emoto, experimented by speaking positive words like *peace, bliss* and *happiness* sitting in front of a few glasses of water labeled with these words. He then spoke negative words like *war, violence,* and *anger* to other glasses containing similar water samples, that were labeled with these negative words.

He then froze all these glasses of water and photographed the ice crystals as seen under a microscope. The results were startling. Those ice crystals from the water that received positive messages appeared as clear as jewels; as beautiful as diamonds! The ice crystals from the water that received negative messages were ugly to look at.

Masaru Emoto repeated these experiments hundreds of times to prove that our thoughts affect water. This is why masters from ancient times taught people to chant *mantras* standing in the sacred river Gaṅgā. The whole river would be energized by the energy of millions of devotees chanting!

The water brought by the Englishmen from Britain in the days of East India Company would usually spoil within a month when they came to India. However, the water carried back with them from Calcutta (Gaṅgā water) would stay fresh even they reached England!

Research conducted on this showed that water from the Gaṅgā had the ability to purify itself. This is why the Gaṅgā is never polluted despite so much polluting material being dumped into it.

Likewise, when food is put before the deity in a temple where *mantras* are chanted constantly, the food absorbs the pure, spiritual energy. It starts radiating the energy of the divine positive qualities. One cannot fall sick by eating *prasād.*

With divine energy, the effect is always positive, never negative. You cannot die in the *amṛtasāgara,* the ocean of nectar. When it comes to the Divine, all you need to do is jump into it with your whole being. All you need to do is to relax into it for transformation.

Arjuna says:

'If You think I am able to behold, O My Lord, master of all mystic power, please show me Your cosmic form.'

There is no such thing as partial surrender to a master. There is no such thing as, 'Please give me what I can take. Let me take a sip and see if I like it. If I do, I shall ask You for more. If not, I shall not take anymore.'

Of course, the master knows your readiness far better than you do. That is why I work on you in stages. As long as you are not ready, what I give you is brain and eye candy, that's all. You can gaze in happiness and go away. The form is all that you can take. It is only when your seriousness of purpose is established, that I can start working on you without the fear that you will run away from the operating table.

The *brahmacāris* who train at the ashram understand the power of the master's words. They listen and listen completely. They listen without applying logic and reason. Logic and reason come with ego. To be egoless, you need to be mindless and shed logic.

Arjuna is in the same mood. 'Let what happens be decided by You,' he says to Kṛṣṇa. What he implies is this: 'I have heard all that You have said. My questions have disappeared and my delusions have evaporated. I truly understand Your greatness. May I see You in Your true form?'

The Divine Eye

11.5 Bhagavān *said:*
O Pārtha, behold My hundreds and thousands of forms,
Of different divine sorts, of various colors and shapes.

11.6 *O Bhārata, see the Āditya, the Vāsu, the Rudrā, the Aśvini, the Marut and many wonders you have never seen before.*

11.7 *O Arjuna, see now in My body, all the moving and the unmoving, Whatever else you wish to see, everything integrated into this body.*

11.8 *But you cannot see Me with these your physical eyes. Let Me give you the divine eye; behold My divine power!*

Kṛṣṇa says, 'O Pārtha, behold the hundreds and thousands of my divine forms. These are diverse divine forms, of diverse colors, shapes and sizes. O Bhārata, see the different manifestations of Āditya, Vāsu, Rudrā, Aśvini Kumāras, Marut and many wonderful beings whom no one has ever seen before.'

But before He gives *darśan* of the universal form, He makes an important and beautiful statement, 'O Arjuna! You cannot see my form with ordinary eyes. To behold this form, you would need *divya netra,* the third eye or the divine eye.

'*Divyaṁ dadāmi te cakṣuḥ...*' Let me give you the divine eye to enable you to see and experience Me.' From this verse He starts giving the *Viśvarūpa darśana* - Vision of His Cosmic Form.

Kṛṣṇa says, 'O Arjuna, may you start seeing whatever exists, the *sthāvara* and the *jaṅgama* (immovable and movable), the universe that no ordinary man can see. Even the great sages have not seen this sight and are not aware of it.'

Arjuna was an intimate friend of Kṛṣṇa and their attachment to each other as friends was deep. They had known each other from their early years and even though Kṛṣṇa was close to all the Pāṇḍavā brothers and also the Kaurava, His bond with Arjuna was special. Over and above their friendship, Arjuna was a very intelligent and learned man in his own right.

But neither the deep friendship nor his intelligence or wisdom could give Arjuna any idea of the real nature, the true nature of Kṛṣṇa, and about His many facets. There are so many forms and manifestations of the different energies that humans have not even heard of. Kṛṣṇa, in His infinite compassion and love for Arjuna, shows him all these wonderful forms.

Now Kṛṣṇa gives Arjuna the power to see what is happening in the whole universe, not only in the present, but in the past and the future also!

Seeing the divine form

Here again are the three questions that are the essence of the whole chapter.

Can the divine form be seen?

What is the qualification to see the divine form?

What really happens when you see the divine form?

I tell you categorically – it *is* possible to see the divine form. There are many enlightened masters who have experienced this consciousness.

Let me give you an instance from my life.

After nine long years of penance, I was completely frustrated at one point. I wondered if I was wasting my whole life reading books, following what the earlier masters said and applying them in my life. I wondered, was there really something called enlightenment or was it a waste of my whole life? At one point I began to fear that I had wasted the very essence of my life, my youth, by pouring all of it into *tapas*, or penance. Was it really worth the sacrifice?

All of a sudden at one point in time, I felt myself going into deep depression. Actually, I later realized that this was not depression. It was a desperate situation, a deep personal quest, and an urge to do or die. Now I know that one needs to reach this stage before one can realize the truth.

Whatever had to be done as spiritual penance, I had done and had not left even an inch untried. For example, at one point in time, I created a wall of fire six feet in diameter, sat inside it and chanted continuously so that I would not fall asleep. In this way, I had tried hundreds of techniques to the best of my ability. Still nothing was happening to me, I concluded that there was either no such thing as enlightenment or it was something I could not achieve.

I strongly began to think that enlightenment was simply something that some people were cheating humanity with, for their own ego-fulfillment. I began to doubt and lose faith in the whole system. The photo of Rāmakṛṣṇa, who had all along been my inspiration, the photo I used to worship everyday, I threw away in disgust, depression and anger and with such force that the glass frame broke.

At that time I was staying in Oṁkāreśvar, in a forest in Madhya Pradesh, on the banks of the holy river Narmadā. I had my rosary, with which I used to say my prayers or do my penance for hours together. It was my constant companion and was something to which I had given utmost respect, almost like my lifeline.

In my anger and depression, I threw the rosary into the river Narmadā and cast the *mantra* out of my mind. I decided, 'No more meditation, no more spirituality. Enough!' I had had enough of the game being played by the so-called enlightened masters. I simply threw everything away, dropped everything.

I then walked into the river Narmadā with my eyes closed. The river was at least sixty feet deep at that point. I just kept walking with my eyes closed. Fear gripped me but I continued. When I opened my eyes, I was on the opposite bank of the river! Till date I have no idea what happened. I have no idea whether there were rocks all-along the path I walked on the river, or whether I floated or whether the river parted. But I did not have the resolve to walk back through the river again, that much I know! To return to the point I started from, I had to walk to the nearest bridge, many miles away!

The seventh day after this incident, I joined the masters in their game! The experience of enlightenment and cosmic consciousness simply happened to me. It never left me afterwards.

So to answer this question, 'Can this be experienced?' The definitive answer is *yes*. As a person who was just like you, I tell you out of courtesy the simple truth, 'Yes, honestly, it can be experienced.'

This is the solid truth; a promise that this can be experienced. Please understand, I have no vested interest in convincing you of this ideology. All I have is simple courtesy, like informing a friend of the traffic situation in a particular place and guiding him through a different route.

It is definitely possible to experience this truth, this cosmic form, in our lives. Never think, 'This is not for me.' It is for everybody! However, unless you are sure of the possibility of having this beautiful, intense experience, listening to all this is a waste of time. If you think this is one more story, do not waste your time here.

The first thing that you need to know is that it *is* possible. Only then what Kṛṣṇa says will work on our being. I will be really happy if you go out after experiencing this cosmic form. At least go out with a glimpse of it. If these words of Kṛṣṇa are to work on you, you must first be convinced ᶜ the possibility of it happening to you and know that these are not just ˉ ᵒᵗ me tell you openly and directly, from my experience, 'It *is*

ou .
ords. ,

These words of Kṛṣṇa are not mere words; they are not mere scriptural words. These words are techniques that go deep inside you and work on you with amazing results. All that you need is complete trust in the master that what He says will happen. I promise you it will.

Who can see the divine form?

Next, what is the qualification?

Basically, by giving this experience to Arjuna, Kṛṣṇa proves that there is no need for any qualifications, because Arjuna himself has no qualifications. Arjuna neither took the responsibility nor understood fully the teachings of Kṛṣṇa. He was simply fortunate to be in the presence of Kṛṣṇa, that's all. Likewise, you too are fortunate to be here and not caught in some traffic jam! There were thousands of possibilities for you to be elsewhere; so many options were available to you. But out of all of them, you chose to be here. This is the only qualification required.

In fact, you are the Arjuna who missed Kṛṣṇa in an earlier form. You are here now, listening or reading, not by any mere accident or divine coincidence. You are here now for a reason. That is qualification enough. Make sure that you do not miss Kṛṣṇa again this time!

By coming here every day, your unconscious and subconscious mind has already accepted whatever is being said here. If this had not happened, you would not return here the following day. You would not be listening to or reading this chapter.

A person told me that when he woke up every day for these few days, he found himself waiting for 5:30 in the evening so that he could attend the discourse! If you are waiting, it means that all these words have already entered your being. So have the trust that you are ready for this experience.

One of the problems is that even if you are qualified, you do not have the trust or belief that you are qualified! This is because society and religious preachers have blamed you continuously for many things and created a kind of guilt in you.

Because of this you have lost faith and confidence in yourself. Now, after having listened for all these days, your still being here is proof that your unconscious mind has accepted these ideas. Your conscious mind may struggle with the question of why you are here, but the fact that you are here shows that unconsciously you have begun enjoying these ideas.

You are fortunate to fall in tune with the great thought of Kṛṣṇa. After understanding the verse, we will enter into a meditation to have at least a glimpse of what the cosmic *Kṛṣṇa* gave Arjuna. Arjuna had no qualification to receive what he got from Kṛṣṇa. When He could give it to Arjuna, why not to us?

First, we acknowledge the possibility of having the experience. We have all understood that it is possible to have it. Next, the qualification: we have all understood that simply by being, here we are qualified for the experience.

Somebody once asked Bhagavān Ramaṇa Maharṣi, enlightened master from India, what was the qualification for enlightenment. Bhagavān replied that merely being alive, simply existing, was the only qualification required!

At the most, the only qualification can be said to be openness. If you did not have it, you would not come here every day. We never allow the belief that we have the qualification to enter into our being. I tell you, drop everything! You are qualified by your very presence here!

Next, what happens when you have the experience?

Kṛṣṇa's words:

'Arjuna, you cannot see Me with these ordinary eyes. You need the divine eye, the third eye, *divyacakṣu.* To see My cosmic form, I give you the divine eye.'

What is this divine eye?

Let me tell you my experience that happened when I was twelve years old.

During that age, I used to do a particular meditation, or rather I used to play with a technique given to me by a master. When I was about ten years old the great master Annamalai Swamigal, disciple of Ramana Maharshi, first taught me the technique of exploring to see where thoughts originated.

Once when I visited him with my parents, he was addressing a group of seekers and was saying, 'We are not the body, we are *ātman*, the spirit. No pain or suffering touches us.'

I wondered how this could be, for if my mother beat me, I could feel the pain! (In India, if kids were mischievous, they would be roundly beaten, you could not call 911!) To experiment, I went home and cut my thigh with a knife to see if I had pain or not. I bled profusely.

Naturally, it not only hurt me, but I had to be taken to the hospital for the wound to be stitched, with more scolding from my mother! I had both pain and suffering. I wondered why this Swami had taught us such a thing as 'no suffering or pain!'

Experimenting on others was easy. Arjuna was intelligent. After understanding everything, he started killing others; he never experimented on himself!

I approached the Swami and related what had happened to me.

First he asked me, 'Did I ask you to go and cut yourself?'

He then made a profound statement that transformed my life. He said, 'You may have pain and suffering now, but do not worry, your attitude of analyzing and searching for the truth, your courage to experiment with truth, will liberate you from all pains, so go ahead!'

He then advised me to start searching for the source of my thoughts. Of course, at that age I was only irritated by his comments and my attention was on the fruits and sweets that devotees had brought him. I was hoping he would give me some in consolation! Honestly, I neither understood nor was convinced of what he said.

However, after a few days I began to playfully and casually try out the technique of trying to see the origin of my thoughts. I did not do this with any expectation or idea. All I knew was what the Swami had told me - that I would go beyond pain or suffering if I did this technique. I had no concept of God, *Brahman, ātman* or *jñāna.*

One evening, at the foothills of the sacred Aruṇācala hill, I was sitting on a rock known locally as the Coral Rock trying out the same technique with eyes closed. I had fallen into deep meditation.

After some time, suddenly something opened, something seemed to happen inside my being, a feeling of being pulled or sucked inside.

The next moment it was as if a door had opened inside me, and I had complete 360-degree vision, both laterally and vertically. I could see on all four sides – the temple that was behind me, the hill that was in front of me, and the city that was on my left and right. I could see vertically too – the sky, the rock on which I was sitting, again the temple behind me.

For normal people who have only a maximum of 120-degree vision, I know this is very difficult to comprehend. All I can do is promise solemnly that it did happen! No other intellectual explanation is possible. Not only was I able to see all around, I was also able to feel that whatever I was seeing was Me. Whether they were plants or rocks or the city or the hill, whatever I could see, I felt they were all just Me. The experience was so intense and ecstatic that it was more than three or four hours before I opened my eyes. I felt feverish with bliss and this mood continued for three days.

But after this, I was overtaken by a fear that there was something wrong with me. I thought a ghost had possessed me and I decided never to go to that rock again. I even began to avoid that route, which I normally took. I related my experience to an elderly *sanyāsini* who was my mentor. She held my hand and seeing the energy, exclaimed, 'You are not possessed by any ghost. You are possessed by God!' She encouraged me to continue with meditation but I never dared to do so for the next six months and was even afraid to close my eyes!

I related my experience to a close friend of mine. I told him about my 360-degree vision and my not knowing what was happening to me, etc. He did not believe me until I proved it to him by telling him about an ant climbing up the tree *behind* me, and correctly telling which side of the coin that he hid in his hand was exposed. He ran away from me in terror!

He was in the ashram recently and said to one of the *ashramites*, 'I was the first person to receive energy *darśan* from him, but I missed it!'

But despite the fear I experienced, the whole body was bubbling with joy and ecstasy.

So welcome was the feeling, that I had a small temptation to go to the rock again. I never really understood what had happened. A year later another enlightened person gave me the explanation; the seeking, however, started after this experience. Nine years of penance followed. All this penance was in order to have this experience again. When it did come the next time, both body and mind were ready and the experience stayed within my being.

The vision of 360 degrees is what Kṛṣṇa means by *divyacakṣu, trinetra,* divine eye or third eye, also called *ājñā cakra.* When this eye opens you will see 360 degrees not only in the horizontal but in the vertical dimension, too. You will see the whole Existence as You, and experience it as You. This experience is what Kṛṣṇa calls as cosmic consciousness.

I felt that everything I saw around me was living, just as how we feel our living bodies, expanding the body consciousness to the universal consciousness. When you feel the whole Universe as you would your own body, it can be called a cosmic experience. Unfortunately, we do not feel alive even within our own bodies!

Just as I was frightened when I had my first experience, Arjuna too was frightened when he started seeing Kṛṣṇa's cosmic form. In such instances, a living master is required for help and guidance. I am often asked this question, 'Who was your master?,' to which I reply, 'Aruṇācala.' Aruṇācala, the sacred hill of Tiruvannamalai, my birthplace, is a living master. For a premature baby to survive, it must be put into the incubator.

Similarly, Aruṇācala is the incubator for the enlightened person-to-be. The energy of Aruṇācala takes care just by your being near it.

'Let me give you the third eye, to enable you to experience the universal consciousness.'

You need to understand that after this verse, neither Kṛṣṇa nor Arjuna speaks. Suddenly, it is Sañjaya who is speaking. After the first chapter in Bhagavad Gītā until now, there is no word from Sañjaya. But here it is he who is speaking. This is a symbolic representation.

Arjuna is unable to speak, because he is in the ecstatic experience. Kṛṣṇa does not speak because His voice is beyond audibility. His voice is in the cosmic frequency, which is not audible to us. So Sañjaya interprets.

A Thousand Blazing Suns

11.9 *Sañjaya said:*
O king, having spoken thus, the great Lord of Yoga, Kṛṣṇa, showed to Arjuna His supreme cosmic form.

11.10 *Numerous mouths and eyes, with numerous wonderful sights, numerous divine ornaments, with numerous divine weapons uplifted,*

11.11 *Arjuna saw this universal form wearing divine garlands and clothing, anointed with celestial fragrances, wonderful, resplendent, endless, with faces on all sides.*

11.12 *If the splendor of a thousand suns were to blaze all together in the sky, it would be like the splendor of that mighty being.*

11.13 *There, in the body of the God of gods, the Pāṇḍavā then saw the whole universe resting in one, with all its infinite parts.*

11.14 *Dhañanjaya, filled with wonder, his hair standing on end, then bowed his head to the God and spoke with joined palms.*

These verses show the unlimited, never-ending, wonderful, all-pervading nature of the Lord. Rāmakṛṣṇa says that when he experienced the form, the cosmic consciousness, he could not pluck a single flower from a plant, because he felt that all the plants were garlands offered to God. In that mood, plucking a flower hurts. A wild animal responds peacefully to your presence. There is no violence in cosmic consciousness. There is only acceptance and inclusion.

This is what Arjuna saw in the universal form, an unlimited number of mouths, eyes, and wonderful visions. The form was decorated with many celestial ornaments and bore many divine upraised weapons. He wore celestial garlands and garments. Many divine scents were smeared all over His body. All was wondrous, brilliant, unlimited, all-expanding.

Here he sees an unlimited number of mouths and eyes in Kṛṣṇa. Now Arjuna sees 360 degrees in both horizontal and vertical dimensions. He sees the whole universe, all the people on the battlefield, all of them inside Kṛṣṇa, as the universal consciousness. He sees the Whole as his own being.

There is no boundary to Kṛṣṇa's universal form. The word Viṣṇu, which is his real form, means one who expands infinitely. The splendor that Sañjaya talks about is beyond anything the mind can comprehend, because it is the source of all splendors.

Notice, it is Sañjaya speaking these words, not Arjuna. Sañjaya is far from the battlefield and has been given the power to see what happens on the battlefield, so that he can describe the events to his king Dhṛtarāṣṭra. Though Kṛṣṇa says that this form is being shown only to Arjuna, by default Sañjaya has the great fortune to witness and participate in this vision.

Arjuna is awestruck and is in silence. He is yet to speak. What he has witnessed is beyond anything that he could have imagined or asked for. But the silence is a very active silence. It is a silence in which he experiences the truth of Kṛṣṇa. It is a silence in which he is actively participating in the process and is being immersed. They say those who experience do not talk. Those who talk have not experienced.

Sañjaya then summarizes Arjuna's reaction to the divine form of Kṛṣṇa in the last few verses. Arjuna is still silent and it is Sañjaya who describes what happens.

What Arjuna saw was beyond his understanding. Wherever he looked was Kṛṣṇa; Kṛṣṇa in many forms, many shapes, many non-forms, and non-shapes. There are no words to describe what Arjuna saw. How does one describe what is beyond the mind, beyond logic, beyond words, beyond all comprehension?

In the body of the supreme Lord, Arjuna saw the whole universe divided in different ways and at the same time united in one form. The universe is divided into many parts such as the sun, moon, earth, planets and other bodies in space. Here he sees all of them as one form. You need to understand this description, which is so beautiful. Later we shall enter into a meditation and pray to the *Parabrahma* Kṛṣṇa to give us all a glimpse of what Arjuna received.

Arjuna is able to see the whole and at the same time all the parts. Even the word hologram, that we now so commonly use to describe the totality of something preserved in a fragment, does no justice to Arjuna's vision. In a hologram, one needs to make the effort to see the whole in the fragment. In this divine vision granted to Arjuna the whole existed with the part with no separation, no discontinuity. The whole was part and the part was whole.

Of all the people on the battlefield of Kurukṣetra, only Arjuna had this great fortune to behold the cosmic vision of Kṛṣṇa. Only he was granted the boon of divine vision to see the entire universe within Kṛṣṇa. The vision that Arjuna beheld enveloped him completely. He was, in fact, part of that vision.

Arjuna and Kṛṣṇa grew up together from childhood. Kṛṣṇa's sister Subhadrā was Arjuna's wife. They had a deep relationship as friends. In this one moment, that relationship was redefined.

Worlds Tremble With Fear

11.15 *Arjuna said;*
O God, I see all the gods in Your body and many types of beings, too.
Brahma, the Lord of creation, seated on the lotus, all the sages, and celestial serpents.

11.16 *I see Your infinite form on every side, with many arms, stomachs, mouths, and eyes;*
Neither the end, nor the middle, nor the beginning do I see, O Lord of the Universe, O cosmic form.

11.17 *I see You with crown, club, and discus; a mass of radiance shining everywhere,*
Difficult to look at, blazing all round like the burning fire and Sun in infinite brilliance.

11.18 *You are the imperishable, the Supreme Being worthy to be known. You are the great treasure house of this Universe.*
You are the imperishable Protector of the eternal order. I believe You are the Eternal Being.

11.19 *I see You without a beginning, middle, or end, infinite in power and with many arms,*
The sun and the moon being Your eyes, the blazing fire your mouth, the whole Universe scorched by Your radiance.

11.20 *This space between earth and the heavens and everything is filled by You alone.*
O Great being, having seen Your wonderful and terrible form, the three worlds tremble with fear.

11.21 *Many celestials enter into You; some praise You in fear with folded hands;*
Many great masters and sages hail and adore You.

11.22 *The Rudrā, Āditya, Vāsu, Sadhya, Vishvadeva, Ashvin, Marut, Ushmapa and a host of Gandharva, Yakṣa, Asura and Siddha are all looking at You in amazement.*

11.23 *Having seen Your immeasurable form with many mouths and eyes, with many arms, thigh, and feet, with many stomach,s and frightening tusks,*
O Mighty-armed, the worlds are terrified and so am I.

11.24 *Seeing You, Your form touching the sky, flaming in many colors, mouths wide open, large fiery eyes, O Viṣṇu,*
I find neither courage nor peace; I am frightened.

As Arjuna is in the same consciousness as the Lord, this verse should actually start with *'Bhagavān uvāca'* meaning 'the Lord said!' These statements are said to come from Him for us to record.

These are beautiful ways that he describes the form. You may wonder why he does so. Please understand, he does so to inspire us to work to achieve this form and this experience, to move in this path. Arjuna is showing us the way.

He says, 'O Lord! I can see all the gods and deities in Your body. I can see the special union of living entities. I can see Brahma seated on the lotus flower. I can see all the sages and divine serpents. O Lord of the universe, I see many arms, stomachs, faces, eyes, and your limitless form. O universal form, I cannot see your beginning, middle, or end.'

As a matter of fact, when you begin to see 360 degrees in both horizontal and vertical dimensions, there really is no beginning, middle, or end to see. It is a continuum. It is like seeing one of these special movies on a circular screen. Where would you describe the beginning to be, the end to be, or the middle to be? It is an infinite circle. The Divine is an infinite circle, with no beginning, no end, and therefore no middle. Without a beginning and an end, to talk about the middle makes no sense.

Part of what Arjuna sees here is the traditional representation of Lord Viṣṇu. Viṣṇu is always depicted with His weapons of mace and discus, the *gada* and *cakra,* and wearing the jewel-studded crown. Viṣṇu is also depicted as resting on the ocean of milk, upon the giant serpent Ādiśeṣa, with Brahma rising from Viṣṇu's navel upon a lotus flower.

Some of what he sees is formless energy. He perceives radiance more powerful than a thousand suns, blazing and dazzling, impossible to look at even with his newly endowed divine eye. What Arjuna sees is beyond any sensory perception, something that could be experienced in that moment in time, impossible to express.

Suddenly the scene changes in these verses. Arjuna is terrified. What he is seeing now is quite different from what he expected when he asked to see Kṛṣṇa's divine form. Arjuna is now incoherent. What he keeps saying is neither logical nor well thought out. What he sees he reproduces to the best of his mental abilities.

He says, 'You are without origin, middle, or end, with unlimited power. You spread throughout the heavens and through all other directions. O Supreme Soul, *Paramātman,* after having seen your wonderful form, all the worlds and the whole Universe are trembling with fear. All the celestial beings are shuddering before this form, and entering into this formless form, some of them afraid, offering prayers with folded hands, along with hosts of realized sages praising this form in silent acceptance and wonderment.'

There is no other record so clear about the cosmic frequency of the universal form as in the *Gītā.* What Arjuna perceives is what is always present, but which he normally has no capability to see. Now he sees Kṛṣṇa in all His manifestations, from the highest to the lowest frequency levels of energy, with nothing filtered.

But suddenly the form seems to change from the magnificent, comforting, and expanded form, to one that is now disturbing. It is still not clear to Arjuna what is happening, but he can anticipate that something he is about to see is not going to be as pleasant as what he had seen so far. What Arjuna sees disturbs him.

'O All pervading Viṣṇu! I see You with your many radiating colors, burning fire in your gaping mouth, heating up the entire Universe with radiance, touching the sky, and Your form unnerves me. My heart trembles in fear, and I have no courage or peace to behold You.' Until now Arjuna was saying there was no beginning, middle, or end. Now he says the form is touching the sky; an indication that he is settling, coming down from the experience.

Arjuna says he wants equilibrium, meaning that he wants his mind to be under his intellectual control. He wants to know the cause and effect, and feel that they are in his control. As long as these are under your control, you feel as if you are a leader; your ego is strong. But the moment these are taken away from you, you feel at a loss and no more a leader. You are just a drop in the ocean. He is afraid of that and is not able to stay in that same state.

The wave in the ocean is part of the ocean. As long as it feels itself to be part of the ocean, there is no separation. However, when the wave experiences its own identity, creates its own identity, it no longer feels itself a part of the ocean. It feels itself to be a separate entity. When it is time to merge back into that ocean, it is afraid. When it looks back at the ocean, with a feeling of separation, it feels afraid.

When Arjuna had his first glimpse of the cosmic Vision of Kṛṣṇa, he identified with the Vision. There was no separation. Now, suddenly there is separation. Along with separation there is fear.

Tell Me Who You Are

11.25 *Having seen your fearsome mouths with blazing tusks like the fire of the end of the Universe,*
I know not the four directions nor do I find peace. O Lord of the Deva, O refuge of the Universe, be gracious.

11.26 *All the sons of Dhṛtarāṣṭra, with many kings of the earth, Bhīṣma, Droṇa, the son of the charioteer, Karṇa, with our warrior chieftains,*

11.27 *Into Your mouths with terrible tusks, fearful to behold, they enter.*
Some are seen caught in the gaps between the tusks and their heads crushed.

11.28 *Even as many torrents of rivers flow towards the ocean,*
So too these warriors in the world of men enter Your flaming mouths.

11.29 *Just as moths hurriedly rush into the fire for their own destruction,*
So too these creatures rush hastily into Your mouths of destruction.

11.30 *Swallowing all worlds on every side with Your flaming mouths, You lick in enjoyment.*
O Viṣṇu, Your fierce rays are burning, filling the whole world with radiance.

11.31 *Tell me who You are, so fierce in form; salutations to You, O supreme; have mercy.*
Indeed I know not Your purpose, but I desire to know You, the Original Being.

In these verses Arjuna expresses his discomfort. Arjuna had earlier said that he beheld all the celestial beings in the cosmic vision of Kṛṣṇa. Then he started feeling disturbed by the terrifying form that this vision changed into. From the high, when his hair stood on end, he slowly comes down. From this verse we should say, 'Arjuna *uvāca*!' meaning Arjuna says... It is no longer the divine state that Arjuna talks from. The moment he started feeling fear he descended to his normal state. You should understand that it is only your fear that separates you from cosmic consciousness.

Fear – The destroyer of ecstacy

There are two things that make you a human – the instinct to possess and the instinct to survive. The instinct to survive arises out of fear, from the *svādiṣṭhāna cakra* (fear energy center in your body), and the instinct to possess comes out of greed, from the *mūlādhāra cakra* (sex energy center in your body). Here the instinct to survive has appeared and he has become Arjuna, the man. We do not understand that when we drop the instinct to survive, we become Kṛṣṇa; we exist forever. We become *Bhagavān,* the universal consciousness. But most often, we hold onto the instinct to survive. Now Arjuna slowly comes down and becomes Arjuna, the man.

Arjuna exclaims, 'I see all the sons of Dhṛtarāṣṭra, along with their allied kings, Bhīṣma, Droṇa, Karṇa, and other chief soldiers rushing into Your fearful mouths. I see some trapped with their heads smashed between Your teeth, ground into nothing.'

He describes the whole scene. He sees the heavy losses on both sides; his own side, his warriors and generals, but even heavier losses on the other side, including Bhīṣma who is invincible, Droṇa and Karṇa who are unconquerable. By inference he sees his own victory in the end.

However, this scene does not fill him with peace and comfort. Arjuna is terrified at this vision of destruction. The destruction of those whom he perceives as his mortal enemies leaves him with no comfort.

The truth is that Arjuna is not in control. He has no clue about what is happening to him and around him. He is in the presence of a primal force, before which all that is obvious is his own insignificance. Victory and defeat seem to make no difference. The vision of destruction implies that he too is mortal. Arjuna is terrified.

Death is the ultimate fear. Even the great warrior Arjuna trembles when faced with death. It is not that Arjuna is not aware of the inevitability of death or the nature of death. Yet Arjuna is petrified. What is Arjuna so afraid of?

One thing, Arjuna does not expect the cosmic form of Kṛṣṇa to be anything but loving and compassionate. Kṛṣṇa can be the friend, the master, the beloved, the child, the mother, and all combined. In every one of these moods, in each *bhāva,* Kṛṣṇa is still lovable, still reachable. However, in the form that Kṛṣṇa has presented now, the all-devouring monster as it were, Arjuna is unable to comprehend any aspect of Kṛṣṇa that he has known.

For the first time, Arjuna realizes that the master cannot be predicted! The primal energy that the master is, has to be experienced in whatever manner it is presented, without expectations and fears.

It is so easy to fall in love with a handsome master. Kṛṣṇa is the most beautiful of all the gods. He is so easy to fall in love with! To fall in love with a terrifying Kālī or an impassive Śiva is far more difficult. But anyone can love Kṛṣṇa, and everyone does. No one expects Kṛṣṇa to be terrifying. So when Kṛṣṇa presents another form to Arjuna, the ground literally slips from under Arjuna's feet. He has no support. He does not know where to turn for help.

So Arjuna pleads, 'Please have mercy upon me. Tell me who You are. Tell me why You are here. I would like to know. I bow down to You.'

Do Not Be Afraid

11.32 Śri Bhagavān *said:*
I am the mighty world-destroying time. I am now destroying the worlds.
Even without you, none of the warriors standing in the hostile armies shall live.

11.33 *Get up and gain glory. Conquer the enemies and enjoy the prosperous kingdom.*
I have slain all these warriors; you are a mere instrument, Arjuna.

11.34 *Droṇa, Bhīṣma, Jayādṛta, Karṇa, and other brave warriors have already been slain by Me; destroy them.*
Do not be afraid; fight and you shall conquer your enemies in battle.

Kṛṣṇa explains in these verses what He really is. 'I am time,' says Kṛṣṇa. 'I devour and destroy the world.'

This is one of the most potent truths uttered by Kṛṣṇa in *Gita*. He has earlier talked to Arjuna about *ātman,* about rebirth, about the nature of *karma,* about doing work without getting attached to the result of work, and about His glories. For the first time, He takes off His mask and says matter-of-factly, 'I am the Destroyer.' He pulls no punches in responding to Arjuna's query, 'Who are you, and what is your purpose?'

Time never stands still. It moves on. Nothing can stop the flow of time. Nothing can bring back time. Nothing can move time forward. Time destroys. The future constantly moves into the present, and then into the past. The sad part is that though we can only experience the present, we constantly try to escape the present. We are forever caught in the fantasies of a future we know nothing about and the regrets of a past we never really lived when it was our present.

The only certainty in our life is that when time moves on it is forever lost. However much we may regret and repent, nothing will change what has happened. But we do have the power, at the moment of the present, to shape our future. Predestination is simply the choice that we did not exercise. Only when we are aware, in the present moment, can we craft our future. Not when it is still the future and not when it slips into the past. We need to use all our intelligence, energy, and creativity to live blissfully in this moment, not in thoughts about the future or regrets about the past.

Kṛṣṇa is stating a simple fact here. 'With or without you,' He says, 'All these warriors will be dead. As time, I shall devour them. It is not you who are the cause. You can be the superficial reason. By being the instrument of their destruction, be the gainer of fame, wealth, and power.'

It is easy to interpret these words of Kṛṣṇa to mean that the future is predestined, since He says all these enemies of Arjuna will be destroyed. From this we can even interpret that His role is to protect the good and destroy the evil. As *Mahākāla*, time personified, Kṛṣṇa destroys all, the good and the bad. Time does not differentiate. Time does not keep accounts of whether you did good deeds or bad. Time moves on and destroys the present into past, future into present and past.

As long as we flow with time, things happen as they should. When we resist and try to have things the way we wish them to be, rather than the way they would be, we get in the way. Like the rock that gets pounded by the river and eventually gets reduced to fine dust, we too get reduced to nothing by time. By imitating the reed in the river that bends offering no resistance, we can flow with time. Struggling to choose is not freedom. It is the bondage of the mind. There is no need to make a choice. Choice happens at the level of the mind, not at the level of the being. Choicelessness can be the choice.

When Kṛṣṇa speaks of destroying and wiping out the world, He is talking about the destruction of the illusory physical and material world. He is the destroyer of fantasies, He is the destroyer of identities, He is the destroyer of egos, and He is the destroyer of all that is unreal. It is important to understand what Kṛṣṇa means in these words. As the supreme consciousness, He too is the energy of Śiva, the Rejuvenator. Śiva is not the Destroyer as He is made out to be. He recreates by destroying. There can be no life without death.

Arjuna's dilemma was his fear of killing all those he loved and respected. He wondered whether he was causing the destruction of his entire lineage by doing this. In truth, Arjuna was fighting against the destruction of his own conditioning. His *saṁskāras,* past memories of parental, teacher related, and other conditionings were difficult to destroy. This great war is really the fight between Arjuna and his *saṁskāras.*

Kṛṣṇa once again takes responsibility for this destruction. Earlier there were only words. Now Arjuna had seen the destruction for himself. He had seen the Kaurava warriors being consumed by the destructive destination that Kṛṣṇa had become. It was impossible for Arjuna to disbelieve what he had seen - Bhīṣma, Droṇa, Karṇa and others disappearing into the vast form of Kṛṣṇa.

Now Kṛṣṇa consoles Arjuna. 'You have seen the truth of what happens. They have been destroyed already. Do not lose heart. Do what you have to do. Fight and destroy what remains, which is just the illusion of your fears.'

You Are Everything And Everywhere

11.35 *Sañjaya said:*
Having heard this speech of Keśava, the crowned Arjuna with joined palms, trembling, prostrating himself,
Again addressed Kṛṣṇa, voice choking, bowing down, overwhelmed with fear.

11.36 *Arjuna said:*
O Hṛṣīkeśā, it is but right that the world delights and rejoices in Your praise.
Rākṣasas fly in fear in all directions and all hosts of sages bow to You.

11.37 *And why should they not bow to Thee, O Great Soul, greater than all else, the Creator of even Brahma the Creator? O Lord of Lords, O Infinite Being, O Abode of the Universe,*
You are the imperishable, that which is beyond both the seen and the unseen.

11.38 *You are the primal God, the Ancient Being, the supreme Refuge of the Universe. You are the Knower and the One to be known.*
You are the supreme Abode, O being of infinite forms, by You alone is the Universe pervaded.

11.39 *You are Vāyu, Yama, Agni, Varuṇa, the moon, Prajapati, and the great-grandfather of all.*
Salutations unto You a thousand times, and again salutations unto You!

11.40 Salutations to You, before and behind! Salutations to You on every side!
O all Infinite in power and Infinite in prowess, You are everything and everywhere.

Arjuna now reaches the third stage of his perception of Kṛṣṇa's cosmic form. In the first stage, Arjuna's expectations of the glorious universal form of Kṛṣṇa were fulfilled. He saw Kṛṣṇa the way He expected: with His crown, discus and mace, with Brahma rising on a lotus flower from Viṣṇu's navel.

Next, as he was getting used to the enormity of the vision that he beheld, Arjuna found this form replaced by a terrible, all-devouring form of Kṛṣṇa that filled Arjuna with fear. Arjuna cries out: 'Who are you? Why are you here?'

Kṛṣṇa explains who He is; that He is the all-devouring time.

Finally, recovering from the primal fear that had overcome him a few moments ago, Arjuna surrenders himself to Kṛṣṇa.

At this stage, Arjuna understands who Kṛṣṇa is. He understands what Kṛṣṇa's purpose is. Arjuna's devotion is at its peak. He salutes Kṛṣṇa as the source of all beings, the creator of Brahma, who in turn created Prajapati, from whom all beings originated. He salutes Kṛṣṇa as the elements of Nature. Since Kṛṣṇa extends everywhere and there is no place where He is not present, Arjuna salutes Him in all directions. Arjuna now truly appreciates the unfathomable magnitude of Kṛṣṇa.

Kṛṣṇa, Yādava, My Friend

11.41 *Arjuna says: Whatever I have rashly said from carelessness or love, addressing You as Kṛṣṇa, Yādava, my Friend.*
Regarding You merely as a friend, unaware of this greatness of Yours.

11.42 *In whatever way I may have insulted You in fun, while at play, resting, sitting, or at meals,*
When alone with You, or in company, O Acyuta, O Immeasurable One, I implore You to forgive me.

11.43 *You are the Father of this world, moving and unmoving. You are to be adored by this world. You are the greatest Guru; there is none who exists equal to You.*
O Being of unequalled power, how then can there be another, superior to You in the three worlds?

11.44 *Therefore, bowing down, I prostrate my body before You and crave Your forgiveness, adorable Lord.*
Even as a father forgives his son, a friend his friend, a lover his beloved, You should, O Deva, forgive me.

Arjuna is afraid again. Having seen what he has seen and understanding the unlimitedness of Kṛṣṇa's form, he remembers that all this while he had treated Kṛṣṇa like a friend, so casually. Instead of fear, guilt and remorse fill his being.

'I called You by Your caste name, Yādava,' Arjuna cries out, 'I called You, 'Hey friend, Hey Kṛṣṇa'. I knew not whom I was addressing, whom I was dealing with. Please forgive me.'

'How could I have done this? Please forgive me for the love I had for You that made me careless in addressing You. Bear with me; forgive me as a father would a son, a lover his beloved and a friend, his mate.

A small story:

With great sincerity and seriousness a devotee of Śiva offered prayers to Śiva's idol at his home altar every day for many years. He had no thought other than Śiva, and all he desired was to have Śiva's vision, His *darśan,* one day or the other.

Since nothing happened year after year and he was getting old, the devotee gave Śiva an ultimatum, 'Either you appear before me, or I will seek an alternative. Before I die I need to have the Lord's *darśan,* so that I may be liberated.'

Śiva still made no appearance.

After a few days the devotee bought and installed an idol of Viṣṇu at his altar, replacing Śiva. But he did not have the heart to throw Śiva away, and merely moved Him to one corner, telling Him, 'See, I waited all this while patiently; all this is Your fault.'

The next morning, he lit incense as usual and placed it before the altar, this time in front of the idol of Viṣṇu. To his irritation he found that the incense smoke was drifting towards the corner where he had cast out Śiva. 'You need no incense!' he cried out, and covered the nose of the idol to prevent it from smelling the incense.

The next moment he felt Śiva standing in front of him, smiling. The devotee was overcome with deep guilt and overwhelming emotion. 'Lord!' he cried, 'All these years I prayed to You without fail and You never appeared to me. Today, when I cast You out and covered Your nose You gave me *darśan.* Why?'

Śiva said: 'It is only today that I became real to you, when you covered My nose. That is why I came to you now.'

As his friend, Kṛṣṇa was the reality to Arjuna. He took liberties with his friend because He was so real to him. But his updated intelligence of

Kṛṣṇa's cosmic form shook him up so badly that he was now consumed by guilt. It was because of the intense devotion that Arjuna had for Kṛṣṇa, that Kṛṣṇa gave him the invaluable gift of His divine form.

All our life, guilt rules us from our past. Whatever we do at a point in time, we do with the intelligence available to us at that point in time. At a later point in time, we look back and remember with the additional knowledge that we have gained since then. Often, what we did before seems wrong to us and we feel guilty. There is no greater sin than carrying such guilt. What we did was not sinful; to carry the guilt with us is sinful.

Arjuna is demonstrating to the rest of us the power of guilt; in this case, guilt that seems to arise from the deepest of love. In one sense he does not wish to carry that guilt with him. He drops it in front of his friend, Lord and master saying, 'Forgive me.' Fear concerns the future. Guilt and remorse plague us from the past. Every single thing that we did could have been done differently. One by one, these negativities pour out of Arjuna and he is getting cleansed in the presence of the master.

Your Familiar Form

11.45 *After seeing this form that I have never seen before, I am filled with gladness but at the same time I am disturbed by fear.*
Please bestow Your grace upon me and show me Your form as the Supreme personality, O Lord of Lords, O refuge of the Universe.

11.46 *O thousand armed universal form! I wish to see Your form with crown, four-armed with mace and disc in Your hand.*
I yearn to see You in that form.

Arjuna now makes his final plea in these verses. 'Show me Your form that I am familiar with,' he says, 'the One that I am comfortable with. I am grateful and overwhelmed by the visions that You have shown me, but what I am comfortable with is Your four-handed form, holding the discus and mace, as the Protector of the Universe. I am not comfortable; I am indeed fearful of the terrifying form of You as the Destroyer, however real it may be.'

All of us are in the same situation as Arjuna. We all have fixed ideas of what divinity is, what motherhood is, what love is, and what friendship is. Existence does not work that way. Existence does not differentiate between good and bad, between beautiful and ugly.

In the Viṣṇu Sahasranāma, which is recited by Bhīṣma as he was awaiting his liberation, he describes Viṣṇu as 'Peaceful, emanating bliss…' If instead, Bhīṣma had used words to describe the fearsome attributes of Viṣṇu such as: 'Frightful destroyer, with burning mouths…' and so on, how many would recite the *Sahasranāma?* It is a different matter that most people who go through the motions of reading and reciting the thousand names of Viṣṇu do not understand a word of what they are saying!

But if you do understand what the words mean, and if you are not in equilibrium, you will be disturbed. These words, understood to be negative by your logical mind, will create severe emotional turbulence within you. A *yogi* is one who has passed beyond these turbulences. Arjuna at this point in time is yet to reach this stage. He still seeks the safety and comfort of the four-handed divine Protector that he is used to, rather than the terrifying *Mahākāla.*

Only You Have Seen This Form

11.47 Bhagavān *said: Dear Arjuna, I have favored you with this Transcendental form within the material world of My internal power.*
No one before you has seen this unlimited, brilliant form.

11.48 *O best among Kuru warriors, no one has ever before seen this universal form of Mine, for neither by studying the* Vedas *nor by performing sacrifices or charities, can this form be seen.*
Only you have seen this form.

11.49 *Do not be disturbed any longer by seeing this terrible form of Mine.*
Dear devotee, be free from all disturbances. With a peaceful mind, you can now see the form you wish to see.

Kṛṣṇa consoles Arjuna in these verses. He is again His compassionate Self to His disturbed disciple.

He tells Arjuna that no one, but no one, has had this great privilege of seeing His cosmic form that He had just displayed to Arjuna. No penances, no rituals, no amount of scriptural reading, and no other charities would gain this Vision for anyone. 'However, you are terrified. That is OK. See Me now in My normal form that you are used to worshipping.'

Kṛṣṇa is clear on this point. It is He who decides how He reveals Himself to His devotees and disciples. It is a gift from the master, from the Divine. It is not earned through effort. Of course, effort prepares one for the receipt of this great gift, but it is not the only necessary condition for the gift to be showered.

Of course, in this chapter Arjuna seeks Kṛṣṇa's vision and it happens. It could have also happened without his seeking. The favor is for the Divine to give, not because we ask. It does not matter to Kṛṣṇa that Arjuna seemingly spurns this gift and would like to see Him as He normally does. A mother's love for her child does not happen as a result of any effort on the child's part. The presence of the child spontaneously evokes the deep unconditional love of the mother for the child.

It is ultimately the surrender of the devotee to the master, like the surrender of the infant to the mother that evokes this unconditional love. The devotee has to return to his original and natural state of surrender to experience unconditional love. To achieve this he has to drop his mind.

Kṛṣṇa leads His disciple in stages through this path of Self-Realization, which is no different from the realization of the Divine.

Only In This Way Can You Reach Me

11.50 *Sañjaya said: Kṛṣṇa, while speaking to Arjuna, revealed His form with four arms,*
Then assuming His human form He consoled the terrified Arjuna.

11.51 *Arjuna said: Seeing this wonderful human form,*
My mind is now calm and I am restored to my original nature.

11.52 Bhagavān *said: The four-armed form that you have seen is rare to behold.*
Even the celestials are forever aspiring to see this form.

11.53 *The four-armed form that you have seen with your transcendental eyes cannot be understood simply by study of the* Vedas, *nor by undergoing penances or charity or worship;*
one cannot see Me as I am by these means.

11.54 *My dear Arjuna, only by undivided devotional service can you understand Me as I am, standing before you, being seen directly.*
Only in this way can you reach Me.

11.55 *My dear Arjuna, one who is engaged entirely in My devotional service, free from attachment, full of love for every entity, surely comes to Me.*

Kṛṣṇa now appears in front of Arjuna first in His four-handed beautiful divine form that Arjuna is comfortable with, and finally as Vāsudeva Kṛṣṇa, in His gentle human form that Arjuna is so familiar with. Arjuna has now seen Kṛṣṇa in all His forms. The true universal form of *virata rūpa* or *viśvarūpa,* that Arjuna found fearsome; the beautiful, much gentler, adorable form with four hands, and finally back to the human form that Arjuna has always known.

Kṛṣṇa says even the great sages, the enlightened masters, have not seen the sights that Arjuna has seen. That is very true. Enlightened masters cannot see visions. When an enlightened being sees another enlightened being, it is in the energy form. To be able to see the gross physical form, both need to readjust their frequencies. No amount of spiritual practices and knowledge can make this happen. This is the space of *bhakti,* pure devotion.

Rāmakṛṣṇa says about one's relationship to a master: 'The love of a chaste wife for her husband, the attachment of a miser to his hoarded wealth, the craving of a pleasure seeker for sensual pleasures, all these rolled into one and directed towards the master is true *bhakti,* devotion.'

Kṛṣṇa concludes this chapter with a clear direction of what a devotee should do to reach Him. It is as simple as one, two, three. 'Work for Me,' He says, 'work for My mission. Surrender to Me as the supreme with no reservations. Have no attachment to whatever you do, leave the results to Me, surrender the fruits of your action to Me. Look upon everyone as your own Self, without dislike and hatred.' All disciples and devotees must understand this.

I tell my disciples:

'If you sit and gaze at me and feel joyful seeing my form, you are chasing me. At best you get eye candy and brain candy, sweet words and a sweet form that makes you feel happy. Then you think I will be leaving soon and feel unhappy. You miss the present moment of my being with you and speculate with regret on my absence that may follow.'

'If instead, you work for my mission, spreading my word and teachings, I shall chase you. I shall always be with you, wherever you are! You do not even need to come to me. I shall come to you.'

May the blessings of the supreme Lord be upon you all!

MEDITATION:

I think it is now time for us to meditate to experience what Arjuna is seeing. Once again the two points:

Is it possible to experience Kṛṣṇa consciousness? Yes, it *is* possible.

What is the qualification? Our being present here is enough.

Now all we need to do is put our whole consciousness intensely into the meditation.

The meditation will take at least 20 minutes. Please sit straight and close your eyes.

Pray intensely to the *Parabrahma Kṛṣṇa,* universal consciousness, in whatever name you know, in whatever form you know. Pray to that energy to give a glimpse of His being to you, a glimpse of the experience that Arjuna received and which all the enlightened masters experienced.

Pray to the universal energy. It responds to your thoughts. Don't think your prayers are dead words. They are living communication.

Inhale and exhale as slowly as possible and as deeply as possible. Concentrate and bring your attention between your eyebrows, on your *ājñā cakra*. Slowly, but very deeply concentrate on your *ājñā cakra*. Without forcing yourself, put your awareness naturally on your *ājñā cakra*.

Slowly start visualizing the whole Universe moving inside your head. Feel this clearly inside your head.

The space that is in front of you, in your inner space, the whole universe is moving. See the sun, moon and all the planets. Visualize this clearly, intensely. Slowly relax the body, be one with the universal consciousness. Feel the experience of being one with the Universe.

You are seeing clearly the sun, moon, stars and planets. Just disappear into the universal consciousness. Forget your name, your form, all the conditionings, your profession, your gender, and your country, everything about yourself. Forget your identity and see the whole universe intensely. Just see the moving universe intensely, all the planets, the stars, all the suns, moons.

Disappear into the universal consciousness. Lose the identity, the root cause of all the thoughts; let it disappear into the universal consciousness. Experience the bliss, the fulfilling bliss of the whole universe. Expand and disappear into that universe.

Dissolve into the universal consciousness. Be in *nityānanda*, eternal bliss!

Thus ends the eleventh chapter named **Viśvarūpa Darśana Yogaḥ** *of the* **Upaniṣad** *of **Bhagavad Gītā**, the scripture of Yoga dealing with the Science of the Absolute, in the form of the dialogue between* **Śrī Kṛṣṇa** *and Arjuna.*

BHAGAVADGĪTĀ

Love Is Your Very Life

BHAKTI YOGAḤ

CHAPTER 12

In love, life comes to its ultimate peak.
It is only in love that we will find God.

Love Is Your Very Life

In the previous chapter Arjuna asks for and receives the *viśvarūpa darśan*, the vision of the universal form of Kṛṣṇa. Kṛṣṇa very patiently resolves Arjuna's doubts and answers all his questions. Arjuna then wishes to see the true reality of Kṛṣṇa, the form behind the formless, the Imperishable, the Eternal. Kṛṣṇa obliges his friend and disciple, Arjuna, the true representative of the human being, *narā*.

Seeing this cosmic form of Kṛṣṇa, and unable to withstand the energy, Arjuna begs Kṛṣṇa to show him the benevolent four-armed form of Viṣṇu that he is used to worshipping with devotion. Finally, Kṛṣṇa reverts to His normal human form as Arjuna's charioteer and the King of Yādavas. After showing His cosmic form and having given the experience of cosmic consciousness to Arjuna, Kṛṣṇa now speaks about *bhakti*, devotional love.

Arjuna's experience of the divine form of Kṛṣṇa raises further questions in his mind.

Is this form that he just witnessed the glorious reality of the cosmos? Is this the true reality that he should focus on? Or is the formless Self, that Kṛṣṇa had talked to him about earlier, more important?

Understanding *bhakti* and love

Usually people think a spiritual experience happens only after *bhakti*, devotional love. However, *bhakti* happens only after a spiritual experience. Real *bhakti* cannot happen to you before a spiritual experience.

Only when a person experiences every being as part of the cosmic consciousness, can he radiate love. Only such a person knows what love is. Nobody else knows what love is. Others *think* that they love, or *act* as if they love. Be very clear, so many people act as if they love. Sometimes by acting they think that they love. Never can we love by acting!

Love must flow from our being. Love happens when we experience cosmic consciousness, when we have a spiritual experience, when our ego disappears. Kṛṣṇa lays out the whole technique for us, step-by-step.

After a spiritual experience, so much gratitude flows from our being, so much love overflows from our being, that we start radiating it. We need not make an effort, it just flows. We cannot stop it. No one can show or experience love unless they have had a spiritual experience.

People ask me, '*Swamiji*, you tell your devotees to meditate, meditate, and meditate. What is the use? Isn't it a selfish practice? Why don't you tell them to do service? That will benefit a lot of people.'

There are many so-called spiritual organizations and organized charities that are caught in social service, just for name, fame and social prestige.

The people running these organizations, the people involved in these organizations, are always preoccupied and busy being photographed for newspapers and magazines. Organized charity is a beautiful way of cheating yourself and others. Your ego is fed well, when you do charity this way.

Charity can never be organized. It just has to flow. It is not an external expression. It is an internal conviction. The moment we try to organize that conviction, the whole thing takes on a different quality, a different color, and a different purpose. Only when it flows after an experience is it a solid expression of love.

Our inner transformation must happen before we help others transform. Unless we feel that we are part of the Whole, unless we feel that every other person is irretrievably linked to us, it is impossible for us to contribute with true love. We will only be hypocrites.

We are part of the cosmic ocean. Each of us is a mere drop. As long as we remain droplets and do not understand the reality of being part of the same ocean, we remain separate, our feelings will be driven by 'I' and 'mine'. As long as this separation remains, there can be no true love. There can be no expression of unconditional love.

Zen Buddhism beautifully says, 'Whatever Buddha does, whatever an enlightened being does, even if he kills someone, it will only do that person good. It will do Buddha, as well as the other person good, because Buddha is driven by cosmic consciousness; therefore, it will always be good for everyone.'

However, whatever an unenlightened man does, even if he does great service, it may or may not do good to him and society. Good or bad is not decided by doing. It is decided by the being!

When an enlightened man acts, even small things lead to great results in the world. When an unenlightened person acts, even great truths may lead to misery and destruction, at times.

Think about the simple words uttered by Buddha, 'Watch your breath, witness your inhaling and exhaling.' Buddha discovered this simple truth through which thousands of people have become enlightened. Through this *vipāssana* meditation technique, the lives of thousands have been transformed. As a result, the entire universe has benefited.

When Buddha uttered an ordinary truth, a simple truth, it led and continues to lead thousands of people into a state of higher consciousness. Yet, when an unenlightened person discovers a great truth, it leads to destruction. For example, the atomic theory is a great truth. The theory of relativity is a great truth. Yet, when it comes from an unenlightened mind, it leads to destruction.

A statistical report in a magazine claims that the governments of all the countries in the world have enough atomic weapons to destroy the planet earth over a thousand times. They have piled up enough atomic weapons to destroy planet earth not once or twice but over 1000 times! And today, there must be twice the power to destroy the world. This is the result of one unenlightened mind.

If a single person with the wrong attitude is allowed to sit in a seat of power, he can endanger the whole of humanity. Everything is ready. All we need is someone to press the button. If he is mad enough and sadistic enough to press the button, global homicide will happen. So many atomic weapons have been piled up.

See, atomic fission is a great truth. Atomic fission says that atoms can be split and thereby made to release massive amounts of energy. It is such a great truth, yet it is an expression of an unenlightened mind. It can be put to many constructive uses. This truth can change the world for the better. However, as long as it is evolved from and operated by unenlightened beings, rooted in their ego, it will naturally lead to destruction.

Deeds or words by themselves don't do good or bad. They do good or bad based upon the consciousness from which they are emitted, based upon the consciousness from which they are expressed. This consciousness, this awareness, is related to the feeling one has for others. The quality of our awareness decides whether the end result benefits or destroys humanity.

Only after a spiritual experience do we feel gratitude at the being level. If it is our solid experience that every living being is God, we radiate love, and our being becomes love. *Bhakti* and love are expressions that flow from that spiritual experience.

Kṛṣṇa's discourse on *Bhakti Yoga* starts after *Viśvarūpa Darśana Yoga.* After the experience He talks about the expression, *Bhakti Yoga*. He talks about the expression of devotional love.

Who Is Perfect?

12.1 Arjuna asks, 'Who are considered perfect, those who are always engaged sincerely in Your worship in form, or those who worship the imperishable, the invisible formless You?'

Arjuna now speaks in a totally different manner. The trend is different now. He asks, 'Which of these two types of people are considered to be better: those who are always engaged in your *bhakti,* devotional love towards You, or those who merge in the *Brahman,* the unmanifest, formless, cosmic consciousness?'

Please be clear, Arjuna is not asking for himself. From here, the discourse becomes a simple discussion. It is more like trying to record the truth for future generations.

The questions from here onward are neither doubts nor enquiries. Arjuna tries to put the whole thing down in the expression form, so that it will be a useful reference for future generations. A flow of Arjuna's love for humanity, an expression of his divine experience, prompts him to seek answers to these vexing questions and record the answers from the godhead Himself.

Arjuna asks, 'Who will be established in You totally? Will it be a devotee or a person who is enlightened?'

Religious people, or so-called religious people, confuse others with this verse about Arjuna's question as to whether worshipping the form or worshipping the formless is right. These people are so confused that they do not know right from wrong. They use their intellectual arrogance and misunderstanding to confuse others. Let me tell you, this is not what Arjuna meant by asking this question. If we look at Kṛṣṇa's answers, we will understand.

Experience or express?

Arjuna asks, 'Is it good to be established in the experience of the divine consciousness and enjoy the resulting eternal bliss? Or is it better to express that love and gratitude created by the conscious experience towards the whole world and every living being? Which one is preferred?'

See, when we have a spiritual experience, some people stay in that experience with closed eyes. Only with eyes closed can they see God. They do not seek to use their senses, since the bliss within is so great that no sensory input even remotely matches that bliss. However, there are others who are impelled to open their eyes, as it were, by the universe, to communicate that blissful experience through their expression to others.

The so-called scholars enter into endless debates on *savikalpa samādhi* and *nirvikalpa samādhi*. *Savikalpa samādhi* is the state where the experience of *samādhi* continues. *Nirvikalpa samādhi* is when the expression of *samādhi* starts. *Savikalpa samādhi* is supposed to be a lower state, and one is supposed to work towards the second and higher state of *nirvikalpa samādhi*. But it is not an ironclad rule. In my case, both happened together. I went through just one and reached the state where the experience was allowed to be expressed. It was the will of the Divine, *Parāśakti*. Please understand that this is not a choice that people make.

Arjuna asks, 'What type of a person is greater? Is it a person who closes his eyes and sees God within himself or a person who opens his eyes and sees God in every being? Who is greater?'

Please understand, he is not asking whether worshiping the form or worshiping the formless is greater. Yet so-called religious people have interpreted it that way, and created problems between the teachings of the great masters Ādi Śaṅkarācārya and Rāmānuja.

Śaṅkara followed *jñāna*, the path of knowledge, which focuses on the formless through intellectual queries. Rāmānuja followed *bhakti*, the path of devotion, which focuses on the form as if the Divine were alive and kicking, as It indeed is! However, those who have studied Śaṅkara and Rāmānuja in depth know that there was much devotion in Śaṅkara's approach and much knowledge in Rāmānuja's approach! Both approaches converge. But the argument goes on and on. But if we see the answers, it is clear that this is not what Arjuna asks. He asks, whether he should be established in that divine experience or whether he should express the gratitude happening within him.

Expressing the gratitude that happens because of the experience, is devotion. Having that experience and rejoicing, staying in that experience, is knowledge. Kṛṣṇa's answer is that both paths are the same. The paths are intertwined. The first one leads to the second one and the second one leads back to first one. We have heard the term vicious circle. First one leads to the second and the second one leads back to the first one.

Now I want to introduce another word 'virtuous circle.' Vicious circle leads to low energy or lower level of consciousness. Virtuous circle leads to high energy, a higher level of consciousness! Bliss leading to devotion and gratitude, devotion and gratitude leading to bliss; these two form the virtuous circle that lead us to higher consciousness.

Dharma means *virtuous circle,* that which leads us to live and express higher and higher levels of consciousness. That in turn leads us to higher and higher levels of blissful experience. Consciousness and bliss lead to expression of that consciousness and bliss, which in turn lead to higher level experiences.

Fix Your Mind On Me

12.2 Lord Kṛṣṇa said, 'Those who fix their mind on Me eternally and those who are steadfast in worshipping Me with supreme faith, I consider them to be perfect in yoga, ready to be united with Me.'

Bhagavān says, 'Those who are established in their consciousness that expresses devotional gratitude, *bhakti,* are always engaged in Me. Those who focus on the transcendental faith, meaning the experience that they undergo at the time of cosmic experience, they are engaged in Me. Both are ultimate. Both are united in Me.

Sanskrit is a beautiful language. We can make any meaning out of any word. That is why thousands of commentaries on the Gītā are possible, yet the Gītā is still new. No book has been commented upon by so many masters, as much as the Gītā has been. Each master gives his own meaning.

Again, I insist that if a person who has not had a spiritual experience starts expressing and lecturing, he will naturally be in trouble and create trouble for others as well. In the same way that the blind leads the blind, both end up in trouble. A person without any spiritual experience, when he translates or talks, he automatically does only 'text torturing.'

Only a person who has had a true spiritual experience and one who is free from inner chatter is true to himself and others. Only then can a person transparently and honestly expose himself to others without thinking what they might say of him. Until then, there is inner chatter and an effort to filter within him. There is an effort to rehearse. We dare not bare the truth of the inner chatter to the outside world. We fear that what may spill out will be unacceptable, so we filter and replace what we feel inside us with lies that will be sociably acceptable. We make our lives into lies.

Real experience is essential

Understand this small example: Let us say I draw a diagram and explain the concept of an experience that I have had to you. After a few days, you present only an audio CD of this session to a friend who did not attend this lecture. You have not had the experience. You are merely translating my experience. How much can you explain? How well will you be able to explain? How much can the other person grasp? He will not be able to grasp much. He will miss many details that are in the diagram. He will miss my body language completely. You cannot explain accurately either, because you are not the one who had the experience.

I am explaining through a picture. If you are here, seeing and listening to me, you will understand. Even then, it is difficult to grasp the truth, to understand it. So if you just give the audio CD to a friend, who has not attended the program, how much will he understand? In the same way, if he tries to understand through the CD and gives a lecture on this subject to someone else, how much of it will be accurate?

A person who has not attended the lecture, who just has the audio recording or a copy of the book, cannot understand much. Like that, the Bhagavad Gītā is a transcription of the audio recording. If the Gītā were an audio recording, at least you would comprehend a bit more from the voice modulation. However, the voice modulation is not there. It is a transcription of an audio recording. How much can you translate or interpret?

That is why Vivekānanda emphasized, again and again, not to read or listen to anything expressed by a person who has not personally experienced the truth. Most importantly, he said, 'Bother about who is speaking, rather than what he is speaking.' He emphasized the personal experience. He added, 'All the books in the libraries in this world cannot lead you to the truth. Once you have realized the truth, you do not need books.'

Intellectual understanding is not experiencing. Understanding is a phenomenon of the mind. It is a byproduct of our ego. The filters of our mind and ego color our understanding.

Experience is the truth felt by the being. Spiritual experience transcends mind and ego. It is pure, uncolored, and permanent. By expressing an understanding of someone's experience, one may express a fact or an opinion at best, but never the truth. Truth must be experienced to be expressed.

Here *Bhagavān* says,

mayyāveśya mano ye māṁ
nitya yuktā upāsate
śraddhayā parayopetās
te me yuktatamā matāḥ

Those who express their experience as devotion, see the world *(upāsate)*. The word *upassana* can be translated in many ways. When we see the Divine in everybody, when we express the truth of the spiritual experience, whatever we do is *upassana*. Please be very clear, when we can't see the Divine in people around us, we can't see the Divine in any statue or any master either. If we don't see the Divine in living beings, we cannot see the Divine in a God or a guru.

If it were not for the great master Rāmānuja, South India would have completely lost its spirituality. Śaṇkara settled in the north, even though he was born and brought up in the south. He spent most of his time in North India. Because of Rāmānuja, devotion and spirituality thrived in South India. Until his end, Rāmānuja stayed in South India. Not only that, Śaṇkara lived only until the age of thirty-two. Rāmānuja lived on planet earth for a long time and inspired thousands of people in the path of spirituality and meditation.

One young man asks Rāmānuja, 'Master, please tell me how I can achieve *bhakti*, achieve God, achieve devotion?' Rāmānuja asks, 'Have you ever loved anybody in your life?' This man was shaken. He said, 'I am a pure *brahmacāri,* a celibate. How can you ask me this question? I came to learn about God and you ask me this question?' Rāmānuja says, 'First go and love somebody. See how you feel when you love somebody. Then come back and I will teach you about God. I will teach you about *bhakti,* devotional love.'

This man was naturally taken aback. He could not understand Rāmānuja. Understand, unless we love the person whom we can see, how will we love an entity that we have never seen? If we can't love human beings whom we see everyday, how can we love the form of God whom we have never seen? What Rāmānuja says is true. We should also understand that unless we radiate love in the space where we stay, we can't love the whole world.

Again and again I tell people, loving the whole world is easy. Loving your wife is difficult. Loving the whole world is easy, because we don't need to do anything to substantiate it! All we must do is to say, 'I love the whole world, and I love the whole world.' But when we love our wife, we must change our attitude. We must change our mind. And we must change our words. We must *do* something. There starts the problem!

Being established in that consciousness or expressing it towards the universe is the same. When a person is merged, when a person is established, he automatically radiates. If the love is not happening, if the expression is not happening, the person has not experienced. When the real experience happens, it automatically expresses. Experience is not something we can possess and keep in our cupboard. No! Experience will possess us and it will radiate through us.

> A disciple asked a Zen master, 'Will an enlightened master speak?' The master said, 'No, an enlightened person never speaks. Only a person who doesn't know speaks.' Then the disciple asked, 'Will an enlightened master keep quiet?' The master said, 'No, an enlightened master never keeps quiet. If he keeps quiet, then he is not enlightened.' The disciple was puzzled, 'You say he neither speaks nor keeps quiet.

What does he do?' The master replied, 'He sings. His being sings. He neither speaks, nor keeps quiet. His very being sings.'

This is because we cannot possess an experience. Only the experience can possess us. When experiences possess us, whatever we do will be a song. Any word that comes out will be a song. Our being will be so light. We will simply float. Our walking will be a dance. Our body language will radiate grace. All our expressions will be a great service to humanity.

The Zen master says beautifully that an enlightened man never keeps quiet nor does he talk, he just sings. That is why the Gītā is given in the form of a song. The Gītā is not prose. It is poetry. Great truths can never be expressed in logic. They can only be expressed through poetry. Prose is logic. It is bound. It is rigid. But poetry is emotion. It is love and it flows.

Kṛṣṇa says that a person established in the consciousness is great; however, the person who expresses, who shares, who automatically radiates is as great as the one who is established. The truth is that if a man is established in consciousness, he will radiate and he will sing.

Let me tell a small story of a great devotee, a *bhakta,* who lived in Vārāṇāsi. This man was a great devotee of Kṛṣṇa. He owned a small copy of the Bhagavad Gītā. That was his entire possession, his only wealth. Every morning he bathed in the sacred river Gaṅgā while reciting the Bhagavad Gītā with devotion. He spent the whole day sitting and meditating on Kṛṣṇa. He was continuously in the ecstasy of Kṛṣṇa. He radiated Kṛṣṇa *bhakti,* devotional love towards Kṛṣṇa.

Of course, we see these types of souls only in India. Society does not disturb people who just sit in ecstasy. Society takes care of them. In any other country such people would be called homeless, hounded by police and the public, put in a shelter and disrespected. Indian culture is beautiful. If we sit in ecstasy, we are respected and worshipped!

This person was in ecstasy, always singing Kṛṣṇa's name, in Kṛṣṇa *dhyāna,* in Kṛṣṇa meditation, in Kṛṣṇa *smaraṇa,* repeating Kṛṣṇa's name. He was lost in Kṛṣṇa consciousness. One day a beggar came and asked, 'Oh Swami, please give me something. For the last three days I have not eaten.' Now this posed a big problem to the *bhakta*. He himself was a beggar and had only one possession, the Gītā. He owned nothing else. If someone gave him food, he ate. Otherwise, he just sang Kṛṣṇa's name. His only property was the Gītā.

When this beggar asked for food after not having eaten for three days, he felt bad. He looked to see if there was something to give. There was only the Bhagavad Gītā, which he had preserved and worshipped for many years. That was his sole possession, akin to God for him. It was everything to him.

Suddenly, he gathered courage and took hold of the book and said, 'I have nothing. I have only this book. However, if you go to the city and tell people that this book was my possession, you will be able to auction it. Surely, someone will buy it. Many people respect me. To some extent, they feel devoted to me. So Kṛṣṇa's blessing is there. Go to the market and auction this book. Take the money and eat and fulfill yourself and be happy.'

The beggar took the book and went away. The next morning, when he was about to chant the Gītā, the *bhakta* said, 'Oh Krsna, I have given away your words to keep your words. What is your word? Your word is to radiate *bhakti*, to radiate devotion, and to radiate service. I gave away your word to keep your word.'

This man was a true devotee. He had seen the truth. He had experienced it. So he was able to express it. He translated his devotion to Krsna as love and service to his fellow men. Keeping Kṛṣṇa's word was more important than keeping Kṛṣṇa's book. Actually, if we use His words properly, we will have the experience. We will radiate His words.

They Too Attain Me

12.3,4 *But those who worship with awareness the imperishable, the unmanifest, that which lies beyond the perception of senses, the all pervading, inconceivable, unchanging, the non-moving and permanent; those who worship by restraining their senses, and are working with even mind for the benefit of mankind, they too attain Me.*

Kṛṣṇa is *saguṇa brahman,* the physical cosmos, who showed Himself in this form to Arjuna in His *viśvarūpa* - cosmic form. Kṛṣṇa is *nirguṇa brahman* as well, the formless consciousness. In both the form and the formless, He is Kṛṣṇa, the divine consciousness who has all the attributes that He talks about here.

The Divine is imperishable. It is *akṣaram*. Everything else in this material universe may come and go, appear and disappear, while the Divine remains forever. It is unique and incomparable and cannot be benchmarked against anything, as it is supreme. It is unmanifest and intangible, and therefore cannot be comprehended by the senses. It cannot be grasped by thoughts and mind, which is why one's mind-body needs to be transcended to glimpse the Divine. The Divine resides everywhere and is omnipresent.

When King Hiraṇyakaśipu, the demonic father of Prahlāda, the young prince and great devotee of Viṣṇu, dares his son to utter the name of Nārāyaṇa whom he hates, Prahlāda says, 'Nārāyaṇa is everywhere. He is in this twig and He is in this pillar.'

Meanwhile in Nārāyaṇa's heavenly abode, Nārāyaṇa jumps up in a hurry from his dalliance. Disturbed by his abrupt movement, his consort Lakṣmī complains, as every wife would, 'Where are you going at this time of the night?' Viṣṇu responds, 'My devotee Prahlāda is about to call me. I do not know whether he will point his finger to a twig or a pillar. Wherever he points, I must be ready to appear. I cannot let him down!'

The true devotee sees his Lord everywhere. Rāmakṛṣṇa describes the love of a true devotee this way: 'It is the love of a chaste wife for her husband, the attachment of a miser towards his hoarded wealth, the craving of a worldly person for sensual pleasures, all rolled into one and directed towards the Lord, creating devotion.'

The true devotee, who follows either path with awareness, with his senses focused on the Lord, experiences Him and also experiences the bliss of serving humanity. The devotee sees the Lord in everyone he meets. His experience of His Lord becomes his expression of love to all.

Kṛṣṇa's beloved Rādhā tells the *gopikās* (women cowherds who were around Kṛṣṇa all the time), 'I don't know what has happened. I don't know what has come over me. I see Kṛṣṇa in everybody. I feel that everybody is Kṛṣṇa. I don't know what is happening.' One of the *gopikās* answers, 'You have devotion as the very black eyeliner in your eyes!'

It is like this: When you wear dark glasses everything appears dark; when you wear green-tinted glasses, everything appears green. In the same way, when you have devotion as your very eyeliner, whomsoever you see, appears as Kṛṣṇa, appears divine! Here, Kṛṣṇa says, the person established in superconsciousness and the person who radiates devotion, are the same. They are not two different groups.

Formless or form?

Kṛṣṇa does not create two groups. Arjuna presents two groups as the reality that he sees: those who are established, and those who are radiating. Kṛṣṇa says both are the same. He does not divide them into two groups, those who are established and those who radiate. Kṛṣṇa says, a person who is established always radiates and the person who radiates is always established. As I said earlier, it is a *virtuous* circle.

Once the experience of the formless divine happens, it is no different from the experience of the form. Both lead to the truth that one is a part of collective consciousness. The expression of this realization is one of deep humility and compassion. It is manifested as deep gratitude and surrender. One learns to flow with the energy of this universe. One no longer struggles against the currents of life.

When we are full of ego we tend to control. We believe we can bring order to an otherwise chaotic world. It takes only a moment to realize that this entire universe and planet earth, function not because of us, but in spite of us. Millions and millions of stars and planets in this universe function in apparent chaos, but understand, the universe is always in order.

We want to be in order, but we are truly chaotic. Only when we surrender to the will of the universe, we fall into the cosmic order. Things go well for us. When we give up wanting, we get what we want. When we get what we truly want, it benefits mankind. Because when we surrender, Kṛṣṇa takes care.

Formless Is Difficult

12.5 For those whose minds are set on the unmanifest, the formless, it is more difficult to advance; attaining the formless, unmanifest, is difficult for the embodied.

Kṛṣṇa says here what many of us know to be true. He says, the intellectual person finds it more difficult to comprehend the Divine. He finds it impossible to shed his ego, in his search for the truth. Therefore he never finds it. The intellect will always try cunning methods to make us believe that we have found the truth

In one's search for the truth, the Divine, which is what the intellectual seeker is focusing on, the intellect, the mind or ego will be the block that makes the path difficult to traverse.

The individual human being carries not only the body but the mind as well. And with the mind, it carries the ego. Unless the mind-body is transcended, spiritual advancement is difficult, as Kṛṣṇa points out.

Shedding the ego is the most difficult thing for the mind-body system. Ego provides the mind-body with its identity, with its existence. The French philosopher Rene Descartes' famous quote, 'I think, therefore I am' is an example of this identification with the intellect.

Whether now or in Kṛṣṇa's time, the world revolved around the power of thought, the power that seems to provide knowledge and skills. It was essential for one's recognition and status in life. Rāmakṛṣṇa Paramahamsa was an incarnation. Yet, in utter humility he accepted three people in his life as his masters. The truth though was that Rāmakṛṣṇa was the means for their liberation, by helping them shed their egos!

It took the no-mind simplicity of a great master to provide guidance to the learned scholars, and to teach them to drop their egos. Dropping the ego is the most difficult thing for the body-mind, especially for one who is focused on the intellect.

Freedom From Birth And Death

12.6,7 *But those who worship me with single-minded devotion, renouncing all activities unto Me, regarding Me as their supreme goal, whose minds are set in Me, I shall deliver them soon from the ocean of the birth and death cycle.*

Kṛṣṇa makes a promise here. Kṛṣṇa says unequivocally, 'I shall deliver them from their material existence, the ocean of *saṁsāra*, the cycle of life and death.' All that the Lord asks is that the devotee be devoted to Him.

Kṛṣṇa says, 'If you surrender to Me, surrender all your actions and the fruits of those actions to Me, do my service, meditate upon Me, remain single-minded upon My consciousness, I shall then redeem you, provide you salvation and liberate you. I shall make sure you never need to be born again.' It is the roar of a lion. It is the roar of the King of this universe. 'Surrender to Me and I shall redeem you. Serve Me and I shall liberate you.'

A small story:

There was once a man who was flying to a foreign country. Midway on the flight, the pilot announced, 'We are in deep trouble. Now, only God can save us. All of you may start praying.'

One passenger did not understand what the pilot said and asked his co-passenger about it. The man replied, 'He says there is no hope.'

All our belief in God is skin deep. First of all, to most of us, God is only a concept and we worship that concept. Most of the time, we beg of that concept. We pray, 'Give me this, O Lord, give me that, O Lord.' When we have one prayer answered, we begin the next. As long as God answers our prayers, as long as the master provides us with what we ask for, our faith in Him lasts. The moment the prayer goes unanswered our faith dissolves. We move on to another God or master. We say, 'Is there anyone else out there who can give me the answer I want?'

We do not realize that often God does not answer our prayers out of sheer compassion, out of sheer love for us. In our ignorant state we keep asking, we keep begging without a break. We do not fully understand the implications of what will happen if our prayers get answered, whether our situation would become better or worse. That is why they say, 'Be careful of what you ask for, you may get it!'

From time to time, God in His infinite wisdom turns down our requests such as wanting to become rich, wanting to be well, wanting to have children, and so on. We then move away from Him. Surrendering to the Divine is not conditional. It must be total. There can be no 'ifs', 'ands', or 'buts'. It cannot be, 'If you grant my prayers, I shall be devoted to you.' That is business. Surrender should be total.

Kṛṣṇa says, 'When you surrender to Me, I shall liberate you.' To reach Him, we must surrender totally. Our senses must be surrendered to Him. Our entire consciousness, our complete awareness must only be of Him and nothing else. Nothing else needs to be done. The technique is so simple. 'Surrender and I shall save you,' says the master. 'I shall save you without delay, immediately.' But we query, 'Is there someone else out there to help me?'

The Lord has made it so simple. Yet, we find it so difficult to believe Him.

Live In Me Always

12.8 You fix your mind on Me alone, establish your mind in Me. You will live in Me always. There is no doubt in it.

'Just fix your mind upon Me, the supreme personality of the Divine and engage all your mind, body and senses in Me and you will thus live in Me always, without a doubt.'

'Na samśayah, without a doubt,' He says. Now He comes to the technique. At one point the *virtuous* circle must begin. First, He explains the virtuous circle of the ultimate experience and expression. Now He comes to the technique.

Please understand that love is not a mood. It is not a mere emotion. It is our very Existence. As long as it is our mood, it will come and go.

There are two kinds of love, horizontal love and vertical love. Let me explain. Horizontal love is like a horizontal line, flat. It is related to time: it starts and ends. Anything that starts must end. If it takes more time to end, don't think it is permanent. Anything that starts must end. It may take a few years or a few months, but it ends. It is impermanent and time bound. This is horizontal love. Horizontal love is related to time.

Vertical love is related to consciousness. Vertical love neither starts nor ends. It does not discriminate. It is our very quality. It flows. If we discriminate and love, it cannot be love. It is an infatuation. As long as the other person fits into our frame, our love grows. The moment the other person doesn't fit into our frame, our love disappears.

In the first session of our meditation camp, I ask people to make an honest list of at least one or two persons in their lives whom they really love. Usually, in the beginning, people come up with a big list: husband, wife, father, mother, brother, sister, and so on. They include people whom they would like to please, or need to please, in order to be happy and undisturbed themselves.

When I begin the discourse, people start crossing out names of people from their list, one by one. Understand, if you cross out something, then it was not love even in the first place; however, people get stuck when they come to the names of their sons or daughters.

I say that all your love is for some reason. For economical benefit or psychological support, you hang onto these relationships. You have somebody as your family or as your community, so that, at the time of trouble, they may support you psychologically or materially.

The next reason we love, is to receive good certificates, positive recognition. Sometimes we share love and show love. We may not do so for economical benefits or psychological support, but we may expect a good certificate or attention for being loving and kind. Some need for attention is always present. There is always some dependent need in us that motivates us to express love. It is never unconditional.

People say, 'No *Swamiji*. I don't love my son or daughter for any of these three reasons.'

I ask them, 'Alright, if suddenly your son starts to decide things on his own, if he doesn't fit into your frame, if he doesn't follow your guidance, if he doesn't live according to your rules, will your love be the same? Enquire honestly.'

Naturally, people say, 'No, it will not be, the love will reduce a little.'

What does this mean? We love our next generation as long as they are extensions of our life. We fulfill our desires through them. We fulfill our lives through them. Whatever we couldn't accomplish, we try to accomplish through them. As long as they act and live as an extension of our life, the relationship is beautiful. But the moment they start deciding on their own, the moment they feel we are suffocating them, the moment they stand up and say 'no,' the relationship takes a different turn.

Children feel they are adults only when they say 'no' to their parents. It is a basic instinct. When they say 'no', they feel they are established as an individual. They don't bother about what you say. All they know is one word, 'no'. They do not know anything else. They feel strong when they say 'no'. That is why, all over the world, youngsters always rebel. Whether it is in the West, or in the East, in all countries, all over the world, in all cultures, the youth say 'no'. When they say 'no', they feel they are strong. The word 'no' gives a certain kind of strength to them.

But our love is dependent only upon 'yes'. As long as we receive 'yes', our love also is 'yes'. When we get a 'no', we too start saying 'no'. This is horizontal love. That is why it ends with some reason. Vertical love never ends because it never starts. Suddenly, at some point we realize, we are living inside everybody just as we live inside our own body.

> There is a beautiful example given in the *Upaniṣads*.
>
> A master asked a disciple, 'Do you enjoy all your five senses'? The disciple said, 'Yes.'
>
> The master asked, 'What if one of your senses was missing, would you have the same amount of joy?'
>
> The disciple replied, 'No, it would be twenty percent less, and if two of my senses were missing, it would be forty percent less.'
>
> The master suddenly said, 'What if you had five more senses?' The disciple answered, 'Naturally my enjoyment would be a hundred percent extra. If I am given one more body, naturally I will enjoy everything twice as much. Or if I am given five bodies, naturally I will enjoy things five times as much.'

If we experience that we are living in all the bodies of this world, how much joy or ecstasy would we experience? It would be immeasurable, eternal, and ultimate. That is what enlightened people experience all the time! When they experience themselves as the whole universe, or as being in every body, they experience tremendous ecstasy, pleasure or bliss. That is why they don't need anything from the outer world.

An elderly person came to one of our programs. Afterward, he said to me with a lot of sympathy, 'You have become a master and an ascetic at such a young age. You have missed life.' He expressed his sympathy. He felt that I had missed out. I told him, 'Don't be sympathetic towards me. Actually I should feel sympathetic towards you. Even after sixty years, you are unable to liberate yourself. Even after sixty years, you are suffering in *saṁsāra*, the illusion of worldly life. Don't be sympathetic towards me. I should be sympathetic towards you!'

When we experience ecstasy and bliss within, we don't feel we are missing anything from the outside world. We don't feel we need something. Real renunciation is not about our renouncing the world. It is about the world renouncing us. When we have that joy, ecstasy and bliss, we automatically radiate that bliss. We never feel that we miss anything or that we have lost something.

Pitfalls and remedies of incorrect renunciation

I tell people not to renounce the world unless they feel ecstasy inside. Never renounce. Work towards ecstasy. When that happens, renunciation automatically happens. If you renounce the outer world without having established the inner world, you will fall into depression.

I have seen many *sanyāsīs* who have taken this path without achieving the inner experience. They are caught in social service and then fall into depression. Around the age of forty to forty-five, they become depressed. They counsel the whole world while they are depressed. So many monks have fallen prey to depression. Never renounce the world, unless you have had a solid experience inside.

When you have had the experience, you don't need to renounce. Automatically, renunciation happens. All these things will drop you. Instead of you dropping them, they will drop you! You dropping these things always creates problems. When *they* drop you, it is the right thing. When you have that joy inside, when you start experiencing the joy in you, nothing needs to be renounced, automatically renunciation happens.

Here, Kṛṣṇa gives techniques to start the virtuous circle. 'Fix your mind on Me. Establish your intelligence in Me. In this way, after acquiring the boundary-less consciousness, you will live in Me always.'

How should we establish our intelligence in Him? Continuously try to put these thoughts and ideas that Kṛṣṇa teaches, inside you. Rāmakṛṣṇa says that what we belch depends upon what we eat. For instance, if we eat some kind of vegetable or fruit, the smell of that comes out when we belch.

In the same way, if we add these ideas continuously to our mind and consciousness, we naturally radiate them. They start shining through our being. When He tells you to let your intelligence be established in Him, it means that when we are in trouble, the solution would automatically come to us based upon these ideas.

As of now, we run and refer to a book, which means we have a guru only in the outer world. If we try and digest these ideas, even when we don't have problems, they will lodge themselves in us, and take us to higher and higher levels of awareness. When we have problems, they will guide us.

If you read books *only* when you are in trouble or when you are seeking a solution, you will not digest the ideas, because your mind will be confused. How will you receive them? How can you digest them when you are troubled and confused? It can't happen this way.

When your mind is in the normal state, receive these ideas as a regular habit. Let it become your normal life style. Just as you eat and bathe everyday, in the same way, absorb these ideas regularly.

In his commentary on the Chāndogya Upaniṣad, Śaṇkara has written beautifully about purification of food.

āhāra śuddho satva śiddho dhruvā smṛtiḥ

When our *āhāra,* food, is purified, our memory is purified.

Please understand, that *āhāra* doesn't mean just the food that we eat. It refers to whatever we take in through the five senses. Television programs that we watch are *āhāra.* Music that we listen to is *āhāra.* The food that we eat is *āhāra.* The odors that we smell are *āhāra.* The touch that we enjoy is *āhāra.*

So all that we take in through the five senses should be pure. Only then can we radiate purity, can we radiate bliss, can we radiate ecstasy, can we radiate divine intelligence. Unless we purify the *āhāras*, that is ingested through the other senses as well, we cannot expect purification of our memories. I feel blessed that when I was born and brought up, there was no television in my village.

People ask me, '*Swamiji* how do you grasp things so easily?' Of course, I somehow pick up things easily, quickly. One small fact: Only a few years ago I started speaking English. I studied some English in school. My native language is Tamil in which I learned everything. I started speaking English regularly only when I came to America in August 2003.

I was asked how I grasp things so quickly. It is because I continuously read. People frequently ask me, 'How do you read so many books?' I never watched television when I was growing up. Television directly destroys our consciousness. Please understand, it affects not only our eyes, it straightaway destroys our consciousness.

Let me tell you an important thing. Understand this example. You are traveling in a vehicle. If you are moving at forty miles per hour, you can see everything on the road, billboards and signboards. Whatever there is to see on the road, you can see them clearly. However, if you drive at 100 miles per hour, will you be able to see anything? You can't. You will not see anything clearly. This is because, you are now seeing an increased number of frames per second. That's why you can't see anything clearly.

On television, you witness many frames per second. Because of the large numbers of frames per second, information is forced upon you, into your unconscious zone, without the control of your logic.

Your logic is analogous to having a security guard outside your home, when a thief turns up. The information on the television is the thief. Logic is your guard on duty. It stands guard. Whatever information comes to you, your logic analyzes it and says, 'This is true. This is a lie. That is a toy, this is a real man. This is a fake, and this is a doll.' The information is analyzed and recorded. But when you watch the television, when the information is forced upon you, your logic loses its ability to analyze. The frames are like the thief who attacks the security guard, your logic. When the logic is put to rest, without delay, the frames reach your unconscious zone and get recorded. The thief enters directly into your unconscious zone. Straightaway, your unconscious is exploited. The information simply penetrates you. It is like a robber walking straight into your bedroom after killing the guard on duty.

Another important point about this is that, because the information reaches you right away, you not only lose your logical and analyzing capacity, you lose your emotional balance as well. That is why, even when you know that the actor is still alive in real life, you weep when you see the actor killed in the movie! Automatically, you start weeping. Tears start rolling even though you know that it is not real, that it is not true. When they laugh, you laugh. When they cry, you cry.

According to the scenes, your moods also change. If you see a depressing scene, you feel depressed. Why? You are an educated person. You know it is a drama. You know the person is alive. You may have seen the actor a few days ago in person, but when you watch the movie and he dies, you experience grief. Why? Because the logic that analyzes this as a truth or lie is put to rest or pushed aside, and information is directly flooded into your system. It is carried straight to your unconsciousness. So, never watch a program that creates depression or misery in you.

Of course, if you watch a program that gives joy, which makes you laugh, that does not hurt your consciousness directly. At the most, you may waste a little time or you may eat a little bit extra while watching the movie. Only the threat of obesity is there. Otherwise, there's no problem. Surveys indicate that 80% of the people eat while they watch television and face obesity problems because of this. This is only a small problem. But never watch anything that creates depression or brings your mood down. Then it becomes a big problem.

The Unknown demystified

Let me answer one important question. People always ask me, '*Swamiji*, is there anything such as spirits or ghosts?' Let me tell you clearly that there is no such thing as ghosts, spirits, demons and no such thing as a devil. You may have one thousand references that say the opposite. I know your minds collect references from movies and books. Your mind is always collecting references. Once your unconscious believes there are spirits, you project it and actually start seeing spirits. Whatever your unconscious believes, you project and see that.

Especially after a lot of research on hypnotism, they are coming up with great truths. If a person is hypnotized and given a hot object to hold and told by the hypnotist, 'You are holding a flower in your hand, you are holding a rose,' not only does his hand not get burned, but after the hot object is removed, the hand smells like a rose!

Hypnotism has so much power, which means your unconscious has so much power. You are unconsciously hypnotized and taught that things like ghosts exist. You end up projecting and seeing ghosts. When you have an experience, it becomes a solid faith.

There is an even more disturbing fact that they have discovered. In the US, in the last decade or so, many cases of childhood trauma have come up, with children claiming sexual abuse by parents. These discoveries are usually made when, as adults, these depressed people go to psychiatrists and such traumatic happenings are discovered under hypnotic states. Cases are reported and investigated by police and regulatory authorities.

In a significant number of these cases, such abuses never really happened. It has been found that the patients developed these ideas under hypnosis as a result of judgmental probing by the psychiatrists.

Treatment that was meant to cure people of their traumas ended up inducing traumas.

If you watch some horror movie continuously for three days, you will start seeing ghosts! Even a screen moving will look like a ghost. Whatever happens around you, you will connect it with the impression of ghosts that was left on your unconscious.

For example, right after watching a horror movie, let us say you feel like drinking some water. You walk into the kitchen and suddenly the cat jumps on you. Now the whole scene is complete! You know for sure that ghosts exist. But it is purely your unconsciousness. Because you start believing it, you start projecting it. Once you start projecting it, your faith is strengthened. It is a vicious circle, and you are caught in it.

Another thing: ghosts as such don't have a physical body. As ordinary humans, you have three bodies - physical, subtle and causal. Even if spirit bodies exist, they don't have a physical body. Of course, first of all, they don't exist. But for argument's sake, if I collect all of your arguments and if I must argue and accept that they do exist, they exist only in the subtle body and causal body. They don't have a physical body.

No ghost comes to you with a physical body except your spouse! If at all it were true that ghosts exist, it means they have only 66% of your capacity since their energy can be only in the two bodies, that is the subtle body and causal body. You have three bodies that equal 100%. Spirits have a maximum of two bodies, so only 66%. It means they are less powerful than you. Even if they exist, you don't have to be afraid of them.

Understand this logically: Even if they exist, you don't need to be afraid of them. They are lower level beings. They are lower level entities. Firstly, they don't exist. But even for argument's sake, if I must argue, they are still lower level entities. You don't have to be afraid of them. So all this about talking to ghosts, mediums, your dead relatives and such, are purely stories. One story is built upon another story. The next story is built upon the third story, purely fictional, nothing but fiction!

A small story:

Once there was a lady who wanted to divorce her husband. She engaged a lawyer to work on her case. After meeting with the couple a few times, the lawyer said to the lady, 'I have made a settlement that is fair to both of you.'

The wife cried, 'What! I could have done that myself. Why do you think I hired a lawyer?'

As long as things support you, any idea is okay; anything is okay. Otherwise, it is a big danger for you! So I tell you, it is better not to believe in mediums and all such things. Don't waste your time talking to people who are dead. We barely have time to talk to people who are alive. Why waste time talking to people who are dead? Let us first talk to people who are directly related to our business and to our lives. Talk to them first. Work with them first. Why should we waste time with other things?

Never allow these horrible things that cause suffering into your consciousness. If you don't allow these things into your consciousness, your intelligence will automatically be established in the Divine. The thoughts that you take in play a major role in the expression of your consciousness. Just take in this one concept that Kṛṣṇa speaks of, 'Establishing your intelligence in Me.' Please understand that whatever you take in as your inputs, you establish your mind only on that. So let your inputs be purified. Let purification of your sensory inputs happen to you. Your consciousness will automatically be established in the Divine.

Again and again, try to absorb these ideas. Let these ideas penetrate you. Don't go behind ideas that make you feel low and that put you into depression. For example, for the last eleven days you have been listening to these ideas. Now, when a problem arises, you will automatically remember, '*Swamiji* said this. I have heard this idea. I think this is what I must understand now.' This will start arising from your being. The truth will begin to support you from within yourself.

If it starts coming up, you have heard what I have said. Otherwise, you are just a silent listener, a silent listener who is sitting here and seriously thinking of something else or passing judgment on my oratorical skills! Whether you are a silent listener or somebody who really heard the discourse, can only be determined by how much these words get repeated in you.

I tell people that when the source of the words is enlightened consciousness, the words simply penetrate you and automatically come into your mind whenever you need their help. People ask me, '*Swamiji*, how can we remember these ideas and practice them?' I tell them, 'Never bother remembering them. Just listen, that's enough. These words are from my experience. So naturally they will penetrate your being.'

Whenever it is necessary, you won't need to remember these words. The words will remember you. Without effort, these words will stay in you and surface. Automatically they will come up when needed. They will erupt into your consciousness, like a pop-up. Similar to the pop-up on your computer monitor, they come up in your consciousness and guide you. You don't need to do anything. All you need to do is listen as a means to put them into your being. Listen to these words repeatedly. Naturally your consciousness will be established in the Divine.

Kṛṣṇa says, 'Immerse your mind completely in Me. Focus your entire attention upon Me. Without a doubt, you will reach the blissful state.'

Practice To Perfection

12.9, 10 *If you are not able to fix your mind upon Me, then Arjuna, with the constant practice of yoga you try to attain Me. If you are not able to practice even this yoga, then performing your duties and surrendering all your actions to Me, you will attain perfection.*

Here Kṛṣṇa talks about *Abhyāsa Yoga*. What is *Abhyāsa Yoga*? *Abhyāsa Yoga* is the practice or method of yoga of holding the mind constantly in a state of union with Divinity. It is the state of complete immersion in the consciousness of Kṛṣṇa.

Why does Kṛṣṇa speak about *Abhyāsa Yoga*? In the last chapter Kṛṣṇa gives Arjuna a glimpse of the universal consciousness, *Viśvarūpa darśan*; however, Arjuna is unable to stay in that state permanently. Arjuna comes out of the experience because of fear or old *saṁskāras,* old embedded memories of past desires. He slips from that state of consciousness. Therefore, Kṛṣṇa speaks about *Abhyāsa Yoga,* how to establish oneself in that consciousness. That's why He speaks about *abhyāsa,* which means practice.

A path for everyone

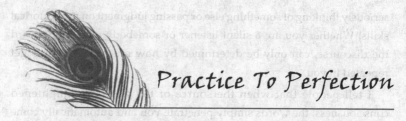

He gives a solid path, or a solid solution to take care of our whole life, to establish ourselves in that consciousness. Continuously, again and again, in our daily life, let us receive these ideas, digest these ideas in our consciousness and let our inner space be filled with these ideas. Let us not waste a few moments. Let our whole inner space be filled with these great thoughts. That is the way to establish us in that superconsciousness.

Kṛṣṇa continues and gives more tips for establishing ourselves in that consciousness and radiating devotion. Kṛṣṇa instructs continuously over the next four verses. He gives various options, step-by-step. He says: If we can't do this, do that. If we can't do that, do this. Kṛṣṇa gives us various options and instructions. The first thing He says is, 'Oh Dhañanjaya, fix your mind upon Me. With constant practice, try to attain Me. If you are not able to practice, then perform actions for Me.'

Rāmakṛṣṇa Paramahamsa had advised a lady to meditate upon the form of goddess Kālī. She said, that however much she tried she was unable to meditate on Kālī. She tried time and again and she was always distracted. She came to Rāmakṛṣṇa upset that she could make no spiritual progress.

Rāmakṛṣṇa enquired whether the lady's attention was diverted to someone or something else. The lady confessed that she was thinking of a young nephew, a child, whom she was fond of. Immediately, Rāmakṛṣṇa advised her, 'Focus your attention on this child whom you love. Meditate upon him.' The lady came back after a few weeks satisfied. Having started her meditation upon the child whom she loved, she could meditate. And once she could meditate, she could transfer her focus to goddess Kālī!

The mind can be trained. What is important, is concentration. Once we learn to focus our attention completely on something, single-pointedly, we can train the mind to be like a laser beam. That laser beam can then be transferred to any object with equal facility and success.

Vivekānanda has said, 'Once you learn all that there is to be known about a handful of clay, by focusing your complete attention on it, you will know about all the clay everywhere in the world.'

Kṛṣṇa refers to controlling the mind through constant practice of meditation, which is part of the yogic path. Meditation is not about sitting down with eyes closed for half an hour every day or every other day or when we get time. Meditation is incessant and obsessive focus upon the Divine. Meditation is a way of life.

Since He knows that we may not be able to lose ourselves in devotion to Him, He offers this as an alternative. 'If the mind cannot be focused on Me,' says the Lord, 'try this. Practice again and again uniting with Me through meditation.' When neither seems possible, Kṛṣṇa offers one more way. 'Do whatever you must. Do your duty as you need to and are able to. But then, surrender what you do to Me. Do what you do for My sake.' By performing whatever we do with total faith in Him, and with a deep feeling of surrender to Him, we reach Him.

Kṛṣṇa implies two things through His statement. First, the results of whatever is done with an attitude of surrender to Him, belong to Him. Our responsibility is to do, and do it well. We have the right to 'doer-ship' not 'owner-ship'. The Lord is the owner of the fruits of actions that we perform on His behalf.

When we learn to do this, we automatically imbibe the concept of non-attachment to the end result. What happens is in His hands, not ours. We then start focusing on the path, not the goal. We focus on the process, not the product. And when we do this, our performance gets better, because we no longer are stressed by what the end result might be. We are no longer worried, since the outcome is in safe hands. Whatever happens is right, and for the common good. If we travel with this awareness, whatever path we take, is the right path. Whatever destination we reach through this right path, is the right destination.

When worship becomes a way of life, when spirituality becomes a part of daily life, there is an attitude of surrender to the Divine. One feels intuitively that whatever happens will be for common good, and whatever happens for the common good, is good for oneself. It does not matter if our neighbor has more than what we have. In fact, we rejoice that the neighbor has more than we have. We no longer have expectations. We have no expectations of what we hope to get. When surrender happens, there is no end-point that one strives for. Wherever the path leads is the right destination. With focus only on the path and not on the goal, expectations of what may happen drop. Whatever happens is good. This non-attachment and lack of expectations is the hallmark of a *karma* yogi, one who has surrendered his actions to the Divine.

I tell people, 'Do not worry about whether I am here physically with you or not. Do not feel unhappy when I leave for another location. If you chase Me, you will never be one with Me. Work on My mission. In whatever way you can, work on activities that benefit humanity. Work on My behalf. Then, instead of you chasing Me, I shall chase you. I shall always be with you.' Working on the mission of the Divine is a sure guarantee to reach Divinity.

Work For Me

12.11 If you are not able to work even this way, surrendering unto Me, give up all the results of your actions to Me without ego.

Kṛṣṇa says, 'Fix your mind upon Me alone. Live in Me.' Then He felt that He had to give Arjuna an option, in case Arjuna could not succeed. 'If you cannot fix your mind upon Me, steadily practice and practice again,' He advised. He relented further, 'If you cannot do this repetitive practice, if this is too much for you, then work on My mission. Whatever you do, do it for Me.'

Kṛṣṇa now says, 'If you are unable to do even this, which is work for My sake, then just abandon your ego and turn over the results of your actions to Me.' Kṛṣṇa relents from His standpoint that Arjuna should work only on those activities that are Kṛṣṇa's. He feels that there may be conditions that may prevent Arjuna from devoting all his time only to those activities that are Kṛṣṇa's.

See how relevant Kṛṣṇa's advice is, even by today's standards. None of us can hope to sit idle and be taken care of. We must do something to occupy ourselves. In our day-to-day reality of life, not all may be able to work on God's mission alone, all the time. We may be able to spend only some time on activities that are selfless activities that benefit humanity overall, and activities that are spiritual. We need to spend a lot of time on activities that are of material benefit to us and to others related to us. Nothing is lost, assures Kṛṣṇa, and He provides the bridge between material pursuits and spiritual pursuits.

Kṛṣṇa brings in the core concept of the Gītā, that of 'renunciation'. He says, 'Do what you must do with an attitude of surrender to Me and sacrifice the results of your actions to Me, with complete control over your self, your ego.'

Kṛṣṇa says, 'If you cannot do whatever else I have told you to do, do this. Drop your ego. Drop the fruits of your actions and renounce them to me.' The freedom that results from what Kṛṣṇa advises is true liberation. Once we realize that we no longer are the masters of our destiny, decision makers of the results of our actions, we feel a weight lifting off our shoulders. It is He who is now responsible for the results of our action. We still are the 'doers', but no longer the 'owners'.

One may wonder, how can I survive in this dog-eat-dog world? How can I succeed in this rat race? Remember that even if you are the winner in this rat race, you are still only a rat!

It is an illusion of our minds that we decide the results of our actions. In each one of our activities there is so much interdependency with others and what they do, on which we have little or no control. It is pure fantasy to believe, that we decide the result of our actions. We cannot even guarantee that we will survive our next breath. Our life is not in our hands. What arrogance, therefore, to imagine that activities in the outer world are subject to our control! There is a power higher than us that decides the results of our actions. Once we realize this and start believing in the wisdom of that higher power, strange and mystical things happen to us.

We just need to let the universe, *Parāśakti*, Kṛṣṇa, the Divine, decide what is best for the rest of humanity and us. Let us surrender the results of all that we do, to this sacred power. Whatever then happens to us is for the good, for our good and the good of everyone in this universe.

'Renounce unto Me,' says Kṛṣṇa, 'surrender yourself to Me, and I shall liberate you.'

Attain Peace

12.12 Knowledge is better than mere practice. Meditation is superior to knowledge. Renouncing the fruit of actions is better than meditation. After renunciation of the fruits of actions, one immediately attains peace.

Kṛṣṇa gives so many instructions. Step-by-step, He gives options. Actually, these are not only for Arjuna's mind. These are for all kinds of minds.

Let me tell a small story from Ramaṇa maharṣi's life:

Somebody goes to him and asks, '*Bhagavān,* what spiritual technique should I use?' He says, 'Do *ātma-vicāranā,* Self-inquiry. Start questioning, *Who am I?*'

After a few days, the devotee comes back and says, 'It is difficult to do Self-enquiry, can I just meditate?' *Bhagavān* says, 'Alright, do meditation.'

After a week, the person returns and says, 'Meditation is also difficult. Can I do *japa,* repetition of *mantras* and recitation of verses?' Bhagavan says, 'Alright, do that.'

A few days pass and he is back again saying, '*Japa* is also difficult. Can I do *pūjā,* the ritual worship?' *Bhagavān* says, 'Alright. Do *pūjā.*'

Within a week the man is there asking, '*Pūjā* is also difficult. Can I start going only to the temple?' *Bhagavān* says, 'Alright, do what you want.'

Masters do not want to close the doors for anybody. Please understand, they give options for everybody. Here, in these verses, Kṛṣṇa gives options to everyone.

We need to have tremendous spontaneity to understand this. Only with spontaneity, will we be able to handle these instructions. For example, if you don't feel like meditating and are in a low mood, don't try sitting in a room with closed doors, forcing yourself to meditate. Just go out, go to the temple. Spend some time freely, walking and moving around. It will relax you. Then you can enter into meditation. And if you are not able to do that also, do something else. Do something that helps to keep you in a relaxed mood that makes you feel relaxed. Then, you can enter into meditation.

Do something

Here, Kṛṣṇa tries to give step-by-step instructions up to the ultimate and last step. The last step, is being in the consciousness, being in bliss. But just because you can't do that, don't stop trying altogether. Do something at least. I have seen people speak about meditation, about *ātma-sādhana* and all sorts of complicated things. But when it comes to practice, just thinking of meditating makes them stop their rituals, everything. In the end they do not even meditate. They say, 'I don't have enough time, *Swamiji*. My mind won't concentrate and I cannot sit quietly, *Swamiji*.'

First they stop everything in the name of meditation. Then they drop meditation because of other reasons! Then they have neither this nor that. Kṛṣṇa doesn't want that to happen. We need spontaneity to decide what we need and what to do at each moment.

Whenever I utter the word 'spontaneity', I remember this personal experience. This is not a story. This happened in my native place. It was a small village, now it has become a district headquarters, a town. They used to stage plays based on the epic Mahābhārata every year. In India, every traditional village would have the recitation of the Mahābhārata once a year. They believed that if they recited the Mahābhārata, it would rain. So they had the habit of reciting the Mahābhārata. In North India, they recite Bhāgavatam, another ancient Hindu epic. In the South, recitation of either Mahābhārata or Rāmāyaṇa takes place. In my village, every year they recited Mahābhārata continuously for sixty days. During the daytime they recited the story. At night, they enacted a small drama based on the story. People from the village staged the drama. More than the drama, their mistakes were most entertaining!

People would gather to watch the drama, not for the drama's sake, but more for the mistakes that were made. The props were limited and what was used as a *vīṇā* (musical stringed instrument) for Sarasvatī, the goddess of knowledge, would be reused as a *gada* (mace) for Bhīma or Hanumān, the monkey-god! Hanumān would use the same device for *gadāyudha* (mace weapon), while Sarasvatī would return with the same thing, using it as a *vīṇā*! It was funny to see and only four or five people would play all the roles! The casting was hilarious as well, with Kṛṣṇa being played by an eighty-five year old man, with one stick in his hand and being quite incapable of walking. He would be assisted onto stage where he would come and say, 'Oh Arjuna, stand up!' By the time he would say, 'Arjuna, stand up' he himself would fall! It was entertaining to watch the whole drama with all their mistakes.

I would watch the drama every night. Only males were allowed to act in the plays. It was also done as a ritual. People who participated wore sacred threads on their wrists, as it was being done as a ritual. They recited the verses in full and only males participated in it; even female roles were played by male members.

One day the scene was about the disrobing of Draupadī , one of the most moving scenes in the Mahābhārata. The man playing the role of Draupadī had donned make-up and wore seven thin saris. In the scene, Duśśāsana, the Kaurava prince, insults Draupadī , the Pāṇḍavās' princess, and attempts to disrobe her in public. He is supposed to pull off six saris and by the time he pulled off the sixth sari, he was expected to act tired and then fall. As soon as Duśśāsana pretends to fall, Draupadī is supposed to shout, 'Kṛṣṇa, Kṛṣṇa, save me.'

On this occasion when the scene started, Duśśāsana forgot to count. He was supposed to pull totally six saris. By the time he came to the sixth sari, he was supposed to fall. As he fell, Draupadī was supposed to call out for Kṛṣṇa and then Kṛṣṇa would appear on stage. This was how the scene was supposed to be. The actor Duśśāsana somehow forgot to count and started to pull the seventh sari also. Draupadī kept trying to indicate with her eyes, 'Hey, seventh sari, seventh sari!' Duśśāsana didn't understand. He thought Draupadī was acting well, so he kept pulling the sari!

Then all of a sudden, Draupadī started beating Duśśāsana, shouting, 'Hey leave my sari alone. Leave my sari! It's my sari, my sari.' Straightaway Draupadī attacked Duśśāsana on stage. All of us were surprised! In the morning, the story read something else and in the evening drama, things were totally different!

But Kṛṣṇa, in this case, was waiting behind the screen. He was standing behind the stage, waiting for Draupadī to call. And Draupadī was shouting, 'Hey Duśśāsana, let go of my sari'. She didn't call Kṛṣṇa. So the actor playing Kṛṣṇa thought that the scene was still going on and that the sixth sari had not yet been pulled. He never arrived on the scene!

This, Duśśāsana didn't understand even after Draupadī kicked him, which made him so angry, that he pulled the sari off completely! Suddenly, he saw Draupadī standing in a blouse and a pair of men's shorts. Below male, above female with complete makeup, long hair and blouse! Luckily the actor playing Draupadī had spontaneity. He quickly turned to the audience and said, 'Kṛṣṇa, You are great. Because You couldn't come to save me, You turned me into a male and saved my dignity!'

Through his spontaneity, he managed the situation, and covered up for Duśśāsana's and Kṛṣṇa's mistakes. When you are spontaneous, you can manage any situation. Whenever I remember the word 'spontaneity', I remember this story!

Actually, spontaneity is a spiritual quality. Only a man who is not caught in his past, who is able to slip away from his past, can be spontaneous. We can be spontaneous only if we don't have a vested interest in our past decisions. This means that we are open to understanding the mistakes we have made in the past and we are ready to update and improve ourselves.

If we have vested interests in the past, we may think, 'No, all these years I have lived believing this idea, and understanding things this way. Today, just because something is said to me I will not change. I cannot! I am not going to change. For the last fifty years of my life, I have lived my life based on this concept, I cannot change it now.' Then we can never be spontaneous. We will miss life and miss it miserably.

The quality of life updates itself. It can be called intelligence only as long as it updates itself. When it stops updating itself, it is intellect. It can no longer be called intelligence. Intelligence is living energy.

The Sanskrit word *dhī* means 'that which is alive'. In Sanskrit, the word for intelligence is *dhī*. *Dhī* is energy that is alive, which continuously updates itself. In the Gāyatrī mantra (a sacred chant) that is central to Hindu worship, we seek to enhance this intelligence-energy when we pray to the Divine.

Only if we don't have a vested interest in our past, in the decisions of our past, or the way in which our past was lived, the way in which we lived our past life (not a different birth, but our life before this moment), will we be spontaneous. Spontaneity is a great spiritual quality.

> Another incident about spontaneity: Once I was giving a discourse on the Īśāvāsya upaniṣad. An elderly person, who looked like a well-read scholar, walked into the hall. After the discourse, without any basic courtesy he stood up and said, 'All these fools have not read anything, which is why you can make them listen to you. Can you

make me listen to you?' I said, 'Please come nearer Sir. I cannot hear what you are saying.' When he came nearer I said, 'Please come to this side and repeat what you said Sir.' He moved to that side. Then I said, 'I think there is a table in the way, please move to the other side Sir.' He moved and came nearer. Then I said, 'You have already listened to me three times. Now sit and listen to what I have to say!'

You can never escape from spontaneity. After this incident, sometime later, I was reading a book about a similar incident that happened in a Zen master's life. I was surprised to see how history repeats itself! When you have spontaneity, nothing can stop you. Spontaneity is a great spiritual quality.

Here Kṛṣṇa gives four different instructions. Either you can establish yourself in *Bhakti Yoga* – Path of Devotion, or live a regular life of spiritual routine, or sacrifice all the fruits of action to God, or live in consciousness and act. You can do whatever you want.

He says, 'If not this, do this. If not these, then that…' Now all that we need to understand is that we should not limit ourselves at one of the lower levels of Kṛṣṇa's instructions. We should always try to move or expand to a higher level. When you can't reach a higher level, at least stay at the lower level, and keep trying without renouncing all efforts completely. Keep at it. You will be surprised at what happens when you put in your sincere effort.

Ultimate freedom

Somebody asked me, '*Swamiji*, why do we have so many gods in India or in the Eastern religions?' All Eastern religions have many gods, whether you consider Hinduism, Buddhism or Jainism. They all have many gods, so many saints and so many gurus, while Western religions have only one God. Why?

Vivekānanda puts it across beautifully in one discourse. Freedom is the basic condition for growth. In any field, if growth has to happen, freedom is the basic condition. In the East they have had inner freedom. No one disturbs your religion here. Spiritual practice is an option. That is why we have the concept of *iṣṭadevatā,* your favorite god. *Iṣṭadevatā* means you can worship whatever form suits your mind.

The scriptures mention 330 million *devatas,* demigods or gods. Actually I think that was probably the size of the population at that time! They wanted each person to have his own customized god. That is why they say 330 million gods! If the scriptures were to be written now, they would say six billion gods. Each one has the freedom to choose their path. Each one has the freedom to choose one's own god. Each one has the freedom to consider himself as God as he realizes the divinity in himself.

People have inner freedom, which is why the East has grown so much spiritually. In the West, you can't have your own god. In India, anyone can declare himself to be a saint overnight. All you need is ten rupees to print a poster or somebody to sponsor the ten rupees. Nothing more is necessary. You can declare yourself a saint, no problem. But in the West, you can't. Only after your death, you can be declared a saint by the religious institution. The institution decides who will be a saint.

The attitudes are totally different. Of course, both have their good and bad.

In the freedom of the East, many good things happen. Tremendous research happened in the inner world because of that freedom. Much research has been done in the inner world and many truths related to the inner world have been brought to light, brought to humanity, because so many people have entered into it. There will always be a few fakes. When so many millions of people take the path, and so many millions of things are expressed, one or two superstitions come about as well.

You may think superstitions exist only in relationship to spirituality. A lot more superstitions exist in science. At least in spirituality the masters do not have any vested interests in declaring something. Nothing significant will be added to their personal lives. They are still going to eat only that much and are going to wear only those few pieces of clothing.

But when it concerns scientists, whatever they declare is going to give them name and fame, money, and additional comfort in their lives. So naturally they have vested interests. With spiritual people, the more they renounce and the less they enjoy the outer world comforts, the more they are respected. So naturally, whatever truths they declare, whatever research they do, will not add anything new to their personal lives. The respect they are given, is based upon their lives, not their words.

With scientists, it is based on their words. So in science, there is a greater possibility for superstitions than in spirituality. And when more and more people take to this spiritual life, there will always be one or two superstitions that result. Just because of this, we can't say that religious freedom is wrong, or that spiritual freedom is wrong. There is a lot of good in it also.

The West has social freedom. You can marry as many times as you want to. You can change your house to your taste. You can change your profession any number of times. You can dress as you wish. Nobody will be bothered. Nobody will mind. Even now, I know people in India who obey family traditions, who have not left their family homes. They don't even shift their houses. They don't change professions and they don't change lifestyles. In the East, they don't have social freedom. They have spiritual freedom. In the West, they have social freedom but not spiritual freedom. For any growth to happen, freedom is a basic necessity.

Here, with these four options, Kṛṣṇa is expressing spiritual freedom. He gives spiritual freedom to us. He says that there are so many paths, and tells us to choose whichever one suits our mentality, and to practice it. He tells us to practice at least one option. It is not so important which option that we choose. It is essential only that we choose something!

In India, at least seventy percent of the population regularly visits a religious place of worship. It might be a nearby temple on their street or something in their neighborhood. Seventy percent of the population is in the habit of visiting a spiritual place regularly. They somehow manage to do it.

Eastern traditions offer many choices. If you are an intellectual person, then Śiva could be your choice and you can continuously sit and meditate. If you are inclined towards devotion, then Viṣṇu could be your choice. The path includes singing and dancing like the great masters Chaitanya and Mīrā. Just sing the glory of the Lord like the *Azhwars,* devotional saints of Tamil Nadu, related with Viṣṇu. If you are inclined towards yoga, if you are a yogi, then Devī is the one for you. Meditate on Her; offer worship and tantric practices.

There are many different kinds of techniques, and the options are many. So you are repeatedly given many options. You have customized ways, customized paths for your personal growth. Thus, naturally wherever one is, one can grow and reach the level one is supposed to reach. There are all sizes of ladders, all kinds of steps. You are continuously given choices, given options. Naturally, one tends to take up something or the other.

The East has explored and done much research on the inner space because of spiritual freedom. The West has achieved so much at a social level because of social freedom. Of course, India has struggled because of the lack of social freedom, but it has gained tremendously because of spiritual freedom. Here, Kṛṣṇa gives many choices in spiritual freedom. One cannot expect any master, other than the Eastern masters, to be so compassionate, concerned, caring, and generous as to give so many options. In the West, the law is compassionate as it gives a lot of options. In the East, the spiritual system is compassionate as it gives a lot of options.

The West has a few areas where you are respected and every individual is respected, such as areas of customer care and other such domains. Many options are given within the social scenario as well. If one is unable to live with their spouse, they can say goodbye. Socially one is not bound. One has freedom.

But in India, spiritual freedom is given more importance. These four options are representative of the spiritual freedom given to society. Here

Kṛṣṇa gives Arjuna the spiritual freedom to choose and of course, not only to Arjuna, but through Arjuna, to all of us.

abhyāsepyasamarthosi mat-karma paramo bhava
madartham api karmāṇi kurvan siddhiṁ avāpsyasi

If you cannot practice the regulations of *Bhakti Yoga,* try to work for Me because by working for me, you will come to the perfect stage, *siddhiṁ avāpsyasi.* Then one by one He gives all options and finally says,

śreyo hi jñānaṁ abhyāsāj jñānād dhyānaṁ viśiṣyate
dhyānāt karma phala tyāgaḥ tyāgāc chāntir anantaram

The last option

'If you can't follow these practices, engage yourself in the cultivation of knowledge.' He says, 'At least collect all these life solutions.' Cultivation of knowledge means collecting solutions to life's mysteries, such as how to avoid depression, how to be more courageous, how to be strong, how to avoid unwanted desires, and how to prevent emotional blocks. This kind of knowledge that you can collect as life solutions can help and protect you.

In the USA, you are familiar with earthquake kits and hurricane kits. You are taught that water bottles and other vital things should be a part of the kit and also present in the cars in Los Angeles. On the fire department's website, there is a big list of things that one must do in order to be prepared in the event of an earthquake. They call it the earthquake kit.

Western society prepares people for these eventualities. But we also need to prepare people to face the earthquakes that happen within, the emotional imbalances that occur within. Just like preparing for an earthquake, one needs to be equipped with an inner earthquake kit. This inner earthquake kit is what I refer to as 'life solutions' or knowledge.

Collect these things now, so that when you face depression you will be prepared. All of us *will* face some sort of inner earthquake at some point in time. If one dies, there is no problem because when one is dead there can be no earthquake. As long as one is alive, naturally at some point, some friends will die, some relatives will die, or some near and dear ones will fall sick or die. All these things are inevitable.

The inevitability of each moment must be understood. Understanding the inevitability of life and collecting knowledge, collecting the tools to support us at those moments, collecting the ideas to balance ourselves at those moments, is *jñāna,* knowledge. We need to prepare 'earthquake kits' for our lives. Otherwise we will be unable to recover. The aftermath will be terrible.

Because authorities never expected category five hurricanes, the aftermath has been terrible in the Gulf Coast of the US. People are struggling and it is difficult. In the same way, if we don't expect life's eventualities, and if we don't anticipate now that inner earthquakes or inner storms will occur, the aftermath will be terrible. Please prepare for the aftermath now. It will lessen the damage.

The Eastern system continuously prepares people for inner hurricanes, inner tornadoes and inner earthquakes. *Jñāna* or knowledge is the earthquake kit. Knowledge is the earthquake kit for the inner space. People are prepared. They do not have to choose between inner and outer spaces. Have an outer earthquake kit in your car, and an inner earthquake kit in your heart. We don't need to choose one or the other. Now we can have both! Because of the worldwide communication systems, even here in the West, we can have both.

Someone asked me, '*Swamiji,* Buddha enlightened ten thousand people. What is your aim?' I replied, 'Without newspapers, without telegrams, without the internet, without airplanes, if Buddha could enlighten ten thousand people, then with all these amenities, we should be able to enlighten at least one million people. Only then, is it worth having all these amenities.'

Now we can have everything in the inner world and the outer world. We can have an earthquake kit in our cars and an inner earthquake kit in our hearts or inner space. Never take inner earthquakes lightly. Taking inner earthquakes lightly means we are acting out of ignorance. It means we are inviting big trouble, without preparing for the aftermath.

When quakes come in the outer world, we can blame government officials, directors, and politicians. We can blame somebody and be rid of the responsibility. We can put the responsibility on someone else's shoulders. But when it comes to the inner world, we can't blame anybody. Each of us must take responsibility.

As Kṛṣṇa says in an earlier chapter:

uddharet ātmanā ātmānaṁ ātmānaṁ avasādhayet
ātmaiva hyātmano bandhuḥ atmaiva ripurātmanaḥ

You must help yourself ascend. If you can help yourself ascend, then you are your best friend. Otherwise you are your worst enemy. He gives options among the different paths, like practicing, cultivation of knowledge, meditation, or renunciation of the fruits of actions, *karma phala tyāga*.

Among these paths, one is better than the other. First, He mentions that the path of meditation is better than knowledge. Better than meditation, is offering everything at the feet of God. He says that by renunciation of the fruits of action, one can immediately achieve peace. As long as we think that 'everything is mine,' we suffer. The moment we surrender, the moment we hand the whole thing over to the Divine, inner healing happens. Our inner space experiences the breeze of divine healing.

Often, people think that surrender is some sort of loss of control. Giving up is an expression of weakness. Letting go is irresponsibility. Understand that control is an expression of ego. All control arises out of the need for 'I' and 'mine'. Control seeks power. Power corrupts.

Surrender is liberation. Surrender is the expression of choicelessness, of leaving the decision to the Divine after doing what one can do. Unless we let go of our expectations and our attachment to the results of our actions, we will continue to build unproductive stress and tension within us, that will reduce and not enhance our performance.

When we learn to focus totally on what we need to do and work on the process, walk the path without worrying about the destination, whatever we do is done better, faster and more effectively. Kṛṣṇa's teaching is not merely spiritual. It is highly practical. It is not only after-life enhancing, but it is present-life enabling.

He says that for the person who renounces the fruits of action, eternal peace is the immediate result. When we renounce ownership to what we do and hand over the ownership to the Divine, peace and bliss descend upon us. There is true liberation in giving up attachment to the results of what we do. This liberation comes from not having expectations of any kind. We are detached from the results of our actions. That allows us to focus totally on what we have in hand, what we have in the present moment. Staying in the present is peace, bliss, liberation, or *mokṣa*.

He Is Very Dear To Me

12.13,14 *One who has no dislike or envy for any being, who is friendly and compassionate to everyone, free from the sense of I and mine, the ego, maintains equanimity of mind both in joy and sorrow, forgiving, ever satisfied, united with Yoga, has a strong commitment to Me and has fixed his mind and intellect upon Me, such a devotee of Mine is very dear to Me.*

In all the previous verses, Kṛṣṇa tells Arjuna to do this or do that. Now, He is not saying, do this or do that. He says, 'Those who do all these things are very dear to Me. If you don't do these, that too is okay. However, if you do them, you will be very dear to Me.' In other words, it is emotional blackmail, not directly but indirectly, but all for a good cause!

'One who is not envious, but is a kind friend to all living entities, who does not think of himself as a proprietor, and who is free from false ego, who is equal in both happiness and distress, who is tolerant, always satisfied, self-controlled, and engaged in devotional service with determination, with intelligence fixed on Me, such a devotee of Mine is very dear to Me.'

Important qualities

Understand here, He says, 'Who is not envious and a kind friend to every living entity.' These are important qualities. Let us analyze our minds. When we honestly analyze our mind, we realize that if somebody came to you and told you he loved you, you wouldn't believe it. The first thing you would do is figure out what he wants from you. You don't believe you are worthy of being loved. Next, you don't believe that somebody can honestly love you, because you don't love anybody honestly. Because you are calculative, you expect the other person also to be calculating. All our love is skin deep, and you know how deep skin is!

Here, He says, 'A person who is a kind friend of everyone, who honestly serves, feels the friendliness in everybody, and is free from false ego.'

Now we should understand the term 'false ego'. Ego not only means showing what you don't have, but also hiding what you have.

There are two types of ego: active ego, and passive ego. Active ego is showing what you have and passive ego is characterized by these kinds of thoughts, 'Oh, what can I do, I am a simple person, I cannot achieve anything, and I cannot do anything.' Hiding oneself is an outcome of the passive ego. An inferiority complex is a manifestation of the passive ego.

At least there is one positive point regarding the superiority complex. With a feeling of superiority, wherever one goes, one gets a big beating. Society tries to cut you down to size. You may then try to overcome your superiority complex. But with inferiority complex, society does not attempt to correct you. It is a cunning way of hiding yourself from life. You will not even know that you have a problem. So a person hiding in the inferior ego, suffers more deeply than someone who hides himself in the superior ego.

A person who looks for fame and name, and a person who doesn't want fame and name are both egoistic. If you ask for name, you are egoistic. And if you don't, it shows passive ego. Whereas a person who lets things happen and a person who allows things to flow, lives in reality.

Kṛṣṇa makes a comment, 'After all, who is going to know who you are? Why do you think you are a big person and your name is so great, and that everybody knows your name? You think you are great, that is why you don't want name and fame. Nobody knows your name, relax.' Kṛṣṇa says clearly, 'Nobody knows your name, relax.'

Nobody knows our name. Asking for name and fame and saying, 'I don't want name and fame,' are different aspects of ego, different varieties of ego. The inferior ego is also ego, which is why he says 'false ego'. You are not only supposed to be free from ego, you are supposed to be free from false ego, as well. You shouldn't hide yourself in inferiority complexes.

A small story:

A master tells a disciple, 'Please press my feet.' The disciple says, 'Oh, I am a sinner, how can I touch Your feet?' He does not want to do it, because he is lazy. So he says, 'I am a great sinner. How can I touch Your feet; how can I do that?'

Later, a devotee brought fruits and *prasād,* offerings. The master put a little in his mouth and left the rest. The next day, he saw nothing on the plate. He asked his disciple, 'What happened to the fruits and *prasād*?' The disciple answered, 'It was *guru prasād,* offering to the master. I could not let it go for a waste. I finished the whole thing because it was *guru prasād.*'

Look at the mind, how nicely it handles situations and different concepts! Wherever we want, we insert whatever is convenient. When he didn't want to work, he said, 'No, how can I touch Your feet. I am not qualified enough. I am not a pure soul.' When he wanted food, it was *guru prasād* and he finished it!

We collect concepts to support our ideology. That is why it is said that the devil quotes the Bible. Only the devil quotes the Bible. When you quote only specifics, you become the devil. But when you understand the essence of the Bible, you become God. You don't need to quote the Bible then. People will quote your words. When you have digested the Bible, you don't need to quote it. People will quote *your* words. When you have not digested the Bible, whenever you quote it without digesting it, you are the devil. Only the devil quotes the Bible, not a person who understands it.

The moment you understand the futility of your goal and wealth, that nothing is going to be with you forever, all of these divine qualities radiate through your being. You will be transformed into a person who is established in forgivingness, who maintains equanimity of mind, who is satisfied and united with yoga. Actually, when you are blissful inside, you radiate these qualities. A man who is totally blissful inside, radiates pleasantness for absolutely no reason.

We continuously carry a sense of slight irritation in our being; we are waiting to pounce on people. The moment we get a chance, we scream, shout, and throw tantrums. We don't know what we are doing. We jump and 'bite' people at the slightest provocation, because we carry some irritation within us. We continuously vomit upon others, the suffering and misery that we feel.

This irritation arises within us out of constant worry and constant inner chatter. We feel we may not get what we are planning for and what we want. All worry, is about the future, based upon what happened in the past. Worry is about expectation of what the future holds for us. Worry arises as a result of the gap between what we expect and what we think we are capable of getting. So we become anxious about whether things will happen the way we expect them to.

Worry is futile, because there are many factors other than our capability that determine the outcome of what we do. The expectation of the outcome is futile, since the future is speculative. We cannot control even our own breath. We cannot say with certainty whether we will take the next breath. What arrogance it is then to think that we can determine our future or the outcome of our actions!

Worry, anxiety, and irritation dissolve once we settle into the present. Only in the present, are we in a position to influence our actions and the immediate outcome of those actions. When we settle into the present, thoughts cease, and worry and irritation disappear. We realize how irrelevant and unproductive worry is.

In meditation courses I ask people to write down whatever they are worried and irritated about at that juncture in their lives. Many write volumes. I tell them to keep the papers and tell me after six months how many of these worries materialized. You will be surprised, less than twenty percent of these worries actually materialize.

Worry and irritation are pointless. Once you understand the futility of irritation, however irritated you are, whatever you create by that irritation or tension will not stay with you. Only how you live, how consciously you live, with what consciousness you choose to live remains with you. When you understand the importance of your state of being, you automatically start radiating pleasantness and joy.

Meditation for devotion

I give people a simple meditation technique to experience *Bhakti Yoga* – the Path of Devotion. Just practice the technique of radiating pleasantness. How does one do it? From morning till night whenever you remember, inhale, exhale, and inhale only the pleasant qualities of bliss. Visualize you are inhaling bliss and exhaling bliss. Your whole being will be filled with joy. In the beginning you will be visualizing, imagining. But in a few days you will realize it is your quality.

One more thing you should know, is that imagination and visualization are two different things. Imagination translates into *kalpanā* in Sanskrit, while visualization translates into *bhāvanā*. *Bhāvanā* is different from *kalpanā*. *Kalpanā* means imagining things that are not there. For example, if you think of an elephant with ten trunks, that is imagination, *kalpanā,* that which is not there. But *bhāvanā* means visualizing, that which is present but may be eluding you.

If you sit during the day and visualize stars in the sky, that is not imagination. It is visualization. Because stars are in the sky, even though you are unable to see them. So visualizing stars is not imagination.

Perceiving what is there, but what you are unable to see at this moment, is visualization. Trying to perceive what can never exist is imagination.

So understand that meditating on gods and goddesses is not imagination. It is visualization. They are there. You cannot see them; that is all. You are supposed to fall in tune with them, like tuning your television. If you tune your television, you can immediately watch many programs. Similarly, visualization is tuning yourself. Just continuously visualize inhaling and exhaling bliss. Visualize *prāṇa* – the life giving energy - going inside and coming out. *Prāṇa* is energy and bliss. Please understand that *prāṇa* is not merely air. *Prāṇa* is the energy that goes through air. For example, a truck comes up to your house and unloads luggage and leaves. The truck is air and the luggage is *prāṇa. Prāṇa* is not just air. Using air as a medium, *prāṇa* enters. *Prāṇa-śakti* is the subtle part of air. *Prāṇa-śakti* is bliss energy, *ananda-śakti.*

So whenever you inhale, visualize yourself inhaling bliss. When you exhale, visualize yourself exhaling bliss. Inhale light and exhale light. Think that your whole body is a beanbag filled with light. Imagine your body is a beanbag filled with bliss and light. You will automatically start radiating bliss, instead of irritation. Instead of vomiting the poison of anger and jealousy on others, you will radiate love and bliss.

'Such a devotee of mine is very dear to Me.' Kṛṣṇa says that if somebody lives in this manner, that devotee is close to Him. He doesn't say 'Do or don't do.' He does not want to make more rules. He is tired of making rules. He has reached a point where his attitude is, 'If you can, do it, otherwise, what can be done?' He is in a relaxed mood.

I think this happens to all masters. All masters come to this point after some time. After some time they say, 'Alright, do whatever you want, what can be done?' They can guide or show you only to a certain extent. Beyond that, if masters persist, people start thinking that the masters have some vested interest in making people enlightened. It is as though if they make ten more people enlightened, they will have a special place in heaven, or god will increase their salary. Understand, they just share what they have, out of joy and bliss.

A small story:

A prisoner was cross-examined in the court.

The lawyer asked, 'Do you know this man?'

The prisoner answered, 'How should I know him?'

The lawyer asked, 'Did he borrow money from you?'

The prisoner replied, 'Why should he borrow money from me?'

The judge was irritated by now and asked the prisoner, 'Why do you ask so many questions? Why can't you just answer the lawyer's questions?'

The prisoner replied, 'Why should I not ask questions?'

Understand, this is exactly what happens in life. You are not ready to trust the master. You keep resisting Him. When the master says drop 'I and mine,' people are afraid that the master may pick them up and take it with him! He may take it away. What to do? They think he is in need of it, which is why he asks them to drop it. They think, 'He is asking us to drop it, so he can take it.' People are suspicious. That is why masters sometimes say, 'This is the right way, but do as you want to do.'

'One who has fixed his mind and intellect upon me,' says Kṛṣṇa. It is difficult for the devotee and disciple to have this attitude of surrender to the master or the universe. As long as things go the way the person wants, as long as the master allows the devotee to do what he wishes, the master is a great master and worthy of celebration. But once the master turns serious, and takes up his responsibility of spiritual surgery on the disciple, he wants to run away.

I tell people, 'Decide well in advance whether I am your right master or not.' A master takes his responsibilities seriously. His major responsibility is surgery; it is the surgery of the cancer of ego. Once the disciple makes a commitment, the master makes his commitment, too. It is dangerous to run away from the operating table. You lose your whole life by running away. You may have to wait many births, before you get another chance.

Here, Kṛṣṇa is in the same mood and He says, 'Such a devotee of Mine is dear to Me,' that's all. He is talking about the commitment that the devotee makes to Him. He says, 'One who makes that commitment to Me and fixes his mind and intellect upon Me, he is dear to Me and will be liberated.' So says the great master.

Be Unaffected

12.15 He, by whom the world is not affected adversely, and who in turn does not affect the world adversely, and he, who is free from joy, anger and anxiety, he is dear to Me.

Kṛṣṇa says, 'He who is not affected adversely or agitated by the world and who in turn does not affect or cause agitation in this world, he who is free from joy, anger and anxiety is dear to Me.'

Only the person who is centered on his being, centered on the ultimate consciousness, does not create havoc in the world. Just by being in the presence of an enlightened person, our minds calm down. We become steady. I can say that not only is the world not adversely affected by such persons, the world is blessed by their presence.

Once a person realizes that they are one with the Divine and all of Existence, how can there be any fight? How can there be any drama? There can't be! There is only the experience of intense love and compassion on its own and towards all beings

.

Move from the periphery to the core

Here Kṛṣṇa is saying that the persons who are expressing from their core, unaffected by the happenings around them, are dear to Him because they are centered on Him.

For most of us, that isn't the case. We live on the periphery of our personalities and make a mess of things wherever we go. To most of us, joy is a period between experiences of sorrow and unhappiness. It is like a period of quiet between two battles that we call peace, just as impermanent and just as unreal.

Joy and temporal pleasure from sensory experiences invariably lead to sorrow. Joy is the by-product of fulfillment, of an expectation. When the expectation is fulfilled the first time, we feel happy. Most likely, this may not happen the next time around. So instead of joy, sorrow follows.

Joy can only be experienced internally if it is to be long lasting. Such joy is more accurately called bliss. Bliss is eternal, unlike joy, which is transient. Bliss is eternal. It arises when we drop expectation, when we stay centered on our being, when we are in the mood and mode of non-attachment.

If we close our eyes and try to focus on an object or event, after a few seconds we see that we can't continue. No thought or idea can control our inner space eternally. Always, there is another thought that comes along to replace the last thought. This is the inner chatter of our mind. Buddha refers to it as the 'monkey mind.'

This chatter is the constant jumping of our mind between past and future. It is the journey that our mind undertakes between what it has experienced and stored as memories, and the unknown, which is full of expectations and speculations, also based upon the past. This jumping, this journey, is what we call thoughts.

Anxiety builds as our ego realizes that what it desires may not happen. This loss of something that has not even happened, the product of pure speculation, causes intense emotions within us. Long before anything happens we anticipate with great anxiety that the worst can happen. Then we wait with bated breath for the event to pass. Quite often you would have experienced a sense of relief when the worst you had imagined had actually come to pass. There is no longer any anxiety when the future has moved into the present.

When Kṛṣṇa says, 'He who is without anxiety will reach Me,' He says that he who is in the present moment will reach Me. In the present moment our thoughts cease and we can see with clarity the truth of our Existence, Kṛṣṇa consciousness, and then we are one with Him.

'Let go of anger,' says Kṛṣṇa. 'He who is without anger shall reach Me.' By the literal understanding of this verse, none of us can reach Kṛṣṇa. All of us express anger at one time or another. Anger is a positive energy. Expressing anger can be positive, both for the person expressing the anger and the one receiving it. This may sound strange but it is true.

Anger is often the product of guilt. We get defensive when our spouse points out something we did not do in the way that they wanted. We move into a defensive position. We feel guilty when we realize we did wrong. But instead of accepting the wrongdoing, we become angry. We would like our wrongdoing to remain our secret and we dislike the other person for bringing it out into the open. It is like a leper not wishing to see his own sores.

In a sense, this anger is also directed at ourselves. The guilt we feel is the result of the internal rage against our own weakness. Guilt is the biggest sin we commit. Whatever we do at a point in time, we do with the knowledge and awareness we possess at that time. Once we have done what we have done, there is nothing within our power to change it.

When we let go of guilt, then we can let go of anger. When we let go of guilt, we let go of our suppressed emotions of anger, regret, defensiveness, and the internal fury. Repressed anger can cause cancer. People who appear calm on the surface, controlling the anger that they feel without expressing it, are sitting on a time bomb. Either it can explode unexpectedly causing grave danger to themselves and others, or it can lead to self-destruction through cancer. It is perfectly possible.

We should learn to direct anger at issues rather than at people. When anger rises against people, divert it to issues, instead of towards a person. The person is only the perceived cause as you see it. The deeper issue remains covered if you direct the anger against the person. It comes back more dangerously. Anger breeds anger. It is a vicious cycle. If, however, we express anger and express it fully against the incident, event, or issue without personalizing it, we can let go of that anger without harm to others and us. It is possible. You need to practice, that's all. When the emotive memory of that anger is expressed, the memory dissolves. No anger remains. Over a period of time, the anger disappears even before it rises. Kṛṣṇa says that one must reach this 'state beyond anger' in order to be able to reach Him.

Selfless In Action

12.16 *He who is free from wants, who is pure and skilled, unconcerned, untroubled, who is selfless in whatever he does, he who is devoted to Me, he is dear to Me.*

Kṛṣna now moves into higher gear. Once you let go of joy, anxiety, and anger, once you transcend these emotions, you reach a state of calmness that takes you close to Him. Now He moves from *'nissaṅgatvaṁ'* to *'nirmohatvaṁ,'* from emotional non-attachment to non-attachment to desires.

We need to understand the difference between 'wants' and 'needs'. Needs are necessary for us to survive on planet earth, like the basic needs of food, shelter, etc. The great Jain master Mahavira says, 'The moment you are born on this planet, the universe sends everything with you that you need.' We just need to trust the universe and we shall get what we need to live. However, we end up seeking more. We see our neighbor. We cannot bear to see that others are happier than we are. We are happy to see people who suffer. This only shows our own state of sorrow in a better light. If a neighbor buys a new air conditioner, the temperature in our house shoots up. If the neighbor buys a new car, our car suddenly slows down. Everything we have is a match for what others have. It is a constant cycle of 'What next? What next?' Even before we start enjoying what we have, we make a plan to get more. There is no joy in having, the joy is in chasing. There is no end point to this chase.

Wants are endless. Wants are suffering. Wants are born out of comparison with others. Needs, our basic needs, carry the energy within them for fulfillment. Wants only carry the seeds of our own suffering.

During our Nithyananda Spurana Program, or LBP Level 2, we take participants through the seven layers of the energy bodies that the spirit passes through when we die. In this process, the departing spirit remembers all that happened during its time in the body until the point of death. It is like a fast replay of all that has happened, every incident that is stored on the hard disk of our memory.

In one of the sessions, I ask people to make a list of their desires, their needs and wants. They fill pages with it. I ask them to review the list many times. Then they do a certain meditation. At the end of the meditation, I ask them to recollect from memory their list of desires. What they can recollect is usually a fraction of what they have written. It is as if they started with a large tree full of leaves, their desires, and during this meditation the tree shed almost all its leaves, as if the leaves were dry and dead. What it retained glowed like golden leaves.

Whatever is left in their memories, those desires glow like gold. They are the ones that carry the energy for their fulfillment! These desires are the true desires that they carry. If the process is done with awareness, these desires are always selfless desires. They may benefit the individual, no doubt, but they always benefit humanity. Only such selfless desires, carry the energy of the universe with them for fulfillment.

When our desires are our own true desires, when they reflect our real needs, when they express themselves in our inner energy, we don't feel any desperation about trying to achieve them. The realization comes that, as a matter of the natural course of events, these desires will be fulfilled. We are not driven, and we are not troubled. We accept that these will happen. Therefore, Kṛṣṇa counsels Arjuna, 'Become free from wants, be selfless and you shall be untroubled, liberated, and you will reach Me.'

Equanimity Of Mind

12.17 *He who does not rejoice or hate, or grieve or desire, renounces both good and evi,l and who is full of devotion, he is dear to Me.*

Kṛṣṇa now goes into another level of controlling the mind. He now refers to one who does not love or hate. He is not talking about not loving anyone. When we love the way we do, with conditionality and expectations, it works well as long as these expectations are fulfilled. When something does not work the way we wish it to, the love disappears like a dewdrop in the sun. In its place, hate appears.

Hatred and love are opposite sides of the same coin, as long as love is conditional. Love can flip into hatred in a moment, the moment we feel that our expectations are threatened. In love of this type, there is external rejoicing, sharing of joy and happiness, and public expression of happiness as long as the emotion remains.

Often, love, or what we believe is love, is related to time and space. So long as the distance is large and the time of contact is minimal we see a few defects in those we profess to love. We aren't together long enough to put expectations on them; however, once we get closer and spend more time, we see the real picture. No wonder they say, 'Familiarity breeds contempt.' It can also convert love into hatred. To transcend love and hatred, which are two different expressions of the same perceived reality, we need to drop expectations. We need to develop a sense of non-attachment. We need to be unconditional in our love.

We all go through several stages of relationships in our lifetime. As children we are totally dependent upon parents.

As we grow into adolescence, we open up to the world and question many things we took for granted as an infant or a child; therefore, teenagers rebel. They wish to be independent. They break rules.

In adulthood, we learn that to survive and coexist we need to follow societal rules and regulations. We develop skills to get along with others. We learn to work and relate with others. As we grow and mature, and the spirit and its development become important, we seek guidance. We look for a master. With the master, the relationship is the reverse of what we started with as a child. We are once again concerned about survival, but it is the survival of the spirit, and not the mind or body. The only relationship that will work with the master is total and unconditional love. It is absolute surrender. Surrender transcends love and hate. When one is in a mood of total surrender to the master or the Divine, both being one and the same, the concept of good and evil, sin and merit disappear.

In a spiritual sense, there is nothing that is a sin. Hell and heaven are not geographical. They are psychological, within our mind and attitude. We commit sins, because we are already in our own hell. We do well to others when we are in our space of heaven or bliss.

Religions try and control us through concepts of sin, original sin, hell and heaven. Please understand that there is no such thing as sin, or hell and heaven. Those who term you sinners are sinners themselves. That's why they call you sinners, because they wish to control you. All religions try to control through fear and greed, through the carrot and stick.

Kṛṣṇa breaks the mold. He tells us, 'Go beyond good and evil.' He says this because there is no such thing as good and evil. It is all in our mind. When we understand this truth we are in His realm. That's His promise.

This Is Whom I Love

12.18,19 *One who treats friends and enemies the same, who faces in the same manner honor and dishonor, heat and cold, happiness and sorrow, fame and infamy; one who is always free from attachment, always silent and satisfied with anything, without a fixed home, who is fixed in mind and who is devoted to Me, such a person is very dear to Me.*

12.20 *Those who truly follow this imperishable path of righteousness with great faith, making Me the supreme goal, are very dear to Me.*

Again Kṛṣṇa says, 'Such a person, full of devotion is dear to Me.' He is not ready to put down any more rules, which means He is almost ending His instructions. He is almost saying, 'This is the way, if somebody is like this, then I love him, that's all. I am not interested in anything else.' He says, 'One who is neutral towards friends and enemies, who is the same in honor and dishonor, heat and cold, joy and pain, free from attachment to the fruits of action, who remains the same in criticism and praise; who is thoughtful, who is content with whatever he gets, who does not care for any house and is resolute in mind, such a man, full of devotion is very dear to Me.'

Let me tell you a story. Rāvaṇa lived for one *kalpa* (many thousands of years). Vyāsa lived for four *kalpas*. Rāvaṇa was building Laṅkāpurī, his capital in Sri Lanka. He got Laṅkāpurī as a gift from Śiva and he was developing it. When Vyāsa came to the city, Rāvaṇa asked him, 'Oh Vyāsa, did you see my palace, and my country? How grand they look.' Vyāsa replied, 'Yes, I have seen them.'

Rāvaṇa showed him everything with pride and asked, 'Why don't you build a house for yourself?'

Vyāsa smiled and said, 'My life is just four *kalpas*. I have no time to waste building houses. After all, I am going to live here for only four *kalpas*, why should I waste time building houses?'

Rāvaṇa lived for only one *kalpa*, for which he built such a big house. Vyāsa whose life was four times as long, thought it was unnecessary to waste part of his life building houses! 'One who is not concerned about owning a house is full of devotion and he is near to Me, dear to Me.' Kṛṣṇa concludes this chapter on *Bhakti Yoga*, Union through Devotion, saying that one who lives in righteousness is devoted to Him.

Dharma is spiritual righteousness. It is not, and has nothing to do with rules and regulations laid down by society and religion. Human tendency is always to break rules. Societal rules, seem to restrict one's freedom of expression and movement.

Understand that you are no sinner! Divinity resides within us. Our only sin, the original sin, is in not recognizing that we are divine; therefore, we don't need to strive to attain salvation. We just need to become aware of our inner divinity. Meditation is a process of shutting the mind down. In this process of reaching the no-mind state, the ego drops. The barrier to the realization that our true nature is divine disappears. We become who we are. We realize we are one with the Divine.

Let us all experience and radiate eternal bliss, *nityānanda*. Thank You.

Thus ends the 12th chapter named* Bhakti Yogaḥ *of the* Upaniṣad *of the* Bhagavad Gītā, *the scripture of Yoga, dealing with the science of the Absolute in the form of the dialogue between* Śrī Kṛṣṇa *and Arjuna.

BHAGAVADGĪTĀ

The Field And The Knower Of The Field

KṢETRA KṢETRAJÑYA VIBHĀGA YOGAḤ

CHAPTER 13

You are a wave in the ocean of Existence.
When the wave understands
that it is not separate from the ocean,
its resistance drops
and it merges with the ocean.

The Field And The Knower Of The Field

In this chapter, Kṛṣṇa speaks to Arjuna about *kṣetra* (Field) and *kṣetrajñya* (Knower of the Field). This chapter is known as the *kṣetra kṣetrajñya vibhāga yoga,* or the yoga of discrimination of the *kṣetra,* the field, and *kṣetrajñya,* the knower of the field.

Kṛṣṇa clearly talks about the physical matter in which we exist, as well as the consciousness that stays in the matter. In some way or other all of us are related to this whole universe, whether we understand it or not, whether we experience it or not. The consciousness is the root cause. It is not only the origin, but also the cause. It is the source from which we come and in which we stay. The whole universe, the universal consciousness, is the space in which we all happen.

Kṛṣṇa uses the wave and the ocean as an analogy. The ocean is the universal consciousness or God, *ātma,* or whatever we may call it. Kṛṣṇa reveals the secret that we are like the waves, and the whole is the ocean. He explains how we can experience oneness with the ocean.

Our only problem in life is that somehow we have forgotten that we are a part of the ocean. We forgot that we belong to the *kṣetrajñya.* The word *kṣetrajñya* means consciousness, which is the cause for the field to function. *Kṣetra* means body and *kṣetrajñya* means the consciousness that knows it has a body. In this chapter, Kṛṣṇa reveals the secrets of *kṣetra* and *kṣetrajñya.* If we don't know the secrets of *kṣetrajñya,* the *kṣetra* acts as if it is the owner.

The body and the mind

A small example:

You buy a new car. You sit in the car and start driving. Suddenly, after ten minutes you realize that you do not know how to stop it. If you don't know how to stop the car you are not driving the car, the car is driving you.

In the same way, we get into this mind and into this body and start living. Suddenly at one point, we find that we are unable to stop the body or mind. It goes on as it wants and is uncontrollable.

Bring the body and mind under your conscious awareness. The body and mind are good servants but not good masters. As servants they are great. Of course, without the body and mind you cannot live life, you cannot enjoy life. They are needed. But unless they are under your control, they will become your masters.

Only two options are possible: either you enjoy them or they enjoy you. In the beginning you may start smoking. After some time you may not really be enjoying the smoke, but the smoke will be enjoying you. Similarly, in the beginning you may start drinking alcohol. After some time the alcohol will be drinking you. In the beginning you start a habit and after some time that habit takes over your life. The habit will be enjoying *your* life. Then you are no longer a person with choices: you are a set of habits that is continuously repeated without your control.

When we start using a car without reading the owner's manual, suddenly we realize that we do not know where the hand brake is. We don't know how to turn left or right. When we enter into the body and mind without knowing how to handle them, we are in the same situation. Bring the body and mind under your control before you are brought under their control.

Whether it is a material life or a spiritual life, unless the body and mind are under our control, whatever we may think or whatever we want to do is of no use. Suppose we sit down in the morning and draw out a big plan for the day, analyzing all the data, 'I must do this,' 'I must do that,' but at the end of the day, beyond our control, we spontaneously indulge in drink and sleep or other things. What is the use of the whole day's plan? Nothing! We go on creating what we want to do in our mind, but at the end of the day, the body behaves the way it wants to. Even the mind behaves as it wants to. We get nowhere!

Until we experience the *kṣetrajñya,* the knower of the field, the real life never begins. This is why the vedic system considers a person to be born only when his individual consciousness is awakened. Until then his physical birth is not accepted, nor is he considered a human being or a *manuṣya.* According to the *Vedas,* only when someone's inner consciousness is awakened he is considered a human being or as a person who has taken birth. Until then, he is one among the animals.

The Sanskrit word *manuṣya* has two meanings. One is 'descendant of Manu,' and the other is 'the man who can handle the mind or one who has gone beyond the mind.' Manu is supposed to be our first forefather. Only when we can handle the mind, we become *manuṣya.* In Sanskrit they say, '*pratyagātma caitanya jāgrataṁ.*' It means that only when the individual consciousness is awakened is one considered to be a person.

In the Indian vedic system, when a child turns seven he is initiated into the Gāyatrī, a sacred *mantra* or chant. You should understand one important thing here. The vedic religion or Hinduism or *Sanātana Dharma,* is the only religion in which there is no baptism, no initiation. You are not given any faith, you are not given any concept, and you are not given any philosophy. You are not asked to believe in anything. You are just given a technique to control your body and mind. That's all. The Gāyatrī mantra is a mere technique with no reference to any deity, taught to the child when he turns six or seven years of age. The Gāyatrī mantra means 'Let me meditate on the energy, which awakens the consciousness in me, and let that consciousness help me to meditate on it.' That's all.

Om bhūr bhuva suvaḥtat savitur vareṇyam |
bhargo devasya dhīmahi
dhiyo yonaḥ prachodayāt ||

This *mantra* does not have any other meaning. There is no mention of Gāyatrī Devī (a Hindu goddess) or any deity with five faces and such things. No. This *mantra* means 'Let me meditate on that consciousness, which awakens my intelligence, and let that consciousness help me to meditate on it.' That's all.

The first thing that our *ṛṣis* or ancient Indian enlightened masters want us to do is to bring our body and mind under our control. They want us to learn how to live with our body and mind. The Gāyatrī *mantra* is like an owner's manual for the body and mind. If we have a car, then an owner's manual is a basic need. Without reading the owner's manual, if we start driving a car, then whose mistake is it? In all vehicles we can see important instructions and warnings on the airbags. 'Airbags may cause serious injury.' 'Kids under the age of twelve should not sit in the front seat.' 'Please read the owner's manual to know more about the airbag.' In the same way, only at around the age of seven do we start to handle our body. Until the age of seven, we live at the instinct level. After the age of seven the intellect starts working and we start making decisions. The moment we start making decisions, we should first know how to bring the body and mind under control. That is why the *vedic* masters teach the technique to awaken the inner intelligence and to master the consciousness. It is similar to reading the owner's manual before using the car.

What You Know Is Not You

13.1 *Arjuna said: O Kṛṣṇa, I wish to know and understand about* prakṛti *and* puruṣa, *passive and active energies, the field and the knower of the field, and of knowledge and of the end of knowledge.*

13.2 *Lord Kṛṣṇa replied to Arjuna saying: This body, O son of Kuntī, is called the field, anyone who knows this body is called the knower of the field.*

13.3 *O Bhārata, we should understand that I am the Knower in all bodies, the Creator. In my opinion knowledge means to understand this body or the field of creation, as well as the Creator, one who knows this field.*

Kṛṣṇa explains, 'O Kaunteya (son of Kuntī), O Arjuna, this body is called the field; the person who knows this body is called the knower of the field or *kṣetrajñya.*'

Whatever you know is not you. If you know something, it is not you. For instance, you can read this book because it is separate and apart from you. Similarly, if you can know your body, then it is not you. If you can know your mind, then it is not you. If you can know your thoughts, then they are not you. Whatever you know is not you. You are separate from that or above that. That is why you are able to know it. Whether it is the body, thoughts, or emotions, whatever you know is not you.

Now we need to separate these two, the field from the knower of the field. Once we separate these two, the body will be blissful and joyful!

Consciousness will be liberated. When these two join, that is where the problem starts.

A one-liner that I read somewhere said: A man tells his friend, 'My sign is earth and my wife's sign is water. Together we make mud!' Water and earth are beautiful as they are. Only when they are mixed do we get mud!

Similarly, consciousness, as it is, is beautiful and so is the body. When the two meet, that is where the trouble starts. All we need to do is understand the field and the knower, that is, what we are and what we are not. The problem in our lives is that when we identify ourselves with something, we believe we are that. Instead of understanding that we possess a mind, we believe we *are* the mind. The mind then becomes 'I'.

As long as I think this table is mine, there is no problem. If I start thinking that I am this table, the problem starts! As long as we think that our body and mind are ours, there is no problem. But the problem appears the moment we identify with them. Kṛṣṇa says, 'We must understand that whatever we know is not us.' Inch by inch He starts to explain the difference between *kṣetra* and *kṣetrajñya.*

One more thing, when we understand that something is separate from us, we never feel that we must renounce it. We simply need to renounce the idea that we are that particular thing, that's all. In fact, we don't even need to renounce; we will simply know that there is nothing to renounce just by being aware of the way in which our body or mind works. Neither will we feel tortured by them, nor will we feel like torturing them. The people who are tortured by the body and mind are caught in this world and its troubles. Another group of people continuously torture the body and mind in the name of *tapas,* penance.

I have seen people in India practicing yoga by sitting or standing on nails for five years! There are people who torture the body by standing on one leg, rolling on the ground, or walking on fire. There is no need to torture the body in such ways. Actually we torture the body because we think that it is torturing us. We take revenge. At one extreme, people are caught in pleasures of the senses and killing themselves. At the other extreme, people torture the body in the name of penance. Neither knows how to handle the body and mind.

A person who knows how to handle his body and mind enjoys the whole thing. He feels completely relaxed with his body and mind. He intensely enjoys all pleasures and comforts, and he never abuses the body.

Enjoying and abusing are two different things. Enjoying is when the mind and the body are in tune with each other. We feel ease, comfort, a deep sense of relaxation, and a feeling of being at home with ourselves.

And then, there is a category of people that tortures the body for the sake of the mind, in the name of penance or *tapas*. These people are in search of peace. They go on disrespecting and torturing the body: going without food for months together, standing on one leg, standing on nails, or walking on fire. They continuously abuse the body or mind in one way or the other.

Sadists are always masochists and masochists are always sadists. Torturing others happens only when we torture ourselves. Please understand that we torture others when we do not feel comfortable within ourselves, when we are in a low or depressed mood. Torturing others is directly related to torturing ourselves.

If we think that we are the mind, we torture our body, and if we think we are the body, we torture our mind. The person who knows the secrets of the body and mind, neither tortures nor abuses them. He knows how to use them and live blissfully with them. Kṛṣṇa reveals the secrets of how to keep the body and mind in beautiful and blissful energy and the inner space flowing in blissful consciousness.

Kṛṣṇa says further, 'O Bhārata, I am also the Knower in all bodies. To understand this body and the knower is called knowledge.'

Beautiful! Here, Krishna says that understanding the field, or the body-mind, and the consciousness is knowledge. He says, 'I myself reside as the consciousness inside the beings.'

Our consciousness is God and there is no separate thing as God. The problem arises when we start thinking that we are the body and the mind. A person who understands that he is consciousness liberates himself. He is enlightened. He becomes the Buddha. Consciousness is God.

The Equation is:

God + body/mind = man

man – body/mind = God!

You are consciousness

Whether we believe it or not, we *are* consciousness. Let us see how we miss it, how we miss and mess our life!

Here is a beautiful story about knowing the body and the mind and how we miss realizing that we are consciousness.

> A pregnant lioness was hunting for food one day when she came across a flock of sheep. She tried to attack the flock, but the effort was too much for her. She fell on the ground, giving birth to a cub and also died due to the pressure she exerted.
>
> The flock of sheep saw the newborn lion cub. They started playing with him. They felt that they should take care of this cub. They just took pity on him and adopted him. The sheep started taking care of the cub in the same way they care for their young ones, feeding him with milk and grass!
>
> The cub started behaving like a sheep and grew up along with the sheep. He lived happily amongst them, not knowing that they were different from him.
>
> After some time the problem started slowly. The mother sheep started receiving complaints about the behavior of the cub, 'He is too arrogant,' 'He is not playing properly with us.' Naturally the cub was sidelined. Whenever any argument arose, they decided to punish him.

After a few days, the lion cub started to wonder, 'What is this? I don't feel that I am really living. Is this all that there is to life - eating grass, jumping around and bleating, just going around the grasslands? I don't feel I am leading a full life.' He felt that he was unlike the others, that somehow he was different. He did not feel that he was being himself.

Whenever he saw a forest, he was tempted to go and explore the forest. But his sheep mother had warned him that it was the one thing he should not do. She forbade him from straying away from the flock, obviously now considering him to be one of the sheep. She cautioned him that if he did so, the lions inside the forest would kill him.

This whole story is actually about the spiritual seeker! It is about how a person takes birth, starts seeking, and how he achieves fulfillment. It's a wonderful story. I love this story. That is why I repeat this story whenever I can!

The mother sheep said, 'You cannot go there, there are lions out there.' The cub somehow managed to suppress his search or feeling of emptiness even though he felt drawn in and was tempted to go into the forest to explore. After some time he decided, 'I think this life is not for me.' But somehow the mother sheep managed to pressurize and control him. She played a big drama - weeping, crying, convincing, and finally she got this lion married!

A small story within this story:

There was a big marriage going on in the forest. The king lion and a lioness were getting married. All the animals of the forest gathered for the ceremony and were celebrating. At the center, there was a dance floor where a big party was going on, but only the lions were dancing and enjoying. The rest of the animals were scared to join them, so they were standing outside and watching. Amidst this celebration, suddenly a rat jumped onto the dance floor and started dancing.

A lion caught the rat and roared, 'How dare you come onto the dance floor? Don't you see that all the animals are standing outside? Only lions dance here!'

The rat sternly said, 'Keep quiet! I was also a lion before I married!'

Now, coming back to the sheep-lion story, the lion cub got married and a few years passed by. After some years he again started thinking and analyzing, 'What is going on? I am leading the same old life: eating, bleating and jumping around! I feel something is seriously missing! I have found whatever best one can get - a good mother, good wife, nice life - but deep inside me there is only emptiness. I don't feel fulfilled. What is happening to me?'

Again he started searching. The seeking started.

Then suddenly one day a lion from the nearby forest attacked the flock of sheep. When this happened all the sheep ran away. This sheep-lion neither felt like running away, nor did he have the courage to stand and face the lion. He knew the lion was trying to attack, but he thought, 'He looks so graceful. Something about him is different.' He had never seen such a majestic beast before. So, slowly, somehow, unconsciously this sheep-lion felt attracted and drawn towards the lion. Because of the attraction, neither did he run away nor did he have the courage to face the lion, because he thought he was a sheep under attack.

He started walking away slowly but kept his face and gaze fixed on the lion. The lion straightaway came near him and caught him. The sheep-lion started bleating, 'Oh, please leave me alone and do not kill me!' The lion said, 'Fool, I have not come to kill you! You are a lion, why are you bleating and shouting for help? Why do you think I will kill you?'

'Lion?' the sheep-lion suspected that the lion was trying to cheat him and take him to the forest. He became frightened and cried, 'No, leave me.' The lion again said, 'Fool! You are a lion, why don't you understand that?' The sheep-lion refused to believe the lion. He escaped and ran away.

Even though he ran away, the sheep-lion was unable to forget the lion. For a week he was afraid. Fear is usually there after the first glimpse, after the first experience. He had had the first glimpse of the lion! This is how Arjuna felt after his first experience of the Divine, his first glimpse of Kṛṣṇa. It is an experience that evokes fear as well as a blissful attraction.

A week passed by and the fear slowly subsided. He felt drawn to the lion once again. The sheep-lion felt like meeting the lion. 'I think I should meet the lion once more,' he thought. One part of his mind was saying, 'No, no, no, I am afraid that he may kill me,' while another part was saying, 'No, it was such a blissful experience with him. He is so graceful and I want to meet him again!'

Please be very clear that unless you have enlightenment within yourself, you will not feel attracted towards an enlightened person. However, if we have not matured or grown to the level of feeling the enlightenment within us, we may not feel even a slight connection with an enlightened person.

There are millions of people living in this city. Why are only a few hundred sitting here for these lectures? Thousands came at least once and have not come back the second time. Why do only a few come regularly? The moment you feel attracted to an enlightened master's teachings, be very clear that the enlightenment in you has started expressing or flowering!

That is the reason why the sheep-lion remembered the lion and felt attracted to it. He felt the intense urge to see the lion again and finally decided to meet him. But how would he meet him? The lion never sent out flyers saying, 'In such and such a place, I am doing a program! You can meet me here.' The sheep-lion came to the edge of the meadow where the forest started, and waited expectantly every day for the lion to appear.

After a few months the lion appeared. The moment the sheep-lion saw him, his fear surfaced and he was caught in the dilemma once again, despite having waited for months to see him. This time the lion came towards him and asked, 'How are you doing?' The sheep-lion started bleating again, 'I am, I am, I am….'

He was unable to answer, but did not run away as he had done earlier. The lion said, 'Don't worry. If you are afraid, I will go away. I am not going to eat you because you are a lion. And because I can't eat you, I won't kill you. Also, since I see no use in you, there is no reason for me to stay here if you are afraid.' Saying this, the lion started walking back towards the forest.

The sheep-lion immediately pleaded with the lion to stay and spend a few moments with him. He also added, 'Don't come too close. You can stand at a distance and talk. Please stand ten feet away and I will stand here. But please spend some time with me.' The sheep-lion was now neither able to forget the lion and escape, nor did he have the courage to go near him!

This is the next phase of growth for a seeker.

With around ten or fifteen feet between them, they stood and talked. However, again and again the lion said, 'You are a lion. Fool! You think you are a sheep! You are not like the friends you live with. This is not the way you are supposed to live.'

The sheep-lion started to think about what the lion said. Slowly the doubt he had that the lion was going to take him to the forest and eat him disappeared. Now the sheep-lion was convinced that the lion did not have an ulterior motive. He understood that the lion did not benefit in any way because of him. He thought, 'I have nothing to offer him and I am of no use to him.'

Only when this confidence comes into the mind of the disciple, he starts trusting the words of the master!

That is why in the vedic system spiritual knowledge is free. We start trusting the master only when we realize that we cannot contribute to the master in any way, that the master has nothing to gain from us, that he is not missing us. The trust between the master and disciple starts when the disciple understands that he has nothing to add to what the master already has in his being. The master is sharing, because he is overflowing. He is not giving in order to take something from us. Only when you understand that, will you start trusting the master's words.

The sheep-lion developed that much trust on the lion. He thought, 'The lion is not going to kill and eat me. If he wanted to do that, he would have done it long ago. One thing is certain. He is not going to gain anything from me. So why does he say I am a lion?'

Then, the sheep-lion thought about what the lion had said. When we understand that we have nothing to give the master, that he is overflowing out of his ecstasy and he is only sharing the joy and bliss, we start experimenting with things more deeply. Until we understand that whatever the master says is only for our own benefit, we never try to experiment with his words.

The sheep-lion thought about the lion, 'He looks so courageous, so graceful, so bold, and he is radiating so much confidence. It doesn't look like he is lying.' We can clearly tell whether someone is lying or not by seeing the eyes of a person. We don't need a lie detector! All we need to do is look into his eyes. So the sheep-lion thought, 'He doesn't look like a liar. Then why is he again and again telling me that I am a lion? I know I am a sheep.'

The lion then said, 'I think you are not interested in believing me. Anyhow, I am not interested in wasting my time. I am going.' But the sheep-lion begged, 'No, no, no! Please, at least give me an appointment.'

The lion asked why he wanted the appointment. The sheep-lion replied, 'I will go home and think about whatever you have told me. Then I will come back and clear my doubts with you.' The lion agreed, saying he would meet him at the same place in one month's time.

The sheep-lion then started to contemplate, 'How can I be a lion? I know for sure I am a sheep. I eat grass. I bleat like a sheep and go around with sheep. So, how can I be a lion?' He thought and thought.

He considered all the great philosophical questions, the very same questions that I have been answering all these days!

There must have been some books: 'sheep-philosophy,' 'sheep-bible,' 'sheep-gita.' The sheep-lion read all of them and thought of all the possible questions. He made a big list of questions that his mother and father never answered. One important thing though is that he never told his mother that he met the lion, because if she knew she would stop him! She would not have allowed him to go to the edge of the forest. She would have told him, 'Never go there! You must stay in the meadows. You cannot go to the other side, into the forest.'

Parents are afraid for their young ones. They send their children to the temples but never to a *Swami*, never to a spiritual master! To them there is always a danger. See, Swami Vivekānanda is great as long as he takes birth in the neighbor's house, not in our house!

Anyhow, finally, after one month the appointment date arrived. The sheep-lion collected whatever he thought was best grass, as an offering to the lion. He gave it to the lion saying, 'Please have all these things. I preserved them carefully for you.' Seeing the love of the sheep-lion, the lion also acted as if he was eating and enjoying the grass, just so that he could please the sheep-lion and make him feel more connected. He was zeroing down the distance. He wanted the sheep-lion to feel comfortable his presence. Only then could any transformation happen.

Naturally, the sheep-lion asked, 'Is it good? Is it tasty?' The lion said, 'Yes, yes, it is tasty. You cook well. You have done a great job.' Some compliment is given!

After accepting the grass offering, the lion started to slowly say the same things to the sheep-lion, 'I am telling you again and again, but you are not ready to listen. You are a lion, not a sheep.'

By now, the sheep-lion knew that what he was thinking was wrong. Still he was unable to accept what the lion was saying as right. How could he be a lion? He knew by now he was not a sheep. He applied logic, 'My color is different. If I am a sheep, I should be like my friends. I think differently. I do not feel satisfied or comfortable with that life. This means I am something more. But I am unable to understand how I could be a lion.' He was not able to comprehend what the lion said. At the same time he was not sure about what he had been thinking all along.

One day, the lion said to him, 'Come, let us go to a nearby lake for a picnic.' By now the sheep-lion was comfortable with the lion and agreed. When they reached the lake, the lion suddenly grabbed the neck of the sheep-lion, dragged him to the water, and told him to look at the reflection in the water.

The lion asked him, 'Do you see an image of a lion in the reflection?'

The sheep-lion replied, 'Yes, I see your reflection. You are standing.'

The lion asked, 'Do you see another reflection?'

The sheep-lion said, 'Yes, I see another small lion, your baby. Where is the baby? Your baby is not here, but his reflection is here. Is he inside the water?'

The lion roared and said, 'Fool, it is you!'

The sheep-lion refused to believe and said, 'No, no, no, maybe your baby is hiding inside the water. Call him.'

The lion said, 'Fool, it is not my baby. It is you.'

The lion then told him, 'Look, I am now moving away. Only you are standing there. See what is happening!'

The sheep-lion then saw the reflection. Suddenly, the first shock happened to him, 'I think there is some truth in what the lion says.'

Again, he was frightened, 'If I am a lion, I must live in the forest. I cannot take that responsibility. If I am a sheep, I am so comfortable. Already, I know all my sheep friends and I get regular food. I know where food is available. I know where I cook. I know where I eat. I know where my house is. I know where my wife is. I know where my life is. I know all these things and I am completely accustomed to the life of a sheep. But if I understand that I am a lion, the whole thing must be dropped. I must renounce the whole thing. I must take a big jump. It's difficult.' That fear came up and he simply ran away; he escaped one more time.

The first experience

After a few months, the lion came in search of the sheep-lion. This time the sheep-lion did not have any grass offerings. Instead the lion brought an offering of meat for the sheep-lion! When he saw the sheep-lion he didn't talk. There were no intellectual discourses, philosophical discussions, or question-and-answer sessions. Straightaway, he caught hold of the sheep-lion, opened his mouth, and put the meat inside.

The moment the sheep-lion tasted the blood, the moment he tasted the meat, something reeled inside him. Something happened to his being. Something happened to his consciousness. Suddenly he swallowed the meat and roared!

The roaring is what we call enlightenment! Most importantly, the sheep-lion realized that he had been a lion from the beginning, from day one!

The same thing happens in our lives. Again and again, we think we are sheep. At some point, we start suspecting, 'I am not feeling satisfied with this life. What is happening?' And after some time, suddenly we see a lion that teaches us, 'You are God. You are that energy. You are consciousness.' We get scared and run away. At home we start thinking, 'I think he has some plans. He wants to build an ashram and he needs me for it. That is why he says these things.'

After a few days we realize that he already has an ashram; we don't need to build one for him or contribute to his ashram. We realize that he has everything and doesn't need anything. Then slowly we start analyzing, 'Why is he coming everyday and saying the same thing?

Everyday he comes, and for two or three hours he says the same thing in a loud voice. Why?' After a few days we think, 'One thing is certain, whatever I think about me is wrong. But I don't know whether whatever he says is right or not.'

During meditation, one glimpse of consciousness happens. When that happens we again run away with the fear. 'No, no. This is not for me. If the same thing happens again, I may leave everything and go after him.' At this stage the master suddenly catches hold of us and puts the meat of solid spiritual experience into our mouth. Something happens in our system, in our consciousness. Suddenly we open our eyes and roar, declaring the experience that happened in our being. We realize that from day one, from the beginning, we have been That. The sheep-lion has always been a lion.

But it requires another lion to make a sheep-lion realize that he is indeed a lion.

From day one, we are the knower or the *kṣetrajñya,* the consciousness. But by mistake we start thinking that we are the body-mind. Suddenly a person who has already experienced that he is consciousness guides us saying, 'This is consciousness and that is body-mind. Understand that you are consciousness.'

Here, the same story is happening between Kṛṣṇa and Arjuna. Kṛṣṇa explains *kṣetra* and *kṣetrajñya.* He tells Arjuna that he is not a sheep but a lion; he is not merely the field, he is the knower of the field.

Consciousness and Conscience

13.4 *Understand my summary of this field of activity and how it is constituted; what its changes are, how it is produced, who that knower of the field of activities is, and what his influences are.*

13.5 *That knowledge of the field of activities and of the knower of activities are described by various sages in the scriptures.*
It is presented with all reasoning as to cause and effect.

13.6,7 *The field of activities and its interactions are said to be: the five elements of nature, false ego, intelligence, the mind, the formless, the ten senses of perception and action, as well as the five objects of senses and desire: hatred, happiness, distress, the aggregate, the life symptoms, and convictions.*

Kṛṣṇa asks Arjuna to listen carefully to His explanation of what constitutes *kṣetra*, body-mind, and its activities, its changes, and how they are produced. These truths have been explained by many *ṛṣis*, sages, from time to time. The vedic scriptures, the Brahma Sūtras for example, express these truths with clarity, using sharp reasoning.

In these verses, Kṛṣṇa takes Arjuna step-by-step into what these activities are and how they interact with each other.

Kṛṣṇa talks about the five great elements, the false ego, the intelligence or the mind that makes decisions, and all ten senses. Please understand, He says, 'ten senses,' *indriyāṇi daśakaṁ ca*. We think we have five senses. No. We have five *karmendriya* and five *jñānendriya. Karmendriya* are the senses or organs responsible for actions such as talking, walking, etc., and they are the mouth, hands and feet, organs of excretion and reproduction. *Jñānendriya* are our five senses that receive knowledge such as smell, taste, sight, touch, and hearing, and they are the nose, tongue, eyes, skin, and ear. So, all the ten senses, plus attachment, aversion, joy, sorrow, the body, mutual attraction, and the consciousness contribute to the field of activities.

Actually the word 'consciousness' cannot be used. When our consciousness becomes rigid, it becomes conscience. There's a difference between conscience and consciousness.

For example, we do something based upon what we think is right or wrong according to our conscience. If we give these same teachings to the next generation, it will not work because something else may be right or wrong for them. When we force them to follow the same thing that we did, we are giving it as just a morality, as just a conscience. We are giving them a law without the spirit. On the other hand, when we give them understanding about life, when we give our next generation an understanding about life, we give them consciousness.

Conscience is suffering

Please be very clear that a person with only conscience always suffers. He can never be happy, whether he enjoys or renounces. If he enjoys, he suffers from guilt. If he renounces, he feels the lack of it. He suffers either way. Never give conscience to the next generation, always give them an understanding about life, what I call consciousness. Let them experience and explore.

I do not believe in morality. I believe in conscious experience. I do not believe in conscientiousness. I believe in consciousness.

Conscience is given to us by society. Consciousness is given to us by God.Conscience is social conditioning. Consciousness is our very nature.

Conscience naturally makes our whole life into a ritual. We should know what we are doing before doing anything. Only then will we do it intensely. If we do not know the logic behind what we are doing, we will not put ourselves completely into it and dedicate ourselves to it.

Kṛṣṇa says that the rigid sense of conscience, all the rules that form the *kṣetra,* are also the field. They are matter. They are not energy. They are not your being. They are not you. Whatever is mentioned here is not you. We should understand we are liberated the moment we know what we are not. We are liberated even if we live with what is not us. Even if we live with our body-mind, if we know that we are not the body and the mind, then we are not their slaves to it!

Please understand that the word 'slavery' can be used as long as something goes against your will. With awareness, even if you live with the body-mind, you are not their slave.

Let me tell you a small story about the life of a Greek sage named Diogenes.

> Diogenes was an enlightened master. A group of people plotted against him and attacked him. He did not react as they had expected. They went prepared to capture him and expected him to retaliate. They were shocked at his response.
>
> He maintained his composure and asked his attackers, 'What do you want?' He asked them like a master.
>
> The attackers were shaken. One of them said that they wanted to capture him and sell him in the slave market.
>
> Diogenes replied, 'Oh, you should have told me that straightaway. Why did you waste your time making plans and discussing? Come, put on the handcuffs. Where are they?'
>
> The attackers were completely taken aback. For the first time they saw a man ordering them to handcuff him! He spoke like a master when he asked them to put the handcuffs on. Finally, they somehow

took out the handcuffs, cuffed his wrist on one side, and locked their own hands on the other side.

Diogenes said, 'Fools, why are you tying up yourselves? Don't you believe me? I was the one who gave the order to handcuff me. Come, let us go wherever you want to take me and sell me. But be very clear, don't run away from me.'

The people who caught him were now slightly frightened. They couldn't understand what was going on. Slowly, they started feeling small and inadequate themselves. Diogenes said, 'Fools, I know the technique of freedom. I know the basic rules of freedom. I constantly experience tremendous inner freedom. Nothing can bind me. Try your best to play your game and let's see where it leads.'

Saying thus, he walked onto the road like a king. His captors followed behind like slaves.

He told the people who were standing on the road and looking at the curious sight, 'They are my slaves because they cannot leave me.' They retorted that Diogenes was the slave.

He replied, 'See, even now if you leave me, I will run away. But now I am letting you go. Can you run away? I am setting you free from this handcuff. Will you run away?' He continued, 'You won't. You need something from me and that makes you my slaves, whereas I want nothing from you. Therefore, I am the master! I am liberated.'

You may not be handcuffed physically, but still you can be a slave by attitude. Slavery is related to the being and not the body.

They took him to the market. Straightaway, he walked to the table where slaves are sold. The auction began. The auctioneer called out, 'Here is a slave. Bidders are welcome and the highest bidder can claim him.'

Diogenes at that point said, 'Stop! Don't say, *Here is a slave.* Say instead, *Here is a master. If you can afford to bid on him, come.*' Nobody dared to bid for a master and therefore nobody bought him. After three days his captors felt burdened that they had to unnecessarily feed him, knowing that nobody would buy him. They felt, 'If we continue to sit here he may sell us. We don't know what he is capable of.'

So they set him free.

This may be a story. Yet the truth behind the story is that nothing can enslave us once we understand that we are not body and mind. We can never become a slave to anything. Even slavery cannot enslave us. Slavery can enslave us as long as we are not ready to cooperate with slavery. This is a subtle point. When we understand that we are beyond body and mind, we will feel no need to resist when somebody tries to enslave us. We know that we can never be slaves.

That is why Kṛṣṇa teaches the secret of understanding the body-mind and consciousness, *kṣetra* and *kṣetrajñya*. In ancient times, man was only subjected to physical slavery. In the present day, man is subjected to psychological slavery. Understand, we are the psychological slaves of countless things that attract us from our environment. As I said earlier, these are our wants that we borrow from others, not the needs we are born with.

When some product is advertised on television, straightaway it sits in our head. Within a few days, we somehow get money and buy that product. We live in a world of psychological slavery. Once we understand that we are not the body-mind, that we are beyond it, we will be totally free from physical and psychological slavery.

See, it is like this. When we badly want a particular object or event to happen, our happiness is in the hands of that object or event. That external object or event has the power to control our happiness. We feel depressed when things turn out other than the way we desired. We feel the world is unfair. Many people ask me, 'Why has God been so unfair to me? Why is it that only I face these difficulties?' Please understand, the moment you place your happiness in the hands of something or someone, you have become their slave. They can exploit you.

One more thing is that even the thought of wanting freedom can exploit us if we allow it. Many times we chase freedom in the name of spiritual seeking. Freedom happens only when we realize that there is no need to chase. We must drop the idea of wanting freedom and just trust the freedom. We will then experience it. Otherwise, craving for freedom can enslave us. We realize the futility of this struggle and experience freedom only when we become aware that we are already free.

The minute we accept whatever we have, we start flowing and stop resisting. We stop giving someone or something the power to control our happiness. Nothing will enslave us. We will experience the consciousness of freedom.

Inner Science Technology

13.8-12 Humility, absence of pride, nonviolence, tolerance, simplicity, service to an enlightened spiritual master, cleanliness, steadiness and self-control; renunciation of the objects of sense gratification; absence of ego, the perception of the pain of the cycle of birth and death, old age and disease;
Nonattachment to children, wife, home and the rest, and even-mindedness amid pleasant and unpleasant events; constant and unalloyed devotion to Me, resorting to solitary places, detachment from the general mass of people; accepting the importance of self realization, and philosophical search for the absolute truth:
All these, I thus declare to be knowledge and anything contrary to these is ignorance.

In these five verses, Kṛṣṇa gives a beautiful technique. Until this point He gave us an intellectual understanding. Now He gives the technique and technology to realize and experience what He says. I call these five verses, the inner science technology to liberate our inner space! It is a precise technique to liberate oneself from the *kṣetra*. It talks about how to be liberated from the body-mind and how to bring them under our control.

First, the moment we understand that we are more powerful than the body-mind, we are liberated from the body and the mind. Here, He beautifully gives the technique to liberate us from the body-mind and therefore, how to experience the consciousness.

Let me first give the translation of the verses:

'Humility, non-violence, tolerance, simplicity, approaching the bona fide spiritual master, cleanliness, steadfastness, self-control, renunciation of the objects of sense gratification, absence of all egos, perception of all the evils of birth and death, old age and diseases, detachment, freedom from all entanglements, even-mindedness amidst pleasant and unpleasant events, constant devotion, aspiring to live in a spiritual way, giving importance to the ultimate truth, and detachment. All these I declare to be knowledge and besides these, whatever there may be, is ignorance.'

Kṛṣṇa mentions a long list of things in these verses with many instructions. Let me be very clear, that if we straightaway try to practice all the qualities He has given here, we will feel we are going mad! We cannot really practice these qualities. All we can do is help the consciousness to happen in us so that we start radiating these qualities. These qualities simply happen in us.

By way of comparison, let us say we want to remove the dirt from a muddy water tank. If we put our hands into the tank and try to take away the mud, what happens? We make it muddier, that's all. All the dirt that is settled below will come up to the surface. Instead, if we sprinkle a handful of lime powder inside the tank, it will absorb the dirt and we can have clean water in the tank.

Our mind is also like a muddy tank. If we try to suppress it and fight with it, we will create more trouble. Instead just add a little meditation, which is like the lime powder, and relax. Just put in your awareness and relax. Automatically the impurities will settle down. The moment we become aware and the witnessing consciousness starts operating, the whole thing settles down. The witnessing consciousness is the lime powder that purifies our being.

Usually, when we read scriptures and books, we start executing them straightaway! For example, if it says, 'Love your neighbor as you love yourself,' we start executing it without understanding. The first difficulty is that we don't understand that we don't love ourselves. And we don't understand that we cannot love somebody unless we first love ourselves. Next, we must have the mood or consciousness from which the loving happens naturally. Love happens as an automatic process.

The minute we impose love on others, it becomes a business transaction. We only know the contaminated version of love. Pure love is not about loving for security or with some other expectation of return. Pure love is an expression of the being. It just happens. If we are true to our being, true to our core, that is enough. Straightaway we will be liberated.

Rāmakṛṣṇa says that if the straight line of honesty connects your mouth and mind, you will be liberated. We cheat ourselves if we engage in an activity because it is appreciated by society and not because we feel it from within. This constant mismatch of internal and external, of what we feel deep within and what we do, creates problems.

Instead of creating consciousness, we start creating the activity. Instead of working on our being, we work on our doing. Our doing is in no way going to help us. Only our being is going to help us. So work on the being and not on the doing. A person who works on his doing may continuously chisel, chisel, and chisel his doing; however, his being will face the same old struggle: suppression, suffering, and fighting. Instead, if we work on our being, we will flower and automatically radiate the right energy, the right consciousness!

You are unique

Normally we believe others' opinions about us. We accept their scale as a standard for measuring ourselves. Then we get into trouble. This is what I call 'guilt'. Guilt is reviewing our past decisions with updated intelligence. If we use our present intelligence to review our past decisions, we create guilt and suffering.

Please be very clear that we are updated every second. Our intelligence is continuously updated. So naturally when we look back and analyze what happened in the past, we feel certain things could have been avoided.

The problem is that we think we are responsible for everything. If we remember that the universe is pure Intelligence, that knows how to take care of our lives, we will simply relax. Also, when we allow the cosmic intelligence to operate, we spontaneously express the beautiful qualities that Kṛṣṇa enumerates.

Kṛṣṇa first talks about humility or *amānitvaṁ*. Humility can never be achieved by effort. If it is attempted through effort, it looks ugly. Humility happens when we feel that every being is unique. It does not come by thinking that everyone is equal. There are no equals! If we deeply understand that every being is unique, we automatically respect everyone. One important thing that you must know is that even our enemy contributes to our growth! He may do it indirectly, but nevertheless he contributes to our growth. We are here as long as we contribute.

Normally we evaluate whether a person is worthy of our respect. We have our own scales to measure this. We will see how well qualified he is, how much society respects him. Then we will decide, 'Okay, I think I can show him some respect.' When we understand that every being is a unique creation of the universe, that the same divinity that is in us is in them also, we automatically radiate humility and the absence of pride. This is what Kṛṣṇa explains.

Another important thing: How should we approach a bona fide spiritual master or *ācāryopāsana?* He talks about this in another verse also: *tad viddhi praṇipātena paripraśnena sevayā.* It means that we should approach the master with questions and request him to answer the questions. Why? Why does Kṛṣṇa say that? What is the need? Again and again, spiritual literature repeatedly emphasizes the master. It is not only in the Bhagavad Gītā. Whether it is Zen Buddhism, Jainism, Judaism, Islam, or Christianity, again and again the master plays an important role. Why? Especially in *Vedānta,* the vedic system, the master plays a major role. Why?

Unless we see someone continuously living in the consciousness and continuously expressing that consciousness, our unconscious refuses to believe it is possible. Our head and heart fight with each other because of this. Our intellect says, 'No, no, no! These are all truths.' Logically we are convinced but emotionally we are unable to experience it.

When we see a living master, our emotions also automatically start experiencing it. Our unconscious, which continuously questions, becomes silent when we see a living master. With books we learn through verbal language; with a master we learn through his body language. He is a living example that proves the truth. He proves that these things can become a reality for us in our life. Three things happen when we meet an enlightened master:

First, we see in front of our own eyes that it is possible to live in eternal bliss or in bliss consciousness all 24 hours of the day. The assurance and inspiration to achieve that state is there. We understand the possibility. Next we ask, 'All right, it is possible for the master, but is it possible for *me?*' That assurance is also given when we reach the master.

The master instills the confidence in us by showing us, 'If I can achieve, why not you?'

It is like this: the seed is afraid to sprout and thinks, 'I may die if I rupture and sprout.' But the tree says, 'No, you must break open. Only when you break open can I happen.' The tree within the seed is waiting for the seed to break so that it can come out, but the seed is waiting for the tree to happen! The seed thinks, 'Who knows whether the tree will happen?' The tree says, 'Open, only then can I happen.' But the seed tells the tree, 'No, let me see you happen and only then will I open.'

We are afraid of the insecurity and uncertainty. But the master offers this guarantee.

A small story:

> A journalist interviews a candidate for the presidential election. While delivering his speech earlier, the candidate had claimed that he could see that his future was bright. So the journalist asked him during the interview, 'If that is so, why do you look worried?'

The candidate said, 'My certainty doesn't come with a warranty. I am optimistic but it is not a guarantee!'

We too are stuck in this way! We are optimistic that we may have the experience. At the same time we are afraid to take the risk.

The master has already become a tree. He gives confidence to the disciple. He says, 'Don't worry, I also struggled like you. Look at me, I have flowered, I have not died. I have become a tree. If you open, you will also become a tree.' He sits with us and assures us that he will take care. He creates the energy and gives confidence to open and become a tree. He reminds us, 'When I have achieved, why not you?'

Third, the master creates the right space or technology for the tree to happen. He creates the right conditions, the right soil, water, etc. All that we need to do is trust the master and break open. That is why masters create ashrams. An ashram is a space that allows us to break open. The seed can open and the tree can happen. It is similar to an operation theatre where you go, open, become a tree and start radiating the experience. The ashram is a space where the conditions are controlled, and in a secure and safe way we can enter into the consciousness.

The master makes us experience the truth, which is in our very being. So first, he assures us of the possibility through his body language. Next, he makes us understand that it is possible for us also. Third, he creates a space in which it can happen. Fourth, he ensures that we are established in that consciousness. These are the responsibilities of a master. That is why the vedic system, the vedic way of life, insists again and again that we reach a living enlightened master. This is what Kṛṣṇa calls *ācāryopāsana*. He gives the important guidelines for us to experiment with the technology.

Consciousness Is Eternal

13.13 *I shall give you the full understanding about the knowable, with which one can taste eternal bliss or the being or the consciousness that has no beginning.*
A life beyond the law of cause, effect, and the material world.

13.14 *With hands and feet everywhere, with eyes, heads, and mouths everywhere, with ears everywhere, He exists in the worlds, enveloping all.*
The Paramātman *(supreme spirit) is all pervading. He exists everywhere.*

13.15 *The* Paramātman *is the original source of all the senses. Yet, He is beyond all the senses. He is unattached.*
Although the consciousness is the maintainer of all the living beings, yet He transcends the modes of nature, and at the same time He is the master of the modes of our material nature.

13.16 *The supreme Truth exists both internally and externally, in the moving and nonmoving. It is beyond the power of the material senses to see or to know Him.*
Although far, far away, He is also near to all.

13.17 *Although the* Paramātman *appears to be divided, He is never divided. He is situated as one.*
Although He is the maintainer of every living entity, it is to be understood that He consumes and creates all.

13.18 *He is the source of light in all luminous objects. He is beyond the darkness of matter and is formless.*
He is knowledge, He is the object of knowledge, and He is the goal of knowledge. He is situated in everyone's heart.

Kṛṣṇa says, 'I shall explain the knowable, knowing which, you will taste the eternal Being, the beginning-less consciousness that lies beyond the causes and effects of this material world.' In the previous verses, Kṛṣṇa talks about the qualities that happen with the flowering of the divine consciousness within. Now He reveals to Arjuna that this consciousness is eternal.

Please understand that our mind associates a time and space with every incident or event. The mind can only think chronologically. It is like an inner reference chart and all incidents are placed in this chart of time and space. Modern science asks questions like, 'How did this happen? What was there before this? What came after this? What triggered this?' When they asked about the creation of this universe, they explained it with the Big Bang theory.

They said that a tiny mass of fire exploded and gave rise to our universe. What they could not answer was, 'What existed before that?' Kṛṣṇa says that this universal energy, the ultimate consciousness, always existed. It manifested in various forms as planets, as humans and so on, but it is eternal. It will continue to manifest itself and return to the Source and it will always exist.

The concept of time and space that we have is based on our mind and senses. Whatever we perceive is a projection of our mind. This understanding of time is different from an enlightened master's understanding. He measures time in terms of *kṣaṇa*. *Kṣaṇa* is the time between two thoughts. It is the space between two thoughts. Buddha referred to this time and space as *śūṇya*. Ādi Śaṅkarācārya referred to it as *pūrṇa*. It is the no-mind zone, the mindful zone, in which we touch base with ourselves. It is the present moment, in which we come face to face with the divinity within, by which we recognize the cosmic energy that is our essential nature.

When we are caught in chasing one material pleasure after another we have so much stress, tension, and worry bombarding our heads every second. Our *kṣaṇa* is very small because of the high number of thoughts inside us. This is why we get a suffocated, panicking feeling. We are running in a rat race. We constantly feel time is running out. We are greedy for more and more experiences before this body dies and we are afraid that we might lose whatever we have come to possess.

We feel this way because we associate ourselves with the *kṣetra,* the temporary body and mind. Please understand that the body and mind are made up of the five elements and they return to their source once they have served their purpose.

On the other hand, an enlightened master knows he is *kṣetrajñya.* He knows that he is not the body-mind system. He has realized that he is the ultimate consciousness. He has no urgency to run in the rat race, because he knows that life goes on, even if this body perishes. He has become a witness to the mind. Any thought that springs up will be only an action-oriented thought, never an unproductive thought. The moment the thought happens, it will immediately expresses itself as an action. No thoughts accumulate inside him. He experiences eternity because of this thoughtless zone that he stays in. This is the beginninglessness of the consciousness that Kṛṣṇa explains here.

The master's help

When we are in front of an enlightened master, one who is in a no-mind state, the number of thoughts in us also comes down and our *kṣaṇa* becomes longer. The gaps between thoughts increase. So without even trying, we become calmer, more peaceful, and more aware!

This positivity and negativity, creation and destruction, are all properties of the changing world around us, of the *kṣetra* that we live in. The minute we know that we are not this changing *kṣetra* but the eternal and unmoving *kṣetrajñya* (the consciousness that runs the *kṣetra),* we are liberated.

Kṛṣṇa calls this eternal bliss *jñeya,* knowable. When the knowing happens, the knowable *(jñeya),* knower *(jñātā),* and the knowledge *(jñāna)* merge. In this experience, the knower, known, and knowledge become one. No separate experience, experiencer, or object of experience exists. It is called *triputi*, where no difference between the three entities exists.

It is like this: Imagine that you love driving and are sitting in a nice new car with all automatic systems and you are driving on a highway at full speed. You are so immersed in that joy of driving the car that you forget yourself. After some time you suddenly realize you are not even driving; the driving is simply happening. You have become the experience of driving and there is no more a sense of you doing the driving. The car is moving forward on its own and you have become the experience. Similarly, if you are immersed and involved deeply in any other passion, the experience, experiencer and object of experience suddenly merge into the eternal consciousness. You call it being 'in the Zone.'

Kṛṣṇa explained that His eternal nature, the eternal Self, is not bound by time. Now He says that He exists everywhere and He is not bound by space. Normally we understand the presence or absence of an object or person in terms of physical attributes. We function in our lives based upon what we see, smell, touch, taste and hear. If our *pañca indriya*, five senses, cannot sense anything, we think nothing exists.

One important and surprising thing is that an enlightened master is more present in his absence than in his physical presence. His energy transcends time and space and is always available everywhere forever!

When you are in the energy field of an enlightened master who is no longer in his body, as in a *jīva samādhi*, the final resting place of the master's body, without even making an effort, you become calmer and experience that space of peace within. Many great temples such as Tirupati, Tiruvannamalai, Mantrālaya and Pazhani in India are built around the final resting places of enlightened masters. That is why these places serve as powerful energy centers today, drawing millions of people every year.

Although physically the master is no longer in the body, we feel his presence. Why? Because he is not bound in space by the body. The cosmic energy that he manifests transcends space and time. Only we know physical barriers. Here, Kṛṣṇa uses the phrase, 'eyes everywhere.'

When Kṛṣṇa says, 'Hands and feet everywhere, eyes, head, ears and mouths everywhere,' what does He mean?

The women who used to look after the cowherds during Kṛṣṇa's time, that is the *gopīs,* were great devotees of Kṛṣṇa. Despite their other household chores, they were soaked in devotion for Kṛṣṇa all the time. It is said in the *rās līlā* - divine play of Kṛṣṇa wherein he gave the experience of universal consciousness to the *gopīs* - that Kṛṣṇa danced with each of the hundred thousand *gopīs* in Brindavan. Kṛṣṇa manifested a form for each of the *gopīs* in order to dance with them individually. It was not merely one form, one body of Kṛṣṇa, but one hundred thousand forms manifesting simultaneously.

Please understand the deeper meaning in this. Each *gopī* was so deeply connected with that divine consciousness, the Kṛṣṇa consciousness, that each one felt His presence. When we go within, into our core, we see divinity in everything. The *gopīs* saw Kṛṣṇa everywhere and in everything they did. This universal consciousness knows no physical barriers. That is why Kṛṣṇa says He is 'all pervading'. He is all enveloping. He is omnipresent.

That is why I say, 'All those who I ordain as healers are my hands, all our *ācāryas* (teachers) are my *vāk* (energy of verbal expression), and all our organizers are my mind.' I can only heal a limited number of people with these two physical hands. I can only conduct a limited number of discourses and programs with this one mouth, and I can only organize a limited number of events with this one brain. That is why I operate through my healers, teachers and organizers. The cosmic Nithyananda operates through them!

For a phone connection to happen from one country to another, we need to have the infrastructure: all the cables installed below the sea and so forth. But for this cosmic connection to happen, nothing is needed. If we simply connect to the Self within, suddenly there will be no barriers. We will simply fly!

Kṛṣṇa goes on to give further qualities of the Self. But understand that all this is said only to inspire us to experience it first hand ourselves. If somebody asks us, 'What does sugar taste like?' and if he has never tasted anything sweet before, how will you explain to him? You may tell him, 'It will be in the form of white cubes, transparent, very sweet.' When he asks, 'What does 'sweet' mean?', what will you say? You can continue to tell him other things about it, 'Sugar is made from sugar cane. Sugar cane is full of sugary syrup, it is fibrous, you can chew on it.' What is the use?

Instead if he puts a handful of sugar in his mouth, he will automatically say, 'This is how sugar tastes! This is how something sweet tastes!' Unless he experiences what 'sweet' means, things will remain a theory for him, although the conviction about sugar might grow in him.

But the problem for intellectuals is that they are clouded with doubts and skepticism, so a theoretical explanation is important. We want to measure everything based on what we know. Kṛṣṇa is compassionate. He is patient.

In Chapter 11, He revealed to Arjuna His cosmic form, the *viśvarūpa darśan*. But soon after that, Arjuna feels intimidated and cannot handle the energy. He pleads with Kṛṣṇa, 'I cannot understand You. I cannot withstand Your glory.' But Arjuna wants to know what Kṛṣṇa is talking about. So once again Kṛṣṇa gives all kinds of descriptions to penetrate Arjuna's doubts and fears.

The compassion of an enlightened master is so great. In spite of the doubts and skepticism, he quietly and patiently sits with the disciple until, one by one, all doubts are washed away. You see, our doubts and questions arise from our mind, forming a thick layer over us. A master's grace gently dissolves this layer.

In this verse, He says that He is responsible for the functioning of all senses, but is beyond them. He is responsible for any life that happens, but is detached from it. He is the one who causes the three main qualities of aggression, laziness, and goodness to happen, but is beyond all three of them.

Kṛṣṇa says all life happens, because of the thread of the universal energy flowing through Him. You see, so many things are happening around us, on their own, beyond our awareness. When we put a piece of bread in our mouth, we chew and swallow it. After that, the whole process of converting this to energy happens without our giving instructions. Forget giving instructions, we don't even know what is happening inside. Today, scientists may understand the chemical reactions, but they still don't know what differentiates a dead cell from a living cell. How then can one understand the universe and all the millions of stars and planets in the galaxies, running in perfect synchronization? Is there any policeman sitting in space and controlling them? No!

Please understand that the life force that conducts the whole show, that controls every breath we take, the same energy that maintains an order in the chaos of the universe, is pure intelligence. In Sanskrit there is a saying that means not even a blade of grass can move without the will of the Divine.

Kṛṣṇa is sending a message to us about how much we depend on Him, who is the cosmic intelligence, for anything to happen. At the same time, without getting involved, the universal energy is a witness to all activities and all life forms.

If we look deeper, we realize that whatever we see and perceive as objects, are creations of the mind along with the senses. We create a world of our own. Deep down, the true Self watches the whole thing without getting involved. Our mind reacts to a particular situation, causing pain or happiness. The mind projects some people as good, some as bad, some incident as painful, others as joyful, etc., and then runs after or away from the people and experiences.

Rāmakṛṣṇa, an enlightened master from West Bengal, India, gives a beautiful analogy. When we stand in a valley, we see pits and depressions on the ground if we look down, and mountain cliffs when we look up. But when we climb up to the summit, we observe that all the ups and downs below no longer matter. We have transcended the ups and downs that we saw when we were on the ground. If we grasp and clutch onto our past, and onto the pains and joys, we keep missing the present moment. We miss eternity. We miss our consciousness inside.

The space within

We see the world full of objects with different qualifiers, because we associate ourselves with a fixed entity. We have created a reference point. Whatever we do, what we think is based on this reference point. We live in this space enclosed by our physical boundary called *ghaṭākāśa*.

There are three spaces we can live in: The space that is covered by the body, the space that is covered by the mind, and the space that cannot be covered by body and mind. The first is *ghaṭākāśa,* or the space enclosed by this physical body. This space exists inside our physical body. Most of us live in this space nearly all the time. The next is *cidākāśa,* the space that you are aware and conscious of. Right now, if you are aware of this hall it is your *cidākāśa*. This is the space of the thoughts and mind. The third is *mahākāśa*. This is the whole space, cosmos, everything put together.

The *ghaṭākāśa* is made up of the five elements that are: earth, water, fire, air, and ether. These elements become subtler as we move up, from earth, to water, to fire, to air, to ether. None of the first four reflect consciousness. Ether, the subtlest element, connects with consciousness. It reflects consciousness. And that is the reason why we are alive. The problem is, we think consciousness is bound by *ghaṭākāśa*. We think it is limited to this body.

That is why we make this body the reference when we view the outer world. We think this body is the 'I' that sees the rest of the world. You see, all science had this as its basic foundation: we are separate entities defined by physical boundaries. Enlightened masters who have moved beyond *ghaṭākāśa* into *mahākāśa* understand that all this division of space is due to our ignorance.

Please understand that space can never be divided. Yet we divide it into boundaries because of our limited understanding. This is the cause for our suffering. Whatever space we may be in, the possibility of achieving a higher space is available to every one of us. Man, as such, is only potentiality. He is not actuality. He is not what he is supposed to be. As of now we are in seed form and have not expressed our potential fully. We have not become trees yet. But that does not mean we cannot grow and become trees. When we transcend these relative boundaries we will understand through experience what Kṛṣṇa says.

Kṛṣṇa says that the supreme truth is inside and outside all living entities. It is moving and non-moving on account of being subtle. This is the space of *mahākāśa,* which includes the space of everything. This space is absolute. Everything is included in this space. When there is no 'two,' how can we compare? How can we say something is near or far when there is only one? The truth is absolute and one.

When we pour water into containers of different shapes and sizes, it takes on their shapes. Water in each of the jars appears to be different from the others. If we carefully examine their contents, all of them contain the same water. Similarly, the world of many forms and shapes, so many species of plants and animals, appears as though there is so much variety. Underlying them all is the same energy. The *prāṇa śakti,* life force, running in each of them is the same. If we understand this simple theory of life - that we came from the same Source and we return to it - we will realize that we are connected to something much greater than our individual self.

A small story:

Once a boy saw a truck being hauled by another truck with the help of a rope. Both the trucks were moving slowly and causing a traffic jam. The boy saw this and started laughing loudly. The truck driver didn't understand what was happening and asked the boy why he laughed. The boy replied, 'You are using two trucks to carry a rope. That is why I am laughing.'

This is how our life is now. When we are in ignorance, we are fooled by everything in the world and we miss what it really is. The universal consciousness manifests in numerous ways and is also responsible for destruction. When the same universal energy is unmanifest, unexpressed, it exists in potential form. This is referred to as *puruṣa* in the scriptures. When this energy manifests itself in this world, taking various names, forms, and shapes, it expresses itself as *prakṛti*. *Prakṛti* is the creative expression of *puruṣa*. The water of the ocean is the *puruṣa* and the waves that dance and play are *prakṛti*. Kṛṣṇa reminds Arjuna that the supreme spirit appears to be divided into *puruṣa* and *prakṛti*, because of the different creations and expressions of *prakṛti*; however, He is beyond all this and exists undivided.

Kṛṣṇa says that He is the supreme Self, or witnessing consciousness that is the source of all light in all luminous objects.

The universal consciousness gives energy to all sources of light such as the sun, moon, stars, and in today's world, artificial lighting. Kṛṣṇa calls this Self the 'Source of light'. The Self is pure intelligence and this knowledge dispels ignorance. An enlightened master sees everything with clarity. He sees the truth as it is. You see, when you are in a dark room you are ignorant of what is present in that room. When the lights are switched on, you become aware of things around you.

An enlightened master uses the lamp of consciousness to see the truth as it is, without any filters. Using this lamp, he experiences his surroundings in totality. This lamp is not like any other lamp; it cuts the layers of ignorance, however deep they may be. That is why the master sees 360 degrees around him. He does not filter what he sees like we do. Please understand, the filtering that we do is the cause of our problems.

We do not see whatever exists *as* it exists. We distort it to suit our ideas that are born out of the ego of our engraved memories.

Forget all about the ego, which is the darkness that obscures our vision. To expel the darkness bring a lamp of awareness into your being. When your entire consciousness has become a flame, the ego is no more.

Understanding The Energy

13.19 *Thus the field of activities, knowledge and the knowable has been summarily described by Me.*
It is only when we can understand the true nature of our supreme Self and the material world with which we have created false identities that we can go beyond this and attain the supreme Self itself.

13.20 Prakṛti *or the field and its attributes and* puruṣa *or the knower or the supreme consciousness are both without beginning.*
All the transformations of nature that we see are produced by the field, or prakṛti.

13.21 *In the production of the body and the senses,* prakṛti *is said to be the cause;*
In the experience of pleasure and pain, puruṣa *is said to be the cause.*

13.22 *The living entity in the material nature follows the way of life, enjoying the moods of nature.*
Due to association with the material nature, it meets the good or evil among various species.

13.23 *Yet, in this body there is a transcendental energy.*
He who is divine, who exists as an owner or the witness, supporter, enjoyer and the pure witnessing consciousness, is known as the Paramātman.

13.24 *One who understands this philosophy concerning material nature, the living entity and the interaction of the modes of nature is sure to attain liberation.*
He will not take birth here again, regardless of his present position.

Kṛṣṇa delivers this discourse of the Bhagavad Gītā to Arjuna standing in a chariot on the battlefield of *kurukṣetra*. If you look a little deeper, this is a beautiful picture of each of us. Kṛṣṇa represents the Self, the charioteer, knower of the field, the one who runs the show. If the charioteer does not know how to take charge, the horses start to pull the chariot in different directions.

These horses symbolize the senses and the mind pulling us to different places as they please, thus leaving us in a state of confusion in everything that we do. If we are not ready to control the horses, the horses will control us. This is what happens in our lives. Due to our lack of understanding about how to drive the chariot, we conveniently give the horses the authority.

The very understanding about the *kṣetra*, meaning the material things around us, teaches us how to control the mind and senses. The minute we understand the *kṣetra*, the body-mind, we realize we are not the *kṣetra*! If we are the *kṣetra*, then how can we understand it? You see, we can read this book because we are not the book, there is a separation between the book and us. In the same way, only when we understand the *kṣetra*, do we understand that we are not the *kṣetra*. This understanding that we are not the *kṣetra* brings with it the understanding that we are the *kṣetrajñya*. When we realize that we are the *kṣetrajñya*, we have transcended the *kṣetra*.

Life is a dream

Actually, there is no such thing as *kṣetra*. It is a projection of the mind, just like a dream. You see, when we go to bed we know that we are so-and-so, husband or wife of so-and-so, working in such-and-such company, etc. We know our whole identity with solid clarity when we go to sleep. We know that even if we have dreams, they are not real. We will wake up the next day and continue our life at the office, with our children and so on.

But the minute we drift into the dream state, we start to think that the dream is real. The more we get into the dream, the more our identity completely changes to suit the role in the dream. What happens in the dream may not be related to what we do in real life. Yet we start to believe it all. If a lion in the dream attacks us, we feel fear and worry and we may even sweat as though it is really happening to us!

In the same way, we think this life is real. If I tell you now that the life that you are leading is nothing but a creation of your mind, will you believe me? No! You are so immersed in this dream that you think is real.

See, when we wake up from a dream, why do we suddenly understand that it was not real? It is because suddenly we perceive a separation between the dream and us. The understanding that it was merely a dream, puts us into reality. Similarly, the understanding that this world is nothing but a projection of the mind, the understanding that this is not our real identity, will put us into reality.

> A small story:
>
> A Zen master woke up crying one morning. His disciples rushed to him. They enquired, 'What happened, master?' The master said, 'In my dream last night, I was a butterfly.'
>
> The disciples did not understand. They asked, 'So what, master? It was a dream and it is over. What bothers you?'
>
> The master replied, 'You do not understand my problem. I am unable to tell whether I am a Zen master who dreamed that I was a butterfly, or whether I am actually a butterfly who is dreaming that I am a Zen master.'

Let us say we dream of winning some award in front of thousands of people. The mind is so powerful that it can create the entire picture including every detail of the auditorium, all the thousand people sitting and clapping, the speeches, everything that we would normally see in an auditorium. The mind is so powerful to be able to give life to the scene around us and not just to our identity in the dream.

This is what the mind does in the so-called real world, also. The only difference is that we wake up easily from our night dreams. However, we do not know how to wake up from this bigger daydream that we now think is reality. As long as we think this world is real, we suffer. The minute we realize this world is not real, we create a distance between the suffering and us. Only an enlightened master who has experienced the truth can awaken us to reality. Out of their compassion, these masters descend on planet earth to tell us that everything we see around us is a projection of our minds.

If a child is constantly reminded about the divinity within, right from birth, it grows up to be a *jīvan mukta*, liberated while still in the body. This is how children were brought up in the vedic tradition. That is why the level of consciousness was so high.

Prakṛti, the material world that we see, is without beginning. *Puruṣa* or supreme consciousness is also without beginning. All changes and transformations are produced by *prakṛti*.

All the transformations that we see, such as the change in seasons, concepts of time and space, our body-mind, or anything that changes, are different attributes of *prakṛti*. It is like the ebb and flow of the waves in an ocean. These attributes rise and fall. The time and space of the rise and fall is totally relative. The duration of the rise and fall of these attributes is also highly relative, because it is purely a concept created by our senses. Our senses perceive time as moving. Our senses perceive the motion of time with respect to the material world, with relation to the speed of the planets, etc. We have created this concept of time for our sensory perceptions. We have created the space and location also with the concept of comparative reality.

For example, if we are sitting with someone we love, no matter how much time passes, we feel as if we were with that person for a short duration. We will not be aware how time passed so quickly. On the other hand, if we are sitting with a person who bores us or bothers us, we will feel like looking at our watch constantly. We would feel that time is not moving at all.

As long as our mind moves, time moves. When we look deeply, we realize that the mind is a constant movement between past and future. The mind is a dilemma; it is constantly reviewing the past and planning for the future. We are constantly pulled towards the past or future and are never in the present moment.

When we fall into the present moment, we fall into eternity and that eternity is a combination of past, present and future. There is no distinction. In this state we become the witness of all time and space-related happenings. We become the witnessing consciousness. We become the knower and we witness the field or *kṣetra* with complete detachment. We realize that everything in the outer world is a drama or a dream, and anything that we attempt to do in our lives is housekeeping in this dream.

Knowledge about the material world is necessary to help us step back from the dream and realize that we are unnecessarily attached and entangled in the field, *kṣetra*. All transformations in the field are related to time and space, which are in turn related to our mind. All transformations are the play of *prakṛti* or the field. Mind is a part of *prakṛti*.

The moment we put our attention on it, the mind ceases. The moment we decide to put our attention on it, we have decided to become the watcher. It then depends on how long we can remain the watcher without becoming entangled in what is being watched. The more we practice this, the longer we experience being the watcher. We realize that we are *puruṣa*.

'Nature is the source of all material causes and their effects, whereas the living entity is the source of things such as *sukha* (pleasure), *duḥkha* (pain) and everything that is of the world.'

Kṛṣṇa puts us back into our consciousness through these words. This contains the gist of what He has been saying in the previous verses. He makes a clear statement that whatever we see, is not us.

He says, 'Go beyond and beyond and beyond and beyond. When you are able to see the body, move beyond. If you are able to witness your thoughts, go further beyond. If you are able to see your moods, go further beyond. If you are able to witness your emotions, go further beyond. You are not that either.'

Watch everything around you as you would the clouds in the sky. Let them pass by without you involved. Even if there is a thought saying that you are witnessing, watch that thought, also. Watch the witnessing until that thought also disappears. Go beyond and beyond, deep into your being.

This last thought that you are witnessing is like a bridge between you and God, between you and the thoughtless zone. Initially, when you try to witness your actions and your thoughts, it is natural to think that you are watching. Let it be, but go beyond. Do not stop there. Witness the thought that you are witnessing. Then the pure, uncorrupted and untouched inner space happens in you. It is only in the uncorrupted and pure inner space that God manifests and the divine consciousness is perceived.

This is the secret or true meaning of the story of Virgin Mary giving birth to Jesus. Understand, when we make our inner space pure like a virgin, we give birth to Christ or the Christ consciousness! We become divine.

Witnessing is the master key

Here Kṛṣṇa gives us a technique. As of now, we are like 18-carat gold, copper and gold mixed together. When we repeatedly put the 18-carat gold into the fire of witnessing consciousness, eventually it becomes 22-carat gold. If we continue to put that gold into the fire, the 22-carat gold becomes pure 24-carat gold. In the same way, if we put ourselves into the fire of witnessing consciousness, we become purified to a certain extent. Again and again, if we constantly put ourselves into this fire of witnessing consciousness, our inner space eventually becomes completely pure, like 24-carat gold.

The essence of all religions and all spirituality, the whole thing is contained in this single verse that Kṛṣṇa presents here. Kṛṣṇa presents the master key that opens all locks, in this chapter: witnessing the body and the mind, witnessing your being. Witnessing is the master key.

A small story:

A man was driving on a highway around midnight. A cop stopped and asked him, 'Sir, I think you are drunk. Have you been drinking?'

The man replied, 'Yes, I have just had six drinks. Do you want the names? A few cans of beer, a few brandies…' He started listing the drinks.

The cop said, 'Stop, I need to take a breath analyzer test. Please get out of the car.'

The man asked, 'Why do you need a test? Don't you believe me?'

The cop was required to do the test whether he believed the driver or not.

Similarly, you cannot just take my word for it. You must do the test. You must test it on yourself. You must test it with your being. Reading or listening will not transform you. Reading or listening is like reading the menu and leaving the restaurant without tasting the food on the menu! If you listen to what I say without testing, it is like going away from a restaurant without eating.

So now since we have read the menu card, it is time to taste the preparation.

Kṛṣṇa goes one step further. All along He told us how to cleanse our inner space and how to realize the divine consciousness within. Now, in the last verse He says that one who does so attains liberation, regardless of his present position.

Every being is moving towards the Divine, whether or not the being is aware of it. We take on this body to fulfill certain desires. If we truly put our energies into dissolving these desires, we have no reason to take another birth to fulfill these desires. The problem happens when we start to lead somebody else's life and forget we are here to live our desires and not others' desires. We constantly borrow other people's desires and accumulate them in us.

Then, before we start realizing our true nature, it becomes time to leave this body. We take with us the entire baggage of unfulfilled desires and take another body again. The universe again and again tries to help us dissolve our desires so that we become free of them. But we resist by not accepting what happens within and around us.

Kṛṣṇa says that an understanding of *kṣetra* or *prakṛti* straightaway liberates us. We are caught up in pursuing sense pleasures and accumulating desires as long as we associate ourselves with this body. The minute we understand that we are beyond the body and mind, we suddenly realize, 'What stupidity to run in this rat race!'

This cognitive shift can happen to anyone at any time. And when it happens, it is a quantum jump in the level of consciousness. It does not happen gradually. It is like pressing a switch and the whole room is lit up in one shot.

So, irrespective of our profession or the level at which we may be spiritually, just an understanding of the play of Existence is enough to heal us. Just an understanding that we are beyond material pursuits is enough to liberate us.

Many People, Many Paths

13.25 *Some perceive the* Paramātman *in their inner psyche through mind and intellect, that have been purified by meditation,*
Or by metaphysical knowledge, or by karma yoga.

13.26 *There are those who, although not conversant in spiritual knowledge, begin to worship the supreme personality upon hearing about Him from others.*
Through the process of hearing about the Supreme Self, they also transcend the path of birth and death.

13.27 *Bhārata, know that whatever is born whether movable or immovable,*
It comes into existence by the combination of kṣetra *and* kṣetrajñya.

In this verse, Kṛṣṇa gives various techniques for the path to Self-realization. He says, various methods or paths may be used to realize our true Self. People say 'As many masters, so many paths.' Actually it should be 'As many disciples, so many paths!' Each disciple can have his own path. This is what Kṛṣṇa says. We can attain the ultimate consciousness through different paths.

Kṛṣṇa says that through meditation or yoga or knowledge or contemplation or surrendering to the Divine, you can attain liberation. All the different methods lead to the same goal. Each chapter of the Bhagavad Gītā gives a different technique to realize the Self.

After our second-level meditation program, Nithyananda Spurana Program, I give spiritual names to those who ask for it. I give the names based on the energies of the devotees. The names depend on how they connect to the cosmic Nithyananda. If I see that individuals act at an emotional level like devotion, I give names that suit that particular energy. The second category is intellectual people. Intellectual people are those who connect at a mental level. They need logical explanations for everything. The third category is of those who connect at the being level.

When I ask for their names, I meditate on their energies and give them the spiritual names. The spiritual name gives them a path, and the path is different for each one. The name has significance. The name reminds you of your path. We generally associate ourselves with our name. So whenever you utter your name or when somebody calls you by your spiritual name, it rings a bell in your head. It guides you to the destination.

Kṛṣṇa tells Arjuna about the paths. He gives options. Kṛṣṇa gives alternatives: meditation, yoga, chanting *mantra,* learning and acquiring knowledge and surrendering to the cosmos.

One important thing is that you should know which path is good for you. There are people who simply follow what others are doing.

Follow your own path

A small story:

On a dark night, a man discovered that the headlights of his car had failed. He decided to follow the car in front of him. It was dark outside and he could not see anything. If the car in front took a turn, he also took that turn. He managed quite well using the light from the car ahead of him.

After some time, the lights of the lead car switched off and came to a sudden halt. The second driver bumped into the car and shouted at the driver of the first car, 'Why did you stop?'

'I've reached my house. What do you expect me to do?' replied the other driver.

You see, if you follow something or someone blindly, you will not reach the correct destination. You must know your own path.

There are different paths to realize the truth. However, we must understand what our path is. This is where a true enlightened master can help. He knows exactly what the path is for you. He corrects you when you are on the wrong path. In our Advanced Healers Program, disciples sit on the stage and answer the audience's questions. When they answer the questions, I know what mistakes they are making and I correct them.

In this verse Kṛṣṇa gives different techniques, like meditation, yoga, knowledge. Lots of people do these things. Some people ask, '*Swamiji*, I am meditating daily for 21 minutes. I am still unable to feel anything. Why is it?' I ask them, 'Tell me honestly, are you meditating with full intensity and full awareness? When you are meditating is your mind with your body or are you thinking about the office?' Naturally, they do not say anything after that.

In this verse Kṛṣṇa talks about *sāṅkhyena* through knowledge or philosophical discussion. You should understand one thing. Gathering knowledge and philosophical discussions can be done in two ways. Many people read lots of books. These people are the intellectuals. But if you look deeper, the knowledge will be just another manifestation of their ego. They would just show off. Only if we internalize them transformation happens in us. If we discuss for the sake of showing our knowledge and ego, we have made no use of that knowledge.

At the end of the verse Kṛṣṇa gives a wonderful technique. He gives the ultimate technique, the technique of surrendering. He says, 'Surrender the outcome of your actions to Me.' This is the most effective technique. He talks about it throughout the Gita.

Just surrender the fruits of your actions to Him, the universal consciousness. Most often, we take responsibility for our actions. That is when our tensions and problems start. Just surrender everything to the cosmic energy of Kṛṣṇa. Once we do, we will feel liberated. We will feel free. This is the easiest path to reach the truth.

A person need not have any spiritual knowledge to start on a particular path. Even if the person is totally new to spirituality, he can follow a spiritual path. Only a cognitive shift must happen. So many enlightened masters did not have any prior knowledge about spirituality.

One important thing to note is that, just because someone has spiritual knowledge, it does not mean that he is actually a seeker. I have seen people read lots of books and discuss spirituality even when it is not needed. They think they have great spiritual knowledge.

When an enlightened master speaks about spirituality, he speaks from his experience of the truth. When a normal person speaks, it is his ego that is speaking. His so-called spiritual knowledge comes from the intellect, from the ego.

People ask me, '*Swamiji*, do you think I should attend this course? Do you think I am capable of doing this course?' I tell them, 'If you are stable and available, I shall make you able.' That is the only prerequisite. If you are stable and available, you are capable of attaining the ultimate truth.

That is what Kṛṣṇa says. You do not need prior knowledge about spirituality to embark on a path. Even if someone simply tells you about it and you start following a path, it is enough. But you should know what you are doing. Don't do anything blindly. That's all.

Whatever you see is a combination of matter and energy. The whole universe is seen as *kṣetra* and *kṣetrajñya, māyā* and *ātman, prakṛti* and *puruṣa,* matter and energy, body-mind and consciousness. Existence as we see it cannot be with only one of them. If we believe that what we see is simply matter we are in illusion or *māyā*.

Kṣetra is the body that we associate ourselves with, and *kṣetrajñya* is the consciousness. What we see as a human body is a combination of both. If there is no consciousness, the body is useless. The matter that we call a body comes to life because of consciousness. Both must be there.

Prakṛti is the manifest and *puruṣa* is the unmanifest. *Kṣetra* is like *prakṛti.* It is the manifested, that which we can see. Along with what you see, there is something behind its existence. It is *puruṣa* or the unmanifest, the energy behind the matter, which we do not normally see.

We have seen in the earlier verses that all the millions of stars, planets and other celestial bodies exist in perfect harmony. There are so many galaxies. They are moving in space that has no bounds. How are they moving in such order? Look at our solar system. All the planets move in perfect paths. If we think they are rocks, dust or ice, if we think they are simply matter, how is such an order maintained in the universe?

They are not solely matter. There is something behind the existence of that matter. There is so much chaos; yet there is a beautiful order in that chaos. Order is present because of *kṣetrajñya.* If it were solely matter or *kṣetra,* there would not be any intelligence. There is intelligence in that matter. That intelligence or consciousness creates this existence. So the combination of *kṣetra* and *kṣetrajñya* is necessary.

Modern science has shown that matter and energy are the same. The outer-world scientists proved this recently. However, the inner-world scientists proved it thousands of years ago. Matter and energy coexist to create existence. Science has proven that every cell in our system has embedded intelligence. Each cell is not made up of simply some chemicals. Each cell also has intelligence or energy. This combination creates the body-mind system.

We should understand that *kṣetra* and *kṣetrajñya* are not separate entities when we analyze them at a deeper level. *Kṣetra* and *kṣetrajñya* are comprised of the same thing. *Kṣetra* is the gross form of the energy that also makes up the subtle form of the *kṣetrajñya.* For existence to happen, both the subtle and gross forms must be there.

We Are Brahman

13.28 *One who sees the supreme spirit accompanying the individual soul in all bodies,*
Who understands that neither the individual soul nor the supreme spirit is ever destroyed, he actually sees.

13.29 *When one does not get degraded or influenced by the mind, and when he can see the supreme spirit in all living and non-living things,*
One reaches the transcendental destination.

13.30 *One who can see that all activities are performed by the body, which is created of material nature,*
Sees that the Self does nothing, he actually sees.

13.31 *When a person can see the supreme Self in all living entities, then he will cease to see the separateness among the living entities.*
He will see that the whole universe is an expansion and expression of the same truth.

Kṛṣṇa says, 'Anyone who has reached Self-realization or the ultimate consciousness sees that the supreme Self is present in all living and non-living entities. He perceives the supreme Self as the indestructible, beginning-less, witnessing consciousness.'

The Existence that we see is not comprised of individual entities. We think that we are separate from others around us. In reality, we are all one. The same supreme Self that Kṛṣṇa speaks about is present in all of us and in everything we see around us.

As I tell everyone, 'I am not here to prove that I am God, I am here to prove that you are God.'

This is the truth. When I say this, people say, 'No, no, *Swamiji*. How can we be God? We have done many sins. We agree that you are God, because you have healing powers. But how can we be God?'

Please understand one thing. It is not that you are not God because you have committed sins. Understand that you do not become a devil if you commit a sin. You are still God. Sins do not qualify or disqualify you from being a God. Your nature is Godliness. Sin is a concept developed by society to control people. The soul of a robber has the same qualification to reach the truth as that of a priest in a temple.

We create a barrier between God and us. We are not ready to believe that what we call God is inside us, also. We happily accept someone else standing in front of us as God; however, we cannot accept that the same God is inside us.

Society would find it difficult to keep us under control if we were to call ourselves gods!

God is everywhere. Divine energy fills and overflows in all places. The only problem is we do not see this, we only see one thing at a time. We see God as someone different and powerful. We create a big gap between God and us.

People in the West call Hindus 'idol worshippers'. They make fun of them. Actually there are people in India too who make fun of idol worship. All the so-called intellectuals and scientific people look down upon people who worship idols. Some so-called neo-vedantis preach *Vedānta* but consider idol worship unscientific. The same is true about performing rituals like *homa* (fire rituals) or *abhiṣekha* (water rituals).

We should understand there is more than an idol in front of us when we worship. When we worship, we worship *through* the idol. We do not worship the idol itself. When we see the energy behind the idol and worship that energy, that worship has value. That is the science also. If we blindly worship the stone without feeling the energy behind the stone, there is no point in it.

Let me ask you, why do we feel a great sense of relief after we pray to God sincerely? Why do we feel a sense of satisfaction when we come out of the temple after prayers? Why do we feel light? When we see the energy behind the idol and worship that energy, we connect to that energy.

When I say we connect to that energy, we create a channel for the soul that is inside us to connect to the supreme Self. This brief time of connection relieves us from our burdens of responsibility. We see the supreme spirit in the idol and pour out our problems in the form of prayers.

We feel relieved because we have full faith in the supreme spirit. We have full confidence that the supreme spirit will take care of us. We believe in the supreme spirit, but we do not believe that the soul that we see in us is also the supreme spirit! We are not able to internalize this truth.

Everything is the supreme spirit

Kṛṣṇa says the soul that is in us and the soul that is in others is the supreme spirit and the supreme soul. But what do we do? We isolate our soul. We define a boundary for our soul and separate it from the supreme spirit. It is like this. There are ten pots of water and there is the reflection of the sun in all the ten pots. Each pot thinks that it holds the sun. All ten pots think that each one is holding a different sun.

In the same way, we think the soul inside us is different from the soul outside us. When we see the same soul everywhere, in everything, when we break the pots, we see what the supreme Self is.

Kṛṣṇa says, 'When we see that the soul that resides in us and in everything around us is indestructible, we see the truth.' The only thing that lives forever is the soul. We should understand that. Everything else must die one day. When we realize this truth, when we understand that only the soul can remain forever, our whole race to get more and more becomes worthless. We realize, 'What is the use of running after things that we know are not going to be with us forever?'

When this is realized, we see the truth.

The mind is the only obstacle on the path to reach the ultimate goal. In the previous verse, Kṛṣṇa tells us how we can see the truth. Here Kṛṣṇa talks about the hurdle that we must cross. He says that when we are not degraded or influenced by the mind, we can see the supreme spirit in everything. Only when we can do that, can we reach the final destination.

We talk about the mind as separate from ourselves. We say, 'It is thinking a lot.' We do not understand what the mind is and we start talking about it. What is the mind actually? It is only an organized structure gifted by God as a tool. The mind is man's servant that helps satisfy his needs and necessities in order to lead a happy life.

The reason for the problems is that the mind, which should be under the control of man, has become a structure that controls man. When our mind acts based on incorrect comprehension or influences, our decisions are degraded. During the first-level meditation program, we discuss how the mind works. We see something and we react to it. The reaction is generally based upon past experiences called *saṁskāras*. If the past experiences were good, the mind decides, 'Okay, good, I can continue.' Otherwise, it rejects it.

Kṛṣṇa says, if our mind comes in the way of seeing what the truth is, our decisions are based on incorrect comprehension. When we are influenced by our mind, we fail to see the supreme soul in everything around us.

If we can keep the mind aside for a while, we see the truth as it is. Our mind cannot accept that the supreme soul is in everything around us. The soul inside us knows the truth. Our soul inside us knows that the supreme soul is everywhere. But our mind creates a strong sheath around it. Our mind takes control over us. It harbors past memories (*saṁskāras*) and creates an illusion that leads to wrong comprehension. The mind creates the illusion that we need the senses and the body to live and enjoy our life.

When we were children, the mind did not have much power. When we were children, we did not build new *saṁskāras*. The conditioning by society builds layers and layers of these *saṁskāras* that give power to the mind. Actually when people say that a child is growing up, it only implies that the child is growing smaller and smaller, only the mind is growing up. The soul is being pushed into a corner and the mind is given more and more power.

This mind prevents us from seeing the truth. It stops us from seeing the supreme soul in everything around us. Be very clear, if we are out of the clutches of the mind, we see reality.

We are safe as long as we can separate the Self from the body and watch as the body reacts to materialistic things. As long as we know that the soul is supreme and the body is a means to fulfill our worldly desires, we are safe. We are on the right path. However, when we place the body over the soul, the problem starts.

We give so much importance to this body, but we don't really respect it. Instead we make use of it. We abuse our body. We watch television for long hours in the night. Our eyes call for rest, but we don't listen because our eyes give us the pleasure of watching programs on the television. Just because there is food in front of us, we continue eating. We may be full, yet we eat because we like the taste. We want to enjoy the taste. So we eat and eat, even if the body rejects it.

So many people go to beauty parlors and spas. That is the fashion these days. Women go to beauty parlors and do their makeup. They put on layers and layers of makeup and artificial nails in an attempt to appear beautiful to others.

A small story:

> A newly married couple visited the husband's village for the first time. The wife was from the city and had never been to a village earlier. They decided to go to the temple at seven o'clock in the morning. Generally in India, people visit the temple early before starting their daily activities. So they wanted to be at the temple at

seven o'clock. The wife started applying her makeup at five o'clock in the morning.

Anyhow, she finished her makeup and they went to the temple. In Indian temples, especially village temples, you can see monkeys, peacocks, rabbits and other animals. This was the first time the wife saw such a temple. She was amused to see all these animals. She commented to her husband about the monkeys.

The husband told her with a smile on his face, 'Yes, I see one big monkey beside me.'

Women compete with the amount of makeup they apply. They think they are taking care of their body by going to beauty parlors and spas. Actually, they only abuse the body. They apply so many chemicals on their skin.

Why do we abuse our body in this fashion? It is because, through the senses of the body, we experience some pleasures. These are sense pleasures. These sense pleasures make us happy. So we hold onto those sense pleasures that we experience through our body.

But we fail to realize that they are momentary. Please be clear, all sense pleasures are momentary. If we feel happy through sense pleasures, the very same senses put you in sadness the next day. It is like those rotating doors. We stand and push one side while the other side pushes us outside the door! If we stay near the door too long, the door will rotate and push us back inside.

We consider our body to be a tool to experience the sense pleasures. We use our body to feel the pleasures from the outside world. We want to feel those sense pleasures again and again. That is why we take care of our body. We want our body to be safe so that we can enjoy. We want our body to look good all the time.

We must understand why we assume this human body form and come to planet earth. Only then will we know the correct way to use the body. Only then we will know our body the right way. First, understand that the body that we have now is one of the many bodies that our soul has assumed. Whether we believe it or not, accept it or not, like it or not, that is the truth. We have taken many births before this life. We have possessed many bodies before this birth. Whether we take another birth, whether we have another body, depends upon how we lead our current life.

This birth that we have taken is to fulfill the carried-over desires of our previous births. These desires are called *prārabdha karma*. Our soul has taken this body to fulfill our *prārabdha karma*. When we die, our last thought decides our next birth. Our soul chooses the body that can fulfill the desires of our last birth. This is the truth.

Understand that we assume a body to fulfill the desires carried over from our previous life. However, what happens is that we create new desires in this life as well. We use our body to experience the sense pleasures and we create more and more desires. Because of this, we fall into the cycle of birth and death. Once we realize that our soul takes this body to complete a mission that it left unfinished in our previous birth, our attitude towards our whole body will change.

Our body is like a cloth. When we wake up early morning, we discard what we were wearing and put on fresh clothes, is it not? In the same way, when we die, we discard this body and take a new body to fulfill our unfulfilled desires, that's all.

People ask me, '*Swamiji*, why do enlightened masters take human birth? Why do they need a body if they are already enlightened, if they have fulfilled all their desires?'

There is a beautiful incident from Rāmakṛṣṇa Paramahamsa's life. Sri Rāmakṛṣṇa was an enlightened master. He told his disciples, 'Once when I was returning from my village in an ox cart, some robbers stopped us. I started repeating all the names of gods so that at least one would work.'

He then explains why even enlightened masters hold onto their body.

He says beautifully, 'A little of my mind is attached to the body so that it can enjoy the love of God and the company of the devotees.'

Please be very clear, an enlightened master holds onto his body out of pure compassion for others. An enlightened master wants to see transformation in others and he can do it more effectively when he is in the body. He does not have any other desire. He can leave his body any time. He holds his body through a thin thread of ego for the benefit of others.

We always want to get more and more out of our body. We want our eyes to see more television; we want our stomach to hold more food; we want our ears to hear louder music. We do all this out of greed. We want to experience more and more sense pleasures.

Instead, if we look at our body with gratitude, when we thank our body every moment for the support it has given us, we connect with our body at a deeper level.

Our body is the temple of our soul. We should respect our body. We should look at our body with gratitude, not greed. We should thank our body for holding our spirit, our soul. Then, we will see a different dimension of our body.

Here Kṛṣṇa says, whatever we think we are enjoying, actually it is the body that is enjoying. Our body enjoys all the material comforts. Our soul can live without them. Our soul is pure consciousness. It does not need anything external to keep it happy.

The problem starts when we think that our soul needs these material things. We associate the happiness from the external materials with our soul. This is where the problem begins. We think the happiness that we gain from material comforts is because our soul feels happy to have them. That is when we accumulate more and more of these material comforts. We run after them.

Kṛṣṇa gives us a technique here. He says, when we watch our body enjoying the sense pleasures, when we watch only our body being associated with the external material comforts and not our soul, we see the truth. Just witness the body. Be aware of your body. Observe the body when it reacts to external things. You will notice a sense of separation from the body. You will see what your body is. You will see that your soul has nothing to do with the pleasures you are enjoying.

Kṛṣṇa gives a great truth in this verse. He talks about collective consciousness. He says when we see the supreme soul in all living beings we no longer see the separateness. We see everything as one single entity. We see the whole universe as one single body, as one entity expressing the same truth.

Please be very clear, we are all connected. Each and every living entity is connected to the other. Your thoughts affect the thoughts of the person sitting beside you. Whether or not you believe it, this is the truth.

We think we are individual consciousness. We think we are separate islands. We think our thoughts are limited to us. We think nobody watches our thoughts. Please understand that the whole universe constantly responds to your thoughts. The whole universe is made up of the same universal consciousness.

Actually there is nothing *but* universal consciousness. Individual consciousness is a piece of the hologram of the universal collective consciousness. Have you seen a hologram? What happens when you break a hologram into five pieces? Each piece becomes a hologram again. Each piece shows the same thing as the whole piece showed you before.

Our individual consciousness is like a hologram. The universal consciousness hologram is broken into many small holograms or individual living things. But each one of us has the same consciousness as the universal consciousness.

You see, your individual consciousness is like an onion. Each one of us is an onion. What do you see in an onion? There are layers over layers of skin. When you peel the onion layer by layer, what is there inside? Nothing! You are just like that onion. You think the onion is solid. Only when you peel, you see that there is nothing inside it. In the same manner, if you peel off the individual body mind layers, you experience that you are the collective consciousness. Once you remove all the layers, you see that every entity around you has the same consciousness. From the beginning, from your birth, society starts creating new layers on you. In the process, the innocent, childlike nature that sees the Self in everything is slowly lost in us. As a child you do lots of things through which you connect to the Self. You do not know you are different from soil or earth. That is why you play with mud. But what do parents do? They scold you. 'Don't do this. Don't do that.' They say, 'You will get dirty. Your clothes will become dirty.'

We continuously impose societal conditions on the child. The child does not know what is dirty or what is clean. The child sees the soil just the same as the floor. He does not see any difference. He connects to the same energy when he plays on the dusty road or inside a clean house. Adults condition children to see a difference.

When we remove the conditionings caused by our body-mind association, we see that everything is pure consciousness. Only then we see that we are all the same. That is what Kṛṣṇa says here. When we see that the supreme soul resides in each of us, we see that all of us are connected to each other. When we see this, we see the truth. We see that the whole universe is the expansion of the same consciousness. The whole universe is the expression of the same truth.

Soul And Body

13.32 Those with the vision of eternity can see that the soul is transcendental, eternal, and beyond the modes of nature.
Despite contact with the material body, O Arjuna, the soul neither does anything nor is attached.

13.33 The sky, due to its subtle nature, does not mix with anything, although it is all pervading.
Similarly, the soul, situated in Brahman, does not mix with the body, though situated in that body.

13.34 O son of Bhārata, as the sun alone illuminates the entire universe, so does the living entity,
One within the body, illuminate the entire consciousness.

13.35 Those who see with the eyes of knowledge, the difference between the body-mind and the Knower of the body-mind, who can understand the process,
are liberated from the bondages of material nature and attain Parāmatman.

Kṛṣṇa again and again talks about the true nature of the Self. He tells Arjuna that the soul is free from all entanglements. It is eternal and transcendental. Kṛṣṇa says that though the soul has come into contact with the material body, it is still free.

In the previous verses, we talked about how the body is the temple of our soul. We saw how the soul takes this body to fulfill the desires of our past birth. The soul actually does nothing. It does not entangle itself in the web of greed and fear. It is the mind that continuously adds new desires to the list and keeps the body running after them. Internally, the soul is always free. It has no bondage.

It is like the lotus plant in a lake. Water droplets that fall on the lotus leaves do not get attached to the leaves. They simply roll off and merge with the water again.

In the same way, the soul that rests inside this body is completely free from worldly joys and sorrows. It is like the drops of water. The soul can simply merge into the supreme soul. Only the body is related to the worldly happenings. The soul is not involved at all.

Kṛṣṇa uses the word *nirguṇa* meaning beyond the three attributes. The three attributes of calmness, passion, and inactivity are related to the mind and body. The soul is free from these attributes. It is neither restless nor is it lazy. It is pure. Actually it is beyond purity. When we use the word pure, then it means that the soul can be associated with the attribute of calmness. But the soul is even beyond calmness. That is why I say it is beyond purity. Nothing can circumscribe it.

One important thing we should know. Only when something is seen by the mind, do words come out. Words are an expression of the chatter that happens in our mind. When there is no mind, there are no words. When you go to the Himalayas surrounded by mountains, the first thing that happens is awe. No words come out. We are silent. Our being enjoys the beauty. Our being does not try to relate it to anything. Our mind has not yet associated any word to it. After a few seconds we experience the 'wow' feeling; it cannot be expressed.

In the same way, enlightenment cannot be expressed in words. There is no enlightened master who can adequately explain what enlightenment is, in words.

Associating the soul with even the word calmness requires the mind. But the soul is beyond this, also. No word can describe it. It just IS, that's all. All enlightened masters are *triguṇa rahita* meaning, residing in a state that is beyond the three attributes. They have gone beyond the three attributes. They know that the soul is free from everything. They know that the body is the temple of the soul. They know that the body does not affect the soul.

Kṛṣṇa gives an example to make this point clear. He says the space that is everywhere is unaffected by anything that is in that space. The subtle energy, space or ether, is present everywhere. Every molecule and atom has this subtle energy. Though it is present in everything that we see, it does not inherit the properties of what it resides in. Even if it is in a flower, it does not take up the scent of the flower.

In the same way, the soul is not affected by where it resides. People think that their soul will go to hell if they have committed sins. They think if they have lived a pious life, their soul will go to heaven. They think that the soul is affected by the deeds of the body. Our sins do not affect the nature of our soul. Please understand that by infusing awareness into what we do, we realize that the body does whatever we do. The soul is completely free from it. Kṛṣṇa says that, just as the sun illuminates our whole world, one supreme Self, that is one *kṣetrajñya*, illuminates all beings in the universe, whether they are animate or inanimate. He says everything has the same consciousness.

Kṛṣṇa gives more and more examples. The sun sheds light on the surrounding planets. The darkness on the planets is removed by the sun's light. In the same way, the supreme Self, *kṣetrajñya*, lights up all beings in the universe. The ultimate consciousness lights up the entire universe. All beings of the universe have this consciousness.

We may wonder why Kṛṣṇa says the same thing over and over again. But He is trying to make the concept of *kṣetra* and *kṣetrajñya* clear to Arjuna. Kṛṣṇa knows that this is important and He wants Arjuna to understand it completely.

Anyhow, Kṛṣṇa says something new here. He says that just as the sun illumines the universe, the soul in this body illumines not only this body, but also everything surrounding it, the entire universe. He says:

yathā prakāśayatyekaḥ kṛtsnaṁ lokaṁ imaṁ raviḥ I
yadā nāhaṁ tadā mokṣo yadāhaṁ bandhanaṁ tadā II 13.34

Kṣetri is the Self. This Self illumines all the *kṣetra,* all the bodies. Not just our body or *kṣetra* is illumined but all the *kṣetra* are illumined. The consciousness present in each of us is the hologram of the supreme Self. So there is no separation between the consciousness present in our body and the consciousness present in a plant or a rock. Everything is the same energy.

The sun lights up everything that is around. There is no partiality. It does not discriminate. Whatever comes its way, it removes the darkness from it. In the same way, the supreme Self present in us illuminates everything in the universe. Our ignorance separates the soul from the supreme soul.

Actually to even use two different words — soul and supreme soul — is not correct. There are no two separate entities called soul and supreme soul. There is only soul. There is only one. Everything in this universe has the supreme soul. We can't even say, 'Everything has the same supreme soul,' because when we use the word same, it means there are copies of the supreme soul in all of us.

No, it is not like that. There is just supreme soul and nothing else. Everything in this universe has the supreme soul. Our mind draws boundaries. It is like creating borders between two countries. So many countries fight over boundaries. One country fights with the other to acquire more land. They are drawing and erasing boundaries all the time.

We think we can draw boundaries between the Self that is present in us, and the supreme Self. We try to put our soul in a tight container made of greed and fear. We close the lid and are afraid to open it. Actually, we fear losing our identity. We associate ourselves with our individual ego. We want to show others how different we are.

Our mind knows that if it opens the lid, the soul and the supreme soul will become one. Our mind knows that the soul in this body and the supreme soul are one and the same; there is no difference between the two. So our mind fears that if it opens the lid, our whole identity will be lost and we will become the same as everyone else. Our mind does not want this to happen.

So we continuously hold onto our individual ego. Only when we realize that we are all connected, that everything in this universe is the same universal consciousness, will we break open the container and merge with the supreme Soul.

Here Kṛṣṇa ends by saying, 'If we can witness as pure consciousness, we will be liberated from the bondages of the body-mind and achieve the eternal consciousness.' Kṛṣṇa gives a technique to realize the eternal consciousness.

Witness and be liberated

Please know that becoming the witness of the *kṣetra* is the only way to keep us away from the bondages of the body-mind. We must witness as the *kṣetrajñya,* consciousness. When we do that we will see the separation of the Self from the body and mind.

Understand that all our movements, reactions and emotions are related to the body-mind system. The way we move our body is a reaction by our body-mind system. Our emotions like anger, laughter, sadness and happiness are reactions of our mind. All of them are movements created by our body-mind system.

When we witness these movements happening in our system, we separate ourselves from the body-mind system. When we watch them like clouds in the sky, when we watch them like a movie on a screen, without getting attached, we see the truth.

Even the thought of witnessing our thoughts and our emotions is a thought that is controlled by our mind. Even that is our thought and implies that mind is still acting. Only when we go beyond that thought, do we experience the eternal consciousness.

Let me explain the technique. The technique may take at least ten minutes.

You are going to witness your body movements, breath movements, and mind movements: movements of your body, movements of your breath, and movements of your mind. You may ask what kind of body movements do we have? Understand that by inhaling and exhaling, your belly will be moving continuously up and down. There will be a slight movement of your belly during your breathing.

Witness that movement.

Next, watch the flow of your breath during inhaling and exhaling, without any attempt to control it.

Third, watch your mind. Thoughts will be going on. Please do not judge your thoughts as right or wrong. For a few minutes, sit next to your mind, like a close friend. Let it tell you whatever it wants to. Let it speak about whatever it wants.

Witness all these with no attachment. Do not stop, control, or go behind anything.

We continuously fight with our body and mind. We cannot get rid of the body and mind by constantly fighting with them. We can only go beyond them through friendliness. Only if we feel deeply friendly towards them, will we be able to go beyond body and mind. If we have a negative emotion towards the body-mind, we will naturally abuse and only have a violent relationship with it. Accept the body and the mind. Witness the mind like a friend. Let whatever is inside come out. There's nothing wrong. Neither support nor suppress. If we support, we will go after the garbage. If we suppress, we will end up analyzing the garbage and pushing it aside. Neither approach is going to work. Just witness.

Witnessing acts like fire. All the thoughts are burned away. Understand, neither suppressing nor supporting your thoughts will work. Only witnessing works.

When we go deep into our being, the witnessing consciousness automatically creates intelligence. Understand that we don't need to be in that mood all twenty-four hours of each day. Even if we get a few glimpses, that is enough. That energy will guide our whole life. If we understand the silence that happens to us when we are witnessing, even for a few seconds, we will taste it and start acting on it. Only out of these few moments does the energy of great achievement happen.

All great things are achieved from the consciousness and intuition that is beyond the body-mind, whether it is Einstein's Theory of Relativity or some other great scientific discovery. They are products of the witnessing consciousness. This is true not only in the field of science but in the arts, spirituality or any field. When we are beyond the body and mind, we bring the maximum out of our being. The ultimate expression of our being happens when we are whole. Whenever we are whole, we are holy. Understand that witnessing is the only path to wholeness or holiness.

Let us pray to the *Parabrahman,* Lord Kṛṣṇa, the ultimate universal consciousness, to give us the inner space of the pure witnessing consciousness; to give us the ultimate experience and establish us in eternal bliss, *nityānanda.*

Thus ends the 13th chapter named* Kṣetra Kṣetrajñya Vibhāga yogaḥ *of the* Upaniṣad *of Bhagavad Gītā, the scripture of Yoga dealing with the science of the Absolute in the form of the dialogue between Śrī Kṛṣṇa and Arjuna.

BHAGAVADGĪTĀ

Drop Your Conditioning

GUṆATRAYA VIBHĀGA YOGAḤ

CHAPTER 14

Human beings have the choice of being ignorant or enlightened. Most often we exercise our freewill and choose to stay ignorant. Krishna explains how to choose to be enlightened!

Drop Your Conditioning

A small story:

On the last day of the school term, students brought gifts to their teacher. The first student presented the teacher with a nicely wrapped gift. The student's father owned the local bakery. The teacher looked at the package, shook it and asked, 'Is this a box of pastries?' The child said, 'Yes.'

Next, a student, whose father was the owner of a clothing store, presented a beautifully decorated gift and again the teacher shook it close to her ears. She then asked, 'Is it a dress?' The child said, 'Yes.'

Another girl came up with a nicely wrapped box. Her father owned a liquor store. The teacher shook the box. She noticed that the package was leaking. She dipped her finger in the leaking fluid and asked the girl curiously, 'Is this some kind of beer?' The child said, 'No.' The teacher dipped her finger again in the fluid, tasted it carefully and asked, 'Ah, this tastes quite exotic. What is it? Is it some kind of wine?' The child again said, 'No.'

Then the teacher said, 'Alright, I give up. Please tell me, what is it?' The child said in a worried tone, 'It is a puppy.'

When we make major decisions through our engraved memories or *saṁskāras*, they lead to problems. The first two guesses of the teacher were correct. The first girl's father was in the business of selling sweets and her gift was a box of sweets. The second child's father owned a clothing store and her gift was a dress. Since the third child's father owned a liquor store, the teacher assumed that the gift was a bottle of liquor!

Engraved memories are stored in our unconscious and drive all our actions. Even though we act according to them, we rarely know or understand where these decisions come from. We think that our actions are based on a logical sequence of thoughts. However, almost all our thoughts and decisions have neither logic nor awareness.

> A real incident:
>
> Our Bidadi ashram is an hour's drive from Bangalore city. In the early days of this ashram, I traveled almost everyday from Bidadi to Bangalore. One day I told the driver to take me to a particular place along the way, near a mosque. The driver was confused. He insisted that there was no mosque on the route that we normally took everyday. I tried to explain that there was one, but he wouldn't believe me. Finally, I mentioned another landmark, a Hindu Hanuman temple. He immediately understood and his face lit up with joy and understanding.
>
> '*Swamiji,* why didn't you tell me that earlier?' he exclaimed, 'Of course I know where you want to go now!'

This Hindu temple was only a small structure compared to the mosque. We traveled past both buildings everyday. Yet, this person was aware of only the Hanumān temple because of his personal preferences. Many memories of experiences are recorded even though we are unconscious of them. In fact, many powerful memories go directly into the unconscious, which we do not recall. They powerfully impact us and influence our decisions and actions. The influence is based on the emotional perception at the time of the experience. What we term perception is not the experience we perceive through the senses; perception is how we respond emotionally to the experience. This response is a conditioned response.

Why Kṛṣṇa Repeats?

14.1 *Kṛṣṇa says, 'I will declare to you again the supreme wisdom,*
The knowledge of which has helped all sages attain supreme perfection.'

14.2 *By becoming fixed in this knowledge, one can attain the transcendental nature, like My own,*
And establish in his eternal consciousness, that one is not born at the time of creation, or destroyed at the time of dissolution.

14.3 *The total material substance, called* Brahman, *is the source of birth,*
It is that Brahman *that I impregnate, making possible the births of all living beings, O son of Bhārata.*

14.4 *Arjuna, understand that all species of life are made possible by birth in this material nature, and I am the seed-giving father.*

By repeating the truth again and again, Kṛṣṇa tries to create an engraved memory of truth in Arjuna's mind.

Please try to understand why Kṛṣṇa repeats Himself. He literally uses the same words again and again. Why? Why should Kṛṣṇa speak the same thing again and again?

Kṛṣṇa is a master who is result-oriented. He persists with what He wants. He is unwilling to compromise. He is not easily satisfied with the attitude, 'I said whatever I had to say; whether he wants to listen or not is up to him.'

No! Again and again, He repeats himself because He wants to create a memory of His teachings in Arjuna's mind. He does this so that even if Arjuna misses a teaching the first time, perhaps he will get it the next time. By creating an engraved memory in Arjuna's mind, He wants Arjuna to follow it. That is why He repeats the truth again.

He says, 'I shall declare once more, I will speak to you about the truth, through the knowledge of which all the sages have attained supreme perfection.'

I repeat certain words and sentences, not because I have nothing else to do. These words and sentences have the power to go deeply within you. If you allow them, they will help you transform. All you need to do is be open and allow these words to sink into you. As you hear these words, let the words penetrate you. These words carry energy to uplift you, to transform you.

Does God exist?

Many religious rituals are designed to build good *saṁskāras* in us. Going to a temple or a church, prayer groups or *satsaṅgs* (spiritual gatherings) reinforce our desire to move forward spiritually. They create the environment, the mood for the right decision to happen. These actions cannot liberate or enlighten us. However, they can condition us and program our unconscious mind to work in a particular way. They can rewire us. Some consider these rituals illogical and unscientific. Science is about facts that can be recorded. Spirituality is about the truth that needs to be experienced. That is why our scriptures never bothered about historical accuracy and factual details. They dealt with issues that affected our consciousness. To understand our scriptures, we cannot use logic. We need to use meditation. Truth has nothing to do with our head. It has everything to do with our being.

People ask me, 'Can you prove the existence of God?'

Before his enlightenment, Vivekānanda, upon meeting his guru Ramakṛṣṇa, asked whether Ramakṛṣṇa could show him God. Vivekānanda asked this question not to embarrass Ramakṛṣṇa but because he felt deeply attracted to this master and wanted help in finding out the truth that had eluded him.

> A young man who had read about Vivekānanda came to one of my discourses in India. I asked him, 'So you read about Vivekānanda?' Unlike Vivekānanda, this young man had no intention of finding the truth. He wanted to show how smart he was.
>
> He proudly said, 'Yes, and I ask you the same question.' Perhaps he thought I would be as humble as Ramakṛṣṇa was!
>
> I caught him by his shirt collar and told him, 'I have not only seen God, but I can show Him to you also. Vivekānanda was prepared to follow Ramakṛṣṇa. Now, you too prepare yourself to come with me, and I will show you God!'
>
> He struggled free of my grip and ran away. He was so scared that he didn't even look back!

God can only be experienced when we drop our mind. He is beyond our mind. How can we prove His existence through the logic of our mind? How can we comprehend the One who is beyond our mind through the powers of our mind? If we can comprehend Him through our mind, our logic, how can He be in any way superior to us? How can He then be God?

When we talk of divinity or God, we struggle with a concept, a theory, with our limited mind-power. We are doing nothing more than that. Because it is only a concept, we can prove or disprove that concept. So we become a devotee or an atheist.

To be an atheist, we need courage. An atheist probably thinks about God more often than the believer who believes and ignores. When we actively disbelieve we will automatically be more aware. An atheist is more aware of God than a believer.

God can only be experienced. Kṛṣṇa wants to take Arjuna to this experience. In fact, He already took him there when He revealed His cosmic form to Arjuna. Now, Kṛṣṇa wants to take the rest of humanity to the same level. So again and again He repeats the techniques so we may realize our divinity. In His deep compassion He gives us a chance to catch the lifeline He is throwing us so that we can be saved.

For the first time, Kṛṣṇa says that we will reach His state. So far He said, 'Worship Me. Surrender unto Me.' Now He says, 'You will achieve the same state in which I am. Anyone can attain the transcendental nature like My own.'

We can achieve the state in which He abides. Kṛṣṇa was the first master courageous and bold enough to declare that enlightenment is available to everybody; anybody can achieve it. Enlightenment is not an accident. It is an incident that we can create.

Until the time of Sri Kṛṣṇa, the *Upaniṣads,* Brahma Sūtra and other scriptures spoke as if enlightenment was an accident. Some people became enlightened; nobody, however, knew why. Nor did they know why others could not get it or how exactly to get it. Nobody knew. They merely knew that some people were blessed, almost as if God was sitting up there and reviewing applications, and to some, He said, 'Alright, yes, granted,' and immediately that person became enlightened!

Kṛṣṇa was the first master who showed how to write the application or present the resume for enlightenment! He showed how to achieve enlightenment, which is not an accident but an incident. We can experience it through our conscious decision. He says that by being fixed in this knowledge, 'One can attain.' He doesn't say, 'You can attain it,' indicating only Arjuna. He says one can attain it, meaning that anybody can attain it.

After the *viśvarūpa darśan* or vision of the cosmic form of Kṛṣṇa, whatever Kṛṣṇa shares with Arjuna is meant for the whole world. Arjuna already achieved what he had to achieve. After that, there was nothing else to say. Arjuna had the vision of Kṛṣṇa's cosmic form. In the eleventh chapter, he experienced *viśvarūpa darśan* and from the twelfth chapter onwards, the teachings were recorded for the benefit of the whole world.

A scientist creates a formula to reproduce things in the outer world. A spiritual master creates a formula to reproduce the experiences of the inner world. Kṛṣṇa says, 'By establishing yourself in this knowledge, you can achieve the experience, or you can establish yourself in the same state in which I am, like My own.' '*Mama*' means 'My own.' Kṛṣṇa declares, 'This truth will directly lead you to the state in which I am established.'

Kṛṣṇa talks about the truth that one is eternal and not limited by birth and death. The state of being eternal transcends creation and dissolution. It transcends the past and future. Eternal is to be here and now. Eternal is the present moment.

Kṛṣṇa is trying to answer philosophical questions that can never really be answered: How is the whole universe created? If everything is God, why is the universe created? How are we born? Whoever tried to answer these questions just created another philosophy.

Out of frustration, someone once asked me such questions: Why are we born? Why should we take birth at all? Why this whole drama of taking birth, meditating, then achieving enlightenment? Why? For whose sake is this drama? If we must end up working out our *karma*, why do we create *karma* in the first place? What is the reason for this? Why does this cycle go on and on?'

Kṛṣṇa tries to answer these questions. However, this answer is not the ultimate Truth. He says, 'Please wait until the teachings are over.' Normally when we don't receive an answer for our philosophical question, we will be stuck with that question and not be able to enter into meditation. Again and again we will think of the question. We will come back to that question. Here, Arjuna also comes back to the same question again and again and gets stuck.

For the sake of meditation or just for the sake of giving him an understanding, Kṛṣṇa gives an answer.

The other day I was sharing the same example using a mathematical formula. Let's say there is a formula 'X + 2 = 4.' In the beginning, the teacher will make an assumption by saying, 'Let us assume that X = 2,' then she replaces X with 2 and goes on to show that 2 + 2 = 4. The problem is solved. Then the teacher says, 'Because the problem is solved, we know that our hypothesis that X = 2 is correct.' But until we come to that conclusion through a process, we can only assume that X = 2.

If we argue about the hypothesis when we make the assumption that X = 2, saying, 'Why should X be equal to 2, why not 3, why don't we assume X = 4?' we will not be able to solve the problem. Once we solve the problem, we know that X is 2. We understand it logically. But before solving, when we start, we must assume that X = 2. Some assumption must be made so that we can proceed to solve the problem.

Kṛṣṇa also makes a small assumption and proceeds to solve the problem. Once He solves the problem, we will understand that what was assumed is the truth. What the teacher assumed was not wrong, but it was still an assumption. Similarly, Kṛṣṇa gives an idea that it is not the ultimate Truth, but a comparative reality. It is a comparative truth. He says, 'I am the father, the *pita*, I am the root cause for everything.'

However, Kṛṣṇa's words can be fully understood only when we experience the consciousness of Kṛṣṇa. Until we experience the consciousness of Kṛṣṇa, they are an assumption.

Even if they are an assumption, it is okay. Proceed with this assumption into the next verses, into the next chapters. Suddenly, when we see the result, we will understand that whatever we have assumed is the truth. Once the problem is solved, all the assumptions that we have made will be understood as the truth. Kṛṣṇa makes this assumption so that we can understand the truth.

Natural Attributes

14.5 *Material nature consists of three modes: goodness, passion and ignorance.*
When the living entity comes in contact with nature, it becomes conditioned by these modes.

14.6 *O Sinless One, the mode of goodness,* satva, *being purer than the others, is illuminating, and it frees one from all sinful reactions.*
Those situated in that mode develop knowledge, but they become conditioned by the concept of happiness.

14.7 *Arjuna, know that the mode of passion,* rajas, *is characterized by intense craving and is the source of desire and attachment.*
Rajas *binds the living entity by attachment to work.*

14.8 *Know, O Arjuna, that the mode of ignorance, tamas, the deluder of the living entity, is born of inertia.*
Tamas *binds the living entity by carelessness, laziness, and excessive sleep.*

We operate through three different types of engraved memories. One is *satva,* the second is *rajas,* and the third is *tamas.* These are roughly translated as goodness, passion and ignorance. *Satva* refers to the *saṁskāras* that lead us to bliss. *Rajas* refers to the engraved memories that lead us to restlessness and make us work intensely. They make us materially productive. The third attribute, *tamas,* refers to the engraved memories that lead us to depression and dullness.

Go beyond your *saṁskāras*

These three different types of engraved memories or *saṁskāras* rule our entire life. Knowledge of these engraved memories is the basic knowledge that must be possessed by anyone who wants to live successfully. Ayurveda is structured around the concept of *guṇas* and their effect on our body-mind system. It is like an owner's manual for using the mind. Without an owner's manual, when we use a product, either we miss the whole thing, or we miss the knowledge of many of the product's applications and features.

There are so many uses and features of a computer. Even the humble calculator has hundreds of applications that we are unaware of. We may use the calculator for basic functions like addition and subtraction; however, we may not take advantage of its other applications. In the same way, if we don't have and don't know the owner's manual for the mind, we do not use it the way we ought to, or to its full potential. Understanding the three different engraved memories or *saṁskāras* is the operating manual for the mind. Because we have never learned or understood about the *guṇas*, we live only a very small fraction of what's possible in life. We miss the beauty and potential of life when we don't have the owner's manual.

At the outset, *saṁskāra* is an active engraved memory that pulls us down and makes us travel the same path again and again. We end up going in dead-end circles. Then, when we do walk down the same path, the engraving becomes even deeper and those memories get further entrenched. Modern science understands this fact. Experiments have shown that repeated emotional experiences create more receptors for that emotion being developed in the brain. Physically, physiologically, the more anger outbursts you have, the more anger receptors your brain develops. The great *ṛṣis*, the inner scientists, have known this for thousands of years. If certain emotions are not expressed, the corresponding brain parts or receptors degenerate and die. So, the more we manage to stay out of negative emotions, the less they bother us. On the contrary, the more we indulge, the more our brain programs the same indulgence. This is the cause of addictions.

Kṛṣṇa explains how we become caught in these three levels of memories and how, again and again, we are pulled and pushed by these memories. It is almost like having three wives. If we have one woman in our life, enlightenment is a luxury. If we have two women, enlightenment is an option. If we have three women in our life, enlightenment is compulsory! With three wives or husbands, one cannot live without enlightenment.

Here, He gives us an understanding of how to live with these engraved memories. Another important point is that because these memories are living energies, they can be used for bad deeds or good deeds.

When a person has energies to do bad deeds, we can tap into those energies and make him do good deeds. From my experiences of conducting meditation programs in prisons, no one puts in as much effort and goes into such deep meditation as a prisoner. We conduct meditation programs in prisons. They are so involved and go into meditation more deeply in comparison to people outside. When prisoners take up meditation, they really take it up. They are intense. They don't do anything half-heartedly. When they are transformed, their whole life is transformed!

If we look at the lives of Indian *ṛṣis* like Vālmīki or the great saint Arunagirinathar, they and many others were sinners. However, a dramatic change occured and a cognitive shift took place in their being. The shift usually happens in the way that our mind receives data, processes it and delivers the result. Once the cognitive shift takes place, we receive data, process it and go inside instead of outside. As long as we react externally, we are working towards depression. However, once we go in, we move into bliss.

For example, the death of someone close to us, our near and dear ones, can lead us to the spiritual path or to frustration. We can think, 'Anyway, I am also going to die, so I should do what I want.' Or we can decide, 'I too will die some day. Let me learn what I can and grow.'

A small story:

A person was about to be hanged. The officer on duty asked him if he had any last wishes. The prisoner said, 'No.' The officer said, 'You can pray to God. You can ask forgiveness and ask for His blessing. We can bring in a priest.'

The prisoner said, 'I want to remember God, but not in the way you suggest. Had I known earlier I would be executed for these crimes, I would have committed a few more sins.'

The prisoner continued, 'If I had known that I was going to be hanged, I would have committed more sins. So if I pray, I will ask God why He didn't let me know earlier that I was going to be hanged. I don't need a priest for that.'

When some people understand that death is the ultimate, they think, 'Death is the ultimate so let me work towards the Divine, achieve God, or realize *ātman*.' Others react differently: anyway we are going to die. Let us do whatever we want and live the way we want to. One group takes the path of meditation and the other takes the path of the outer world. The path we choose is up to us.

Kṛṣṇa explains how engraved memories disturb our mind and through this understanding, we can transform our being.

Before explaining these verses, let me present a small diagram through which we can understand how engrams affect our decisions and how to come out of the influence of engrams.

Please understand how we receive information or data from the outer world, how we process it and how we make decisions. First, we see something through the eyes. I have taken the example of sight, but we can replace it with any other sense, such as hearing, smelling, tasting or touching. Among these five *jñānendriya* (senses of perception), any one can be used here.

How the mind works?

There are five *jñānendriya* and five *karmendriya* (senses of action) that are the means of communication between the external world and us. *Jñānendriya* are the senses of perception, the five senses of smell, taste, sight, touch and hearing. The *karmendriya* are five actions of elimination, procreation, locomotion, grasping and speaking. Each sense is related to one of the energy centers *(cakras)* in our body-mind system. For instance, locomotion is related to the *maṇipūraka cakra* (energy center located in the stomach region) and the energy of fire.

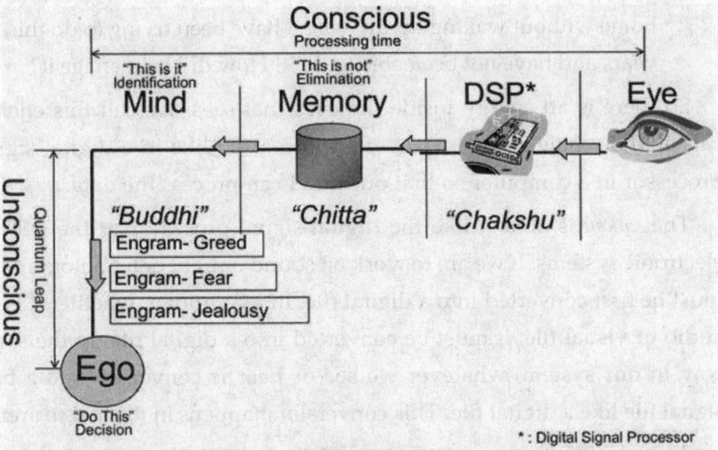

LBP Techniques help in removing negative engraved memories and add positive energy using meditation techniques

We can take any of the five *jñānendriya* to replace the eyes in this example. Through the eyes we see a scene. Let us say we see this scene of this discourse is happening. You see me talking to you. First your eye captures this whole scene like a picture and this picture goes to the *cakṣu* (the energy behind the eyes). Understand, we don't see *with* the eye, we see *through* the eye. There is an energy that is inside or behind the eye that actually sees. There is an energy inside or behind the ears that hears. The ears by themselves cannot hear. That is why when we are engrossed in a book we may not hear the alarm or doorbell ring. If we are reading, we may not know if our spouse walks into the room. Of course, if it is late at night, all wives know when their husbands sneak into the house. That is a different matter!

A small story:

A man goes to the police station to meet a thief who had burgled his home the previous night and taken all the cash. The officer on duty refuses to allow him to meet the thief, saying, 'You cannot talk to him now. You can meet him in court tomorrow.' The man pleads, 'I don't want to disturb him. All I want to know is how he entered my home without waking up my wife. I have been trying to do this for years and have not been able to do it! How did he manage it?'

So there is an energy inside the eyes that sees. We call this energy *cakṣu.* The whole scene is converted into a file like in a digital signal processor in a computer so that our mind can process the data.

The *cakṣu* is almost like the digital signal processor or the DSP in electronic systems. If we are to work on sound or light or a photograph, it must be first converted into a digital file. In a computer, whether it is an audio or visual file, it must be converted into a digital file. In the same way in our system, whatever we see or hear is converted into a bio-signal file like a digital file. This conversion happens in this *cakṣu* area.

Then the file starts moving up, step-by-step. The file goes to the part of the mind called *citta* (memory). If we understand this, our whole life can be transformed. We will know where and how we react. We will realize how we make big decisions based upon our assumptions and consequently suffer.

This is what happened in the story where the teacher imagined that alcohol was the liquid leaking from her gift and tasted it without thinking. We can understand how these mistakes happen by analyzing the diagram.

The file goes to *citta,* the place where past memories are collected. This area is where the work of excluding happens. When the file reaches this place, the excluding process starts - *Na iti, Na iti* - not this. The process of *neti neti* (this is not, this is not) takes place in this area. Upon seeing this file, our *citta* starts eliminating whatever the object is not.

Take the example of this scene: First you see me, the whole scene is photographed. It goes to *cakṣu* and becomes a bio-signal file. The file is then taken to *citta. Citta* says, 'This is not a tree. This is not an animal. This is not a plant. This is not this. This is not that.' The excluding process happens in *citta.*

It is like searching for the word 'cow' in a dictionary. You first eliminate all other letters to reach 'c.' Then you search for 'o' and eliminate all other letters. Then you reach 'w' by eliminating all other letters. In this manner, you reach the word 'cow.' This is how *citta* works.

Next, the file goes to *manas,* another part of the mind. The *manas* tries to positively identify, 'This is a human being. He is wearing a saffron robe. He is standing on a stage.' The identification process, *'iti, iti'* (this is it, this is it) happens in *manas.* In *citta,* '*neti, neti*' or the 'not this, not this,' elimination occurs.

Once the positive identification happens, the file goes to a third part of the mind called *buddhi* or intelligence. *Buddhi* is where the trouble starts. Here the analysis starts, 'How am I related to this file? How am I connected to this scene? How is it relevant to me? How should I respond to this scene?'

If past memories about me have been good or pleasant according to your intelligence, you respond in a positive way. You immediately refer to those past memories and review, 'It was so good at yesterday's discourse.' Your intelligence refers to the past memory and makes a decision based upon these experiences. If past experiences with me have been positive, your intelligence tells you to stay and listen. If past experiences have been unpleasant and you felt bored, your intelligence tells you that this is not the place for you and that you should leave. These are logical decisions based on conscious memories retained by your mind.

Up to this point, transmission of what is perceived by the senses and what is registered by the mind are relatively straightforward. It is a conscious process. I explained earlier about conscious and unconscious minds. Psychologists talk about a subconscious mind as well. This does not exist. This is a term used to further confuse you.

If the processing of sensory data is stopped at this conscious level, at the intelligence level, we make decisions at the conscious level by using our intellect. This is alright; it is limiting, however, because the conscious mind is still only ten percent of the total mind capacity. This is what we call intellect-based decision-making. These decisions are based on logic and a rationale. We are proud of this achievement. The French philosopher Descartes said, 'I think therefore I am.' He didn't realize that he limited his potential to only ten percent. What a sad state!

Because of the limited capacity of our conscious mind, nature wires us to use our unconscious mind to decide many things. Unfortunately this unconscious mind is a conditioned mind. It is full of engraved memories, beliefs and value systems drilled into us from childhood. All that parents and elders have taught us plus all that we have been force-fed by religion and society from a deeply impressionable age are stored in this vault that is never open to us. It opens on its own when it chooses to, especially in moments of stress and trauma. Just as viruses and bacteria attack when our immune system is down, the virus of engrams and *saṁskāras* influence us when our emotional systems are weakened.

Ego decides

Saṁskāras do not accumulate only during this lifetime. The mental attitudes are carried over from previous births. Neural scientists tell us about the part of our brain called the reptilian brain that stores memories of our evolution from marine and amphibian creatures.

From the conscious mind, the information is passed to the unconscious region of the mind, the ego.

I call this unconscious region of the mind *ego* not because it is arrogant, but because it provides you the identity of who you are. The word 'ego' is derived from a Greek word that means 'a mask.' Your identity is a mask that you wear. It is not you.

Your identity stems from your unconscious. You project who you wish to be, never who you are. You do not even know who you are. Who you are is deeply buried in your unconscious. All the major decisions that shape your life are consigned to this unconscious zone. This is the repository of all those emotionally-filled memories and beliefs about yourself, which constitute what you are and, therefore, create your identity. This is what I call the *ego*.

The conscious mind does not make important decisions. It makes a few decisions that can be reached by its limited intellect. Anything important moves to the unconscious ego. Our unconscious handles all life-threatening situations, the so-called fight-or-flight decisions. Our conscious mind is too slow to handle them.

Let us go back to the incident of your watching me here. The problem arises if your conscious mind does not make a direct decision. If you have had past experiences with other persons wearing saffron robes, you will have engrams about that experience. You will not bother to see who this person is. You decide based on that memory that says, 'No, with that master I suffered like this; with some other master, I suffered like that.' It will be a generalized memory. You make a decision based on your collected past *saṁskāras*.

That is where we create trouble. When decisions are made with a straight understanding, there is no major problem. However, most of the time we collect and react based on engrams that are unrelated to each other.

For example, you see someone wearing a white dress. You may have been hurt in the past by someone wearing a white dress. The moment you see a white dress, the memory comes back even if you don't want it to.

In the same way, if we are abused or disrespected in a house, the memory comes up automatically the next time we visit that house, even if the person who did it is not there. We experience the same feeling, feel depressed and go into a low mood.

We connect and associate things with places, with triggers, with memories, and put them into memory files. We are not able to work spontaneously. We must rely on some technique, some method to reduce our processing work. Naturally, we opt for some kind of arrangement in our memory. Consequently, we miss out on real life.

Only in the first few days of marriage do we respond spontaneously to our spouse. Within the first few months of living with our spouse, we form a clear idea about him or her. After that, we don't really live with him or her. We live with our imagination of him or her. We live with our understanding of him or her. After that, whatever our spouse does is wrong. We come to a predetermined conclusion that the spouse is always wrong. If our spouse does something right, we say that it happened by mistake!

So after a few months, we come to a conclusion about the other persons in our life. We create an engram related to them based on our judgment. After that, we judge whatever he or she does through the filter of the engram or engraved memory. Sometimes we create engraved memories in our system based on experiences that others have or from media influences.

> A small story:
>
> One day, a funeral procession slowly made its way down the road. A man walking two bulldogs as he moved along ahead of the body of the dead woman. There was a long queue of people following slowly behind him.
>
> An onlooker observed the number of people in the procession and thought, 'She must have been a famous woman.' He approached the

man with the bulldogs and asked, 'Who is the dead lady?'

The man replied, 'She is my mother-in-law.'

The onlooker asked if the two dogs were the dead woman's pets. The man replied, 'No. They attacked and killed her.'

'Killed her?' the onlooker asked. 'Yes,' said the man. The onlooker asked, 'Can I borrow the dogs for two days?'

The man pointed to the people following him and said, 'Join the queue.'

When we enter into relationships with preconceived notions, this is what happens! We collect so many memories that we never relate to people as they are. We only relate with the preconceived memory we have of the person.

People ask me, '*Swamiji*, is our life pre-destined or open to free will?' Understand, the more engrams we have, the more our life is predestined. This is because we will go along the same route repeatedly. The fewer engrams we have, the more freedom we enjoy.

The number of *saṁskāras* determines whether we have free will or if our life is predestined. For example, the file travels to the ego, and the ego gives the decision, and we execute it. If there are more engrams, the file travels to every table as in a bureaucratic office. Each engram places its stamp, puts its signature and writes its opinion.

People with many engrams never relax. They don't sit quietly. So much physical restlessness is due to many decisions taking place inside their unconscious.

Take the example of smoking: According to the data collected at the conscious level, we know smoking is injurious to health. According to simple, straightforward data that we have assimilated, we know smoking is injurious to health; however, when the time comes, suddenly we decide to smoke.

How does the file take such a quantum leap? How is the decision totally changed? When the file travels to the unconscious area, engrams say, 'No, no! The last time I smoked, I felt really good; I felt relieved from all the stress.'

If you want to eliminate stress, wear a tight shoe instead of smoking. When you wear a tight shoe, you forget other worries. By creating bigger problems, we try to forget the smaller problems. If we wear tight shoes, we automatically forget smaller worries.

Here, in the unconscious area, all the past memories reside: 'I smoked. I felt good. I felt relieved. All the stress disappeared.' We suddenly make a decision that we did not want to make, because of these unconscious memories.

We make countless decisions based upon engraved memories. Suddenly we shout and after ten minutes, we repent, 'Why did I shout? I always wanted to keep a smiling face. I wanted people to acknowledge that I have a smiling face. Why did I shout?' We repent. We made a sudden decision. We reacted suddenly due to these engrams.

Kṛṣṇa speaks of *satva guṇa saṁskāras* that lead us to bliss and peace, *rajasic guṇa saṁskāras* that lead to restlessness and violence and *tamasic saṁskāras* that lead to depression. He further explains how these *saṁskāras* influence our decision-making process.

Let us say our radio suddenly stops working properly and we simultaneously connect with frequencies from three channels: One channel is playing an advertisement for a cosmetic product. The second channel gives instructions for farming. The third channel is playing a comedy drama. The result will sound like this to us, 'Please spray a little bit of pesticide. After that wipe your face clean. Now brush your teeth properly and put on a little more pesticide. Finally jump up and down and laugh flailing your arms and legs!'

If we try to execute decisions based on these mixed, cross-wired instructions, just imagine what our plight would be! Similarly, when we try to work with different types of engrams - *satva, rajas* and *tamas* - and all three cross each other, they create hell in our lives. Please understand that intelligent people collect arguments to arrive at a fresh judgment while most of us collect arguments to support a pre-existing judgment.

If we look into our life we will know how many times have we accepted our mistakes? Of course, even to look into our lives and see how many times we have erred needs intelligence. We usually react out of arrogance or guilt. We say, 'So what if I made a mistake?' We brush it aside. This is one kind of attitude, the attitude of might is right. The other attitude is that of suffering from guilt.

Please understand that an unintelligent man never feels guilty. Of course I tell you to drop your guilt as well. That is in a different context. Only an intelligent man who thinks of *dharma* (righteousness) suffers from guilt. Only he feels guilt. A person who lives and feels only at the instinct level never feels guilty. An Arjuna or a Yudhiṣtra feels guilty. A Duryodhana will not feel guilty.

A person at the intellect level suffers guilt. Someone at the level of intuition goes beyond guilt. He understands the truth as it is. Kṛṣṇa speaks of how to handle these three *guṇas* properly and use them to the maximum. Getting the maximum out of them is an intelligent process.

A small story:

A young child swallowed a coin and was taken to the doctor. The doctor used different methods to no avail. The nurse also tried; still the coin didn't come out. A friend standing nearby made an attempt without success. A passerby observed this and offered his assistance. The doctor asked, 'What can you do?' The passerby said, 'Give me one moment.' He spoke to the child and came back smiling with the coin. The surprised doctor asked, 'I am a doctor. I could not take the coin out. How did you do it?'

The passerby said, 'I am a con artist. I can extract money out of anybody.'

Kṛṣṇa gives tips and techniques to get the maximum out of all the three *guṇas!* Before entering into these three layers of engrams, *saṁskāras* related to *satva, rajas* and *tamas,* let me illustrate how we are caught in them and how they work. Then, we will enter into each technique.

Seven energy layers of the body

These are the seven energy layers of our body-mind system. These are seven parts of our being.

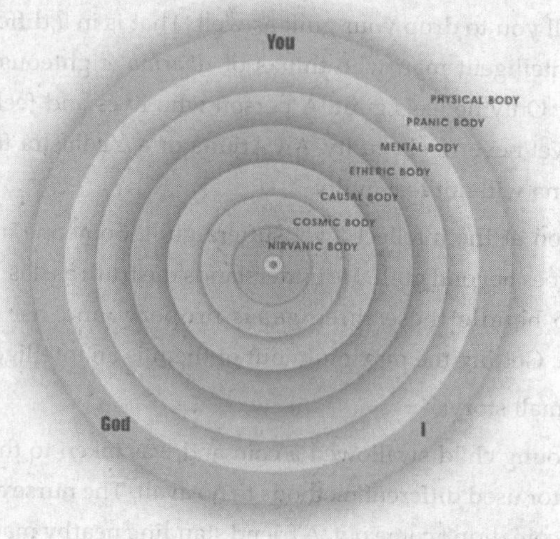

The first is the physical body, our flesh and bones. Next is the *pranic* layer, the energies of *prāna, vyāna, udāna, apāna* and *samāna,* or the five air movements that take place in our body-mind system. The third is the mental body. This is where our mental inner chattering continuously takes place. A continuous recorder goes on as inner chatter inside us whether we are standing, sitting or doing nothing. Sometimes we open our mouth and chatter. At other times, we close our mouth and continue to chatter. Whether we open our mouth or not, talking continues. This is inner chattering or the mental body or *cancala,* which means inner movement.

The fourth is the etheric body. This is the space where our intense emotions and painful experiences are stored. Usually intense emotions involve pain and suffering. We do not know any other intense emotion. If we do, we are a spiritual person.

When we look into life, we see that pain gives such an intense feeling. When we are depressed or in pain, we become intense and our whole mind is centered. Our mind does not move towards anything else.

Have you experienced bliss to the same extent or depth that you have experienced pain? No. All we know is pain.

We cannot intellectually understand the three bodies beyond the etheric body. They can only be experienced spiritually through meditation.

The pranic layer is filled with desires. The mental body is filled with 'I should have' or guilt feelings. The etheric body is pain. Understand these three. Desire, guilt and pain are the feelings or the experiences stored in these layers.

When emotions, desires and feelings arising out of these three attributes are pure, they are called *satva, rajas* and *tamas* depending on the quality of the emotion. Usually, they are impure. They are mixed with each other. We should know how to purify them. If we can purify our desires, we will be liberated. We can only cleanse and purify the desires, directing them towards the right path. Without desires, we can't breathe. Even inhaling and exhaling cannot happen without desires. We cannot live without desires. Desires must be handled properly. Desires must be straightened. That's what we need to work towards, *satva.*

Next comes guilt or *rajas.* Our restlessness is created by thoughts like, 'I should have done that', 'I should have lived like that', 'Because I did not do it then, let me do it now', 'I should have reacted in a certain manner; however, at that time, I did not have the intelligence. Let me teach him a lesson, I know what to do now.' This is how restlessness or *rajas* operates.

The third is pain. Whether we do right or wrong, we know how to make it painful. Whatever it is, we know how to create suffering through *tamas.*

The first four body-mind layers are influenced by the three *guṇas.* The mind cannot experience the remaining three layers beyond the fourth layer. They can be experienced only through meditation. In the fifth layer, the causal body, we sleep soundly without dreams. It is called *kāraṇa śarīra,* the energy layer that we experience during deep sleep. The sixth layer is the cosmic layer, filled with joyful memories, and the seventh is the nirvanic layer or the bliss body.

Just remember the first four layers of physical, pranic, mental and etheric energy. That's enough, because we will work only on these now. Kṛṣṇa has already spoken about the physical layer. Now He works on the other three *guṇas* of *satva, rajas* and *tamas. Satva* is related to the second layer, which is the pranic layer; *rajas* is related to the third layer, which is the mental body; and the fourth layer is the etheric layer of *tamas.* As I was saying, *satva* is related to desires and the *prāna śarīra.* When our desires change, our *prāna* flow or our airflow changes. *Prāna* is the life giving energy that we inhale along with the air that we take in. Air is only a medium to take in *prāna.* It is *prāna* that sustains life in us. This *prāna* is affected by the changing desires in us. For example, if we are caught in lust or an intense desire, our inhaling and exhaling becomes intense. The *prāna* going in and coming out increases. With any desire, the *prāna* flow totally changes. If we are in a silent, peaceful mood, the *prāna* flow will be so mild, we will not know *prāna* is flowing.

Understand that this *pranic* layer is filled with desires. What should we learn about *satva,* about this *pranic* layer? Let me explain.

You are pure consciousness

Whether we believe it or not, we are God. We are pure consciousness. Whatever thoughts we create in our pure consciousness gain power. This space exists in all of us and is called Self, *ātman,* or inner divinity. Whatever thoughts we create in this space, the deeper they are, the more power they get from this consciousness. It is like placing a slide in front of the bulb in a slide projector. That slide becomes reality on the screen. This inner Self is also light and any slide we create in this area becomes reality in the outer world.

But the problem is we create self-contradictory desires. We suffer with our desires because of this. Whether our desires are fulfilled or not, the resulting suffering is inevitable. If the desires are fulfilled, there will be emptiness, and if they are unfulfilled, there will be restlessness. In both cases, we move towards *tamas.* Why?

Why should we suffer because of desires? First, understand self-contradicting desires. For instance, if we want to get rid of a headache, normally we create an engram that continuously says, 'I should get rid of this headache. I should get rid of this headache.' We repeat the same words constantly in our unconscious. By continuously thinking that we want to get rid of the headache, we will never be able to get rid of it. When we repeat a word, in this case 'headache', we actually give power to it. The headache intensifies instead of disappearing.

It is a subtle understanding. Whatever words we repeat unconsciously become reality in our body, mind and in our world. It is because we have the power to give life to any word. If the words 'Let me get up and go', come to our mind, with those words, immediately our body will move; we will stand up and start going.

One word can make us do whatever we want. Words that appear in our mind are important. Words that appear in our mind are *mantra* (sacred sounds). When put together, all the words that appear in our mind form our life, especially the words that we repeat unconsciously.

For example, if we observe what happens when we brush our teeth in the morning, we see that our mind is somewhere else. When we are in the shower, the mind is elsewhere. Especially when we take a cold water shower, we sometimes even sing to divert our mind. Cold showers and singing are closely connected! Since nobody is watching us in the bathroom, we talk or sing freely. Sometimes people even argue with themselves loudly in the bathroom.

> A man was standing near the bathroom when his wife came out. He asked, 'Who were you arguing with in the bathroom?'
>
> She said, 'I was talking to myself.'
>
> He asked, 'Why were you arguing?'
>
> She said, 'I know what I was doing, so stay out of it.'
>
> He continued, 'I can understand that you were talking to yourself, but why were you arguing with yourself?'
>
> She said, 'You know me. I don't accept stupid logic. That is why I was arguing with myself!'

We play games all the time! We continuously talk without coming to reality. We utter the same words when brushing our teeth every day of the week. The moment we start brushing our teeth, we will have the same trend of thoughts. Every time we shower, we have the same type of thoughts too. If we observe ourselves closely, we will realize these things.

Thoughts that we repeat unconsciously are more powerful than words we use consciously. We create many thoughts, many *saṁskāras* that are self-contradictory. 'I should get rid of this headache' is a self-contradictory thought. When we repeat those words we remember the headache as well. By remembering the word 'headache' again and again, we bring back that memory and we bring back that headache into our mind. How do we expect to get rid of the headache then?

If we constantly repeat, 'I should get rid of this headache,' we bring that memory back every time we utter the word 'headache.' We bring that whole file of suffering back to our mind. How can we get rid of the headache then? Instead of using the word headache, create a *saṁskāra* such as, 'I should become healthy' again and again. Then we can remember the idea of health!

Whatever *mantra* or word we use, that *dhyāna* or meditation automatically happens in our unconscious. If we use the word 'headache' again and again, we will be meditating on the headache again and again. If we use the word 'health' again and again, we will be meditating on health again and again.

That is why when we start to meditate upon God, we start with a *dhyāna śloka* - meditation verse. Before meditating, we recite the *dhyāna śloka.* It is like the invocation verses that invoke God with the right words. In these verses we verbalize what good things we wish to visualize in our lives.

The power of visualization

Verbalization of visualization is the *dhyāna śloka.* Now, if again and again we verbalize the word headache, headache, headache, what will we visualize? We will visualize the person who gives us a headache, or what we feel like when we get a headache. We will continuously visualize the headache scene and the related mood.

Whatever we visualize again and again will be inscribed or engraved in our memory, in our inner space, in our inner being. If we have a disease, please never create and repeat a word that carries the name of the disease. For example, never say, 'Let me get rid of this heart problem. Let me get rid of this diabetes. Let me get rid of this high blood pressure' Use straight words, not self-contradictory words. If we have pain or an illness, use words like 'Let me become healthy.' Words create a visualization and energy of what we want to happen.

Always use these words, 'Let me become healthy.' Never use words like, 'Let me get rid of this back pain.'

Never use self-contradicting engrams. The more we use self-contradicting engrams, the more we engrave that disease into our inner space. The more we engrave, the more powerful the engrams become. Please do not abuse the inner space or *icchā śakti* (power of creation). The *pranic* layer is our *icchā śakti.* It has the energy to make things happen. It has the energy to fulfill our desires. Do not waste *icchā śakti* by creating self-contradicting thoughts or self-contradicting engrams.

Self-contradicting thoughts corrupt our whole *satva* space. When you go home today, spend just ten minutes to do this exercise. Sit for ten minutes with yourself and write down the thoughts that come to your mind regularly. Then see where you are creating self-contradicting engrams and edit them, clear them. Don't bring self-contradicting thoughts into your mind.

We continuously allow ourselves to be exploited by what we hear and see. People who don't know the truth of the mind and consciousness influence us. All these problems arise because we don't know that pure joy of inner space is possible.

Let me make the bold statement that no medicine or chemical can help our mind. All anti-anxiety medicines, all anti-depression medicines are consolations. First, we visualized that we suffered from depression and now we visualize that we have taken some medicine, that's all.

Let me share another important secret. It is a business secret! Many people say, '*Swamiji*, that person has done some black magic on me. He has laid a spell on me. Someone has put an evil spirit behind me. Some evil being possesses me.' There are many people who exploit this kind of fear in others, cashing in on this fear. Understand: All such negativity has only one power, our faith in it.

All negative thoughts, such as black magic or evil or demonic acts, have only one power and that is our faith in them. Our faith in them gives them power. Because we believe in them, we connect all the incidents and make trouble for ourselves. And then we struggle to free ourselves.

When people come to me with these fears, I say, 'There is nothing, don't worry. There is no problem.' Then they think, 'This master is young. He doesn't know much. Let's go to an older person who will give us some counter-spells, some talisman, someone who will do some exorcism and remove this negativity and blockage.'

They think I don't know anything. Then what do I do to help them? I give them some talisman and say, 'You don't have to pay. Just put this under your pillow and you will be healed. You will be cured.' The talisman, the *yantra,* has nothing in it. I am clear that the *yantra* has nothing in it. The person has created an idea within himself. He has this negativity. By giving him the *yantra,* I create an idea in him that he doesn't have any negativity. It is like using one thorn to remove another thorn. There is nothing else in this.

I tell people, 'Don't think that by having these *yantras* something will shower from your roof. Nothing can shower from your house except rats!' These *yantras* are antidotes for their negative faith. They already created the faith that they have certain problems. I just tell them honestly, 'You created this trouble, and now I am your help to undo it.' So understand: All negativity has only one power: our faith in it.

If the person who exploits these fears only takes money for them, that's fine; we can earn back that money. The danger is that he also creates an engram in us. He creates a *saṁskāra* that continuously haunts us. For anything and everything, we run to him like slaves. It is better to be caught in the hands of the ghost than in the hands of a sorcerer! At least, the ghost will trouble us only once in a while; this person, however, will exploit us completely.

Now, when we create self-contradicting thoughts, we start believing them. Especially when they name a disease in psychoanalysis, it is like the fashion business. In the fashion business, every week they launch a new dress. Similarly here, every month they invent a new disease.

By repeating that negative idea, by meditating on the symptom, we start creating that symptom in us. It is a dangerous game. Don't be caught in that game. We disturb the *satva,* the pure space of our being, by creating self-contradicting thoughts. So write down your major thoughts and desires and analyze them. This is the first step. Next, let us see how two desires contradict one another. For instance, we want to lead a peaceful life and we want wealth. Either decide to take responsibility and be happy with that responsibility, or decide to relax and accept whatever happens.

Only one thought should be strengthened when two desires conflict. When we have both, we have a self-contradicting mental setup. In the *satva* space, in the *satva* energy, when we create self-contradicting engraved memories, we are automatically thrown into *rajas.*

The mode of passion is born of unlimited desires and longings. This is a beautiful verse. Because of these desires and longings, Kṛṣṇa says, the embodied living entity is bound to doing result-oriented actions.

He talks about desires and longings. What is the difference? Desires and longings - *rāga* means desire; *tṛṣṇā* means craving, longing. What is the difference? Some memories have our emotional support whereas some memories have been inserted into our being by advertisements.

Self-contradicting desires

Advertisements are not only on the television or in a movie theatre. If our father repeats something time and again, that is an advertisement. Some desires have our mental support. We feel these will give us fulfillment; we feel these are our genuine needs. Some desires have been sold to us by someone else. That is the difference between desires and longings.

Desires are ours and longings have been given to us by society. They are a social conditioning. Desires are inborn. They are our nature. If we fulfill desires, we feel fulfilled and relaxed. With longings, the moment we fulfill them, we feel empty. This is the difference between desire and longing. Desire gives us fulfillment. Longing gives us emptiness.

Kṛṣṇa shows us how self-contradicting desires lead us to *rajas.* When desires contradict each other, we get confused. We fall into restlessness. When the information about an object comes into our system, it passes through *cakṣu, citta, buddhi* and then goes to the ego. On its way, before this file reaches the ego, it passes through the unconscious space of engrams that write their opinions on this file.

Let us say ten engrams write a decision saying, 'I want to sit and listen to the discourse' and another ten engrams write, 'No, let us go watch a movie. After all, it is the weekend.' Ten engrams write similar decisions on the file, and another ten engrams write another kind of decision on the file. By the time the file reaches the ego, we are confused. As a result of these contradicting opinions from our engrams, we have inner restlessness.

The more engrams, the more time it takes to make a decision. We will suffer and be in a dilemma. Man *is* a dilemma. Continuously we think, 'I should have done this,' or 'I should have done that.' Dilemma is due to too many engrams.

Dilemma is what Kṛṣṇa calls *rajas* and restlessness. In *rajas,* we have tremendous anger, violence and inner restlessness. A *rajasic* person shouts at others and experiences an irritable mood. He waits to vomit out his irritation and anger on others.

Once we remove these engrams, we can make one thousand decisions without getting stressed. The file will go straight to the ego without interruption. To make a decision we don't need to cross three hundred desks as in an Indian government office. Instead there will be only two or three tables. One says, 'Yes,' the other says, 'Okay.' By the time the file reaches the ego, there will not be many differing opinions. It can decide instantly and send the file back for action. The process will be easy. Making decisions will be easy and our time and energy will not be wasted.

That is why Kṛṣṇa says that when we don't expect the result, when we don't think of *karma phala* (result of the work done), we can do the work intensely. There are fewer engrams and we will not be tortured by them.

In the next verse Kṛṣṇa talks about *tamas.* He addresses Arjuna, 'Oh son of Bhārata, know that the mode of darkness, *tamas,* is born out of ignorance. The results of this mode are madness, indolence and sleep, which bind the conditioned soul.' This is a beautiful explanation of *tamas.*

If there are more *saṁskāras* or engrams, the file does not reach the ego easily. In fact, the file may not reach the ego fully. A powerful engram may make the decision on the way. It is similar to a 'non application of mind' in legal terminology.

Why does this happen? Why do you decide unconsciously and regret later?

This unconscious zone is filled with negative memories and restlessness. All our past memories and past thought patterns, *saṁskāras* or engrams, are stored in this zone as files. So many files are stored in this zone without any logical connection between them.

This is what happens. When the file takes a quantum leap to this zone, it does not reach the ego properly for a decision because this zone is where all the data that causes restlessness in you is stored. It is as if your computer hard disk is loaded with high-resolution photographs and there is no further space to work on your hard disk. Like that, when your unconscious is loaded with past thought patterns and memories, it becomes inefficient and makes superficial, illogical decisions.

Take this example: According to data that you have collected, smoking is injurious to health. It is not good for your body or mind. You can hold onto this decision as long as you are at the conscious level. But once the mind takes the leap to the ego, the engrams instruct you to smoke; you simply decide to smoke! The conscious process says, 'No, it is not good for health.' Yet the unconscious process just makes the decision and you execute it! It is a pure instinct-level decision.

When we have more engrams, we don't know what decision will come out. It is like a Pandora's box. We don't know what will come out since the inner space is full of engrams and *saṁskāras*. We are at the level of an animal. We act on instinct.

When there are only a few engrams, it is like not having three hundred desks for the file to have to move through. There are only a few desks, similar to a private corporation. This is the human level or the level of intellect.

When there are no engrams, there will be no need for the file to drop into the unconscious zone for a decision. It straightaway meets the *buddhi* and ego after the mind. There are no blocks. The time taken for the unconscious process will be less than the conscious process. We will be intuitive or at the level of God.

The level of an animal is the level of instinct; the level of man is the level of intellect; the level of God is the level of intuition. The level of instinct is the level of *tamas*; the level of intellect is the level of *rajas*; the level of intuition is the level of *satva*.

In *satva*, our mind works continuously and we make decisions. We can be active twenty-four hours and yet remain peaceful. This is what I call action in inaction and inaction in action. Kṛṣṇa says we will be centered when we are in *satva*. We will remain utterly relaxed in the midst of activity.

The whole thing is dependent on one thing: our engrams or engraved memories. The number of engraved memories determines whether we are caught in *satva*, *rajas* or *tamas*. These three are not enlightened states. Enlightenment is beyond these three. If we are caught in *tamas*, we need to move towards *rajas*. If we are caught in *rajas*, move towards *satva*. If we are caught in *satva*, it will automatically lead us to enlightenment. *Tamas* is also not taking up enough responsibility. For example, we are in *tamas* if we studied to become a doctor and we do not practice our profession out of laziness. If we don't practice for some other reason, that is fine. Don't drop out from anything due to *tamas*. If we drop out because of a spiritual reason, that is different. Some people drop out to meditate, go on a pilgrimage or to do spiritual work. That is fine. However, we are caught in *tamas* when we drop out due to laziness or for no reason at all.

Dropping out due to *tamas* means that we don't have enough energy and we cannot make a responsible decision. Why? Too many engrams block our decision process. By the time we make one decision, we feel tired and want to sleep. That is why we attempt to escape from life. Escapists are *tamasic* people.

Guarding the Senses

14.9 *The mode of goodness conditions one to happiness, Passion conditions him to fruits of action, and ignorance to madness.*

14.10 *Sometimes the mode of passion becomes prominent, defeating the mode of goodness, O son of Bhārata. And sometimes the mode of goodness defeats passion, and at other times the mode of ignorance defeats goodness and passion. In this way there is always competition for supremacy.*

14.11 *When the light of Self-knowledge illuminates all the senses (or gates) in the body, Then it should be known that goodness is predominant.*

14.12 *O chief of Bhārata, when there is an increase in the mode of passion, the symptoms of great attachment, uncontrollable desire, hankering, and intense endeavor develop.*

Kṛṣṇa further explains the three modes. 'O Bhārata, sometimes the mode of goodness, *satva*, becomes prominent, defeating the modes of passion and ignorance, and at other times, ignorance defeats goodness and passion. In this way, there is always competition for supremacy.'

All of us are not completely caught in *satva* or *rajas* or *tamas.* We swing between *satva, rajas* and *tamas.* We go from this end to that end, and from that end to this end.

Sometimes we get up in the morning and feel fresh. We feel as if all our questions are answered; we are fresh, alive and we think we have become almost enlightened! Everything goes beautifully until evening. Suddenly we become restless. The very next day, we are in *tamas.* We don't want to do anything. These mood swings take place continuously.

Obesity and mood swings are closely related. When we allow these mood swings to happen, we torture ourselves. Sometimes we are restless, sometimes we are peaceful and sometimes we are in *tamas.* When we are in *tamas* we don't want to do anything; we want to escape from everything; we want to dump everything and run away. We are caught in these three modes of nature: sometimes in instinct, sometimes in intellect and sometimes in intelligence.

Why do we have mood swings?

Why? This happens if we have collected too many *saṁskāras* about something over many years. For example, we have many engrams about drinking if, from a young age, we were repeatedly taught not to drink and that drinking is a sin. This raises our curiosity and we are tempted to taste alcohol at least once. Never give a law to children. Instead give them understanding and the spirit behind the law.

If we want to bring up children blissfully, we need to bring them up without guilt. Following rules without understanding them leads to breaking the rules. Breaking rules creates guilt. Guilt is the worst imaginable sin. To give understanding, we need two things. First we need to be intelligent enough to understand the meaning behind the rules we are trying to enforce. Next we need patience to explain it all to them. Even though it takes more time and energy, focus on giving them understanding.

Never give rules if you want people to follow them! If we give a rule, they will do the opposite of the rule. Furthermore, we can't even predict that they will do the exact opposite. Even though it requires time and energy, take time and raise children with understanding.

People complain to me, '*Swamiji*, in these modern times, there is no time. My daughter goes to school. I have a job. How do we find time to make her understand?' I say, 'Why did you give birth to your child if you don't have time to bring her up? You should have become a *sanyāsi* like me! You should have decided earlier in life.'

> A mother brought her child to me and said, '*Swamiji*, please advise him. Please ask him to obey me.'
>
> I was not keen on giving that advice because I myself didn't listen to or obey my mother when I was young! How could I give that advice? But I could not say that to the woman. So I decided to make her happy by advising her son.
>
> She continued, '*Swamiji*, you must advise him.'
>
> I tried to escape two or three times, but to no avail. Finally I called the boy and gently said, 'Why don't you obey your mother? I am also obeying her right now! Why don't you listen to what she says?'
>
> You will be surprised to hear the boy's reply. He explained, '*Swamiji*, she is not happy. If I listen to her advice I will become like her. Why are you asking me to listen to her?'
>
> I was taken aback. He was speaking the truth.

I somehow convinced him and sent him away; however, I was not convinced. He said the truth. If the mother was unhappy how could the son follow her advice?

In the near future, children will sue parents if they don't bring them up properly. They have already started doing it. Kids who are depressed or in prison claim their problems are due to their parents raising them improperly. Instead of bringing them up, they brought them down.

Before deciding to have children, become enlightened. That is the only qualification we need. Unless we are clear as to how to guide them, we should not plan to have children. The world is populated enough. We have brought many billions of people to planet earth. If we can't provide food, medicine and shelter to those already here, why bring in more people? Where is the place? Where are the resources?

If you decide to have children, have the intelligence to give them the understanding behind all that you tell them. Whatever you give in the form of understanding gets recorded in the *satva* layer. This understanding becomes intelligence. Whatever you give as a rule and command sits in the *rajas* and *tamas* layers. Even if it is good advice, don't give it as a rule. If good advice is given as a rule, it creates an aversion in them.

When parents bring their kids to me, they force them to touch my feet. I say, 'Never do that. This is your greed.' These parents think that they and their children get *puṇya* or good credits by touching my feet. They impose this idea on their kids, an idea based on their greed.

By forcing the kids, they make the kids hate me. Some parents push their kids' heads down to my feet, as if they will receive positive current from my feet! I ask these parents not to force them. *Namaskār* (joining your hands in respect) is more than enough. By forcing them, they make the kids hate me. The next time these kids see the orange robe, they will grumble, 'Oh, now we must do that exercise.'

Never force rules on kids. We are suffering from rules given to us by our parents. The rules given by our parents are in our *rajas* and *tamas* layers. They lead us to restlessness and deep depression again and again. They create more and more trouble for us.

Desire and guilt

Desire and guilt are two forms of the same energy. One is related to the future. The other is related to the past. Desire is related to the future. Guilt is related to the past. 'I should have done that' plays a major role in our 'I should do this.' 'I should do this' is determined by 'I should have done that.'

Guilt that is created by rules handed down to us by our elders creates hell in our life and leads us to *tamas*. Kṛṣṇa says we are led to *antaha* (the end). We fall into ignorance or into the end.

Kṛṣṇa says the manifestations of the modes of goodness can be experienced when all the gates of the body are illuminated by knowledge.

This is the technique. The gates of the body are the gates through which we receive knowledge or information: eyes, ears, nose, tongue and the sense of touch or physical pleasure. These are the files through which we receive information from outside. He says that we should keep these five carefully guarded by *prakāśa* (illuminated knowledge). We should ensure security at these gates and knowledge is that security.

We should have knowledge about what should be taken in and what should not be taken in. Knowing this, we will reside in *satva* forever. We will reside in bliss forever. He says we should appoint a guard for the gates of our body. There is no security system for our body. We have security for our home. People spend a maximum of twelve hours at their home and they spend the remaining twelve hours outside the home. We reside twenty-four hours every day in this house called our body, yet we don't have a security system!

Ramaṇa Maharṣi sings in beautiful homage to the sacred Arunachala Hill in Tiruvannamalai in his famous song 'Arunachala Aksharamanamalai,' 'When these thieves, the five senses, have entered into the house, Oh Arunachala, were you not at home? How did they enter?' He asks Śiva, 'When these five senses entered the house (body-mind), were you not there? Why did you let them enter?'

Kṛṣṇa says, let us have the security, the protection of knowledge at the five gates, and we will reside in continuous bliss.

This means that we should not allow thoughts that create suffering to enter our mind through the eyes and other senses. This means, avoid the television. At least do not watch programs that create depression. We should only watch programs that give joy and make us blissful. We should never watch anything that makes us cunning, that gives us suffering or makes us feel violent.

When we protect our senses with *satva,* we will not allow negative engrams to come in. People immediately ask me, 'If we don't know what is happening in society, how can we live?'

Don't worry about those things. Any important or urgent news will reach us through somebody in some way. We are not living on an island. Moreover, by gaining knowledge of criminal activities through media, there is nothing much we can do. Newspapers carry the same news everyday. Most of it is about murder, rape, theft, and accidents. The only difference lies in the city or country where it takes place. Instead of reading the news everyday, we can predict what is going to happen and where! Why do we want to read and verify this? Only the place and numbers vary anyway.

What difference will it make to our lines? If the people who handle the situation know about it, that is enough. When we imbibe continuous information of this kind, we create engrams. We create fear strokes and suffering. If we continuously read about kidnapping, if our husband or kid is late by a few minutes, we start worrying. We become restless. If something wrong really happens, we will suffer only on the day when it happens. However, when we create engrams that generate anxiety, we suffer everyday. Can we stop it from happening, and if we can, how?

If we can stop it, no problem; then it is intelligence. Whatever can stop this worry from materializing is intelligence. But most of the time we collect these engrams that we can neither stop nor do anything with. We simply suffer. We put ourselves into *rajas* and *tamas* again and again.

Please do not infuse your consciousness with thoughts that create suffering in you. Continuously add thoughts that give bliss and peace. We may think this is impractical. We may think, 'How can we live in society without knowing what's going on in the world?' Be very clear, knowing what's going on in the world is a disease. Collecting information is a disease. The other day, someone said, '*Swamiji*, we should watch television to get an idea of the culture.' These television shows, however, are trash. They are nonsensical. The more we watch, the more negativity we imbibe.

Watching television shows creates engrams in our unconscious mind about the standard of life. If we continuously see and listen to these negative things, we belch all that negativity into our lives. We set unreasonable standards for ourselves based on what input goes inside us.

Life is much too valuable and too short to be spent worrying. Do not allow thoughts that create depression, low mood and longing, into your system, especially at *sandhyā* time - the twilight time at which day and night meet. Our ancient masters knew that *sandhyā* time, when day and night meet, is a critical time. There are two *sandhyās,* dawn and dusk. Our masters knew that whatever thought-seeds are sown inside our being at *sandhyā* come out as full-blown trees. That is why the masters insisted that at *sandhyā* time, one should spend time in a temple, praying, listening to prayers, reading devotional material or meditating. These spiritual ideas go inside as seeds and become a valuable tree in our life.

These days, we watch television at *sandhyā* time. We put all the trash inside like in a trashcan and the next day we get the smell of it. Never put negative *saṁskāras* inside yourself especially this time.

Protect your senses twenty-four hours a day. If you cannot then at least protect yourself at least during *sandhyā* time. *Sandhyā* is the one-and-half hours of clairvoyance when day and night meet. In India it is 6:00 – 7:30 in the morning and evening, at sunrise and sunset. This period varies from country to country. During *sandhyā* we should not allow negative engrams to enter our being. Whatever enters our being during *sandhyā* exists or radiates throughout our life. Kṛṣṇa gives this one advice, this one technique because this is the way we can turn it around. Using this technique we transform and the cognitive shift can happen.

As of now, cognition happens in our mind based upon our negative engrams. If we change the input, if we move our mental setup into a different energy zone or vibration, the cognitive shift happens. We process data with positive engrams, with a positive base.

Kṛṣṇa gives one technique, one suggestion: Protect the five senses from negative ideas and infuse positive ideas through the five senses. Whatever we feed upon becomes our being and we radiate that energy. Spend *sandhyā* time in a good way. Meditate at home during this time. If you don't meditate, go to a temple or church and do something spiritual at this time. Recite a verse, say prayers or do some good work instead of wasting time and adding negative engrams. The more negative engrams we put inside, the more we move towards depression.

The more money we deposit into the bank, the higher our bank balance. The more negative engrams we have, the more our depression. Our masters knew where man would collect positive engrams and where man would collect negative engrams. They created many spaces where man could collect positive engrams and protect himself. Please understand this one suggestion from Kṛṣṇa and save the body with pure satvic security, and experience bliss.

Kṛṣṇa explained earlier that when one is aware, one is in *satva.* Now He explains what happens to someone in *rajas.*

Kṛṣṇa says that attachment, greed, craving and restless action are indications of rajasic behavior. This fits most people, but it fits most aptly anyone in business or a corporate career.

Greed is the corporate creed. People who recruit and train employees use motivation as their only tool. What is motivation?

The whole idea of motivating someone is ill-motivated. To motivate someone, we must hold a carrot in front of him or her. Then the carrot becomes the goal. If we are donkeys, we follow the carrot. If we have any intelligence, we will realize that the carrot will always be dangled in front of us just out of reach!

The donkey runs after the carrot in restless action. It cannot stay still. The carrot is so near and yet so far. So how can it stay still? This is the story of the corporate people. Business people complain, '*Swamiji,* business is so tough. No one is honest these days. Everyone is a cheat. I cannot trust anyone. I am experiencing financial losses. I do not know how long I can afford to continue. Please advise me.'

They are smart. They do not say, 'Please help me.' They say, 'Please advise me.' Then I am caught! If I advise them to do something, they can hold me responsible later. They can come back and say, '*Swamiji*, you told me to do that. It did not work. Now please help me out.'

I tell them, 'If business is difficult, and you cannot trust anybody and you are making no money, what is the point? Stop doing business. Close your business. Relax.'

They explode, 'Oh my God, *Swamiji*, how can you say that? What will I do then? How will I live?'

On the one hand, they say that they are losing money. On the other hand, when I tell them how to stop the losses, they ask how they will live! What kind of a drama is this? We may laugh, yet each of us is in this kind of a drama, a psychodrama of our own making.

We are like a wind-up toy. We have been fully wound and each time the spring relaxes, something inside winds us up again. We are like that battery bunny in television advertisements. We move continuously. We cannot rest. We think this movement is the purpose of our life.

Our life has no purpose. There is no goal to life. Living itself is the path and the goal. If we are aware, in *satva*, we enjoy the path; we enjoy the journey. We do not care where we are going, so long as the path is enjoyable. So long as we enjoy the path, it is the right path and our destination will be right.

But instead of enjoying the path, we worry about the goal. We worry about when we will reach, where we will reach. In the process, we do not notice how we are traveling. We miss the beauty of the path.

When we enjoy our path, we will enjoy our work. Whatever destination we reach will be the right destination.

That is why people who are successful are passionate about what they do. They do not care what happens in the end as long as what they do is enjoyable. If we are passionate about what we do, we will enjoy what we do. Whatever we do will be wonderful and successful.

However, as long as we struggle, we suffer even if we make money. The goal that we are chasing will be a mirage, an illusion. As soon as we reach that goal, we will be forced to chase another goal. We will not have a minute to pause, to rest and enjoy what we have achieved. Acquisition becomes the goal, not enjoyment.

We can never be happy in *rajas*. It drives us like a donkey until we are exhausted and we collapse. We need to decide whether or not this is the way we want to live. Ask: Do I wish to be a donkey driven by a carrot's dangling in front of me all my life? When we decide, 'No, this is not what I want,' it is time to break away from *rajas* and move towards bliss.

The Depression of Success

14.13 *O son of Kuru, when there is an increase in the mode of ignorance,*
Madness, illusion, inertia and darkness are manifested.

14.14 *When one dies in the mode of goodness,*
He goes where the realized souls are.

14.15 *When one dies in the mode of passion, he takes birth among those engaged in activities.*
When he dies in the mode of ignorance, he takes birth in the space of the ignorant.

14.16 *By acting in the mode of goodness, one becomes purified.*
Work done in the mode of passion results in distress, and actions performed in the mode of ignorance result in foolishness.

14.17 *From the mode of goodness, real knowledge develops;*
From the mode of passion, greed develops;
From the mode of ignorance develops foolishness, madness and illusion.

We act like a wind-up toy when we are steeped in *rajas,* and like a battery-operated toy with a dead battery when we are in *tamas.* Kṛṣṇa uses powerful words to drive home how desperate that state is: ignorance, madness, illusion, inertia and darkness.

It is surprising how quickly one can slip from *rajas* to *tamas.* To slip from restless activity into inactivity and inertia is simple. Activity without meaning, activity with tension and stress and activity totally focused on sensual satisfaction quickly leads to deep fatigue. The activity without any meaning that we find in *tamas* is not the same as activity without a purpose and goal that we experience in *satva*. Please do not confuse the two.

The purpose of life

I mentioned earlier that the real danger of *rajas* is that we are constantly focused on a goal and we forget to enjoy the path as we pursue a meaningless purpose. Life has no purpose. It only has meaning. The meaning of life is to be aware, to be conscious, and to realize our inner divinity. That is why I say that I am here not to prove my divinity, but to prove your divinity.

To be divine and to realize that inner divinity is our true meaning in life. Anything less than that is meaningless. Being aggressive, being restlessly active, or being constantly on the move does not help us understand or realize this meaning. We will be running after one thing or another. We are just plain greedy. Ramana Maharishi says that a mustard seed looks like a mountain when we want it desperately; however, even a mountain becomes as insignificant as a mustard seed once we achieve it.

If we are driven by mere possessive obsession, we are bound to become tired sooner or later. Aggression results in deep depression. This is what I call the 'depression of success.' I see this often in countries like the USA. People struggle to increase their material wealth, disregarding everything else. People change cars every year, houses every third year and their spouses every fifth year!

People run after material possessions and trophies without knowing why. One day when they have acquired and reacquired so many things and still feel unhappy, uneasy and listless, they wonder why they acquired the things that they struggled for. They go into deep depression, what we call *tamas*.

In poor countries like India, people have little and are desperate to acquire minimal comforts. Just to have three meals a day, wear footwear or go to school is a great luxury for many. For those who miss out on essentials, their suffering arises out of the depression of failure. That is relatively easy to cure. All they need is some success and they are happy.

The depression of success is more difficult to address. To experience failure when we have been always successful and we have worked so hard is difficult to accept. What results then is depression, *tamas*.

Tamas is generally born out of the ignorance of our true self. This is the original sin. The original sin of Adam and Eve was not listening to the snake or having sex; rather, it was the lack of understanding of their own inner divinity.

Sometimes *tamas* can arise out of an effort to move out of that ignorance. When moving into a spiritual path, a highly rajasic person, one who has been aggressively pursuing material gains, can easily move into *tamas* for a while. I see this in our ashram. When a person accustomed to restless and meaningless activity is becoming centered, the body-mind system initially rejects activity and sinks deep into inactivity, into *tamas*.

People literally sleep day and night, not wanting to do anything. However, this does not last long. The negativities get worked out and they settle into a sattvic mode of meaningful activity, that does not pursue goals.

Tamas is darkness. It is negative. We can only remove darkness by bringing in light. In the same way, we dispel ignorance by bringing in awareness. The *Upaniṣad* says *tamaso mā jyotirgamaya* meaning, 'Let my darkness be removed by light'.

Let the light and wisdom of Kṛṣṇa, the *Jagatguru,* dispel your darkness and *tamas.*

In these verses, Kṛṣṇa tells us where the person goes after death when steeped in these attributes of *satva, rajas* and *tamas.* A *satvic* person becomes divine. A *tamasic* person chooses a lower life. A *rajasic* person continues to suffer due to greed.

In another verse in Gītā, Kṛṣṇa tells Arjuna that a person is reborn based on the last thought before death. Here Kṛṣṇa explains how that last thought is not an accident. It is based on one's *guṇa*, one's nature.

People tell me, 'Oh *Swamiji*, why should we worry about spiritual stuff now? This is the time to enjoy. When we get old, we can think about spirituality. After all, Kṛṣṇa declared that our last thought redeems us. All we have to say is Ram or Kṛṣṇa as we take our last breath.'

If only it were that easy, then all of us would never be reborn! If throughout life you run after money and material possessions, do you think your last thought will be about anything other than money? If throughout life you were obsessed with wine, women and song, only those thoughts fill your mind when you die. How we live life now determines how we will be reborn.

Kṛṣṇa says that a person living in *satva* goes to higher spaces, the abodes of the realized sages. He becomes divine. When we are steeped in *satva,* we live in awareness. We live in the present moment. We are no longer attached. We are no longer obsessed with the results of our action and we are no longer controlled by fear and greed. We stop thinking about ourselves and we start living for others. It is no longer me and me alone, but me and you, and eventually just you that includes me as well. All transactions become unconditional.

The present state is eternal. That is the state of the higher planets, of the heaven that one talks about. We can be in heaven even when we are alive. When our spirit moves beyond the body, it has the potential to move beyond its *saṁskāras,* the conditioning, into its true potential of self-realization.

When one is in *tamas,* in deep ignorance and darkness, one sinks lower in rebirth. Kṛṣṇa says such a person is reborn as an animal. The lowest energy center of a human being is the *mūlādhāra cakra,* the root center at the base of the spine which is the sex center. And this is the highest center at which animal energy operates. All animals operate out of pure survival instinct. Their nature is conditioned for that. There is nothing wrong or inferior about that. That is their nature.

Human beings are provided with intelligence to move upward in consciousness. We have the freedom to make mistakes and we do make mistakes. When Kṛṣṇa talks about being reborn in ignorance and as animals, it is not to denigrate animals. He means, a human being who behaves instinctively, out of a blocked *mūlādhāra cakra,* and out of an animalistic nature, is ignorant of his potential as a human.

We are not human beings striving for a spiritual experience. We are spiritual beings enjoying a human experience. That is the truth.

We can be in this state only when we are in *satva.* When we are in *tamas,* we forget our spiritual nature. When we are in *rajas,* we have a vague idea; however, even that spiritual experience becomes an attachment, another goal and desire. We become attached to something that is beyond attachment. Kṛṣṇa says that we are reborn into this human form, back into this cycle of life and death, this cycle of *saṁsāra,* with all its suffering.

It is our choice to be instinctive and unconscious, in deep *tamas,* like an animal, or to be logical and chasing objects out of *rajas.* The third choice is to be beyond attachments, in a superconscious state, in an intuitive state, in tune with our sublime *satva* nature. This choice determines our next birth. In fact, it determines whether we will even be born again.

Kṛṣṇa the master psychologist is right on the mark: Purification and knowledge from *satva,* distress and greed from *rajas,* and foolishness, madness and illusion from *tamas*! Moving from ignorance to wisdom, from greed to gratitude is the movement to satva, the center.

Our center is our true nature. Our true nature is divine. We are one with the universal energy, God, *Parāśakti* or whatever we want to call it. We cannot describe it. We can just experience it. We experience bliss when our focus is in that central core and not out at the edges of our personality.

Throughout life we run away from that center, that core of bliss. Our senses lead us towards the periphery where material objects are. Our inner core is empty: it is *śūṇya.* But it is also *pūrṇa,* complete by itself with nothing else needed to top off the bliss. The outer periphery, however, is forever changing. Nothing is eternal about it. Even when objects are the same, our perceptions keep changing. This periphery is *māyā,* illusion and *tamas,* ignorance.

Our *rajasic* nature, the restless activity that strives to introduce purpose into something that is essentially without purpose, keeps driving us away from the center into this peripheral darkness of *tamas* and *māyā. Rajas* always drives us into *tamas.* Aggression, passion, attachment and aversion eventually take us into delusion and ignorance.

But from time to time we get that spark of intelligence that says life does not need to be this way. There is more meaning to life than fantasies. We start searching. When we seek our true nature, we move towards our center, the core of bliss. Then something in the external space attracts us and we move out to the periphery. We keep moving in and out, from center to periphery, from periphery back to center.

That is why I call human beings eccentric! They can neither be in the center nor in the periphery. They settle in between and keep oscillating. They are eccentric. They are neither in complete madness nor centered in their divine consciousness.

The movement towards our core, our true self, is driven by *satva.* The movement outwards is driven by *rajas.* When we are fully settled in the periphery, we are caught in *tamas.* We are no longer human. When we settle into the center, we go beyond the three *guṇas.* We become the *triguṇa rahita,* the divine one who is beyond the three attributes.

Where Do We Go from Here?

14.18 *Those situated in the mode of goodness gradually go upward to the higher planes; those in the mode of passion live on the earthly planets; and those in the mode of ignorance go down to the worlds below.*

14.19 *When we see that there is nothing beyond these modes of nature in all activities and that the supreme Lord is transcendental to all these modes, then we can know our spiritual nature.*

14.20 *When the embodied being is able to transcend these three modes, he can become free from birth, death, old age and their distresses and can enjoy nectar even in this life.*

Kṛṣṇa provides the key to liberation here. Those who go beyond the three *guṇas* become free of bondage and enjoy bliss in this world. This is the assurance of the master.

Step one is when we realize that each of our activities arises from one of the three *guṇas: satva, rajas* and *tamas.* Step two is the understanding about which *guṇa* it is and exactly what that *guṇa* is doing to us. Step three is to move out of that *guṇa* into the *satva guṇa.* Finally we transcend *satva guṇa* and enter into *nirguṇa* or 'no-*guṇa* state'.

Whatever we are doing we need to become aware of the *guṇa* driving us. If it is a fantasy, we work out of *tamas.* If it is fear and greed, we work out of *rajas.* And if we are unattached and undisturbed by all that is happening around us, we act out of *satva.*

Moving out of fear or fantasy requires de-conditioning from *saṁskāras*, the embedded memories in our unconscious. This is difficult to do at the conscious level and dangerous to do at the unconscious level. It needs to be done at the superconscious level through meditative practices such as we have in our NSP courses.

What do I mean by this? We have talked about the *saṁskāras* that are engraved memories buried in our unconscious. They drive us through one of these attributes *(guṇas)*. We think and act out of one attribute or a mixture of attributes. These thoughts and actions when repeated again and again furrow the *saṁskāras,* or its subtler mindset, *vāsanās,* deep into our psyche. Conscious, logical and analytical procedures cannot easily identify them, let alone remove or repair them. That is why so-called catharsis processes that aim to rid us of negative emotions give only temporary relief. The basic negativity remains buried.

So first become aware of your thoughts and actions. Identify which *guṇa* they come from. If it is a fantasy, rooted in *tamas,* drop the fantasy and move into the present reality. The problem that you face is that fantasies are more interesting than the way you lead your lives! That is why you prefer to stay in fantasy and out of touch with reality. You need to realize that you are operating out of sheer ignorance and that this will not help you in any way. This realization and awareness that will help you move out of the zone of fantasies, can only come as a result of meditation, which leads to self-awareness.

Similarly, we are driven by *rajas* when we run after something that attracts us or run away from something that disturbs us. We need to realize that this is a vicious cycle: this cycle of attachment and aversion, of greed and fear. More and more of what we desire will give us less and less happiness. Unless we turn and face what we are afraid of, the fear remains rooted. Again, meditation is the key. It leads to the awareness of this vicious cycle and helps us stay detached.

Through repeated practice of meditation techniques, we can burn out our *saṁskāras* and shift out of the *guṇas* that we are currently rooted in.

We can move into a state of non-attachment by dropping the emotional load of our memories. We can be cleansed of negativities and unblock and energize our *cakras* through meditation. That is the key.

Someone in the Hollywood film industry told me that all movie plots are based upon one of these *cakra* emotional blocks. This is what we teach in our first level Life Bliss Programs. It is not merely our real life that is affected, even our fantasy life revolves around the *cakras*! To understand the *cakras* and their emotional blocks is to understand our *guṇas*. And to understand our *guṇas* is to find the way and open the door to bliss.

Going Beyond the Guṇas

14.21 *Arjuna inquired: O my Lord, by what symptoms is one known who is transcendental to those modes? What is his behavior? And how does he transcend the modes of nature?*

14.22, 23, 24, 25

The Blessed Lord said: He who does not hate illumination, attachment and delusion when they are present, nor longs for them when they disappear; who is seated like one unconcerned, being situated beyond these material reactions of the modes of nature, who remains firm, knowing that the modes alone are active;

He who regards alike pleasure and pain, and looks on a lump of earth, a stone and a piece of gold with an equal eye; who is wise and holds praise and blame to be the same; who is unchanged in honor and dishonor, who treats friend and foe alike, who has abandoned all result-based undertakings - such a man is said to have transcended the modes of nature.

With great clarity the master tells us what to do. He uses specific terms that cannot be misunderstood or misinterpreted. Kṛṣṇa explains the nature of one who has transcended the three *guṇas,* one who has gone beyond his natural attributes. He explains what we need to do to become a *triguṇa rahita,* to become liberated from the influence of the three *guṇas.*

One who is beyond the three *guṇas* is unaffected by their play. He is beyond the play of emotions. Whatever happens is right for him. Success and failure mean the same. Friend and foe make no difference. Poverty or richness has no influence.

Such an attitude of total detachment requires one thing: complete trust. When we trust that whatever happens is what needs to happen and we accept whatever happens as it arises, we are totally detached. Then whatever happens will be right. Such trust can only come from surrender.

I tell my disciples that because I have no home, every home that I visit is my home. Anywhere and everywhere I stay, whether it is under a tree or out in the open, is my home. Four walls, a door and a lock do not create a home for me. People ask why I wear jewelry or different kind of clothing. What difference does it make? This body itself is not mine. This skin is not mine. What difference would it make if I wore this or that?

There is neither attraction nor aversion. Just as people admire the clothes or accessories on a mannequin, I admire the clothes and jewelry on this body. They have no connection to me.

Every movement I make is at the order of Existence. I cannot move a finger without the permission of that universal energy. Usually when people talk about God, it is a concept to them, a theory to prove or disprove. For enlightened beings, it is reality; it is the reality of their existence every moment. When people look at themselves, the 'I', the identity, drives them. For enlightened beings, that identity is not real. 'I' does not exist.

When we are one with Existence, one with nature, nothing affects us. I walked tens of thousands of miles barefoot across the length and breadth of India. People ask, 'How is it your feet are so soft, not calloused and broken as ours would be if we walked barefoot even ten miles?' I tell you: If we trust Nature, Nature looks after us.

Pain and pleasure are part of our conditioning. During my *parivrājaka* (monastic wandering) days, I happened to visit a village in Central India. I came across a strange characteristic in the lives of women there: painless delivery of babies. The women used to enter huts specially built for that purpose. There were no cries and no shrieks. They went in alone, needed no help and simply came out smiling with a baby. I was surprised! When

I asked an elder how it was that they had no pain and did not need a doctor or midwife, he did not understand my question. 'Pain?' he asked, 'What pain? Why should women feel pain at childbirth? It is a celebration!'

We create pain and pleasure through association, through conditioning. We create greed and fear through association. Our *saṁskāras*, our conditioned memories, create pain and pleasure.

Our conditioning, our upbringing, should be called 'down-bringing' since it drags us down and does not raise us up. Our conditioning inculcates these negativities in us. This is how society ensures its survival through controlling us with fear and greed.

Our NSP meditations are designed to dissolve our conditioning, our embedded memories. At the end of the four-day course in India (which is a two-day course overseas), people prostrate at each other's feet with no differentiation of age, gender, wealth or class. Their negativities disappear and, at that heightened energy level, all that one can see is the divinity in others. I have seen fathers-in-law prostrate at the feet of their daughters-in-law, something nobody would believe in the context of the Indian culture!

Expression Of The Divine

14.26 *One who engages in full devotional service, who does not fall down in any circumstance, at once transcends the modes of material nature and thus comes to the level of* Brahman.

14.27 *And I am the basis of impersonal* Brahman, *which is the rightful state of ultimate happiness, and which is immortal, imperishable and eternal.*

Kṛṣṇa concludes the chapter by saying that the transcendental state beyond the three attributes of nature, the *guṇas,* is *Brahman,* the ultimate cosmic consciousness. He says you reach this through devotion. He says that He is that *Brahman,* the Source of eternal bliss.

Kṛṣṇa speaks as *Parabrahma* Kṛṣṇa, the supreme energy and not as Vāsudeva Kṛṣṇa, the individual. What is the difference between *Parabrahma* Kṛṣṇa (ultimate consciousness) and Vāsudeva Kṛṣṇa (the physical person, the son of Vāsudeva)? In the case of an ordinary human being, even though he has the potential of divinity, he has not realized it. So he is different. That is the difference between you and an enlightened master. Both are equally divine. Yet, you are unaware of your divinity, whereas the enlightened master is fully aware of it.

In the case of Kṛṣṇa, he is the master. Why then the difference? The difference is not to do with Him. It is to do with us. The frequency of *Parabrahma* Kṛṣṇa is not visible to and approachable by mortals. That is why Arjuna had to be given the divine vision to perceive *Parabrahma rūpa* or *viśvarūpa,* the cosmic form of Kṛṣṇa. Even Arjuna, His closest mortal friend, His mirror as the human, could not perceive Him in that cosmic form until he was permitted.

In order for humans to perceive Him and interact with Him, *Parabrahma* Kṛṣṇa must become Vāsudeva Kṛṣṇa. To a certain extent He must subject Himself to the play of the *guṇas.*

Each enlightened master is unique in his expression of his experience as the Divine. Our scriptures say that if two enlightened masters say the same thing, one is a fake! The experience is the same, yet the expression is different. Kṛṣṇa is different from Buddha and Christ. Each has the same theme of compassion, yet the way the compassion is expressed is different. Buddha expressed it as contemplation and Kṛṣṇa in joyous abandon. So we choose a master based upon how we vibrate to his expression. If our path is devotion, we gravitate to Kṛṣṇa; He is lovable. If we are the meditative type, we go to Śiva, the master who taught in silence.

It does not matter who our master is. What matters is our faith, trust and the attitude of surrender. Our master can be an unenlightened being. If we trust him, we can become enlightened, even though he may not be. What matters more is our attitude and approach, our *guṇa,* and not the master's state. Even if we worship a stone and surrender to it, imagining it to be our ultimate savior, we will be liberated. It is true.

Let us pray to *Parabrahma* Kṛṣṇa, the universal consciousness, the ultimate energy, to give us all this understanding in our life, to make us experience the truth that He teaches and to establish us in and make us radiate eternal bliss, *nityānanda.*

Thus ends the fourteenth chapter named **Guṇatraya Vibhāga Yogaḥ** *of the* **Upaniṣad** *of* ***Bhagavad Gītā****, the scripture of Yoga, dealing with the science of the Absolute in the form of the dialogue between* **Śrī Kṛṣṇa** *and Arjuna.*

BhagavadGītā

No Questions, Only Doubts

Puruṣottama Yogaḥ

Chapter 15

When we question,
we reveal our arrogance and aggression.
When we doubt,
we exhibit our ignorance and seek clarity.

No Questions, Only Doubts

Only Kṛṣṇa speaks in Chapter 15 of Bhagavad Gītā. Arjuna does not utter a word. Arjuna's inner chatter has been silenced. As a result, his questions have disappeared.

Kṛṣṇa expounds upon who He is and what He is. This chapter is traditionally titled *Puruṣottama* Yoga, yoga of the supreme Self. Kṛṣṇa unveils the reasons why He is *Puruṣottama,* supreme amongst beings and explains that what He has imparted to Arjuna is the most profound secret. Kṛṣṇa is convinced that Arjuna is ready to receive the Truth.

Arjuna has settled into his Self. His confusions have disappeared; questions have dissolved due to his cosmic experience in *Viśvarūpa Darśana Yoga* - having the Vision of Kṛṣṇa's cosmic form - and his direct spiritual experience. He has achieved the depth of knowledge and clear understanding required to internalize whatever Kṛṣṇa has taught him so far. He has achieved the intensity of spiritual experience. He is a new being.

Arjuna doesn't have any more intellectual questions. He has reached a point where he is totally ready to receive Kṛṣṇa. He has moved forward from a state of thoughtfulness, where he is confused and full of questions, to a no-thought state, a no-mind state where questions disappear.

As long as we have questions, we will not receive the answer. Questions are about defending our prejudice and defending our limited understanding. Questions act as a barrier between knowledge and us, between the master and us. All great masters, including Buddha and Lao Tse, had an aversion to questions.

Doubts are necessary

Masters convey their experience. It is an energy transmission that occurs. To convey an experience in words denies the experience. Once verbalized, the experience loses meaning. Lao Tse says, 'If it is really truth that was experienced, it cannot be communicated. If it can be communicated, it is not the truth.'

Arjuna's questions arose out of confusion. As a warrior, a *kṣatriya,* Arjuna was accustomed to killing. His confusion on that battlefield of *Kurukṣetra* was not about killing per se; rather it was about killing kinsmen, teachers and friends. Arjuna's confusion did not arise from a principle of non-violence; if it had, it is doubtful that Kṛṣṇa would have persuaded him to fight.

Arjuna's confusion, depression, doubts and questions arose from his ego, his feeling of 'I' and 'mine'. The warriors assembled in front of him, those men whom he had to fight and kill or be killed by were kith and kin. They were not strangers. It was possessiveness, not non-violence that created confusion in Arjuna's mind.

Arjuna's illusion caused confusion. His view that these warriors assembled in front of him were relatives, teachers and friends meant that he had no societal right to kill them. As a warrior, Arjuna had no qualms or moral issues about killing people. Therefore, the violence of his ego, the violence born out of possession acted as a barrier; it was not a moral principle of non-violence.

What remains with Arjuna are not questions that he has for himself, but doubts that he would like to clear on behalf of mankind. These questions now have a completely different focus. They do not pertain to what he should do or not do. After seeing Kṛṣṇa's cosmic form, his questions are about the nature of the divine Kṛṣṇa and how to approach Him. Kṛṣṇa now explains to Arjuna what He is and how to reach Him. Kṛṣṇa is convinced that Arjuna is through with his intellectual questions. What remain are only doubts.

Doubt means a person is ready to digest the master, receive the master, and imbibe the master. Whatever word comes out of the master clears doubt. Doubt makes the master express himself. Questions make the master close himself. Almost all questions are violence.

Words can be categorized into two streams. One stream consists of questions, another of doubts. A question means violence; it is arrogance to express that we know something or to defend what we know as truth. Most of the time we ask questions to show that we know something. People often ask me big questions.

A person asked me, '*Swamiji,* the Brahma Sūtra says *Brahman* is beyond comprehension. He is beyond understanding and beyond intellect. Is that right?'

The purpose of this statement is to show that he has read Brahma Sūtra. This is not a question. There is no quest in it.

Doubt without quest is question. Question with quest is doubt. Questions do not seek truth; doubts do.

Man cannot handle too much truth. He can handle half-truths. Beyond that, truth starts transforming him. He feels that the ground he is standing on is slipping away. None of us wants to know the truth. If truth is given honestly, only a few will be willing to listen. People become frightened the moment honest truths are given. Truth frightens them. So, they question the truth.

We hide the truth in numerous ways. Why do we have so many social courtesies? We respect each other. For social courtesies, we do many formalities. We are taught from childhood to say 'Please' and 'Thank you,' irrespective of whether we mean it, irrespective of whether the situation demands it, rather because social etiquette says so. Whenever we meet someone, we say 'It's nice to meet you,' even though we may not feel so nice!

Even I am sometimes forced to play this game. When people initially meet me, when they do not know me well, it is best for me to be socially polite to them. Otherwise they get hurt. They are not ready to face the truth. Whatever words they might express to me, their mind is not ready to accept the truth. It will be too harsh. So I offer them brain candy. Why disturb them from their socially comfortable situation when they are not yet ready?

If we really feel 'nice,' our whole body, our being shows it. Must we say 'It's nice to meet you,' for the other person to understand that we are happy to meet him? Our whole body language, our smile, our sheer pleasure at meeting that person makes that obvious. We don't need to use words.

We know that the truth is something else. We dare not face the truth. We feel that we cannot afford to be truthful in verbal language as well as body language. The truth straightaway gives us enlightenment. It transforms us.

The moment someone honestly imbibes or catches a single point of truth or a single dimension of truth, it does wonders.

Vivekānanda says beautifully, 'Even if you memorize each book in all the libraries of the world, it will not help you except to increase your ego about the bookish knowledge you acquire. Take one idea and imbibe it in your being, experience it. Your life will be transformed by a single idea, just one idea!'

A book from Tamilnadu, South India describes the life of sixty-three enlightened masters. The name of this Tamil book is Periapuranam, meaning 'Great Epic'.

If we study this book, we find masters who apparently haven't done anything worthwhile, nothing at all. Nothing happened in their lives. Some masters just picked flowers and offered them to God, nothing else. Yet, they achieved enlightenment. What we do is unimportant. How honest we are with our action matters. When they offered flowers, they were true and honest to the action.

We may also offer flowers everyday and do everything to please God, yet we aren't enlightened. We only incur an added expense of maintaining a garden or buying flowers! The problem is, we are not honest. When these masters pick flowers to offer to God, they continuously think about the deity to whom they are offering the flowers. They are totally devoted to the thought of the deity. Nothing distracts them.

When we pick flowers to offer to a favorite deity, we think of something else, somebody else. I have seen people do rituals regularly. But their thoughts are on office work or something else in their life.

When our heart is not in it, worship becomes a chore. When our heart is in it, even hard work becomes joyful worship.

If we scan our day from the moment we get out of bed until the end of the day, it is filled with lies. Our smiles are false. When we smile, we don't want the other person to know what is in our mind; so we don't look into each other's eyes. Why? We fear that the other person will read our mind. We can present a big smile on our lips when our heart boils; however, in our eyes, we cannot hide anything.

Just open up, whatever comes out is your experience. For example, if someone asks our name, do we prepare? Do we need to carry clues for that? Of course not! It's our experience. If something has not become our experience, we need to prepare to deliver a lecture. If we must prepare to deliver a lecture, or if we fear public speaking, this means we are filled with lies. Our whole being is a lie; our life is a lie.

Why do people fear public speaking? We fear that we may speak what we think. We fear that whatever is going on inside might spill out. We know that there is so much dirt inside that something might erupt, some garbage might tumble out and we are scared. That is why we prepare what and how we speak.

Why do we lie?

We must be certain that we don't speak something else; we need to remember the points one by one. If we forget, we are afraid that we may say something that is really in our mind. Preparation is done to ensure that we don't say something else. Preparation is nothing but trying to hide our true inner chatter.

If a professional speaker must prepare all his talks, whatever he says is a lie. It has not become his experience. It has not become a part of his being. It has not been internalized as a part of his being. It has just been memorized and delivered.

Not only for public speaking or discourses, even when we meet friends or we are with our spouse, we plan and rehearse words. We rehearse how we will start, what we will begin with and how we will continue the topic. We do a full dress rehearsal. If the other person starts talking on a different topic, we are lost; we have no idea what to say. We have done a complete rehearsal only of what we know and want to talk about.

If we need to be prepared in order to speak to our boss that is okay. We must be courteous; otherwise we may lose our job. That is at least a basic need and part of the social game. Let us accept it, forget about it and move on. But the situation is much worse than that. We continuously prepare dialogues for friends and family. If we must always prepare, whatever we prepare is a lie. Even if we say it as if it is a fact, it is not the truth. Stating a fact is not being truthful.

In real life, why do we lie so much? Why does a husband always tell his wife that he loves her? If he loves her, his body language should show that. But when he verbalizes it, he actually reminds himself. He must remind himself that he is supposed to love her. When we speak too many words, we are lying. We are not speaking the truth. We are covering a lie with a lot of decorations.

Speaking the truth is dangerous. If we speak the truth, we have space among enlightened people but not other folks. It is so dangerous.

Truth endures logical questions and arguments. It withstands the test of logical analysis. If someone needs to verify whether something is pure gold, we must put it in acid to test it. An acid test is required to test the truth of gold. In the same manner, if we wish to know whether something is pure truth, we must put it to an acid test of logical analysis. Our logic will simply fall and fail.

When our logic falls before it, you can be sure it's the truth. Anything that is truth destroys our logic; it means that our logic will become so tired that it will fall by itself. If it is the ultimate Truth, it must stand the test of logical analysis. It must withstand all the logical acid tests that it is put through.

If the disciple is in the questioning mood, the master must prove his words. He must be prepared to go through the acid tests demanded by the questioning disciple. It is a big load.

If the disciple is in doubt, the master will open up with the truth. He will not cover the truth with words. He will not play with words. The naked truth will be told directly. Any truth can be served and explained to a mind with doubt. To a questioning mind, nothing can be explained.

The disciple's mood decides whether the master's words will be advice or a powerful transformational technique. If the disciple is completely tuned, the master can help him. The master need not even be enlightened.

A small story:

A scholar lived on the banks of the Yamunā River. Daily he offered ritual worship to Kṛṣṇa. A milkmaid brought milk for the scholar on a regular basis. One day, she did not come because it had rained heavily the previous night and the river had flooded.

The following day when she arrived at the scholar's home, he asked, 'Why didn't you bring my milk yesterday?' She replied, 'The river was flooded and I was unable to cross it.'

The scholar told her, 'Many have crossed the *saṁsāra sāgara* (ocean of worldly life) by chanting Kṛṣṇa's name. Yet you can't cross a small river. Chant His name and cross!'

Like a typical scholar, he showed off his dry knowledge to impress the poor milkmaid while simultaneously scolding her for missing a day of service. The milkmaid received his words as absolute truth.

From that day onwards, the milkmaid was on time.

Sometime later, the river flooded again. The milkmaid shocked the scholar by arriving at the usual hour. He asked her, 'How did you manage to cross the river?'

The milkmaid replied, 'Due to your guidance, master. I chanted Kṛṣṇa's name and walked upon the water as you told me.'

The scholar could not digest it. He demanded proof. The milkmaid agreed. They went down to the riverbank. The milkmaid chanted Kṛṣṇa's name and walked upon the water. She just floated and crossed the river.

The scholar could not believe what was happening. He thought, 'If an ignorant milkmaid can walk on water based on my teachings, why can't I, a great scholar?'

He started chanting Kṛṣṇa's name. However, as he approached the water, he lifted his waistcloth so as not to wet it. He stepped into the water and sank.

He didn't actually have any belief in what he told the milkmaid. He just spoke those words to show off his knowledge.

But if the disciple is in a receptive mood, even casual words of the master can be techniques for his growth; it will benefit him. Even if the master is unenlightened or if the master has no belief or experience of his own words, the disciple's belief surmounts any obstacle.

Doubt and faith are two sides of the same coin. We cannot have faith without doubt. That is why, however much people wish to believe my words, they have doubts. I tell them it is okay to have doubts. They are going through a process, a cycle of faith and doubt. As doubt is cleared, a greater faith develops. Then, the next level of doubt occurs. A new layer of understanding is revealed and faith is restored.

Ultimately, the disciple, the devotee, transcends doubt and faith. He reaches the truth. Until such time, it is normal to have recurring doubt and faith.

Now, Arjuna has come to an understanding. Because of his firsthand spiritual experience, he has come to the level of doubt. No more questions. He does not ask what is beneficial for him. Those self-serving calculations have gone. No more questions like *kim tad brahma kimadhyātmaṁ kim karma puruṣottama.*

He was playing with words then. Now everything has disappeared. In the first chapter, Kṛṣṇa was totally silent. Arjuna spoke at length. He quoted on righteousness and from ancient scriptures. In this chapter, Arjuna is completely silent.

This is a problem faced by every master descending on planet earth. An innocent disciple is better than an ignorant disciple.

Unlearn to learn

A small story:

A man approached a music teacher and asked, 'Master, I have studied music for four years. Now I want to learn from you. How long will it take?'

Master replied, 'It may take six years.'

Another guy came and asked, 'I have studied music for two years. How long it will take for me to learn?'

The master said, 'Two years.'

A third guy came, 'Master, I know nothing about music. How long must I spend to learn music?'

The master replied, 'No time. You can pick it up from me in no time at all.'

A fresh, innocent disciple immediately imbibes the master. He just picks up from the master. He directly absorbs the master into his own being. However, for those with partial knowledge, the master must do something to undo what they have learned.

All masters descending on planet earth bring the same *śāstra,* the knowledge that is written down. But they also bring the life that is infused in this knowledge. What we read in books are just words. They never bring transformation for the reader. No book can give us the truth. They are not designed for that.

A small incident:

Rāmakṛṣṇa Paramahamsa dictated a book while a disciple took notes. At one point, the disciple asked, 'Master, please repeat that.' The master repeated the statement.

The disciple stopped writing and said, 'Master, this statement contradicts your statement in the previous chapter. This is confusing.'

Rāmakṛṣṇa told him, 'Don't worry. Write down what I dictate.'

The disciple was unconvinced. Rāmakṛṣṇa explained, 'The purpose of the book is not to present facts, but to state the truth and bring about transformation. It is to inspire people to move towards a living master.'

The master's words are not related to facts; they are truth. Facts record; truth resonates.

This is true regarding all scriptures and books. No book can give the ultimate Truth. The problem is that some people take books as the ultimate authority. They take their intellect as authority. Instead of living the truth, they take books as authority. They demand proof for the masters' words based on books and scriptures they have read.

The main problem is the meaning of words. For example, if a master utters the word *'ātman,'* he says it from the Sanskrit dictionary. But we look for *'ātman'* in our own Oxford dictionary! Naturally the problem starts.

When we are in the presence of a living master, we can seek clarification. We can immediately clear doubts. A master knows by seeing our faces that we are unable to understand. He explains further till things fit together.

When we read books we are playing with our mind. That is why many feel more comfortable with books than listening to a living master. This is the difference between real seekers and pseudo seekers.

If our search is real, if it is an urge, we will be seeking a living master. On the other hand, if our search is an entertainment, just passing time, we feel comfortable with books and old masters' photographs.

If our search is intense, we feel deeply connected with a living master. He is the Truth.

Truth is like lightning. It is instantaneous; it is quantum. It is not evolutionary. Facts are logical, step-by-step, and evolutionary. Each part must be understood before the next is understood. With truth, absorption is total, instantaneous and holistic. That's why it is difficult to grasp the truth through the intellect. It does not seem logical; it is not rational.

Throughout the centuries people have suffered misgivings because the truth they saw within their beings did not match the truth accepted by society and organized religion. Society and religion have established rules and regulations that have nothing to do with truth since it is difficult to interpret and regulate truth. Rules and regulations are based only upon facts.

Facts and truth do not always go together. Facts are one-dimensional, relating only to time, whereas the truth is space *and* time; it is multidimensional.

Here, Arjuna has come to a level of maturity that is no longer satisfied with factual information. His quest is for the Truth. His confusions have disappeared. He has no more questions. Only doubts. Doubts are great. They are clear indicators that the disciple is ready to receive and imbibe the master. Doubts are green signals whereas questions are red signals.

Questions prevent the master from opening up further. They interrupt the master and demand His reply to our words. Furthermore, when we are unable to follow, we question the authority of the living master, the living energy itself. We measure him with our limited intellect. We limit him with the limitations of our intellect and we use our intellect as the benchmark to judge him.

A small story:

A young man approached an elderly person sitting under a tree near his village and told him that he was in search of a guru. The old man replied that he knew of a guru. He described him in detail, how he looked, where to locate him and so forth. The young man thanked him and moved on. For thirty years, he searched. Unable to find the guru, he gave up and headed back to his hometown.

Before reaching home, he saw an old man who exactly matched the description of the guru. Approaching closer, the young man realized that he was none other than the old man with whom he started his search. The young man asked, 'Why did you allow me to waste thirty years looking for you?'

The old man replied, 'Those years were not wasted. They molded you. When you came to me thirty years ago, I described myself, including the tree under which I sat. You were unable to recognize me. You were in a hurry to travel, wander and satisfy your ego. Your searching was necessary in order to dissolve questions that arose from your ego. Now you are ripe and ready to receive me.'

If the disciple is not in a receptive state, he is even unable to recognize his guru. Questions arise from ego. Doubts arise from consciousness.

Arjuna did everything. In the second chapter, when Kṛṣṇa spoke about *ātma,* saying *nainaṁ chindanti śastrāṇi nainaṁ dahati pavakaḥ* (Ch.2, verse 23) (The soul cannot be touched by any weapon or be burned by fire), Arjuna immediately asks: How will an enlightened man speak?

Why? Why did he ask that question? It was out of pure ego, to judge Kṛṣṇa, to see whether Kṛṣṇa was enlightened. Arjuna was checking the authority of the master. It started with violence, with questions.

Gradually, by Chapter 9 when Kṛṣṇa revealed *rājavidyā rāja guhyaṁ,* royal knowledge and royal secret, that Existence is intelligence, that the cosmic energy is intelligence, Arjuna's questions very slowly settle down.

When he heard the glory of Kṛṣṇa, love started flowering in him. When Kṛṣṇa revealed His cosmic form, the *viśvarūpa,* Arjuna experienced the ultimate consciousness.

In Chapter 9, with the revelation of divine knowledge and secrets, intelligence happened. In Chapter 10, with *Vibhūti Yoga,* divine manifestation, devotion started flowering. In Chapter 11, with *viśvarūpa darśan,* Arjuna had the experience. Now all questions are over.

RamaKṛṣṇa Paramahamsa says beautifully, 'In a party, until the food is served, conversations and noise happen. Once the food is served, only the noise of serving and eating will be heard! Till the ultimate experience, questions will be there. After that, the expression of that experience alone will be there. All other noise will disappear.'

Arjuna first questioned the authority of Kṛṣṇa. Then he moved into calculation of his own benefits. Now it is acceptance. First it was resistance, then indifference and finally acceptance.

Creative energy is different from accounting. Only God can create. If anybody creates anything, he experiences divinity at that moment. That is why pregnant ladies were worshipped in India during vedic times. It was believed that they healed people, just by their touch. Architects are creators. Engineers make good money, but architects have the satisfaction. They are creative. Without creativity, we miss life.

Here, Arjuna has finished everything. His calculations are over. He has come down to the level of doubts. With questions, the tone is different. Questions demand proof from the master. Doubts are not like that. They are just asking for some tips. Arjuna has come to the level of complete acceptance of the master. That is why, throughout this chapter, Arjuna is silent. He is ready to imbibe the master. He is ready to take everything thrown to him.

Journey Into The Causal Body

15.1 Bhagavān *says,*
'It is said that there is an imperishable banyan tree whose roots are on the outside; leaves and branches are under the earth.
The leaves are said to be the vedic hymns. He who knows this tree knows the Vedas.*'*

15.2 *The branches of this tree extend below and above the earth, nourished by the three human attributes,* guṇas.
Its buds are the sense objects.
This tree also has roots going down and these are bound to the resultant actions of humans.

Kṛṣṇa refers to the causal body as the banyan tree. This is a continuation of the previous chapter. Chapters 14 to 17 are interconnected. They are connected discourses. In this chapter, *Puruṣottama Yoga,* yoga of the supreme Self, He refers to the fifth layer.

The fifth layer is the causal body where all *saṁskāras* are stored in seed form. We enter this layer in deep sleep. We take *saṁskāras* out from this layer and create the world.

Desire is an energy. That energy is abused by creating self-contradicting desires. Self-contradicting desires put us into restlessness. After that, if we don't correct ourselves, we fall into depression. He gave techniques to clear self-contradicting desires.

Desires

Our own desires, born out of our *vāsanās*, carry their own energy for fulfillment, as they are the basic needs and purpose with which we were born.

The universe blesses us with the power to meet all our real needs. However, once here, we accumulate other desires. These desires are the wants that we borrow from others by comparing, copying and envying others.

Ramana Maharṣi says, 'This universe can fulfill the needs of all its inhabitants; but it cannot fulfill the wants of even a single person.' How true!

When desires are borrowed, when they are based on coveting other people's belongings, there will be a serious contradiction between our wants and needs. Fulfillment of our needs gives happiness, true joy. That is why a poor man eats his simple meal with such gusto.

Chasing wants, our borrowed desires, causes sorrow. Have you ever seen a rich man eat with true happiness? His accumulated wealth invariably gives him. diseases He needs personal trainers and dieticians to keep him fit and healthy.

Desires are caused by *saṁskāras,* which are stored in our unconscious mind layer. Our mind finds it difficult to cope with even the remaining ten percent of sensory inputs that are fed into its conscious realm.

Embedded memories, *saṁskāras,* drive our actions. We do not realize that these desires are not the true desires that carry energy to be fulfilled. They are simply picked up from others, based upon jealousy and comparison. But for the most part, our *saṁskāras* define us.

Now Kṛṣṇa moves on to the next layer, where *saṁskāras* are stored in the seed form. Even if we move beyond the three layers of desire, restlessness and depression, these *saṁskāras* in seed form (called *bīja saṁskāra, bīja* meaning 'seed') need to be cleared.

Kṛṣṇa speaks of techniques to destroy these *saṁskāras*. These may not express themselves in us right now. Yet if they are allowed to be there in seed form, at one time or another, they will exploit us.

In an office, some files are on the table, some are in the archives, while others are in the safety vault. The previous three layers are like the office table and archived material. This causal layer is the office safety vault. The next two layers are the external vaults. In the previous chapter, Kṛṣṇa explains techniques to clear the table. Now He gives techniques to empty the office safety vault.

Kṛṣṇa says, 'The roots of the tree are on the outside; the branches are inside.' From the causal body, if the roots are taken to be outside, it should be in the earlier three layers ending with the physical body. In a tree, the roots feed nutrients to the tree. The tree takes water and minerals through the roots. The roots decide the condition and growth of a tree. That is why Kṛṣṇa says the roots of the tree are in the physical body. The tree of *saṁskāra* is watered by the five senses of the physical body and our actions. The *saṁskāras* in seed form in the causal body are formed and watered by the five senses of the physical body.

Kṛṣṇa further says that the leaves are the *vedic* hymns and one who knows the tree is knower of the *Vedas*. He says *saṁskāras* are the *vedic* hymns, the *mantras*. *Mantras* are defined as *manasasya sthiraha iti mantraḥ,* whatever controls or stabilizes the mind, or *manaḥ trāyate iti mantraḥ,* that which redeems the life of man.

Words that are settled in our inner selves pave our road. Words expressed or coming out when we are alone, are the *saṁskāras* printed in the causal body. Our lives revolve them.

Words are double-edged swords. Whatever words we use to offend others settle in our inner self. They emerge whenever they find a chance to push out of our inner self. No man is intelligent enough to use harsh words on others and smooth words inside. It is an unconscious action. That is why, in ancient Indian society, the usage of harsh words was controlled by various customs.

Our mind is constantly occupied in inner chatter. Eventually we express part of this chatter in words. Part of it we suppress for fear of societal repercussions. We do not express what we fear would hurt others or what might be unacceptable to others. All these words settle deep inside our *maṇipūraka cakra,* the navel energy center, which is the seat of words.

There are words we feel comfortable using based on our position relative to the listener. We may say harsh things to subordinates, spouses, children and others whom we think we control. We dare not dream of saying those words to superiors and strangers. Words that are harsh, whether expressed externally or internally, settle down within us. What goes out also goes in. These settle within our navel energy center. Both expressed and unexpressed words build our bank of *saṁskāras.*

Every word we speak affects us and affects those who listen to them or at whom they are directed. The same effect happens with thoughts.

One who understands this can influence other people through his thoughts and words, perhaps more effectively than through his actions. Even we do not know how our thoughts and words influence and affect other people; they may not be as focused and effective, but they will still affect others and us.

In this area, we have good news as well as bad news. The good news is that at any time we can reorganize our causal body. The bad news is that our present negativity is responsible for any suffering that we go through.

> A woman telephoned her husband at his office. Her husband explained that he was too busy to talk. The wife said, 'It won't take long. I have one piece of good news and one bit of bad news.'
>
> Her husband replied, 'Tell me the good news because the bad news can be handled later.'
>
> She said, 'I have just discovered that the airbag in our car is working perfectly.'
>
> The bad news was obviously that she had an accident; that is why the airbag in the car inflated!

Every piece of good news has hidden bad news. So we have good news and bad news about the causal body.

Kṛṣṇa further states that one who knows this tree is the knower of the *Vedas*. He says one who has the knowledge that *saṁskāras,* which constitute the causal body, are the result of the five senses, knows the *Vedas* or has the knowledge of life's guiding force.

The transient and the permanent

The water a tree receives through its roots mainly decides the condition of the tree. If good water and manure are available, the tree flourishes. The leaves will be green. If poison is poured on it, the tree sheds its leaves and slowly dies.

This tree of *saṁskāras,* which is in the causal body, lives mainly due to the five senses. Kṛṣṇa uses the word *aśvattha,* which also means that which is transient, that which is not today as it was yesterday and which will not be tomorrow as it is today. It refers to material life where nothing is what it seems to be. As Buddha says, everything is temporary - '*anicca,*' impermanent.

Life, as people say, is not unreal. If it were truly unreal, we would not be able to experience it. The fact that we experience material life and seem to enjoy it, even if temporarily, means it is real. It is unreal to the extent that whatever we experience is transient and impermanent.

Unreal does not mean nonexistent. If something is nonexistent, we cannot perceive it or experience it, even temporarily. Even a dream is real. We say dreams are unreal, but we cannot deny that we experience dreams. People recollect some dreams vividly. How can dreams be unreal? However, it is a fact that we do not have self-awareness while dreaming.

Once we become aware, we wake up from the dream. It has never happened that a lion or a murderer chasing a person has caught that person in a dream. It may happen in a movie, but not in real life. As soon as we are threatened, as soon as we become aware of ourselves, we wake up and the dream ends.

Dreams are not unreal in the sense that they are nonexistent; they are unreal to the extent that we are unaware. In the same manner, sages tell us that we are unaware even when we are awake. *'Jagrat, jagrat,'* they say, 'wake up, wake up.' They do not ask us to wake up from sleep. They ask us to wake up from our unaware wakefulness into an aware wakefulness.

Aśvattha signifies this state of unawareness. To understand this unawareness produced by our senses and directed by our *saṁskāras,* is to gain knowledge, the *Vedas*. Kṛṣṇa goes on to explain more about this state of unawareness.

Kṛṣṇa says the roots go upwards as well as downwards. He says the leaves of the tree are decided by the tricks of the five senses and the resultant action of mankind. The roots are not only in the physical body, but also in the action. Kṛṣṇa says the tree is deeply rooted because the action of the entire mankind is always result-oriented. It is always guided by greed and fear.

The *aśvattha* tree, the banyan tree, is like a human body. Its roots, like in a human being, are above, like our hair. The hair is said to be a channel to draw in cosmic energy. Our limbs, hands and legs are like branches of the banyan tree. The human system is truly upside down!

Kṛṣṇa gives a beautiful tip to clear the *saṁskāras*. If we are not guided by greed and fear, if our actions are not result-oriented, no *saṁskāras* will be created. If you serve selflessly for at least half an hour a day, it will do you a lot of good.

While doing service, don't plan anything. Don't even plan to have a group of volunteers do the service. Just do any work that you can do. It may seem silly and a waste of time. But at a later date, this time alone will be felt as purposeful. If your service is fueled by greed or fear, you may end up in a mess and be a nuisance to others, too. We can never experience fulfillment when our selfish desires are met. They are food for our ego and they serve no universal cause.

A small story:

> The boy scouts in a school were required to do one act of social service daily and report it to their scoutmaster. Three boys jointly said that they helped an elderly lady cross the street. The master was not able to understand. He was puzzled. 'Helping an old lady cross the road is a good service, but it does not require three boys. One is sufficient. Why three of you?'
>
> The boys said, 'No sir, it was a job for three of us because the old lady did not want to cross the street. We had to carry her!'

Systemized service often leads to such a situation. So don't plan anything. Just do service anywhere. Then the service you do will infuse enormous power into your being. For at least half an hour a day do something selflessly. I tell my devotees to contribute service to the mission for at least half an hour a day. This service is meditation. It inculcates the spirit of collective consciousness and lays the path to realizing the divinity underlying the service.

Bhagavan says, '*karmānubandhīni manuṣya loke.*' All our actions revolve around results. So, at least in this service, don't think of dollars or fame. Don't plan to impress. Don't plan to make your presence felt. Do the work for its own sake.

Even when we do so-called philanthropic or charitable work, we must be careful not to bind ourselves to the results of our actions. People ask, 'What is the point of meditation when the rest of the world suffers?' It is good if we can genuinely feel the suffering of humanity and wish to do work to help end that suffering. However, we must have the sense of this expanded consciousness to feel this compassion.

Mostly we do charitable work based on notions of earning brownie points that will do us good in our afterlife, whether we believe in rebirth or not. Or we would like to see ourselves in the media and feel good. It fulfills our need for attention either in this world or in another world after death.

There is no concept of sin or merit on the spiritual path. No one, neither a Citragupta nor a Saint Peter stands at the Pearly Gates enquiring as to whether you have done your necessary quota of charity work down below.

When you work, whether it is charitable as you and society define it, or commercial and mercenary, as long you do it with no expectation of results, your actions will be selfless. These actions are not motivated by fear and greed. They will not result in the hangover of *saṁskāras*.

This may seem difficult for the intellect to accept. When individuals and corporations embark upon philanthropic activities, they measure the success of their input, whether in terms of money or effort, by what has been achieved. Objectives need to be well defined, budgets need to be created, results need to be analyzed and the course must be corrected.

Yet, there is a way in which the process is defined and not the results. When a defined process is followed, results naturally follow. If we follow the right path, we reach the right destination. It takes courage to believe and implement this. It takes courage to say that we will work without expecting rewards. It takes a truly confident person to accept that what is important is 'doing' and not 'doership' and that status is not as important as the state of doing.

What needs to be done is to focus on the present, define a path and a process; then see to it that the process is followed. If this is done with awareness, results will follow.

Cutting the Tree Down

15.3 *The real form of this tree cannot be perceived. No one can understand where it ends, where it begins, or where its foundation is.*
But with determination one must cut down this strongly rooted tree with the weapon of detachment.

15.4 *One must then seek that place from which having gone, one never returns, and surrender to the supreme Being from whom all activities started in ancient times.*

Kṛṣṇa speaks further about the causal body where *saṁskāras* are stored. He is an extraordinary scientist. A scientist can honestly search for the truth; he can give up his own faith and belief for the cause of this search and is courageous enough to express the secrets that he discovers step-by-step.

We see these qualities in Kṛṣṇa. He is honest in His expression or search. He is ready to give up His small understandings for the bigger truth. He is ready to give up yesterday's truth for today's updated intelligence.

We can't wait for a train by looking at last year's timetable. Kṛṣṇa continuously updates Himself. Lastly, He is courageous to open up the secrets in public. He is not worried about copyright and intellectual property rights.

The ancient vedic society in India believed that knowledge was free. The idea of copyright did not exist. Kṛṣṇa is courageous enough to open up all the secrets.

He beautifully says, '*narūpamasyeha tatopalabhyate.*' No one can perceive the real form of this tree. No one can understand where it begins, where it ends or where its foundation is. However, with determination one should cut down this tree with the weapon of strong will and detachment.

No one can see what one has stored in one's causal body. It is like Pandora's Box. All the *saṁskāras* stored in the causal layer reveal themselves one by one. When we erase four of them, ten will surface. What is inside nobody knows. Only one thing is possible. All the *saṁskāras* can be cut by a strong will of detachment. With a strong will, with intelligence, the entire causal layer can be cleared.

People ask a master to show them how to get rid of *saṁskāras.* Only strong will and intelligence can do that. Do we ask the master's help to take our hands out of the fire? No! We know fire burns. So we withdraw our hands immediately. We ask the master only because the understanding is not there.

If the understanding is present, right action follows. If right action does not happen, be very clear that the understanding has not happened. Similarly, *saṁskāras* are dangerous. All that is needed is intelligence and a strong will of detachment.

Kṛṣṇa explains that after cutting the tree of *saṁskāras,* surrender to the space of eternal silence, from where there is no coming back. This is the space in which the whole of Existence is established.

One's identity is the collection of one's *saṁskāras,* past memories and desires that are stored in the unconscious mind. This is in the causal layer of our energy. Through deep and focused meditation, we can access this unconscious causal layer and dissolve the *saṁskāras* stored here. Once done, we no longer return as the same person. We are free of *saṁskāras* and liberated.

The spirit that leaves the body goes through a comatose state when it passes through this causal body layer. As long as the spirit has not crossed this layer, it can return to the body. This is the power of *saṁskāras.* These engraved memories or desires can pull the spirit back. That is why sometimes after many years in a coma, people return to consciousness. They are pulled back by unfulfilled desires. However, once the spirit crosses the causal layer, it cannot return to the body. It must move on to the next layer, the cosmic layer.

Once we access this point of dissolution of *saṁskāras* and move on to the cosmic layer, we no longer operate unconsciously at the behest of our stored memories. We move into a state of intuition, as opposed to our earlier state of instinct. We are no longer in an ignorant wakeful state, but in the truly awakened state of consciousness.

Bringing awareness into the unconscious through the super-conscious meditative route is the only correct way to dissolve accumulated *saṁskāras*.

Cleansing Techniques

15.5 *Those who are free from pride, delusion, and attachment, those who dwell in the Self, who are done with lust, who are free from the dualities of joy and sorrow, who are not confused, and who know how to surrender to the supreme person, attain the eternal consciousness.*

15.6 *That supreme space of eternal consciousness, My consciousness, is not illuminated by the Sun or the Moon, or by fire.*
Those who enter that space never return to this material world.

Kṛṣṇa explains the same truth again at a deeper level. He had expressed the same idea in earlier chapters. But Arjuna was unable to understand. At that time, Arjuna was in the questioning mood. In the questioning mood, we miss the whole subject and are busy preparing questions. Now that mood has gone and there are only doubts, no questions.

With doubt, the disciple is open. He is open with his being waiting for the master to flow into him. Arjuna is ready to imbibe Kṛṣṇa. He is waiting for the master's words. His inner chatter has ceased so there are no more questions. He now has the inner space and awareness to receive Kṛṣṇa. That is why he is now able to understand.

Zen Buddhism calls it a *koan,* a riddle of sorts. Just one word is given. One famous Zen *koan* goes like this: 'What is the sound of one hand clapping?' Another says: 'What was your face before your mother and father were born?'

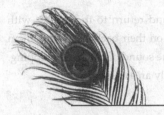

Disciples meditate upon these *koans* and return to the master with answers. The master gives them a whack on their back and sends them on their way. Ultimately they experience the sound of one hand clapping. There is no expressed answer to a *koan*, only an experience.

Beyond attachment

Here Kṛṣṇa says, 'Those who are free from pride, delusion, and attachment, those who dwell in the Self, who are done with lust, who are free from the dualities of joy and sorrow, who are not confused, and who know how to surrender to the supreme person, attain the eternal consciousness.'

What wonderful usage of words!

He does not say who have 'renounced' lust. No, because renunciation won't do. *Vairāgya* means beyond attachment and detachment. *Rāga* means attachment. *Arāga* means detachment. *Virāga* or *vairāgya* means beyond attachment and detachment. It is nonattachment.

Until the age of seven, we are attached to toys. By age eight or nine we are forced to be detached from these. By twenty, most people are beyond attachment or detachment to children's toys. With detachment, we might have renounced it externally. But the inner urge for it prevails.

That is why Kṛṣṇa uses fitting words: those who are 'done' with lust. In this state, we know what we can afford. We know it is there. We can use it or throw it away based on the need. Life is also like a toy. If this is fully understood, you will live like a king, not an ordinary materialistic king, but an enlightened king, *a rājarṣi.*

This is a Zen *koan*. This is not for understanding. This is to be meditated upon. On meditating upon this technique, these characteristics will start flowering in you and give you a clear-cut idea about the causal body.

Earlier, Kṛṣṇa explained ways to erase *saṁskāras*. Now He speaks on the construction of a proper layer. It is about re-programming your causal layer.

Kṛṣṇa gives techniques for construction of the causal body.

Kṛṣṇa's words are like Zen *koans*. Actually Kṛṣṇa uses the same words again. Not only words and expressions, He uses the same letters again. Earlier He used these words as advice. Now He uses same words as programming techniques. This chapter is about programming our causal layer, programming our *saṁskāras*. This program creates positive *saṁskāras* in our causal layer. As long as Arjuna was in the questioning mood, these same words were spelt out as advice. When he enters into the mood of doubts, he receives the same words as techniques. When the disciple is in a questioning mood, the master's words will be taken as advice. Only when the disciple stops questioning and starts listening, these same words will be techniques.

With advice, you need keys to open the door. Techniques are the keys themselves. They are ready to open the door.

Arjuna now receives the gist of earlier chapters. He receives the juice in this chapter. In North Indian monasteries, this chapter is chanted before every meal. This 15th chapter must be chanted before meals, since this chapter is a programming tool of the inner space. The mere words of this chapter can do wonders in re-programming your causal layer.

It takes less than five minutes to chant it. Anybody can do it. Don't worry about the meaning. If you understand the meaning, it is good. Yet, it is highly useful even if chanted without understanding. Repeating these words can program your causal layer. Especially, when you chant them in a mood of surrender, with due respect to the master, it directly touches the causal layer.

Arjuna is completely in a receiving mood. He is fully tuned to the master. If the disciple is completely tuned to the master, Existence helps him through the master. Arjuna needs no explanations, no logic. He is ready to imbibe the master.

Hence, Kṛṣṇa utters the following words to program the causal layer. He gives techniques to create positive *saṁskāras*.

He says, 'Those who are free from pride, delusion, and attachment, those who dwell in the Self, who are done with lust, who are free from the dualities of joy and sorrow, who are not confused, and who know how to surrender to the supreme person, attain eternal consciousness.'

Lust is difficult for a man to shed. Even the greatest of sages have succumbed to lust. Lust is of the body and as long as body consciousness remains, lust will stay. Only a person who has gone beyond body consciousness can drop lust.

A small story:

A small boy went to a kids' movie with his parents. It was about a lion cub and other animals in a jungle. The boy was thoroughly enjoying it. Suddenly there was a scene where the lion cub was trapped by a hunter and became terrified.

The boy was not able to bear this scene. He just jumped from his seat and ran down the hall towards the movie screen. He started throwing up his hands and legs as if in a fight with the hunter in the movie who was about to cage the lion cub. Soon the other animals in the jungle joined together and drove away the hunter and rescued the cub.

The boy came back to his seat and proudly told his mother, 'See how I went first and all the animals followed me and we saved the cub!'

Just as the boy thought that the movie was real, we believe that the input perceived by our senses is also real. We are caught in the *māyā* or illusion created by our senses. The most powerful illusion is the lust within us.

An enlightened master transcends sex and lust. He is genderless. He becomes an *ardhanārīśvara,* a man-woman, a person who expresses both traditionally male and female qualities or attributes. One key attribute of enlightenment is genderlessness.

Kṛṣṇa is direct. He does not believe in giving brain candy to keep you happy. He is brutally direct. He says, 'He who has conquered lust.' Lust is a primal emotion provided by nature for continuation of the species. Going beyond lust, conquering lust, is the first major step in realizing super-consciousness.

Humans are forever confused between love and lust. They think only animals are lustful. Actually, only animals are capable of *pure* lust when they mate. Humans, with their rationalization, can neither be lustful nor loving. So, they are forever in the twilight zone, dissatisfied and unfulfilled.

In the Vedic marriage ritual of *saptapadi,* the seven steps that the couple takes together after tying the wedding knot in Hindu marriage ceremonies, sacred *mantras* are chanted in front of the fire-witness wherein the wife says to the husband, 'Become my eleventh son' and the husband says to the wife, 'Become my eleventh daughter.' It means that in the eleventh year of marriage, their intimacy would be so great that they become each other's child! There is a deep intimacy; there is a wonderful relationship. These words were not poems. They were the guidelines for living.

Add friendliness to love. As of now, our love and lust are deep-rooted violence, to own the other person, to conquer the other person while he or she resists. It's a war. Instead, add friendliness to relationships. Welcome the partner as he or she is; do not just accept him or her. Welcome and accept the mind, body and being as it is.

Are we friendly even to our own body? No, we are not. If we watch carefully, we disrespect and abuse our body. We stay up late and watch television even if our body cries out for sleep. We gorge ourselves on food even if our stomach is full. We smoke even if our lungs cry out. We drink ourselves to unconsciousness. We treat our body like a garbage dump. We are like the pig that shoves its nose into filth thinking it can escape the smell of the filth. We torture our body for what we feel is enjoyment.

We are bothered about terrorism around the globe. Yet we ignore violence at home and violence against our own body. Sadism and masochism do not bother us, terrorism does. But we torture ourselves with guilt and others with our perfectionism. This is also violence, a subtle form of terrorism.

A man once told me, 'My wife is a lawyer.' I asked, 'Does she go to court?' He replied, 'No, she argues at home.'

Drop your imagination and dreams. Add friendliness towards yourself and others, towards their body, mind and being. Carry words that heal others. Carry your body in a way that heals others. Carry friendliness with you always. This is a spiritual process. Carry the grace and goodwill of Lakṣmī instead of observing fasts and *pūjā*.

Kṛṣṇa says, 'That supreme space of eternal consciousness, My consciousness, is not illuminated by the sun or the moon, or by fire. Those who enter that space never return to this material world.'

These words are not advice. They are for contemplation. Advice is the only thing everybody gives and nobody takes! Kṛṣṇa gives these words to program our causal layer. These are words to contemplate, to meditate upon. They are the hymns to be meditated upon.

The causal layer of energy is the passage through which the spirit passes on its last leg before it leaves the material world. When the spirit is stuck in this causal layer, one is in coma. One can be stuck in this layer for a long time.

Those who go past the causal layer, this layer of energetic darkness, where neither the sun nor the moon shines, nor fire warms, progress onwards to the cosmic layer and then to the nirvanic layer, which signifies true liberation.

One can meditate upon this technique, upon this truth expounded by Kṛṣṇa, through the darkness meditation that teachers teach in some of our meditation programs. This meditation, which focuses on darkness, liberates one from the fear of death and the fear of loss of identity that causes the fear of death.

Death is not an option. Death of the body is certain. Separation of the spirit from the body-mind is painful. Vivekānanda says it is like a thousand scorpions stinging at once.

At death the spirit leaves the body shell and merges into infinite energy. It then reappears in another shell, another body. Individual self merges with universal Self. When the spirit is such that it has gone beyond attachment and lust and is constantly focused on the Self, then there is no return for that spirit into another body-mind complex. Else it returns.

Kṛṣṇa points out that the death of the body is a certainty, however, the death of the spirit is impossible. The spirit lives on. When the spirit is evolved it doesn't revert to a mental setup that it transcended in the previous birth, that's all.

Conditioning

15.7 *The living entities in this conditioned material world are a portion of My eternal Self.*
In this conditioned material world they are attracted by the six senses, which include the mind, dwelling in prakṛti, *the active energy principle.*

15.8 *The spirit in the body-mind living in this material world moves from one body to another carrying these just as wind carries fragrance.*

Kṛṣṇa uses a new word, 'conditioning'. Recent research tells us that human beings walk on two legs due to conditioning. A group of scientists recently found a seventeen-year-old boy in a forest. Wolves had raised him. The scientists tried to teach him how to walk on two legs and speak a few words. They were unable to do this and he died within a year.

Man walks on two legs due to conditioning. Everything we consider as human nature is nothing but conditioning.

Zen Buddhism has a beautiful technique for de-conditioning. For twenty-one days, the aspirant has to remain in a room. He can eat and sleep. But he must throw away everything he has seen or heard from his mind. Nothing he has seen or heard should enter his mind. They say within twenty-one days he will be enlightened. It is a tough job. It is tough to be in such a position even for twenty-one minutes.

Here Kṛṣṇa says, 'conditioned world'. Everything is conditioning. Right and wrong, honor and dishonor, are all conditioning. We think of honor or dishonor because we are taught that way.

We are conditioned. If a group of people gives us a certificate and clap their hands, we take it as an honor. That is the way we are taught. But never judge yourself by others' applause. This idea of honor drives many people mad. Never accept the judgment of the crowd.

Integrity decides your worth

A small story:

Winston Churchill was delivering a lecture. About 10,000 people were listening. A press person asked Churchill what he felt about such a huge gathering. Churchill replied, 'Never judge my importance by the crowd. Today there are 10,000 persons. If you announce that I will be hung in public tomorrow, there will be 100,000 people. It will be a scene to be seen.'

The crowd cannot decide right and wrong or honor and dishonor. Your integrity, your honesty, your depth of self-awareness alone can decide your worth.

Here Kṛṣṇa gives these meditation hymns to re-program your causal layer, your *saṁskāra*. Only those who don't know themselves worry about others knowing them. After crossing the three layers and going beyond the causal layer, you enter a space where you are free from conditioning. May you be free from all conditioning!

Kṛṣṇa says, 'They are attracted by the six senses that include the mind.'

There are five physical senses and the sixth sense is the mind. However, according to me, the mind is the only sense and the so-called five physical senses are slaves to it. If the mind can be handled, all the other five can be handled.

A small story:

Queen Madalasa gave birth to seven children. Each child became enlightened by the age of seven and moved out of the kingdom. Their father, the king, was puzzled. How did seven children in a row become enlightened? He probed into the issue and found that

Madalasa had taught them one phrase, *tat tvam asi* (You are That). Just by internalizing *tat tvam asi*, their mental setup changed. They were cleared of *saṁskāras* in the causal layer. They became enlightened.

Enlightenment is the removal of *saṁskāras* and the dissolution of conditioning. We return to our pure original state. This is why enlightenment is referred to as *samādhi*. *Samādhi* means 'returning to the original state'.

The spirit in the body-mind living in this material world, moves from one body to another carrying these *saṁskāras* just as the wind carries fragrance. *Saṁskāras* in one body quit that body and take shelter in another. This continuous vicious cycle of movement of *saṁskāras* is what Kṛṣṇa refers to as *saṁsāra*, the life-and-death cycle.

Kṛṣṇa says 'taking these'. What does He mean by 'these'? In the previous verse, Kṛṣṇa talked about the six senses, including the mind. He refers to them here. When the spirit leaves one body and moves to another body, it carries the six senses, the five physical senses and the mind. Just as the wind carries fragrances, the consciousness carries *saṁskāras*, causal level imprints, from body to body.

Kṛṣṇa answers a frequently asked question about sin. People ask whether sins come with them from one birth to another. Sins never follow. Only imprints travel. For example, if a man commits one hundred murders, the quantity will not follow, but the basic mentality of violence accompanies and tortures him. Only the mental setup is carried.

The concept of *karma* is often used to justify actions, by saying, 'It is our *karma*. It is our destiny, what can be done?', 'Whatever had to happen has happened.' This is pure fabrication and justification of our negative deeds.

We have the freedom to act: the free will to decide and act. Ironically, only an enlightened master has no freedom. Enlightened masters are driven by *Parāśakti's* will; they are guided by Her, that universal power, into doing what they must do. Understand: I cannot take a single step on my own. My limbs move in accordance with Her wishes.

Rāmakṛṣṇa beautifully says that the soul travels from one body to another like we move from one room to another. When He left His physical body, His wife Śāradā devī was about to remove her jewelry. (Traditional Hindu families never allow a widow to wear jewels, especially the sacred thread signifying marital status, and bracelets.)

Just as she was about to remove the sacred thread, Rāmakṛṣṇa appeared and told her not to remove it. He said, 'Where have I gone? Just to another room. Don't remove your jewelry.' From that time till her end, Śāradā devī followed His words. This may seem easier today. But in those days, in an orthodox Hindu family in a small village, it was not so. She was highly courageous.

Someone who leaves all social conditioning, who sheds all *saṁskāras* in his causal layer, moves from body to body as easily as moving from one room to another.

We create big buildings. We accumulate a good bank balance. We have friends. Just as we start enjoying life, suddenly death appears before us. We fear death only because it takes everything away from us. We will not fear death if we are unattached, if our causal layer is not filled with *saṁskāras*, if we are not gripped by social conditioning. We know it is like moving from one room to another.

As Kṛṣṇa says elsewhere, 'It is like changing one dress for another.'

The *saṁskāras* of this life are the result of *prārabdha karma*, the mindset, along with the spirit from the *vāsanas* of the past birth that are carried into this birth. It is always a mix of pain and pleasure.

You Are Your Saṁskāras

15.9 *The living entity, the spirit, leaves one body, takes another body and gets new eyes, ears, nose, tongue and sensing body according to the* saṁskāras *it had in its causal layer and enjoys the new mental setup.*

15.10 *Fools can neither understand how a living entity can quit his body nor what sort of a body he enjoys under the spell of* guṇas, *the attributes and moods of nature. Only those whose eyes are trained by knowledge can see these things.*

'The living entity, the spirit, leaves one body, takes another body and gets new eyes, ears, nose, tongue and sensing body according to the *saṁskāras* it had in its causal layer and enjoys the new mental setup.'

Here Kṛṣṇa reveals another secret. He says, 'You create a body according to the *saṁskāras* in the causal layer.'

There is an Indian science called *sāmudrikā lakṣaṇa śāstra,* the technique of studying body features. By observing our physical body structure, experts can read and reveal our mental setup. They know the relationship between mind and body.

Kṛṣṇa says that we create our sensory organs, according to *saṁskāras* in our causal layer. Kṛṣṇa says that living entities create all five senses through the mind or mental setup. This happens not only when we take another body. Everyday when we wake up from deep sleep, our senses are recreated. If we change our mental setup, within a short time, our face changes.

You create yourself

Our 'mind' is the intelligence spread all over our body. It is the intelligence that resides in our cells. In a period of a little under two years, every part of our body, every cell in our body, gets renewed. Our body as it was a year ago is not the body it is today. Our present body is not the body it will be a year from now. This is not fiction; it is a proven scientific fact.

Then why do we behave the same way as we have for years? Why do illnesses plague us for years, even though the cells are no longer the same?

Each cell as it dies, leaves behind a memory that the newly created cell follows. That is the *saṁskāras* within us. The *saṁskāras* ensures the continuation of a pattern despite complete changes in the body-mind system. This *saṁskāras* are more powerful than the rest of the body-mind system. It decides and drives.

The deep sleep we go into everyday is a rehearsal of our death process. We die and are reborn. Our subtle body leaves the gross body and returns reenergized if we allow it to. It is in our hands to maximize this process of rejuvenation that happens automatically everyday.

Through meditation we can clear our *saṁskāras* and be reborn. We can change our features, our character and behavior, all by reprogramming our *saṁskāras*.

That is why people radiate grace after they start meditation. Beauty is created by make-up. Grace is radiated by meditation. Grace makes the occupant feel at home. It soothes the atmosphere. Beauty creates excitement. Beauty moves the other person into *rajas* (restlessness). Grace creates calmness, *satva*. Grace puts the other person in energy.

People reminisce about great masters like Ramaṇa Maharṣi and say that He imparted wisdom through silence. It is the enlightened master's grace that penetrates the other person's energy and changes that person's *saṁskāras*.

All that we need to do in an enlightened master's presence is just be, be open and silent and allow the master's grace to penetrate us. There is nothing that we need to do. The master's grace does whatever is needed.

One version of the great Indian epic Rāmāyaṇa says that when princess Sīta, the leading lady of the epic, entered the court of King Janaka, her father, all the great kings, monks and mystics stood up automatically. This was not protocol. The grace she radiated caused this response in them. Beauty can create only temptation in the other person. Only grace can create respect. The grace radiating from Sīta's being made everybody stand up.

Zen Buddhism says that if we can walk on a lawn without killing the grass or creating a path with our footsteps, we are eligible for *sanyās*. I doubted this. I thought it was impossible. After all, the whole body weight is there. How can grass bear such a load and not leave imprints?

As I said earlier, I went on a safari in South India. I sat on an elephant and the caretaker came along with me. It was evening. It became dark. The caretaker had no torch or light. I asked him how he would find his way back home. He replied, 'I have created a path by my daily walk that I can follow even in darkness.'

I asked about the elephant because it traveled with him everyday. He said, 'The elephant's feet do not create a path. The elephant and other animals do not destroy grass as they walk over it.' I started calculating the load exerted by one foot of the elephant. At the least, it works out to four times that of an average man. However, it did not create a path. It did not kill a single blade of grass. In spite of the physical mass, there was no damage to the environment.

That is why Zen Buddhism says we are eligible for *sanyas* only when we can walk on the lawn without killing a blade of grass. The negativity, arrogance, violence, negative *saṁskāras* in our causal layer, makes us feel heavy on earth. If we feel heavy around our navel area, we carry negative *saṁskāras*. The feeling of heaviness is not connected to our weight. It is due to imprints in our inner space. A person who feels light radiates grace from his being and he never creates a path on a lawn. He never kills a blade of grass by his walk.

Zen says we are spiritually evolved souls only when our feet do not create a path, when we float while we walk, when we do not go against Nature. Man is the only animal who has gone against Nature.

> A small story:
>
> A man wanted to do away with his wife and her pet cat. In India, there used to be no way to divorce one's wife. So he decided to at least get rid of the cat. He took the cat ten miles away in his car, dropped it off and returned home. Just as he entered his house, the cat also arrived. He was shocked.
>
> The next day he took the cat and traveled forty minutes away. He reached a thick forest he had never seen before. He abandoned the cat there.
>
> He started his return trip and reached home. To his utter amazement, the cat was standing at the doorway.
>
> The third day, he took the cat, blindfolded it, put it in a sack, drove a very circuitous route, left it in a certain spot and started driving back. He drove for one hour and then called up his wife and asked, 'Dear, is the cat at home by any chance?' The wife replied that the cat had just returned. The man said, 'Please can you somehow find out how to get home. I have lost my way.'

Animals are one with Nature. It is human beings who have gone against Nature, who have lost their way.

Here Kṛṣṇa says, we create our senses according to our *saṁskāras*. This happens not only when we die and take birth; we redesign our senses to suit our *saṁskāras* everyday, when we wake up too. If we wake up with the right mental setup, we will have our senses accordingly and for the whole day we can enjoy it. If on the other hand, we get up with negativity, we suffer.

The few moments immediately after we wake up are crucial. Whatever we feel will be reflected the rest of the day. If we radiate joy, our whole day will be joyful. If we are irritable, our whole day will be irritable.

Kṛṣṇa further says that the type of senses we create determines the type of sensory objects we enjoy. If we create positive senses, we enjoy a positive life. If we create negative senses, we suffer a negative life. The type of senses we create determines what type of objects or pleasures attract us, and we experience that.

Our senses, intelligence and our body-mind system create the energy field around us. This energy field attracts similar energy fields. If we are negative, if our perceptions are negative, we attract people with negative mindsets and descend into a vicious cycle. However, if we convert negativity into positive emotions and positive perceptions, we attract like-minded, positive people.

This is extremely important in spiritual progress. It is easy to make progress and evolve when we are with a master. However, when we get into the company of people who are not following the path, it is easy to slip from our path.

That is why I am keen to create ashrams or communities where like-minded people can live together and grow in spirituality. The energy created in this process cannot be created in the external world. We can be idealistic and say that we can meditate anywhere; however, in reality, spirituality thrives either in aloneness or in like-minded communities. Like energies attract one another and enhance one another.

Kṛṣṇa provides a wonderful punch line in the middle of this chapter.

'Fools,' He says. Kṛṣṇa uses the Sanskrit word *mūḍhaḥ* , which means 'fool'. Fools can neither understand how a living entity can quit his body nor what sort of a body he enjoys under the spell of *guṇa*, the attributes and moods of Nature. Only those whose eyes are trained by knowledge can see these things.

Life – a gift from the Divine

The first thought with which we get up from our bed plays a major role in our enjoyment throughout the day. What is our first thought usually? First we feel awake. We feel our body. Then it may be the fear that we must go to our office or it may be the greed to finish some work. At the stroke of the thought, fear or greed, our body jumps out of bed. We connect to our body through fear or greed.

Kṛṣṇa says that if we catch our body with fear or greed, we attract more and more fear or greed throughout the day.

There are many gates to enter the body. Never enter through the fear or greed gate. Get up with a spiritual thought. Remember your master or favorite God. Practice it consciously for a few days. Then it will become your routine. Don't connect to your body with fear or greed; you will attract more and more greed or fear.

Let your first thought be spiritual. Remember your master or God or anyone divine and thank Him. Thank Him for the extended life. Everyday that you wake up is an extension to your life on planet earth. Thank Divinity for the grace, for the extension.

Waking up from bed is not our birthright. Of course, birth itself is not our right. It is a pure gift from Existence. Be grateful to the Divine for this day and extension here.

If we wake up from bed with spiritual thoughts, that consciousness stays with us the whole day. If we are made to get up from bed by material thoughts, we start our day with irritation. The entire day we carry the same irritated mood.

When we are in deep sleep, we are in touch with the causal layer. While waking up, we travel along the other three layers and reach the physical body. The three layers are like a shopping mall with various *saṁskāras*. According to our causal layer, we pick up the related *saṁskāras* and contact our physical body and design our senses accordingly.

Just for twenty-one days, wake up with a spiritual thought and check your face. It will be changed. Your eyes will have a new look.

I am not putting forward a theory. I have experienced this. A few hundred thousand people around the world practice these words. From that authority, I tell you, this is a vibrant technique.

Don't conduct the body with *tamas or rajas* (depression or restlessness). If you wake up with greed or fear, you design a body that radiates greed or fear and thereby attracts incidents that put you in greed or fear.

When you travel from the causal layer to the physical body, pick up *satva* (peaceful or blissful) *saṁskāras.* Have a spiritual thought as the first thought. Think of your master or God or anything that gives you a spiritual memory. That is why in India, ancient mystics tell us to meditate early in the morning. At least for a few seconds be in a blissful mood. Your inner space will be fresh and new.

Kṛṣṇa says, 'Only those whose eyes are trained by knowledge can see the truth of this science.' The whole thing is before you. He says fools cannot understand and only those with eyes of knowledge can see. The choice of being a fool or a man with eyes of knowledge is left to us. The choice is completely ours.

Awareness, Not Achievement

15.11 *The serious practitioner of yoga, with an understanding of his Self, can see all this clearly.*
But those who do not have an understanding of the Self, however much they try, cannot see.

15.12 *The light of the sun, the light of the moon and the light of fire, all their radiance is also from Me.*

15.13 *Entering into earth, I support all beings with My energy; becoming the watery moon, I nourish all plant life.*

15.14 *I am the fire of digestion in every living body and I am the breath of life, exhaled and inhaled, with which I digest the four-fold food.*

Kṛṣṇa uses '*yoginaḥ*' in this verse. Yoga has become a buzzword for cool people. I recently read an advertisement offering super-deluxe Kundalini Yoga that provides instant liberation! I have never read about super-deluxe yogic practices offering instant liberation yoga mentioned in the scriptures.

Yoga is the link, the union, between the individual self, *ātman,* and universal Self, cosmic consciousness, *Brahman*. Awareness of this link, awareness that the self is the same as the Self, leads to liberation. Patañjali, the great scientist sage of ancient India, lays down eight paths to this union, the liberation, and the awareness that we are divine.

In today's world, my opinion is that *dhyāna,* meditation, which is one of the eight limbs, is best suited for spiritual progress and for the realization that one's self is part of that cosmic Self.

Kṛṣṇa says that until that awareness happens, however much one may strive, one will not reach Him.

Understand, here we are talking about awareness, not achievement. The truth is that our individual self is an integral part of the universal consciousness, the Self. This truth is not something that we need to work towards. It exists. It is. We are blinded by individual ego, *māyā,* the illusion of our individual identity, in forgetting that we are part of the collective consciousness.

Yogis, sincere spiritual practitioners, lift this veil of *māyā,* destroy the illusion, to see beyond into the truth of their oneness with the Divine. Meditation is the path and technique to lift this veil. Meditation enables the practitioner to go deeper and deeper into himself. Meditation brings about awareness of what is.

Master – the dispeller of darkness

Light is awareness. Light is the sustainer of life. The Bible says, 'God said, *Let there be light and there was light.*' Light is one of the first manifestations of the Divine in creation. Without light and heat from the sun, life as we know it would be impossible. Everything in this world revolves around energy received from the sun in the form of light and heat.

The sun is also the dispeller of darkness. Not only does Kṛṣṇa establish that He is the creator of this universe - the solar system, sun, moon and the fire that sustain our lives, but He also tells us that He is the Dispeller of darkness.

Kṛṣṇa, as the master, as the guru, is the Dispeller of darkness. *Guru* means one who dispels darkness. As the sun, moon and the fire, Kṛṣṇa is the ultimate master who leads us into awareness.

Kṛṣṇa is the destroyer of our *saṁskāras. Saṁskāras* are products of darkness, our unconscious. Darkness is not a positive entity. It cannot be shifted from point to point. However, it can be destroyed by light. The presence of light dissolves darkness. The presence of awareness destroys *saṁskāras.* Darkness has no existence of its own. It only exists when there is no light. We cannot create darkness. It is the absence of something.

When someone cannot see, he is not bothered by darkness. He is not afraid of darkness. To a blind man, darkness is his nature. A blind man will not say that he sees ghosts and spirits in darkness. Darkness is the state that he exists in.

A truly courageous man is also not disturbed by darkness. Someone who is not afraid of anything does not fear the loss of ego, loss of identity and death. To him, darkness poses no fear as well. He can equally handle darkness and light, without fear or attraction.

Other than these two classes of people, darkness poses problems and presents fears for everyone else.

Kṛṣṇa is not only the Lord of light, but of darkness as well.

Kṛṣṇa further expands on His pervasiveness. In the form of light and heat, He is the Sustainer of all beings within this universe. As we have seen, He is the dispeller of darkness, the dissolver of *saṁskāras.*

He says that He is the energy of the watery moon and through this energy He is the life energy within plant life.

Kṛṣṇa affirms that He is *Brahman* and through His manifestation of the various natural elements of space, air, fire, water and earth, He is responsible for plant life and therefore for food and human beings.

Without plant life, there is no food. Without food, there is no body and mind. Body and mind become food for others after death. Food is an expression of divinity. The energy behind food is both the creator and destroyer of *saṁskāras.*

Most of us treat food as a basic necessity or an object of sensual pleasure. We ignore it or become addicted to it. We need to be aware of what we eat.

A disciple asked a Zen master, 'Master, what changed in you when you became enlightened?'

The master said, 'Now that I have become enlightened, I eat when I eat and sleep when I sleep.'

This may sound confusing. How many of us eat when we eat? How many of us focus on the food that we eat? While eating, we focus on everything except food. We talk, dream, read, watch television, fight and do everything except be aware of the food.

We treat food as garbage and it turns into garbage inside us. Once we treat food as energy, the life energy that it is, we experience a transformation inside us. Saying grace before meals as Christians do is a wonderful custom.

Before eating, offer gratitude to the universe for what you have received and meditate upon the food. Traditionally, Hindus offer oblations to the Divine and chant prayers before eating. Major changes happen when you follow these customs with awareness.

A person who can be so settled in the present is one who is aware. He is one with Kṛṣṇa.

The role of the sun as the giver of light and heat energies is obvious. It is also obvious that without the sun, all life forms will cease to exist. However, the fact that the moon is a nourishing energy providing life energy to plants and therefore to humans is not that well appreciated.

The moon controls our behavior, moods and minds. *Soma*, the name for the moon, refers to its fluidity and the transient nature of waxing and waning.

Kṛṣṇa then talks about *vaiśvānara, prāṇa* and *apāna*.

The Bṛhadāraṇyaka Upaniṣad says:

'This fire that is within the human being and which digests the food that he eats is *vaiśvānara*. The sound of this fire *vaiśvānara* is that which one hears by closing the ears. When death nears and the spirit is about to leave the body, he no longer hears this sound.'

This *Upaniṣad* goes on to say that neither *āhāra* (food), nor *prāṇa* (breath), can function alone, one without the other. Food will decay without breath and breath will dry up without food. Together, when the awareness of their union happens, true consciousness results.

What Kṛṣṇa implies here as well is that food is divine since it has His imprint on it. We tend to take food for granted. Only when food is scarce, is it appreciated and enjoyed.

A small story:

> A teacher was teaching a little boy good habits at nursery school: how to sit properly at the table, fold the napkin on his lap, pick up the fork and spoon and so on.
>
> As the boy was about to gulp down what was set in front of him, she asked, 'Haven't we forgotten something?'
>
> The boy replied, 'What now?'
>
> The teacher said, 'Don't you pray before you start eating?'
>
> 'No,' said the boy. 'My mom's a good cook!'

The Way Our Mind Functions

15.15 *I am seated in everyone's heart and from Me came memory, knowledge and their loss. I am known by the* Vedas; *indeed, I am the creator of* vedānta *and I am the knower of the* Vedas.

15.16 *There are two things, the perishable and the imperishable, in this world. There are the living beings who are perishable while there is the unchangeable, the imperishable.*

Kṛṣṇa says that He is memory and He is knowledge. What does this mean? How does our mind work? How does it invent beliefs? We don't even know where our mind is. If I ask you where your mind is, you will point to your head. That's not your mind.

Every cell in our body has inbuilt intelligence. These cells constantly regenerate themselves. These cells make up our body-mind system. Therefore, there is not one place where our mind is definitely located; certainly it is not in our head!

Intellect and intuition

All our decisions are influenced by our past experiences that are stored as *samskāra*s in our unconscious mind. This unconscious area is powerful. It can be used in three ways: at the instinct level, intellect level or intuition level. As long as the unconscious is overloaded with negative memories and restlessness, it works at the instinct level. We decide instinctively, unconsciously, just like an animal does and end up regretting most decisions.

Next is the intellect level. Here, we are conscious and make decisions logically, but we don't have extra enthusiasm or energy. We are not creative or innovative; we don't grow.

When we are at the intellect level, we are not tired; yet we are not energetic either. We are in a break-even state. At this level, we do not use our potential to the maximum.

The level where we can actualize our entire potential is the intuition level. If we can infuse deep silence and awareness into the unconscious zone and replace engraved memories or files with silence and awareness, we are at the intuition level.

The greatest wealth lies within, not outside. The greatest joy lies within, not outside. In the outside world, every experience of joy is followed by sorrow. Joy creates expectations and when expectations are not fulfilled, they lead to sorrow. When the search begins inside, expectations drop, attachments drop and a new joy happens. That joy is eternal, never ending. It is *ānanda, nityānanda,* eternal bliss.

Because we are unaware of this, we search outside for happiness, because that is the only way we know.

A small story:

One boy used to always sleep during the guest lectures in college. One day his friend asked him, 'Why do you come to the guest lectures? You only sleep here.'

The boy replied, 'I suffer from insomnia and this is the only place where I am able to sleep.'

Understand: like this boy who went to the guest lecture to sleep, we too go to so many places outside of us in search of happiness. We search for the right thing but in the wrong places. We have been conditioned that way. All we need to do is turn inward.

In his commentary on the Gītā, Śaṅkara says that memory and knowledge come from Kṛṣṇa to those who do good deeds and loss of memory and knowledge to those who do evil deeds. The reference to memory and knowledge here is to the understanding of our true nature, the understanding and realization that we are one with the Divine, that Kṛṣṇa is seated in our hearts.

Kṛṣṇa takes Arjuna into a deeper understanding. Kṛṣṇa talks about *puruṣa,* the principle of energy that underlies our existence. *Sāṅkhya* philosophy talks about *puruṣa* and *prakṛti. Puruṣa,* in one sense is energy, and *prakṛti* is matter. *Puruṣa* is the unmoving, passive energy principle, whereas *prakṛti* is the active material principle. *Puruṣa* is the male principle; *prakṛti* is the female principle. *Puruṣa* is Śiva and *prakṛti* is Śakti.

Kṛṣṇa goes beyond that philosophy. He says *Puruṣa* is twofold, one imperishable and the other perishable. He says all living beings are the perishable *puruṣa* and they are situated in the imperishable energy.

In earlier chapters, Kṛṣṇa has covered in depth these aspects of *prakṛti,* which operate through the mind, senses and the attributes, the three types of *guṇa.* Here, He expands upon *puruṣa. Puruṣa* is the ultimate energy from which all emanates. *'Īśā vāsyaṁ idaṁ sarvaṁ'* says the Īśāvāsya upaniṣad, 'All that exists is energy.'

The great scientist, Einstein became depressed when the findings from his theory of relativity and his discovery that matter can release energy resulted in nuclear bombs. He was shocked at the destruction he had unwittingly caused and turned to spirituality for solace.

When Einstein read this verse from the *Upaniṣads,* written possibly five to ten thousand years ago, he said, 'I felt proud that I had discovered that matter is energy. Many thousand years ago, these sages knew this, and also knew that matter arises from energy. The last step in science is the first step in spirituality.'

The primal energy principle, *puruṣa* is like potential energy. It is energy, but passive. It is the operating principle behind the entire universe. Without this energy, nothing will exist. Nothing will live.

Kṛṣṇa says that there are two kinds of *puruṣa*: one is eternal and one perishes.

The *puruṣa* that perishes is the body-mind energy embedded in all beings, including humans. This energy has a definite, limited lifetime. It is always changing. There is nothing permanent about it. It is programmed for deterioration and destruction.

The *puruṣa* that is *kūtastha* is the imperishable aspect of this energy. It is the energy of the spirit that is indestructible. It is the soul that is forever, that which cannot be destroyed.

Kṛṣṇa points out that primal energy manifests in different ways, as perishable and imperishable. Both are aspects of primal energy. One is destroyed and the other lives. One who realizes this difference and understands the true nature of *puruṣa* is liberated.

RamaKṛṣṇa Paramahamsa says:

An arrogant scholar was very proud of his learning. He was a great *advaitic* (subject of non-duality) scholar and did not believe in the various forms of God. God came to him one day.

The mother goddess appeared before him in all Her splendor. She came as the primal energy, *Parāśakti*. The scholar was in a swoon for a long time. When he woke up, he shouted, 'Ka, Ka, Ka.' He could not fully pronounce 'Kālī,' the name of the goddess whom he had seen. Words cannot describe the Divine!

Collective Consciousness

15.17 *Besides these two, there is the supreme* Puruṣa, *the Lord Himself, who pervades and sustains these three worlds.*

15.18 *As I am transcendental, beyond both the perishable and the imperishable, and the best, I am declared both in the world and in the* Vedas *as that supreme person,* Puruṣottama.

15.19 *Whoever knows Me as the Supreme, without a doubt, is to be understood as the knower of everything, and he worships Me with all his being, O son of Bhārata.*

15.20 *This is the most profound teaching taught by Me, O Sinless One, and whoever knows this will become wise and his actions will bear fruit.*

Kṛṣṇa says that beyond these two aspects of *puruṣa,* the perishable body-mind energy and the imperishable spirit energy, there lies another level of energy that is the supreme *puruṣa.* He goes on to say that He is that supreme *puruṣa, Puruṣottama.*

Puruṣa is the energy that pervades us. *Puruṣottama* is the energy that pervades the entire universe. *Puruṣottama* in that sense is no different from *Parāśakti,* the cosmic energy. It is only a play of words to separate *Puruṣa* as male and *Śakti* as female, while describing the ultimate cosmic consciousness.

The energy behind life

Buddha says, 'The universe creates itself. There was never a time that the universe was not there. There never will be a time when the universe will not be there.'

The universe is imperishable. The energy behind the universe is imperishable. Kṛṣṇa says that He is that energy, the *Puruṣottama* that drives the universe eternally.

A beautiful verse from the *Upaniṣads* used as the invocation verse in many rituals:

Om pūrṇamadaḥ pūrṇamidaṁ pūrṇāt pūrṇamudacyate |
pūrṇasya pūrṇamādāya pūrṇameva avaśiṣyate ||

'All is Fullness. From fullness, fullness results. When fullness is removed from fullness, what remains is still fullness.'

It refers to this aspect of what Kṛṣṇa is saying. From the Infinite sprang this universe and many other universes.

No proof exists as to how the universe was created. The biblical story of creation or the story of Brahma and *pralaya,* the great deluge, are metaphorical stories that essentially point towards a supreme energy responsible for the universe. However, the universe was always there.

The Big Bang theory does not explain how big bangs still continue if that was what caused the universe. For every big bang that creates new stars and galaxies in some part of the universe, there is a black hole somewhere else resulting in disappearance of stars and galaxies. For every birth, there is a death. Yet, how did the original birth happen? It never did. It was always there.

Kṛṣṇa says, 'Beyond the perishable and imperishable am I, *Puruṣottama.*' He is not talking about the Yādava king Kṛṣṇa, Vāsudeva Kṛṣṇa, son of Vāsudeva and Devaki. He is talking about *Parabrahma* Kṛṣṇa, the *Īśvara.* He is *Saguṇa,* the universal form and *nirguṇa,* the formless energy. He is that *Brahman* into whom the soul, the individual imperishable Self and the perishable body-mind, merge.

He is the *Brahman* into whom the six-billion humans and countless billion living beings on planet earth as well as countless trillion upon trillion entities in all the universes merge. He is *Puruṣa,* the energy, and *Prakṛti,* the matter. Without Him, nothing moves.

We see *Puruṣottama* in different ways, depending upon our upbringing and capabilities. We see Him as the six-headed, twelve-handed Kartikeya or Muruga, or the four-handed Bālāji or the two-handed, peacock-feather-adorned, flute-playing Kṛṣṇa. We see Him in a way that is comfortable for us to see Him, so that we can reach Him.

> A great scholar and devotee prayed for years to Śiva to receive His *darśan,* His divine appearance. Nothing happened. One day, fearing that he may not live much longer, the devotee decided that he would no longer worship Śiva, but turn to Viṣṇu, whom he heard was kinder.
>
> He placed Śiva's statue to one side of his altar and replaced Śiva with a beautiful Viṣṇu statue. He did not have the heart to throw the Śiva statue away, because in his heart of hearts, he still was a devotee of Śiva. He lit incense in front of the Viṣṇu statue as he started his worship.
>
> He became annoyed when the incense smoke began drifting towards the Śiva statue instead of Viṣṇu. He stood up and covered the nose of Śiva saying, 'This is not for you. I don't pray to you anymore.'
>
> The moment he did this, he felt Śiva's presence and had His *darśan*! He broke down and cried, 'Oh Lord! For years I worshipped you according to the rules. You never appeared. Now, I cast you away. Worse yet, I insulted you by covering your nose. Still, you appeared. Why?'
>
> Śiva said, 'Only now you have felt Me as reality. You felt Me so strongly that you covered My nose. Till now, I was only a concept to you.'

To most of us, God is a mere concept, a theory. He is a convenient theory to hide behind, to cover our fears and anxieties and to show off our knowledge by expounding upon complex concepts and philosophies.

What difference does it make whether we call Kṛṣṇa '*Brahman, Puruṣottama, Parabrahma, Prakṛti,*' or any other name? By whatever name He is called, He is the supreme energy who causes us to move.

It is the unbounded authority of Kṛṣṇa, with which He declares Himself to be *Puruṣottama* that makes Gītā a scriptural authority. It is not the wisdom contained in it, nor the eternal truths, but the courage of that one person, who declared Himself to be the Transcendental Being that defines this work as an eternal scriptural truth. May that *Puruṣottama*, that *Parabrahma* Kṛṣṇa, bless us all!

Now, Kṛṣṇa presents the great truths about His true representation as the collective consciousness.

This may surprise you or it may be something you already know. Irrespective of whether this concept is new or old, analyze this truth, internalize as much as you can, question it until your logic fails.

The first truth: All our minds are not individually separated pieces of the universe. They are all one and the same.

All our minds are interlinked. Not only interlinked, they directly affect each other. They straightaway affect each other. This is what I call collective consciousness. Our thoughts are as infectious as our colds. People may escape from someone else's cold. A cold may not be so infectious; however, our thoughts are more infectious than a cold!

If we catch someone's cold, we may suffer physically for a few days and then get over it. When we catch thoughts from people, not only do we suffer mentally, the suffering is long-term as well. Anything we think affects people around us. Not only are those near us touched by our thoughts, so is everyone living on planet earth.

Understand, our intellect will definitely resist this now; we will analyze this later. How can this be true? We shall analyze during the question and answer sessions, one by one, inch by inch.

I have declared the first truth: All of us are not different beings, different minds. We are all totally interlinked, closely networked. Any of my thoughts can transform you; any of your thoughts can touch me. We are not separated individuals.

Please be very clear, we are not individual islands, separated from each other and uninfluenced by each other. Only one truth called collective consciousness links all of us.

The next truth: Not only at the mental level, even at the deeper level of consciousness, the deeper we go, the deeper we are connected.

Understand that as long as we hold onto the concept of individual consciousness, we will be continuously suffering, physically or mentally or on the being level. Why do we continuously resist Nature? Whatever Nature offers, we resist.

You are a part of the Whole

Yes! We are a part of the Whole. If we fall in tune with the Whole, the Whole behaves as a friend. The moment we think, discriminate or behave with the Whole in the opposite way, it acts like an enemy. Be very clear, the Whole is not here to kill or destroy us.

The Whole, the universe, is a hologram of which we are a part. Just as in a hologram, every part of the hologram, even if it splits off, reflects the totality of that hologram, we reflect the totality of the Whole that is the universe.

Another example is what happens when a person dies of drowning. The dead body floats. The dead body is heavier than water. Yet, it floats. On the other hand, a living body that is lighter than water does not float. It drowns. Why is this so? As long as we are living, we are unable to relate with water. Our ego prevents that. Our mind prevents that. In the dead body, there is no mind and no ego. It is the mind and ego that causes our heaviness.

I recently read an interesting interview with a man who survived jumping into the Niagara Falls. Imagine someone surviving a jump into the Niagara Falls! If you have been to the Niagara Falls, you know the magnitude of the Falls. All kinds of journalists questioned him about this unusual and daring feat. This man said beautifully, 'When I jumped I became a part of the Niagara Falls. I felt I was a part of it. I never felt different from the Falls.'

When we are in tune with the collective consciousness, when we become a part of the collective consciousness, Nature is with us, Nature is our friend and Nature protects us. Nature will not harm us. When we think that we are different from Nature, as long as we think that we are an individual consciousness, Nature protests against us. As long as we are in tune with the collective consciousness, Nature protects us.

Whenever we want to achieve social or economic success, we achieve our goal only when we feel in tune with the whole group. We must fall in tune with the collective consciousness. We will be resisted and we will resist as long as we feel individual, as long as we have an idea that we are somebody, an identity. Whether it is home or office or workplace or industry, this will happen.

If we disappear into the collective consciousness, we are protected and taken care of. We attain complete success, not only socially and economically, but we experience it as well. It will be a feeling of fulfillment. The feeling will be inexplicable. The moment we resist, we make a hellish experience out of it.

A small story:

Once there were two ants sitting on the rim of a cup that contained *amṛta,* the nectar of immortality. As they were talking, one of the ants lost his balance and was about to fall into the cup. He somehow balanced himself and managed to get back on the rim. The other ant asked him, 'Why don't you want to fall into the cup? Even if you drown, you will only become immortal.'

The first ant replied, 'But I *don't want* to drown!'

We don't realize that merging with the collective consciousness will liberate us in totality. We resist and hold on to ourselves. As long as we do not disappear into the collective consciousness, we continuously create hell for ourselves and for others.

This same teaching is contained in Taoism, the ancient Chinese philosophy. Tao is about flowing with Nature. Water is the greatest illustration of natural flow. It flows with the landline. It flows around obstacles, smoothly, energetically. Tao talks about reeds in water that bend with the flow and straighten up once the flow is less. This happens when we do not imagine ourselves to be different from our environment.

The third truth: At the ultimate level, at the spiritual level, the moment we understand that we are deeply connected, totally connected, intensely connected to the whole group, to the whole universe, not only do we experience bliss, but we really live, opening many dimensions of our being.

Right now we are stressed out and disturbed continuously and we need to think too much. With our separate body-mind, we need to think too much, we need to try too hard to enjoy life.

If we disappear into collective consciousness, we open many dimensions, many possibilities. See, now with only this one body that we have, it is a feeling of joy and we can enjoy so much. Imagine what we can do if we have two bodies? Imagine what we can do when we have many bodies!

If the multitudes of bodies increase, so does the joy, the bliss. This is our experience when we realize we are a part of the collective consciousness.

We are not an individual consciousness as we think. Layer by layer, when we go deeper and deeper, we realize that we are one with everything. So, automatically, diseases disappear. We feel well being in our mental layer, pranic layer, *etheric* layer, physical layer and all other layers.

When we experience that we are boundary-less consciousness, it is an unbelievable experience. It is difficult to imagine. I have seen people at the end of the program in such ecstasy that they forget their name, identity, social status, education, qualifications, wealth, religion, everything that they are and they have. They respect the other person; they respect everyone. They prostrate at each other's feet.

I have seen the father-in-law prostrating before his daughter-in-law! In India this never happens. This has happened at the end of the program because he sees the divinity in her. The mother-in-law sees the divinity in her son-in-law and touches his feet. Grandparents touch the feet of their granddaughter. The bosses or owners touch the feet of their staff or people working under them.

Experience and realize

When we experience the feeling of oneness or collective consciousness, when we experience the bliss or experience of collective consciousness, we forget differences of name, wealth, social status and prestige; whatever we think of as ourselves disappears. The truth of who we are is revealed.

I have seen that by touching the feet of their worst enemies, or people much younger or at a much lower economic level, people forget their identity. They are elevated spiritually. They experience a deep level of consciousness, such intense bliss, that their ego disappears. They see God in everyone and they are in bliss, in ecstasy, in collective consciousness.

They are not visualizing. When the experience happens, the whole group realizes that they are all One and the same. They understand that they are not different entities. Only when we experience collective consciousness can we say, can we realize, and can we experience the meaning of the word bliss, eternal bliss, *nityānanda*.

Kṛṣṇa says, 'I am seated in the hearts of all.' He is in the hearts of all of us, all of you, every single person in this universe. The difference between the self and the Self, the difference between the imperishable and the perishable, are for the 'deluded' and 'confused' as Kṛṣṇa says. Once one has the awareness of collective consciousness, there is no difference. Everyone merges into the collective consciousness.

The wave thinks that it is separate from the ocean. It does not realize that it comes from the ocean and goes back to the ocean, that it is the ocean. Just as the wave is part of the ocean, we are part of Existence. How can we attain or reach *Puruṣottama*, when we are already a part of Him? We can only gain awareness that we are a part of Him.

This is the profound teaching of Kṛṣṇa. In this chapter, Kṛṣṇa becomes the ultimate master. Arjuna is completely in silence, the best way to imbibe the master.

The master removes the ultimate cancerous tumor that happens to our being, which we call ego.

A master does surgery on that tumor. He never allows us to be stuck or comfortable with anything less than the enlightened state. Even when we progress spiritually, we get stuck in some layer. We don't know we are stuck and not progressing. In these situations, the master pushes us again and again to move forward. He transforms our whole life.

When we see the surgeon's knife, we think he will hurt us, but the knife of a surgeon is not for killing; it is for healing. In India, gods have swords and other weapons. These are symbolic representations of them as the surgeons who remove our ego. Goddess Kālī has a big knife in one hand and a severed head in the other hand. The severed head represents the ego and the sword represents knowledge or wisdom that has destroyed the ego.

The master makes sure that we are not stuck anywhere and that we reach the ultimate. That's why in the East so much importance is given to the master. The West only knows teachers. In the West, the idea of a spiritual master doesn't exist. In the East, in *gurukuls*, traditional schools that impart spiritual education, even the regular, non-spiritual education was given by spiritual masters, not teachers.

What is the difference between a master and a teacher? A teacher knows intellectually; a master knows experientially. A master has experienced what he is speaking, the truth. If Indian kings wanted to learn archery, they went to a master. You may wonder what enlightened persons know about agriculture, archery or business. Every art and science has a technique. In the *gurukul*, at the age of seven, all children were initiated into meditation, which they practiced until the age of fourteen. If they had their first spiritual experience by then, they studied Brahma Sūtra, which imparted advanced spiritual truths, and took up a renunciate life, *sanyās*. Otherwise they studied the intricacies of life through the Kāmasūtra and entered into married life.

Everyone was happy because they were properly guided by enlightened masters to live the life best suited to them. A teacher teaches through verbal language; a master teaches through his body language. It is known now that ninety percent of our communication is through nonverbal communication, through the body language. The direct touch and presence of a master transforms and awakens a person by creating such a space.

Once we see the master, he says we are not what we imagine ourselves to be. He tells us that we are not human beings seeking a spiritual experience; we are spiritual beings having a human experience. Not only are we not ready to believe this; we are also acutely uncomfortable with it. We feel he is preaching his ideas, trying to convert us. We become frightened and want to run away.

We want to be happy with our sheep life and be stuck with our regular things like wife, children, work and pleasure. After some time, when the master continues to give us the same idea, we stop resisting, but we are not yet convinced. After some more time, the energy of the master attracts us and we start remembering him. He becomes a part of our being. Still, we are not ready to accept what he says. We play a game of hide and seek.

At some point, when we trust him, he shows us that we are the same as him. He shows us that we can realize the truth and eventually be like him. Again we get frightened and act like a sheep. Then the master also acts like a sheep to make us comfortable, and make us feel that he is one among us. Once we relate to him and trust him, he forces us to experience that we are lions. This is what I call initiation, or the first experience. He forces us to experience that we are lions, but even after that experience, we again deny it.

After a long time, the master makes us experience our true nature and gives us the ultimate freedom. Then, only then, do we realize that we were always lions.

We don't have to become something new; we need to wake up and realize what we already are. The master never allows us to stop at any step before the full flowering. Again and again, he inspires and takes us to higher levels of conscious experience, until we realize we are that eternal consciousness, until we realize our true potentiality, the ultimate Truth.

The more we allow his surgery, the more we realize the truth. A few people run away from the operating table during surgery; that's dangerous. Before surrendering, do all the checking, verifying, window-shopping. But once you surrender, allow him to work on you.

Let us pray to Kṛṣṇa, the ultimate energy, the universal consciousness, the cosmic intelligence, to give us the experience of eternal consciousness; to make us beings with *jñāna cakṣu,* eyes of knowledge, and establish us in *nitya ānanda,* eternal bliss. Thank you!

Thus ends the fifteenth chapter named **Puruṣottama Yogaḥ** *of the* **Upaniṣad** *of* ***Bhagavad Gītā,*** *the scripture of yoga dealing with the science of the Absolute in the form of the dialogue between* ***Śrī Kṛṣṇa*** *and Arjuna*

BhagavadGītā

You And Me

Daivāsura Saṁpad Vibhāga Yogaḥ

Chapter 16

Human beings are born
with innate divine nature;
they are not sinners!
Yet, worldly conditioning turns them demonic.
How do we become divine again?
Krishna explains!

You And Me

This chapter is traditionally called *Daivāsura Sampad Vibhāga Yoga*, or the yoga of divine and demonic nature. Here Krṣṇa explains the concept of *saṁskāras* (engraved memories) from an even deeper level. He moves into the deeper energy layers of the body-mind system and takes us to the cosmic layer. The energy that pervades this space, this universe, this cosmos, is the energy of *ākāśa* - ether.

Divine or demon?

Krṣṇa speaks about the qualities of the divine and the demonic. The beauty is that both these words have the same root. Of course, it is not accidental; both qualities are rooted in the same energy. It is just a simple decision. When you choose the word 'you', you become divine, and when you choose the word 'me', you become a demon. That's all.

Śrī Rāmakṛṣṇa Paramahamsa, enlightened master of ancient India, speaks beautifully of the same energy. No energy can be destroyed; your love can never be destroyed. It can only be converted. He says that as long as the calf says, *'ahaṁ, ahaṁ'* ('me, me'), it must work, suffer, get beaten and tortured. Once it is killed, musical instruments are made out of its skin; then when we beat the instrument, it says, *'tumi, 'Tumi'* or *'tum'* ('you, you'). As long as it says, *'ahaṁ, ahaṁ'* it suffers; when it says, *'tuṁ, tuṁ,'* it starts being used for wonderful purposes like singing the glory of the Divine!

This is a beautiful metaphor from colloquial Bengali (the language of West Bengal). Rāmakṛṣṇa explains that as long as we have the idea '*ahaṁ, ahaṁ*' or '*ami, ami,*' (me, me), we will continuously be a demon to ourselves and to others. The moment the cognitive shift happens in us, that is, when the '*tumi, tumi*' ('you, you') occurs. We will be a blessing for ourselves and for others.

All the engraved memories, the *saṁskāras,* are stored in the causal layer. They operate without our control. Decisions are made without our knowledge. However, at the deeper level, in the cosmic layer, we decide consciously: you or me, divine or demon.

When we make the decision of 'You,' we radiate divine qualities. When we make the decision of 'me,' we radiate demonic qualities. Actually, most people sit here because it strengthens their egos. At the end of this discourse, they know much more than others! They can tell others what they know. Many times, we sit and listen for the ego's satisfaction. So if we sit and listen for this purpose, even if we listen to Gītā, be very clear, it will just create trouble for our being. We will not be helped in any way.

The decision about 'You' or 'me' is made in the cosmic layer. If we decide with the attitude of 'you,' the whole thing becomes divine; if we decide with the attitude of 'me,' the whole thing becomes demonic. The mind is neither negative nor positive; *citta* is neither negative nor positive. None of these, including the *guṇa* (attributes), are negative or positive. Even tamasic qualities, such as laziness, are neither negative nor positive. Many enlightened masters seem passive, not doing anything at all. We cannot differentiate between their attitude and laziness. For instance, Bhagavān Ramana Maharishi sat throughout his life in one little town, Tiruvannamalai. He never moved out of there. He was mostly in silence. Yet we cannot say he was in *tamas,* since he never made any decision out of 'me.' The whole process was happening with 'you' as a center, not 'me.'

We cannot call the *citta,* the mind, or *samskāra* good or bad. In the superficial layers, they are neither. However, the decisions we make in the cosmic layer, in the deeper layer, determine whether they are good or bad. The energy behind passion and compassion is really one and the same. When we decide based on 'me', it is passion; when we decide based on 'You', it is compassion.

We need to understand one important thing. If we feel passion strongly in our being, but our compassion has only a little intensity, then our compassion is just a pseudo-expression, perhaps for the sake of name and fame, not for anything else. If we don't have compassion as intensely as our passion, all our activities are based on ego. Even this Gītā discourse can become food for the ego, if the decision is taken out of 'I' and 'me'. When the decision happens out of 'You,' even ordinary daily activities can become divine, not just Gītā discourses.

We need not work on the 'doing'; we need to work on the 'being.' Doing can never lead us to anything. As long as we believe that *doing* can lead us to the Ultimate, we have *karma*. This is called *pūrva mimāṁsi* (those who interpret the *vedic* rituals literally). Only when we understand that only *being* can lead us to the Ultimate, we are called *uttara mimāṁsi* (those who interpret the *vedic* scriptures according to *vedānta*-based non-duality).

According to the *Vedas*, there are two major types of people: People who believe in doing and people who believe in being. People who believe in transforming the 'Being' are *vedantins*; people who believe that the transformation to the Ultimate can be achieved by 'doing' are *karmakandis.* Of course, the Ultimate can be achieved only by working on the being, not by working on the doing. If we work on the doing, we either suppress or express. We continuously fight with ourselves; nothing else is achieved. Only a man who transforms his being can achieve the Ultimate.

Whether to be a demonic or divine, we decide at that one point. When we receive the data, process it and deliver the result or command, how is the command delivered? What is the center from which the command emerges? If the command comes out with the thinking, 'What is there for me, what is there for me?' then whatever we do, including meditation, will be only ego-satisfying.

Many people ask, '*Swamiji*, at some point, I felt such deep ecstasy in meditation, such beautiful bliss. But suddenly, within two hours it disappeared, it never came back! Why is this so? How can we get it back?'

Please understand that bliss is choicelessness. When we are absent, when our identity disappears, we experience bliss. The moment we want the bliss back, the moment we covet bliss, we have already chosen. The moment we choose, we will always choose suffering. *All choices are suffering, because choice is based on the mind.* It is based on duality. Bliss is choicelessness. It is beyond duality; therefore, there is nothing to choose 'between'. Bliss occurs beyond the level of mind and choice. But the moment we want to grab or have bliss, we suffer because we have dropped to the level of the mind, comparison and duality. Bliss can never be experienced this way.

When we are blissful, we allow bliss to possess us. The moment we want to possess bliss, we turn it into suffering. When we want to possess in order to strengthen our ego, the decision is from the attitude of 'me'. The moment the attitude of 'me' or 'mine' appears and decides, it destroys the bliss. We can no longer be divine. When we are blissful, we have said, 'No' to 'me'; we are relaxed in the 'You' idea. The moment we want to possess bliss, we have said, 'Yes' to 'me'.

'You' and 'Me'

We need to understand 'You' and 'me' properly. The word 'me' means ego; the word 'You' means the whole of Existence. When our identity evaporates, when our ego dissolves, whatever is left is Existence; it is the Divine. We create the demon by bringing in the idea of 'me'. With the 'me' idea, whatever we do, be it meditation, rituals, learning, or knowledge, it will only strengthen the ego. naturally leads to more ignorance and suffering. Anything done with the attitude of 'You,' whatever it is, naturally becomes divine and leads to bliss.

In Sanskrit, we have two words: *nivritti* and *pravritti*. *Nivritti* - looking inwards, or liberation - is centered on the idea of 'You'. *Pravritti* -

looking outwards, or bondage - is centered on the idea of 'me'. Whatever is done out of 'You,' leads to liberation; whatever we do out of the idea of 'Me,' leads to bondage.

As long as we are centered in ourselves, we are in the bondage of attraction and aversion, greed and fear. Both these bind us, block us, and keep us firmly locked in the material world. These are creations of our ego or identity.

When we shed our ego, we become boundary-less. We are no longer limited by selfish thoughts about 'me' and 'mine', our kith and kin. The whole world is ours to care for. Kṛṣṇa refers to this as *vasudaiva kuṭuṁbakaṁ*, 'the whole world is one family'. As long as we feel that our body-mind is our boundary, that we are separate from the rest of the universe, we will continuously fight with Existence, we will continuously fight with nature, and we will continuously fight with the Whole. Please understand that the 'part' can never succeed when it fights with the 'Whole'.

Whatever we think, speak or do based upon the idea 'me' leads to more and more complications, more and more suffering.

Here, Kṛṣṇa beautifully explains the demonic and divine natures.

In earlier chapters, Arjuna spoke. Arjuna was expressing his ego, and a catharsis was happening. Slowly he came to the next level, allowing Kṛṣṇa to speak, and the conversation began to happen. Now in the 15th and 16th chapters, Arjuna is practically silent; he is listening. No questions, only doubts. He is asking for clarifications and more understanding from his master.

Qualifications Of Divinity

16.1,2,3 Bhagavān *Kṛṣṇa says, 'Fearlessness, purification of the being, cultivation of spiritual knowledge, charity, and being centered on the being, performance of sacrifices, and accumulation of knowledge, austerity, simplicity, non-violence, truthfulness, freedom from anger, renunciation, tranquility, aversion to fault-finding, compassion for all living entities, freedom from covetousness, gentleness, modesty, studied determination, vigor, more forgiveness, fortitude, cleanliness, freedom from envy, and from the passion for honor - these transcendental qualities, O Son of Bhārata (Arjuna), belong to divine men, endowed with divine nature.'*

Kṛṣṇa lists a number of qualities that take us to a higher plane of consciousness, qualities that make us divine.

Attitude matters

Now when we listen to this list of qualities with the attitude of 'me', what do we usually do? We start practicing all these virtues. Be clear that if we try to practice all of these qualities, one thing is sure: we will become mad. We will not be able to do anything because we will be fighting with ourselves. We will be controlling our senses to strengthen our ego. When we try to understand these ideas with our ego, with the attitude of 'me,' we practice them to strengthen the idea of 'me,' to improve ourselves and become better beings. Again and again, masters prove that they are not better beings; they are totally transformed beings. There is a difference between better beings and transformed beings.

The other day I shared the story of the lion and the sheep-lion told by Swami Vivekānanda. It is a beautiful story. The sheep-lion does not want to realize that he is a lion. He wants to be a good, strong sheep. He asks the lion to give him a technique for becoming a strong sheep.

Similarly, if we start practicing these qualities listed by Kṛṣṇa, we may have a stronger ego. That is why so-called *tapasvi* (ascetics, people performing penances), people who repress themselves, have a strong ego. People who perform penances or repress desires, radiate ego. We clearly see that they do these things to strengthen their ego.

When we are completely blissful and relaxed, austerity happens. I have seen many *sanyāsīs* (ascetics), especially in India, who blame householders for not being pure, for being sinners. When we force ourselves to do penance, we continuously burn inside; as a side effect we often have doubts about our path and ourselves. This doubt causes us to continuously do something; we then make others guilty about the path that they are following.

We make others feel guilty that they are doing the wrong thing, when we feel what we are doing is right. This happens particularly when people come to us and admit their wrongdoings.

Listening to confessions makes a person's ego strong. The listener feels strong. He feels that the people confessing are doing wrong, whereas he is pure. When we do penance out of ego, we want others to feel guilty and we want others to confess to us. We feel strengthened listening to others' mistakes. We feel strong when we address others as sinners.

Swami Vivekānanda says that calling man a sinner is the only sin. Penance is supposed to happen naturally out of joy and bliss, just as a natural thing. Anything done by force is not going to help us or society.

Society teaches us that we are sinners. First of all, this is not true. No enlightened master who has realized the divinity within is capable of saying this. Secondly, who gains anything at all by calling everyone a sinner?

If a religious organization convinces people that they are sinners, that organization can control people. Unless an organization controls people, it cannot survive. There are only two methods that an organization can use to survive and grow: greed and fear. Either it attracts people by instilling greed in them, or makes them afraid by instilling fear.

Kṛṣṇa tells us to be without fear and greed. He also says to be without anger. He tells to be truthful, simple, meek, gentle, non-violent, and to be without expectations, and to renounce. These are qualities of the Divine; these are qualities that you express when you are focused not on your own self but on others. These are qualities that arise from the heart and not from the mind. These are qualities that arise from love and not from desire.

God, the very idea of God, should evoke love, not fear. God in any religion should be portrayed as compassionate. No enlightened master has experienced otherwise or expressed otherwise. The concept of a fearsome God with vengeance is a man made myth. It is created by man, to set one man against another, to divide, control, and conquer.

God resides in you and me. We know everything that we do. When we do wrong, we know. No one has to tell us. That becomes our sin. The guilt makes our life hell, nothing else.

God is merely that energy of inner, higher intelligence. That same intelligent energy that is within us also drives the entire universe. The energy that powers us is the same energy that powers the sun. There is no difference at all.

As human beings we have the opportunity to expand into this energy, into this higher intelligence. Unfortunately, animals do not have this ability, this consciousness. Humans do. To ignore this gift, this opportunity, this consciousness, is our original sin. The entire meaning of our life is to discover this truth and become divine. That is why, if we die without realizing this truth, we are born again.

We go through this cycle of life and death again and again, because we do not recognize who we are. As Buddha says, that is the cause of our suffering. When we realize our own Self, our true divine potential, we realize the meaning of our life, and there is no need to be born again. We become liberated.

You Are A Demon If...

16.4 Pride, arrogance, conceit, anger, harshness or cruelty, and ignorance - these qualities belong to those born with demonic nature, O Son of Pritā

16.5 The transcendental qualities are conducive to liberation, whereas the demonic qualities make for bondage. Do not worry, Pāṇḍavā, you are born with divine qualities.

16.6 Pārtha, in this world there are two kinds of created beings, one is divine and the other demonic. I have explained at length to you the divine qualities. Now hear about the demonic qualities also, so that you will understand and live your life blissfully and happily.

16.7 Persons with demonic nature do not know what is bondage and what is liberation; nor what is cleanliness; truthful behavior is not in them.

What is demonic nature? Kṛṣṇa says that all actions done out of arrogance, out of pride, out of ego, for name and fame, and for power, are demonic in nature. As in the case of Rāvaṇa, they benefit neither the person himself nor others. Their actions are performed out of ignorance and ultimately lead to their own downfall.

I have seen many people do penance like Rāvaṇa (King of Lanka who abducted Rāma's wife, in the Indian epic, the Rāmāyaṇa). Rāvaṇa did penance; however, his powers neither helped him nor others. He became a demon for others and for himself. He killed others and finally destroyed himself. His penance was done with the attitude of 'me' and 'what is there in it for me?' The whole story happened to strengthen the 'I' and 'mine'. Please understand that whatever we do, whether we study the scriptures, do charity or social service, or perform *pūjā* (prayer), rituals, or meditation, if they are done to strengthen the 'I' and 'mine', they always lead to suffering.

Focusing on the 'I' is instinctive. It is a call for survival. It is a call for our survival based on our conditioning and insecurities. The instinct to survive is what is called 'I', and the instinct to possess is what is referred to as 'mine'. The person who understands that both are illusions is an aware person. Such a person realizes that the instinct to survive does not help, and no matter what one may have, one still cannot survive forever.

The instinct to survive is pure illusion. At the most we can survive perhaps for 70 to 80 years. Sometimes a person lives to be 90 to 100 years with the same identity. Yet the instinct to survive tries to extend itself. It wants to make life eternal. No one wants to die. Naturally we are then walking towards suffering. As long as we carry this instinct to survive, we repeatedly hurt ourselves.

This morning an *ashramite* complained that she is hurt by small and well-meaning criticisms from others. She said she is sensitive. I asked her to stop using that word. I said, 'You are not sensitive. A sensitive person is porous; he allows the words to pass through him. Only arrogant people get hurt. If we are hurt, please understand that we are arrogant. We are impenetrable like stone, which is why words come and hit us. Don't say that you are sensitive.'

A sensitive person lets words pass through him. He never suffers. Suffering is from arrogance, never from sensitivity. A person who is sensitive never suffers. We suffer from words when we stop them, when we resist them, when we make our own meaning out of them. When we do not make meanings out of words, we do not suffer. It is like playing with words. We choose nice words to support our ego. We do not say, 'I am hurt because I am arrogant.' We use polished words such as, 'I am hurt because I am sensitive.'

Please don't cheat yourself with words. Let straight words be used. I hear many polished words around the world. People easily cheat themselves with such words. Don't cheat yourself with polished words. Let things be straight and clear. We can use polished words to cheat others, but please let us not use them to cheat ourselves.

> Let me tell you a small story…
>
> A contractor wanted to donate a sports car to an official.
>
> The official refused, saying, 'I am an honest person and I cannot think of accepting this gift.'
>
> The contractor asked him, 'In that case, how about if I sell this car to you for ten dollars?'
>
> The official replied immediately, 'In that case, I will buy two cars!'
>
> Be clear and do not play with words. Let us not cheat ourselves with words.

Let us be clear about what we mean. Let us use the same honest words to express what we really are and what we really feel. Rāmakṛṣna says, 'Let your words and mind be straightened.' Whatever is, let it be expressed with straight words. At least we will know that we have a problem. When we use colorful, polished words, by and by, we forget we have a problem. When we play with words, we forget that we have a problem. And this is very dangerous.

Understand: when we know that we don't know, at least we know that we don't know. When we don't know that we don't know, then we don't even know that we don't know! We then have a problem. Be very clear. At least let us know that we have a problem.

Let us use straight words. The shortest distance between two points is a straight line. To achieve anything, the shortest way is straightforwardness. Nothing else can work.

Living the Divine

Here Kṛṣṇa gives all the divine qualities, one by one. It is not necessary to explain all the qualities. Let us take a few. Let us take fearlessness, for example.

As long as we carry the instinct to survive, we have fear. Fear can never be taken away from our being, as long as we want to survive. Surrendering to Existence, surrendering to death is the one and only way to achieve fearlessness.

There is a beautiful *Upaniṣad* (part of the Hindu scriptures), the Kaṭhopaniṣad, that you must read. It is from the wonderful system of *vedānta* (essence of the *Vedas* including the *Upaniṣads*), founded by the *vedic ṛṣis* (sages). They have gone deep into the science of death. The West has dedicated its entire energy to understand life, whereas the East has dedicated its energy to understanding death! That is why *ṛṣis* live even after they die. They live after death, too. They exist; they discovered the art of living even after death. People who are caught in the material world, however, die each moment, even as they live. This Kaṭhopaniṣad is the science of death.

There is a beautiful story of a young boy, Naciketa, who goes to the abode of Yama, the Lord of death. Yama was not there when Naciketa went to meet Him; His servants try to receive him, but the boy insists on waiting for Yama. Yama receives him after three days. Yama welcomes him. At this point, we must understand that no one goes to Yama's abode; *He* comes to our abode! Always it is He who comes! When we try to escape from Him, He is death as we know it ordinarily; He will take away our 'I' and 'mine' - all our possessions and relationships; we cannot sign our check or drive our car, once He takes us. We cannot have our relations anymore. Whatever we think is ours will be taken away: wealth, relationships, bank balance - everything. What we think is 'I' - the body, even that will be taken away. When death comes to us, everything is taken away. To the contrary, when *we go to death* like Naciketa did, fearlessly, death welcomes us! Yama becomes our host!

In this story, Yama receives Naciketa with love and care. Immediately, He becomes a loving host. Next, He offers him three boons (wishes). Naciketa first asks for good relationships. He says, 'When I go back to my family, my father should accept me, love me and take me back.' Yama blesses him with good relationships. After that Yama blesses him with wealth, and shows him how to create wealth, pleasure and comforts. Now Yama is behaving like a God. First, He behaved like a loving host, and then He behaves like a God. Ultimately, Yama gives him *ātmajñāna* - knowledge of the Self. Now, He is behaving like an enlightened master himself! The third boon he gives because Naciketa asks Him for the secret of death. Pleased with the boy's sincerity and courage, Yama blesses him with enlightenment itself.

Look at the paradox of life: When we run away from death, Death or Yama chases us, wherever we are. Death takes away all our wealth, our relationships, whatever we think of as 'I' and 'mine'. But here, with Naciketa, the whole situation is just the opposite! When we surrender to Yama, when we go to Him, He is a loving host. He is not something terrible as we imagine Him to be. We always portray Yama as a huge form, black in color, with a big moustache, traveling slowly on a buffalo, with a rope in His hands and a terrible, arrogant and egoistic demeanor!

Here the whole scene is different. He says, 'Welcome! You are the form of *Agni*, fire.' A guest is considered to be the form of fire that we worship.

The vedic culture says, '*Atithi devo bhava*' - the guest is God. In *vedic* culture, the guest or *atithi* is respected as God. *Atithi* means a person who arrives without telling us in which *thiti* (time or date) he will come. Not the person who sends us an email, then a phone call, a fax, and then expects that we pick him up at the airport! Such a person is not an *atithi*. No! He is our relative! We must take care of him. He must be received; it is pure business. But *atithi* is different.

Please understand that all our relationships are more or less business relationships. *Atithi* means a person who comes straightaway into our lives with an openness. The big problem is, today the *atithi* concept is lost. People cannot believe that in Indian villages, the doors of all homes are kept open in the daytime. At least in the village in which I was brought up, all the doors of all the houses were open. I could go to any home on that street and eat. A child can go to any house and eat! The very idea of *atithi,* the unannounced guest, has disappeared in most places. When people call India a poor country, I tell them, 'No. You don't know the value of Indian culture.'

For example, when we travel to a developed country and go to a new city for business purposes, how much can we afford to spend on hotels and lodges? On the contrary, at least in India, if we have one friend, just a phone call is enough, and all arrangements are taken care of! There too, due to the cultural invasion, this hospitality is diminishing. At least in the villages where vedic culture is alive, this *atithi* culture is alive. *Atithi devo bhava* is where we respect any guest as God.

Yama tells Naciketa, 'You are my guest and you have come to my house in the form of '*vaiśvānarāgnī*' (the fire that we worship). The (priest) is considered to be the embodiment of *Agni*, the divine *Agni*. You have come to my house as the embodiment of the Divine. You are here. Let me pay my respects to you. I was not here to receive you when you arrived. Please forgive me for not being here for three days to receive you.'

Usually we postpone *Yama* (death). Usually we try to escape from Him. But when we go in search of Him, He will not be there, as we feared! That is the essence of this whole story.

Usually He chases us. We run away from Him, and He is behind us! But when we turn and go towards Him, we suddenly find that He is not there! For three days, Naciketa could not find Yama. Understand this important point. This story is significant; it has a tremendous truth. When Naciketa went to death, death was not there. This means when we turn towards death, we will not find death as we imagined it to be. Whatever imagination we have about death will not be there when we surrender to death. Now, because of our fear, we try to escape; because we try to escape, He chases us.

It is like a vicious cycle. If we understand that, at the moment we surrender, He will not be there as we imagined Him, as we expected Him to be, we will get tremendous courage. That courage makes us face Him more clearly. When we face Him more clearly, we get more courage. When we follow this circle, it is called a virtuous circle; what we experience presently is the vicious cycle. Let us turn our vicious cycle into a virtuous circle.

If we can understand this Kaṭhopaniṣad story, our whole idea of death will be transformed. First of all, when we seek Him, He is not there. Second, when He appears He is not as we imagined Him to be. Rather than being an arrogant, terrifying form waiting to take our possessions, He is a humble host, welcoming us graciously. He then behaves like a God and blesses us with relationships, wealth and ultimately *ātmajñāna*, knowledge of the Self, enlightenment.

We may ask how to go towards death. For example: 'Should we commit suicide?' Please understand that committing suicide is not facing death. Be very clear that people who commit suicide are not fearless. They are the most cowardly people. They commit suicide because they are unable to live this life. Rather than facing death, they escape from life. Suicide is not facing death, but escaping from life. Escaping from life is one thing; facing death is another. These two are very different from each other.

When fear is created in our system or when fear happens, the only way to face the fear is to just go through it. Don't allow it to frighten you. Some people tell me that they are afraid of their fears. Fear is enough trouble, why be afraid of fear as well? Don't allow the fear to overshadow you. Sit with yourself; be with yourself. Let the fears come up. How long can you postpone your fears? How long can you control your fears? How long can you escape from your fears? Allow them to surface. Your whole being will shake, tears may roll, and you may have a deep depression. Let everything happen. Whether you consciously allow the fear to happen or not, the fearful incidents will happen. So it is better to face it with clarity and courage.

Our fears can be classified into five major categories. The first is the fear of losing wealth and comforts. The second is the fear of losing some part of our body due to an accident or disease. The third is the fear of losing our near and dear ones. The fourth is the fear of losing our mental well-being. The fifth is the fear of the unknown, that is, the fear of death, ghosts, God, hell, heaven, and such things. These are the five major categories of fears we face in life. All our fears can be brought under these five categories.

Allow all of them to surface. Sit with yourself. Let everything come out; let your mind face the fears. Let your mind speak everything; let everything come out. Give it half an hour. Let it happen. You may feel depressed, tears may roll, and your whole body may shake. Let everything come out. What can be done? If you could do anything, you would have done it. Very clearly, your very existence proves that you are not able to do anything. That is why you are just keeping quiet. Allow the fear to happen. Let the fear come into your being.

Let the fear come up to your conscious layer without being suppressed. Accept that there is a possibility for all these fears to come true: your wealth may be stolen, you may have an accident, a near or dear one may die, or you may die. All these possibilities are real. Yes. What can be done? This is life. This is what is called facing reality as it is.

Only small kids need fantasies and imagination to face reality as it is. However, we need to understand the truth as it is. We can't escape from reality; we can't escape from the truth. The more we try to escape, the more it haunts us; the more it chases us. When we allow the fears to come out, suddenly we will see that they leave us, and we become more responsible, more intense.

From ingratitude to gratitude

When there is a possibility that our good health may be taken away from us, we will not take our health for granted; we will start living life intensely. We will not take things for granted when the possibility of life's being taken away from us, when the possibility of death enters our being. We will realize our responsibility and the gift of life that Existence has bestowed upon us.

Let me tell you a small story to show how we take things for granted.

There was a king who felt completely bored after forty-five years of the good life. He had whatever he wanted: wealth, luxuries, and other pleasures. Whatever was there to enjoy, he had it all. There was nothing for him to do. All the excitement was lost; he was bored.

Let me tell you, when you have all material comforts, when you have everything that you want in the material plane, tremendous boredom will happen within you.

If we don't already have everything, we at least have the excitement of something left to achieve; we work for that. There is a need for continuity. There is a need to live. We will have some goal. When we have everything, what should we live for? Nothing! So never imagine that when we have everything, we will be happy.

This king entered hell simply because he had everything. He was totally depressed, bored. He didn't wish to come out of his room; he was lying there the entire day through the year. His ministers tried their best to bring him out, to enliven him, and to give him a little excitement. They brought the best comforts and luxuries from all over the country, all possible pleasures. Nothing worked on the king. He said, 'No, I don't care for anything.'

Finally they decided to do one thing. They said, 'O King, there is an enlightened master in the forest. He may be able to help you. Why don't you meet him? He will bring you out of your depression. Many have been helped by him.'

The king said, 'I am not interested in going anywhere.' The ministers asked him to try just once. He agreed saying, 'You are telling me so much about him, let me give him a try.'

He went to meet the master. The king was full of doubts and questions and unwilling to trust the master. He thought, 'Who knows if he is enlightened or not?' He asked the master straightaway, 'Can you help me come out of my depression?'

That is the way people question when they come just to check a master out. They don't come to learn; they come to verify. Many people ask me, 'Can you show us some path to achieve God?' I tell them, 'I will try; why don't you be seated?' They question me as if they have come to check me out!

Similarly, the king just wanted to check out that enlightened master. He asked straightaway, 'Can you do something to get me out of this depression?'

The master told him that if he could bring all his wealth in one bag, he could teach him.

Immediately the king decided that this master had nothing to do with enlightenment. 'He is a cheat, a bogus fellow; he is asking for my wealth.'

He went away without giving a reply. However, that night he wondered why the master asked for his wealth. 'In spite of my doubt about him, there is some grace, there is something about him working on me,' he thought.

People ask me how to find out if someone is enlightened. We can never find out using the intellect. Always try your best to suspect the person. If he is really enlightened, then his form, his very being, will impress us! We will not be able to forget him. That is the scale to check if a person is enlightened or not. People ask me if they should remember me all the time. I say, 'No. Try your best to forget me, to doubt me. If you have been really touched by me, you will not be able to do so, try as you might!' My presence will work beyond your intellect. If you are going to be helped by me, you will simply fall in tune with me.

Let me state very clearly: You will simply fall in tune! Through intellect we can never analyze or understand. With your intellect, try your best to say 'No.' If you always say 'No,' you will never be cheated, so that is the best thing to do. If the person is enlightened, he will be able to penetrate you beyond your intellect. He will be there in your being. He will be there in your mind in the day and in your dreams in the night. He will be haunting you. You cannot escape from him.

> So this king felt he was being haunted by the master. The king was lying on his bed, rolling from side to side. 'Shall I try? If he takes away my wealth, I can easily catch him. After all, it's my kingdom.' He did all the calculations. 'In any case, I am not happy with this wealth; if he takes it away, what is there to lose? It is not useful to me, so let him have it.'
>
> So the king decided to take the risk. The next day he converted his wealth into diamonds, put them all in one bag, and brought the bag to the master. He stood in front of the master. Without saying a single word, the master suddenly snatched the bag and started running. The king understood that this master really was a cheat. He started chasing the master.

We cannot successfully chase someone who lives in the forest since he knows the secrets of the forest. That is why professional people never catch bandits. Not only in this country, but all over the world, professional police never catch bandits. The bandits know the secrets of the landscape.

> The master ran this way and that, since he knew the forest very well. The king was new to the forest and tried his best to follow. This chase went on and on. The king wondered why he had taken such a risk. He was blaming himself and suffering. 'When I return to the country, I will have nothing. I will be a beggar. I will need to beg in order to eat,' he thought. He visualized scenes of his poverty. He began suffering his poverty. Poverty had already entered his mind. When he was rich, he was suffering; now he was suffering due to poverty. That is the paradox of money: When it is there, it gives suffering; when it not there, again it gives suffering.

When it became evening, the king was about to give up. He thought, 'Now I cannot do anything. This master knows the forest too well.' At this point, the master stopped running. The moment the king saw that the master had stopped, he quickly caught up with him and grabbed the bag.

The master laughed. The king could not understand what was going on. The master said, 'Fool, now take this and enjoy.'

Suddenly, the king felt that he had become rich! Just because he had missed his wealth for one day, he felt he had become rich!

The master said, 'Fool, you were depressed because you took everything for granted. Now the same wealth that you lost for one day, you have back again; go and enjoy it.' The king came out of his depression just by being made to miss his wealth for one day!

In our life, also, we undergo the same thing when we allow the 'consciousness of insecurity' to happen to us. Please understand that I am using the word 'consciousness'. The feeling of insecurity is a consciousness; it is the truth. If we allow this feeling to happen in us we will never take life for granted. We will start enjoying life intensely. If for just one day we intensely miss what we have, we will never take life for granted again.

For example, try to live for even twelve hours without opening your eyes. Keep them closed. You will then never take your eyes for granted! Similarly, we will never take our life for granted if we know it will be taken away from us. We forget that it will be taken away from us one day, that is the problem. We suppress the fear, the insecurity about losing our lives; that is why we never enjoy life, and we take it for granted.

The moment we experience insecurity, when we understand that life might be taken away from us any moment, we start living intensely! If we are depressed or bored, and we lose everything for just twelve hours, we will suddenly understand this truth. We will never again take life for granted.

The king felt bored because he took life for granted. When we face death, when we face insecurity, immediately we understand how we have been taking life for granted, and we start living intensely. That is what this story means.

Yama gave relationships, wealth, and finally enlightenment to Naciketa. When people come out of the darkness or death meditation in the NSP, they tell me that they understand the real meaning of relationships; this means Yama has blessed them! They know the value of their wealth now; it means Yama has blessed them with wealth and now they will start living. They realize that life is the ultimate blessing, and naturally Yama has showered that blessing on them. They understand that the body may die and that there is something beyond the body and mind that exists in them; that is what I call *ātmajñāna* (Self-knowledge).

We have the blessings of relationships, wealth and enlightenment when we face fear and death with clarity. Here, when Kṛṣṇa speaks of fearlessness, He means, 'Face it, face the fear; only then fearlessness can happen.' Only when we face the instinct to survive and the instinct to possess, will we enter the zone of fearlessness.

Until then it can never happen. You can face the instinct for survival or the instinct for possession only by making decisions based on the concept of 'You,' not on the concept of 'me.'

As long as you work, act, speak and think centered on 'me, me, me,' you will be a demon; you will work out of the instinct for survival and the instinct for possession. When you work based on the concept of 'You, you, you,' you will radiate a new energy.

Try this simple experiment: Try living for others' sake for just one week. I am not asking you to give away your property or any such thing.

Usually we think, 'What is there in this for me?' For example, if your wife calls you up to see a movie, you say, 'No, I want to go to the beach.' You always force your preference. Just for one week, in your office, in your house, wherever you go, decide to be with the attitude of 'you' instead of 'me.' Try this with simple, day-to-day life decisions, not things like giving away your property. Immediately the mind thinks, 'If I start thinking based on 'you', people will take me for granted, people may exploit me, people may cheat me.'

Alright, that is fine. Now nobody is cheating you. You are living centered on the idea of 'me'. You are protecting yourself. Are you happy? Come on, be frank, are you happy? Not really! So why not then take a chance to be centered on 'You'? We live all our life with this '*āsuri saṁpat,*' what Kṛṣṇa calls demonic nature, the attitude of 'me, me, me.'

Living beyond 'Me'

Now just for one week, why not try this? These workshops and your time in the ashram is such a great chance to practice this. At present, when you come back into the hall for the next session, what do you do? You grab your seat. You leave your kerchief, also, to block the seat! First, you grab your seat. When *prasād* (blessed food) is given, you grab your plate first . For one week, take your plate after another person receives the food. See that the person next to you is comfortable. When you get up in the morning ask the other person, 'Are you okay? Why don't you use the bathroom first, then I will use it.' We always say, 'Wait, I have to go first. I have some urgent work.' Instead of that attitude, try this experiment of letting others use or talk first with simple, small things. 'Please go ahead and use that. I will use it after you.' Or, 'You have been working continuously; let me help you with this small task.'

For one week, put that 'You' into your being. You will not know from where the bliss suddenly comes! Suddenly you will feel that your whole being is relaxed. When you don't give attention to 'me,' you will never be 'in tension.' As long as you are giving attention to 'me,' you will be continuously in tension.

When you replace 'me' with 'You,' a deep inner healing happens in you.

What I am talking about is not morality. Please don't think I am teaching you how to live happily. There are many who write books like, *How to*

Stop Worrying and Start Living. I am not the person to teach 'how-to stuff.' I am not giving this as morality; I am giving this as a spiritual practice. If you are working towards spiritual growth, if you are a 'professional seeker,' please try this one practice. I use the term 'professional seeker,' because there is always a group of people who are professional seekers. If any *swami* (holy man) comes they attend his programs. Any *swami*, any book, any spiritual event - they will always be present. People come to me and say, '*Swamiji*, for the last thirty years I have been seeking.' Don't feel proud about that.

Don't be proud that you are a professional seeker. Please be clear that if you have pride that you are a professional seeker, or that you know some *swami* or other, or that you have attended some discourse or other, some meditation program or other, you are not on the true spiritual path; you are just window shopping, that's all.

If you are really a seeker, if you think you are seeking spirituality, then do this one spiritual practice. Try this single spiritual practice for seven days. If you think there is any way I can help you, take this single statement and forget about everything else. Work based on this single statement: instead of deciding based on 'me, me, me,' decide based on 'You, you, you.'

I am not asking you to give away or renounce anything; just try this with simple, day-to-day decisions. You will see something happening in your being. The tension, that solid weight in you, will melt, loosen up; you will experience inner healing and a tremendous and cool, blissful breeze will happen in you. Naturally when you get a glimpse of this mood, you automatically start expressing this attitude in day-to-day life, everyday and every moment.

We always choose words and actions based on 'me.' For instance, when we shout at somebody we say, 'I am doing it for his good, for his sake.' When someone is angry, we say, 'See, he is like a demon, he is mad at others, he is shouting.' When someone else is angry we say he is a demon; when we get angry we say it is for that person's good! 'If I don't teach him, who will teach him? I am doing it only for his good.'

Please understand, don't play with words; be straight. Experiment with this for the next week, not longer. After that you can become your old self. You can't become, that is a different issue! Try it on simple things. Instead of deciding based on 'me,' decide based on 'You.' The irritation that you continuously carry will disappear. The instinct to survive, to possess, will disappear. You will become an empty being.

You will become a hollow bamboo. Whenever you become a hollow bamboo, you are a flute in the hands of the Divine. Whatever happens through you will be divine; you will imbibe the divine nature.

Kṛṣṇa further explains step-by-step how to imbibe divine nature: How to cause the cognitive shift at the deep, subtle level.

Please understand that working at the level of *satva* (equanimity), *rajas* (aggression), or *tamas* (slothfulness) is difficult. It is akin to changing all the servants in order to change the master. We will never be able to do that. Just change the master and all the servants will be transformed.

Here, Kṛṣṇa gives the technique to change the master, the ego that makes decisions. He gives the straight technique for the cognitive shift to happen. At present, cognition happens in us keeping the 'I' as the center; He gives a simple technique to replace the 'I' with 'You' so that the cognitive shift happens. This same system will be used for the divine nature.

Rāma and Rāvaṇa in the Hindu epic Rāmāyaṇa are both energetic; both have the *brahmāstra* (high energy weapon). The only difference is that one is centered on 'I,' the other one is centered on 'you.' That is the only thing that makes one person divine and the other demonic. Rāma is divine; Rāvaṇa is demonic.

Kṛṣṇa goes further to give subtle techniques to experience the consciousness of 'You,' the ultimate consciousness, the consciousness of the Whole, the '*daivika saṁpat*' or divine nature of your being, through this cognitive shift.

Step-by-step Kṛṣṇa explains all these great qualities. As I mentioned, please don't try to practice these qualities as a separate effort. The more we try to practice these separately, the more schizophrenic we will become. We will be fighting with ourselves. Do something that will make you express these qualities in life. Automatically you will become blissful, free from anger, and full of *dharmic* (righteous) qualities.

When we do anything including charity by force or social conditioning, merely because we have been told that we will go to heaven, we will have trouble. Never do *dāna* (charity) if you feel something is being taken from you. The word *dāna,* giving or donating, is wrong; *sharing* is the right word. Because we feel we have enough, we share with others. With the word *dāna,* there is ego, the thought, 'I am higher, the giver; you are lower, the receiver.' With sharing the idea of donation does not exist. The thought is, 'We have got it, let us share.'

Sharing is the right attitude. If we do charity with the attitude of 'I,' we will later check whether our name has appeared on the plaque! 'Has my name been spelled correctly? Is it the right size? Is the font larger or smaller than that of someone else's name?' Especially in India, even if a tube light is presented to a temple it will be inscribed with the words 'Rāmanāthan, son of Somanāthan, in the memory of his mother, Saundarya Lakṣmī, who passed away on this date, presented this to this temple on this day.' It will be painted with black paint. When we switch on the tube light we will just see a black line on the wall – no light!

Ramana Maharshi says beautifully, 'When you don't ask, you will be given.' I tell people, 'When *you* don't tell what good things you do, *I* will tell.' When people do things for the ashram, but do not tell anyone about them, *I* tell the whole world about them. However, when they tell, I keep quiet. When you don't do from the attitude of 'I,' you won't feel like something is being taken away from you. Above all, you will feel tremendous fulfillment. Anything you do with the attitude of 'you' will make you radiate these beautiful, divine qualities

Service is not always devotion

Even Yaśodā (the foster mother of Kṛṣṇa) had the idea of 'I.'

Let me tell you a lovely story. It is about a great devotee named Taraṅgiṇi. It is a wonderful expression of love; the 'I' and 'you' are expressed truly here.

The story goes that within twelve hours of Kṛṣṇa's birth He was handed over to Yaśodā. He took birth at midnight, and before sunrise He was brought to Yaśodā. This was because of a prophecy that Kamsa, His uncle, would come to kill Him at sunrise. Yaśodā brought Him up until He left his home, Vṛdāvan. Despite her bringing Him up, when Yaśodā asked Him to sing or play the flute, He would not play.

However, when Taraṅgiṇi, a devotee of Kṛṣṇa from a lower caste asked Kṛṣṇa to play, He would play for her. She would stand in a corner and would not come in front of Him. She would quietly enjoy His presence and music from a distance. Once Kṛṣṇa had gone, Taraṅgiṇi would touch the dust in the place where He had stood and played.

One day Kṛṣṇa forgot the flute and went away. Of course, He did not forget, He must have pretended to have forgotten it. Would Kṛṣṇa forget? He would make others forget, but He would never forget anything! He pretended to have forgotten the flute. Taraṅgiṇi noticed the flute and with love and care, kept it in her home to hand over to Kṛṣṇa.

The next day Kṛṣṇa said, 'Someone has taken My flute.' He pretended to search for it. He learned that Taraṅgiṇi had the flute and went to her house. Since He was from a higher caste, He needed a reason to go to the area of the lower community people. Yaśodā would ask Him why he had gone there. She would punish Him, since higher caste people did not go to that area. Kṛṣṇa went to the area. It was full of mud, dirty roads, and a hut in which a thousand suns were shining, meaning that there were a thousand holes in the hut! Kṛṣṇa entered the house and asked for His flute.

Taraṅgiṇi was totally shaken to see Kṛṣṇa in her house. She was overwhelmed; she was unable to speak. She ran and brought the flute to Him. Kṛṣṇa continued His act, asking if He should play the flute. And who can refuse when Kṛṣṇa asks?

She replied, 'My Lord, even Gods and *ṛṣis* come down to listen to Your music, how can I say no?'

He sat on the steps, and started playing; she sat in a corner filled with ecstasy. Yaśodā arrived at that moment. She felt terribly upset because He had never played the flute for her.

She said, 'I take care of you; I give you food and look after you completely. You never play for me. Yet you come and play here for this urchin girl!'

Please understand that the attitude of Taraṅgiṇi is 'you,' and the attitude of Yaśodā is 'me.' Due to this, all Yaśodā's service had no positive result for her. Since Yaśodā disturbed him, Kṛṣṇa stopped playing. The tune that Kṛṣṇa played to Taraṅgiṇi is known as *punnagavarali*, 'the broken tune'.

Kṛṣṇa told Yaśodā, 'You served Me, no doubt, but with the attitude of 'I'. Taraṅgiṇi is devoted to Me; you are devoted to yourself. As long as I am your Kṛṣṇa you take care of Me; that means you are devoted to yourself, you are centered on yourself and not on Me. That is why you are unable to digest five minutes of separation.'

This is the instinct to possess. Kṛṣṇa continued, 'You have come all the way here; you are not even giving five minutes of My space to her. Taraṅgiṇi never asked Me to come to her house. She never expected that I would play for her. She is totally dedicated with only the attitude of 'you.'

Then Kṛṣṇa blessed Taraṅgiṇi saying, 'You will have *sāmīpya mukti;* you will become a *shanbaga* flower and reside in My garland. You will stay with Me forever.'

There are four *muktis* or levels of liberation: *sālokya mukti, sārūpya mukti, sāmīpya mukti* and *sāyujya mukti. Sālokya* means 'same place'; it means we will be allowed to stay in *Vaikunṭa*, Viṣṇu's abode. We will have a residence in heaven. *Sārūpya* means we will have the same form as the Lord. For example, we can see *Jaya-Vijaya*, the gatekeepers of heaven; they have the same *śankh* (conch), *cakra* (discus), *gada* (mace), *padma* (lotus) - all the accessories of Viṣṇu in the same *svarūpa* (form).

Sāmīpya (being near) is being in the inner circle; the *cakra* that Viṣṇu is carrying has achieved *sāmīpya mukti!* Becoming enlightened oneself is *sāyujya mukti. Sāmīpya mukti* is the best enlightenment, because we can enjoy Him forever! It is like an ant forever enjoying the sugar candy.

Sāyujya mukti is like *becoming* the sugar candy. This is for all the *ṛṣis.* For devotees, the ultimate state is *sāmīpya mukti.* So Kṛṣṇa blessed Taraṅgiṇi with *sāmīpya mukti.*

He said, 'May you become a flower in My garland and be on My body. May you be on Me.' He then turned to Yaśodā and said, 'Because you served with the attitude of 'me, me, me,' may you not have any temple on planet earth.'

Yaśodā served Kṛṣṇa so much, but have you seen a single Yaśodā temple? No! Everywhere you see Radha temples. If you go to Vṛdāvan, Radha is worshipped more than Kṛṣṇa. Even a milkman when selling milk will call out, 'Rādhe, Rādhe,' not 'Kṛṣṇa, Kṛṣṇa.' Despite all her service, since it was centered on 'me', Yaśodā was unable to achieve enlightenment.

On the other hand, Taraṅgiṇi, being born of a lower community was never even close to Kṛṣṇa. She was not allowed to serve Him; however, because she lived with the attitude of 'you, you, you', Kṛṣṇa went to her home, blessed her with eternal closeness to Him, and gave her liberation.

Even if they run after the Divine, people with the attitude of 'I' can never reach the Divine, because the Divine runs away from them. If we live with the attitude of 'you', even if we live in a hut with a thousand holes, Kṛṣṇa waits for us at our doorstep. Many stories illustrate how the

'I' drives the Divine away, and the 'you' attracts the Divine. One small attitude change can take care of the cognitive shift.

Let me tell you one more small story. It is about the fight between the *śankh* (conch), *cakra* (discus) and *pādukā* (sandals) of Viṣṇu.

Viṣṇu has a *śankh*, *cakra*, and *pādukā*. One day He returns home after having gone out. Viṣṇu is blissful energy, and likes to go around and enjoy!

Vaikuṇṭa, Viṣṇu's abode is totally different from Śiva's abode. It is a fun place. Continuously dance goes on and all varieties of food are served!

Anyhow, Viṣṇu returns and leaves his sandals outside His bedroom and goes in to rest on his beautiful serpent bed, *Ādiśeṣa*. The conch and discus look at the sandals and laugh. 'See, you may carry Viṣṇu all day long, but when He comes into the room, you must stay out. Only we can enter with Him. You have not really achieved *sāmīpya mukti* (close to the Lord). We are with him twenty-four hours a day. For the twelve hours of the night you are outside. So you have half *sāmīpya mukti*; we have full *sāmīpya mukti*.â

The sandal replies, 'Alright, what can I do? Whatever Viṣṇu wants, let it be.' The next morning when Viṣṇu comes out, the sandals ask Him, 'Lord, the conch and discus are making fun of me. Is it true that You are unhappy with me? Is it true that I have only fifty percent *sāmīpya mukti*? What mistake have I made?'

Lord Viṣṇu laughs and tells the sandals, 'Attitude and time do not mean that you are unimportant or they are important. Attitude and time do not show favoritism. I have no favoritism; each of you has a different place, work, and thing to do.'

He then adds, 'By worshipping the conch and discus people cannot get liberation. However, by worshipping you they can get liberation! The sandals when worshiped can give enlightenment. The discus kills; the conch declares victory in war. These are their roles;

worshipping them cannot give liberation. Your duties are different. Your place is different. Only by holding you people can attain liberation. Since they have made funs of you, let them be born on planet earth and worship you for fourteen years. The conch and discus will take birth as Bhārata and Śatrughna (brothers of Lord Rāma, in the Indian epic Rāmāyaṇa) and worship the sandals of Lord Rāma for fourteen years when He is exiled to the forest. Let them worship you and understand that only you can liberate them.'

We must understand that people around the master have different responsibilities. If we think that some are important and others unimportant, we will face difficulties. The person who thinks he is important will be made to kneel in front of the person whom he thinks is unimportant.

The conch and the discus started thinking 'me, me, me' and so naturally they had to suffer. The sandals thought, 'You, You, You' and were therefore worshipped. Viṣṇu blessed the sandals saying, 'Let the conch and discus worship you and attain liberation, and then they will never talk about you like this.'

How we are centered and where our attention is focused are what makes our life demonic or divine. Divine or demon's is determined only by one concept: 'You' or 'me.'

Are you divine or demonic?

Now, here is another important point. After hearing about 'You' and 'me', the next thought that may come to our mind is, '*Swamiji,* I do not know whether I am working based on 'You' or based on 'me.' I am worried about whether I am a demon or divine. Please guide me, tell me, based on which quality I am working.'

Let me assure you that if this fear arises in you, you are divine. The person who is ready to look into his mind, the person who is afraid about whether he is living rightly or wrongly, always lives rightly. Only the person who is arrogant is demonic. The person who is demonic never considers whether he does right or wrong. He thinks that he is always right.

Arjuna also has that fear, '*Bhagavān,* am I living with divine or demonic nature?' He is not expressing that feeling, but his face reveals his fear.

Now Lord Kṛṣṇa explains that living with transcendental qualities, that is, the attitude of 'you,' one achieves liberation or enlightenment - *nivritti.* By living with the idea of 'I' we create more bondage. The demonic qualities make for bondage, meaning *pravritti.*

Lord Kṛṣṇa assures Arjuna that he is born with divine qualities.

If we have ever contemplated whether we were living with 'You' or 'I', if the doubt ever arose, if we have suffered, if we have felt fear or guilt, be clear that we are born with divine nature. On the other hand, if we feel that we are living properly, and that we came here because we had no other entertainment, with the thought, 'Let me listen to whatever master is saying,' if we have that attitude, then we know our nature!

If we have looked once into our being, considered and thought, 'Am I living with demonic nature, or am I living with divine nature? What is my nature?' If we looked even once into our being and tried to measure ourselves with this scale, we are in the position of Arjuna. Be very clear that we too are born with divine qualities. So if you are worried after hearing the qualities, then be sure you are born with divine qualities and you don't need to worry about it any further.

When a person who is righteous listens to such words, he will try to verify his own nature, since he is centered on *dharma,* righteousness. People who are *adharmic,* non-righteous, even if they listen to such discourses think, 'Oh, *Swamiji* speaks about all these things as though he lives them. Let us see how he lives them. Let us see if his living is in tune with his ideas.' A person who is divine tries to chisel or correct himself, whereas a person who is demonic tries to correct others. With demonic nature, the person holds the hammer and chisel towards others, whereas with the divine nature, he holds the hammer and chisel towards himself.

When we carve ourselves we become God. If we have ever looked within ourselves, then we are born with the divine nature. Now Arjuna has become mature; the moment he hears these truths he looks into his being. Naturally, then Lord Kṛṣṇa tells him that he is born with divine nature.

Kṛṣṇa describes the qualities of a person who lives based on 'I, I, I.' I don't think we need to understand these qualities because we already have these qualities, which is why we still feel we are suffering. There is no need to read these qualities, because we know enough of them. All that we need to know is how to live with the attitude of 'You, You, You'.

Please understand that when we live with the attitude of 'You, You, You,' we completely forget ourselves; we disappear into Existence; we are in bliss.

Let me share an important technique that Lord Kṛṣṇa speaks about. For three days, think you are somebody else. It may seem funny! For instance, if you are a doctor, for three days think you are a beach freak. Clearly visualize yourself as somebody else, not a doctor. The moment you change the idea about yourself, a tremendous freedom happens to you. Your tension disappears.

Before taking *sanyās* aspirants undergo a meditation called '*bhūta śarīra vāsa*', meaning they are giving up their entire past. They perform the death ceremony of their parents, *śrāddhā,* even if their parents are alive. This is because if the parents die after the person takes *sanyās* (renunciation), who will do the death rituals for them? Therefore they do it now itself. They also do their own *śrāddhā* (death rituals) since they will have no children and there will be no one to do it for them!

After the *śrāddhā* they must lose their identity, whatever they may have been - doctor, lawyer, or engineer. To do that they smear their entire body with sacred ash, and like a ghost they put on *rudrākṣamālā* (necklace of the holy *rudrākṣ* seeds) and celebrate! Their identity is completely lost and they beg for alms. They do not associate with their identity. They completely break their identity. For three days they meditate that they are somebody else. Only if they pass this meditation and break from their identity for three days, are they given *sanyās*.

This is '*bhūta śarīra vāsa*,' breaking away from our past identity.

For three days try this meditation. For three days think you are somebody else. Whatever you think of as your property, forget it; whatever you think are your problems, throw them out; whatever you think of as your profession, give it up. You can pick it up later, but for three days throw it all away.

You will see a new consciousness rising in you. If you throw away the 'me,' that alone liberates you, and if you start working on 'You,' you experience tremendous bliss. When you drop 'me,' you experience peace; when you start working with 'You,' you experience peace and bliss. This is the straight path to peace and bliss.

How To Save Our Planet?

16.8 People with such demonic qualities think there is no ultimate energy or intelligence that is running this planet earth, that is running the universe, and that this whole creation is produced out of lust and desire, and is unreal.

16.9 Following this material view of creation, these degraded souls with small intellect, lost in themselves and committing cruel deeds, are engaged in the destruction of the world.

Please understand, the energy that is within us, the energy that drives us is the same energy that drives this universe, this solar system, and planet earth. This energy is intelligence, the highest intelligence.

Kṛṣṇa says that when we are unable to recognize this energy, we are demonic. We do not believe everything operates out of this energy; instead we believe we make things happen with our greed, lust, and desires. We believe we run this world with our puny intellect that we consider intelligence.

People who think the world is pure chemistry become demons. Naturally, if we think this whole world is just inert matter, we try to acquire more and more by killing everybody, by hook or by crook, by right or wrong means, and we do what we want to. Only when we understand that this universe is intelligence, and that it responds to our thoughts and activities will we live properly, or start really living.

A small story:

A group of scientists thought they could do anything and everything. They challenged God, 'Now you are unnecessary. Whatever you do, we can do. We can even clone human beings. What do you say? Now we can also develop whatever you have created on earth. Our department has developed everything. We can do anything.'

God was surprised to see all the scientists' creations - the sizes of the bananas and other fruit they had created, and so forth!

The scientists then challenged God to a competition. 'Come face us. We will do whatever you do. We are better than you; you can go and rest. We don't need you anymore.'

God agreed to face the scientists.

God created a plant, and immediately the scientists created the same plant in a better way. One by one, they created the same thing God created. Suddenly, God took a little dust and created a man.

The scientists said, 'This is not a big deal, now that we have the ability to clone.' They took some dust and were about to create a man.

God said 'Stop. Bring your own dust and create. Don't use My dust!'

Whatever we may achieve, wherever science may go, the Divine is alive. God exists and the cosmic intelligence runs this whole universe. We may create man out of dust, but where will we get the dust from? We cannot create dust! It *has* to be God's dust! Be clear that there is a pure energy and intelligence that is the source, the underpinning of the whole universe.

When a person is living within the limits of the intellect and 'me,' he cannot experience the Whole. He knows only logic and calculation, and with that arrogance thinks he knows everything.

Many young people come to me with their parents, who force them to prostrate at my feet. I never like people being forced to fall at my feet. If these young people want they can leave, but they stand there and ask questions such as, 'Why should I fall at your feet?' I tell them, 'I have not asked you to. Why should you stand here and argue?' Yet their arrogance is so much that they stand and argue. I think to myself, 'They should probably get married.' After a year when they return as married people, without prompting they simply do a *sāṣṭānga namaskār,* a full prostration, because in one year they would have been completely trained to surrender!

What we cannot do in ten years, can be done in one year of marriage! Those same people fall flat on the ground and know how to listen. They are polite. They say, 'Yes, *Swamiji*!' They know the power of the 'Yes' *mantra*!

That is what should be done to demonic people: Simply get them married and the demonic qualities will disappear. Perhaps that is why God created the institution of marriage!

People with demonic qualities say the world is produced out of sexual desire and lust. Lust is the reason for the whole universe, they say.

Please be clear that lust cannot be the reason. Intelligence, divine energy is the cause and effect of this whole universe; the cause and effect that is responsible for the universe is the Divine . However, when we think it is lust or that we are responsible, we live with the idea of 'me, me, me.'

Kṛṣṇa says firmly that when we believe that we are the cause of this universe, this Existence, we are so deluded and locked in our own identities, we destroy the world and ourselves as well.

Our ancient sages, the great *ṛṣis,* were not fools. They did not retire to forests because they had nowhere else to go. Many were great kings, rulers of this planet, and they voluntarily left behind all that they had, so that they could understand where they came from. It was not enough for them to read and listen to the experiences of others; they chose to experience the truth themselves.

In the process, they realized themselves and became liberated. What they realized in one sense was simple. As many others over thousands of years have discovered, they discovered that they were part of this cosmic Existence. They realized and experienced that they, too, were Gods. They found that the same energy that operated in this universe operated within them. They experienced that every living being on earth came from the same energy source.

The environment we live in, the oxygen we breathe, the water we drink, the soil that produces the food we eat, all this is the same energy source. This is what we call *panca bhūta* in Sanskrit, the five elemental energies that sustain us. When these are destroyed by our low intelligence, out of our selfishness, the world around us collapses.

How To Save Ourselves?

16.10 Filled with insatiable desires, hypocrisy, pride, and arrogance; holding wrong views due to delusion, they act with impure motives and for impermanent objectives.

16.11,12 Obsessed with endless anxiety lasting until death, considering sense gratification their highest aim, and convinced that sense pleasure is everything; bound by hundreds of ties of desire and enslaved and filled with anger, they strive to obtain wealth by unlawful means, to fulfill sensual pleasures.

What Kṛṣṇa says here is applicable to a vast majority of people today.

Times have changed since the days of the vedic educational system where, from childhood, one was guided toward self-awareness. Modern-day education is based upon logic, science, and rules, and is short on self-awareness and *dharma*, righteousness.

When we are caught in the material world, focused on 'I' and 'me,' we are stuck in the *mūlādhāra* and *svādiṣṭhāna cakras*. Greed and fear rule us, and we are forever in the bondage of attachment and aversion. Whatever we do is done with selfish and impure motives and results in consequences that are mostly illusionary.

In an earlier verse Kṛṣṇa explained how a person with demonic nature could destroy this world. Here, He shows how such a person can destroy himself. Out of pride, arrogance, and hypocrisy, such a person moves in a path directed by purely selfish and material objectives, and derives results that produce suffering.

When we focus on matter, we tend to lose sight of the energy inherent in matter. When we focus on the form, we cannot see the formless that enables the form. What is permanent in both cases is the formless energy that drives the form and matter.

Science has moved a long way from the Newtonian model based on matter and form. This model is no longer relevant. From the days of Einstein, when matter and energy were linked inextricably, the concept has changed. Today all sciences accept that matter and energy not only co-exist, but also that the same object or event can be perceived or experienced by the observer as matter or energy or both.

So, we are back to the Indian master Ādi Śaṅkarācārya's theory that the observer determines what is being observed. We may think this is fanciful. However, this is an accepted theory in the most advanced form of Quantum Physics today. Elementary subatomic particles, when observed in identical conditions with identical tools, appear differently to different observers. As yet there is no explanation for this phenomenon.

Our ancient sages explained that this happens based on our deep-rooted conditioning, which colors our perceptions. When science is sufficiently advanced, it will accept this truth.

Events that happen around us, as well as objects that surround us, can be viewed in different ways. Everything depends upon our conditioning, our *saṁskāras.*

> A couple with young children was driving along the beach one warm summer evening. A young woman in the convertible ahead of them stood up and waved. She had no clothes on!
>
> The parents pretended nothing was amiss.
>
> A small, shrill voice piped up from the backseat, 'Mom, Dad, look! The lady is not wearing a seatbelt!'

Perceptions differ based on our experience bank. A child's perception is innocent and without negativity. It is totally objective. Over time, we accumulate feelings of guilt, shame, fear, arrogance, hypocrisy, greed, and irritation. Our responses to situations are tinged by these negative emotions.

As I have explained before, most humans live in their *mūlādhāra cakra,* unable to rise beyond their survival needs. Their entire focus is on survival and their emotions are anger, greed, and lust. Everything is physical, material, and self-centered. It is all business.

A few are caught in their *svādiṣṭhāna cakra* and stay there bound by insecurities. Fears of various kinds control them. Men are more prone to stay blocked in *mūlādhāra* and women in *svādiṣṭhāna.* Both are unfulfilling. Both are unreal from a spiritual perspective. In *mūlādhāra* we are caught in fantasies. Our entire life is based on how we wish it were, rather than enjoying it as it is. This only leads to suffering.

Once we know how to lead our life without fantasies the fear of death disappears. Then suffering and misery dissolve automatically. We move from the demonic into the divine realm.

Here Lord Krṣṇa explains the same concept in a deeper way and gives a beautiful punch line.

Many take shelter in pleasures and pain that end only with their death. With some, even at that time it doesn't end. They think of the money they paid for insurance, casket, marble gravestone, etc. They regard gratification of desires as the sole objective in life.

Many people ask me, '*Swamiji,* in Gītā, Krṣṇa says that the last thought before death determines how we are born in the next birth. Can we find a way to have good thoughts at the time of death?'

I agree that this is a practical question. Unfortunately, there is no practical answer. There is a word called *vāsanā* in Sanskrit that refers to our mental attitude. *Vāsanā* is built up over our entire life beginning in childhood, some of it even from before birth. It is the accumulated software of our mind that drives us; it is our operational system, the Microsoft-Vista equivalent in our mind-ware.

Vāsanās are the compilation of all our value systems and beliefs, that define our mental attitude, that in turn drives our actions. Unfortunately, *vāsanās,* along with their counterpart *saṁskāras,* memories, are part of our unconscious mind and we have no easy way to access them. Therefore, we have no means to control them and make things happen the way we want them to. It is as if we are on autopilot, with our *vāsanās* and *saṁskāras* driving us through life until we die.

The nature of the unconscious mind is to react to the senses. We may think we respond consciously. But almost all the time our reactions are instinctive, decided by *vāsanās* and *saṁskāras,* rather than by conscious application of our rational mind. This is what Kṛṣṇa refers to as the nature of a demonic person. Instinct is the nature of animals, and because it is their nature, it works well for them. They flow with nature.

Instinct is not the nature of humans. Human consciousness can rise to the intuitive level, in which awareness results in high action. This is the potential of the Divine inherent in all of us. Instead of rising to the intuitive level, the superconscious level, most people find it easier to descend into the instinctive or unconscious level.

We rush towards pleasure and away from pain. We are so eager to fulfill our desires that we go to any length to amass wealth and do any deed, however questionable it may seem. As Kṛṣṇa says, this goes on until we die. If we expect that we will suddenly be filled with thoughts of the Divine at death, even though our whole life we chased only pleasures, this is another foolish fantasy.

Sensory Trap

16.13 *They think: This has been gained by me today; I shall fulfill this desire; I have this much wealth and will have more wealth in the future;*

16.14 *That enemy has been slain by me, and I shall slay others, also. I am the Lord. I am the enjoyer. I am successful, powerful, and happy.*

16.15 *I am rich and born in a noble family. Who is equal to me? I shall perform sacrifice, I shall give charity, and I shall rejoice. Thus deluded by ignorance,*

16.16 *Thus confused by various anxieties and caught in a net of illusions, one becomes too deeply attached to sensory pleasures and falls into hell.*

Kṛṣṇa does not let go. He wants Arjuna and mankind to understand how deeply the human psyche is damaged by the ego.

In one of his commentaries, Śaṅkarā defines *āhāra* to mean all sensory inputs whereas traditionally *āhāra* is translated as food. Food, as we normally understand it, is what the mouth consumes. This is the sustenance upon which the physical body feeds and grows. Many live only to eat, but a few aware ones eat only enough to sustain themselves, so that they can live.

Every sensory organ has its own *āhāra,* input, upon which it feeds. Based on these inputs, the eye, ear, tongue, nose, and skin develop their desires and convey these desires to the body-mind system. Control of these senses and the desires that they weave is what Sage Patañjali prescribed as *pratyāhāra,* one of the eight methods of his Aṣṭāṅga yoga.

Pratyāhāra is not suppression of the senses. *Pratyāhāra* is not starving the senses. Just as we need to eat in order to live, the senses need inputs to function. However, these inputs can be regulated so that the fantasies they weave are kept in control.

The average human is led by his senses; he does not lead his senses. His *karmendriya,* the organs of action that are responsible for movements, are driven by these senses without the need for input from the conscious mind. Instinctively, they avoid pain and welcome pleasure.

A small story:

Two friends met in the street. One of them looked sad and almost on the verge of tears. The other one asked, 'What happened? Why do you look so sad?'

He replied, 'My uncle passed away three weeks ago. He left me fifty thousand dollars.'

His friend said, 'That's not bad.'

He continued, 'Two weeks ago my cousin died, and he left me ninety thousand dollars.'

His friend cried, 'This is great!'

He went on, 'Last week my grandfather died. He left me a million.'

His friend asked, 'Then why are you so sad?'

He replied, 'Because this week, nobody died.'

Understand: Once we allow our mind to get driven away by the senses, there is no stopping. So we continue with our fantasies. We fantasize about accumulating wealth. Unfortunately for us, the purpose of gaining wealth is rarely to enjoy it. In most cases, the joy of acquisition becomes the drive for the person rather than the joy of using the wealth. It has nothing to do with what one can do with the wealth. It has to do with how much more we have than all the other people that we know. The day our neighbor buys a new air-conditioner, the temperature in our house goes up! The day our neighbor buys a new car, our car, which till that day ran well, will stall. As soon as we see another woman wearing the latest style shoes, our shoes that had fit absolutely fine, start pinching.

We are driven by comparison and envy. We are not merely fulfilling our needs, we are actually fulfilling other people's wants and desires. From childhood, we are taught to grab. Nothing we have is enough. Nothing fulfills us. Until death, we are driven by greed.

Existence is waiting to shower us with all that we need. The problem is that we never stop to understand what we need. All the time we are caught in the web of our sensory fantasies, and we run after what others own; we let our senses lead us. After doing these programs and becoming healers, these people spend more time meditating and being aware of who they are. They develop an understanding of their real needs. It is no longer necessary to run after empty wants. What they need comes to them; their needs follow them.

Our body-mind system carries within it the energy required to fulfill the desires that we were born with. Nature, as Mahāvīra and other great masters have said, brings us into this world having already made sure that all our needs will be fulfilled. However, we develop wants and desires that we borrow from others; these are not our needs.

Once we move from the 'me' - focused demonic state into the 'you' - based divine state, we no longer need to worry about creating wealth, developing a power base, establishing relationships, or whatever else we have focused attention upon all our lives. Existence takes care of all that we really need.

If instead we are focused on our own self, 'me,' be sure we are moving in a downward spiral that Kṛṣṇa says takes us into hell.

Cast into Suffering

16.17 Self-complacent and always conceited, deluded by wealth and false pride, they perform superficial sacrifices in name only, without following the vedic rules or regulations.

16.18 The demonic person, consumed by ego, power, pride, lust, and anger, becomes envious of the supreme personality of godhead, who is situated in his own body and in the bodies of others, and blasphemes against Him.

16.19 Those who are envious (of Him) and cruel, who are the lowest among men, I repeatedly cast into the ocean of material existence, into various lowly, demonic forms of life.

16.20 These foolish beings attain repeated births amongst the species of demonic life. Without ever achieving Me, O Son of Kuntī, they sink into the most abominable existence.

Kṛṣṇa has said in other verses that He will receive anyone with compassion and redeem them. Here He says He will cast them aside into suffering. How do we reconcile these two positions?

Both positions are true! After all, every word that an enlightened master utters is true. It is our understanding that needs to improve.

Kṛṣṇa is compassion incarnate. Anyone who surrenders to Him is redeemed, liberated. That is the absolute truth. The problem is that we only pretend to surrender. What we have are mere words. Our thoughts do not match our words, and our words do not match our actions.

People come to me and say, '*Swamiji*, we surrender to you. Please help us and relieve us of our suffering.' When I tell them to attend the meditation program the following week, they say they need to check their appointment book! They still think that they have surrendered!

People tell me, '*Swamiji*, you say visualization helps make things happen. We have tried; nothing happens.'

Nothing happens because you are full of self-contradiction. If we wish to get rid of back pain, and we keep saying, 'Let this back pain go,' it will never go. Every time we utter the words *back pain*, our mind latches more firmly onto the concept of pain. If we want to get rid of pain, we must visualize health, not pain, not getting rid of pain, but feeling healthy.

When we surrender to Kṛṣṇa, our surrender must be total. There can be nothing between Him and us. Then, He surely liberates us, because then we are already liberated; we are in Kṛṣṇa consciousness.

Here, He talks about people who feel no need to surrender to Him. They are so full of ego that they feel He is their competitor. He says He will cast them into the material world. In this material world they can follow their senses, sense objects, and what they consider to be sensual pleasures till death. As I said before, it is our decision. Even Kṛṣṇa is helpless to change it, because He has given us the power to decide. He has handed over the decision to us; to decide whether we want to be 'me'- or 'you'-focused, demonic or divine.

With devotion and surrender we grow. We grow in love to a master and to *God*. Most of us look to God as a person to pray to, to worship. We feel God is a third person. He is not us. Prayer and worship become important pathways to reach this form. The moment we drop the idea of a person, prayer disappears; instead, meditation becomes significant.

In prayer, we worship God. In meditation, we *become* God. It is easy to resort to worship, as it is external. We are used to focusing on externals. Meditation is going inwards. So, it is more difficult for many who are educated rationally. That's why meditation never became the central core of religion in the West. In the East all the great masters founded their teachings on meditation. They taught followers to turn inwards. They taught them to be God, not to worship God.

Meditation leads us to surrender. Meditation is the creation of awareness. Awareness is the knowledge that we are one with the universe. It is then about 'you' instead of 'me.' The feeling of 'you' and the absence of 'me' dissolve the idea of 'I' as identity. This is the foundation of surrender.

This is what Kṛṣṇa talks about in this chapter. The courage to move from 'me' to 'you' is the courage to trust, love, and surrender. When that happens there is nothing else but Him. We become Kṛṣṇa.

When we are one with the universe, one with Kṛṣṇa, there is nothing else we need to look up to. There is nothing else to look for. We have reached eternal bliss - *nityānanda.*

Of Gold And Women

16.21 *There are three gates leading to this hell: lust, anger, and greed.*
As they lead to the degradation of the soul, these three are to be abandoned.

16.22 *Those who have escaped these three gates of hell, O son of Kuntī, behave in a manner beneficial to the (evolution of the) soul, and thus (gradually) attain the supreme destination.*

16.23 *But he who discards scriptural injunctions, and acts according to his base impulses, attains neither perfection, nor happiness, nor the supreme destination.*

16.24 *By the regulations of the scriptures, one should understand what is duty and what is not duty. After being versed in scriptural injunctions, one should act accordingly.*

Kṛṣṇa ends the chapter with this advice: Shed anger, greed, and lust and we will be saved. He calls them gates to hell.

These are the qualities of the blocked *mūlādhāra cakra*. These are attributes that bind us to 'me' and 'mine.' We mistakenly believe that these qualities are essential for our life on this planet. Nothing can be more wrong.

As long as we are bound by anger, lust, and greed, what He calls the three gateways to hell, we are in bondage; we are in suffering. We do not need to die and be escorted to someplace called hell. We live in it day after day and suffer.

Kāma, krodha, and *lobha*: lust, anger, and greed. When we shed these we are liberated. Rāmakṛṣṇa says again and again, drop *kāñcana* and *kāminī*, gold and women, greed and lust, and we will be liberated. Lust for women, and greed for gold, these two desires more than anything else cause all our sufferings.

Krodha, anger, arises out of the suffering. We feel thwarted and we feel angry. The cycle goes on. When these three combine they create *moha*, or delusion. There is nothing real about *kāñcana* - gold and *kāminī* - woman, because these are impermanent; they cannot give abiding joy. We may feel the pleasure for awhile. After that, we will take them for granted.

At one level these emotions are desires. Anger, greed, and lust are expressions related to desires. Desires are energy. Lust is what drives us into reproduction and it is essential for the survival of the species. Greed is the extreme expression of our survival needs. Anger is often the driving force to get things done. The three achieve positive results, too.

Kṛṣṇa refers to the expression of these emotions, however, in the context of self-gratification. He refers to the gratification of base impulses. The baseness of the impulse is related to the intention. As long as these are expressed with the attitude of 'me,' they are base and demonic impulses. There are no redeeming features.

Lust can be transformed when it is expressed in an unselfish and unattached way. Lust will then totally disappear. Compassion and caring will be in its place. Every woman, including his own wife, was 'mother' to Rāmakṛṣṇa Paramahamsa, enlightened master from India. That was the extent of his purity and devotion. Of course, such people are exceptions.

Lust is one aspect of the broad spectrum of desires. Unending desire is greed. When a desire is truly fulfilled, it leaves us. *Karma* consists of unfulfilled desires that goad us into action. We can never fulfill our desires, because many of these desires are not truly ours. We borrow these desires from other people. We need a bigger house, fancier car, or younger wife because our friend, neighbor, or cousin has one.

Even if we acquire one, the satisfaction will be temporary. There is never contentment. Each desire is the seed of suffering. That is why Kṛṣṇa calls it a gateway to hell. But how do we get rid of these desires?

This is what we teach at our second level Life Bliss Program, the Nithyananda Spurana Program or NSP. We help identify true desires, the *prārabdha karma,* with which we are born into this world. These are our true needs, not borrowed wants. We have the energy to fulfill them and discard them. Our *karma* dissolves.

The NSP course leaves us free of negativities. People who attend this program say that they cannot hate or even dislike anyone. The 'I' blossoms into 'you' effortlessly.

At this stage we shed anger as well. Anger and guilt are byproducts of desires. What we cannot acquire makes us angry. Anger produces guilt. Being angry towards a person is fruitless. Much of the negativity expressed towards others comes back to us. It depletes our energy. Anger or even guilt is also often an expression of one's inability to do something. It is a self-centered emotion born of one's weakness.

Suppression of anger does not help. It can actually lead to chronic diseases like cancer. When we learn to turn the emotion of anger towards an issue instead of a person, it becomes energy instead of a disability. Anger needs to be transformed into the positive energy of action.

What Kṛṣṇa asks us to do is to transform negative emotions like lust, greed, and anger into positive energies. He tells us that these are gateways to hell, so long as we use them from the attitude of 'me.' When we transform these emotions into energy, by shifting to the attitude of 'you,' these same emotions become gateways to heaven.

Thus ends the sixteenth chapter named **Daivāsura Sampad Vibhāga Yogaḥ** *of the* **Upaniṣad** *of Bhagavad* ***Gītā****, the scripture of yoga, dealing with the science of the Absolute in the form of the dialogue between* **Śrī Kṛṣṇa** *and Arjuna.*

BHAGAVADGĪTĀ

SINCERITY: THE STRAIGHT WAY TO LIBERATION

ŚRADDHĀTRAYA VIBHĀGA YOGAḤ

CHAPTER 17

Living is about experimenting with the truth.
It is about having the courage
to experiment with the truth.
Just reading or listening and thinking
one has understood it, is meaningless.
The understanding
must be applied with courage.

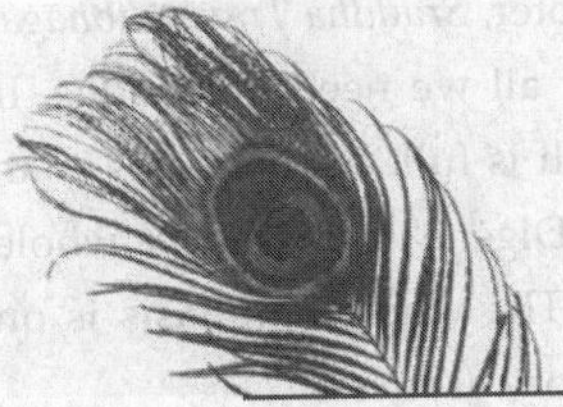

Sincerity: The Straight Way To Liberation

In the seventeenth chapter, Kṛṣṇa straightaway gives the methodology or technique to imbibe whatever He speaks in *Śraddhā Traya Vibhāga Yoga,* the Yoga of Discerning the Three-Fold Faith. After all the words that Kṛṣṇa expressed in earlier chapters, no new teaching is given here. All that Kṛṣṇa has spoken and taught so far is a prelude to what He is speaking now. Here, Kṛṣṇa speaks about sincerity.

Let me explain the meaning of the word *śraddha.* Please understand that *śraddha* is not faith; always the word *śraddha* is translated as faith. This is not correct.

The power to transform

Śraddha means faith plus the courage to experiment with the truth. *Śraddha* means faith plus the courage to experiment with what we believe in. With *śraddha* we will never fail. Understand that there is a possibility that we may fail with faith alone. When we have faith without the courage to experiment with the truth, it is like going to a restaurant, reading the menu card and just leaving. We miss eating. We never taste the food. We never experience it. However, when we have *śraddha* with sincerity, there is no chance of missing the truth. A person never misses when he has *śraddha* with sincerity.

Lord Kṛṣṇa explains and now puts all His emphasis on *śraddha.* After sixteen chapters of teachings, He has nothing new to add. He has said whatever can be said. He has explained all the seven layers of energy.

Now Kṛṣṇa comes to the seventeenth chapter, *Śraddha Traya Vibhāga.* Whatever can be said has been said. Now all we need is *śraddha.* If somebody has had a good feast, his stomach is full. All he needs is an antacid, 'Digene'. All Arjuna needs now is 'Digene' to digest the whole thing and enjoy. This chapter is 'Digene'. The whole emphasis is on *śraddha*: honesty, truthfulness and straightforwardness.

We may question, 'Why would He devote one full chapter for *śraddha*?' Please understand that we invariably miss enlightenment because of lack of understanding of this subject, *śraddha.* Let me be very clear, it is not that we don't know the truth that Lord Kṛṣṇa speaks. We know whatever Lord Kṛṣṇa speaks of and all that He has spoken so far. We know it all. It's not that we don't know. Yet why have we not become Kṛṣṇa?

We miss one thing - *śraddha.* That's the only thing we need. Our problem is not that we don't know. Our problem is that we know too much and we are unable to digest and implement it.

Swami Vivekānanda says beautifully that instead of knowing the whole library, we should know just five concepts. We should experiment with these five concepts with *śraddha.* Let the five concepts become your life. That is enough. Nothing else is necessary. Instead of having the whole library in your head, have the five concepts in your heart. Here, Kṛṣṇa emphasizes the importance of *śraddha*: how *śraddha* and **only** *śraddha* can transform your whole life. Understand, whatever you believe, if you have *śraddha,* if you have sincerity in the concept, you will achieve the ultimate. Even if you believe in atheism, there is no problem.

Many people have achieved God and attained the Truth through the path of atheism. Buddha never spoke of God. He never spoke about God. Yet not only did He become enlightened, thousands attained enlightenment because of Him. In modern times, J.Kṛṣṇamūrti did not mention God in his philosophy. He was an enlightened master. He radiated enlightenment. George Gurdjieff became enlightened with no concept or idea of God. What you believe is not important. How intense you are is important.

People use the title *Mahātma* to describe Mahātma Gandhi because he was intense in whatever he believed in. He was sincere to the core. Whatever he believed in, he experimented with the truth of it. The title of his autobiography, *The Story of My Experiments with Truth,* depicts his life. He experimented with the truth. He allowed the truth to work on him. He worked with the truth. Working with the truth is what I call sincerity. Sincerity is not just listening, reading or believing in the truth. Sincerity is working with the truths. It is straightaway executing them, experimenting with them and having the courage to play with them.

Both meditation and gambling require courage. We need courage for gambling. And we also need courage for meditation. Meditation is the ultimate gamble. With ordinary gambling, we gamble with money. In meditation we gamble with our ego. We gamble with our whole being. But one thing is for sure in the gamble of meditation: if we lose, we win. Only losers win in this game!

In ordinary gambling, the more we get, the more we win. In the gamble of meditation, when we put the ego at stake, we win the whole game. We put our whole ego at stake. Spiritual life needs courage. That is why Swami Vivekānanda calls his spiritual disciples *'dhīraḥ'*. *Dhīrā* means someone who is courageous, who is courage personified.

We might ask, 'Why do spiritual people need courage? For the spiritual life, don't we need to be silent?' No! Spiritual life calls for courage. To experiment with these truths, we need courage. In the past sixteen chapters we have heard many different teachings, different understandings and so many different techniques. We have heard everything. All of this can help transform our life only if we have the courage to experiment with them. Otherwise they add more weight to our head, that's all.

Please understand that if we receive these teachings and store them in our head, we gain more head weight, nothing else. Now we think, 'I know Gītā.' However, we need to experiment with Gītā. We need to experience it.

For example, if we eat too much food and we are unable to digest it, what happens? We vomit it out. We end up with a stomach ache and we vomit. Similarly, if we hear all these things and we don't experience them, we will get a headache. We will catch people and vomit all these things on them. Please be very clear that unless we have sincerity, unless we experiment with these truths, listening to these truths is dangerous.

Now I am giving one more step. Here it says, 'If you don't practice, listening to these truths is dangerous.' We may ask, 'Why?' Because now, by and by, even after so many days of listening or reading these great truths, we will start hallucinating that we know, without knowing. That is the most dangerous game.

Never ever get caught in that game!

Spiritual life needs courage, sincerity, and the consciousness of *dhIraḥ*.

The Bharaṇi – killer of thousand minds

A small story:

The great saint Dakṣiṇāmūrti Swamigal lived in Tamilnadu, South India, near a place called Tiruvaroor. Let me share a historical incident from his life.

A poet from the king's court met Dakṣiṇāmūrti Swamigal and was inspired by his presence. Consequently, the poet wrote one thousand songs in the Bharaṇi style in the saint's honor. Bharaṇi is a special style of poetry involving one thousand verses. The rule is that only someone who shows courage and power and kills one thousand elephants in war is qualified to have such a song written about him. Here, this poet was so inspired by the saint's presence that he simply wrote the songs about him on the spot.

The king also considered himself to be Bharaṇi. I don't know if he killed one thousand elephants in war. He may have just paid a poet to write one thousand songs about him!

Anyway, suddenly, one day in court, out of ego and pride, the king announced, 'I am the only Bharaṇi in this whole country, in this whole region!' One of his poets stood up and said, 'No O King, you are wrong. Dakṣiṇāmūrti Swamigal is also a Bharaṇi. One of your court poets has sung a Bharaṇi about him.'

The king's ego was hurt. He said, 'What? Who is this person deserving Bharaṇi? Bring him here.' The poet said, 'No, no, he is a beggar. He will not come here.' Beggars can never be forced. We can never force homeless people. We can force anybody but a homeless person to do what we want, because he has no desire. We can't do anything about him. As long as someone has some desire, he obeys the social system. So we can't do anything about a homeless person. He does not care for name, home, fame or security. So we cannot bind him. In this case, this man was a beggar and a *saint*. They could not bring him to the king.

The king felt deeply offended. He said, 'What? For a beggar, Bharaṇi! Which fool sang the songs? Call him to me right now.'

The poet was summoned to the court. The king said, 'Fool, how dare you sing Bharaṇi for a beggar.' The poet replied, 'O King, please forgive me. Before you say anything, before you abuse that master, it would be nice if you would go to see him.'

The king said, 'What kind of advice are you giving me? Tomorrow morning your head will be cut off.'

That was the king's usual trend, direct violence. Only foolish people immediately express violence. When they can't behave in an intelligent way, when they don't know the truth and they don't have enough energy to convince the other person of the truth, they take to the sword.

Take for example the history of Buddhism or Hinduism. They never converted anyone with the sword. They had intelligence. They converted through logic, analysis and convincing the other person of the truth.

For example, great masters like Ādi Śaṇkara and Maṇḍana Miśra had different views on a particular subject; still they did not fight with each other. Śaṇkara did not say, 'If you don't convert to *Vedānta*, I will kill you.' They sat together and analyzed what they knew. It was a loving discussion. It was a beautiful scene. Śaṇkara and Maṇḍana Miśra sorted out their differences with deep respect by discussing without rancor.

The person who acted as judge in the discussion was Maṇḍana Miśra's wife. What a beautiful, loving atmosphere it must have been! Can you believe that the wife of one of the competitors was the judge? Never! And here, Śaṇkara appointed Maṇḍana Miśra's wife as the judge. Bhārati judged the discussion between Śaṇkara and Maṇḍana Miśra. And finally, she passed judgment in favor of Śaṇkara. She declared that Śaṇkara won the debate. The whole thing happened out of love. There was no violence, no cutting, no killing, nothing. It was just a simple discussion.

Throughout the history of Eastern religions, there was never any cutting or killing. They never converted through the sword because they did not believe in killing. They had enough intelligence to express the concept. And one more thing, the loser automatically joined the group that expressed the truth more clearly!

When Śaṇkara convinced Maṇḍana Miśra, Mishra dropped everything and surrendered his life to Śaṇkara! He became a disciple of Śaṇkara and took the spiritual name Sureśvarācārya. He followed the path of Śaṇkara's teachings. People who use the sword prove that they are foolish. Because they lack intelligence, they must attack. Those who convert people through the sword prove they do not have enough clarity or courage to perceive the truth. We can never achieve anything by the sword. Only destruction is possible through the sword, never construction.

> The king, foolish as he was, straightaway said, 'Kill him. Tomorrow morning the poet should be killed.' The poet replied, 'I have no

problem. I have experienced Truth through this master. I am ready to die; however, if you are really intelligent, meet this master at least once. Don't punish me until you have seen him. Then I will be ready to die.'

The king agreed, 'Alright, I will see him. If he is not a real *Bharaṇi,* we will kill him also.'

The king set off to meet the master with all his paraphernalia: chariots, foot soldiers, elephants, armies and all his warriors. Kings always travel with their paraphernalia because they lose their identity without their paraphernalia. In contrast, Dakṣiṇāmūrti Swamigal was a *paramahamsa,* an enlightened master. Masters always live by themselves. They do not need any paraphernalia. This master was an *avadhūt,* which means he never wore clothes. The king found him sitting under a big banyan tree. Without any paraphernalia, he was sitting under the banyan tree and the king arrived with his paraphernalia to see him.

This was the scene: This simple beggar sat in a corner without any clothes. He was in bliss and peace, completely lost in Existence, in *brahmajñāna* (knowledge of the Supreme). He sat in intense silence and peace. This silence penetrated anyone in his presence. The king appeared with his warriors and entire army to confront this yogi who sat in profound silence.

The king jumped down from his chariot and advanced towards the master. The master did not move. There was no movement in him even after seeing the king and his army and hearing all the commotion. He opened his eyes and looked straight into the king's eyes. It was the first time that someone looked straight into the king's eyes. The king had always looked at others straight in their eyes and they had always put their heads down. For the first time somebody looked straight into the eyes of the king. After a few seconds, the king put his head down. The king clearly felt something happening inside his being. He felt like a mere beggar in the master's presence. He did not know how to act. He did not know how to react. It was a strange situation. He was at a loss. He could not decide what to do. He felt overwhelmed.

Dakṣiṇāmūrti Swamigal signaled to the king to sit down. There were no words from him. He simply made a sign asking the king to sit. All the ministers and the army dropped their weapons and also sat in silence. In ten minutes the whole army was sitting down. It is impossible to make an army sit. Even the leader of the army can't make the army sit. That is why they say we must continuously give a task to the Devil. If we don't give any task to the devil, it will eat us! Similarly, we cannot make the army keep quiet. But here the whole army sat in silence.

One hour passed. Then two hours passed; three hours; then the evening also passed; one day elapsed. The master, the king and the entire army sat in silence. Not a single word was exchanged. There were no instructions, nothing. They did not even greet each other. They were merely sitting. Two days elapsed; then three days. Now the master thought, 'This is too much. The poor man and his entire army have been simply sitting for three days without food and even without toilet visits! These people must return to their kingdom, to the palace. The king must take care of the country. He has been just sitting here for three days.

The master opened his eyes and said, 'Now you can go.' The king fell flat at the master's feet, did *namaskār* (obeisance) and came out of the forest.

Then the king summoned the poet and said, 'Forget one thousand elephants. You may sing praises for the master that you usually sing for the one who has killed ten thousand elephants!'

The poet made a beautiful statement, 'Killing ten thousand elephants is easy. It is not a big deal. You just need the weapons and you can simply kill; however, killing one's mind is the real achievement.'

This master had killed the king's mind. Not only had Dakṣiṇāmūrti Swamigal killed his own mind, he could kill anybody else's mind if they sat in his presence. Killing ten thousand elephants doesn't take courage, but killing your mind requires courage.

Courage and sincerity are the only pre-requisites

All we need for real spiritual life is courage and sincerity to experiment with the truth. We typically lack that quality. We listen to everything. Wherever there are discourses and lectures, we go and listen to anyone who speaks. We read all the books. When it comes to facing the reality of putting this knowledge to test, there is no action. Then you tell me, 'For practical purposes, *Swamiji*, we must have our possessions. Otherwise how can we survive in this world?' You just compromise cunningly.

Compromising is cowardice. Please understand that the person who compromises *never* experiences anything in his life. Not only in the spiritual life, even in the outer world life. He can never experience life itself.

Sincerity to experience a single truth is enough. Nothing else is necessary. We don't need to do big things. Please be very clear, we can't call somebody 'a big person' if he does something big. What he does is unimportant; *how* he does it is important.

As an example, throughout his life the great saint Nammalvar, who lived in Tamilnadu, made garlands for Viṣṇu. He did nothing else. He picked flowers from a garden, made garlands and gave it to God. All he did was make garlands. He became enlightened. So many enlightened masters did not do big things. They did small things in a big way. They had deep trust.

Another enlightened person did not even do that. He did not make garlands to offer God. Instead he threw a stone towards the Śiva *liṅga* everyday. His name was Sakyanayanar (Sakya refers to the clan of the Buddha, and Nayanar is a name for devotees of Śiva). Somehow he became a Buddhist monk. Because he was a Buddhist monk, he could not worship the Śiva *liṅga* in public. Yet he had tremendous respect and devotion for Śiva.

In Buddhism, at least one son from every family is given to the monastery at a young age. They bring him up and make him a Buddhist monk. Like that, Sakyanayanar was given away to a monastery. Still, he had deep devotion to Śiva. Everyday he went near the Śiva temple. It was not even a regular temple; it was just a small Śiva *liṅga* under a tree. From a distance he took a stone, visualized it as a flower and threw the stone at the Śiva *liṅga*. If someone observed him and asked, 'What are you doing?' he would say, 'I am only throwing stones at the Śiva *liṅga*.' He would throw the stones and leave that place.

One day when he threw a stone, an old man suddenly appeared and asked, 'What are you doing?' He replied, 'I am only throwing stones at the *liṅga*.' The old man said, 'No, the way in which you throw shows your devotion. You may be throwing stones, but the way in which you are throwing shows devotion. Tell me who you are?'

Sakyanayanar replied, 'Somehow I was born in a Buddhist family, yet I am deeply devoted to Śiva. Everyday I come and offer my Being to him by throwing a stone. Immediately the old man turned around, gave *darśan* (vision) as Śiva and blessed him with enlightenment.

Understand that what we do is unimportant. Even if we sweep our home, even if we just clean our house, it is okay as long as we do it with complete and intense sincerity in that moment.

Live in the moment.

Understand that spiritual practice does not mean you need to go into a deep forest, hold your nose ten times, and breathe this way and that way. You will only torture yourself. Do anything, but do it with intensity and sincerity. Have courage to express whatever you believe. Have courage to work and experiment with whatever you believe. Whatever your beliefs may be, have the courage to experiment with them.

Don't bother whether the truth you believe is the ultimate Truth. You will never know whether it is ultimate unless you have the courage to experiment with it. Without experimenting, you cannot conclude. If you conclude without experimenting, it is prejudice. You cannot conclude without experimenting. All you need is courage to experiment with the truth that you believe.

Tamil has three words for *satya* (truth). One word is *vaaimai,* which means speaking the truth through the mouth. Another word is *unmai,* which is speaking the truth through your mind or heart. The third beautiful word is *meimai,* which means living the truth through your body.

In Tamil, *'mai'* means body. Truth means living the truth through the body. All of us understand speaking the truth through the mouth and speaking the truth through the mind. However, what does 'living the truth through the body' mean? We have never heard this before.

This is where we miss the boat. We continuously think about the truth from morning till night. We speak what we think is the truth. Nonetheless, we forget one important thing: executing the truth in life, living the truth in life. That is where we miss. Living the truth in life is the essence.

Patañjali gives *satya* as the first instruction in his Aṣṭāṅga yoga. It is *vaaymai, unmai* and *maimai,* all the three combined.

When practiced sincerely, any part of the eight limbs or even a part of a part can lead to enlightenment. In reality we become aware of *satya,* that ultimate truth, upon enlightenment, and not before.

That is why I have said time and again that it is not necessary to have an enlightened master as our *guru* to become enlightened. Any master whom we follow sincerely can lead us to enlightenment. Even if we truly believe a stone idol will deliver us into liberation, it will do so.

Our approach, our conviction, our courage and our trust elevate us.

Śraddha is total conviction in what we are doing. There should be no doubt in our mind about the path that we are following and why we are following. All great masters had undivided focus in whatever they did. They never swerved from their chosen path no matter what challenges and problems they faced, including threats to their lives.

Śraddha will also deliver whatever else we need, including material benefits. Here Kṛṣṇa speaks of spiritual enhancement. We can use the same technique to achieve whatever else we need. *Śraddha* works equally well in material pursuits. That is what I call Quantum Spirituality. Spirituality is not separate from materialism. Spiritual wellbeing is not divorced from material wellbeing. Material wellbeing is part of overall spiritual wellbeing. And that is Quantum Spirituality.

Be very clear, spirituality is not about renouncing everything and going off to a forest or a mountain. If we do this without cleansing our mind, we will only live our fantasies in the forest or on the mountain. We need not go anywhere to practice spirituality. We can stay where we are and enjoy whatever we have without regrets and guilt. All we must do is give up and renounce our fantasies about what we do not have.

To accomplish this, to focus on what we have, to enjoy what we have and to renounce greed and expectation, requires courage, determination, single-minded focus and discipline. It requires *śraddha*.

Understand that the ultimate step or the straight way to enlightenment is honesty and sincerity towards our beliefs. Whatever we believe is not the issue. We must have the courage to experiment with it.

Way To Worship

17.1 Arjuna said: What is the mode of devotion of those who perform spiritual practices with sincerity, but without following the scriptural injunctions, O Kṛṣṇa? Is it in the mode of goodness, aggression or ignorance?

Arjuna asks a beautiful question. Arjuna asks: 'Kṛṣṇa, those who discard the ordinances of the scriptures but perform sacrifices, what is their position? Is it *satvic, rajasic or tamasic*? What is the state of people who don't follow the instructions of the scriptures, the ancient books, and instead worship according to their own beliefs? Is it *rajas, tamas or satva*? Are they in a peaceful (*satvic*) state, a restless (*rajasic*) state or an ignorant (*tamasic*) state?'

Worship can occur at many levels. Arjuna's question is based upon the three attributes or *guṇas.* Worship is also dependent on our energy levels. Many people are comfortable worshipping at the physical level, the gross level, through techniques such as *pūjā,* going to temples to worship the deities, bathing in holy rivers, etc. From an energy point of view, these are linked to the earth energy and the water energy.

At another level of energy, one may perform fire sacrifices such as *yajña* or *homa.* These are related to the fire energy. Typically the energy of the fire is transferred to water pots that are placed around the sacrificial fireplace. This water, which is energized by the ritual, is then poured over idols, or sprinkled over people or upon the earth to energize them.

The energy of air can be accessed through breathing techniques such as *prāṇāyāma* or the chanting of verses. In the first nine verses of Śiva

Sūtra, Lord Śiva explains about these types of techniques to Devī, His disciple.

It is possible to access the etheric energy through meditation, though this requires understanding and awareness.

Each form of worship or sacrifice is based upon one's aptitude and inclination. Each of these is guided by scriptural instructions as to how to perform the worship, when and where, etc.

Arjuna asks, 'How important is it to follow these instructions? What happens when one follows one's own inclinations and worships?'

This is an interesting question. A saint in Tamilnadu worshipped Śiva with such intensity that he cut out his eyes and placed them on the Śiva liṅga. Other masters placed all kinds of material at the altar including raw meat. Rāmakṛṣṇa placed a thread under the nose of Kālī's idol to check whether She was breathing before he offered Her the ritual food!

Many masters have followed their inclination when worshipping their favorite deity. Scriptures never stood in their way of worship. However, these masters were focused on what they were doing. They had *śraddha.* That is important.

Arjuna's query is in this connection.

Don't Torture Me

17.2 The supreme Lord said: The natural faith of embodied beings is of three kinds: Goodness, aggression, and ignorance. Now hear about these from Me.

17.3 O Arjuna, the sincerity of each is in accordance with one's own natural disposition. One is known by one's sincerity. One can become whatever one wants to be.

17.4 Men in the nature of goodness worship the deities; those in the nature of aggression worship the demons, and those in the nature of ignorance worship ghosts and spirits.

17.5, 6 Ignorant persons of demonic nature are those who practice severe austerities without following the prescription of the scriptures, who are full of hypocrisy and egotism, who are impelled by the force of desire and attachment and who senselessly torture the elements in their body and also Me who dwells within the body.

Kṛṣṇa explains that the way we worship depends upon our natural disposition, the *guṇa*, attributes that we are born with.

When we are born, we carry within us the *vāsanā*, the essence of the mental attitude from our past lives. This comes with the *prārabdha karma* (unfulfilled actions from past lives) and the *saṁskāras* (deeply engraved memories), that drive our mental makeup and actions throughout our present lives. In turn, *guṇas* or the attributes we are born with are determined.

We are born with a natural inclination based upon our last life and attitude. Depending on the attitude, we may have the attribute of *satva, rajas* or *tamas* as our driving nature.

All societies, religions, faiths, castes or creeds are simply translations of these basic natures or traits or mental conditionings, nothing more. After taking birth on planet earth, we adopt the nature into which we are born that is according to our past attitude. In our new birth, we settle into a religious belief dictated by that natural attribute.

However, we do not realize that we are a part of the Whole, a fragment of Existence or the supreme consciousness. We do not realize that our true nature transcends all material associations and conditionings. When this relationship with Existence is forgotten, we give energy to our associations in material life. We develop allegiance to the blind rules of some religion. Such an existence is purely materialistic and the association itself is artificial. To come out of this, we must break out of our material bonds and enter the path of Self-realization.

Śraddha here refers to the faith that comes out of good work. Yet pure goodness goes beyond all material acts. It is transcendental. Hence there is nothing like the fully good, the completely good in material life.

Please be very clear, only a person whose nature is pure goodness can connect with the Divine, with Existence.

An enlightened master goes beyond the three *guṇas*. He transcends these attributes because he burns out all his *vāsanās, saṁskāras,* and *karmas*. Unbound by desires, greed, fear, or attachment, he is beyond the illusion of material existence. He dissolves into the cosmic energy when he chooses to leave the body.

When the energy of an enlightened master is reborn on this planet, when it takes human form, it is imbued with some *satva guṇa,* since all beings in physical form must by nature have an attribute.

Such a being is an incarnation, an *avatār*. Upon realization by the incarnation of the being's enlightened state, that incarnation reverts to its transcendental state of being without attributes or *guṇa*. In some cases, the incarnation continues upon this planet to fulfill the mission that Existence has sent it to accomplish. In other cases, upon realization of its true nature, the incarnation reverts to its original cosmic state.

If a *tamasic* person becomes enlightened, he goes through the stages of *rajas* and *satva* before the realization happens. The transition may happen quickly but it must happen. Vālmīki (an Indian sage) was a robber who terrorized and killed people. His nature was deep *tamas* with a layer of *rajas*. When he caught hold of Nārada and demanded money, Nārada offered him the name Nārāyaṇa. He was transformed the moment Vālmīki uttered the name of the Lord. He shifted to *satva* and became the enlightened master who wrote the *Rāmāyaṇa* epic.

Kṛṣṇa says that our style of worship depends upon our nature. A person established in *satva* worships *devatas* (deities, gods) who are peaceful. A person established in *rajas* worships *yakṣas* (supernatural beings) and *rākṣasas* (demons). A person established in *tamas* (ignorance) worships *pretas* (spirits of the dead) and *bhūtas* (ghosts).

Please understand, whatever is your ideal, whatever you hold in high esteem, whoever you follow, whatever you worship, that is your nature and that decides your quality. If we worship the right ideal, we are established in *satva*. If we have Swami Vivekānanda's poster in our room, we are in *satva*. If we have an actor's photo or poster in our room, we are in *rajas* and *tamas*. *Tamas* is like watching a violent fighting show. Please be very clear that if you continuously sit in front of the television and watch fighting, you are established in *tamas*.

Kṛṣṇa says that based upon our ideal, our *guṇa* (attributes) can be described.

In the last verse, He says, 'Please do not punish your body. You not only punish yourself, but you also punish me because I reside in you!'

Do not abuse your body

The scriptures do not recommend severe austerities and penances. Walking on fire and such other things are unnecessary. When I make you do these things once in a while, it is to make you break the pattern that you have always lived your life in. But you should not subject yourself to these as daily rituals, 'Every morning when I wake up, I should walk on ten feet of fire...' No!

Kṛṣṇa says there is no need for all these things. People perform them out of pride and ego, merely to show, 'I did all these things.' They are done out of pride and egoism. They are done out of lust and attachment. For example, some people sit for years on a bed of nails or sit with one hand raised. All these painful contortions are foolish. These people torture their bodies and the material elements as well as the *Paramātman* (supreme consciousness) dwelling inside them. Beautifully Lord Kṛṣṇa says, 'Please do not torture the soul inside your body. Don't abuse your body. The body is the temple of God.

By torturing the temple of God, you torture the supreme consciousness residing inside. He says that those who torture the supreme consciousness inside the body are demons. Rāvaṇa did penance. He cut off his heads and put them into the fire. This is a demon's penance, torturing the body and torturing the supreme consciousness residing in the body. There is no need to do self-torture. Kṛṣṇa says, 'Don't torture yourself.' God never asked you to torture yourself. These people wanted to destroy somebody all the time. That is why they did these violent things even to themselves. The entire purpose of this penance and self-torture was to boost the ego, to seek power.

No scripture expects or teaches us how to kill others, torture others or do black magic to others. The other day I spoke to somebody about *yantras* as a remedy. *Yantra* is a metal plate with a diagrammatic representation of a powerful *mantra* (chant) that is sanctified through rituals. After that lecture someone told me, 'I bought a *yantra,* but when I wanted to return it to the person I bought it from, he threatened to curse me.'

You need to understand that only an enlightened being can curse. Only he has that power. But an enlightened person will never curse. Please be very clear that only an enlightened person can make his curse effective. Others cannot. It is not that anybody can curse and it will become reality. No, only an enlightened person can curse, and an enlightened person will never curse. If he curses, he is not enlightened. *Nobody* can curse you. If he is not enlightened, don't be concerned about it. It will never work because for a curse you need *satya-saṅkalpa,* the backing of Truth.

Only the words of a person who has achieved the ultimate energy can become reality. I will say again that only an enlightened person can curse, and an enlightened person will never curse. Because the enlightened person is in universal consciousness, cursing another person is the same as cursing himself!

Never be afraid of curses! Nobody can curse you. One thing is sure, if someone curses, he hurts himself more than he hurts others. So never be afraid of curses.

Spiritual relationships can never exist out of fear or greed. Never be obedient to somebody out of fear. Simply throw things out if it is forced on you out of fear. Never be afraid of anything.

Here Kṛṣṇa says that there is no need for all this penance. Out of pride and ego you cheat yourself with all this penance but you never really achieve anything. The person who does these things out of ego and pride is a demon, a *rākṣasa.*

A demon is in deep *tamas,* in ignorance. All that drives such a person is the boost to his ego without consideration for himself and others. Such a person is a spiritual cipher.

Believe And Practice

17.7 Food that we consume is of three kinds, according to the three types of material nature. These are sacrifice, austerity and charity. Hear the difference between these three.

Kṛṣṇa now speaks about food. Three different types of people enjoy three different types of food. Before we discuss these verses, let me explain the three different types of *śraddha* based on what we are.

Please understand that one group of people is completely negative. They only doubt and doubt and doubt. They have decided not to believe in anything. They have decided not to raise themselves in their lives. They remain dumb. We can't do anything with them. This is the first group.

The second group consists of people who believe, but do not practice. The third group of people believes and practices sincerely.

There are three groups. One group doubts. Even the word doubting is too good to describe it. They are prejudiced. This group is in *tamas*. The next group is the believers. They are in *rajas*. The third group is sincere. This group is in *satva*. Kṛṣṇa beautifully explains the differences between the prejudiced group, the believers and the sincere group. He then talks about their ways of life, character and how we can achieve the sincerity of *satva* and imbibe the truths explained in the Gītā.

He gives beautiful step-by-step explanations and teachings on how to raise ourselves from the prejudiced level to the believing level, and from the believing level to the sincerity level. All those here are already at the believing level.

If you are prejudiced, you will not sit here everyday. You would merely stand there, listen to two or three words and go away. Many people come just to check out what is going on. They stand here for two or three minutes and look at their watch. And even in those few minutes, their feet will shuffle ten times this way and that, and they will say, 'Alright, enough. I think he is just a young *swami*. What can he say that I do not already know?' They just walk out.

If you are not at least at the level of belief, you will not sit here. Coming regularly and sitting through these lectures shows that you are at least at the level of belief.

Now all you need to do is jump into the level of sincerity. The moment we jump into the level of sincerity, we experience the truth. We become Kṛṣṇa. We experience Kṛṣṇa consciousness.

Now we will enter into the technology of experiencing the sincerity, the technology of Kṛṣṇa consciousness.

You see, there is an important choice that you must make. Either you should be completely sincere and trust what I say as the truth, or be very clear that whatever I am saying is just lies. If you can't practice what I am saying, whatever I am saying is a lie. If you are unable to practice, what is the use of this truth? Whether I am saying the truth or not, you will decide. Only you can decide that. No one else can decide for you. I cannot decide for you. If you can execute what I tell you, if you are able to imbibe it, I am speaking the truth. If you are unable to do it, what is the use of the whole thing? Nothing. There's no use. For eighteen days, it's a waste of three hours of your time and three hours of mine, that's all. If you don't imbibe, if it does not transform your life, then it is only a waste of time and whatever has happened here is not the truth.

The courage to experiment is enough

Please be very clear that the result of my words on your consciousness decides whether what I spoke is the truth or a lie. One more thing you must understand is that you don't need to do it completely or perfectly.

Having the courage to experiment is enough. After my talking all these days, if you say, 'Why not test for two or three days?'; if you have that much courage, that is enough.

If that doesn't happen, then my sitting and shouting and talking is just like an Indian political meeting speaker! If you are in South India, whether you want it or not, you must listen to some political speaker every year, maybe every month. They air the politician's talk on the loudspeaker throughout the city. No one can escape hearing him.

Let me share a real incident that happened some time ago. One day I was traveling from Pudukottai in Tamilnadu to our Bangalore ashram. We suddenly started hearing a voice over a loudspeaker. The person speaking used slang words, not a single decent word, except two or three, 'hmmm, hmmm.' There were no other decent words. We couldn't escape from his slang words for ten kilometers, which means half an hour. The roads were also horrible. For half an hour, he was shouting. Unfortunately, we had to drive past the stage where he was speaking. I was surprised that only four ladies were sitting in front of the stage. There were more people on the stage than in the audience!

I asked one *brahmacāri* (unmarried boy training on the path of *sanyās*) traveling with me, 'What is going on? Why is he using all these slang words?'

The *brahmacāri* said, 'What is this, *Swamiji*? He is speaking decently. Why are you blaming him?'

I asked, 'Is this decency?'

He said, '*Swamiji*, you have not been present at these kinds of meetings. That is why you call this slang. It is actually decent.'

I asked, 'Then why are there only four ladies in the audience?'

He said, 'Because of the loudspeakers, people can listen to the speech from their homes for a radius of ten kilometers. They don't need to attend the meeting.'

In that political meeting, the speaker told the crowd, 'O dear people who are here, like an ocean you have gathered…' Only four ladies were listening to him and he called them an ocean. And these four ladies were chewing betel nut and betel leaves and spitting on the ground continuously.

These old ladies must have had some arguments with their daughters-in-law at home. Where else could they go after that? There was some entertainment here, so they must have come here. They must have thought, 'Let us go and sit there. Maybe at the end of the talk, they will give some clothes or gifts. If we don't get anything, we can remove a few flags and take them home. We can use them to clean the house!' This was why these ladies probably decided to come.

Please understand that our meeting will become one more such meeting if we don't have the courage to experiment with the truth that we learned here. If we don't practice, if don't allow Kṛṣṇa's words to work on us, if we don't work with these words, this meeting will be another political meeting, maybe a polite political meeting. Please don't make this a political meeting. Let these words penetrate you. May you experiment with the truth. If you don't experiment, at least it will be mentally clear to you that this is not the truth.

You might think, 'This *swami* was simply saying what he has read somewhere.' But if you believe this is the truth, you will be here. If you think this is not the truth, you will not be here. You will not come everyday and sit for three hours, even if you do not have any other work to do. You have a television at home. You could have sat in front of the television. There are many other places to go; yet you chose to be here. You chose to listen. This shows that you think there is truth behind these words. So when you think there is some truth, never wait to experiment with it.

Have courage and experiment. Take one single idea. You don't need to experiment with the whole Gītā. Take one single concept and imbibe that to the core. Let your whole being vibrate with that single thought.

Swami Vivekānanda says, 'When you commit to a single idea, your blood should boil with that single idea. Even your hair should stand in that direction. Your bones, your thoughts, your body and your mind should all stand for it. Your whole being should be directed towards that concept. Only then success is certain.'

Please understand, take one concept and work with it. If you fail, there is nothing wrong. But have courage to work with it. If you succeed, you will know it is the truth, and you will be liberated. You will have bliss. If it fails, you will know that it is not the truth and you will be clear. You can continue your search elsewhere. So be very clear about it. The basic truth Kṛṣṇa is telling you is about sincerity.

There are three groups of people. The *tamasic* group is prejudiced, meaning negative. The *rajasic* group believes intellectually. The *satva* group has sincerity. They not only believe, but they have courage to play with the words and ideas as well. Please do not miss the courage. Let these words penetrate you.

We Are What We Eat

17.8 *The foods that promote longevity, virtue, strength, health, happiness and joy are juicy, smooth, substantial and nutritious.*
Such foods are liked by persons in the mode of goodness.

17.9 *People in the mode of aggression like foods that are very bitter, sour, salty, hot, pungent, dry, and burning, and which cause pain, grief and disease.*

17.10 *People in the mode of ignorance like foods that are stale, tasteless, putrid, rotten, refuse and of impure energy.*

Kṛṣṇa talks about the nature of food consumed by people of *satva*, *rajas* and *tamas* temperaments.

He explains what kind of food these people like, what kind of lives these people lead and what kind of understanding these people experience in their lives. The most important thing is what kind of understanding they acquire. See, the same words can be understood in many different ways.

The other day, I related the story of a scholar who narrated the story of Hariścandra, a king who sacrificed his wife and child in order to keep his word. At the end of the story the narrator asked two people, 'What did you understand from the story?'

One person said, 'Even if you die, you must speak the truth.'

The other person said, 'If it is an emergency, you can sell your wife. There is nothing wrong with that!'

From the same story, two different understandings arose. In the story of the great king Hariścandra, he gave away his kingdom, sold his wife, and allowed himself and his son to be killed in order to fulfill his promise and uphold the truth of his commitments. We need to understand the word in the context of its spirit.

Words can easily be misunderstood! Please don't miss the essence of the words. It is easy to miss the spirit behind the words, the true meaning behind the words. Experiment with courage. And if you can't, if this is not the truth for you, forget about it. At least you will be free to search somewhere else.

Experiment and experience

If you think that it is the truth and you don't execute it or experiment with it in your life, then drop it! Otherwise it will become a habit to listen to the truth and not practice it. It will become a mental setup. It is the *most* dangerous mental setup. People ask me, '*Swamiji,* should I renounce everything to become enlightened? Should I become a *sanyāsi,* a monk?'

I tell them, 'No. There is no need. Just do one thing. Don't have the mental setup of receiving the truth and not practicing it, that's all.' That is the most dangerous thing that can happen to any being. Please be very clear, receiving the truth and understanding it intellectually without having the courage to practice it is the worst possible mental setup. That is the worst devil or demon that can catch hold of you. So at least have the courage to decide, 'This is not for me because this is not the truth.' If you believe this is the truth, then have the courage to experiment with it.

You have heard many things. Kṛṣṇa does not say anything new in this chapter. He says only one thing, 'Be sincere.' Sincerity is the straight way. I tell people, 'Honesty is the basic spiritual virtue. Sincerity is the basic spiritual virtue.' First be a gentleman, then you can be a spiritual man. Gentleman means to be honest to what you believe, truthful to the core. Never do anything without being clear about the truth, and never stop doing anything if you know it is the truth. The scientist is courageous enough to go after the truth. Wherever the research takes him, he is ready to experiment.

In the same way, you must become an inner scientist, a spiritual scientist. You must have the courage to go behind the experience within the words. You must be able to play with them.

A small story:

An enlightened Zen master and his disciple went to the river to bathe. Suddenly, the disciple fell into the river and shouted, 'Master, save me, save me.'

The Zen master said, 'You are *ātman* (soul), save yourself. You are God, save yourself.'

The disciple shouted, 'Master, first save me, then you can teach me philosophy. Then you can teach me meditation. First, please save me.'

The master replied, 'Stand up and save yourself.'

The disciple shouted, 'No, No, Master, save me! Then you can teach me.'

The master shouted back, 'Fool, I am telling you to stand up.'

The disciple became frightened. Just out of fear, he simply stood up, and realized that the water was only up to his knees!

When you stand up, you understand the whole *samsāra sāgara,* the ocean of life. Whatever you consider to be the great worries of your life are not even up to your knee level. They are just up to the ankle level. Because you are lying down, because you never stand up, you think you are drowning; you think you are going to die.

I tell you from my personal experience, if you stand up, you will realize that the water is only knee-deep. Whatever you regard as the *samsāra sāgara* (the ocean of life) is only knee deep. It is nothing. There is no way it can affect you. But you need courage to stand up.

For example, if the disciple had decided, 'No, no, I am drowning and instead of pulling me out and helping me, Master is teaching me impractical things. What kind of a master is he?' If he simply blamed the master, he would have gone with the river.

He had the courage and in a minute, he got the guts to experiment with the master's words and was saved. You need the guts. You need the courage to stand up and see the truth by yourself. It is having the courage to experiment. Nothing will be lost. If something can be lost, it is better to lose it as soon as possible. May you be rid of that thing or situation. If something can be lost by practicing the truth, may it be lost as early as possible. The earlier it is lost, the better for you.

May you flood your being with the truth. Whatever cannot stand, whatever is washed away, let it be washed away. May it be lost from your being as early as possible.

Kṛṣṇa explains here about the energy of various food substances. Generally, all food that is not from plants i.e., from animal origin, has negative energy. Food that is hot and spicy tends to aggravate desires. Vegetarian food that is fresh and not spicy is ideal for spiritual practices.

In our Nithya Spiritual Healing system, it is essential that the healers become vegetarians and give up substances such as alcohol, tobacco, drugs, etc. I have nothing against alcohol or meat. I have no theories about cruelty to animals and so on. Plants also have life, just perhaps not at the same frequency. So if one argues from the point of cruelty to animals, eating vegetables also is cruelty to plants.

The Nithya Spiritual Healing system is based on deep meditative techniques. For the meditative energy to be effective, negative energy substances should not be used. I have seen that these meditations do not go together with meat as well as with tobacco and alcohol. If healers eat meat, smoke or drink, they are affected physiologically and psychologically.

Many people complain that this condition is restrictive. What can I do? To satisfy the followers who wish to become healers, I have modified the system for self-healing, which allows them to eat meat, drink or smoke. But the interesting development is that many of these healers drop meat, cigarettes and liquor on their own! After a while the mind-body system rejects these low energy food substances automatically.

Any serious meditation technique requires one to be in the energy field. The word '*āhāra*' used by Kṛṣṇa can be expanded to mean food for all senses, not merely for the tongue. All sensory inputs need to be of the same description that Kṛṣṇa uses here, promoting 'longevity, virtue, strength, health, happiness and joy' to aid one's progress in one's spiritual path by the *satvic* route.

Charity Without Expectations

17.11 *Sacrifice without expectation of results, as stipulated in the scriptures, with a firm belief and conviction that it is a duty, is in the mode of goodness.*

17.12 *O Arjuna, that sacrifice that is performed with expectation of result or for show out of pride, is of the nature of aggression.*

17.13 *Sacrifice that is performed without following the scripture, in which no food is distributed, which is devoid of mantra, sincerity, and gift, is said to be in the mode of ignorance.*

Kṛṣṇa talks about how to give, how to sacrifice and how to serve others. In the *vedic* tradition, sacrifices such as fire rituals (*yajña* and *homa)* were not mere rituals to worship celestial beings. They had the far deeper meaning of benefiting the living and the poor.

Every ritualistic offering had a major element of gifting the deserving poor. Whoever came to such a ritual never went away empty-handed. When the great *ṛṣis,* the masters, performed rituals, they had nothing to seek. They performed these in line with the truth of their experiences, which were the scriptural understandings. They expected nothing. They performed rituals as a day-to-day living expression. These rituals were conducted so that the celestial beings and nature were pleased and humanity benefited. These were selfless offerings of *satva guṇa* (good nature).

Great kings also practiced these rituals. Kings performed fire rituals to display power and to show that they controlled other kings. These were a display of ego. Kings such as Yudhiṣtra performed the horse sacrifice, *Aṣvamedha Yāga,* and the *Rājasūya Yāga* to announce their supremacy over other kings. However, these were required of kings and were also occasions to give their wealth away generously. These were performed in the mode of aggression, *rajas.*

Demonic creatures also performed other extreme sacrifices with no concern for anything except to show their brute strength. These did not involve charity or generosity. These did not follow the scriptural guidelines. These were carried out purely for selfish reasons.

When young Naciketa's father gave away useless old cows that no longer produced milk as fire offerings, the young lad protested. 'What are you doing?' he asked his father. 'Why are you giving away useless things in a sacrifice that is meant for giving away valuable material? If you want to give nothing else, then give me away,' Naciketa said. As a result, in deep ignorance and anger, his father offered his son to Yama, god of death.

Please understand that a sacrifice is not measured by how much we give. It is measured by how much we give that we cannot afford to give. It is measured by how much we give when it hurts us to give and that too without any expectation in return. Such a sacrifice straightaway leads to liberation.

Many people give with wonderful intent. It is not charity if they give part of their wealth without it affecting their lifestyle. It is no sacrifice. Many people tell me, '*Swamiji*, I am writing a legal will leaving all my possessions to this ashram, temple or your mission.' What is the big deal in giving away after death? You cannot carry it with you anyway.

A sacrifice must hurt to be genuine. It must cause you discomfort and yet be given with total pleasure and without expectations. That is the spirit of genuine surrender. That is the spirit of doing things without expectation of the fruits of action.

I am not denouncing the wonderful charity that many wealthy people do without posing for photographs. They do it with good intentions of helping the disadvantaged. That mental attitude of giving and sharing what they have with the needy benefits them. That *vāsanā* of generosity stays with their spirit. There is no doubt in this.

However, that charity will be in the mode of *rajas,* not *satva.* When people move from this *rajas* state of giving to the *satva* state of giving, wealth seeks them out. Lakṣmī, the goddess of wealth, comes to them without being asked! She knows these people will be the route for benefiting mankind.

There is nothing degrading about wealth and power. They are great energies. Like all great energies, the problem is handling them without letting them go to one's head. As an example, look at the difference between Rāvaṇa and Janaka. Janaka was a *rājarṣi,* the king who was also a sage. He ruled a kingdom, but treated the power and wealth as if they belonged to someone else. He was a mere keeper, a mere witness. On the other hand, although highly gifted and a great *tapasvi* who undertook many severe penances, Rāvaṇa was ruled by his ego and senses. That brought about his ruin.

The universe operates on the principle of abundance. There is no shortage of anything in the universe. What we need, we get. The trouble is that we are dissatisfied with what we need. Our wants are immeasurable. Great masters have said that it is possible for the universe to fulfill the needs of all the people on planet earth, but not the wants of one single person. Our greed has no limits.

May your desire to give away be limitless. May your desire to acquire become zero. You will be amazed at how wealth seeks you.

Deeds, Words, And Thoughts

17.14 *The worship of deities, the priest, the guru, and the wise; purity, honesty, living in reality, and nonviolence are said to be austerity of deed.*

17.15 *Speech that is non-offensive, truthful, pleasant, beneficial, and is used for the regular study of scriptures is called austerity of word.*

17.16 *Serenity of mind, gentleness, equanimity, self-control, and purity of thought are called austerity of thought.*

17.17 *The above mentioned threefold austerity (of thought, word and deed), practiced by yogis with supreme sincerity, without a desire for the fruit, is said to be in the mode of goodness.*

17.18 *Austerity that is performed for gaining respect, honor, reverence, and for the sake of show, yielding an uncertain and temporary result, is said to be in the mode of aggression.*

17.19 *Austerity performed with foolish stubbornness or with self-torture or for harming others, is said to be in the mode of ignorance.*

Kṛṣṇa defines austerity of deeds, words and thoughts. *Tapas* or penance is the austere, simple way of living, the mode of *aparigraha* (simplicity). It is based upon what one needs and not what one craves for. One who successfully practices this is a *tapasvi.*

Kṛṣṇa explained earlier and repeats here that *tapasya,* austerity or penance, doesn't mean inflicting pain or torturing oneself and others. This includes not merely physical torture and pain, but also takes into account pain through words and thoughts. Penance undertaken in this manner is abusing oneself and the God who resides within, forgetting that the body is a temple of God.

Penance performed out of foolishness and self-torture destroys or injures others. Please understand, such acts are done out of ignorance. That's what I explained earlier with regard to black magic. No black magic can be done. No evil spirit can be sent to you. No one but an enlightened master can curse, and an enlightened master cannot curse. He can only bless.

Forget these negative things. Never be concerned about these things. All such actions are out of *tamas.* They never work and they disturb only the person who initiates them. They can never disturb others.

Lord Kṛṣṇa says that the people who are in *rajas* carry out sacrifices for the sake of respect, honor and worship. When they do penance or sacrifice in this manner, it is unstable. When people don't respect them, they stop doing it. They do it as long as people fall at their feet. If the respect is lost, they stop their *tapasya.*

Penance performed with the view of obtaining any result, (and even a noble ideal like enlightenment is a result) is in the mode of *rajas,* aggression or passion. Only when it is in the nature of total surrender, with no expectation of any results, it is in *satva* and of spiritual value.

When I talk about my *tapas* during my days of wandering all over India, I did difficult things. I realize now that many of these could have been dispensed with.

I experimented with ten thousand keys before I found the key to unlock the door to enlightenment. I tell my disciples that they do not need to go through that. There is an easier, faster and simpler way!

As long as I struggled towards enlightenment in my spiritual practices, it eluded me. I was able to realize myself only when I threw away my rosary and the photograph of Śrī RamaKṛṣṇa Paramahamsa that I had with me all those years, and sat down in meditation, with the feeling, 'Let what may happen, happen.'

Here, Kṛṣṇa uses the word *saumyatvaṁ* beautifully.

We have no exact English translation for this word *saumyatva*. *Saumyatvaṁ* refers to satisfaction and a feeling that is completely comfortable. It refers to one whose presence makes you feel totally relaxed, and induces thoughts that calm and center the mind. Please understand *saumyatva* and pleasing words are basic qualities to be practiced by a spiritual person.

Some people become enlightened, yet they can't help others. For example, I saw a great, enlightened swami living in the Himalayas who spent the whole day smoking *ganja*. No doubt he was enlightened. He put a copper coin in the *chillum* pipe with which he smoked *ganja*. You will be surprised that when he emptied the *chillum* pipe, a gold coin fell out! I witnessed this happen many times. He sold that coin to buy more *ganja*. He lived in Uttarkāśī (in Uttaranchal, North India). Of course, I had great respect for him because he was a *tapasvi*. He never wore any clothes. He was a *nāga-sādhu*.

Nāga means a *sanyāsi* who does not wear clothes. In that cold weather they lived without clothes. They are also called *paramahamsa*. *Paramahamsa sanyāsīs* do not wear clothing except to go into the city to spread the divine mission. Otherwise they are not supposed to wear clothes.

Paramahamsas live like children. When this *swami*, a great *paramahamsa*, emptied his *chillum*, there would be a gold coin in it. I asked him, 'Baba, you are a great *tapasvi*, an *atmajñāni* (one who has Self-knowledge) and a *brahmajñāni* (one who has knowledge of the *Brahman*), why are you smoking *ganja*?'

He said, 'A big elephant cannot be tied to a small hut. We must make it a little dull and silent. Only then can the elephant stay in the small hut. After enlightenment, the soul cannot stay in this small body. I must bring it down and make it dull. Then it can stay in this body. To bring it down, I do these things.' Of course, their smoking is different from an ordinary man's smoking.

Someone asked me, '*Swamiji*, Swami Vivekānanda and Rāmakṛṣṇa Paramahamsa used to smoke. Why can't I smoke?'

I explained to him, 'Swami Vivekānanda became enlightened before he started smoking. Become enlightened and then you can smoke and do whatever you want. Without achieving what they achieved, doing what they did is wrong.' Please understand that whatever enlightened masters do is totally different from what you are supposed to do. Actually, they do things opposite of what you are supposed to do. You must do things to elevate yourself. They must do things to bring themselves down!

This *nāga-sādhu* in Uttarkāśī is enlightened; however, he cannot help everybody. His type is such he will not help people. He is a mystic. He will not teach anybody and he will not make anybody enlightened. He does not work with people. He is that type.

On the other hand, some people who experience the truth share the truth with the world. Swami Vivekānanda and Paramahamsa Yogānanda were great souls who shared their experiences for the benefit of others. That was their mission. Bhāgavatam says that people who explain or share the truth, such as Kṛṣṇa, are incarnations.

Sukha Brahma was the son of Vyāsa, the compiler of the *Vedas* and author of Bhāgavatam and Mahābhārata. Sukha Brahma *ṛṣi* was an enlightened master who wore no clothes.

Sukha Brahma was questioned, 'What is the difference between enlightened people and *avatārs* or incarnations?'

Sukha Brahma says beautifully: *soundaryatva, tejavastva, sārasvatya,* and the power, *lakṣmītva. Soundaryatva* means that if we see them, we will automatically feel like sitting and listening to them. We will automatically feel like turning around once more to capture their grace! That which simply attracts our mind is *soundaryatva.*

The next attribute is *tejas*, a sharp radiating energy and clarity. The third is *sārasvatya*. This means that no matter how difficult a concept or idea is, they can explain it in a simple way. It merely flows from their tongue where Saraswatī (goddess of knowledge) resides.

Above all is *lakṣmītva*. This means that just by their thought, wealth and work will happen. Everything happens according to how they want it to happen. When somebody radiates all four of these qualities, he is an incarnation.

Radiating enlightenment

Here, Kṛṣṇa says the same thing, *saumyatva*. Please understand, even for incarnations, *soundarya* and *saumyatva* are necessary qualities. Now surely we should imbibe these qualities in our lives.

The penance that is supposed to be done by words is speaking the truth and speaking pleasing words, *priyahitaṁ ca yat*. Please understand, creating a healing effect through words is important. Creating a healing effect through our words is basic for a spiritual practitioner. We should not utter words that hurt others. Our presence should be healing.

Always use pleasing words. Never use sharp or disturbing words.

One more thing, sometimes we don't understand how our words disturb others. We do not know how our words disrespect or emotionally disturb other beings. We must be careful about our speech.

When we sit with somebody, that person should feel, 'Can I sit for a longer time with him? Can I spend more time with him? Can I meet him tomorrow? Will I see him again?' We should create that healing feeling in the other person. People should wait for us rather than run away from us. Usually we create a negative effect. We create an uncomfortable feeling. People just run away from us. A simple, single word if used improperly, can destroy a whole relationship.

Lord Kṛṣṇa says a spiritual person should use pleasing words and not agitate others. When we do not agitate others, we will not be arrogant. See, this is not even social morality. This is a spiritual practice.

As I explained the other day, the same words we use to hurt others will hurt us as well. We will use these same words towards ourselves as well. This truth is embedded in the science of energy and vibration. So we must be clear about the words we use. Kṛṣṇa says to study spiritual literature regularly. By regularly studying scriptural literature, these ideas go again and again into our brain. Consequently, we acquire courage to experiment with the truth. We acquire courage to work with these truths.

I ask you to take up any truth and practice it at least a few times. For example, yesterday I told you not to continuously function based on the idea 'me, me, me.' Instead try the idea 'you, you, you.' Try that at least ten times and see the effect in your life. If it does not work out, you can throw it away, it's up to you, but at least try it out ten times. You will glimpse the truth expressed by Kṛṣṇa.

Intellectuals have two weapons: words and logic. They can be helpful teaching tools if properly used or they can be frightening weapons. It is up to us to choose how to use them: whether in the mode of ignorance, aggression or goodness.

Our words and thoughts can affect water and we are composed almost entirely of water. That is why words hurt us so much or they heal us so much. Through words we can work miracles.

Kṛṣṇa talks about austerity in action as well. He speaks about the five conditions that are also in Patañjali's Ashtanga Yoga as the five disciplines of *yama: satya, ahiṁsā, asteya, aparigraha* and *brahmacarya.* These mean truth in thoughts, words and deeds embodying nonviolence, non-covetousness, simplicity and living in reality with the focus on the Supreme as the ultimate in any kind of penance.

Many feel that the truth must be told even if it hurts. Please understand that if it hurts someone, it cannot be the truth. It is only our perception of the truth. It is only a reflection of our ego presented by our mind as truth. We are not in the truth if we perceive something with our senses and we draw conclusions with our limited knowledge based upon those perceptions, and then express these as our truth and hurt someone. If we do this, be very clear, we are in aggression and ignorance. We are not in the truth. We are not in goodness.

Truth is a reflection of compassion. Truth is an expression of compassion. Truth and compassion always go together. For that reason, truth can never hurt. It can only heal.

How To Give?

17.20 *Charity that is given at the right place and time as a matter of duty to a deserving candidate who does nothing in return is considered to be in the mode of goodness.*

17.21 *Charity that is given unwillingly or to get something in return or to gain some result is in the mode of aggression.*

17.22 *Charity that is given at a wrong place and time to unworthy persons or without paying respect to the receiver or with ridicule is in the mode of ignorance.*

Kṛṣṇa speaks about the concept of *dāna* (charity), which I explained earlier. Charity is sharing. It is not done with the attitude of giving. It is done with the attitude of sharing and not expecting good results because of it or some easy route into heaven because of it. Charity is done out of love and gratitude.

'O God, you have given me so much, now let me share a little bit with society and with the world.' Charity is the attitude of sharing. Charity that is done out of duty, without any expectation means feeling committed to the Whole, to God, and with that feeling, giving as a natural commitment. It is given with the attitude that 'It is my quality and I have to do it.' Only then it becomes real *dāna*. Sharing at the proper time and place and to a worthy person is charity in the mode of goodness.

There are three kinds of *dāna*. Understand, *annadāna* means giving food, clothes and whatever is related for someone's physical needs. Next is *vidyādāna.* This means giving education and also whatever someone needs for mental growth. For example, when somebody is depressed, if you give him or her some consoling ideas, that is *vidyādāna.* If somebody does not know how to clean a room and you teach him or her, that is *vidyādāna.* If somebody does not know how to cut grass and you teach him, that is *vidyādāna.*

The ultimate charity - *jñānadāna*

And the third kind is *jñānadāna,* giving spiritual knowledge.

If we give *annadāna,* we satisfy a person for three hours. After three hours, again he needs food. If we give *vidyādāna,* education or knowledge, he will have food for himself for one life. If we give education, he can earn food for himself. He will make money and buy food for himself. If we give *jñānadāna,* we will satisfy that person birth after birth! *Annadāna* satisfies for three hours. *Vidyādāna* satisfies the receiver for one life. If we give *jñānadāna,* it fulfills that person for life after life. He will never fall into depression or the ocean of material world, birth after birth.

Jñānadāna is the ultimate charity.

The common expression says, 'If a person needs fish and we feed or buy him a fish, he can be satisfied for one meal.' This is *annadāna.* 'If we teach him how to fish, he can manage his whole life without hunger.' This is *vidyādāna.* This is where the expression stops.

In our Healer's Initiation Program, we tell them to stop eating fish! That solves their problem for many cycles of birth. This is *jñānadāna*!

Understand one thing: even if you have come and sat here accidentally after looking at my pictures saying, 'I saw a cutout or poster. He is so young. The poster says that he is speaking on Bhagavad Gītā. Let me see what he is saying...' Even if you have come just to check it out, and you land up hearing the whole Gītā, it will help you. At some point in time, you will remember these truths and execute them. Naturally you cannot be the same person again. At some point in time when you are about to make a mistake, you will remember these truths. These thoughts have gone inside you. They will make you correct yourself choicelessly. This is *jñānadāna*.

The knowledge that you have received now will transform your whole life even if you don't practice it. These words are so powerful that automatically they will start working on you. You will not remain the same person. Your depth of depression will be reduced. Your depth of suffering will be reduced. You will feel that you are entering a new life. Your life will become courageous and a new confidence will enter your life. This is *jñānadāna*. This is the ultimate *puṇya* (virtuous deed) of giving knowledge. No other good deed is equivalent to giving spiritual knowledge.

Giving food bestows three hours of satisfaction. Giving education gives satisfaction for this one life. Giving spiritual knowledge satisfies souls life after life. Kṛṣṇa says when charity is done purely out of a feeling of sharing, it is *satvika*, the ultimate good, the ultimate purity.

One more point is that the person who gives loses nothing with *jñānadāna*. With all other *dāna*, the person who gives has a little less. In *annadāna*, he who gives will lose and he who receives will gain. In *vidyādāna*, the giver does not lose. He retains the same level. In *jñānadāna*, I tell you a secret: the more you share, the more it grows in you! It is a win-win situation. Here, you receive automatically. It grows in the person who shares it.

And I tell you another important secret: Don't think you are the only one benefiting by hearing me now. By expressing these things, even I am benefited.

A simple analogy will help explain how this happens. When a woman gives birth to a child, not only is the child born, the woman too takes birth as a mother. Until then she is only a woman. Once she gives birth, she is called 'mother.' When a child takes birth, not only does the child take birth, even the mother takes birth. Before that she is not a mother.

She is only a woman. The moment she gives birth to a child, both the child and the mother are born.

In the same way, when you receive spiritual knowledge from me, I also grow!

That is why in the *vedic* system, they recite the following *mantra* before spiritual lessons:

Oṁ sahanāvavatu sahanau bhunaktu

saha vīryam karavāvahai

tejasvi nāvadhītamastu mā vidvishāvahai

Oṁ śhānti śhānti śhāntih

This *śhānti* or peace *mantra* means: may we both (master and disciple) achieve perfection. May both of us grow. May both of us help each other. May we not have enmity towards each other.

Understand, the *mantra* doesn't say, 'May *you* learn.' It says, 'May *both of us* learn.' The *vedic* system is so humble. To tell you the truth, when I speak, I also learn.

Somebody asked me, '*Swamiji*, what are you going to speak about?'

I said, 'Who knows? Just like you, I also sit and listen!'

Here all I have in front of me are Sanskrit verses. I read the verse and speak whatever comes forth spontaneously; that's all. Just like you, I also sit and listen. Just as you are benefited, I am also benefited. Both of us grow. Only an egoistic person thinks that only the disciple is benefited. No! The master also benefits. He can become a master only when a disciple happens!

Only when a child is born is the woman called a mother. Only when a disciple becomes enlightened, the *guru* becomes a master. Otherwise, he is not a master. If the woman is unable to give birth to a child, she cannot be a mother. Similarly, until *you* become enlightened, I cannot be called a master. Be very clear, by sharing this knowledge, I also grow. The person who shares with simplicity and humility, who is very clear and honest about the whole truth of sharing and is not caught in the false ego, his *dāna,* his sharing of thoughts is *satvika* and is related to *satva guṇa* – the attribute of goodness.

When you ask questions, if I don't know the answer, I say I don't know the answer. People ask, 'What is this? *Swamiji,* you are enlightened and you say you don't know.'

I tell them, 'Only an enlightened master says 'I don't know.' Only he has the courage to accept the truth. If a normal person doesn't know, he minces words. He puts some words here and there and confuses the audience.'

Confusing the audience is not a complicated job. It is easy because they are already confused! There is nothing more to be done. Just use some words. That's all. And it's not a big thing. Only an enlightened person is courageous enough to say, 'I don't know' when he doesn't know.

To answer a question without knowledge doesn't require enlightenment. It needs foolish hypocrisy. The straightforward, honest approach to the truth is what Kṛṣṇa calls *satvika dāna.*

Here, in whatever way I experience the truth, I simply express it and share it - honestly, without reservation. That is *satvika dāna* according to Kṛṣṇa. And He goes on to explain *rajas dāna* and *tamas dāna.*

Many times, the *dāna* is not given voluntarily. Or they may give something away as a part of a ritual. For example, in a Hindu wedding the giving away of a bride is called *kanya dāna.*

Earlier I spoke about people who give their property for charitable purposes in their will. What choice do they have? They cannot carry it with them. In many cases they may have fought with their children and decided not to leave them anything. Probably the son or daughter did not listen to their arranged marriage proposal and instead married by falling in love. So instead of giving away the wealth to their children, these people give it away as charity. Such acts are not acts of charity. They are done with ulterior motives.

There are others whose charity it is better not to accept. Kṛṣṇa refers to this as giving in ignorance. People will come with money not declared for tax as earned income and gift that to the ashram. They will use it as a tax saving strategy. What for?

Often, disciples ask why do I not accept donations from very wealthy people who come to the ashram seeking help. Unless the person stays with me for a year or more and shows his sincerity towards the mission, it is difficult to accept anything from that person. Why become bonded to people whose motives are not merely selfish but self-defeating?

Parāśakti (Existence) guides the mission and She takes care. What She cannot give, no one else can give. What She decides not to give, who else can give?

Thou Art That

17.23 'Om̐ Tat Sat' is said to be the threefold name of the Eternal Being (Brahma). Persons with good (brahmanic) qualities, the Vedas, and the selfless service (seva, yajña) *were created by and from Brahma in the ancient times.*
17.24 Therefore, acts of sacrifice, charity, and austerity prescribed in the scriptures are always commenced by uttering 'OṀ ' by the knowers of the Supreme being.
17.25 Various types of sacrifice, charity, and austerity are performed by the seekers of liberation by uttering 'Tat' (or He is all) without seeking a reward.
17.26 The word 'Sat' is used in the sense of Reality and goodness. The word 'Sat' is also used for an auspicious act, O Arjuna.
17.27 Sincerity in sacrifice, charity, and austerity is also called 'Sat'. Selfless service for the sake of the Supreme is, in truth, termed as 'Sat'.
17.28 Whatever is done without sincerity, whether it is sacrifice, charity, austerity, or any other act is called 'Asat.' It has no value here or hereafter, O Arjuna.

In conclusion, Kṛṣṇa moves on to a different plane altogether. So far He explained sacrifice, austerity and charity. He clarified what needs to be done and how. He spelled out the different modes based on the nature of people in relation to performing sacrifice, austerity and charity.

Please understand that all kinds of food, penance, sacrifice or charity fall into the basic three categories explained by Kṛṣṇa - *satvic, rajasic* and *tamasic*. These translate as the modes of goodness, passion and ignorance.

But the important thing is that as long as they are done in the materialistic world, they are conditioned. When they are done with the attitude of gratitude to the Divine and Existence, only then you encounter spiritual progress or spiritual elevation. Our scriptures explain that anything done in the nature of *rajas* or *tamas* cannot give the ultimate result. Only the act done in the attitude of *satva* or goodness gives the final result. One who does such acts without this awareness has temporary results but not the final result.

In the days of Mahābhārata, sacrificial rituals were part and parcel of daily life. This is not the case today. The *brāhmaṇas* (highly learned sect of people) were the keepers of the sacred knowledge that connected the physical ritual with the metaphysical truth expressed by the great sages in the *Vedas*. They were the keepers of the flame, in a real sense, since most *vedic* rituals invoked and addressed the fire energy. Sacrifices were directed towards elemental energies and celestial beings. Austerity was directed towards your own self. Charity was directed towards those around you.

The *brāhmaṇas* were expected to lead an austere and charitable life in keeping with the spirit of their profession. In this chapter Kṛṣṇa elaborates on these concepts so that everyone can move forward on the path to liberation. It is not only for the *brāhmaṇas,* it is also for *kṣatriyas, vaiśyas* and *śūdras* - the other castes. Any member of any caste is qualified for liberation if he follows these principles. Liberation has nothing to do with birth.

The prime requirement is sincerity, *śraddha. Śraddha* refers as well to the understanding that sacrifice, austerity or charity is not directed towards oneself or a material goal. They are directed to the Ssupreme consciousness.

In the last three verses Kṛṣṇa provides the technique to achieve this transfer of focus from self to Self. He provides the method by which anyone can surrender the results of his activities, the fruits of his action (called *karma phala)* to the Divine. He provides the tool in the form of the invocation, *Oṁ Tat Sat.*

The three words *Oṁ Tat Sat* are the words of the Divine — *Om iti etat brahmano nedistham namaḥ,* shows the first goal, the beginning. *Tat tvam asi* indicates the second goal, the continuation. *Sat eva saumya* is the third goal or final result. All three combined give the words *Oṁ Tat Sat.*

This is why these words have such great importance or significance. Any person doing charity or work with the attitude of addressing *Oṁ Tat Sat* will be with Existence, the divine consciousness.

These three words simply imply: 'I offer all to that Truth. I surrender everything to that Divine. Let that be the Truth.' This is the *mahāvākya,* the great truth, handed down by the master to Arjuna as the technique to ensure sincerity in all activities of sacrifice, austerity and charity.

Please understand that any action, whether penance, charity or sacrifice, has no meaning when the purpose is not to achieve the Ultimate, the Divine.

The final aim in all the *Vedas* is to gain the experience of Kṛṣṇa or the supreme consciousness. No success, fulfillment or happiness is possible without following this principle.

The *guru* or spiritual master is the only being who can help you and guide you to make your life successful and fulfilled.

Understand, people are conditioned to worship all kinds of deities or demi-gods or spirits right from birth based on the nature of their *guṇas.* But the path of achieving the ultimate consciousness, the understanding of Kṛṣṇa, goes beyond and transcends all three *guṇas*.

This is where the role of a *guru* or spiritual master is important. He directs and leads you on the path of proper understanding for an experience of the ultimate consciousness. Such an understanding, such a perception, leads to faith and ultimately to love of the Divine. This is the purpose and final goal of life.

Let us all pray to *Parabrahma* Kṛṣṇa with all sincerity to give us the experience of this chapter of Gītā that leads to attainment of the ultimate consciousness, *nityānanda*!

Let us all experience the sincerity and imbibe and experience the truths of *Parabrahma* Kṛṣṇa (cosmic Kṛṣṇa). Let us pray to Him to give us all the sincerity and experience of the truth that He is teaching through the Gītā to all of us, and let Him make us experience and establish ourselves in eternal bliss, *nityānanda*!

Thus ends the seventeenth chapter named **Śraddhātraya Vibhāga Yogaḥ** *of the* **Upaniṣad** *of the* ***Bhagavad Gītā****, the scripture of Yoga, dealing with the science of the Absolute in the form of the dialogue between* ***Śrī Kṛṣṇa*** *and Arjuna.*

BhagavadGītā

Drop Everything And Surrender

Mokṣa Sanyāsa Yogaḥ

Chapter 18

*There is nothing to surrender except the 'I' and 'mine'. **Kṛṣṇa** explains how surrender brings the ultimate freedom - Enlightenment.*

Drop Everything And Surrender

Drop everything and surrender. This is the gist not only of this final chapter of Bhagavad Gītā, it is also the essence of the entire Bhagavad Gītā.

Drop everything, whatever you know as *dharma*, whatever you know as life, whatever you think you know, just drop it. Whatever you know is only your knowledge; it is just what *you* know. It is not what *is*.

Knowledge doesn't prove Existence

In fact, wisdom and truth are about what we do not know. Knowledge of the mind, which we take so much pride in, functions like blinders that we wear to shut out the truth of Existence. The French philosopher Rene Descartes said, 'I think, therefore I am.' The mind is not the scale of measure of existence.

What we are has nothing to do with our thoughts. If our thoughts alone could circumscribe what we are, we would be nothing more than a biomechanical machine.

Animals have greater innate intelligence than humans. Animals do not clutter their minds with fantasies like humans do. They simply flow with nature.

A lion or tiger hunts for food when it is hungry. It eats when it must eat and sleeps when it is tired. No wild animal stores food, except in rare cases when dictated by Nature. No animal in the wild becomes obese.

Humans think. That is the problem. Our great sages, the ancient *ṛṣis*, declared the opposite of Descartes. They say, 'Drop your mind and you will be aware. You will realize your true potential as a human.'

Ādi Śaṅkarācārya, one of the greatest Hindu philosophers, proclaims this so beautifully in the verses of his Ātma Ṣaṭakam. To define what he truly is, his inner divinity, Śaṅkara negates his body, mind, senses, emotions, and all his relationships.

Understand, we are spiritual beings in human form and not human beings striving to be spiritual. Our intelligence is unlimited. But our intellect *is* limited.

Knowledge is of three kinds. The first, and the least relevant type, is acquired through the mind and intellect. Scientific knowledge such as physics, math, medicine, etc., falls into this category. We believe this knowledge enhances the quality of our lives. The more we acquire knowledge belonging to this first category, the more disturbed we become.

The second type of knowledge cannot be taught in the same way as intellectual knowledge. This type of knowledge must be learned. Creative arts belong to this type. We cannot learn to sing, dance, or write by reading a book. We must first imbibe and then we must express. In addition to the head and intellect, one's heart and emotions must be involved. Knowledge based on the heart is based upon intellect plus something more.

The third and highest type of knowledge is from the being. It is conveyed from the being to the being. This knowledge is the 'aha' experience that happens so rarely. The greatest discoveries and inventions are this type of knowledge. This is communion, as opposed to communication at the intellectual level and collaboration at the emotional level. Knowledge at the being level is a combination of knowledge of the head, knowledge of the heart, plus something more.

Even knowledge about God creates bondage when it is merely intellectual, because we will only know about God. Knowing *about* God is not the same as *knowing* God. When we completely surrender everything we will not even have the idea that we know God. When that idea does not exist in us, we know God.

Words do not express God. God manifests when expressions cease. Zen masters say that the finger pointing to the moon is not the moon. Words about God in any form, however sincere they may be, are mere pointers and reminders.

The problem with religions is that they teach us *about* God. They do not teach us how to know God. Religions tell us a few things about God and instill fear and greed in us.

How many religions have helped enlighten people? Millions of people have been massacred in the name of preserving and propagating religions. Religions caused destruction and death, not enlightenment.

Spiritual masters never preached that one should kill another, or cajole, coerce, and convert. No spiritual master preached violence. If he did, he would be no master!

Great spiritual masters aim to awaken individual consciousness, so that we become aware that we are part of the collective consciousness of this universe. They come with a mission to make us understand that we must move from the attitude of 'I' to 'you' and 'us.'

The ignorant followers of the great masters built religious institutions based upon their limited understanding of the truths that the masters expressed. Unlike spirituality that spreads love among people, religion fosters violence.

Enlightenment is a gift. It makes no difference what effort we put in. We may have stood on one leg for hundreds of years or may have done other penances. These are equivalent to buying the one-dollar lottery ticket. What we receive in return is a pure gift. Whatever we do is within the dream. How can that get us something beyond the dream?

Kṛṣṇa says, 'Drop everything and surrender.' The word surrender itself frightens people. We must understand that we are not going to lose anything when we surrender. We are only going to gain everything.

Surrender and understand

Realize first of all that we have nothing of any value to surrender! We only think we do. We simply need to open our eyes and see that everything that *is*, is divine. The 'I' and 'mine' that we hold onto are mere lies. The moment we understand this, we surrender. The moment we surrender, we understand.

When we call something 'mine,' legally it may belong to us, but existentially it does not. Legally we can fence off a piece of land and call it ours. But Nature or Existence does not know that it is ours. When a cyclone hits, it does not care whose property it is. For Existence there is no law.

Our idea of 'mine' is protected by the laws of society. We cannot truly use the term 'law of the land.' The land has no laws. Only society has laws. The land can have an earthquake at any time. We cannot have laws to govern Nature. As long as you are caught with the concept of 'I' and 'mine,' you will not understand the truth about Existence.

When Kṛṣṇa tells us to drop everything and surrender, He asks us to open our eyes and see the foolishness of the drama we play with our possessions and expectations. It is one thing if you play the game to cheat others; however, do not cheat yourself.

Can whatever you think of as 'I,' either your body or mind, function without air? Can you say that the air belongs to you? This basic energy, *prāna,* which goes in and comes out, does not belong to you. If *prāna* stops happening what you think of as 'you' disappears.

It is like saying that the foundation does not belong to me, but the first floor of the house is mine! You can do that legally, but it is impossible existentially. The earth that it sits on does not belong to you either. The earth can give one small shake, and whatever you thought was yours just disappears!

The very foundation of whatever you think is 'you' does not belong to you. The base or root of what you think of as 'you' does not belong to you, but belongs to Nature.

We take for granted the air that continuously goes in and comes out. Maybe if God called a strike, like a workers' union strike, we would understand that we cannot take even the air for granted. But He is a *Karuṇāmūrti,* god of mercy. Out of His compassion He never goes on strike! That is why we take life for granted. Just because certain things belong to us legally, we think that the concept of 'mine' is solid.

Anybody who is intelligent enough to open his eyes and see realizes that 'I' and 'mine' are a drama. The moment the air that goes in does not come out, it is over. 'I' disappears. Immediately your name will be taken from the name board outside your house and put on your tombstone. You will be taken to the place where you can rest forever!

Sometimes even the piece of land that we think belongs to us we may find doesn't, when we see the papers of that land! Our life itself is built on paper. The moment we have the intelligence to see this, the moment we wake up to this reality, we achieve the state of surrender. We immediately experience tremendous relief from the need to continuously protect ourselves.

The two instincts to hold onto 'I' and 'mine' are the reasons for physical and mental problems. The instinct to survive and the instinct to possess are the root cause of our problems. On the other hand, when we realize that the 'I' and 'mine' do not exist, we realize how foolish we have been in spending our whole life and energy in building sandcastles.

A small Zen story:

Some children were playing on the beach, making sandcastles the whole day. At the end of the day they jumped on the castles and destroyed everything that they had taken the whole day to make. And they enjoyed that, too! A Zen master sat nearby and watched the whole scene. He merely said, 'This is life.'

A king also watched this scene. Then one child started crying because another child smashed his sandcastle. The king laughed and said, 'How foolish to cry over a sandcastle.'

> The Zen master laughed at the king. The king became angry and asked, 'Why are you laughing?'
>
> The master explained, 'At least these kids know that they are playing when they make and break sandcastles. In contrast, when you make and break stone castles you think you are doing something real. The children are more aware than you; yet you call them foolish. That is why I am laughing.'

Actually, our life is pseudo-life. The way children live is real life. They understand that it has no value intrinsically. One day it will be built and the next day destroyed. They are not emotionally disturbed. But if our castles are shaken we have a problem. The whole thing is pure fun! We must understand that whatever way we live and whatever we may build does not belong to us. If we do not internalize the outer incidents, and treat them with the indifference they deserve, we experience what I call surrender.

Do not internalize sensory input and do not take things too seriously. When you take life too seriously you can be sure of one thing, and that is sickness. The moment you believe that there is an 'I' in your being you start moving away from life.

The idea that you have of yourself has no base, whatever you may think of as you. Sometimes you think you are the body. Sometimes you think you are the mind, and other times, you think you are the senses. No matter what you identify yourself with, it is baseless.

Whatever aspect you think of as 'you' will not grow. If you think you are the body, you stop the growth of the body, because you do not like change. When you think you are the mind, you stop the growth of the mind. That is the reason egoistic people cannot listen to new ideas or read about them. They think that they already know and have nothing more to learn. When you think that your mind is you, the very attitude of learning, the beginner's mind, is lost.

If you think you are the body, you do not let the body rejuvenate itself. You do not let your body do its regular work. If you think you are the mind, you do not let it learn anything new. You do not allow anything new to enter. That is a sure way of destroying it.

The same applies to what you consider as 'mine.' This is based on the laws of society. In no way is it related to the laws of Existence.

You are not who you think you are

It is well known to science that of the trillions of cells in our body-mind system, millions of cells die each day and millions of cells are reborn. After a few years, there isn't a single cell in our body that existed two years earlier. Every single entity in the body is new. This means that the constant 'I' that we imagine to be does not exist. Yet, we carry that label proudly.

All we are is a bunch of memories, value systems, and beliefs, collectively known as *saṁskāras*. Our *saṁskāras* define us. And our *saṁskāras* make decisions for us. That is what this 'I' is all about.

We conduct Life Bliss Programs on meditation to eliminate these *saṁskāras*, because *saṁskāras* rule us and we make our decisions unconsciously. We live unconsciously and instinctively, instead of consciously and intuitively. When we are focused on the 'I', our responses are unconscious and instinctive. They are defensive and protective. Studies have shown that when cells are in a protective mode they cannot grow. As long as we are focused on 'I,' we never grow.

The feeling of 'I' arises from the *svādiṣṭhāna cakra,* the spleen energy center, where the Self is established. This is the seat of insecurity. Until we relinquish our fears by energizing this *cakra,* we desperately grasp the apparent security of 'I.'

The feeling of 'mine' is more primal than that of 'I.' 'Mine,' the ideas of survival and possession, precedes the identity of 'I.' It arises from the *mūlādhāra cakra,* the root energy center. All emotional blocks like lust, greed, and anger arise through this feeling of possession.

Giving up possessiveness and identity are difficult when we are conditioned the way we are, yet it is not impossible. In the Nithyananda Order, all the teachers who take up mission work and conduct the Life Bliss Programs change their names to spiritual names that I give them.

Why do they change their names, sometimes even at the age of sixty? They will tell you that for the first time in their lives they feel a sense of liberation and freedom. They feel reborn and they celebrate. Initially people told me that it would be difficult to find teachers who are willing to change their names, since most people would not like to give up their past identity. The truth is that when you truly understand what this is, you sincerely wish to give up your past identity.

Similarly, when we give up our possessions and attachment to possessions, we feel liberation. When I walked out of my home for spiritual wandering I felt no loss. Today the whole world is my home!

This does not mean that all of you need to become monks, renunciants, and *sanyāsīs*. You can happily continue your normal life, but drop your attachments, fantasies, speculations, greed, and fear.

You need not renounce what you already have. All you need to do to achieve happiness is to renounce what you *do not* have.

This one statement has been a clarion call for awakening thousands of people. For the first time in their lives, they understood the mistakes they were making. By dropping fantasies about the future, which had no existence, and by dropping regrets and guilt about their past, about which nothing could be done, they reached a state of happiness that had thus far eluded them.

Renunciation does not mean sitting cross-legged with a tense look and eyes closed. Renunciation is a state of mind and not a mere state of the body. It is a state of being. We can renounce attachments to relationships and possessions while being involved in material life. On the other hand, we could take *sanyās,* go to the distant Himalayas, and every time we close our eyes our inner television would switch on.

The surrender that Kṛṣṇa talks about involves dropping fantasies and surrendering to reality. The true reality, the only truth, is that we are part of the collective consciousness. When we have this awareness, there is no room for the individual 'I' and 'mine' to rule our actions.

Again and again Kṛṣṇa speaks about renunciation: How we should surrender the fruits of action to Him without renouncing the action itself, and how all knowledge and action should be surrendered at His feet. He prepares Arjuna for this final moment when He tells him that all that needs to be done is to surrender.

Surrender is of three kinds. The first step is the surrender of the intellect. For most people, especially intellectuals, this is the easiest. Your ego must be ripe before it can fall. The more stuff you pack into your thick skull, the more bloated it becomes. When someone appears on the scene and proves that intellectual knowledge is a pile of garbage, a person with a truly ripe intellectual ego understands and accepts the truth. When this happens, such a person surrenders his intellect to the master who shows him the way. Only those with half-baked knowledge, who pretend to have intellectual status, have a problem in understanding such a truth. Many intellectual seekers and spiritual shoppers come to me with loads of questions. After spending time with me, most of them tell me, with great surprise, that they no longer have questions. I don't take the trouble to answer their questions. All I do is add more words to them. They struggle with the new words and ultimately find the right answers themselves!

When I do answer, I answer the questioner. I look into his being and provide the solution.

The next step in surrender is the surrender of the heart. People ask how they will remember me when they go away from the ashram. I tell them that if I am their master they will have trouble forgetting me! The thought of the master will melt your heart. You will become emotional. You do not need to be in the master's physical presence. The mere thought is enough. Tears will flow from your eyes. Ramakṛṣṇa says, 'Know this for sure: When the mere thought of your *iṣṭadevatā* (favorite deity) or your master reduces you to tears, you are in your final *janma*, your final birth.'

What an enlightened master says is always true. So powerful is this surrender that it can liberate you, enlighten you. This is the power of devotion, *bhakti*. Kṛṣṇa keeps repeating that this is the easiest way to reach Him. He says, 'Just be devoted to Me and Me alone, and I shall save you.'

The third and final form of surrender is the surrender of the senses. When the surrender of senses happens, enlightenment happens, and when enlightenment happens, the surrender of the senses happens.

Walking with Arjuna after the Mahābhārata war, Kṛṣṇa points to a bird on a tree and remarks, 'Arjuna, look at that green crow!'

Arjuna responds, 'Yes, Kṛṣṇa, I see the green crow.'

Kṛṣṇa says, 'What a fool you are! How can a crow be green?'

Arjuna simply says, 'Kṛṣṇa, when you told me to look at that green crow, what I saw was indeed a green crow.'

Such was the state of Arjuna's surrender to his master, whatever He said was what Arjuna's eyes saw. This is the final state of surrender.

It may surprise you that an enlightened master has no freedom to do what he wishes. Ordinary people have the freedom to do what they wish. Each of you has full freedom to do what you wish. After doing what you want and then suffering, you claim it was because of your destiny! In contrast, every word I utter is at the command of *Parāśakti*, the cosmic energy.

Kṛṣṇa's advice to Arjuna, and to all seekers, is to drop everything and surrender unto Him. That is the only and final solution.

The Act And The Actor

18.1 *Arjuna said, 'Kṛṣṇa, Killer of the demon Keśī, I wish to understand what the essence of renunciation is and what being a monk is.'*

Arjuna speaks now, after being silent for a long time. He will stop speaking soon. He is not questioning. He just expresses a few doubts. The arrogance or violence in Arjuna's being has disappeared. He has become like a flower due tothe experience of the cosmic vision that Kṛṣṇa showered on him.

Sometimes after listening to the whole discourse, disciples ask me to repeat a joke or a story once more! They have heard it once but want to hear it again. Especially from the master, listening to certain things again and again gives great joy.

The words of a master are energy. These words drill deep into you and transform you. At the time of listening, you may not realize their impact. Arjuna asks some of these questions in order to hear Kṛṣṇa again.

Arjuna says, 'O Mighty One, I wish to understand the purpose of renunciation and of the monastic life of *sanyās.* Please tell me the truth.'

A small story:

A man calls the lawyer's office and asks to speak to his ex-wife's lawyer.

The secretary says, 'I'm sorry Sir, but the lawyer passed away yesterday.'

The man expresses the usual condolences and disconnects. Ten minutes later, for the second time, he calls and asks to speak to his ex-wife's lawyer.

The secretary says, 'I told you ten minutes ago that he passed away last night.' Once more the man thanks her and disconnects.

Again, after ten minutes, he calls the lawyer's office and asks to talk to his ex-wife's lawyer. Now the secretary becomes a little angry and says, 'I already told you that you cannot talk to him. He died yesterday. Can't you understand?'

The man replies, 'Yes ma'am, I understand. But it gives me such joy to hear it that I am calling again and again!'

Arjuna too wants to listen to the same truth again and again.

In India it is often difficult to distinguish a renunciant, a *sanyāsi,* from a common beggar. Both seek alms. Both possess very little. And both are homeless. Many people take the easy path and treat the *sanyāsi* like a beggar and shoo him off.

I tell my disciples, 'When in doubt treat the beggar as if he were a monk. Some people tell me, 'But *Swamiji,* they are cheating us!'

Get cheated, that's all. When you give, give unconditionally or don't give at all. If you expect that a monk will bless you if you give and that the blessing will have effect, why can't the blessing of a beggar have the same effect?

Quite often people give to those wearing a monk's garb because they are conditioned to give to them and they are afraid to refuse. They believe that if the monk curses them they will have problems. So, giving alms to a *sanyāsi* is like taking out insurance. You are afraid you may go to hell.

Please understand, there is no hell or heaven. These are illusions used by religions to control you through fear of hell and greed for heaven. No one keeps a list of your merits and offences. God does not pronounce judgment based on a list.

I tell people who wish to donate to my mission and ashram, not to do it hoping that they will be guaranteed a place in heaven. 'There will be no Nithyananda waiting to guide you into heavenly suites when you die,' I tell them. When you do good deeds in this world, you are already in heaven. When you cause problems to everyone and yourself, you are in hell.

Give unconditionally if you can afford it. Give even if you cannot afford it. That is when giving becomes truly effective. When you sacrifice what you cannot afford to sacrifice, by the mere act of giving you become a renunciant, a *sanyāsi.*

Arjuna is confused about the act and the actor. What is important is the act. Anyone can be the actor.

Charity Must Be Selfless

18.2 *Kṛṣṇa said, the wise describe the essence of sanyās as giving up all selfish work based on desire, and renunciation as the freedom from all attachment to the results of one's actions.*

18.3 *Some learned men say that all kinds of result-based activities are sins and should be given up, but there are yet other sages who maintain that acts of service, charity, and austerity should never be given up.*

18.4 *Arjuna, here is what I say about renunciation; there are three kinds of renunciation explained.*

18.5 *Acts of service, charity, and austerity are not to be given up; they should be performed. Even the sages are purified by sacrifice, charity, and penance.*

18.6 *Arjuna, all acts of duty must also be performed without any expectation of result. That is My considered opinion.*

Kṛṣṇa replies: 'Bhārata, now hear my judgment about renunciation. Renunciation is of many types. Let me explain the truth.'

Bhagavān says that some learned masters say that giving up activities based on material desires is renunciation. Others say that giving up the results is renunciation, *tyāg*.

No other master is as compassionate as Kṛṣṇa. Again and again He comes down and explains the truths step-by-step.

Some learned people recommend ritualistic actions, such as killing an animal for a sacrifice. Other learned people denounce that act. Kṛṣṇa clarifies these opinions now.

Sacrifice defined

After all, it is Kṛṣṇa in the form of the Ultimate who originally created the scriptures and laws; therefore, any explanation from Him should be considered the last word. He says that any process of renunciation should be considered within the context in which it is performed. Renunciation can be of three types: sacrifice, charity, and penance. These purify even those who are already evolved and pure.

It must be understood that the purpose of performing sacrifices is the purification, or upliftment, of the human being on the spiritual path. Kṛṣṇa says that any sacrifice done for the welfare of humanity is not to be given up. As sacrifices are meant to achieve the supreme, performing charity is recommended to purify one's heart and put one on the path of spiritual progress.

Sacrifice is normally understood to be rituals such as *yajña* and *homa,* etc. These are the fire rituals prescribed in Vedic literature to propitiate the deities. When carried out with awareness, these powerful techniques link us to the cosmic energy.

Whatever we do for others without expecting anything in return is a sacrifice. Charitable service is giving with no expectation in return. Those who are truly charitable never allow others to know what they are doing. Only then charity achieves its purpose.

Charity should also involve pain. You can call it charity when you cannot afford to give something away and yet you give it away. Charity must become a penance and lead to austerity if it is to be real.

Penance is denying oneself sense pleasures. Penance is turning inwards, whereas sacrifice and charity are focused outwards.

'All these activities should be performed without attachment or expectation of results. They should be performed as a matter of duty and this is My final opinion,' says the master.

This must be understood in-depth. Whether it is spiritual or worldly activity, as long as you struggle with a purpose and a goal, you can *never* relax. The person who surrenders to the flow of life experiences the inner space and outer space at the same time.

Let me explain what I mean by the word surrender. Think of two intersecting lines, axes.

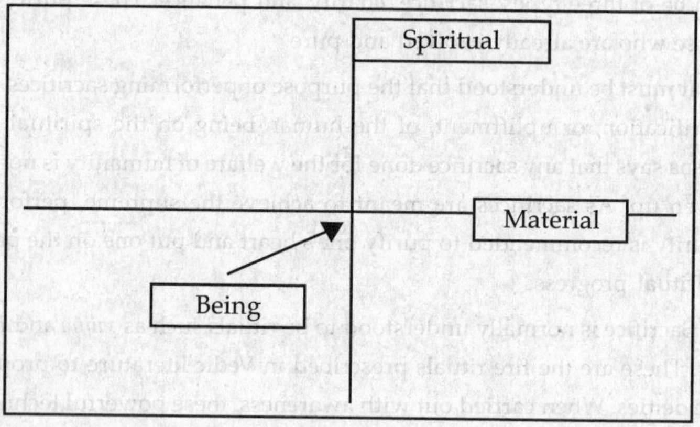

The vertical axis is spiritual life. The horizontal axis is material life. The point of intersection is your being. This is the goal you have. You have some goal in your material life and also in your spiritual life. To achieve your goal in your material life, you are continuously struggling and working. To achieve your spiritual goal, you are again working intensely doing yoga, *prāṇāyāma, pratyāhāra,* etc. When you struggle with material goals, you are on the horizontal line whereas when you struggle with spiritual goals, you are on the vertical line.

As long as you struggle in material life, you avoid spiritual life. As long as you struggle in spiritual life, you avoid material life. Both are a struggle.

Kṛṣṇa says, 'Relax from both.' You may think, 'What is this funny instruction He is giving?' You think that if you relax in both you will lose both. However, the truth is, that when you relax in both you fall into your inner consciousness, your being or your inner space. When you experience this inner consciousness you will suddenly realize that you can explode in all directions. You do not need to choose between horizontal and vertical lines. You can travel on both lines at the same time!

In the material world, the world of 'mine,' your properties are your goal. In the spiritual world, also, you have certain goals, such as enlightenment. Actually, spiritual goals create more ego than material goals. At least with material goals, at some point, you realize that you cannot achieve real happiness by running after them. But with spiritual goals you do not even understand what you are doing. Both goals take your being away from your being. When you surrender and relax into your being, you suddenly realize you are neither the body nor the mind.

As long as you believe you are the mind, you will be forced to choose between the vertical and horizontal lines. You will be in a dilemma, because the mind wants to choose. The mind and dilemma are the same thing. The mind ceases to exist once dilemmas vanish. You continuously worry about whether to choose this or that.

A small story:

> A man was sitting at home crying loudly. Usually men do not cry and especially not loudly!
>
> His wife asks, 'Why are you crying?'
>
> He says, 'Do you remember when your father caught us red-handed when we were together twenty years ago? He threatened me that if I did not marry you he would have me put in jail.'

The wife replies, 'Of course I remember. Why are you crying for that?'

The man says, 'If I hadn't done what he said I would be a free man today!'

Whenever you choose something, someday you will definitely wonder about the choice you made. The people who choose material goals will feel that they are missing spiritual life. And those who pick spiritual goals will feel they are missing material life. For the first time, Kṛṣṇa gives the ultimate technique for Quantum Spirituality. He is the first quantum scientist of the inner world. He says relax and surrender, and you will experience the intensity of your inner consciousness. You will understand that you do not need to choose between the horizontal and vertical lines. You can explode in all 360 degrees. You experience choicelessness. Choicelessness does not mean that you do not choose anything. When you stop choosing, you will choose everything.

Similarly, surrender does not mean passive surrender or pretending to give up. Many people claim, '*Swamiji*, I have surrendered everything to God. Bless me so that I get a better paying job!'

A woman told me, '*Swamiji*, you must take care of me because I have totally surrendered to you. Please give me mental peace.'

I said, 'Okay, attend the next meditation program and we will see.'

Immediately she replied, 'I cannot spare two days!' She had just told me that she had surrendered to me!

Before making any statement, know the situation. Otherwise you will suffer! With real surrender you do not exclude anything. You include everything. You do not need to choose between horizontal and vertical lines. You can experience both and something more. You can explode in different dimensions of your being!

Again, when I say surrender, you do not need to surrender to any god or guru. Just surrender to your own being, to your own consciousness, to your own inner space. The problem is you do not respect your inner space. That is why in the initial level you need an entity called god or guru.

Somebody asked me, '*Swamiji*, I have surrendered to you. What should I do?'

I told him, 'If you really surrender, you will not have that question! You will be guided from within. As long as you have doubts, you have not surrendered.'

Duty Without Delusion

18.7 *Prescribed duties should never be renounced. If one gives up his prescribed duties through the illusion of renunciation, this is said to be in the state of ignorance.*

18.8 *Anyone who gives up prescribed duties as troublesome, or out of fear, is said to be in the state of aggression, and does not benefit from renunciation.*

18.9 *But he who performs what is prescribed as a matter of duty, without expectation or attachment to the results, his renunciation is of the nature of* satva, *goodness, O Arjuna.*

18.10 *Those who neither hate disagreeable work, nor are attached to pleasant work are in a state of intelligence, goodness, and renunciation, free of all doubts.*

18.11 *Human beings cannot give up all activities; therefore, the one who has renounced the fruits of such activity is one who has truly renounced.*

18.12 *To one who has not renounced, the three kinds of fruits of action — desirable, undesirable, and mixed — accrue after death, but not to one who has renounced.*

Kṛṣṇa says that *nitya karma* or obligatory duties must be followed with discipline and consistency. Not doing these takes us into the state of *tamas,* inaction born out of ignorance and laziness.

Nitya karmas vary from person to person. The duties of a householder are different from those of a monk or a student. Each has clear guidelines in terms of what one should and should not do.

Many times the idea of dropping our responsibilities and taking up a different role is more attractive than growing in awareness, so that we can perform our own duties well and without attachment. Be very clear, without the right attitude and awareness, no role that we take up will work out for us.

In our *ashram* routine, everyone must attend *Guru pūjā* at six a.m. This includes permanent residents and *brahmacāris*, as well as those who stay there for courses or healing. You should see the reluctance with which some outsiders attend the *pūjā*. Of course quite a few are still asleep at six a.m. and we do not have a police force to find them and wake them up!

Giving up what needs to be done because it is uncomfortable is not renunciation! That is convenient inaction, born out of *rajas*. After attending a course many ask how many meditation techniques they can do each day. I tell them, 'Do at least one properly.' A week later, after the fervor has cooled down, if I ask, they sheepishly say, 'I do not have time to practice even one meditation, *Swamiji*.'

All of us find time for everything except meditation. We find time to give appointments to everyone else except ourselves! Who is the loser?

Kṛṣṇa says that doing what needs to be done because that is what is recommended, without attachment to the action and without desire, is the ideal condition of *satva*.

Kṛṣṇa has said this many times in Gītā so that the message sinks in. Do what your duty is, based on your societal or religious beliefs and codes. However, do it without attachment and expectation of results.

The consciousness of 'I' and 'mine,' in terms of the performance of the activity should be absent.

Often in traditional homes people chant prayers or *mantras* as a mere chore. They try to concentrate, yet they are disturbed by every activity happening in the house. These people are so attached to 'their' doing it and 'their' doing it well, that everything disturbs them. On the other hand, watch a child recite a *mantra*. He plays with it and has fun!

Annamalai Swamigal in Tiruvannamalai initiated me into a meditation technique when I was not even ten. For two years all I did was play with that technique. In two years the technique had its effect!

Kṛṣṇa says that a person in the satvic mode of calmness and awareness is undisturbed by external conditions. He is not bothered whether someone appreciates or condemns what he does. Renunciation is in the true spirit and is done out of goodness only when a person renounces the expectation of result.

It is natural that a human being cannot remain still without doing some work. If not physically, at least mentally he does something. Even in sleep, he dreams. If we close our eyes we watch our inner television. If we plug our ears and close our eyes and stay in an insulated room, we are still filled with inner chatter.

This being the case, the only way man can be comfortable and at peace with himself is by not having any expectation of the result of his thoughts or words or actions. This can be achieved by every one of us. Kṛṣṇa says that one who is not concerned about the fruits of his action has truly renounced.

Even when an action has been completed and the expected result achieved, as long as one is attached to that action and its result another desire crops up. This is what I call *karma*. *Karma* is nothing but unfulfilled desires. As long as we have attachment to the action as 'doer,' which in turns creates an expectation of reward or punishment, we are caught in the cycle of *karma* and *saṁsāra*. Our concern about whether an action or the result is good, bad or a mix of both follows us as our mental attitude or *vāsanā* after death.

Please understand that no one is 'up there' keeping an account of our deeds and misdeeds. Our own spirit does that job. So we can never escape! When we die the body perishes, but the spirit moves on to another body. That spirit carries its earlier mental attitude, its *vāsanā*. There is no exception to this rule. *Saṁskāras* are the carried-over desires and they cause the cycle of *saṁsāra:* birth, death and rebirth.

However, we have no unfulfilled desires - *karma, saṁskāra* or *vāsanā* - left when we renounce attachment to 'doership' and become a mere witness to both the action and the result. Such a person breaks out of this cycle of *saṁsāra*.

Technology Of Surrender

18.13,14 Learn from Me, Arjuna, there are five causes that bring about the accomplishment of all action, as described in **Sāṅkhya** *philosophy.*
These are the physical body that is the seat of action; the attributes of nature or guṇa *that are the Doer; the eleven organs of perceptions; action by the life forces; and finally the Divine.*

18.15 These five factors are responsible for whatever right or wrong actions a man performs by deed, word, and thought.

18.16 Those who think they, their body and spirit, are the doers, are ignorant and do not see things as they are.

In these verses, Kṛṣṇa gives the exact technology of surrender. Kṛṣṇa lists five factors from *Sāṅkhya* philosophy responsible for our activities. These are the body-mind system, the operator of the body-mind system (that is the individual), the senses, different efforts causing the activities, and finally the ultimate power of God. All activities, right or wrong, good or bad, are caused by these five factors. If however, the individual considers himself to be the doer, his body and mind, he is not aware.

Kṛṣṇa uses the word *ātman* when saying that one who perceives one's spirit or Self as the agent, the doer or the performer, does not see and is not aware. Kṛṣṇa draws a distinction between the individual Self and the cosmic energy. He differentiates between *ātman* and *Brahman, mānava* and *Deva,* Narā and Nārāyaṇa, self and *Parāśakti.*

Kṛṣṇa concludes that while philosophical discussion mentions five players in all activities, the ultimate controller is the Divine. We are immersed in our body-mind-spirit system and caught in our sensory perceptions, and believe that we are the power behind all that we do. So long as we have this deluded belief, we are rooted in ignorance.

Whatever you may understand as yourself, your body-mind-spirit system, is the totality of many things. And individually each is responsible for something. In spite of this, you think that 'you' are responsible for the whole thing. That is where the trouble starts. As we saw earlier, there are three levels of surrender, at the levels of intellect, emotion, and being.

Surrendering the intellect is easy because it continuously tortures you. When you see somebody more intelligent and with clearer thinking you just surrender. Most of the time you want to get rid of your intellect. Finding somebody to dump your intellect on allows you to relax from it.

Next, emotional surrender happens when you feel deeply connected to the master after experiencing some meditation or understanding. The master's emotions mean the things he guides you in, the way he wants you to live. The master becomes the number one priority at the emotional level.

Next is a deeper level of surrender at the level of the senses. The surrender of the senses means that your senses listen to what he says. Normally, when you listen to me, a filter in your mind discounts what you do not agree with. You hear what you want to hear. However, when intellectual surrender and emotional surrender happen, you are ready to surrender this disbelief and unblock your senses.

Once a disciple asked his master, 'Why should I surrender?'

The master asked, 'How do you know whatever you think you know about yourself?'

The disciple replied, 'I know myself through my senses.'

The master asked, 'Who do you think you are according to your senses?'

The disciple said, 'As far as I know, I am the body and mind.'

His master responded, 'You are God, not just body and mind.'

The master said, 'Only when you surrender your senses, will you realize the truth of what I am saying. The moment you trust me more than your senses you experience that you are God. You then understand the meaning of *tatvamasi* (literally '*You Are That*', meaning 'you are divine').'

I keep saying, 'I am not here to prove that I am God. I am here to prove that you are God.'

The master stands for the idea that you are the infinite. He shows you various dimensions of your inner self that you have not explored or experienced. He shows that if it is possible for him, it is possible for you, also. But as long as you believe your senses, you think that you are the body and mind.

When you trust the master more than your senses, you understand that the master's words and not your senses are the truth. When the master says you are God, you suddenly realize the truth for yourself. You realize that you are not the body or mind as your senses have led you to believe.

Two voices are speaking from two different levels. On the one hand, your senses tell you that you are the body and mind. On the other hand, the master tells you that you are God. As long as you listen to your senses you will not even hear what the master says. When you move away from your senses and come to the master, you hear him and experience the truth that you are divine.

The final surrender

In the inner world, the first and last tool you need is complete surrender. Only then can you wake up to the truth. You can experience Kṛṣṇa consciousness not just by surrendering the intellect and emotions, but by surrendering the root of the intellect and emotions, that is, the senses. The senses supply the data. When you surrender them the source of the data is surrendered.

You receive all information about yourself through the senses. You respect yourself because of data you collect about yourself through the senses of others. If somebody says, 'You are beautiful,' you make an entry in a notebook. When you are told that you are dumb, another entry is made!

At the end of the day you make a survey and assess what everybody said. You see that seventy-two percent of the people say that you are intelligent; twenty percent say that you are dumb, and the rest do not know. You decide that if seventy-two percent of the people say that you are intelligent, all of them cannot be fools. Therefore, you must be intelligent! Thus your conclusion about yourself is based on what others say about you.

You continuously go around asking people to tell you something about yourself. As a result, the senses give you an idea of what you are. Kṛṣṇa asks Arjuna to surrender these senses.

When you surrender your senses, the root of your idea of yourself, you lose your identification with the body and mind. As long as you believe your senses you think that you are the body and mind. Only when you believe the master's words more than your senses do you realize the truth that you are divine.

It is up to you to choose. If you believe the senses, you cannot believe the master. And if you believe the master, you cannot believe your senses. It is for you to decide.

Kṛṣṇa says that only when you surrender at all three levels do you have the ultimate experience. Let me tell you this: surrender itself is enlightenment. At that moment you experience the Truth.

Usually we play with words. People tell me that they have surrendered their life to Kṛṣṇa, Venkateshwara, or Śiva. Then they say that their only wish is to be happy. If they have truly surrendered, surrender is enough. They will not need to ask for anything else. As long as doubts remain, surrender has not happened, because the moment you surrender, *you* disappear.

In surrender, you have nothing to lose and everything to gain. Surrendering does not mean giving up everything. Keep all your possessions; take care however, that you do not internalize them. Do not judge yourself based on your properties. You are far greater than you think. You are greater than your bank balance, name and fame, relationships and all these things put together.

As long as you judge yourself based on these things, these become the central points in your life. Understand that you are something beyond these things. The moment you wake up to this truth you will not allow yourself to be put into any frame based upon bank balance, relationships, attitudes, or name and fame. You have then surrendered. I simply ask you to surrender these small ideas you have about yourself.

On the surface of the vast ocean of life, small bubbles are formed. One bubble starts thinking that it is an individual, long-lasting entity. It lasts only for a few moments. Yet within those few moments it collects other bubbles around it. One bubble is its wife, another bubble is its son, and so on. Some are called parents or relatives, still others are friends, and so on. It collects bubbles on all sides to protect itself.

It collects a few grains of sand from the beach and thinks these are its property. It thinks one grain of sand is its bank balance, another is its jewelry and treasures, and so on. Then it builds a fence to protect its property. How long can the bubble play this game? Only for a few seconds! Before it can complete its game, it disappears back into the ocean.

The bubble was part of the ocean in all three instances: when it was created, when it existed, and when it disappeared. Even though it claimed to be different from the ocean, even though it thought it was an individual, and even though it thought many people and things belonged to it, it was always part of the ocean and very soon disappeared into it, also!

In the same way, for a few moments you think you exist as an individual being in this universal consciousness. Within those few moments you catch hold of a few people as your relatives and friends. This makes you feel safe. You collect a few things as possessions. You feel secure with these things around you. With these things you form an opinion about yourself. You play the same game as the bubble.

Experiencing surrender

Suddenly the whole thing disappears. Before the game started, while the game is going on, and when the game ends, whether you understand it or not, realize it or not, experience it or not, you belong to the ocean. You are God. You are one with Existence.

When I say surrender, I mean wake up to the truth that you are the ocean. When you are born, when you think you are an individual, or when you become enlightened, you are always the ocean. Waking up to this ultimate Truth is surrender. Surrender these small ideas about yourself and wake up to reality. Otherwise you just play with the word surrender.

We use inflated words when we define ourselves. We do not realize that we are beyond these descriptions. One day a follower used exaggerated words about himself in front of me. After he left I told my disciple that he seemed to be suffering from an inferiority complex. I said, any estimation you have of yourself, except that you are God, is an underestimation!

Some fish swim along with the current. Others swim against the current. Whether they go with or against the current, all the fish are in the water. Whether you flow with Existence or fight it, you are one with it. Whether or not you have realized you are divine, you are divine. There is no choice in this. You can make only one choice, realize and enjoy or continue to struggle and suffer; that's all! You may try to create stronger fences around yourself or collect more bubbles around you, but can you ask the wave not to come? Whatever you may do the whole thing is only a drama of a few seconds.

The next problem is what to do if you cannot surrender.

Some people tell me, '*Swamiji,* I am unable to surrender. What can I do?' Do not worry because you have nothing to surrender. By understanding that you have nothing to surrender, you have already surrendered. Just relax. Whether you surrender or not, Existence will take care. Automatically life continues and you will relax. That relaxation itself is surrender.

Relax into the flow of life and wake up to the truth that you are something greater than your body and mind as suggested by your senses. You are led by society to think that you are something. Now wake up to the truth that you are greater than what you can imagine. Surrendering will give you a new consciousness. You will be a new being.

There are three levels of birth, three types of *garbha* or wombs, according to the ancient scriptures. The first is the *bhū garbha.* This is the womb of a woman that gives birth to an infant. This is connected to the *mūlādhāra cakra,* the lowest of the seven *cakras* or energy centers in the human body.

Next is the *hṛt garbha.* This is the womb of the heart and is witnessed in the case of real artists. A singer or a painter for example, conceives the song or picture in his heart and then delivers it.

A woman feels fulfillment when she gives birth to a child and becomes a mother. In the same way, when an artist creates a painting, poem, sculpture, or song, he feels an overwhelming satisfaction and fulfillment. For the poet, the womb is in his heart, the *hṛt garbha.*

The ultimate is the *jñāna garbha,* which happens in the highest energy center, the *sahasrāra cakra* - on the top of the head. In the *jñāna garbha,* all the spiritual ideas are conceived in the head and worked on. Suddenly one moment you give birth to a new you, to an enlightened being.

When you receive this concept of surrender and work on it, you will wake up and give birth to yourself as an enlightened being. As long as you identify with the bubble you feel insecure. The instinct to survive and the instinct to possess torture you. The moment you understand you belong to the ocean, that you are from it, that you are in it, and that you will disappear into it, you will realize that you will never die, because you are the ocean.

The moment you realize that you are the ocean there is nothing to possess, because everything belongs to you. Hence, the instinct to possess disappears. I am not asking you to legally throw away your possessions. You do not need to throw away whatever you have. Just do not internalize them. Within yourself be aware that you are something greater than anything you can possibly possess.

At the age of seven your toys are important to you. Do they hold the same importance today? You have neither renounced them nor are you attached to them. They are just there. You have grown beyond them.

Rāga means attachment. *Arāga* means detachment. *Virāga* (or *Vairāgya)* means beyond attachment and detachment. As you grew up, *vairāgya* naturally happened towards your toys. So also, when you realize that you are the ocean, *vairāgya* will happen towards the few sand particles and bubbles that you have collected and gathered around yourself. You will have gone beyond these things.

The instincts to survive and possess would no longer be relevant to you. Your property does not suddenly disappear. They are there, but you live with them and enjoy them more intensely.

When you realize that they may be taken from you at any moment, you do not take them for granted. When you realize that you are the ocean and that they are also of the same ocean, you value them more. When you realize this, you are transformed at the level of body, mind, and consciousness. When consciousness is transformed, you give birth to a new you.

Kṛṣṇa goes much deeper than these three levels of surrender. He gives Arjuna a glimpse of the ultimate experience itself. Kṛṣṇa already gave Arjuna the experience during *Viśvarūpa darśan,* the vision of His cosmic form. Even so, Arjuna was unable to establish himself in that experience due to fear.

Always you miss the first experience because of fear. Now Arjuna is more mature and capable of being established in the experience. Kṛṣṇa gives Arjuna the experience that will stay with him forever. In the next few verses Kṛṣṇa puts Arjuna into the experience of enlightenment.

A small story:

A man asked a Zen master how to become Buddha. The master just slapped him! In that instant, the man became enlightened. He experienced Buddhahood in himself. The slap simply showed him that he was already That. He merely needed to wake up from sleep.

Kṛṣṇa is waking Arjuna up from the long slumber called *saṁsāra sāgara.* This can also be called unconsciousness or *tamas.* Kṛṣṇa gives him a good shake by giving him the ultimate experience and Arjuna is established into that final level or highest level of surrender.

Extreme Statement

18.17 One who is egoless, whose intelligence is not of attachment, though he may kill, is not the slayer, and is never bound by his actions.

A very dangerous statement! No master except Kṛṣṇa can make such a courageous statement. Of course one who has reached that level of awareness does not think of killing. As long as we have the idea of 'I' and 'mine' we attack or kill. On the other hand, when we surrender we learn to include everything.

We kill others only when we feel insecure. We do not need courage to make war. We only need cowardice. The person who is courageous never kills others. He is established in non-violence. That is the reason Kṛṣṇa makes this bold statement — one who is not entangled in ego, even if he kills, does not kill.

Kṛṣṇa emphasizes here: May you liberate yourself from ego. He does not ask Arjuna to kill. One problem is that people give their own meaning to words. They have their own understanding.

A small story:

Once there was a little boy in a Zen monastery training to be a monk. One day, when he was cleaning his master's room, he accidentally broke his master's favorite teacup.

He wanted to confess to his master about the teacup, but was scared that he would punish him. He approached the master and asked him, 'Master, isn't it true that everything that was born has to die someday?'

The master replied, 'Yes.'

The boy then showed him the fragments of the broken cup and said, 'It was time for your teacup to die.'

Do not give your own meaning to what Kṛṣṇa has said! He is asking you to be liberated from ego. The person who has realized that he is part of a whole will not kill, even if he kills. Kṛṣṇa asks you to experience the truth about yourself. Recognize the correct meaning. Kṛṣṇa asks you to liberate yourself from your ego. He does not ask you to go around killing people.

Kṛṣṇa uses killing as an extreme example to make Arjuna think. When one no longer feels the need to survive, anything that one does is without attachment and without expectation. When a person is in that state, he is truly in tune with Existence. If such a person destroys, it is similar to the destruction caused by Nature, which happens at a different frequency and understanding level as I explained earlier.

Kṛṣṇa makes this statement to drive the point home to Arjuna, that it is his duty to stand up and fight instead of running away from the battlefield.

Components Of Action

18.18 *Knowledge, the object of the knowledge, and the subject of the knowledge, the knower, are the three factors that stimulate action; the senses, the action, and the performer comprise the three components of action.*

18.19 *According to the guṇa theory of Sāṅkhya, there are three types in knowledge, action, and performers of action. Listen as I describe them.*

18.20 *That knowledge by which the one imperishable reality is seen in all Existence, undivided in the divided, is knowledge in the state of goodness.*

18.21 *The knowledge by which one sees different realities of various types among all beings, as separate from one another, such knowledge is in the mode of aggression.*

18.22 *The irrational, baseless, and worthless knowledge by which one clings to one single effect as if it is everything; such knowledge is in the mode of darkness or ignorance.*

18.23 *Obligatory duty performed without likes and dislikes, and without selfish motives and attachment to the fruit, is in the mode of goodness.*

18.24 *Action performed with ego, with selfish motives, and with too much effort, is in the mode of aggression.*

18.25 *Action that is undertaken because of delusion, disregarding consequences, loss, injury to others, as well as one's own ability, is in the mode of ignorance.*

18.26 *The performer who is free from attachment, non-egoistic, endowed with resolve and enthusiasm, and unperturbed in success or failure is called good.*

18.27 *The performer who is impassioned, who desires the fruits of work, who is greedy, violent, impure, and affected by joy and sorrow, is called aggressive.*

18.28 *The performer who is undisciplined, vulgar, stubborn, wicked, malicious, lazy, depressed, and procrastinating is called ignorant.*

In these verses Kṛṣṇa explains the nature of man. Kṛṣṇa has already said that the final performer is not man, Narā, but the divine, Narayana. Even so, the human is still the subject, the medium that we are dealing with. All the frailties that we have are inherent in our nature. These are the *guṇas*, or attributes, that define our behavior. These attributes control our thoughts, words, and actions. One is not all the time, from birth to death, in one *guṇa* or attribute.

The *guṇas* are of three kinds: *satva, rajas and tamas. Satva* is defined as calm, peaceful, spiritual, and good, etc. This is generally the attribute of spiritually inclined persons. *Rajas* is translated as aggressive, passionate, and active, etc. This is the primary attribute of kings, warriors, and business people. *Tamas* is lazy, ignorant, and passive, etc. *Tamas* is seen as the inactive component that many of us experience at times. It is the active component of those who live to eat and sleep.

In these verses Kṛṣṇa beautifully defines, in detail, the qualities and effects of these *guṇas* upon us to make us aware of what happens within us. As the master explains in these words, and once we understand how we react, we can move to the next level of understanding and shift to a superior attribute.

Yes, all of us must be *rajasic*, or aggressive, part of the time to accomplish things. Even so, if we can act aggressively without greed, anger or fear affecting us, as well as acting without attachment, we are in the *satvic* mode, although superficially we seem to be in the *rajasic* mode.

Kṛṣṇa defines a *satvic* person as one who sees the collective consciousness, the whole, in the parts. He understands that he is not alone and not an island; rather he is linked with everyone and everything in this universe. He understands his connection with the cosmic energy.

A *satvic* person is not focused on himself. He realizes that his survival and possessions, the 'I' and 'mine,' are meaningless. His activities are selfless without expectation of praise or reward, and without attachment to the process or result as success or failure. There is no feeling of 'I' and 'mine' involved in his actions.

It is not that difficult to move into a *satvic* state. True, you may not be able to stay there all the time, but once you understand how this state liberates you, you try more and more to stay there.

To be in the *satvic* state is to understand that past and future are mere illusions. They do not exist. Past is gone, never to return. Why worry? Future is a mirage. All you can do is activate your present moment. The present moment determines your future. Once you focus on the present, your awareness increases manifold and you drop expectations and attachment. You respond to the reality of now. You are in *satva*.

You fall into a *rajasic* state when you distinguish between you and me. There is really no differentiation. Your mind, the ego, and your *saṁskāras* bring up this differentiation between you and others. A *rajasic* person does everything expecting a reward. He is selfish, aggressive, and impatient. Failure is a blow to his ego.

A *rajasic* person can never be happy. Almost all of you are driven by *rajas*. This is the predominant attribute in modern times. Rich or poor, intelligent or foolish, educated or uneducated, almost everyone compares himself with the next person and wants what the other person has. As long as you are driven by your desires and not satisfied with what you have, you are in *rajas*.

Rajas corrodes you. It eats up your soul. There is no end to greed and no limit to fear. These are the driving forces of *rajas*. *Rajas* is about trying to attain what you don't have, not being happy with what you have, not being happy about where you are, and not being happy when you are in the present moment. You are either constantly in the future, imagining what you would like to be and what you would like to have, or you are in the past, thinking about how you could have done better. *Rajas* is living in a fantasy world.

In *tamas* one is fully in delusion. One sticks to embedded beliefs, knowledge, or conditions without making an effort to verify whether they are right or wrong, appropriate or not, harmful or not. Religious zealots and gangsters are in *tamas.* There is no difference between them; only their objectives are different. Both are dogmatic, violent and totally selfish. They adopt any means, even criminal, to achieve their objectives.

Tamas does not just mean inactivity, laziness and procrastination. Yes, it is all that; however, it also includes mindless action performed without realizing that one is part of a whole. The ego is so enlarged that it believes it is the whole. It believes nothing else of significance exists; others are of no consequence. Hitler, who destroyed millions of people believing that they were inferior, was in deep *tamas. Tamas* is an animal at its worst, when it stops heeding the laws of Nature. And only a human can be in *tamas.* An animal can never be in *tamas*, because it is directed by the intelligence of Nature.

Meanings Of Life

18.29 *Now hear Me explain, fully and separately, the threefold division of intellect and resolve, based on modes of material nature, O Arjuna.*

18.30 *O Arjuna, that intellect is in the mode of goodness that understands the path of work and the path of renunciation, right and wrong action, fear and fearlessness, bondage and liberation.*

18.31 *That intellect is in the mode of passion that cannot distinguish between principles of right conduct and wrongdoing, and right and wrong action, O Arjuna.*

18.32 *That intellect is in the mode of ignorance that accepts unrighteousness as righteousness and thinks everything to be that which it is not, O Arjuna.*

18.33 *Consistent and continuous determination in controlling mind, breath, and senses for uniting with the Divine is goodness, Arjuna.*

18.34 *Craving for results of action while clinging to goals of proper conduct, pleasure and wealth is the state of passion.*

18.35 *Ignorant resolve that cannot go beyond dreaming, fear, grief, despair, and delusion — such is in darkness, Arjuna.*

Here Kṛṣṇa refers to the approach known as defining the *puruṣārtha* or meanings of life.

Dharma, artha, kāma and *mokṣa* are the four *puruṣārtha*. These can be translated as righteousness, wealth, desire or lust, and liberation. These are the four-fold meanings of life. I prefer not to call them the purposes of life. There is no purpose to life. Once we fix a purpose to life it becomes a goalpost and attachments and expectations result.

Life is a path without a destination. Once we assume there is a destination, we hurry. The future becomes a stress-inducing factor. Let us say we travel from New York to Washington. Once we fix Washington as our destination, the next issue is, 'When will we reach there?' In the process we do not enjoy the journey. The journey becomes an irritation that we must cross in order to reach our destination.

In life, do not fix a destination. Each journey must be enjoyed. Enjoy the people you meet, the experiences you have and what you pick up on the way, without being greedy to acquire more. The journey, the path, becomes so enjoyable that whatever destination you reach is the right destination.

People who attach a purpose to life are disturbed. Philosophers who have no other work create false purposes to life. When we let life lead us, when we take life as it comes, we enjoy every moment. We truly live in the present, like a god.

Puruṣārtha provides four meanings to life:

Dharma is right conduct or virtue. Buddha preached this as the middle path.

Artha is the stuff that we pick up on our path and journey, the material things that we need to sustain ourselves.

Kāma is the pleasure of the senses we experience and enjoy on this journey. These are rightful acquisitions and pleasurable experiences. Do not feel disturbed by the need for these. But do not become caught up in them and forget to move on the path and enjoy the journey to the fullest.

Mokṣa, or liberation, is the ultimate meaning to life. This is the culmination of the liberation from expectation, desires, greed and fear, and liberation from attachment to desires. This understanding that non-attachment and absence of expectation leads to liberation can fill us with bliss.

Here Kṛṣṇa gives the essence of how we should lead our lives to make it meaningful. He says that goodness or *satva* is the state in which there is clarity about right and wrong, and whatever we do with our body, mind, and senses is done with a view to liberate ourselves from attachment and desires in order to realize that we are divine.

Delusion Of Senses

18.36,37 And now hear from Me, O Arjuna, about three kinds of pleasure. The pleasure that one enjoys from spiritual practice results in cessation of all sorrows. The pleasure that appears as poison in the beginning, but is like nectar in the end, comes by the grace of Self-knowledge and is in the mode of goodness.

18.38 Sensual pleasures that appear as nectar in the beginning, but become poison in the end, are in the mode of passion.

18.39 Pleasure that is delusion from beginning to end, and born out of sleep, laziness, and illusion is said to be of the nature of ignorance.

18.40 No one, either here or among the celestials in the higher planetary systems, is free from these three states of material nature.

Earlier Kṛṣṇa spoke about the influence of *guṇas* (attributes) on the intellect, that in turn defines the way we act. Now He talks about how we respond as a result of our behavior.

Kṛṣṇa says that spiritual practice, that is the state of *satva,* is difficult in the beginning and is bitter like poison; however, it becomes life-giving nectar in the end. Sensual pleasures born out of *rajas,* on the other hand, seem like nectar in the beginning, but become poisonous. In the *tamasic* state, Kṛṣṇa says, one is deluded as if in sleep, laziness, and illusion. Every human is in one state or another. Not merely humans, even the celestials, who are supposedly more evolved, are in the same modes.

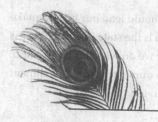

How beautifully the master summarizes how we become deluded by our senses! It is not easy to begin spiritual practice. In the *vedic* tradition, in the *gurukul* schools, from a young age children were brought up in an environment of spirituality. They learned to control their mind and senses at an early age and to focus upon Self-realization. They understood, by the example of their masters, that there was something more pleasurable than sensory pleasures. This gave them courage.

In today's age, this education system is considered impractical. Invading Moguls and the colonizing British destroyed the *vedic* culture, especially the *gurukul* tradition. This was not accidental or incidental. It was a deliberate strategy. What we have today is a mass of literate Indians who are uneducated. They are totally unaware of the great tradition of our *vedic* culture. They think rituals are meaningless. We have lost the knowledge of the connection between these rituals and spirituality. Rituals, when carried out meaningfully, are the basis of spirituality.

We are all in the *rajasic* mode now and only sensory pleasures of the body matter. In the *tamasic* mode, we don't even know we are in deep ignorance. The sensory organs are our windows to the external world. They are trained to run away from pain and chase pleasure. Bodily pleasure gives mental pleasure and therefore emotional satisfaction. Once we experience the mental pleasure, we constantly rewind and replay that pleasure. Our past drives our future.

If you lead your life with awareness, you won't get caught in the illusions of attachment and expectations driving your actions.

A small story:

A three-year-old boy asked his aunt who was pregnant, 'Why is your stomach so big?'

She replied, 'I am having a baby.'

The boy was surprised and asked, 'Is it a good baby?'

She replied, 'Oh, yes, it is a real good baby.'

The boy was shocked and asked, 'Then why did you eat him?'

Often in life, we too jump to the wrong conclusions when we are led by our senses! We try to keep on experiencing pain and pleasure alternately. Either way it is only an illusion.

Kṛṣṇa describes the *tamasic* person with great insight. He does not use the word poison in describing the state of such a person. A *tamasic* person is like a drug addict, He says. At least a *rajasic* person enjoys the experience now, and suffers later. A *tamasic* person has no enjoyment. He suffers without knowing that he is suffering. That is why he passes his suffering on to others with no compunction. That is how ignorant people, who rise to become leaders, act.

Rightful Conduct, Not To Perfection

18.41 *Brāhmaṇas, kṣatriyas, vaiśyas and sūdras are divided in the work they do based on their nature, Arjuna.*

18.42 *The nature of Brāhmaṇa is characterized by calmness, discipline, austerity, tolerance, honesty, knowledge, wisdom, and belief in God.*

18.43 *Kṣatriya are characterized by their qualities of heroism, vigor, firmness, dexterity, and steadfastness in battle, leadership, and generosity.*

18.44 *Those who are good at cultivation, cattle rearin,g and trade are known as Vaiśya. Those who are very good in service are classified as Sūdra.*

18.45 *One can attain the highest perfection by devotion to one's natural work. Listen to Me about how one attains perfection while engaged in one's natural work.*

18.46 *One attains perfection by worshipping the supreme Being, from whom all beings originate and by whom this entire universe is pervaded, through performance of one's natural duty for Him.*

18.47 *It is better to engage in one's rightful conduct, even though one may not perform it to perfection, rather than to accept another's conduct and perform it perfectly. Duties prescribed according to one's nature are never affected by sinful reactions.*

18.48 *Every work has some defect, just as fire is covered by smoke. One should not give up the work that is born of his own nature, even if such work is full of fault, Arjuna.*

'Śreyān svadharmo viguṇaḥ paradharmāt svanuṣṭhitāt,' says Kṛṣṇa.

Here Kṛṣṇa says that it is better to do one's assigned work imperfectly, rather than do another's work perfectly. It is possible that one can perform elements of another's work well. A *brāhmaṇa,* being a scholar, may excel as a *vaiśya* in commercial calculations; however, he will have neither the heart nor the head to be a businessman.

In the *gurukul* system, along with the master, the child also was allowed to select his vocation. The child could express its passion and decide.

With time, this classification of selection and training became corrupted. Those who were *brāhmaṇa* wanted their children to be *brāhmaṇa,* and so on. The *varṇa* or caste system that had originally been a selection and training system in education, led to the stratification of society based upon birth.

Before we condemn the caste system, realize that every society has stratification. In *Vedic* India this classification was based upon talents and intelligence. In modern society it is based on money and power. Which is better?

Without the *brāhmaṇa* being the keepers of knowledge our *Vedic* treasures would have disappeared thousands of years ago. The people who denounce the system do it for power and money, not for any selfless reasons. They recommend no alternative means of preserving traditional knowledge.

I am not a *brāhmaṇa. Brāhmaṇas* have come to me and hinted at their discomfort at being termed *brāhmaṇas.* They are well-educated people. I tell them, 'Be proud of your culture, your tradition. Without *brāhmaṇa,* the *Vedic* tradition would have died long ago.'

This praise is for those *brāhmaṇas* who have remained true to their scholarship. Those who have succumbed to the lure of wealth have no right to be called *brāhmaṇas.*

This is where the *varṇa* system has failed. From a scientific and efficient work system, it has deteriorated into a power-broking system. We need to fix that. Those who are true to their tradition are poor and disrespected. Only those who use their scholarly skills to become *kṣatriyas* and *vaiśyas* have gained power, money, and respect. The problem with society and the societal structure is that they become exclusive; good societies should be inclusive. Today in the West, as well as in other places including India, if we have money or power we are respected. Does anyone rebel against that? No! How can we call a society advanced or progressive when its main criterion for respect is money?

By that logic, I would have been denounced had I been born in any country other than India. For nearly ten years I was homeless! For nine years I traveled the length and breadth of India without carrying money. People welcomed me and offered me transport, shelter, and food. In the West I would have been locked up in a jail or a shelter!

When you see a homeless person approaching your car in the USA, you instinctively raise your windows and lock your doors. You are so afraid. In India, is anyone afraid of a beggar coming and standing in front of them? Why? There is acceptance. People in the West say that acceptance is weakness, not violence. How strange societal values have become! You respect a person only when you are afraid of him.

We cannot evolve unless there is a fundamental change in our thinking. We have come to a stage where negative qualities are the hallmark of respectability. Violence and aggression can never win. Acceptance and compassion alone will.

Instructions For Enlightenment

8.49 *One whose mind is always free from selfish attachment, who has controlled the mind and who is free from desires, who attains perfection of freedom from selfish attachment to the fruits of work, is one who has renounced.*

18.50 *Understand from Me how one can achieve the state of Truth, Brahman, by acting in the way I shall now summarize, Arjuna.*

18.51,52,53
Endowed with purified intellect; subduing the mind with firm resolve; turning away from objects of the senses; giving up likes and dislikes; living in solitude; eating lightly; controlling the mind, speech, and organs of action; being ever absorbed in meditation; taking refuge in detachment, and relinquishing egotism, violence, pride, lust, anger, and proprietorship, one becomes peaceful, free from the notion of 'I' and 'mine', and fit for attaining oneness with the supreme Being.

These verses are the ultimate *sūtra,* the technique to liberate oneself and realize *Brahman,* ultimate Truth. Kṛṣṇa describes how to reach the ultimate Truth.

Arjuna is full of questions, and so are all of you. Questions are born out of ignorance and never out of wisdom. They raise more questions when they are answered, because people don't listen. His compassion drives Him to repeat His answers to ensure that Arjuna understands.

As long as we question why, we never get a clear answer. Especially with Existence, the question 'Why?' has no relevance. As I said earlier, we operate at a different frequency from the Divine, so even if it is explained we will not understand. Spirituality is an inner science, not an outer science - and that is fortunate! In the outer sciences, we keep asking 'Why?' and when we cannot get answers we get stuck. Then, we produce half-baked theories that convince no one. Spirituality does not concern itself with 'Why?' It is about 'How?'. 'Why?' is about logic. 'How?' is about realism. *Śāstras* answer the 'Why?' *Sūtras* answer the 'How?' Once in a while the master delivers the *sūtra* amidst the *śāstra* that He must deliver to keep Arjuna quiet.

He says, 'Settle the mind and control the senses.' Can you do that while sitting in the middle of a traffic intersection? No. That is why He says to go into solitude and cut yourself off from disturbances. Eat little, so that you are not disturbed. Go into meditation and shut your senses to external objects.

These are the clearest instructions on how to meditate. Prepare yourself to be away from potential disturbances. There is no point in meditating when you are sure the phone will ring or a guest will be arriving. You are only wasting time. Fix a time and place when you will be alone and undisturbed.

There are simple ways to reduce sensory disturbances. Closing the eyes is insufficient. Your eyeballs will still move and an inner television will still play. Mentally freeze your eyeballs. Think they are made of stone and still them. At the same time place your tongue on your upper palate and lock it. If there is movement of the tongue, that creates verbalization, then visualization is difficult. These two tools of mentally freezing your eyeball movement and locking your tongue substantially reduce the wandering of the mind due to sensory disturbances.

Meditate on an empty stomach. A full stomach makes us sleepy; it will not take us into realization. Ideally one should meditate in the same location regularly to preserve the energy raised in meditation.

These are the physical requirements. Next Kṛṣṇa repeats what He has been emphasizing all along.

Drop your personality, He says, drop your ego, your attachments, your ideas of 'I' and 'mine,' as well as the emotions that bind you to survival and possession. Then you will be liberated and ready to reach the supreme Being.

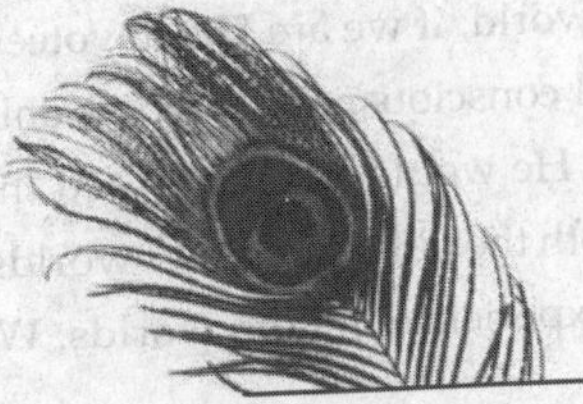

You Are Not The Master Of Your Destiny

18.54 Absorbed in the Supreme Being, the serene one neither grieves nor desires. Becoming impartial to all beings, one obtains the highest devotional love for Me.

18.55 By devotion one truly understands what and who I am in essence. Having known Me in essence, one immediately merges with Me.

18.56 My devotee, occupied with everyday life, still remains under My protection, the imperishable ultimate abode, through My mercy, through devotion to Me.

18.57 While being engaged in activities, just depend upon Me, and being fully conscious of Me, work always under My protection.

18.58 When your mind becomes fixed on Me, you shall overcome all difficulties by My grace. But if you do not listen to Me due to ego, you shall perish.

Kṛṣṇa explains how devotion is reached and how He protects the devotee. Developing the state of non-attachment, being impartial to all beings, being unconcerned by success and failure, fully absorbed in Godhood, one becomes His devotee. Once one understands this, one merges into Kṛṣṇa consciousness. When one is in Kṛṣṇa consciousness, the devotee, even if he is engaged in worldly activities, is protected by the grace and compassion of Kṛṣṇa.

Recently I expressed this concept to some devotees. When we relax from the instinct that constantly works to protect us, the space created allows the power of coincidence to happen. Kṛṣṇa says that even though we may be engaged in the activities of the world, if we are His devotees, under His protection we experience eternal consciousness. If Kṛṣṇa only wanted to give us the spiritual experience, He would not have used the word 'protection.' So Kṛṣṇa is referring to both the outer and inner worlds. The person who surrenders gets the best experience in both worlds. We simply need to get out and He will get in.

A small story:

One day Viṣṇu was resting on *Ādiśeṣa,* His bed that is actually a big serpent. Lakṣmī, His consort, was pressing His feet. This is known as *pādaseva* - service to the feet. In those days women actually served their husbands! Suddenly, Viṣṇu called for His vehicle, Garuḍa. He stood up, ran a few steps, stopped and then walked back. Lakṣmī was puzzled and asked what had happened. Viṣṇu explained that He had seen a man throwing stones at one of His devotees who was meditating. He jumped up, intending to protect him: however, He saw the devotee open his eyes and pick up a stone to defend himself. When Viṣṇu saw that the man could protect himself, He decided not to go!

Thus, when you protect yourself and your property He withdraws. To protect does not mean that you should not lock your house. It means that you should drop the instinct of survival. The instinct to survive kills you every moment. When you surrender this instinct, Kṛṣṇa will protect you. Intellectually you cannot understand this. You think, 'How can somebody who made a statement thousands of years ago give me protection?' You think that the survival instinct is essential in order to exist. You will realize the futility of the survival instinct only when you surrender. After that, you will automatically realize that you can live without the instinct to survive or the instinct to possess. When you surrender, a space is created that allows the power of coincidence to happen. Automatically you are taken care of by the energy of Kṛṣṇa.

When you believe that you are intelligent enough to use your mind and go your own way, you are asking for trouble. Kṛṣṇa says you will perish if you follow your mind and senses, instead of listening to Him.

Understand surrender

We must understand two things. The first is about listening to one's mind and the second is about not listening to the master.

Many people have an issue about accepting another human as superior, as someone to whom they should defer, let alone surrender. They think that prostrating at another person's feet is disrespecting themselves and quite uncivilized.

When I heal someone, if the pain is in the leg, I normally bend down and touch the person's feet. Once someone asked me, '*Swamiji*, how can you touch someone's feet? You are lowering yourself.'

I said, 'When I touch someone's feet, I am raising them to my level. When you fall at my feet, you surrender your ego!'

When you fall at someone's feet, you surrender your ego. It is good for you. It does not matter to whom you surrender. Whether you surrender to a stone or a human being, surrendering your ego raises you spiritually. This is the absolute Truth. You do not need to discriminate, search, filter and go through a lot of effort and time to surrender to an enlightened master.

Someone asked me, 'What do you mean by surrender?' Surrender is when you find someone whom you can unconditionally love and you have no problem if it is obvious that you are in love with that person. Your identity then merges with that person.

I tell them, 'Think of the person whom you would like to be with if God told you that the entire Earth is about to be destroyed. Only you and one other person will survive and you can choose that person. Who will that person be? That person is the one you have surrendered to!'

Vedic chants end with the word *namaḥ*. What does this mean? It means 'I surrender to You.' Each time you utter a *Vedic* prayer, you say, 'I surrender to You, my Lord.' Is there another system of prayer that so thoroughly destroys your ego?

So, just because you do not surrender to a master or a favorite deity, because one is human and the other is stone, do you think you are the master, free and independent? You surrender to someone else for money, power, or lust. One of these will surely happen. People run after someone, because that person carries something that they want.

How much more sensible it is to follow and surrender to someone out of intelligence, because that person is more aware and can guide you on the path to awareness?

Why are we reluctant to surrender to another person? It is because we have been captured by our mind and senses. We fear losing the identity that our mind and senses have created for us. Our mind fights against shifting our allegiance from that ego and identity to someone else.

Realize that you are a slave to your senses and not the master of your destiny as you imagine. Be aware that your pains and sorrows arise from the mistaken belief that you are the master of your destiny. Once you realize this, you will look for an alternative.

You then understand what the greatest master of all says: If you listen to Me, I shall protect you, whatever may happen. If you do not, and you follow your mind, you shall perish.

Energy darśan

18.59 *If, due to ego, you think: 'I shall not fight,' your resolve is useless, and your own nature will compel you.*

18.60 *O Arjuna, you are controlled by your own natural conditioning. Therefore you shall do, even against your will, what out of delusion you wish not to do.*

18.61 *The supreme Lord resides in everyone's heart, O Arjuna, and is directing the activities of all living entities that are acting as machines under His illusive material power.*

18.62 *Surrender to Him completely. By His grace you will attain supreme peace and the eternal abode.*

Kṛṣṇa first delivers an ultimatum to Arjuna. 'Whether you like it or not, Arjuna,' He says, 'you will fight. In seeming intelligence, your ego tells you that you should not fight. You are under the illusion of your superficial knowledge that it is not right to wage war against friends, relatives, and teachers. But you forget that your nature and your conditioning as a warrior drive you. You are a puppet in the hands of Existence. You will fight.'

Nothing can be clearer. The law of nature drives us to fulfill our unfulfilled desires. Our past conditioning invokes these desires. Even though they may be in our unconscious, inaccessible to us, they determine what we do. The master sees this even if we cannot. That is why Kṛṣṇa makes this bold statement.

Kṛṣṇa then switches gears and starts giving Arjuna the experience. He starts radiating eternal consciousness to place Arjuna into the experience of enlightenment.

Just relax for a few minutes. Relax from all the thoughts and ideas going on in your head. Drop your thoughts from your inner space, so that you may glimpse that consciousness. There is a distinct possibility that you may experience what Arjuna experienced by the grace of Kṛṣṇa.

Throughout Bhagavad Gītā, Kṛṣṇa has been saying, 'Surrender to Me.' He has been saying 'I' and 'Me,' meaning that He represents the Divine. Now, suddenly, He changes that and says surrender unto Him as a third person. For the first time He refers to the Divine in this way. This means that He has expanded beyond the body. He now speaks as *Parabrahma Kṛṣṇa,* the universal Kṛṣṇa. He speaks from the eternal consciousness. In order to give a disciple the experience, the master must be in the same state, too. That is why Kṛṣṇa went into that expanded state.

He has expanded into that consciousness and is about to give energy *darśan.* He is ready to shower His energy on Arjuna.

Surrender To Me

18.63 *I have explained the knowledge that is the secret of secrets. After fully reflecting on this, do as you wish.*

18.64 *Because you are dear friend, I express this truth to you. This is the most confidential of all knowledge. Hear this from Me. It is for your benefit.*

18.65 *Always think of Me and become devotee. Worship Me and offer your homage unto Me. Thus you will certainly attain Me. This I promise you because you are very dear friend.*

18.66 *Abandon all principles and concepts of right conduct and simply surrender unto Me. I shall deliver you from all sinful reaction. Have no worry.*

What powerful words! Only the Divine can speak these words of absolute authority.

Now He comes to the ultimate teaching. This is the essence of all His teachings, the quintessence of Bhagavad Gītā. He wakes up Arjuna with this verse and puts him into Kṛṣṇa consciousness or enlightenment. He says, 'Give up everything, whatever you know as *dharma,* the rules and regulations of the outer life and of the inner life. Drop everything that you know and surrender unto Me. I shall deliver you from everything. Do not fear.' Kṛṣṇa gives him *abhaya,* complete protection.

With this verse, Kṛṣṇa makes Arjuna drop everything and liberates him. He gives him a conscious experience of the ocean. Kṛṣṇa gives Arjuna the ultimate experience permanently. We cannot call him Arjuna any longer, because he has become Kṛṣṇa. He has achieved Kṛṣṇa-consciousness. Now only Kṛṣṇa exists. Kṛṣṇa and Arjuna have become one, neither exists. It is only energy.

Forget about *dharma,* the codes of conduct laid down by religions, and turn to Me. I shall be your savior, says Kṛṣṇa.

Do not misunderstand, misquote, and misuse these words. You will do yourself the greatest disservice. The Divine does not care whether you are good or evil, a saint or a sinner. All have equal chances of reaching the Divine. This is the truth. Of course, when you come close to the Divine, the energy transforms you. You are reborn. Religion is the creation of men. Spirituality is the creation of enlightened masters who live in the energy of the Divine with total awareness. Kṛṣṇa, Śiva, Buddha, Mahavira and Jesus were enlightened masters. It is their followers, who interpreted them to the best or worst of their understanding, created religions. The followers established *dharma,* the codes of righteous conduct. The master is only interested in putting you on the right path. Thus, Kṛṣṇa says with absolute conviction and authority: Forget all codes of conduct, give up all religions and come to Me with awareness. If you understand this verse and act accordingly, you will be liberated. That is Kṛṣṇa's promise.

Take a few moments now to pray to *Parabrahma* Kṛṣṇa, the universal Kṛṣṇa, who showered enlightenment on Arjuna and gave him the ultimate experience. Pray that He may shower the same experience on us or give us a glimpse of the ultimate Truth. Take a few moments to pray. Do not think that He is unavailable now. He is always available to everybody on planet earth. He may not have the body, but He is available in the form of energy.

I Shall Not Leave

18.67 This knowledge should never be spoken by you to one who is devoid of austerity, who is without devotion, who does not desire to listen, or who speaks ill of Me.

18.68 One who communicates the supreme secret to the devotees performs the highest devotional service to Me, and at the end he will without doubt come back to Me.

18.69 No other person shall do a more pleasing service to Me, and no one on the earth shall be more dear to Me.

18.70 I say that One who studies this sacred dialogue worships Me with the sacrifice of his intelligence.

18.71 One who listens with faith and without envy becomes free from sinful reactions and attains to the planets where those of merit dwell.

18.72 O Arjuna, did you listen to this with single-minded attention? Has your delusion born of ignorance been completely destroyed?

These words are meant not merely for Arjuna, but for all of humanity. Kṛṣṇa says here that we should read, listen and understand this dialogue between Arjuna and Kṛṣṇa, between Narā and Narayana. Nothing more needs to be read or listened to. Everything we need is here.

Only one who is in deep devotion to Me should read this. I have conveyed here that which is most beneficial, the secret of how to live and how to reach Me. One who understands this and drops his mind, with his focus entirely upon Me, shall reach Me without a doubt.

This is Kṛṣṇa's promise.

He blessed the whole universe with His grace and compassion. He showered His blessing on Arjuna and made him merge with Him. The same consciousness is being showered on the whole universe. He declares that whoever studies this sacred conversation will achieve His eternal consciousness. When we put anything into the fire, it disappears. In the same way, when we immerse ourselves in the study of Gītā, we will not remain as we are. We will disappear into Him. Only He remains, only He exists.

Earlier Kṛṣṇa said that He would appear again and again whenever He is needed to restore equilibrium between good and bad. He is the only great master who has the courage to say, 'I am not the last master; it is not that there will be no one after Me.' Kṛṣṇa will not reappear in his Vāsudeva Kṛṣṇa form, with peacock feathers and a flute! That is the mistake we make in our assumption. His energy will reappear in the form of enlightened masters, time and again. He will come again and again to restore the balance, redeem the good, and destroy the evil.

This is the last time Kṛṣṇa speaks in Bhagavad Gītā. He asks, 'Arjuna, have you listened to me with attention? Has your delusion disappeared?'

Until the end He is the teacher. He is full of compassion. His concern is only for Arjuna and the rest of humanity. 'Have you understood?' He asks. 'Have your doubts disappeared? Do you need anything more?'

This is the greatness of masters. Nothing concerns them except the deliverance of their disciples. That is why they have come here. Otherwise why should they waste their time on planet earth? They can be immersed in the blissful energy that they are part of without disturbance.

My disciples understand when I tell them that the only time I feel anything like sadness is when a disciple leaves me. It saddens me because he is losing a great opportunity. His spirit brought him to me for redemption. If the body-mind does not cooperate, the spirit must live again and again until it gets the opportunity to be liberated. In each cycle of birth that the spirit undertakes, it suffers, and regrets not having taken that final step.

No one who has crossed my ashram gates can ever leave me. Even if they leave, I shall not leave them. I shall be with them. That one moment of intelligence that brought them in is enough for me to care of them.

Those who have understood the formless form that resides in me know that I am part of them. Wherever they are, I am part of them.

This is Kṛṣṇa's promise: Listen to Me, understand Me and come to Me; then you are a part of Me.

Kṛṣṇa Is Present

18.73 *Arjuna said: O Lord, my illusion is now gone. I have regained my memory by Your mercy, and I am now firm and free from doubt and ready to obey you.*

18.74 *Sañjaya said: Thus have I heard the conversation of two great souls, Kṛṣṇa and Arjuna. And so wonderful is that message that my hair stands on end.*

18.75 *By the mercy of Vyāsa, I have heard these most confidential words directly from Kṛṣṇa, the master of all mysticism, who was speaking personally to Arjuna.*

18.76 *O King, as I repeatedly recall this wondrous and holy dialogue between Kṛṣṇa and Arjuna, I take pleasure, being thrilled every moment.*

18.77 *O King, when I remember the wonderful form of Lord Kṛṣṇa, I am struck with even greater wonder, and I rejoice again and again.*

18.78 *Wherever there is Kṛṣṇa, the master of all mystics, and wherever there is Partha, the supreme carrier of bow and arrow, there will certainly be opulence, victory, extraordinary power, and morality. That is my opinion.*

In these last verses Arjuna and Sañjaya take over. Arjuna bows down to the master and says, 'All my doubts are gone; I understand. I am ready. I shall obey whatever you say and I shall fight.'

The rest is history. Under the guidance of Arjuna, the Kaurava army is annihilated. All the Kaurava brothers, all the great teachers, and all the great warriors perish. It is also history that in due course all the Pāṇḍavā brothers die, as does the great master Kṛṣṇa. He gives up His mortal form. As long as you are in any form, the form will perish. The energy lives on. That is what Kṛṣṇa taught in these chapters and verses. Sacrifice your form and gain the formless.

Now Sañjaya comes back into the picture. Arjuna has disappeared and Kṛṣṇa is in ecstasy. Both are in no mood to speak. Sañjaya started speaking when Arjuna was in depression and Kṛṣṇa had nothing to say at that time. Then when Kṛṣṇa was giving the first experience to Arjuna, Kṛṣṇa was in higher consciousness and Arjuna was in ecstasy. Sañjaya came in to speak at that time because both were not in a mood to speak. Now Sañjaya comes back again. Not only are Kṛṣṇa and Arjuna not in a mood to speak, they are both no longer there. Sañjaya addresses Dhṛtarāṣṭra, 'O King, as I repeatedly recall this wondrous spiritual dialogue between Kṛṣṇa and Arjuna, I feel a great joy or ecstasy at every moment.'

Sañjaya says, 'By the mercy of Vyāsa, I heard these confidential talks directly from the master of all mysticism, Sri Kṛṣṇa.' Sañjaya expresses gratitude and joy at hearing this by the grace of Vyāsa, who is the author of Mahābhārata, in which the Bhagavad Gītā is recounted. 'Wherever there is Kṛṣṇa, the master of all mystics, and wherever there is Arjuna, the supreme archer, there will certainly be opulence, victory, extraordinary power and morality. This is my opinion.' He ends the whole thing with a beautiful auspicious blessing.

Whenever we read, teach or listen to Bhagavad Gītā, Kṛṣṇa and Arjuna are present. They are present in their formless form. They have been here throughout these eighteen days.

You are the fortunate listeners and readers of this mystic dialogue between the two great souls, the master and the disciple. You are blessed with wealth, health, and success in whatever you undertake. Go with Kṛṣṇa consciousness and you will be in *nityānanda*, eternal bliss.

Thus ends the eighteenth chapter named **Mokṣa Sanyāsa Yogaḥ** *of the* **Upaniṣad** *of Bhagavad Gītā, the scripture of yoga, dealing with the science of the Absolute in the form of the dialogue between* **Śrī Kṛṣṇa and Arjuna.**

BHAGAVADGĪTĀ

Verses

Invocation Verses

ॐ पार्थाय प्रतिबोधितां भगवता नारायणेन स्वयं
व्यासेन ग्रथितां पुराणमुनिना मध्ये महाभारतम्
अद्वैतामृतवर्षिणीं भगवतीं अष्टादशाध्यायिनीं
अम्ब त्वमनुसन्दधामि भगवद्गीते भवद्वेषिणीम्

Om pārthāya pratibodhitāṁ bhagavatā nārāyaṇena svayaṁ
vyāsena gratitāṁ purāṇa muninā madhye mahābhāratam I
advaitāmṛtavarṣiṇīṁ bhagavatīṁ aṣṭādaśādhyāyinīṁ
amba tvām anusandadhāmi bhagavadgīte bhavadveṣiṇīm II

Om, I medidate upon you, Bhagavad Gītā the affectionate Mother, the Divine Mother showering the nectar of non duality and destroying rebirth, (who was) incorporated into the **Mahābhārata** *of eighteen chapters by sage* **Vyāsa**, *the author of the* **purāṇas** *and imparted to Arjuna by Lord* **Nārāyaṇa**, *Himself.*

वसुदेवसुतं देवं कंसचाणूरमर्दनम् ।
देवकीपरमानन्दं कृष्णं वन्दे जगद्गुरुम् ॥

vasudeva sutaṁ devaṁ kamsa cāṇūra mardanam I
devakī paramānandaṁ kṛṣṇam vande jagad gurum II

I salute you Lord **Kṛṣṇa**, *Teacher to the world, son of* **Vāsudeva**, *supreme bliss of* **Devakī**, *destoryer of Kamsa and* **Cāṇūra**

Verses of Gita Chapter - 1

अथ प्रथमोऽध्यायः

अर्जुनविषादयोगः

Arjunaviṣāda Yogaḥ

धृतराष्ट्र उवाच
धर्मक्षेत्रे कुरुक्षेत्रे समवेता युयुत्सवः ।
मामकाः पाण्डवाश्चैव किमकुर्वत सञ्जय ॥ १.१

dhṛtarāṣṭra uvāca
dharmakṣetre kurukṣetre samavetā yuyutsavaḥ /
māmakāḥ pāṇḍavāś caiva kim akurvata sañjaya // 1.1

dhṛtarāṣṭra: Dhṛtarāṣṭra; *uvāca*: said; *dharmakṣetre*: in the place of righteousness; *kurukṣetre*: in this location of kurukṣetra; *samavetāḥ*: gathered; *yuyutsavaḥ*: desiring to fight; *māmakāḥ*: my people; *pāṇḍavāḥ*: the sons of Pāṇḍu; *ca*: and; *eva*: also; *kiṁ*: what; *akurvata*: did they do; *sañjaya*: O Sañjaya

1.1 Dhṛtarāṣṭra said: O Sañjaya, on this righteous location of Kurukṣetra, *what did my sons and those of Pāṇḍu ready to fight, do?*

सञ्जय उवाच
दृष्ट्वा तु पाण्डवानीकं व्यूढं दुर्योधनस्तदा ।
आचार्यमुपसङ्गम्य राजा वचनमब्रवीत् ॥ १.२

sañjaya uvāca
dṛṣṭvā tu pāṇḍavānīkaṁ vyūḍhaṁ duryodhanas tadā /
ācāryam upasaṅgamya rājā vacanam abravīt // 1.2

sañjaya: Sañjaya; *uvāca*: said; *dṛṣṭvā*: having seen; *tu*: indeed; *pāṇḍavānīkaṁ*: the Pāṇḍavā army; *vyūḍhaṁ*: arranged in formation; *duryodhanaḥ*: Duryodhana; *tadā*: then; *ācāryam*: the teacher; *upasaṅgamya*: approaching; *rājā*: the king; *vacanam*: words; *abravīt*: said

1.2 Sañjaya said: O king, looking at the Pāṇḍavā army in full formation, Duryodhana went to his teacher and spoke.

पश्यैतां पाण्डुपुत्राणामाचार्य महतीं चमूम् ।
व्यूढां द्रुपदपुत्रेण तव शिष्येण धीमता ॥ १.३

pasyai 'tāṁ pāṇḍuputrāṇām ācārya mahatīṁ camūm **/**
vyūḍhām drupada putreṇa tava śiṣyeṇa dhīmatā **//** 1.3

pasya: behold; *etāṁ*: this; *pāṇḍuputrāṇām*: of the sons of Pāṇḍu; *ācārya*: O teacher; *mahatīṁ*: great; *camūm*: army; *vyūḍhām*: formed; *drupada-putreṇa*: by the son of Drupada; *tava śiṣyeṇa*: by your disciple; *dhīmatā*: intelligent

1.3 O my teacher, behold the great army of the sons of Pāṇḍu, arrayed for battle by your intelligent disciple, the son of Drupada.

अत्र शूरा महेष्वासा भीमार्जुनसमा युधि ।
युयुधानो विराटश्च द्रुपदश्च महारथः ॥ १.४

atra śūrā maheṣvāsā bhīmārjunasamā yudhi **/**
yuyudhāno virāṭaś ca drupadaś ca mahā rathaḥ **//** 1.4

atra: here; *śūrāḥ*: heroes; *maheṣvāsāḥ*: mighty archers; *bhīmārjuna*: Bhīma and Arjuna; *samāḥ*: equal; *yudhi*: in battle; *yuyudhānaḥ*: Yuyudhana; *virāṭaḥ*: Virāṭa; *ca*: and; *drupadaḥ*: Drupada; *ca*: and; *mahārathaḥ*: great charioteers

1.4 Here in this army there are many heroes wielding mighty bows, and equal in military prowess to Bhīma and Arjuna - Yuyudhāna, Virāṭa, and the great chariot warrior Drupada.

धृष्टकेतुश्चेकितानः काशिराजश्च वीर्यवान् ।
पुरुजित् कुन्तिभोजश्च शैब्यश्च नरपुङ्गवः ॥ १.५

dhṛṣṭaketuś cekitānaḥ kāśirājaś ca vīryavān **/**
purujit kuntibhojaś ca śaibyaś ca narapuṅgavaḥ **//** 1.5

dhṛṣṭaketuḥ: Dṛṣthtaketu; *cekitānaḥ*: Cekitāna; *kāśirājaḥ*: Kāśirāja; *ca*: and; *vīryavān*: courageous; *purujit*: Purujit; *kuntibhojaḥ*: Kuntibhoja; *ca*: and; *śaibyaḥ*: Śaibya; *ca*: and; *narapuṅgavaḥ*: best of men

1.5 There are courageous warriors like Dṛṣṭaketu, Cekitāna, the couragious Kāśīrāja, Purujit, Kuntibhoja and Śaibya, the best of men.

युधामन्युश्च विक्रान्त उत्तमौजाश्च वीर्यवान् ।
सौभद्रो द्रौपदेयाश्च सर्व एव महारथाः ॥ १.६

yudhāmanyuś ca vikrānta uttamaujāś ca vīryavān |
saubhadro draupadeyāś ca sarva eva mahārathāḥ || 1.6

yudhāmanyuḥ: Yudhāmanyu; *ca*: and; *vikrāntaḥ*: mighty; *uttamaujāḥ*: Uttamauja; *ca*: and; *vīryavān*: brave; *saubhadraḥ*: the son of Subhadrā; *draupadeyāḥ*: the sons of Draupadī ; *ca*: and; *sarva*: all; *eva*: certainly; *mahārathāḥ*: great chariot fighters.

1.6 There are the mighty Yudhāmanyu, *the brave Uttamauja, Abhimanyu, the son of* Subhadrā *and the sons of* Draupadī *, all of them great chariot warriors.*

अस्माकं तु विशिष्टा ये तान्निबोध द्विजोत्तम ।
नायका मम सैन्यस्य संज्ञार्थं तान् ब्रवीमि ते ॥ १.७

asmākaṁ tu viśiṣṭā ye tān nibodha dvijottama |
nāyakā mama sainyasya saṁjñārthaṁ tān bravīmi te || 1.7

asmākaṁ: our; *tu*: also; *viśiṣṭāḥ*: important; *ye*: who; *tān*: those; *nibodha*: know; *dvijottama*: the best of the *brāhmaṇas*; *nāyakāḥ*: leaders; *mama*: my; *sainyasya*: of the army; *saṁjñārthaṁ*: for information; *tān*: them; *bravīmi*: I speak; *te*: to you.

1.7 O best of the brāhmaṇas, *know them also, who are the principal warriors on our side the generals of my army; for your information, I mention them.*

भवान् भीष्मश्च कर्णश्च कृपश्च समितिञ्जयः ।
अश्वत्थामा विकर्णश्च सौमदत्तिस्तथैव च ॥ १.८

bhavān bhīṣmaś ca karṇaś ca kṛ paś ca samitiṁjayaḥ |
aśvatthāmā vikarṇaś ca saumadattis tathai 'va ca || 1.8

bhavān: your self; *bhīṣmaḥ*: grandfather Bhīṣma; *ca*: and; *karṇaḥ*: Karṇa; *ca*: and; *kṛpaḥ*: Kṛpa; *ca*: and; *samitiṁjayaḥ*: victorious in war; *aśvatthāmā*: Aśvattāma; *vikarṇaḥ*: Vikarṇa; *ca*: and; *saumadattiḥ*: the son of Somadatta; *tathā*: thus as; *eva*: only; *ca*: and

1.8 They are yourself, Bhīṣma, Karṇa, Kṛpa who is ever victorious in battle and even so Aśvattāma, Vikarṇa and the son of Somadatta.

अन्ये च बहवः शूरा मदर्थे त्यक्तजीविताः ।
नानाशस्त्रप्रहरणाः सर्वे युद्धविशारदाः ॥ १.९

anye ca bahavaḥ śūrā mad arthe tyakta jīvitāḥ I
nānā śastra praharaṇāḥ sarve yuddha viśāradāḥ II 1.9

anye: many others; *ca*: also; *bahavaḥ*: in great numbers; *śūrāḥ*: heroes; *mad arthe*: for my sake; *tyakta jīvitāḥ*: prepared to risk life; *nānā*: many; *śastra*: weapons; *praharaṇāḥ*: equipped with; *sarve*: all of them; *yuddha*: battle; *viśāradāḥ*: experienced in military science.

1.9 There are many other heroes who are prepared to lay down their lives for my sake. All of them are well equipped with different kinds of weapons, and all are experienced in military science.

अपर्याप्तं तदस्माकं बलं भीष्माभिरक्षितम् ।
पर्याप्तं त्विदमेतेषां बलं भीमाभिरक्षितम् ॥ १.१०

aparyāptaṁ tad asmākaṁ balaṁ bhīṣmābhi rakṣitam I
paryāptaṁ tvidam eteṣāṁ balaṁ bhīmābhi rakṣitam II 1.10

aparyāptaṁ: unlimited; *tat*: that; *asmākaṁ*: of ours; *balaṁ*: strength; *bhīṣmābhi rakṣitam*: presided over and protected by Bhīṣma; *paryāptaṁ*: limited; *tu*: but; *idaṁ*: all this; *eteṣāṁ*: their; *balaṁ*: strength; *bhīmābhi rakṣitam*: presided over and protected by Bhīma

1.10 This army of ours protected by Bhīṣma is invincible whereas their army protected by Bhīma is conquerable.

अयनेषु च सर्वेषु यथाभागमवस्थिताः ।
भीष्ममेवाभिरक्षन्तु भवन्तः सर्व एव हि ॥ १.११

ayaneṣu ca sarveṣu yathā bhāgam avasthitāḥ I
bhīṣmam evā bhirakṣantu bhavantaḥ sarva eva hi II 1.11

ayaneṣu: in the divisions; *ca*: and; *sarveṣu*: everywhere; *yathā bhāgam*: as per the divisions; *avasthitāḥ*: situated; *bhīṣmam*: to Bhisma; *eva*: alone; *abhi rakṣantu*: protect; *bhavantaḥ*: you; *sarva*: all; *eva*: only; *hi*: indeed

1.11 Stationed in your respective divisions on all fronts, all of you must give full protection to Bhīṣma.

तस्य सञ्जनयन् हर्षं कुरुवृद्धः पितामहः ।
सिंहनादं विनद्योच्चैः शङ्खं दध्मौ प्रतापवान् ॥ १.१२

tasya sañjanayan harṣaṁ kuru vṛddhaḥ pitāmahaḥ I
siṁha nādaṁ vinadyoccaiḥ śaṇkhaṁ dadhmau pratāpavān II 1.12

tasya: his; *sañjanayan*: causing; *harṣaṁ*: joy; *kuru vṛddhaḥ*: old man of the Kuru dynasty; *pitāmahaḥ*: the grandfather; *siṁha nādaṁ*: lion's roar; *vinadya*: causing to sound; *uccaiḥ*: loudly; *śaṇkhaṁ*: conch; *dadhmau*: blew; *pratāpavān*: mighty

1.12 Then Bhīṣma, the grand old man of the Kuru dynasty, their glorious grandfather, roared like a lion and blew his conch, giving Duryodhana joy.

ततः शङ्खाश्च भेर्यश्च पणवानकगोमुखाः ।
सहसैवाभ्यहन्यन्त स शब्दस्तुमुलोऽभवत् ॥ १.१३

tataḥśaṇkhāś ca bheryaś ca paṇavānaka gomukhāḥ I
sahasaivābhyahanyanta sa śabdas tumulo 'bhavat II 1.13

tataḥ: then; *śaṇkhāḥ*: conches; *ca*: and; *bheryaś ca paṇavānaka*: drums, bugles, horns and trumpets; *gomukhāḥ*: cow horns; *sahasā eva:* quite suddenly *abhyahanyanta*: blared; *saḥ*: that; *śabdaḥ*: sound; *tumulaḥ*: tumultuous; *abhavat*: became

1.13 Then, conches, bugles, trumpets, drums and horns were all suddenly sounded, and the combined sound was tumultuous.

ततःश्वेतैर्हयैर्युक्ते महति स्यन्दने स्थितौ ।
माधवः पाण्डवश्चैव दिव्यौ शङ्खौ प्रदध्मतुः ॥ १.१४

tataḥ śvetair hayair yukte mahati syandane sthitau I
mādhavaḥ pāṇḍavaś caiva divyau śaṇkhau pradadhmatuḥ II 1.14

tataḥ: then; *śvetaiḥ*: by white; *hayaiḥ*: horses; *yukte*: being yoked; *mahati*: magnificent; *syandane*: chariot; *sthitau*: seated; *mādhavaḥ*: Mādhava, Śrī Kṛṣṇa; *pāṇḍavaḥ*: son of Pāṇḍu; *ca*: and; *eva*: only; *divyau*: divine; *śaṇkhau*: conches; *pradadhmatuḥ*: blew

1.14 Then, seated on a magnificent chariot drawn by white horses, both Kṛṣṇa and Arjuna sounded their divine conches.

पाञ्चजन्यं हृषीकेशो देवदत्तं धनञ्जयः ।
पौण्ड्रं दध्मौ महाशङ्खं भीमकर्मा वृकोदरः ॥ १.१५

pāñcajanyaṁ hṛṣīkeśo devadattaṁ dhanaṁjayaḥ /
pauṇḍraṁ dadhmau mahā śaṅkhaṁ bhīma karmā vṛkodaraḥ // 1.15

pāñcajanyaṁ: the conch named Pāñcajanya; *hṛṣīkeśaḥ*: One who has mastered the senses (Kṛṣṇa) ; *devadattaṁ*: the conch named Devadatta; *dhanaṁjayaḥ*: Dhañanjaya, the winner of wealth; *pauṇḍraṁ*: the conch named Pauṇḍra; *dadhmau*: blew; *mahā-śaṅkhaṁ*: the great conch; *bhīma karmā*: one who performs terrible tasks; *vṛkodaraḥ*: one with the belly of a wolf

1.15 Then, Kṛṣṇa blew His conch, called Pāñcajanya; Arjuna blew his, called Devadatta; and Bhīma blew his mighty conch called Pauṇḍra.

अनन्तविजयं राजा कुन्तीपुत्रो युधिष्ठिरः ।
नकुलः सहदेवश्च सुघोषमणिपुष्पकौ ॥ १.१६

anantavijayaṁ rājā kuntī putro yudhiṣṭhiraḥ /
nakulaḥ sahadevaś ca sughoṣa maṇipuṣpakau // 1.16

काश्यश्च परमेष्वासः शिखण्डी च महारथः ।
धृष्टद्युम्नो विराटश्च सात्यकिश्चापराजितः ॥ १.१७

kāśyaś ca parameṣvāsaḥ śikhaṇḍī ca mahā rathaḥ /
dhṛṣṭadyumno virāṭaś ca sātyakiś cāparājitaḥ // 1.17

द्रुपदो द्रौपदेयाश्च सर्वशः पृथिवीपते ।
सौभद्रश्च महाबाहुः शङ्खान् दध्मुः पृथक् पृथक् ॥ १.१८

drupado draupadeyāś ca sarvaśaḥ pṛthivī pate /
saubhadraś ca mahābāhuh śaṅkhān dadhmuḥ pṛthak-pṛthak // 1.18

anantavijayaṁ: the conch named Ananta-vijaya; *rājā*: the king; *kuntī putraḥ*: the son of Kuntī; *yudhiṣṭhiraḥ*: Yudhistra; *nakulaḥ*: Nakula; *sahadevaḥ*: Sahadeva; *ca*: and; *sughoṣa maṇipuṣpakau*: the conches named Sughośa and Maṇipuṣpaka; *kāśyaḥ*: the king of Kāśī (Vārаṇāsi); *ca*: and; *parameṣvāsaḥ*: the great archer; *śikhaṇḍī*: Śikhaṇḍī; *ca*: and; *mahā rathaḥ*: great chariot warrior; *dhṛṣṭadyumnaḥ*: Dhṛṣṭadyumna; *virāṭaḥ*: Virāṭa; *ca*: and; *sātyakiḥ*: Sātyaki; *ca*: and; *aparājitaḥ*: invincible; *drupadaḥ*: Drupada; *draupadeyāḥ*: the sons of Draupadī ; *ca*: also; *sarvaśaḥ*: all; *pṛthivīpate*: O' king of earth;

saubhadraḥ: the son of Subhadrā (Abhimanyu); *ca*: and; *mahā bāhuḥ*: mighty-armed; *śaṅkhān*: conches; *dadhmuḥ* blew; *pṛthak pṛthak*: severally

1.16, 17, 18 King Yudhisṭra, the son of Kuntī, blew his conch, the Anantavijaya, and Nakula and Sahadeva blew theirs known as Sughośa and Maṇipuṣpaka. The excellent archer, the king of Kāśī, the great chariot-fighter Śikhaṇḍī, Dhṛṣṭadyumna, Virāṭa and the invincible Sātyaki, Drupada, the sons of Draupadī , and the mighty-armed Abhimanyu, son of Subhadrā, all of them, O king, blew their own conches.

स घोषो धार्तराष्ट्राणां हृदयानि व्यदारयत् ।
नभश्च पृथिवीं चैव तुमुलो व्यनुनादयन् ॥ १.१९

sa ghoṣo dhārtarāṣṭrāṇāṁ hṛdayāni vyadārayat |
nabhaś ca pṛthivīṁ caiva tumulo vyanunādayan || 1.19

saḥ: that; *ghoṣaḥ*: uproar; *dhārtarāṣṭrāṇāṁ*: of the sons of Dhṛtarāṣṭra; *hṛdayāni*: hearts; *vyadārayat*: broke; *nabhaḥ*: the sky; *ca*: and; *pṛthivīṁ*: the earth; *ca*: and; *eva*: only; *tumulaḥ*: tumultous; *vyanunādayan*: resounding

1.19 The terrible sound echoing through the sky and the earth rent the hearts of the sons of Dhṛtarāṣṭra.

अथ व्यवस्थितान्दृष्ट्वा धार्तराष्ट्रान् कपिध्वजः ।
प्रवृत्ते शस्त्रसम्पाते धनुरुद्यम्य पाण्डवः ॥ १.२०
हृषीकेशं तदा वाक्यमिदमाह महीपते ।

atha vyavasthitān dṛṣṭvā dhārtarāṣṭrān kapidhvajaḥ |
pravṛtte śastrasaṁpāte dhanur udyamya pāṇḍavaḥ || 1.20
hṛṣīkeśaṁ tadā vākyam idam āha mahīpate |

atha: then; *vyavasthitān*: stationed; *dṛṣṭvā*: seeing; *dhārtarāṣṭrān*: the sons of Dhṛtarāṣṭra; *kapidhvajaḥ*: one whose flag is marked with the ape; *pravṛtte*: about to begin; *śastrasaṁpāte*: the arrows released; *dhanuḥ*: bow; *udyamya*: after taking up; *pāṇḍavaḥ*: the son of Pāṇḍu; *hṛṣīkeśaṁ*: to Kṛṣṇa; *tadā*: then; *vākyam*: words; *idaṁ*: this; *āha*: said; *mahī pate*: O Lord of the earth

1.20 Seeing the sons of Dhṛtarāṣṭra arrayed in the battle field, Arjuna, the son of Pāṇḍu, who was seated in his chariot, bearing the flag marked with Hanumān, took up his bow.

अर्जुन उवाच
सेनयोरुभयोर्मध्ये रथं स्थापय मेऽच्युत ॥ १.२१

यावदेतान्निरीक्षेऽहं योद्धुकामानवस्थितान् ।
कैर्मया सह योद्धव्यमस्मिन् रणसमुद्यमे ॥ १.२२

arjuna uvāca
senayor ubhayor madhye rathaṁ sthāpaya me 'cyuta // 1.21

yāvad etān nirīkṣe 'haṁ yoddhu kāmān avasthitān /
kair mayā saha yoddhavyam asmin raṇasamudyame // 1.22

arjuna: Arjuna; *uvāca*: said; *senayoḥ*: of the armies; *ubhayoḥ*: of both; *madhye*: in between; *rathaṁ*: the chariot; *sthāpaya*: position; *me*: my; *acyuta*: O infallible one; *yāvat*: while; *etān*: all these; *nirīkṣe*: behold; *ahaṁ*: I; *yoddhu kāmān*: desiring to fight; *avasthitān*: standing; *kaiḥ*: with whom; *mayā*: by me; *saha*: with; *yoddhavyam*: to be fought; *asmin*: in this; *raṇasamudyame*: situation of war;

1.21, 22 Arjuna said: O Infallible One, please place my chariot between the two armies while I may observe these warriors arrayed for battle and with whom I have to engage in fight.

योत्स्यमानानवेक्षेऽहं य एतेऽत्र समागताः ।
धार्तराष्ट्रस्य दुर्बुद्धेर्युद्धे प्रियचिकीर्षवः ॥ १.२३

yotsyamānān avekṣe 'haṁ ya ete 'tra samāgatāḥ /
dhārtarāṣṭrasya durbuddher yuddhe priyacikīrṣavaḥ // 1.23

yotsyamānān: those who wish to fight; *avekṣe*: see; *ahaṁ*: I; *yaḥ*: who; *ete*: these; *atra*: here; *samāgatāḥ*: assembled; *dhārtarāṣṭrasya*: the son of Dhṛtarāṣṭra; *durbuddheḥ*: evil-minded; *yuddhe*: in the fight; *priyacikīrṣavaḥ*: wishing to please

1.23 Let me see these well wishers in this war of the evil-minded Duryodhana, who have come together here to fight.

सञ्जय उवाच
एवमुक्तो हृषीकेशो गुडाकेशेन भारत ।
सेनयोरुभयोर्मध्ये स्थापयित्वा रथोत्तमम् ॥ १.२४

भीष्मद्रोणप्रमुखतः सर्वेषां च महीक्षिताम् ।
उवाच पार्थ पश्यैतान्समवेतान्कुरूनिति ॥ १.२५

sañjaya uvāca
evam ukto hṛṣīkeśo guḍākeśena bhārata I
senayor ubhayor madhye sthāpayitvā rathottamam II 1.24

bhīṣma droṇa pramukhataḥ sarveṣāṁ ca mahīkṣitām I
uvāca pārtha paśyaitān samavetānkurūniti II 1.25

sañjaya: Sañjaya; *uvāca*: said; *evaṁ*: thus; *uktaḥ*: addressed; *hṛṣīkeśaḥ*: Krishna (Lord of senses); *guḍākeśena*: Arjuna (one who has conquered sleep); *bhārata*: O Bhārata; *senayoḥ*: of armies; *ubhayoḥ*: of both; *madhye*: in the middle of; *sthāpayitvā*: having placed; *rathottamam*: the finest chariot

bhīṣma: grandfather Bhīṣma; *droṇa*: the teacher Droṇa; *pramukhataḥ*: in front of; *sarveṣāṁ*: of all; *ca*: and; *mahīkṣitām*: of rulers of the world; *uvāca*: said; *pārtha*: O Pārtha; *paśyai*: see; *etān*: these; *samavetān*: assembled; *kurūn*: the Kurus; *iti*: thus

1.24, 25 Sañjaya said: O descendant of Bhārata, *being thus addressed by Arjuna, Kṛṣṇa then drew up the fine chariot to the middle of both the armies in front of Bhīṣma, Droṇa and all the kings and said, 'Arjuna, behold the Kauravas assembled here.'*

तत्रापश्यत् स्थितान् पार्थः पितॄनथ पितामहान् ।
आचार्यान्मातुलान्भ्रातॄन् पुत्रान्पौत्रान्सखींस्तथा ॥ १.२६
श्वशुरान्सुहृदश्चैव सेनयोरुभयोरपि ।

tatrā paśyat sthitān pārthaḥ pitṝn atha pitāmahān I
ācāryān mātulān bhrātṝn putrān pautrān sakhīṁs tathā II 1.26
śvaśurān suhṛdaś caiva senayorubhayorapi I

tatra: there; *apaśyat*: saw; *sthitān*: positioned; *pārthaḥ*: Arjuna; *pitṝn*: fathers; *atha*: also; *pitāmahān*: grandfathers; *ācāryān*: teachers; *mātulān*: maternal uncles; *bhrātṝn*: brothers; *putrān*: sons; *pautrān*: grandsons; *sakhīn*: friends; *tathā*: too; *śvaśurān*: fathers-in-law; *suhṛdaḥ*: well-wishers; *ca*: and; *eva*: only; *senayoḥ*: of the armies; *ubhayoḥ*: of both ; *api*: also

1.26 There Arjuna saw, stationed there in both the armies his uncles, grand uncles, teachers, maternal uncles, brothers, sons, grandsons, and friends, as well as his fathers-in-law and well-wishers.

तान् समीक्ष्य स कौन्तेयः सर्वान्बन्धूनवस्थितान् ॥ १.२७
कृपया परयाऽऽविष्टो विषीदन्निदमब्रवीत् ।

tān samīkṣya sa kaunteyaḥ sarvān bandhūn avasthitān // 1.27
kṛpayā parayā 'viṣṭo viṣīdann idam abravīt /

tān: those; *samīkṣya*: after seeing; *sa*: he; *kaunteyaḥ*: kaunteya; *sarvān*: all; *bandhūn*: relatives; *avasthitān*: standing; *kṛpayā*: by pity; *parayā*: deep; *āviṣṭaḥ*: filled; *viṣīdan*: lamenting; *idaṁ*: thus; *abravīt*: spoke

1.27 Seeing all those relatives present there, Arjuna was overwhelmed with deep pity and spoke in sadness.

अर्जुन उवाच
दृष्ट्वेमं स्वजनं कृष्ण युयुत्सुं समुपस्थितम् ॥ १.२८
सीदन्ति मम गात्राणि मुखं च परिशुष्यति ।

arjuna uvāca
dṛṣṭvemaṁ svajanaṁ kṛṣṇa yuyutsuṁ samupasthitam // 1.28
sīdanti mama gātrāṇi mukhaṁ ca pariśuṣyati /

arjuna: Arjuna; *uvāca*: said; *dṛṣtvā*: after seeing; *imaṁ*: all these; *svajanaṁ*: kinsmen; *kṛṣṇa*: Kṛṣṇa; *yuyutsuṁ*: all eager to do battle; *samupasthitam*: arranged in form; *sīdanti*: fail; *mama*: my; *gātrāṇi*: limbs; *mukhaṁ*: mouth; *ca*: and; *pariśuṣyati*: is parching

वेपथुश्च शरीरे मे रोमहर्षश्च जायते ॥ १.२९
गाण्डीवं स्रंसते हस्तात्त्वक्चैव परिदह्यते ।

vepathuś ca śarīre me romaharṣaś ca jāyate // 1.29
gāṇḍīvaṁ sraṁsate hastāt tvak caiva paridahyate /

vepathuḥ: trembling; *ca*: and; *śarīre*: in body; *me*: my; *romaharṣaḥ*: hair standing on end; *ca*: and; *jāyate*: happens; *gāṇḍīvaṁ*: Gāṇḍīva; *sraṁsate*: slips; *hastāt*: from the hands; *tvak*: skin; *ca*: and; *eva*: only; *paridahyate*: is burning

1.28, 29 Arjuna said: Kṛṣṇa, seeing my friends and relatives present before me, eager to wage war, my limbs are giving way, my mouth is parching and a shiver is running through my body, my hair is standing on end.

न च शक्नोम्यवस्थातुं भ्रमतीव च मे मनः ॥ १.३०
निमित्तानि च पश्यामि विपरीतानि केशव ।

na ca śaknomy avasthātuṁ bhramatīva ca me manaḥ ॥ 1.30
nimittāni ca paśyāmi viparī tāni keśava ।

na: not; *ca*: and; *śaknomi*: am able; *avasthātuṁ*: to stand; *bhramatīva*: as if whirling; *ca*: and; *me*: my; *manaḥ*: mind; *nimittāni*: portents; *ca*: also; *paśyāmi*: I see; *viparī tāni*: just the opposite; *keśava*: O Keśava, killer of demon Kesin

1.30 My bow gāṇḍīva *is slipping from my hands and my skin is burning all over. My mind is whirling as it were, and I am now unable to stand here any longer.*

न च श्रेयोऽनुपश्यामि हत्वा स्वजनमाहवे ॥ १.३१
न काङ्क्षे विजयं कृष्ण न च राज्यं सुखानि च ।

na ca śreyo 'nupaśyāmi hatvā svajanam āhave ॥ 1.31
na kāṅkṣe vijayaṁ kṛṣṇa na ca rājyaṁ sukhāni ca ।

na: not; *ca*: and; *śreyaḥ*: good; *anupaśyāmi*: I see; *hatvā*: after killing; *svajanam*: own kinsmen; *āhave*: in battle; *na*: not; *kāṅkṣe*: I desire; *vijayaṁ*: victory; *kṛṣṇa*: O Kṛṣṇa; *na*: not; *ca*: and; *rājyaṁ*: kingdom; *sukhāni*: pleasures; *ca*: and

1.31 I foresee only evil omens, O Kṛṣṇa, I do not see any good coming out of killing one's own kinsmen in this battle. I do not covet my dear Kṛṣṇa, victory or kingdom or pleasures.

किं नो राज्येन गोविन्द किं भोगैर्जीवितेन वा ॥ १.३२

kiṁ no rājyena govinda kiṁ bhogair jīvitena vā ॥ 1.32

kiṁ: what; *no*: to us; *rājyena*: by kingdom; *govinda*: Govinda; *kiṁ*: what; *bhogaiḥ*: by pleasures; *jīvitena*: life; *vā*: or

1.32 Of what use will kingdom or happiness or even life be to us?

येषामर्थे काङ्क्षितं नो राज्यं भोगाः सुखानि च ।
त इमेऽवस्थिता युद्धे प्राणांस्त्यक्त्वा धनानि च ॥ १.३३

yeṣām arthe kāṅkṣitaṁ no rājyaṁ bhogāḥ sukhāni ca |
ta ime 'vasthitā yuddhe prāṇāṁs tyaktvā dhanāni ca || 1.33

yeṣām: for whose; *arthe*: sake; *kāṅkṣitam*: desired; *no*: by us; *rājyaṁ*: kingdom; *bhogāḥ*: enjoyment; *sukhāni*: happiness; *ca*: and; *te*: they; *ime*: these; *avasthitāḥ*: stand; *yuddhe*: in battle; *prāṇān*: lives; *tyaktvā*: giving up; *dhanāni*: wealth; *ca*: and

1.33 For whose sake we desire this kingdom, enjoyment and happiness, they stand in battle staking their lives and property.

आचार्याः पितरः पुत्राः तथैव च पितामहाः ।
मातुलाः श्वशुराः पौत्राः श्यालाः संबन्धिनस्तथा ॥ १.३४

ācāryāḥ pitaraḥ putrāḥ tathaiva ca pitāmahāḥ |
mātulāḥ śvaśurāḥ pautrāḥ śyālāḥ saṁbandhinas tathā || 1.34

ācāryāḥ: teachers; *pitaraḥ*: fathers; *putrāḥ*: sons; *tathā eva*: like that; *ca*: and; *pitāmahāḥ*: grandfathers; *mātulāḥ*: maternal uncles; *śvaśurāḥ*: fathers-in-law; *pautrāḥ*: grandsons; *śyālāḥ*: brothers-in-law; *saṁbandhinaḥ*: relatives; *tathā*: as well as

1.34 Teachers, fathers, sons as well as grandfathers, maternal uncles, fathers-in-law, grandsons, brothers-in-law and other relatives.

एतान्न हन्तुमिच्छामि घ्नतोऽपि मधुसूदन ।
अपि त्रैलोक्यराज्यस्य हेतोः किं नु महीकृते ॥ १.३५

etān na hantum icchāmi ghnato 'pi madhusūdana |
api trailokyarājyasya hetoḥ kiṁ nu mahīkṛ te || 1.35

etān: these; *na*: not; *hantum*: for killing; *icchāmi*: I wish; *ghnataḥ*: killed; *api*: even; *madhusūdana*: O killer of the demon Madhu; *api*: even; *trailokya*: of the three worlds; *rājyasya*: of the kingdoms; *hetoḥ*: in exchange; *kiṁ*: what; *nu*: then; *mahīkṛte*: for the sake of the earth

1.35 Madhusūdana (Kṛṣṇa), even if I am killed (by them) I do not want to kill these ones even to gain control of all three worlds, much less for the earthly lordship.

निहत्य धार्तराष्ट्रान्नः का प्रीतिः स्याज्जनार्दन ।
पापमेवाश्रयेदस्मान्हत्वैतानाततायिनः ॥ १.३६

nihatya dhārtarāṣṭrān naḥ kā prī tiḥ syāj janārdana /
pāpam evāśrayed asmān hatvaitān ātatāyinaḥ // 1.36

nihatya: after slaying; *dhārtarāṣṭrān*: sons of Dhṛtarāṣṭra; *naḥ*: to us; *kā*: what; *prītiḥ*: pleasure; *syāt*: may be; *janārdana*: *Janārdana*; *pāpaṁ*: sins; *eva*: only; *āśrayet*: will take hold; *asmān*: us; *hatvā*: after killing; *etān*: these; *ātatāyinaḥ*: wrong-doers

1.36 What pleasure will we get by destroying the sons of Dhṛtarāṣṭra, Janārdana? Only sin will overcome us if we slay these wrong doers.

तस्मान्नार्हा वयं हन्तुं धार्तराष्ट्रान्स्वबान्धवान् ।
स्वजनं हि कथं हत्वा सुखिनः स्याम माधव ॥ १.३७

tasmān nārhā vayaṁ hantuṁ dhārtarāṣṭrān svabāndhavān /
svajanaṁ hi kathaṁ hatvā sukhinaḥ syāma mādhava // 1.37

tasmāt: therefore; *na*: not; *arhāḥ*: justified; *vayaṁ*: we; *hantuṁ*: to kill; *dhārtarāṣṭrān*: the sons of Dhṛtarāṣṭra; *svabāndhavān*: our friends; *svajanaṁ*: kinsmen; *hi*: for; *kathaṁ*: how; *hatvā*: after killing; *sukhinaḥ*: happy; *syāma*: may be; *mādhava*: O *Mādhava* (Kṛṣṇa)

1.37 Therefore, it is not proper for us to kill the sons of Dhṛtarāṣṭra and our relations, for how could we be happy after killing our own kinsmen, Mādhava?

यद्यप्येते न पश्यन्ति लोभोपहतचेतसः ।
कुलक्षयकृतं दोषं मित्रद्रोहे च पातकम् ॥ १.३८

yadyapyete na paśyanti lobhopahata cetasaḥ /
kulakṣayakṛtaṁ doṣaṁ mitradrohe ca pātakam // 1.38

yadyapi: even if; *ete*: these; *na*: not; *paśyanti*: see; *lobhopahata*: greed overtaken; *cetasaḥ*: intelligence; *kulakṣayakṛtaṁ*: in killing the race done; *doṣaṁ*: fault; *mitradrohe*: treason to friends; *ca*: and; *pātakam*: sin

1.38 O Janārdana, these men, blinded by greed, see no fault in killing one's family or being treasonable to friends, incur sin.

कथं न ज्ञेयमस्माभिः पापादस्मान्निवर्तितुम् ।
कुलक्षयकृतं दोषं प्रपश्यद्भिर्जनार्दन ॥ १.३९

katham na jñeyam asmābhiḥ pāpād asmān nivartitum |
kulakṣaya kṛ taṁ doṣaṁ prapaśyadbhir janārdana || 1.39

kathaṁ: why; *na*: not; *jñeyam*: to be understood; *asmābhiḥ*: by us; *pāpāt*: from sins; *asmāt*: from this; *nivartitum*: to turn away; *kulakṣaya kṛtaṁ*: destruction of a dynasty; *doṣaṁ*: evil; *prapaśyadbhiḥ*: by the witnessing; *janārdana*: Janārdana (Kṛṣṇa)

1.39 Why should we, who clearly see the sin in the destruction of a dynasty, not turn away from this crime?

कुलक्षये प्रणश्यन्ति कुलधर्माः सनातनाः ।
धर्मे नष्टे कुलं कृत्स्नमधर्मोऽभिभवत्युत ॥ १.४०

kulakṣaye praṇaśyanti kuladharmāḥ sanātanāḥ |
dharme naṣṭe kulaṁ kṛ tsnam adharmo 'bhibhavatyuta || 1.40

kulakṣaye: in destroying the family; *praṇaśyanti*: perish; *kuladharmāḥ*: the family traditions; *sanātanāḥ*: age-old; *dharme*: virtue; *naṣṭe*: destroyed; *kulaṁ*: family; *kṛtsnam*: whole; *adharmaḥ*: non-righteousness; *abhibhavati*: overtakes; *uta*: and

1.40 With the destruction of the dynasty, the age-old family traditions die and virtue having been lost, vice overtakes the entire race.

अधर्माभिभवात्कृष्ण प्रदुष्यन्ति कुलस्त्रियः ।
स्त्रीषु दुष्टासु वार्ष्णेय जायते वर्णसङ्करः ॥ १.४१

adharmābhibhavāt kṛṣṇa praduṣyanti kula striyaḥ |
strīṣu duṣṭāsu vārṣṇeya jāyate varṇasaṁkaraḥ || 1.41

adharma: non-righteousness; *abhi bhavāt*: from the preponderance; *kṛṣṇa*: O Kṛṣṇa; *praduṣyanti*: become corrupt; *kula striyaḥ*: family women; *strīṣu duṣṭāsu*: when women become corrupt; *vārṣṇeya*: O Vārṣṇeya (Kṛṣṇa); *jāyate*: arises; *varṇasaṁkaraḥ*: intermixture of castes

1.41 When non-righteous practices become common, O Kṛṣṇa, the women of the family become corrupt, and with the degradation of womanhood, O Descendant of Vṛṣṇi, ensues intermixture of castes.

सङ्करो नरकायैव कुलघ्नानां कुलस्य च ।
पतन्ति पितरो ह्येषां लुप्तपिण्डोदकक्रियाः ॥ १.४२

saṁkaro narakāyaiva kulaghnānāṁ kulasya ca |
patanti pitaro hyeṣāṁ lupta piṇḍodaka kriyāḥ || 1.42

saṁkaraḥ: mixture; *narakāya*: for hell; *eva*: only; *kulaghnānāṁ*: of the killers of the family; *kulasya*: of the family; *ca*: and; *patanti*: fall; *pitaraḥ*: forefathers; *hi*: also; *eṣāṁ*: their; *lupta*: deprived; *piṇḍodaka*: offering of rice and water to the departed souls; *kriyāḥ*: performances

दोषैरेतैः कुलघ्नानां वर्णसङ्करकारकैः ।
उत्साद्यन्ते जातिधर्माः कुलधर्माश्च शाश्वताः ॥ १.४३

doṣair etaiḥ kulaghnānāṁ varṇa saṁkarakārakaiḥ |
utsādyante jātidharmāḥ kuladharmāś ca śāśvatāḥ || 1.43

doṣaiḥ: faults; *etaiḥ*: these; *kulaghnānāṁ*: of the destroyer of the family; *varṇa saṁkara*: mixture of castes; *kārakaiḥ*: by the doers; *utsādyante*: are destroyed; *jāti dharmāḥ*: caste rituals; *kula dharmāḥ*: family traditions; *ca*: and; *śāśvatāḥ*: age-old

1.42, 43 A mixture of blood damns the destroyers of race and the race itself. Deprived of offering of oblations of rice and water the departed souls of the race also fall, the age-long caste traditions and family customs of the killers of kinsmen become extinct.

उत्सन्नकुलधर्माणां मनुष्याणां जनार्दन ।
नरकेऽनियतं वासो भवतीत्यनुशुश्रुम ॥ १.४४

utsannakula dharmāṇāṁ manuṣyāṇāṁ janārdana |
narake 'niyataṁ vāso bhavatītyanuśuśruma || 1.44

utsanna: spoiled; *kula dharmāṇāṁ*: of those who have the family traditions; *manuṣyāṇāṁ*: of such men; *janārdana*: O Kṛṣṇa; *narake*: in hell; *aniyataṁ*: always; *vāsaḥ*: residence; *bhavati*: becomes; *iti*: thus; *anuśuśruma*: we hear

1.44 O Janārdana, we hear that those who have lost family traditions dwell in hell for an indefinite period of time.

अहो बत महत् पापं कर्तुं व्यवसिता वयम् ।
यद्राज्यसुखलोभेन हन्तुं स्वजनमुद्यताः ॥ १.४५

aho bata mahat pāpaṁ kartuṁ vyavasitā vayaṁ /
yad rājya sukha lobhena hantuṁ svajanam udyatāḥ // 1.45

aho bata: alas; *mahat*: great; *pāpaṁ*: sins; *kartuṁ*: to do; *vyavasitā*: prepared; *vayaṁ*: we; *yat*: that; *rājya*: kingdom; *sukha lobhena*: by greed for kingdom; *hantuṁ*: to kill; *svajanaṁ*: kinsmen; *udyatāḥ*: prepared

1.45 Alas, we are prepared to commit greatly sinful acts of killing our kinsmen, driven by the desire to enjoy royal happiness.

यदि मामप्रतीकारमशस्त्रं शस्त्रपाणयः ।
धार्तराष्ट्रा रणे हन्युस्तन्मे क्षेमतरं भवेत् ॥ १.४६

yadi mām apratīkāram aśastraṁ śastrapāṇayaḥ /
dhārtarāṣṭrā raṇe hanyuḥ tan me kṣemataraṁ bhavet // 1.46

yadi: if; *māṁ*: me; *apratīkāraṁ*: not resistant; *aśastraṁ*: unarmed; *śastrapāṇayaḥ*: with weapons in hand; *dhārtarāṣṭrāḥ*: the sons of Dhṛtarāṣṭra; *raṇe*: in the battle; *hanyuḥ*: may kill; *tat*: that; *me*: mine; *kṣemataraṁ*: better; *bhavet*: will be

1.46 It would be better if the sons of Dhṛtarāṣṭra, armed with weapons, killed me in battle while I am unarmed and unresisting.

सञ्जय उवाच
एवमुक्त्वार्जुनः सङ्ख्ये रथोपस्थ उपाविशत् ।
विसृज्य सशरं चापं शोकसंविग्नमानसः ॥ १.४७

sañjaya uvāca
evam uktvārjunaḥ saṁkhye rathopastha upāviśat /
visṛ jya saśaraṁ cāpaṁ śokasaṁvignamānasaḥ // 1.47

sañjaya: Sañjaya; *uvāca*: said; *evaṁ*: thus; *uktvā*: having said; *arjunaḥ*: Arjuna; *saṁkhye*: in the battle field; *rathopastha*: chariot at the rear side;

upāviśat: sat down; *visṛ jya*: having cast aside; *saśaraṁ*: with the arrow; *cāpaṁ*: the bow; *śoka*: sorrow; *saṁvigna*: distressed; *mānasaḥ*: with a mind

1.47 Sañjaya said: Arjuna, whose mind was agitated by grief on the battle field, having spoken thus, cast aside his bow along with the arrow and sat down at the rear portion of the chariot.

इति श्रीमद्भगवद्गीतासूपनिषत्सु ब्रह्मविद्यायां योगशास्त्रे
श्रीकृष्णार्जुनसंवादे अर्जुनविषादयोगो नाम प्रथमोऽध्याय:

iti śrī mad bhagavadgītāsūpaniṣatsu brahmavidyāyām
yogaśāstre śrīkṛṣṇārjuna saṁvāde arjuna visāda yogo nāma
prathamo 'dhyāyaḥ ||

In the Upaniṣad *of the Bhagavad Gītā, the knowledge of* Brahman, *the Supreme, the science of Yoga and the dialogue between Śrī Kṛṣṇa and Arjuna, this is the first discourse designated:*

Arjunaviṣāda Yogaḥ

Verses Of Gita Chapter - 2

अथ द्वितीयोऽध्याय:

सांख्य योग:

Sāṅkhya Yogaḥ

सञ्जय उवाच ।
तं तथा कृपयाविष्टमश्रुपूर्णाकुलेक्षणम् ।
विषीदन्तमिदं वाक्यमुवाच मधुसूदन: ॥ २.१ ॥

sañjaya uvāca
taṁ tathākṛpayāviṣṭamaśrupūrṇākulekṣaṇam I
viṣīdantamidam vākyamuvāca madhusūdanaḥ II 2.1

sañjaya uvāca: Sañjaya said; *taṁ*: to him; *tathā:* thus; *kṛpayā*: by pity; *āviṣṭam*: overcome; *aśrupūrṇā*: full of tears; *ākula*: agitated; *īkṣaṇam*: (one with) eyes; *viṣīdantaṁ*: sorrowing; *idaṁ*: this; *vākyam*: word; *uvāca*: said; *madhu-sūdanaḥ*: the killer of Madhu

2.1 Sañjaya said: As Arjuna's eyes overflowed with tears of pity and despair, Kṛṣṇa spoke to him thus

श्री भगवानुवाच
कुतस्त्वा कश्मलमिदं विषमे समुपस्थितम् ।
अनार्यजुष्टमस्वर्ग्यमकीर्तिकरमर्जुन ॥ २.२

śrībhagavānuvāca
kutastvā kaśmalamidaṁ viṣame samupasthitam I
anāryajuṣṭamasvargyamakīrtikaram arjuna II 2.2

śrī bhagavān uvāca: Lord said; *kutaḥ*: why; *tvā*: upon you; *kaśmalam*: delusion; *idaṁ*: this; *viṣame*: in this critical time; *samupasthitam*: arrived; *anārya juṣṭam*: unworthy of a noble soul; *asvargyam*: not leading to heaven; *akīrtikaram*: disgraceful; *arjuna*: O Arjuna

2.2 Kṛṣṇa said: Where from has this dejection descended on you at this critical time, Arjuna! You behave unlike a noble man and this will keep you away from realization.

क्लैब्यं मा स्म गमः पार्थ नैतत्त्वय्युपपद्यते ।
क्षुद्रं हृदयदौर्बल्यं त्यक्त्वोत्तिष्ठ परन्तप ॥ २.३

klaibyaṁ mā sma gamaḥ pārtha naitattvayyupapadyate I
kṣudraṁ hṛdayadaurbalyaṁ tyaktvottiṣṭha parantapa II 2.3

klaibyaṁ: impotence; *mā*: do not; *sma gamaḥ*: yield; *pārtha*: son of Pritā; *na*: not; *etat*: this; *tvayi*: in you; *upapadyate*: is fitting; *kṣudraṁ*: mean; *hṛdaya daurbalyaṁ*: weakness of heart; *tyaktvaa*: after abandoning; *uttiṣṭha*: get up; *paraṁtapa*: O destroyer of enemies

2.3 Do not yield to fear, Pārtha! It does not befit you. Drop this faint-heartedness and stand up, O destroyer of enemies!

अर्जुन उवाच
कथं भीष्ममहं सङ्ख्ये द्रोणं च मधुसूदन ।
इषुभिः प्रतियोत्स्यामि पूजार्हावरिसूदन ॥ २.४

arjuna uvāca
katham bhīṣmamahaṁ saṅkhye droṇaṁ ca madhusūdana I
iṣubhiḥ pratiyotsyāmi pūjārhāvarisūdana II 2.4

arjuna uvāca: Arjuna said; *katham*: how; *bhīṣmam*: Bhīṣma; *ahaṁ*: I; *saṁkhye*: in battle; *droṇaṁ*: Droṇa; *ca*: also; *madhusūdana*: O killer of Madhu; *iṣubhiḥ*: with arrows; *pratiyotsyāmi*: shall counterattack; *pūjārhāu*: the two worthy of worship; *arisūdana*: O killer of the enemies

2.4 Arjuna said: O killer of Madhu, how can I oppose, in battle, Bhīṣma and Droṇa who are worthy of my worship?

गुरूनहत्वा हि महानुभावान् श्रेयो भोक्तुं भैक्ष्यमपीह लोके ।
हत्वाऽर्थकामांस्तु गुरूनिहैव भुञ्जीय भोगान् रुधिरप्रदिग्धान् ॥ २.५

gurūnahatvā hi mahānubhāvān śreyo bhoktuṁ bhaikṣyamapīha loke I
hatvārthakāmāṁs tu gurūnihaiva bhuñjīya bhogānrudhirapradigdhān II 2.5

gurūn: the elders; *ahatvā*: not having killed; *hi*: indeed; *mahānubhāvān*: great souls; *śreyah*: it is better; *bhoktuṁ*: to enjoy life; *bhaikṣyam*: begging; *api*: even; *iha*: in this life; *loke*: in this world; *hatvā*: after killing; *arthakāmān*: wealth and enjoyment; *tu*: but; *gurūn*: elders; *iha*: in this world; *eva*: only;

bhuñjīya: has to enjoy; *bhogān*: enjoyable things; *rudhira*: blood; *pradigdhān*: tainted with

2.5 I would rather beg for my food in this world than kill the most noble of teachers. If I kill them, all my enjoyment of wealth and desires will be stained with blood.

न चैतद्विद्मः कतरन्नो गरीयो यद्वा जयेम यदि वा नो जयेयुः ।
यानेव हत्वा न जिजीविषामस्तेऽवस्थिताः प्रमुखे धार्तराष्ट्राः ॥ २.६

na caitadvidmaḥ kataranno garīyo yadvā jayema yadi vā no jayeyuḥ I
yāneva hatvā na jijīviṣāmaste'vasthitāḥ pramukhe dhārtarāṣṭrāḥ II 2.6

na: nor; *cha*: also; *etat*: this; *vidmaḥ*: do know; *katarat*: which; *naḥ*: us; *garīyah*: better; *yat*: what; *vā*: either; *jayema*: shall conquer; *yadi*: if; *vā*: or; *naḥ*: us; *jayeyuḥ*: shall conquer; *yān*: those whom; *eva*: only; *hatvā*: after killing; *na*: never; *jijīviṣāmaḥ*: want to live; *te*: all of them; *avasthitāḥ*: assembled; *pramukhe*: in front of; *dhārtarāṣṭrāḥ*: the sons of Dhṛtarāṣṭra

2.6 I cannot say which is better; their defeating us or us defeating them. We do not wish to live after slaying the sons of Dhṛtarāṣṭra who stand before us.

कार्पण्यदोषोपहतस्वभावः पृच्छामि त्वां धर्मसम्मूढचेताः ।
यच्छ्रेयः स्यान्निश्चितं ब्रूहि तन्मे शिष्यस्तेऽहं शाधि मां त्वां प्रपन्नम् ॥ २.७

kārpaṇyadoṣopahatasvabhāvaḥ pṛcchāmi tvāṁ dharmasaṁmūḍhacetāḥ I
yacchreyaḥ syānniścitaṁ brūhi tanme śiṣyaste'ham śādhi māṁ
tvāṁ prapannam II 2.7

kārpaṇya: miserly; *doṣa*: weakness; *upahata*: being inflicted by; *svabhāvaḥ*: characteristics; *pṛcchāmi*: I am asking; *tvāṁ*: you; *dharma*: religion; *saṁmūḍha cetāḥ*: bewildered mind; *yat*: what; *śreyaḥ*: good; *syāt*: may be; *niścitaṁ*: decidedly; *brūhi*: tell; *tat*: that; *me*: unto me; *śiṣyaḥ*: disciple; *te*: your; *aham*: I am; *śādhi*: just instruct; *māṁ*: me; *tvāṁ*: you; *prapannam*: surrendered

2.7 My heart is overwhelmed with pity and my mind is confused about what my duty is. I beg of you, please tell me what is best for me. I am your disciple. Instruct me as I seek refuge in you.

न हि प्रपश्यामि ममापनुद्याद् यच्छोकमुच्छोषणमिन्द्रियाणाम् ।
अवाप्य भूमावसपत्नमृद्धं राज्यं सुराणामपि चाधिपत्यम् ॥ २.८

na hi prapaśyāmi mamāpanudyād yacchokamucchoṣaṇamindriyāṇām |
avāpya bhūmāvasapatnamṛddhaṁ rājyaṁ surāṇāmapi cādhipatyam || 2.8

na: do not; *hi*: indeed; *prapaśyāmi*: I see; *mama*: my; *apanudyāt*: can drive away; *yat*: that; *śokam*: lamentation; *ucchoṣaṇam*: drying up; *indriyāṇām*: of the senses; *avāpya*: after achieving; *bhūmau*: on the earth; *asapatnam*: without rival; *ṛddhaṁ*: prosperous; *rājyam*: kingdom; *surāṇām*: of the demigods; *api*: even; *ca*: also; *ādhipatyam*: supremacy

2.8 Even if I were to attain unrivalled dominion and prosperity on earth or even lordship over the Gods, how would that remove this sorrow that burns my senses?

सञ्जय उवाच
एवमुक्त्वा हृषीकेशं गुडाकेश: परन्तप ।
न योत्स्य इति गोविन्दमुक्त्वा तूष्णीं बभूव ह ॥ २.९

sañjaya uvāca
evamuktvā hṛṣīkeśaṁ guḍākeśaḥ parantapa |
na yotsya iti govindamuktvā tūṣṇīṁ babhūva ha || 2.9

sañjaya uvācha: Sañjaya said; *evam*: thus; *uktvā*: after speaking; *hṛṣīkeśam*: unto Kṛṣṇa, the master of the senses; *guḍākeśaḥ*: one who has won over sleep (Arjuna); *parantapa*: destroyer of the enemies; *na yotsye*: I shall not fight; *iti*: thus; *govindam*: unto Kṛṣṇa, the giver of pleasure; *uktvā*: having said; *tūṣṇīṁ*: silent; *babhūva*: became; *ha*: clearly

2.9 *Sañjaya said: Arjuna then said to Kṛṣṇa, 'Govinda, I shall not fight,' and fell silent.*

तमुवाच हृषीकेश: प्रहसन्निव भारत ।
सेनयोरुभयोर्मध्ये विषीदन्तमिदं वच: ॥ २.१०

tamuvāca hṛṣīkeśaḥ prahasanniva bhārata |
senayorubhayormadhye viṣīdantamidaṁ vacaḥ || 2.10

tam: unto him; *uvācha*: said; *hṛṣīkeśaḥ*: the master of the senses, Kṛṣṇa; *prahasan*: smiling; *iva*: as if; *bhārata*: O Dhṛtarāṣṭra, descendant of Bhārata; *senayoḥ*: of the armies; *ubhayoḥ*: of both; *madhye*: between; *viṣīdantam* : unto the lamenting one; *idaṁ*: the following; *vachaḥ*: words

2.10 Kṛṣṇa, smilingly spoke the following words to the grief-stricken Arjuna, as they were placed in the middle of both armies.

श्री भगवानुवाच ।
अशोच्यानन्वशोचस्त्वं प्रज्ञावादांश्च भाषसे ।
गतासूनगतासूंश्च नानुशोचन्ति पण्डिताः ॥ २.११

śrībhagavānuvāca
aśocyānanvaśocastvaṁ prajñāvādāṁś ca bhāṣase I
gatāsūnagatāsūṁśca nānuśocanti paṇḍitāḥ II 2.11

śrī bhagavān uvāca: the Lord said; *aśocyān*: those not worthy of lamentation; *anvaśocas*: you are lamenting; *tvaṁ*: you; *prajñāvādāṁ*: learned talks; *ca*: also; *bhāṣase*: you are speaking; *gatāsūn*: lost life; *agatāsūn*: not past life; *ca*: also; *na*: never; *anuśocanti*: lament; *paṇḍitāḥ*: the learned

2.11 Bhagavān *said: You grieve for those that should not be grieved for and yet, you speak words of wisdom. The wise grieve neither for the living nor for the dead.*

न त्वेवाहं जातु नासं न त्वं नेमे जनाधिपाः ।
न चैव न भविष्यामः सर्वे वयमतः परम् ॥ २.१२

na tvevāhaṁ jātu nāsaṁ na tvaṁ neme janādhipāḥ I
na caiva na bhaviṣyāmaḥ sarve vayam ataḥ param II 2.12

na: not; *tu*: but; *eva*: only; *ahaṁ*: I; *jātu*: at any time; *na*: not; *āsaṁ*: existed; *na*: it is not so; *tvaṁ*: yourself; *na*: not; *ime*: all these; *janādhipāḥ*: kings; *na*: never; *ca:* also; *eva*: only; *na*: not like that; *bhaviṣyāmaḥ*: shall exist; *sarve*: all of us; *vayaṁ*: we; *ataḥ paraṁ*: hereafter

2.12 It is not that at anytime in the past I did not exist. So did you and these rulers exist, and we shall not ever cease to be hereafter.

देहिनोऽस्मिन्यथा देहे कौमारं यौवनं जरा ।
तथा देहान्तरप्राप्तिर्धीरस्तत्र न मुह्यति ॥ २.१३

dehino'sminyathā dehe kaumāraṁ yauvanaṁ jarā /
tathā dehāntara prāptirdhīras tatra na muhyati // 2.13

dehinaḥ: of the embodied soul; *asmin*: in this; *yathā*: as; *dehe*: in the body; *kaumāraṁ*: boyhood; *yauvanaṁ*: youth; *jarā*: old age; *tathā*: similarly; *dehāntara*: transference of the body; *prāptiḥ*: achievement; *dhīraḥ*: the brave; *tatra*: thereupon; *na*: never; *muhyati*: is deluded

2.13 Just as the spirit in this body passes through childhood, youth and old age, so does it pass into another body; the man centered in himself does not fear this.

मात्रास्पर्शास्तु कौन्तेय शीतोष्णसुखदुःखदाः ।
आगमापायिनोऽनित्यास्तांस्तितिक्षस्व भारत ॥ २.१४

mātrāsparśāstu kaunteya śītoṣṇasukhaduḥkadāḥ /
āgamāpāyino'nityāstāṁstitikṣasva bhārata // 2.14

mātrā: of the senses; *spārśāḥ*: contact; *tu*: only; *kaunteya*: O son of Kuntī; *śīta*: cold; *uṣṇa*: hot; *sukha*: pleasure; *dukkha-dah*: giving pain; *āgama*: appearing; *apāyinaḥ*: disappearing; *anityāḥ*: nonpermanent; *tān*: all of them; *titikṣasva*: tolerate; *bhārata*: O descendant of the Bhārata dynasty

2.14 O son of Kuntī, contact with sense objects causes heat and cold, pleasure and pain, and these have a beginning and an end. O Bhārata, these are not permanent; endure them bravely.

यं हि न व्यथयन्त्येते पुरुषं पुरुषर्षभ ।
समदुःखसुखं धीरं सोऽमृतत्वाय कल्पते ॥ २.१५

yaṁ hi na vyathayantyete puruṣam puruṣarṣabha /
samaduḥkhasukhaṁ dhīraṁ so'mṛtatvāya kalpate // 2.15

yaṁ: whom; *hi*: indeed; *na*: never; *vyathayanti*: are distressing; *ete*: all these; *puruṣam*: to a person; *puruṣarṣabha*: O best among men; *sama*: equal; *duḥkha*: sorrow; *sukhaṁ*: happiness; *dhīraṁ*: brave; *saḥ*: he; *amṛtatvāya*: for liberation; *kalpate*: is fit

2.15 O chief among men, the brave person to whom all these are not distressing, for whom sorrow and happiness are equal, is fit for liberation.

नासतो विद्यते भावो नाभावो विद्यते सत: ।
उभयोरपि दृष्टोऽन्तस्त्वनयोस्तत्त्वदर्शिभि: ॥ २.१६

nāsato vidyate bhāvo nābhāvo vidyate satah I
ubhayorapi drṣṭontastvanayostattvadarśibhih II 2.16

na: never; *asataḥ*: of the nonexistent; *vidyate*: there is; *bhāvaḥ*: existence; *na*: never; *abhāvaḥ*: non existence; *vidyate*: there is; *satạh*: of the eternal; *ubhayoḥ*: of the two; *api*: verily; *drṣtaḥ*: observed; *antaḥ*: essence; *tu*: but; *anayoḥ*: of them; *tattvadarśibhiḥ*: truth by the seers

2.16 The nonexistent has no being; that which exists never ceases to exist. This truth about both is perceived by those who know the Truth.

अविनाशि तु तद्विद्धि येन सर्वमिदं ततम् ।
विनाशमव्ययस्यास्य न कश्चित्कर्तुमर्हति ॥ २.१७

avināśi tu tadviddhi yena sarvamidaṁ tatam I
vināśamavyayasyāsya na kaścitkartumarhati II 2.17

avināśi: imperishable; *tu*: but; *tat*: that; *viddhi*: know it; *yena*: by whom; *sarvaṁ*: all of the body; *idaṁ*: this; *tataṁ*: pervaded; *vināśaṁ*: destruction; *avyayasya*: of the imperishable; *asya*: of it; *na kaścit*: no one; *kartuṁ*: to do; *arhati*: is able

2.17 Know It to be indestructible by which all this body is pervaded. Nothing can destroy It, the Imperishable.

अन्तवन्त इमे देहा नित्यस्योक्ता: शरीरिण: ।
अनाशिनोऽप्रमेयस्य तस्माद्युध्यस्व भारत ॥ २.१८

antavanta ime dehā nityasyoktāḥ śarīriṇaḥ I
anāśino 'prameyasya tasmādyudhyasva bhārata II 2.18

antavantaḥ: perishable; *ime*: all these; *dehāḥ*: bodies; *nityasya*: eternal in existence; *uktāḥ*: it is so said; *śarīriṇaḥ*: of the embodied soul; *anāśinaḥ*: never to be destroyed; *aprameyasya*: immeasurable; *tasmāt*: therefore; *yudhyasva*: fight; *bhārata*: O descendant of Bhārata

2.18 These bodies of the material energy are perishable. The energy itself is eternal, incomprehensible and indestructible. Therefore, fight, O Bhārata.

य एनं वेत्ति हन्तारं यश्चैनं मन्यते हतम्
उभौ तौ न विजानीतो नायं हन्ति न हन्यते ॥ २.१९

ya enaṁ vetti hantāraṁ yaścainaṁ manyate hatam I
ubhau tau na vijānīto nāyaṁ hanti na hanyate II 2.19

yaḥ: anyone; *enaṁ*: this; *vetti*: knows; *hantāraṁ*: the killer; *yaḥ*: anyone; *ca*: also; *enaṁ*: this; *manyate*: thinks; *hatam*: killed; *ubhau*: both of them; *tau*: they; *na*: not; *vijānītaḥ*: know; *na*: never; *ayaṁ*: this; *hanti*: kills; *na*: nor; *hanyate*: be killed

2.19 Neither understands; he who takes the Self to be the slayer nor he who thinks he is slain. He who knows the truth understands that the Self does not slay, nor is It slain.

न जायते म्रियते वा कदाचित् नायं भूत्वा भविता वा न भूयः ।
अजो नित्यः शाश्वतोऽयं पुराणो न हन्यते हन्यमाने शरीरे ॥ २.२०

na jāyate mriyate vā kadācit
nāyaṁ bhūtvā bhavitā vā na bhūyaḥ I
ajo nityaḥ śāśvato 'yaṁ purāṇo
na hanyate hanyamāne śarīre II 2.20

na: never; *jāyate*: takes birth; *mriyate*: dies; *vā*: either; *kadācit*: at any time (past, present or future); *na*: never; *ayaṁ*: this; *bhūtvā*: having come into being; *bhavitā*: will come to be; *vā*: or; *na*: not; *bhūyaḥ*: after; *ajaḥ*: unborn; *nityaḥ*: eternal; *śāśvataḥ*: permanent; *ayaṁ*: this; *purāṇaḥ*: the oldest; *na*: never; *hanyate*: is killed; *hanyamāne śarīre*: when the body is killed

2.20 The Self is neither born nor does It ever die. After having been, It never ceases not to be. It is unborn, eternal, changeless and ancient. It is not killed when the body is killed.

वेदाविनाशिनं नित्यं य एनमजमव्ययम् ।
कथं स पुरुषः पार्थ कं घातयति हन्ति कम् ॥ २.२१

vedāvināśinaṁ nityaṁ ya enamajamavyayam I
kathaṁ sa puruṣaḥ pārtha kaṁ ghātayati hanti kam II 2.21

veda: knows; *avināśinaṁ*: indestructible; *nityaṁ*: permanent; *yaḥ*: one who; *enaṁ*: this (soul); *ajam*: unborn; *avyayam*: immutable; *kathaṁ*: how; *saḥ*: he; *puruṣaḥ*: person; *pārtha*: O Pārtha (Arjuna); *kaṁ*: whom; *ghātayati*: hurts; *hanti*: kills; *kaṁ*: whom

2.21 *O Pārtha, how can man slay or cause others to be slain, when he knows It to be indestructible, eternal, unborn, and unchangeable?*

वासांसि जीर्णानि यथा विहाय नवानि गृह्णाति नरोऽपराणि ।
तथा शरीराणि विहाय जीर्णान्यन्यानि संयाति नवानि देही ॥ २.२२

vāsāṁsi jīrṇāni yathā vihāya navāni gṛhṇāti naro 'parāṇi I
tathā śarīrāṇi vihāya jīrṇā nyanyāni saṁyāti navāni dehī II 2.22

vāsāṁsi: garments; *jīrṇāni*: old and worn out; *yathā*: as; *vihāya*: after giving up; *navāni*: new garments; *gṛhṇāti*: does accept; *naraḥ*: a man; *aparāṇi*: others; *tathā*: in the same way; *śarīrāṇi*: bodies; *vihāya*: after giving up; *jīrṇāni*: old and useless; *anyāni*: different; *saṁyāti*: accepts; *navāni*: new sets; *dehī*: the embodied soul

2.22 *Just as man casts off his worn out clothes and puts on new ones, the Self casts off worn out bodies and enters newer ones.*

नैनं छिन्दन्ति शस्त्राणि नैनं दहति पावकः ।
न चैनं क्लेदयन्त्यापो न शोषयति मारुतः ॥ २.२३

nainaṁ chindanti śastrāṇi nainaṁ dahati pāvakaḥ I
na cainaṁ kledayantyāpo na śoṣayati mārutaḥ II 2.23

na: not; *enaṁ*: this (soul); *chindanti*: cut to pieces; *śastrāṇi*: weapons; *na*: not; *enaṁ*: this soul; *dahati*: burns; *pāvakaḥ*: fire; *na*: not; *ca*: also; *enaṁ*: this soul; *kledayanti*: moistens; *āpaḥ*: water; *na*: not; *śoṣayati*: dries; *mārutaḥ*: wind

2.23 *Weapons do not cleave the Self, fire does not burn It, water does not moisten It and wind does not dry It.*

अच्छेद्योऽयमदाह्योऽयं अक्लेद्योऽशोष्य एव च ।
नित्य: सर्वगत: स्थाणु: अचलोऽयं सनातन: ॥ २.२४

acchedyo'yamadāhyo'yamakledyo'śoṣya eva ca |
nityaḥ sarvagataḥ sthāṇuracalo'yaṁ sanātanaḥ || 2.24

acchedyaḥ: incapable of being cut; *ayaṁ*: this soul; *adāhyaḥ*: cannot be burned; *ayaṁ*: this soul; *akledyaḥ*: insoluble; *aśoṣyaḥ*: cannot be dried; *eva*: certainly; *ca*: and; *nityaḥ*: everlasting; *sarvagataḥ*: all-pervading; *sthāṇuḥ*: unchangeable; *acalaḥ*: immovable; *ayaṁ*: this soul; *sanātanaḥ*: eternally the same

2.24 The Self cannot be broken nor burnt nor dissolved nor dried up. It is eternal, all-pervading, stable, immovable and ancient.

अव्यक्तोऽयमचिन्त्योऽयं अविकार्योऽयमुच्यते ।
तस्मादेवं विदित्वैनं नानुशोचितुमर्हसि ॥ २.२५

avyakto'yamacintyo'yamavikāryo'yamucyate |
tasmādevaṁ viditvainaṁ nānuśocitumarhasi || 2.25

avyaktaḥ: unmanifest; *ayaṁ*: this; *acintyaḥ*: unthinkable; *ayaṁ*: this; *avikāryaḥ*: immutable; *ayaṁ*: this; *ucyate*: is spoken of; *tasmāt*: therefore; *evaṁ*: as such; *viditvā*: having known; *enaṁ*: this; *na*: not; *anuśocituṁ arhasi*: (you) should not grieve

2.5 The Self is said to be unmanifest, unthinkable and unchangeable and able. Knowing this to be such, you should not grieve.

अथ चैनं नित्यजातं नित्यं वा मन्यसे मृतम् ।
तथापि त्वं महाबाहो नैवं शोचितुमर्हसि ॥ २.२६

atha cainaṁ nityajātaṁ nityaṁ vā manyase mṛtam |
tathāpi tvaṁ mahābāho naivaṁ śocitum arhasi || 2.26

atha: however; *ca*: also; *enaṁ*: this soul; *nityajātaṁ*: always born; *nityaṁ*: forever; *vā*: either; *manyase*: think; *mṛtaṁ*: dead; *tathā api*: still; *tvaṁ*: you; *mahābāho*: O mighty-armed one; *na*: not; *enaṁ*: like this ; *śocituṁ arhasi*: you lament

2.26 O mighty-armed, even if you should think of the soul as being constantly born and constantly dying, even then, you should not lament.

जातस्य हि ध्रुवो मृत्यु ध्रुवं जन्म मृतस्य च ।
तस्मादपरिहार्येऽर्थे न त्वं शोचितुमर्हसि ॥ २.२७

jātasya hi dhruvo mṛtyurdhruvaṁ janma mṛtasya ca |
tasmādaparihārye'rthe na tvaṁ śocitumarhasi || 2.27

jātasya: one who has taken his birth; *hi*: indeed; *dhruvo*: certain; *mṛtyuḥ*: death; *dhruvaṁ*: certain; *janma*: birth; *mṛtasya*: of the dead; *ca*: also; *tasmāt*: therefore; *aparihārye*: for that which is unavoidable; *arthe*: in the matter of; *na*: do not; *tvaṁ*: you; *śocituṁ arhasi*: you lament

2.27 Indeed, death is certain for the born and birth is certain for the dead. Therefore, you should not grieve over the inevitable.

अव्यक्तादीनि भूतानि व्यक्तमध्यानि भारत ।
अव्यक्तनिधनान्येव तत्र का परिदेवना ॥ २.२८

avyaktādīni bhūtāni vyaktamadhyāni bhārata |
avyaktanidhanānyeva tatra kā paridevanā || 2.28

avyaktādīni: unmanifest in the beginning; *bhūtāni*: living beings; *vyakta*: manifest; *madhyāni*: in the middle; *bhārata*: O descendant of Bhārata; *avyakta nidhanāni*: unmanifest after death; *eva*: like that; *tatra*: therefore; *kā*: what; *paridevanā*: lamentation

2.28 O Bhārata, being intangible in the beginning, being intangible again in their end, seemingly tangible in the middle, what are we grieving about?

आश्चर्यवत्पश्यति कश्चिदेनं आश्चर्यवद्वदति तथैव चान्यः ।
आश्चर्यवच्चैनमन्यः शृणोति श्रुत्वाप्येनं वेद न चैव कश्चित् ॥ २.२९

āścaryavatpaśyati kaścidena māścaryavadvadati tathaiva cānyaḥ |
āścaryavaccainamanyaḥ śṛṇoti śrutvāpyenaṁ veda na caiva kaścit || 2.29

āścaryavat: amazingly; *paśyati*: see; *kaścit*: some one; *enaṁ*: this soul; *āścaryavac*: amazingly; *vadati*: speaks; *tathā*: like that; *eva*: only; *ca*: also; *anyaḥ*: another; *āścaryavat*: amazingly; *ca*: also; *enaṁ*: this soul; *anyaḥ*: another; *śṛṇoti*: hear; *śrutvā*: having heard; *api*: even; *enaṁ*: this soul; *veda*: do know; *na*: not; *ca*: and; *eva*: only; *kaścit*: someone

2.29 One sees It as a wonder, another speaks of It as a wonder, another hears of It as a wonder. Yet, having heard, none understands It at all.

देही नित्यमवध्योऽयं देहे सर्वस्य भारत ।
तस्मात्सर्वाणि भूतानि न त्वं शोचितुमर्हसि ॥ २.३०

dehī nityamavadhyo 'yaṁ dehe sarvasya bhārata I
tasmātsarvāni bhūtāni na tvaṁ śocitumarhasi II 2.30

dehī: the soul; *nityaṁ*: eternally; *avadhyaḥ*: cannot be killed; *ayaṁ*: this soul; *dehe*: in the body; *sarvasya*: of everyone; *bhārata*: O descendant of Bhārata; *tasmāt*: therefore; *sarvāṇi*: all; *bhūtāni*: living entities (that are born); *na*: not; *tvaṁ*: yourself; *śocituṁ arhasi*: should grieve

2.30 *O Bhārata, This that dwells in the body of everyone can never be destroyed; do not grieve for any creature.*

स्वधर्ममपि चावेक्ष्य न विकम्पितुमर्हसि ।
धर्म्याद्धि युद्धाच्छ्रेयोऽन्यत्क्षत्रियस्य न विद्यते ॥ २.३१

svadharmamapi cāvekṣya na vikampitumarhasi I
dharmyāddhi yuddhācchreyo'nyat kṣatriyasya na vidyate II 2.31

svadharmaṁ: one's own duty; *api*: also; *ca*: and; *avekṣya*: considering; *na*: not; *vikampitum*: to hesitate; *arhasi*: you deserve; *dharmyāt hi yuddhāt*: from righteous war indeed; *śreyaḥ*: better; *anyat*: anything else; *kṣatriyasya*: of the kṣatriya; *na*: does not; *vidyate*: exist

2.31 *You should look at your own duty as a* kṣatriya. *There is nothing higher for a* kṣatriya *than a righteous war. You ought not to hesitate.*

यदृच्छया चोपपन्नं स्वर्गद्वारमपावृतम् ।
सुखिनः क्षत्रियाः पार्थ लभन्ते युद्धमीदृशम् ॥ २.३२

yadṛcchayā copapannaṁ svargadvāramapāvṛtam I
sukhinaḥ kṣatriyāḥ pārtha labhante yuddhamīdṛśam II 2.32

yadṛcchayā: by its own accord; *ca*: also; *upapannaṁ*: arrived; *svargadvāraṁ*: gate of heaven; *apāvṛtaṁ*: wide open; *sukhinaḥ*: happy; *kṣatriyāḥ*: the members of the royal order; *pārtha*: O son of Pritā; *labhante*: achieve; *yuddhaṁ*: war; *īdṛśaṁ*: like this

2.32 *O Pārtha, happy indeed are the* kṣatriyas *who are called to fight in such a battle without seeking. This opens for them the door to heaven.*

अथ चेत्त्वमिमं धर्म्यं सङ्ग्रामं न करिष्यसि ।
ततः स्वधर्मं कीर्तिं च हित्वा पापमवाप्स्यसि ॥ २.३३

atha cettvamimaṁ dharmyaṁ saṅgrāmaṁ na kariṣyasi **/**
tataḥ svadharmaṁ kīrtiṁ ca hitvā pāpamavāpsyasi **//** 2.33

atha: therefore; *cet*: if; *tvaṁ*: you; *imaṁ*: this; *dharmyaṁ*: righteous; *saṅgrāmaṁ*: war; *na*: do not; *kariṣyasi*: you will perform; *tataḥ*: then; *svadharmaṁ*: your duty; *kīrtiṁ*: reputation; *ca*: also; *hitvā*: having lost; *pāpaṁ*: sin; *avāpsyasi*: do gain

2.33 If you will not fight this righteous war, then you will incur sin having abandoned your own duty, and you will lose your reputation.

अकीर्तिंचापि भूतानि कथयिष्यन्ति तेऽव्ययाम् ।
संभावितस्य चाकीर्तिः मरणादतिरिच्यते ॥ २.३४

akīrtiṁ cāpi bhūtāni kathayiṣyanti te'vyayām **/**
saṁbhāvitasya cākīrtirmaraṇādatiricyate **//** 2.34

akīrtiṁ: infamy; *ca*: also; *api*: also; *bhūtāni*: all people; *kathayiṣyanti*: will speak; *te*: of you; *avyayāṁ*: undying; *saṁbhāvitasya*: of a respectable man; *ca*: also; *akīrtiḥ*: ill-fame; *maraṇāt*: than death; *atiricyate*: becomes more than

2.34 People too will remember your everlasting dishonor and to one who has been honored, dishonor is worse than death.

भयाद्रणादुपरतं मंस्यन्ते त्वां महारथाः ।
येषां च त्वं बहुमतो भूत्वा यास्यसि लाघवम् ॥ २.३५

bhayādraṇāduparataṁ maṁsyante tvāṁ mahārathāḥ **/**
yeṣāṁ ca tvaṁ bahumato bhūtvā yāsyasi lāghavam **//** 2.35

bhayāt: out of fear; *raṇāt*: from war; *uparataṁ*: retired; *maṁsyante*: will consider; *tvāṁ*: you; *mahārathāḥ*: the great generals; *yeṣāṁ*: of those who; *ca*: also; *tvaṁ*: you; *bahumataḥ*: in great estimation; *bhūtvā*: having become; *yāsyasi*: will get; *lāghavaṁ*: decreased in value

2.35 The great generals will think that you have withdrawn from the battle because you are a coward. You will be looked down upon by those who had thought much of you and your heroism in the past.

अवाच्यवादांश्च बहून्वदिष्यन्ति तवाहिताः ।
निन्दन्तस्तव सामर्थ्यं ततो दुःखतरं नु किम् ॥ २.३६

avācyavādāṁśca bahūn vadiṣyanti tavāhitāḥ I
nindantastava sāmarthyaṁ tato duḥkhataraṁ nu kim II 2.36

avācyavādān: unspeakable words; *ca*: also; *bahūn*: many; *vadiṣyanti*: will say; *tava*: your; *ahitāḥ*: enemies; *nindantaḥ*: while vilifying; *tava*: your; *sāmarthyaṁ*: ability; *tataḥ*: than that; *duḥkhataraṁ*: more painful; *nu*: of course; *kiṁ*: what

2.36 Many unspeakable words would be spoken by your enemies reviling your power. Can there be anything more painful than this?

हतो वा प्राप्स्यसि स्वर्गं जित्वा वा भोक्ष्यसे महीम् ।
तस्मादुत्तिष्ठ कौन्तेय युद्धाय कृतनिश्चयः ॥ २.३७

hato vā prāpsyasi svargaṁ jitvā vā bhokṣyase mahīm I
tasmāduttiṣṭha kaunteya yuddhāya kṛtaniścayaḥ II 2.37

hataḥ: being killed; *vā*: either; *prāpsyasi*: you will gain; *svargaṁ*: heaven; *jitvā*: after conquering; *vā*: or; *bhokṣyase*: you will enjoy; *mahīṁ*: the world; *tasmāt*: therefore; *uttiṣṭha*: get up; *kaunteya*: O son of Kuntī; *yuddhāya*: for war; *kṛta niścayaḥ*: determined

2.37 Slain, you will achieve heaven; victorious, you will enjoy the earth. O son of Kuntī, stand up determined to fight.

सुखदुःखे समे कृत्वा लाभालाभौ जयाजयौ ।
ततो युद्धाय युज्यस्व नैवं पापमवाप्स्यसि ॥ २.३८

sukhaduḥkhe same kṛtvā lābhālābhau jayājayau I
tato yuddhāya yujyasva naivaṁ pāpamavāpsyasi II 2.38

sukha duḥkhe: in happiness as well as in distress; *same*: equal; *kṛtvā*: doing so; *lābhālābhau*: gain and loss; *jayājayau*: victory and defeat; *tataḥ*: thereafter; *yuddhāya*: for war; *yujyasva*: get ready; *na*: not; *evaṁ*: in this way; *pāpaṁ*: sin; *avāpsyasi*: you will gain

2.38 Pleasure and pain, gain and loss, victory and defeat – treat them all the same. Do battle for the sake of battle and you shall incur no sin.

एषा तेऽभिहिता सांख्ये बुद्धिर्योगे त्विमां श्रृणु ।
बुद्ध्या युक्तो यया पार्थ कर्मबन्धं प्रहास्यसि ॥ २.३९

eṣā tebhihitā sānkhye buddhiryoge tvimāṁ śṛṇu I
buddhyā yukto yayā pārtha karmabandhaṁ prahāsyasi II 2.39

eṣā: all these; *te*: you; *abhihitā*: described; *sāṁkhye*: in the *Sāṅkhya Yoga* (yoga of knowledge); *buddhiḥ*: intelligence; *yoge*: in the Karma Yoga of selfless action; *tu*: but; *imāṁ*: this; *śṛṇu*: hear; *buddhyā*: by intelligence; *yuktaḥ*: equipped; *yayā*: by which; *pārtha*: O son of Pritā; *karma bandhaṁ*: bondage of action; *prahāsyasi*: you shall throw off

2.39 What has been taught to you concerns the wisdom of Sāṅkhya. *Now, listen to the wisdom of yoga. Having known this, O Pārtha, you shall cast off the bonds of action.*

नेहाभिक्रमनाशोऽस्ति प्रत्यवायो न विद्यते ।
स्वल्पमप्यस्य धर्मस्य त्रायते महतो भयात् ॥ २.४०

nehābhikramanāśo 'sti pratyavāyo na vidyate I
svalpamapyasya dharmasya trāyate mahato bhayāt II 2.40

na: there is not; *iha*: in this path (of selfless action); *abhikramanāśaḥ*: loss of effort; *asti*: there is; *pratyavāyaḥ*: contrary result; *na*: not; *vidyate*: there is; *svalpaṁ*: a little; *api*: also; *asya*: of this discipline; *dharmasya*: of this occupation; *trāyate*: releases; *mahataḥ*: of very great; *bhayāt*: from fear

2.40 There is no wasted effort or dangerous effect from this. Even a little knowledge of this, even a little practice of yoga, protects one from great fear.

व्यवसायात्मिका बुद्धिरेकेह कुरुनन्दन ।
बहुशाखा ह्यनन्ताश्च बुद्धयोऽव्यवसायिनाम् ॥ २.४१

vyavasāyātmikā buddhirekeha kurunandana I
bahuśākhā hyanantāśca buddhayovyavasāyinām II 2.41

vyavasāyātmikā: fixed resolve; *buddhiḥ*: intelligence; *ekā*: only one; *iha*: in this (Karma Yoga); *kuru nandana*: O son of the Kurus; *bahuśākhāḥ*: various branches; *hi*: indeed; *anantāḥ*: unlimited; *ca*: also; *buddhayaḥ*: intelligence; *avyavasāyināṁ*: of the undecided (ignorant men moved by desires)

2.41 *Joy of the Kurus, all you need is single-pointed determination. Thoughts of the irresolute are many, branched and endless.*

यामिमां पुष्पितां वाचं प्रवदन्त्यविपश्चितः ।
वेदवादरताः पार्थ नान्यदस्तीतिवादिनः ॥ २.४२

yāmimāṁ puṣpitāṁ vācaṁ pravadantyavipaścitaḥ I
vedavādaratāḥ pārtha nānyadastīti vādinaḥ II 2.42

yāṁ imāṁ: all these; *puṣpitāṁ*: flowery; *vācaṁ*: words; *pravadanti*: say; *avipaścitaḥ*: ignorant men; *vedavādaratāḥ*: devoted to the letter of the Veda; *pārtha*: O son of Pārtha; *na*: not; *anyat*: anything else; *asti*: there is; *iti*: thus; *vādinaḥ*: advocates

2.42 *Foolish ones speak a lot, taking pleasure in the eulogizing words of* Vedas, *O Pārtha, saying, 'There is nothing else.'*

कामात्मानः स्वर्गपरा जन्मकर्मफलप्रदाम् ।
क्रियाविशेषबहुलां भोगैश्वर्यगतिं प्रति ॥ २.४३

kāmātmānaḥ svargaparā janmakarmaphalapradām I
kriyāviśeṣabahulāṁ bhogaiśvaryagatiṁ prati II 2.43

kāmātmānaḥ: desirous of sense gratification; *svargaparāḥ*: aiming at heaven as supreme goal; *janma karma phala pradām*: resulting in rebirth as the fruit; *kriyā viśeṣa bahulāṁ*: many rituals of various kinds; *bhogaiśvarya*: sense enjoyment opulence; *gatiṁ*: way; *prati*: towards

2.43 *Men of little knowledge are very much attached to the flowery words of the* Vedas *which recommend various fruitful activities for elevation to heavenly planets, resulting in good birth, power, and so forth. Being desirous of sense gratification and opulent life, they say that there is nothing more than this to living.*

भोगैश्वर्यप्रसक्तानां तयापहृतचेतसाम् ।
व्यवसायात्मिका बुद्धिः समाधौ न विधीयते ॥ २.४४

bhogaiśvaryaprasaktānāṁ tayāpahṛtacetasām I
vyavasāyātmikā buddhiḥ samādhau na vidhīyate II 2.44

bhogaiśvarya: material enjoyment opulence; *prasaktānāṁ*: of those who are so attached; *tayā*: by such words; *apahṛta cetasāṁ*: bewildered in mind; *vyavasāyātmikā*: fixed determination; *buddhiḥ*: intellect; *samādhau*: in the supreme goal; *na*: not; *vidhīyate*: centers on

2.44 Those whose minds are diverted and who are not determined are not fit for steady meditation and samādhi.

त्रैगुण्यविषया वेदा निस्त्रैगुण्यो भवार्जुन ।
निर्द्वन्द्वो नित्यसत्त्वस्थो निर्योगक्षेम आत्मवान् ॥ २.४५

traiguṇyaviṣayā vedā nistraiguṇyo bhavārjuna |
nirdvandvo nityasattvastho niryogakṣema ātmavān || 2.45

traiguṇya viṣayā: pertaining to the three modes of material nature and the means of achieving them; *vedā*: Vedic literature; *nistraiguṇyaḥ*: indifferent to the material enjoyments and their means; *bhava*: be; *arjuna*: O Arjuna; *nirdvandvaḥ*: free from the pairs of opposites; *nitya sattvasthaḥ*: ever remaining in *satva* (eternal existence); *niryogakṣemaḥ*: free from (the thought of) acquisition and preservation; *ātmavān*: established in the Self

2.45 O Arjuna! Be you above the three attributes that the Vedas *deal in; free yourself from the pairs-of-opposites and be always in* satva *(goodness), free from all thoughts of acquisition or preservation and be established in the Self.*

यावानर्थ उदपाने सर्वतः सम्प्लुतोदके ।
तावान्सर्वेषु वेदेषु ब्राह्मणस्य विजानतः ॥ २.४६

yāvānartha udapāne sarvataḥ saṁplutodake |
tāvānsarveṣu vedeṣu brāhmaṇasya vijānataḥ || 2.46

yāvān: how much; *arthaḥ*: means; *udapāne*: in a well of water; *sarvataḥ*: on all sides; *saṁplutodake*: in a great reservoir of water; *tāvān*: that much; *sarveṣu*: in all; *vedeṣu*: in the Veda; *brāhmaṇasya*: of the man who knows the supreme Brahman; *vijānataḥ*: of one who has achieved enlightenment

2.46 The sage who has known the Self has little use for the vedic scriptures *as these are like a pool of water in a place which is already in flood.*

कर्मण्येवाधिकारस्ते मा फलेषु कदाचन ।
मा कर्मफलहेतुर्भूर्मा ते सङ्गोऽस्त्वकर्मणि ॥ २.४७

karmaṇyevādhikāraste mā phaleṣu kadācana I
mā karmaphalaheturbhūrmā te saṅgo 'stvakarmaṇi II 2.47

karmaṇi: in the duties; *eva*: only; *adhikāraḥ*: right; *te*: of you; *mā*: never; *phaleṣu*: in the fruits; *kadācana*: at any time; *mā*: do not; *karma phala*: in the result of action; *hetuḥ*: cause; *bhūḥ*: let be; *mā*: never; *te*: of you; *saṅgaḥ*: attachment; *astu*: be there; *akarmaṇi*: in inaction

2.47 *You have a right only to work, but never to the outcome. Let not the outcome be your motive; but do not move into inaction.*

योगस्थ: कुरु कर्माणि सङ्गं त्यक्त्वा धनञ्जय ।
सिद्ध्यसिद्ध्यो: समो भूत्वा समत्वं योग उच्यते ॥ २.४८

yogasthaḥ kuru karmāṇi saṅgaṁ tyaktvā dhañanjaya I
siddhyasiddhyoḥ samo bhūtvā samatvaṁ yoga ucyate II 2.48

yogasthaḥ: steadfast in yoga; *kuru*: perform; *karmāṇi*: duties; *saṅgaṁ*: attachment; *tyaktvā*: having abandoned; *dhañajaya*: O Dhañanjaya; *siddhyasiddhyoḥ*: success and failure; *samaḥ*: the same; *bhūtvā*: having become; *samatvaṁ*: evenness of mind; *yoga*: yoga; *ucyate*: is called

2.48 *O Dhañanjaya! Do what you have to do with no attachment to outcome, being centered in yoga. Be balanced in success and failure. Evenness of mind is yoga.*

दूरेण ह्यवरं कर्म बुद्धियोगाद्धनञ्जय ।
बुद्धौ शरणमन्विच्छ कृपणा: फलहेतव: ॥ २.४९

dūreṇa hyavaraṁ karma buddhiyogād dhanañjaya I
buddhau śaraṇamanviccha kṛpaṇāḥ phalahetavaḥ II 2.49

dūreṇa hi avaraṁ: far superior; *karma*: activities; *buddhiyogāt*: based on the yoga of knowledge; *dhanaṁjaya*: O conqueror of wealth; *buddhau*: in such wisdom; *śaraṇam*: full surrender; *anviccha*: desire; *kṛpaṇāḥ*: wretched; *phalahetavaḥ*: those desiring fruit of action

2.49 O Dhañanjaya, beyond the yoga of wisdom, is action. Wretched are those whose motive is the outcome; surrender yourself to wisdom.

बुद्धियुक्तो जहातीह उभे सुकृतदुष्कृते ।
तस्माद्योगाय युज्यस्व योगः कर्मसु कौशलम् ॥ २.५०

buddhiyukto jahātīha ubhe sukṛtaduṣkṛte |
tasmādyogāya yujyasva yogaḥ karmasu kauśalam || 2.50

buddhiyuktaḥ: even minded person; *jahāti*: gives up; *iha*: in this life; *ubhe*: both; *sukṛta duṣkṛte*: good and bad results; *tasmāt*: therefore; *yogāya*: for the sake of yoga; *yujyasva*: be so engaged; *yogaḥ*: yoga; *karmasu*: in all activities; *kauśalam*: art (of freeing the Self from the bondage of action)

2.50 Endowed with the wisdom of evenness of mind, move away from both good and evil deeds in this life. Devote yourself to yoga. Skill in action is yoga.

कर्मजं बुद्धियुक्ता हि फलं त्यक्त्वा मनीषिणः ।
जन्मबन्धविनिर्मुक्ताः पदं गच्छन्त्यनामयम् ॥ २.५१

karmajaṁ buddhiyuktā hi phalaṁ tyaktvā manīṣiṇaḥ |
janmabandhavinirmuktāḥ padaṁ gacchantyanāmayam || 2.51

karmajaṁ: born of action; *buddhiyuktā*: even minded ones; *hi*: indeed; *phalaṁ*: results; *tyaktvā*: after giving up; *manīṣiṇaḥ*: sages; *janma bandha vinirmuktāḥ*: free from the bondage of birth; *padaṁ*: position; *gacchanti*: reach; *anāmayaṁ*: without ills

2.51 The wise, having abondoned the outcome of their actions and possessed of knowledge, are freed from the cycle of birth and death. They go to the state which is beyond all sorrow.

यदा ते मोहकलिलं बुद्धिर्व्यतितरिष्यति ।
तदा गन्तासि निर्वेदं श्रोतव्यस्य श्रुतस्य च ॥ २.५२

yadā te mohakalilaṁ buddhirvyatitariṣyati |
tadā gantāsi nirvedaṁ śrotavyasya śrutasya ca || 2.52

yadā: when; *te*: they; *moha kalilaṁ*: slough of delusion; *buddhiḥ*: understanding; *vyatitariṣyati*: will pass through; *tadā*: at that time; *gantāsi*: you shall attain; *nirvedaṁ*: cheerlessness; *śrotavyasya*: all that is to be heard; *śrutasya*: all that is already heard; *ca*: also

2.52 When your wisdom takes you beyond delusion, you shall be indifferent to what has been heard and what is yet to be heard.

श्रुतिविप्रतिन्ना ते यदा स्थास्यति निश्चला ।
समाधावचला बुद्धिस्तदा योगमवाप्स्यसि ॥ २.५३

śrutivipratipannā te yadā sthāsyati niścalā |
samādhāvacalā buddhistadā yogamavāpsyasi || 2.53

śrutivipratipannā: confused by much hearing; *te*: this; *yadā*: when; *sthāsyati*: rests; *niścalā*: steady; *samādhau*: on God; *acalā*: unflinching; *buddhiḥ*: intellect; *tadā*: at that time; *yogaṁ*: self-realization; *avāpsyasi*: you will achieve

2.53 When you are not confused by what you have heard and your wisdom stands steady and unmoving in the Self, you shall attain Self–realization.

अर्जुन उवाच
स्थितप्रज्ञस्य का भाषा समाधिस्थस्य केशव ।
स्थितधीः किं प्रभाषेत किमासीत व्रजेत किम् ॥ २.५४

arjuna uvāca
sthitaprajñasya kā bhāṣā samādhisthasya keśava |
sthitadhīḥ kiṁ prabhāṣeta kimāsīta vrajeta kim || 2.54

arjuna uvāca: Arjuna said; *sthitaprajñasya*: of one who is of secure mind; *kā*: what; *bhāṣā*: language; *samādhisthasya*: of one established in the tranquility of mind; *keśava*: O Kṛṣṇa; *sthitadhīḥ*: one with stable mind; *kiṁ*: how; *prabhāṣeta*: speak; *kim*: how; *āsīta*: sits; *vrajeta*: walks; *kim*: how

2.54 O Keśava! *What is the description of one who stays in the present moment and is merged in the awareness of truth and wisdom? How does one of steady wisdom speak, how does he sit, how does he walk?*

श्री भगवानुवाच ।
प्रजहाति यदा कामान्सर्वान्पार्थ मनोगतान् ।
आत्मन्येवात्मना तुष्टः स्थितप्रज्ञस्तदोच्यते ॥ २.५५

śrībhagavānuvāca

prajahāti yadā kāmānsarvānpārtha manogatān |

ātmanyevātmanā tuṣṭaḥ sthitaprajñastadocyate || 2.55

śrī bhagavān uvāca: The Lord said; *prajahāti*: gives up; *yadā*: when; *kāmān*: desires; *sarvān*: of all varieties; *pārtha*: O son of Pritā; *manogatān*: existing in mind; *ātmani*: in the soul; *eva*: only; *ātmanā*: by the self; *tuṣṭaḥ*: satisfied; *sthitaprajñaḥ*: one of secure understanding; *tadā*: at that time; *ucyate*: is said

2.55 Śrī Bhagavān *said: O Pārtha, a man who casts off completely all the desires of the mind and is satisfied in the Self by the Self, He is said to be one of steady wisdom.*

दुःखेष्वनुद्विग्नमनाः सुखेषु विगतस्पृहः ।

वीतरागभयक्रोधः स्थितधीर्मुनिरुच्यते ॥ २.५६

duḥkheṣvanudvignamanāḥ sukheṣu vigataspṛhaḥ /

vītarāgabhayakrodhaḥ sthitadhīrmunirucyate // 2.56

duḥkheṣu: in sorrow; *anudvignamanāḥ*: without being agitated in mind; *sukheṣu*: in happiness; *vigataspṛhaḥ*: without being interested; *vīta*: free from; *rāga*: passion; *bhaya*: fear; *krodhaḥ*: anger; *sthitadhīḥ*: one who is steady in mind; *muniḥ*: a sage; *ucyate*: is called

2.56 He whose mind is not disturbed by adversity and who, in prosperity, does not go after other pleasures, he who is free from attachment, fear or anger is called a sage of steady wisdom.

यः सर्वत्रानभिस्नेहस्तत्तत्प्राप्य शुभाशुभम् ।

नाभिनन्दति न द्वेष्टि तस्य प्रज्ञा प्रतिष्ठिता ॥ २.५७

yaḥ sarvatrānabhisnehastattatprāpya śubhāśubham /

nābhinandati na dveṣṭi tasya prajñā pratiṣṭhitā // 2.57

yaḥ: one who; *sarvatra*: everywhere; *anabhisnehaḥ*: without affection; *tat*: that; *tat*: that; *prāpya*: after achieving; *śubhāśubhaṁ*: good evil; *na*: not; *abhinandati*: rejoices; *na*: not; *dveṣṭi*: resents; *tasya*: his; *prajñā*: knowledge; *pratiṣṭhitā*: fixed

2.57 His wisdom is fixed who is everywhere without attachment, meeting with anything good or bad and who neither rejoices nor hates.

यदा संहरते चायं कूर्मोऽङ्गानीव सर्वशः ।
इन्द्रियाणीन्द्रियार्थेभ्यस्तस्य प्रज्ञा प्रतिष्ठिता ॥ २.५८

yadā saṁharate cāyaṁ kūrmo 'ṅgānīva sarvaśaḥ I
indriyāṇīndriyārthebhyastasya prajñā pratiṣṭhitā II 2.58

yadā: when; *saṁharate*: withdraws; *ca*: also; *ayaṁ*: this; *kūrmaḥ*: tortoise; *aṅgānī*: limbs; *iva*: like; *sarvaśaḥ*: altogether; *indriyāṇi*: senses; *indriyārthebhyaḥ*: from the sense objects; *tasya*: his; *prajñā*: consciousness; *pratiṣṭhitā*: fixed

2.58 As the tortoise withdraws its limbs from all sides, when a person withdraws his senses from the sense-objects, his wisdom becomes steady.

विषया विनिवर्तन्ते निराहारस्य देहिनः ।
रसवर्जं रसोऽप्यस्य परं दृष्ट्वा निवर्तते ॥ २.५९

viṣayā vinivartante nirāhārasya dehinaḥ I
rasavarjaṁ raso'pyasya paraṁ dṛṣṭvā nivartate II 2.59

viṣayāḥ: sense objects; *vinivartante*: turn away; *nirāhārasya*: of one who does not enjoy them with his senses; *dehinaḥ*: of the embodied; *rasavarjaṁ*: yearning, persisting; *rasaḥ*: yearning; *api*: although there is; *asya*: his; *paraṁ*: the supreme; *dṛṣṭvā*: after seeing; *nivartate*: returns

2.59 From the body, the sense objects turn away, but the desires remain; his desires also leave him on seeing the Supreme.

यततो ह्यपि कौन्तेय पुरुषस्य विपश्चितः ।
इन्द्रियाणि प्रमाथीनि हरन्ति प्रसभं मनः ॥ २.६०

yatato hyapi kaunteya puruṣasya vipaścitaḥ I
indriyāṇi pramāthīni haranti prasabhaṁ manaḥ II 2.60

yatataḥ: while endeavoring; *hi*: indeed; *api*: also; *kaunteya*: O son of Kuntī; *puruṣasya*: of the man; *vipaścitaḥ*: the wise; *indriyāṇi*: the senses; *pramāthīni*: turbulent; *haranti*: carry away; *prasabhaṁ*: by force; *manaḥ*: the mind

2.60 O son of Kuntī, the turbulent senses carry away the mind of a wise man, though he is striving to be in control.

तानि सर्वाणि संयम्य युक्त आसीत मत्परः ।
वशे हि यस्येन्द्रियाणि तस्य प्रज्ञा प्रतिष्ठिता ॥ २.६१

tāni sarvāṇi saṁyamya yukta āsīta matparaḥ I
vaśe hi yasyendriyāṇi tasya prajñāpratiṣṭhitā II 2.61

tāni: those senses; *sarvāṇi*: all; *saṁyamya*: keeping under control; *yuktaḥ*: yogi; *āsīta*: sitting; *matparaḥ*: devoted to Me; *vaśe*: in full subjugation; *hi*: indeed; *yasya*: one whose; *indriyāṇi*: senses; *tasya*: his; *prajñā*; mind; *pratiṣṭhitā*: stable

2.61 Having restrained them all, he should sit steadfast, intent on Me. His mind is steady in the present whose senses are under control.

ध्यायतो विषयान्पुंसः सङ्गस्तेषूपजायते।
सङ्गात् सञ्जायते कामः कामात्क्रोधोऽभिजायते ॥ २.६२

dhyāyato viṣayānpuṁsaḥ saṅgasteṣūpajāyate I
saṅgātsañjāyate kāmaḥ kāmātkrodhobhijāyate II 2.62

dhyāyataḥ: contemplating; *viṣayān*: sense objects; *puṁsaḥ*: of the person; *saṅgaḥ*: attachment; *teṣu*: in these sense objects; *upajāyate*: develops; *saṅgāt*: from attachment; *saṁjāyate*: develops; *kāmaḥ*: desire; *kāmāt*: from desire; *krodhaḥ*: anger; *abhijāyate*: ensues

2.62 When a man thinks of objects, it gives rise to attachment for them. From attachment, desire arises; from desire, anger is born.

क्रोधाद्भवति संमोहः संमोहात्स्मृतिविभ्रमः ।
स्मृतिभ्रंशाद् बुद्धिनाशो बुद्धिनाशात्प्रणश्यति ॥ २.६३

krodhād bhavati saṁmohaḥ saṁmohāt smṛtivibhramaḥ I
smṛtibhraṁśād buddhināśo buddhināśātpraṇaśyati II 2.63

krodhāt: from anger; *bhavati*: takes place; *saṁmohaḥ*: illusion; *saṁmohāt*: from illusion; *smṛti*: of memory; *vibhramaḥ*: loss; *smṛti bhraṁśāt*: from loss of memory; *buddhi nāśaḥ*: loss of reason; *buddhināśāt*: from loss of reason; *praṇaśyati*: perishes

2.63 From anger arises delusion, from delusion, loss of memory, from loss of memory, the destruction of discrimination, from destruction of discrimination, he perishes.

रागद्वेषवियुक्तैस्तु विषयानिन्द्रियैश्चरन् ।
आत्मवश्यैर्विधेयात्मा प्रसादमधिगच्छति ॥ २.६४

rāgadveṣaviyuktaistu viṣayānindriyaiścaran |
ātmavaśyairvidheyātmā prasādamadhigacchati || 2.64

rāga dveṣa: likes and disklikes; *viyuktaiḥ*: by those free from such things; *tu*: but; *viṣayān*: sense objects; *indriyaiḥ*: by the senses; *caran*: enjoying; *ātmavaśyaih*: by the disciplined; *vidheyātmā*: self controlled; *prasādaṁ*: placidity of mind; *adhigacchati*: attains

2.64 The self-controlled man, moving among objects with his senses under control, free from both attraction and repulsion, attains peace.

प्रसादे सर्वदुःखानां हानिरस्योपजायते ।
प्रसन्नचेतसो ह्याशु बुद्धिः पर्यवतिष्ठते ॥ २.६५ ॥

prasāde sarvaduḥkhānāṁ hānirasyopajāyate |
prasannacetaso hyāśu buddhiḥ paryavatiṣṭhate || 2.65

prasāde: with achieving peace of mind; *sarva*: of all; *duḥkhānāṁ*: of miseries; *hāniḥ*: destruction; *asya*: his; *upajāyate*: takes place; *prasannacetasaḥ*: of the happy-minded; *hi*: indeed; *āśu*: very soon; *buddhiḥ*: intelligence; *paryavatiṣṭhate*: firmly established

2.65 All pains are destroyed in that peace, for the intellect of the tranquil-minded soon becomes steady.

नास्ति बुद्धिरयुक्तस्य न चायुक्तस्य भावना ।
न चाभावयतः शान्तिरशान्तस्य कुतः सुखम् ॥ २.६६ ॥

nāsti buddhirayuktasya na cāyuktasya bhāvanā |
na cābhāvayataḥ śāntiraśāntasya kutaḥ sukham || 2.66

na asti: there is not; *buddhiḥ*: wisdom; *ayuktasya*: of one who is not connected to Self; *na*: neither; *ca*: and; *ayuktasya*: of one devoid of Self awareness; *bhāvanā*: devotion; *na*: neither; *ca*: and; *abhāvayataḥ*: for the indisciplined; *śāntiḥ*: peace; *aśāntasya*: of the indisciplined; *kutaḥ*: how; *sukhaṁ*: happiness

2.66 A person not in self awareness cannot be wise or happy or peaceful. How can there be happiness to one without peace?

इन्द्रियाणां हि चरतां यन्मनोऽनुविधीयते ।
तदस्य हरति प्रज्ञां वायुर्नावमिवांभसि ॥ २.६७ ॥

indriyāṇāṁ hi caratāṁ yanmano 'nuvidhīyate I
tadasya harati prajñāṁ vāyurnāvamivāmbhasi II 2.67

indriyāṇāṁ: of the senses; *hi*: indeed; *caratāṁ*: moving among objects; *yat*: that; *manaḥ*: mind; *anu: with; vidhīyate*: joined; *tat*: that; *asya*: his; *harati*: takes away; *prajñāṁ*: discrimination; *vāyuḥ*: wind; *nāvaṁ*: a boat; *iva*: like; *ambhasi*: on the water

2.67 He loses his awareness of the present moment when his mind follows the wandering senses, just as the wind carries away a boat on the waters.

तस्माद्यस्य महाबाहो निगृहीतानि सर्वशः ।
इन्द्रियाणीन्द्रियार्थेभ्यस्तस्य प्रज्ञा प्रतिष्ठिता ॥ २.६८ ॥

tasmādyasya mahābāho nigṛhītāni sarvaśaḥ I
indriyāṇīndriyārthebhyastasya prajñā pratiṣṭhitā II 2.68

tasmāt: therefore; *yasya*: of one's; *mahābāho*: O mighty-armed one; *nigṛhītāni*: so curbed down; *sarvaśaḥ*: in all respects; *indriyāṇi*: the senses; *indriyārthebhyaḥ*: from the sense objects; *tasya*: his; *prajñā*: intelligence; *pratiṣṭhitā*: fixed

2.68 O Mighty-armed one, his knowledge is therefore steady whose senses are completely detached from sense objects.

या निशा सर्वभूतानां तस्यां जागर्ति संयमी ।
यस्यां जाग्रति भूतानि सा निशा पश्यतो मुनेः ॥ २.६९ ॥

yā niśā sarvabhūtānāṁ tasyāṁ jāgarti saṁyamī I
yasyāṁ jāgrati bhūtāni sā niśā paśyato muneḥ II 2.69

yā: what; *niśā*: is night; *sarva*: all; *bhūtānāṁ*: of living entities; *tasyāṁ*: in that; *jāgarti*: wakeful; *saṁyamī*: the self-controlled; *yasyāṁ*: in which; *jāgrati*: awake; *bhūtāni*: all beings; *sā*: that is; *niśā*: night; *paśyataḥ*: for the seer; *muneḥ*: for the sage

2.69 The self–controlled man lies awake in that which is night to all beings. That in which all beings are awake is the night for the sage who sees.

आपूर्यमाणमचलप्रतिष्ठं समुद्रमापः प्रविशन्ति यद्वत् ।
तद्वत्कामा यं प्रविशन्ति सर्वे स शान्तिमाप्नोति न कामकामी ॥ २.७० ॥

āpūryamāṇamacalapratiṣṭhaṁ samudramāpaḥ praviśanti yadvat I
tadvatkāmā yaṁ praviśanti sarve sa śāntimāpnoti na kāmakāmī II 2.70

āpūryamāṇam: always filled; *acalapratiṣṭham*: steadily established; *samudram*: the ocean; *āpaḥ*: water; *praviśanti*: enter; *yadvat*: as; *tadvat*: so; *kāmāḥ*: desires; *yaṁ*: one; *praviśanti*: enter; *sarve*: all; *saḥ*: that person; *śāntim*: peace; *āpnoti*: achieves; *na*: not; *kāmakāmī*: one who cherishes longings

2.70 Just as all waters enter the ocean, he attains peace into whom all desires enter, which when filled from all sides, remains unmoved; not the desirer of desires.

विहाय कामान्यः सर्वान् पुमांश्चरति निःस्पृहः ।
निर्ममो निरहङ्कारः स शान्तिमधिगच्छति ॥ २.७१ ॥

vihāya kāmānyaḥ sarvān pumāṁścarati niḥspṛhaḥ I
nirmamo nirahañkāraḥ sa śāntimadhigacchati II 2.71

vihāya: after giving up; *kāmān*: desires for sense gratification; *yaḥ*: the person; *sarvān*: all; *pumān*: a person; *carati*: moves; *niḥspṛhaḥ*: desireless; *nir mamaḥ*: without a sense of proprietorship; *nir ahaṁkāraḥ*: without false ego; *saḥ*: he; *śāntim*: peace; *adhigacchati*: attains

2.71 The man who moves about abandoning all desires, without longing, without the sense of I and mine, attains peace.

एषा ब्राह्मी स्थितिः पार्थ नैनां प्राप्य विमुह्यति ।
स्थित्वाऽस्यामन्तकालेऽपि ब्रह्मनिर्वाणमृच्छति ॥ २.७२ ॥

eṣā brāhmī sthitiḥ pārtha naināṁ prāpya vimuhyati I
sthitvāsyāmantakālepi 'brahmanirvāṇamṛcchati II 2.72

eṣā: this; *brāhmī*: God-realised soul; *sthitiḥ*: situation; *pārtha*: O son of Pritā; *na*: not; *enāṁ*: this; *prāpya*: after achieving; *vimuhyati*: get deluded; *sthitvā*: being so situated; *asyāṁ*: in this state; *antakāle*: at the end of life; *api*: also; *brahma nirvāṇaṁ*: passing into one with the ultimate Reality; *ṛcchati*: attains

2.72 *O Pārtha, this is the state of* Brahman; *none is deluded after attaining this. Even at the end of life, one attains oneness with Brahman when established in this state.*

इति श्रीमद्भगवद्गीतासूपनिषत्सु ब्रह्मविद्यायां योगशास्त्रे
श्रीकृष्णार्जुनसंवादे साङ्ख्ययोगो नाम द्वितीयोऽध्यायः ॥२॥

iti śrī mad bhagavadgītāsūpaniṣatsu brahmavidyāyām
yogaśāstre śrīkṛṣṇārjuna saṁvāde sāṅkhya yogo nāma dvitīyo'dhyāyaḥ ||

In the Upaniṣad *of the Bhagavad Gītā, the knowledge of* Brahman, *the Supreme, the science of Yoga and the dialogue between Śrī Kṛṣṇa and Arjuna, this is the second discourse designated:*

Sāṅkhya Yogaḥ

Verses Of Gita Chapter - 3

अथ तृतीयोऽध्याय:

कर्मयोग:

Karma Yogaḥ

अर्जुन उवाच
ज्यायसी चेत्कर्मणस्ते मता बुद्धिर्जनार्दन ।
तत्किं कर्मणि घोरे मां नियोजयसि केशव ॥ ३.१

arjuna uvāca
jyāyasī cetkarmaṇaste matā buddhirjanārdana **/**
tatkiṁ karmaṇi ghore māṁ niyojayasi keśava **//** 3.1

arjuna: Arjuna; *uvāca*: said; *jyāyasī*: speaking highly; *cet*: although; *karmaṇaḥ*: action; *te*: your; *matā*: opinion; *buddhir*: knowledge; *janārdana*: Janārdana; *tat*: therefore; *kiṁ*: why; *karmaṇi*: in action; *ghore*: terrible; *māṁ*: me; *niyojayasi*: engaging me; *keśava*: Keśava (slayer of the demon *Keshi*)

3.1 Arjuna said: O Janārdana, O Keśava, *Why do You make me engage in this terrible war if You think that knowledge is superior to action?*

व्यामिश्रेणेव वाक्येन बुद्धिं मोहयसीव मे ।
तदेकं वद निश्चित्य येन श्रेयोऽहमाप्नुयाम् ॥ ३.२

vyāmiśreṇeva vākyena buddhiṁ mohayasīva me **/**
tadekaṁ vada niścitya yena śreyohamāpnuyām **//** 3.2

vyāmiśreṇa: by ambiguous; *iva*: as; *vākyena*: words; *buddhiṁ*: intelligence; *mohayasi*: confusing; *iva*: as; *me*: my; *tat*: therefore; *ekaṁ*: one; *vada*: tell; *niścitya*: for certain; *yena*: by which; *śreyaḥ*: benefit; *ahaṁ*: I; *āpnuyāṁ*: may have

3.2 My intelligence is confused by Your conflicting words. Tell me clearly what is best for me.

श्रीभगवानुवाच
लोकेऽस्मिन्द्विविधा निष्ठा पुरा प्रोक्ता मयानघ ।
ज्ञानयोगेन साङ्ख्यानां कर्मयोगेन योगिनाम् ॥ ३.३

śrībhagavānuvāca

loke'smindvividhā niṣṭhā purā proktā mayānagha |
jñānayogena sāṁkhyānāṁ karmayogena yoginām || 3.3

śrī bhagavān uvāca: the Lord said; *loke*: in the world; *asmin*: this; *dvividhā*: two kinds of; *niṣṭhā*: faith; *purā*: before; *proktā*: were said; *mayā*: by Me; *anagha*: O sinless one; *jñānayogena*: by the yoga of knowledge; *sāṁkhyānāṁ*: of the Sāṅkhya; *karmayogena*: by the yoga of action; *yoginām*: of the yoga practitioners

3.3 The Lord said, 'O sinless Arjuna, as I said before, in this world there are two paths; Self knowledge for the intellectual and the path of action of the knowing.

न कर्मणामनारम्भान्नैष्कर्म्यं पुरुषोऽश्नुते ।
न च सन्न्यसनादेव सिद्धिं समधिगच्छति ॥ ३.४

na karmaṇāmanārambhānnaiṣkarmyaṁ puruṣo'śnute |
na ca sannyasanādeva siddhiṁ samadhigacchati || 3.4

na: without; *karmaṇām*: of the actions; *anārambhāt*: abstaining; *naiṣkarmyaṁ*: freedom from action; *puruṣaḥ*: man; *aśnute*: achieve; *na*: not; *ca*: also; *sannyasanāt*: by renunciation; *eva*: surely; *siddhiṁ*: success; *samadhigacchati*: attain

3.4 A person does not attain freedom from action by abstaining from work, nor does he attain fulfillment by giving up action.

न हि कश्चित्क्षणमपि जातु तिष्ठत्यकर्मकृत् ।
कार्यते ह्यवशः कर्म सर्वः प्रकृतिजैर्गुणैः ॥ ३.५

na hi kaścitkṣaṇamapi jātu tiṣṭhatyakarmakṛt |
kāryate hyavaśaḥ karma sarvaḥ prakṛtijairguṇaiḥ || 3.5

na: not; *hi*: surely; *kaścit*: anyone; *kṣaṇam*: for a moment; *api*: also; *jātu*: even; *tiṣṭhati*: stands; *akarmakṛt*: without doing something; *kāryate*: forced to work; *hi*: surely; *avaśaḥ*: helplessly; *karma*: action; *sarvaḥ*: all; *prakṛtijaih*: of the modes of material nature; *guṇaiḥ*: by the attributes

3.5 Surely, not even for a moment can anyone stand without doing something. He is always in action, despite himself, as this is his very nature.

कर्मेन्द्रियाणि संयम्य य आस्ते मनसा स्मरन् ।
इन्द्रियार्थान्विमूढात्मा मिथ्याचारः स उच्यते ॥ ३.६

karmendriyāṇi saṁyamya ya āste manasā smaran /
indriyārthānvimūḍhātmā mithyācāraḥ sa ucyate // 3.6

karmendriyāṇi: the five working sense organs; *saṁyamya*: restraining; *ya*: who; *āste*: remains; *manasā*: mentally; *smaran*: recollecting; *indriyārthān*: objects of the senses; *vimūḍha*: foolish; *atma*: soul; *mithyācāraḥ*: hypocrite; *saḥ*: he; *ucyate*: is called

3.6 He who restrains the sense organs, but who still thinks of the objects of the senses is deluded and is called a hypocrite.

यस्त्विन्द्रियाणि मनसा नियम्यारभतेऽर्जुन ।
कर्मेन्द्रियैः कर्मयोगमसक्तः स विशिष्यते ॥ ३.७

yastvindriyāṇi manasā niyamyārabhate 'rjuna /
karmendriyaiḥ karmayogamasaktaḥ sa viśiṣyate // 3.7

yaḥ: who; *tu*: but; *indriyāṇi*: senses; *manasā*: by the mind; *niyamya*: controlling; *ārabhate*: begins; *arjuna*: O Arjuna; *karmendriyaiḥ*: by the active sense organs; *karmayogam*: work of devotion; *asaktaḥ*: without attachment; *saḥ*: he; *viśiṣyate*: superior

3.7 He who begins controlling the senses by the mind and performs selfless work through the sense organs is superior, O Arjuna.

नियतं कुरु कर्म त्वं कर्म ज्यायो ह्यकर्मणः
शरीरयात्रापि च ते न प्रसिद्ध्येदकर्मणः ॥ ३.८

niyataṁ kuru karma tvaṁ karma jyāyo hyakarmaṇaḥ /
śarīrayātrāpi ca te na prasiddhyedakarmaṇaḥ // 3.8

niyataṁ: prescribed; *kuru*: do; *karma*: work; *tvaṁ*: you; *karma*: work; *jyāyaḥ*: better; *hi*: than; *akarmaṇaḥ*: without work; *śarīra*: body; *yātrā*: maintenance; *api*: even; *ca*: also; *te*: your; *na*: never; *prasiddhyet*: possible; *akarmaṇaḥ*: without work

3.8 Do your prescribed work, as doing work is better than being idle. Even your own body cannot be maintained without work.

यज्ञार्थात्कर्मणोऽन्यत्र लोकोऽयं कर्मबन्धनः ।
तदर्थं कर्म कौन्तेय मुक्तसङ्गः समाचर ॥ ३.९

yajñārthātkarmaṇo'nyatra loko'yam karmabandhanaḥ |
tadarthaṁ karma kaunteya mukta saṅgaḥ samācara || 3.9

yajñārthāt: sacrifice for; *karmaṇaḥ*: work done; *anyatra*: otherwise; *lokaḥ*: world; *ayaṁ*: this; *karma bandhanaḥ*: bondage by work; *tad*: that; *arthaṁ*: for; *karma*: work; *kaunteya*: O son of Kuntī; *mukta*: liberated; *saṅgaḥ*: attachment; *samācara*: do perfectly

3.9 *Work has to be performed selflessly; otherwise, work binds one to this world. O son of* Kuntī, *perform your work for Me and you will do it perfectly, liberated and without attachment.*

सहयज्ञाः प्रजाः सृष्ट्वा पुरोवाच प्रजापतिः ।
अनेन प्रसविष्यध्वमेष वोऽस्त्विष्टकामधुक् ॥ ३.१०

sahayajñāḥ prajāḥ sṛṣṭvā puro'vāca prajāpatiḥ |
anena prasaviṣyadhvameṣa vo'stviṣṭakāmadhuk || 3.10

sah: along with; *yajñāḥ*: sacrifices; *prajāḥ*: people; *sṛṣṭvā*: creating; *purā*: before; *uvāca*: said; *prajāpatiḥ*: the lord of creation; *anena*: by this; *prasaviṣyadhvaṁ*: be more and more prosperous; *eṣaḥ*: certainly; *vaḥ*: your; *astu*: let it be; *iṣṭa*: desired; *kāma dhuk*: bestower of gifts

3.10 Brahma, *the lord of creation before creating human kind as selfless sacrifice said, 'By this selfless service, be more and more prosperous and let it bestow all the desired gifts.'*

देवान्भावयतानेन ते देवा भावयन्तु वः ।
परस्परं भावयन्तः श्रेयः परमवाप्स्यथ ॥ ३.११

devān bhāvayatā'nena te devā bhāvayantu vaḥ |
parasparaṁ bhāvayantaḥ śreyaḥ paramavāpsyatha || 3.11

devān: celestial beings; *bhāvayata*: having pleased; *anena*: by this sacrifice; *te*: those; *devāḥ*: demigods; *bhāvayantu*: will please; *vaḥ*: you; *parasparaṁ*: mutual; *bhāvayantaḥ*: pleasing one another; *śreyaḥ*: prosperity; *paraṁ*: supreme; *avāpsyatha*: achieve

3.11 *The celestial beings, being pleased by this sacrifice, will also nourish you; with this mutual nourishing of one another, you will achieve supreme prosperity.*

इष्टान्भोगान्हि वो देवा दास्यन्ते यज्ञभाविताः ।
तैर्दत्तानप्रदायैभ्यो यो भुङ्क्ते स्तेन एव सः ॥ ३.१२

iṣṭānbhogān hi vo devā dāsyante yajñabhāvitāḥ I
tairdattānapradāyaibhyo yo bhuṅkte stena eva saḥ II 3.12

iṣṭān: desired; *bhogān*: necessities of life; *hi*: certainly; *vaḥ*: to you; *devāḥ*: demigods; *dāsyante*: award; *yajña*: sacrifice; *bhāvitāḥ*: satisfied; *taiḥ*: by them; *dattān*: things given; *apradāya*: without offering; *ebhyaḥ*: to the celestial beings; *yaḥ*: who; *bhuṅkte*: enjoys; *stenaḥ*: thief; *eva*: certainly; *saḥ*: he

3.12 Satisfied with the selfless service, the celestial beings certainly award you the desired necessities of life. He who enjoys the things given by them without offering to the celestial beings is certainly a thief.

यज्ञशिष्टाशिनः सन्तो मुच्यन्ते सर्वकिल्बिषैः ।
भुञ्जते ते त्वघं पापा ये पचन्त्यात्मकारणात् ॥ ३.१३

yajñaśiṣṭāśinaḥ santo mucyante sarvakilbiṣaiḥ I
bhuñjate te tvaghaṁ pāpā ye pacantyātmakāraṇāt II 3.13

yajñaśiṣṭāśinaḥ: those who eat the food remnants of sacrifice; *santaḥ*: devotees; *mucyante*: get relief from; *sarva*: all; *kilbiṣaiḥ*: sins; *bhuñjate*: enjoy; *te*: they; *tu*: but; *aghaṁ*: grievous; *pāpāḥ*: sins; *ye*: those; *pacanti*: prepare food; *ātmakāraṇāt*: for sense enjoyment

3.13 Those who eat food after selfless service are free of all sins. Those who prepare food for sense enjoyment do grievous sin.

अन्नाद्भवन्ति भूतानि पर्जन्यादन्नसम्भवः ।
यज्ञाद्भवति पर्जन्यो यज्ञः कर्मसमुद्भवः ॥ ३.१४

annādbhavanti bhūtāni parjanyādannasaṁbhavaḥ I
yajñādbhavati parjanyo yajñaḥ karmasamudbhavaḥ II 3.14

annāt: from grains; *bhavanti*: grow; *bhūtāni*: beings; *parjanyāt*: from rains; *anna*: food grains; *saṁbhavaḥ*: possible; *yajñāt*: from sacrifice; *bhavati*: becomes possible; *parjanyaḥ*: rains; *yajñaḥ*: sacrifice; *karma*: work; *samudbhavaḥ*: born of

3.14 All beings grow from food grains, from rains the food grains become possible, the rains become possible from selfless sacrifice.

कर्म ब्रह्मोद्भवं विद्धि ब्रह्माक्षरसमुद्भवम् ।
तस्मात्सर्वगतं ब्रह्म नित्यं यज्ञे प्रतिष्ठितम् ॥ ३.१५

karma brahmodbhavaṁ viddhi brahmākṣarasamudbhavam /
tasmātsarvagataṁ brahma nityaṁ yajñe pratiṣṭhitam // 3.15

karma: work; *brahmodbhavaṁ*: Creator born of; *viddhi*: know; *brahma*: Creator; *akṣarasamudbhavaṁ*: Supreme born of; *tasmāt*: therefore; *sarvagataṁ*: all-pervading; *brahma*: Supreme; *nityaṁ*: eternally; *yajñe*: in sacrifice; *pratiṣṭhitaṁ*: situated

3.15 Know that work is born of the Creator and He is born of the Supreme. The all-pervading Supreme is eternally situated in sacrifice.

एवं प्रवर्तितं चक्रं नानुवर्तयतीह यः ।
अघायुरिन्द्रियारामो मोघं पार्थ स जीवति ॥ ३.१६

evaṁ pravartitaṁ cakraṁ nānuvartayatīha yaḥ /
aghāyurindriyārāmo moghaṁ pārtha sa jīvati // 3.16

evaṁ: prescribed; *pravartitaṁ*: established; *cakraṁ*: cycle; *na*: not; *anuvartayati*: adopt; *iha*: in this; *yaḥ*: who; *aghāyuḥ*: life full of sins; *indriyārāmaḥ*: satisfied in sense gratification; *moghaṁ*: useless; *pārtha*: O son of Pritā; *saḥ*: he; *jīvati*: lives

3.16 O Pārtha, he who does not adopt the prescribed, established cycle lives a life full of sins. Rejoicing in sense gratification, he lives a useless life.

यस्त्वात्मरतिरेव स्यादात्मतृप्तश्च मानवः ।
आत्मन्येव च सन्तुष्टस्तस्य कार्यं न विद्यते ॥ ३.१७

yastvātmaratireva syādātmatṛptaśca mānavaḥ /
ātmanyeva ca santuṣṭastasya kāryaṁ na vidyate // 3.17

yaḥ: who; *tu*: but; *ātmaratiḥ*: takes pleasure; *eva*: certainly; *syāt*: remains; *ātmatṛptaḥ*: satisfied in self; *ca*: and; *mānavaḥ*: man; *ātmani*: in oneself; *eva*: certainly; *ca*: and; *saṁtuṣṭaḥ*: satiated; *tasya*: his; *kāryaṁ*: work; *na*: not; *vidyate*: exist

3.17 One who takes pleasure in the self, who is satisfied in the self and who is satiated in oneself, for him certainly, no work exists.

नैव तस्य कृतेनार्थो नाकृतेनेह कश्चन ।
न चास्य सर्वभूतेषु कश्चिदर्थव्यपाश्रयः ॥ ३.१८

naiva tasya kṛtenārtho nākṛteneha kaścana |
na cāsya sarvabhūteṣu kaścidarthavyapāśrayaḥ || 3.18

na: never; *eva*: certainly; *tasya*: his; *kṛtena*: by doing duty; *arthaḥ*: purpose; *na*: not; *akṛtena*: without doing duty; *iha*: in this world; *kaścana*: whatever; *na*: never; *ca*: and; *asya*: of him; *sarvabhūteṣu*: all living beings; *kaścit*: any; *artha*: purpose; *vyapāśrayaḥ*: taking shelter of

3.18 Certainly, he never has any purpose for doing his duty or for not doing his duty in this world. He does not depend on any living being.

तस्मादसक्तः सततं कार्यं कर्म समाचर ।
असक्तो ह्याचरन्कर्म परमाप्नोति पूरुषः ॥ ३.१९

tasmādasaktaḥ satataṁ kāryaṁ karma samācara |
asakto hyācaran karma paramāpnoti pūruṣaḥ || 3.19

tasmāt: therefore, *asaktaḥ*: without attachment, *satataṁ*: always, *kāryaṁ*: work, *karma*: work, *samācara*: perform, *asaktaḥ*: not attached, *hi*: certainly, *ācaran*: performing, *karma*: work, *paraṁ*: supreme, *āpnoti*: achieves, *pūruṣaḥ*: man

3.19 Therefore, one should work always without attachment. Performing work without attachment, certainly, man achieves the Supreme.

कर्मणैव हि संसिद्धिमास्थिता जनकादयः ।
लोकसंग्रहमेवापि संपश्यन्कर्तुमर्हसि ॥ ३.२०

karmaṇaiva hi saṁsiddhimāsthitā janakādayaḥ |
lokasaṁgrahamevāpi sampaśyankartumarhasi || 3.20

karmaṇā: by work; *eva*: also; *hi*: certainly; *saṁsiddhiṁ*: perfection; *āsthitāḥ*: situated; *janakādayaḥ*: Janaka and other kings; *lokasaṁgrahaṁ*: educating people; *eva*: also; *api*: therefore; *saṁpaśyan*: considering; *kartuṁ*: act; *arhasi*: deserve

3.20 King Janaka and others attained perfection by selfless service. To guide others you too must act selflessly.

यद्यदाचरति श्रेष्ठस्तत्तदेवेतरो जनः ।
स यत्प्रमाणं कुरुते लोकस्तदनुवर्तते ॥ ३.२१

yad yad ācarati śreṣṭhas tat tad evetaro janaḥ |
sa yatpramāṇaṁ kurute lokastadanuvartate || 3.21

yad-yat: what; *ācarati*: act; *śreṣṭhaḥ*: great; *tat-tat*: that; *eva*: certainly; *itaraḥ*: common; *janaḥ*: persons; *saḥ*: he; *yat*: what; *pramāṇam*: evidence; *kurute*: perform; *lokaḥ*: world; *tat*: that; *anuvartate*: follow in footsteps

3.21 *Whatever action is performed by a great person, others follow. They follow the example set by him.*

न मे पार्थास्ति कर्तव्यं त्रिषु लोकेषु किञ्चन ।
नानवाप्तमवाप्तव्यं वर्त एव च कर्मणि ॥ ३.२२

na me pārthāsti kartavyaṁ triṣu lokeṣu kiñcana |
nānavāptamavāptavyaṁ varta eva ca karmaṇi || 3.22

na: not; *me*: mine; *pārtha*: O son of Pritā; *asti*: is; *kartavyaṁ*: duty; *triṣu*: in the three; *lokeṣu*: worlds; *kiṁcana*: anything; *na*: no; *anavāptam*: in want; *avāptavyaṁ*: to be gained; *varte*: engaged; *eva*: only; *ca*: and; *karmaṇi*: work

3.22 O *Pārtha, there is nothing that I must do in the three worlds. Neither am I in want of anything nor do I have anything to gain. Yet, I am always in action.*

यदि ह्यहं न वर्तेयं जातु कर्मण्यतन्द्रितः ।
मम वर्त्मानुवर्तन्ते मनुष्याः पार्थ सर्वशः ॥ ३.२३

yadi hyahaṁ na varteyaṁ jātu karmaṇyatandritaḥ |
mama vartmānuvartante manuṣyāḥ pārtha sarvaśaḥ || 3.23

yadi: if; *hi*: certainly; *ahaṁ*: I; *na*: not; *varteyaṁ*: engage; *jātu*: ever; *karmaṇi*: work; *atandritaḥ*: with care; *mama*: My; *vartma*: path; *anuvartante*: follow; *manuṣyāḥ*: persons; *pārtha*: Pārtha; *sarvaśaḥ*: in all respects

3.23 *If I did not engage in work with care, O Pārtha, certainly, people would follow My path in all respects.*

उत्सीदेयुरिमे लोका न कुर्यां कर्म चेदहम् ।
सङ्करस्य च कर्ता स्यामुपहन्यामिमाः प्रजाः ॥ ३.२४

utsīdeyurime lokā na kuryāṁ karma cedaham /
saṅkarasya ca kartā syāmupahanyāmimāḥ prajāḥ // 3.24

utsīdeyuḥ: ruin; *ime*: these; *lokāḥ*: worlds; *na*: not; *kuryāṁ*: do; *karma*: work; *cet*: if; *ahaṁ*: I; *saṅkarasya*: confusion of species; *ca*: and; *kartā*: doer; *syāṁ*: shall be; *upahanyāṁ*: destroy; *imāḥ*: these; *prajāḥ*: beings

3.24 If I do not work, then these worlds would be ruined. I would be the cause of creating confusion and destruction.

सक्ताः कर्मण्यविद्वांसो यथा कुर्वन्ति भारत ।
कुर्याद्विद्वांस्तथासक्तश्चिकीर्षुर्लोकसंग्रहम् ॥ ३.२५

saktāḥ karmaṇyavidvāṁso yathā kurvanti bhārata /
kuryādvidvāṁstathāsaktaścikīrṣurlokasaṁgraham // 3.25

saktāḥ: attached; *karmaṇi*: work; *avidvāṁsaḥ*: ignorant; *yathā*: as; *kurvanti*: do; *bhārata*: Bhārata; *kuryāt*: do; *vidvān*: wise; *tathā*: and; *asaktaḥ*: without attachment; *cikīrṣuḥ*: desiring; *lokasaṁgrahaṁ*: leading people

3.25 As the ignorant do their work with attachment to the results, O Bhārata, the wise do so without attachment, for the welfare of people.

न बुद्धिभेदं जनयेदज्ञानां कर्मसङ्गिनाम् ।
जोषयेत्सर्वकर्माणि विद्वान्युक्तः समाचरन् ॥ ३.२६

na buddhi bhedaṁ janayedajñānāṁ karmasaṅginām /
joṣayetsarvakarmāṇi vidvānyuktaḥ samācaran // 3.26

na: not; *buddhi*: intelligence; *bhedaṁ*: disrupt; *janayet*: do; *ajñānāṁ*: ignorant; *karma*: work *saṅgināṁ*: attached; *joṣayet*: engaged; *sarva*: all; *karmāṇi*: work; *vidvān*: wise; *yuktaḥ*: balanced; *samācaran*: practising

3.26 Let not the wise disturb the minds of the ignorant who are attached to the results of work. They should encourage them to act without attachment.

प्रकृतेः क्रियमाणानि गुणैः कर्माणि सर्वशः ।
अहङ्कारविमूढात्मा कर्ताहमिति मन्यते ॥ ३.२७

prakṛteḥ kriyamāṇāni guṇaiḥ karmāṇi sarvaśaḥ /
ahaṅkāravimūḍhātmā kartāhamiti manyate // 3.27

prakṛteḥ: of material nature; *kriyamāṇāni*: all being done; *guṇaiḥ*: by the attributes; *karmāṇi*: work; *sarvaśaḥ*: all kinds of; *ahaṁkāra*: ego; *vimūḍhātmā*: confused being; *kartā*: doer; *ahaṁ*: I; *iti*: thus; *manyate*: thinks

3.27 People, confused by ego, think they are the doers of all kinds of work while it is being done by the energy of nature.

तत्त्ववित्तु महाबाहो गुणकर्मविभागयो: ।
गुणा गुणेषु वर्तन्त इति मत्वा न सज्जते ॥ ३.२८

tattvavittu mahābāho guṇakarmavibhāgayoḥ I
guṇā guṇeṣu vartanta iti matvā na sajjate II 3.28

tattvavit: one who knows the truth; *tu*: but; *mahābāho*: mighty-armed one; *guṇa*: attributes; *karma*: work; *vibhāgayoḥ*: differences; *guṇāḥ*: attributes; *guṇeṣu*: in sense gratification; *vartante*: engaged; *iti*: thus; *matvā*: thinking; *na*: never; *sajjate*: becomes attached

3.28 One who knows the Truth, O mighty-armed one, knows the differences between the attributes of nature and work. Knowing well about the attributes and sense gratification, he never becomes attached.

प्रकृतेर्गुणसंमूढा: सज्जन्ते गुणकर्मसु ।
तानकृत्स्नविदो मन्दान्कृत्स्नविन्न विचालयेत् ॥ ३.२९

prakṛterguṇasaṁmūḍhāḥ sajjante guṇa karmasu I
tānakṛtsnavido mandānkṛtsnavinna vicālayet II 3.29

prakṛteḥ: by the material nature; *guṇa*: attributes; *saṁmūḍhāḥ*: fooled; *sajjante*: become engaged; *guṇa*: attributes; *karmasu*: actions; *tān*: those; *akṛtsnavidaḥ*: persons with less wisdom; *mandān*: lazy; *kṛtsnavit*: who has wisdom; *na*: not; *vicālayet*: unsettle

3.29 Fooled by the attributes of nature, those people with less wisdom or who are lazy become engaged in actions driven by these attributes. But, the wise should not unsettle them.

मयि सर्वाणि कर्माणि संन्यस्याध्यात्मचेतसा ।
निराशीर्निर्ममो भूत्वा युध्यस्व विगतज्वर: ॥ ३.३०

mayi sarvāṇi karmāṇi sannyasyādhyātmacetasā I
nirāśīrnirmamo bhūtvā yudhyasva vigatajvaraḥ II 3.30

mayi: to Me; *sarvāṇi*: all kinds of; *karmāṇi*: work; *saṁnyasya*: renouncing; *adhyātma*: spiritual knowledge; *cetasā*: consciousness; *nirāśīḥ*: without desire for gain; *nir mamaḥ*: without sense of ownership; *bhūtvā*: being; *yudhyasva*: fight; *vigatajvaraḥ*: without being lazy

3.30 Dedicating the results of work to Me, with consciousness filled with spiritual knowledge, without desire for gain and without sense of ownership, without being lazy, do what you have to do.

ये मे मतमिदं नित्यमनुतिष्ठन्ति मानवाः ।
श्रद्धावन्तोऽनसूयन्तो मुच्यन्ते तेऽपि कर्मभिः ॥ ३.३१

ye me matamidaṁ nityamanutiṣṭhanti mānavāḥ /
śraddhāvanto 'nasūyanto mucyante tepi karmabhiḥ // 3.31

ye: who; *me*: My; *matam*: teaching; *idaṁ*: these; *nityaṁ*: always; *anutiṣṭhanti*: execute regularly; *mānavāḥ*: persons; *śraddhāvantaḥ*: with faith; *anasūyantaḥ*: without envy; *mucyante*: become free; *te*: all of them; *api*: even; *karmabhiḥ*: from the bondage of fruitive actions

3.31 Those persons who execute their duties according to My teaching and who follow these teachings faithfully, without envy, become free from the bondage of actions.

ये त्वेतदभ्यसूयन्तो नानुतिष्ठन्ति मे मतम् ।
सर्वज्ञानविमूढांस्तान्विद्धि नष्टानचेतसः ॥ ३.३२

ye tvetad abhyasūyanto nānutiṣṭhanti me matam /
sarvajñānavimūḍhāṁstānviddhi naṣṭānacetasaḥ // 3.32

ye: those; *tu*: but; *etat*: this; *abhyasūyantaḥ*: out of envy; *na*: not; *anutiṣṭhanti*: regularly perform; *me*: My; *mataṁ*: teaching; *sarvajñāna*: all kinds of knowledge; *vimūḍhān*: fooled; *tān*: they; *viddhi*: know; *naṣṭān*: ruined; *acetasaḥ*: without Consciousness

3.32 But those who do not regularly perform their duty according to My teaching, are ignorant, senseless and ruined.

सदृशं चेष्टते स्वस्याः प्रकृतेर्ज्ञानवानपि ।
प्रकृतिं यान्ति भूतानि निग्रहः किं करिष्यति ॥ ३.३३

sadṛśaṁ ceṣṭate svasyāḥ prakṛterjñānavānapi /
prakṛtiṁ yānti bhūtāni nigrahaḥ kiṁ kariṣyati // 3.33

sadṛśaṁ: according to; *ceṣṭate*: tries; *svasyāḥ*: by one's nature; *prakṛteḥ*: modes; *jñānavān*: wise; *api*: even; *prakṛtiṁ*: nature; *yānti*: goes through; *bhūtāni*: living beings; *nigrahaḥ*: suppression; *kiṁ*: what; *kariṣyati*: can do

3.33 Even the wise person tries to act according to the modes of his own nature, for all living beings go through their nature. What can restraint of the senses do?

इन्द्रियस्येन्द्रियस्यार्थे रागद्वेषौ व्यवस्थितौ ।
तयोर्न वशमागच्छेत्तौ ह्यस्य परिपन्थिनौ ॥ ३.३४

indriyasyendriyasyārthe rāgadveṣau vyavasthitau |
tayorna vaśamāgacchet tau hyasya paripanthinau || 3.34

indriyasya: of the senses; *indriyasya arthe*: for sense objects; *rāga*: attachment; *dveṣau*: repulsion; *vyavasthitau*: put under control; *tayoḥ*: of them; *na*: never; *vaśaṁ*: control; *āgacchet*: come; *tau*: those; *hi*: certainly; *asya*: his; *paripanthinau*: stumbling blocks

3.34 Attachment and repulsion of the senses for sense objects should be put under control. One should never come under their control as they certainly are the stumbling blocks on the path of self-realization.

श्रेयान्स्वधर्मो विगुणः परधर्मात्स्वनुष्ठितात् ।
स्वधर्मे निधनं श्रेयः परधर्मो भयावहः ॥ ३.३५

śreyānsvadharmo viguṇahparadharmātsvanuṣṭhitāt |
svadharme nidhanaṁ śreyaḥ paradharmo bhayāvahaḥ || 3.35

śreyān: better; *svadharmaḥ*: own duty; *viguṇaḥ*: in a faulty manner; *paradharmāt*: other's duty; *svanuṣṭhitāt*: perfectly done; *svadharme*: in one's duty; *nidhanaṁ*: death; *śreyaḥ*: better; *paradhamaḥ*: other's duty; *bhayāvahaḥ*: dangerous

3.35 It is better to do one's own duty, even if it is in a faulty manner, than to do someone else's duty perfectly. Death in the course of performing one's own duty is better than doing another's duty, as this can be dangerous.

अर्जुन उवाच
अथ केन प्रयुक्तोऽयं पापं चरति पूरुषः ।
अनिच्छन्नपि वार्ष्णेय बलादिव नियोजितः ॥ ३.३६

arjuna uvāca

atha kena prayukto'yaṁ pāpaṁ carati pūruṣaḥ |
anicchannapi vārṣṇeya balādiva niyojitaḥ || 3.36

arjuna uvāca: Arjuna said; *atha*: then; *kena*: by what; *prayuktaḥ*: forced; *ayaṁ*: this (person); *pāpaṁ*: sins; *carati*: acts; *pūruṣaḥ*: man; *anicchan*: without desiring; *api*: though; *vārṣṇeya*: O descendant of Vrishni; *balāt*: by force; *iva*: as if; *niyojitaḥ*: engaged

3.36 Arjuna said, 'O descendant of Vṛṣṇi, then, by what is man forced to sinful acts, even without desiring, as if engaged by force?'

श्री भगवानुवाच

काम एष क्रोध एष रजोगुणसमुद्भवः ।
महाशनो महापाप्मा विद्ध्येनमिह वैरिणम् ॥ ३.३७

śrībhagavānuvāca

kāma eṣa krodha eṣa rajoguṇasamudbhavaḥ |
mahāśano mahāpāpmā viddhyenamiha vairiṇam || 3.37

śrī bhagavān uvāca: the Lord said; *kāma*: lust; *eṣa*: these; *krodha*: anger; *eṣa*: these; *rajoguṇa*: attribute of passion; *samudbhavaḥ*: born of; *mahāśanaḥ*: all-devouring; *mahāpāpmā*: greatly sinful; *viddhi*: know; *enaṁ*: this; *iha*: in the world; *vairiṇaṁ*: greatest enemy

3.37 The Lord said, 'It is lust and anger born of the attribute of passion, all-devouring and sinful, which is one's greatest enemy in this world.'

धूमेनाव्रियते वह्निर्यथादर्शो मलेन च ।
यथोल्बेनावृतो गर्भस्तथा तेनेदमावृतम् ॥ ३.३८

dhūmenāvriyate vanhiryathādarśo malena ca |
yatholbenāvṛto garbhastathā tenedamāvṛtam || 3.38

dhūmena: by smoke; *āvriyate*: covered; *vahniḥ*: fire; *yathā*: as; *ādarśaḥ*: mirror; *malena*: by dust; *ca*: also; *yathā*: as; *ulbena*: by the womb; *āvṛtaḥ*: covered; *garbhaḥ*: embryo; *tathā*: so; *tena*: by that; *idaṁ*: this; *āvṛtaṁ*: covered

3.38 As fire is covered by smoke, as a mirror is covered by dust, or as the embryo is covered by the womb, so also, the living being is covered by lust.

आवृतं ज्ञानमेतेन ज्ञानिनो नित्यवैरिणा ।
कामरूपेण कौन्तेय दुष्पूरेणानलेन च ॥ ३.३९

āvṛtaṁ jñānametena jñānino nityavairiṇā /
kāmarūpeṇa kaunteya duṣpūreṇānalena ca // 3.39

āvṛtaṁ: covered; *jñānam*: knowledge; *etena*: by this; *jñāninaḥ*: of the knower; *nitya*: eternal; *vairiṇā*: enemy; *kāma*: desire; *rū peṇa*: in the form of; *kaunteya*: O son of Kuntī; *duṣpūreṇa*: never satisfied; *analena*: by fire; *ca*: and

3.39 The knowledge of the knower is covered by this eternal enemy in the form of lust, which is never satisfied and burns like fire, O son of Kuntī

इन्द्रियाणि मनो बुद्धिरस्याधिष्ठानमुच्यते ।
एतैर्विमोहयत्येष ज्ञानमावृत्य देहिनम् ॥ ३.४०

indriyāṇi mano buddhirasyādhiṣṭhānamucyate /
etairvimohayatyeṣa jñānamāvṛtya dehinam // 3.40

indriyāṇi: senses; *manaḥ*: mind; *buddhiḥ*: intelligence; *asya*: of; *adhiṣṭhānaṁ*: sitting place; *ucyate*: called; *etaiḥ*: by these; *vimohayati*: confuses; *eṣaḥ*: this; *jñānaṁ*: knowledge; *āvṛtya*: covering; *dehinam*: embodied being

3.40 The senses, the mind and the intelligence are the locations of this lust, which confuses the embodied being and covers the knowledge.

तस्मात्त्वमिन्द्रियाण्यादौ नियम्य भरतर्षभ ।
पाप्मानं प्रजहि ह्येनं ज्ञानविज्ञाननाशनम् ॥ ३.४१

tasmāttvamindriyāṇyādau niyamya bhāratarṣabha /
pāpmānaṁ prajahi hyenaṁ jñānavijñānanāśanam // 3.41

tasmāt: therefore; *tvam*: you; *indriyāṇi*: senses; *ādau*: in the beginning; *niyamya*: by controlling; *Bhārata ṛṣabha*: O chief amongst the descendants of Bhārata; *pāpmānaṁ*: symbol of sin; *prajahi*: curb; *hi*: certainly; *enaṁ*: this; *jñāna*: knowledge; *vijñāna*: consciousness; *nāśanaṁ*: destroyer

3.41 Therefore, O chief amongst the descendants of Bhārata, in the very beginning, control the senses and curb the symbol of sin, which is certainly the destroyer of knowledge and consciousness.

इन्द्रियाणि पराण्याहुरिन्द्रियेभ्यः परं मनः ।
मनसस्तु परा बुद्धिर्यो बुद्धेः परतस्तु सः ॥ ३.४२

indriyāṇi parāṇyāhurindriyebhyaḥ paraṁ manaḥ |
manasastu parā buddhiryo buddheḥ paratastu saḥ || 3.42

indriyāṇi: senses; *parāṇi*: superior; *āhuḥ*: is said; *indriyebhyaḥ*: more than the senses; *paraṁ*: superior; *manaḥ*: mind; *manasaḥ*: more than the mind; *tu*: also; *parā*: superior; *buddhiḥ*: intelligence; *yaḥ*: who; *buddheḥ*: more than intelligence; *parataḥ*: superior; *tu*: but; *saḥ*: he

3.42 It is said that the senses are superior to the body. The mind is superior to the senses. The intelligence is still higher than the mind and the consciousness is even higher than intelligence.

एवं बुद्धेः परं बुद्ध्वा संस्तभ्यात्मानमात्मना ।
जहि शत्रुं महाबाहो कामरूपं दुरासदम् ॥ ३.४३

evaṁ buddheḥ paraṁ buddhvā saṁstabhyātmānamātmanā |
jahi śatruṁ māhābāho kāmarūpaṁ durāsadam || 3.43

evaṁ: and; *buddheḥ*: of intelligence; *paraṁ*: superior; *buddhvā*: knowing; *saṁstabhya*: by steadying; *ātmānaṁ*: of the mind; *ātmanā*: by intelligence; *jahi*: conquer; *śatruṁ*: enemy; *māhābāho*: O mighty-armed one; *kāma*: lust; *rūpaṁ*: in the form of; *durāsadaṁ*: insatiable

3.43 Knowing the Self to be superior to mind and intelligence, by steadying the mind by intelligence, conquer the insatiable enemy in the form of lust, O mighty-armed one.

इति श्रीमद्भगवद्गीतासूपनिषत्सु ब्रह्मविद्यायां योगशास्त्रे
श्रीकृष्णार्जुनसंवादे कर्मयोगो नाम तृतीयोऽध्यायः ॥२

iti śrī mad bhagavadgītāsūpaniṣatsu brahmavidyāyām
yogaśāstre śrīkṛṣṇārjuna saṁvāde karmayogo nāma tṛtīyo'dhyāyaḥ ||

In the Upaniṣad *of the Bhagavad Gītā, the knowledge of* Brahman, *the Supreme, the science of Yoga and the dialogue between Śrī Kṛṣṇa and Arjuna, this is the third discourse designated:*

Karma Yogaḥ

Verses Of Gita Chapter - 4

अथ चतुर्थोऽध्याय:

ज्ञानकर्मसंन्यासयोग:

Jñānakarmasanyāsa Yogaḥ

श्री भगवानुवाच ।
इमं विवस्वते योगं प्रोक्तवानहमव्ययम् ।
विवस्वान्मनवे प्राह मनुरिक्ष्वाकवेऽब्रवीत् ॥४.१

śrībhagavānuvāca
imaṁ vivasvate yogaṁ proktavānaham avyayaṁ **I**
vivasvānmanave prāha manurikṣvākave'bravīt **II** 4.1

śrī bhagavān uvāca: the Lord said; *imaṁ*: this; *vivasvate*: to the Sun god; *yogaṁ*: the science of yoga; *proktavān*: instructed; *ahaṁ*: I; *avyayaṁ*: imperishable; *vivasvān*: sun god; *manave*: to Manu, the father of mankind; *prāha*: told; *manuḥ*: Manu; *ikṣvākave*: to King Ikṣvāku; *abravīt*: said

4.1 The Lord said: 'I taught the sun god, Vivasvān, the imperishable science of yoga and Vivasvān taught Manu, the father of mankind and Manu in turn taught Ikṣvāku.'

एवं परम्पराप्राप्तमिमं राजर्षयो विदुः ।
स कालेनेह महता योगो नष्टः परन्तप ॥४.२

evaṁ paraṁparāprāptamimaṁ rājarṣayo viduḥ **I**
sa kāleneha mahatā yogo naṣṭaḥ parantapa **II** 4.2

evaṁ: thus; *paraṁparā*: Master-disciple succession; *prāptaṁ*: received; *imaṁ*: this science; *rājarṣayaḥ*: the saintly kings; *viduḥ*: understood; *saḥ*: that knowledge; *kālena*: in the course of time; *iha*: in this world; *mahatā*: by great; *yogaḥ*: the science of yoga; *naṣṭaḥ*: lost; *paraṁtapa*: subduer of the enemies

4.2 The supreme science was thus received through the chain of master-disciple succession and the saintly kings understood it in that way. In the course of time, the succession was broken and therefore the science as it was appears to have been lost.

स एवायं मया तेऽद्य योगः प्रोक्तः पुरातनः ।
भक्तोऽसि मे सखा चेति रहस्यं ह्येतदुत्तमम् ॥ ४.३

sa evāyaṁ mayā te'dya yogaḥ proktaḥ purātanaḥ |
bhakto 'si me sakhā ceti rahasyaṁ hyetaduttamam || 4.3

saḥ: that; *eva*: only; *ayaṁ*: this; *mayā* : by Me; *te*: to you; *adya*: today; *yogaḥ*: the science of yoga; *proktaḥ*: spoken; *purātanaḥ*: very old; *bhaktaḥ*: devotee; *asi*: you are; *me*: My; *sakhā* : friend; *ca*: also; *iti*: therefore; *rahasyaṁ*: mystery; *hi*: because *etat*: this; *uttamaṁ*: supreme

4.3 That ancient science of enlightenment, or entering into eternal bliss, is today taught by me to you because you are my devotee as well as my friend. You will certainly understand the supreme mystery of this science.

अर्जुन उवाच ।
अपरं भवतो जन्म परं जन्म विवस्वतः ।
कथमेतद्विजानीयां त्वमादौ प्रोक्तवानिति ॥ ४.४

arjuna uvāca
aparaṁ bhavato janma paraṁ janma vivasvataḥ |
kathametad vijānīyāṁ tvamādau proktavāniti || 4.4

arjuna uvāca: Arjuna said; *aparaṁ*: of recent origin; *bhavataḥ*: Your; *janma*: birth; *paraṁ*: very old; *janma*: birth; *vivasvataḥ*: of the Sun god; *kathaṁ*: how; *etat*: this; *vijānīyāṁ*: can I understand; *tvaṁ*: You; *ādau*: in the beginning; *proktavān*: instructed; *iti*: thus

4.4 Arjuna said: 'Oh Kṛṣṇa, you are younger to the sun god Vivasvān by birth. How am I to understand that in the beginning you instructed this science to him?'

श्री भगवानुवाच
बहूनि मे व्यतीतानि जन्मानि तव चार्जुन ।
तान्यहं वेद सर्वाणि न त्वं वेत्थ परन्तप ॥ ४.५

śrībhagavānuvāca
bahuni me vyatītāni janmāni tava cārjuna |
tānyahaṁ veda sarvāṇi na tvaṁ vettha parantapa || 4.5

śrī bhagavān uvāca: The Lord said; *bahūni:* many; *me*: of Mine; *vyatī tā ni*: have passed; *janmāni*: births; *tava*: yours; *ca*: also; *arjuna*: O Arjuna; *tā ni*:

all of those; *ahaṁ*: I; *veda*: do know; *sarvāṇi*: all; *na*: not; *tvaṁ*: yourself; *vettha*: know; *paraṁtapa*: O scorcher of the foes

4.5 The Lord said: Many many births both you and I have passed. I can remember all of them, but you cannot, O Parantapa!

अजोऽपि सन्नव्ययात्मा भूतानामीश्वरोऽपि सन् ।
प्रकृतिं स्वामधिष्ठाय संभवाम्यात्ममायया ॥४.६

ajo 'pi sannavyayātmā bhūtānām īśvaro 'pi san I
prakṛtiṁ svāmadhiṣṭhāya saṁbhavāmyātmamāyayā II 4.6

ajaḥ: unborn; *api*: also; *san*: being so; *avyaya*: instructible; *atmā:* spirit; *bhūtānāṁ:* living entities; *īśvaraḥ*: supreme Lord; *api*: also; *san*: being so; *prakṛtiṁ*: nature; *svāṁ*: of Myself; *adhiṣṭhāya*: keeping under control; *saṁbhavāmi*: I come into being; *ātmamāyayā*: by My divine potency.

4.6 Although I am unborn, imperishable and the lord of all living entities, by ruling my nature I reappear by my own māyā.

यदा यदा हि धर्मस्य ग्लानिर्भवति भारत ।
अभ्युत्थानमधर्मस्य तदात्मानं सृजाम्यहम् ॥४.७

yadā yadā hi dharmasya glānirbhavati bhārata I
abhyutthānamadharmasya tadātmānaṁ sṛjāmyaham II 4.7

yadā -yadā : whenever; *hi*: well; *dharmasya*: of righteousness; *glāniḥ*: decline; *bhavati*: takes place; *bhārata*: O descendant of Bhārata; *abhyutthānaṁ*: predominance; *adharmasya*: of unrighteousness; *tadā* : at that time; *ātmānaṁ*: self; *sṛjāmi*: bring forth; *ahaṁ*: I

4.7 When positive consciousness declines, when collective negativity rises, Again and again, at these times, I am reborn.

परित्राणाय साधूनां विनाशाय च दुष्कृताम् ।
धर्मसंस्थापनार्थाय संभवामि युगे युगे ॥४.८

paritrāṇāya sādhūnāṁ vināśāya ca duṣkṛtām I
dharmasaṁsthāpanārthāya saṁbhavāmi yuge-yuge II 4.8

paritrāṇāya: for the protection of; *sādhūnāṁ*: of the pious; *vināśāya*: to destroy; *ca*: also; *duṣkṛtāṁ*: of the wicked; *dharma*: righteousness; *saṁsthāpanārthāya*: to establish; *saṁbhavāmi*: I manifest; *yuge-yuge*: age after age

4.8 To nurture the pious and to annihilate the wicked, to re-establish righteousness I am reborn, age after age.

जन्म कर्म च मे दिव्यमेवं यो वेत्ति तत्त्वतः ।
त्यक्त्वा देहं पुनर्जन्म नैति मामेति सोऽर्जुन ॥ ४.९

janma karma ca me divyamevaṁ yo vetti tattvataḥ |
tyaktvā dehaṁ punarjanma naiti māmeti so 'rjuna || 4.9

janma: birth; *karma*: work; *ca*: and; *me*: of Mine; *divyaṁ*: divine; *evaṁ*: so also; *yaḥ*: anyone whoever; *vetti*: knows; *tattvataḥ*: in reality; *tyaktvā*: after leaving aside; *dehaṁ*: body; *punaḥ*: again; *janma*: birth; *na*: never; *eti*: attains; *māṁ*: unto Me; *eti*: does attain; *saḥ*: he; *arjuna*: Arjuna

4.9 One who knows or experiences my divine appearance and activities does not take birth again in this material world after leaving the body but attains me, o Arjuna.

वीतरागभयक्रोधा मन्मया मामुपाश्रिताः ।
बहवो ज्ञानतपसा पूता मद्भावमागताः ॥ ४.१०

vītarāgabhayakrodhā manmayā māmupāśritāḥ |
bahavo jñānatapasā pūtā madbhāvamāgatāḥ || 4.10

vīta: free from; *rāga*: passion; *bhaya*: fear; *krodhāḥ*: anger; *manmayā*: fully absorbed in Me; *māṁ*: unto Me; *upāśritāḥ*: taking refuge; *bahavaḥ*: many beings; *jñāna*: wisdom; *tapasā*: by penance; *pūtāḥ*: sanctified; *mad bhāvaṁ*: My nature; *āgatāḥ*: attained

4.10 Being freed from attachment, fear and anger, being filled with me and by taking refuge in me, many beings in the past have become sanctified by the knowledge of me and have realized me.

ये यथा मां प्रपद्यन्ते तांस्तथैव भजाम्यहम् ।
मम वर्त्मानुवर्तन्ते मनुष्याः पार्थ सर्वशः ॥ ४.११

ye yathā māṁ prapadyante tāṁstathaiva bhajāmyaham |
mama vartmānuvartante manuṣyāḥ pārtha sarvaśah || 4.11

ye: whoever; *yathā*: whatever way; *māṁ*: unto Me; *prapadyante*: seek; *tān*: unto them; *tathā eva*: in the same way; *bhajāmi*: I approach; *ahaṁ*: I; *mama*: My; *vartma*: of the path; *anuvartante*: follow; *manuṣyāḥ*: people; *pārtha*: son of Pritā; *sarvaśaḥ*: in all respects

4.11 I reward everyone, I show myself to all people, according to the manner in which they surrender unto me, in the manner that they are devoted to me, O Pārtha!

काङ्क्षन्तः कर्मणां सिद्धिं यजन्त इह देवताः ।
क्षिप्रं हि मानुषे लोके सिद्धिर्भवति कर्मजा ॥४.१२

kāṅkṣantaḥ karmaṇāṁ siddhiṁ yajanta iha devatāḥ I
kṣipraṁ hi mānuṣe loke siddhirbhavati karmajā II 4.12

kāṅkṣantaḥ: desiring; *karmaṇāṁ*: of activities; *siddhiṁ*: success; *yajante*: worship; *iha*: in this world; *devatāḥ*: gods; *kṣipraṁ*: quickly; *hi*: for; *mānuṣe loke*: in human society; *siddhiḥ bhavati*: success comes; *karmajā* : born of action

4.12 Men in this world desire success from activities and therefore they worship the gods. Men get instant results from active work in this world.

चातुर्वर्ण्यं मया सृष्टं गुणकर्मविभागशः।
तस्य कर्तारमपि मां विद्ध्यकर्तारमव्ययम् ॥४.१३

cāturvarṇyaṁ mayā sṛṣṭaṁ guṇakarma vibhāgaśaḥ I
tasya kartāram api māṁ viddhyakartāramavyayam II 4.13

cāturvarṇyaṁ: the four divisions of human society; *mayā*: by Me; *sṛṣṭaṁ*: created; *guṇa*: attribute; *karma*: work; *vibhāgaśaḥ*: in terms of division; *tasya*: of that; *kartāraṁ*: doer; *api*: although; *māṁ*: Me; *viddhi*: know; *akartāraṁ*: as the non-doer; *avyayaṁ*: immortal

4.13 Depending upon the distribution of the three attributes or guṇas *and action, I have created the four castes. Yet, I am to be known as the non-doer, the unchangeable.*

न मां कर्माणि लिम्पन्ति न मे कर्मफले स्पृहा ।
इति मां योऽभिजानाति कर्मभिर्न स बध्यते ॥४.१४

na māṁ karmāṇi limpanti na me karmaphale spṛhā I
iti māṁ yo'bhijānāti karmabhirna sa badhyate II 4.14

na: never; *māṁ*: Me; *karmāṇi*: work; *limpanti*: affect; *na*: not; *me*: My; *karmaphale*: in fruits of action; *spṛhā* : longing for; *iti*: thus; *māṁ*: Me; *yaḥ*: one who; *abhijānāti*: understands; *karmabhiḥ* : by the action; *na*: never; *saḥ*: he; *badhyate*: is bound.

4.14 I am not affected by any work; nor do I long for the outcome of such work. One who understands this truth about me also does not get caught in the bondage of work.

एवं ज्ञात्वा कृतं कर्म पूर्वैरपि मुमुक्षुभिः ।
कुरु कर्मैव तस्मात्त्वं पूर्वैः पूर्वतरं कृतम् ॥ ४.१५

evaṁ jñātvā kṛtaṁ karma pūrvairapi mumukṣubhiḥ |
kuru karmaiva tasmāttvaṁ pūrvaiḥ pūrvataraṁ kṛtam || 4.15

evaṁ: thus; *jñātvā*: knowing well; *kṛtaṁ*: performed; *karma*: work; *pūrvaiḥ*: by the ancient people; *api*: also; *mumukṣubhiḥ*: by those seeking liberation; *kuru*: perform; *karma*: prescribed duty; *eva*: only; *tasmāt*: therefore; *tvaṁ*: you; *pūrvaiḥ*: by the predecessors; *pūrvataraṁ*: as in the past; *kṛtaṁ*: as performed

4.15 All the wise and liberated souls of ancient times have acted with this understanding and thus attained liberation. Just as the ancients did, perform your duty with this understanding.

किं कर्म किमकर्मेति कवयोऽप्यत्र मोहिताः ।
तत्ते कर्म प्रवक्ष्यामि यज्ज्ञात्वा मोक्ष्यसेऽशुभात् ॥ ४.१६

kiṁ karma kimakarmeti kavayo'pyatra mohitāḥ |
tat te karma pravakṣyāmi yaj jñātvā mokṣyase'śubhāt || 4.16

kiṁ: what; *karma*: action; *kiṁ*: what; *akarma*: inaction; *iti*: thus; *kavayaḥ*: the wise; *api*: also; *atra*: in this matter; *mohitāḥ*: confused; *tat*: that; *te*: unto you; *karma*: action; *pravakṣyāmi*: I shall explain; *yat*: which; *jñātvā*: after knowing; *mokṣyase*: be liberated; *aśubhāt*: from ills

What is action and what is inaction, even the wise are confused. Let me explain to you what action is, knowing which you shall be liberated from all ills.

कर्मणो ह्यपि बोद्धव्यं बोद्धव्यं च विकर्मणः ।
अकर्मणश्च बोद्धव्यं गहना कर्मणो गतिः ॥ ४.१७

karmaṇo hyapi boddhavyaṁ boddhavyaṁ ca vikarmaṇaḥ |
akarmaṇaśca boddhavyaṁ gahanā karmaṇo gatiḥ || 4.17

karmaṇaḥ: of action; *hi*: for; *api*: also; *boddhavyaṁ*: should be understood; *boddhavyaṁ*: to be understood; *ca*: also; *vikarmaṇaḥ*: wrong action; *akarmaṇaḥ*: inaction; *ca*: also; *boddhavyaṁ*: should be understood; *gahanā*: mysterious; *karmaṇaḥ*: of action; *gatiḥ*: way.

4.17 The complexities of action are very difficult to understand. Understand fully the nature of proper action by understanding the nature of wrong action and inaction.

कर्मण्यकर्म यः पश्येदकर्मणि च कर्म यः ।
स बुद्धिमान्मनुष्येषु स युक्तः कृत्स्नकर्मकृत् ॥४.१८

karmaṇyakarma yaḥ paśyedakarmaṇi ca karma yaḥ I
sa buddhimān manuṣyeṣu sa yuktaḥ kṛtsnakarmakṛt II 4.18

karmaṇi: in action; *akarma*: inaction; *yaḥ*: one who; *paśyet*: sees; *akarmaṇi*: in inaction; *ca*: also; *karma*: action; *yaḥ*: one who; *saḥ*: he; *buddhimān*: wise; *manuṣyeṣu*: among men; *saḥ*: he; *yuktaḥ*: yogi; *kṛtsnakarmakṛt*: engaged in all activities

4.18 He who sees inaction in action and action in inaction, is wise and a yogi, Even if engaged in all activities.

यस्य सर्वे समारम्भाः कामसङ्कल्पवर्जिताः ।
ज्ञानाग्निदग्धकर्माणं तमाहुः पण्डितं बुधाः ॥४.१९

yasya sarve samārambhāḥ kāmasaṅkalpavarjitāḥ I
jñānāgnidagdhakarmāṇaṁ tam āhuḥ paṇḍitaṁ budhāḥ II 4.19

yasya: one whose; *sarve*: all kinds of; *samārambhāḥ*: in all situations; *kāma*: desire for sense gratification; *saṅkalpa*: purpose; *varjitāḥ*: devoid of; *jñāna*: of perfect knowledge; *agni*: fire; *dagdhakarmāṇaṁ*: whose actions have been burnt; *taṁ*: him; *āhuḥ*: declare; *paṇḍitaṁ*: wise; *budhāḥ*: the wise.

4.19 He who is determined and devoid of all desires for sense gratification, he is of perfect knowledge. The sages declare such a person wise whose actions are burnt by the fire of knowledge.

त्यक्त्वा कर्मफलासङ्गं नित्यतृप्तो निराश्रयः ।
कर्मण्यभिप्रवृत्तोऽपि नैव किञ्चित्करोति सः ॥४.२०

tyaktvā karmaphalāsaṅgaṁ nityatṛpto nirāśrayaḥ I
karmaṇyabhipravṛtto'pi naiva kiñcitkaroti saḥ II 4.20

tyaktvā : having given up; *karmaphalāsaṅgaṁ*: attachment to results of action; *nitya*: always; *tṛptaḥ*: satisfied; *nirāśrayaḥ*: without shelter; *karmaṇi*: in action; *abhipravṛttaḥ*: being fully engaged; *api*: although; *na*: does not; *eva*: verily; *kiñcit:* anything; *karoti*: does; *saḥ*: he

4.20 Having given up all attachment to the results of his action, always satisfied and independent, the wise man does not act, though he is engaged in all kinds of action.

निराशीर्यतचित्तात्मा त्यक्तसर्वपरिग्रहः ।
शारीरं केवलं कर्म कुर्वन्नाप्नोति किल्बिषम् ॥ ४.२१

nirāśī ryatacittātmā tyaktasarvaparigrahaḥ **/**
śārīraṁ kevalaṁ karma kurvannāpnoti kilbiṣam **//** 4.21

nirāśīḥ: without desire for the result; *yata*: controlled; *cittātmā*: mind and consciousness; *tyakta*: giving up; *sarva*: all; *parigrahaḥ*: sense of ownership; *śārīraṁ*: bodily effort; *kevalaṁ*: only; *karma*: work; *kurvan*: doing so; *na*: never; *āpnoti*: acquire; *kilbiṣaṁ*: sin

4.21 The person who acts without desire for the result; with his consciousness controlling the mind, giving up all sense of ownership over his possessions and body and only working, incurs no sin.

यदृच्छालाभसन्तुष्टो द्वन्द्वातीतो विमत्सरः ।
समः सिद्धावसिद्धौ च कृत्वापि न निबध्यते ॥ ४.२२

yadṛcchālābhasantuṣṭo dvandvātī to vimatsaraḥ **/**
samaḥ siddhāvasiddhau ca kṛtvāpi na nibadhyate **//** 4.22

yadṛcchā lābha: what is obtained unsought; *santuṣta*: satisfied; *dvandva*: pairs of opposites; *atī taḥ*: surpassed; *vimatsaraḥ*: free from envy; *samaḥ*: equal; *siddhau*: in success; *asiddhau*: in failure; *ca*: also; *kṛtvā*: after doing; *api*: even; *na*: never; *nibadhyate*: bound

4.22 He who is satisfied with profit which comes of its own accord and who has gone beyond duality, who is free from envy, who is in equanimity both in success and failure, such a person though doing action, is never affected.

गतसङ्गस्य मुक्तस्य ज्ञानावस्थितचेतसः ।
यज्ञायाचरतः कर्म समग्रं प्रविलीयते ॥ ४.२३

gatasaṅgasya muktasya jñānāvasthitacetasaḥ **/**
yajñāyācarataḥ karma samagraṁ pravilī yate **//** 4.23

gatasaṅgasya: unattached to the modes of material nature; *muktasya*: of the liberated; *jñānā*: knowledge; *avasthita*: established; *cetasaḥ*: of such spirit; *yajñāya*: for the sake of sacrifice; *ācarataḥ*: practice; *karma*: work; *samagraṁ*: in total; *pravilī yate*: melts away.

4.23 The work of a liberated man who is unattached to the modes of material nature and who is fully centered in the ultimate knowledge, who works totally for the sake of sacrifice, merges entirely into the knowledge.

ब्रह्मार्पणं ब्रह्महविर्ब्रह्माग्नौ ब्रह्मणा हुतम् ।
ब्रह्मैव तेन गन्तव्यं ब्रह्मकर्मसमाधिना ॥ ४.२४

brahmārpaṇaṁ brahmahavirbrahmāgnau brahmaṇā hutam I
brahmaiva tena gantavyaṁ brahmakarmasamādhinā II 4.24

brahma: supreme; *arpaṇaṁ*: offering; *brahma*: supreme; *haviḥ*: oblation; *brahma*: supreme; *agnau*: in the fire of; *brahmaṇā*: by the supreme; *hutaṁ*: offered; *brahma*: supreme; *eva*: only; *tena*: by him; *gantavyaṁ*: to be reached; *brahma*: supreme; *karma*: action; *samādhinā*: by complete absorption

4.24 The offering, the offered butter to the supreme in the fire of the supreme is offered by the supreme. Certainly, the supreme can be reached by him who is absorbed completely in action.

दैवमेवापरे यज्ञं योगिनः पर्युपासते ।
ब्रह्माग्नावपरे यज्ञं यज्ञेनैवोपजुह्वति ॥ ४.२५

daivamevāpare yajñaṁ yoginaḥ paryupāsate I
brahmāgnāvapare yajñaṁ yajñenaivopajuhvati II 4.25

daivaṁ: gods; *eva*: only; *apare*: others; *yajñaṁ*: sacrifices; *yoginaḥ*: yogis; *paryupāsate*: worship; *brahma*: supreme; *agnau*: in the fire; *apare*: others; *yajñaṁ*: sacrifice; *yajñena*: by sacrifice; *eva*: only; *upajuhvati*: offer as sacrifice.

4.25 Some yogis worship the gods by offering various sacrifices to them, While others worship by offering sacrifices in the fire of the supreme.

श्रोत्रादीनीन्द्रियाण्यन्ये संयमाग्निषु जुह्वति ।
शब्दादीन्विषयानन्य इन्द्रियाग्निषु जुह्वति ॥ ४.२६

śrotrādī nīndriyāṇyanye saṁyamāgniṣu juhvati I
śabdādī nviṣayānanya indriyāgniṣu juhvati II 4.26

śrotrādīnī : organ of hearing; *indriyāṇi*: senses; *anye*: others; *saṁyama* : self discipline; *agniṣu*: in the fire; *juhvati*: offer as sacrifice; *śabdādī n*: sound vibrations; *viṣayān*: objects of sense gratification; *anye*: others; *indriya*: of sense organs; *agniṣu*: in the fire; *juhvati*: sacrifice

4.26 Some sacrifice the hearing process and other senses in the fire of equanimity and others offer as sacrifice the objects of the senses, such as sound in the fire of the sacrifice.

सर्वाणीन्द्रियकर्माणि प्राणकर्माणि चापरे ।
आत्मसंयमयोगाग्नौ जुह्वति ज्ञानदीपिते ॥ ४.२७

sarvāṇīndriyakarmāṇi prāṇakarmāṇi cāpare I
ātmasaṁyamayogāgnau juhvati jñānadīpite II 4.27

sarvāṇi: all; *indriya*: senses; *karmāṇi*: actions; *prāṇakarmāṇi*: activities of the life breath; *ca*: also; *apare*: others; *ātmasaṁyama*: self control; *yoga*: yoga; *agnau*: in the fire of; *juhvati*: offer; *jñāna dīpite*: kindled by wisdom.

4.27 One who is interested in knowledge offers all the actions due to the senses, including the action of taking in the life breath into the fire of Yoga and is engaged in the yoga of the equanimity of the mind.

द्रव्ययज्ञास्तपोयज्ञा योगयज्ञास्तथापरे ।
स्वाध्यायज्ञानयज्ञाश्च यतयः संशितव्रताः ॥ ४.२८

dravyayajñāstapoyajñā yogayajñāstathāpare I
svādhyāyajñānayajñāśca yatayaḥ saṁśitavratāḥ II 4.28

dravya: material wealth; *yajñāḥ* : sacrifice; *tapo*: penance; *yajñāḥ* : sacrifice; *yoga*: yoga; *yajñāḥ*: sacrifice; *tathā* : and; *apare*: others; *svādhyāya*: self-study; *jñāna*: knowledge; *yajñāḥ*: sacrifice; *ca*: and; *yatayaḥ*: striving souls; *saṁśita vratāḥ*: those of strict vows.

4.28 There is the sacrifice of material wealth, sacrifice through penance, sacrifice through yoga and other sacrifices while there is sacrifice through self-study and through strict vows.

अपाने जुह्वति प्राणं प्राणेऽपानं तथापरे ।
प्राणापानगती रुद्ध्वा प्राणायामपरायणाः ॥ ४.२९

apāne juhvati prāṇaṁ prāṇe 'pānaṁ tathāpare I
prāṇāpānagatī ruddhvā prāṇāyāmaparāyaṇāḥ II 4.29

apāne: in the out going breath; *juhvati*: sacrifice; *prāṇaṁ*: life energy; *prāṇe*: in the life energy; *apānaṁ*: the outgoing breath; *tathā* : thus; *apare*: others; *prāṇa*: inhaling; *apāna*: exhaling; *gatī* : movement; *ruddhvā* : after restraining;

prāṇāyāma: breath control; *parāyaṇāḥ* : so inclined

4.29 There are others who sacrifice the life energy in the form of incoming breath and outgoing breath, thus checking the movement of the incoming and outgoing breaths and controlling the breath.

अपरे नियताहाराः प्राणान्प्राणेषु जुह्वति ।
सर्वेऽप्येते यज्ञविदो यज्ञक्षपितकल्मषाः ॥४.३०

apare niyatāhārāḥ prāṇānprāṇeṣu juhvati |
sarve'pyete yajñavido yajñakṣapitakalmaṣāḥ || 4.30

apare: others; *niyata*: controlled; *āhārāḥ*: eating; *prāṇān*: vital energy; *prāṇeṣu*: in the vital energy; *juhvati*: sacrifice; *sarve api ete*: all of these; *yajñavidaḥ*: those knowing sacrifice; *yajña kṣapita kalmaṣāḥ*: those destroying their sins through sacrifice.

4.30 There are others who sacrifice through controlled eating and offering the outgoing breath, life energy. All these people know the meaning of sacrifice and are purified of sin or karma.

यज्ञशिष्टामृतभुजो यान्ति ब्रह्म सनातनम् ।
नायं लोकोऽस्त्ययज्ञस्य कुतोऽन्यः कुरुसत्तम ॥४.३१

yajñaśiṣṭāmṛtabhujo yānti brahma sanātanam |
nāyaṁ loko'styayajñasya kuto'nyaḥ kurusattama || 4.31

yajñaśiṣṭa: left over of sacrifice; *amṛta*: nectar; *bhujaḥ*: one who enjoys; *yānti*: attain; *brahma*: supreme; *sanātanaṁ*: eternal; *na*: not; *ayaṁ*: this; *lokah*: world; *asti*: is; *ayajñasya*: to one who does not sacrifice; *kutaḥ*: where; *anyaḥ*: other; *kuru sattama*: O best among the Kurus

4.31 Having tasted the nectar of the results of such sacrifices, they go to the supreme eternal consciousness. This world is not for those who have not sacrificed. How can the other be, Arjuna?

एवं बहुविधा यज्ञा वितता ब्रह्मणो मुखे ।
कर्मजान्विद्धि तान्सर्वानेवं ज्ञात्वा विमोक्ष्यसे ॥४.३२

evaṁ bahuvidhā yajñā vitatā brahmaṇo mukhe |
karmajānviddhi tānsarvānevaṁ jñātvā vimokṣyase || 4.32

evaṁ: thus; *bahu*: many; *vidhāḥ*: kinds of; *yajñāḥ*: sacrifices; *vitatā*: explained; *brahmaṇaḥ mukhe*: in the words of the Veda; *karmajān*: born of actions of mind, sense and body; *viddhi*: know; *tān*: those; *sarvān*: all; *evaṁ*: thus; *jñātvā*: after knowing; *vimokṣyase*: will be liberated

4.32 Thus, there are many kinds of sacrifices born of work mentioned in the Vedas. *Thus, knowing these, one will be liberated.*

श्रेयान्द्रव्यमयाद्यज्ञाज्ज्ञानयज्ञः परंतप ।
सर्वं कर्माखिलं पार्थ ज्ञाने परिसमाप्यते ॥ ४.३३

śreyāndravyamayādyajñājjñānayajñaḥ parantapa |
sarvaṁ karmā'khilaṁ pārtha jñāne parisamāpyate || 4.33

śreyān: superior; *dravyamayāt*: material wealth; *yajñāt*: sacrifice; *jñāna yajñaḥ*: sacrifice in wisdom; *paraṁtapa*: O subduer of foes; *sarvaṁ*: all; *karma*: activities; *akhilaṁ*: in totality; *pārtha*: O son of Pritā; *jñāne*: in wisdom; *parisamāpyate*: ends in

4.33 O conqueror of foes, the sacrifice of wisdom is superior to the sacrifice of material wealth. After all, all activities totally end in wisdom.

तद्विद्धि प्रणिपातेन परिप्रश्नेन सेवया ।
उपदेक्ष्यन्ति ते ज्ञानं ज्ञानिनस्तत्त्वदर्शिनः ॥ ४.३४

tadviddhi praṇipātena paripraśnena sevayā |
upadekṣyanti te jñānaṁ jñāninastattvadarśinaḥ || 4.34

tat: that; *viddhi*: understand; *praṇipātena*: by approaching a spiritual master; *paripraśnena*: by questioning; *sevayā*: by offering service; *upadekṣyanti*: will advise; *te*: unto you; *jñānaṁ*: knowledge; *jñāninaḥ* : the enlightened; *tattva darśinaḥ*: the spiritual seers.

4.34 Understand these truths by approaching a spiritual master, by asking him your questions, by offering service. The enlightened person can initiate the wisdom unto you because he has seen the truth

यज्ज्ञात्वा न पुनर्मोहमेवं यास्यसि पाण्डव ।
येन भूतान्यशेषेण द्रक्ष्यस्यात्मन्यथो मयि ॥ ४.३५

yajjñātvā na punarmohamevaṁ yāsyasi pāṇḍava |
yena bhūtānyaśeṣeṇa drakṣyasyātmanyatho mayi || 4.35

yat: which; *jñātvā*: after knowing; *na*: not; *punaḥ*: again; *mohaṁ*: desire; *evaṁ*: thus; *yāsyasi*: shall attain; *pāṇḍava*: O son of Pāṇḍu; *yena*: by which; *bhūtāni*: living entities; *aśeṣeṇa*: totally; *drakṣyasi*: will see; *ātmani*: within yourself; *atho*: then; *mayi*: in Me

4.35 O Pāṇḍavā, knowing this you will never suffer from desire or illusion, you will know that all living beings are in the supreme, in Me.

अपि चेदसि पापेभ्य: सर्वेभ्य: पापकृत्तम: ।
सर्वं ज्ञानप्लवेनैव वृजिनं संतरिष्यसि ॥ ४.३६

api cedasi pāpebhyaḥ sarvebhyaḥ pāpakṛttamaḥ I
sarvaṁ jñānaplavenaiva vṛjinaṁ santariṣyasi II 4.36

api: even; *cet*: if; *asi*: you are; *pāpebhyaḥ*: of sinners; *sarvebhyaḥ*: of all; *pāpakṛttamaḥ*: greatest sinner; *sarvaṁ*: all; *jñāna plavena*: by the boat of knowledge; *eva*: only; *vṛjinaṁ*: the ocean of miseries; *santariṣyasi*: you will cross.

4.36 Even if you are the most sinful of all sinners, you will certainly cross completely the ocean of miseries through the boat of knowledge.

यथैधांसि समिद्धोऽग्निर्भस्मसात्कुरुतेऽर्जुन ।
ज्ञानाग्निः सर्वकर्माणि भस्मसात्कुरुते तथा ॥ ४.३७

yathaidhāṁsi samiddho'gnir bhasmasātkurute'rjuna I
jñānāgniḥ sarvakarmāṇi bhasmasātkurute tathā II 4.37

yathā: as; *edhāṁsi*: firewood; *samiddhaḥ* : blazing; *agniḥ*: fire; *bhasmasāt*: ashes; *kurute*: does; *arjuna*: O Arjuna; *jñāna*: knowledge; *agniḥ*: fire; *sarva*: all; *karmāṇi*: actions; *bhasmasāt*: ashes; *kurute*: does; *tathā*: in the same way.

4.37 Just as a blazing fire turns firewood to ashes, O Arjuna, so does the fire of wisdom burn to ashes all actions, all your karma.

न हि ज्ञानेन सदृशं पवित्रमिह विद्यते ।
तत्स्वयं योगसंसिद्धः कालेनात्मनि विन्दति ॥ ४.३८

na hi jñānena sadṛśaṁ pavitramiha vidyate I
tatsvayaṁ yogasaṁsiddhah kālenātmani vindati II 4.38

na: not; *hi*: certainly; *jñānena*: with knowledge; *sadṛśaṁ*: similar; *pavitraṁ*: pure; *iha*: here; *vidyate*: exists; *tat*: that; *svayaṁ*: himself; *yoga*: in devotion; *saṁsiddhaḥ*: purified; *kālena*: in course time; *ātmani*: within self; *vindati*: acquires.

4.38 Truly, in this world, there is nothing as pure as wisdom. One who has matured to know this enjoys in himself in due course of time.

श्रद्धावाँल्लभते ज्ञानं तत्परः संयतेन्द्रियः ।
ज्ञानं लब्ध्वा परां शान्तिमचिरेणाधिगच्छति ॥ ४.३९

śraddhāvāllabhate jñānaṁ tatparaḥ saṁyatendriyaḥ |
jñānaṁ labdhvā parāṁ śāntimacireṇādhigacchati || 4.39

śraddhāvān: faithful person; *labhate*: achieves; *jñānaṁ*: knowledge; *tatparaḥ*: attached; *saṁyata*: controlled; *indriyaḥ*: senses; *jñānaṁ*: knowledge; *labdhvā*: having achieved; *parāṁ*: supreme; *śāntiṁ*: peace; *acireṇa*: without delay; *adhigacchati*: attains

4.39 A person with śraddhā (courageous faith) achieves wisdom and has control over the senses. Achieving wisdom, without delay, he attains supreme peace.

अज्ञश्चाश्रद्दधानश्च संशयात्मा विनश्यति ।
नायं लोकोऽस्ति न परो न सुखं संशयात्मनः ॥ ४.४०

ajñaścāśraddadhānaśca saṁśayātmā vinaśyati |
nāyaṁ loko 'sti na paro na sukhaṁ saṁśayātmanaḥ || 4.40

ajñaḥ: ignorant; *ca*: and; *aśraddadhānaḥ*: one having no faith; *ca*: and; *saṁśayātmā*: doubting soul; *vinaśyati*: perish; *na*: not; *ayaṁ*: this; *lokah*: world; *asti*: is; *na*: not; *paraḥ*: next; *na*: not; *sukhaṁ*: happiness; *saṁśayātmanaḥ*: of the doubting soul.

4.40 Those who have no wisdom and faith, who always have doubts, are destroyed. There is no happiness in this world or the next.

योगसंन्यस्तकर्माणं ज्ञानसंछिन्नसंशयम् ।
आत्मवन्तं न कर्माणि निबध्नन्ति धनञ्जय ॥ ४.४१

yogasannyastakarmāṇaṁ jñānasaṁchinnasaṁśayam |
ātmavantaṁ na karmāṇi nibadhnanti dhañanjaya || 4.41

yogasannyastakarmāṇaṁ: one who has dedicated his actions to god according to Karma yoga; *jñānasaṁchinna saṁśayaṁ*: whose doubts have been cleared by knowledge; *ātmavantaṁ*: self possessed; *na*: not; *karmāṇi*: actions; *nibadhnanti*: bind; *dhañanjaya*: O Dhañanjaya

4.41 O winner of riches, one who has renounced the fruits of his actions, whose doubts are destroyed, who is well-situated in the Self, is not bound by his actions.

तस्मादज्ञानसंम्भूतं हृत्स्थं ज्ञानासिनात्मनः ।
छित्त्वैनं संशयं योगमातिष्ठोत्तिष्ठ भारत ॥४.४२

tasmādajñānasaṁbhūtaṁ hṛtsthaṁ jñānāsinātmanaḥ /
chittvainaṁ saṁśayaṁ yogamātiṣṭhottiṣṭha bhārata // 4.42

tasmāt: therefore; *ajñāna*: ignorance; *saṁbhūtaṁ*: born of; *hṛtsthaṁ*: situated in the heart; *jñānāsinā*: by the sword of knowledge; *ātmanaḥ*: of the self; *chittvā*: having cutting off; *enaṁ*: this; *saṁśayaṁ*: doubt; *yogaṁ*: in yoga; *ātiṣṭha*: be firm; *uttiṣṭha*: stand up; *bhārata*: O descendant of Bhārata

4.42 *O descendant of Bhārata, therefore, stand up, be situated in yoga. Armed with the sword of knowledge; cut the doubt born of ignorance that exists in your heart.*

इति श्रीमद्भगवद्गीतासूपनिषत्सु ब्रह्मविद्यायां योगशास्त्रे
श्रीकृष्णार्जुनसंवादे ज्ञानकर्मसंन्यासयोगो नाम चतुर्थोऽध्यायः ॥२

iti śrī mad bhagavadgītāsūpaniṣatsu brahmavidyāyām
yogaśāstre śrī kṛṣṇārjuna saṁvāde jñānakarmasannyāsa yogo nāma
caturtho'dhyāyaḥ //

In the Upaniṣad *of the Bhagavad Gītā, the knowledge of* Brahman, *the Supreme, the science of Yoga and the dialogue between Śrī Kṛṣṇa and Arjuna, this is the fourth discourse designated:*

Jñānakarmasanyāsa Yogaḥ

Verses Of Gita Chapter - 5

अथ पञ्चमोऽध्यायः

संन्यासयोगः

Sanyāsa Yogaḥ

अर्जुन उवाच ।
सन्न्यासं कर्मणां कृष्ण पुनर्योगं च शंससि ।
यच्छ्रेय एतयोरेकं तन्मे ब्रूहि सुनिश्चितम् ॥ ५.१

arjuna uvāca
sannyāsaṁ karmaṇāṁ kṛṣṇa punaryogaṁ ca śaṁsasi **/**
yacchreya etayorekaṁ tanme brūhi suniścitaṁ **//** 5.1

arjuna uvāca: Arjuna said; *sannyāsaṁ*: renunciation; *karmaṇāṁ*: of all actions; *kṛṣṇa*: O Kṛṣṇa; *punaḥ*: again; *yogaṁ*: devotion; *ca*: also; *śaṁsasi*: praising; *yat*: which; *śreyaḥ*: beneficial; *etayoḥ*: of the two; *ekaṁ*: one; *tat*: that; *me*: to me; *brūhi*: please tell; *suniścitaṁ*: definitely

5.1 Arjuna said: Oh Kṛṣṇa, you asked me to renounce work first and then you ask me to work with devotion. Will you now please tell me, one way or the other, which of the two will work for me?

श्री भगवानुवाच ।
सन्न्यास: कर्मयोगश्च नि:श्रेयसकरावुभौ ।
तयोस्तु कर्मसंन्यासात्कर्मयोगो विशिष्यते ॥ ५.२

śrībhagavānuvāca
sannyāsaḥ karmayogaśca niḥśreyasakarāvubhau **/**
tayostu karmasannyāsātkarmayogo viśiṣyate **//** 5.2

śrī bhagavān uvāca: Lord Kṛṣṇa said; *sannyāsah*: renunciation; *karmayogaḥ*: work in devotion; *ca*: also; *niḥśreyasakarāv*: for liberation; *ubhau*: both; *tayoḥ*: of the two; *tu*: but; *karmasannyāsāt*: between work and renunciation; *karmayogaḥ*: work in devotion; *viśiṣyate*: better

5.2 Kṛṣṇa says: The renunciation of work and work in devotion are both good for liberation. But, of the two, work in devotional service is better than renunciation of work.

ज्ञेय: स नित्यसंन्यासी यो न द्वेष्टि न काङ्क्षति ।
निर्द्वन्द्वो हि महाबाहो सुखं बन्धात्प्रमुच्यते ॥५.३

jñeyaḥ sa nityasannyāsī yo na dveṣṭi na kāṅkṣati I
nirdvandvo hi mahābāho sukhaṁ bandhātpramucyate II 5.3

jñeyaḥ: should be known; *saḥ*: he; *nitya*: always; *saṁnyāsī* : renouncer; *yaḥ*: who; *na*: never; *dveṣṭi*: hates; *na*: never; *kāṅkṣati*: desires; *nirdvandvaḥ*: free from all dualities; *hi*: certainly; *mahābāho*: mighty-armed one; *sukham*: easily; *bandhāt*: from bondage; *pramucyate*: completely liberated

5.3 He who neither hates nor desires the fruits of his activities has renounced. Such a person, free from all dualities, easily overcomes material bondage and is completely liberated, Oh Arjuna!

साङ्ख्ययोगौ पृथग्बाला: प्रवदन्ति न पण्डिता: ।
एकमप्यास्थित: सम्यगुभयोर्विन्दते फलम् ॥५.४

sāṅkhyayogau pṛthagbālāḥ pravadanti na paṇḍitāḥ I
ekamapyāsthitaḥ samyagubhayorvindate phalam II 5.4

sāṁkhyayogau: sāṁkhya system and yoga; *pṛthak*: different; *bālāḥ*: less intelligent; *pravadanti*: say; *na*: not; *paṇḍitāḥ*: learned; *ekaṁ*: one; *api*: even; *āsthitaḥ*: situated; *samyak*: complete; *ubhayoḥ*: of both; *vindate*: enjoys; *phalaṁ*: result

5.4 Only the ignorant speaks of the path of action to be different from the path of renunciation, those who are actually learned say that both action and renunciation lead to the same truth.

यत्साङ्ख्यै: प्राप्यते स्थानं तद्योगैरपि गम्यते ।
एकं साङ्ख्यं च योगं च य: पश्यति स पश्यति ॥५.५

yat sāṅkhyaiḥ prāpyate sthānaṁ tadyogairapi gamyate I
ekaṁ sāṅkhyaṁ ca yogaṁ ca yaḥ paśyati sa paśyati II 5.5

yat: what; *sāṅkhyaiḥ*: by Sāṅkhya system; *prāpyate*: get; *sthānaṁ*: position; *tat*: that; *yogaiḥ*: by work in devotion; *api*: also; *gamyate*: can reach; *ekam*: one; *sāṅkhyaṁ*: Sāṅkhya system; *ca*: and; *yogaṁ*: work in devotion; *ca*: and; *yaḥ*: who; *paśyati*: sees; *saḥ*: he; *paśyati*: sees

5.5 He who knows, knows that the state reached by renunciation and action are one and the same. State reached by renunciation can also be achieved by action, know them to be at same level and see them as they are.

संन्यासस्तु महाबाहो दुःखमाप्तुमयोगतः ।
योगयुक्तो मुनिर्ब्रह्म नचिरेणाधिगच्छति ॥ ५.६

sannyāsastu mahābāho duḥkhamāptumayogataḥ |
yogayukto munirbrahma nacireṇādhigacchati || 5.6

sannyāsaḥ: renunciation; *tu*: but; *mahābāho*: mighty-armed one; *duḥkhaṁ*: misery; *āptuṁ*: afflicts with; *ayogataḥ*: without devotion; *yogayuktaḥ*: engaged in devotion; *muniḥ*: wise; *brahma*: supreme; *nacireṇa*: without delay; *adhigacchati*: attains

5.6 Renunciation without devotional service afflicts one with misery, Oh mighty-armed one. The wise person engaged in devotional service attains the Supreme without delay.

योगयुक्तो विशुद्धात्मा विजितात्मा जितेन्द्रियः ।
सर्वभूतात्मभूतात्मा कुर्वन्नपि न लिप्यते ॥ ५.७

yogayukto viśuddhātmā vijitātmā jitendriyaḥ |
sarvabhūtātmabhūtātmā kurvannapi na lipyate || 5.7

yogayuktaḥ: engaged in work with devotion; *viśuddhātmā* : a man of purified mind; *vijita*: self-controlled; *atma*: soul; *jitendriyaḥ*: conquered the senses; *sarvabhūtātma*: to all living beings; *bhūtātma*: compassionate; *kurvan api*: though engaged in work, *na*: never; *lipyate*: entangled

5.7 The person engaged in devoted service, beyond concepts pure and impure, self-controlled and who has conquered the senses is compassionate and loves everyone, although engaged in work, he is never entangled.

नैव किञ्चित्करोमीति युक्तो मन्येत तत्त्ववित् ।
पश्यञ्श्रुण्वन्स्पृशञ्जिघ्रन्नश्नन्गाच्छन्स्वपञ्श्वसन् ॥ ५.८

naiva kiñcitkaromīti yukto manyeta tattvavit |
paśyanśṛṇvanspṛśañjighrannaśnangacchansvapañśvasan || 5.8

na: never; *eva*: certainly; *kiṁcit*: anything; *karomi*: I do; *iti*: thus; *yuktaḥ*: engaged; *manyeta*: thinks; *tattvavit*: one who knows the truth; *paśyan*: seeing; *śṛṇvan*: hearing; *spṛśan*: touching; *jighran*: smelling; *aśnan*: eating; *gacchan*: going; *svapan*: dreaming; *śvasan*: breathing

प्रलपन्विसृजन्गृह्णन्नुन्मिषन्निमिषन्नपि ।
इन्द्रियाणीन्द्रियार्थेषु वर्तन्त इति धारयन् ॥ ५.९

pralapanvisṛjangṛhṇannunmiṣannimiṣannapi **/**
indriyāṇīndriyārtheṣu vartanta iti dhārayan **//** 5.9

pralapan: talking; *visṛjan*: giving up; *gṛihṇan*: accepting; *unmishan*: opening; *nimiṣan*: closing; *api*: though; *indriyāṇi*: the senses; *indriyārtheṣu*: in gratifying senses; *vartanta*: are engaged; *iti*: thus; *dhārayan*: considering

5.8, 9 One who knows the truth, though engaged in seeing, hearing, touching, smelling, eating, going, dreaming and breathing knows that he never does anything. While talking, letting go, receiving, opening, closing, he considers that the senses are engaged in gratification.

ब्रह्मण्याधाय कर्माणि सङ्गँ त्यक्त्वा करोति यः ।
लिप्यते न स पापेन पद्मपत्रमिवाम्भसा ॥ ५.१०

brahmaṇyādhāya karmāṇi saṅgaṁ tyaktvā karoti yaḥ **/**
lipyate na sa pāpena padmapatramivāmbhasā **//** 5.10

brahmaṇi: Eternal Consciousness; *ādhāya*: surrendering to; *karmāṇi*: actions; *saṅgaṁ*: attachment; *tyaktvā* : giving up; *karoti*: does; *yaḥ*: who; *lipyate*: affected; *na*: never; *saḥ*: he; *pāpena*: by sin; *padma*: lotus; *patraṁ*: leaf; *iva*: like; *ambhasā*: water

5.10 He, who acts without attachment, giving up and surrendering to the eternal consciousness, He is never affected by sin, in the same way that the lotus leaf is not affected by water.

कायेन मनसा बुद्ध्या केवलैरिन्द्रियैरपि ।
योगिन: कर्म कुर्वन्ति सङ्गं त्यक्त्वात्मशुद्धये ॥ ५.११

kāyena manasā buddhyā kevalairindriyairapi **/**
yoginaḥ karma kurvanti saṅgaṁ tyaktvātmaśuddhaye **//** 5.11

kāyena: by the body; *manasā*: by the mind; *buddhyā*: by the intellect; *kevalaiḥ*: only; *indriyaiḥ*: by the senses; *api* also: *yoginaḥ*: yogis; *karma*: action; *kurvanti*: perform; *saṅgaṁ*: attachment; *tyaktvā*; having abandoned; *ātmaśuddhaye*: for the purification of the self

5.11 The yogis, giving up attachment, act with the body, mind, intelligence, even with the senses for the purpose of self-purification.

युक्त: कर्मफलं त्यक्त्वा शान्तिमाप्नोति नैष्ठिकीम्
अयुक्त: कामकारेण फले सक्तो निबध्यते ॥ ५.१२

yuktaḥ karmaphalaṁ tyaktvā śāntimāpnoti naiṣṭhikīm /
ayuktaḥ kāmakāreṇa phale sakto nibadhyate // 5.12

yuktaḥ: one steadfast in devotion; *karma*: action; *phalaṁ*: fruit: *tyaktvā*: giving up; *śāntiṁ*: peace; *āpnoti*: achieves: *naiṣṭhikīṁ*: established; *ayuktaḥ*: one not steadfast in devotion; *kāmakāreṇa*: for enjoying the fruits of the action; *phale*: fruit; *saktaḥ*: attached; *nibadhyate*: becomes entangled

5.12 One who is engaged in devotion, gives up attachment to outcome of one's actions and is centered, is at peace. One who is not engaged in devotion, attached to the outcome of one's action becomes entangled.

सर्वकर्माणि मनसा संन्यस्यास्ते सुखं वशी ।
नवद्वारे पुरे देही नैव कुर्वन्न कारयन् ॥५.१३

sarvakarmāṇi manasā sannyasyāste sukhaṁ vaśī /
navadvāre pure dehī naiva kurvanna kārayan // 5.13

sarva: all; *karmāṇi*: activities; *manasā*: by the mind; *sannyasya*: giving up; *āste*: remains; *sukhaṁ*: in happiness; *vaśī* : who is controlled; *navadvāre*: of nine gates; *pure*: in the city; *dehī* : body; *na*: never; *eva*: surely; *kurvan*: doing; *na*: never: *kārayan*: causing to be done

5.13 One who is controlled, giving up all the activities of the mind, surely remains in happiness in the city of nine gates (body), neither doing anything nor causing anything to be done.

न कर्तृत्वं न कर्माणि लोकस्य सृजति प्रभुः ।
न कर्मफलसंयोगं स्वभावस्तु प्रवर्तते ॥५.१४

na kartṛtvaṁ na karmāṇi lokasya sṛjati prabhuḥ /
na karmaphalasaṁyogaṁ svabhāvas tu pravartate // 5.14

na: never; *kartṛtvaṁ*: of doing; *na*: not; *karmāṇi*: activities; *lokasya*: of the people; *sṛjati*: creates; *prabhuḥ*: master; *na*: not; *karma*: activities; *phala*: fruit; *saṁyogaṁ*: connection; *svabhāvaḥ*: nature; *tu*: but; *pravartate*: act

5.14 The master does not create activities nor makes people do nor connects with the outcome of the actions. All this is enacted by the material nature.

नादत्ते कस्यचित्पापं न चैव सुकृतं विभुः ।
अज्ञानेनावृतं ज्ञानं तेन मुह्यन्ति जन्तवः ॥५.१५

nādatte kasyacitpāpaṁ na caiva sukṛtaṁ vibhuḥ I
ajñānenāvṛtaṁ jñānaṁ tena muhyanti jantavaḥ II 5.15

na: never; *ādatte*: accepts; *kasyacit*: anyone's; *pāpaṁ*: sins; *na*: not; *ca*: and; *eva*: surely; *sukṛtaṁ*: good deeds; *vibhuḥ*: lord; *ajñānena*: by ignorance; *āvṛtaṁ*: covered; *jñānaṁ*: knowledge; *tena*: by that; *muhyanti*: are confused; *jantavaḥ*: living beings

5.15 The Lord, surely, neither accepts anyone's sins nor good deeds. Living beings are confused by the ignorance that covers the knowledge.

ज्ञानेन तु तदज्ञानं येषां नाशितमात्मनः ।
तेषामादित्यवज्ज्ञानं प्रकाशयति तत्परम् ॥५.१६

jñānena tu tadajñānaṁ yeṣāṁ nāśitamātmanaḥ I
teṣāmādityavajjñānaṁ prakāśayati tatparam II 5.16

jñānena: by knowledge; *tu*: but; *tad*: that; *ajñānaṁ*: ignorance; *yeṣāṁ*: whose; *nāśitaṁ*: destroyed; *ātmanaḥ*: of the self; *teṣām*: their; *ādityavat*: like the rising sun; *jñānaṁ*: knowledge; *prakāśayati*: throws light on; *tat param*: that supreme consciousness

5.16 Whose ignorance is destroyed by the knowledge, their knowledge, like the rising sun, throws light on the supreme consciousness.

तद्बुद्धयस्तदात्मानस्तन्निष्ठास्तत्परायणाः ।
गच्छन्त्यपुनरावृत्तिं ज्ञाननिर्धूतकल्मषाः ॥५.१७

tadbuddhayastadātmānastanniṣṭhāstatparāyaṇāḥ I
gacchantyapunarāvṛttiṁ jñānanirdhūtakalmaṣāḥ II 5.17

tad buddhyaḥ: one whose intelligence is in the supreme; *tad ātmānaḥ*: whose mind is in the supreme; *tanniṣṭhāḥ*: whose faith is in the supreme; *tat parāyaṇāḥ*: who has surrendered to the supreme; *gacchanti*: go; *apunarāvṛittiṁ*: liberation; *jñāna*: knowledge; *nirdhūta*: cleansed; *kalmaṣāḥ*: sins

5.17 One whose intelligence, mind, faith are in the Supreme and one who has surrendered to the Supreme, his misunderstandings are cleansed through knowledge and he goes towards liberation.

विद्याविनयसंपन्ने ब्राह्मणे गवि हस्तिनि ।
शुनि चैव श्वपाके च पण्डिताः समदर्शिनः ॥५.१८

vidyāvinayasaṁpanne brāhmaṇe gavi hastini |
śuni caiva śvapāke ca paṇḍitāḥ samadarśinaḥ || 5.18

vidyā: knowledge; *vinaya*: compassion; *saṁpanne*: full with; *brāhmaṇe*: in the brahmana; *gavi*: in the cow; *hastini*: in the elephant; *śuni*: in the dog; *ca*: and; *eva*: surely; *śvapāke*: in the dog-eater; *ca*: and; *paṇḍitāḥ*: learned; *sama*: equal; *darśinaḥ*: see

5.18 One who is full of knowledge and compassion sees equally the learned brāhmaṇa, *the cow, the elephant, the dog and the dog-eater.*

इहैव तैर्जितः सर्गो येषां साम्ये स्थितं मनः ।
निर्दोषं हि समं ब्रह्म तस्माद्ब्रह्मणि ते स्थिताः ॥ ५.१९

ihaiva tairjitaḥ sargo yeṣāṁ sāmye sthitaṁ manaḥ |
nirdoṣaṁ hi samaṁ brahma tasmād brahmaṇi te sthitāḥ || 5.19

iha: in this life; *eva*: surely; *taiḥ*: by them; *jitaḥ*: conquered; *sargaḥ*: birth and death; *yeṣāṁ*: of whose; *sāmye*: in equanimity; *sthitaṁ*: situated; *manaḥ*: mind; *nir doṣaṁ*: flawless; *hi*: surely; *samaṁ*: in equanimity; *brahma*: supreme; *tasmāt*: therefore; *brahmaṇi*: in the supreme; *te*: they; *sthitāḥ*: situated

5.19 In this life, surely, those whose minds are situated in equanimity have conquered birth and death. They are flawless like the Supreme and therefore, are situated in the Supreme.'

न प्रहृष्येत्प्रियं प्राप्य नोद्विजेत्प्राप्य चाप्रियम् ।
स्थिरबुद्धिरसंमूढो ब्रह्मविद्ब्रह्मणि स्थितः ॥ ५.२०

na prahṛṣyetpriyaṁ prāpya nodvijet prāpya cāpriyam |
sthirabuddhirasaṁmūḍho brahmavid brahmaṇi sthitaḥ || 5.20

na: never; *prahṛṣyet*: rejoice; *priyaṁ*: like; *prāpya*: achieving; *no*: not; *udvijet*: agitated; *prāpya*: achieving; *ca*: and; *apriyaṁ*: the unpleasant; *sthirabuddhiḥ*: steady intelligence; *asaṁmūḍhaḥ*: undeluded; *brahmavid*: one who knows the Supreme; *brahmaṇi*: in the Supreme; *sthitaḥ*: situated

5.20 One who does not rejoice at achieving something he likes nor gets agitated on getting something he does not like, who is of steady intelligence, who is not deluded, one who knows the Supreme, is situated in the Supreme.

बाह्यस्पर्शेष्वसक्तात्मा विन्दत्यात्मनि यत्सुखम् ।
स ब्रह्मयोगयुक्तात्मा सुखमक्षयमश्नुते ॥ ५.२१

bāhyasparśeṣvasaktātmā vindatyātmani yatsukham |
sa brahmayogayuktātmā sukhamakṣayamaśnute || 5.21

bāhya: outer; *sparśeṣu*: sense pleasures; *asaktātmā* : not attached; *vindati*: enjoys; *ātmani*: in the Self; *yat*: that; *sukhaṁ*: happiness; *saḥ*: he; *brahma yoga*: engaged in the Supreme; *yuktātmā*: self-connected; *sukhaṁ*: happiness; *akṣayaṁ*: unlimited; *aśnute*: enjoys

5.21 One who is not attached to the outer world sense pleasures, who enjoys in the Self, in that happiness, he is self-connected and engaged in the Supreme and enjoys unlimited happiness.

ये हि संस्पर्शजा भोगा दुःखयोनय एव ते ।
आद्यन्तवन्तः कौन्तेय न तेषु रमते बुधः ॥ ५.२२

ye hi saṁsparśajā bhogā duḥkhayonaya eva te |
ādyantavantaḥ kaunteya na teṣu ramate budhaḥ || 5.22

ye: those; *hi*: surely; *saṁsparśajāḥ*: by contact with the senses; *bhogāḥ*: enjoyments; *duḥkha*: misery; *yonayaḥ*: sources of; *eva*: surely; *te*: they are; *ādya*: beginning; *antavantaḥ*: subject to end; *kaunteya*: son of Kuntī; *na*: not; *teṣu*: in those; *ramate*: enjoys; *budhaḥ*: intelligent person

5.22 The intelligent person surely does not enjoy the sense pleasures, enjoyments which are sources of misery and which are subject to beginning and end.

शक्नोतीहैव यः सोढुं प्राक्शरीरविमोक्षणात् ।
कामक्रोधोद्भवं वेगं स युक्तः स सुखी नरः ॥ ५.२३

śaknotīhaiva yaḥ soḍhuṁ prākśarīravimokṣaṇāt |
kāmakrodhodbhavaṁ vegaṁ sa yuktaḥ sa sukhī naraḥ || 5.23

śaknoti: able to do; *iha eva*: in this body; *yaḥ*: one who; *soḍhuṁ*: tolerate; *prāk*: before; *śarīra*: body; *vimokṣaṇāt*: give up; *kāma*: desire; *krodha*: anger; *udbhavaṁ*: generated from; *vegaṁ*: urge; *sa*: he; *yuktaḥ*: well-situated; *saḥ*: he; *sukhī* : happy; *naraḥ*: man

5.23 Before leaving this present body, if one is able to tolerate the urges of material senses and check the force of desire and anger, he is well situated and he is happy in this world.

योऽन्तःसुखोऽन्तरारामस्तथान्तर्ज्योतिरेव यः ।
स योगी ब्रह्मनिर्वाणं ब्रह्मभूतोऽधिगच्छति ॥ ५.२४

yo'ntaḥsukho'ntarārāmastathāntarjyotireva yaḥ I
sa yogī brahmanirvāṇaṁ brahmabhūto'dhigacchati II 5.24

yaḥ: who; *antaḥ sukhaḥ*: happy from within; *antarārāmaḥ*: active within; *tathā* : as well as; *antarjyotiḥ*: illumined within; *eva*: surely; *yaḥ*: who; *saḥ*: he; *yogī* : mystic; *brahma nirvāṇaṁ*: liberated in the Supreme; *brahma bhūtaḥ*: self realized; *adhigacchati*: attains

5.24 One who is happy from within, active within as well as illumined within, surely, is a yogi (united in mind body and spirit) and he is liberated in the Supreme, is self-realized and attains the Supreme.

लभन्ते ब्रह्मनिर्वाणमृषयः क्षीणकल्मषाः ।
छिन्नद्वैधा यतात्मानः सर्वभूतहिते रताः ॥ ५.२५

labhante brahmanirvāṇamṛṣayaḥ kṣīṇakalmaṣāḥ I
chinnadvaidhā yatātmānaḥ sarvabhūtahite ratāḥ II 5.25

labhante: achieve; *brahma nirvāṇaṁ*: liberation in the Supreme; *ṛṣayaḥ*: who are active within; *kṣīṇakalmaṣāḥ*: devoid of sins; *chinna*: torn off; *dvaidāḥ*: duality; *yatātmānaḥ*: engaged in self-realization; *sarva*: all; *bhūta*: living beings; *hite*: for the welfare; *ratāḥ*: engaged

5.25 The holy men whose sins have been destroyed are working for the welfare of other beings, those who are self-restrained and have cleared all their doubts and dualities attain the eternal happiness of God, Nityānanda *of Divine.*

कामक्रोधवियुक्तानां यतीनां यतचेतसाम् ।
अभितो ब्रह्मनिर्वाणं वर्तते विदितात्मनाम् ॥ ५.२६

kāmakrodhaviyuktānāṁ yatīnāṁ yatacetasām I
abhito brahmanirvāṇaṁ vartate viditātmanām II 5.26

kāma: desire; *krodha*: anger; *viyuktānāṁ*; one freed from; *yatīnāṁ*; of the ascetics; *yata cetasāṁ*: with the thoughts controlled; *abhitaḥ*: on all sides; *brahma nirvāṇaṁ*: absolute freedom; *vartate*: exists; *viditātmanāṁ*: of those who have realized the Self

5.26 They who are free from lust and anger, who have subdued the mind and senses, and who have known the Self, easily attain liberation.

स्पर्शान्कृत्वा बहिर्बाह्यांश्चक्षुश्चैवान्तरे भ्रुवोः ।
प्राणापानौ समौ कृत्वा नासाभ्यन्तरचारिणौ ॥ ५.२७

sparśānkṛtvā bahirbāhyāṁścakṣuścaivāntare bhruvoḥ /
prāṇāpānau samau kṛtvā nāsābhyantaracāriṇau // 5.27

sparśān: external sense objects; *kṛtvā* : keeping; *bahiḥ*: external; *bāhyān*: external; *cakṣuḥ*: eyes; *ca*: and; *eva*: surely; *antare*: within; *bhruvoḥ*: eyebrows; *prāṇāpānau*: inward and outward breath; *samau*: suspending; *kṛtvā* : doing; *nāsābhyantara*: within the nostrils; *cārinau*: moving

यतेन्द्रियमनोबुद्धिर्मुनिर्मोक्षपरायणः ।
विगतेच्छाभयक्रोधो यः सदा मुक्त एव सः ॥ ५.२८

yatendriyamanobuddhirmunir mokṣaparāyaṇaḥ /
vigatecchābhayakrodho yaḥ sadā mukta eva saḥ // 5.28

yata: controlled; *indriya*: senses; *mano*: mind; *buddhiḥ*: intelligence; *muniḥ* the sage; *mokṣa*: liberation; *parāyaṇaḥ*: aiming; *vigata*: free from; *icchā*: desires; *bhaya*: fear; *krodah*: anger; *yaḥ*: one who; *sadā*: always; *muktaḥ*: liberated; *eva*: certainly; *saḥ*: he is

5.27,28 Shutting out all external sense objects, keeping the eyes and vision concentrated between the two eyebrows, suspending the inward and outward breaths within the nostrils and thus controlling the mind, senses and intelligence, the transcendental who is aiming at liberation, becomes free from desire, fear and the by-product of desire and fear, anger all three. One who is always in this state is certainly liberated.

भोक्तारं यज्ञतपसां सर्वलोकमहेश्वरम् ।
सुहृदं सर्वभूतानां ज्ञात्वा मां शान्तिमृच्छति ॥ ५.२९

bhoktāraṁ yajñatapasāṁ sarvalokamaheśvaram /
suhṛdaṁ sarvabhūtānāṁ jñātvā māṁ śāntimṛcchati // 5.29

bhoktāraṁ: one who enjoys; *yajña*: sacrifice; *tapasāṁ*: penance; *ṣarva*: all; *loka*: worlds; *maheśvārāṁ*: lord; *suhṛdaṁ*: benefactor; *sarva*: all; *bhūtānāṁ*: living beings; *jñātvā*: knowing; *māṁ*: me; *śāntiṁ*: peace; *ṛcchati*: achieves

5.29 One who knowing Me as the purpose of sacrifice and penance, as the lord of all the worlds and the benefactor of all the living beings, achieves peace.

इति श्रीमद्भगवद्गीतासूपनिषत्सु ब्रह्मविद्यायां योगशास्त्रे
श्रीकृष्णार्जुनसंवादे संन्यासयोगो नाम पञ्चमोऽध्याय: ॥२

iti śrīmad bhagavadgītāsūpaniṣatsu brahmavidyāyām
yogaśāstre śrīkṛṣṇārjuna saṁvāde sannyāsayogo nāma
pañcamo 'dhyāyaḥ ||

In the Upaniṣad *of the Bhagavad Gītā, the knowledge of* Brahman, *the Supreme, the science of Yoga and the dialogue between Śrī Kṛṣṇa and Arjuna, this is the fifth discourse designated:*

Sanyāsa Yogaḥ

Verses Of Gita Chapter - 6

अथ षष्ठोऽध्याय:

ध्यानयोग:

Dhyāna Yogaḥ

श्री भगवानुवाच

अनाश्रित: कर्मफलं कार्यं कर्म करोति य: ।

स संन्यासी च योगी च न निरग्निर्न चाक्रिय: ॥ ६.१

śrībhagavānuvāca

anāśritaḥ karmaphalaṁ kāryaṁ karma karoti yaḥ I

sa sanyāsī ca yogī ca na niragnirna cā'kriyaḥ II 6.1

śrī bhagavān uvāca: the Lord said; *anāśritaḥ*: without shelter; *karma*: action; *phalaṁ*: fruit; *kāryaṁ*: obligated; *karma*: work; *karoti*: performs; *yaḥ*: who; *saḥ*: he; *sannyāsī*: ascetic; *ca*: and; *yogī*: one engaged in yoga; *ca*: and; *na*: not; *nir*: without; *agniḥ*: fire; *na*: not; *ca*: and; *akriyaḥ*: without work

6.1 Bhagavān *says: One who performs actions without being attached to its outcome is an ascetic. He is a religious performer of purification of mind.*

One who has stopped performing any actions, one who doesn't accept the sacred fire and doesn't perform his rituals is neither an ascetic nor a karma yogi, a sage immersed in action.

यं संन्यासमिति प्राहुर्योगं तं विद्धि पाण्डव ।

न ह्यसंन्यस्तसङ्कल्पो योगी भवति कश्चन ॥ ६.२

yaṁ sannyāsamiti prāhuryogaṁ taṁ viddhi pāṇḍava I

na hyasannyastasaṅkalpo yogī bhavati kaścana II 6.2

yaṁ: what; *sannyāsam*: renunciation; *iti*: thus; *prāhuḥ*: they say; *yogaṁ*: linking with the Supreme; *taṁ*: that; *viddhi*: you should know; *pāṇḍava*: O son of Pāṇḍu; *na*: never; *hi*: certainly; *asannyasta*: without renouncing; *saṅkalpaḥ*: self interest; *yogī*: one engaged in yoga; *bhavati*: becomes; *kaścana*: anyone

6.2 O Pāṇḍavā, renunciation leads to the state of yoga where one is linking oneself with the Supreme. This union with the Divine can happen only when you renounce self interest.

आरुरुक्षोर्मुनेर्योगं कर्म कारणमुच्यते ।
योगारूढस्य तस्यैव शमः कारणमुच्यते ॥ ६.३

ārurukṣormuner yogaṁ karma kāraṇamucyate /
yogārūḍhasya tasyaiva śamaḥ kāraṇamucyate // 6.3

ārurukṣoḥ: one wishing to ascend to the state of yoga (no-mind state); *muneḥ*: of the sage; *yogaṁ*: yoga system; *karma*: work; *kāraṇaṁ*: cause; *ucyate*: is said to be; *yoga*: yoga; *arūḍhasya*: of one who has attained; *tasya*: his; *eva*: certainly; *śamaḥ*: cessation of all activities; *kāraṇaṁ*: cause; *ucyate*: is said to be

6.3 For one desirous of achieving the state of yoga or no-mind state action is the means and after ascendance cessation from all actions happens.

यदा हि नेन्द्रियार्थेषु न कर्मस्वनुषज्जते ।
सर्वसङ्कल्पसंन्यासी योगारूढस्तदोच्यते ॥ ६.४

yadā hi nendriyārtheṣu na karmasvanuṣajjate /
sarvasankalpasannyāsī yogārūḍhastadocyate // 6.4

yadā: when; *hi*: certainly; *na*: not; *indriyārtheṣu*: in sense gratification; *na*: never; *karmasu*: in fruitive activities; *anuṣajjate*: does necessarily engage; *sarva sankalpa*: all material desires; *sannyāsī*: renouncer; *yogārūḍhaḥ*: elevated in yoga; *tadā*: at that time; *ucyate*: is said to be

6.4 Any one is said to have attained the state of yoga when, having renounced all material desires, he neither acts for sense gratification nor engages in result focused activities.

उद्धरेदात्मनात्मानं नात्मानमवसादयेत्
आत्मैव ह्यात्मनो बन्धुरात्मैव रिपुरात्मनः ॥ ६.५

uddharedātmanātmānaṁ natmānamavasādayet /
ātmaiva hyātmano bandhurātmaiva ripurātmanaḥ // 6.5

uddharet: one must deliver; *ātmanā*: by the mind; *ātmānaṁ*: the conditioned soul; *na*: never; *ātmānaṁ*: the conditioned soul; *avasādayet*: put into degradation; *ātmā*: mind; *eva*: certainly; *hi*: surely; *ātmanaḥ*: of the conditioned soul; *bandhuḥ*: friend; *ātmā*: mind; *eva*: certainly; *ripuḥ*: enemy; *ātmanaḥ*: of the conditioned soul

6.5 You are your own friend; you are your own enemy. Evolve yourself through the Self and do not degrade yourself.

बन्धुरात्मात्मनस्तस्य येनात्मैवात्मना जितः ।
अनात्मनस्तु शत्रुत्वे वर्तेतात्मैव शत्रुवत् ॥ ६.६

bandhurātmātmanastasyayenātmaivātmanā jitaḥ |
anātmanastu śatrutve vartetātmaiva śatruvat || 6.6

bandhuḥ: friend; *ātmā*: the Self; *ātmanaḥ*: of the living entity; *tasya*: of him; *yena*: by whom; *ātmā*: the Self; *eva*: certainly; *ātmanā*: by the living entity; *jitaḥ*: conquered; *anātmanaḥ*: of one who has failed to control the Self; *tu*: but; *śatrutve*: because of enmity; *varteta*: remains; *ātmā eva*: the very mind; *śatruvat*: as an enemy

6.6 For him who has conquered the self, the Self is the best of friends; for one who has failed to do so, his self will remain the greatest enemy.

जितात्मनः प्रशान्तस्य परमात्मा समाहितः ।
शीतोष्णसुखदुःखेषु तथा मानापमानयोः ॥ ६.७

jitātmanaḥ praśāntasya paramātmā samāhitaḥ |
śītoṣṇasukhaduḥkheṣu tathā mānāpamānayoḥ || 6.7

jitātmanaḥ: of one who has conquered his self; *praśāntasya*: who has attained tranquility; *paramātmā*: Supreme; *samāhitaḥ*: approached completely; *śītoṣṇa*: in cold heat; *sukha*: happiness; *duḥkheṣu*: and distress; *tathā*: also; *māna*: in honor; *apamānayoḥ*: dishonor

6.7 For one who has conquered the self, who has attained tranquility, the Supreme is already reached. Such a person remains in this state in happiness or distress, heat or cold, honor or dishonor.

ज्ञानविज्ञानतृप्तात्मा कूटस्थो विजितेन्द्रियः ।
युक्त इत्युच्यते योगी समलोष्टाश्मकाञ्चनः ॥ ६.८

jñānavijñānatṛptātmā kūṭastho vijitendriyaḥ |
yukta ityucyate yogī samaloṣṭāśmakāñcanaḥ || 6.8

jñāna: acquired knowledge; *vijñāna*: realized knowledge; *tṛptātmā*: contented self; *kūṭasthaḥ*: established in Self-realization; *vijitendriyaḥ*: one who has subdued his senses; *yukta*: competent for self-realization; *iti*: thus; *ucyate*: is said; *yogī*: one established in yoga; *sama*: equipoised; *loṣṭāśma*: lump of earth, stone; *kāñcanaḥ*: gold

6.8 A person whose mind is contented because of spiritual knowledge, who has subdued his senses and to whom stone and gold are same and who is satisfied

with what he is having, is said to be established in Self-realization and is called an enlightened being.

सुहृन्मित्रार्युदासीन मध्यस्थद्वेष्यबन्धुषु ।
साधुष्वपि च पापेषु समबुद्धिर्विशिष्यते ॥ ६.९

suhṛnmitrāryudāsīnamadhyasthadveṣya bandhuṣu /
sadhuṣvapi ca pāpeṣu samabuddhirviśiṣyate // 6.9

suhṛt: to well-wishers by nature; *mitra*: affectionate benefactors; *ari*: enemies; *udāsīna*: neutral; *madhyastha*: mediators; *dveṣya*: envious; *bandhuṣu*: friends; *sādhuṣu*: pious; *api*: also; *ca*: and; *pāpeṣu*: sinners; *sama*: equal *buddhiḥ*: with equal mind; *viśiṣyate*: is further advanced

6.9 A person is considered truly advanced when he regards honest well-wishers, affectionate benefactors, the neutral, mediators, the envious, friends and enemies, the pious and the sinners all with an equal mind.

योगी युञ्जीत सततमात्मानं रहसि स्थित: ।
एकाकी यतचित्तात्मा निराशीरपरिग्रह: ॥ ६.१०

yogī yuñjīta satatamātmānaṁ rahasi sthitaḥ /
ekākī yatachittātmā nirāśīraparigrahaḥ // 6.10

yogī: yogi; *yuñjīta*: concentrate; *satataṁ*: always; *ātmānaṁ*: himself; *rahasi*: in a secluded place; *sthitaḥ*: situated; *ekākī* : alone; *yatachittātmā* : careful in mind; *nir āśīḥ*: without being attracted by anything else; *aparigrahaḥ*: free from the feeling of possessiveness

6.10 A yogi should always try to concentrate his mind on the supreme Self; situated in a secluded place, he should carefully control his mind without being attracted by anything and should be free from the feeling of possessiveness.

शुचौ देशे प्रतिष्ठाप्य स्थिरमासनमात्मन: ।
नात्युच्छ्रितं नातिनीचं चैलाजिनकुशोत्तरम् ॥ ६.११

śucau deśe pratiṣṭhāpya sthiramāsanamātmanaḥ /
nātyucchritaṁ nātinīcaṁ cailājinakuśottaram // 6.11

śucau: in a clean state; *deśe*: land; *pratiṣṭhāpya*: placing; *sthiraṁ*: stable; *āsanaṁ*: seat; *ātmanaḥ*: own; *na*: not; *ati*: very low; *ucchritaṁ*: high; *na*: not; *nīcaṁ*: low; *caila ajina*: of soft cloth and deerskin; *kuśa*: kuśa grass; *uttaraṁ*: covering

6.11 On a clean and pure place, one should establish his seat by laying **kuśa** *grass, a deer skin and a cloth, one over another, neither too high nor too low.*

तत्रैकाग्रं मनः कृत्वा यतचित्तेन्द्रियक्रियः ।
उपविश्यासने युञ्ज्याद्योगमात्मविशुद्धये ॥ ६.१२

tatraikāgraṁ manaḥ kṛtvā yatacittendriyakriyaḥ |
upaviśyāsane yuñjyādyogamātmaviśuddhaye || 6.12

tatra: then; *ekāgraṁ*: with one focus; *manaḥ*: mind; *kṛtvā*: making; *yata cittendriya kriyaḥ*: having restrained the functions of the mind and senses; *upaviśya*: sitting; *āsane*: on the seat; *yuñjyāt*: should execute; *yogaṁ*: yoga; *ātma*: oneself; *viśuddhaye*: to purify

6.12 Sitting firmly on that pure seat, the yogi should practice the purification of the self by controlling the activities of mind and the senses.

समं कायशिरोग्रीवं धारयन्नचलं स्थिरः
सम्प्रेक्ष्य नासिकाग्रं स्वं दिशश्चानवलोकयन् ॥ ६.१३

samaṁ kāyaśirogrīvaṁ dhārayannacalaṁ sthiraḥ |
samprekṣya nāsikāgraṁ svaṁ diśaścānavalokayan || 6.13

samaṁ: straight; *kāya*: body; *śiraḥ*: head; *grīvaṁ*: neck; *dhārayan*: holding; *acalaṁ*: steady; *sthiraḥ*: still; *saṁprekṣya*: looking; *nāsika*: nose; *agraṁ*: at the tip; *svaṁ*: own; *diśaḥ*: directions; *ca*: and; *anavalokayan*: not looking

6.13 Holding the body, head and neck steady, look at the tip of your nose without looking in any other direction.

प्रशान्तात्मा विगतभीर्ब्रह्मचारिव्रते स्थितः ।
मनः संयम्य मच्चित्तो युक्त आसीत मत्परः ॥ ६.१४

praśāntātmā vigatabhīrbrahmacārivrate sthitaḥ |
manaḥ saṁyamya maccitto yukta āsīta matparaḥ || 6.14

praśāntātmā: unagitated mind; *vigatabhīḥ*: free from fear; *brahmachārivrate*: in the vow of living with Existence; *sthitaḥ*: situated; *manaḥ*: mind; *saṁyamya*: controlling; *maccittaḥ*: mind fixed in Me; *yuktaḥ*: balanced; *āsīta*: sit; *matparaḥ*: Me supreme goal

6.14 Sit with an unagitated mind, free from fear and in tune with Existence, controlling the mind, focusing it on Me and make Me the supreme goal.

युञ्जन्नेवं सदात्मानं योगी नियतमानसः ।
शान्तिं निर्वाणपरमां मत्संस्थामधिगच्छति ॥ ६.१५

yuñjannevaṁ sadātmānaṁ yogī niyatamānasaḥ /
śāntiṁ nirvāṇaparamāṁ matsaṁsthāmadhigacchati // 6.15

yuñjan: practicing; *evaṁ*: thus; *sadā*: always; *ātmānaṁ*: Self; *yogī* : yogi; *niyata*: controlled; *mānasaḥ*: mind; *śāntiṁ*: peace; *nirvāṇa*: liberation; *paramāṁ*: supreme; *matsaṁsthāṁ*: My kingdom; *adhigacchati*: attain

6.15 Always practising control over the mind and situated in the Self, the yogi attains peace, the supreme liberation and My kingdom.

नात्यश्नतस्तु योगोऽस्ति न चैकान्तमनश्नतः ।
न चाति स्वप्नशीलस्य जाग्रतो नैव चार्जुन ॥ ६.१६

nātyaśnatastu yogosti na caikāntamanaśnataḥ /
na cāti svapnaśīlasya jāgrato naiva cārjuna // 6.16

na: never; *atyaśnataḥ*: too much eats; *tu*: but; *yogaḥ*: yoga; *asti*: is; *na*: not; *ca*: and; *ekāntaṁ*: on the one side; *anaśnataḥ*: not eat; *na*: not; *ca*: and; *ati*: too much; *svapna śīlasya*: sleep; *jāgrataḥ*: awake; *na*: not; *eva*: also; *ca*: and; *arjuna*: Oh Arjuna

6.16 Yoga is neither eating too much nor eating too little; it is neither sleeping too much nor sleeping too little, Oh Arjuna.

युक्ताहारविहारस्य युक्तचेष्टस्य कर्मसु ।
युक्तस्वप्नावबोधस्य योगो भवति दुःखहा ॥ ६.१७

yuktāhāravihārasya yuktaceṣṭasya karmasu /
yuktasvapnāvabodhasya yogo bhavati duḥkhahā // 6.17

yukta: regulated; *āhāra*: food; *vihārasya*: rest; *yukta*: regulated; *ceṣṭasya*: exertion; *karmasu*: work; *yukta*: regulated; *svapna avabodhasya*: sleep and wakefulness; *yogaḥ*: yoga; *bhavati*: becomes; *duḥkhahā* : reduced misery

6.17 One who is regulated in food, rest, recreation and work, sleep and wakefulness, can reduce misery.

यदा विनियतं चित्तमात्मन्येवावतिष्ठते ।
निःस्पृहः सर्वकामेभ्यो युक्त इत्युच्यते तदा ॥ ६.१८

yadā viniyataṁ cittamātmanyevāvatiṣṭhate |
niḥspṛhaḥ sarvakāmebhyo yukta ityucyate tadā || 6.18

yadā: when; *viniyataṁ*: disciplined; *cittaṁ*: mind; *ātmani*: situated in the Self; *eva*: certainly; *avatiṣṭhate*: situated; *niḥspṛhaḥ*: free of desire; *sarva*: all; *kāmebhyaḥ*: material desires; *yuktaḥ*: situated; *iti*: thus; *ucyate*: said to be; *tadā* : then

6.18 When the mind is disciplined and one is situated in the Self, free from all desires, then one is said to be situated in yoga.

यथा दीपो निवातस्थो नेङ्गते सोपमा स्मृता ।
योगिनो यतचित्तस्य युञ्जतो योगमात्मनः ॥ ६.१९

yathā dīpo nivātastho neṅgate sopamā smṛtā |
yogino yatacittasya yuñjato yogamātmanaḥ || 6.19

yathā: as; *dīpaḥ*: lamp; *nivātasthaḥ*: in a place without wind; *na*: not; *iṅgate*: waver; *sā*: this; *upamā*: comparison; *smṛtā*: is considered; *yoginaḥ*: of the yogi; *yata cittasya*: whose mind is controlled; *yuñjataḥ*: engaged; *yogaṁ*: in yoga; *ātmanaḥ*: in the Self

6.19 As a lamp in a place without wind does not waver, so also the yogi, whose mind is controlled remains steady, engaged in yoga, in the Self.

यत्रोपरमते चित्तं निरुद्धं योगसेवया ।
यत्र चैवात्मनात्मानं पश्यन्नात्मनि तुष्यति ॥ ६.२०

yatroparamate cittaṁ niruddhaṁ yogasevayā |
yatra caivātmanātmānaṁ paśyannātmani tuṣyati || 6.20

yatra: there; *uparamate*: quietened; *cittaṁ*: mind; *niruddhaṁ*: stop; *yoga*: yoga; *sevayā*: work; *yatra*: there; *ca*: and; *eva*: certainly; *ātmanā*: by the Self; *ātmānaṁ*: Self; *paśyan*: seeing; *ātmani*: in the Self; *tuṣyati*: satisfied

6.20 In yoga, the mind becomes quiet and the Self is satisfied by the Self in the Self.

सुखमात्यन्तिकं यत्तद्बुद्धिग्राह्यमतीन्द्रियम् ।
वेत्ति यत्र न चैवायं स्थितश्चलति तत्त्वतः ॥ ६.२१

sukhamātyantikaṁ yattadbuddhigrāhyamatīndriyam |
vetti yatra na caivāyaṁ sthitaścalati tattvataḥ || 6.21

sukhaṁ: happiness; *ātyantikaṁ*: supreme; *yat*: which; *tad*: that; *buddhi*: intelligence; *grāhyaṁ*: grasped; *atīndriyaṁ*: beyond the senses; *vetti*: know; *yatra*: where; *na*: not; *ca*: and; *eva*: certainly; *ayaṁ*: he; *sthitaḥ*: situated; *calati*: moves; *tattvataḥ*: from truth

6.21 Supreme bliss is grasped by intelligence transcending the senses. The person who knows this is based in reality.

यं लब्ध्वा चापरं लाभं मन्यते नाधिकं ततः
यस्मिन्स्थितो न दुःखेन गुरुणापि विचाल्यते ॥ ६.२२

yaṁ labdhvā cāparaṁ lābhaṁ manyate nādhikaṁ tataḥ |
yasminsthito na duḥkhena guruṇāpi vicālyate || 6.22

yaṁ: that which; *labdhvā*: by attaining; *ca*: and; *aparaṁ*: any other; *lābhaṁ*: gain; *manyate*: considers; *na*: not; *adhikaṁ*: more; *tataḥ*: than that; *yasmin*: in which; *sthitaḥ*: situated; *na*: not; *duḥkhena*: by misery; *guruṇā api*: though difficult; *vicālyate*: becomes shaken

6.22 By attaining that Supreme, one does not consider any other gain as being greater. By being situated in the Supreme, one is not shaken by the greatest of misery.

तं विद्याद् दुःखसंयोगवियोगं योगसंज्ञितम् ।
स निश्चयेन योक्तव्यो योगोऽनिर्विण्णचेतसा ॥ ६.२३

taṁ vidyād duḥkhasaṁyogaviyogaṁ yogasaṁjñitam |
sa niścayena yoktavyo yogo'nirviṇṇacetasā || 6.23

taṁ: that; *vidyāt*: know; *duḥkha*: misery; *saṁyoga*: contact; *viyogaṁ*: removal; *yoga*: yoga; *saṁjñitaṁ*: is termed as; *saḥ*: he; *niśchayena*: with determination; *yoktavyaḥ*: practiced; *yogaḥ*; yoga; *anirviṇṇa cetasā*: without deviating

6.23 When yoga is practiced with determination without deviating, the misery by contact with material senses is removed.

सङ्कल्पप्रभवान्कामांस्त्यक्त्वा सर्वानशेषतः
मनसैवेन्द्रियग्रामं विनियम्य समन्ततः ॥ ६.२४

saṅkalpaprabhavānkāmāṁstyaktvā sarvānaśeṣataḥ |
manasaivendriyagrāmaṁ viniyamya samantataḥ || 6.24

saṁkalpa: thought; *prabhavān*: born of; *kāmān*: desires; *tyaktvā*: give up; *sarvān*: all; *aśeṣataḥ*: completely; *manasā*: mind; *eva*: certainly; *indriya grāmaṁ*: all senses; *viniyamya*: regulating; *samantataḥ*: from all sides

6.24 Giving up completely all the fantasies born of the mind, one can regulate all the senses from all the sides by the mind.

शनैः शनैरुपरमेद् बुद्ध्या धृतिगृहीतया ।
आत्मसंस्थं मनः कृत्वा न किञ्चिदपि चिन्तयेत् ॥ ६.२५

śanaiḥ śanairuparamedbuddhyā dhṛtigṛhītayā |
ātmasaṁsthaṁ manaḥ kṛtvā na kiñcidapi cintayet || 6.25

śanaiḥ: gradually; *śanaiḥ*: step by step; *uparamet*: hold; *buddhyā*: by intelligence; *dhṛti gṛhītayā*: held by conviction; *ātma*: Self; *saṁsthaṁ*: established; *manaḥ*: mind; *kṛtvā*: doing; *na*: not; *kiṁcit*: other; *api*: also; *cintayet*: thinking of

6.25 Gradually, step by step, one should become established in the Self, held by the conviction of intelligence, with the mind not thinking of anything else.

यतो यतो निश्चरति मनश्चञ्चलमस्थिरम् ।
ततस्ततो नियम्यैतदात्मन्येव वशं नयेत् ॥ ६.२६

yato yato niścarati manaścañcalamasthiram |
tatastato niyamyaitadātmanyeva vaśaṁ nayet || 6.26

yataḥ-yataḥ: wherever; *niścarati*: becomes agitated; *manaḥ*: mind; *cañcalaṁ*: moving; *asthiraṁ*: not steady; *tataḥ-tataḥ*: there; *niyamya*: control; *etat*: this; *ātmani*: in the Self; *eva*: certainly; *vaśaṁ*: under control; *nayet*: must bring under

6.26 From wherever the mind becomes agitated due to its wandering and unsteady nature, from there, one must certainly bring it under the control of the Self.

प्रशान्तमनसं ह्येनं योगिनं सुखमुत्तमम् ।
उपैति शान्तरजसं ब्रह्मभूतमकल्मषम् ॥ ६.२७

praśāntamanasaṁ hyenaṁ yoginaṁ sukhamuttamam |
upaiti śāntarajasaṁ brahmabhūtamakalmaṣam || 6.27

praśānta: peaceful; *manasaṁ*: mind; *hi*: certainly; *enaṁ*: this; *yoginaṁ*: yogi; *sukhaṁ*: happiness; *uttamaṁ*: highest; *upaiti*: attains; *śānta rajasaṁ*: passion pacified; *brahma bhūtaṁ*: liberated by the Supreme; *akalmaṣaṁ*: free from sins

6.27 The yogi whose mind is peaceful attains the highest happiness; his passion is pacified and he is free from sins as he is liberated by the Supreme.

युञ्जन्नेवं सदात्मानं योगी विगतकल्मषः ।
सुखेन ब्रह्मसंस्पर्शमत्यन्तं सुखमश्नुते ॥ ६.२८

yuñjannevaṁ sadātmānaṁ yogī vigatakalmaṣaḥ |
sukhena brahmasaṁsparśamatyantaṁ sukhamaśnute || 6.28

yuñjan: being engaged; *evaṁ*: in this way; *sadā* : always; *ātmānaṁ*: Self; *yogī* : yogi; *vigata*: free from; *kalmaṣaḥ*: material contamination; *sukhena*: in happiness; *brahma saṁsparśaṁ*: in touch with the Supreme; *atyantaṁ*: highest; *sukhaṁ*: happiness; *aśnute*: attains

6.28 The yogi always engaged in the Self and free from material contamination, is in touch with the Supreme and attains the highest happiness.

सर्वभूतस्थमात्मानं सर्वभूतानि चात्मनि ।
ईक्षते योगयुक्तात्मा सर्वत्र समदर्शनः ॥ ६.२९

sarvabhūtasthamātmānaṁ sarvabhūtāni cātmani |
īkṣate yogayuktātmā sarvatra samadarśanaḥ || 6.29

sarva: all; *bhūta*: living beings; *sthaṁ*: situated; *ātmānaṁ*: Supreme; *sarva*: all; *bhūtāni*: living beings; *ca*: and; *ātmani*: in the Supreme; *īkṣate*: sees; *yoga*: yoga; *yuktātmā*: engaged Self; *sarvatra*: everywhere; *sama*: equal; *darśanaḥ*: seeing

6.29 The yogi sees the Supreme situated in all beings and also all beings situated in the Supreme. One engaged in the Self sees the Supreme everywhere.

यो मां पशयति सर्वत्र सर्वं च मयि पश्यति ।
तस्याहं न प्रणश्यामि स च मे न प्रणश्यति ॥ ६.३०

yo māṁ paśyati sarvatra sarvaṁ ca mayi paśyati |
tasyāhaṁ na praṇaśyāmi sa ca me na praṇaśyati || 6.30

yaḥ: who; *māṁ*: Me; *paśyati*: sees; *sarvatra*: everywhere; *sarvaṁ*: everything; *ca*: and; *mayi*: in Me; *paśyati*: sees; *tasya*: for him; *ahaṁ*: I; *na*: not; *praṇaśyāmi*: lost; *saḥ*: he; *ca*: and; *me*: Me; *na*: not; *praṇaśyati*: lost

6.30 For one who sees Me everywhere and who sees everything in Me, for him I am never lost nor is he lost to Me.

सर्वभूतस्थितं यो मां भजत्येकत्वमास्थितः ।
सर्वथा वर्तमानोऽपि स योगी मयि वर्तते ॥ ६.३१

sarvabhūtasthitaṁ yo māṁ bhajatyekatvamāsthitaḥ I
sarvathā vartamānopi sa yogī mayi vartate II 6.31

sarva: all; *bhūta*: beings; *sthitaṁ*: situated; *yaḥ*: who; *māṁ*: Me; *bhajati*: worships; *ekatvaṁ*: in oneness; *āsthitaḥ*: situated; *sarvathā* : in all respects; *vartamānaḥ*: present; *api*: though; *saḥ*: he; *yogī* : yogi; *mayi* : in Me; *vartate*: remains

6.31 He who is in oneness with Me in all respects, worships Me situated in all beings and remains present in Me.

आत्मौपम्येन सर्वत्र समं पश्यति योऽर्जुन ।
सुखं वा यदि वा दुःखं स योगी परमो मतः ॥ ६.३२

ātmaupamyena sarvatra samaṁ paśyati yorjuna I
sukhaṁ vā yadi vā duḥkhaṁ sa yogī paramo mataḥ II 6.32

ātmaupamyena: self by comparison; *sarvatra*: everywhere; *samaṁ*: equal; *paśyati*: see; *yaḥ*: who; *arjuna*: Oh Arjuna; *sukhaṁ*: happiness; *vā*: or; *yadi*: if; *vā*: or; *duḥkhaṁ*: misery; *saḥ*: such; *yogī* : yogi; *paramaḥ*: supreme; *mataḥ*: opinion

6.32 One who can feel the happiness or misery of others equally as he can feel his own happiness and misery is the supreme yogi in My opinion, Oh Arjuna.

अर्जुन उवाच ।
योऽयं योगस्त्वया प्रोक्तः साम्येन मधुसूदन ।
एतस्याहं न पश्यामि चञ्चलत्वात्स्थितिं स्थिराम् ॥ ६.३३

arjuna uvāca

yoyaṁ yogastvayā proktaḥ sāmyena madhusūdana I
etasyāhaṁ na paśyāmi cañcalatvātsthitiṁ sthirām II 6.33

arjuna uvāca: Arjuna said; *yaḥ*: this; *ayaṁ*: system; *yogaḥ*: yoga; *tvayā* : by You; *proktaḥ*: said; *sāmyena*: generally; *madhusūdana*: O killer of Madhu; *etasya*: of this; *ahaṁ*: I; *na*: not; *paśyāmi*: see; *cañcalatvāt*: due to being restless; *sthitiṁ*: situation; *sthirāṁ*: steady

6.33 Arjuna said: O Madhusūdana, I am not able to see this system of yoga as told by You in the situation of the mind being restless and not steady.

चञ्चलं हि मन: कृष्ण प्रमाथि बलवद्दृढम् ।
तस्याहं निग्रहं मन्ये वायोरिव सुदुष्करम् ॥ ६.३४

cañcalaṁ hi manaḥ kṛṣṇa pramāthī balavad dṛḍham I
tasyāhaṁ nigrahaṁ manye vāyoriva suduṣkaram II 6.34

cañcalaṁ: wavering; *hi*: certainly; *manaḥ*: mind; *kṛṣṇa*: O Kṛṣṇa; *pramāthī*: agitating; *balavat*: strong; *dṛḍhaṁ*: firm; *tasya*: its; *ahaṁ*: I; *nigrahaṁ*: controlling; *manye*: think; *vāyoḥ*: of the wind; *iva*: like; *suduṣkaraṁ*: difficult

6.34 O Kṛṣṇa, the wavering mind is agitating, strong and firm. I think it is difficult to control the mind like it is difficult to control the wind.

श्री भगवानुवाच
असंशयं महाबाहो मनो दुर्निग्रहं चलम् ।
अभ्यासेन तु कौन्तेय वैराग्येण च गृह्यते ॥ ६.३५

śrībhagavānuvāca
asaṁśayaṁ mahābāho mano durnigrahaṁ calam I
abhyāsena tu kaunteya vairāgyeṇa ca gṛhyate II 6.35

śrī bhagavān uvāca: the Lord said; *asaṁśayaṁ*: without doubt; *mahābāho*: O mighty-armed one; *manaḥ*: mind; *durnigrahaṁ*: difficult to control; *calaṁ*: wavering; *abhyāsena*: by practice; *tu*: but; *kaunteya*: O son of Kuntī; *vairāgyeṇa*: by detachment; *ca*: and; *gṛhyate*: is controlled

6.35 The Lord said: O mighty-armed son of Kuntī, it is undoubtedly difficult to control the wavering mind but by practice and detachment, it can be controlled.

असंयतात्मना योगो दुष्प्राप इति मे मति: ।
वश्यात्मना तु यतता शक्योऽवाप्तुमुपायत: ॥ ६.३६

asaṁyatātmanā yogo duṣprāpa iti me matiḥ I
vaśyātmanā tu yatatā śakyovāptumupāyataḥ II 6.36

asaṁyatātmanā: uncontrolled by the mind; *yogaḥ*: yoga; *duṣprāpaḥ*: difficult to attain; *iti*: thus; *me*: My; *matiḥ*: opinion; *vaśyātmanā*: controlled by the mind; *tu*: but; *yatatā*: by one engaged in practise; *śakyaḥ*: practical; *avāptuṁ*: to achieve; *upāyataḥ*: by appropriate means

6.36 For one whose mind is uncontrolled, it is difficult to attain yoga in My opinion. But, it is practical to achieve control over the mind by appropriate means.

अर्जुन उवाच

अयतिः श्रद्धयोपेतो योगाच्चलितमानसः ।

अप्राप्य योगसंसिद्धिं कां गतिं कृष्ण गच्छति ॥ ६.३७

arjuna uvāca

ayatiḥ śraddhayopeto yogāccalitamānasaḥ I

aprāpya yogasaṁsiddhiṁ kāṁ gatiṁ kṛṣṇa gacchati II 6.37

arjuna uvāca: Arjuna said; *ayatiḥ*: the uncontrolled person; *śraddhyā*: with faith; *upetaḥ*: engaged; *yogāt*: from yoga; *calita*: wavered; *mānasaḥ*: mind; *aprāpya*: not getting; *yoga*: yoga; *saṁsiddhiṁ*: achieve; *kāṁ*: which; *gatiṁ*: destination; *kṛṣṇa*: O Kṛṣṇa; *gacchati*: achieve

6.37 Arjuna said: O Kṛṣṇa, if a person is engaged in yoga with faith but does not attain yoga because of the wavering mind, what destination does he achieve

कच्चिन्नोभयविभ्रष्टश्छिन्नाभ्रमिव नश्यति ।

अप्रतिष्ठो महाबाहो विमूढो ब्रह्मणः पथि ॥ ६.३८

kaccinnobhayavibhraṣṭaśchinnābhramiva naśyati I

apratiṣṭho mahābāho vimūḍho brahmaṇaḥ pathi II 6.38

kaccit: whether; *na*: not; *ubhaya*: both; *vibhraṣṭaḥ*: deviated from; *chinna*: torn; *abhraṁ*: cloud; *iva*: like; *naśyati*: perish; *apratiṣṭhaḥ*: without any position; *mahābāho*: O mighty-armed one; *vimūḍhaḥ*: confused; *brahmaṇaḥ*: Supreme; *pathi*: on the path

6.38 O mighty-armed Kṛṣṇa, does the person who deviated from the path perish, torn like a cloud without any position?

एतन्मे संशयं कृष्ण छेत्तुमर्हस्यशेषतः ।

त्वदन्यः संशयस्यास्य छेत्ता न ह्युपपद्यते ॥ ६.३९

etanme saṁśayaṁ kṛṣṇa chettumarhasyaśeṣataḥ I

tvadanyaḥ saṁśayasyāsya chettā na hyupapadyate II 6.39

etat: this; *me*: My; *saṁśayaṁ*: doubt; *kṛṣṇa*: O Kṛṣṇa; *chettuṁ*: dispel; *arhasi*: deserve; *aśeṣataḥ*: completely; *tvat*: than You; *anyaḥ*: another; *saṁśayasya*: of the doubt; *asya*: of this; *chettā* : remover; *na*: not; *hi*: certainly; *upapadyate*: to be found

6.39 This is my doubt, O Kṛṣṇa and I request You to dispel it completely. Certainly, there is no one to be found other than You who can remove this doubt.

श्री भगवानुवाच ।
पार्थ नैवेह नामुत्र विनाशस्तस्य विद्यते ।
न हि कल्याणकृत्कश्चिद् दुर्गतिं तात गच्छति ॥ ६.४०

śrībhagavānuvāca
pārtha naiveha nāmutra vināśastasya vidyate I
na hi kalyāṇakṛtkaściddurgatiṁ tāta gacchati II 6.40

śrī bhagavān uvāca: the Lord said; *pārtha*: O son of Pritā; *na*: not; *eva*: thus; *iha*: in this; *na*: not; *amutra*: in the next life; *vināśaḥ*: destruction; *tasya*: his; *vidyate*: exists; *na*: not; *hi*: certainly; *kalyāṇakṛt*: doing activities for the good; *kaścit*: anyone; *durgatiṁ*: degradation; *tāta*: then; *gacchati*: goes

6.40 The Lord said: O son of Pritā, the person engaged in activities for good does not meet with destruction either in this world or the next life; he never faces degradation.

प्राप्य पुण्यकृतां लोकानुषित्वा शाश्वती: समा: ।
शुचीनां श्रीमतां गेहे योगभ्रष्टोऽभिजायते ॥ ६.४१

prāpya puṇyakṛtāṁ lokānuṣitvā śāśvatiḥ samāḥ I
śucīnāṁ śrī matāṁ gehe yogabhraṣṭo'bhijāyate II 6.41

prāpya: after achieving; *puṇyakṛtāṁ*: one who has done virtuous deeds; *lokān*: worlds; *uṣitvā* : after living; *śāśvatīḥ*: many; *samāḥ*: years; *śucīnāṁ*: of the virtuous; *śrī matāṁ*: of the prosperous; *gehe*: in the house; *yoga bhraṣṭaḥ*: one who has fallen from yoga; *abhijāyate*: takes birth

6.41 The person who has fallen from yoga after many years of living in the world and doing virtuous deeds takes birth in the house of the virtuous and prosperous.

अथवा योगिनामेव कुले भवति धीमताम् ।
एतद्धि दुर्लभतरं लोके जन्म यदीदृशम् ॥ ६.४२

athavā yogināmeva kule bhavati dhī matām I
etaddhi durlabhataraṁ loke janma yadīdṛśam II 6.42

athavā : or; *yogināṁ*: yogis'; *eva*: certainly; *kule*: in the family; *bhavati*: becomes; *dhīmatāṁ*: wise; *etat*: this; *hi*: certainly; *durlabhataraṁ*: rare; *loke*: in the world; *janma*: birth; *yat*: which; *īdṛśaṁ*: like this

6.42 Or the yogi certainly takes birth in a family of wise people. Certainly, such a birth is rare in this world.

तत्र तं बुद्धिसंयोगं लभते पौर्वदेहिकम् ।
यतते च ततो भूयः संसिद्धौ कुरुनन्दन ॥ ६.४३

tatra taṁ buddhisaṁyogaṁ labhate paurva dehikam |
yatate ca tato bhūyaḥ saṁsiddhau kurunandana || 6.43

tatra: then; *taṁ*: that; *buddhi*: intelligence; *saṁyogaṁ*: united with; *labhate*: gains; *paurva*: previous; *dehikaṁ*: body; *yatate*: try; *ca*: and; *tataḥ*: then; *bhūyaḥ*: again; *saṁsiddhau*: for attaining; *kuru nandana*: O son of Kuru

6.43 O son of Kuru, on taking such a birth, the person gains the intelligence of the previous body and tries again to attain yoga.

पूर्वाभ्यासेन तेनैव ह्रियते ह्यवशोऽपि सः ।
जिज्ञासुरपि योगस्य शब्दब्रह्मातिवर्तते ॥ ६.४४

pūrvābhyāsena tenaiva hriyate hyavaśo'pi saḥ |
jijñāsurapi yogasya śabdabrahmātivartate || 6.44

pūrva: previous; *abhyāsena*: by practice; *tena*: by that; *eva*: certainly; *hriyate*: is attracted; *hi*: certainly; *avaśaḥ*: automatically; *api*: also; *saḥ*: he; *jijñāsuḥ*: inquisitive; *api*: also; *yogasya*: about yoga; *śabda brahma*: scriptures; *ativartate*: transcends

6.44 Due to the practice in his previous life, he certainly gets attracted automatically to yoga and he is inquisitive about yoga and transcends the scriptures.

प्रयत्नाद्यतमानस्तु योगी संशुद्धकिल्बिषः ।
अनेकजन्मसंसिद्धस्ततो याति परां गतिम् ॥ ६.४५

prayatnādyatamānastu yogī saṁśuddhakilbiṣaḥ |
anekajanmasaṁsiddhastato yāti parāṁ gatim || 6.45

prayatnāt: by trying; *yatamānaḥ*: endeavor; *tu*: and; *yogī*: yogi; *saṁśuddha*: cleaned; *kilbiṣaḥ*: sins; *aneka*: many; *janma*: births; *saṁsiddhaḥ*: achieved; *tataḥ*: then; *yāti*: achieves; *paraṁ*: highest; *gatiṁ*: state

6.45 A yogi by trying and practicing, after many births, is cleaned of all sins and achieves the highest state.

तपस्विभ्योऽधिको योगी ज्ञानिभ्योऽपि मतोऽधिकः ।
कर्मिभ्यश्चाधिको योगी तस्माद्योगी भवार्जुन ॥ ६.४६

tapasvibhyodhiko yogī jñānibhyo'pi mato 'dhikaḥ I
karmibhyaścādhiko yogī tasmādyogī bhavārjuna II 6.46

tapasvibhyaḥ: than the ascetic; *adhikaḥ*: greater; *yogī* : yogi; *jñānibhyoḥ*: than the wise; *api*: also; *mataḥ*: opinion; *adhikaḥ*: greater; *karmibhyaḥ*: than person who works for the fruit of action; *ca*: and; *adhikaḥ*: greater; *yogī* : yogi; *tasmāt*: so; *yogī* : yogi; *bhava*: become; *arjuna*: O Arjuna

6.46 A yogi is greater than the ascetic, than the wise and the person who works for the fruit of the action. So, become a yogi, O Arjuna.

योगिनामपि सर्वेषां मद्गतेनान्तरात्मना ।
श्रद्धावान्भजते यो मां स मे युक्ततमो मतः ॥ ६.४७

yogināmapi sarveṣāṁ madgatenāntarātmanā I
śraddhāvān bhajate yo māṁ sa me yuktatamo mataḥ II 6.47

yogināṁ: yogis; *api*: also; *sarveṣāṁ*: all kinds of; *madgatena*: living in Me; *antarātmanā*: thinking of Me; *śraddhāvān*: in full faith; *bhajate*: worship; *yaḥ*: who; *māṁ*: Me; *saḥ*: he; *me*: Me; *yuktatamaḥ*: engaged; *mataḥ*: opinion

6.47 Of all yogis, one who always lives in Me, thinking of Me, who worships Me in full faith, he is considered engaged in Me.

इति श्रीमद्भगवद्गीतासूपनिषत्सु ब्रह्मविद्यायां योगशास्त्रे
श्रीकृष्णार्जुनसंवादे ध्यानयोगो नाम षष्ठोऽध्यायः ॥ २

iti śrīmad bhagavadgītāsūpaniṣatsu brahmavidyāyām
yogaśāstre śrīkṛṣṇārjuna saṁvāde dhyānayogo nāma
ṣaṣtho'dhyāyaḥ II

In the Upaniṣad *of the Bhagavad Gītā, the knowledge of* Brahman, *the Supreme, the science of Yoga and the dialogue between Śrī Kṛṣṇa and Arjuna, this is the sixth discourse designated:*

Dhyāna Yogaḥ

Verses Of Gita Chapter - 7

अथ सप्तमोऽध्याय:

ज्ञानविज्ञानयोग:

Jñānavijñāna Yogaḥ

श्री भगवानुवाच।
मय्यासक्तमना: पार्थ योगं युञ्जन्मदाश्रय: ।
असंशयं समग्रं मां यथा ज्ञास्यसि तच्छृणु ॥७.१

śrībhagavānuvāca
mayyāsaktamanāḥ pārtha yogaṁ yuñjanmadāśrayaḥ I
asaṁśayaṁ samagraṁ māṁ yathā jñāsyasi tacchṛṇu II 7.1

śrībhagavānuvāca: Kṛṣṇa said; *mayi*: in Me; *āsaktamanāḥ*: mind attached; *pārtha*: Arjuna, O son of Pritā; *yogaṁ*: union; *yuñjan*: so practising; *madāśrayaḥ*: in My shelter; *asaṁśayaṁ*: without doubt; *samagraṁ*: completely; *māṁ*: to Me; *yathā*: how, in what manner; *jñāsyasi*: you can know; *tat*: that; *śṛṇu*: hear

7.1 Kṛṣṇa says, Arjuna, Listen to Me, you can know Me completely and without doubt by practicing yoga in true consciousness of Me, with your mind attached to Me.

ज्ञानं तेऽहं सविज्ञानमिदं वक्ष्याम्यशेषत: ।
यज्ज्ञात्वा नेह भूयोऽन्यज्ज्ञातव्यमवशिष्यते ॥७.२

jñānaṁ te'haṁ savijñānamidaṁ vakṣyāmyaśeṣataḥ I
yajjñātvā neha bhūyo'nyajjñātavyamavaśiṣyate II 7.2

jñānaṁ: phenomenal knowledge; *te*: unto you; *ahaṁ*: I; *sa*: with; *vijñānaṁ*: absolute knowledge; *idaṁ*: this; *vakṣyāmi*: shall explain; *aśeṣataḥ*: in full; *yat*: which; *jñātvā*: knowing; *na*: not; *iha*: in this world; *bhūyaḥ*: further; *anyat*: anything more; *jñātavyaṁ*: knowable; *avaśiṣyate*: remains to be known

7.2 Let Me explain to you in detail this phenomenal and absolute knowledge along with its realization; by knowing which, there shall remain nothing further to be known.

मनुष्याणां सहस्रेषु कश्चिद्यतति सिद्धये ।
यततामपि सिद्धानां कश्चिन्मां वेत्ति तत्त्वत: ॥ ७.३

manuṣyāṇāṁ sahasreṣu kaścidyatati siddhaye ।
yatatāmapi siddhānāṁ kaścinmāṁ vetti tattvataḥ ॥ 7.3

manuṣyāṇāṁ: of men; *sahasreṣu*: out of many thousands; *kaścit*: hardly one; *yatati*: endeavors; *siddhaye*: for perfection of self-realization; *yatatāṁ*: of those so endeavoring; *api*: indeed; *siddhānāṁ*: of those who have achieved perfection; *kaścit*: hardly one; *māṁ*: Me; *vetti*: does know; *tattvataḥ*: in truth

7.3 Out of many thousands of men, hardly one endeavors or strives to achieve perfection of self-realization; of those so endeavoring, hardly one achieves the perfection of self-realization and of those, hardly one knows Me in truth or reaches that state of oneness with Me.

भूमिरापोऽनलो वायु: खं मनो बुद्धिरेव च ।
अहंङ्कार इतीयं मे भिन्ना प्रकृतिरष्टधा ॥ ७.४

bhūmirāpo'nalo vāyuḥ khaṁ mano buddhireva ca ।
ahankāra itīyaṁ me bhinnā prakṛtiraṣṭadhā ॥ 7.4

bhūmiḥ: earth; *āpaḥ*: water; *analah*: fire; *vāyuḥ*: air; *khaṁ*: ether; *manaḥ*: mind; *buddhiḥ*: intelligence; *eva*: certainly; *ca*: and; *ahaṁkāraḥ*: ego; *iti*: thus; *iyaṁ*: all these; *me*: My; *bhinnā*: separated, various; *prakṛtiḥ*: external energies; *aṣṭadhā*: total eight

7.4 Earth, water, fire, air, ether, mind, intelligence and false ego all together these eight constitute My separated external energies.

अपरेयमितस्त्वन्यां प्रकृतिं विद्धि मे पराम् ।
जीवभूतां महाबाहो ययेदं धार्यते जगत् ॥ ७.५

apare'yamitastvanyāṁ prakṛtiṁ viddhi me parām ।
jīvabhūtāṁ mahābāho yayedaṁ dhāryate jagat ॥ 7.5

aparā: inferior; *iyaṁ*: this; *itaḥ*: besides this; *tu*: but; *anyāṁ*: another; *prakṛtiṁ*: energy; *viddhi*: understand; *me*: my; *parāṁ*: superior; *jīvabhūtāṁ*: the living entities; *mahā-bāho*: O mighty armed one; *yayā*: by whom; *idaṁ*: this; *dhāryate*: bearing; *jagat*: the material world

7.5 Besides these external energies, which are inferior in nature, O mighty-armed Arjuna, there is a superior energy of Mine. This comprises all the embodied souls of all the living entities by which this material world is being utilized or exploited.

एतद्योनीनि भूतानि सर्वाणीत्युपधारय ।
अहं कृत्स्नस्य जगतः प्रभवः प्रलयस्तथा ॥ ७.६

etadyonīni bhūtāni sarvāṇītyupadhāraya /
ahaṁ kṛtsnasya jagataḥ prabhavaḥ pralayastathā // 7.6

etad: these two natures; *yonīni*: source of birth; *bhūtāni*: everything created; *sarvāṇī*: all; *iti*: thus; *upadhāraya*: know; *ahaṁ*: I; *kṛtsnasya*: all-inclusive; *jagataḥ*: of the world; *prabhavaḥ*: source of manifestation; *pralayaḥ*: annihilation; *tathā*: as well as

7.6 Know for certain that everything living is manifested by these two energies of Mine. I am the Creator, the Sustainer and the Destroyer of them.

मत्तः परतरं नान्यत्किञ्चिदस्ति धनञ्जय ।
मयि सर्वमिदं प्रोतं सूत्रे मणिगणा इव ॥ ७.७

mattaḥ parataraṁ nānyatkiñcidasti dhanañjaya /
mayi sarvamidaṁ protaṁ sūtre maṇigaṇā iva // 7.7

mattaḥ: beyond Myself; *parataraṁ*: superior; *na*: not; *anyat kiñcit*: anything else; *asti*: there is; *dhanañjaya*: O conqueror of wealth; *mayi*: in Me; *sarvaṁ*: all that be; *idaṁ*: which we see; *protaṁ*: strung; *sūtre*: on a thread; *maṇigaṇāḥ*: pearls; *iva*: likened

7.7 O conqueror of wealth [Arjuna], there is no truth superior to Me. Everything hangs upon Me, as pearls are strung on a thread.

रसोऽहमप्सु कौन्तेय प्रभास्मि शशिसूर्ययोः ।
प्रणवः सर्ववेदेषु शब्दः खे पौरुषं नृषु ॥ ७.८

raso'hamapsu kaunteya prabhāsmi śaśisūryayoḥ /
praṇavaḥ sarvavedeṣu śabdaḥ khe pauruṣaṁ nṛṣu // 7.8

rasaḥ: taste; *ahaṁ*: I; *apsu*: in water; *kaunteya*: O son of Kuntī; *prabhā*: light; *asmi:* I am; *śaśisūryayoḥ*: in the sun and the moon; *praṇavaḥ*: the letters a-u-m; *sarva*: in all; *vedeṣu*: in the Vedas; *śabdaḥ*: sound vibration; *khe*: in the ether; *pauruṣaṁ*: virility, manliness; *nṛṣu*: in man

7.8 O son of Kuntī [Arjuna], I am the taste of water, the radiance of the sun and the moon, the sacred syllable 'Om' in the vedic mantras. *I am the sound in ether and ability in man.*

पुण्यो गन्धः पृथिव्यां च तेजश्चास्मि विभावसौ ।
जीवनं सर्वभूतेषु तपश्चास्मि तपस्विषु ॥ ७.९

puṇyo gandhaḥ pṛthivyāṁ ca tejaścāsmi vibhāvasau |
jīvanaṁ sarvabhūteṣu tapaścāsmi tapasviṣu || 7.9

puṇyaḥ: original; *gandhaḥ*: fragrance; *pṛthivyām*: in the earth; *ca*: also; *tejaḥ*: temperature; *ca*: also; *asmi*: I am; *vibhāvasau*: in the fire; *jīvanaṁ*: life; *sarva*: all; *bhūteṣu*: living entities; *tapaḥ*: penance; *ca*: also; *asmi*: I am; *tapasviṣu*: in those who practice penance.

7.9 I am the original fragrance of the earth, and I am the heat in fire. I am the life of all living beings, and I am the penances of all ascetics.

बीजं मां सर्वभूतानां विद्धि पार्थ सनातनम् ।
बुद्धिर्बुद्धिमतामस्मि तेजस्तेजस्विनामहम् ॥ ७.१०

bījaṁ māṁ sarvabhūtānāṁ viddhi pārtha sanātanam |
buddhirbuddhimatāmasmi tejastejasvināmaham || 7.10

bī jaṁ: the seed; *māṁ*: Me; *sarvabhūtānāṁ*: of all living entities; *viddhi*: understand; *pārtha*: O son of Pritā; *sanātanaṁ*: original, eternal; *buddhiḥ*: intelligence; *buddhimatāṁ*: of the intelligent; *asmi*: I am; *tejaḥ*: prowess; *tejasvināṁ*: of the powerful; *ahaṁ*: I am

7.10 O son of Pritā, I am the eternal source of all creatures, the intelligence of the intelligent, and the brilliance of all those who are brilliant.

बलं बलवतां चाहं कामरागविवर्जितम् ।
धर्माविरुद्धो भूतेषु कामोऽस्मि भरतर्षभ ॥ ७.११

balaṁ balavatāṁ cāhaṁ kāmarāgavivarjitaṁ |
dharmāviruddho bhūteṣu kāmo'smi bharatarṣabha || 7.11

balaṁ: strength; *balavatāṁ*: of the strong; *cāham*: I am; *kāma*: desire; *rāga*: attachment; *vivarjitaṁ*: devoid of; *dharma:* religious principle; *aviruddhaḥ*: not against the religious principles; *bhūteṣu*: in all beings; *kāmaḥ*: lust; *asmi*: I am; *Bhārata ṛṣabha*: O Lord of the Bhāratas

7.11 I am the strength of the strong, and I am procreative energy in living beings, devoid of lust and in accordance with religious principles, O Lord of the Bhārata.

ये चैव सात्त्विका भावा राजसास्तामसाश्च ये ।
मत्त एवेति तान्विद्धि न त्वहं तेषु ते मयि ॥७.१२

ye caiva sāttvikā bhāvā rājasāstāmasāśca ye |
matta eveti tānviddhi na tvahaṁ teṣu te mayi || 7.12

ye: all those; *ca*: and; *eva*: certainly; *sāttvikāḥ*: in goodness; *bhāvāḥ*: states of being; *rājasāḥ*: mode of passion; *tāmasāḥ*: mode of ignorance; *ca*: and; *ye*: although; *mattaḥ*: from Me; *eva*: certainly; *iti*: thus; *tān*: those; *viddhi*: try to know; *na*: not; *tu*: but; *ahaṁ*: I; *teṣu*: in those; *te*: they; *mayi*: unto Me

7.12 All states of being - be they of goodness, passion or ignorance - all emanate from Me. I am independent of them but they are dependent on Me.

त्रिभिर्गुणमयैर्भावैरेभिः सर्वमिदं जगत् ।
मोहितं नाभिजानाति मामेभ्यः परमव्ययम् ॥७.१३

tribhirguṇamayairbhāvairebhiḥ sarvamidaṁ jagat |
mohitaṁ nābhijānāti māmebhyaḥ paramavyayam || 7.13

tribhiḥ: three; *guṇamayaiḥ*: by the three gunas; *bhāvaiḥ*: state of being; *ebhiḥ*: all these; *sarvaṁ*: the whole world; *idaṁ*: this; *jagat*: universe; *mohitaṁ*: deluded; *nābhijānāti*: do not know; *māṁ*: Me; *ebhyaḥ*: above these; *paraṁ*: the Supreme; *avyayaṁ*: immutable

7.13 The whole world is deluded by the three modes (goodness, passion and ignorance), and thus does not know Me. I am above the modes and unchangeable

दैवी ह्येषा गुणमयी मम माया दुरत्यया ।
मामेव ये प्रपद्यन्ते मायामेतां तरन्ति ते ॥७.१४

daivī hyeṣā guṇamayī mama māyā duratyayā |
māmeva ye prapadyante māyāmetām taranti te || 7.14

daivī: transcendental; *hi*: certainly; *eṣā*: this; *guṇamayī*: consisting of the three modes of material nature; *mama*: My; *māyā*: energy; *duratyayā*: very difficult to overcome; *māṁ*: unto Me; *eva*: certainly; *ye*: those; *prapadyante*: surrender; *māyāmetāṁ*: this illusory energy; *taranti*: overcome; *te*: they

7.14 My divine energy, consisting of the three modes of material nature, is difficult to overcome. But those who surrender unto Me can cross beyond it with ease.

न मां दुष्कृतिनो मूढाः प्रपद्यन्ते नराधमाः ।
माययापहृतज्ञाना आसुरं भावमाश्रिताः ॥ ७.१५

na māṁ duṣkṛ tino mūḍhāḥ prapadyante narādhamāḥ /
māyayāpahṛtajñānā āsuraṁ bhāvamāśritāḥ // 7.15

na: not; *māṁ*: unto Me; *duṣkṛtinaḥ*: miscreants; *mūḍhāḥ*: foolish; *prapadyante*: surrender; *nara adhamāḥ*: lowest among mankind; *māyayā* : by the illusory energy; *apahṛta*: stolen by illusion; *jñānāḥ*: knowledge; *āsuraṁ*: demonic; *bhāvaṁ*: nature; *āśritāḥ*: accepting.

7.15 Those miscreants who are foolish, lowest among mankind, whose knowledge is stolen by māyā *(that which is not real), and who have taken shelter in demonic nature, do not surrender unto Me.*

चतुर्विधा भजन्ते मां जनाः सुकृतिनोऽर्जुन ।
आर्तो जिज्ञासुरर्थार्थी ज्ञानी च भरतर्षभ ॥ ७.१६

caturvidhā bhajante māṁ janāḥ sukṛtino'rjuna /
ārto jijñāsurarthārthī jñānī ca bharatarṣabha // 7.16

caturvidhāḥ: four kinds of; *bhajante*: render services; *māṁ*: unto Me; *janāḥ*: persons; *sukṛtinaḥ*: those who are pious; *arjuna*: O Arjuna; *ārtaḥ*: the distressed; *jijñāsuḥ*: the inquisitive; *arthārthī* : one who desires material gain; *jñānī*: one who knows things as they are; *ca*: also; *bharatarṣabha*: O great one amongst the descendants of Bhārata.

7.16 O best among the Bhārata, four kinds of pious men begin to render devotional service unto Me. They are: the distressed, the desirer of wealth, the inquisitive, and those searching for knowledge of the Absolute.

तेषां ज्ञानी नित्ययुक्त एकभक्तिर्विशिष्यते ।
प्रियो हि ज्ञानिनोऽत्यर्थमहं स च मम प्रियः ॥ ७.१७

teṣāṁ jñānī nityayukta ekabhaktirviśiṣyate /
priyo hi jñānino'tyarthamahaṁ sa ca mama priyaḥ // 7.17

teṣāṁ: of them; *jñānī*: the wise; *nityayuktaḥ*: ever steadfast; *eka bhaktiḥ*: whose devotion is to the one; *viśiṣyate*: better; *priyaḥ*: dear; *hi*: verily; *jñāninaḥ*: of the wise; *atyarthaṁ*: exceedingly; *ahaṁ*: I; *saḥ*: he; *ca*: and; *mama*: to me; *priyaḥ*: dear

7.17 Of these, the wise one who is in full knowledge and ever united with Me through single-minded devotion is the best. I am very dear to him, and he is dear to Me

उदाराः सर्व एवैते ज्ञानीत्वात्मैव मे मतम् ।
आस्थितः स हि युक्तात्मा मामेवानुत्तमां गतिम् ॥७.१८

udārāḥ sarva evaite jñānītvātmaiva me matam /
āsthitaḥ sa hi yuktātmā māmevānuttamāṁ gatim // 7.18

udārāḥ: noble; *sarve*: all; *eva*: certainly; *ete*: these; *jñānī*: one who is in knowledge; *tu*: but; *ātmā eva*: just like Myself; *me*: My; *mataṁ*: opinion; *āsthitaḥ*: situated; *saḥ*: he; *hi*: certainly; *yuktātmā*: engaged in devotional service; *māṁ*: unto Me; *eva*: certainly; *anuttamāṁ*: the highest goal; *gatiṁ*: destination

7.18 All these devotees are indeed noble; one who knows Me, dwells in Me. Being engaged in My mission, he attains Me.

बहूनां जन्मनामन्ते ज्ञानवान्मां प्रपद्यते ।
वासुदेवः सर्वमिति स महात्मा सुदुर्लभः ॥७.१९

bahūnāṁ janmanāmante jñānavānmāṁ prapadyate /
vāsudevaḥ sarvamiti sa mahātmā sudurlabhaḥ // 7.19

bahūnāṁ: many; *janmanāṁ*: births; *ante*: after; *jñānavān*: he possessing knowledge; *māṁ*: unto Me; *prapadyate*: surrenders; *vāsudevaḥ*: cause of all causes; *sarvaṁ*: all; *iti*: thus; *saḥ*: such; *mahātmā* : great soul; *sudurlabhaḥ*: very rare.

7.19 After many births and deaths, he who knows Me surrenders to Me, knowing Me to be the cause of all causes and all that is. Such a great soul is very rare.

कामैस्तैस्तैर्हृतज्ञानाः प्रपद्यन्तेऽन्यदेवताः ।
तं तं नियममास्थाय प्रकृत्या नियताः स्वया ॥७.२०

kāmaistaistairhṛtajñānāḥ prapadyante'nyadevatāḥ /
taṁ taṁ niyamamāsthāya prakṛtyā niyatāḥ svayā // 7.20

kāmaiḥ: by desires; *taiḥ*: by those; *taiḥ*: by those; *hṛta*: distorted; *jñānāḥ*: knowledge; *prapadyante*: surrender; *anya*: other; *devatāḥ*: deities; *taṁ-taṁ*: that; *niyamaṁ*: rules; *āsthāya*: following; *prakṛtyā*: by nature; *niyatāḥ*: controlled; *svayā*: by their own.

7.20 Those whose discrimination has been distorted by various desires, surrender unto deities. They follow specific rules and regulations of worship according to their own nature.

यो यो यां यां तनुं भक्तः श्रद्धयार्चितुमिच्छति ।
तस्य तस्याचलां श्रद्धां तामेव विदधाम्यहम् ॥ ७.२१

yo yo yāṁ yāṁ tanuṁ bhaktaḥ śraddhayārcitumicchati |
tasya tasyācalāṁ śraddhāṁ tāmeva vidadhāmyaham || 7.21

yaḥ: that; *yaḥ*: that; *yāṁ*: which; *yāṁ*: which; *tanuṁ*: form of the deities; *bhaktaḥ*: devotee; *śraddhayā*: with faith; *arcituṁ*: to worship; *icchati*: desires; *tasya*: of that; *tasya*: of that; *acalāṁ*: steady; *śraddhāṁ*: faith; *tāṁ*: him; *eva*: surely; *vidadhāmi*: give; *ahaṁ*: I

7.21 I am in everyone's heart as the super soul. As soon as one desires to worship some deity, I make his faith steady so that he can devote himself to that particular deity.

स तया श्रद्धया युक्तस्तस्याराधनमीहते ।
लभते च ततः कामान्मयैवविहितान्हि तान् ॥ ७.२२

sa tayā śraddhayā yuktastasyārādhanamīhate |
labhate ca tataḥ kāmānmayaiva vihitānhi tān || 7.22

saḥ: he; *tayā*: with that; *śraddhayā*: with faith; *yuktaḥ*: endowed; *tasya*: his; *ārādhanaṁ*: worship; *īhate*: endeavors; *labhate*: obtains; *ca*: and; *tataḥ*: from that; *kāmān*: desires; *mayā*: by Me; *eva*: alone; *vihitān*: bestowed; *hi*: for; *tān*: those.

7.22 Endowed with such a faith, he endeavors to worship a particular demigod and obtains his desires; In reality, these benefits are granted by Me alone.

अन्तवत्तु फलं तेषां तद्भवत्यल्पमेधसाम् ।
देवान्देवयजो यान्ति मद्भक्ता यान्ति मामपि ॥ ७.२३

antavattu phalaṁ teṣāṁ tadbhavatyalpamedhasām |
devāndevayajo yānti madbhaktā yānti māmapi || 7.23

antavat tu: limited and temporary; *phalaṁ*: fruits; *teṣāṁ*: their; *tat*: that; *bhavati*: becomes; *alpa medhasāṁ*: of those of small intelligence; *devān*: demigods' planets; *devayajaḥ*: worshipers of demigods; *yānti*: achieve; *mad*: My; *bhaktāḥ*: devotees; *yānti*: attain; *māṁ*: to Me; *api*: surely

7.23 Men of limited intelligence worship the demigods and their fruits are limited and temporary. Those who worship the demigods go only to the planets of the demigods, but My devotees reach My supreme planet.

अव्यक्तं व्यक्तिमापन्नं मन्यन्ते मामबुद्धयः ।
परं भावमजानन्तो ममाव्ययमनुत्तमम् ॥७.२४

avyaktaṁ vyaktimāpannaṁ manyante māmabuddhayaḥ I
paraṁ bhāvamajānanto mamāvyayamanuttamam II 7.24

avyaktaṁ: nonmanifested; *vyaktiṁ*: personality; *āpannaṁ*: achieved; *manyante*: think; *māṁ*: unto Me; *abuddhayaḥ*: less intelligent persons; *paraṁ*: supreme; *bhāvaṁ*: state of being; *ajānantaḥ*: without knowing; *mama*: My; *avyayaṁ*: imperishable; *anuttamaṁ*: the finest.

7.24 Unintelligent men, who do not know Me perfectly, think that I, the supreme personality of godhead, the Bhagavān, *who was impersonal before, have become a human being now. They do not know that I am imperishable and supreme, even when I assume the body.*

नाहं प्रकाशः सर्वस्य योगमायासमावृतः ।
मूढोऽयं नाभिजानाति लोको मामजमव्ययम् ॥७.२५

nāhaṁ prakāśaḥ sarvasya yogamāyāsamāvṛtaḥ I
mūḍhoyaṁ nābhijānāti loko māmajamavyayam II 7.25

na: nor; *ahaṁ*: I; *prakāśaḥ*: manifest; *sarvasya*: to everyone; *yoga māyā*: internal potency; *samāvṛtaḥ*: covered; *mūḍhaḥ*: foolish; *ayaṁ*: this; *na*: not; *abhijānāti*: can understand; *lokaḥ*: such less intelligent persons; *māṁ*: Me; *ajaṁ*: unborn; *avyayaṁ*: immutable.

7.25 I am never revealed to the foolish and unintelligent, covered as I am by My divine power ; the ignorant do not know Me, unborn and eternal.

वेदाहं समतीतानि वर्तमानानि चाऽर्जुन ।
भविष्याणि च भूतानि मां तु वेद न कश्चन ॥७.२६

vedāhaṁ samatītāni vartamānāni cārjuna I
bhaviṣyāṇi ca bhūtāni māṁ tu veda na kaścana II 7.26

veda: know; *ahaṁ*: I; *sama*: equally; *atītāni*: past; *vartamānāni*: present; *ca*: and; *arjuna*: O Arjuna; *bhaviṣyāṇi*: future; *ca*: also; *bhūtāni*: living entities; *māṁ*: Me; *tu*: but; *veda*: knows; *na*: not; *kaścana*: anyone

7.26 O Arjuna, as the supreme personality of Godhead, I know all that has happened, all that is happening, and all that is to happen. I also know all living entities; but no one knows Me.

इच्छाद्वेषसमुत्थेन द्वन्द्वमोहेन भारत ।
सर्वभूतानि संमोहं सर्गे यान्ति परन्तप ॥ ७.२७

icchādveṣasamutthena dvandvamohena bhārata ।
sarvabhūtāni sammohaṁ sarge yānti parantapa ॥ 7.27

icchā: desire; *dveṣa*: hate; *samutthena*: born; *dvandva*: duality; *mohena*: overcome; *bhārata*: O scion of Bhārata; *sarva*: all; *bhūtāni*: living entities; *sammohaṁ*: into delusion; *sarge*: in creation; *yānti*: go; *parantapa*: O conqueror of enemies.

7.27 O scion of Bhārata [Arjuna], O conqueror of the foe, all living entities are born into delusion, overcome by the dualities of attachment and aversion.

येषां त्वन्तगतं पापं जनानां पुण्यकर्मणाम् ।
ते द्वन्द्वमोहनिर्मुक्ता भजन्ते मां दृढव्रताः ॥ ७.२८

yeṣāṁ tvantagataṁ pāpaṁ janānāṁ puṇyakarmaṇām ।
te dvandvamohanirmuktā bhajante māṁ dṛḍhavratāḥ ॥ 7.28

yeṣāṁ: whose; *tu*: but; *antagataṁ*: completely eradicated; *pāpaṁ*: sin; *janānāṁ*: of the persons; *puṇya*: pious; *karmaṇāṁ*: previous activities; *te*: they; *dvandva*: duality; *moha*: delusion; *nirmuktāḥ*: free from; *bhajante*: worship; *māṁ*: Me; *dṛḍhavratāḥ*: with determination.

7.28 Persons who have acted virtuously, whose sinful actions are completely eradicated and who are freed from the duality of reality and unreality, engage themselves in My worship with firm resolve.

जरामरणमोक्षाय मामाश्रित्य यतन्ति ये ।
ते ब्रह्म तद्विदुः कृत्स्नमध्यात्मं कर्म चाखिलम् ॥ ७.२९

jarāmaraṇa mokṣāya māmāśritya yatanti ye ।
te brahma tadviduḥ kṛtsnamadhyātmaṁ karma cākhilam ॥ 7.29

jarā: old age; *maraṇa*: death; *mokṣāya*: for the purpose of liberation; *māṁ*: unto Me; *āśritya*: taking shelter of; *yatanti*: endeavor; *ye*: all those; *te*: such persons; *brahma*: Brahman; *tat*: actually that; *viduḥ*: they know; *kṛtsnaṁ*: everything; *adhyātmaṁ*: transcendental; *karma*: activities; *ca*: and; *akhilaṁ*: entirely

7.29 Persons who are striving for liberation from the cycle of birth, old age and death, take refuge in Me. They are actually Brahman *because they comprehend everything about activities that transcend these.*

साधिभूताधिदैवं मां साधियज्ञं च ये विदुः ।
प्रयाणकालेऽपि च मां ते विदुर्युक्तचेतसः ॥ ७.३०

sādhibhūtādhidaivaṁ māṁ sādhiyajñaṁ ca ye viduḥ **/**
prayāṇakāle 'pi ca māṁ te vidur yuktacetasaḥ **//** 7.30

sādhibhūta: the governing principle of the material manifestation; *adhidaivaṁ*: underlying all the demigods; *māṁ*: Me; *sādhiyajñaṁ*: sustaining all sacrifices; *ca*: and; *ye*: those; *viduḥ*: know; *prayāṇa*: of death; *kāle*: at the time; *api*: even; *ca*: and; *māṁ*: Me; *te*: they; *viduḥ*: know; *yukta cetasaḥ*: with steadfast minds.

7.30 Those who know Me as the Supreme Lord, as the governing principle of the material manifestation, who know Me as the one underlying all the demigods and as the one sustaining all sacrifices, can with steadfast mind, understand and know Me, even at the time of death.

इति श्रीमद्भगवद्गीतासूपनिषत्सु ब्रह्मविद्यायां योगशास्त्रे
श्रीकृष्णार्जुनसंवादे ज्ञानविज्ञानयोगो नाम सप्तमोऽध्यायः ॥ २

iti śrīmad bhagavadgītāsūpaniṣatsu brahmavidyāyāṁ
yogaśāstre śrīkṛṣṇārjuna saṁvāde jñānavijñāna yogo nāma
saptamo'dhyāyaḥ **//**

In the Upaniṣad *of the Bhagavad Gītā, the knowledge of* Brahman, *the Supreme, the science of Yoga and the dialogue between Śrī Kṛṣṇa and Arjuna, this is the seventh discourse designated:*

Jñānavijñāna Yogaḥ

Verses Of Gita Chapter - 8

अथ अष्टमोऽध्याय:

अक्षरब्रह्मयोग:

Akṣarabrahma Yogaḥ

अर्जुन उवाच ।
किं तद् ब्रह्म किमध्यात्मं किं कर्म पुरुषोत्तम ।
अधिभूतं च किं प्रोक्तमधिदैवं किमुच्यते ॥८.१

arjuna uvāca
kiṁ tadbrahma kimadhyātmaṁ kiṁ karma puruṣottama **/**
adhibhūtaṁ ca kiṁ proktamadhidaivaṁ kimucyate **//** *8.1*

arjuna uvāca: Arjuna said; *kiṁ*: what; *tat*: that; *brahma*: Brahman; *kiṁ*: what; *adhyātmaṁ*: the self; *kiṁ*: what; *karma*: fruitive activities; *puruṣottama*: O Supreme Person; *adhibhūtaṁ*: the material manifestation; *ca*: and; *kiṁ*: what; *proktaṁ*: is called; *adhidaivaṁ*: the demigods; *kiṁ*: what; *ucyate*: is called.

8.1 Arjuna said: O my Lord, O supreme person, what is Brahman? *What is the Self? What are result-based actions? What is this material manifestation? And what are the demigods? Please explain all this to me.*

अधियज्ञ: कथं कोऽत्र देहेऽस्मिन्मधुसूदन ।
प्रयाणकाले च कथं ज्ञेयोऽसि नियतात्मभि: ॥८.२

adhiyajñaḥ kathaṁ ko'tra dehe'sminmadhusūdana **/**
prayāṇakāle ca kathaṁ jñeyo'si niyatātmabhiḥ **//** *8.2*

adhiyajñaḥ: the Lord of sacrifice; *kathaṁ*: how; *kaḥ*: who; *atra*: here; *dehe*: in the body; *asmin*: in this; *madhusūdana*: O Madhusudana; *prayāṇakāle*: at the time of death; *ca*: and; *kathaṁ*: how; *jñeyaḥ*: be known; *asi*: You can; *niyatātmabhiḥ*: by the self-controlled.

8.2 How does this Lord of sacrifice live in the body, and in which part does He live, O Madhusūdana? *How can those engaged in devotional service know You at the time of their death?*

श्री भगवानुवाच ।
अक्षरं ब्रह्म परमं स्वभावोऽध्यात्ममुच्यते ।
भूतभावोद्भवकरो विसर्गः कर्मसंज्ञितः ॥ ८.३

śrībhagavānuvāca
akṣaraṁ brahma paramaṁ svabhāvo'dhyātmamucyate /
bhūtabhāvodbhavakaro visargaḥ karmasañjñitaḥ // *8.3*

śrībhagavānuvāca: Bhagavān said; *akṣaraṁ*: indestructible; *brahma*: Brahman; *paramaṁ*: transcendental; *svabhāvaḥ*: eternal nature; *adhyātmaṁ*: the self; *ucyate*: is called; *bhūtabhāva-udbhavakaraḥ*: action producing the material bodies of the living entities; *visargaḥ*: creation; *karma*: fruitive activities; *samñitaḥ*: is called.

8.3 Bhagavān *said: The indestructible, transcendental living entity is called* Brahman *and his eternal nature is called the self. Action pertaining to the development of the material bodies is called* karma, *or result based activities.*

अधिभूतं क्षरो भावः पुरुषश्चाधिदैवतम् ।
अधियज्ञोऽहमेवात्र देहे देहभृतां वर ॥ ८.४

adhibhūtaṁ kṣaro bhāvaḥ puruṣaścādhidaivatam /
adhiyajño'hamevātra dehe dehabhṛtāṁ vara // *8.4*

adhibhūtaṁ: the physical manifestation; *kṣaraḥ*: constantly changing; *bhāvaḥ*: nature; *puruṣaḥ*: the universal form; *ca*: and; *adhidaivataṁ*: including all demigods like the sun and moon; *adhiyajñaḥ*: the Supersoul; *ahaṁ*: I (Kṛṣṇa); *eva*: alone; *atra*: in this; *dehe*: body; *dehabhṛtāṁ*: of the embodied; *vara*: the Supreme.

8.4 Physical nature is known to be endlessly changing. The universe is the cosmic form of the supreme Lord, and I am that Lord represented as the super soul, dwelling in the heart of every being that dwells in a body.

अन्तकाले च मामेव स्मरन्मुक्त्वा कलेवरम् ।
यः प्रयाति स मद्भावं याति नास्त्यत्र संशयः ॥ ८.५

antakāle ca māmeva smaranmuktvā kalevaram /
yaḥ prayāti sa madbhāvaṁ yāti nā'styatra saṁśayaḥ // *8.5*

antakāle: at the end of life; *ca*: also; *māṁ*: unto Me; *eva*: only; *smaran*: remembering; *muktvā*: quitting; *kalevaraṁ*: the body; *yaḥ*: he who; *prayāti*: goes; *saḥ*: he; *madbhāvaṁ*: My nature; *yāti*: achieves; *na*: not; *asti*: there is; *atra*: here; *saṁśayaḥ*: doubt.

8.5 Whoever, at the time of death, quits his body, remembering Me alone, attains My nature immediately. Of this there is no doubt.

यं यं वापि स्मरन्भावं त्यजत्यन्ते कलेवरम् ।
तं तमेवैति कौन्तेय सदा तद्भावभावितः ॥ ८.६

yaṁ yaṁ vāpi smaranbhāvaṁ tyajatyante kalevaram |
taṁ taṁ evaiti kaunteya sadā tadbhāvabhāvitaḥ || 8.6

yaṁ yaṁ: whatever; *vā*: either; *api*: also; *smaran*: *remembering*; *bhāvaṁ*: nature; *tyajati*: give up; *ante*: at the end; *kalevaraṁ*: this body; *taṁ taṁ*: similar; *eva*: certainly; *eti*: gets; *kaunteya*: O son of Kuntī; *sadā*: always; *tat*: that; *bhāva*: state of being; *bhāvitaḥ*: remembering.

8.6 Whatever state of being one remembers when he quits his body, it is that state one will attain without fail.

तस्मात्सर्वेषु कालेषु मामनुस्मर युध्य च ।
मय्यर्पितमनोबुद्धिर्मामेवैष्यस्यसंशयम् ॥ ८.७

tasmātsarveṣu kāleṣu māmanusmara yudhya ca |
mayyarpitamanobuddhirmāmevaiṣyasyasaṁśayam || 8.7

tasmāt: therefore; *sarveṣu*: always; *kāleṣu*: time; *māṁ*: unto Me; *anusmara*: go on remembering; *yudhya*: fight; *ca*: also; *mayi*: unto Me; *arpita*: surrender; *manaḥ*: mind; *buddhiḥ*: intellect; *māṁ*: unto Me; *eva*: alone; *eṣyasi*: will attain; *asaṁśayaḥ*: beyond a doubt.

8.7 Arjuna, think of Me in the form of Kṛṣṇa always, while continuing with your prescribed duty of fighting. With your activities dedicated to Me and your mind and intelligence fixed on. Me, you will attain Me without doubt.

अभ्यासयोगयुक्तेन चेतसा नान्यगामिना ।
परमं पुरुषं दिव्यं याति पार्थानुचिन्तयन् ॥ ८.८

abhyāsayogayuktena cetasā nānyagāminā |
paramaṁ puruṣaṁ divyaṁ yāti pārthānucintayan || 8.8

abhyāsa: practice; *yoga yuktena*: being engaged in meditation; *cetasā*: by the mind and intelligence; *nā 'nyagāminā*: without their being deviated; *paramaṁ*: the Supreme; *puruṣaṁ*: personality of godhead; *divyaṁ*: transcendental; *yāti*: achieves; *pārtha*: O son of Pritā; *anucintayan*: constantly thinking of

8.8 He who meditates on the supreme person, his mind constantly engaged in remembering Me, not deviating from the path, O Pārtha, He is sure to reach Me.

कविं पुराणमनुशासितारमणोरणीयांसमनुस्मरेद्यः
सर्वस्य धातारमचिन्त्यरूपमादित्यवर्णं तमसः परस्तात् ॥ ८.९

kaviṁ purāṇamanuśāsitāramaṇoraṇī yāṁsamanusmaredyaḥ |
sarvasya dhātāramacintyarūpamādityavarṇaṁ tamasaḥ parastāt || 8.9

kaviṁ: one who knows everything; *purāṇaṁ*: the oldest; *anuśāsitāraṁ*: the controller; *aṇoḥ*: of the atom; *aṇīyāṁsaṁ*: smaller than; *anusmaret*: always thinking; *yaḥ*: one who; *sarvasya*: of everything; *dhātāraṁ*: the maintainer; *acintya*: inconceivable; *rūpaṁ*: form; *āditya varṇaṁ*: illuminated like the sun; *tamasaḥ*: of the darkness; *parastāt*: transcendental

8.9 One should meditate on the Supreme as the one who knows everything, as He is the most ancient, who is the controller, who is smaller than the smallest, who is the maintainer of everything, who is beyond all material conception, who is inconceivable, and who is always a person.

प्रयाणकाले मनसाऽचलेन भक्त्या युक्तो योगबलेन चैव ।
भ्रुवोर्मध्ये प्राणमावेश्य सम्यक् स तं परं पुरुषमुपैति दिव्यम् ॥ ८.१०

prayāṇakāle manasācalena bhaktyā yukto yogabalena caiva |
bhruvormadhye prāṇamāveśya samyak sa taṁ paraṁ puruṣamupaiti divyam || 8.10

prayāṇa kāle: at the time of death; *manasā*: by the mind; *acalena*: without being deviated; *bhaktyā*: in full devotion; *yuktaḥ*: engaged; *yoga balena*: by the power of mystic yoga; *ca*: also; *eva*: certainly; *bhruvoḥ*: between the two eyebrows; *madhye*: in; *prāṇaṁ*: the life air; *āveśya*: establishing; *samyak*: completely; *saḥ*: he; *taṁ*: that; *paraṁ*: transcendental; *puruṣaṁ*: personality of godhead; *upaiti*: achieves; *divyaṁ*: in the spiritual kingdom.

8.10 One, who at the time of death, fixes his mind and life air between the eyebrows without being distracted, by the power of yoga and in full devotion, engages himself in dwelling on Me, He will certainly attain Me.

यदक्षरं वेदविदो वदन्ति विशन्ति यद्यतयो वीतरागाः ।
यदिच्छन्तो ब्रह्मचर्यं चरन्ति तत्ते पदं संग्रहेण प्रवक्ष्ये ॥ ८.११

yadakṣaraṁ vedavido vadanti viśanti yadyatayo vītarāgāḥ |

yadicchanto brahmacaryaṁ caranti tatte padaṁ sangraheṇa
pravakṣye || *8.11*

yat: that which; *akṣaraṁ*: inexhaustible; *vedavidaḥ*: a person conversant with the Vedas; *vadanti*: say; *viśanti*: enters; *yat*: in which; *yatayaḥ*: great sages; *vītarāgāḥ*: in the renounced order of life; *yat*: that which; *icchantaḥ*: desiring; *brahmacaryaṁ*: celibacy; *caranti*: practices; *tat*: that; *te*: unto you; *padaṁ*: situation; *sangraheṇa*: in summary; *pravakṣye*: I shall explain.

8.11 Persons who are learned in the Veda *and who are great sages in the renounced order, enter into* Brahman. *Desiring such perfection, one practices* brahmacarya. *I shall now explain to you this process by which one may attain liberation.*

सर्वद्वाराणि संयम्य मनो हृदि निरुध्य च ।
मूर्ध्न्याधायात्मनः प्राणमास्थितो योगधारणाम् ॥ ८.१२

sarvadvārāṇi saṁyamya mano hṛdi nirudhya ca |
mūrdhnyādhāyātmanaḥ prāṇamāsthito yogadhāraṇām || *8.12*

sarva dvārāṇi: all the doors of the body; *saṁyamya*: controlling; *manaḥ*: mind; *hṛdi*: in the heart; *nirudhya*: confined; *ca*: also; *mūrdhni*: on the head; *ādhāya*: fixed; *ātmanaḥ*: soul; *prāṇaṁ*: the life air; *āsthitaḥ*: situated; *yoga dhāraṇāṁ*: the yogic situation

8.12 Closing all the doors of the senses and fixing the mind on the heart and the life air at the top of the head, one establishes himself in yoga.

ओमित्येकाक्षरं ब्रह्म व्याहरन्मामनुस्मरन् ।
यः प्रयाति त्यजन्देहं स याति परमां गतिम् ॥ ८.१३

omityekākṣaraṁ brahma vyāharanmāmanusmaran |
yaḥ prayāti tyajandehaṁ sa yāti paramāṁ gatiṁ || *8.13*

om: the combination of letters om (omkāra); *iti*: thus; *ekākṣaraṁ*: supreme indestructible; *brahma*: absolute; *vyāharan*: vibrating; *māṁ*: Me (Kṛṣṇa); *anusmaran*: remembering; *yaḥ*: anyone; *prayāti*: leaves; *tyajan*: quitting; *dehaṁ*: this body; *saḥ*: he; *yāti*: achieves; *paramāṁ*: supreme; *gatiṁ*: destination

8.13 Centered in this yoga practice and vibrating the sacred syllable OM, the supreme combination of letters, if one dwells in the Supreme and quits his body, he certainly achieves the supreme destination.

अनन्यचेता: सततं यो मां स्मरति नित्यश: ।
तस्याहं सुलभ: पार्थ नित्ययुक्तस्य योगिन: ॥ ८.१४

ananyacetāḥ satatam yo mām smarati nityaśaḥ /
tasyāham sulabhaḥ pārtha nityayuktasya yoginaḥ // 8.14

ananyacetāḥ: without deviation; *satatam*: always; *yaḥ*: anyone; *mām*: Me (Kṛṣṇa); *smarati*: remembers; *nityaśaḥ*: regularly; *tasya*: to him; *aham*: I am; *sulabhaḥ*: very easy to achieve; *pārtha*: O son of Pritā; *nitya*: regularly; *yuktasya*: engaged; *yoginaḥ*: of the devotee.

8.14 I am always available to anyone who remembers Me constantly Pārtha, because of his constant engagement in devotional service.

मामुपेत्य पुनर्जन्म दु:खालयमशाश्वतम् ।
नाप्नुवन्ति महात्मान: संसिद्धिं परमां गता: ॥ ८.१५

māmupetya punarjanma duḥkhālayamaśāśvatam /
nāpnuvanti mahātmānaḥ saṁsiddhim paramām gatāḥ // 8.15

mām: unto Me; *upetya*: achieving; *punaḥ*: again; *janma*: birth; *duḥkhālayam*: a place of miseries; *aśāśvatam*: temporary; *na*: never; *āpnuvanti*: attain; *mahātmanaḥ*: the great souls; *saṁsiddhim*: perfection; *paramām*: ultimate; *gatāḥ*: achieved.

8.15 After attaining Me, the great souls who are devoted to Me in yoga are never reborn in this world. This world is temporary and full of miseries and they have attained the highest perfection.

आब्रह्मभुवनाल्लोका: पुनरावर्तिनोऽर्जुन ।
मामुपेत्य तु कौन्तेय पुनर्जन्म न विद्यते ॥ ८.१६

ābrahmabhuvanāllokāḥ punarāvartinorjuna /
māmupetya tu kaunteya punarjanma na vidyate // 8.16

ābrahmabhuvanātlokāḥ: upto the world of Brahma; *punarāvartinaḥ*: again returning; *arjuna*: O Arjuna; *mām*: unto Me; *upetya*: arriving; *tu*: but; *kaunteya*: O son of Kuntī; *punar janma*: rebirth; *na*: never; *vidyate*: takes to

8.16 From the highest planet in the material world down to the lowest, all are places of misery wherein repeated birth and death take place. One who reaches My abode, O son of Kuntī, is never reborn.

सहस्रयुगपर्यन्तमहर्यद् ब्रह्मणो विदुः ।
रात्रिं युगसहस्रान्तां तेऽहोरात्रविदो जनाः ॥ ८.१७

sahasrayugaparyantamaharyad brahmaṇo viduḥ |
rātriṁ yugasahasrāntāṁ te'horātravido janāḥ || *8.17*

sahasra: thousand; *yuga*: millenniums; *paryantaṁ*: including; *ahaḥ*: day; *yat*: that; *brahmaṇaḥ*: of Brahma; *viduḥ*: they know; *rātriṁ*: night; *yuga*: millenniums; *sahasrāntāṁ*: similarly, at the end of one thousand; *te*: that; *aho rātra*: day and night; *vidaḥ*: understand; *janāḥ*: people

8.17 By human calculation, a thousand ages taken together is the duration of Brahma's *one day. His night is just as long.*

अव्यक्ताद् व्यक्तयः सर्वाः प्रभवन्त्यहरागमे ।
रात्र्यागमे प्रलीयन्ते तत्रैवाव्यक्तसंज्ञके ॥ ८.१८

avyaktādvyaktayaḥ sarvāḥ prabhavantyaharāgame |
rātryāgame pralīyante tatraivāvyaktasaṁjñake || *8.18*

avyaktāt: from the unmanifest; *vyaktayaḥ*: living entities; *sarvāḥ*: all; *prabhavanti*: come into being; *aharāgame*: at the beginning of the day; *rātryāgame*: at the fall of night; *pralīyante*: are annihilated; *tatra*: there; *eva*: certainly; *avyakta*: the unmanifest; *saṁjñake*: called

8.18 From the intangible all living entities come into being at the beginning of Brahma's *day. During* Brahma's *night all that are called intangible are annihilated.*

भूतग्रामः स एवायं भूत्वा भूत्वा प्रलीयते ।
रात्र्यागमेऽवशः पार्थ प्रभवत्यहरागमे ॥ ८.१९

bhūtagrāmaḥ sa evāyaṁ bhūtvā bhūtvā pralīyate |
rātryāgame'vaśaḥ pārtha prabhavatyaharāgame || *8.19*

bhūtagrāmaḥ: the aggregate of all living entities; *saḥ*: they; *eva*: certainly; *ayaṁ*: this; *bhūtvā bhūtvā* : taking birth; *pralī yate*: annihilate; *rātri*: night; *āgame*: on arrival; *avaśaḥ*: automatically; *pārtha*: O son of Pritā; *prabhavati*: manifest; *ahar*: during daytime; *āgame*: on arrival.

8.19 Again and again the day comes, and this host of beings is active; and again the night falls, O son of Pritā, and they are automatically annihilated.

परस्तस्मात्तु भावोऽन्योऽव्यक्तोऽव्यक्तात्सनातन: ।
य: स सर्वेषु भूतेषु नश्यत्सु न विनश्यति ॥ ८.२०

parastasmāttu bhāvo'nyo'vyakto'vyaktātsanātanaḥ /
yaḥ sa sarveṣu bhūteṣu naśyatsu na vinaśyati // 8.20

paraḥ: transcendental; *tasmāt*: from that; *tu*: but; *bhāvaḥ*: nature; *anyaḥ*: another; *avyaktaḥ*: unmanifest; *avyaktāt*: from the unmanifest; *sanātanaḥ*: eternal; *yaḥ*: that; *saḥ*: which; *sarveṣu*: all; *bhūteṣu*: manifestation; *naśyatsu*: being annihilated; *na*: never; *vinaśyati*: annihilated.

8.20 Yet there is another nature, which is eternal and is beyond this tangible and intangible matter. It is supreme and is never annihilated. When all in this world is annihilated, that part remains the same.

अव्यक्तोऽक्षर इत्युक्तस्तमाहु: परमां गतिम् ।
यं प्राप्य न निवर्तन्ते तद्धाम परमं मम ॥ ८.२१

avyakto'kṣara ityuktastamāhuḥ paramāṁ gatim /
yaṁ prāpya na nivartante taddhāma paramaṁ mama // 8.21

avyaktaḥ: unmanifested; *akṣaraḥ*: infallible; *iti*: thus; *uktaḥ*: said; *taṁ*: that which; *āhuḥ*: is known; *paramāṁ*: ultimate; *gatiṁ*: destination; *yaṁ*: that which; *prāpya*: gaining; *na*: never; *nivartante*: comes back; *tat dhāma*: that abode; *paramaṁ*: supreme; *mama*: Mine

8.21 That supreme abode is said to be intangible and infallible and is the supreme destination. When one gains this state one never comes back. That is My supreme abode.

पुरुष: स पर: पार्थ भक्त्या लभ्यस्त्वनन्यया ।
यस्यान्त:स्थानि भूतानि येन सर्वमिदं ततम् ॥ ८.२२

puruṣaḥ sa paraḥ pārtha bhaktyā labhyastvananyayā /
yasyāntaḥsthāni bhūtāni yena sarvamidaṁ tatam // 8.22

puruṣaḥ: that supreme power; *saḥ*: He; *paraḥ*: the Supreme, than whom no one is greater; *pārtha*: O son of Pritā; *bhaktyā*: by devotional service; *labhyaḥ*: can be achieved; *tu*: but; *ananyayā*: unalloyed, undeviating devotion; *yasya*: whom; *antaḥ sthāni*: within; *bhūtāni*: all of this material manifestation; *yena*: by whom; *sarvaṁ*: all; *idaṁ*: whatever we can see; *tataṁ*: distributed

8.22 Son of Pritā, the supreme person, who is greater than all, is attainable by undeviating devotion. Although He is present in His abode, He is all-pervading, and everything is situated within Him.

यत्र काले त्वनावृत्तिमावृत्तिं चैव योगिनः ।
प्रयाता यान्ति तं कालं वक्ष्यामि भरतर्षभ ॥ ८.२३

yatra kāle tvanāvṛttimāvṛttim caiva yoginaḥ I
prayātā yānti taṁ kālaṁ vakṣyāmi bharatarṣabha II 8.23

yatra: in that; *kāle*: time; *tu*: but; *anāvṛttiṁ*: no return; *āvṛttiṁ*: return; *ca*: also; *eva*: certainly; *yoginaḥ*: of different kinds of mystics; *prayātāḥ*: one who goes; *yānti*: departs; *taṁ*: that; *kālaṁ*: time; *vaksyāmi*: describing; *bharatarṣabha*: O best of the Bhāratas.

8.23 O best of the Bhārata, I shall now explain to you the different times when passing away from this world, one returns or does not return.

अग्निर्जोतिरहः शुक्लः षण्मासा उत्तरायणम् ।
तत्र प्रयाता गच्छन्ति ब्रह्म ब्रह्मविदो जनाः ॥ ८.२४

agnirjyotirahaḥ śuklaḥ ṣaṇmāsā uttarāyaṇam I
tatra prayātā gacchanti brahma brahmavido janāḥ II 8.24

agniḥ: fire; *jyotiḥ*: light; *ahaḥ*: day; *śuklaḥ*: white; *ṣaṇmāsāḥ*: six months; *uttarāyaṇaṁ*: when the sun passes on the northern side; *tatra*: there; *prayātāḥ*: one who goes; *gacchanti*: passes away; *brahma*: to the Absolute; *brahmavidaḥ*: one who knows the Absolute; *janāḥ*: person

8.24 Those who pass away from the world during the influence of the fire god, during light, at an auspicious moment, during the fortnight of the moon ascending and the six months when the sun travels in the north, and have realized the supreme Brahman *do not return.*

धूमो रात्रिस्तथा कृष्णः षण्मासा दक्षिणायनम् ।
तत्र चान्द्रमसं ज्योतिर्योगी प्राप्य निवर्तते ॥ ८.२५

dhūmo rātristathā kṛṣṇaḥ ṣaṇmāsā dakṣiṇāyanam I
tatra cāndramasaṁ jyotiryogī prāpya nivartate II 8.25

dhūmaḥ: smoke; *rātriḥ*: night; *tathā*: also; *kṛṣṇaḥ*: the fortnight of the dark moon; *ṣaṇmāsāḥ*: the six months; *dakṣiṇāyanaṁ*: when the sun passes on the southern side; *tatra*: there; *cāndramasaṁ*: the moon planet; *jyotiḥ*: light; *yogī*: the mystic; *prāpya*: achieves; *nivartate*: comes back.

8.25 The mystic who passes away from this world during the smoke, the night, the moonless fortnight, or the six months when the sun passes to the south, have done good deeds go to the cosmic layer and again comes back.

शुक्लकृष्णे गती ह्येते जगतः शाश्वते मते ।
एकया यात्यनावृत्तिमन्ययावर्तते पुनः ॥ ८.२६

śukla kṛṣṇe gatī hyete jagataḥ śāśvate mate /
ekayā yātyanāvṛttimanyayāvartate punaḥ // *8.26*

śukla: light; *kṛṣṇe*: darkness; *gatī*: passing away; *hi*: certainly; *ete*: all these; *jagataḥ*: of the material world; *śāśvate*: of the Vedas; *mate*: in the opinion; *ekayā*: by one; *yāti*: goes; *anāvṛttiṁ*: no return; *anyayā*: by the other; *āvartate*: comes back; *punaḥ*: again

8.26 According to the Vedas, *there are two ways of passing from this world: one in the light and one in darkness. When one passes in light, he does not return; but when one passes in darkness, he again comes back.*

नैते सृती पार्थ जानन्योगी मुह्यति कश्चन ।
तस्मात्सर्वेषु कालेषु योगयुक्तो भवार्जुन ॥ ८.२७

naite sṛtī pārtha jānanyogī muhyati kaścana /
tasmātsarveṣu kāleṣu yogayukto bhavārjuna // *8.27*

na: never; *ete*: all these; *sṛtī* : different paths; *pārtha*: O son of Pritā; *jānan*: even if they know; *yogī* : the devotees of the Lord; *muhyati*: bewildered; *kaścana*: anyone; *tasmāt*: therefore; *sarveṣu kāleṣu*: always; *yoga yuktaḥ*: being engaged in Kṛṣṇa consciousness; *bhava*: just become; *arjuna*: O Arjuna

8.27 O son of Pritā, the devotees who know these different paths are never bewildered. O Arjuna, be always fixed in devotion.

वेदेषु यज्ञेषु तपःसु चैव दानेषु यत्पुण्यफलं प्रदिष्टम् ।
अत्येति तत्सर्वमिदं विदित्वा योगी परं स्थानमुपैति चाद्यम् ॥ ८.२८

vedeṣu yajñeṣu tapaḥsu caiva dāneṣu yat puṇyaphalaṁ pradiṣṭam /
atyeti tatsarvamidaṁ viditvā yogī paraṁ sthānamupaiti cādyam // *8.28*

vedeṣu: in the study of the Vedas; *yajñeṣu*: in the performances of yajna, sacrifice; *tapaḥsu*: undergoing different types of austerities; *ca*: also; *eva*:

certainly; *dāneṣu*: in giving charities; *yat*: that which; *puṇya phalaṁ*: the result of pious work; *pradiṣṭaṁ*: directed; *atyeti*: surpasses; *tat*: all those; *sarvaṁ idaṁ*: all those described above; *viditvā*: knowing; *yogī*: the devotee; *paraṁ*: supreme; *sthānaṁ*: abode; *upaiti*: achieves peace; *ca*: also; *ādyaṁ*: original.

8.28 A person who accepts the path of devotional service is not denied the results derived from studying the Vedas, *performing austerities and sacrifices, giving charity or pursuing pious and result based activities. At the end he reaches the supreme abode.*

इति श्रीमद्भगवद्गीतासूपनिषत्सु ब्रह्मविद्यायां योगशास्त्रे
श्रीकृष्णार्जुनसंवादे अक्षरब्रह्मयोगो नाम अष्टमोऽध्यायः ॥ २

iti śrīmad bhagavadgītāsūpaniṣatsu brahmavidyāyāṁ
yogaśāstre śrīkṛṣṇārjuna saṁvāde akṣarabrahmayogo
nāma aṣṭamo'dhyāyaḥ //

In the Upaniṣad *of the Bhagavad Gītā, the knowledge of* Brahman, *the Supreme, the science of Yoga and the dialogue between Śrī Kṛṣṇa and Arjuna, this is the eighth discourse designated:*

Akṣarabrahma Yogaḥ

Verses Of Gita Chapter - 9

अथ नवमोऽध्याय:

राजविद्याराजगुह्ययोग:

Rājavidyā-Rājaguhya Yogaḥ

श्री भगवानुवाच

इदं तु ते गुह्यतमं प्रवक्ष्याम्यनसूयवे ।

ज्ञानं विज्ञानसहितं यज्ज्ञात्वा मोक्ष्यसेऽशुभात् ॥ ९.१

śrī bhagavānuvāca

idaṁ tu te guhyatamaṁ pravakṣyāmyanasūyave I

jñānaṁ vijñānasahitaṁ yajjñātvā mokṣyase'śubhāt II 9.1

śrī bhagavān uvāca: the supreme personality of godhead said; *idaṁ*: this; *tu*: but; *te*: unto you; *guhyatamaṁ*: the most confidential; *pravakṣyāmi*: I am speaking; *anasūyave*: to the non-envious; *jñānaṁ*: knowledge; *vijñāna*: realized knowledge; *sahitaṁ*: with; *yat*: which; *jñātvā*: knowing; *mokṣyase*: be released; *aśubhāt*: from this miserable material existence.

9.1 Kṛṣṇa said: Arjuna, you trust Me and you are not envious of Me; I shall therefore impart to you this profound and secret wisdom and experience; This will free you of all miseries of material existence.

राजविद्या राजगुह्यं पवित्रमिदमुत्तमम् ।

प्रत्यक्षावगमं धर्म्यं सुसुखं कर्तुमव्ययम् ॥ ९.२

rājavidyā rājaguhyaṁ pavitramidamuttamam I

pratyakṣāvagamaṁ dharmyaṁ susukhaṁ kartumavyayam II 9.2

rājavidyā: the king of education; *rājaguhyaṁ*: the king of confidential knowledge; *pavitraṁ*: the purest; *idaṁ*: this; *uttamaṁ*: transcendental; *pratyakṣa*: directly experienced; *avagamaṁ*: understood; *dharmyaṁ*: the principle of religion; *susukhaṁ*: very happy; *kartuṁ*: to execute; *avyayaṁ*: everlasting.

9.2 This knowledge is king of all knowledge and the most secret of all secrets. It is the purest knowledge, sacred and gives direct perception of Self realization. It is eternal and easy to practice.

अश्रद्दधानाः पुरुषा धर्मस्यास्य परन्तप ।
अप्राप्य मां निवर्तन्ते मृत्युसंसारवर्त्मनि ॥९.३

aśraddadhānāḥ puruṣā dharmasyāsya parantapa |
aprāpya māṁ nivartante mṛtyusaṁsāravartmani || 9.3

aśraddadhānāḥ: those who are faithless; *puruṣāḥ*: such persons; *dharmasya*: of this process of religion; *asya*: of it; *parantapa*: O killer of the enemies; *aprāpya*: without obtaining; *māṁ*: Me; *nivartante*: come back; *mṛtyu*: death; *saṁsāra*: material existence; *vartmani*: on the path of.

9.3 Those who have no faith in this knowledge cannot attain Me, O conqueror of foes

मया ततमिदं सर्वं जगदव्यक्तमूर्तिना ।
मत्स्थानि सर्वभूतानि न चाहं तेष्ववस्थितः ॥९.४

mayā tatamidaṁ sarvam jagadavyakta mūrtinā |
matsthāni sarvabhūtāni na cahaṁ teṣvavasthitaḥ || 9.4

mayā: by Me; *tataṁ*: spread; *idaṁ*: all these manifestations; *sarvaṁ*: all; *jagat*: cosmic manifestation; *avyakta mūrtinā*: unmanifested form; *matsthāni*: unto Me; *sarvabhūtāni*: all living entities; *na*: not; *ca*: also; *ahaṁ*: I; *teṣu*: in them; *avasthitaḥ*: situated.

9.4 The entire universe is pervaded by Me in My formless form. All beings are based in Me, but I am not in them.

न च मत्स्थानि भूतानि पश्य मे योगमैश्वरम् ।
भूतभृन्न च भूतस्थो ममात्मा भूतभावनः ॥९.५

na ca matsthāni bhūtāni paśya me yogamaiśvaram |
bhūtabhṛnna ca bhūtastho mamātmā bhūtabhāvanaḥ || 9.5

na: never; *ca*: also; *matsthāni*: situated in Me; *bhūtāni*: all creations; *paśya*: just see; me: My; *yogaṁ aiśvaraṁ*: inconceivable mystic power; *bhūtabhṛt*: maintainer of all living entities; *na*: never; *ca*: also; *bhūtasthaḥ*: in the cosmic manifestation; *mama*: My; *ātmā*: Self; *bhūtabhāvanaḥ*: is the source of all manifestations.

9. 5 Look at My mystic powers! I create and sustain all living entities but do not depend on them, nor do they depend on Me.

यथाकाशस्थितो नित्यं वायुः सर्वत्रगो महान् ।
तथा सर्वाणि भूतानि मत्स्थानीत्युपधारय ॥ ९.६

yathākāśasthito nityaṁ vāyuḥ sarvatrago mahān |
tathā sarvāṇi bhūtāni matsthānītyupadhāraya || 9.6

yathā: as much as; *ākāśasthitaḥ*: situated in space; *nityaṁ*: always; *vāyuḥ*: wind; *sarvatragaḥ*: blowing everywhere; *mahān*: mighty; *tathā*: similarly; *sarvāṇi*: everything; *bhūtāni*: created beings; *matsthānī*: situated in Me; *iti*: thus; *upadhāraya*: try to understand.

9.6 As the mighty wind, blowing everywhere, always rests in eternal space, all beings rest in Me.

सर्वभूतानि कौन्तेय प्रकृतिं यान्ति मामिकाम् ।
कल्पक्षये पुनस्तानि कल्पादौ विसृजाम्यहम् ॥ ९.७

sarvabhūtāni kaunteya prakṛtiṁ yānti māmikām |
kalpakṣaye punastāni kalpādau visṛjāmyaham || 9.7

sarva bhūtāni: all created entities; *kaunteya*: O son of Kuntī; *prakṛtim*: nature; *yānti*: enter; *māmikām*: unto Me; *kalpakṣaye*: at the end of the millennium; *punaḥ*: again; *tāni*: all those; *kalpādau*: in the beginning of the millennium; *visṛ jāmi*: I create; *ahaṁ*: I.

9.7 O son of Kuntī, at the end of every age all beings merge into Me, at the beginning of every new age I create them again.

प्रकृतिं स्वामवष्टभ्य विसृजामि पुनः पुनः ।
भूतग्राममिमं कृत्स्नमवशं प्रकृतेर्वशात् ॥ ९.८

prakṛtiṁ svāmavaṣṭabhya visṛjāmi punaḥ punaḥ |
bhūtagrāmamimaṁ kṛtsnamavaśaṁ prakṛtervaśāt || 9.8

prakṛtiṁ: material nature; *svāṁ*: of My personal Self; *avaṣṭabhya*: enter in; *visṛjāmi*: create; *punaḥ punaḥ*: again and again; *bhūta grāmaṁ*: all these cosmic manifestations; *imaṁ*: this; *kṛtsnaṁ*: total; *avaśaṁ*: automatically; *prakṛteḥ*: by the force of nature; *vaśāt*: under obligation.

9.8 My material nature creates the beings again and again. They are controlled by My material nature.

न च मां तानि कर्माणि निबध्नन्ति धनञ्जय ।
उदासीनवदासीनमसक्तं तेषु कर्मसु ॥ ९.९

na ca māṁ tāni karmāṇi nibadhnanti dhanañjaya |
udāsīnavadāsīnamasaktaṁ teṣu karmasu || 9.9

na: never; *ca*: also; *māṁ*: Me; *tāni*: all those; *karmāṇi*: activities; *nibadhnanti*: bind; *dhanañjaya*: O conqueror of riches; *udāsī navat*: as neutral; *āsīnaṁ*: situated; *asaktaṁ*: without attraction; *teṣu*: in them; *karmasu*: in activities.

9.9 O Dhañanjaya, all this work does not bind Me. I am ever unattached and indifferent.

मयाध्यक्षेण प्रकृतिः सूयते सचराचरम् ।
हेतुनानेन कौन्तेय जगद्विपरिवर्तते ॥ ९.१०

mayādhyakṣeṇa prakṛtiḥ sūyate sacarācaram |
hetunānena kaunteya jagadviparivartate || 9.10

mayā: by Me; *adhyakṣeṇa*: by superintendence; *prakṛtiḥ*: material nature; *sūyate*: manifests; *sacarācaraṁ*: with the moving and the nonmoving; *hetunā*: for this reason; *anena*: this; *kaunteya*: O son of Kuntī; *jagat*: the cosmic manifestation; *viparivartate*: is working.

9.10 The material nature of prakṛti *works under My direction, O son of Kuntī, and creates all moving and unmoving beings through My energy of* māyā. *By its rule this manifestation is created and annihilated again and again.*

अवजानन्ति मां मूढा मानुषीं तनुमाश्रितम् ।
परं भावमजानन्तो मम भूतमहेश्वरम् ॥ ९.११

avajānanti māṁ mūḍhā mānuṣīṁ tanumāśritam |
paraṁ bhāvamajānanto mama bhūtamaheśvaram || 9.11

avajānanti: deride; *māṁ*: Me; *mūḍhāḥ*: foolish men; *mānuṣīṁ*: in human form; *tanuṁ*: body; *āśritaṁ*: assuming; *paraṁ*: transcendental; *bhāvaṁ*: nature; *ajānantaḥ*: not knowing; *mama*: Mine; *bhūta*: everything that be; *maheśvaraṁ*: the supreme proprietor.

9.11 Fools deride Me when I descend in the human form. They do not know My transcendental nature and My supreme dominion over all that is.

मोघाशा मोघकर्माणो मोघज्ञाना विचेतसः ।
राक्षसीमासुरीं चैव प्रकृतिं मोहिनीं श्रिताः ॥ ९.१२

moghāśā moghakarmāṇo moghajñānā vicetasaḥ /
rākṣasīmāsurīṁ caiva prakṛtiṁ mohinīṁ śritāḥ // 9.12

moghāśāḥ: baffled hope; *moghakarmāṇaḥ*: baffled in fruitive activities; *mogha jñānāḥ*: baffled in knowledge; *vicetasaḥ*: bewildered; *rākṣasīṁ*: demonic; *āsurīṁ*: atheistic; *ca*: and; *eva*: certainly; *prakṛtiṁ*: nature; *mohinīṁ*: bewildering; *śritāḥ*: taking shelter of.

9.12 Those who are thus deluded are demonic and atheistic. In their deluded condition, their hopes for liberation, their result oriented actions and their culture of knowledge become false and useless.

महात्मानस्तु मां पार्थ दैवीं प्रकृतिमाश्रिताः ।
भजन्त्यनन्यमनसो ज्ञात्वा भूतादिमव्ययम् ॥ ९.१३

mahātmānastu māṁ pārtha daivīṁ prakṛtimāśritāḥ /
bhajantyananyamanaso jñātvā bhūtādimavyayam // 9.13

mahātmānaḥ: the great souls; *tu*: but; *māṁ*: unto Me; *pārtha*: O son of Pritā; *daivīṁ*: divine; *prakṛtiṁ*: nature; *āśritāḥ*: taken shelter of; *bhajanti*: render service; *ananya manasaḥ*: without deviation of the mind; *jñātvā*: knowing; *bhūta*: creation; *ādiṁ*: original; *avyayaṁ*: inexhaustible.

9.13 O son of Pritā, the great souls who are not deluded know me as unchangeable. They are devoted to Me as they know as the cause of all creation.

सततं कीर्तयन्तो मां यतन्तश्च दृढव्रताः ।
नमस्यन्तश्च मां भक्त्या नित्ययुक्ता उपासते ॥ ९.१४

satataṁ kīrtayanto māṁ yatantaśca dṛḍhavratāḥ /
namasyantaśca māṁ bhaktyā nityayuktā upāsate // 9.14

satataṁ: always; *kīrtayantaḥ*: chanting; *māṁ*: Me; *yatantaḥ ca*: fully endeavoring also; *dṛḍha vratāḥ*: with determination; *namasyantah ca*: offering obeisance; *māṁ*: unto Me; *bhaktyā*: in devotion; *nitya yuktā*: perpetually engaged; *upāsate*: worship.

9.14 Those with firm resolve perpetually worship Me with devotion. They sing My glories, striving with determination, prostrating to Me.

ज्ञानयज्ञेन चाप्यन्ये यजन्तो मामुपासते ।
एकत्वेन पृथक्त्वेन बहुधा विश्वतोमुखम् ॥ ९.१५

jñānayajñena cāpyanye yajanto māmupāsate |
ekatvena pṛthaktvena bahudhā viśvatomukham || 9.15

jñāna yajñena: by cultivation of knowledge; *ca*: also; *api*: certainly; *anye*: others; *yajantaḥ*: worshiping; *māṁ*: Me; *upāsate*: worship; *ekatvena*: in oneness; *pṛthaktvena*: in duality; *bahudhā*: diversity; *viśvato mukhaṁ*: in the universal form.

9.15 Some worship Me by acquiring and spreading wisdom of the Self. Others worship Me in my non dual form, or dual form or universal form.

अहं क्रतुरहं यज्ञः स्वधाहमहमौषधम् ।
मन्त्रोऽहमहमेवाज्यमहमग्निरहं हुतम् ॥ ९.१६

ahaṁ kraturahaṁ yajñaḥ svadhāham ahamauṣadham |
mantro 'hamahamevājyaṁ ahamagnirahaṁ hutam || 9.16

ahaṁ: I; *kratuḥ*: ritual; *ahaṁ*: I; *yajñaḥ*: sacrifice; *svadhā*: oblation; *ahaṁ*: I; *auṣadhaṁ*: healing herb; *mantraḥ*: transcendental chant; *ahaṁ*: I; *eva*: certainly; *ājyaṁ*: melted butter; *ahaṁ*: I; *agniḥ*: fire; *ahaṁ*: I; *hutaṁ*: offering.

पिताहमस्य जगतो माता धाता पितामहः ।
वेद्यं पवित्रमोङ्कार ऋक्साम यजुरेव च ॥ ९.१७

pitāhamasya jagato mātā dhātā pitāmahaḥ |
vedyaṁ pavitramoṇkāra ṛksāma yajureva ca || 9.17

pitā: father; *ahaṁ*: I; *asya*: of this; *jagataḥ*: of the universe; *mātā*: mother; *dhātā*: supporter; *pitāmahaḥ*: grandfather; *vedyaṁ*: what is to be known; *pavitraṁ*: that which purifies; *oṁkāraḥ*: the syllable om; *ṛk*: the Rig Veda; *sāma*: the Sama Veda; *yajuḥ*: the Yajur Veda; *eva*: certainly; *ca*: and

गतिर्भर्ता प्रभुः साक्षी निवासः शरणं सुहृत् ।
प्रभवः प्रलयः स्थानं निधानं बीजमव्ययम् ॥ ९.१८

gatirbhartā prabhuḥ sākṣī nivāsaḥ śaraṇaṁ suhṛt |
prabhavaḥ pralayaḥ sthānaṁ nidhānaṁ bījamavyayam || 9.18

gatiḥ: goal; *bhartā*: sustainer; *prabhuḥ*: Lord; *sākṣī*: witness; *nivāsaḥ*: abode; *śaraṇaṁ*: refuge; *suhṛt*: most intimate friend; *prabhavaḥ*: creation; *pralayaḥ*: dissolution; *sthānaṁ*: ground; *nidhānaṁ*: resting place; *bījaṁ*: seed; *avyayaṁ*: imperishable.

तपाम्यहमहं वर्षं निगृह्णाम्युत्सृजामि च ।
अमृतं चैव मृत्युश्च सदसच्चाहमर्जुन ॥ ९.१९

tapāmyahamahaṁ varṣaṁ nigṛhṇāmyutsṛjāmi ca **/**
amṛtaṁ caiva mṛtyuśca sadasaccāhamarjuna **//** 9.19

tapāmi: give heat; *ahaṁ*: I; *ahaṁ*: I; *varṣaṁ*: rain; *nigṛhṇāmi*: withhold; *utsṛjāmi*: send forth; *ca*: and; *amṛtaṁ*: immortality; *ca*: and; *eva*: certainly; *mṛtyuḥ*: death; *ca*: and; *sat*: being; *asat*: nonbeing; *ca*: and; *ahaṁ*: I; *arjuna*: O Arjuna.

9.16, 17, 18, 19

I am the ritual, I am the sacrifice, I am the offering, I am the herb, I am the mantra, I am the clarified butter, I am the fire, and I am the oblation.

I am the supporter of the universe, the father, the mother, and the grandfather. I am the object of knowledge, the sacred syllable "OM", and also the Rig, the Yajur, and the Sāma Vedas.

I am the goal, the supporter, the Lord, the witness, the abode, the refuge, the friend, the origin, the dissolution, the foundation, the substratum, and the immutable seed. I give heat. I send, as well as withhold, the rain.

I am immortality, as well as death. I am also both the Eternal and the temporal, O Arjuna.

त्रैविद्या मां सोमपाः पूतपापा यज्ञैरिष्ट्वा स्वर्गतिं प्रार्थयन्ते ।
ते पुण्यमासाद्य सुरेन्द्रलोकमश्नन्ति दिव्यान्दिवि देवभोगान् ॥ ९.२०

traividyā māṁ somapāḥ pūtapāpā yajñairiṣṭvā svargatiṁ prārthayante **/**
te puṇyamāsādya surendralokamaśnanti divyāndivi devabhogān **//** 9.20

traividyāḥ: the knowers of the three Vedas; *māṁ*: unto Me; *somapāḥ*: drinkers of soma juice; *pūta*: purified; *pāpāḥ*: sins; *yajñaiḥ*: with sacrifices; *iṣṭvā*: after worshiping; *svargatiṁ*: passage to heaven; *prārthayante*: pray; *te*: they; *puṇyaṁ*: virtue; *āsādya*: enjoying; *surendra*: of Indra; *lokaṁ*: the world; *aśnanti*: enjoy; *divyān*: celestial; *divi*: in heaven; *devabhogān*: pleasures of the gods.

9.20 Those who practice the vedic *rituals and drink the soma juice worship Me indirectly seeking the heavenly pleasures. They go to heaven and enjoy sensual delights.*

ते तं भुक्त्वा स्वर्गलोकं विशालं क्षीणे पुण्ये मर्त्यलोकं विशन्ति।
एवं त्रयीधर्ममनुप्रपन्ना गतागतं कामकामा लभन्ते ॥ ९.२१

te taṁ bhuktvā svargalokaṁ viśālaṁ kṣīṇe puṇye martyalokaṁ viśanti I
evaṁ trayīdharmamanuprapannā gatāgataṁ kāmakāmā labhante II 9.21

te: they; *taṁ*: that; *bhuktvā*: enjoying; *svargalokaṁ*: heaven; *viśālaṁ*: vast; *kṣīṇe*: being exhausted; *puṇye*: merits; *martya lokaṁ*: mortal earth; *viśanti*: fall down; *evaṁ*: thus; *trayī*: three Vedas; *dharmaṁ*: doctrines; *anuprapannāḥ*: following; *gatāgataṁ*: death and birth; *kāma kāmāḥ*: desiring sense enjoyments; *labhante*: attain

9.21 Once they have thus enjoyed heavenly sense pleasure, they are reborn on this planet again. By practicing vedic *rituals as result oriented actions, they are bound by the cycle of birth and death.*

अनन्याश्चिन्तयन्तो मां ये जनाः पर्युपासते ।
तेषां नित्याभियुक्तानां योगक्षेमं वहाम्यहम् ॥ ९.२२

ananyāścintayanto māṁ ye janāḥ paryupāsate I
teṣāṁ nityābhiyuktānāṁ yogakṣemaṁ vahāmyaham II 9.22

ananyāḥ: no other; *cintayantaḥ*: concentrating; *māṁ*: unto Me; *ye*: who; *janāḥ*: persons; *paryupāsate*: properly worship; *teṣāṁ*: their; *nityābhiyuktānāṁ*: always fixed in devotion; *yogakṣemaṁ*: requirements; *vahāmi*: carry; *ahaṁ*: I.

9.22 When you reside in My consciousness, whatever you lack I give. And whatever you have, I preserve

येऽप्यन्यदेवता भक्ता यजन्ते श्रद्धयान्विताः ।
तेऽपि मामेव कौन्तेय यजन्त्यविधिपूर्वकम् ॥ ९.२३

ye'pyanyadevatā bhaktā yajante śraddhayā'nvitāḥ I
te'pi māmeva kaunteya yajantyavidhipūrvakam II 9.23

ye: those; *api*: also; *anya*: other; *devatāḥ*: demigods; *bhaktāḥ*: devotees; *yajante*: worship; *śraddhayā anvitāḥ*: with faith; *te*: they; *api*: also; *māṁ*: Me; *eva*: even; *kaunteya*: O son of Kuntī; *yajanti*: sacrifice; *avidhi pūrvakaṁ*: in an improper manner.

9.23 Even those who worship other deities, they too worship Me, O son of Kuntī but without true understanding.

अहं हि सर्वयज्ञानां भोक्ता च प्रभुरेव च ।
न तु मामभिजानन्ति तत्त्वेनातश्च्यवन्ति ते ॥ ९.२४

ahaṁ hi sarvayajñānāṁ bhoktā ca prabhureva ca I
na tu māmabhijānanti tattvenātaścyavanti te II 9.24

ahaṁ: I; *hi*: surely; *sarva*: of all; *yajñānāṁ*: sacrifices; *bhoktā*: enjoyer; *ca*: and; *prabhuḥ*: Lord; *eva*: also; *ca*: and; *na*: not; *tu*: but; *māṁ*: Me; *abhijānanti*: know; *tattvena*: in reality; *atah*: therefore; *cyavanti*: fall down; *te*: they

9.24 I am the only enjoyer and the only object of sacrifice. Those who do not recognize My true transcendental nature are born again and again.

यान्ति देवव्रता देवान्पितॄन्यान्ति पितृव्रताः ।
भूतानि यान्ति भूतेज्या यान्ति मद्याजिनोपि माम् ॥ ९.२५

yānti devavratā devān pitṝnyānti pitṛvratāḥ I
bhūtāni yānti bhūtejyā yānti madyājino'pi mām II 9.25

yānti: achieve; *deva vratāḥ*: worshipers of demigods; *devān*: to demigods; *pitṝn*: to ancestors; *yānti*: go; *pitṛ vratāḥ*: worshipers of the ancestors; *bhūtāni*: to ghosts and spirits; *yānti*: go; *bhūtejyāḥ*: worshippers of ghosts and spirits; *yānti*: go; *mad*: My; *yājinaḥ*: devotees; *api*: also; *māṁ*: unto Me.

9.25 Those who worship the deities will take birth among the deities; those who worship ghosts and spirits will take birth among such beings; those who worship ancestors go to the ancestors; those who worship Me will live with Me.

पत्रं पुष्पं फलं तोयं यो मे भक्त्या प्रयच्छति ।
तदहं भक्त्युपहृतमश्नामि प्रयतात्मनः ॥ ९.२६

patraṁ puṣpaṁ phalaṁ toyaṁ yo me bhaktyā prayacchati I
tadahaṁ bhaktyupahṛtamaśnāmi prayatātmanaḥ II 9.26

patraṁ: a leaf; *puṣpaṁ*: a flower; *phalaṁ*: a fruit; *toyaṁ*: water; *yaḥ*: whoever; *me*: unto Me; *bhaktyā*: with devotion; *prayacchati*: offers; *tat*: that; *ahaṁ*: I; *bhaktyupahṛtaṁ*: offered in devotion; *aśnāmi*: accept; *prayatātmanaḥ*: of one in pure consciousness.

9.26 Whoever offers Me with love and devotion a leaf, a flower, fruit or water, I will accept and consume what is offered by the pure-hearted

यत्करोषि यदश्नासि यज्जुहोषि ददासि यत् ।
यत्तपस्यसि कौन्तेय तत्कुरुष्व मदर्पणम् ॥ ९.२७

yatkaroṣi yadaśnāsi yajjuhoṣi dadāsi yat |
yattapasyasi kaunteya tatkuruṣva madarpaṇam || 9.27

yat: whatever; *karoṣi*: you do; *yat*: whatever; *aśnāsi*: you eat; *yat*: whatever; *juhoṣi*: you offer; *dadāsi*: you give away; *yat*: whatever; *tapasyasi*: austerities you perform; *kaunteya*: O son of Kuntī; *tat*: that; *kuruṣva*: make; *mat*: unto Me; *arpaṇaṁ*: offering.

9.27 O son of Kuntī, all that you do, all that you eat, all that you offer and give away, as well as all austerities that you may perform, give them as an offering to Me.

शुभाशुभफलैरेवं मोक्ष्यसे कर्मबन्धनैः ।
संन्यासयोगयुक्तात्मा विमुक्तो मामुपैष्यसि ॥ ९.२८

śubhāśubhaphalairevaṁ mokṣyase karmabandhanaiḥ |
sannyāsayogayuktātmā vimukto māmupaiṣyasi || 9.28

śubha: good; *aśubha*: evil; *phalaiḥ*: results; *evaṁ*: thus; *mokṣyase*: free; *karma*: action; *bandhanaiḥ*: bondage; *sannyāsa*: of renunciation; *yoga*: the yoga; *yuktātmā*: having the mind firmly set on; *vimuktaḥ*: liberated; *māṁ*: to Me; *upaiṣyasi*: you will attain.

9.28 You will be freed from all reactions to good and evil deeds by this renunciation, You will be liberated and come to Me.

समोऽहं सर्वभूतेषु न मे द्वेष्योऽस्ति न प्रियः ।
ये भजन्ति तु मां भक्त्या मयि ते तेषु चाप्यहम् ॥ ९.२९

samo'haṁ sarvabhūteṣu na me dveṣyo'sti na priyaḥ |
ye bhajanti tu māṁ bhaktyā mayi te teṣu cā'pyaham || 9.29

samaḥ: equally disposed; *ahaṁ*: I; *sarva bhūteṣu*: to all living entities; *na*: no one; *me*: Mine; *dveṣyaḥ*: hateful; *asti*: is; *na*: nor; *priyaḥ*: dear; *ye*: those; *bhajanti*: render transcendental service; *tu*: yet; *māṁ*: unto Me; *bhaktyā*: in devotion; *mayi*: unto Me; *te*: such persons; *teṣu*: in them; *ca*: also; *api*: certainly; *ahaṁ*: I.

9.29 I dislike no one, nor am I partial to anyone. I am equal to all. Whoever is devoted to Me is a friend, is in Me, and I am also a friend to him.

अपि चेत्सुदुराचारो भजते मामनन्यभाक् ।
साधुरेव स मन्तव्य: सम्यग्व्यवसितो हि स: ॥ ९.३०

api cetsudurācāro bhajate māmananyabhāk |
sādhureva sa mantavyaḥ samyagvyavasito hi saḥ || 9.30

api: in spite of; *cet*: although; *sudurācāraḥ*: one committing the most abominable actions; *bhajate*: engaged in devotional service; *māṁ*: unto Me; *ananyabhāk*: without deviation; *sādhuḥ*: saint; *eva*: certainly; *saḥ: he*; *mantavyaḥ*: to be considered; *samyak*: completely; *vyavasitaḥ*: situated; *hi*: certainly; *saḥ*: he.

9.30 Even if the most sinful person engages himself in devotional service, He is to be considered saintly because he is properly situated

क्षिप्रं भवति धर्मात्मा शश्वच्छान्तिं निगच्छति ।
कौन्तेय प्रतिजानीहि न मे भक्त: प्रणश्यति ॥ ९.३१

kṣipraṁ bhavati dharmātmā śaśvacchāntiṁ nigacchati |
kaunteya pratijānīhi na me bhaktaḥ praṇaśyati || 9.31

kṣipraṁ: very soon; *bhavati*: becomes; *dharmātmā*: righteous; *śaśvat śāntiṁ*: lasting peace; *nigacchati*: attains; *kaunteya*: O son of Kuntī; *pratijānīhi*: justly declare; *na*: never; *me*: Mine; *bhaktaḥ*: devotees; *praṇaśyati*: perishes.

9.31 He quickly becomes righteous and attains lasting peace. O son of Kuntī, declare it boldly that My devotee never perishes.

मां हि पार्थ व्यपाश्रित्य येऽपि स्यु: पापयोनय: ।
स्त्रियो वैश्यास्तथा शूद्रास्तेऽपि यान्ति परां गतिम् ॥ ९.३२

mām hi pārtha vyapāśritya ye'pi syuḥ pāpayonayaḥ |
striyo vaiśyāstathā śūdrāste'pi yānti parāṁ gatim || 9.32

mām: unto Me; *hi*: certainly; *pārtha*: O son of Prtha; *vyapāśritya*: particularly taking shelter; *ye*: anyone; *api*: also; *syuḥ*: becomes; *pāpayonayaḥ*: born of a lower family; *striyaḥ*: women; *vaiśyāḥ*: mercantile people; *tathā*: also; *śūdrāḥ*: people considered low-born; *te api*: even they; *yānti*: go; *parām*: supreme; *gatim*: destination.

9.32 *O son of Pritā, anyone who takes shelter in Me, women, traders, workers or even sinners can approach the supreme destination.*

किं पुनर्ब्राह्मणा: पुण्या भक्ता राजर्षयस्तथा ।
अनित्यमसुखं लोकमिमं प्राप्य भजस्व माम् ॥ ९.३३

kiṁ punarbrāhmaṇāḥ puṇyā bhaktā rājarṣayastathā |
anityamasukhaṁ lokamimaṁ prāpya bhajasva mām || 9.33

kiṁ: how much; *punaḥ*: again; *brāhmaṇāḥ*: brahmanas; *puṇyāḥ*: righteous; *bhaktāḥ*: devotees; *rājarṣayaḥ*: saintly kings; *tathā*: also; *anityaṁ*: temporary; *asukhaṁ*: sorrowful; *lokaṁ*: planet; *imaṁ*: this; *prāpya*: gaining; *bhajasva*: are engaged in loving service; *mām*: unto Me.

9.33 *How easier then it is for the learned, the righteous, the devotees and saintly kings who in this temporary miserable world engage in loving service unto Me.*

मन्मना भव मद्भक्तो मद्याजी मां नमस्कुरु ।
मामेवैष्यसि युक्त्वैवमात्मानं मत्परायण: ॥ ९.३४

manmanā bhava madbhakto madyājī māṁ namaskuru |
māmevaiṣyasi yuktvaivamātmānaṁ matparāyaṇaḥ || 9.34

manmanāḥ: always thinking of Me; *bhava*: become; *mad*: My; *bhaktaḥ*: devotee; *madyājī*: My worshiper; *māṁ*: unto Me; *namaskuru*: offer obeisances; *māṁ*: unto Me; *eva*: completely; *eṣyasi*: come; *yuktvā evaṁ*: being absorbed; *ātmānaṁ*: your soul; *matparāyaṇaḥ*: devoted to Me.

9.34 *Fix your mind on Me, be devoted to Me, worship Me, and bow down to Me. Thus, uniting yourself with Me by setting Me as the supreme goal and the sole refuge, you shall certainly come to Me.*

इति श्रीमद्भगवद्गीतासूपनिषत्सु ब्रह्मविद्यायां योगशास्त्रे
श्रीकृष्णार्जुनसंवादे राजविद्याराजगुह्ययोगो नाम नवमोऽध्याय: ॥

iti śrīmad bhagavadgītāsūpaniṣatsu brahmavidyāyām
yogaśāstre śrīkṛṣṇārjuna saṁvāde rājavidyā rājaguhyayogo nāma
navamo'dhyāyaḥ ||

In the Upaniṣad *of the Bhagavad Gītā, the knowledge of* Brahman, *the Supreme, the science of Yoga and the dialogue between Śrī Kṛṣṇa and Arjuna, this is the ninth discourse designated:*

Rājavidyā-Rājaguhya Yogaḥ

Verses Of Gita Chapter - 10

अथ दशमोऽध्यायः

विभूतियोगः

Vibhūthi Yogaḥ

श्री भगवानुवाच ।
भूय एव महाबाहो शृणु मे परमं वचः ।
यत्तेऽहं प्रीयमाणाय वक्ष्यामि हितकाम्यया ॥ १

Śrībhagavānuvāca
bhūya eva mahābāho śṛṇu me paramaṁ vacaḥ I
yatte'haṁ prīyamāṇāya vakṣyāmi hitakāmyayā II 10.1

śrī bhagavān uvāca: Lord Krṣna said; *bhūyaḥ:* again; *eva:* surely; *mahābāho:* mighty-armed; *śṛnu:* hear; *me:* My; *paramaṁ:* supreme; *vacaḥ:* words; *yat:* that which; *te:* to you; *ahaṁ:* I; *prīyamāṇāya:* dear to Me; *vakṣyāmi:* say; *hitakāmyayā:* with the desire for your benefit.

10.1 Lord Kṛṣṇa said: Listen again, Oh Arjuna! You are My dear friend, Listen carefully again, I shall speak further on knowledge for your welfare.

न मे विदुः सुरगणाः प्रभवं न महर्षयः ।
अहमादिर्हि देवानां महर्षीणां च सर्वशः ॥ २

na me viduḥ suragaṇāḥ prabhavaṁ na maharṣayaḥ I
ahamādirhi devānāṁ maharṣīṇāṁ ca sarvaśaḥ II 10.2

na: not; *me:* My; *viduḥ:* know; *suragaṇāḥ:* demigods; *prabhavaṁ:* glories; *na:* not; *maharṣayaḥ:* great sages; *ahaṁ:* I; *ādiḥ:* origin; *hi:* certainly; *devānāṁ:* of the gods; *maharṣīṇāṁ:* of the great sages; *ca:* and; *sarvaśaḥ:* in all respects.

10.2 Neither the hosts of deities nor the great sages know My origin, My opulence. I am the source of the deities and the sages.

यो मामजमनादिं च वेत्ति लोकमहेश्वरम् ।
असंमूढः स मर्त्येषु सर्वपापैः प्रमुच्यते ॥ ३

yo māmajamanādiṁ ca vetti lokamaheśvaram I
asaṁmūḍhaḥ sa martyeṣu sarvapāpaiḥ pramucyate II 10.3

yo: who; *mām:* to Me; *ajaṁ:* unborn; *anādiṁ:* without beginning; *ca:* and; *vetti:* know; *loka:* worlds; *maheśvaram:* supreme lord; *asaṁmūḍhaḥ:* without doubt; *sa:* he; *martyeṣu:* mortal; *sarva:* all; *pāpaiḥ:* sins; *pramucyate:* delivered.

10.3 He who knows Me as the unborn, without beginning, and supreme Lord of all the worlds, Only he, who has this clarity, is wise and freed from all bondage.

बुद्धिर्ज्ञानमसम्मोहः क्षमा सत्यं दमः शमः ।
सुखं दुःखं भवोऽभावो भयं चाभयमेव च ॥ ४

buddhirjñānam asaṁmohaḥ kṣamā satyaṁ damaḥ śamaḥ /
sukhaṁ duḥkhaṁ bhavo 'bhāvo bhayaṁ cābhayameva ca // 10.4

buddhiḥ: intelligence; *jñānam:* knowledge; *asaṁmohaḥ:* free from doubt; *kṣamā:* forgiveness; *satyaṁ:* truthfulness; *damaḥ:* control of senses; *śamaḥ:* control of mind; *sukhaṁ:* happiness; *duḥkhaṁ:* distress; *bhavo 'bhāvo:* birth and death; *bhayaṁ:* fear; *cā:* and; *abhayaṁ:* fearlessness; *eva:* also; *ca:* and

अहिंसा समता तुष्टिस्तपो दानं यशोऽयशः ।
भवन्ति भावा भूतानां मत्त एव पृथग्विधाः ॥ ५

ahiṁsā samatā tuṣṭistapo dānaṁ yaśo 'yaśaḥ /
bhavanti bhāvā bhūtānāṁ matta eva pṛthagvidhāḥ // 10.5

ahiṁsā: non-violence; *samatā:* equanimity; *tuṣṭis:* satisfaction; *tapo:* austerity; *dānaṁ:* charity; *yaśo:* fame; *ayaśaḥ:* infamy; *bhavanti:* become; *bhāvā:* nature; *bhūtānāṁ:* living beings; *matta:* from me; *eva:* surely; *pṛthagvidhāḥ:* in various forms

10.4,5 Intelligence, knowledge, freedom from doubt and delusion, forgiveness, truthfulness, control of the senses, control of the mind, happiness, distress, birth, death, fear, fearlessness, non-violence, equanimity, satisfaction, austerity, charity, fame and infamy, all these various qualities of living beings are created by Me alone.

महर्षयः सप्त पूर्वे चत्वारो मनवस्तथा ।
मद्भावा मानसा जाता येषां लोक इमाः प्रजाः ॥ ६

maharṣayaḥ sapta pūrve catvāro manavastathā /
madbhāvā mānasā jātā yeṣāṁ loka imāḥ prajāḥ // 10.6

maharṣayaḥ: great sages; *sapta:* seven; *pūrve:* before; *catvāro:* four; *manavas:* Manus; *tathā:* and; *madbhāvā:* endowed with My power; *mānasā:* from the mind; *jātā:* born; *yeṣāṁ:* of them; *loka:* worlds; *imāḥ:* all this; *prajāḥ:* living beings.

10.6 The seven great sages and before them, the four great Manus, endowed with My power, They arose from My mind and all the living beings populating the planet descend from them.

एतां विभूतिं योगं च मम यो वेत्ति तत्त्वतः ।
सोऽविकम्पेन योगेन युज्यते नात्र संशयः ॥ ७

etām vibhūtiṁ yogaṁ ca mama yo vetti tattvataḥ I
so 'vikampena yogena yujyate nātra saṁśayaḥ II 10.7

etāṁ: all this; *vibhūtiṁ:* glory; *yogaṁ:* powers; *ca:* and; *mama:* My; *yo:* who; *vetti:* knows; *tattvataḥ:* truth; *so:* he; *'vikampena:* without distraction; *yogena:* in yoga; *yujyate:* engaged; *nā:* not; *atra:* here; *saṁśayaḥ:* doubt.

10.7 He who knows all this glory and powers of mine, truly, he is fully united in Me; Of that there is no doubt.

अहं सर्वस्य प्रभवो मत्तः सर्वं प्रवर्तते ।
इति मत्वा भजन्ते मां बुधा भावसमन्विताः ॥ ८

ahaṁ sarvasya prabhavo mattaḥ sarvaṁ pravartate I
iti matvā bhajante māṁ budhā bhāvasamanvitāḥ II 10.8

ahaṁ: I; *sarvasya:* all; *prabhavo;* source; *mattaḥ:* from Me; *sarvaṁ:* all; *pravartate:* emanates; *iti:* thus; *matvā:* knowing; *bhajante:* pray; *māṁ:* to Me; *budhā:* wise; *bhāvasamanvitāḥ:* surrender

10.8 I am the source of all the spiritual and material worlds. Everything arises from Me. The wise who know this are devoted to Me and surrender their heart to Me.

मच्चित्ता मद्गतप्राणा बोधयन्तः परस्परम् ।
कथयन्तश्च मां नित्यं तुष्यन्ति च रमन्ति च ॥ ९

maccittā madgataprāṇā bodhayantaḥ parasparam I
kathayantaśca māṁ nityaṁ tuṣyanti ca ramanti ca II 10.9

maccittā: with mind engaged in Me; *madgataprāṇā:* lives absorbed in Me; *bodhayantaḥ:* enlightening; *parasparam:* one another; *kathayantaḥ:* talking about My glories; *ca:* and; *mām:* about Me; *nityam:* always; *tuṣyanti:* satisfied; *ca:* and; *ramanti:* enjoy bliss; *ca:* and

10.9 With mind and lives absorbed on Me, always enlightening one another and talking about My glories, the wise are content and blissful.

तेषां सततयुक्तानां भजतां प्रीतिपूर्वकम् ।
ददामि बुद्धियोगं तं येन मामुपयान्ति ते ॥ १०

teṣāṁ satatayuktānāṁ bhajatāṁ prītipūrvakam **I**
dadāmi buddhiyogaṁ taṁ yena māmupayānti te **II** 10.10

teṣāṁ: to them; *satatayuktānāṁ:* always engaged; *bhajatāṁ:* praying; *prītipūrvakam:* with love; *dadāmi:* I give; *buddhiyogaṁ:* intelligence; *taṁ:* that; *yena:* by which; *māṁ:* to Me; *upayānti:* come; *te:* they

10.10 To those who are always engaged in Me with love, I give them enlightenment by which they come to Me.

तेषामेवानुकम्पार्थमहमज्ञानजं तमः ।
नाशयाम्यात्मभावस्थो ज्ञानदीपेन भास्वता ॥ ११

teṣāmevānukampārthamahamajñānajaṁ tamaḥ **I**
nāśayāmyātmabhāvastho jñānadīpena bhāsvatā **II** 10.11

teṣāṁ: to them; *evā:* also; *anukampārtham:* out of compassion; *aham:* I; *ajñānajaṁ:* born of ignorance; *tamaḥ:* darkness; *nāśayāmi:* destroy; *ātma:* within; *bhāvasthaḥ:* themselves; *jñānadīpena:* lamp of knowledge; *bhāsvatā:* shining

10.11 Out of compassion to them, I destroy the darkness born out of their ignorance by the shining lamp of knowledge.

अर्जुन उवाच
परं ब्रह्म परं धाम पवित्रं परमं भवान् ।
पुरुषं शाश्वतं दिव्यमादिदेवमजं विभुम् ॥ १२

Arjuna uvāca
paraṁ brahma paraṁ dhāma pavitraṁ paramaṁ bhavān **I**
puruṣaṁ śāśvataṁ divyamādidevamajaṁ vibhum **II** 10.12

Arjuna uvāca: Arjuna said; *paraṁ:* supreme; *brahman:* truth; *paraṁ:* supreme; *dhāma:* light; *pavitraṁ:* pure; *paramaṁ:* supreme; *bhavān:* yourself; *puruṣaṁ:* person; *śāśvataṁ:* original; *divyam:* godly; *ādidevam:* original god; *ajaṁ:* unborn; *vibhum:* glorious

10.12 Arjuna said: You are the supreme truth, supreme sustenance, supremely purifier, the primal, eternal and glorious Lord.

आहुस्त्वामृषयः सर्वे देवर्षिर्नारदस्तथा ।
असितो देवलो व्यासः स्वयं चैव ब्रवीषि मे ॥ १३

āhustvāmṛṣayaḥ sarve devarṣirnāradastathā I
asito devalo vyāsaḥ svayaṁ caiva bravīṣi me II 10.13

āhuh: say; *tvām:* to you; *ṛṣayaḥ:* sages; *sarve:* all; *devarṣiḥ:* sage of gods; *nāradaḥ:* Nārada; *tathā:* and; *asitaḥ:* Asita; *devalaḥ:* Devala; *vyāsaḥ:* Vyāsa; *svayaṁ:* personally; *ca:* and; *eva:* surely; *bravīṣi:* explain; *me:* to me

10.13 All the sages like Nārada, Asita, Devala, and Vyāsa have explained this. Now you are personally explaining to me.

सर्वमेतदृतं मन्ये यन्मां वदसि केशव ।
न हि ते भगवन्व्यक्तिं विदुर्देवा न दानवाः ॥ १४

sarvametadṛtaṁ manye yanmāṁ vadasi keśava I
na hi te bhagavanvyaktiṁ vidurdevā na dānavāḥ II 10.14

sarvam: all; *etad:* these; *ṛtaṁ:* truths; *manye:* accept; *yan:* which; *māṁ:* to me; *vadasi:* say; *keśava:* Keshava; *na:* not; *hi:* surely; *te:* your; *bhagavan:* lord; *vyaktiṁ* : express; *viduḥ:* know; *devā:* gods; *na:* nor; *dānavāḥ:* demons

10.14 Oh Keśava, I accept all these truths that You have told me. Oh Lord, neither the gods nor the demons know You.

स्वयमेवात्मनात्मानं वेत्थ त्वं पुरुषोत्तम ।
भूतभावन भूतेश देवदेव जगत्पते ॥ १५

svayamevātmanātmānaṁ vettha tvaṁ puruṣottama I
bhūtabhāvana bhūteśa devadeva jagatpate II 10.15

svayam: own; *evā:* surely; *atmanā:* by yourself; *atmānaṁ:* yourself; *vettha:* know; *tvaṁ:* you; *puruṣottama:* perfect man; *bhūtabhāvana:* origin of beings; *bhūteśa:* lord of beings; *devadeva:* god of gods; *jagatpate:* lord of the world

10.15 Surely, You alone know Yourself by Yourself, Oh Perfect One, the origin of beings, Oh Lord of beings, Oh God of gods, Oh Lord of the world.

वक्तुमर्हस्यशेषेण दिव्या ह्यात्मविभूतयः ।
याभिर्विभूतिभिर्लोकानिमांस्त्वं व्याप्य तिष्ठसि ॥ १६

vaktumarhasyaśeṣeṇa divyā hyātmavibhūtayaḥ I
yābhirvibhūtibhirlokānimāṁstvaṁ vyāpya tiṣṭhasi II 10.16

vaktum: say; *arhasi:* deserve; *aśeṣeṇa:* in detail; *divyā:* divine; *hi:* surely; *ātma:* Your; *vibhūtayaḥ:* glories; *yābhir:* by which; *vibhūtibhiḥ:* glories; *lokān:* worlds; *imān:* these; *tvaṁ:* You; *vyāpya:* pervade; *tiṣṭhasi:* remain

10.16 Only You can describe in detail Your divine glories by which You pervade this universe.

कथं विद्यामहं योगिंस्त्वां सदा परिचिन्तयन् ।
केषु केषु च भावेषु चिन्त्योऽसि भगवन्मया ॥ १७

kathaṁ vidyāmahaṁ yogiṁstvāṁ sadā paricintayan I
keṣu keṣu ca bhāveṣu cintyo'si bhagavanmayā II 10.17

kathaṁ: how; *vidyām:* know; *ahaṁ:* I; *yogins:* yogi; *tvāṁ:* you; *sadā:* always; *paricintayan:* contemplation; *keṣu-keṣu:* in which; *ca:* and; *bhāveṣu:* nature; *cintyo'si:* contemplated; *bhagavan:* lord; *mayā:* by me

10.17 How may I know You by contemplation? In which forms should I contemplate on You, Oh Lord?

विस्तरेणात्मनो योगं विभूतिं च जनार्दन ।
भूयः कथय तृप्तिर्हि शृण्वतो नास्ति मेऽमृतम् ॥ १८

vistareṇātmano yogaṁ vibhūtiṁ ca janārdana I
bhūyaḥ kathaya tṛptirhi śṛṇvato nāsti me'mṛtam II 10.18

vistareṇā: in detail; *atmano:* of Yourself; *yogaṁ:* powers; *vibhūtiṁ:* glories; *ca:* and; *janārdana:* Janārdana; *bhūyaḥ:* again; *kathaya:* say; *tṛptiḥ:* satisfaction; *hi:* surely; *śṛṇvato:* hear; *nā:* not; *asti:* is; *me:* my; *amṛtam:* nectar

10.18 Tell me in detail of your powers and glories, Oh Janārdana. Again, please tell for my satisfaction as I do not tire of hearing your sweet words.

श्री भगवानुवाच ।
हन्त ते कथयिष्यामि दिव्या ह्यात्मविभूतयः ।
प्राधान्यतः कुरुश्रेष्ठ नास्त्यन्तो विस्तरस्य मे ॥ १९

Śrībhagavānuvāca
hanta te kathayiṣyāmi divyā hyātmavibhūtayaḥ /
prādhānyataḥ kuruśreṣtha nāstyanto vistarasya me // 10.19

śrī bhagavān uvāca: The Lord said; *hanta:* yes; *te:* to you; *kathayiṣyāmi:* I will talk; *divyā:* divine; *hi:* surely; *ātma:* My; *vibhūtayaḥ:* glories; *prādhānyataḥ:* main; *kuruśreṣtha:* great among the Kurus; *na:* not; *asti:* there; *antaḥ:* end; *vistarasya:* detail; *me:* My

10.19 Kṛṣṇa said, 'Yes, Oh kuruśreṣtha, I will talk to you surely of My divine glories; but only of the main ones as there is no end to the details of My glories.

अहमात्मा गुडाकेश सर्वभूताशयस्थितः ।
अहमादिश्च मध्यं च भूतानामन्त एव च ॥ २०

ahamātmā guḍākeśa sarvabhūtāśayasthitaḥ /
ahamādiśca madhyaṁ ca bhūtānāmanta eva ca // 10.20

aham: I; *ātmā:* soul; *guḍākeśa:* Arjuna; *sarva:* all; *bhūtā:* living beings; *aśayasthitaḥ:* situated in; *aham:* I; *ādiḥ:* beginning; *ca:* and; *madhyaṁ:* middle; *ca:* and; *bhūtānām:* of living beings; *anta:* end; *eva:* also; *ca:* and

10.20 I am the Spirit, Oh Guḍākeśā, situated in all living beings. I am surely the beginning, middle and end of all beings.

आदित्यानामहं विष्णुर्ज्योतिषां रविरंशुमान् ।
मरीचिर्मरुतामस्मि नक्षत्राणामहं शशी ॥ २१

ādityānāmahaṁ viṣṇurjyotiṣāṁ raviraṁśumān /
marīcirmarutāmasmi nakṣatrāṇāmahaṁ śaśī // 10.21

ādityānām: of the Ādityas; *ahaṁ:* I; *viṣṇuḥ: Viṣṇu*; *jyotiṣāṁ:* of the luminaries; *raviḥ :* the sun; *aṁśumān:* bright; *marīciḥ:* Marīcī; *marutām:* of the Maruts; *asmi:* am; *nakṣatrāṇāṁ:* of the Nakṣatras; *ahaṁ:* I; *śaśī:* the moon

10.21 Of the Ādityas, I am Viṣṇu. Of the luminaries, I am the bright sun. Of the Maruts, I am Marīcī. Of the Nakṣatras, I am the moon.

वेदानां सामवेदोऽस्मि देवानामस्मि वासवः ।
इन्द्रियाणां मनश्चास्मि भूतानामस्मि चेतना ॥ २२

vedānāṁ sāmavedo'smi devānāmasmi vāsavaḥ I
indriyāṇāṁ manaścāsmi bhūtānāmasmi cetanā II 10.22

vedānāṁ: of the Vedas; *sāmavedaḥ:* Sāma Veda; *asmi:* I am; *devānām:* of the gods; *asmi:* I am; *vāsavaḥ:* Vasava; *indriyāṇāṁ:* of the senses; *manaḥ:* mind; *ca:* and; *asmi:* I am; *bhūtānām:* of living beings; *asmi:* I am; *cetanā:* consciousness

10.22 Of the Vedas, *I am the Sāma Veda. Of the gods, I am Indra. Of the senses, I am the mind and in living beings, I am the consciousness.*

रुद्राणां शङ्करश्चास्मि वित्तेशो यक्षरक्षसाम् ।
वसूनां पावकश्चास्मि मेरुः शिखरिणामहम् ॥ २३

rudrāṇāṁ śaṅkaraścāsmi vitteśo yakṣarakṣasām I
vasūnāṁ pāvakaścāsmi meruḥ śikhariṇāmaham II 10.23

rudrāṇāṁ: of the rudras; *śaṅkaraḥ:* Shankara; *ca:* and; *asmi:* I am; *vitteśaḥ:* god of wealth; *yakṣa:* demigods; *rakṣasām:* demons; *vasūnāṁ:* of the Vasus; *pāvakaḥ:* fire; *ca:* and; *asmi:* I am; *meruḥ:* Meru; *śikhariṇām:* of the peaks; *aham:* I

10.23 Of the Rudras, I am Sankara and of the Yakṣas *and* Rākṣasas, *I am Kubera, god of wealth. Of the Vasus, I am fire and of the peaks, I am Meru.*

पुरोधसां च मुख्यं मां विद्धि पार्थ बृहस्पतिम् ।
सेनानीनामहं स्कन्दः सरसामस्मि सागरः ॥ २४

purodhasāṁ ca mukhyaṁ māṁ viddhi pārtha bṛhaspatim I
senānīnāmahaṁ skandaḥ sarasāmasmi sāgaraḥ II 10.24

purodhasāṁ: of the priests; *ca:* and; *mukhyaṁ:* main; *māṁ:* Me; *viddhi:* understand; *pārtha:* Pārtha; *bṛhaspatim:* Brihaspati; *senānīnām:* of the warriors; *ahaṁ:* I am; *skandaḥ:* Skanda; *sarasām:* of the water bodies; *asmi:* I am; *sāgaraḥ:* the ocean

10.24 Of the priests, understand, O Pārtha, that I am the chief Brihaspati. Of the warriors, I am Skanda. Of the water bodies, I am the ocean.

महर्षीणां भृगुरहं गिरामस्म्येकमक्षरम् ।
यज्ञानां जपयज्ञोऽस्मि स्थावराणां हिमालयः ॥ २५

maharṣīṇāṁ bhṛgurahaṁ girāmasmyekamakṣaram /
yajñānāṁ japayajño'smi sthāvarāṇāṁ himālayaḥ // 10.25

maharṣīṇāṁ: of the great sages; *bhṛguḥ:* Bhrigu; *ahaṁ:* I; *girām:* of the vibrations; *asmi:* I am; *ekam akṣaram:* single letter (Om); *yajñānāṁ:* of the yajnas (sacrifices); *japayagñaḥ:* chanting of holy names; *asmi:* I am; *sthāvarāṇāṁ:* of the immovables; *himālayaḥ:* Himalayas

10.25 Of the great sages, I am Bhrigu. Of the vibrations, I am the OM. Of the sacrifices, I am the chanting of holy names. Of the immovable objects, I am the Himalayas.

अश्वत्थः सर्ववृक्षाणां देवर्षीणां च नारदः ।
गन्धर्वाणां चित्ररथः सिद्धानां कपिलो मुनिः ॥ २६

aśvatthaḥ sarvavṛkṣāṇāṁ devarṣīṇāṁ ca nāradaḥ /
gandharvāṇāṁ citrarathaḥ siddhānāṁ kapilo muniḥ // 10.26

aśvatthaḥ: banyan tree; *sarva:* all; *vṛkṣāṇāṁ:* of the trees; *devarṣīṇāṁ:* of the sages of the gods; *ca:* and; *nāradaḥ:* Nārada; *gandharvāṇaṁ:* of the Gandharvas; *citrarathaḥ:* Chitraratha; *siddhānāṁ:* of the Siddhas; *kapilaḥ:* Kapila; *muniḥ:* sage

10.26 Of all the trees, I am the Banyan tree and of all the sages of the gods, I am Nārada. Of the Gandharvas, I am Chitraratha. Of the realized souls, I am the sage Kapila.

उच्चैःश्रवसमश्वानां विद्धि माममृतोद्भवम् ।
ऐरावतं गजेन्द्राणां नराणां च नराधिपम् ॥ २७

uccaiḥśravasamaśvānāṁ viddhi māmamṛtodbhavam /
airāvataṁ gajendrāṇāṁ narāṇāṁ ca narādhipam // 10.27

uccaiḥśravasaṁ: Ucchaishravas; *aśvānāṁ:* of the horses; *viddhi:* know; *māṁ:* Me; *amṛtodbhavam:* Born of nectar produced from the churning of the ocean; *airāvataṁ:* Airavata; *gajendrāṇāṁ:* of the elephants; *narāṇāṁ:* of men; *ca:* and; *narādhipam:* king

10.27 Of the horses, know me to be Ucchaishravas born of the nectar generated from the churning of the ocean; Of the elephants, Airavata and of men, the king.

आयुधानामहं वज्रं धेनूनामस्मि कामधुक् ।
प्रजनश्चास्मि कन्दर्पः सर्पाणामस्मि वासुकिः ॥ २८

āyudhānāmahaṁ vajraṁ dhenūnāmasmi kāmadhuk |
prajanaścāsmi kandarpaḥ sarpāṇāmasmi vāsukiḥ || 10.28

āyudhānām: of the weapons; *ahaṁ:* I am; *vajraṁ:* thunderbolt; *dhenūnām:* of the cows; *asmi:* I am; *kāmadhuk:* Kamadhenu; *prajanaḥ:* for begetting children; *cā:* and; *asmi:* I am; *kandarpaḥ:* god of love; *sarpāṇāṁ:* of the snakes; *asmi:* I am; *vāsukiḥ:* Vasuki

10.28 Of the weapons, I am the thunderbolt. Of the cows, I am Kamadhenu; For begetting children, I am the god of love. Of the snakes, I am Vasuki.

अनन्तश्चास्मि नागानां वरुणो यादसामहम् ।
पितॄणामर्यमा चास्मि यमः संयमतामहम् ॥ २९

anantaścāsmi nāgānāṁ varuṇo yādasām aham |
pitṛṇāmaryamā cāsmi yamaḥ saṁyamatāmaham || 10.29

anantaḥ: Ananta; *ca:* and; *asmi:* I am; *nāgānāṁ:* of the serpents; *varuṇaḥ:* Varuṇa; *yādasām:* of the water deities; *aham:* I am; *pitṛṇām:* of the ancestors; *aryamā:* Aryama; *ca:* and; *asmi:* I am; *yamaḥ:* Yama; *saṁyamatām:* of the ones who ensure discipline; *aham:* I

10.29 Of the serpents, I am Ananta. Of the water deities, I am Varuṇa. Of the ancestors, I am Aryama and of the ones who ensure discipline, I am Yama.

प्रह्लादश्चास्मि दैत्यानां कालः कलयतामहम् ।
मृगाणां च मृगेन्द्रोऽहं वैनतेयश्च पक्षिणाम् ॥ ३०

prahlādaścāsmi daityānāṁ kālaḥ kalayatāmaham |
mṛgāṇāṁ ca mṛgendro'haṁ vainateyaśca pakṣiṇām || 10.30

prahlādaḥ: Prahlada; *ca:* and; *asmi:* I am; *daityānāṁ:* of the Daityas; *kālaḥ:* time; *kalayatām:* of the subduers; *aham:* I; *mṛgāṇāṁ:* of the animals; *ca:* and; *mṛgendraḥ:* king of animals; *ahaṁ:* I; *vainateyaḥ:* Garuda; *ca:* and; *pakṣiṇām:* of the bird

10.30 Of the Daitya (demons), I am Prahlad and of the reckoners, I am time. Of the animals, I am the king of animals (lion) and of the birds, I am Garuda.

पवन: पवतामस्मि राम: शस्त्रभृतामहम् ।
झषाणां मकरश्चास्मि स्रोतसामस्मि जाह्नवी ॥ ३१

pavanaḥ pavatāmasmi rāmaḥ śastrabhṛtāmaham I
jhaṣāṇāṁ makaraścāsmi srotasāmasmi jānhavī II 10.31

pavanaḥ: wind; *pavatāṁ:* that which purifies; *asmi:* I am; *rāmaḥ:* Rama; *śastrabhṛitām:* wielders of weapons; *ahaṁ:* I; *jhaṣāṇāṁ:* of the water beings; *makaraḥ :* fish; *cā:* and; *asmi:* I am; *srotasām:* of the flowing rivers; *asmi:* I am; *jānhavī:* Jahnavi (Ganga)

10.31 Of the purifiers, I am the wind. Of the wielders of weapons, I am Rama. Of the water beings, I am the shark and of the flowing rivers, I am Jahnavi (Ganga).

सर्गाणामादिरन्तश्च मध्यं चैवाहमर्जुन ।
अध्यात्मविद्या विद्यानां वाद: प्रवदतामहम् ॥ ३२

sargāṇāmādirantaśca madhyaṁ caivāhamarjuna I
adhyātmavidyā vidyānāṁ vādaḥ pravadatāmaham II 10.32

sargāṇāṁ: of all creations; *ādiḥ:* beginning; *antaḥ:* end; *ca:* and; *madhyaṁ:* middle; *ca:* and; *eva:* surely; *aham:* I; *arjuna:* Arjuna; *adhyātmavidyā:* spiritual knowledge; *vidyānāṁ:* of all knowledge; *vādaḥ:* logic; *pravadatām:* of arguments; *aham*: I

10.32 Of all creations, I am surely the beginning and end and the middle, O Arjuna. Of all knowledge, I am the spiritual knowledge of the Self. Of all arguments, I am the logic.

अक्षराणामकारोऽस्मि द्वन्द्व: सामासिकस्य च ।
अहमेवाक्षय: कालो धाताहं विश्वतोमुख: ॥ ३३

akṣarāṇāmakāro'smi dvandvaḥ sāmāsikasya ca I
ahamevākṣayaḥ kālo dhātāhaṁ viśvatomukhaḥ II 10.33

akṣarāṇām: of the letters; *akāraḥ:* The letter A; *asmi:* I am; dvandvaḥ: of the dual words; *sāmāsikasya:* compounds; *ca:* and; *ahaṁ:* I; *evā:* surely; *akṣayaḥ:* never-ending; *kālo:* time; *dhātā:* creator; *ahaṁ:* I; *viśvatomukhaḥ:* faces facing the world (Brahma)

10.33 Of the letters, I am the 'A'. Of the dual words, I am the compounds and surely I am the never-ending time. I am the Omniscient who sees everything.

मृत्यु: सर्वहरश्चाहं उद्भवश्च भविष्यताम् ।
कीर्ति: श्रीर्वाक्च नारीणां स्मृतिर्मेधा धृति: क्षमा ॥ ३४

mṛtyuḥ sarvaharaścāhamudbhavaśca bhaviṣyatāṃ I
kīrtiḥ śrīrvākca nāriṇāṁ smṛtirmedhā dhṛtiḥ kṣamā II 10.34

mṛtyuḥ: death; *sarvaharaḥ:* all-devouring; *ca:* and; *aham:* I; *udbhavaḥ:* creation; *ca:* and; *bhaviṣyatāṃ:* of the future; *kīrtiḥ:* fame; *śrīr vāk:* wealth of words; *ca:* and; *nāriṇāṁ:* of the feminine; *smṛtiḥ:* memory; *medhā:* intelligence; *dhṛtiḥ:* faithfulness; *kṣamā:* patience

10.34 I am the all-devouring death and I am the creator of all things of the future. Of the feminine, I am fame, fortune, beautiful speech, memory, intelligence, faithfulness and patience.

बृहत्साम तथा साम्नां गायत्री छन्दसामहम् ।
मासानां मार्गशीर्षोऽहं ऋतूनां कुसुमाकर: ॥ ३५

bṛhatsāma tathā sāmnāṁ gāyatrī chandasāmaham I
māsānāṁ mārgaśīrṣo'hamṛtūnāṁ kusumākaraḥ II 10.35

bṛhatsāma: Bṛhat Sāma; *tathā:* and; *sāmnāṁ:* of the Sāma Veda; *gāyatrī:* Gāyatrī; *chandasām:* of all poetry; *aham:* I; *māsānāṁ:* of the months; *mārgaśīrṣaḥ:* Mārgaśīrṣa; *aham:* I; *ṛtūnāṁ:* of the seasons; *kusumākaraḥ:* spring

10.35 Of the **Sāma** *Veda hymns, I am the Bṛhat* **Sāma** *and of all poetry, I am the Gāyatrī. Of the months, I am Mārgaśīrṣa and of the seasons, I am spring.*

द्यूतं छलयतामस्मि तेजस्तेजस्विनामहम् ।
जयोऽस्मि व्यवसायोऽस्मि सत्त्वं सत्त्ववतामहम् ॥ ३६

dyūtaṁ chalayatāmasmi tejastejasvināmaham I
jayo'smi vyavasāyo'smi sattvaṁ sattvavatāmaham II 10.36

dyūtaṁ: gambling; *chalayatām:* of all cheating; *asmi:* I am; *tejaḥ:* effulgence; *tejasvināṁ:* of all the effulgent things; *aham:* I; *jayaḥ:* victory; *asmi:* I am; *vyavasāyaḥ:* of all adventure; *asmi:* I am; *sattvaṁ:* the satvic nature; *sattvavatām:* of those who are tranquil; *aham:* I

10.36 I am the sattva quality of those who are of tranquil nature.

वृष्णीनां वासुदेवोऽस्मि पाण्डवानां धनञ्जयः ।
मुनीनामप्यहं व्यासः कवीनामुशना कविः ॥ ३७

vṛṣṇīnāṁ vāsudevo'smi pāṇḍavānāṁ dhanañjayaḥ I
munīnāmapyahaṁ vyāsaḥ kavīnāmuśanā kaviḥ II 10.37

vṛṣṇīnāṁ: of the Vṛṣnis; *vāsudevaḥ:* Vāsudeva; *asmi:* I am; *pāṇḍavānāṁ:* of the Pāṇḍavās; *dhanañjayaḥ:* Dhañanjaya; *munīnām:* of the sages; *api:* also; *ahaṁ:* I; *vyāsaḥ:* Vyāsa; *kavīnām:* of the thinkers; *uśanā:* Usana; *kaviḥ:* seer

10.37 Of the descendants of Vṛṣṇi, I am Vāsudeva Kṛṣṇa. Of the Pāṇḍavās, I am Arjuna. Of the sages, I am also Vyāsa and of the seer, I am Usana.

दण्डो दमयतामस्मि नीतिरस्मि जिगीषताम् ।
मौनं चैवास्मि गुह्यानां ज्ञानं ज्ञानवतामहम् ॥ ३८

daṇḍo damayatāmasmi nītirasmi jigīṣatām I
maunaṁ caivāsmi guhyānāṁ jñānaṁ jñānavatāmaham II 10.38

daṇḍaḥ: rod of punishment; *damayatām:* of all punishments; *asmi:* I am; *nītiḥ:* morality; *asmi:* I am; *jigīṣatām:* of the victorious; *maunaṁ:* silence; *ca:* and; *evā:* also; *asmi:* I am; *guhyānāṁ:* of the secrets; *jñānaṁ:* knowledge; *jñānavatāṁ*: of the wise; *aham:* I

10.38 Of rulers, I am their sceptre. Of the victorious, I am statesmanship. Of all secrets, I am also silence. Of the wise, I am wisdom.

यच्चापि सर्वभूतानां बीजं तदहमर्जुन ।
न तदस्ति विना यत्स्यान्मया भूतं चराचरम् ॥ ३९

yaccāpi sarvabhūtānāṁ bījaṁ tadahamarjuna I
na tadasti vinā yatsyānmayā bhūtaṁ carācaram II 10.39

yat: what; *cā:* and; *api:* also; *sarva:* all; *bhūtānāṁ:* beings; *bījaṁ:* seed; *tat:* that; *aham:* I; *arjuna:* Arjuna; *na:* not; *tat:* that; *asti:* is; *vinā:* without; *yat:* that; *syān:* exists; *mayā:* by Me; *bhūtaṁ:* created; *cara:* moving; *acaram:* unmoving

10.39 Also, of whatever beings exist, I am the seed, O Arjuna. There is nothing that exists without Me in all creations, moving and unmoving.

नान्तोऽस्ति मम दिव्यानां विभूतीनां परन्तप ।
एष तूद्देशतः प्रोक्तो विभूतेर्विस्तरो मया ॥ ४०

nānto'sti mama divyānāṁ vibhūtīnāṁ parantapa |
eṣa tūddeśataḥ prokto vibhūtervistaro mayā || 10.40

na: not; *antaḥ:* end; *asti:* is; *mama:* My; *divyānāṁ:* divine; *vibhūtīnāṁ:* glories; *parantapa:* Supreme Lord; *eṣa:* all this; *tu:* that; *uddeśataḥ:* examples; *proktaḥ:* said; *vibhūteḥ:* glories; *vistaraḥ:* detailed; *mayā:* by Me

10.40 There is no end to My divine glories, Oh Parantapa. What have been said by Me are examples of My detailed glories.

यद्यद्विभूतिमत्सत्त्वं श्रीमदूर्जितमेव वा ।
तत्तदेवावगच्छ त्वं मम तेजोंशसंभवम् ॥ ४१

yad yad vibhūtimatsattvaṁ śrīmadūrjitameva vā |
tat tad evā'vagaccha tvaṁ mama tejoṁśasaṁbhavam || 10.41

yad-yad: whatever; *vibhūtimat:* glorious; *sattvaṁ:* existence; *śrīmad:* beautiful; *ūrjitam:* glorious; *eva:* also; *vā:* or; *tat-tad:* all that; *eva:* surely; *avagaccha:* you should know; *tvaṁ:* you; *mama:* My; *tejaḥ:* splendour; *aṁśa:* part; *saṁbhavam:* born of

10.41 You should know that whatever glories exist or whatever beautiful and glorious exists, all that surely is born of just a portion of My splendour.

अथवा बहुनैतेन किं ज्ञातेन तवार्जुन ।
विष्टभ्याहमिदं कृत्स्नमेकांशेन स्थितो जगत् ॥ ४२

athavā bahunaitena kiṁ jñātena tavārjuna |
viṣṭabhyāhamidaṁ kṛtsnamekāṁśena sthito jagat || 10.42

athavā: or; *bahunā:* many; *etena:* of this kind; *kiṁ:* what; *jñātena:* know; *tava:* you; *arjuna:* Arjuna; *viṣṭabhya:* full; *aham:* I; *idaṁ:* this; *kṛtsnam*: of all manifestations; *eka:* one; *aṁśena:* part; *sthito:* situated; *jagat:* world

10.42 Of what use is to know about the many manifestations of this kind, O Arjuna? I pervade this entire world with just a part of Myself.

इति श्रीमद्भगवद्गीतासूपनिषत्सु ब्रह्मविद्यायां योगशास्त्रे
श्रीकृष्णार्जुनसंवादे विभूतियोगो नाम दशमोऽध्यायः ॥

iti śrīmad bhagavadgītāsūpaniṣatsu brahmavidyāyām
yogaśāstre śrīkṛṣṇārjuna saṁvāde vibhūtiyogo nāma
daśamo'dhyāyaḥ ||

In the Upaniṣad *of the Bhagavad Gītā, the knowledge of* Brahman, *the Supreme, the science of Yoga and the dialogue between Śrī Kṛṣṇa and Arjuna, this is the tenth discourse designated:*

Vibhūthi Yogaḥ

Verses Of Gita Chapter - 11

अथ एकादशोऽध्यायः

विश्वरूपदर्शनयोगः

Viśvarūpa darśana Yogaḥ

अर्जुन उवाच
मदनुग्रहाय परमं गुह्यमध्यात्मसंज्ञितम् ।
यत्त्वयोक्तं वचस्तेन मोहोऽयं विगतो मम ॥ १

Arjuna uvāca
madanugrahāya paramaṁ guhyaṁ adhyātmasaṁjñitam **/**
yattvayoktaṁ vacastena moho'yaṁ vigato mama **//** 11.1

Arjuna uvāca: Arjuna said; *madanugrahāya:* out of compassion for me; *paramaṁ:* supreme; *guhyaṁ:* confidential; *adhyātma:* spiritual; *saṁjñitam:* in the matter of; *yat:* what; *tvayā:* by You; *uktaṁ:* said; *vacaḥ:* words; *tena:* by that; *mohaḥ:* delusion; *ayaṁ*: this; *vigataḥ:* removed; *mama:* my

11.1 Arjuna says: 'O Lord! By listening to Your wisdom on the supreme secret of Existence and your glory, I feel that my delusion has disappeared.'

भवाप्ययौ हि भूतानां श्रुतौ विस्तरशो मया ।
त्वत्तः कमलपत्राक्ष माहात्म्यमपि चाव्ययम् ॥ २

bhavāpyayau hi bhūtānāṁ śrutau vistaraśo mayā **/**
tvattaḥ kamalapatrākṣa māhātmyamapi cāvyayam **//** 11.2

bhava: creation; *apyayau:* dissolution; *hi:* certainly; *bhūtānāṁ:* of all living entities; *śrutau:* have heard; *vistaraśaḥ:* detail; *mayā:* by me; *tvattaḥ:* from You; *kamalapatrākṣa*: O lotus-eyed one; *māhātmyam:* glories; *api:* also; *cā:* and; *avyayam*: inexhaustible

11.2 O Kṛṣṇa! I have heard from you about the creation and destruction of all beings, Also, Your inexhaustible greatness.

एवमेतद्यथात्थ त्वमात्मानं परमेश्वर ।
द्रष्टुमिच्छामि ते रूपमैश्वरं पुरुषोत्तम ॥ ३

evaṁetadyathāttha tvamātmānaṁ parameśvara |
draṣṭumicchāmi te rūpamaiśvaraṁ puruṣottama || 11.3

evaṁ: thus; *etat:* this; *yathā:* as it is; *āttha:* have spoken; *tvaṁ:* You; *ātmānaṁ:* the soul; *parameśvara:* the Supreme Lord; *draṣṭuṁ:* to see; *icchāmi:* I wish; *te:* You; *rūpaṁ:* form; *aiśvaraṁ:* divine; *puruṣottama:* best of manifested forms

11.3 Puruṣottama! You have declared what You are, O Lord supreme, I wish to see the divine form of yours.

मन्यसे यदि तच्छक्यं मया द्रष्टुमिति प्रभो।
योगेश्वर ततो मे त्वं दर्शयात्मानमव्ययम् ॥ ४

manyase yadi tacchakyaṁ mayā draṣṭumiti prabho |
yogeśvara tato me tvaṁ darśayātmānamavyayam || 11.4

manyase: You think; *yadi:* if; *tat:* that; *śakyaṁ:* able; *mayā:* by me; *draṣṭum:* to see; *iti:* thus; *prabho:* O Lord; *yogeśvara:* O Lord of all mystic power; *tataḥ:* then; *me*: unto me; *tvaṁ:* You; *darśaya:* show; *ātmānaṁ:* Yourself; *avyayaṁ:* imperishable

11.4 If you think it is possible for me to see it, then please, O Lord of Yoga and all mystic power, show me Your form of eternal universal Self.

श्री भगवानुवाच
पश्य मे पार्थ रूपाणि शतशोऽथ सहस्रशः।
नानाविधानि दिव्यानि नानावर्णाकृतीनि च ॥ ५

Srībhagavānuvāca
paśya me pārtha rūpāṇi śataśo'tha sahasraśaḥ |
nānāvidhāni divyāni nānāvarṇākṛtīni ca || 11.5

śrī bhagavān uvāca: Kṛṣṇa said; *paśya:* behold; *me*: Mine; *pārtha:* arjuna; *rūpāṇi*: forms; *śataśaḥ:* hundreds; *atha:* also; *sahasraśaḥ:* thousands; *nānāvidhāni:* of different nature; *divyāni:* divine; *nānā:* various; *varṇa*: colors; *ākṛtīni:* shapes; *ca*: also

11.5 Bhagavān *said: O Pārtha, behold my hundreds and thousands of forms, of different divine sorts, of various colors and shapes.*

पश्यादित्यान्वसून्वरुद्रानश्विनौ मरुतस्तथा।
बहून्यदृष्टपूर्वाणि पश्याश्चर्याणि भारत ॥ ६

paśyādityānvasūnrudrānaśvinau marutastathā |
bahūnyadṛṣṭapūrvāṇi paśyāścaryāṇi bhārata || 11.6

paśya: see; *adityān*: the twelve sons of Aditi; *vasūn*: the eight Vasus; *rudrān:* the eleven forms of Rudra; *aśvinau:* the two Aśvinis; *marutaḥ:* the forty-nine Maruts (wind deities); *tathā:* also; *bahūni:* many; *adṛṣṭa*: that you have never seen; *pūrvāṇi:* before; *paśya:* see; *āścaryāṇi:* wonderful; *bhārata:* O best of the Bhāratas

*11.6 O Bhārata, see the Ādityas, the Vasus, the Rudras, the **Aśvins,** the Maruts and many wonders you have never seen before.*

इहैकस्थं जगत्कृत्स्नं पश्याद्य सचराचरम्।
मम देहे गुडाकेश यच्चान्यद्द्रष्टुमिच्छसि ॥ ७

ihaikasthaṁ jagatkṛtsnaṁ paśyādya sacarācaram |
mama dehe guḍākeśa yaccānyad draṣṭumicchasi || 11.7

iha: in this; *ekasthaṁ:* situated in one; *jagat:* the universe; *kṛtsnaṁ:* whole; *paśya*: see; *adya*: now; *sa:* with; *carā*: moving; *acaram*: not moving; *mama*: My; *dehe:* in this body; *guḍākeśa*: O Arjuna; *yat:* that; *ca:* also; *anyat*: other; *draṣṭum:* to see; *icchasi*: you like

11.7 O Arjuna, now in My body, all the moving and the unmoving, whatever else you wish to see, everything integrated into this body.

न तु मां शक्यसे द्रष्टुमनेनैव स्वचक्षुषा।
दिव्यं ददामि ते चक्षुः पश्य मे योगमैश्वरम् ॥ ८

na tu māṁ śakyase draṣṭumanenaiva svacakṣuṣā |
divyaṁ dadāmi te cakṣuḥ paśya me yogamaiśvaram || 11.8

na: never; *tu:* but; *māṁ:* Me; *śakyase:* able; *draṣṭum*: to see; *anena:* by this; *eva:* certainly; *svacakṣuṣā:* with your own eyes; *divyaṁ:* divine; *dadāmi:* I give; *te:* to you; *cakṣuḥ:* eyes; *paśya:* see; *me*: My; *yogam aiśvaram:* divine powers

11.8 But you cannot see Me with these your physical eyes. Let Me give you the divine eye; behold my divine power.

सञ्जय उवाच

एवमुक्त्वा ततो राजन्महायोगेश्वरो हरिः।
दर्शयामास पार्थाय परमं रूपमैश्वरम् ॥ ९

Sañjaya uvāca

evamuktvā tato rājanmahāyogeśvaro hariḥ |

darśayāmāsa pārthāya paramaṁ rūpamaiśvaram || 11.9

Sañjaya uvāca: Sañjaya said; *evam:* thus; *uktvā:* having said; *tataḥ:* thereafter; *rājan:* O King; *mahāyogeśvaraḥ*: the great Lord of Yoga; *hariḥ:* Kṛṣṇa; *darśayāmāsa:* showed; *pārthāya:* to Arjuna; *paramaṁ*: divine; *rūpam:* form; *aiśvaram:* opulences

11.9 Sañjaya said: O King, having spoken thus, the great Lord of Yoga, Kṛṣṇa, showed to Arjuna His supreme cosmic form.

अनेकवक्त्रनयनमनेकाद्भुतदर्शनम् ।
अनेकदिव्याभरणं दिव्यानेकोद्यतायुधम् ॥ १०

anekavaktranayanamanekādbhuta darśanam |

anekadivyābharaṇaṁ divyānekodyatāyudham || 11.10

aneka: various; *vaktra:* mouths; *nayanam:* eyes; *aneka:* various; *adbhuta*: wonderful; *darśanam:* sights; *aneka*: many; *divya:* divine; *ābharaṇaṁ:* ornaments; *divya*: divine; *aneka:* various; *udyata:* uplifted; *āyudham:* weapons

11.10 Numerous mouths and eyes, with numerous wonderful sights, numerous divine ornaments, with numerous divine weapons uplifted.

दिव्यमाल्याम्बरधरं दिव्यगन्धानुलेपनम् ।
सर्वाश्चर्यमयं देवमनन्तं विश्वतोमुखम् ॥ ११

divyamālyāmbaradharaṁ divyagandhānulepanam |

sarvāścaryamayaṁ devamanantaṁ viśvatomukham || 11.11

divya: divine; *mālya:* garlands; *ambaradharaṁ*: covered with the dresses; *divya:* divine; *gandha:* fragrance; *anulepanam*: smeared; *sarva:* all; *aścaryamayaṁ:* wonderful; *devaṁ:* shining; *anantaṁ:* endless; *viśvatomukham:* with faces on all sides

11.11 Arjuna saw this universal form wearing divine garlands and clothing, anointed with celestial fragrances, wonderful, resplendent, endless, with faces on all sides.

दिवि सूर्यसहस्रस्य भवेद्युगपदुत्थिता ।
यदि भा: सदृशी सा स्याद्भासस्तस्य महात्मन: ॥ १२

divi sūryasahasrasya bhavedyugapadutthitā |
yadi bhāḥ sadṛśī sā syādbhāsastasya mahātmanaḥ || 11.12

divi: in the sky; *sūrya:* sun; *sahasrasya:* of many thousands; *bhaved:* there were; *yugapad:* simultaneously; *utthitā:* present; *yadi:* if; *bhāḥ:* splendor; *sadṛśī:* like; *sā*: that; *syād:* may be; *bhāsaḥ:* effulgence; *tasya:* there is; *mahātmanaḥ:* of the great Lord

11.12 If the splendor of a thousand suns were to blaze all together in the sky, it would be like the splendor of that mighty Being.

तत्रैकस्थं जगत्कृत्स्नं प्रविभक्तमनेकधा।
अपश्यद्देवदेवस्य शरीरे पाण्डवस्तदा॥ १३

tatraikasthaṁ jagatkṛtsnaṁ pravibhaktamanekadhā |
apaśyad devadevasya śarīre pāṇḍavastadā || 11.13

tatra: there; *ekasthaṁ:* in one place; *jagat:* universe; *kṛtsnaṁ:* completely; *pravibhaktam:* divided in; *anekadhā:* many groups; *apaśyat:* saw; *devadevasya:* God of gods; *śarīre:* in the body; *pāṇḍavaḥ:* Arjuna; *tadā*: at that time

11.13 There, in the body of the God of gods, the Pāṇḍavā then saw the whole universe resting in one, with all its infinite parts.

ततः स विस्मयाविष्टो हृष्टरोमा धनञ्जयः।
प्रणम्य शिरसा देवं कृताञ्जलिरभाषत॥ १४

tataḥ sa vismayāviṣṭo hṛṣṭaromā dhanañjayaḥ |
praṇamya śirasā devaṁ kṛtāñjalirabhāṣata || 11.14

tataḥ: thereafter; *saḥ:* he; *vismayāviṣṭaḥ:* being overwhelmed with wonder; *hṛṣṭaromā*: with his bodily hair standing on end; *dhanañjayaḥ:* Arjuna; *praṇamya:* offering obeisances; *śirasā:* with the head; *devaṁ:* to God; *kṛtāñjaliḥ*: with folded palms; *abhāṣata:* said

11.14 Dhañanjaya, filled with wonder, his hair standing on end, then bowed his head to the God and spoke with joined palms.

अर्जुन उवाच।
पश्यामि देवांस्तव देव देहे सर्वांस्तथा भूतविशेषसङ्घान्।
ब्रह्माणमीशं कमलासनस्थम् ऋषींश्च सर्वानुरगांश्च दिव्यान्॥ १५

arjuna uvāca

paśyāmi devāṁstava deva dehe sarvāṁstathā bhūtaviśeṣasaṅghān I

brahmāṇamīśaṁ kamalāsanasthaṁ ṛṣīṁścasarvānuragāṁśca divyān II 11.15

arjuna uvāca: Arjuna said; *paśyāmi:* I see; *devān:* all the gods; *tava:* Your; *deva*: O Lord; *dehe*: in the body; *sarvān:* all; *tathā:* also; *bhūta:* living entities; *viśeṣa saṅghān:* specifically assembled; *brahmāṇam:* Brahma; *īśaṁ:* Lord; *kamalāsanastham*: sitting on the lotus flower; *ṛṣīn:* great sages; *ca:* also; *sarvān:* all; *uragān:* serpents; *ca:* also; *divyān:* divine

11.15 Arjuna said; O God, I see all the gods in Your body and many types of beings. Brahma, the Lord of creation seated on the lotus, all the sages and celestial serpents.

अनेक बाहूदरवक्त्रनेत्रं पश्यामि त्वां सर्वतोऽनन्तरूपम् ।

नान्तं न मध्यं न पुनस्तवादिं पश्यामि विश्वेश्वर विश्वरूप ॥ १६

anekabāhūdaravaktranetraṁ paśyāmi tvām sarvato'nantarūpam I

nāntaṁ na madhyaṁ na punastavādiṁ paśyāmi viśveśvara viśvarūpa II 11.16

aneka: many; *bāhu:* arms; *udara:* bellies; *vaktra:* mouths; *netraṁ:* eyes; *paśyāmi*: I see; *tvām:* unto You; *sarvataḥ*: from all sides; *anantarūpam:* endless form; *nā 'ntaṁ*: there is no end; *na madhyaṁ:* there is no middle; *na punaḥ:* nor again; *tava:* Your; *ādiṁ*: beginning; *paśyāmi:* I see; *viśveśvara*: O Lord of the universe; *viśvarūpa:* in the form of the universe

11.16 I see Your infinite form on every side, with many arms, stomachs, mouths and eyes; Neither the end, nor the middle nor the beginning do I see, O Lord of the Universe, O cosmic form.

किरीटिनं गदिनं चक्रिणं च तेजोराशिं सर्वतो दीप्तिमन्तम् ।

पश्यामि त्वां दुर्निरीक्ष्यं समन्ताद्दीप्तानलार्कद्युतिमप्रमेयम् ॥ १७

kirīṭinaṁ gadinaṁ cakriṇaṁ ca tejorāśiṁ sarvato dīptimantam I

paśyāmi tvāṁ durnirīkṣyaṁ samantāddīptānalārkadyutimaprameyam II 11 .17

kirīṭinaṁ: with helmets; *gadinaṁ:* with maces; *cakriṇaṁ:* with discs; *ca:* and; *tejorāśiṁ:* radiance; *sarvataḥ:* all sides; *dīptimantam:* glowing; *paśyāmi*: I see; *tvāṁ*: You; *durnirīkṣyaṁ:* difficult to see; *samantāt:* spreading; *dīptānala:* blazing fire; *arka*: sun; *dyutiṁ:* sunshine; *aprameyam:* immeasurable

11.17 I see You with crown, club and discus; a mass of radiance shining everywhere, difficult to look at, blazing all round like the burning fire and sun in infinite brilliance.

त्वमक्षरं परमं वेदितव्यं त्वमस्य विश्वस्य परं निधानम्।
त्वमव्यय: शाश्वतधर्मगोप्ता सनातनस्त्वं पुरुषो मतो मे ॥ १८

tvamakṣaraṁ paramaṁ veditavyaṁ tvamasya viśvasya paraṁ nidhānam I
tvamavyayaḥ śāśvatadharmagoptā sanātanastvaṁ puruṣo mato me II 11.18

tvaṁ: You; *akṣaraṁ:* inexhaustible; *paramaṁ:* supreme; *veditavyaṁ:* to be understood; *tvaṁ:* You; *asya:* of this; *viśvasya:* of the universe; *paraṁ:* supreme; *nidhānam:* basis; *tvaṁ:* You are; *avyayaḥ*: inexhaustible; *śāśvata dharma goptā*: maintainer of the eternal religion; *sanātanaḥ:* eternal; *tvaṁ:* You; *puruṣaḥ:* supreme personality; *mato me:* is my opinion

11.18 You are the imperishable; the supreme being worthy to be known. You are the great treasure house of this universe. You are the imperishable protector of the eternal order. I believe You are the eternal being.

अनादिमध्यान्तमनन्तवीर्यं अनन्तबाहुं शशिसूर्यनेत्रम्।
पश्यामि त्वां दीप्तहुताशवक्त्रं स्वतेजसा विश्वमिदं तपन्तम् ॥ १९

anādimadhyāntamanantavīryamanantabāhuṁ śaśisūrya netram I
paśyāmi tvāṁ dīptahutāśavaktraṁ svatejasā viśvamidaṁ tapantam II 11.19

anādi: without beginning; *madhya:* middle; *antaṁ:* end; *ananta*: unlimited; *vīryaṁ:* glorious; *ananta:* unlimited; *bāhuṁ:* arms; *śaśi:* moon; *sūrya:* sun; *netram*: eyes; *paśyāmi:* I see; *tvāṁ:* You; *dīpta:* blazing; *hutāśa vaktraṁ:* fire coming out of Your mouth; *svatejasā:* by Your; *viśvam*: this universe; *idaṁ:* this; *tapantaṁ:* scortching

11.19 I see you without a beginning, middle or end, infinite in power and many arms, The sun and the moon being Your eyes, the blazing fire your mouth, the whole universe scorched by Your radiance.

द्यावापृथिव्योरिदमन्तरं हि व्याप्तं त्वयैकेन दिशश्च सर्वा:।
दृष्ट्वाद्भुतं रूपमुग्रं तवेदं लोकत्रयं प्रव्यथितं महात्मन् ॥ २०

dyāvāpṛthivyoridamantaraṁ hi vyāptaṁ tvayaikena diśaśca sarvāḥ I
dṛṣṭvādbhutaṁ rūpamugraṁ tavedaṁ lokatrayaṁ pravyathitaṁ mahātman II 11.20

dyāvā: in outer space; *pṛthivyoḥ:* of the earth; *idaṁ:* this; *antaraṁ:* unlimited; *hi*: certainly; *vyāptaṁ:* pervaded; *tvaya* : by You; *ekena:* by one; *diśaḥ:* directions; *ca*: and; *sarvāḥ*: all; *dṛṣṭvā:* by seeing; *adbhutaṁ:* wonderful; *rūpaṁ:* form; *ugraṁ:* terrible; *tava*: Your; *idaṁ:* this; *loka:* three world; *trayaṁ:* three; *pravyathitaṁ:* perturbed; *mahātman*: O great one

11.20 This space between earth and the heavens and everything is filled by You alone. O great Being, having seen Your wonderful and terrible form, the three worlds tremble with fear.

अमी हि त्वां सुरसङ्घा विशन्ति केचिद्भीताः प्राञ्जलयो गृणन्ति।
स्वस्तीत्युक्त्वा महर्षिसिद्धसङ्घाः स्तुवन्ति त्वां स्तुतिभिः पुष्कलाभिः ॥ २१

amī hi tvāṁ surasaṅghā viśanti kecidbhītāḥ prāñjalayo gṛṇanti I
svastī tyuktvā maharṣisiddhasaṅghāḥ stuvanti tvāṁ stutibhiḥ puṣkalābhiḥ II 11.21

amī: all those; *hi:* certainly; *tvāṁ:* unto You; *surasaṁghā:* groups of celestials; *viśanti:* entering; *kecit:* some of them; *bhītāḥ:* out of fear; *prāñjalayaḥ:* with folded hands; *gṛṇanti:* offering prayers unto; *svastī:* all peace; *iti:* thus; *uktvā:* speaking like that; *maharṣi:* great sages; *siddhasaṁghāḥ:* realized sages; *stuvanti:* singing hymns; *tvāṁ:* unto You; *stutibhiḥ:* with hymns; *puṣkalābhiḥ:* sublime

11.21 Many celestials enter into You; some praise You in fear with folded hands; many great masters and sages hail and adore you.

रुद्रादित्या वसवो ये च साध्या विश्वेऽश्विनौ मरुतश्चोष्मपाश्च।
गन्धर्वयक्षासुरसिद्धसङ्घा वीक्षन्ते त्वां विस्मिताश्चैव सर्वे ॥ २२

rudrādityā vasavo ye ca sādhyā viśve'śvinau marutaścoṣmapāśca I
gandharvayakṣāsura siddhasaṅghā vīkṣante tvaṁ vismitāś caiva sarve II 11.22

rudra: manifestations of Lord Śiva; *ādityāḥ:* the Āditya; *vasavaḥ:* the Vasu; *ye:* all those; *ca:* and; *sādhyāḥ:* the Sādhyā; *viśve:* the Visvedeva; *aśvinau:* the aśvini-kumāra; *marutaḥ:* the Marut; *ca*: and; *ūṣmapāḥ:* the forefathers; *ca:* and; *gandharva*: of the Gandharva; *yakṣa*: the Yakṣa; *asura siddha:* the demons and the perfected demigods; *saṅghāḥ:* assemblies; *vīkṣante:* are seeing; *tvāṁ:* You; *vismitāḥ:* in wonder; *ca:* also; *eva:* certainly; *sarve:* all

11.22 The Rudra, Āditya, Vasu, Sādhyā, Viśvedeva, aśvin, Marut, Ūṣmapa and a host of Gandharva, yakṣa, Asura and Sidhha are all looking at You in amazement.

रूपं महत्ते बहुवक्त्रनेत्रं महाबाहो बहुबाहुरुपादम्।
बहूदरं बहुदंष्ट्राकरालं दृष्ट्वा लोकाः प्रव्यथितास्तथाहम् ॥ २३

rūpaṁ mahatte bahuvaktranetraṁ mahābāho bahubāhūrupādam **/**
bahūdaraṁ bahudaṁṣṭrākarālaṁ dṛṣṭvā lokāḥ pravyathitāstathāham **//** 11.23

rūpaṁ: form; *mahat:* very great; *te:* of You; *bahu:* many; *vaktra:* faces; *netraṁ:* eyes; *mahābāho:* O mighty-armed one; *bahu:* many; *bāhu:* arms; *ūru:* thighs; *pādam* : legs; *bahūdaraṁ:* many bellies; *bahu daṁṣṭrā:* many teeth; *karālaṁ:* horrible; *dṛṣṭvā*: seeing; *lokāḥ:* all the world; *pravyathitāḥ:* perturbed; *tathā:* similarly; *aham:* I

11.23 Having seen Your immeasurable form with many mouths and eyes, with many arms, thighs and feet, with many stomachs and frightening tusks, O mighty-armed, the worlds are terrified and so am I.

नभःस्पृशं दीप्तमनेकवर्णं व्यात्ताननं दीप्तविशालनेत्रम् ।
दृष्ट्वा हि त्वां प्रव्यथितान्तरात्मा धृतिं न विन्दामि शमं च विष्णो ॥ २४

nabhaḥspṛśaṁ dīptamanekavarṇaṁ vyāttānanaṁ dīptaviśāla netram **/**
dṛṣṭvā hi tvāṁ pravyathitāntarātmā dhṛtiṁ na vindāmi śamaṁ ca viṣṇo **//** 11.24

nabhaḥ spṛśaṁ: touching the sky; *dīptaṁ:* glowing; *aneka:* many; *varṇaṁ:* color; *vyāttā:* open; *ānanaṁ:* mouth; *dīpta:* shining; *viśāla:* very great; *netraṁ:* eyes; *dṛṣṭvā* : by seeing; *hi:* certainly; *tvāṁ:* You; *pravyathita:* perturbed; *antarātmā*: soul; *dhṛtiṁ:* steadiness; *na:* no; *vindāmi:* find; *śamaṁ:* peace; *ca:* also; *viṣṇo*: O Lord Viṣṇu

11.24 Seeing You, Your form touching the sky, flaming in many colors, mouths wide open, large fiery eyes, O Viṣṇu, I find neither courage nor peace; I am frightened.

दंष्ट्राकरालानि च ते मुखानि दृष्ट्वैव कालानलसन्निभानि ।
दिशो न जाने न लभे च शर्म प्रसीद देवेश जगन्निवास ॥ २५

daṁṣṭrākarālāni ca te mukhāni dṛṣṭvaiva kālānalasannibhāni **/**
diśo na jāne na labhe ca śarma prasīda deveśa jagannivāsa **//** 11.25

daṁṣṭrā: teeth; *karālāni*: ferocious; *ca:* also; *te:* Your; *mukhāni:* faces; *dṛṣṭvā*: seeing; *eva*: thus; *kālānala:* the fire of death; *sannibhāni:* as if blazing; *diśaḥ:* directions; *na jāne*: do not know; *na labhe:* nor obtain; *ca śarma:* and grace; *prasīda:* be pleased; *deveśa*: O Lord of all lords; *jagannivāsa:* refuge of the worlds

11.25 Having seen your fearsome mouths with blazing tusks like the fire of the end of the universe, I know not the four directions nor do I find peace. O Lord of the Deva, O refuge of the Universe, be gracious.

अमी च त्वां धृतराष्ट्रस्य पुत्राः सर्वे सहैवावनिपालसङ्घैः ।
भीष्मो द्रोणः सूतपुत्रस्तथासौ सहास्मदीयैरपि योधमुख्यैः ॥ २६

amī ca tvāṁ dhṛtarāṣṭrasya putrāḥ sarve sahaivāvanipālasaṅghaiḥ ।
bhīṣmo droṇaḥ sūtaputrastathāsau sahāsmadīyairapi yodhamukhyaiḥ ॥ 11.26

amī: all those; *ca:* also; *tvāṁ:* You; *dhṛtarāṣṭrasya:* of Dhṛtarāṣṭra; *putrāḥ:* sons; *sarve:* all; *sahaiva:* along with; *avanipāla*: warrior kings; *saṁghaiḥ:* the groups; *bhīṣm*: Bhīṣma; *droṇaḥ*: Droṇācārya; *sūtaputraḥ:* Karṇa; *tathā:* also; *asau*: that; *saha*: with; *asmadīyaiḥ:* our; *api:* also; *yodhamukhyaiḥ:* chief among the warriors

11.26 All the sons of Dhṛtarāṣṭra with many kings of the earth, Bhīṣma, Droṇa, the son of the charioteer, Karṇa, with our warrior chieftains.

वक्त्राणि ते त्वरमाणा विशन्ति दंष्ट्राकरालानि भयानकानि ।
केचिद्विलग्ना दशनान्तरेषु संदृश्यन्ते चूर्णितैरुत्तमाङ्गैः ॥ २७

vaktrāṇi te tvaramāṇā viśanti daṁṣṭrākarālāni bhayānakāni ।
kecidvilagnā daśanāntareṣu sandṛśyante cūrṇitairuttamāñgaiḥ ॥ 11.27

vaktrāṇi: mouths; *te*: Your; *tvaramāṇḥ*: hurrying; *viśanti:* entering; *daṁṣṭrā:* teeth; *karālāni:* terrible; *bhayānakāni:* very fearful; *kecit:* some of them; *vilagnā:* being attacked; *daśanāntareṣu:* between the teeth; *saṁdṛśyante:* found; *cūrṇitaiḥ:* crushed; *uttamāñgaiḥ:* by the head

11.27 Into Your mouths with terrible tusks, fearful to behold, they enter. Some are seen caught in the gaps between the tusks and their heads crushed.

यथा नदीनां बहवोऽम्बुवेगाः समुद्रमेवाभिमुखा द्रवन्ति ।
तथा तवामी नरलोकवीरा विशन्ति वक्त्राण्यभिज्वलन्ति ॥ २८

yathā nadīnāṁ bahavo'mbuvegāḥ samudramevābhimukhā dravanti ।
tathā tavāmī naralokavīrā viśanti vaktrāṇyabhivijvalanti ॥ 11.28

yathā: as; *nadīnāṁ:* of the rivers; *bahavaḥ:* many; *ambuvegāḥ*: waves of the waters; *samudram*: ocean; *eva:* certainly; *abhimukhāḥ:* towards; *dravanti:* gliding; *tathā:* similarly; *tava:* Your; *amī:* all those; *naralokavīrāḥ:* the human kings; *viśanti:* entering; *vaktrāṇi:* into the mouths; *abhivijvalanti:* blazing

11.28 Even as many torrents of rivers flow towards the ocean, so too these warriors in the world of men enter Your flaming mouths.

यथा प्रदीप्तं ज्वलनं पतङ्गा विशन्ति नाशाय समृद्धवेगाः ।
तथैव नाशाय विशन्ति लोकास्तवापि वक्त्राणि समृद्धवेगाः ॥ २९

yathā pradīptaṁ jvalanaṁ pataṅgā viśanti nāśāya samṛddhavegāḥ I
tathaiva nāśāya viśanti lokāstavāpi vaktrāṇi samṛddhavegāḥ II 11.29

yathā: as; *pradīptaṁ:* blazing; *jvalanaṁ:* fire; *pataṅgāḥ*: moths; *viśanti:* enters; *nāśāya*: destruction; *samṛddha:* full; *vegāḥ:* speed; *tathai 'va*: similarly; *nāśāya*: for destruction; *viśanti:* entering; *lokāḥ:* all people; *tava:* unto You; *api*: also; *vaktrāṇi:* in the mouths; *samṛddhavegāḥ:* with full speed

11.29 Just as moths hurriedly rush into the fire for their own destruction, So too these creatures rush hastily into Your mouths of destruction.

लेलिह्यसे ग्रसमानः समन्ताल्लोकान्समग्रान्वदनैर्ज्वलद्भिः ।
तेजोभिरापूर्य जगत्समग्रं भासस्तवोग्राः प्रतपन्ति विष्णो ॥ ३०

lelihyase grasamānaḥ samantāllokānsamagrānvadanairjvaladbhiḥ I
tejobhirāpūrya jagatsamagraṁ bhāsastavo'grāḥ pratapanti viṣṇo II 11.30

lelihyase: licking; *grasamānaḥ:* devouring; *samantāt:* from all directions; *lokān*: people; *samagrān:* completely; *vadanaiḥ:* by the mouth; *jvaladbhiḥ:* with blazing; *tejobhiḥ*: by effulgence; *āpūrya:* covering; *jagat:* the universe; *samagraṁ:* all; *bhāsas*: illuminating; *tava:* Your; *ugrāḥ:* terrible; *paratapanti:* scorching; *viṣṇo*: O all pervading Lord

11.30 Swallowing all worlds on every side with your flaming mouths You lick in enjoyment. O Viṣṇu, Your fierce rays are burning, filling the whole world with radiance.

आख्याहि मे को भवानुग्ररूपो नमोऽस्तु ते देववर प्रसीद ।
विज्ञातुमिच्छामि भवन्तमाद्यं न हि प्रजानामि तव प्रवृत्तिम् ॥ ३१

ākhyāhi me ko bhavānugrarūpo namo'stu te devavara prasīda I
vijñātumicchāmi bhavantamādyaṁ na hi prajānāmi tava pravṛttim II 11.31

ākhyāhi: please explain; *me:* unto me; *kaḥ:* who; *bhavān:* You; *ugrarūpaḥ:* fierce form; *namaḥ astu:* obeisances; *te:* unto You; *devavara:* the great one amongst the gods; *prasīda:* be gracious; *vijñātum:* just to know; *icchāmi:* I wish; *bhavantaṁ:* You; *ādyaṁ*: the original; *na:* never; *hi:* certainly; *prajānāmi:* do I know; *tava:* Your; *pravṛttim:* purpose

11.31 Tell me who You are, so fierce in form; salutations to You, O Supreme; have mercy. Indeed I know not Your purpose but I desire to know You, the Original Being.

श्री भगवानुवाच

कालोऽस्मि लोकक्षयकृत्प्रवृद्धो लोकान् समाहर्तुमिह प्रवृत्तः ।

ऋतेऽपि त्वां न भविष्यन्ति सर्वे येऽवस्थिताः प्रत्यनीकेषु योधाः ॥ ३२

Śrībhagavānuvāca

kālo'smi lokakṣayakṛtpravṛddho lokānsamāhartumiha pravṛttaḥ **/**

ṛte'pi tvāṁ na bhaviṣyanti sarve ye'vasthitāḥ pratyanīkeṣu yodhāḥ **// 11.32**

śrī bhagavān uvāca: Kṛṣṇa said; *kālaḥ:* time; *asmi*: I am; *loka:* the worlds; *kṣayakṛt*: destroyer; *pravṛddhaḥ*: to engage; *lokān*: all people; *samāhartuṁ:* to destroy; *iha*: in this world; *pravṛttaḥ:* to engage; *ṛte 'pi:* without even; *tvāṁ:* you; *na*: never; *bhaviṣyanti:* will be; *sarve:* all; *ye:* who; *avasthitāḥ*: situated; *pratyanīkeṣu*: on the opposite side; *yodhāh:* the soldiers

11.32 Śrī Bhagavān *said: I am the mighty world-destroying Time, I am now destroying the worlds. Even without you, none of the warriors standing in the hostile armies shall live.*

तस्मात्त्वमुत्तिष्ठ यशो लभस्व जित्वा शत्रून् भुङ्क्ष्व राज्यं समृद्धम् ।

मयैवैते निहताः पूर्वमेव निमित्तमात्रं भव सव्यसाचिन् ॥ ३३

tasmāttvamuttiṣṭha yaśo labhasva jitvā śatrūn bhuṅkṣva rājyaṁ samṛddham **/**

mayaivaite nihatāḥ pūrvameva nimittamātraṁ bhava savyasācin **// 11.33**

tasmāt: therefore; *tvaṁ:* you; *uttiṣṭha:* get up; *yaśaḥ:* fame; *labhasva:* gain; *jitvā*: conquering; *satrūn*: enemies; *bhuṅkṣva:* enjoy; *rājyaṁ:* kingdom; *samṛddham:* flourishing; *maya:* by Me; *eva*: certainly; *ete*: all these; *nihatāḥ*: already killed; *pūrvameva*: by previous arrangement; *nimittamātraṁ*: just an instrument; *bhava*: become; *savyasācin*: O Arjuna (one who can use both the hands equally)

11.33 Get up and gain glory. Conquer the enemies and enjoy the prosperous kingdom. I have slain all these warriors; you are a mere instrument, Arjuna.

द्रोणं च भीष्मं च जयद्रथं च कर्णं तथान्यानपि योधवीरान् ।

मया हतांस्त्वं जहि मा व्यथिष्ठा युध्यस्व जेतासि रणे सपत्नान् ॥ ३४

droṇaṁ ca bhīṣmaṁ ca jayadrathaṁ ca karṇaṁ tathānyānapi yodhavīrān |
mayā hatāṁstvaṁ jahi mā vyathiṣṭā yudhyasva jetāsi raṇe sapatnān || 11.34

droṇaṁ ca: also Droṇa; *bhīṣmaṁ ca:* also Bhisma; *jayadrathaṁ ca:* also Jayadratha; *karṇaṁ:* also Karṇa; *tathā:* also; *anyān*: others; *api:* certainly; *yodhavīrān*: great warriors; *mayā:* by Me; *hatān:* already killed; *tvaṁ:* you; *jahi:* becomes victorious; *mā*: never; *vyathiṣṭā:* be disturbed; *yudhyasva:* just fight; *jetāsi*: just conquer; *raṇe:* in the fight; *sapatnān:* enemies

11.34 Droṇa, Bhīṣma, Jayadratha, Karṇa and other brave warriors have already been slain by Me; destroy them. Do not be be afraid; fight and you shall conquer your enemies in battle.

सञ्जय उवाच
एतच्छुत्वा वचनं केशवस्य कृताञ्जलिर्वेपमानः किरीटी ।
नमस्कृत्वा भूय एवाह कृष्णं सगद्गदं भीतभीतः प्रणम्य ॥ ३५

sañjaya uvāca
etacchrutvā vacanaṁ keśavasya kṛtāñjalirvepamānaḥ kirīṭī |
namaskṛtvā bhūya evāha kṛṣṇaṁ sagadgadaṁ bhītabhītah praṇamya || 11.35

sañjaya uvāca: Sañjaya said; *etat*: thus; *śrutvā:* hearing; *vacanaṁ:* speech; *keśavasya:* of Kṛṣṇa; *kṛtāñjaliḥ:* with folded hands; *vepamānaḥ:* trembling; *kirīṭī*: Arjuna; *namaskṛtvā:* offering obeisances; *bhūya:* again; *eva:* also; *āha kṛṣṇaṁ*: said unto Kṛṣṇa; *sagadgadaṁ:* faltering; *bhītabhītaḥ:* fearful; *praṇamya:* offering obeisances

11.35 Sañjaya said: Having heard this speech of Keśava, the crowned Arjuna with joined palms, trembling, prostrating himself, again addressed Kṛṣṇa, voice choking, bowing down, overwhelmed with fear.

अर्जुन उवाच
स्थाने हृषीकेश तव प्रकीर्त्या जगत्प्रहृष्यत्यनुरज्यते च ।
रक्षांसि भीतानि दिशो द्रवन्ति सर्वे नमस्यन्ति च सिद्धसङ्घाः ॥ ३६

arjuna uvāca
sthāne hṛṣīkeśa tava prakīrtyā jagatprahṛṣyatyanurajyate ca |
rakṣāṁsi bhītāni diśo dravanti sarve namasyanti ca siddhasaṅghāḥ || 11.36

arjuna uvāca: Arjuna said; *sthāne:* rightly; *hṛṣīkeśa*: O master of all senses; *tava*: Your; *prakīrtyā*: glories; *jagat:* the entire world; *prahṛṣyati* : rejoicing; *anurajyate*: becoming attached; *ca:* and; *rakṣāṁsi:* the demons; *bhītāni:* out of fear; *diśaḥ*: directions; *dravanti*: fleeing; *sarve*: all; *namasyanti*: offering respect; *ca*: also; *siddhasaṅghāḥ*: the perfect human beings

11.36 Arjuna said: O Hṛṣīkeśā, it is but right that the world delights and rejoices in Your praise. Rākṣasas fly in fear in all directions and all hosts of sages bow to You.

कस्माच्च ते न नमेरन्महात्मन् गरीयसे ब्रह्मणोऽप्यादिकर्त्रे ।
अनन्त देवेश जगन्निवास त्वमक्षरं सदसत्तत्परं यत् ॥ ३७

kasmācca te na nameranmahātman garīyase brahmaṇo'pyādikartre |
ananta deveśa jagannivāsa tvamakṣaraṁ sadasattatparaṁ yat || 11.37

kasmāt: why; *ca:* also; *te:* unto You; *na:* not; *nameran:* offer proper obeisances; *mahātman:* O great one; *garīyase:* You are better than; *brahmaṇaḥ*: Brahma; *api:* although; *ādikartre:* the supreme creator; *ananta:* unlimited; *deveśa*: God of the gods; *jagannivāsa:* O refuge of the universe; *tvaṁ:* You are; *akṣaraṁ*: imperishable; *sadasat*: cause and effect; *tat paraṁ:* transcendental; *yat:* because

11.37 And why should they not bow to Thee, O great soul, greater than all else, the Creator of even Brahma the Creator. O Lord of Lords, O infinite Being, O Abode of the Universe, You are the imperishable, that which is beyond both seen and the unseen.

त्वमादिदेव: पुरुष: पुराणस्त्वमस्य विश्वस्य परं निधानम् ।
वेत्तासि वेद्यं च परं च धाम त्वया ततं विश्वमनन्तरूप ॥ ३८

tvamādidevaḥ puruṣaḥ purāṇastvamasya viśvasya paraṁ nidhānam |
vettāsi vedyaṁ ca paraṁ ca dhāma tvayā tataṁ viśvamanantarūpa || 11.38

tvaṁ: You; *ādidevaḥ:* the original supreme God; *puruṣaḥ:* the supreme being; *purāṇaḥ:* old; *tvaṁ:* You; *asya:* this; *viśvasya:* universe; *paraṁ:* transcendental; *nidhānam*: refuge; *vettā*: knower; *asi*: You are; *vedyaṁ ca*: and the knowable; *paraṁ ca*: and transcendental; *dhāma:* refuge; *tvayā:* by You; *tataṁ:* pervaded; *viśvaṁ:* universe; *anantarūpa*: unlimited form

11.38 You are the primal God, the ancient Being, the supreme refuge of the universe. You are the knower and the One to be known. You are the supreme abode. O Being of infinite forms, by You alone is the universe pervaded.

वायुर्यमोऽग्निर्वरुण: शशाङ्क: प्रजापतिस्त्वं प्रपितामहश्च ।
नमो नमस्तेऽस्तु सहस्रकृत्व: पुनश्च भूयोऽपि नमो नमस्ते ॥ ३९

vāyuryamognirvaruṇaḥ śaśāṅkaḥ prajāpatistvaṁ prapitāmahaśca **/**
namo namaste'stu sahasrakṛtvaḥ punaśca bhūyo'pi namo namaste **//** *11.39*

vāyuḥ: air; *yamaḥ:* controller; *agniḥ:* fire; *varuṇaḥ:* water; *śaśāṅkaḥ:* moon; *prajāpatiḥ*: Brahma; *tvaṁ*: You; *prapitāmahaḥ*: grandfather; *ca:* also; *namaḥ*: offering respects; *namas te*: again my respects unto You; *astu*: be; *sahasrakṛtvaḥ*: a thousand times; *punaḥ ca:* and again; *bhūyaḥ*: again; *api*: also; *namaḥ*: offer my respects; *namas te*: offering my respects unto You

11.39 You are Vayu, Yama, Agni, Varuṇa, the moon, Prajapati and the great-grandfather of all. Salutations unto You a thousand times and again, salutations unto You!

नमः पुरस्तादथ पृष्ठतस्ते नमोऽस्तु ते सर्वत एव सर्व ।
अनन्तवीर्यामितविक्रमस्त्वं सर्वं समाप्नोषि ततोऽसि सर्वः ॥ ४०

namaḥ purastādatha pṛṣṭataste namo'stu te sarvata eva sarva **/**
anantavīryāmitavikramastvaṁ sarvaṁ samāpnoṣi tato'si sarvaḥ **//** *11.40*

namaḥ: offering obeisances; *purastāt*: from the front; *atha*: also; *pṛṣṭhataḥ:* from behind; *te*: You; *namo 'stu:* offer my respects; *te:* unto You; *sarvata:* from all sides; *eva sarva*: because You are everything; *ananta vīrya:* unlimited potency; *amita vikramaḥ*: unlimited force; *tvaṁ:* You; *sarvaṁ:* everything; *samāpnoṣi*: cover; *tato 'si*: therefore You are; *sarvaḥ* : everything

11.40 Salutations to You, before and behind! Salutations to You on every side! O All! Infinite in power and Infinite in prowess, You are everything and everywhere.

सखेति मत्वा प्रसभं यदुक्तं हे कृष्ण हे यादव हे सखेति ।
अजानता महिमानं तवेदं मया प्रमादात्प्रणयेन वापि ॥ ४१

sakheti matvā prasabhaṁ yaduktaṁ he Kṛṣna he yādava he sakheti **/**
ajānatā mahimānaṁ tavedaṁ mayā pramādātpraṇayena vāpi **//** *11.41*

sakha: friend; *iti*: thus; *matvā*: thinking; *prasabhaṁ:* easy familiarity; *yat:* whatever; *uktaṁ*: said; *he Kṛṣṇa*: O Kṛṣṇa; *he yādava:* O Yadava; *he sakhe 'ti*: O my dear friend; *ajānatā*: without knowing; *mahimānaṁ:* glories; *tava:* Your; *idaṁ*: this; *mayā:* by me; *pramādāt:* out of foolishness; *praṇayena:* out of love; *vā 'pi:* either

11.41 Whatever I have rashly said from carelessness or love, addressing You as Kṛṣṇa, Yadava, my friend regarding You merely as a friend, unaware of this greatness of Yours.

यच्चावहासार्थमसत्कृतोऽसि विहारशय्यासनभोजनेषु ।
एकोऽथवाप्यच्युत तत्समक्षं तत्क्षामये त्वामहमप्रमेयम् ॥ ४२

yaccāvahāsārthamasatkṛto'si vihāraśayyāsana bhojaneṣu /
eko'thava'pyacyuta tat samakṣaṁ tatkṣāmaye tvāmahamaprameyam // 11.42

yat: whatever; *ca:* also; *avahāsārthum*: for joking; *asatkṛtaḥ*: dishonor; *asi*: have been done; *vihāra*: in relaxation; *śayyā:* while lying on the bed; *āsana:* in a sitting place; *bhojaneṣu:* or while eating together; *ekaḥ*: alone; *athava:* or; *api:* others; *acyuta:* O infallible one; *tatsamakṣaṁ*: in their presence; *tat*: all those; *kṣāmaye:* excuse; *tvām*: from You; *aham:* I; *aprameyam:* immeasurable

11.42 In whatever way I may have insulted You in fun, while at play, resting, sitting or at meals, when alone with You or in company, O Acyuta, O immeasurable One, I implore You to forgive me.

पितासि लोकस्य चराचरस्य त्वमस्य पूज्यश्च गुरुर्गरीयान् ।
न त्वत्समोऽस्त्यभ्यधिकः कुतोऽन्यो लोकत्रयेऽप्यप्रतिमप्रभाव ॥ ४३

Pitāsi lokasya carācarasya tvamasya pūjyaśca gururgarīyān /
na tvatsamo'styabhyadhikaḥ kuto'nyo lokatraye'pyapratimaprabhāva // 11.43

Pitā: father; *asi*: You are; *lokasya*: of all the world; *cara*: moving; *acarasya*: nonmoving; *tvaṁ*: You are; *asya*: of this; *pūjyaḥ*: worshipable; *ca*: also; *guruḥ*: master; *garīyan*: glorious; *na*: never; *tvatsamaḥ*: equal to You; *asti:* there is; *abhyadhikaḥ*: greater; *kutaḥ*: how is it possible; *anyo*: other; *lokatraye*: in three planetary systems; *api:* also; *apratima*: immeasurable; *prabhāva*: power

11.43 You are the father of this world, moving and unmoving. You are to be adored by this world. You are the greatest guru; there is none who exists equal to You. O Being of unequalled power, how then can there be another, superior to You in the three worlds?

तस्मात्प्रणम्य प्रणिधाय कायं प्रसादये त्वामहमीशमीड्यम् ।
पितेव पुत्रस्य सखेव सख्युः प्रियः प्रियायार्हसि देव सोढुम् ॥ ४४

tasmātpraṇamya praṇidhāya kāyaṁ prasādaye tvāmahamīśamīḍyam /
pite'va putrasya sakhe'va sakhyuḥ priyaḥ priyāyārhasi deva soḍhum // 11.44

tasmāt: therefore; *praṇamya:* after offering obeisances; *praṇidhāya:* laying down; *kāyaṁ*: body; *prasādaye:* to beg mercy; *tvāṁ*: unto You; *ahaṁ:* I;

īśaṁ: unto the Supreme Lord; *īḍyam:* who is worshipable; *pite 'va*: like a father; *putrasya:* of a son; *sakhe 'va*: like a friend; *sakhyuḥ:* of a friend; *priyaḥ*: lover; *priyāya*: of the dearmost; *arhasi:* You should; *deva*: my Lord; *soḍhum:* tolerate

11.44 Therefore, bowing down, I prostrate my body before You and crave Your forgiveness, adorable Lord. Even as a father forgives his son, a friend his friend, a lover his beloved, You should, O Deva, forgive me.

अदृष्टपूर्वं हृषितोऽस्मि दृष्ट्वा भयेन च प्रव्यथितं मनो मे।
तदेव मे दर्शय देव रूपं प्रसीद देवेश जगन्निवास ॥ ४५

adṛṣṭapūrvaṁ hṛṣito'smi dṛṣṭvā bhayena ca pravyathitaṁ mano me **/**
tadeva me darśaya devarūpaṁ prasīda deveśa jagannivāsa **//** 11.45

adṛṣṭapūrvaṁ: never seen before; *hṛṣito*: gladdened; *asmi*: I am; *dṛṣṭvā:* by seeing; *bhayena:* out of fear; *ca:* also; *pravyathitaṁ:* perturbed; *mano:* mind; *me:* my; *tad*: therefore; *eva*: certainly; *me:* unto me; *darśaya:* show; *deva*: O Lord; *rūpaṁ*: the form; *prasīda*: just be gracious; *deveśa*: O Lord of lords; *jagannivāsa*: the refuge of the universe

11.45 After seeing this form that I have never seen before, I am filled with gladness but at the same time I am disturbed by fear. Please bestow Your grace upon me and show me Your form as the supreme personality, O Lord of Lords, O refuge of the Universe.

किरीटिनं गदिनं चक्रहस्तमिच्छामि त्वां द्रष्टुमहं तथैव।
तेनैव रूपेण चतुर्भुजेन सहस्रबाहो भव विश्वमूर्ते ॥ ४६

kirīṭinaṁ gadinaṁ cakrahastamicchāmi tvāṁ draṣṭumahaṁ tathaiva **/**
tenaiva rūpeṇa caturbhujena sahasrabāho bhava viśvamūrte **//** 11.46

kirīṭinaṁ: crowned; *gadinaṁ*: with club; *cakrahastam*: disc in hand; *icchāmi*: I wish; *tvāṁ*: You; *draṣṭum*: to see; *ahaṁ*: I; *tathai' va*: in that form; *tenai 'va*: by that; *rūpeṇa*: with form; *caturbhujena*: four-handed; *sahasrabāho:* O thousand-handed one; *bhava:* just become; *viśvamūrte*: O universal form

11.46 O thousand armed Universal Form! I wish to see Your form with crown, four-armed with mace, disc in Your hand. I yearn to see You in that form.

श्रीभगवानुवाच
मया प्रसन्नेन तवार्जुनेदं रूपं परं दर्शितमात्मयोगात्।
तेजोमयं विश्वमनन्तमाद्यं यन्मे त्वदन्येन न दृष्टपूर्वम् ॥ ४७

śrībhagavānuvāca

mayā prasannena tavārjunedaṁ rūpaṁ paraṁ darśitamātmayogāt I
tejomayaṁ viśvamanantamādyaṁ yanme tvadanyena na dṛṣṭapūrvam II 11.47

śrī bhagavān uvāca: Śrī bhagavan said; *mayā*: by Me; *prasannena:* happily; *tava:* unto you; *arjuna*: O Arjuna; *idam*: this; *rūpaṁ:* form; *paraṁ*: transcendental; *darśitaṁ*: shown; *ātmayogāt:* by My internal power; *tejomayaṁ*: full of effulgence; *viśvaṁ:* the entire universe; *anantaṁ*: unlimited; *ādyaṁ*: original; *yan me*: that which is Mine; *tvad anyena:* besides you; *na dṛṣṭapūrvam:* no one has previously seen

11.47 Bhagavān *said: Dear Arjuna, I happily show you this transcendental form within the material world of My internal power. No one before you has seen this unlimited, brilliant form.*

न वेदयज्ञाध्ययनैर्न दानैः न च क्रियाभिर्न तपोभिरुग्रैः ।
एवं रूपः शक्य अहं नृलोके द्रष्टुं त्वदन्येन कुरुप्रवीर ॥ ४८

na vedayajñādhyayanairna dānaiḥ na ca kriyābhirna tapobhirugraiḥ I
evaṁrūpaḥ śakya ahaṁ nṛloke draṣṭuṁ tvadanyena kurupravīra II 11.48

na: never; *veda*: by Vedic study; *yajña:* sacrifice; *ādhyayanaiḥ:* study; *na dānaiḥ:* not by charity; *na*: never; *ca:* also; *kriyābhiḥ:* by pious activities; *na tapobhiḥ:* by serious penances; *ugraiḥ:* severe; *evaṁ:* thus; *rūpaḥ:* form; *śakyaḥ:* can be seen; *ahaṁ:* I; *nṛloke*: in this material world; *draṣṭuṁ*: to see; *tvad:* you; *anyena:* by another; *kurupravīra:* O best among the Kuru warriors

11.48 O best among Kuru warriors, no one had ever before seen this Universal form of mine, for neither by studying the Vedas *nor by performing sacrifices or charities, can this form be seen. Only you have seen this form.*

मा ते व्यथा मा च विमूढभावो दृष्ट्वा रूपं घोरमीदृङ्ममेदम् ।
व्यपेतभीः प्रीतमनाः पुनस्त्वं तदेव मे रूपमिदं प्रपश्य ॥ ४९

mā te vyathā mā ca vimūḍhabhāvo dṛṣṭvā rūpaṁ ghoramīdṛṅmamedam I
vyapetabhīḥ prītamanāḥ punastvaṁ tadeva me rūpamidaṁ prapaśya II 11.49

mā: let it not be; *te:* unto you; *vyathā:* trouble; *mā*: let it not be; *ca*: also; *vimūḍhabhāvaḥ*: bewilderment; *dṛṣṭvā:* by seeing; *rūpaṁ:* form; *ghoraṁ:* terrible; *īdṛk:* like this; *mama*: My; *idaṁ*: as it is; *vyapetabhīḥ:* just become free from all fear; *prītamanāḥ*: be pleased in mind; *punaḥ*: again; *tvaṁ:* you;

tat: that; *eva:* thus; *me*: My; *rūpam:* form; *idaṁ:* this; *prapaśya:* just see

11.49 Do not be disturbed any longer by seeing this terrible form of Mine. Dear devotee, be free from all disturbances. With a peaceful mind, you can now see the form you wish to see.

सञ्जय उवाच।
इत्यर्जुनं वासुदेवस्तथोक्त्वा स्वकं रूपं दर्शयामास भूयः।
आश्वसयामास च भीतमेनं भूत्वा पुनः सौम्यवपुर्महात्मा ॥ ५०

sañjaya uvāca
ityarjunaṁ vāsudevastatho'ktvā svakaṁ rūpaṁ darśayāmāsa bhūyaḥ /
āśvasayāmāsa ca bhītamenaṁ bhūtvā punaḥ saumyavapurmahātmā // 11.50

saṅjaya uvāca: Sañjaya said; *iti:* thus; *arjunaṁ:* unto Arjuna; *vāsudevaḥ:* Kṛṣṇa; *tathā*: that way; *uktvā:* saying; *svakaṁ*: His own; *rūpaṁ*: form; *darśayāmāsa*: showed; *bhūyaḥ*: again; *āśvāsayāmāsa:* also convinced him; *ca:* also; *bhītam:* fearful; *enaṁ:* him; *bhūtvā punaḥ:* becoming again; *saumyavapuḥ:* beautiful form; *mahātmā:* the great one

11.50 Sañjaya said: Kṛṣṇa, while speaking to Arjuna, revealed His form with four arms, Then assuming His human form He consoled the terrified Arjuna.

अर्जुन उवाच।
दृष्ट्वेदं मानुषं रूपं तव सौम्यं जनार्दन।
इदानीमस्मि संवृत्तः सचेताः प्रकृतिं गतः॥ ५१

arjuna uvāca
dṛṣṭvedaṁ mānuṣaṁ rūpaṁ tava saumyaṁ janārdana /
idānīmasmi saṁvṛttaḥ sacetāḥ prakṛtiṁ gataḥ // 11.51

arjuna uvāca: Arjuna said; *dṛṣṭvā*: seeing; *idaṁ*: this; *mānuṣaṁ:* human being; *rūpam*: form; *tava:* Your; *saumyaṁ:* very beautiful; *janārdana:* O chastiser of the enemies; *idānīm*: just now; *asmi:* I am; *saṁvṛttaḥ*: settled; *sacetāh:* in my consciousness; *prakṛtiṁ:* my own; *gataḥ:* I

11.51 Arjuna said: Seeing this wonderful human form, My mind is now calm and I am restored to my original nature.

श्री भगवानुवाच
सुदुर्दर्शमिदं रूपं दृष्टवानसि यन्मम ।
देवा अप्यस्य रूपस्य नित्यं दर्शनकाङ्क्षिणः ॥ ५२

śrībhagavānuvāca
sudurdarśamidaṁ rūpaṁ dṛṣṭavānasi yanmama |
devā apyasya rūpasya nityaṁ darśanakāṅkṣiṇaḥ || 11.52

śrī bhagavān uvāca: Kṛṣṇa said; *sudurdarśaṁ:* very difficult to be seen; *idaṁ:* this; *rūpaṁ:* form; *dṛṣṭavān asi:* you have seen; *yat:* which; *mama:* of Mine; *devāḥ:* the celestials; *apyasya:* also this; *rūpasya:* form; *nityaṁ:* eternally; *darśana kāṅkṣiṇaḥ*: always aspire to see

11.52 Bhagavān *said: The four-armed form that you have seen is rare to behold. Even the celestials are forever aspiring to see this form.*

नाहं वेदैर्न तपसा न दानेन न चेज्यया ।
शक्य एवंविधो द्रष्टुं दृष्ट्वानसि मां यथा ॥ ५३

nāhaṁ vedairna tapasā na dānena na cejyayā |
śakya evaṁvidho draṣṭuṁ dṛṣṭavānasi māṁ yathā || 11.53

nā: never; *ahaṁ*: I; *vedaiḥ*: by study of the *Vedas*; *na*: never; *tapasā*: by serious penances; *na*: never; *dānena*: by charity; *na:* never; *ca:* also; *ijyayā*: by worship; *śakyaḥ*: it is possible; *evaṁvidhaḥ*: like this; *draṣṭuṁ*: to see; *dṛṣṭavān*: seeing; *asi:* you are; *māṁ*: Me; *yathā:* as.

11.53 *The four armed form which you have seen with your transcendental eyes cannot be understood simply by study of the* Vedas, *nor by undergoing penances or charity or worship; one cannot see Me as I am by these means.*

भक्त्या त्वनन्यया शक्य अहमेवंविधोऽर्जुन ।
ज्ञातुं द्रष्टुं च तत्त्वेन प्रवेष्टुं च परन्तप ॥ ५४

bhaktyā tvananyayā śakya ahamevaṁvidho'rjuna |
jñātuṁ draṣṭuṁ ca tattvena praveṣṭuṁ ca parantapa || 11.54

bhaktyā: by devotional service; *tu:* but; *ananyayā*: without being mixed with fruitive activities or speculative knowledge; *śakyaḥ*: possible; *aham*: I; *evaṁvidhaḥ*: like this; *arjuna*: O Arjuna; *jñātuṁ*: to know; *draṣṭuṁ:* to see; *ca:* and; *tattvena*: in fact; *praveṣṭuṁ:* and to enter into; *ca:* also; *paraṁtapa:* O mighty-armed one

11.54 My dear Arjuna, only by undivided devotional service can you understand Me as I am, standing before you, be seen directly. Only in this way can you reach Me.

मत्कर्मकृन्मत्परमो मद्भक्तः संङ्गवर्जितः ।
निर्वैरः सर्वभूतेषु यः स मामेति पाण्डव ॥ ५५

matkarmakṛnmatparamo madbhaktaḥ saṅgavarjitaḥ |
nirvairaḥ sarvabhūteṣu yaḥ sa māmeti pāṇḍava || 11.55

matkarmakṛt: engaged in doing My work; *matparamaḥ*: considering Me the Supreme; *madbhaktaḥ*: engaged in My devotional service; *saṅgavarjitaḥ*: freed from the contamination of previous activities and mental speculation; *nirvairaḥ*: without an enemy; *sarvabhūteṣu:* to every living entity; *yaḥ*: one who; *sa:* he; *mām:* unto Me; *eti*: comes; *pāṇḍava:* O son of Pāṇḍu

11.55 My dear Arjuna, one who is engaged entirely in My devotional service, free from attachment, full of love for every entity, surely comes to Me.

इति श्रीमद्भगवद्गीतासूपनिषत्सु ब्रह्मविद्यायां योगशास्त्रे
श्रीकृष्णार्जुनसंवादे विश्वरूपदर्शनयोगो नाम एकादशोऽध्यायः ॥

iti śrīmad bhagavadgītāsūpaniṣatsu brahmavidyāyām
yogaśāstre śrīkṛṣṇārjuna saṁvāde viśvarūpadarśanayogo
nāmaekādaśo'dhyāyaḥ ||

In the Upaniṣad *of the Bhagavad Gītā, the knowledge of* Brahman, *the Supreme, the science of Yoga and the dialogue between Śrī Kṛṣṇa and Arjuna, this is the eleventh discourse designated:*

Viśvarūpa darśana yogaḥ

Verses Of Gita Chapter 12

अथ द्वादशोऽध्यायः

भक्तियोगः

Bhakti Yogaḥ

अर्जुन उवाच

एवं सततयुक्ता ये भक्तास्त्वां पर्युपासते ।

ये चाप्यक्षरमव्यक्तं तेषां के योगवित्तमाः ॥ १

arjuna uvāca

evaṁ satatayuktā ye bhaktāstvāṁ paryupāsate I

ye cā'pyakṣaramavyaktaṁ teṣāṁ ke yogavittamāh II 12.1

arjuna uvāca: Arjuna said; *evaṁ:* thus; *satata:* always; *yuktāḥ:* engaged; *ye:* those; *bhaktāḥ:* devotees; *tvāṁ:* you; *paryupāsate:* worship; ye: those; *cā:* and; *api*: also; *akṣaraṁ:* imperishable; *avyaktaṁ:* the unmanifest; *teṣāṁ:* of these; *ke:* who; *yogavittamāḥ:* perfect in knowledge of yoga

12.1 Arjuna asked: Who are considered perfect, those who are always engaged sincerely in Your worship in form, or those who worship the imperishable, the invisible formless You?

श्री भगवानुवाच

मय्यावेश्य मनो ये मां नित्ययुक्ता उपासते ।

श्रद्धया परयोपेतास्ते मे युक्ततमा मताः ॥ २

śrī Bhagavānuvāca

mayyāveśya mano ye māṁ nityayuktā upāsate I

śraddhayā parayo'petāste me yuktatamā matāḥ II 12.2

śrī bhagavān uvāca: Lord Kṛṣṇa says; *mayi:* on Me; *āveśya*: fixing; *manaḥ*: the mind; *ye*: those; *māṁ*: Me; *nitya*: eternally; *yuktāḥ*: engaged; *upāsate*: worship; *śraddhayā*: with faith; *parayā:* supreme; *upetāḥ*: endowed; *te:* these; *me:* by Me; *yuktatamāḥ:* perfect in yoga; *matāḥ:* opinion

12.2 Lord Kṛṣṇa said: Those, who by fixing their mind on Me eternally, and those who are steadfast in worshipping Me with supreme faith, I consider them to be perfect in Yoga, ready to be united with Me.

ये त्वक्षरमनिर्देश्यमव्यक्तं पर्युपासते ।
सर्वत्रगमचिन्त्यं च कूटस्थमचलं ध्रुवम् ॥ ३

ye tvakṣaramanirdeśyamavyaktaṁ paryupāsate |
sarvatragamacintyaṁ ca kūṭasthamacalaṁ dhruvam || 12.3

ye: those; *tu*: but; *akṣaraṁ*: imperishable; *anirdeśyaṁ*: indefinable; *avyaktaṁ*: unmanifest; *paryupāsate*: worship; *sarvatragaṁ*: all pervading; *acintyaṁ*: inconceivable; *ca*: also; *kūṭasthaṁ*: unchanging; *achalaṁ*: immovable; *dhruvam:* fixed

सन्नियम्येन्द्रियग्रामं सर्वत्र समबुद्धयः ।
ते प्राप्नुवन्ति मामेव सर्वभूतहिते रताः ॥ ४

sanniyamyendriyagrāmaṁ sarvatra samabuddhayaḥ |
te prāpnuvanti māmeva sarvabhūtahite ratāḥ || 12.4

sanniyamya: restrained; *indriyagrāmaṁ:* all the senses; *sarvatra:* everywhere; *samabuddhayaḥ:* equally disposed; *te*: they; *prāpnuvanti:* achieve; *mām:* Me; *eva:* only; *sarvabhūta hite:* for the welfare of all living beings; *ratāḥ:* engaged

12.3,4 But those who worship with awareness the imperishable, the unmanifest, that which lies beyond the perception of senses, the all pervading, inconceivable, unchanging, the non-moving and permanent, those who worship by restraining their senses, and are working with even mind for the benefit of mankind, they too attain Me.

क्लेशोऽधिकतरस्तेषामव्यक्तासक्तचेतसाम् ।
अव्यक्ता हि गतिर्दुःखं देहवद्भिरवाप्यते ॥ ५

kleśo'dhikatarasteṣāmavyaktāsaktacetasām |
avyaktā hi gatirduḥkhaṁ dehavadbhiravāpyate || 12.5

kleśaḥ: trouble; *adhikataraḥ*: greater; *teṣām*: of those; *avyaktāsaktacetasām*: whose minds are set on the unmanifest; *avyaktā:* unmanifest; *hi:* for; *gatiḥ:* goal; *duḥkhaṁ*: sorrow; *dehavadbhiḥ:* for the embodied; *avāpyate:* is attained

12.5 For those whose minds are set on the unmanifest, the formless, it is more difficult to advance; attaining the formless unmanifest is difficult for the embodied.

ये तु सर्वाणि कर्माणि मयि संन्यस्य मत्पराः ।
अनन्येनैव योगेन मां ध्यायन्त उपासते ॥ ६

ye tu sarvāṇi karmāṇi mayi sannyasya matparāḥ **/**
ananyenaiva yogena māṁ dhyāyanta upāsate **//** 12.6

ye: who; *tu*: but; *sarvāṇi*: all; *karmāṇi*: actions; *mayi:* in me; *sannyasya:* renouncing; *matparāḥ:* regarding me as the supreme goal; *ananyena:* focussed; *eva*: even; *yogena*: with yoga; *māṁ*: me; *dhyāyantaḥ:* meditating; *upāsate:* worship

तेषामहं समुद्धर्ता मृत्युसंसारसागरात् ।
भवामि नचिरात्पार्थ मय्यावेशितचेतसाम् ॥ ७

teṣāmahaṁ samuddhartā mṛtyusaṁsārasāgarāt **/**
bhavāmi nacirātpārtha mayyāveśitacetasām **//** 12.7

teṣām: for them; *ahaṁ:* I; *samuddhartā:* the savior; *mṛtyu saṁsāra sāgarāt:* from the ocean of life and death cycle; *bhavāmi:* become; *na cirāt:* before long; *pārtha:* Arjuna; *mayi:* in me; *āveśita cetasām:* of those whose minds are set

12.6,7 But those who worship me with single minded devotion, renouncing all activities unto Me, regarding Me as their supreme goal, whose minds are set in Me, I shall deliver them soon from their ocean of the birth and death cycle.

मय्येव मन आधत्स्व मयि बुद्धिं निवेशय ।
निवसिष्यसि मय्येव अत ऊर्ध्वं न संशयः ॥ ८

mayyeva mana ādhatsva mayi buddhiṁ niveśaya **/**
nivasiṣyasi mayyeva ata ūrdhvaṁ na saṁśayaḥ **//** 12.8

mayi: upon Me; *eva:* only; *manaḥ:* mind; *ādhatsva:* fix; *mayi:* upon Me; *buddhiṁ:* mind; *niveśaya:* apply; *nivasiṣyasi:* you will live; *mayi:* in Me; *eva:* alone; *ata ūrdhvaṁ*: thereafter; *na:* no; *saṁśayaḥ:* doubt

12.8 You fix your mind on Me alone, establish your mind in Me. You will live in Me always. There is no doubt in it.

अथ चित्तं समाधातुं न शक्नोषि मयि स्थिरम् ।
अभ्यासयोगेन ततो मामिच्छाप्तुं धनञ्जय ॥ ९

atha cittaṁ samādhātuṁ na śaknoṣi mayi sthiram **/**
abhyāsayogena tato māmicchāptuṁ dhanañjaya **//** 12.9

atha: if; *cittaṁ:* mind; *samādhātuṁ:* to fix; *na:* not; *śaknoṣi:* you are able; *mayi*: upon Me; *sthiram:* steadily; *abhyāsa yogena:* by the practice of yoga; *tataḥ:* then; *mām*: Me; *iccha*: desire; *āptuṁ*: to get; *dhanañjaya:* Arjuna

12.9 If you are not able to fix your mind upon Me then Arjuna, with the constant practice of Yoga, you try to attain Me.

अभ्यासेऽप्यसमर्थोऽसि मत्कर्मपरमो भव ।
मदर्थमपि कर्माणि कुर्वन्सिद्धिमवाप्स्यसि ॥ १०

abhyāse'pyasamartho'si matkarmaparamo bhava /
madarthamapi karmāṇi kurvansiddhimavāpsyasi // 12.10

abhyāse: in practice; *api:* even if; *asamarthaḥ:* unable; *asi*: you are; *matkarma*: My work; *paramaḥ:* dedicated to; *bhava*: become; *madarthaṁ:* for Me; *api:* even; *karmāṇi*: work; *kurvan*: performing; *siddhim:* perfection; *avāpsyasi:* you will achieve

12.10 If you are not able to practice even this yoga then performing your duties and surrendering all your actions to Me, you will attain perfection.

अथैतदप्यशक्तोऽसि कर्तुं मद्योगमाश्रितः ।
सर्वकर्मफलत्यागं ततः कुरु यतात्मवान् ॥ ११

athaitadapyaśakto'si kartuṁ madyogamāśritaḥ /
sarvakarmaphalatyāgaṁ tataḥ kuru yatātmavān // 12.11

atha: even though; *etad*: this; *api:* also; *aśaktaḥ*: unable; *asi:* you are; *kartuṁ*: to perform; *madyogam:* My yoga; *āśritaḥ:* taking refuge in; *sarva karma:* of all activities; *phala:* of the results; *tyāgaṁ:* renunciation; *tataḥ:* then; *kuru:* do; *yatātmavān:* self controlled.

12.11 If you are not able to work even this way, surrendering unto Me, give up all the results of your actions to Me without ego.

श्रेयो हि ज्ञानमभ्यासात् ज्ञानाद्ध्यानं विशिष्यते ।
ध्यानात्कर्मफलत्यागस्त्यागाच्छान्तिरनन्तरम् ॥ १२

śreyo hi jñānamabhyāsājjñānāddhyānaṁ viśiṣyate /
dhyānātkarmaphalatyāgastyāgācchāntiranantaram // 12.12

śreyo: better; *hi:* indeed; *jnānam:* knowledge; *abhyāsāt:* than practice; *jñānāt:* than knowledge; *dhyānaṁ:* meditation; *viśiṣyate:* superior; *dhyānāt:* than meditation; *karmaphala tyāgaḥ*: renunciation of the fruits of action; *tyāgāt:* than such renunciation; *śāntiḥ*: peace; *anantaram*: thereafter

12.12 Knowledge is better than mere practice. Meditation is superior to knowledge. Renunciating the fruit of actions is better than meditation. After renouncing of fruits of actions, one immediately attains peace.

अद्वेष्टा सर्वभूतानां मैत्रः करुण एव च ।
निर्ममो निरहङ्कारः समदुःखसुखः क्षमी ॥ १३

adveṣṭā sarvabhūtānāṁ maitraḥ karuṇa eva ca **/**
nirmamo nirahaṅkāraḥ samaduḥkhasukhaḥ kṣamī **//** 12.13

adveṣṭā: non envious; *sarvabhūtānāṁ:* toward all living entities; *maitraḥ:* friendly; *karuṇa:* kindly; *eva:* certainly; *ca:* also; *nirmamaḥ:* with no sense of proprietorship; *nirahankāraḥ:* without false ego; *sama:* equal; *duḥkha:* in distress; *sukhaḥ:* and happiness; *kṣamī:* forgiving.

सन्तुष्टः सततं योगी यतात्मा दृढनिश्चयः ।
मय्यर्पितमनोबुद्धिर्यो मद्भक्तः स मे प्रियः ॥ १४

santuṣṭaḥ satataṁ yogī yatātmā dṛḍhaniścayaḥ **/**
mayyarpitamanobuddhiryo madbhaktaḥ sa me priyaḥ **//** 12.14

santuṣṭaḥ: satisfied; *satataṁ:* always; *yogī*: one engaged in yoga; *yatātmā:* self controlled; *dṛḍhaniścayaḥ:* with determination; *mayi*: upon Me; *arpita:* engaged; *manaḥ*: mind; *buddhiḥ:* and intelligence; *yaḥ:* one who; *madbhaktaḥ:* My devotee; *saḥ:* he; *me*: to Me; *priyaḥ:* dear.

12.13,14 One who has no dislike or envy for any being, who is friendly and compassionate to everyone, free from the sense of I and mine, the ego, maintains equanimity of mind both in joy and sorrow, forgiving, ever satisfied, united with Yoga, has a strong commitment to Me and has fixed his mind and intellect upon Me, such a devotee of Mine is very dear to Me.

यस्मान्नोद्विजते लोको लोकान्नोद्विजते च यः ।
हर्षामर्षभयोद्वेगैर्मुक्तो यः स च मे प्रियः ॥ १५

yasmānnodvijate loko lokānnodvijate ca yaḥ **/**
harṣāmarṣabhayodvegairmukto yaḥ sa ca me priyaḥ **//** 12.15

yasmāt: from whom; *na:* not; *udvijate*: is agitated; *lokaḥ:* the world; *lokāt:* from the world; *na*: not; *udvijate*: is agitated; *ca:* and; *yaḥ:* who; *harṣāmarṣabhayodvegaiḥ:* from joy; envy; fear and anxiety; *muktaḥ:* freed; *yaḥ:* who; *sa:* he; *ca:* and; *me:* to me; *priyaḥ:* dear

12.15 He, by whom the world is not affected adversely, and who in turn does not affect the world adversely, and he, who is free from joy, anger, and anxiety, he is dear to Me.

अनपेक्ष: शुचिर्दक्ष उदासीनो गतव्यथ: ।
सर्वारम्भपरित्यागी यो मद्भक्त: स मे प्रिय: ॥ १६

anapekṣaḥ śucirdakṣaḥ udāsīno gatavyathaḥ **/**
sarvārambhaparityāgī yo madbhaktaḥ sa me priyaḥ **//** 12.16

anapekṣaḥ: free from expectations; *śuciḥ:* pure; *dakṣa:* expert; *udāsīnaḥ:* unconcerned; *gatavyathaḥ:* untroubled; *sarvārambha parityāgī:* renouncing all undertakings; *yo:* who; *madbhaktaḥ:* my devotee; *saḥ:* he; *me:* to me; *priyaḥ:* dear

12.16 He, who is free from wants, who is pure and skilled, unconcerned, untroubled, who is selfless in whatever he does, he who is devoted to Me, he is dear to Me.

यो न हृष्यति न द्वेष्टि न शोचति न काङ्क्षति ।
शुभाशुभपरित्यागी भक्तिमान्य: स मे प्रिय: ॥ १७

yo na hṛṣyati na dveṣṭi na śocati na kāṅkṣati **/**
śubhāśubhaparityāgi bhaktimānyaḥ sa me priyaḥ **//** 12.17

yaḥ: who; *na:* not; *hṛṣyati:* rejoices; *na:* not; *dveṣṭi:* hates; *na:* not; *śocati:* grieves; *na:* not; *kāṅkṣati:* desires; *subhāśubha parityāgī:* renouncing good and evil; *bhaktimān:* full of devotion; *yaḥ:* who; *sa*: he; *me:* to me; *priyaḥ:* dear

12.17 He who does not rejoice or hate or grieve or desire, renounces both good and evil and who is full of devotion, he is dear to Me.

सम: शत्रौ च मित्रे च तथा मानापमानयो: ।
शीतोष्णसुखदु:खेषु सम: सङ्गविवर्जित: ॥ १८

samaḥ śatrau ca mitre ca tathā mānāpamānayoḥ **/**
śītoṣṇasukhaduḥkheṣu samaḥ saṅgavivarjitaḥ **//** 12.18

samaḥ: equal; *śatrau:* to an enemy; *ca:* also; *mitre:* to a friend; *ca:* also; *tathā:* so; *māna:* in honor; *apamānayoḥ:* and dishonour; *śīta:* in cold; *uṣṇa*:

heat; *sukha*: happiness; *duḥkheṣu:* and sorrow; *samaḥ:* same; *saṅgavivarjitaḥ:* free from all association

तुल्यनिन्दास्तुतिर्मौनी संतुष्टो येन केनचित् ।
अनिकेतः स्थिरमतिर्भक्तिमान्मे प्रियो नरः ॥ १९

tulyanindāstutirmaunī santuṣṭo yena kenacit **I**
aniketaḥ sthiramatirbhaktimānme priyo naraḥ **II** 12.19

tulya: equal; *nindā:* in defamation; *stutiḥ:* and repute; *maunī:* silent; *santuṣṭaḥ:* satisfied; *yena kenacit:* with anything; *aniketaḥ:* having no residence; *sthira*: fixed; *matiḥ:* mind; *bhaktimān*: engaged in devotion; *me:* to Me; *priyaḥ:* dear; *naraḥ:* a man

12.18,19 One who treats friends and enemies the same, who faces in the same manner honor and dishonor, heat and cold, happiness and sorrow, fame and infamy, one who is always free from attachment, always silent and satisfied with anything, without a fixed home, who is fixed in mind and who is devoted to Me, such a person is very dear to Me.

ये तु धर्म्यामृतमिदं यथोक्तं पर्युपासते ।
श्रद्दधाना मत्परमा भक्तास्तेऽतीव मे प्रियाः ॥ २०

ye tu dharmyāmṛtamidaṁ yathoktaṁ paryupāsate **I**
śraddadhānā matparamā bhaktāste 'tīva me priyāḥ **II** 12.20

ye: who; *tu:* indeed; *dharmya:* righteous path; *amṛtam:* nectar; *idaṁ:* this; *yathā:* as; *uktaṁ:* said; *paryupāsate:* follow; *śraddadhānā:* with faith; *matparamā:* taking Me as the Supreme Lord; *bhaktāḥ:* devotees; *te:* they; *atīva*: very much; *me:* to Me; *priyāḥ:* dear

12.20 Those who truly follow this imperishable path of righteousness with great faith, making Me the supreme goal, are very dear to Me.

इति श्रीमद्भगवद्गीतासूपनिषत्सु ब्रह्मविद्यायां योगशास्त्रे
श्रीकृष्णार्जुनसंवादे भक्तियोगो नाम द्वादशोऽध्यायः ॥

iti śrīmad bhagavadgītāsūpaniṣatsu brahmavidyāyām
yogaśāstre śrīkṛṣṇārjuna saṁvāde bhaktiyogo nāma
dvādaśo'dhyāyaḥ **II**

In the Upaniṣad *of the Bhagavad Gītā, the knowledge of* Brahman, *the Supreme, the science of Yoga and the dialogue between Śrī Kṛṣṇa and Arjuna, this is the twelfth discourse designated:*

Bhakti Yogaḥ

Verses Of Gita Chapter - 13

अथ त्रयोदशोऽध्यायः

क्षेत्रक्षेत्रज्ञविभागयोगः

Kṣetra Kṣetrajñya Vibhāga Yogaḥ

अर्जुन उवाच
प्रकृतिं पुरुषं चैव क्षेत्रं क्षेत्रज्ञमेव च ।
एतद्वेदितुमिच्छामि ज्ञानं ज्ञेयं च केशव ॥ १

arjuna uvāca
prakṛtiṁ puruṣaṁ caiva kṣetraṁ kṣetrajñameva ca **/**
etadveditumicchāmi jñānaṁ jñeyaṁ ca keśava **//** *13.1*

arjuna uvāca: Arjuna said; *prakṛtiṁ:* nature; *puruṣaṁ:* the enjoyer; *ca:* also; *eva*: certainly; *kṣetraṁ:* body; *kṣetrajñam:* knower of the body; *eva:* certainly; *ca:* also; *etad:* all this; *vedituṁ:* to understand; *icchāmi:* I wish; *jñānaṁ:* knowledge; *jñeyaṁ:* the object of knowledge; *ca:* also; *keśava:* O Kṛṣṇa.

13.1 Arjuna said: O Kṛṣṇa, I wish to know and understand about prakṛti *and* puruṣa, *passive and active energies. The field and the knower of the field, and of knowledge and of the end of knowledge.*

श्री भगवानुवाच ।
इदं शरीरं कौन्तेय क्षेत्रमित्यभिधीयते ।
एतद्यो वेत्ति तं प्राहुः क्षेत्रज्ञ इति तद्विदः ॥ १

śrībhagavānuvāca
idam śarīraṁ kaunteya kṣetramityabhidhīyate **/**
etadyo vetti taṁ prāhuḥ kṣetrajña iti tadvidaḥ **//** *13.2*

śrī bhagavān uvāca: the personality of godhead said; *idaṁ:* this; *śarīraṁ:* body; *kaunteya:* O son of Kuntī; *kṣetraṁ:* the field; *iti:* thus; *abhidhīyate:* is called; *etat:* this; *yaḥ:* anyone; *vetti:* knows; *taṁ:* he; *prāhuḥ:* is called; *kṣetrajña:* knower of the body; *iti:* thus; *tadvidaḥ:* one who knows

13.2 Lord Kṛṣṇa replies to Arjuna saying: This body, O son of Kuntī, is called the field, anyone who knows this body is called the knower of the field.

क्षेत्रज्ञं चापि मां विद्धि सर्वक्षेत्रेषु भारत ।
क्षेत्रक्षेत्रज्ञयोर्ज्ञानं यत्तज्ज्ञानं मतं मम ॥ २

kṣetrajñaṁ cāpi māṁ viddhi sarvakṣetreṣu bhārata |
kṣetrakṣetrajñayorjñānaṁ yattajjñānaṁ mataṁ mama || 13.3

kṣetrajñaṁ: the knower; *ca:* also; *api:* certainly; *māṁ:* Me; *viddhi:* know; *sarva:* all; *kṣetreṣu:* in bodily fields; *bhārata:* O son of Bhārata; *kṣetra:* field of activities (the body); *kṣetrajñayoḥ:* the knower of the field; *jñānaṁ:* knowledge; *yat:* that which is taught; *tat:* that; *jñānaṁ:* knowledge; *mataṁ:* opinion; *mama:* that

13.3 O Bhārata, know that I am the Knower in all bodies, the witness. In my opinion knowledge means the understanding of this body or the field of activity as well as the Knower of this field.

तत्क्षेत्रं यच्च यादृक्च यद्विकारि यतश्च यत् ।
स च यो यत्प्रभावश्च तत्समासेन मे श्रृणु ॥ ३

tat kṣetraṁ yac ca yādṛk ca yadvikāri yataś ca yat |
sa ca yo yat prabhāvaś ca tat samāsena me sṛṇu || 13.4

tat: that; *kṣetraṁ:* field of activities; *yah:* as; *ca:* and; *yādṛk:* as it is; *ca:* and; *yat*: what is; *vikāri:* changes; *yataḥ:* from which; *ca:* and; *yat:* which; *sa:* he; *ca:* also; *yaḥ:* one; *yat:* which; *prabhāvaśca:* influence also; *tat:* that; *samāsena:* in summary; *me:* from Me; *sṛṇu:* understand

13.4 Understand my summary of this field of activity and how it is constituted, what its changes are, how it is produced, who that knower of the field of activities is, and what his influences are.

ऋषिभिर्बहुधा गीतं छन्दोभिर्विविधैः पृथक् ।
ब्रह्मसूत्रपदैश्चैव हेतुमद्भिर्विनिश्चितैः ॥ ४

ṛsibhirbahudhā gītaṁ chandobhirvividhaiḥ pṛthak |
brahmasūtra padaiścaiva hetumadbhirviniścitaiḥ || 13.5

ṛsibhir: by the wise sages; *bahudhā:* in many ways; *gītaṁ:* described; *chandobhiḥ*: Vedic hymns; *vividhaiḥ:* in various; *pṛthak:* variously; *brahmasūtra:* the Vedanta; *padaiḥ*: aphorisms; *ca:* also; *eva*: certainly; *hetumadbhir:* with cause and effect; *viniścitaiḥ*: ascertained

13.5 That knowledge of the field of activities and of the knower of activities is described by various sages with chants in the scriptures It is presented with all reasoning as to cause and effect.

महाभूतान्यहङ्कारो बुद्धिरव्यक्तमेव च ।
इन्द्रियाणि दशैकं च पञ्च चेन्द्रियगोचराः ॥ ५

mahābhūtānyahaṅkāro buddhiravyaktameva ca |
indriyāṇi daśaikaṁ ca pañca cendriyagocarāḥ || 13.6

इच्छा द्वेषः सुखं दुःखं सङ्घातश्चेतना धृतिः ।
एतत्क्षेत्रं समासेन सविकारमुदाहृतम् ॥ ६

icchādveṣaḥ sukhaṁ duḥkhaṁ saṅghātaścetanā dhṛtiḥ |
etatkṣetraṁ samāsena savikāramudāhṛtam || 13.7

mahābhūtāni: great elements; *ahaṅkāraḥ:* ego; *buddhiḥ:* intelligence; *avyaktaṁ:* the unmanifested; *eva:* certainly; *ca:* also; *indriyāṇi*: senses; *daśaikaṁ:* eleven; *ca:* also; *pañca:* five; *ca:* also; *indriyagocarāḥ:* objects of the senses; *icchā:* desire; *dveṣaḥ*: hatred; *sukhaṁ:* happiness; *duḥkhaṁ:* distress; *saṅghātaḥ:* the aggregate; *cetanā*: living symptoms; *dhṛtiḥ:* conviction; *etat:* all this; *kṣetraṁ:* the field of activities; *samāsena:* in summary; *savikāraṁ:* with its modifications; *udāhṛtam:* exemplified

13.6,7 The field of activities and its interactions are said to be: the five elements of nature, ego, intelligence, the mind, the formless, the ten senses of perception and action, as well as the five objects of senses and desire, hatred, happiness, distress, the aggregate, the life symptoms, and convictions.

अमानित्वमदम्भित्वमहिंसा क्षान्तिरार्जवम् ।
आचार्योपासनं शौचं स्थैर्यमात्मविनिग्रहः ॥ ७

amānitvamadambhitvamahimsā kṣāntirārjavam |
ācāryopāsanaṁ śaucaṁ sthairyamātmavinigrahaḥ || 13.8

amānitvaṁ: humility; *adambhitvaṁ:* pridelessness; *ahimsā:* nonviolence; *kṣāntiḥ*: tolerance; *ārjavam:* simplicity; *ācāryopāsanaṁ:* approaching a bonafide spiritual master; *śaucaṁ:* cleanliness; *sthairyaṁ:* steadfastness; *ātmavinigrahaḥ:* control

इन्द्रियार्थेषु वैराग्यमनहङ्कार एव च ।
जन्ममृत्युजराव्याधिदुःखदोषानुदर्शनम् ॥ ८

indriyārtheṣu vairāgyamanahaṁkāra eva ca |
janmamṛtyujarāvyādhi-duḥkhadoṣānudarśanam || 13.9

indriyārtheṣu: in the matter of the senses; *vairāgyaṁ:* renunciation; *anahaṁkāra*: being without egoism; *eva:* certainly; *ca:* also; *janma:* birth;

mṛtyu: death; *jarā:* old age; *vyādhi:* disease; *duḥkha:* distress; *doṣa:* fault; *anudarśanam:* observing

असक्तिरनभिष्वङ्गः पुत्रदारगृहादिषु ।
नित्यं च समचित्तत्वमिष्टानिष्टोपपत्तिषु ॥ ९

asaktiranabhiṣvaṅgaḥ putradāragṛhādiṣu /
nityaṁ ca samacittatvamiṣṭāniṣṭopapattiṣu // 13.10

asaktiḥ: without attachment; *anabhiṣvaṅgaḥ:* without association; *putra:* sons; *dāra*: wife; *gṛhādiṣu:* home, etc.; *nityaṁ:* eternal; *ca:* also; *samacittatvaṁ:* equilibrium; *iṣṭā:* desirable; *aniṣṭa*: undesirable; *upapattiṣu*: having obtained

मयि चानन्ययोगेन भक्तिरव्यभिचारिणी ।
विविक्तदेशसेवित्वमरतिर्जनसंसदि ॥ १०

mayi cānanyayogena bhaktiravyabhicāriṇī /
vivikta deśasevitvamaratirjana saṁsadi // 13.11

mayi: unto Me; *ca:* also; *ananyayogena:* by devotional service; *bhaktiḥ:* devotion; *avyabhicāriṇī:* constant, unalloyed; *vivikta:* solitary; *deśa:* place; *sevitvaṁ:* resorting to; *aratiḥ:* without attachment; *jana:* to people in general; *saṁsadi:* mass

अध्यात्मज्ञाननित्यत्वं तत्त्वज्ञानार्थदर्शनम् ।
एतज्ज्ञानमिति प्रोक्तमज्ञानं यदतोऽन्यथा ॥ ११

adhyātmajñānanityatvaṁ tattvajñānārthadarśanam /
etajjñānamiti proktamajñānaṁ yadatonyathā // 13.12

adhyātma: pertaining to the self; *jñāna:* knowledge; *nityatvaṁ:* eternity; *tattva jñānā*: knowledge of the truth; *artha*: for the purpose of; *darśanam*: philosophy; *etat*: all this; *jñānam*: knowledge; *iti:* thus; *proktam:* declared; *ajñānaṁ:* ignorance; *yat:* that which; *ataḥ:* from this; *anyathā*: others

13.8,9,10,11,12 Humility, absence of pride, nonviolence, tolerance, simplicity, service to an enlightened spiritual master, cleanliness, steadiness and self-control; renunciation of the objects of sense gratification; absence of ego, the perception of the pain of the cycle of birth and death, old age and disease; nonattachment to children, wife, home and the rest and even-mindedness amid pleasant and unpleasant events; constant and unalloyed devotion to Me, resorting to solitary places, detachment from the general mass of people; accepting the importance of self realization, and philosophical search for the absolute truth: All these I thus declare to be knowledge and anything contrary to these is ignorance.

ज्ञेयं यत्तत्प्रवक्ष्यामि यज्ज्ञात्वामृतमश्नुते ।
अनादिमत्परं ब्रह्म न सत्तन्नासदुच्यते ॥ १२

jñeyaṁ yattatpravakṣyāmi yajjñātvāmṛtamaśnute |
anādimatparaṁ brahma na sattannāsaducyate || 13.13

jñeyaṁ: knowable; *yat:* that; *tat:* which; *pravakṣyāmi:* I shall now explain; *yat*: which; *jñātvā:* knowing; *amṛtaṁ*: nectar; *aśnute*: taste; *anādimat:* that which has no beginning; *paraṁ*: the supreme; *brahma:* spirit; *na:* neither; *sat:* cause; *tat:* that; *nā:* nor; *asat*: effect; *ucyate:* is called

13.13 I shall fully give you the understanding about the knowable with which one can taste eternal bliss or the being or the consciousness that has no beginning. A life beyond the cause and effect and the material world.

सर्वत: पाणिपादं तत्सर्वतोऽक्षिशिरोमुखम् ।
सर्वत: श्रुतिमल्लोके सर्वमावृत्य तिष्ठति ॥ १३

sarvataḥ pāṇipādaṁ tat sarvato 'kṣiśiromukham |
sarvataḥ śrutimalloke sarvamāvṛtya tiṣṭhati || 13.14

sarvataḥ: everywhere; *pāṇi:* hands; *pādaṁ:* legs; *tat:* that; *sarvataḥ:* everywhere; *akṣi*: eyes; *śiro*: head; *mukham:* face; *sarvataḥ:* everywhere; *śrutimat*: hearing; *loke:* in the world; *sarvaṁ:* everything; *āvṛtya:* covering; *tiṣṭhati:* exists

13.14 With hands and feet everywhere, with eyes, heads and mouths everywhere, with ears everywhere, He exists in the worlds, enveloping all. The Paramātman *(supreme spirit) is all pervading.*

सर्वेन्द्रियगुणाभासं सर्वेन्द्रियविवर्जितम् ।
असक्तं सर्वभृच्चैव निर्गुणं गुणभोक्तृ च ॥ १४

sarvendriyaguṇābhāsaṁ sarvendriyavivarjitam |
asaktaṁ sarvabhṛccaiva nirguṇaṁ guṇabhoktṛ ca || 13.15

sarva: all; *indriya*: senses; *guṇa*: qualities; *ābhāsaṁ*: original source; *sarva:* all; *indriya*: senses; *vivarjitam:* being without; *asaktaṁ*: without attachment; *sarvabhṛt*: maintainer of everyone; *ca:* also; *eva:* certainly; *nirguṇaṁ:* without material qualities; *guṇabhoktṛ*: simultaneously master of the gunas; *ca:* also

13.15 The Paramātman *is the original source of all the senses. Yet, He is beyond all the senses. He is unattached. Although the consciousness is the maintainer of all the living beings, yet He transcends the modes of the nature and at the same time He is the master of the modes of our material nature.*

बहिरन्तश्च भूतानामचरं चरमेव च ।
सूक्ष्मत्वात्तदविज्ञेयं दूरस्थं चान्तिके च तत् ॥ १६

bahir antaśca bhūtānām acaraṁ carameva ca **/**
sūkṣmatvāttadavijñeyaṁ dūrasthaṁ cāntike ca tat **//** *13.16*

bahiḥ: outside; *antaḥ:* inside; *ca:* also; *bhūtānām:* of all living entities; *acaraṁ:* not moving; *caraṁ:* moving; *eva:* also; *ca:* and; *sūkṣmatvāt:* on account of being subtle; *tat:* that; *avijñeyaṁ:* unknowable; *dūrasthaṁ:* far away; *ca:* also; *antike*: near; *ca:* and; *tat:* that

13.16 The supreme truth exists both within and without, it is present in everything mobile or immobile. It is not knowable through the senses as it is very subtle. Though far, yet it is the nearest.

अविभक्तं च भूतेषु विभक्तमिव च स्थितम् ।
भूतभर्तृ च तज्ज्ञेयं ग्रसिष्णु प्रभविष्णु च ॥ १६

avibhaktaṁ ca bhūteṣu vibhaktamiva ca sthitam **/**
bhūtabhartṛ ca tajjñeyaṁ grasiṣṇu prabhaviṣṇu ca **//** *13.17*

avibhaktaṁ: without division; *ca:* also; *bhūteṣu:* in every living being; *vibhaktaṁ*: divided; *iva:* as if; *ca:* also; *sthitam:* situated; *bhūta bhartṛ:* maintainer of all living entities; *ca:* also; *tat:* that; *jñeyaṁ:* to be understood; *grasiṣṇu*: devours; *prabhaviṣṇu*: develops; *ca:* also

13.17 Though appearing fragmented it is indivisible whole. Though He is the maintainer of every living entity, it is to be understood that He consumes and creates all.

ज्योतिषामपि तज्ज्योतिस्तमसः परमुच्यते ।
ज्ञानं ज्ञेयं ज्ञानगम्यं हृदि सर्वस्य विष्ठितम् ॥ १७

jyotiṣāmapi tajjyotistamasaḥ paramucyate **/**
jñānaṁ jñeyaṁ jñānagamyaṁ hṛdi sarvasya viṣṭhitam **//** *13.18*

jyotiṣām: in all luminous objects; *api:* also; *tat:* that; *jyotiḥ:* source of light; *tamasaḥ*: of the darkness; *paraṁ:* beyond; *ucyate:* is said; *jñānaṁ*: knowledge; *jñeyaṁ:* to be known; *jñānagamyaṁ:* to be approached by knowledge; *hṛdi:* in the heart; *sarvasya*: of everyone; *viṣṭhitam:* situated

13.18 He is the source of light in all luminous objects. He is beyond the darkness of matter and is formless. He is knowledge, He is the object of knowledge, and He is the goal of knowledge. He is situated in everyone's heart.

इति क्षेत्रं तथा ज्ञानं ज्ञेयं चोक्तं समासतः ।
मद्भक्त एतद्विज्ञाय मद्भावायोपपद्यते ॥ १८

iti kṣetraṁ tathā jñānaṁ jñeyaṁ co 'ktaṁ samāsataḥ I
madbhakta etadvijñāya madbhāvāyopapadyate II 13.19

iti: thus; *kṣetraṁ:* the field of activities (the body); *tathā:* also; *jñānaṁ:* knowledge; *jñeyaṁ:* the knowable; *ca:* also; *uktaṁ*: described; *samāsataḥ*: in summary; *madbhaktaḥ*: My devotee; *etad:* all this; *vijñāya:* after understanding; *madbhāvāya:* My nature; *upapadyate:* attains

13.19 Thus the field of activities, knowledge and the knowable has been summarily described by Me. It is only when we can understand the true nature of our supreme Self and the material world with which we have created false identities that we can go beyond this and attain the supreme Self itself.

प्रकृतिं पुरुषं चैव विद्धयनादी उभावपि ।
विकारांश्च गुणांश्चैव विद्धि प्रकृतिसंभवान् ॥ १९

prakṛtiṁ puruṣaṁ caiva viddhyanādī ubhāvapi I
vikārāṁśca guṇāṁścaiva viddhi prakṛti saṁbhavān II 13.20

prakṛtiṁ: material nature; *puruṣaṁ:* living entity; *ca:* also; *eva*: certainly; *viddhi*: must know; *anādī:* without beginning; *ubhāu:* both; *api:* also; *vikārān:* transformations; *ca:* also; *guṇān:* three modes of nature; *ca:* also; *eva*: certainly; *viddhi:* know; *prakṛti:* material nature; *saṁbhavān:* produced of

13.20 Prakṛti *or the field and its attributes and the* puruṣa *or the knower or the supreme consciousness are both without beginning. All the transformations of nature that we see are produced by the field or* prakṛti.

कार्यकारणकर्तृत्वे हेतुः प्रकृतिरुच्यते ।
पुरुषः सुखदुःखानां भोक्तृत्वे हेतुरुच्यते ॥ २०

kāryakāraṇakartṛtve hetuḥ prakṛtirucyate I
puruṣaḥ sukhaduḥkhānāṁ bhoktṛtve heturucyate II 13.21

kārya: effect; *kāraṇa:* cause; *kartṛtve:* in the matter of creation; *hetuḥ:* instrument; *prakṛtiḥ:* material nature; *ucyate:* is said to be; *puruṣaḥ*: the living entity; *sukha:* of happiness; *duḥkhānāṁ:* and distress; *bhoktṛtve:* in enjoyment; *hetuḥ:* the instrument; *ucyate:* is said to be

13.21 In the production of the body and the senses, prakṛti *is said to be the cause; In the experience of pleasure and pain,* puruṣa *is said to be the cause.*

पुरुषः प्रकृतिस्थो हि भुङ्क्ते प्रकृतिजान्गुणान्।
कारणं गुणसङ्गोऽस्य सदसद्योनिजन्मसु ॥ २१

puruṣaḥ prakṛtistho hi bhuṅkte prakṛtijānguṇān /
kāraṇaṁ guṇasaṅgosya sadasadyonijanmasu // *13.22*

puruṣaha: the living entity; *prakṛtisthaḥ:* being situated in the material energy; *hi:* certainly; *bhuṅkte:* enjoys; *prakṛtijān:* produced by the material nature; *guṇān:* modes of nature; *kāraṇaṁ:* cause; *guṇasaṅgaḥ:* association with the modes of nature; *asya:* of the living entity; *sadasad:* good and bad; *yoni:* species of life; *janmasu:* births

13.22 The living entity in the material nature follows the way of life, enjoying the moods of nature. Due to association with the material nature it meets the good or evil among various species.

उपद्रष्टानुमन्ता च भर्ता भोक्ता महेश्वरः।
परमात्मेति चाप्युक्तो देहेऽस्मिन्पुरुषः परः ॥ २३

upadraṣṭānumantā ca bhartā bhoktā maheśvaraḥ /
paramātmeti cāpyukto dehesminpuruṣaḥ paraḥ // *13.23*

upadraṣṭā: overseer; *anumantā*: permitter; *ca:* also; *bhartā:* master; *bhoktā:* supreme enjoyer; *maheśvaraḥ:* the supreme Lord; *paramātmā:* supersoul; *iti*: also; *ca* : and; *apyuktaḥ*: is said; *dehe:* in this body; *asmin*: this; *puruṣaḥ:* enjoyer; *paraḥ*: transcendental

13.23 Yet, in this body there is a transcendental energy. He who is divine, who exists as a owner or the witness, supporter, enjoyer and the pure witnessing consciousness, is known as the Paramātman.

य एवं वेत्ति पुरुषं प्रकृतिं च गुणैः सह।
सर्वथा वर्तमानोऽपि न स भूयोऽभिजायते ॥ २४

ya evaṁ vetti puruṣaṁ prakṛtiṁ ca guṇaiḥ saha /
sarvathā vartamānopi na sa bhūyobhijāyate // *13.24*

yaḥ: he who; *evaṁ:* thus; *vetti:* understands; *puruṣaṁ:* the living entity; *prakṛtiṁ*: material nature; *ca:* and; *guṇaiḥ:* modes of material nature; *saha:* with; *sarvathā:* by all means; *vartamānaḥ:* situated; *api*: in spite of; *na*: never; *saḥ*: he; *bhūyaḥ:* again; *abhijāyate*: takes his birth

13.24 One who understands this philosophy concerning material nature, the living entity and the interaction of the modes of nature is sure to attain liberation. He will not take birth here again, regardless of his present position.

ध्यानेनात्मनि पश्यन्ति केचिदात्मानमात्मना।
अन्ये साङ्ख्येन योगेन कर्मयोगेन चापरे ॥ २५

dhyānenātmani paśyanti kecidātmānamātmanā |
anye sāṅkhyena yogena karmayogena cāpare || 13.25

dhyānena: by meditation; *ātmani*: in one self; *paśyanti:* see; *kecit:* some; *ātmānam*: Supersoul; *ātmanā:* by the mind; *anye:* others; *sāṅkhyena:* by philosophical discussion; *yogena:* by the yoga system; *karmayogena:* by activities without fruitive desire; *ca:* also; *apare:* others

13.25 Some perceive the Paramātman *in their inner psyche through mind and intellect that have been purified by meditation or by metaphysical knowledge or by* karma yoga.

अन्ये त्वेवमजानन्तः श्रुत्वान्येभ्य उपासते।
तेऽपि चातितरन्त्येव मृत्युं श्रुतिपरायणाः ॥ २६

anye tvevamajānantaḥ śrutvānyebhya upāsate |
te 'pi 'cātitarantyeva mṛtyuṁ śrutiparāyaṇāḥ || 13.26

anye: others; *tu:* but; *evaṁ:* thus; *ajānantaḥ*: without spiritual knowledge; *śrutvā:* by hearing; *anyebhyaḥ:* from others; *upāsate:* begin to worship; *te:* they; *api:* also; *ca*: and; *atitaranti:* transcend; *eva:* certainly; *mṛtyuṁ:* the path of death; *śrutiparāyaṇāḥ* : inclined to the process of hearing

13.26 There are those who, although not conversant in spiritual knowledge, begin to worship the supreme personality upon hearing about Him from others. Through the process of hearing about the supreme Self, they also transcend the path of birth and death.

यावत्सञ्जायते किञ्चित्सत्त्वं स्थावरजङ्गमम्।
क्षेत्रक्षेत्रज्ञसंयोगात्तद्विद्धि भरतर्षभ ॥ २७

yāvatsañjāyate kiñcit sattvaṁ sthāvarajaṅgamam |
kṣetrakṣetrajñasaṁyogāttadviddhi bharatarṣabha || 13.27

yāvat: whatever; *sañjāyate:* takes place; *kiñcit:* anything; *sattvaṁ:* existence; *sthāvara:* not moving; *jaṅgamam:* moving; *kṣetra:* the body; *kṣetrajña*: knower of the body; *saṁyogāt:* union between; *tadviddhi:* you must know it; *bharatarṣabha:* O chief of the Bhāratas

13.27 Bhārata, know that whatever that is movable or immovable is born, It comes into existence by combination of kṣetra *and* kṣetrajñya

समं सर्वेषु भूतेषु तिष्ठन्तं परमेश्वरम् ।
विनश्यत्स्वविनश्यन्तं यः पश्यति स पश्यति ॥ २८

samaṁ sarveṣu bhūteṣu tiṣṭhantaṁ parameśvaram |
vinaśyatsvavinaśyantaṁ yaḥ paśyati sa paśyati || 13.28

samaṁ: equally; *sarveṣu:* in all; *bhūteṣu*: living entities; *tiṣṭhantaṁ:* residing; *parameśvaram*: the supersoul; *vinaśyatsu:* in the destructible; *avinaśyantaṁ* : not destroyed; *yaḥ*: anyone; *paśyati:* sees; *saḥ:* he; *paśyati:* actually sees

13.28 One who sees the supreme Spirit accompanying the individual soul in all bodies, who understands that neither the individual soul nor the supreme Spirit is ever destroyed, actually sees.

समं पश्यन्हि सर्वत्र समवस्थितमीश्वरम् ।
न हिनस्त्यात्मनात्मानं ततो याति परां गतिम् ॥ २९

samaṁ paśyanhi sarvatra samavasthitamīsvaram |
na hinastyātmanā 'tmanaṁ tato yāti parāṁ gatim || 13.29

samaṁ: equally; *paśyan:* seeing; *hi:* certainly; *sarvatra:* everywhere; *samavasthitam*: equally situated; *īsvaraṁ:* Supersoul; *na:* does not; *hinasti:* degrade; *ātmanā:* by the mind; *atmanaṁ:* the soul; *tato yāti*: then reaches; *parāṁ:* the transcendental; *gatim:* destination

13.29 When one does not get degraded or influenced by the mind and when he can see the supreme Spirit in all living and non-living things, One reaches the transcendental destination.

प्रकृत्यैव च कर्माणि क्रियमाणानि सर्वशः ।
यः पश्यति तथात्मानमकर्तारं स पश्यति ॥ ३०

prakṛtyaiva ca karmāṇi kriyamāṇāni sarvaśaḥ |
yaḥ paśyati tathātmānamakartāraṁ sa paśyati || 13.30

prakṛtyā: by material nature; *eva:* certainly; *ca*: also; *karmāṇi:* activities; *kriyamāṇāni:* engaged in performing; *sarvaśaḥ*: in all respects; *yaḥ:* anyone who; *paśyati:* sees; *tathā:* so also; *atmānaṁ:* himself; *akartāraṁ:* non-doer; *saḥ*: he; *paśyati:* sees perfectly

13.30 One who can see that all activities are performed by the body, which is created of material nature, sees that the Self does nothing, actually sees.

यदा भूतपृथग्भावमेकस्थमनुपश्यति ।
तत एव च विस्तारं ब्रह्म सम्पद्यते तदा ॥ ३१

yadā bhūtapṛthagbhāvamekasthamanupaśyati |
tata eva ca vistāraṁ brahma saṁpadyate tadā || 13.31

yadā: when; *bhūta:* living entities; *pṛthagbhāvaṁ:* separated identities; *ekasthaṁ*: situated in one; *anupaśyati:* tries to see through authority; *tata eva:* thereafter; *ca*: also; *vistāraṁ:* expanded; *brahma:* the Absolute; *saṁpadyate:* attains; *tadā:* at that time

13.31 When a person can see the supreme Self in all living entities then he will cease to see the separateness among the living entities. He will see that the whole universe is an expansion and expression of the same truth.

अनादित्वान्निर्गुणत्वात्परमात्मायमव्ययः ।
शरीरस्थोऽपि कौन्तेय न करोति न लिप्यते ॥ ३२

anāditvānnirguṇatvātparamātmāyamavyayaḥ |
śarīrastho'pi kaunteya na karoti na lipyate || 13.32

anāditvāt: due to eternity; *nirguṇatvāt:* due to transcendental; *paramātmā:* supreme soul; *ayaṁ*: this; *avyayaḥ:* inexhaustible; *śarīrastho 'pi:* though dwelling in the body; *kaunteya:* O son of Kuntī; *na karoti:* never does anything; *na lipyate* : nor is he entangled

13.32 Those with the vision of eternity can see that the soul is transcendental, eternal, and beyond the modes of nature. Despite contact with the material body, O Arjuna, the soul neither does anything nor is attached.

यथा सर्वगतं सौक्ष्म्यादाकाशं नोपलिप्यते ।
सर्वत्रावस्थितो देहे तथात्मा नोपलिप्यते ॥ ३३

yathā sarvagataṁ saukṣmyādākāśaṁ nopalipyate |
sarvatrāvasthito dehe tathātmā nopalipyate || 13.33

yathā: as; *sarvagataṁ:* all-pervading; *saukṣmyād:* due to being subtle; *ākāśaṁ:* the sky; *na:* never; *upalipyate:* mixes; *sarvatra:* everywhere; *avasthitaḥ:* situated; *dehe:* in the body; *tathā:* such; *ātmā*: the self; *na:* never; *upalipyate:* mixes.

13.33 The sky, due to its subtle nature, does not mix with anything, although it is all-pervading. Similarly, the soul, situated in Brahman, *does not mix with the body, though situated in that body.*

यथाप्रकाशयत्येकः कृत्स्नं लोकमिमं रविः ।
क्षेत्रं क्षेत्री तथा कृतस्नं प्रकाशयति भारत ॥ ३४

yathā prakāśayatyekaḥ kṛtsnaṁ lokamimaṁ raviḥ |
kṣetraṁ kṣetrī tathā kṛtsnaṁ prakāśayati bhārata || *13.34*

yathā: as; *prakāśayati:* illumines; *ekaḥ:* one; *kṛtsnaṁ:* the whole; *lokaṁ*: universe; *imaṁ:* this; *raviḥ:* the sun; *kṣetraṁ:* this body; *kṣetrī*: the soul; *tathā:* similarly; *kṛtsnaṁ:* all; *prakāśayati:* illumines; *bhārata:* O son of Bhārata

13.34 O son of Bhārata, as the Sun alone illumines the universe, so does the living entity, one within the body, illumines the consciousness.

क्षेत्रक्षेत्रज्ञयोरेवमन्तरं ज्ञानचक्षुषा।
भूतप्रकृतिमोक्षं च ये विदुर्यान्ति ते परम्॥ ३५

kṣetrakṣetrajñayorevamantaraṁ jñāna cakṣuṣā |
bhūtaprakṛtimokṣaṁ ca ye viduryānti te param || *13.35*

kṣetra: body; *kṣetrajñayoḥ:* of the proprietor of the body; *evaṁ:* that; *antaraṁ:* difference; *jñānacakṣuṣā:* by vision of knowledge; *bhūta:* living entity; *prakṛti*: material nature; *mokṣaṁ:* liberation; *ca:* also; *ye:* one who; *viduḥ:* knows; *yānti:* approaches; *te*: they; *param:* supreme

13.35 Those, who see with the eyes of knowledge the difference between the body-mind and the knower of the body-mind, can understand the process. Are liberated from the bondages of the material nature and attain the Paramātman.

इति श्रीमद्भगवद्गीतासूपनिषत्सु ब्रह्मविद्यायां योगशास्त्रे
श्रीकृष्णार्जुनसंवादे क्षेत्रक्षेत्रज्ञविभागयोगो नाम त्रयोदशोऽध्याय: ॥

iti śrīmad bhagavadgītāsūpaniṣatsu brahmavidyāyām
yogaśāstre śrīkṛṣṇārjuna saṁvāde kṣetra kṣetrajña vibhāgayogo nāma trayodaśo'dhyāyaḥ ||

In the Upaniṣad *of the Bhagavad Gītā, the knowledge of* Brahman, *the Supreme, the science of Yoga and the dialogue between Śrī Kṛṣṇa and Arjuna, this is the thirteenth discourse designated:*

Kṣetra kṣetrajñya Vibhāga Yogaḥ

Verses Of Gita Chapter - 14

अथ चतुर्दशोऽध्यायः

गुणत्रयविभागयोगः

Guṇatraya Vibhāga Yogaḥ

श्री भगवानुवाच ।

परं भूयः प्रवक्ष्यामि ज्ञानानां ज्ञानमुत्तमम् ।

यज्ज्ञात्वा मुनयः सर्वे परां सिद्धिमितो गताः ॥ १

śrībhagavānuvāca

paraṁ bhūyaḥ pravakṣyāmi jñānānāṁ jñānamuttamam I

yajjñātvā munayaḥ sarve parāṁ siddhimito gatāḥ II 14.1

śrī bhagavān uvāca: Kṛṣṇa said; *paraṁ*: supreme; *bhūyaḥ*: again; *pravakṣyāmi*: I shall speak; *jñānānāṁ*: of all knowledge; *jñānaṁ*: knowledge; *uttamam*: the supreme; *yat*: which; *jñātvā*: knowing; *munayaḥ*: the sages; *sarve*: all; *parāṁ*: supreme; *siddhiṁ*: perfection; *itaḥ*: from this world; *gatāḥ*: attained

14.1 Kṛṣṇa says, 'I will declare to you again the supreme wisdom, The knowledge of which has helped all sages attain supreme perfection.'

इदं ज्ञानमुपाश्रित्य मम साधर्म्यमागताः ।

सर्गेऽपि नोपजायन्ते प्रलये न व्यथन्ति च ॥ २

idaṁ jñānamupāśritya mama sādharmyamāgatāḥ I

sarge'pi nopajāyante pralaye na vyathanti ca II 14.2

idaṁ: this; *jñānam:* knowledge; *upāśritya:* taking shelter of; *mama*: My; *sādharmyam*: nature; *āgatāḥ:* attained; *sarge 'pi:* even in the creation; *na:* never; *upajāyante*: comes in; *pralaye:* in the annihilation; *na:* nor; *vyathanti:* disturbed; *ca:* also

14.2 By becoming fixed in this knowledge, one can attain the transcendental nature, like my own, and establish in his eternal consciousness, that one is not born at the time of creation, or disturbed at the time of dissolution.

मम योनिर्महद्ब्रह्म तस्मिन्गर्भं दधाम्यहम् ।

संभवः सर्वभूतानां ततो भवति भारत ॥ ३

mama yonirmahadbrahma tasmingarbhaṁ dadhāmyaham **/**
saṁbhavaḥ sarvabhūtānāṁ tato bhavati bhārata **//** 14.3

mama: My; *yoniḥ:* source of birth; *mahad brahma:* material cause of the entire creation called mahat brahma; *tasmin:* in that; *garbhaṁ:* pregnancy; *dadhāmi:* create; *ahaṁ*: I; *saṁbhavaḥ*: possibility; *sarvabhūtānāṁ:* of all living entities; *tataḥ:* thereafter; *bhavati:* becomes; *bhārata:* O son of Bhārata

14.3 The total material substance, called Brahman, *is the source of birth, It is that* Brahman *that I impregnate, making possible the births of all living beings, O son of Bhārata.*

सर्वयोनिषु कौन्तेय मूर्तय: सम्भवन्ति या: ।
तासां ब्रह्म महद्योनिरहं बीजप्रद: पिता ॥ ४

sarvayoniṣu kaunteya mūrtayaḥ saṁbhavanti yāḥ **/**
tāsāṁ brahma mahadyonirahaṁ bījapradaḥ pitā **//** 14.4

sarva yoniṣu: in all species of life; *kaunteya:* O son of Kuntī; *mūrtayaḥ:* forms; *saṁbhavanti*: as they appear; *yāḥ*: which; *tāsāṁ:* all of them; *brahma*: supreme; *mahad yoniḥ*: the source of birth in the material substance; *ahaṁ*: Myself; *bījapradaḥ:* seed-giving; *pitā:* father

14.4 Arjuna, understand that all species of life are made possible by birth in this material nature, and I am the seed-giving father.

सत्त्वं रजस्तम इंति गुणा: प्रकृतिसंभवा: ।
निबध्नन्ति महाबाहो देहे देहिनमव्ययम् ॥ ५

sattvaṁ rajastama iti guṇāḥ prakṛtisaṁbhavāḥ **/**
nibadhnanti mahābāho dehe dehinamavyayam **//** 14.5

sattvaṁ: mode of goodness; *rajaḥ:* mode of passion; *tamaḥ:* mode of ignorance; *iti*: thus; *guṇāḥ*: qualities; *prakṛti*: material nature; *saṁbhavāḥ:* produced of; *nibadhananti*: does condition; *mahābāho*: O mighty-armed one; *dehe*: in this body; *dehinaṁ*: the living entity; *avyayaṁ*: eternal

14.5 Material nature consists of the three modes—goodness, passion and ignorance. When the living entity comes in contact with nature, it becomes conditioned by these modes.

तत्र सत्त्वं निर्मलत्वात्प्रकाशकमनामयम् ।
सुखसङ्गेन बध्नाति ज्ञानसंङ्गेन चानघ ॥ ६

tatra sattvaṁ nirmalatvāt prakāśakamanāmayam **/**
sukhasaṅgena badhnāti jñānasaṅgena cānagha **//** 14.6

tatra: thereafter; *sattvaṁ*: mode of goodness; *nirmalatvāt*: being purest in the material world; *prakāśakaṁ*: illuminating; *anāmayam*: without any sinful reaction; *sukha*: happiness; *saṅgena*: association; *badhnāti*: conditions; *jñāna*: knowledge; *saṅgena:* association; *ca*: also; *anagha*: O sinless one

14.6 O sinless One, the mode of goodness, satva, *being purer than the others, is illuminating, and it frees one from all sinful reactions. Those situated in that mode develop knowledge, but they become conditioned by the concept of happiness.*

रजो रागात्मकं विद्धि तृष्णासङ्गसमुद्भवम् ।
तन्निबध्नाति कौन्तेय कर्मसङ्गेन देहिनम् ॥ ७

rajo rāgātmakaṁ viddhi tṛṣṇāsaṅgasamudbhavam **/**
tannibadhnāti kaunteya karmasaṅgena dehinam **//** 14.7

rajaḥ: the mode of passion; *rāgātmakaṁ:* born of desire or lust; *viddhi:* know; *tṛṣṇā*: with craving; *saṅga*: association; *samudbhavam:* produced of; *tan*: that; *nibadhnāti*: binds; *kaunteya*: O son of Kuntī; *karmasaṅgena*: by association with fruitive activity; *dehinam*: the embodied

14.7 Arjuna, know that the mode of passion, rajas, *is characterized by intense craving and is the source of desire and attachment.* Rajas *binds the living entity by attachment to work.*

तमस्त्वज्ञानजं विद्धि मोहनं सर्वदेहिनाम् ।
प्रमादालस्यनिद्राभिस्तन्निबध्नाति भारत ॥ ८

tamastvajñānajaṁ viddhi mohanaṁ sarvadehinām **/**
pramādālasyanidrābhistannibadhnāti bhārata **//** 14.8

tamaḥ: mode of ignorance; *tu:* but; *ajñānajaṁ*: products of ignorance; *viddhi*: know; *mohanaṁ:* delusion; *sarvadehinām*: of all embodied beings; *pramāda*: madness; *ālasya*: indolence; *nidrābhiḥ:* sleep; *tat:* that; *nibadhnāti:* binds; *bhārata* : O son of Bhārata

14.8 Know, O Arjuna, that the mode of ignorance, tamas, *the deluder of the living entity is born of inertia.* Tamas *binds the living entity by carelessness, laziness, and excessive sleep.*

सत्त्वं सुखे सञ्जयति रजः कर्मणि भारत ।
ज्ञानमावृत्य तु तमः प्रमादे सञ्जयत्युत ॥ ९

sattvaṁ sukhe sañjayati rajaḥ karmaṇi bhārata /
jñānamāvṛtya tu tamaḥ pramāde sañjayatyuta // 14.9

sattvaṁ: mode of goodness; *sukhe:* in happiness; *sañjayati:* develops; *rajaḥ:* mode of passion; *karmaṇi:* fruits of activities; *bhārata:* O son of Bhārata; *jñānam*: knowledge; *āvṛtya:* covering; *tu:* but; *tamaḥ*: the mode of ignorance; *pramāde*: in madness; *sañjayati:* develops; *uta:* it is said

14.9 The mode of goodness conditions one to happiness, passion conditions him to fruits of action, and veiling the knowledge, tamas binds one to carelessness.

रजस्तमश्चाभिभूय सत्त्वं भवति भारत ।
रजः सत्त्वं तमश्चैव तमः सत्त्वं रजस्तथा ॥ १०

rajastamaścābhibhūya sattvaṁ bhavati bhārata /
rajaḥ sattvaṁ tamaścaiva tamaḥ sattvaṁ rajastathā // 14.10

rajaḥ: mode of passion; *tamaḥ:* mode of ignorance; *ca:* also; *abhibhūya*: also surpassing; *sattvaṁ*: mode of goodness; *bhavati:* becomes prominent; *bhārata:* O son of Bhārata; *rajaḥ:* mode of passion; *sattvaṁ:* mode of goodness; *tamaḥ*: mode of ignorance; *ca:* also; *eva*: like that; *tamaḥ*: mode of ignorance; *sattvaṁ*: mode of goodness; *rajaḥ*: mode of passion; *tathā:* as in this

14.10 Sometimes the mode of passion becomes prominent, defeating the mode of goodness, O son of Bhārata. And sometimes the mode of goodness defeats passion, and at other times the mode of ignorance defeats goodness and passion. In this way there is always competition for supremacy.

सर्वद्वारेषु देहेऽस्मिन्प्रकाश उपजायते ।
ज्ञानं यदा तदा विद्याद्विवृद्धं सत्त्वमित्युत ॥ ११

sarvadvāreṣu dehesminprakāśa upajāyate /
jñanaṁ yadā tadā vidyādvivṛddhaṁ sattvamityuta // 14.11

sarvadvāreṣu: all the gates; *dehe 'smin*: in this body; *prakāśaḥ:* quality of illumines; *upajāyate*: develops; *jñanaṁ*: knowledge; *yadā*: when; *tadā*: at that time; *vidyāt*: must know; *vivṛddhaṁ*: increased; *sattvam:* the mode of goodness; *iti:* thus; *uta*: said

14.11 When the light of Self-knowledge illumines all the senses (or gates) in the body, then it should be known that goodness is predominant.

लोभ: प्रवृत्तिरारम्भ: कर्मणामशम: स्पृहा ।
रजस्येतानि जायन्ते विवृद्धे भरतर्षभ ॥ १२

lobhaḥ pravṛttirārambhaḥ karmaṇāmaśamaḥ spṛhā /
rajasyetāni jāyante vivṛddhe bharatarṣabha // 14.12

lobhaḥ: greed; *pravṛttiḥ*: hankering; *ārambhaḥ*: endeavor; *karmaṇām:* of activities; *aśamaḥ*: uncontrollable; *spṛhā*: desire; *rajasi:* in the mode of passion; *etāni*: all this; *jāyante*: develop; *vivṛddhe*: when there is excess; *bharatarṣabha*: O chief of the descendants of Bhārata

14.12 O chief of the Bhārata, when there is an increase in the mode of passion, the symptoms of great attachment, uncontrollable desire, hankering, and intense endeavor develop.

अप्रकाशोऽप्रवृत्तिश्च प्रमादो मोह एव च ।
तमस्येतानि जायन्ते विवृद्धे कुरुनन्दन ॥ १३

aprakāśo'pravṛttiśca pramādo moha eva ca /
tamasyetāni jāyante vivṛddhe kurunandana // 14.13

aprakāśaḥ: darkness; *apravṛttiḥ*: inactivity; *ca*: and; *pramādaḥ*: madness; *mohaḥ*: illusion; *eva*: certainly; *ca*: and; *tamasi*: in the mode of ignorance; *etāni*: these; *jāyante*: are manifested; *vivṛddhe:* is developed; *kurunandana:* O son of Kuru

14.13 O son of Kuru, when there is an increase in the mode of ignorance, madness, illusion, inertia and darkness are manifested.

यदा सत्त्वे प्रवृद्धे तु प्रलयं याति देहभृत् ।
तदोत्तमविदां लोकानमलान्प्रतिपद्यते ॥ १४

yadā sattve pravṛddhe tu pralayaṁ yāti dehabhṛt /
tadottamavidāṁ lokānamalānpratipadyate // 14.14

yadā: when; *sattve:* mode of goodness; *pravṛddhe:* in development; *tu*: but; *pralayaṁ*: dissolution; *yāti:* goes; *dehabhṛt:* embodied; *tadā:* at that time; *uttamavidāṁ*: of the great sages; *lokān:* the planets; *amalān*: pure; *pratipadyate:* attains.

14.14 When one dies in the mode of goodness, He goes to the highest of worlds.

रजसि प्रलयं गत्वा कर्मसङ्गिषु जायते ।
तथा प्रलीनस्तमसि मूढयोनिषु जायते ॥ १५

rajasi pralayaṁ gatvā karmasaṅgiṣu jāyate I
tathā pralīnastamasi mūḍhayoniṣu jāyate II 14.15

rajasi: in passion; *pralayaṁ:* dissolution; *gatvā:* attaining; *karmasaṅgiṣu:* in the pursuit of activities; *jāyate:* takes birth; *tathā:* thereafter; *pralīnaḥ:* being dissolved; *tamasi:* in ignorance; *mūḍha:* ignorant; *yoniṣu*: species; *jāyate*: take birth

14.15 When one dies in the mode of passion, he takes birth among those engaged in activities. When he dies in the mode of ignorance, he takes birth in the space of the ignorant.

कर्मणः सुकृतस्याहुः सात्त्विकं निर्मलं फलम् ।
रजसस्तु फलं दुःखमज्ञानं तमसः फलम् ॥ १६

karmaṇaḥ sukṛtasyāhuḥ sāttvikaṁ nirmalaṁ phalam I
rajasastu phalaṁ duḥkhamajñānaṁ tamasaḥ phalam II 14.16

karmaṇaḥ: of work; *sukṛtasya*: in the mode of goodness; *āhuḥ*: said; *sāttvikaṁ:* mode of goodness; *nirmalaṁ:* purified; *phalam:* result; *rajasaḥ:* of the mode of passion; *tu:* but; *phalaṁ:* result; *duḥkham:* misery; *ajñānaṁ:* nonsense; *tamasaḥ:* of the mode of ignorance; *phalam:* result

14.16 By acting in the mode of goodness, one becomes purified. Work done in the mode of passion results in distress, and actions performed in the mode of ignorance result in foolishness.

सत्त्वात्सञ्जायते ज्ञानं रजसो लोभ एव च ।
प्रमादमोहौ तमसो भवतोऽज्ञानमेव च ॥ १७

sattvātsañjāyate jñānaṁ rajaso lobha eva ca I
pramādamohau tamaso bhavato'jñānameva ca II 14.17

sattvāt: from the mode of goodness; *sañjāyate*: develops; *jñānaṁ*: knowledge; *rajasaḥ*: from the mode of passion; *lobhaḥ*: greed; *eva*: certainly; *ca*: also; *pramāda*: madness; *mohau*: illusion; *tamasaḥ*: from the mode of ignorance; *bhavataḥ*: develops; *ajñānam*: ignorance; *eva:* certainly; *ca:* also

14.17 From the mode of goodness, real knowledge develops; from the mode of passion, greed develops; from the mode of ignorance develops foolishness, madness and illusion.

ऊर्ध्वं गच्छन्ति सत्त्वस्था मध्ये तिष्ठन्ति राजसाः ।
जघन्यगुणवृत्तिस्था अधो गच्छन्ति तामसाः ॥ १८

ūrdhvaṁ gacchanti sattvasthā madhye tiṣṭhanti rājasāḥ I
jaghanyaguṇavṛttisthā adho gacchanti tāmasāḥ II 14.18

ūrdhvaṁ: upwards; *gacchanti*: go; *sattvasthāḥ*: one who is situated in the mode of goodness; *madhye:* in the middle; *tiṣṭhanti:* dwell; *rājasāḥ:* those who are situated in the mode of passion; *jaghanya:* abominable; *guṇa:* quality; *vṛttisthāḥ:* occupation; *adhaḥ*: down; *gacchanti:* go; *tāmasāḥ:* people in the mode of ignorance

14.18 Those situated in the mode of goodness gradually go upward to the higher world ; those in the mode of passion live on the earthly planets; and those in the mode of ignorance go down to the worlds below.

नान्यं गुणेभ्यः कर्तारं यदा द्रष्टानुपश्यति ।
गुणेभ्यश्च परं वेत्ति मद्भावं सोऽधिगच्छति ॥ १९

nānyaṁ guṇebhyaḥ kartāraṁ yadā draṣṭānupaśyati I
guṇebhyaśca paraṁ vetti madbhāvaṁ so'dhigacchati II 14.19

na: never; *anyaṁ*: other than; *guṇebhyaḥ*: from the qualities; *kartāraṁ:* the performer; *yadā:* when; *draṣṭā'nupaśyati:* he who sees properly; *guṇebhyaśca*: from the modes of nature; *paraṁ:* transcendental; *vetti:* know; *madbhāvaṁ:* My spiritual nature; *saḥ:* he; *adhigacchati:* is promoted

14.19 When we see that there is nothing beyond these modes of nature in all activities and that the supreme Lord is transcendental to all these modes, the seeker can know My spiritual nature.

गुणानेतानतीत्य त्रीन्देही देहसमुद्भवान् ।
जन्ममृत्युजरादुःखैर्विमुक्तोऽमृतमश्नुते ॥ २०

guṇānetānatītya trīndehī dehasamudbhavān I
janmamṛtyujarāduḥkhairvimukto'mṛtamaśnute II 14.20

guṇān: qualities; *etān:* all these; *atītya*: transcending; *trīn*: three; *dehī*: embodied; *deha*: body; *samudbhavān*: produced of; *janma*: birth; *mṛtyu:* death; *jarā*: old age; *duḥkhaiḥ*: distresses; *vimuktaḥ:* being freed from; *amṛtam*: nectar; *aśnute:* enjoys

14.20 When the embodied being is able to transcend these three modes, he can become free from birth, death, old age and their distresses and can enjoy nectar even in this life.

अर्जुन उवाच
कैर्लिङ्गैस्त्रीन्गुणानेतानतीतो भवति प्रभो ।
किमाचारः कथं चैतांस्त्रीन्गुणानतिवर्तते ॥ २१

arjuna uvāca
kairliṅgaistrīnguṇānetānatīto bhavati prabho I
kimācāraḥ kathaṁ caitāṁstrīnguṇānativartate II 14.21

arjuna uvāca: Arjuna said; *kaiḥ:* by which; *liṅgaiḥ:* symptoms; *trīn:* three; *guṇān*: qualities; *etān:* all these; *atītaḥ:* having transcended; *bhavati:* become; *prabho*: my Lord; *kim:* what; *ācāraḥ:* behavior; *kathaṁ:* what; *ca:* also; *etāṁ*: these; *trīn:* three; *guṇān:* qualities; *ativartate:* transcend

14.21 Arjuna inquired: O my Lord, by what symptoms is one known who is transcendental to those modes? What is his behavior? And how does he transcend the modes of nature?

श्री भगवानुवाच
प्रकाशं च प्रवृत्तिं च मोहमेव च पाण्डव ।
न द्वेष्टि सम्प्रवृत्तानि न निवृत्तानि काङ्क्षति ॥ २२

śrībhagavānuvāca
prakāśaṁ ca pravṛttiṁ ca mohameva ca pāṇḍava I
na dveṣṭi sampravṛttāni na nivṛttāni kāṅkṣati II 14.22

śrībhagavānuvāca: the supreme personality of godhead said; *prakāśaṁ ca:* and illumination; *pravṛttiṁ ca:* and attachment; *mohaṁ:* illusion; *eva ca:* also; *pāṇḍava*: O son of Pāṇḍu; *na dveṣṭi:* does not hate; *saṁpravṛttāni:* although developed; *na nivṛttāni*: nor stop development; *kāṅkṣati*: desires

उदासीनवदासीनो गुणैर्यो न विचाल्यते ।
गुणा वर्तन्त इत्येव योऽवतिष्ठति नेङ्गते ॥ २३

udāsīnavadāsīno guṇairyo na vicālyate I
guṇā vartanta ityeva yo'vatiṣṭhati neṅgate II 14.23

udāsīnavat: as if neutral; *āsīnaḥ*: situated; *guṇaiḥ:* by the qualities; *yaḥ:* one who; *na*: never; *vicālyate:* is agitated; *guṇāḥ:* the qualities; *vartante:* is situated; *ityeva:* knowing thus; *yaḥ:* one who; *avatiṣṭhati:* remains; *na*: never; *eṅgati:* flickering

समदु:खसुख: स्वस्थ: समलोष्टाश्मकाञ्चन: ।
तुल्यप्रियाप्रियो धीरस्तुल्यनिन्दात्मसंस्तुति: ॥ २४

samaduḥkhasukhaḥ svasthaḥ samaloṣṭāśmakāñcanaḥ /
tulyapriyāpriyo dhīrastulyanindātmasaṁstutiḥ // 14.24

sama: equal; *duḥkha:* in distress; *sukhaḥ:* in happiness; *svasthaḥ:* being situated himself; *sama:* equally; *loṣṭa*: a lump of earth; *aśma:* stone; *kāñcanaḥ:* gold; *tulya*: equally disposed; *priya:* dear; *apriyo:* undesirable; *dhīraḥ:* steady; *tulya*: equally; *nindā*: in defamation; *ātmasaṁstutiḥ:* in praise of himself

मानापमानयोस्तुल्यस्तुल्यो मित्रारिपक्षयो: ।
सर्वारम्भपरित्यागी गुणातीत: स उच्यते ॥ २५

mānāpamānyostulyastulyo mitrāripakṣayoḥ /
sarvārambhaparityāgī guṇātitaḥ sa ucyate // 14.25

māna: in honor; *apamānyoḥ:* dishonor; *tulyaḥ:* equally; *tulyaḥ:* equally; *mitra*: friend; *ari*: enemy; *pakṣayoḥ*: in parties; *sarva*: all; *ārambha*: endeavor; *parityāgī*: renouncer; *guṇātītaḥ*: transcendental to the material modes of nature; *saḥ:* he; *ucyate*: is said to be

14.22,23,24,25 The Blessed Lord said: He who does not hate illumination, attachment and delusion when they are present, nor longs for them when they disappear; who is seated like one unconcerned, being situated beyond these material reactions of the modes of nature, who remains firm, knowing that the modes alone are active; He who regards alike pleasure and pain, and looks on a lump of earth, a stone and a piece of gold with an equal eye; who is wise and holds praise and blame to be the same; who is unchanged in honor and dishonor, who treats friend and foe alike, who has abandoned all result based undertakings—such a man is said to have transcended the modes of nature.

मां च योऽव्यभिचारेण भक्तियोगेन सेवते ।
स गुणान्समतीत्यैतान्ब्रह्मभूयाय कल्पते ॥ २६

maṁ ca yo'vyabhicāreṇa bhaktiyogena sevate /
sa guṇānsamatītyaitānbrahmabhūyāya kalpate // 14.26

maṁ: unto Me; *ca:* also; *yaḥ:* person; *avyabhicāreṇa:* without fail; *bhaktiyogena*: by devotional service; *sevate:* renders service; *saḥ:* he; *guṇān:* all the modes of material nature; *samatītya:* transcending; *etān*: all this; *brahmabhūyāya:* to be elevated to the Brahman; *kalpate:* is considered.

14.26 One who engages in full devotional service, who does not fall down in any circumstance, at once transcends the modes of material nature and thus comes to the level of Brahman.

ब्रह्मणो हि प्रतिष्ठाहममृतस्याव्ययस्य च ।
शाश्वतस्य च धर्मस्य सुखस्यैकान्तिकस्य च ॥ २७

brahmaṇo hi pratiṣṭhāhamamṛtasyāvyayasya ca **/**
śāśvatasya ca dharmasya sukhasyaikāntikasya ca **//** 14.27

brahmaṇaḥ: of the impersonal brahma; *hi:* certainly; *pratiṣṭhā*: the rest; *aham:* I am; *amṛtasya*: of the immortal; *avyayasya*: of the imperishable; *ca:* also; *śāśvatasya:* of the eternal; *ca:* and; *dharmasya:* of the rightful state; *sukhasya:* happiness; *aikāntikasya*: ultimate; *ca:* also.

14.27 And I am the basis of Brahman, *which is the rightful state of ultimate happiness, and which is immortal, imperishable and eternal.*

इति श्रीमद्भगवद्गीतासूपनिषत्सु ब्रह्मविद्यायां योगशास्त्रे
श्रीकृष्णार्जुनसंवादे गुणत्रयविभागयोगो नाम चतुर्दशोऽध्यायः ॥

iti śrīmad bhagavadgītāsūpaniṣatsu brahmavidyāyām
yogaśāstre śrīkṛṣṇārjuna saṁvāde Guṇatraya Vibhāgayogo nāma
caturdaśo'dhyāyaḥ **//**

In the Upaniṣad *of the Bhagavad Gītā, the knowledge of* Brahman, *the Supreme, the science of Yoga and the dialogue between Śrī Kṛṣṇa and Arjuna, this is the fourteenth discourse designated:*

Guṇatraya Vibhāga Yogaḥ

Verses Of Gita Chapter - 15

अथ पञ्चदशोऽध्यायः

पुरुषोत्तमयोगः

Puruṣottama Yogaḥ

श्री भगवानुवाच
ऊर्ध्वमूलमधःशाखमश्वत्थं प्राहुरव्ययम् ।
छन्दांसि यस्य पर्णानि यस्तं वेद स वेदवित् ॥ १

śrī bhagavan uvāca
ūrdhvamūlamadhaḥ śākhamaśvattham prāhuravyayam I
chandāṁsi yasya parṇāni yastaṁ veda sa vedavit II 15.1

śrī bhagavan uvāca: the Lord said; *ūrdhvamūlam:* with roots above; *adhaḥ*: downwards; *śākham:* branches; *aśvattham:* banyan tree; *prāhuḥ:* is said; *avyayam*: eternal; *chandāṁsi:* the vedic hymns; *yasya:* of which; *parṇāni*: leaves; *yaḥ*: anyone who; *taṁ:* that; *veda*: knows; *saḥ:* he; *vedavit:* knower of the Vedas

15.1 Bhagavān *says, 'The imperishable tree of life symbolized by the Asvatta has its root above with the branches spreading below. It has the leaves in the form of the* Vedic *chants. The one who knows this eternal tree becomes the knower of Veda.*

अधश्चोर्ध्वं प्रसृतास्तस्य शाखा गुणप्रवृद्धा विषयप्रवालाः ।
अधश्च मूलान्यनुसंततानि कर्मानुबन्धीनि मनुष्यलोके ॥ २

adhaścordhvaṁ prasṛtāstasya śākhā guṇapravṛddhā viṣayapravālāḥ I
adhaśca mūlānyanusaṁtatāni karmānubandhīni manuṣyaloke II 15.2

adhaḥ: below; *ca:* and; *urdhvaṁ*: above; *prasṛtāḥ*: extended; *tasya:* its; *śākhāḥ*: branches; *guṇa:* by the human attributes; *pravṛddhāḥ*: nourished; *viṣaya:* sense objects; *pravālāḥ*: buds; *adhaḥ:* downward; *ca:* and; *mūlani:* roots; *anusaṁtatāni:* extended; *karma:* action; *anubandhīni:* bound; *manuṣyaloke:* in the world of men

15.2 The branches of this tree extend below and above the earth, nourished by the three human attributes, guṇa. *Its buds are the sense objects. This tree also has roots going down and these are bound to the resultant actions of humans.*

न रूपमस्येह तथोपलभ्यते नान्तो न चादिर्न च संप्रतिष्ठा ।
अश्वत्थमेनं सुविरूढमूलमसङ्गशस्त्रेण दृढेन छित्त्वा ॥ ३

na rūpamasyeha tathopalabhyate nānto na cādirna ca saṁpratiṣṭhā |
aśvatthamenaṁ suvirūḍhamūlamasaṅgaśastreṇa dṛḍhena chittvā || 15.3

na: not; *rūpam:* form; *asya:* its; *iha*: here; *tathā:* as such; *upalabhyate:* can be perceived; *na:* not; *antaḥ*: end; *na:* not; *ca:* and; *ādiḥr:* beginning; *na:* not; *ca:* and; *saṁpratiṣṭhā:* foundation; *aśvatthaṁ:* banyan tree; *enaṁ:* this; *suvirūḍha*: strongly; *mūlaṁ*: rooted; *asaṅgaśastreṇa:* by the weapon of detachment; *dṛḍhena:* strong; *chittvā*: cut down

15.3 The real form of this tree cannot be perceived. No one can understand where it ends, where it begins, or where its foundation is. But with determination one must cut down this strongly rooted tree with the weapon of detachment.

ततः पदं तत्परिमार्गितव्यं यस्मिन्गता न निवर्तन्ति भूयः ।
तमेव चाद्यं पुरुषं प्रपद्ये यतः प्रवृत्तिः प्रसृता पुराणी ॥ ४

tataḥ padaṁ tatparimārgitavyaṁ yasmingatā na nivartanti bhūyaḥ |
tameva cādyaṁ puruṣaṁ prapadye yataḥ pravṛittiḥ prasṛtā purāṇī || 15.4

tataḥ: thereafter; *padaṁ:* goal; *tat*: that; *parimārgitavyaṁ:* has to be searched out; *yasmin:* where; *gatāḥ:* going; *na:* not; *nivartanti:* return; *bhūyaḥ:* again; *taṁ:* in that; *eva*: even; *ca*: and; *ādyaṁ:* original; *puruṣaṁ:* supreme; *prapadye:* surrender; *yataḥ*: from whom; *pravṛittiḥ:* activity; *prasṛtā:* began; *purāṇī:* ancient

15.4 One must then seek that place from which having gone, one never returns and surrender to the supreme Being from whom all activities started from ancient times.

निर्मानमोहा जितसङ्गदोषा अध्यात्मनित्या विनिवृत्तकामाः ।
द्वन्द्वैर्विमुक्ताः सुखदुःखसंज्ञैर्गच्छन्त्यमूढाः पदमव्ययं तत् ॥ ५

nirmānamohā jitasaṅgadoṣā adhyātmanityā vinivṛittakāmāḥ |
dvandvairvimuktāḥ sukhaduḥkhsañjñairgacchanty-
amūḍhāḥ padamavyayaṁ tat || 15.5

nirmāna: without pride; *mohāḥ:* delusion; *jita:* having conquered; *saṅga*: attachment; *doṣāḥ*: defects; *adhyātma*: in the Self; *nityāḥ:* eternally; *vinivṛitta:* detached; *kāmāḥ*: from desires; *dvandvaiḥ*: from the dualities; *vimuktāḥ*: liberated; *sukha*: happiness; *duḥkha*: sorrow; *sañjñaiḥ:* known; *gacchanti:* reach; *amūḍhāḥ:* not confused; *padam:* goal; *avyayaṁ:* eternal; *tat:* that

15.5 Those who are free from pride, delusion, and attachment, those who dwell in the Self, who are done with lust, who are free from dualities of joy and sorrow, not confused and those who know how to surrender to the supreme person, attain the eternal consciousness.

न तद्भासयते सूर्यो न शशाङ्को न पावकः ।
यद्गत्वा न निवर्तन्ते तद्धाम परमं मम ॥ ६

na tadbhāsayate sūryo na śaśāṅko na pāvakaḥ /
yadgatvā na nivartante taddhāma paramaṁ mama // 15.6

na: not; *tat:* that; *bhāsayate*: illuminates; *sūryaḥ*: the sun; *na*: not; *śaśāṅkaḥ*: the moon; *na:* not; *pāvakaḥ*: fire; *yat:* where; *gatvā:* going; *na:* not; *nivartante:* return; *tad dhāma*: that abode; *paramaṁ:* supreme; *mama:* My

15.6 That supreme space of eternal consciousness, My consciousness, is not illumined by the Sun or the Moon, or by fire. Those who enter that space never return to this material world.

ममैवांशो जीवलोके जीवभूतः सनातनः ।
मनःषष्ठानीन्द्रियाणि प्रकृतिस्थानि कर्षति ॥ ७

mamai'vā'ṁśo jīvaloke jīvabhūtaḥ sanātanaḥ /
manaḥ ṣaṣṭhānī'ndriyāṇi prakṛtisthāni karṣati // 15.7

mama: My; *eva:* even; *aṁśaḥ*: portion; *jīvaloke*: in the world of life; *jīvabhūtaḥ*: the living entity; *sanātanaḥ:* eternal; *manaḥ:* with the mind; *ṣaṣṭāni:* six; *indriyāṇi*: senses; *prakṛiti*: active principle; *sthāni:* staying; *karṣati:* attract

15.7 The living entities in this conditioned material world are a portion of My eternal Self; in this conditioned material world they are attracted by the six senses, which include the mind, dwelling in prakṛti, *the active energy principle.*

शरीरं यदवाप्नोति यच्चाप्युत्क्रामतीश्वरः ।
गृहीत्वैतानि संयाति वायुर्गन्धानिवाशयात् ॥ ८

śarīraṁ yadavāpnoti yaccāpyutkrāmatīśvaraḥ /
gṛihītvai'tāni saṁyāti vāyurgandhānivāśayāt // 15.8

śarīraṁ: body; *yat:* when; *avāpnoti:* gets; *yat:* when; *cāpi:* and also; *utkrāmati:* leaves; *īśvaraḥ*: the lord of the mind body; *gṛihītvā:* taking; *etāni*: all these; *saṁyāti*: goes away; *vāyuḥ:* the wind; *gandhān:* smells; *iva:* like; *āśayāt:* from their source

15.8 The spirit in the mind-body living in this material world moves from one body to another carrying these just as air carries aroma.

श्रोत्रं चक्षुः स्पर्शनं च रसनं घ्राणमेव च ।
अधिष्ठाय मनश्चायं विषयानुपसेवते ॥ ९

śrotraṁ cakṣuḥ sparśanaṁ ca rasanaṁ ghrāṇaṁ eva ca **/**
adhiṣṭhāya manaścāyaṁ viṣayānupasevate **//** 15.9

śrotraṁ: ears; *cakṣuḥ:* eyes; *sparśanaṁ:* touch; *ca*: and; *rasanaṁ:* tongue; *ghrāṇaṁ*: smelling power; *eva:* even; *ca:* and; *adhiṣṭhāya:* presiding over; *manaḥ*: mind; *ca:* and; *ayaṁ*: he; *viṣayān:* sense objects; *upasevate:* enjoys

15.9 The living entity, the spirit, leaves one body, takes some other body and gets new eyes, ears, nose, tongue and sensing body according to the samskāras *it had in its causal layer and enjoys the new mental setup.*

उत्क्रामन्तं स्थितं वापि भुञ्जानं वा गुणान्वितम् ।
विमूढा नानुपश्यन्ति पश्यन्ति ज्ञानचक्षुषः ॥ १०

utkrāmantaṁ sthitaṁ vāpi bhuñjānaṁ vā guṇānvitam **/**
vimūḍhā nānupaśyanti paśyanti jñānacakṣuṣah **//** 15.10

utkrāmantaṁ: departing; *sthitaṁ*: staying; *vāpi:* or also; *bhuñjānaṁ:* enjoying; *vā:* or; *guṇānvitam:* united with attributes; *vimūḍhā:* foolish persons; *na:* not; *anupaśyanti:* see; *paśyanti*: see; *jñānacakṣuṣah:* those who have the eyes of knowledge

15.10 Fools in ignorance do not perceive the spirit being conjunction with the guṇās *as its enters, enjoys and leaves the body. The one whose inner eye is open clearly perceives everything.*

यतन्तो योगिनश्चैनं पश्यन्त्यात्मन्यवस्थितम् ।
यतन्तोऽप्यकृतात्मानो नैनं पश्यन्त्यचेतसः ॥ ११

yatanto yoginaścainaṁ paśyantyātmanyavasthitam **/**
yatanto'pyakṛtātmāno nainaṁ paśyantyacetasah **//** 15.11

yatantaḥ: trying; *yoginaḥ:* those who practice yoga; *ca:* and; *enaṁ:* this; *paśyanti*: can see; *ātmani:* in the self; *avasthitam:* situated; *yatantaḥ:* trying; *api:* also; *akṛtātmānaḥ*: without an understanding of the self; *na:* not; *enaṁ:* this; *paśyanti:* see; *acetasaḥ*: unintelligent

15.11 The serious practitioner of Yoga, with an understanding of his self, can see all this clearly. But those who do not have an understanding of the self, however much they try, cannot see.

यदादित्यगतं तेजो जगद्भासयतेऽखिलम् ।

यच्चन्द्रमसि यच्चाग्नौ तत्तेजो विद्धि मामकम् ॥ १२

yadādityagataṁ tejo jagadbhāsayate'khilam **|**

yaccandramasi yaccāgnau tattejo viddhi māmakam **||** 15.12

yat: which; *ādityagataṁ:* residing in the sun; *tejaḥ:* light; *jagat:* world; *bhāsayate:* lights up; *akhilam:* completely; *yat:* which; *candramasi:* in the moon; *yat:* which; *ca:* and; *agnau:* in the fire; *tat:* that; *tejaḥ:* light; *viddhi:* know; *māmakam:* from me

15.12 The light of the sun, the light of the moon and the light of fire, all their radiance is also from Me.

गामाविश्य च भूतानि धारयाम्यहमोजसा ।

पुष्णामि चौषधी: सर्वा: सोमो भूत्वा रसात्मक: ॥ १३

gāmāviśya ca bhūtāni dhārayāmyahamojasā **|**

puṣṇāmi causadhīḥ sarvāḥ somo bhūtvā rasātmakaḥ **||** 15.13

gām: the earth; *āviśya:* entering; *ca:* and; *bhūtāni:* living beings; *dhārayāmi:* sustaining; *aham:* I; *ojasā:* by energy; *puṣṇāmi:* nourishing; *ca:* and; *oṣadhīḥ:* plant life; *sarvāḥ:* all; *somaḥ:* the Moon; *bhūtvā:* becoming; *rasātmakaḥ:* watery

15.13 Entering into earth, I support all beings with My energy; becoming the watery moon I nourish all plant life.

अहं वैश्वानरो भूत्वा प्राणिनां देहमाश्रित: ।

प्राणापानसमायुक्त: पचाम्यन्नं चतुर्विधम् ॥ १४

ahaṁ vaiśvānaro bhūtvā prāṇināṁ dehamāśritaḥ **|**

prāṇāpānasamāyuktaḥ pacāmyannaṁ caturvidham **||** 15.14

ahaṁ: I; *vaiśvānaro:* as the digestive fire; *bhūtvā:* becoming; *prāṇināṁ:* of all living beings; *dehaṁ:* body; *āśritaḥ:* situated; *prāṇā:* exhaled breath; *apāna:* inhaled breath; *samāyuktaḥ:* associated; *pacāmi:* digest; *annaṁ:* food; *caturvidham:* fourfold

15.14 I am the fire of digestion in every living body and I am the breath of life, exhaled and inhaled, with which I digest the four-fold food.

सर्वस्य चाहं हृदि सन्निविष्टो मत्तः स्मृतिर्ज्ञानमपोहनं च ।
वेदैश्च सर्वैरहमेव वेद्यो वेदान्तकृद्वेदविदेव चाहम् ॥ १५

sarvasya cāhaṁ hṛdi sanniviṣṭo mattaḥ smṛtirjñānamapohanaṁ ca /
vedaiśca sarvairahameva vedyo vedāntakṛdvedavideva cāham // 15.15

sarvasya: of all; *ca:* and; *ahaṁ:* I; *hṛdi:* in the heart; *sanniviṣṭo:* seated; *mattaḥ*: from Me; *smṛtiḥ:* memory; *jñānaṁ:* knowledge; *apohanaṁ ca:* and loss; *vedaiḥ:* by the Vedas; *ca:* also; *sarvaiḥ:* all; *aham:* I; *eva:* even; *vedyaḥ:* to be known; *vedāntakṛt*: creator of the *Vedānta*; *vedavit:* the knower of the Veda; *eva:* even; *ca:* and; *aham*: I

15.15 I am seated in everyone's heart and from Me came memory, knowledge and their loss. I am known by the Vedas; *indeed, I am the Creator of* Vedānta *and I am the knower of the* Vedas.

द्वाविमौ पुरुषौ लोके क्षरश्चाक्षर एव च ।
क्षरः सर्वाणि भूतानि कूटस्थोऽक्षर उच्यते ॥ १६

dvāvimau puruṣau loke kṣaraścākṣara eva ca /
kṣaraḥ sarvāṇi bhūtāni kūṭasthokṣara ucyate // 15.16

dvāu: two; *imau:* these; *puruṣau:* puruṣa; *loke:* in the world; *kṣaraḥ:* perishable; *ca:* and; *akṣara:* imperishable; *eva:* even; *ca:* and; *kṣaraḥ:* the perishable; *sarvāṇi*: all; *bhūtāni:* living being; *kūṭasthaḥ:* unchangeable; *akṣara:* imperishable; *ucyate:* is said

15.16 There are two things, the perishable and the imperishable, in this world. There are the living beings who are perishable while there is the unchangeable, the imperishable.

उत्तमः पुरुषस्त्वन्यः परमात्मेत्युदाहृतः ।
यो लोकत्रयमाविश्य बिभर्त्यव्यय ईश्वरः ॥ १७

uttamaḥ puruṣastvanyaḥ paramātmetyudāhṛtaḥ /
yo lokatrayamāviśya bibhartyavyaya īśvaraḥ // 15.17

uttamaḥ: the best; *puruṣaḥ:* puruṣa; *tu:* but; *anyaḥ:* another; *paramātmā:* the Supreme Self; *iti:* thus; *udāhṛtaḥ:* is said; *yaḥ:* who; *lokatrayaṁ:* the three worlds; *āviśya*: pervading; *bibharti:* sustaining; *avyayaḥ:* indestructible; *īśvaraḥ:* the Lord

15.17 Besides these two, there is the supreme Puruṣa *the Lord Himself, who pervades and sustains these three worlds.*

यस्मात्क्षरमतीतोऽहमक्षरादपि चोत्तमः ।
अतोऽस्मि लोके वेदे च प्रथितः पुरुषोत्तमः ॥ १८

yasmātkṣaramatītohamakṣarādapi cottamaḥ I
atosmi loke vede ca prathitaḥ puruṣottamaḥ II 15.18

yasmāt: from which; *kṣaram:* the perishable; *atītaḥ:* transcendental; *aham:* I; *akṣarāt:* from the impersishable; *api:* also; *ca:* and; *uttamaḥ:* the best; *ataḥ:* therefore; *asmi*: I am; *loke:* in the world; *vede:* in the Veda; *ca:* and; *prathitaḥ:* declared; *puruṣottamaḥ*: as the Supreme Purusha

15.18 As I am transcendental, beyond both the perishable and the imperishable, and the best, I am declared both in the world and in the Vedas *as that supreme person,* Puruṣottama.

यो मामेवमसंमूढो जानाति पुरुषोत्तमम् ।
स सर्वविद्भजति मां सर्वभावेन भारत ॥ १९

yo māmevamasammūḍho jānāti puruṣottamam I
sa sarvavidbhajati mām sarvabhāvena bhārata II 15.19

yaḥ: who; *mām:* Me; *evam:* thus; *asammūḍhaḥ:* without a doubt; *jānāti:* knows; *puruṣottamam*: the supreme Puruṣa; *saḥ:* he; *sarvavid:* knower of everything; *bhajati*: worships; *mām:* Me; *sarva bhāvena:* with all being; *bhārata*: O son of Bhārata

15.19 Whoever knows Me as the supreme without a doubt, is to be understood as the knower of everything and he worships Me with all his being, O son of Bhārata.

इति गुह्यतमं शास्त्रमिदमुक्तं मयाऽनघ ।
एतद्बुद्ध्वा बुद्धिमान्स्यात्कृतकृत्यश्च भारत ॥ २०

iti guhyatamaṁ śāstramidamuktaṁ mayānagha I
etadbuddhvā buddhimānsyātkṛtakṛtyaśca bhārata II 15.20

iti: thus; *guhyatamaṁ:* secret; *śāstraṁ:* science; *idaṁ:* this; *uktaṁ:* taught; *mayā:* by Me; *anagha:* O sinless one; *etat:* this; *buddhvā:* knowing; *buddhimān:* wise; *syāt:* becomes; *kṛtakṛtyaḥ:* accomplished all actions; *ca:* and; *bhārata:* O son of Bhārata

15.20 This is the most profound teaching taught by Me, O Sinless One and whoever knows this will become wise and his actions will bear fruit.

इति श्रीमद्भगवद्गीतासूपनिषत्सु ब्रह्मविद्यायां योगशास्त्रे
श्रीकृष्णार्जुनसंवादे पुरुषोत्तमयोगो नाम पञ्चदशोऽध्यायः ॥

iti śrīmad bhagavadgītāsūpaniṣatsu brahmavidyāyām
yogaśāstre śrīkṛṣṇārjuna saṁvāde puruṣottamayogo nāma
pañcadaśo 'dhyāyaḥ ||

In the Upaniṣad *of the Bhagavad Gītā, the knowledge of* Brahman, *the Supreme, the science of Yoga and the dialogue between Śrī Kṛṣṇa and Arjuna, this is the fifteenth discourse designated:*

Puruṣottama Yogaḥ

Verses Of Gita Chapter - 16

अथ षोडशोऽध्यायः

दैवासुरसम्पद्विभागयोगः

Daivāsura Sampad Vibhāga Yogaḥ

श्री भगवानुवाच
अभयं सत्त्वसंशुद्धिर्ज्ञानयोगव्यवस्थितिः ।
दानं दमश्च यज्ञश्च स्वाध्यायस्तप आर्जवम् ॥ १

śrī bhagavan uvāca
abhayaṁ sattvasaṁśuddhirjñānayogavyavasthitiḥ **/**
dānaṁ damaśca yajñaśca svādhyāyastapa ārjavam **//** 16.1

अहिंसा सत्यमक्रोधस्त्यागः शान्तिरपैशुनम् ।
दया भूतेष्वलोलुप्त्वं मार्दवं ह्रीरचापलम् ॥ २

ahiṁsā satyamakrodhastyāgaḥ śāntirapaiśunam **/**
dayā bhūteṣvaloluptvaṁ mārdavaṁ hrīracāpalam **//** 16.2

तेजः क्षमा धृतिः शौचमद्रोहो नातिमानिता ।
भवन्ति संपदं दैवीमभिजातस्य भारत ॥ ३

tejaḥ kṣamā dhṛtiḥ śaucamadroho nātimānitā **/**
bhavanti sampadaṁ daivīmabhijātasya bhārata **//** 16.3

śrī bhagavan uvāca: Lord Kṛṣṇa said; *abhayaṁ*: fearlessness; *sattvasaṁśuddhiḥ*: purification of one's existence; *jñāna*: knowledge; *yoga*: of linking up; *vyavasthitiḥ*: remaining engaged in; *dānaṁ*: charity; *damaś ca*: and controlling the mind; *yajñaś ca*: and performance of sacrifice; *svādhyāyaḥ*: study of vedic literature; *tapaḥ*: austerity; *ārjavam*: simplicity; *ahiṁsā*: nonviolence; *satyaṁ*: truthfulness; *akrodhaḥ*: freedom from anger; *tyāgaḥ*: renunciation; *sāntiḥ*: tranquillity; *apaiśunaṁ*: aversion to fault-finding; *dayā*: mercy; *bhūteṣu*: towards all living entities; *aloluptvaṁ*: freedom from greed; *mārdavaṁ*: gentleness; *hrīḥ*: modesty; *acāpalam*: determination; *tejaḥ*: vigor; *kṣamā*: forgiveness; *dhṛtiḥ*: fortitude; *śaucaṁ*: cleanliness; *adrohaḥ*: freedom from envy; *na*: not; *atimānitā*: expectation of honor; *bhavanti*: become; *saṁpadaṁ*: qualities; *daivīṁ*: transcendental; *abhijātasya*: of one who is born of; *bhārata*: O son of Bhārata (Arjuna).

16.1,2,3 Bhagavān *Kṛṣṇa says, 'Fearlessness, purification of the being, cultivation of spiritual knowledge, charity and being centered on the being, performance of sacrifices, and accumulation of knowledge, austerity, simplicity, non-violence, truthfulness, freedom from anger, renunciation, tranquility, aversion to fault finding, compassion for all living entities, freedom from covetousness, gentleness, modesty, studied determination, vigor, more forgiveness, fortitude, cleanliness, freedom from envy, and from the passion of honor, these transcendental qualities, O Son of Bhārata (Arjuna), belong to divine men, endowed with divine nature.'*

दम्भो दर्पोऽभिमानश्च क्रोधः पारुष्यमेव च ।
अज्ञानं चाभिजातस्य पार्थ सम्पदमासुरीम् ॥ ४

dambho darpo'bhimānaśca krodhaḥ pāruṣyameva ca |
ajñānaṁ cābhijātasya pārtha sampadamāsurīm || 16.4

dambhaḥ: pride; *darpaḥ*: arrogance; *abhimānaḥ*: conceit; *ca*: and; *krodhaḥ*: anger; *pāruṣyaṁ*: harshness; *eva*: certainly; *ca*: and; *ajñānaṁ*: ignorance; *ca*: and; *abhijātasya*: one who is born of; *pārtha*: O son of Pritā; *saṁpadaṁ*: nature; *āsurīm*: demonic.

16.4 Pride, arrogance, conceit, anger, harshness or cruelty, and ignorance - these qualities belong to those born with demonic nature, O son of Pritā (Arjuna).

दैवी सम्पद्विमोक्षाय निबन्धायासुरी मता ।
मा शुचः सम्पदं दैवीमभिजातोऽसि पाण्डव ॥ ५

daivī sampadvimokṣāya nibandhayāsuri matā |
mā śucāḥ sampadaṁ daivīmabhijātosi pāṇḍava || 16.5

daivī: transcendental, divine; *saṁpat*: nature; *vimokṣāya*: for liberation; *nibandhaya*: for bondage; *asuri*: demonic qualities; *matā*: it is considered; *mā*: do not; *śucāḥ*: worry; *saṁpadaṁ*: nature; *daivīm*: transcendental, divine; *abhijātaḥ*: born; *asi*: you are; *pāṇḍava*: O son of Pāṇḍu.

16.5 The transcendental qualities are conducive to liberation, whereas the demonic qualities make for bondage. Do not worry, Pāṇḍavā (Arjuna), you are born with divine qualities.

द्वौ भूतसर्गौ लोकेऽस्मिन्दैव आसुर एव च ।
दैवो विस्तरशः प्रोक्त आसुरं पार्थ मे श्रृणु ॥ ६

dvau bhūtasargau loke'smin daiva āsura eva ca |
daivo vistaraśaḥ prokta āsuraṁ pārtha me śṛṇu || 16.6

dvau: two; *bhūtasargau*: created living beings; *loke*: in the world; *asmin:* in this; *daiva*: godly; *āsura*: demonic; *eva*: certainly; *ca*: and; *daivaḥ*: divine; *vistaraśaḥ*: in great detail; *proktaḥ*: said; *āsuraṁ*: demonic; *pārtha*: O son of *Pritā*; *me*: from Me; *śṛṇu*: hear.

16.6 Pārtha (Arjuna), in this world there are two kinds of created beings, one is divine and the other, demonic. I have explained at length to you the divine qualities, now understand the demonic qualities also, so that you will understand and live your life blissfully and happily.

प्रवृत्तिं च निवृत्तिं च जना न विदुरासुराः ।
न शौचं नापि चाचारो न सत्यं तेषु विद्यते ॥ ७

pravṛttiṁ ca nivṛttiṁ ca janā na vidurāsurāḥ /
na śaucaṁ nāpi cācāro na satyaṁ teṣu vidyate // 16.7

pravṛttiṁ: bondages; *ca*: also; *nivṛttiṁ*: liberation; *ca*: and; *janāḥ*: persons; *na*: never; *viduḥ*: know; *āsurāḥ*: demoniac qualities; *na*: never; *śaucaṁ*: cleanliness; *na*: nor; *api*: also; *ca*: and; *ācāraḥ*: behavior; *na*: never; *satyaṁ*: truth; *teṣu*: in them; *vidyate*: there is.

16.7 Persons with demonic nature do not know what is bondage and what is liberation; not what is cleanliness; truthful behavior is not in them.

असत्यमप्रतिष्ठं ते जगदाहुरनीश्वरम् ।
अपरस्परसंभूतं किमन्यत्कामहैतुकम् ॥ ८

asatyamapratiṣṭhaṁ te jagadāhuranīśvaram /
aparasparasaṁbhūtaṁ kimanyatkāmahaitukam // 16.8

asatyaṁ: unreal; *apratiṣṭhaṁ*: without foundation; *te*: they; *jagat*: the cosmic manifestation; *āhuḥ*: is said; *anīśvaram*: with no controller; *aparasparasaṁbhūtaṁ*: born of mutual union; *kimanyat*: there is no other cause; *kāmahaitukam*: it is due to lust only.

16.8 People with such qualities think there is no ultimate energy or intelligence that is running this planet earth, that is running the universe, and that this whole creation is produced out of lust and desire, and is unreal.

एतां दृष्टिमवष्टभ्य नष्टात्मानोऽल्पबुद्धयः ।
प्रभवन्त्युग्रकर्माणः क्षयाय जगतोऽहिताः ॥ ९

etāṁ dṛṣṭimavaṣṭabhya naṣṭātmāno'lpabuddhayaḥ /
prabhavantyugrakarmāṇaḥ kṣayāya jagato'hitāḥ // 16.9

etāṁ: thus; *dṛṣṭim*: vision; *avaṣṭabhya*: accepting; *naṣṭa*: lost; *ātmānaḥ*: self; *alpabuddhayaḥ*: less intelligent; *prabhavanti: come forth; ugrakarmāṇaḥ*: in painful activities; *kṣayāya*: for the destruction; *jagataḥ*: of the world; *ahitāḥ*: unbeneficial.

16.9 Following this material view of creation, these degraded souls with small intellect, lost in themselves and committing cruel deeds are engaged in the destruction of the world.

कामममाश्रित्य दुष्पूरं दम्भमानमदान्विताः।
मोहाद्गृहीत्वाऽसद्ग्राहान्प्रवर्तन्तेऽशुचिव्रताः॥ १०

kāmamāśritya duṣpūraṁ dambhamānamadānvitāḥ I
mohādgṛhītvā 'sadgrāhānpravartante'śucivratāḥ II 16.10

kāmaṁ: lust; *āśritya*: taking shelter of; *duṣpūraṁ*: insatiable; *dambha*: pride; *māna*: false prestige; *madānvitāḥ*: absorbed in conceit; *mohāt*: by illusion; *gṛhītvā*: taking; *asat*: nonpermanent; *grāhān*: things; *pravartante*: flourish; *aśuci*: unclean; *vratāḥ*: avowed.

16.10 Filled with insatiable desires, hypocrisy, pride, and arrogance; holding wrong views due to delusion, they act with impure motives and for impermanent objectives.

चिन्तामपरिमेयां च प्रलयान्तामुपाश्रिताः।
कामोपभोगपरमा एतावदिति निश्चिताः॥ ११

cintāmaparimeyāṁ ca pralayāntāmupāśritāḥ I
kāmopabhogaparamā etāvaditi niścitāḥ II 16.11

आशापाशशतैर्बद्धाः कामक्रोधपरायणाः।
ईहन्ते कामभोगार्थमन्यायेनार्थसञ्चयान्॥ १२

āśāpāśaśatairbaddhāḥ kāmakrodhaparāyaṇāḥ I
īhante kāmabhogārthamanyāyenā'rthasañcayān II 16.12

cintāṁ: fears and anxieties; *aparimeyāṁ*: unmeasurable; *ca*: and; *pralayāntāṁ*: unto the point of death; *upāśritāḥ*: having taken shelter of them; *kāmopabhoga*: sense gratification; *paramāḥ*: the highest goal of life; *etavad*: thus; *iti*: in this way; *niścitāḥ*: ascertained; *āśāpāśa*: entanglements in the network of hope; *śataiḥ*: by hundreds; *baddhāḥ*: being bound; *kāma*: lust; *krodha*: anger; *parāyaṇāḥ*: always situated in that mentality; *īhante*: desire; *kāma*: lust; *bhogā*: sense enjoyment; *arthaṁ*: for that purpose; *anyāyenā*: illegally; *artha*: wealth; *sañcayān*: accumulate.

16.11,12 Obsessed with endless anxiety lasting until death, considering sense gratification their highest aim, and convinced that sense pleasure is everything; bound by hundreds of ties of desire and enslaved and filled with anger, they strive to obtain wealth by unlawful means to fulfill sensual pleasures.

इदमद्य मया लब्धमिमं प्राप्स्ये मनोरथम् ।
इदमस्तीदमपि मे भविष्यति पुनर्धनम् ॥ १३

idamadya mayā labdhamimaṁ prāpsye manoratham /
idamastīdamapi me bhaviṣyati punardhanam // 16.13

idaṁ: this; *adya*: today, now; *mayā*: by me; *labdhaṁ*: attained; *imaṁ*: this; *prāpsye*: I shall gain; *manoratham*: according to my desires; *idaṁ*: this; *asti*: there is; *idaṁ*: this; *api*: also; *me*: mine; *bhaviṣyati*: will increase in the future; *punaḥ*: again; *dhanaṁ*: wealth.

16.13 They think: This has been gained by me today; I shall fulfill this desire; I have this much wealth and will have more wealth in the future;

असौ मया हतः शत्रुर्हनिष्ये चापरानपि ।
ईश्वरोऽहमहं भोगी सिद्धोऽहं बलवान्सुखी ॥ १४

asau mayā hataḥ śatrurhaniṣye cāparānapi /
īśvaro'hamahaṁ bhogī siddho'haṁ balavānsukhī // 16.14

आढ्योऽभिजनवानस्मि कोऽन्योऽस्ति सदृशो मया ।
यक्ष्ये दास्यामि मोदिष्य इत्यज्ञानविमोहिताः ॥ १५

ādhyo'bhijanavānasmi ko'nyo'sti sadṛśo mayā /
yakṣye dāsyāmi modiṣya ityajñānavimohitāḥ // 16.15

asau: that; *mayā*: by me; *hataḥ*: has been killed; *śatruḥ*: enemy; *haniṣye*: I shall kill; *ca*: also; *aparān*: others; *api*: certainly; *īśvaro*: the lord; *ahaṁ*: I am; *ahaṁ*: I am; *bhogī*: the enjoyer; *siddhaḥ*: complete, perfect; *ahaṁ*: I am; *balavān*: powerful; *sukhī*: happy; *ādhyaḥ*: wealthy; *abhijanavān:* surrounded by aristocratic relatives; *asmi*: I am; *kaḥ*: who else; *anyaḥ*: other; *asti*: there is; *sadṛśo*: like; *mayā*: me; *yakṣye*: I shall sacrifice; *dāsyāmi*: I shall give charity; *modiṣya*: I shall rejoice; *iti*: thus; *ajñāna*: by ignorance; *vimohitāḥ*: misled, deluded by.

16.14, 15 That enemy has been slain by me, and I shall slay others also. I am the Lord. I am the enjoyer. I am successful, powerful, and happy; I am rich and born in a noble family. Who is equal to me? I shall perform sacrifice, I shall give charity, and I shall rejoice. Thus deluded by ignorance.

अनेकचित्तविभ्रान्ता मोहजालसमावृताः ।
प्रसक्ताः कामभोगेषु पतन्ति नरकेऽशुचौ ॥ १६

anekacittavibhrāntā mohajālasamāvṛtāḥ /
prasaktāḥ kāmabhogeṣu patanti narake'śucau // 16. 16

aneka: many; *citta vibhrāntāḥ*: perplexed by anxieties; *moha jāla*: by a net of illusions; *samāvṛtāḥ*: surrounded; *prasaktāḥ*: attached; *kāma*: lust; *bhogeṣu*: sense gratification; *patanti*: slides down; *narake*: into hell; *aśucau*: unclean.

16.16 Thus confused by various anxieties and caught in a net of illusions, one becomes too deeply attached to sensory pleasures and falls into hell.

आत्मसम्भाविताः स्तब्धा धनमानमदान्विताः ।
यजन्ते नामयज्ञैस्ते दम्भेनाविधिपूर्वकम् ॥ १७

ātmasaṁbhāvitāḥ stabdhā dhanamānamadānvitāḥ /
yajante nāmayajñaiste dambhenā'vidhipūrvakam // 16.17

ātmasaṁbhāvitāḥ: self-complacent; *stabdhāḥ*: conceited; *dhanamāna*: wealth and false pride; *madānvitāḥ*: absorbed in pride; *yajante*: perform sacrifices; *nāma*: in name only; *yajñaiḥ*: with such a sacrifice; *te*: they; *dambhena*: out of pride; *avidhipūrvakaṁ*: without following regulations.

16.17 Self-complacent and always conceited, deluded by wealth and false pride, they perform superficial sacrifices in name only, without following the vedic *rules or regulations.*

अहंकारं बलं दर्पं कामं क्रोधं च संश्रिताः ।
मामात्मपरदेहेषु प्रद्विषन्तोऽभ्यसूयकाः ॥ १८

ahaṅkāraṁ balaṁ darpaṁ kāmaṁ krodhaṁ ca saṁśritāḥ /
māmātmaparadeheṣu pradviṣanto'bhyasūyakāḥ // 16.18

ahaṁkāraṁ: false ego; *balaṁ*: power, strength; *darpaṁ*: arrogance, pride; *kāmaṁ*: lust; *krodhaṁ*: anger; *ca*: also; *saṁśritāḥ*: having taken shelter; *māṁ*: of Me; *ātma*: one's own; *paradeheṣu*: in other bodies; *pradviṣantaḥ*: blasphemes against God; *abhyasūyakāḥ*: envious.

16.18 The demonic person, consumed by ego, power, pride, lust and anger, becomes envious of the supreme personality of godhead, who is situated in his own body and in the bodies of others, and blasphemes against Him.

तानहं द्विषतः क्रूरान्संसारेषु नराधमान् ।
क्षिपाम्यजस्रमशुभानासुरीष्वेव योनिषु ॥ १९

tānahaṁ dviṣataḥ krūrānsaṁsāreṣu narādhamān /
kṣipāmyajasramaśubhānāsurīṣveva yoniṣu // 16.19

tān: those; *ahaṁ*: I; *dviṣataḥ*: envious; *krūrān*: cruel, wicked; *saṁsāreṣu*: into the ocean of material existence; *narādhamān*: the lowest of mankind; *kṣipāmi:* put; *ajasraṁ*: repeatedly; *aśubhān*: inauspicious; *āsurīṣu*: demonic; *eva*: certainly; *yoniṣu*: in the wombs.

16.19 Those who are envious (of Him) and cruel, who are the lowest among men, I repeatedly cast into the ocean of material existence, into various lowly, demonic forms of life.

आसुरीं योनिमापन्ना मूढा जन्मनि जन्मनि ।
मामप्राप्यैव कौन्तेय ततो यान्त्यधमां गतिम् ॥ २०

āsurīṁ yonimapannā mūḍhā janmani janmani /
māmaprāpyaiva kaunteya tato yāntyadhamāṁ gatim // 16.20

āsurīṁ: demonic; *yoniṁ*: species; *apannā*: gaining; *mūḍhāḥ*: the foolish; *janmani janmani*: in birth after birth; *mām*: unto Me; *aprāpya*: without achieving; *eva*: certainly; *kaunteya*: O son of Kuntī; *tataḥ:* thereafter; *yānti:* goes; *adhamāṁ*: condemned; *gatim*: destination.

16.20 These foolish beings attain repeated birth amongst the species of demoniac life. Without ever achieving Me, O Son of Kuntī, they sink into the most abominable existence.

त्रिविधं नरकस्येदं द्वारं नाशनमात्मनः ।
कामः क्रोधस्तथा लोभस्तस्मादेतत्त्रयं त्यजेत् ॥ २१

trividhaṁ narakasyedaṁ dvāraṁ nāśanamātmanaḥ /
kāmaḥ krodhastathā lobhastasmādetattrayaṁ tyajet // 16.21

trividhaṁ: three kinds of; *narakasya*: hellish; *idaṁ*: this; *dvāraṁ*: gate; *nāśanaṁ*: ruin, destruction; *ātmanaḥ*: of the self; *kāmaḥ*: lust; *krodhaḥ*: anger; *tathā*: as well as; *lobhaḥ*: greed; *tasmāt*: therefore; *etat*: these; *trayaṁ*: three; *tyajet*: give up.

16.21 There are three gates leading to this hell: lust, anger and greed. As they lead to the degradation of the soul, these three are to be abandoned.

एतैर्विमुक्तः कौन्तेय तमोद्वारैस्त्रिभिर्नरः ।
आचरत्यात्मनः श्रेयस्ततो याति परां गतिम् ॥ २२

etairvimuktaḥ kaunteya tamodvāraistribhirnaraḥ /
ācaratyātmanaḥ śreyastato yāti paraṁ gatim // 16.22

etaiḥ: by these; *vimuktaḥ*: escaped; *kaunteya*: O son of Kuntī; *tamodvāraiḥ*: the gates of darkness; *tribhiḥ*: three kinds of; *naraḥ*: a person; *ācarati:* acts, behaves; *ātmanaḥ*: self; *śreyaḥ*: benediction; *tataḥ*: thereafter; *yāti*: goes; *paraṁ*: supreme; *gatim*: destination

16.22 Those who have escaped these three gates of hell, O son of Kuntī, behave in a manner beneficial to the (evolution of the) soul, and thus (gradually) attain the supreme destination.

यः शास्त्रविधिमुत्सृज्य वर्तते कामकारतः ।
न स सिद्धिमवाप्नोति न सुखं न परां गतिम् ॥ २३

yaḥ śāstravidhimutsṛjya vartate kāmakārataḥ /
na sa siddhimavāpnoti na sukhaṁ na paraṁ gatim // 16.23

yaḥ: anyone; *śāstravidhiṁ*: the injunctions of the scriptures; *utsṛjya*: giving up; *vartate*: remains; *kāmakārataḥ*: acting whimsically in lust; *na*: never; *saḥ*: he; *siddhiṁ*: perfection; *avāpnoti*: achieves; *na*: never; *sukhaṁ*: happiness; *na*: never; *paraṁ*: the supreme; *gatim*: destination.

16.23 But he who discards scriptural injunctions and acts according to his base impulses attains neither perfection, nor happiness, nor the supreme destination.

तस्माच्छास्त्रं प्रमाणं ते कार्याकार्यव्यवस्थितौ ।
ज्ञात्वा शास्त्रविधानोक्तं कर्म कर्तुमिहार्हसि ॥ २४

tasmācchāstraṁ pramāṇaṁ te kāryākāryavyavasthitau /
jñātvā śāstravidhānoktaṁ karma kartumihārhasi // 16.24

tasmāt: therefore; *śāstraṁ*: scriptures; *pramāṇaṁ*: evidence; *te*: your; *kārya*: duty; *akārya*: forbidden activities; *vyavasthitau*: in determining; *jñātvā*: knowing; *śāstra*: of scripture; *vidhāna*: regulations; *uktaṁ*: as declared; *karma*: work; *kartuṁ*: to do; *ihā'rhasi*: you should do it

16.24 By the regulations of the scriptures, one should understand what is duty and what is not duty. After being versed in scriptural injunctions, one should act accordingly.

इति श्रीमद्भगवद्गीतासूपनिषत्सु ब्रह्मविद्यायां योगशास्त्रे
श्रीकृष्णार्जुनसंवादे दैवासुरसम्पद्विभागयोगो नाम षोडशोऽध्यायः ॥

iti śrīmad bhagavadgītāsūpaniṣatsu brahmavidyāyām
yogaśāstre śrīkṛṣṇārjuna saṁvāde daivāsurasaṁpad vibhāgayogo nāma
ṣoḍaśo'dhyāyaḥ ||

In the Upaniṣad *of the Bhagavad Gītā, the knowledge of* Brahman, *the Supreme, the science of Yoga and the dialogue between Śrī Kṛṣṇa and Arjuna, this is the sixteenth discourse designated:*

Daivāsura Saṁpad Vibhāga Yogaḥ

Verses Of Gita Chapter - 17

अथ सप्तदशोऽध्यायः

श्रद्धात्रयविभागयोगः

Śraddhātraya Vibhāga Yogaḥ

अर्जुन उवाच
ये शास्त्रविधिमुत्सृज्य यजन्ते श्रद्धयान्विताः ।
तेषां निष्ठा तु का कृष्ण सत्त्वमाहो रजस्तमः ॥ १

arjuna uvāca
ye śāstravidhim utsṛjya yajante śraddhayānvitāḥ /
teṣāṁ niṣṭhā tu kā kṛṣṇa sattvamāho rajastamaḥ // 17.1

arjuna uvāca: Arjuna said; *ye:* those; *śāstravidhiṁ:* the regulations of scripture; *utsṛjya:* giving up; *yajante:* worship; *śraddhayā:* sincerity; *anvitāḥ:* possessed of; *teṣāṁ*: of them; *niṣṭhā:* faith; *tu:* but; *kā:* what is that; *Kṛṣṇa:* O Kṛṣṇa; *sattvaṁ:* in goodness; *āho*: said; *rajas*: in aggression; *tamaḥ:* in ignorance.

17.1 Arjuna said: What is the mode of devotion of those who perform spiritual practices with sincerity, but without following the scriptural injunctions, O Kṛṣṇa? Is it in the mode of goodness, aggression or ignorance?

श्री भगवानुवाच ।
त्रिविधा भवति श्रद्धा देहिनां सा स्वभावजा ।
सात्त्विकी राजसी चैव तामसी चेति तां श्रृणु ॥ २

śrībhagavānuvāca
trividhā bhavati śraddhā dehināṁ sā svabhāvajā /
sāttvikī rājasī caiva tāmasī ceti tāṁ śṛṇu // 17.2

śrī bhagavan uvāca: Kṛṣṇa said; *trividhā:* three kinds; *bhavati:* become; *śraddhā:* sincerity; *dehināṁ:* of the body; *sā:* that; *svabhāvajā:* according to his nature; *sāttvikī* : nature of goodness; *rājasī:* nature of aggression; *ca:* also; *eva*: certainly; *tāmasī:* nature of ignorance; *ca*: and; *iti*: thus; *tāṁ*: that; *śṛṇu*: hear from Me.

17.2 The Supreme Lord said: The natural faith of embodied beings is of three kinds: goodness, aggression, and ignorance. Now hear about these from Me.

सत्त्वानुरूपा सर्वस्य श्रद्धा भवति भारत ।
श्रद्धामयोऽयं पुरुषो यो यच्छ्रद्धः स एव सः ॥ ३

sattvānurūpā sarvasya śraddhā bhavati bhārata /
śraddhāmayo'yam puruṣo yo yacchraddhaḥ sa eva saḥ // 17.3

satvānurūpā: according to the existence; *sarvasya:* of everyone; *śraddhā*: sincerity; *bhavati*: becomes; *bhārata*: O son of Bhārata; *śraddhā:* sincerity; *mayaḥ:* full; *ayam*: this; *puruṣaḥ:* living entity; *yaḥ:* anyone; *yat*: that; *śraddhaḥ*: sincerity; *saḥ:* that; *eva*: certainly; *saḥ:* he.

17.3 O Arjuna, the sincerity of each is in accordance with one's own natural disposition. One is known by one's sincerity. One can become whatever one wants to be.

यजन्ते सात्त्विका देवान्यक्षरक्षांसि राजसाः ।
प्रेतान्भूतगणांश्चान्ये यजन्ते तामसा जनाः ॥ ४

yajante sāttvikā devānyakṣarakṣāṁsi rājasāḥ /
pretānbhūtagaṇāṁścānye yajante tāmasā janāḥ // 17.4

yajante: worship; *sāttvikāḥ:* those who are in the mode of goodness; *devān:* deities; *yakṣarakṣāṁsi rājasāḥ:* those who are in the mode of aggression worship demons; *pretān:* dead spirits; *bhūtagaṇān:* ghosts; *cā 'nye:* and others; *yajante:* worship; *tāmasāḥ:* in the mode of ignorance; *janāḥ:* people.

17.4 Men in the nature of goodness worship the deities; those in the nature of aggression worship the demons and those in the nature of ignorance worship ghosts and spirits.

अशास्त्रविहितं घोरं तप्यन्ते ये तपो जनाः ।
दम्भाहङ्कारसंयुक्ताः कामरागबलान्विताः ॥ ५

aśāstravihitaṁ ghoraṁ tapyante ye tapo janāḥ /
dambhāhaṅkārasaṁyuktāḥ kāmarāgabalānvitāḥ // 17.5

कर्शयन्तः शरीरस्थं भूतग्राममचेतसः ।
मां चैवान्तः शरीरस्थं तान्विद्ध्यासुरनिश्चयान् ॥ ६

karśayantaḥ śarīrasthaṁ bhūtagrāmamacetasaḥ /
mām caivāntah śarīrasthaṁ tānviddhyāsuraniścayān // 17.6

aśāstra: not mentioned in the scriptures; *vihitaṁ:* directed; *ghoraṁ:* harmful to others; *tapyante:* undergo penances; *ye:* those; *tapaḥ:* austerities; *janāḥ:* persons; *dambha*: pride; *ahaṁkāra*: egoism; *saṁyuktāḥ:* engaged; *kāma:* lust; *rāga:* attachment; *bala*: force; *anvitāḥ:* impelled by; *karṣayantaḥ:* tormenting; *śarīrasthaṁ*: situated within the body; *bhūtagrāmaṁ:* combination of material elements; *acetasaḥ:* by such a misled mentality; *mām:* to Me; *ca:* also; *eva:* certainly; *antaḥ:* within; *śarīrastham:* situated in the body; *tān:* them; *viddhi:* understand; *āsura:* demons; *niścayān:* certainly.

17.5,6 Ignorant persons of demonic nature are those who practice severe austerities without following the prescription of the scriptures, who are full of hypocrisy and egotism, who are impelled by the force of desire and attachment and who senselessly torture the elements in their body and also Me who dwells within the body.

आहारस्त्वपि सर्वस्य त्रिविधो भवति प्रियः ।
यज्ञस्तपस्तथा दानं तेषां भेदमिमं श्रृणु ॥ ७

āhārastvapi sarvasya trividho bhavati priyaḥ I
yajñastapastathā dānaṁ teṣāṁ bhedamimaṁ śṛṇu II 17.7

āhāra: eating; *tu:* certainly; *api:* also; *sarvasya:* of everyone; *trividhaḥ:* three kinds; *bhavati*: there are; *priyaḥ:* dear; *yajñaḥ:* sacrifice; *tapaḥ:* austerity; *tathā:* also; *dānaṁ*: charity; *teṣāṁ:* of them; *bhedaṁ:* differences; *imaṁ:* thus; *śṛṇu:* hear.

17.7 Food that we consume is of three kinds, according to the three types of material nature. So are the sacrifice, austerity and charity. Hear the difference between these three.

आयुःसत्त्वबलारोग्यसुखप्रीतिविवर्धनाः ।
रस्याः स्निग्धाः स्थिरा हृद्या आहाराः सात्त्विकप्रियाः ॥ ८

āyuḥsattvabalārogyasukhaprītivivardhanāḥ I
rasyāḥ snigdhāḥ sthirā hṛdyā āhārāḥ sāttvikapriyāḥ II 17.8

āyuḥ: duration of life; *sattva:* existence; *bala:* strength; *ārogya:* health; *sukha*: happiness; *prīti:* satisfaction; *vivardhanāḥ:* increasing; *rasyāḥ:* juicy; *snigdhāḥ:* fatty; *sthirāḥ:* enduring; *hṛdyāḥ:* pleasing to the heart; *āhārāḥ:* food; *sāttvika:* goodness; *priyāḥ*: palatable.

17.8 The foods that promote longevity, virtue, strength, health, happiness, and joy are juicy, smooth, substantial, and nutritious. Such foods are liked by persons in the mode of goodness.

कट्वम्ललवणात्युष्णतीक्ष्णरूक्षविदाहिनः ।
आहारा राजसस्येष्टा दुःखशोकामयप्रदाः ॥ ९

kaṭvamlalavaṇātyuṣṇa tīkṣṇa rūkṣa vidāhinaḥ I
āhārā rājasasyeṣṭā duḥkhaśokāmayapradāḥ II 17.9

kaṭu: bitter; *amla*: sour; *lavaṇa:* salty; *atyuṣṇa:* very hot; *tīkṣṇa:* pungent; *rūkṣa:* dry; *vidāhinaḥ:* burning; *āhārāḥ:* food; *rājasasya:* in the mode of aggression; *iṣṭāḥ:* palatable; *duḥkha:* distress; *śoka:* misery; *āmaya pradāḥ:* causing disease.

17.9 People in the mode of aggression like foods that are very bitter, sour, salty, hot, pungent, dry, and burning, and cause pain, grief, and disease.

यातयामं गतरसं पूति पर्युषितं च यत् ।
उच्छिष्टमपि चामेध्यं भोजनं तामसप्रियम् ॥ १०

yātayāmaṁ gatarasaṁ pūti paryuṣitaṁ ca yat |
ucchiṣṭamapi cāmedhyaṁ bhojanaṁ tāmasapriyam || 17.10

yātayāmaṁ: food cooked three hours before being eaten; *gatarasaṁ:* tasteless; *pūti*: bad smelling; *paryuṣitaṁ*: decomposed; *ca*: also; *yat:* that which; *ucchiṣṭam*: remnants of food eaten by others; *api*: also; *ca:* and; *amedhyaṁ:* untouchable; *bhojanaṁ:* eating; *tāmasa:* in the mode of darkness; *priyam:* dear

17.10 People in the mode of ignorance like foods that are stale, tasteless, putrid, rotten, refuse, and of impure energy.

अफलाकाङ्क्षिभिर्यज्ञो विधिदृष्टो य इज्यते ।
यष्टव्यमेवेति मनः समाधाय स सात्त्विकः ॥ ११

aphalākāṅkṣibhiryajño vidhidṛṣto ya ijyate |
yaṣṭavyameveti manaḥ samādhāya sa sāttvikaḥ || 17.11

aphalākāṅkṣibhiḥ: without desire for result; *yajñaḥ:* sacrifice; *vidhi*: accordingly; *dṛṣtaḥ*: direction; *yaḥ:* anyone; *ijyate:* performs; *yaṣṭavyaṁ:* must be performed; *eva:* certainly; *iti*: thus; *manaḥ:* mind; *samādhāya:* fixed in; *saḥ:* he; *sāttvikaḥ:* in the nature of goodness

17.11 Sacrifice without expectation of results, as stipulated in the scriptures, with a firm belief and conviction that it is a duty, is in the mode of goodness.

अभिसन्धाय तु फलं दम्भार्थमपि चैव यत् ।
इज्यते भरतश्रेष्ठ तं यज्ञं विद्धि राजसम् ॥ १२

abhisandhāya tu phalaṁ dambhārthamapi caiva yat |
ijyate Bhārataśreṣtha taṁ yajñaṁ viddhi rājasam || 17.12

abhisandhāya: desiring; *tu:* but; *phalaṁ:* the result; *dambha:* pride; *arthaṁ:* for the sake of; *api:* also; *ca:* and; *eva:* certainly; *yat:* that which; *ijyate:* is offered; *bharataśreṣṭha:* O chief of the Bhāratas; *taṁ:* that; *yajñaṁ:* sacrifice; *viddhi:* know; *rājasam* : in the mode of aggression

17.12 O Arjuna, that sacrifice that is performed with expectation of result or for show out of pride, is of the nature of aggression.

विधिहीनमसृष्टान्नं मन्त्रहीनमदक्षिणम् ।
श्रद्धाविरहितं यज्ञं तामसं परिचक्षते ॥ १३

vidhihīnamasṛṣṭānnaṁ mantrahīnamadakṣiṇam I
śraddhāvirahitaṁ yajñaṁ tāmasaṁ paricakṣate II 17.13

vidhihīnaṁ: without scriptural direction; *asṛṣṭānnaṁ:* without distribution of prasadam; *mantrahīnaṁ*: with no chanting of the vedic hymns; *adakṣiṇam*: with no remunerations to the priests; *śraddhā:* sincerity; *virahitaṁ:* without; *yajñaṁ:* sacrifice; *tāmasaṁ:* in the mode of ignorance; *paricakṣate:* is to be considered

17.13 Sacrifice that is performed without following the scripture, in which no food is distributed, which is devoid of mantra, sincerity, and gift, is said to be in the mode of ignorance.

देवद्विजगुरुप्राज्ञपूजनं शौचमार्जवम् ।
ब्रह्मचर्यमहिंसा च शारीरं तप उच्यते ॥ १४

devadvijaguruprājñapūjanaṁ śaucamārjavam I
brahmacaryamahiṁsā ca śārīraṁ tapa ucyate II 17.14

deva: deities; *dvija:* the priest; *guru:* the master; *prājña:* worshipable personalities; *pūjanaṁ:* worship; *śaucaṁ:* cleanliness; *ārjavam:* simplicity; *brahmacaryaṁ:* living in reality; *ahiṁsā:* nonviolence; *ca:* also; *śārīraṁ:* pertaining to the body; *tapa*: austerity; *ucyate*: is said to be

17.14 The worship of deities, the priest, the guru, and the wise; purity, honesty, living in reality, and nonviolence are said to be austerity of deed.

अनुद्वेगकरं वाक्यं सत्यं प्रियहितं च यत् ।
स्वाध्यायाभ्यसनं चैव वाङ्मयं तप उच्यते ॥ १५

anudvegakaraṁ vākyaṁ satyaṁ priyahitaṁ ca yat I
svādhyāyābhyasanaṁ caiva vāṅmayaṁ tapa ucyate II 17.15

anudvega: not agitating; *karaṁ:* producing; *vākyaṁ:* words; *satyaṁ:* truthful; *priya*: dear; *hitaṁ*: beneficial; *ca:* also; *yat:* which; *svādhyāya:* vedic study; *abhyasanaṁ*: practice; *ca:* also; *eva*: certainly; *vāṅmayaṁ:* of the voice; *tapa:* austerity; *ucyate:* is said to be

17.15 Speech that is non-offensive, truthful, pleasant, beneficial, and is used for the regular study of scriptures is called austerity of word.

मन: प्रसाद: सौम्यत्वं मौनमात्मविनिग्रह: ।
भावसंशुद्धिरित्येतत्तपो मानसमुच्यते ॥ १६

manaḥ prasādaḥ saumyatvaṁ maunamātmavinigrahaḥ I
bhāvasaṁśuddhirityetattapo mānasamucyate II 17.16

manaḥ prasādaḥ: fulfillment of the mind; *saumyatvaṁ:* satisfied; *maunaṁ:* gravity; *ātma*: self; *vinigrahaḥ:* control; *bhāva:* nature; *saṁśuddhiḥ:* purification; *iti:* thus; *etat:* that is; *tapaḥ:* austerity; *mānasaṁ:* of the mind; *ucyate:* is said to be.

17.16 Serenity of mind, gentleness, equanimity, self-control, and purity of thought are called austerity of thought.

श्रद्धया परया तप्तं तपस्तत्त्रिविधं नरै: ।
अफलाकाङ्क्षिभिर्युक्तै: सात्त्विकं परिचक्षते ॥ १७

śraddhayā parayā taptaṁ tapastattrividhaṁ naraiḥ I
aphalākāṅkṣibhiryuktaiḥ sāttvikaṁ paricakṣate II 17.17

śraddhayā: with sincerity; *parayā:* transcendental; *taptaṁ*: execution; *tapaḥ:* austerity; *tat:* that; *trividhaṁ:* three kinds; *naraiḥ:* by men; *aphalākāṅkṣibhiḥ*: without desires for fruits; *yuktaiḥ:* engaged; *sāttvikaṁ:* in the mode of goodness; *paricakṣate:* is called

17.17 The above mentioned threefold austerity (of thought, word, and deed), practiced by yogis with supreme sincerity, without a desire for the fruit, is said to be in the mode of goodness.

सत्कारमानपूजार्थं तपो दम्भेन चैव यत् ।
क्रियते तदिह प्रोक्तं राजसं चलमध्रुवम् ॥ १८

satkāramānapūjārthaṁ tapo dambhena caiva yat I
kriyate tadiha proktaṁ rājasaṁ calamadhruvam II 17.18

satkāra: respect; *māna:* honor; *pūjārthaṁ:* for worship; *tapaḥ:* austerity; *dambhena:* pride; *ca:* also; *eva:* certainly; *yat:* which is; *kriyate:* performed; *tat:* that; *iha:* in this world; *proktaṁ:* is said; *rājasaṁ:* in the mode of aggression; *calaṁ:* flickering; *adhruvam*: temporary

17.18 Austerity that is performed for gaining respect, honor, reverence, and for the sake of show, yielding an uncertain and temporary result, is said to be in the mode of aggression.

मूढग्राहेणात्मनो यत्पीडया क्रियते तपः ।
परस्योत्सादनार्थं वा तत्तामसमुदाहृतम् ॥ १९

mūḍhagrāheṇātmano yatpīḍayā kriyate tapaḥ /
parasyotsādanārthaṁ vā tattāmasamudāhṛtam // 17.19

mūḍha: foolish; *grāheṇā:* with endeavor; *atmanaḥ:* of one's own self; *yat:* which; *pīḍayā*: by torture; *kriyate:* is performed; *tapaḥ:* penance; *parasya:* to others; *utsādanārthaṁ:* causing annihilation; *vā*: or; *tat*: that; *tāmasaṁ:* in the mode of darkness; *udāhṛtam:* is said to be

17.19 Austerity performed with foolish stubbornness or with self-torture or for harming others, is said to be in the mode of ignorance.

दातव्यमिति यद्दानं दीयतेऽनुपकारिणे ।
देशे काले च पात्रे च तद्दानं सात्त्विकं स्मृतम् ॥ २०

dātavyamiti yaddānaṁ dīyate'nupakāriṇe /
deśe kāle ca pātre ca taddānaṁ sāttvikaṁ smṛtam // 17.20

dātavyaṁ: worth giving; *iti*: thus; *yat:* that which; *dānaṁ:* charity; *dīyate:* given; *anupakāriṇe*: to person who does no service in return; *deśe:* in place; *kāle:* in time; *ca*: also; *pātre:* suitable person; *ca:* and; *tat:* that; *dānaṁ:* charity; *sāttvikaṁ:* in the mode of goodness; *smṛtam:* consider

17.20 Charity that is given at the right place and time as a matter of duty to a deserving candidate who does nothing in return, is considered to be in the mode of goodness.

यत्तु प्रत्युपकारार्थं फलमुद्दिश्य वा पुनः ।
दीयते च परिक्लिष्टं तद्दानं राजसं स्मृतम् ॥ २१

yattu pratyupakārārthaṁ phalamuddiśya vā punaḥ /
dīyate ca parikliṣṭaṁ taddānaṁ rājasaṁ smṛtam // 17.21

yat: that which; *tu*: but; *pratyupakārārthaṁ:* for the sake of getting some return; *phalaṁ:* result; *uddiśya:* desiring; *vā:* or; *punaḥ:* again; *dīyate:* is given in charity; *ca*: also; *parikliṣṭaṁ:* grudgingly; *tat:* that; *dānaṁ:* charity; *rājasaṁ:* in the mode of aggression; *smṛtam:* is understood to be

17.21 Charity that is given unwillingly or to get something in return or to gain some result is in the mode of aggression.

अदेशकाले यद्दानमपात्रेभ्यश्च दीयते ।
असत्कृतमवज्ञातं तत्तामसमुदाहृतम् ॥ २२

adeśakāle yaddānamapātrebhyaśca dīyate /
asatkṛtamavajñātaṁ tattāmasamudāhṛtam // 17.22

adeśa: unpurified place; *kāle:* unpurified time; *yat:* that which; *dānaṁ:* charity; *apātrebhyaḥ:* to unworthy persons; *ca:* also; *dīyate:* is given; *asatkṛtaṁ:* without respect; *avajñātaṁ:* without proper attention; *tat:* that; *tāmasaṁ:* in the mode of darkness; *udāhṛtam:* is said to be

17.22 Charity that is given at a wrong place and time to unworthy persons or without paying respect to the receiver or with ridicule is in the mode of ignorance.

ॐ तत्सदिति निर्देशो ब्रह्मणस्त्रिविधः स्मृतः ।
ब्राह्मणास्तेन वेदाश्च यज्ञाश्च विहिताः पुरा ॥ २३

Om tatsaditi nirdeśo brahmaṇastrividhaḥ smṛtaḥ /
brāhmaṇāstena vedāsca yajñāśca vihitāḥ purā // 17.23

Om: indication of the Supreme; *tat:* that; *sat:* eternal; *iti:* that; *nirdeśaḥ*: indication; *brahmaṇaḥ:* of the Supreme; *trividhaḥ:* three kinds; *smṛtaḥ:* consider; *brāhmaṇāḥ:* the brahmaṇas; *tena:* therefore; *vedāḥ:* the vedic literature; *ca:* also; *yajñāḥ:* sacrifice; *ca:* also; *vihitāḥ:* used; *purā:* formerly

*17. 23 'OM Tat Sat' is said to be the threefold name of the eternal Being (*Brahma*). Persons with good (*brahminic*) qualities, the* Vedas, *and the selfless service* (seva, yajña) *were created by and from* Brahma *in the ancient time.*

तस्मादोमित्युदाहृत्य यज्ञदानतपःक्रियाः ।
प्रवर्तन्ते विधानोक्ताः सततं ब्रह्मवादिनाम् ॥ २४

tasmādomityudāhṛtya yajñadānatapaḥkriyāḥ /
pravartante vidhānoktāḥ satataṁ brahmavādinām // 17.24

tasmāt: therefore; *Om*: beginning with om; *iti:* thus; *udāhṛtya:* indicating; *yajña:* sacrifice; *dāna:* charity; *tapaḥ:* penance; *kriyāḥ:* performances; *pravartante:* begin; *vidhānoktāḥ:* according to scriptural regulation; *satataṁ:* always; *brahmavādinām:* of the transcendentalists

17.24 Therefore, acts of sacrifice, charity, and austerity prescribed in the scriptures are always commenced by uttering 'OM' by the knowers of the supreme Being.

तदित्यनभिसंधाय फलं यज्ञतपःक्रियाः ।
दानक्रियाश्च विविधाः क्रियन्ते मोक्षकाङ्क्षिभिः ॥ २५

tadityanabhisandhāya phalaṁ yajñatapaḥkriyāḥ /
dānakriyāśca vividhāḥ kriyante mokṣakāṅkṣibhiḥ // 17.25

tat: that; *iti:* they; *anabhisandhāya:* without fruitive result; *phalaṁ:* result of sacrifice; *yajña:* sacrifice; *tapaḥ:* penance; *kriyāḥ:* activities; *dāna:* charity; *kriyāḥ:* activities; *ca:* also; *vividhāḥ:* varieties; *kriyante:* done; *mokṣakāṅkṣibhiḥ:* those who actually desire liberation.

17.25 Various types of sacrifice, charity, and austerity are performed by the seekers of liberation by uttering 'Tat' (or He is all) without seeking a reward.

सद्भावे साधुभावे च सदित्येतत्प्रयुज्यते ।
प्रशस्ते कर्मणि तथा सच्छब्दः पार्थ युज्यते ॥ २६

sadbhāve sādhubhāve ca sadityetatprayujyate /
praśaste karmaṇi tathā sacchabdaḥ pārtha yujyate // 17.26

यज्ञे तपसि दाने च स्थितिः सदिति चोच्यते ।
कर्म चैव तदर्थीयं सदित्येवाभिधीयते ॥ २७

yajñe tapasi dāne ca sthitiḥ sad iti cocyate /
karma caiva tadarthīyaṁ sadityevābhidhīyate // 17.27

sadbhāve: in the sense of the nature of the Truth; *sādhubhāve:* in the sense of the nature of devotion; *ca:* also; *sat:* the Truth; *iti:* thus; *etat:* this; *prayujyate:* is used; *praśaste:* auspicious; *karmaṇi:* activities; *tathā:* also; *sacchabdaḥ:* the sound *sat*; *pārtha*: O son of Pritā; *yujyate:* is used; *yajñe:* sacrifice; *tapasi:* in penance; *dāne*: charity; *ca:* also; *sthitiḥ:* situated; *sat*: the Truth; *iti*: thus; *ca*: and; *ucyate:* pronounced; *karma:* work; *ca:* also; *eva*: certainly; *tad:* that; *arthīyaṁ:* are meant; *sat*: Truth; *iti:* thus; *eva:* certainly; *abhidhīyate:* is called.

17.26,27 The word 'Sat' is used in the sense of reality and goodness. The word 'Sat' is also used for an auspicious act, O Arjuna. Sincerity in sacrifice, charity, and austerity is also called 'Sat'. Selfless service for the sake of the supreme is, in truth, termed as 'Sat'.

अश्रद्धया हुतं दत्तं तपस्तप्तं कृतं च यत् ।
असदित्युच्यते पार्थ न च तत्प्रेत्य नो इह ॥ २८

aśraddhayā hutaṁ dattaṁ tapastaptaṁ kṛtaṁ ca yat **/**
asadityucyate pārtha na ca tatpretya no iha **//** 17.28

aśraddhayā: without sincerity; *hutaṁ:* offered in sacrifice; *dattaṁ*: given; *tapaḥ*: penance; *taptaṁ:* executed; *kṛtaṁ:* performed; *ca:* also; *yat:* that which; *asat:* not Truth; *iti:* thus; *ucyate:* is said to be; *pārtha:* O son of Pritā; *no:* never; *ca:* also; *tat:* that; *pretya:* after death; *na:* nor; *iha:* in this life.

17. 28 Whatever is done without sincerity whether it is sacrifice, charity, austerity, or any other act is called 'asat'. It has no value here or hereafter, O Arjuna.

इति श्रीमद्भगवद्गीतासूपनिषत्सु ब्रह्मविद्यायां योगशास्त्रे
श्रीकृष्णार्जुनसंवादे श्रद्धात्रयविभागयोगो नाम सप्तदशोऽध्यायः ॥

iti śrīmad bhagavadgītāsūpaniṣatsu brahmavidyāyām yogaśāstre
śrīkṛṣṇārjuna saṁvāde śraddhātrayavibhāgayogo nāma saptadaśodhyāyaḥ **//**

In the Upaniṣad *of the Bhagavad Gītā, the knowledge of* Brahman, *the Supreme, the science of Yoga and the dialogue between Śrī Kṛṣṇa and Arjuna, this is the seventeenth discourse designated:*

Śraddhatraya vibhāga Yogaḥ

Verses Of Gita Chapter - 18

अथ अष्टादशोऽध्यायः

मोक्षसंन्यासयोगः

Mokṣa Sanyāsa Yogaḥ

अर्जुन उवाच

सन्न्यासस्य महाबाहो तत्त्वमिच्छामि वेदितुम् ।
त्यागस्य च हृषीकेश पृथक्केशिनिषूदन ॥ १

arjuna uvāca
sannyāsasya mahābāho tattvamicchāmi veditum /
tyāgasya ca hṛṣīkeśa pṛthakkeśiniṣūdana // 18.1

arjuna uvāca: Arjuna said; *sannyāsasya:* monkhood; *mahābāho:* O mighty-armed one; *tattvaṁ:* truth; *icchāmi:* I wish; *veditum:* to understand; *tyāgasya:* of renunciation; *ca*: also; *hṛṣīkeśa*: O master of the senses; *pṛthak*: differently; *keśiniṣūdana*: O killer of the Kesi demon

18.1 Arjuna said, 'Kṛṣṇa, killer of the demon Kesi, I wish to understand what the purpose of renunciation is and about monkhood, and the difference between the two.'

श्री भगवानुवाच
काम्यानां कर्मणां न्यासं सन्न्यासं कवयो विदुः ।
सर्वकर्मफलत्यागं प्राहुस्त्यागं विचक्षणाः ॥ २

śrībhagavānuvāca
kāmyānāṁ karmaṇāṁ nyāsaṁ sannyāsaṁ kavayo viduḥ /
sarvakarmaphalatyāgaṁ prāhustyāgaṁ vicakṣaṇāḥ // 18.2

śrībhagavānuvāca: Śrī Bhagavān said; *kāmyānāṁ:* with desire; *karmaṇāṁ*: activities; *nyāsaṁ*: renunciation; *sannyāsaṁ*: renounced order of life; *kavayaḥ*: the learned; *viduḥ*: know; *sarva:* of all; *karma:* activities; *phala*: of results; *tyāgaṁ*: renunciation; *prāhuḥ:* call; *tyāgaṁ:* renunciation; *vicakṣaṇāḥ:* the experienced

18.2 Kṛṣṇa said, the wise say that the purpose of monkhood as giving up all selfish work based on desire, and renunciation as the freedom from all attachment to the results of one's actions.

त्याज्यं दोषवदित्येके कर्म प्राहुर्मनीषिणः ।
यज्ञदानतपःकर्म न त्याज्यमिति चापरे ॥ ३

tyājyaṁ doṣavadityeke karma prāhurmanīṣiṇaḥ |
yajñadānatapaḥkarma na tyājyamiticāpare || 18.3

tyājyaṁ: must be given up; *doṣavad:* like sins; *iti:* thus; *eke:* one group; *karma*: work; *prāhuḥ:* said; *manīṣiṇaḥ:* of great thinkers; *yajña:* sacrifice or service; *dāna*: charity; *tapaḥ:* penance or austerity; *karma:* work; *na:* never; *tyājyaṁ:* is to be given up; *iti:* thus; *ca:* certainly; *apare:* others

18.3 Some learned men say that all kinds of result-based activities are sins and should be given up, but there are yet other sages who maintain that acts of service, charity and austerity should never be given up.

निश्चयं श्रृणु मे तत्र त्यागे भरतसत्तम ।
त्यागो हि पुरुषव्याघ्र त्रिविधः सम्प्रकीर्तितः ॥ ४

niścayaṁ śṛṇu me tatra tyāge bharatasattama |
tyāgo hi puruṣavyāghra trividhaḥ samprakīrtitaḥ || 18.4

niścayaṁ: certainty; *śṛṇu:* hear; *me:* from Me; *tatra:* there; *tyāge:* in the matter of renunciation; *bharata sattama:* O best of the Bhāratas; *tyāgaḥ:* renunciation; *hi*: certainly; *puruṣavyāghra:* O tiger among human beings; *trividhaḥ:* three kinds; *samprakīrtitaḥ* : is declared

18.4 Arjuna, here is what I say about renunciation. There are three kinds of renunciation explained.

यज्ञदानतपःकर्म न त्याज्यं कार्यमेव तत् ।
यज्ञो दानं तपश्चैव पावनानि मनीषिणाम् ॥ ५

yajñadānatapaḥ karma na tyājyaṁ kāryameva tat |
yajño dānaṁ tapaścaiva pāvanāni manīṣiṇām || 18.5

yajña: sacrifice; *dāna:* charity; *tapaḥ:* penance; *karma:* activities; *na:* never; *tyājyaṁ*: to be given up; *kāryaṁ:* must be done; *eva:* certainly; *tat:* that; *yajñaḥ:* service; *dānaṁ:* charity; *tapaḥ:* austerity; *ca:* also; *eva*: certainly; *pāvanāni:* purifying; *manīṣiṇām:* even of the great souls

18.5 Acts of service, charity and austerity are not to be given up; they should be performed. Even the sages are purified by sacrifice, charity and penance.

एतान्यपि तु कर्माणि सङ्गं त्यक्त्वा फलानि च ।
कर्तव्यानीति मे पार्थ निश्चितं मतमुत्तमम् ॥ ६

etānyapi tu karmāṇi saṅgaṁ tyaktvā phalāni ca /
kartavyānīti me pārtha niścitaṁ matamuttamam // 18.6

etāni: all this; *api:* certainly; *tu:* must; *karmāṇi:* activities; *saṅgaṁ:* association; *tyaktvā:* renouncing; *phalāni:* results; *ca:* also; *kartavyāni:* as duty; *iti:* thus; *me*: My; *pārtha*: O son of Pritā; *niścitaṁ*: definite; *mataṁ:* opinion; *uttamam:* the best

18.6 Arjuna, all these actions of duty must also be performed without any expectation of result. That is My considered opinion.

नियतस्य तु संन्यासः कर्मणो नोपपद्यते ।
मोहात्तस्य परित्यागस्तामसः परिकीर्तितः ॥ ७

niyatasya tu sannyāsaḥ karmaṇo nopapadyate /
mohāttasya parityāgastāmasaḥ parikīrtitaḥ // 18.7

niyatasya: prescribed duties; *tu:* but; *sannyāsaḥ:* renunciation; *karmaṇaḥ:* activities; *na*: never; *upapadyate*: is deserved; *mohāt:* by illusion; *tasya:* of which; *parityāgaḥ*: renunciation; *tāmasaḥ:* in the mode of ignorance; *parikīrtitaḥ*: is declared

18.7 Prescribed duties should never be renounced. If one gives up his prescribed duties through the illusion of renunciation, this is said to be in the state of ignorance.

दुःखमित्येव यत्कर्म कायक्लेशभयात्त्यजेत् ।
स कृत्वा राजसं त्यागं नैव त्यागफलं लभेत् ॥ ८

duḥkhamityeva yatkarma kāyakleśabhayāttyajet /
sa kṛtvā rājāsaṁ tyāgaṁ nai'va tyāgaphalaṁ labhet // 18.8

duḥkhaṁ: unhappy; *iti:* thus; *eva:* certainly; *yat:* that which; *karma:* work; *kāya*: body; *kleśa:* troublesome; *bhayāt:* out of fear; *tyajet:* gives up; *sa:* that; *kṛtvā:* after doing; *rājāsaṁ:* in the mode of aggression; *tyāgaṁ:* renunciation; *nai'va:* certainly not; *tyāga:* renounced; *phalaṁ:* results; *labhet:* gain

18.8 Anyone who gives up prescribed duties as troublesome, or out of fear, is said to be in the state of aggression, does not benefit from renunciation.

कार्यमित्येव यत्कर्म नियतं क्रियतेऽर्जुन ।
सङ्गं त्यक्त्वा फलं चैव स त्यागः सात्त्विको मतः ॥ ९

kāryamityeva yatkarma niyataṁ kriyate'rjuna /
saṅgaṁ tyaktvā phalaṁ caiva sa tyāgaḥ sāttviko mataḥ // 18.9

kāryaṁ: must be done; *iti*: thus; *eva*: thus; *yat*: that which; *karma:* work; *niyataṁ*: prescribed; *kriyate*: performed; *arjuna:* O Arjuna; *saṅgaṁ:* association; *tyaktvā:* giving up; *phalaṁ:* result; *ca:* also; *eva:* certainly; *saḥ:* that; *tyāgaḥ:* renunciation; *sāttvikaḥ*: in the mode of goodness; *mataḥ:* in My opinion.

18.9 But he who performs what is prescribed, as a matter of duty, without expectation or attachment to the results, his renunciation is of the nature of satva, goodness, O Arjuna.

न द्वेष्ट्यकुशलं कर्म कुशले नानुषज्जते ।
त्यागी सत्त्वसमाविष्टो मेधावी छिन्नसंशयः ॥ १०

na dveṣṭyakuśalaṁ karma kuśale nā'nuṣajjate /
tyāgī sattvasamāviṣṭo medhāvī chinnasaṁśayaḥ // 18.10

na: never; *dveṣti:* hates; *akuśalaṁ:* inauspicious; *karma:* work; *kuśale:* in the auspicious; *na:* nor; *anuṣajjate:* becomes attached; *tyāgī:* the renouncer; *sattva*: goodness; *samāviṣṭaḥ:* absorbed in; *medhāvī:* intelligent; *chinna:* cut up; *saṁśayaḥ:* all doubts

18.10 Those who neither hate disagreeable work nor are attached to pleasant work are in a state of intelligence, goodness and renunciation, free of all doubts.

न हि देहभृता शक्यं त्यक्तुं कर्माण्यशेषतः ।
यस्तु कर्मफलत्यागी स त्यागीत्यभिधीयते ॥ ११

na hi dehabhṛtā śakyaṁ tyaktuṁ karmāṇyaśeṣataḥ /
yastu karmaphalatyāgī sa tyāgītyabhidhīyate // 18.11

na: never; *hi:* certainly; *dehabhṛtā:* of the embodied; *śakyaṁ:* possible; *tyaktuṁ:* to renounce; *karmāṇi:* activities of; *aśeṣataḥ:* altogether; *yastu:* anyone who; *karma*: work; *phala*: results; *tyāgī:* renouncer; *sa tyāgī:* the renouncer; *iti:* thus; *abhidhīyate* : it is said

18.11 Human beings cannot give up all activities. Therefore the one who has renounced the fruits of such activity is one who has truly renounced.

अनिष्टमिष्टं मिश्रं च त्रिविधं कर्मणः फलम् ।
भवत्यत्यागिनां प्रेत्य न तु सन्न्यासिनां क्वचित् ॥ १२

aniṣṭamiṣṭaṁ miśraṁ ca trividhaṁ karmaṇaḥ phalam /
bhavatyatyāgināṁ pretya na tu sannyāsināṁ kvacit // 18.12

aniṣṭaṁ: undesirable; *iṣṭaṁ:* desirable; *miśraṁ ca:* or mixture; *trividhaṁ:* three kinds; *karmaṇaḥ*: work; *phalam:* result; *bhavati:* becomes; *atyāgināṁ:* of the non-renouncer; *pretya:* after death; *na tu:* but not; *sannyāsināṁ:* of the renounced order; *kvacit:* at any time

18.12 For one who is not renounced, the three kinds of fruits of action—desirable, undesirable and mixed—acrue after death, but not to one who has renounced.

पञ्चैतानि महाबाहो कारणानि निबोध मे।
साङ्ख्ये कृतान्ते प्रोक्तानि सिद्धये सर्वकर्मणाम् ॥ १३

pañcai'tāni mahābāho kāraṇāni nibodha me /
sāṅkhye kṛtānte proktāni siddhaye sarvakarmaṇām // 18.13

अधिष्ठानं तथा कर्ता करणं च पृथग्विधम्।
विविधाश्च पृथक्चेष्टा दैवं चैवात्र पञ्चमम् ॥ १४

adhiṣṭhānaṁ tathā kartā karaṇaṁ ca pṛthagvidham /
vividhāśca pṛthakceṣṭā daivaṁ caivātra pañcamam // 18.14

pañca: five; *etāni*: all these; *mahābāho:* O mighty-armed one; *kāraṇāni:* causes; *nibodha*: just understand; *me:* from Me; *sāṁkhya:* in the Sāṅkhya philosophy; *kṛtānte*: after performance; *proktāni:* said; *siddhaye:* perfection; *sarva*: all; *karmaṇām*: actuated. *adhiṣṭhānaṁ*: place; *tathā*: also; *kartā:* worker; *karaṇaṁ ca:* and instruments; *pṛthagvidham*: different kinds; *vividhāś ca:* varieties; *pṛthak*: separately; *ceṣṭā:* endeavor; *daivaṁ:* the supreme; *ca:* also; *eva*: certainly; *atra*: here; *pañcamam:* five

18.13,14 Learn from Me Arjuna, the five causes that bring about the accomplishment of all action, as described in Sāṅkhya *philosophy. These are: physical body that is the seat of action; the attributes of nature or* guṇa, *which is the doer; the eleven organs of perception and action by the life forces and finally the Divine.*

शरीरवाङ्मनोभिर्यत्कर्म प्रारभते नरः।
न्याय्यं वा विपरीतं वा पञ्चैते तस्य हेतवः ॥ १५

śarīravāṅmanobhir yat karma prārabhate naraḥ /
nyāyyaṁ vā viparītaṁ vā pañcai 'te tasya hetavaḥ // 18.15

śarīra: body; *vāk*: speech; *manobhiḥ*: by the mind; *yat*: anything; *karma*: work; *prārabhate*: begins; *naraḥ*: a person; *nyāyyaṁ*: right; *vā:* or; *viparītaṁ*: the opposite; *vā*: or; *pañca*: five; *ete*: all these; *tasya:* its; *hetavaḥ:* causes

18.15 These five factors are responsible for whatever right or wrong actions a man performs by deed, word and thought.

तत्रैवं सति कर्तारमात्मानं केवलं तु यः ।
पश्यत्यकृतबुद्धित्वान्न स पश्यति दुर्मतिः ॥ १६

tatraivam sati kartāramātmānaṁ kevalaṁ tu yaḥ /
paśyatyakṛtabuddhitvānna sa paśyati durmatiḥ // 18.16

tatra: there; *evaṁ*: certainly; *sati:* being; *kartāraṁ*: of the worker; *ātmānaṁ*: the self; *kevalaṁ*: only; *tu*: but; *yaḥ:* anyone; *paśyati:* sees; *akṛta buddhitvāt*: due to unintelligence; *na:* never; *saḥ:* he; *paśyati:* sees; *durmatiḥ:* foolish

18.16 Those who think they, their spirit, are the doers, are ignorant and do not see things as they are.

यस्य नाहङ्कृतो भावो बुद्धिर्यस्य न लिप्यते ।
हत्वाऽपि स इमाँल्लोकान्न हन्ति न निबध्यते ॥ १७

yasya nāhaṅkṛto bhāvo buddhir yasya na lipyate /
hatvā 'pi sa imāṁllokān na hanti na nibadhyate // 18.17

yasya: of one who; *nā:* never; *ahaṁkṛtaḥ*: ego; *bhāvaḥ*: nature; *buddhiḥ*: intelligence; *yasya*: one who; *na*: never; *lipyate:* is attached; *hatvā 'pi*: even killing; *saḥ*: he; *imān*: this; *lokān:* world; *na:* never; *hanti:* kills; *na:* never; *nibadhyate:* becomes entangled

18.17 One who is egoless, whose intelligence is not of attachment, though he may kill, is not the slayer and is never bound by his actions.

ज्ञानं ज्ञेयं परिज्ञाता त्रिविधा कर्मचोदना ।
करणं कर्म कर्तेति त्रिविधः कर्मसंग्रहः ॥ १८

jñānaṁ jñeyaṁ parijñātā trividhā karmacodanā /
karaṇaṁ karma karteti trividhaḥ karmasaṁgrahaḥ // 18.18

jñānaṁ: knowledge; *jñeyaṁ:* objective; *parijñātā:* the knower; *trividhā:* three kinds; *karma*: work; *codanā:* impetus; *karaṇaṁ:* the senses; *karmā:* work; *kartā:* the doer; *iti*: thus; *trividhaḥ*: three kinds; *karma*: work; *saṁgrahaḥ*: accumulation

18.18 Knowledge, object of the knowledge and the subject of the knowledge, the knower, are the three factors that stimulate action; the senses, the action and the performer comprise the three components of action.

ज्ञानं कर्म च कर्ता च त्रिधैव गुणभेदतः ।
प्रोच्यते गुणसङ्ख्याने यथावच्छृणु तान्यपि ॥ १९

jñānaṁ karma ca kartā ca tridhaiva guṇabhedataḥ I
procyate guṇasaṅkhyāne yathāvacchṛṇu tānyapi II 18.19

jñānaṁ: knowledge; *karma:* work; *ca:* also; *kartā:* worker; *ca:* also; *tridha:* three kinds; *eva:* certainly; *guṇabhedataḥ*: in terms of different modes of material nature; *procyate*: is said; *guṇasaṅkhyāne:* in terms of different modes; *yathāvat:* as they act; *śṛṇu*: hear; *tāni:* all of them; *api:* also

18.19 According to the science of guṇas, *there are three types in knowledge, action, and performers of action. Listen as I describe them.*

सर्वभूतेषु येनैकं भावमव्ययमीक्षते ।
अविभक्तं विभक्तेषु तज्ज्ञानं विद्धि सात्त्विकम् ॥ २०

sarvabhūteṣu yenaikaṁ bhāvamavyayamīkṣate I
avibhaktaṁ vibhakteṣu tajjñānaṁ viddhi sāttvikam II 18.20

sarvabhūteṣu: in all living entities; *yena*: by whom; *ekaṁ*: one; *bhāvaṁ*: situation; *avyayaṁ*: imperishable; *īkṣate:* does see; *avibhaktaṁ*: undivided; *vibhakteṣu:* in the numberless divided; *tat:* that; *jñānaṁ:* knowledge; *viddhi:* know; *sāttvikam:* in the mode of goodness

18.20 That knowledge by which one imperishable reality is seen in all Existence, undivided in the divided, is knowledge in the state of goodness.

पृथक्त्वेन तु यज्ज्ञानं नानाभावान्पृथग्विधान् ।
वेत्ति सर्वेषु भूतेषु तज्ज्ञानं विद्धि राजसम् ॥ २१

pṛthaktvena tu yajjñānaṁ nānābhāvān pṛthagvidhān I
vetti sarveṣu bhūteṣu tajjñānaṁ viddhi rājasam II 18.21

pṛthaktvena: because of division; *tu:* but; *yajjñānaṁ:* which knowledge; *nānābhāvān*: various situations; *pṛthagvidhān*: differently; *vetti:* one who knows; *sarveṣu*: in all; *bhūteṣu*: living entities; *tajjñānaṁ:* that knowledge; *viddhi:* must be known; *rājasam:* in terms of aggression

18.21 The knowledge by which one sees different realities of various types among all beings as separate from one another; such knowledge is in the mode of aggression.

यत्तु कृत्स्नवदेकस्मिन्कार्ये सक्तमहैतुकम् ।
अतत्त्वार्थवदल्पं च तत्तामसमुदाहृतम् ॥ २२

yat tu kṛtsnavad ekasmin kārye saktaṁ ahaitukam **/**
atattvārthavadalpaṁ ca tat tāmasamudāhṛtam **//** 18.22

yat: that which; *tu:* but; *kṛtsnavat:* all in all; *ekasmin:* in one; *kārye:* work; *saktaṁ*: attached; *ahaitukam:* without cause; *atattvārthavat:* without reality; *alpaṁ:* very meager; *ca:* and; *tat:* that; *tāmasaṁ:* in the mode of darkness; *udāhṛtam:* is spoken

18.22 The irrational, baseless, and worthless knowledge by which one clings to one single effect as if it is everything, such knowledge is in the mode of darkness of ignorance.

नियतं सङ्गरहितमरागद्वेषतः कृतम् ।
अफलप्रेप्सुना कर्म यत्तत्सात्त्विकमुच्यते ॥ २३

niyataṁ saṅgarahitamarāgadveṣataḥ kṛtam **/**
aphalaprepsunā karma yat tat sāttvikamucyate **//** 18.23

niyataṁ: regulative; *saṅgarahitaṁ:* without attachment; *arāgadveṣataḥ*: without love or hatred; *kṛtam:* done; *aphalaprepsunā:* without fruitive result; *karma:* acts; *yat:* which; *tat:* that; *sāttvikaṁ:* in the mode of goodness; *ucyate:* is called

18.23 Obligatory duty performed without likes and dislikes and without selfish motives and attachment to the fruit, is in the mode of goodness.

यत्तु कामेप्सुना कर्म साहङ्कारेण वा पुनः ।
क्रियते बहुलायासं तद्राजसमुदाहृतम् ॥ २४

yat tu kāmepsunā karma sāhaṁkāreṇa vā punaḥ **/**
kriyate bahulāyāsaṁ tad rājasamudāhṛtam **//** 18.24

yat: that which; *tu:* but; *kāmepsunā:* with fruitive result; *karma:* work; *sāhaṁkāreṇa*: with ego; *vā:* or; *punaḥ:* again; *kriyate:* performed; *bahulāyāsaṁ:* with great labor; *tat*: that; *rājasaṁ:* in the mode of passion; *udāhṛtam:* is said to be

18.24 Action performed with ego, with selfish motives, and with too much effort, is in the mode of aggression.

अनुबन्धं क्षयं हिंसामनपेक्ष्य च पौरुषम् ।
मोहादारभ्यते कर्म यत्तत्तामसमुच्यते ॥ २५

anubandhaṁ kṣayaṁ hiṁsāmanapekṣya ca pauruṣam **/**
mohād ārabhyate karma yat tat tāmasamucyate **//** 18.25

anubandhaṁ: future bondage; *kṣayaṁ:* destruction; *hiṁsām:* violence; *anapekṣya:* without consideration of consequences; *ca:* also; *pauruṣam:* ability; *mohāt:* by illusion; *ārabhyate:* begun; *karma:* work; *yat:* which; *tat:* that; *tāmasaṁ:* in the mode of ignorance; *ucyate:* is said to be

18.25 Action that is undertaken because of delusion, disregarding consequences, loss, injury to others, as well as one's own ability, is in the mode of ignorance.

मुक्तसङ्गोऽनहंवादी धृत्युत्साहसमन्वित: ।
सिद्ध्यसिद्ध्योर्निर्विकार: कर्ता सात्त्विक उच्यते ॥ २६

muktasaṅgo'nahaṁvādī dhṛtyutsāhasamanvitaḥ /
siddhyasiddhyor nirvikāraḥ kartā sāttvika ucyate // 18.26

muktasaṅgaḥ: liberated from all material association; *anahaṁvādī*: without false ego; *dhṛtyutsāha*: with great enthusiasm; *samanvitaḥ*: qualified in that way; *siddhi:* perfection; *asiddhyoḥ*: failure; *nirvikāraḥ*: without change; *kartā:* worker; *sāttvikaḥ:* in the mode of goodness; *ucyate:* is said to be

18.26 The performer who is free from attachment, non-egotistic, endowed with resolve and enthusiasm, and unperturbed in success or failure is called sātvika.

रागी कर्मफलप्रेप्सुर्लुब्धो हिंसात्मकोऽशुचि: ।
हर्षशोकान्वित: कर्ता राजस: परिकीर्तित: ॥ २७

rāgī karmaphalaprepsurlubdho hiṁsātmako 'śuciḥ /
harṣaśokānvitaḥ kartā rājasaḥ parikīrtitaḥ // 18.27

rāgī: very much attached; *karmaphala:* to the fruit of the work; *prepsuḥ:* desiring; *lubdhaḥ*: greedy; *hiṁsātmakaḥ:* and always envious; *aśuciḥ*: unclean; *harṣaśokānvitaḥ*: complicated, with joy and sorrow; *kartā*: such a worker; *rājasaḥ*: in the mode of passion; *parikīrtitaḥ*: is declared

18.27 The performer who is impassioned, who desires the fruits of work, who is greedy, violent, impure, and affected by joy and sorrow, is called aggressive.

अयुक्त: प्राकृत: स्तब्ध: शठोऽनैष्कृतिकोऽलस: ।
विषादी दीर्घसूत्री च कर्ता तामस उच्यते ॥ २८

ayuktaḥ prākṛtaḥ stabdhaḥ śaṭho naiṣkṛtiko 'lasaḥ /
viṣādī dīrghasūtrī ca kartā tāmasa ucyate // 18.28

ayuktaḥ: without reference to scriptural injunctions; *prākṛtaḥ:* materialistic; *stabdhaḥ*: obstinate; *śaṭhaḥ:* deceitful; *naiṣkṛtikaḥ*: expert in insulting others;

alasaḥ: lazy; *viṣādī*: morose; *dīrghasūtrī:* procrastinating; *ca:* also; *kartā:* worker; *tāmasa:* in the mode of ignorance; *ucyate:* is said to be

18.28 The performer who is undisciplined, vulgar, stubborn, wicked, malicious, lazy, depressed, and procrastinating is called ignorant or tamasic.

बुद्धेर्भेदं धृतेश्चैव गुणतस्त्रिविधं शृणु।
प्रोच्यमानमशेषेण पृथक्त्वेन धनञ्जय॥ २९

buddherbhedaṁ dhṛteś cai 'va guṇatastrividhaṁ śṛṇu /
procyamānamaśeṣeṇa pṛthaktvena dhanañjaya // 18.29

buddheḥ: of intelligence; *bhedaṁ:* differences; *dhṛteḥ:* of steadiness; *ca*: also; *eva*: certainly; *guṇataḥ:* by the modes of material nature; *trividhaṁ:* the three kinds of; *śṛṇu*: just hear; *procyamānaṁ:* as described by Me; *aśeṣeṇa:* in detail; *pṛthaktvena*: differently; *dhanañjaya:* O winner of wealth

18.29 Now hear Me explain, fully and separately, the threefold division of intellect and resolve, based on modes of material Nature, O Arjuna.

प्रवृत्तिं च निवृत्तिं च कार्याकार्ये भयाभये।
बन्धं मोक्षं च या वेत्ति बुद्धिः सा पार्थ सात्त्विकी॥ ३०

pravṛttiṁ ca nivṛttiṁ ca kāryakārye bhayābhaye /
bandhaṁ mokṣaṁ ca yā vetti buddhiḥ sā pārtha sāttvikī // 18.30

pravṛttiṁ: the path of work; *ca:* also; *nivṛttiṁ:* the path of renunciation; *ca:* and; *kārya*: work that is to be done; *akārye*: prohibited action; *bhaya*: fearful; *abhaye:* fearlessness; *bandhaṁ:* obligation; *mokṣaṁ ca:* and liberation; *yā:* that which; *vetti*: knows; *buddhiḥ:* understanding; *sā:* that; *pārtha:* O son of Pritā; *sāttvikī*: in the mode of goodness

18.30 O Arjuna, that intellect is in the mode of goodness which understands the path of work and the path of renunciation, right and wrong action, fear and fearlessness, bondage and liberation.

यया धर्ममधर्मं च कार्यं चाकार्यमेव च।
अयथावत्प्रजानाति बुद्धिः सा पार्थ राजसी॥ ३१

yayā dharmamadharmaṁ ca kāryaṁ cākāryam eva ca /
ayathāvat prajānāti buddhiḥ sā pārtha rājasī // 18.31

yayā: by which; *dharmaṁ:* right conduct; *adharmaṁ:* what is not right conduct; *ca*: and; *kāryaṁ:* work; *ca*: also; *akāryaṁ*: what ought not to be done; *eva:* certainly; *ca:* also; *ayathāvat:* not perfectly; *prajānāti:* knows; *buddhiḥ:* intelligence; *sā*: that; *pārtha*: O son of Pritā; *rājasī:* in the mode of passion

18.31 That intellect is in the mode of passion that cannot distinguish between principles of right conduct and wrong doing, and right and wrong action, O Arjuna.

अधर्मं धर्ममिति या मन्यते तमसावृता ।
सर्वार्थान्विपरीतांश्च बुद्धिः सा पार्थ तामसी ॥ ३२

adharmaṁ dharmamiti yā manyate tamasā 'vṛtā I
sarvārthānviparītāṁśca buddhiḥ sā pārtha tāmasī II 18.32

adharmaṁ: what is not right conduct; *dharmaṁ:* right conduct; *iti:* thus; *yā:* which; *manyate*: thinks; *tamasā:* by ignorance; *avṛtā:* covered; *sarvārthān:* all things; *viparītāṁ*: the wrong direction; *ca:* also; *buddhiḥ:* intelligence; *sā:* that; *pārtha:* O son of Pritā; *tāmasī:* the mode of ignorance

18.32 That intellect is in the mode of ignorance that accepts unrighteousness as righteousness and thinks everything to be that which it is not, O Arjuna.

धृत्या यया धारयते मनःप्राणेन्द्रियक्रियाः ।
योगेनाव्यभिचारिण्या धृतिः सा पार्थ सात्त्विकी ॥ ३३

dhṛtyā yayā dhārayate manaḥ prāṇendriyakriyāḥ I
yogenāvyabhicāriṇyā dhṛtiḥ sā pārtha sāttvikī II 18.33

dhṛtyā: determination; *yayā:* by which; *dhārayate:* continued; *manaḥ:* mind; *prāṇa*: life energy; *indriya*: senses; *kriyāḥ*: activities; *yogena:* uniting with God; *avyabhicāriṇyā*: without any break; *dhṛtiḥ*: such determination; *sā*: that; *pārtha*: O son of Pritā; *sāttvikī*: in the mode of goodness

18.33 Consistent and continuous determination in controlling the mind, breath and senses for uniting with the Divine is goodness, Arjuna

यया तु धर्मकामार्थान्धृत्या धारयतेऽर्जुन ।
प्रसङ्गेन फलाकाङ्क्षी धृतिः सा पार्थ राजसी ॥ ३४

yayā tu dharma kāmārthān dhṛtyā dhārayate 'rjuna I
prasaṅgena phalākāṅkṣī dhṛtiḥ sā pārtha rājasī II 18.34

yayā: by which; *tu:* but; *dharma kāmārthān:* for the three goals in life, right conduct, sense pleasure and wealth; *dhṛtyā*: by determination; *dhārayate*: continuously; *arjuna*: O Arjuna; *prasaṅgena:* for that; *phalākāṅkṣī:* desiring fruitive results; *dhṛtiḥ*: determination; *sā*: that; *pārtha:* O son of Pritā; *rājasī:* in the mode of passion

18.34 Craving for results of action while clinging to goals of proper conduct, pleasure and wealth is the state of passion.

यया स्वप्नं भयं शोकं विषादं मदमेव च ।
न विमुञ्चति दुर्मेधा धृतिः सा पार्थ तामसी ॥ ३५

yayā svapnaṁ bhayaṁ śokaṁ viṣādaṁ madameva ca **/**
na vimuñcati durmedhā dhṛtiḥ sā pārtha tāmasī **//** 18.35

yayā: by which; *svapnaṁ:* dream; *bhayaṁ:* fearfulness; *śokaṁ:* lamentation; *viṣādaṁ*: moroseness; *madaṁ:* delusion; *eva:* certainly; *ca:* also; *na:* never; *vimuñcati*: is liberated; *durmedhā:* unintelligent; *dhṛtiḥ*: determination; *sā:* that; *pārtha:* O son of Pritā; *tāmasī:* in the mode of ignorance

18.35 Ignorant resolve which cannot go beyond dreaming, fear, grief, despair and, delusion—such is in darkness, Arjuna.

सुखं त्विदानीं त्रिविधं श्रृणु मे भरतर्षभ ।
अभ्यासाद्रमते यत्र दुःखान्तं च निगच्छति ॥ ३६

sukhaṁ tvidānīṁ trividhaṁ śṛṇu me bharatarṣabha **/**
abhyāsād ramate yatra duḥkhāntaṁ ca nigacchati **//** 18.36

यत्तदग्रे विषमिव परिणामेऽमृतोपमम् ।
तत्सुखं सात्त्विकं प्रोक्तमात्मबुद्धिप्रसादजम् ॥ ३७

yat tad agre viṣaṁ iva pariṇāme 'mṛtopamam **/**
tat sukhaṁ sāttvikaṁ proktaṁ ātmabuddhiprasādajam **//** 18.37

sukhaṁ: happiness; *tu:* but; *idānīṁ:* now; *trividhaṁ:* three kinds; *śṛṇu:* hear; *me*: from Me; *bharatarṣabha:* O best amongst the Bhāratas; *abhyāsāt:* by practice; *ramate*: enjoyer; *yatra:* where; *duḥkha:* distress; *antaṁ*: end; *ca:* also; *nigacchati:* gains; *yat*: that which; *tat*: that; *agre:* in the beginning; *viṣaṁ iva:* like poison; *pariṇāme:* at the end; *amṛta:* nectar; *upamam*: compared to; *tat:* that; *sukhaṁ:* happiness; *sāttvikaṁ*: in the mode of goodness; *proktaṁ*: is said; *ātma:* self; *buddhi*: intelligence; *prasādajam*: satisfactory

18.36,37 And now hear from Me, O Arjuna, about three kinds of pleasure. The pleasure that one enjoys from spiritual practice results in cessation of all sorrows. The pleasure that appears as poison in the beginning, but is like nectar in the end, comes by the grace of Self-knowledge and is in the mode of goodness.

विषयेन्द्रियसंयोगाद्यत्तदग्रेऽमृतोपमम् ।
परिणामे विषमिव तत्सुखं राजसं स्मृतम् ॥ ३८

viṣayendriyasaṁyogadyat tad agre 'mṛtopamam **/**
pariṇāme visamiva tat sukhaṁ rājasaṁ smṛtam **//** 18.38

viṣaya: objects of the senses; *indriya:* senses; *saṁyogat:* combination; *yat:* which; *tat*: that; *agre*: in the beginning; *amṛtopamam:* just like nectar; *pariṇāme:* at the end; *visamiva*: like poison; *tat:* that; *sukhaṁ*: happiness; *rājasaṁ*: in the mode of passion; *smṛtam*: is considered

18.38 Sensual pleasures that appear as nectar in the beginning, but become poison in the end, are in the mode of passion.

यदग्रे चानुबन्धे च सुखं मोहनमात्मनः ।
निद्रालस्यप्रमादोत्थं तत्तामसमुदाहृतम् ॥ ३९

yadagre cānubandhe ca sukhaṁ mohanamātmanaḥ **/**
nidrālasyapramādotthaṁ tat tāmasamudāhṛtam **//** 18.39

yat: that which; *agre:* in the beginning; *ca:* also; *anubandhe:* by binding; *ca:* also; *sukhaṁ:* happiness; *mohanaṁ:* illusion; *ātmanaḥ:* of the self; *nidrā*: sleeping; *ālasya*: laziness; *pramāda*: illusion; *utthaṁ:* produced of; *tat:* that; *tāmasaṁ:* in the mode of ignorance; *udāhṛtam:* is said to be

18.39 Pleasure that is delusion from beginning to end and born out of sleep, laziness and illusion is said to be of the nature of ignorance.

न तदस्ति पृथिव्यां वा दिवि देवेषु वा पुनः ।
सत्त्वं प्रकृतिजैर्मुक्तं यदेभिः स्यात्त्रिभिर्गुणैः ॥ ४०

na tad asti pṛthivyāṁ vā divi deveṣu vā punaḥ **/**
sattvaṁ prakṛtijairmuktaṁ yadebhiḥ syāttribhirguṇaiḥ **//** 18.40

na: not; *tad:* that; *asti:* there is; *pṛthivyām:* within the universe; *vā:* or; *divi:* in the higher planetary system; *deveṣu:* amongst the demigods; *vā:* or; *punaḥ:* again; *sattvaṁ:* existence; *prakṛtijaiḥ:* under the influence of material nature; *muktaṁ*: liberated; *yat:* that; *ebhiḥ:* by this; *syāt:* so becomes; *tribhiḥ:* by three; *guṇaiḥ* : modes of material nature

18.40 No one, either here or among the celestials in the higher planetary systems, is free from these three states of material nature.

ब्राह्मणक्षत्रियविशां शूद्राणां च परन्तप ।
कर्माणि प्रविभक्तानि स्वभावप्रभवैर्गुणैः ॥ ४१

brāhmaṇakṣatriyaviśāṁ śūdrāṇāṁ ca parantapa I
karmāṇi pravibhaktāni svabhāvaprabhavairguṇaiḥ II 18.41

brāhmaṇa: the *brāhmaṇas*; *kṣatriya:* the *kṣatriyas*; *visāṁ:* the vaiśyas; *śūdrāṇāṁ*: the śūdras; *ca*: and; *parantapa:* O subduer of the enemies; *karmāṇi*: activities; *pravibhaktāni*: are divided; *svabhāva*: own nature; *prabhavaiḥ*: born of; *guṇaiḥ*: by the modes of material nature

18.41 Brāhmaṇas, kṣatriyas, vaiśya*s and* śūdras *are divided in the work they do based on their nature, Arjuna.*

शमो दमस्तपः शौचं क्षान्तिरार्जवमेव च ।
ज्ञानं विज्ञानमास्तिक्यं ब्रह्मकर्म स्वभावजम् ॥ ४२

śamo damastapaḥ śaucaṁ kṣāntirārjavameva ca I
jñānaṁ vijñānamāstikyaṁ brahmakarma svabhāvajaṁ II 18.42

śamaḥ: peacefulness; *damaḥ:* self-control; *tapaḥ:* austerity; *śaucaṁ:* purity; *kṣāntiḥ*: tolerance; *ārjavaṁ*: honesty; *eva:* certainly; *ca:* and; *jñānaṁ:* knowledge; *vijñānaṁ:* wisdom; *āstikyaṁ:* belief in God; *brahma:* of a brahmana; *karma:* duty; *svabhāvajaṁ*: born of his own nature

18.42 The nature of Brāhmaṇa *is characterized by their calmness, discipline, austerity, tolerance, honesty, knowledge, wisdom and belief in God.*

शौर्यं तेजो धृतिर्दाक्ष्यं युद्धे चाप्यपलायनम् ।
दानमीश्वरभावश्च क्षात्रं कर्म स्वभावजम् ॥ ४३

śauryaṁ tejo dhṛtir dākṣyaṁ yuddhe cāpyapalāyanam I
dānamīśvarabhāvaśca kṣātraṁ karma svabhāvajam II 18.43

śauryaṁ: heroism; *tejaḥ:* power; *dhṛtir:* determination; *dākṣyaṁ:* resourcefulness; *yuddhe:* in battle; *ca:* and; *api:* also; *apalāyanam:* not fleeing; *dānam*: generosity; *īśvara:* leadership; *bhāvaḥ:* nature; *ca:* and; *kṣātraṁ:* kṣatriya; *karma:* duty; *svabhāvajam:* born of his own nature

18.43 Kṣatriya *are characterized by their qualities of heroism, vigor, firmness, dexterity, steadfastness in battle, leadership and generosity.*

कृषिगौरक्ष्यवाणिज्यं वैश्यकर्म स्वभावजम् ।
परिचर्यात्मकं कर्म शूद्रस्यापि स्वभावजम् ॥ ४४

kṛṣi gaurakṣya vāṇijyaṁ vaiśyakarmasvabhāvajam /
paricaryātmakaṁ karma śūdrasyā api śvabhāvajam // 18.44

kṛṣi: plowing; *gaurakṣyaṁ:* protecting cows; *vāṇijyaṁ:* trade; *vaiśya:* vaiśyas; *karma*: duty; *svabhāvajam:* born of his own nature; *paricaryā:* service; *atmakaṁ:* nature; *karma:* duty; *śūdrasyā:* of the śūdra; *api:* also; *svabhāvajaṁ:* born of his own nature

18.44 Those who are good at cultivation, cattle rearing, and trade are known as Vaiśya. *Those who are very good in service are classed as* śūdra.

स्वे स्वे कर्मण्यभिरतः संसिद्धिं लभते नरः ।
स्वकर्मनिरतः सिद्धिं यथा विन्दति तच्छुणु ॥ ४५

sve sve karmaṇyabhirataḥ saṁsiddhiṁ labhate naraḥ /
svakarmanirataḥ siddhiṁ yathā vindati tacchṛṇu // 18.45

sve: own; *sve*: own; *karmaṇi:* in work; *abhirataḥ:* following; *saṁsiddhiṁ:* perfection; *labhate*: achieves; *naraḥ:* a man; *svakarma:* by his own duty; *nirataḥ:* engaged; *siddhiṁ*: perfection; *yathā:* as; *vindati:* attains; *tat:* that; *śṛṇu:* listen

18.45 One can attain the highest perfection by devotion to one's natural work. Listen to Me how one attains perfection while engaged in one's natural work.

यतः प्रवृत्तिर्भूतानां येन सर्वमिदं ततम् ।
स्वकर्मणा तमभ्यर्च्य सिद्धिं विन्दति मानवः ॥ ४६

yataḥ pravṛttirbhūtānāṁ yena sarvamidaṁ tatam /
svakarmaṇā tamabhyarcya siddhiṁ vindati mānavaḥ // 18.46

yataḥ: from whom; *pravṛttiḥ:* the emanation; *bhūtānāṁ:* of all living entities; *yena:* by whom; *sarvaṁ:* all; *idaṁ:* this; *tatam:* is pervaded; *svakarmaṇā:* in his own duties; *taṁ:* Him; *abhyarcya:* by worshiping; *siddhiṁ:* perfection; *vindati:* achieves; *mānavaḥ*: a man

18.46 One attains perfection by worshipping the supreme Being from whom all beings originate and by whom all this universe is pervaded through performance of one's natural duty for Him.

श्रेयान्स्वधर्मो विगुणः परधर्मात्स्वनुष्ठितात् ।
स्वभावनियतं कर्म कुर्वन्नाप्नोति किल्बिषम् ॥ ४७

śreyān svadharmo viguṇaḥ paradharmāt svanuṣṭhitāt /
svabhāvaniyataṁ karma kurvannāpnoti kilbiṣam // 18.47

śreyān: better; *svadharmaḥ:* one's own rightful conduct; *viguṇaḥ*: imperfectly performed; *paradharmāt:* another's conduct; *svanuṣṭhitāt:* perfectly done; *svabhāvaniyataṁ*: prescribed duties according to one's nature; *karma:* work; *kurvan*: performing; *na:* never; *āpnoti:* achieve; *kilbiṣam*: sinful reactions

18.47 It is better to engage in one's rightful conduct, even though one may not perform it to perfection, rather than to accept another's conduct and perform it perfectly. Duties prescribed according to one's nature, are never affected by sinful reactions.

सहजं कर्म कौन्तेय सदोषमपि न त्यजेत् ।
सर्वारम्भा हि दोषेण धूमेनाग्निरिवावृताः ॥ ४८

sahajaṁ karma kaunteya sadoṣamapi na tyajet /
sarvārambhā hi doṣeṇa dhūmenā gnirivā vṛtāḥ // 18.48

sahajaṁ: born simultaneously; *karma:* work; *kaunteya:* O son of Kuntī; *sadoṣaṁ*: with fault; *api:* although; *na:* never; *tyajet:* to be given up; *sarvārambhāḥ:* any venture; *hi*: certainly; *doṣeṇa:* with fault; *dhūmenāgniḥivāvṛtāḥ*: being covered like the smoke around the fire

18.48 Every work has some defect, just as fire is covered by smoke. One should not give up the work that is born of his own nature, even if such work is full of fault, Arjuna.

असक्तबुद्धिः सर्वत्र जितात्मा विगतस्पृहः ।
नैष्कर्म्यसिद्धिं परमां सन्न्यासेनाधिगच्छति ॥ ४९

asaktabuddhiḥ sarvatra jitātmā vigataspṛhaḥ /
naiṣkarmyasiddhiṁ paramāṁ sannyāsenādhigacchati // 18.49

asaktabuddhiḥ: unattached intelligence; *sarvatra:* everywhere; *jitātmā:* control of the mind; *vigataspṛhaḥ:* without material desires; *naiṣkarmyasiddhiṁ:* perfection through the realisation of state of Brahman; *paramāṁ:* supreme; *saṁyāsena:* by the renounced order of life; *adhigacchati*: attains

18.49 One whose mind is always free from selfish attachment, who has controlled the mind and who is free from desires, he, by renunciation, attains perfection of freedom from selfish attachment to the fruits of work.

सिद्धिं प्राप्तो यथा ब्रह्म तथाप्नोति निबोध मे।
समासेनैव कौन्तेय निष्ठा ज्ञानस्य या परा॥ ५०

siddhiṁ prāpto yathā brahma tathāpnoti nibodha me |
samāsenaiva kaunteya niṣṭhā jñānasya yā parā || 18.50

siddhiṁ: perfection; *prāptaḥ:* achieving; *yathā:* as; *brahma:* the supreme; *tathā:* so; *apnoti*: achieves; *nibodha:* try to understand; *me:* from Me; *samāsena:* summarily; *eva*: certainly; *kaunteya:* O son of Kuntī; *niṣṭhā:* stage; *jñānasya:* of knowledge; *yā:* which; *parā*: transcendental

18.50 Understand from Me how one can achieve the state of Truth, Brahman, *by acting in the way I shall now summarize, Arjuna.*

बुद्ध्या विशुद्धया युक्तो धृत्यात्मानं नियम्य च।
शब्दादीन्विषयांस्त्यक्त्वा रागद्वेषौ व्युदस्य च॥ ५१

buddhyā viśuddhayā yukto dhṛtyātmānaṁ niyamya ca |
śabādīnviṣayāṁstyaktvā rāgadveṣau vyudasya ca || 18.51

विविक्तसेवी लघ्वाशी यतवाक्कायमानसः।
ध्यानयोगपरो नित्यं वैराग्यं समुपाश्रितः॥ ५२

viviktasevī laghvāśī yatavākkāyamānasaḥ |
dhyānayogaparo nityaṁ vairāgyaṁ samupāśritaḥ || 18.52

अहङ्कारं बलं दर्पं कामं क्रोधं परिग्रहम्।
विमुच्य निर्ममः शान्तो बह्मभूयाय कल्पते॥ ५३

ahaṁkāraṁ balaṁ darpaṁ kāmaṁ krodhaṁ parigraham |
vimucya nirmamaḥ śānto brahmabhūyāya kalpate || 18.53

buddhyā: *by the intelligence;* viśuddhayā: *fully purified;* yuktaḥ: *such engagement;* dhṛtyā*: determination;* atmānaṁ: *self;* niyamya*: regulated;* ca*: also;* śabdādīn*: the sense objects, such as sound, etc.;* viṣayān*: sense objects;* tyaktvā*: giving up;* rāga*: attachment;* dveṣau*: hatred;* vyudasya*: having laid aside;* ca*: also;* viviktasevī*: living in a secluded place;* laghvāśī: *eating a small quantity;* yatavāk*: control of speech;* kāya*: body;* mānasaḥ*: control of the mind;* dhyānayogaparaḥ*: always absorbed in trance;* nityaṁ*: twenty-four hours a day;* vairāgyaṁ*: detachment;* samupāśritaḥ*: taken shelter of;* ahaṁkāraṁ*: false ego;* balaṁ: *false strength;* darpaṁ: *false pride;* kāmaṁ*: lust;* krodhaṁ*: anger;* parigraham: *acceptance of material things;* vimucya: *being delivered;* nirmamaḥ: *without proprietorship;* sāntaḥ: *peaceful;* brahmabhūyāya: *to become self-realized;* kalpate: *is understood*

18.51,52,53 Endowed with purified intellect; subduing the mind with firm resolve; turning away from the objects of senses; giving up likes and dislikes; living in solitude; eating lightly; controlling the mind, speech, and organs of action; ever absorbed in meditation; taking refuge in detachment; and relinquishing egotism, violence, pride, lust, anger, and proprietorship, one becomes peaceful, free from the notion of "I" and "mine", and fit for attaining oneness with the supreme Being.

ब्रह्मभूत: प्रसन्नात्मा न शोचति न काङ्क्षति ।
सम: सर्वेषु भूतेषु मद्भक्तिं लभते पराम् ॥ ५४

brahmabhūtaḥ prasannātmā na śocati na kāṅkṣati **/**
samaḥ sarveṣu bhūteṣu madbhaktiṁ labhate parāṁ **//** 18.54

brahmabhūtaḥ: being one with the Absolute; *prasannātmā:* fully joyful; *na:* never; *śocati*: laments; *na:* never; *kāṅkṣati:* desires; *samaḥ:* equally disposed; *sarveṣu:* all; *bhūteṣu:* living entities; *madbhaktiṁ*: My devotion; *labhate*: gains; *parāṁ*: transcendental

18.54 Absorbed in the supreme Being, the serene one neither grieves nor desires. Becoming impartial to all beings, one obtains My highest devotional love.

भक्त्या मामभिजानाति यावान्यश्चास्मि तत्त्वत: ।
ततो मां तत्त्वतो ज्ञात्वा विशते तदनन्तरम् ॥ ५५

bhaktyā mām abhijānāti yāvān yaścāsmi tattvataḥ **/**
tato māṁ tattvato jñātvā viśate tadanantaram **//** 18.55

bhaktyā: by pure devotional service; *mām:* Me; *abhijānāti:* one can know; *yāvān*: as much as; *yaścāsmi:* as I am; *tattvataḥ:* in truth; *tataḥ:* thereafter; *māṁ*: Me; *tattvataḥ*: by truth; *jñātvā*: knowing; *viśate:* enters; *tadanantaram:* thereafter

18.55 By devotion one truly understands what and who I am in essence. Having known Me in essence, one immediately merges with Me.

सर्वकर्माण्यपि सदा कुर्वाणो मद्व्यपाश्रय: ।
मत्प्रसादादवाप्नोति शाश्वतं पदमव्ययम् ॥ ५६

sarvakarmāṇyapi sadā kurvāṇo madvyapāśrayaḥ **/**
matprasādādavāpnoti śāśvataṁ padamavyayam **//** 18.56

sarva: all; *karmāṇi:* activities; *api:* although; *sadā*: always; *kurvāṇaḥ*: performing; *mat*: under My; *vyapāśrayaḥ*: protection; *mat:* My; *prasādāt:* mercy; *avāpnoti:* achieves; *śāśvataṁ*: eternal; *padaṁ:* abode; *avyayam:* imperishable

18.56 My devotee occupied in everyday life still reaches under My protection the imperishable ultimate abode through my mercy, through devotion to Me.

चेतसा सर्वकर्माणि मयि सन्न्यस्य मत्परः ।
बुद्धियोगमुपाश्रित्य मच्चित्तः सततं भव ॥ ५७

cetasā sarvakarmāṇi mayi sannyasya matparaḥ I
buddhiyogamupāśritya maccittaḥ satataṁ bhava II 18.57

cetasā: by intelligence; *sarvakarmāṇi:* all kinds of activities; *mayi:* unto Me; *sannyasya:* giving up; *matparaḥ:* My protection; *buddhiyogaṁ:* devotional activities; *upāśritya*: taking shelter of; *maccittaḥ:* consciousness; *satataṁ:* always; *bhava:* just become

18.57 While being engaged in activities just depend upon Me, and being fully conscious of Me, work always under My protection.

मच्चित्तः सर्वदुर्गाणि मत्प्रसादात्तरिष्यसि ।
अथ चेत्त्वमहङ्कारान्न श्रोष्यसि विनङ्क्ष्यसि ॥ ५८

maccittaḥ sarvadurgāṇi matprasādāt tariṣyasi I
atha cet tvamahaṁkārānna śroṣyasi vinaṅkṣyasi II 18.58

mat: My; *cittaḥ:* consciousness; *sarva:* all; *durgāṇi:* impediments; *mat:* My; *prasādāt:* My mercy; *tariṣyasi:* you will overcome; *atha:* therefore; *cet:* if; *tvaṁ:* you; *ahaṁkārāt*: by false ego; *na:* not; *śroṣyasi:* do not hear; *vinaṅkṣyasi:* then lose yourself

18.58 When your mind becomes fixed on Me, you shall overcome all difficulties by My grace. But if you do not listen to Me due to ego, you shall perish.

यदहङ्कारमाश्रित्य न योत्स्य इति मन्यसे ।
मिथ्यैष व्यवसायस्ते प्रकृतिस्त्वां नियोक्ष्यति ॥ ५९

yadahaṁkāramāśritya na yotsya iti manyase I
mithyaiṣa vyavasāyaste prakṛtistvāṁ niyokṣyati II 18.59

yat: therefore; *ahaṁkāram:* false ego; *āśritya:* taking shelter; *na:* not; *yotsye*: shall fight; *iti:* thus; *manyase:* think; *mithyaiṣa:* this is all false; *vyavasāyaste:* your determination; *prakṛtiḥ:* material nature; *tvāṁ:* you; *niyokṣyati:* will engage you

18.59 If due to ego you think: 'I shall not fight,' your resolve is useless, and your own nature will compel you.

स्वभावजेन कौन्तेय निबद्धः स्वेन कर्मणा।
कर्तुं नेच्छसि यन्मोहात्करिष्यस्यवशोऽपि तत्॥ ६०

svabhāvajena kaunteya nibaddhaḥ svena karmaṇa /
kartuṁ necchasi yan mohāt kariṣyasyavaśo 'pi tat // 18.60

svabhāvajena: by one's own nature; *kaunteya:* O son of Kuntī; *nibaddhaḥ*: conditioned; *svena:* by one's own; *karmaṇa:* activities; *kartuṁ:* to do; *na*: not; *icchasi*: like; *yat:* that; *mohāt:* by illusion; *kariṣyasi:* you will act; *avaśo:* imperceptibly; *api*: even; *tat:* that

18.60 O Arjuna, you are controlled by your own natural conditioning. Therefore, you shall do even against your will, what you do not wish to do out of delusion.

ईश्वरः सर्वभूतानां हृद्देशेऽर्जुन तिष्ठति।
भ्रामयन्सर्वभूतानि यन्त्रारूढानि मायया॥ ६१

īśvaraḥ sarvabhūtānāṁ hṛddeśe 'rjuna tiṣṭhati /
bhrāmayan sarvabhūtāni yantrārūḍhāni māyayā // 18.61

īśvaraḥ: the Supreme Lord; *sarvabhūtānāṁ:* of all living entities; *hṛddeśe:* in the heart; *arjuna:* O Arjuna; *tiṣṭhati:* resides; *bhrāmayan:* causing to travel; *sarvabhūtāni* : all living entities; *yantra:* machine; *ārūḍhāni:* being so placed; *māyayā:* under the illusion

18.61 The supreme Lord resides in everyone's heart, O Arjuna, and is directing the activities of all living entities who are acting as machines under the illusion of the material world.

तमेव शरणं गच्छ सर्वभावेन भारत।
तत्प्रसादात्परां शान्तिं स्थानं प्राप्स्यसि शाश्वतम्॥ ६२

tameva śaraṇaṁ gaccha sarvabhāvena bhārata /
tatprasādātparāṁ śāntiṁ sthānaṁ prāpsyasi śāśvatam // 18.62

taṁ: unto Him; *eva:* certainly; *śaraṇaṁ:* surrender; *gaccha:* go; *sarvabhāvena:* in all respects; *bhārata:* O son of Bhārata; *tatprasādāt:* by His grace; *parāṁ:* supreme; *śāntiṁ:* in peace; *sthānaṁ:* abode; *prāpsyasi:* you will get; *śāśvatam:* eternal

18.62 Surrender to Him completely. By His grace you will attain supreme peace and the eternal abode.

इति ते ज्ञानमाख्यातं गुह्याद्गुह्यतरं मया ।
विमृश्यैतदशेषेण यथेच्छसि तथा कुरु ॥ ६३

iti te jñānamākhyātaṁ guhyād guhyataraṁ mayā /
vimṛśyai tadaśeṣeṇa yathecchasi tathā kuru // 18.63

iti: thus; *te*: unto you; *jñānaṁ:* knowledge; *ākhyātaṁ*: described; *guhyāt*: confidential; *guhyataraṁ:* still more confidential; *mayā:* by Me; *vimṛśya:* by deliberation; *etat*: that; *aśeṣeṇa:* fully; *yathā*: as you; *icchasi*: you like; *tathā*: that; *kuru:* perform

18.63 I have explained the knowledge that is the secret of secrets. After fully reflecting on this, do as you wish.

सर्वगुह्यतमं भूयः शृणु मे परमं वचः ।
इष्टोऽसि मे दृढमिति ततो वक्ष्यामि ते हितम् ॥ ६४

sarvaguhyatamaṁ bhūyaḥ śṛṇu me paramaṁ vacaḥ /
iṣṭo 'si me dṛḍhamiti tato vakṣyāmi te hitam // 18.64

sarvaguhyatamaṁ: the most confidential of all; *bhūyaḥ:* again; *śṛṇu:* just hear; *me*: from Me; *paramaṁ*: the supreme; *vacaḥ*: instruction; *iṣṭo 'si:* you are very dear to Me; *me*: of Me; *dṛḍhaṁ*: very; *iti:* thus; *tataḥ:* therefore; *vakṣyāmi:* I am speaking; *te:* for your; *hitam:* benefit

18.64 Because you are My dear friend, I express this truth to you. This is the most confidential of all knowledge. Hear this from Me. It is for your benefit.

मन्मना भव मद्भक्तो मद्याजी मां नमस्कुरु ।
मामेवैष्यसि सत्यं ते प्रतिजाने प्रियोऽसि मे ॥ ६५

manmanā bhava madbhakto madyājī māṁ namaskuru /
māmevaiṣyasi satyaṁ te pratijāne priyo 'si me // 18.65

manmanāḥ: thinking of Me; *bhava:* just become; *madbhaktaḥ:* My devotee; *madyājī*: My worshiper; *māṁ*: unto Me; *namaskuru*: offer your obeisances; *mām*: unto Me; *eva*: certainly; *eṣyasi:* come; *satyaṁ:* truly; *te:* to you; *pratijāne*: I promise; *priyaḥ:* dear; *asi*: you are; *me:* Mine

18.65 Always think of Me and become My devotee. Worship Me and offer your homage unto Me. Thus you will certainly attain to Me. This I promise you because you are My very dear friend.

सर्वधर्मान्परित्यज्य मामेकं शरणं व्रज ।
अहं त्वा सर्वपापेभ्यो मोक्षयिष्यामि मा शुचः ॥ ६६

sarvadharmān parityajya māmekaṁ śaraṇaṁ vraja **/**
ahaṁ tvā sarvapāpebhyo mokṣayiṣyāmi mā śucaḥ **//** 18.66

sarvadharmān: all principles of right conduct; *parityajya:* abandoning; *mām:* unto Me; *ekaṁ:* only; *śaraṇaṁ:* surrender; *vraja:* go; *ahaṁ:* I; *tvā*: you; *sarva:* all; *pāpebhyaḥ*: from sinful reactions; *mokṣayiṣyāmi:* deliver; *mā:* not; *śucaḥ:* worry

18.66 Abandon all principles and concepts of right conduct and simply surrender unto Me. I shall deliver you from all sinful reaction. Have no worry.

इदं ते नातपस्काय नाभक्ताय कदाचन ।
न चाशुश्रूषवे वाच्यं न च मां योऽभ्यसूयति ॥ ६७

idaṁ te nā 'tapaskāya nā 'bhaktāya kadācana **/**
na cā 'śuśrūṣave vācyaṁ na ca māṁ yo 'bhyasūyati **//** 18.67

idaṁ: this; *te:* you; *na:* never; *atapaskāya*: one who is not austere; *na:* never; *abhaktāya*: one who is not a devotee; *kadācana*: at any time; *na:* never; *ca:* also; *aśuśrūṣave*: one who is not engaged in devotional service; *vācyaṁ:* to be spoken; *na*: never; *ca:* also; *māṁ:* unto Me; *yaḥ:* anyone; *abhyasūyati:* envious

18.67 This knowledge should never be spoken by you to one who is devoid of austerity, who is without devotion, who does not desire to listen, or who speaks ill of Me.

य इमं परमं गुह्यं मद्भक्तेष्वभिधास्यति ।
भक्तिं मयि परां कृत्वा मामेवैष्यत्यसंशयः ॥ ६८

ya idaṁ paramaṁ guhyaṁ madbhakteṣvabhidhāsyati **/**
bhaktiṁ mayi parāṁ kṛtvā māmevaiṣyaty asaṁśayaḥ **//** 18.68

yaḥ: anyone; *idaṁ:* this; *paramaṁ:* most; *guhyaṁ:* confidential; *mat:* Mine; *bhakteṣu*: amongst devotees of; *abhidhāsyati*: explains; *bhaktiṁ*: devotional service; *mayi*: unto Me; *parāṁ:* transcendental; *kṛtvā*: having done; *mām:* unto Me; *eva:* certainly; *eṣyati:* comes; *asaṁśayaḥ:* without doubt

18.68 One who communicates the supreme secret to the devotees performs the highest devotional service to Me, and at the end he will without doubt, come back to Me.

न च तस्मान्मनुष्येषु कश्चिन्मे प्रियकृत्तमः ।
भविता न च मे तस्मादन्यः प्रियतरो भुवि ॥ ६९

na ca tasmānmanuṣyeṣu kaścin me priya kṛttamaḥ I
bhavitā na ca me tasmādanyaḥ priyataro bhuvi II 18.69

na: never; *ca:* and; *tasmāt:* therefore; *manuṣyeṣu:* among mankind; *kaścit*: anyone; *me:* My; *priyakṛttamaḥ:* more dear; *bhavitā:* will become; *na:* nor; *ca:* and; *me*: My; *tasmāt:* than him; *anyaḥ:* other; *priyataraḥ:* dearer; *bhuvi:* in this world

18.69 No other person shall do a more pleasing service to Me, and no one on the earth shall be more dear to Me.

अध्येष्यते च य इमं धर्म्यं संवादमावयोः ।
ज्ञानयज्ञेन तेनाहमिष्टः स्यामिति मे मतिः ॥ ७०

adhyeṣyate ca ya imaṁ dharmyaṁ saṁvādamāvayoḥ I
jñānayajñena tenāhamiṣṭaḥ syāmiti me matiḥ II 18.70

adhyeṣyate: will study; *ca:* also; *yaḥ:* he; *imaṁ:* this; *dharmyaṁ*: sacred; *saṁvādaṁ*: conversation; *āvayoḥ:* of ours; *jñāna:* knowledge; *yajñena:* by sacrifice; *tena*: by him; *ahaṁ*: I; *iṣṭaḥ*: worshiped; *syām:* shall be; *iti*: thus; *me:* My; *matiḥ*: opinion

18.70 I say that One who studies this sacred dialogue worships Me by sacrifice of his intelligence.

श्रद्धावाननसूयश्च शृणुयादपि यो नरः ।
सोऽपि मुक्तः शुभाँल्लोकान्प्राप्नुयात्पुण्यकर्मणाम् ॥ ७१

śraddhāvānanasūyaśca śṛṇuyādapi yo naraḥ I
so 'pi muktaḥ śubhāṁl lokān prāpnuyāt puṇyakarmaṇām II 18.71

śraddhāvān: faithful; *anasūyaś ca:* and not envious; *śṛṇuyāt:* does hear; *api*: certainly; *yaḥ:* who; *naraḥ:* a man; *saḥ:* he; *api*: also; *muktaḥ:* being liberated; *śubhān*: auspicious; *lokān:* planets; *prāpnuyāt:* attains; *puṇyakarmaṇām:* of those with merit

18.71 One who listens with faith and without envy becomes free from sinful reactions and attains to the planets where those of merit dwell.

कच्चिदेतच्छ्रुतं पार्थ त्वयैकाग्रेण चेतसा ।
कच्चिदज्ञानसम्मोहः प्रनष्टस्ते धनञ्जय ॥ ७२

kaccid etacchrutaṁ pārtha tvayaikāgreṇa cetasā I
kaccid ajñānasaṁmohaḥ pranaṣṭaste dhanañjaya II 18.72

kaccit: whether; *etat:* this; *śrutaṁ:* heard; *pārtha:* O son of Pritā; *tvaya:* by you; *ekāgreṇa*: with full attention; *cetasā:* by the mind; *kaccit:* whether; *ajñāna*: ignorant; *saṁmohaḥ:* illusion; *pranaṣṭaḥ:* dispelled; *te:* of you; *dhanañjaya:* O conqueror of wealth (Arjuna)

18.72 O Arjuna, did you listen to this with single-minded attention? Has your delusion born of ignorance been completely destroyed?

अर्जुन उवाच
नष्टो मोहः स्मृतिर्लब्धा त्वत्प्रसादान्मयाऽच्युत ।
स्थितोऽस्मि गतसन्देहः करिष्ये वचनं तव ॥ ७३

Arjuna uvāca
naṣṭo mohaḥ smṛtirlabdhā tvatprasādānmayā'cyuta I
sthito 'smi gatasandehaḥ kariṣye vacanaṁ tava II 18.73

Arjuna uvāca: Arjuna said; *naṣṭaḥ:* dispelled; *mohaḥ:* illusion; *smṛtiḥ:* memory; *labdhā*: regained; *tvatprasādāt*: by Your mercy; *mayā:* by me; *acyuta*: O infallible Kṛṣṇa; *sthitaḥ*: situated; *asmi*: I am; *gata*: removed; *sandehaḥ:* all doubts; *kariṣye:* I shall execute; *vacanaṁ*: order; *tava:* Your

18.73 Arjuna said: O Lord, my illusion is now gone. I have regained my memory by Your mercy, and I am now firm and free from doubt and ready to obey you.

संजय उवाच
इत्यहं वासुदेवस्य पार्थस्य च महात्मनः ।
संवादमिममश्रौषमद्भुतं रोमहर्षणम् ॥ ७४

Sañjaya uvāca
ityahaṁ vāsudevasya pārthasya ca mahātmanaḥ I
saṁvādamimamaśrauṣamadbhutaṁ romaharṣaṇam II *18.74*

Sañjaya uvāca: Sañjaya said; *iti:* thus; *ahaṁ:* I; *vāsudevasya:* of Kṛṣṇa; *pārthasya*: of Arjuna; *ca:* also; *mahātmanaḥ:* two great souls; *saṁvādaṁ*: discussion; *imaṁ*: this; *aśrauṣaṁ:* heard; *adbhutaṁ:* wonder; *romaharṣaṇam:* hair standing on end

18.74 Sañjaya said: Thus have I heard the conversation of two great souls, Kṛṣṇa and Arjuna. And so wonderful is that message that my hair stands on end.

व्यासप्रसादाच्छ्रुतवानेतद्गुह्यमहं परम् ।
योगं योगेश्वरात्कृष्णात्साक्षात्कथयतः स्वयम् ॥ ७५

vyasāprasādācchrutavānetadguhyamahaṁ param /
yogaṁ yogeśvarāt kṛṣṇāt sākṣāt kathayataḥ svayam // 18.75

vyasāprasādāt: by the mercy of Vyāsadeva; *śrutavān:* heard; *etat:* this; *guhyaṁ*: confidential; *ahaṁ*: I; *param:* the supreme; *yogaṁ:* mysticism; *yogeśvarāt:* from the master of all mysticism; *kṛṣnāt:* from Kṛṣṇa; *sākṣāt:* directly; *kathayataḥ:* speaking; *svayam:* personally

18.75 By the mercy of Vyāsa, I have heard these most confidential words directly from Kṛṣṇa, the master of all mysticism, who was speaking personally to Arjuna.

राजन्संस्मृत्य संस्मृत्य संवादमिममद्भुतम् ।
केशवार्जुनयोः पुण्यं हृष्यामि च मुहुर्मुहुः ॥ ७६

rājan saṁsmṛtya-saṁsmṛtya saṁvādamimamadbhutam /
keśavārjunayoḥ puṇyaṁ hṛṣyāmi ca muhur-muhuḥ // 18.76

rājan: O King; *saṁsmṛtya:* remembering; *saṁsmṛtya:* remembering; *saṁvādaṁ*: discussion; *imaṁ:* this; *adbhutam:* wonderful; *keśava:* Lord Kṛṣṇa; *arjunayoḥ*: and Arjuna; *puṇyaṁ:* pious; *hṛṣyāmi:* taking pleasure; *ca:* also; *muhur-muhuḥ:* always, repeatedly

18.76 O King, as I repeatedly recall this wondrous and holy dialogue between Kṛṣṇa and Arjuna, I take pleasure, being thrilled every moment.

तच्च संस्मृत्य संस्मृत्य रूपमत्यद्भुतं हरेः ।
विस्मयो मे महान् राजन्हृष्यामि च पुनः पुनः ॥ ७७

tacca saṁsmṛtya-saṁsmṛtya rūpam atyadbhutaṁ hareḥ /
vismayo me mahān rājan hṛṣyāmi ca punaḥ-punaḥ // 18.77

tat: that; *ca:* also; *saṁsmṛtya:* remembering; *saṁsmṛtya:* remembering; *rūpaṁ:* form; *ati:* great; *adbhutaṁ:* wonderful; *hareḥ:* of Lord Kṛṣṇa; *vismayaḥ:* wonder; *me*: my; *mahān:* great; *rājan:* O King; *hṛṣyāmi:* enjoying; *ca:* also; *punaḥ-punaḥ*: repeatedly

18.77 O King, when I remember the wonderful form of Lord Kṛṣṇa, I am struck with even greater wonder, and I rejoice again and again.

यत्र योगेश्वरः कृष्णो यत्र पार्थो धनुर्धरः ।
तत्र श्रीर्विजयो भूतिर्ध्रुवा नीतिर्मतिर्मम ॥ ७८

yatra yogeśvaraḥ kṛṣṇo yatra pārtho dhanurdharaḥ I
tatra śrīrvijayo bhūtirdhruvā nītirmatirmama II 18.78

yatra: where; *yogeśvaraḥ:* the master of mysticism; *kṛṣṇaḥ:* Lord Kṛṣṇa; *yatra*: where; *pārthaḥ:* the son of Pritā; *dhanurdharaḥ:* the carrier of the bow and arrow; *tatra*: there; *śrīḥ:* opulence; *vijayaḥ:* victory; *bhūtiḥ:* exceptional power; *dhruvā:* certain; *nītiḥ:* morality; *matirmama:* is my opinion.

18.78 Wherever there is Kṛṣṇa, the master of all mystics, and wherever there is Pārtha, the supreme carrier of bow and arrow, there will certainly be opulence, victory, extraordinary power, and morality. That is my opinion.

इति श्रीमद्भगवद्गीतासूपनिषत्सु ब्रह्मविद्यायां योगशास्त्रे
श्रीकृष्णार्जुनसंवादे मोक्षसंन्यासयोगो नाम अष्टादशोऽध्यायः ॥

iti śrīmadbhagavadgītāsūpaniṣatsu brahmavidyāyāṁ yogaśāstre
śrī kṛṣṇārjunasaṁvāde mokṣasaṁnyāsa yogo nāma aṣṭādaśo 'dhyāyaḥ II

In the Upaniṣad *of the Bhagavad Gītā, the knowledge of* Brahman, *the Supreme, the science of Yoga and the dialogue between Śrī Kṛṣṇa and Arjuna, this is the eighteenth discourse designated:*

Mokṣa Sanyāsa Yogaḥ

BhagavadGītā

Appendix

Scientific Research on Bhagavad Gītā

Several institutions have conducted experiments using scientific and statistically supported techniques to verify the truth behind Bhagavad Gītā. Notable amongst them is the work carried out by Maharṣi Maheśa yogi, whose findings are published through Maharṣi ved vijñān viśva vidyāpīṭaṁ.

Studies conducted using meditation techniques related to truths expressed in the verses of Bhagavad Gītā have shown that the quality of life is significantly improved through meditation. These studies have found that meditators experience a greater sense of peace resulting in a reduced tendency towards conflict.

Meditators gain greater respect for and appreciation of others. Their own inner fulfilment increases resulting in improved self-respect and self-reliance, leading to Self Actualization.

One's ability to focus along with brain function integration is enhanced. These have resulted in greater comprehension, creativity, faster response time in decision-making and superior psychomotor coordination.

Stress levels have been shown to decrease with enhanced sensory perception and overall health. The tendency towards depression has been clearly shown to decrease.

There is enough evidence to show that as a result of meditation, individuals gain a better ethical lifestyle that in turn improves their interaction with others in the community, resulting in less conflict and crime. Group meditation of 7000 people (square root of 1% of world population at the time of the study) was significantly correlated to a reduction in conflict worldwide.

Meditation leads to higher levels of consciousness. Through the research tools of Applied Kinesiology, Dr. David Hawkins (author of the book *Power vs. Force*) and others have shown that human consciousness has risen in the last few decades, crossing a critical milestone for the first time in human history. Dr. Hawkins' research also documents that Bhagavad Gītā is at the very highest level of Truth conveyed to humanity.

We acknowledge with gratitude the work done by the Maharṣi Maheś yogi institutions and Dr. David Hawkins in establishing the truth of this great scripture.

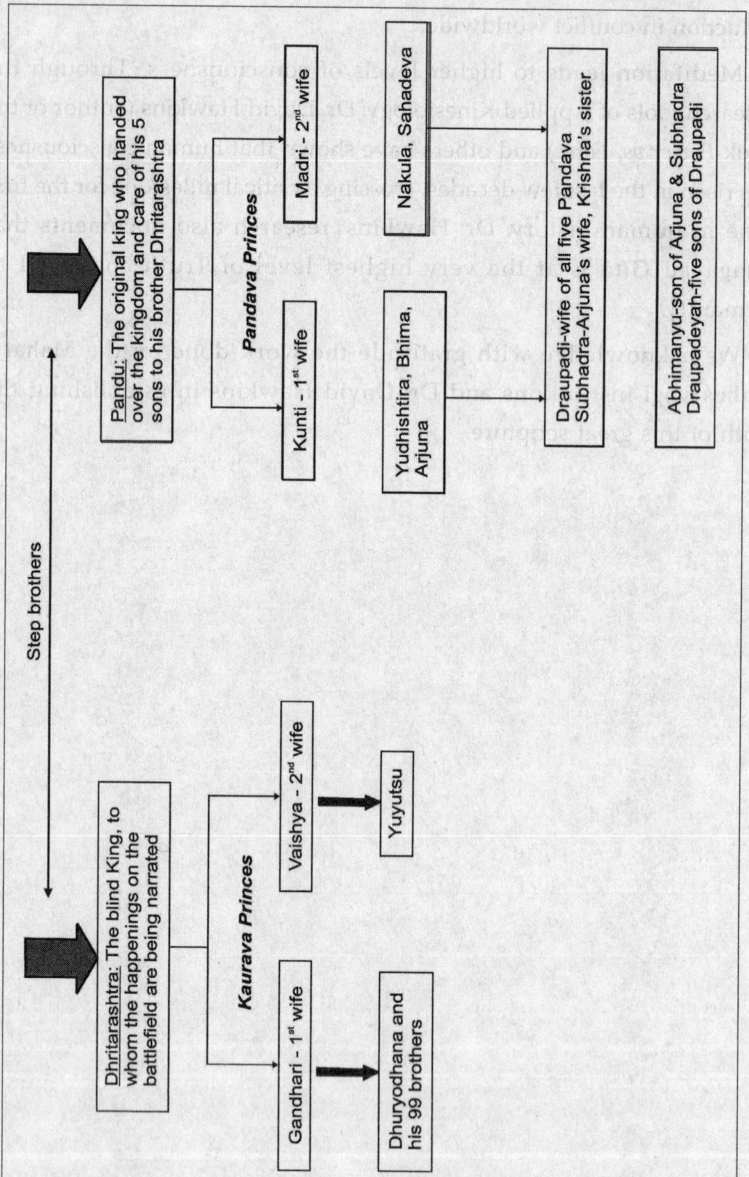
Dhritarashtra: The blind King, to whom the happenings on the battlefield are being narrated
Step brothers
Pandu: The original king who handed over the kingdom and care of his 5 sons to his brother Dhritarashtra
Kaurava Princes
Gandhari - 1st wife
Vaishya - 2nd wife
Dhuryodhana and his 99 brothers
Yuyutsu
Pandava Princes
Kunti - 1st wife
Madri - 2nd wife
Yudhishtira, Bhima, Arjuna
Nakula, Sahadeva
Draupadi-wife of all five Pandava
Subhadra-Arjuna's wife, Krishna's sister
Abhimanyu-son of Arjuna & Subhadra
Draupadeyah-five sons of Draupadi

Key Characters in Bhagavad Gītā

Kṛṣṇa :	god incarnate; related to both Kauravas and Pāṇḍavās; Arjuna's charioteer in the war
Arjuna :	the most illustrious of the Pāṇḍavā brothers; expert wielder of the bow
Yudhiṣṭhira :	eldest of Pāṇḍavās, renowned for his unflinching adherence to truth and righteousness which earned him the title 'Dharmarāja'
Bhīma :	The 2nd of the Pāṇḍavā brothers; distinguished from his brothers by his great stature and unimaginable strength.
Nakula and Sahadeva :	twin sons of Mādri; expert swordsmen; expert swordsmen
Duryodhana :	son of Dhṛtarāṣṭra, the Kaurava King
Karṇa :	son of Kuntī from the Sun god; renowned for his sacrifice and generosity
Duśśāsana :	brother of Duryodhana, is killed by Bhīma in the war
Bhīṣma :	great grandfather of the Kaurava & Pāṇḍavā; great warrior
Droṇa :	a great archer and teacher of both Kauravas and Pāṇḍavās
Pāṇḍu :	father of Pāṇḍavās, husband of Kuntī

Mādrī	:	2nd wife of Pāṇḍu; mother of Sahadeva and Nakula
Kuntī	:	wife of Pāṇḍu, mother of Pāṇḍavās
Gāndhārī	:	mother of Kauravas; voluntarily blindfolded herself throughout her married life since her husband Dhṛtarāṣṭra was born blind
Śakuni	:	brother of Gāndhārī; Duryodhana's maternal uncle
Drupada	:	a great warrior and father of Draupadī
Dṛṣṭadyumna	:	son of king Drupada and brother of Draupadī
Dṛṣṭaketu	:	king of Chedis, an ally of the Pāṇḍavās.
Śikhaṇḍi	:	a mighty archer and a transsexual person
Virāṭa	:	Abhimanyu's father-in-law; king of a neighboring kingdom
Yuyudhāna	:	Kṛṣṇa's charioteer and a great warrior
Kāśirāja	:	king of the neighboring kingdom of Kāśī
Cekitāna	:	an ally of the Pāṇḍavās, a great warrior
Kuntībhoja	:	adoptive father of Kuntī, the mother of the first three Pāṇḍavā princes
Purujit	:	brother of Kuntibhoj,
Śaibya	:	a ruler friendly to the Pāṇḍavās, leader of the Śibi tribe
Uttamouja	:	a great warrior
Sañjaya	:	minister and narrator of events to Dhṛtarāṣtra
Vikarṇa	:	third of the Kaurava brothers
Aśvattāma	:	Droṇa's son and Achilles heel; said to always speak the truth
Kṛpācārya	:	teacher of martial arts to both Kaurava and Pāṇḍavā
Śalya	:	king of neighboring kingdom and brother of Mādri, Nakula and Sahadeva's mother

Somadatta	:	king of Bahikas
Duśśāsana	:	one of Kaurava brothers; responsible for insulting Draupadī
Śantanu	:	Arjuna's great grandfather
Subhadrā	:	Lord Kṛṣṇa's sister; wife of Arjuna
Vicitravīrya	:	Śikhaṇḍi's step brother
Vyāsa	:	author of Mahābhārata and Brahma Sūtras; grandfather to the Pāṇḍavās.
Yudhāmanyu	:	an ally of Pāṇḍavās, prince of Pāñcāla
Yuyudhāna	:	another name for Sātyaki

Glossary

Abhaya: complete protection

Ābharaṇa: adornment

Abhin: an opium variant

Abhiṣeka: water rituals involving pouring of water on the deity

Abhaya hasta: the hand of the deity showing protection and grace

Abhyāsa yoga: practise of yoga of holding the mind in a state of union with divinity

Āditya: the Sun

Advaita anubhava: Non duality experience

Añjana: collyrium, black pigment used to paint the eye lashes

Aśraya doṣa: defect related to reality

Āśīrvāda: blessing

Aṣṭāṇga Yoga: eight fold path to enlightenment prescribed by Patañjali in his Yoga Sūtra

Aṣṭāvakra: an enlightened sage of ancient India, authored Aṣṭāvakra Samhita

Āgāmya karma: karma we accumulate in the present birth

Agarbathis: incense Sticks

Agni: fire, also 'god of fire'

Aham: me

Ahaṅkāra: ego, identity which we project to the world

Āhāra: food

Āhāra śuddhi: purity of food

Ahimsā: non violence

Ahirbudhnya: one of the Rudras or the celestial beings

Airāvata: the elephant of Indra, king of celestial beings

Aja: one of the Rudras or the celestial beings

Ājñā cakra: the sixth energy center located between the eyebrows. Means 'command' or 'will' in Sanskrit. This cakra is blocked by one's own ego.

Ākāśa: space, sky; subtlest form of energy of universe

Akṣaram: imperishable

Ālahāla: a deadly poison obtained during churning of the milky oceans by the gods and demons. It was consumed by Lord Śiva to save mankind.

Ālvārs: Tamil poet saints of south India who lived between the sixth and ninth centuries and espoused emotional devotion or bhakti to Viṣṇu-Kṛṣṇa in their songs of longing, ecstasy and service.

Amānitvam: humility

Ambā: the eldest daughter of King of Kāśi

Ambaravānnan: one of the names of Lord Śiva

Ambikāpati, Amarāvati: eternal lovers who lived during the period of Kulothunga Chola, an ancient ruler in South India

Amṛta dhāra: flow of nectar

Amṛta: divine nectar whose consumption leads to immortality

Amṛtatva: immortality

Anāhata cakra: subtle energy center in the heart region related to love.

Ānanda darśan: the blessing given by enlightened master imparting energy to the recipient.

Ānanda Sabha: meditation hall at Nithyananda Dhyanapeetam, Bidadi

Ānanda spuraṇa: fountain of bliss

Ānandamaya Kośa: the fifth and final energy layer in the five layers known as kośas. A meditative journey through the five kośas is the essence of Nithyananda's Ātma Spuraṇa Program.

Anantavijaya: Yudhiṣṭhira's conch

Anasūyanto: without enemy

Anitya: transient

Annadāna: donation of food

Annāmalai swamigal: enlightened disciple and personal assistant of enlightened master Bhagavān Ramaṇa Maharṣi

Annamaya kośa: food or Physical sheath, the first of the five kośas or energy sheaths.

Antarikṣa: space

Antima Sanyās: renunciation at the time of death

Anubhūti: inner experience

Āpas: water

Apāna: part of prāna that works downwards and is responsible for the excretory and reproductory organs

Aparājita: form of rudra; also means 'invincible' or 'unconquered'

Aparigraha: concept of non-possessiveness

Arāga: detachment

Āraṇyaka: part of the vedic literature which describes the significance of rituals. Since they are voluminous they are referred as āranyakas which means forest.

Ārati: a Hindu ritual, in which light from wicks soaked in ghee (purified butter) or camphor is offered to one or more deities.

Arcāvatara: descent of the divine into the deity for purpose of worship

Ardha Kumbhamela: spiritual gathering which happens once in three years in India at one of the four places of Prayāg, Haridvār, Ujjain and Nāsik on the banks of sacred rivers.

Ardhanārīśvara: a form of Lord Śiva that is half-man and half-woman

Artha: a person who is in distress and suffering

Aruṇācala hill: a holy hill in the city of Tiruvannamalai, Tamil Nadu, South India

Aruṇācala akṣaramanamalai: the soul stirring hymn to Aruṇācala Śiva, composed by the enlightened master Bhagavān Śrī Ramaṇa Maharṣi

Aruṇagirināthar: a Tamil poet who lived in the 15th century in Tamil Nadu, India. Authored Tirupugazh, a book of hymns in praise of Lord Muruga, a Hindu god

Aryamā: one of the adityās

Āsana: physical posture

Ashramites: those who live in the ashram

Astra: a thought or word that is given an enormous power to destroy by its creator

Āsurī sampat: demonic nature

Aśvatta: banyan tree

Aśvinī: it is the very first of the 27th constellation of stars in Hindu astronomy

Aśvinī kumāras: divine twin horsemen who were also the physicians of the Devas

Atharva veda: the last of the vedas, which are ancient Hindu texts

Atithi devo bhava : consider the guest as God

Ātma Bhūti: state of Divine

Ātma sādhana: self effort

Ātma vicāraṇa: self enquiry

Ātma vidya: knowledge of the self

Ātma jñāna: Self realization

Ayyā: refers to Śrī Nithya Sadhānanda, Secretary to Swamiji

Āzhwars: devotional saints of Tamilnadu, India

Bālāji: one of the names of the presiding deity of Tirumala Tirupati

Bali: a king of the demon race

Beedi: local Indian cigarette

Bīja: seed; bīja-mantra refers to the single syllable mantras used to invoke certain deities

Bhaga: a form of Śiva; a form of the sun

Bhagavān: literally god; often used for an enlightened Master

Bhāgavatam: Devotional stories on Lord Kṛṣṇa, compiled by Veda Vyāsa.

Bhāvanā: visualization

Bhakti: devotion

Bhakta: a devotee

Bhagīratha: ruler of Kośala, a kingdom in ancient India. He performed intense tapas to bring river Ganges to the Earth from the Heavens

Bhaja govindam: collection of 32 (sometimes 34) devotional verses composed by enlightened master Ādi Śaṅkarā. This is considered to be the essence of Vedānta and Advaita

Bharaṇi: a form of poetry in the Tamil Sangam literature

Bharata: brother of lord Rāma in Rāmāyaṇa

Bhāva roga: emotional diseases

Bhāvana: visualization

Bhū garbha: womb of the mother

Bhūta śarīra vāsa: life in the earlier body or the previous birth

Big Bang: one of the cosmological models of the Universe; proposed by Georges Lemaitre, a Roman Catholic priest

Bodhi Dharma: Bodhi Dharma was a Buddhist monk from southern India who lived during the early 5th century and is traditionally credited as the transmitter of Zen to China.

Brahma Jñāna: Self Realization

Brahma sūtra: ancient spiritual treatise

Brahmaloka: the highest of the celestial worlds

Brahmāṇḍa: cosmos

Brahmāstra: nuclear weapon

Bhṛgu: great sage of the Vedic tradition

Brihat sāma: a part of the Chāndogya Upaniṣad

Brindāvan: place where Kṛṣṇa grew up

Caitanya Mahāprabhu: a 15th century mystic from Bengal, India steeped in devotion to enlightened master Kṛṣṇa. His followers are known as Gaudīya Vaiśṇavas.

Cakra: energy centers in the body. Literally means 'wheel' based on the experience of mystics who perceived these energy centers as whirlpools of energy. There are seven major chakras along the spine: Mūlādhāra, Svādhiṣṭhāna, Maṇipūraka, Anāhata, Viśuddhi, Ājñā and Sahasrāra.

Cakṣu: energy behind the power of sight.

Candāla: low caste person

Cār dhām: four sacred pilgrim centres in the Himālayas, namely Haridvār, Riśikeś, Kedārnath and Badrināth

Candramā: moon

Charles Townes: an American Nobel Prize-winning physicist and educator; well-known for his work in Maser and Quantum electronics

Cidākāśa : the space in the surrounding(eg. as in a room). The other two being ghaṭākāśa and mahākāśa. Mahākāśa is the third infinite space of Consciousness.

Citragupta: a Hindu god assigned with the task of keeping complete records of actions of human beings on the earth, and upon their death, deciding as regards sending them to the heaven or the hell,

Citraratha: a gandharva, a celestial being

Dadhīci: a great sage

Daityas: race of beings that fought against demi gods

Daivī sampath: divine nature

Dakṣiṇāmūrti swamigal: great south indian saint

Dakṣiṇāyanam: the six months in the year when the sun moves to the southern hemisphere

Dakṣiṇeśvar: a small town in West Bengal, famous for its Kālī temple where Rāmakṛṣṇa Paramahamsa lived

Dāna: sharing

Dānava: a race of the asuras or deamons

Darśan: vision; usually referred to seeing divinity

Dāsa bhāva: feeling that you are a servant of the master

Dasa graha: ten major heavenly bodies

Devadās, Pārvati: eternal lovers

Devaki: Lord Kṛṣṇa's mother

Devatas: demigods

Devī: supreme goddess in Hinduism, cosmic mother.

Devī Gāyatrī: godess of knowledge

Dharma: righteousness

Dharmakṣetra: holy land

Dhanañjaya: the name of a vital air nourishing the body; a name of Arjuna

Dhāraṇa: collection or concentration of the mind (joined with the retention of breath)

Dhee: intellect

Dhīraḥ: courageous person. Term used by Svami Vivekānanda in exhorting his followers

Dhyāna: meditation

Dhyāna yoga: path of meditation techniques

Dīkṣa: grace bestowed by the master and the energy transferred by the master to the disciple at initiation or any other time, may be through a mantra, a touch, a glance or even a thought.

Divya cakṣu: divine eye. Also called divya netra

Doṣa: defect

Dr. Brian Weiss: a Pshychotherapist, famous for his book, 'Many Lives, Many Masters'

Dṛṣṭi: sight, seeing with mental eye

Dṛṣṭi Sṛṣṭi: seeing the world as we wish to see it

Drupada: king of Pāñcāla, a great warrior, father of Draupadī

Duḥkha: pain

Dvaita: school of thought that says the individual self is separate from existence

Dveśa: aversion

Dvija: twice born. Refers to the state of awakening of Consciousness.

Ekapāda: form of rudra

Ekādaśi: eleventh day of every lunar month in the Hindu calendar. Normally people fast on this day for spiritual benefits

Ellarum Vaango: a Tamil sentence meaning, 'All of you please come.'

Gadā: weapon similar to a mace; also gadhāyudaḥ

Gandharvas: celestial beings with superb musical skills; act as messengers between God and man

Gaṅgā: the most celebrated river in India, considered holy by all Hindus.

Gaṅgotri: a famous pilgrim town where the river Gaṅgā originates.

Garuḍa: eagle; Lord Viṣṇu's vehicle

Ghaṭākāśa: the space enclosed by our physical body

Ghee: clarified butter

Giriśa: a form of Rudra, Lord Śiva

Girivala: circumambulating Aruṇācala, the holy hill of Tiruvannamalai for spiritual benefits

Gomukh: holy place in Himālayas. River Gaṅgā originates from the snout of Gomukh glacier

Gongura chutney: spicy south indian side dish

Gopikās: cow herdess who were Kṛṣṇa's playmates

Gopura, gopuram: temple tower

Govinda: another name for Lord Kṛṣṇa

Govindapāda: the guru of enlightened master Ādi Śaṅkara

Gṛhasta: a householder, a married person; coming from the word gṛha, meaning house

Guṇa: the three human behavioural characteristics or predispositions; satva, rajas and tamas.

Guru: master; literally one who leads from gu (darkness) to ru (light)

Gurukul, Gurukulam: literally 'tradition of guru', refers to the ancient education system in which children were handed over to a guru at a very young age by parents for upbringing and education

Guḍākeśā: one who has transcended sleep; refers to Arjuna

Gurudakṣiṇā: offering to the Guru

Guruji: master

Guru Pūjā: ritual worship of the master.

Guru Svāmi: a person who leads a holy trip to Śabrimala

Hammurabhi: ancient king of Mesopatamia, known for his Hammurabhi's code, one of the first written books on codes of Law

Hanuman: the monkey god from the epic Rāmāyaṇa

Hara: a form of Rudra, Lord Śiva

Hare Kṛṣṇa: a holy chant on Lord Kṛṣṇa

Haridvār: temple town in North India; one of the holiest places for Hindus

Hariścāndra: a famous king of the Solar dynasty renowned for his piety and justice. He sacrificed his wife and child to keep his word

Hastināpura: a town in the state of Uttar Pradesh. It was the capital of the kingdom of the Kauravas

Hiraṇyakaśipu: a demonic king

Holi: Indian festival celebrated with colors

Homa: ritual to Agni, the god of fire; metaphorically represents the transfer of energy from the energy of Ākāśa (space), through Vāyu (Air), Agni (Fire), Āpas (Water), and Pṛthvī (Earth) to humans. Also yāga, yajña

Homa kuṇḍa: sacrificial fire pit

Hṛd garbha: womb of the heart

Hṛṣīkeśa: controller of the senses and superconscious, refers to Lord Kṛṣṇa

Icchā śakti: energy of desire. The other two are kriya śakti, energy of action and jñāna śakti, energy of knowledge.

Icchā: desire

I Ching: one of the oldest of Chinese classical texts, describes Cosmology and philosophy

Iḍā: along with piṅgala and suṣuṁna, the virtual energy pathway through which pranic energy flows

Ikṣvāku: was the first king of the Ikṣvāku dynasty and founder of the Solar Dynasty of kṣatriyas in vedic civilization in ancient India.

Indra: god of all divine beings

Indra loka: the abode of Indra, heaven

Itihāsa: legend, epic, mythological stories; also purāṇa

Iṣṭadevatā: favourite deity

Īśvara: Lord of the Universe

Jagat: Universe

Jagat guru: master of the whole universe

Jahnu: a sage

Janaka: a noble and benevolent king who ruled Mithila; father of princess Sītā in the epic Rāmāyaṇa.

Janārdana: another name for Lord Kṛṣṇa

Janmas: births

Japa: repetition of mantras either silently or loudly

Jāṭarāgni: digestive fire inside our body

Jayanti: the Sanskrit word for birth anniversary

Jiḍḍu Kṛṣṇamurti: renowned Indian philosopher

Jāgrata: wakefulness

Jāti: birth

jāti-doṣa: defect related to birth

Jīva samādhi: burial place of an enlightened master, where his spirit lives on

Jīvātman: the ordinary soul

Jñāna: knowledge

Jñāna garbha: womb of the knowledge

Jñānendriya: organs of knowledge

Jyotiṣa: Astrology; jyotiṣi is an astrologer

Kailāśa: A part of Himālayas in Tibet, considered to the abode of Lord Śiva and a place of eternal bliss

Kaivalya: liberation; same as mokṣa, nirvāṇa

Kāla: time

Kālī: a Hindu goddess

Kalpa: many thousands of years

Kalpana: imagination

Kāma: sensory pleasures, also means lust

Kāmadhenu: sacred cow

Kāminī: women

Kāñcana: gold

Kanyādāna: giving away a bride

Kāraṇa śarīra: causal body

Karma: spiritual law of cause and effect, driven by vāsana and samskāra

Karma kāndis: seekers who follow the path to achieve the ultimate through action

Karmaphala : outcome of action

Karmendriya: organs of action

Karmī: one driven by desire

Karṇa: son of Kuntī, also is a step brother to the Pāṇḍavās; renowned for his generosity

Kārthigai Deepam: Festival of lights celebrated on full moon day in month of November/December in South India

Karuṇāmūrti: god of mercy

Kāśī: holy place on the banks of river Ganges

Kaśyapa: an ancient sage believed to be the father of devas (celestial beings), asuras (demons) and the humans

Kathāmṛtam: words of immortality describing your life

Kaurava: one of the two principal clans in the epic, Mahābhārata

Kāvi vastra: saffron cloth usually worn by mendicants

Keśava: another name for Lord Kṛṣṇa

Keśī: a demon, was slain by Lord Kṛṣṇa

Khadga : sword

Kīrtans: devotional songs

Koan: Zen parables, an anecdote or riddle without any solution to show the inadequacy of logical reasoning

Kośa: energy layer surrounding body; there are 5 such layers. These are: annamaya or body, prānamaya or breath, manomaya or thoughts, vijñānamaya or sleep and ānandamaya or bliss kośas

Kriya śakti: energy of action. Other two energies are energy of desire and energy of knowledge.

Krodha: anger

Kṛpā: grace

Kṛpācārya: a great general who fought in the battle of Kurukṣetra on the side of the Kauravas

Kṣaṇa: moment in time; refers to time between two thoughts

Kṣatriya: warrior class

Kṣema: success

Kṣipram: instant

Kubera: Lord of Wealth

Kumbh Mela: large spiritual gathering in India that occurs four times every twelve years, attracting millions of people. The four locations of Kumbh Mela are Prayāg in Allahabad at the confluence of Gaṅgā, Yamuna and the underground Sarasvati river; Haridwar on the banks of Gaṅgā; Ujjain along the Kṣipra river and Nasik along the Godāvarī river.

Kuṇḍalinī: energy that resides at the root chakra 'mūlādhāra'

Kurukṣetra: the land where the great war of Mahābharata was fought between the Pāṇḍavās and the Kauravas in the Haryana state of India

Kuṣa grass: sacred grass used in the Vedic tradition for various religious ceremonies. The seat made of Kuṣa grass and covered with a skin and a cloth is considered ideal for meditation.

Lakṣmī: goddess of wealth and fortune

Lakṣmī Yantra: the divine mystical drawing that bestows wealth

Līlā: divine play

Lobha: greed

Mādhava: another name for Lord Kṛṣṇa

Madhura bhāva: the relationship of beloved between master and disciple

Madhusūdana: another name for Kṛṣṇa, slayer of the demon madhu

Mahā Samādhi: Attaining Enlightenment and leaving the body; the final Liberation

Mahā: great

Maharṣi: great sage

Mahābhārata: the Hindu epic whose central characters are the five Pāṇḍavā princes, their hundred Kaurava cousins and enlightened master Kṛṣṇa.

Mahākaśa: the whole cosmos

Mahāmaṇḍaleśwar: title given to the leader of a very large religious organization; signifies the highest level of traditional spiritual Hindu guardianship

Mahāmeru: a mountain

Mahāparinirvāṇa: day of enlightened souls

Mahāvākya: great sayings from the Upaniṣads. There are four: Aham Brahmāsmi, Tat Tvam Asi, Ayam Ātma Brahma and Prājñānam Brahma. All four mean that You are the Divine.

Mahāvīra: Varthamana Mahāvira was the 24th and last tīrthaṅkara or enlightened one, and established the tenets of the religion of Jainism, founded in India and now practiced by millions worldwide.

Makara: name of a fish

Mālā: a garland, a necklace; rudrākṣamālā is a garland made of the seeds of the rudrākṣa tree

Mama: my own

Mamakāra: inner ego that constantly says that you are smaller than what you think you are

Mana śarīra: mental layer

Manana: thinking, contemplating

Manas: mind

Mānava: humans

Mandir: temple

Maṇḍana Miśra: a contemporary of Ādi Śaṅkarā who later became his disciple

Maṅgala: auspicious; maṅgala sūtra, literally auspicious thread, the yellow or gold thread or necklace, a married Hindu woman wears

Maṇipūraka cakra: subtle energy center located near the navel region, related to the emotion of worry.

Mānickavāsagar: one of the 63 Nāyanmars, authored Thiruvasagam, a collection of hymns in praise of Lord Śiva.

Manipuṣpaka: Sahādeva's conch

Manomaya Kośa: the third mental energy sheath in the five Kośas or energy sheaths

Mantra: a sound, a formula; sometimes a word or a set of words, which because of their inherent sounds, have energizing properties. Mantras are used as sacred chants to worship the Divine

Manu: father of mankind

Manusmṛti: code of conduct written by Manu, the father of mankind for harmonious existence

Marut: storm dieties

Mārgazhi: refers to the month of January in Tamil

Mātṛ bhāva: feeling that the master is like the mother

Māyā: that which is not, not reality, illusion; all life is māyā according to advaita

Meimai: living the truth through your body

Melkote: holy town in Karnataka, India where Śrī Rāmānujacārya, the great saint lived

Menakā: a celestial maiden

Mīmāmsā: a system of ancient Indian philosophy

Mīrā: a great devotee of Lord Kṛṣṇa

Mitya: transient

Mohinī: the only female incarnation of Lord Viṣṇu, a femme fatale

Mokṣa: liberation; same as nirvāṇa, samādhi, turīya etc.

Mṛtyuñjaya Homa: fire ritual done to avoid untimely death and improve longevity of life.

Muṇḍa : the shaven head

Muni: realized being

Mūdhaḥ: fool

Mūlādhāra cakra: energy center located at the base of the spine

Nārī: woman

Nārada: a divine sage and the greatest devotee of Lord Viṣṇu; he playfully causes quarrels among Gods

Nāyanmārs: Tamil devotee saints of enlightened master Śiva, 63 in number, whose life stories are told in the book Peria Puranam

Nīlakaṇṭha: the one with the 'blue throat,' refers to Lord Śiva

Na iti: not this

Naciketa: lead character in Kaṭhopaniṣad, believed to have learnt the secret of death from Lord Yama (god of death) himself.

Nadi: river

Nāḍī: nerve; also an energy pathway that is not physical

Nāga sādhu: ascetic who does not wear clothes

Nāga: a snake

Nakṣatrāṇi: stars

Namaḥ: I surrender to you

Namaskār: traditional greeting with raised hands, with palms brought together

Nānta: without end

Nārāyaṇa: another name for Lord Viṣṇu

Nara: man; also depicts the human aspect of lord Viṣṇu

Narmadā: a holy river in central India

Naropa: an Indian Buddhist monk

Naṭarāja: a depiction of Lord Śiva as the cosmic dancer, main deity in the famous temple at Chidambaram

Navagraha: nine major heavenly bodies as defined in Hindu Mythology

Neeru: water in Kannada

Neti neti: this is not

Nididhyāsana: expressing in your life

Nirguṇa: formless

Nirguṇa brahman: consciousness that cannot be limited to a form

Nirmohatvam: non attachment to desires

Nirvāṇa : liberation; same as mokṣa, samādhi

Nirvāṇi akhāda: the Saṅgha of Nāga sādhus

Nirvikalpa samādhi: the state of deep meditation wherein one transcends the form of the deity

Nisargadatta Mahāraj: an enlightened master who lived in Mumbai. Passed away on 8th September 1981, at the age of 84.

Nissaṅgatvam: a state of being non-attached

Nityānanda: eternal bliss

Nitya kīrtans: holy hymns

Nivṛtti: inward looking

Niyama: moral discipline, the second of eight paths of Patañjali's Aṣṭāṇga Yoga; refers to a number of day-to-day rules of observance for a spiritual path

Nṛsimha Avatār: incarnation of Lord Viṣṇu in which he is half-lion and half-human

Nyāya Śāstra: scripture of logic

Nyāya: logic

Om: sacred syllable; the primordial sound

Oṁkāreśvar: a Hindu temple, located in Shivapuri island on Narmada river; shaped like the sacred symbol 'Om'

Pāda: feet, also means quarter of a poem

Pādaseva: service to the feet; usually to that of the Master

Padārtha: word meaning

Pāduka: sandals

Pāṇḍavās: five brothers in Mahābharata, also sons of Pāṇḍu

Pāñcāla: an ancient region in North India, around the rivers Ganges and Yamuna

Pāñcāli: another name for Draupadī , the wife of the Pāṇḍavās

Pāni: water in hindi language

Paṇḍit: scholar

Pañca bhūta: five elemental energies that sustain us, namely, earth, water, fire, air and ether

Pañca indriya: five senses

Pāñcajanya: Lord Kṛṣṇa's conch

Pāpa: sin

Pārtha: Arjuna

Parabrahma Kṛṣṇa: Kṛṣṇa as the cosmic energy

Paramahamsa Yogānanda: an enlightened master, advocated practice of Kriya Yoga to attain Self-realization.

Paramahamsa: literally the 'supreme swan'; refers to an enlightened being

Parantapa: another name of Arjuna

Parikrama: the ritual of going around a holy location, such as a hill or water body

Parivrājaka: wandering by an ascetic monk

Patañjali: father of Yoga, famous for his treatise on yoga called Patañjali's Yoga Sūtras

Pauṇḍra: Bhīma's conch

Pazhani: a famous pilgrim town in south india

Periyapurānam: A Tamil classic by Sekkizhar on the lives of the 63 Nāyanmārs, the devotee saints of enlightened master Śiva.

Phala: fruit; phalāśruti refers to the assumed benefits of worship

Piṇḍāṇḍa: individual microcosm as against Brahmānda or universe

Piṅgala: please see idā

Prāṇāyāma: breath control

Prāṇa śakti: bliss energy

Prāṇa Pratiṣṭha: installation of energy in the main diety

Prāṇa: life energy; also refers to breath; prāṇāyāma is control of breath

Prāṇamaya kośa: The second sheath of energy in the 5 layer kośa system

Prārabdha karma: karmas based on which this life has been assumed

Praṇava: mystic symbol 'Om'

Prahlāda: a great devotee of lord Viṣṇu and son of Hiranyakaśīpu, the demon king

Prajāpati: a Hindu diety from whom all beings are believed to originate

Prakṛti: Nature

Prakāśa: illuminated knowledge

Prakaśānanda Sarasvati: a Rasik saint in the tradition of Caitanya Mahāprabhu, his teachings are mainly based on the Bhagavad Gītā.

Pralaya: the great deluge

Prasād: food offered to God and eaten by devotees with his blessings

Pratijānīhi: declare it boldly

Pratyāhāra: fifth limb of Patañjali's Aṣṭaṇga Yoga referring to turning away from sensory inputs

Pratyāhāra: literally 'staying away from food'; in this case refers to control of all senses as part of the eight fold Aṣṭaṇga Yoga

Pravṛitti: looking outward (the worldly life)

Prayāg: city in the North Indian state of Uttar Pradesh, one of four sites of the mass Hindu pilgrimage Kumbh Mela, the others being Haridwar, Ujjain and Nāsik. It is situated at the confluence of the three rivers Ganga, Yamuna and Sarasvati

Pritha: another name for Kuntī

Pṛthvī: earth energy

Pūjā: form of ritual worship

Punnāgavarāli: a tune in carnatic music, believed to be a melody that can mesmerize snakes

Puṇya: merit, beneficence

Purāṇa: mythological stories

Purohit: priest

Puruṣa: the personification of the Supreme energy

Puruśottama: means Supreme Being; one of the names of Lord Viṣṇu

Puṣpaka vimānam: mythological Aircraft

Pūrṇāvatār: complete incarnation

Pūrṇa: literally 'complete'; refers in the advaita context to reality

Pūrva mīmāmsa: one of the six branches of vedic knowledge that accepts only the karma kāṇḍa as the supreme authority

Putra: son; putrī: daughter

Rāga: attachment

Rājarṣi: king who is also a sage

Rājasūya yāga: sacrifice performed to celebrate victory

Rājasannyāsi: king of saints

Rajas, rajasic: the second characteristic of the three human guṇa or behaviour modes, referring to passionate action

Raktha: blood

Rākṣasa: demon

Ramaṇa Purānam: verses in praise of Ramaṇa Maharṣi, an enlightened master from Tiruvannamalai

Ramaṇa Maharshi: an enlightened master from Tiruvannamalai

Rāmānuja: founder of the Viśiṣṭādvaita or qualified non-duality principle. One of the greatest teachers of Hindu philosophy

Rāmāyaṇa: famous Indian epic authored by Vālmiki, a robber-turned-saint

Rāmakṛṣṇa Paramahamsa: An enlightenend master from Dakṣiṇeśvar, West Bengal, India.

Rāsa līlā: divine dance of the gopīs, Kṛṣṇa's devotees

Rātri: night

Rāvaṇa: mighty emperor of Lanka, the villain in Rāmāyaṇa, who abducted princess Sītā in the Indian historical epic Rāmāyaṇa.

Rene Descartes: French philosopher and mathematician, father of Modern philosophy

Ṛg Veda: the oldest of the 4 vedas

Rotis: flat circular Indian bread made usually from wheat

Ṛṣīkeśa: pilgrimage in Himālayas

Ṛṣi: a sage

Rudrākṣa: beads of the Rudrākṣa tree, literally means 'Śiva's tears'

Rudrākṣamāla: necklace of holy rudrākṣa seeds

Rudra: another name for Lord Śiva

Rudras: elemental powers

Śabarimala: a famous pilgrim centre in Kerala, India

Śabda Tattva: principle of sound

Sadāśiva Brahmendra: 18th century Tamil saint and music composer

Śadhana Sadan: Śankar Mahāraj's ashram

Sādhu: literally a 'good person'; refers to an ascetic; same as sannyāsī

Saguṇa: with form

Saguṇa brahman: the formless in form

Sahasranāma: 1000 names invoking a particular deity which devotees recite

Sahasrāra: lotus with thousand petals; the crown energy centre

Saivism: a sect that reveres Lord Śiva as the Supreme Being

Sakha bhāva: the relationship of friendship between the Master and the disciple

Śakti: energy; intelligent energy; Parāśakti refers to universal energy, divinity; considered feminine; masculine aspect of Śakti is Śiva

Sākyanāyanār: originally a Buddhist monk who became an ardent devotee of Śiva in the later part of his life

Sālokya mukti: residence in the same abode of the Lord

Sāma veda: one of the Vedas, the ancient core Hindu scriptures

Samādhi: state of no-mind, no-thoughts; literally, becoming one's original state; liberated, enlightened state.

Śambāla: place where one is in peace and security; space of ultimate freedom

Śambhu: form of rudra

Saṁśaya: doubt

Saṁskāra: embedded memories of unfulfilled desires stored in the subconscious that drive one into decisions, into karmic action

Saṁyama: complete concentration

Samāna: part of prāṇa responsible for digestion and assimilation of food

Sāmīpya mukti: enlightenment whereby one is very near to the Lord

Saṁsāra Sāgara: ocean of wordly life

Saṁsāra māya: illusion of life

Sāmudrika lakṣana Śāstra: technique of studying body features

Sanātana dharma: eternal path of righteousness

Sañcita karma: our complete bank of unfulfilled karmas

Sandhyā: twilight; sandhyā kāl refers to evening

Sañjaya: the narrator who tells blind Dhṛtarāṣṭra the progress of the war from day to day.

Saṅkalpa: vow or promise; also means conscious decision

Śankar Maharāj: a young sanyāsi

Śaṅkha: conch

Śānti: peace

Śaṅkarā: an enlightened master from Kālady, Kerala. Exponent of Advaita vedānta

Sāṅkhya philosophy: one of the six schools of classical system of orthodox Indian philosophy. Sāṅkhya philosophy regards the universe as consisting of two realities: puruṣa (self) and prakṛti (matter).

Sannyās: giving up worldly life; sannyāsi or sannyāsin, a monk, an ascetic

Sannyāsini: refers to a female monk

Saptapadi: the seven steps taken by the couple after tying the wedding knot in Hindu marriages

Saptaṛṣīs: the 7 sages who control the world

Śāradā Devī: wife of Rāmakṛṣṇa

Sārasvatya: explain a difficult idea very simply

Saree: traditional attire of Indian women

Śarīra: body

Śāstra: sacred texts

Ṣāṣṭāṅga namskāra: full prostration

Sat cit ānanda: existence, knowledge, bliss

Satori: high state of consciousness

Śatrughna: brother of lord Rāma in the Hindu epic, Rāmāyaṇa

Satsang: spiritual gatherings

Sātyaki: name of a great warrior

Satyavatī: Arjuna's great grandmother

Savikalpa samādhi: is one of the highest forms of minor state of samādhi meditation. In Savikalpa samādhi, the human consciousness is dissolved and lost for a short period of time

Sāyujya mukti: becoming enlightened oneself

Satva, satvic: the highest attribute or guṇa of spiritual calmness

Siddhi: extraordinary powers attained through spiritual practice

Śikhaṇḍi: daughter-son of King Drupada, a girl-turned-man, warrior on the Pāṇḍavā side. He had been born in an earlier lifetime as a woman named Ambā, who was rejected by Bhīśma for marriage.

Siṁha: lion

Siṁha svapna: nightmare

Sītā: wife of Lord Rāma in Rāmāyaṇa

Śiṣya: disciple

Śiva: rejuvenator in the trinity; often spelt as Śiva. Śiva also means 'causeless auspiciousness'

Skandha: Another name for Lord Subrahmaṇya

Smaraṇa: remembrance; constantly remembering the Divine

Smṛti: literally 'that which is remembered'; refers to later day Hindu works which are rules, regulations, laws and epics, such as Manu's works, Purāṇas etc.

Śraddhā: trust, faith, belief, confidence

Śravaṇa: listening

Sṛṣṭi: creation, which is created

Śruti: literally 'that which is heard'; refers to the ancient scriptures of Vedas, Upaniṣads and Bhagavad Gītā; considered to be revealed scriptures

Stotras: devotional verses, to be recited or sung

Śūdra: the caste of manual labourers

Sumerian civilization: an ancient civilization that existed in the Mesopatamia till the 2nd millennium BC

Sūtra: literally 'thread'; refers to epigrams, short verses which impart spiritual techniques

Śūnya: literally zero; however, Buddha uses this word to mean reality

Suṣuṁna: Please see 'iḍa'

Svādhiṣṭhāna: where Self is established; the groin or spleen energy centre

Svapna: dream

Svatantra: free

Socrates: a famous Greek philosopher; one of the founders of Western philosophy

Soma: wine of the gods

Somadatta: a kinsman of the Kuru clan

Soundaryatva: that which attracts our mind

Śraddhā: faith with courage to experiment with the Truth

Sṛṣṭi dṛṣṭi: accept the world and life as it is

Sthira: stable

Sthūla śarīra: physical Body

Subramanya: a Lord, also is son of Śiva

Sudarśana homa: fire ritual done for success in an undertaking

Śūdras: workers

Sūfi: sect of divine mystics in Islam

Sughoṣa: Nakula's conch

Sukha: happiness

Śukrācārya: guru of asuras

Sūkṣma śarīra: subtle body

Suptacittam: state of being aware even in sleep

Sūrya: the son god

Suṣupti: deep sleep

Sūtradhāra: controller and director of the technique

Svapna: dream state

Svayaṁvara: choosing of the husband by a woman by her own choice

Svāmi Brahmānanda: disciple of Śrī Rāmakṛṣṇa Paramahamsa

Svarūpa: form

Tamas, tamasic: the guṇa of laziness or inaction

Tantra: esoteric techniques used in spiritual evolution

Tapas: severe spiritual endeavour, penance

Tapovan: a holy place in the Himalayas

Tapasvī: one who undertakes severe penance

Tārakāsura: a demon

Tarangini: great devotee of Kṛṣṇa

Tat tvam asi: that art thou

Tataḥ kim: what next

Tejas: glow, grace

Tejavastva: sharp radiating energy and clarity

Thatāgata: Buddhahood, a pāli word

Tiruvannamalai: temple town in South India, the birth-place of Paramahamsa Nithyananda

Tīrtha: water; tīrthaṁ is a holy river and a pilgrimage centre

Trikāla: all three time zones, past, present and future; trikālajñāni is one who can see all three at the same time; an enlightened being is beyond time and space

Tirupati: temple town in south india where the presiding diety is Lord Veṅkateśwara

Tiruvaroor: a place in Tamil Nadu, India where Lord Dakṣiṇāmūrti, an enlightened master lived

Triguṇa rahita: beyond the three guṇas of rajas, tamas and satva

Triputi: the triad of knower, known and knowledge

Tṛṣṇa: craving or longing

Turīya: state of samādhi, no-mind

Turīya avastha: state that persists through all the 3 states of consciousness- waking, dream and deep sleep

Tyāg: renunciation

Ucchaiśravas: the legendary snow white horse in the Hindu Mythology

Udāna: part of prāṇa that helps the soul leave the body at the time of death

Uṇmai: 'Truth' in Tamil

Upāsanā: literally means 'sitting near,' denotes a prescribed method for approaching a deity or God

Upaniṣads: the essence of the vedas

Uśana: guru of asuras, Śukrācārya

Uttamauja: a Pāñcāla prince, son of subhadrā

Uttar kāśī: a town in North India

Uttarāyaṇam: six months that the sun travels in the north

Uttara mimāmsi: those who interpret vedic scriptures according to vedānta

Vaikuṇṭha: the abode of lord Viṣṇu

Vāimai: truth spoken through the mouth

Vairāgya: beyond attachment and detachment

Vaiśvānarāgni: fire that we worship

Vaiśyas: business community

Vajra: thunderbolt

Vāli: monkey king in the Hindu epic Rāmāyaṇa who is killed by prince Rāma

Vālmīki: author of the famous epic, Rāmāyaṇa.

Vārаṇāsi: famous pilgrimage centre and temple town of North India

Varṇa dharma: duty of one's caste

Varada hasta: boon-giving hand

Varuṇa: god of the ocean

Vāsanā: mental set up

Vāstu Śāstra: an ancient vedic science related to the science of architecture

Vasu: means 'Dweller' or 'Dwelling'

Vasudeva: father of Lord Kṛṣṇa

Vāsudeva Kṛṣṇa: Kṛṣṇa, the mortal being, the son of Vāsudeva

Vāsuki: the serpent with which the Gods and the demons churned the milky ocean in the Hindu mythology

Vāyu: lord of wind

Vedānta: describes a group of philosophical traditions concerned with the Self-realisation by which one understands the ultimate nature of reality (Brahman). Also was originally a word used in Hindu philosophy as a synonym for that part of the Veda texts known also as the Upaniṣads

Venkaṭeśvara: the presiding diety in Tirupati, a temple in South India

Verandah: porch

Vidyādāna: giving education to meet someone's mental growth

Vijñānabhairava tantra: classical text in Tantra

Vijñānamaya kośa: knowledge layer

Vijitendriya: one who has won over his senses

Vikarṇa: a Kaurava warrior

Vīṇa: a musical stringed instrument

Vipāsana meditation: Buddhist meditation technique

Virāṭa rupa: true universal form of Kṛṣṇa

Virāṭa: king of Matsya region

Vīrabhadra: form of Rudra

Viṣṇu sahasranāma: thousand names of Viṣṇu

Viṣṇu: supreme god in the Vaiśnavite tradition of Hinduism.

Viśāda: grief

Viśiṣṭādvaita: school of thought that says the individual self is a part of existence with its own attributes

Viśvāmitra: great sage

Viśvanāth: name of a temple in Kāśī

Vivekānanda: primary disciple of Rāmakṛṣṇa Paramahamsa and Founder of the Rāmakṛṣṇa Order. 19th century Eastern mystic considered a key figure in spreading awareness of Hinduism and Yoga in Europe and America.

Vrajā homa: a fire ritual of purification

Vṛikodara: one with the stomach of the wolf; another name for Bhīma, one of the Pāndava brothers

Vyādha Gītā: literally means 'song of a butcher.' Consists if the teachings imparted by Vyādh (a butcher) to a monk

Vṛṣṇi: king of the yadu dynasty

Vṛtrāsura: evil being

Vyāna: the energy that pervades the whole body. Its major function is circulation

Yādava: the clan to which Kṛṣṇa belonged

Yajur veda: one of the 4 vedas

Yakṣa: demigod who according to Hindu mythology guards wealth.

Yama dharma: the lord of death

Yama: Lord of death, also refers to inner discipline

Yantra: a tool for liberation

Yayāti: an illustrious king

Yogabhraṣṭha: fallen away from the path of Yoga

Yogi: practitioner of yoga

Upaniṣads: scriptures that form the essence of the ancient texts of the Vedas. Literally means 'sitting with the master'. There are eleven main Upaniṣads that have been commented on by enlightened master Ādi Śaṅkara.

Appendix

H.H. Paramahamsa Nithyananda & His Spiritual Mission

His Holiness Paramahamsa Nithyananda is a world teacher in the science of living enlightenment. As a spiritual head of the world's oldest apex body of Hinduism, he is revered as a living incarnation of superconsciousness by millions worldwide.

Paramahamsa Nithyananda's morning satsangs (spiritual sessions) are viewed live in over 30 countries every day via TV and video-conferencing. He is also the most watched spiritual teacher on YouTube.com, with nearly 16 million views. He is also the author of more than 300 books published in 27 global languages.

A spiritual genius with an enlightened insight into everything from management to meditation, relationships to religion, success to spirituality, Paramahamsa Nithyananda brings to us a wealth of practical wisdom and techniques for lasting inner change.

Paramahamsa Nithyananda is the spiritual head of several non-profit organizations worldwide which enrich lives through personal transformation programs and courses, publications, spiritual healing and humanitarian services.

As a global humanitarian, Paramahamsa Nithyananda is working to promoting global peace, through transformation of the individual. His spiritual mission includes ashrams and centres worldwide which serve as spiritual laboratories where inner growth is profound and outer growth is a natural consequence.

Service activities include conducting meditation and de-addiction camps worldwide, free medical camps and artificial limb donation for the needy, support to children in rural areas, conducting meditation camps for prisoners, relief work and disaster recovery management in flood hit areas.

Paramahamsa Nithyananda is also deeply committed to creating international awareness about Indian culture and the ancient Vedic tradition. As an enlightened mystic, a spiritual evolutionary, a trained yogi, a powerful healer and a siddha, Paramahamsa Nithyananda is actively involved with scientists and researchers worldwide to decode the mystical yogic sciences of the East, including levitation, teleportation and manifestation (materialization).

Today, Paramahamsa Nithyananda is an inspiring personality for millions of people worldwide. His authenticity, depth of experience and his rare gift for making spirituality both practical and enjoyable have allowed His teachings to reach far and wide. He has healed thousands of people of diseases ranging from depression to cancer, often with a single touch. Working and sharing with over 10 million people worldwide every year, Paramahamsa Nithyananda and His mission are committed to help humanity make the next big breakthrough: into super-consciousness, and bring about an enlightened humanity!

Programs

Inner Awakening – Awaken The Right Intelligence For Life!

A unique 21-day yoga and meditation retreat with Enlightened Master Paramahamsa Nithyananda.

Imagine,

- Being the master of your destiny
- Being the leader that you know you are
- Having the successful life you deserve
- Falling in love with life again!

STOP IMAGINING. CREATE YOUR REALITY!

Learn,

the ancient science and secrets:

- to awaken your kundalini energy
- to heal your mind, body, soul & relationships
- to activate your hidden potential for greatness
- to hand-craft a successful future, and...

... to TASTE ENLIGHTENMENT!

Nithya Kriya Yoga - Live Life At Your Peak

Our ability to live life to its fullest is blocked as we engage with life in a very limited way. In this 2 day intensive program, we learn to apply the techniques from the essence of all spiritual wisdom: the four sacred principles that reveal the secrets of life and death. Not adapting these principles in our life is the root of all conflicts we face with life. Through this program, you will be initiated into these four principles and learn powerful techniques to overcome -

- Any kind of fear, especially fear of death
- Unconscious conflicting desires
- Guilts due to social conditioning
- Past traumas and pains and
- Live your life at its peak!

Nithya Dhyaan Yoga - Break Free Of Limitations!

Have you wondered why the experience we receive from life is always the same, no matter how much we strive to alter it? Our endeavors to find happiness, success and better relationships may yield varied results, but at the end we are almost always left with the feeling that nothing has changed. The reason for this limited experience of life is the behavioural patterns which are deeply engraved in us. Each pattern is associated with one of the seven major energy centres (chakras) in our system, which subtly influence our emotional behaviour. In this intensive 2-day workshop, we learn to apply the four sacred principles of blissful living (integrity, authenticity, responsibility and enriching), to heal our chakras and go beyond the influence of these limiting behavioural patterns.

Kalpataru - Manifest Your Destiny!

The Kalpataru is a powerful workshop that aligns your actions with your true intentions. It is a simple method that allows you to awaken your innate power so that you can manifest your own destiny. Chronic diseases are miraculously healed, financial or relationship problems are sorted out effortlessly., mracles of transformation happen and a deep sense of fulfillment and joy is experienced. Receive a personal blessing from a rare living incarnation H.H. Paramahamsa Nithyananda and empower your true intentions to transform into your reality!

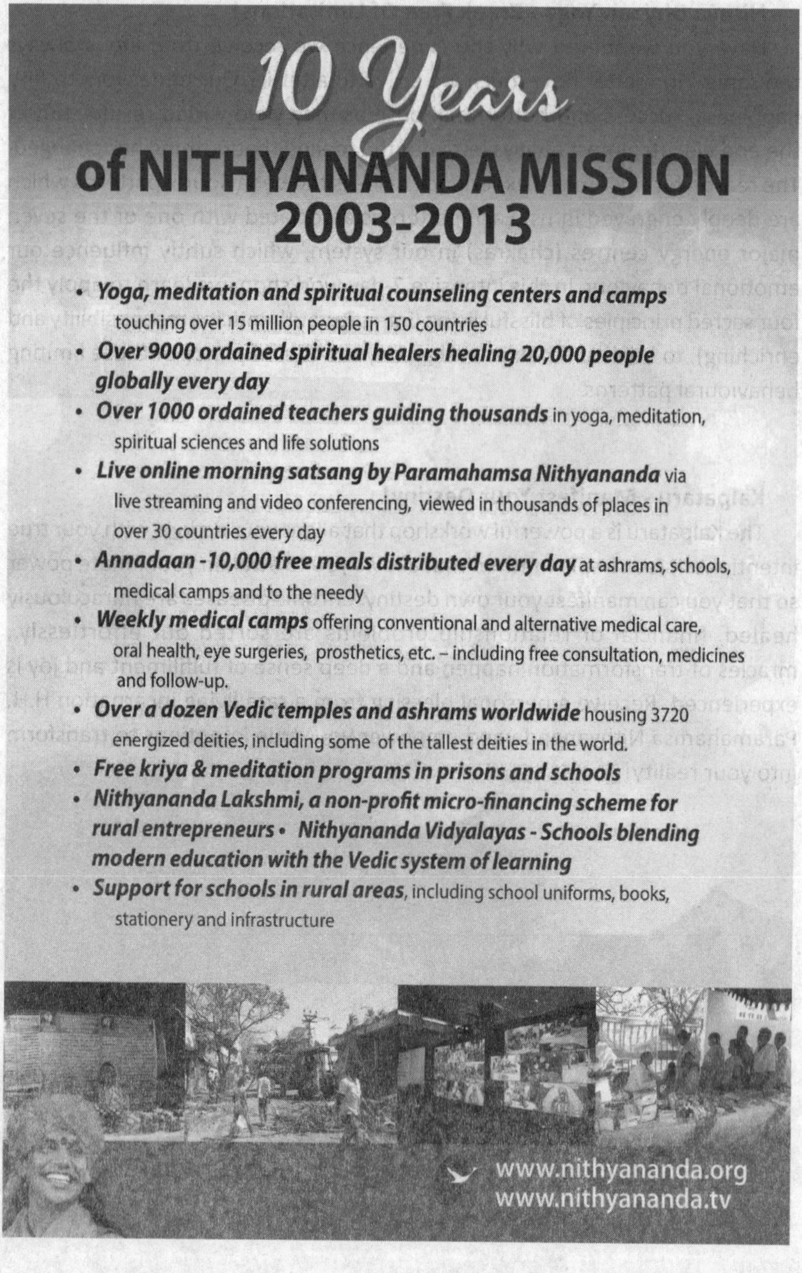
10 Years
of NITHYANANDA MISSION
2003-2013
• Yoga, meditation and spiritual counseling centers and camps touching over 15 million people in 150 countries
• Over 9000 ordained spiritual healers healing 20,000 people globally every day
• Over 1000 ordained teachers guiding thousands in yoga, meditation, spiritual sciences and life solutions
• Live online morning satsang by Paramahamsa Nithyananda via live streaming and video conferencing, viewed in thousands of places in over 30 countries every day
• Annadaan - 10,000 free meals distributed every day at ashrams, schools, medical camps and to the needy
• Weekly medical camps offering conventional and alternative medical care, oral health, eye surgeries, prosthetics, etc. – including free consultation, medicines and follow-up.
• Over a dozen Vedic temples and ashrams worldwide housing 3720 energized deities, including some of the tallest deities in the world.
• Free kriya & meditation programs in prisons and schools
• Nithyananda Lakshmi, a non-profit micro-financing scheme for rural entrepreneurs • Nithyananda Vidyalayas - Schools blending modern education with the Vedic system of learning
• Support for schools in rural areas, including school uniforms, books, stationery and infrastructure
www.nithyananda.org
www.nithyananda.tv

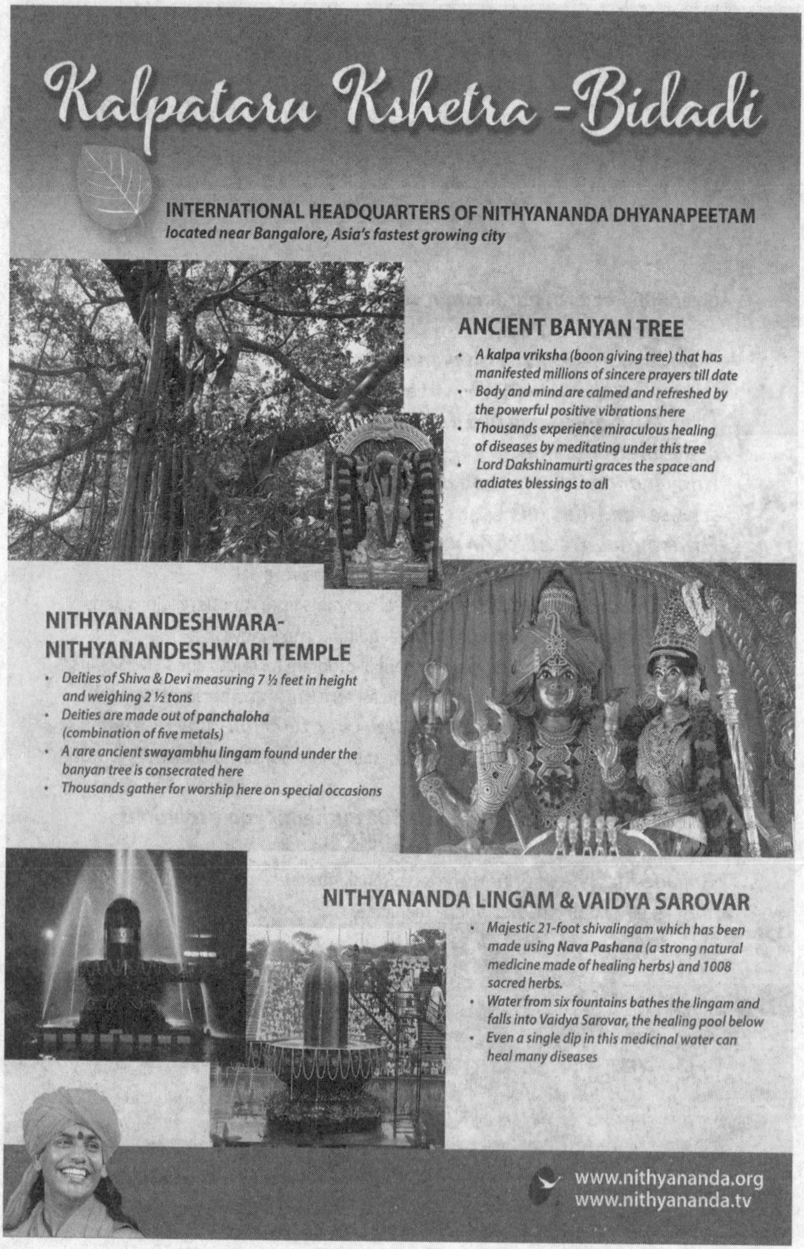

Kalpataru Kshetra - Bidadi
INTERNATIONAL HEADQUARTERS OF NITHYANANDA DHYANAPEETAM
located near Bangalore, Asia's fastest growing city
ANCIENT BANYAN TREE
• A kalpa vriksha (boon giving tree) that has manifested millions of sincere prayers till date
• Body and mind are calmed and refreshed by the powerful positive vibrations here
• Thousands experience miraculous healing of diseases by meditating under this tree
• Lord Dakshinamurti graces the space and radiates blessings to all
NITHYANANDESHWARA-NITHYANANDESHWARI TEMPLE
• Deities of Shiva & Devi measuring 7 ½ feet in height and weighing 2 ½ tons
• Deities are made out of panchaloha (combination of five metals)
• A rare ancient swayambhu lingam found under the banyan tree is consecrated here
• Thousands gather for worship here on special occasions
NITHYANANDA LINGAM & VAIDYA SAROVAR
• Majestic 21-foot shivalingam which has been made using Nava Pashana (a strong natural medicine made of healing herbs) and 1008 sacred herbs.
• Water from six fountains bathes the lingam and falls into Vaidya Sarovar, the healing pool below
• Even a single dip in this medicinal water can heal many diseases
www.nithyananda.org
www.nithyananda.tv

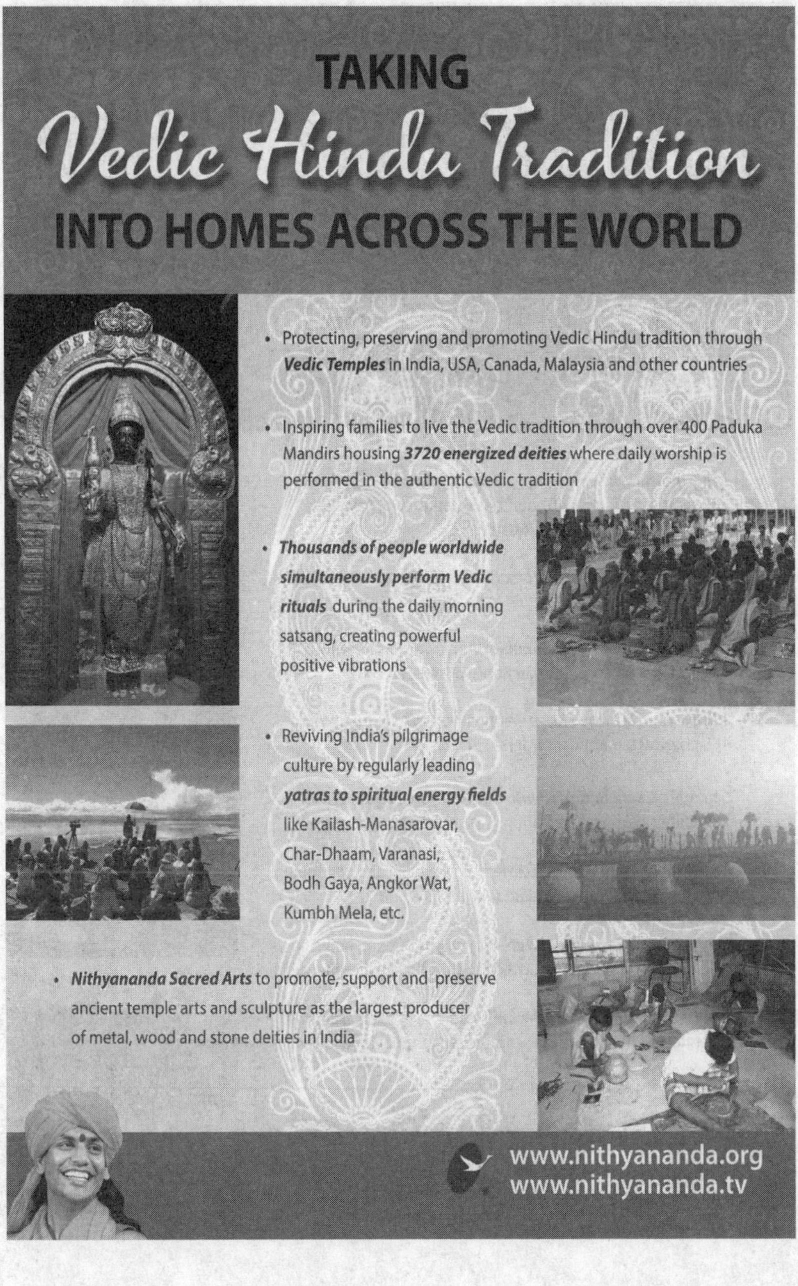
TAKING
Vedic Hindu Tradition
INTO HOMES ACROSS THE WORLD
• Protecting, preserving and promoting Vedic Hindu tradition through *Vedic Temples* in India, USA, Canada, Malaysia and other countries
• Inspiring families to live the Vedic tradition through over 400 Paduka Mandirs housing *3720 energized deities* where daily worship is performed in the authentic Vedic tradition
• *Thousands of people worldwide simultaneously perform Vedic rituals* during the daily morning satsang, creating powerful positive vibrations
• Reviving India's pilgrimage culture by regularly leading *yatras to spiritual energy fields* like Kailash-Manasarovar, Char-Dhaam, Varanasi, Bodh Gaya, Angkor Wat, Kumbh Mela, etc.
• *Nithyananda Sacred Arts* to promote, support and preserve ancient temple arts and sculpture as the largest producer of metal, wood and stone deities in India
www.nithyananda.org
www.nithyananda.tv

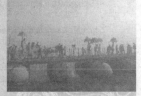

INSPIRING A GLOBAL
Vedic Renaissance
Daily morning live satsang by Paramahamsa Nithyananda viewed online in over 40 countries through two-way video conferencing and Nithyananda TV.
Daily spiritual talks by Paramahamsa Nithyananda viewed on various TV channels
Over 20 different types of meditation programs at various levels offered in corporates, schools, prisons, etc.
Nithya Yoga & Nithya Kriya – authentic yogic solutions for 108 physical & mental disorders
Scientific & safe initiation into mystical yogic sciences like kundalini awakening, levitation, hunger-free Sammyama etc.
The Nithyananda Sannyas Order for spreading and continuing the sannyas parampara (tradition)
Nithyananda Gurukuls and eN-Vidyalayas offering holistic traditional and modern education in a healthy environment
Inspiring the youth to be the ambassadors of Vedic tradition by enriching them through scripture study, rituals and kriyas
www.nithyananda.org
www.nithyananda.tv

Reaching Out to Serve the World
ANNADAAN : FREE FOOD FOR ALL
• More than 10,000 free meals served each day in Nithyananda ashrams and centers worldwide.
• Nutritious vegetarian meals cooked using authentic sattvic methods in a hygienic environment
• Chanting of vedic mantras or keertans while cooking infuse high-energy vibrations into the food.
• Free meal schemes are also offered in schools, prisons and temples.
FREE MEDICAL SERVICES : HEALTH WITH CARE
• Fortnightly and monthly multispecialty medical camps offering all services
• Weekly mobile medical services including free consultation and medicines in rural areas
• A 100% free dialysis clinic with 47 dialysis machines catering to 250 patients per day in the pipeline
• Free 100-bed hospital with all amenities planned for the needy
DISASTER RELIEF : HELPING TO HEAL
• Emergency relief to victims of natural calamities such as tsunami, earthquake, floods etc
• Distribution of free through various relief measures, by offering clothes, food, water and most importantly, psychological support and trauma counseling.
www.nithyananda.org
www.nithyananda.tv

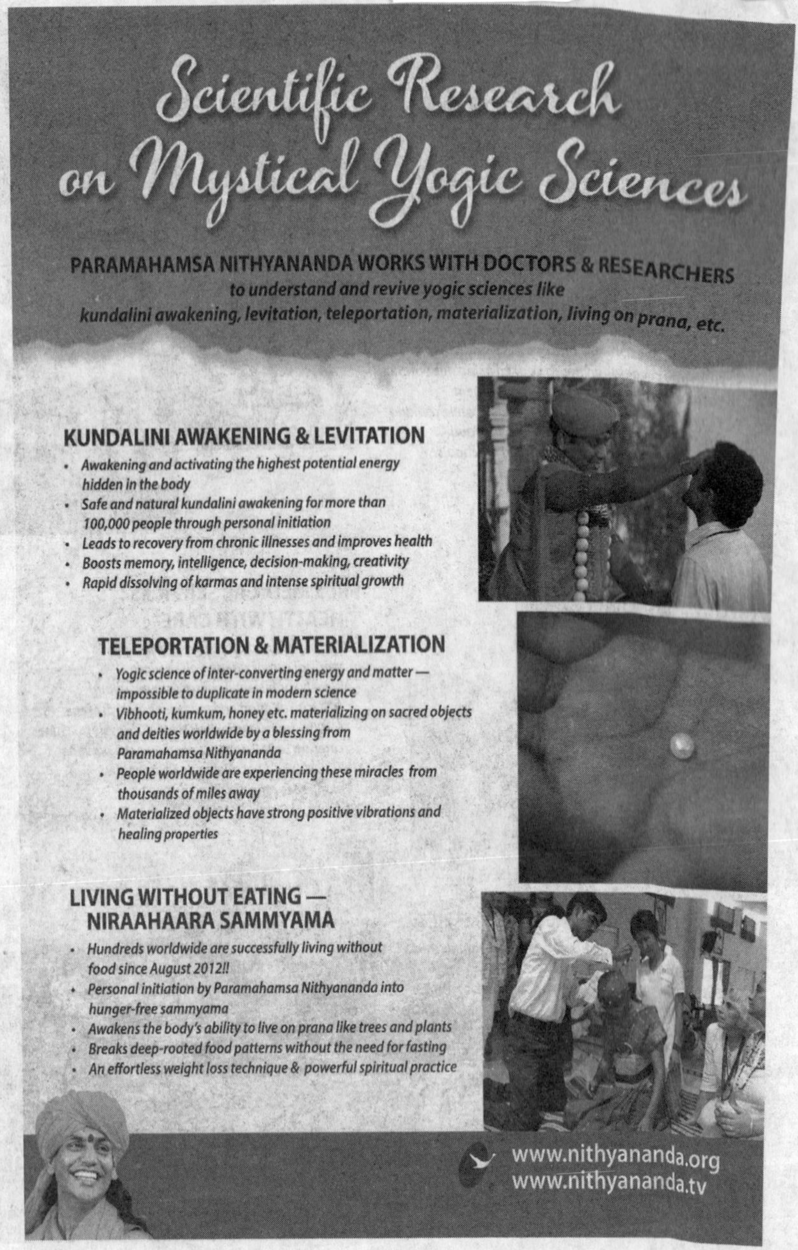
Scientific Research on Mystical Yogic Sciences
PARAMAHAMSA NITHYANANDA WORKS WITH DOCTORS & RESEARCHERS
to understand and revive yogic sciences like
kundalini awakening, levitation, teleportation, materialization, living on prana, etc.
KUNDALINI AWAKENING & LEVITATION
• Awakening and activating the highest potential energy hidden in the body
• Safe and natural kundalini awakening for more than 100,000 people through personal initiation
• Leads to recovery from chronic illnesses and improves health
• Boosts memory, intelligence, decision-making, creativity
• Rapid dissolving of karmas and intense spiritual growth
TELEPORTATION & MATERIALIZATION
• Yogic science of inter-converting energy and matter — impossible to duplicate in modern science
• Vibhooti, kumkum, honey etc. materializing on sacred objects and deities worldwide by a blessing from Paramahamsa Nithyananda
• People worldwide are experiencing these miracles from thousands of miles away
• Materialized objects have strong positive vibrations and healing properties
LIVING WITHOUT EATING — NIRAAHAARA SAMMYAMA
• Hundreds worldwide are successfully living without food since August 2012!!
• Personal initiation by Paramahamsa Nithyananda into hunger-free sammyama
• Awakens the body's ability to live on prana like trees and plants
• Breaks deep-rooted food patterns without the need for fasting
• An effortless weight loss technique & powerful spiritual practice
www.nithyananda.org
www.nithyananda.tv